Introduction to Formal Language Theory

MICHAEL A. HARRISON
University of California
Berkeley, California

Introduction to Formal Language Theory

ADDISON-WESLEY PUBLISHING COMPANY
Reading, Massachusetts
Menlo Park, California
London
Amsterdam
Don Mills, Ontario
Sydney

This book is in the
ADDISON-WESLEY SERIES IN COMPUTER SCIENCE

Consulting editor:
Michael A. Harrison

 Printed in the United States of America. Published simultaneously in Canada. Library of Congress Catalog Card No. 77–81196.

ISBN 0-201-02955-3
CDEFGHIJKL-MA-89876543

To Susan and Craig

Preface

Formal language theory was first developed in the mid 1950's in an attempt to develop theories of natural language acquisition. It was soon realized that this theory (particularly the context-free portion) was quite relevant to the artificial languages that had originated in computer science. Since those days, the theory of formal languages has been developed extensively, and has several discernible trends, which include applications to the syntactic analysis of programming languages, program schemes, models of biological systems, and relationships with natural languages. In addition, basic research into the abstract properties of families of languages has continued.

The primary goal of this book is to give an account of the basic theory. My personal interests are in those applications of the subject to syntactic analysis, and some material on that subject is included. The temptation to write about Lindenmayer systems, program schemes, AFL's, and natural-language processing has been resisted. There are now specialized books available on those topics.

This book is written for advanced undergraduates or graduate students. It is assumed that the student has previously studied finite automata, Turing machines, and computer programming. Experience has shown that the material in this book is easily accessible to mathematics students who do not know any computer science. Although no single academic course is prerequisite to the study of the material in this book, it has been my experience that students who have had no background in constructing proofs do have difficulty with the material. Any junior or senior who is majoring in computer science should be able to read the book.

One of the problems facing any person teaching formal language theory is how to present the results. The proofs in language theory are often constructive and the verifications that the constructions work can be long. One approach is to give the intuitive idea and omit a formal proof. This leads to an entertaining course, but some students are unable to carry out such proofs and soon learn to claim all sorts of false results. On the other hand, if one attempts to prove everything thoroughly, the course goes slowly and becomes one interminable induction proof after another. The few students who survive such a course are capable of doing research and writing proofs. The presentation in this book is designed to help the instructor to strike a compromise between the two extremes. When I teach the course, I try to give the intuitive versions of the constructions and proofs in class and to depend on the text for the details. There are a lot of exercises, particularly of the "prove something" variety, in the text and I assign a good many of these when I teach the material. The student who wants to be a specialist can become well versed in all the techniques; yet it is still possible to accommodate students who have a more casual interest in the subject.

A few sections are marked with an asterisk to indicate that they may be skimmed on a first reading. Just because a section is "starred" does not mean it is difficult. It means that it can be omitted if an instructor becomes pressed for time.

There is enough material in the book for a two-course sequence. In a one-quarter introductory course, the following sections should be covered:

Chapter 1, Sections 1.1, 1.2, 1.4, 1.5, 1.6.
Chapter 2, Section 2.5 if the students are well prepared. If not, everything.
Chapter 3, Sections 3.1–3.4.
Chapter 4, Sections 4.1–4.4, 4.6.
Chapter 5, Sections 5.1–5.4.
Chapter 6, Sections 6.1, 6.2, 6.4, 6.5, 6.7.
Chapter 7, Sections 7.1, 7.2.
Chapter 8, Sections 8.1–8.4.
Chapter 9.
Chapter 12, Sections 12.1, 12.2, 12.4, 12.6, 12.7.

If an instructor has additional time, a good strategy would be to choose additional material from the non-starred sections.

Sometimes a proof will depend on an earlier exercise. However, all the proofs needed to develop basic results are given in the book; consequently, the instructor can feel confident that he or she will not run into an unpleasant surprise while preparing a lecture. Not all of the exercises are straightforward and particularly difficult ones are starred.

An attempt has been made to credit results to their authors in the historical summaries at the end of each chapter. There are some cases in which priority is in doubt, and then the first published paper or thesis is referenced. The literature on formal language theory is extensive and I have limited the bibliography to papers whose results have been used or which I have read and found interesting and/or useful. No attempt has been made to include papers on program schemes or biologically motivated automata theory. Some papers on AFL theory and Turing complexity have been included. I apologize in advance to those who may feel that their work was inadequately referenced, and hope they understand the limitations of both space and time.

I have had a great deal of help in the preparation of this book. Most of this assistance came from students who took notes, read drafts, corrected error or constructed improved proofs. I want to thank them all but especially Douglas J. Albert, John C. Beatty, John Foderaro, Matthew M. Geller, Ivan M. Havel, Robert Henry, Richard B. Hull, William N. Joy, Kimberly N. King, Arnaldo Moura, John D. Revelle, Walter L. Ruzzo, Donald Sannella, Barbara Simons, Neil Wagoner, Timothy C. Winkler, Paul Winsburg, and Amiram Yehudai.

The continuous support of the National Science Foundation is gratefully acknowledged.

I want to express my deep appreciation to the many people at Addison Wesley who assisted in the preparation of the book. Special thanks must go to Mary A. Cafarella who edited the manuscript and to William B. Gruener who is the finest Computer Science editor that I have ever known.

The special assistance of Ralph L. Coffman, Anthony M. Harrison, John E. Hopcroft, and Joan M. Sautter made the whole project even more worthwhile.

Susan L. Graham taught from a draft of the manuscript and her suggestions were very helpful. Ruth Suzuki typed the manuscript and course notes. Somehow she converted a nearly illegible handwritten manuscript into beautifully typed notes so that student feedback was possible, all in realtime. Her contribution is greatly appreciated. Both Dorian Bikle and Caryn Dombroski helped with other aspects of the production. Caryn also drew the cover design which is based on a pun by Susan L. Graham.

Berkeley
May 1978

Michael A. Harrison

Contents

one

Foundations of Language Theory— Strings and How to Generate Them

1.1 INTRODUCTION

Formal language theory concerns itself with sets of strings called "languages" and different mechanisms for generating and recognizing them. Certain finitary processes for generating these sets are called "grammars." A mathematical theory of such objects was proposed in the latter 1950's and has been extensively developed since that time for application both to natural languages and to computer languages. The aim of this book is to give a fairly complete account of the basic theory and to go beyond it somewhat into its applications to computer science.

In the present chapter, we begin in Section 1.2 by giving the basic string-theoretic notation and concepts that will be used throughout. Section 1.3 gives a number of useful results for dealing with strings. Many of those results will not be needed until later and so the section has an asterisk after its number. Sections which are starred in this manner may be read lightly. When references to a theorem from that section occur later, the reader is advised to return to the starred section and read it more thoroughly.

Section 1.4 introduces the family of phrase-structure grammars, which are fundamental objects of our study. A number of examples from natural language and programming languages help to motivate the study. Section 1.5 introduces many other families of grammars and indicates intuitively how their languages may also be characterized by different types of automata.

Section 1.6 is devoted to trees and their relation to context-free grammars. The intuition developed in that section will be important in subsequent chapters.

Section 1.7 is devoted to Ramsey's Theorem, which is a deep and very general combinatorial theorem. It is used to show relationships that must hold in any sufficiently long word. Section 1.8 is devoted to showing how to construct words with no repeated subwords.

Section 1.9 proves a classical theorem of analysis due to Lagrange. In later sections, this can be applied to power series generated by context-free grammars and can be used to solve for the "degree of ambiguity."

1.2 BASIC DEFINITIONS AND NOTATION

A formalism is required to deal with strings and sets of strings. Let us fix a finite nonempty set Σ called an *alphabet*. The elements of Σ are assumed to be *indivisible symbols*.

Examples $\Sigma = \{0, 1\}$ or $\Sigma = \{a, b\}$.

In certain applications to compiling, we might have an alphabet which contains **begin, end**. These are assumed to be indivisible symbols in the applications. A set $X = \{1, 10, 100\}$ is not an alphabet since the elements of X are made up of other basic symbols.

Definition A *word* (or *string*) over an alphabet Σ is a finite-length Σ-sequence.

A typical word can be written as $x = a_1 \cdots a_k$, $k \geqslant 0$, $a_i \in \Sigma$ for $1 \leqslant i \leqslant k$. We allow $k = 0$, which gives the *null* (or *empty*) *word,* which is denoted by Λ. k is called the *length* of x, written $\lg(x)$, and is the number of occurrences of letters of Σ in x.

Let Σ^* denote the set of all finite-length Σ-sequences.

Let x and y be in Σ^*. Define a binary operation of *concatenation*, where we form the new word xy.

Example Let $\Sigma = \{0, 1\}$ and

$$x = 010 \qquad y = 1$$

Then

$$xy = 0101 \quad \text{and} \quad yx = 1010$$

The following proposition summarizes the basic properties of concatenation.

Proposition 1.2.1 Let Σ be an alphabet.

a) Concatenation is *associative*; i.e., for each x, y, z in Σ^*,

$$x(yz) = (xy)z$$

b) Λ is a two-sided identity for Σ^*; i.e., for each $x \in \Sigma^*$,

$$x\Lambda = \Lambda x = x$$

c) Σ^* is a monoid† under concatenation and Λ is the identity element.
d) Σ^* has left and right cancellation. For each $x, y, z \in \Sigma^*$,
   i) $zx = zy$ implies $x = y$, and
   ii) $xz = yz$ implies $x = y$.
e) For any $x, y \in \Sigma^*$,

$$\lg(xy) = \lg(x) + \lg(y).$$

It is necessary to extend our operations on strings to sets. Let X, Y be sets of words. Hereafter, one writes $X, Y \subseteq \Sigma^*$. Then the *product* of two sets is:

$$XY = \{xy \mid x \in X, y \in Y\}.$$

Exponent notation can be used in an advantageous fashion for sets. Let $X \subseteq \Sigma^*$. Define

$$X^0 = \{\Lambda\} \qquad \text{and} \qquad X^{i+1} = X^i X \qquad \text{for all } i \geq 0.$$

Define *monoid* (or *Kleene*) *closure* of a set $X \subseteq \Sigma^*$ by

$$X^* = \bigcup_{i \geq 0} X^i,$$

and *semigroup closure* by

$$X^+ = X^* X = \bigcup_{i \geq 1} X^i.$$

Examples Let $\Sigma = \{0, 1\}$. In general,

$$\Sigma^i = \{x \in \Sigma^* \mid \lg(x) = i\}.$$

Thus‡

$$\Sigma^* = (\Sigma)^*.$$

Note that

$$\Sigma^+ = \Sigma^* - \{\Lambda\}.$$

Also, if

$$X = \{\Lambda, 01\} \qquad \text{and} \qquad Y = \{010, 0\},$$

then

$$XY = \{0, 010, 01010\}.$$

Proposition 1.2.2 For each $X \subseteq \Sigma^*$,

a) for each $i \geq 0$, $X^i \subseteq X^*$;
b) for each $i \geq 1$, $X^i \subseteq X^+$;
c) $\Lambda \in X^*$;
d) $\Lambda \in X^+$ if and only if $\Lambda \in X$.

---

† A *semigroup* consists of a set S with a binary associative operation $\cdot$ defined on S. A *monoid* is a semigroup which possesses a two-sided identity. The set of functions on a set is a monoid under the operation of functional composition.

‡ The set of all Σ-words can be obtained by applying the star operation to Σ.

The product, exponent, and star notation has a counterpart in the monoid of binary relations on a set which we will mention.

Definition Let $\rho \subseteq X \times Y$ and $\sigma \subseteq Y \times Z$ be binary relations. The *composition* of ρ and σ is:

$$\rho\sigma = \{(x, z) \mid (x, y) \in \rho \quad \text{and} \quad (y, z) \in \sigma \quad \text{for some } y \in Y\} \subseteq X \times Z.$$

If we specialize to binary relations on a set – that is, $\rho \subseteq X \times X$ – we can define

$$\rho^0 = \{(x, x) \mid x \in X\} \qquad \text{(the equality or diagonal relation).}$$

For each $i \geqslant 0$,

$$\rho^{i+1} = \rho^i \rho.$$

The reflexive–transitive closure of ρ is:

$$\rho^* = \bigcup_{i \geqslant 0} \rho^i,$$

while the transitive closure of ρ is:

$$\rho^+ = \rho^* \rho = \bigcup_{i \geqslant 1} \rho^i.$$

It is easy to verify the following property of ρ^*, which is usually taken as the definition of reflexive–transitive closure.

Fact Let ρ be a binary relation on X and let x, x' be in X. Then $(x, x') \in \rho^*$ if and only if there exists $r \geqslant 0; z_0, \ldots, z_r$ in X such that:

i) $x = z_0$;

ii) $z_r = x'$;

iii) $(z_i, z_{i+1}) \in \rho \quad$ for each $0 \leqslant i < r$.

A similar statement holds for transitive closures. Just replace "*" by "+" and "$r \geqslant 0$" by "$r \geqslant 1$."

Another useful operation on strings is transposing or reversing them. That is, if $x = 011$, then define $x^T = 110$. A more formal definition, useful in proofs, is now given.

Definition The *transpose* operator is defined on strings in Σ^* as follows:

$$\Lambda^T = \Lambda$$

For any x in Σ^*, a in Σ,

$$(xa)^T = a(x^T)$$

The notation is extended to sets in Σ^* "pointwise":

$$X^T = \{x^T \mid x \in X\}.$$

Examples Let $\Sigma = \{a, b\}$ and $L = ab^* = \{ab^i \mid i \geqslant 0\}$. Then

$$L^T = b^*a = \{b^ia \mid i \geqslant 0\}.$$

Also, the following sequence of containments is a good test of familiarity with the notation:

$$\{a^ib^i \mid i \geqslant 0\} \subseteq a^*b^* = \{a^ib^j \mid i, j \geqslant 0\} \subseteq \{a, b\}^*;$$

$$P = \{ww^T \mid w \in \{a, b\}^*\}.$$

P is the set of even-length "palindromes." A palindrome is a string that is the same whether written forwards or backward. We conclude this section by giving some natural-language examples.†

RADAR
ABLE WAS I ERE I SAW ELBA
MADAM IM ADAM
A MAN A PLAN A CANAL PANAMA

1.3* Σ* REVISITED – A COMBINATORIAL VIEW

In this section, we shall take a brief, more algebraic look at the monoid Σ^*. We begin by recalling some concepts from semigroup theory.

If we have some semigroup S, let T be a subset of S (not necessarily a subsemigroup). T is contained in at least one subsemigroup, namely S. Let T^+ be the least subsemigroup containing T (i.e., the intersection of all subsemigroups of S containing T). We say that T^+ is the *semigroup generated by* T. If $T^+ = S$, we say that T is a *set of generators for* S. Similar remarks hold for monoids, except that we would write T^* instead of T^+. There is another important type of generation.

Definition Let T be a set of generators of a semigroup (monoid) S. S is *free* over T if each element of S has a unique representation as a product of elements from T.

Fact Σ^* is free over Σ.

Thus if we have $x, y \in \Sigma^*$, where $x = a_1 \cdots a_m$, $a_i \in \Sigma$, $m \geqslant 0$, and $y = b_1 \cdots b_n$, $b_i \in \Sigma$, $n \geqslant 0$, then we may have $x = y$ if and only if $m = n$ and $a_i = b_i$ for all i, $1 \leqslant i \leqslant m = n$.

There is an important but simple theorem that lies at the root of the study of equations in Σ^*.

Theorem 1.3.1 (*Levi*) Let v, w, x, and y be words in Σ^*. If $vw = xy$, then:

i) if $\lg(v) \geqslant \lg(x)$, then there exists a unique word $z \in \Sigma^*$ such that $v = xz$ and $y = zw$;
ii) if $\lg(v) = \lg(x)$, then $v = x$ and $w = y$;

† The spaces between words are included only for clarity in the last two examples.

iii) if $\lg(v) \leqslant \lg(x)$, then there exists a unique word $z \in \Sigma^*$ such that $x = vz$ and $w = zy$.

Proof The most intuitive way to deal with general problems of this type is to draw a picture of the strings, as follows:

CASE i)

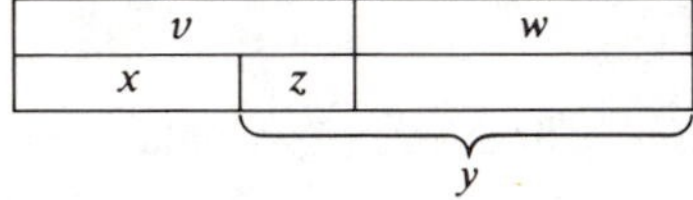

From the picture, it is clear that the desired relationships hold.

The proof follows by considering whether the line between x and y in the second row of the picture goes to the left or right of the line between v and w.

A formal proof of the result would proceed by an induction on $\lg(vw)$, and is omitted. □

Definition Let w and y be in Σ^*. Write $w \leqslant y$, w is a *prefix* of y, if there exists y' in Σ^* so that

$$y = wy'$$

Also, w is a *suffix* of y if $y = y'w$ for some $y' \in \Sigma^*$.

This allows us to state a corollary to Theorem 1.3.1.

Corollary Let v, w, x, and y be in Σ^*. If $vw = xy$, then

$$x \leqslant v \qquad \text{or} \qquad v \leqslant x$$

As an example of the usefulness of these little results, we prove the following easy proposition.

Proposition 1.3.1 Let w, x, y and z be in Σ^*. If $w \leqslant y$ and $x \leqslant yz$ then either $w \leqslant x$ or $x \leqslant w$.

Proof $w \leqslant y$ and $x \leqslant yz$ imply that there exist y' and x' so that

$$y = wy' \tag{1.3.1}$$

$$yz = xx' \tag{1.3.2}$$

Thus (1.3.1) and (1.3.2) imply that

$$yz = wy'z = xx'$$

but $w(y'z) = xx'$ implies that

$$x \leqslant w \qquad \text{or} \qquad w \leqslant x. \qquad \square$$

A more interesting and useful result is the following.

Theorem 1.3.2 Let $y \in \Sigma^*$ and $x, z \in \Sigma^+$ such that $xy = yz$. Then there exist $u, v \in \Sigma^*$ and $p \geqslant 0$ such that $x = uv$, $z = vu$, and $y = (uv)^p u = u(vu)^p$.

Proof We induct on the length of y.

Basis. If $\lg(y) = 0$, we have $u = \Lambda = y$, $v = x = z$, and $p = 0$.

Induction step. There are two cases depending on the comparative lengths of x and y.

CASE 1. $\lg(x) \geqslant \lg(y)$.

By Theorem 1.3.1 applied to $xy = yz$, we know that there is $v \in \Sigma^*$ so that

$$x = yv \qquad \text{and} \qquad z = vy$$

We may choose $p = 0$ and $u = y$ and the result is proven. Note that if $\lg(x) = \lg(y)$, then $v = \Lambda$, but the proof is still valid.

CASE 2. $\lg(x) < \lg(y)$.

Again by Theorem 1.3.1, there exists $w \in \Sigma^*$ so that

$$y = xw \qquad \text{and} \qquad y = wz$$

and $\lg(w) < \lg(y)$. Since we have

$$xw = wz$$

with $\lg(w) < \lg(y)$, we can assert, by the induction hypothesis, that there exist u, $v \in \Sigma^*$ and $p \geqslant 0$ so that $x = uv$, $z = vu$, and $w = (uv)^p u$. From the above, we have

$$y = xw = uvw = uv(uv)^p u = (uv)^{p+1} u.$$

The induction has been extended. □

Now we approach a very useful theorem which has many applications. The sufficient condition is particularly valuable.

Theorem 1.3.3 Let $u, v \in \Sigma^*$. $u = w^m$ and $v = w^n$ for some $w \in \Sigma^*$, m, $n \geqslant 0$, if and only if there exist $p, q \geqslant 0$ so that u^p and v^q contain a common prefix (suffix) of length $\lg(u) + \lg(v) - (\lg(u), \lg(v))$, where (i, j) denotes the greatest common divisor of i and j.

Proof Let $\lg(u) = s$ and $\lg(v) = t$. Let

$$\left.\begin{aligned} u &= a_0 \cdots a_{s-1} \\ v &= b_0 \cdots b_{t-1} \end{aligned}\right\} \text{with } a_i, b_j \in \Sigma,$$

and suppose that $s < t$.

Let us first suppose that the second condition is satisfied, that is, we deal with sufficiency first. Suppose that $(s, t) = 1$.

Claim $a_i = b_0$ for each $0 \leqslant i < s$. That is, all the a_i are equal and thus $\lg(w) = 1$.

Proof We simply begin to pair off the first $s + t - 1$ letters of u^p and v^q, and we get:

i	$u^p \quad v^q$
0	$a_0 = b_0$
1	$a_1 = b_1$
	$\vdots$
$s+t-2$	$a_h = b_k$

It is clear that

$$a_i = b_i \quad \text{for each } i, \qquad 0 \leqslant i < s.$$

Moreover, the following is true.

Fact For each i, $0 \leqslant i < s - 1$,

$$a_{(i+t) \bmod s} = b_i.$$

This fact is easily seen to be true for $i = 0$. From that, the case of $i > 0$ follows easily from the form of u^p and v^q. Now let us consider the set of letters

$$A = \{a_{kt \bmod s} \mid 0 \leqslant k < s\}.$$

Since $(s, t) = 1$, we have $\{kt \bmod s \mid 0 \leqslant k < s\} = \{0, 1, \ldots, s-1\}$. By this fact, every letter in u is in A and equals b_0. Thus all the letters in u are identical.

Therefore $u = b_0^s$ and $v = b_0^t$ since every letter in v is equal to some letter in u.

To extend the result to the case where $d = (s, t) > 1$, simply take words of length d and work over Σ^d, using the previous case.

Necessity. Let $u = w^m$ and $v = w^n$ for some $w \in \Sigma^*$; $m, n \geqslant 0$. Let†

$$p = \left\lceil \frac{m + n - (m, n)}{m} \right\rceil$$

and

$$q = \left\lceil \frac{m + n - (m, n)}{n} \right\rceil.$$

Then we have

$$u^p = w^{mp}$$

$$v^q = w^{nq}$$

† The notation $\lceil x \rceil$ denotes the "ceiling" of x, the smallest integer $\geqslant x$.

but $mp \geqslant m+n-(m,n)$ and $nq \geqslant m+n-(m,n)$ so that u^p and v^q have a common prefix of length

$$\geqslant \lg(w)(m+n-(m,n)) = \lg(u)+\lg(v)-(\lg(u),\lg(v)). \qquad \square$$

Corollary If $uv = vu$, where $u, v \in \Sigma^*$, then there is $w \in \Sigma^*$ so that $u = w^m$ and $v = w^n$ for some $m, n \geqslant 0$.

Now, an application of the previous theorem will be presented.

Theorem 1.3.4 Let $X = \{x,y\} \subseteq \Sigma^+$ with $x \neq y$. X^+ is free if and only if $xy \neq yx$.

Proof If X^+ is free, then $xy \neq yx$.

Conversely, suppose $xy \neq yx$ with $\Lambda \neq x \neq y \neq \Lambda$. Assume, for the sake of contradiction, that there is a nontrivial relation involving x and y, say,

$$x^{n_1}y^{n_2}\cdots x^{n_{k-1}}y^{n_k} = y^{m_1}x^{m_2}\cdots y^{m_{\ell-1}}x^{m_\ell} \tag{1.3.3}$$

with n_i, $m_i > 0$ for all i. [Note that (1.3.3) can be assumed to begin (end) with different words by left (right) cancellation.] We may assume that $\lg(y) \leqslant \lg(x)$. This and (1.3.3) imply that y is a prefix of x. Thus,

$$x = y^q t_0 \tag{1.3.4}$$

for some $t_0 \in \Sigma^*$, where $q \geqslant 1$ is the largest power of y that is a prefix of x. Substituting (1.3.4) in (1.3.3) yields:

$$y^q t_0 y \cdots y^{n_k} = y^{m_1} y^q t_0 \cdots x^{m_\ell}.$$

By left cancellation,

$$t_0 y \cdots y^{n_k} = y^{m_1} t_0 \cdots x^{m_\ell}. \tag{1.3.5}$$

Note that y cannot be a prefix of t_0 because, if it were, the definition of q would be contradicted. By (1.3.5), we know that t_0 is a prefix of y. Hence,

$$y = t_0 t_1$$

for some $t_1 \in \Sigma^*$. From (1.3.3) we must have that y is a suffix of x. [Recall that $\lg(y) \leqslant \lg(x)$]. Since $y = t_0 t_1$ is a suffix of x and $\lg(y) = \lg(t_0 t_1)$, we must have, from Eq. (1.3.4), that:

$$y = t_1 t_0 = t_0 t_1 \tag{1.3.6}$$

From the Corollary to Theorem 1.3.3 and Eq. (1.3.6), we know that there exists $z \in \Sigma^*$ so that

$$t_0 = z^{p_0}, \qquad t_1 = z^{p_1}, \qquad y = z^{p_2}$$

for some $p_0, p_1, p_2 \geq 0, p_0 + p_1 = p_2 > 0$. But now we know from (1.3.4) that

$$\begin{aligned} x &= y^q t_0 = (t_0 t_1)^q t_0 \\ &= z^{p_2 q + p_0}. \end{aligned}$$

Since both x and y are powers of z, we know that:

$$xy = yx = z^{(q+1)p_2 + p_0}$$

which is a contradiction. □

In certain applications, it is useful to order strings.

Definition Let S be any set. A binary relation, to be written $\leqslant$, is a *partial order* on S if it is reflexive, antisymmetric, and transitive, that is, if for each a, b, c in S,

1) $a \leqslant a$;
2) if $a \leqslant b$ and $b \leqslant a$, then $a = b$;
3) if $a \leqslant b$ and $b \leqslant c$, then $a \leqslant c$.

Moreover, $\leqslant$ is said to be a *total order* if it is a partial order which satisfies the following additional property: For each $a, b \in S$, either

$$a \leqslant b \qquad \text{or} \qquad b \leqslant a.$$

where the relation $a < b$ is an abbreviation for $a \leqslant b$ and $a \neq b$.

For example, the "prefix relation" is a partial ordering of Σ^*. The ordinary relation $<$ on natural numbers is an example of a total order. Now we introduce a mathematical counterpart to a dictionary ordering.

Definition Let Σ be any alphabet and suppose that Σ is totally ordered by $\prec$. Let $x = x_1 \cdots x_r$, $y = y_1 \cdots y_s$, where $r, s \geqslant 0$, $x_i, y_j \in \Sigma$. We say that $x \prec y$ if

i) $x_i = y_i$ for $1 \leqslant i \leqslant r$ and $r < s$; or
ii) there exists $k \geqslant 1$ so that $x_i = y_i$ for $1 \leqslant i < k$ and $x_k \prec y_k$. $\prec$ is referred to as *lexicographic order.*

This definition is not hard to understand:

i) says that if x is a proper prefix of y (that is, $y \in \{x\}\Sigma^+$), then $x \prec y$;
ii) says that if there exist $u, v, v' \in \Sigma^*$; $a, b, \in \Sigma$ so that $x = uav$, $y = ubv'$ and $a \prec b$, then $x \prec y$.

Note that if $\Sigma = \{a, b, \ldots, z\}$ and the total order is alphabetical, then the lexicographic order on Σ^* is the usual dictionary order.

Example Consider $\Sigma = \{0,1\}$. We begin to enumerate the elements of Σ^* in lexicographic order.

$$\begin{array}{l} \Lambda \\ 0 \\ 00 \\ 000 \\ \vdots \\ 01 \\ \vdots \\ 1 \\ \vdots \\ 11 \\ \vdots \end{array}$$

First we justify that $\prec$ is a total order on Σ^*.

Proposition 1.3.2 Let $x, y, z \in \Sigma^*$.

1 If $x \prec y$, $y \prec z$, then $x \prec z$.
2 If $x \preceq y$ and $y \preceq x$, then $x = y$.
3 For every $x, y \in \Sigma^*$, either $x = y$, $x \prec y$, or $y \prec x$.

This proposition establishes $\prec$ as a total order on Σ^*. Next we establish the connection between concatenation and lexicographic order.

Proposition 1.3.3 Let $x, y, z \in \Sigma^*$. $\quad x \prec y$ if and only if $zx \prec zy$.

Next we show that things are different on the right.

Proposition 1.3.4 Concatenation is not "monotone" on the right. That is, there exist $x, y, z \in \Sigma^*$, such that $x \prec y$ but $xz \not\prec yz$.

Proof Let $\Sigma = \{0,1,2\}$. Choose $x = 0$, $y = 01$, and $z = 2$. Clearly $x \prec y$, but $xz = 02 \succ 012 = yz$. □

Now we will state and prove one of the main properties of lexicographic order.

Theorem 1.3.5 Let $x, y \in \Sigma^*$ and $x \prec y$. Either

i) x is a prefix of y, or
ii) for any $z, z' \in \Sigma^*$, $xz \prec yz'$.

Proof Suppose x is not a proper prefix of y. Then, since $x \prec y$, there exists $u, v, v' \in \Sigma^*$; $a, b \in \Sigma$, so that

$$x = uav$$

$$y = ubv'$$

with $a \prec b$. But $xz = uavz$ and $yz = ubv'z$, so that $xz \prec yz$. □

PROBLEMS

1 Two words x and $z \in \Sigma^*$ are said to be *conjugates* if there exists $y \in \Sigma^*$ so that $xy = yz$. Show that x and z are conjugate if and only if there exist $u, v \in \Sigma^*$ so that $x = uv$ and $z = vu$.

2 Show that the conjugate relation is an equivalence relation on Σ^*.

3 Show that, if x is conjugate to y in Σ^*, then x is obtained from y by a circular permutation of letters of y.

4 Let $x, w \in \Sigma^*$. Show that, if $x = w^n$ for some $n \geqslant 0$, then every conjugate x' is of the form $x' = (w')^n$ for some $n' \geqslant 0$ and some $w' \in \Sigma^*$ which is conjugate to w.

5 Let $w, z \in \Sigma^*$. z is a *root* of w if $w = z^n$ for some $n \geqslant 0$. The root of w of minimal length is a *primitive root* of w, and is denoted by $\rho(w)$. Show that the following proposition is true.

Proposition Let $x, y \in \Sigma^+$. We have $xy = yx$ if and only if $\rho(x) = \rho(y)$.

6 Show that, for any $w \in \Sigma^*$, we have $\rho(w^k) = \rho(w)$ for any $k \geqslant 1$ where $\rho(w)$ is the primitive root of w.

7 Prove Proposition 1.3.2.

8 Let $\prec$ be the lexicographic order on Σ^*. Prove that, if $y \prec x \prec yz$, then there exists $w \in \Sigma^*$ such that $x = yw$, where $w \prec z$.

9 Let Σ be of finite cardinality n and let ω be any map of Σ onto $\{1, \ldots, n\}$. This provides a standard way of totally ordering Σ. Extend the order to Σ^* as follows: Let $x = x_1 \cdots x_k$, $x_k \in \Sigma$ for $1 \leqslant i \leqslant k$. Define

$$\omega(x) = \sum_{i=1}^{k} \frac{\omega(x_i)}{(n+1)^{i-1}} .$$

For example, if $\Sigma = \{0, 1\}$ and $\omega(0) = 1$ and $\omega(1) = 2$, then we have

$$\omega(00) = \tfrac{3}{2}, \qquad \omega(\Lambda) = 0, \qquad \omega(01) = 2, \qquad \omega(011) = \tfrac{5}{2}.$$

Give maximum and minimum values of $\omega(x)$ as a function of n and k.

10 Prove that, for any strings x and y, $\omega(x) \leqslant \omega(y)$ if and only if $x \preceq y$.

11 Suppose we redefined the ω function to be

$$\omega'(x) = \sum_{i=1}^{k} \frac{\omega(x_i)}{n^{i-1}} .$$

Would Problem 10 still be valid?

12 Show that Theorem 1.3.3 is best possible by showing that the bound $\lg(u) + \lg(v) - (\lg(u), \lg(v))$ cannot be improved.

1.4 PHRASE-STRUCTURE GRAMMARS

There is an underlying framework for describing "grammars." Our intuitive concept of a grammar is as a (finite) mechanism for producing sets of strings. The following concept has proved to be very useful in linguistics, in programming languages and even in biology.

Definition A *phrase-structure grammar* is a 4-tuple: $G = (V, \Sigma, P, S)$, where:
V is a finite nonempty set called the *total vocabulary*;
$\Sigma \subseteq V$ is a finite nonempty set called the *terminal alphabet;*
$S \in V - \Sigma = N$ is called the *start symbol;*†
P is a finite set of *rules* (or *productions*) of the form

$$\alpha \to \beta \qquad \text{where} \qquad \alpha \in V^*NV^* \qquad \text{and} \qquad \beta \in V^*.$$

Some examples will help to motivate and clarify these concepts.

Example of natural language The alphabet Σ would consist of all words in the language. Although large, Σ is finite. N would contain variables which stand for concepts that need to be added to a grammar to understand its structure, for example‡ ⟨noun phrase⟩ and ⟨verb phrase⟩. The start symbol would be ⟨sentence⟩ and a typical rule might be:

⟨sentence⟩ → ⟨noun phrase⟩ ⟨verb phrase⟩

Example from programming languages Here Σ would be all the symbols in the language. For some reasonable language, it might contain

A, B, C, . . . , Z, :=, **begin**, **end**, **if**, **then**, etc.

The set of variables would contain the start symbol ⟨program⟩, as well as others like ⟨compound-statement⟩, ⟨block⟩, etc. A typical rule might be as follows:

⟨for statement⟩ → **for** ⟨control variable⟩ := ⟨for list⟩ **do** ⟨statement⟩

Example 1.4.1 (of a more abstract grammar) Let $\Sigma = \{a, b\}$, $N = V - \Sigma = \{A, S\}$ with the productions:

$$S \to ab \qquad AS \to bSb$$
$$S \to aASb \qquad A \to \Lambda$$
$$A \to bSb \qquad aASAb \to aa$$

Note that a phrase-structure grammar has very general rules. The only requirement is that the lefthand side has at least one variable.

Grammars are made for "rewriting" or "generation," as given by the following definition.

---

† N is called the set of *nonterminals*, or the set of *variables*.

‡ For the moment only, variables are being written in angled brackets to distinguish them.

Definition Let $G = (V, \Sigma, P, S)$ be a phrase-structure grammar and let $\alpha', \beta' \in V^*$. α' is said to *directly generate* β', written $\alpha' \Rightarrow \beta'$ if there exist $\alpha_1, \alpha_2, \alpha, \beta \in V^*$, such that $\alpha' = \alpha_1 \alpha \alpha_2$, $\beta' = \alpha_1 \beta \alpha_2$ and $\alpha \to \beta$ is in P. We write $\overset{*}{\Rightarrow}$ for the reflexive–transitive closure of $\Rightarrow$.

Example We use the grammar of Example 1.4.1:

$$S \Rightarrow ab$$

$$S \Rightarrow \underline{aA}Sb \Rightarrow ab\underline{S}bb \Rightarrow ababbb \tag{1.4.1}$$

$$S \overset{*}{\Rightarrow} (ab)^2 b^2$$

A sequence like (1.4.1) is called a *generation* or *derivation.* It is convenient in displaying derivations, to underline the subword being rewritten, as is done in (1.4.1).

Certain conventions are adopted in usage of symbols. Capital letters near the beginning of the alphabet are used for elements of V or N. Lower-case elements like a, b, c designate elements of Σ or $\Sigma_\Lambda = \Sigma \cup \{\Lambda\}$. One uses $\alpha, \beta, \gamma, \ldots$ for elements of V^* and $u, v, w, \ldots$ for elements of Σ^*.

Definition Let $G = (V, \Sigma, P, S)$ be a phrase-structure grammar. The set of *sentential forms* of G, written $S(G)$, is the set:

$$S(G) = \{\alpha \in V^* \mid S \overset{*}{\Rightarrow} \alpha\}.$$

Intuitively, a sentential form is something derivable from S. Historically, S stood for "sentencehood" and so, potentially, a sentential form could be expanded to a sentence. The set of sentences can be defined as the language generated by the grammar, as is done in the following definition.

Definition Let $G = (V, \Sigma, P, S)$ be a phrase-structure grammar. The *language generated by* G, written $L(G)$, is the set:

$$L(G) = S(G) \cap \Sigma^* = \{w \in \Sigma^* \mid S \overset{*}{\Rightarrow} w\}.$$

An important concept is expressed when we say that two grammars are "equivalent." Since there are a number of concepts of equivalence which make sense, the term *weak equivalence* is sometimes used for this concept.

Definition If G and G' are phrase-structure grammars, then G is said to be (*weakly*) *equivalent to* G' if $L(G) = L(G')$.

Let us work more closely with a grammar in order to get a feeling for what is involved. The example will show that these constructs do possess a certain complexity. Let $G = (V, \Sigma, P, S)$, where

$$\Sigma = \{0, 1\}, \qquad V = \Sigma \cup \{A, B, C, D, S\}.$$

The rules of P are listed in Table 1.1, with numbers and explanatory comments.

TABLE 1.1

Number	*Rule*	*Comments*
1	$S \rightarrow ABC$	start
2	$AB \rightarrow 0AD$	add a 0
3	$AB \rightarrow 1AE$	add a 1
4	$DC \rightarrow B0C$	drop a 0
5	$EC \rightarrow B1C$	drop a 1
6	$D0 \rightarrow 0D$	skip right
7	$D1 \rightarrow 1D$	remembering a 0
8	$E0 \rightarrow 0E$	skip right
9	$E1 \rightarrow 1E$	remembering a 1
10	$AB \rightarrow \Lambda$	terminate
11	$C \rightarrow \Lambda$	
12	$0B \rightarrow B0$	move B left to
13	$1B \rightarrow B1$	continue

What is $L(G)$ for this grammar? At this point, the answer is not clear, and even the intuitive comments given in the grammatical description do not help very much. It turns out that

$$L(G) = \{xx \mid x \in \{0,1\}^*\}. \tag{1.4.2}$$

Even knowing the answer is of little help, since we must prove it. Proofs of this kind are important because we must verify that:

i) xx is in $L(G)$ for each $x \in \{0, 1\}^*$;

ii) every string in $L(G)$ is of the form xx, where $x \in \{0,1\}^*$.

Step (i) is not too hard in general. Step (ii) is necessary for making sure that a construction is correct.

Let us now work out some of the propositions needed to prove (1.4.2).

Consider derivations that start from the string $xABxC$, where $x \in \{0,1\}^*$. We will determine all the ways in which the derivation can continue and ultimately be able to generate a sentence.

First of all, these considerations suffice to deal with (1.4.2), since

$$S \Rightarrow ABC = \Lambda AB\Lambda C$$

Now consider

$$xABxC \tag{1.4.3}$$

How shall we continue?

CASE 1. Apply production 10 to (1.4.3). We get:

$$xABxC \Rightarrow xxC \tag{1.4.4}$$

Our only choice is to use production 11, to get:

$$xx \in L(G).$$

This is fine, since we need this string in the language.

CASE 2. Apply production 11 to (1.4.3). We get:

$$xABxC \Rightarrow xABx$$

We could again apply production 10 but that would reproduce Case 1. So we'll use one of productions 2 or 3, say 2. Then we get:

$$xABx \Rightarrow x0ADx$$

Now rules 6 and 7 are applicable (depending on the structure of x). There is no way that the D can ever be made to go away, because it will never find a C with which to "collaborate" (as in rule 4). Thus the initial choice of rule 11 leads us to block. (The argument would be the same if production 3 instead of production 2 had been employed.)

CASE 3. Apply production 2 to (1.4.3). (There is an analogous argument for production 3 by the symmetry of the rules.)

$$\begin{aligned} x\underline{AB}xC &\Rightarrow x0A\underline{Dx}C && \\ &\overset{*}{\Rightarrow} x0Ax\underline{DC} && \text{rules 6 and 7} \\ &\Rightarrow x0AxB0C && \text{drop a 0} \\ &\overset{*}{\Rightarrow} x0ABx0C && \text{continue} \end{aligned}$$

In this case, a string was found which is one longer than x and of the same form.

The cases we have studied exhaust all possible rewritings of $xABxC$, and it now follows that (1.4.2) is true. □

Doing these proofs is important because it helps to prevent errors. In the example, note that rules 12 and 13 occur after the termination rules. The reason is that the grammar was designed first. When the proof was carried out, it became apparent that omissions had been made.

Writing a grammar for a problem is very much like composing a program (in a primitive programming language). The techniques for writing an understandable or structured program are even more useful here and should be employed.

PROBLEM

1 Give a phrase-structure grammar that generates the set

$$L = \{a^i b^j a^i b^j \mid i, j \geqslant 1\}.$$

Explain clearly how the grammar is supposed to work, and also prove that it generates L; i.e., every string in $L(G)$ is in L and every string in L is in $L(G)$.

1.5 OTHER FAMILIES OF GRAMMARS – THE CHOMSKY HIERARCHY

We shall now survey some of the other families of grammars which are known, and characterize some of them by automata. This will be a somewhat informal survey. In later chapters, these devices will be studied in great detail and the actual characterizations will be proved.

First, we consider some variations on phrase-structure grammars.

Definition A phrase-structure grammar $G = (V, \Sigma, P, S)$ is said to be of *type 0* if each rule is of the form

$$\alpha \to \beta$$

where $\alpha \in N^+$ and $\beta \in V^*$.

We shall see that type 0 and phrase-structure grammars are equivalent. This is, in fact, a general theme that will run throughout the book. For a given family of languages, $\mathscr{L}$, we will be interested in very powerful types of grammars that generate $\mathscr{L}$. Moreover, we are very interested in the weakest family of grammars that also generates $\mathscr{L}$. When we have some particular set L and wish to show it is in $\mathscr{L}$, we use a powerful type of grammar. On the other, if we wish to show that some given set L' is *not* in $\mathscr{L}$, then it is convenient to assume it is in $\mathscr{L}$ and is generated by a very constrained type of grammar. It then becomes much easier to find a contradiction.

Definition A phrase-structure grammar $G = (V, \Sigma, P, S)$ is said to be *context-sensitive with erasing* if each rule is of the form

$$\alpha A \gamma \to \alpha \beta \gamma$$

where $A \in N$ and $\alpha, \beta, \gamma \in V^*$.

Examples Consider the grammar G_1 given by the following rules:

$$S \to ABC$$

$$A \to a$$

$$aB \to b$$

$$C \to c$$

This grammar is neither type 0 nor context-sensitive with erasing, but is phrase-structure. Of course, every type 0 grammar and context-sensitive with erasing grammar must be phrase-structure.

Now consider grammar G_2 shown below:

$$S \to AB \qquad A \to a$$

$$AB \to BA \qquad B \to b$$

G_2 is type 0 but not context-sensitive with erasing. It is easy to modify G_1 to obtain a grammar G_3 which is context-sensitive with erasing but not type 0. This is left to the reader.

The next definition will lead to a different family of languages.

Definition A phrase-structure grammar $G = (V, \Sigma, P, S)$ is *context-sensitive* if each rule is of the form

i) $$\alpha A \gamma \rightarrow \alpha\beta\gamma$$

where $A \in N; \alpha, \gamma \in V^*, \beta \in V^+$; or

ii) $$S \rightarrow \Lambda$$

If this rule occurs, then S does not appear in the righthand side of any rule.

The motivation for the term context-sensitive comes from rules like

$$\alpha A \gamma \rightarrow \alpha\beta\gamma$$

The idea is that A is rewritten by β only if it occurs in the context of α on the left and γ on the right.

The purpose of the restriction $\beta \in V^+$ is to ensure that when A is rewritten, it has an effect. But this condition alone would rule out Λ from being a sentence. For certain technical reasons and for certain applications, we would like to include Λ. This leads to condition (ii) in the definition. We must constrain the appearance of S in the rules; otherwise erasing could be simulated by a construction using rules $\alpha A \gamma \rightarrow \alpha S \gamma$ and $S \rightarrow \Lambda$, to yield

$$\alpha A \gamma \Rightarrow \alpha S \gamma \Rightarrow \alpha\gamma$$

Now we give a definition of context-free grammars, which will be one of the main topics of this book.

Definition A phrase-structure grammar $G = (V, \Sigma, P, S)$ is a *context-free grammar* if each rule is of the form

$$A \rightarrow \alpha$$

where $A \in N, \alpha \in V^*$.

The term "context free" means that A can be replaced by α wherever it appears, no matter the context.

Some authors given an alternative definition in which $\alpha \in V^+$, which prohibits Λ rules. The presence of Λ rules in our definition must be accounted for eventually; and indeed it will be shown that, for each language L generated by a context-free grammar with Λ rules, there exists a Λ-free, context-free grammar that generates $L - \{\Lambda\}$. In the meantime Λ rules will play an important role in proofs, since they frequently give rise to special cases that must be carefully checked. Because Λ rules do cause technical problems, their omission is a common suggestion of novices and a temptation to specialists. Systematic omission of Λ rules changes the class of theorems one can prove. We shall include them.

There is an alternative form of context-free grammar which is used in the specification of programming languages. This system is called the Backus normal form or Backus–Naur form; in either case it is commonly abbreviated BNF. The form uses four meta characters which are not in the working vocabulary. These are

$$\langle \qquad \rangle \qquad ::= \qquad |$$

The idea is that strings (which do not contain the meta characters) are enclosed by ⟨ and ⟩ and denote variables. The symbol ::= serves as a replacement operator just like → and | is read "or".

Example An ordinary context-free grammar for unsigned digits in a programming language might be as follows, where D stands for the class of digits and U stands for the class of unsigned integers:

$$\begin{array}{ll} D \to 0 & D \to 5 \\ D \to 1 & D \to 6 \\ D \to 2 & D \to 7 \\ D \to 3 & D \to 8 \\ D \to 4 & D \to 9 \\ U \to D & U \to UD \end{array}$$

The example, when rewritten in BNF, becomes

⟨digit⟩ ::= 0|1|2|3|4|5|6|7|8|9

⟨unsigned integer⟩ ::= ⟨digit⟩|⟨unsigned integer⟩ ⟨digit⟩

In this book, we will adopt a blend of the two notations. We shall use | but not the other metacharacters. This allows for the compact representation of context-free grammars.

There are a few special classes of context-free grammars which will now be singled out.

Definition A context-free grammar $G = (V, \Sigma, P, S)$ is *linear* if each rule is of the form

$$A \to uBv \quad \text{or} \quad A \to u$$

where $A, B \in N$ and $u, v \in \Sigma^*$.

In a linear grammar, there is at most one variable on the right side of each rule.

In a linear grammar, if the one variable that appears is on the right end of the word, the grammar is called "right linear." A left linear grammar is defined in analogous fashion.

Definition A context-free grammar $G = (V, \Sigma, P, S)$ is *right linear* if each rule is of the form

$$A \to uB \qquad A, B \in N$$

or

$$A \to u \qquad u \in \Sigma^*$$

Examples $S \to aSa|bSb|\Lambda$ is a linear context-free grammar for the even-length palindromes; that is,

$$L(G) = \{ww^T \mid w \in \{a, b\}^*\}.$$

The grammar G' given by

$$S \to aS|a$$

is a right linear grammar which generates

$$L(G') = a^+$$

Any of these families of grammars gives rise to a family of languages. The following definition makes the connection more precise.

Definition A language L is said to be of type X (e.g., phrase-structure, context-sensitive, etc.) if there exists a type-X grammar G such that $L(G) = L$.

For any language, there will be infinitely many grammars generating it.

Example Let G_1 be the following grammar:

$$S \to aSa$$
$$S \to aa$$
$$S \to a$$

Clearly, $L(G_1) = a^+$.

This example shows that a^+ is a linear language, but we know still more. The previous example establishes that a^+ is a right linear language.

A great deal is known about these classes of languages and grammars. In the rest of this section, we shall give an outline. To summarize the material, we use Table 1.2. The undefined terms in the table will be explained subsequently.

TABLE 1.2 The Chomsky Hierarchy

Grammars	*Languages*	*Automata*
Phrase-structure Type 0 Context-sensitive with erasing	Recursively enumerable sets	Nondeterministic or deterministic Turing machines
Context-sensitive Monotonic	Context-sensitive	Nondeterministic linearly space-bounded Turing machines, or lba's, for short
Context-free	Context-free	Nondeterministic pushdown automata
$LR(k)$	Deterministic context-free	Deterministic pushdown automata
Linear	Linear context-free	Two-tape nondeterministic finite automata of a special type or 1-turn pda's
Right linear Left linear	Regular sets	Nondeterministic or deterministic, one-way or two-way finite automata

We shall now try to give some intuitive meaning to the technical terms in this table. (This organization is sometimes called the Chomsky hierarchy.) The reader who has trouble understanding the table should not be distressed. The definitions will be given later in full detail, and the results will be carefully proven.

A *deterministic* automaton which is in a given state reading a given input always does the same thing (i.e., transfers to the same new state, writes the same output, etc.). On the other hand, a *nondeterministic* automaton may "choose" any one of a finite set of actions. A nondeterministic automaton is said to *accept* a string x if there exists some sequence of transitions which start from an initial configuration, end in a final configuration, and are "controlled by x".

A *recursive set* is a set for which there exists an algorithm for deciding set membership. That is, for any string x, the algorithm will halt in a finite amount of time, either accepting or rejecting x. A *recursively enumerable* set is a set for which there exists a procedure for recognizing the set. That is, given a string x in the set, the procedure will halt after a finite length of time, accepting x. On the other hand, if x is not in the set, the procedure may either halt, rejecting x, or never halt.

Recursive sets are a proper subset of the recursively enumerable sets.

A *Turing machine* is simply a finite-state control device with a finite but potentially unbounded read–write tape. The sets accepted by deterministic and nondeterministic Turing machines are the same.

A *l*inear *b*ounded *a*utomaton (lba) is a Turing machine with a bounded tape. It should be noted that if the automaton is limited to n squares of tape, by suitably enlarging its alphabet to k-tuples, it can increase its effective tape size to kn for any fixed k. Hence the word *linear*.

While many properties of context-sensitive languages and deterministic context-sensitive languages (languages accepted by deterministic lba's) are known, it is an open question as to whether the two families of languages are equivalent.

A *p*ush*d*own *a*utomaton (pda) has a finite-state control with an input tape and an auxiliary pushdown store (LIFO, or *l*ast-*i*n, *f*irst-*o*ut, store). In a given state, reading a given input and the symbol from the top of its pushdown store, it will make a transition to a new state, writing $n \geqslant 0$ symbols on the top of its pushdown store ($n = 0$, corresponding to erasing the top symbol of the pushdown store).

LR(k) *grammars* are grammars that may be parsed from left to right, with k symbols lookahead, by working from the bottom to the top. This class of grammar is rich enough to contain the syntax of many programming languages but restrictive enough to be parsable in "linear" time.

The deterministic context-free languages are characterized by the automata which accept them. It will be shown that they are a proper subset of the family of context-free languages.

PROBLEMS

Definition A phrase-structure grammar $G = (V, \Sigma, P, S)$ is called *monotonic* if each rule is of the form:

i) $\alpha \to \beta$ where $\alpha \in V^*NV^*$, $\beta \in V^*$, and $\lg(\alpha) \leqslant \lg(\beta)$;

ii) $S \to \Lambda$ and if this rule occurs, then S does not appear on the righthand side of any rule in P.

1 Given a phrase-structure (context-sensitive with erasing) [context-sensitive] {monotonic} grammar, show that there is a phrase-structure (context-sensitive with erasing) [context-sensitive] {monotonic} grammar $G' = (V', \Sigma, P', S')$ with $L(G') = L(G)$ and for each rule $\alpha \to \beta$ in P', we have $\alpha \in N^+$.

2 Prove the following statement (if it is true; if not give a counter example).

Fact For each phrase-structure (context-sensitive with erasing) [context-sensitive] {monotonic} grammar $G = (V, \Sigma, P, S)$, there is a phrase-structure (context-sensitive with erasing) [context-sensitive] {monotonic} grammar $G' = (V', \Sigma, P', S')$ such that $L(G') = L(G)$ and each rule in P' is of the form

$$\alpha \to \beta$$

with $\alpha \in N^+$, $\beta \in N^*$, or

$$A \to a$$

with $A \in N$ and $a \in \Sigma \cup \{\Lambda\}$.

In the next few problems, we shall show that the family of monotonic languages is coextensive with the family of context-sensitive languages.

Definition For any phrase-structure grammar $G = (V, \Sigma, P, S)$, let the *weight* of G be $\max \{\lg(\beta) \mid \alpha \to \beta \text{ is in } P\}$.

3 Prove the following fact.

Fact For each monotonic grammar $G = (V, \Sigma, P, S)$, there is a monotonic grammar $G' = (V', \Sigma, P', S)$ of weight at most 2, so that $L(G') = L(G)$.

4 Prove the following statement.

Fact For each monotonic grammar $G = (V, \Sigma, P, S)$, there is a context-sensitive grammar $G' = (V', \Sigma, P', S)$ such that $L(G') = L(G)$.

5 Consider the following "proof" of Problem 4:

Assume without loss of generality that the weight of G is 2.

i) If a production $\pi \in P$ has weight < 2, then $\pi \in P'$.
ii) If $\pi = AB \to CD$ and $C = A$ or $B = D$, then $\pi \in P'$.
iii) If $\pi = AB \to CD$ with $C \neq A$ and $D \neq B$, then the following productions are in P':

$$AB \to (\pi, A)B$$
$$(\pi, A)B \to (\pi, A)D$$
$$(\pi, A)D \to CD$$

where (π, A) is a new variable.

Surely P' is a finite set of context-sensitive rules, and since

$$AB \underset{G'}{\Rightarrow} (\pi, A)B \underset{G'}{\Rightarrow} (\pi, A)D \underset{G'}{\Rightarrow} CD$$

we have that $L(G') = L(G)$

a) Is this proof correct? If not, explain in detail.
b) If the proof is correct, is the argument incomplete in some way? If there are any gaps, complete the proof.

c) If your answer to (a) was yes and to (b) was no, then what do you think is the point of this problem?

6 Give a context-sensitive or monotonic grammar which generates

$$\{xx \mid x \in \{a, b\}^*\}$$

Be sure to explain your grammar and prove that it works.

7 Show that the family of languages generated by context-sensitive grammars with erasing is identical to the phrase-structure languages.

1.6 CONTEXT-FREE GRAMMARS AND TREES

The systematic use of trees to illustrate context-free derivations is an important device that greatly sharpens our intuition. Since we use these concepts in formal proofs, it is necessary to have precise formal definitions of the concepts. It turns out that the usual graph-theoretic terminology is insufficient for our purposes. On the other hand, a completely formal treatment becomes tedious and obscures the very intuition we wish to develop. For these reasons, a semiformal approach is developed here, which can be completely formalized. We leave a number of alternative approaches for the exercises.

An example of a tree T is given in Fig. 1.1. It has one or more *nodes* (x_0, $x_1, \ldots, x_{10}$), one of which is the *root* (x_0). We denote the relation of *immediate descendancy* by $\ulcorner$ (thus, on Fig. 1.1(a), $x_2 \ulcorner x_4$ but not $x_2 \ulcorner x_{10}$). The *descendancy* relation is the reflexive and transitive closure $\overset{*}{\ulcorner}$ of $\ulcorner$ (now $x_2 \overset{*}{\ulcorner} x_{10}$). If $x \overset{*}{\ulcorner} y$, then the *path from x to y* (or *path to y* if x is the root) is the sequence of all nodes between and including x and y (for example, (x_0, x_2, x_4, x_8) is the path from x_0 to x_8

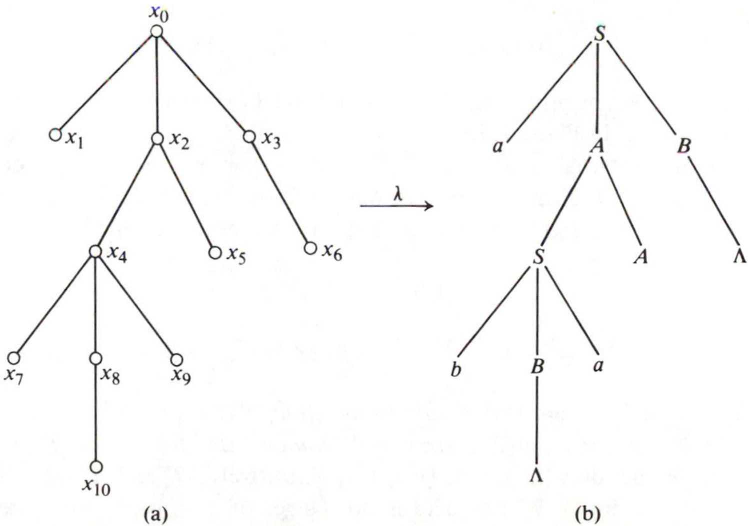

FIG. 1.1

in Fig. 1.1(a)). If n is the number of nodes in one of the longest paths in T, then the *height of* T is, by definition, $n-1$ (the tree in Fig. 1.1(a) has height 4). A node x is a *leaf* in T if for no y in T, $x \ulcorner y$. Nodes that are not leaves are called *internal*.

We must pay attention to the left–right order of nodes. Let

$$y_1, y_2, \ldots, y_m, \qquad m \geqslant 1 \tag{1.6.1}$$

be a sequence of all the leaves in T without repetition. (There is no other restriction on this sequence except the informal assumption that sequence (1.6.1) represents the intuitive left-to-right orders of leaves.) Now we define a special relation $\llcorner$ between certain pairs of nodes in T.

For any x, y in T,

$$x \llcorner y$$

if and only if

i) x and y are not on the same path, and
ii) for some leaves y_i, y_{i+1} $(1 \leqslant i < m)$ in (1.6.1) we have $x \overset{*}{\ulcorner} y_i$ and $y \overset{*}{\ulcorner} y_{i+1}$.

Thus, in particular, there is no leaf "between" x and y. (Thus, for instance, we have $x_2 \llcorner x_6$ but not $x_9 \llcorner x_6$ in Fig. 1.1(a).) Note that relation $\llcorner$ is determined uniquely by (1.6.1). The *left-to-right order* is then the reflexive and transitive closure $\llcorner^*$ of $\llcorner$.

Note that we have $\ulcorner^+ \cap \llcorner^+ = \emptyset$. On the other hand, one of the two relations $\llcorner^*$ or $\ulcorner^*$ (or their inverses) holds between any two nodes of a tree.

Every node $x \in T$ has a *label* $\lambda(x)$ from a given finite set of labels – in our cases it is always the set $V_\Lambda = V \cup \{\Lambda\}$, where V is the alphabet of a given grammar. The corresponding function λ: $T \mapsto V_\Lambda$: $x \mapsto \lambda(x)$ is the labeling (thus Fig. 1.1(a) $\overset{\lambda}{\mapsto}$ Fig. 1.1(b)). Of special importance are the *root label of* T, $\mathbf{rt}(T)$, and the *frontier* of T, $\mathbf{fr}(T)$. The latter is defined as a concatenation of labels of leaves in (1.6.1):

$$\mathbf{fr}(T) = \lambda(y_1)\,\lambda(y_2)\cdots\lambda(y_m) \in V^*.$$

Note that some leaves may be labeled by Λ and thus $\mathbf{fr}(T)$ may be shorter than sequence (1.6.1) (for instance, in Fig. 1.1, $\mathbf{fr}(T) = abaA$).

For any internal node x in T the set $\{y \mid y = x \quad \text{or} \quad x \ulcorner y\}$ defines an *elementary subtree of* T in an obvious way. A *cross section in* T is any maximal sequence of nodes in T (with respect to the partial ordering obtained from the prefix relation)

$$\xi = (x_1, x_2, \ldots, x_n)$$

such that $x_1 \llcorner x_2 \llcorner \cdots \llcorner x_n$ $(n \geqslant 1)$. Thus, in particular, sequence (1.6.1) is a cross section in T.

Two trees T, T' are *structurally isomorphic*, $T \cong T'$, if and only if there is a bijection $T \mapsto T'$: $x \mapsto x'$, called a *structural isomorphism from* T *to* T', such that $x \ulcorner y$ $(x \llcorner y)$ if and only if $x' \ulcorner y'$ $(x' \llcorner y')$; (intuitively, T and T' are "identical except for the labeling"). Where there is no danger of confusion, we write $T = T'$ when $T \cong T'$, and the labeling is preserved (this is in agreement with the customary understanding that T and T' are "identical," but not with the algebraic definition of trees). Also we use the same symbols $\ulcorner$, $\llcorner$, λ, even for different trees.

We now define certain trees and sets of trees related to grammars. Let $G = (V, \Sigma, P, S)$ be a context-free grammar. We interpret the productions of G as trees (of height 1) in a natural way: The production $A_0 \to A_1 A_2 \cdots A_n$ corresponds to the tree shown in Fig. 1.2 (or, formally, $x_0 \ulcorner x_1, x_0 \ulcorner x_2, \ldots, x_0 \ulcorner x_m, x_1 \llcorner x_2 \llcorner \cdots \llcorner x_n$, and $\lambda(x_i) = A_i$, $0 \leqslant i \leqslant n$). We make a convention that, in this correspondence, $\lambda(x_i) = \Lambda$ if and only if $i = n = 1$ and $A_0 \to \Lambda$ is in P.

Definition Let $G = (V, \Sigma, P, S)$ be a context-free grammar and let T be a tree with labeling λ: $T \mapsto V_\Lambda$. T is said to be a *grammatical tree of G* if and only if, for every elementary subtree T' of T, there exists a production $p \in P$ corresponding to T'. Moreover, a *derivation tree T* is a grammatical tree such that $\mathbf{fr}(T) \in \Sigma^*$.

Consequently, the leaves in a derivation tree are precisely the nodes labeled by letters in Σ (called the *terminal nodes*) or by Λ (the *Λ-nodes*). All other nodes are labeled by letters in $N = V - \Sigma$ (and are accordingly called the *nonterminal nodes*). Note, that in particular, a trivial tree consisting of a single node, labeled by $a \in \Sigma$ or by Λ, is a derivation tree of G.

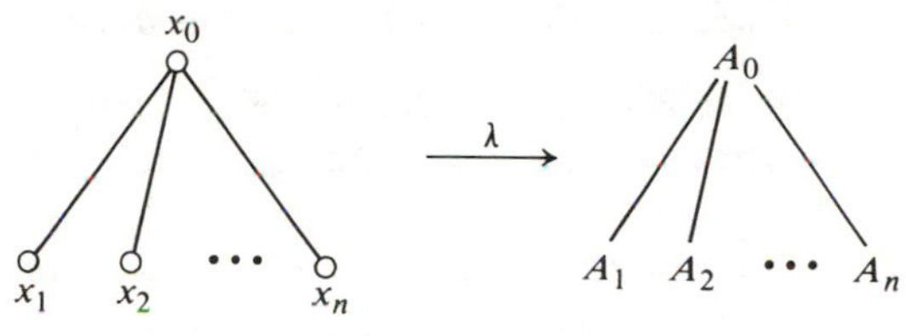

FIG. 1.2

The tree in Fig. 1.1 may serve as an example of a grammatical tree for any grammar with productions

$$S \to aAB \mid bBa$$

$$A \to SA$$

$$B \to \Lambda$$

Now let us turn to the question of relating these trees to the properties of the relation $\Rightarrow$.

Example Let G be

$$S \to AB$$

$$A \to a$$

$$B \to b$$

then the derivation

$$S \Rightarrow AB \Rightarrow Ab \Rightarrow ab \tag{1.6.2}$$

is associated with the tree

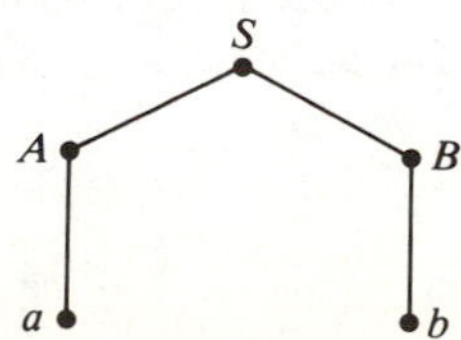

Note that the derivation

$$S \Rightarrow AB \Rightarrow aB \Rightarrow ab \tag{1.6.3}$$

is also a derivation of ab, and the same tree is associated with it. Thus there are many different derivations associated with the same tree.

Example If G is the grammar

$$S \rightarrow aSa$$
$$S \rightarrow bSb$$
$$S \rightarrow \Lambda$$

which may be compactly written

$$S \rightarrow aSa \mid bSb \mid \Lambda$$

then the derivation

$$S \Rightarrow aSa \Rightarrow abSba \Rightarrow abaSaba \Rightarrow abaaba$$

is represented by the tree in Fig. 1.3, where the derived string may be read off by concatenating in left-to-right order the symbols on the frontier of the tree; i.e., "reading the tree leaves."

Since many derivations may correspond to the same tree, we would like to identify one of these as *canonical* so as to set up a one-to-one correspondence between trees and derivations.

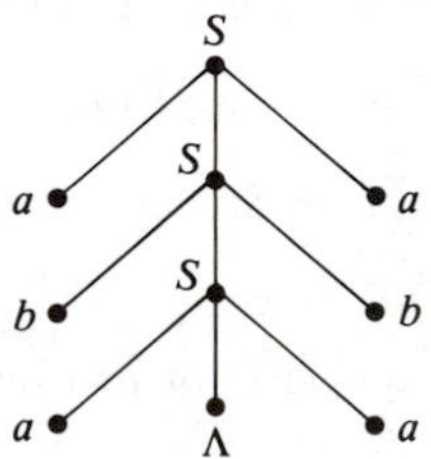

FIG. 1.3

Definition Let $G = (V, \Sigma, P, S)$ be a context-free grammar and let $\alpha, \beta \in V^*$. If

$$\alpha \Rightarrow \beta \tag{1.6.4}$$

then there exist $\alpha_1, \alpha_2, A, \theta$, so that $\alpha = \alpha_1 A \alpha_2$, $\beta = \alpha_1 \theta \alpha_2$, and $A \rightarrow \theta$ is in P. If $\alpha_2 \in \Sigma^*$, then (1.6.4) is called a *rightmost* (or *canonical*) generation. If $\alpha_1 \in \Sigma^*$, then (1.6.4) is a *leftmost generation*. The notation

$$\alpha \underset{R}{\Rightarrow} \beta \qquad \text{or} \qquad \alpha \underset{L}{\Rightarrow} \beta$$

is used in the respective cases.

Note that (1.6.2) and (1.6.3) provide examples of rightmost and leftmost derivations.

Now we can state the correspondence between trees and rightmost derivations.

Theorem 1.6.1 Let $G = (V, \Sigma, P, S)$ be a context-free grammar. There is a one-to-one correspondence between rightmost (leftmost) derivations of a string $w \in \Sigma^*$ and the derivation trees of w with root labeled S.

Proof The proof is obvious intuitively, the correspondence being the natural one. A formal proof is omitted, since trees have been introduced only informally. □

The condition in Theorem 1.6.1 that $w \in \Sigma^*$ is necessary. To illustrate this point, consider the grammar:

$$S \to ABC \qquad B \to b$$

$$A \to a \qquad C \to c$$

The tree

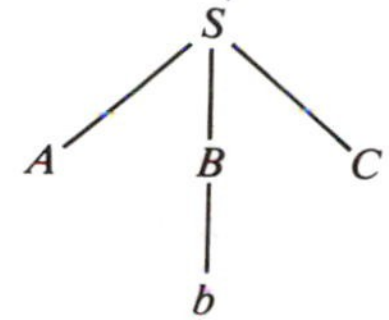

has frontier AbC. There is no rightmost or leftmost derivation that contains that string.

Definition Let $G = (V, \Sigma, P, S)$ be a context-free grammar; $\alpha \in V^*$ is a *canonical sentential form* if $S \underset{R}{\overset{*}{\Rightarrow}} \alpha$.

Not every sentential form is canonical, as the following trivial example shows. Let G be

$$S \to AA$$

$$A \to a$$

then $aA \in S(G)$ but is not canonical.

Definition A context-free grammar $G = (V, \Sigma, P, S)$ is *ambiguous* if there exists $x \in L(G)$ such that x has at least two rightmost generations from S. A grammar that is not ambiguous is said to be *unambiguous*. Alternatively, G is *unambiguous* if, for any two derivation trees T and T' (from S), $\mathbf{fr}(T) = \mathbf{fr}(T')$ implies $T = T'$.

Example Let G be $S \to SbS|a$. Then G is ambiguous, since the string $(ab)^2a$ has the two rightmost generations shown in Fig. 1.4.

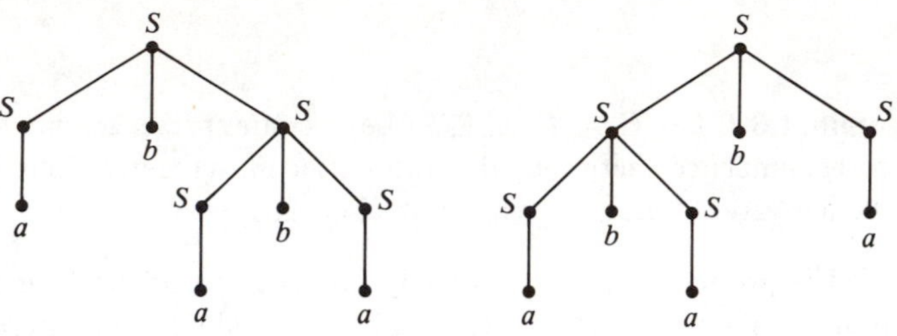

FIG. 1.4

Definition A context-free language L is *unambiguous* if there exists an unambiguous context-free grammar G such that $L = L(G)$.

It can easily be shown that the language generated by the grammar in the preceding example is

$$L(G) = \{(ab)^n a \mid n \geqslant 0\}.$$

Consider the grammar G':

$$S \to Ta$$

$$T \to abT \mid \Lambda$$

Then we have

$$S \underset{R}{\Rightarrow} Ta$$

$$T \underset{R}{\Rightarrow} abT \overset{*}{\underset{R}{\Rightarrow}} (ab)^n T \underset{R}{\Rightarrow} (ab)^n$$

$$S \overset{*}{\underset{R}{\Rightarrow}} (ab)^n a, \qquad n \geqslant 0$$

We have that $L(G) = L(G')$ and hence the language $L = \{(ab)^n a \mid n \geqslant 0\}$ is unambiguous.

This discussion raises a deep question. Can ambiguity always be disposed of by changing grammars? Assuming the worst, the following definition would be useful.

Definition A context-free language is *inherently ambiguous* if L is not unambiguous (i.e., there does not exist any unambiguous grammar G such that $L = L(G)$).

In a later chapter, it will be shown that there exist inherently ambiguous context-free languages. The following is an example.

$$L = \{a^i b^j c^k \mid i = j \quad \text{or} \quad j = k, \text{ where } i, j, k \geqslant 1\}$$

Returning to the relationship between trees and grammars we note that if $G = (V, \Sigma, P, S)$ is linear, then each rule in G is of the form

$$A \to a_1 a_2 \cdots a_i B a_{i+1} \cdots a_k \qquad B \in N, \qquad a_i \in \Sigma,$$

or

$$A \to a_1 a_2 \cdots a_k \qquad k \geqslant 0.$$

Thus trees associated with a linear grammar have a special form. At each level, at most one node may have descendants. An example of such a tree is shown in Fig. 1.5.

Example Let G be $S \to aSb \mid \Lambda$, which is a "minimal linear" grammar in that it has only one variable. Then

$$L(G) = \{a^i b^i \mid i \geqslant 0\}.$$

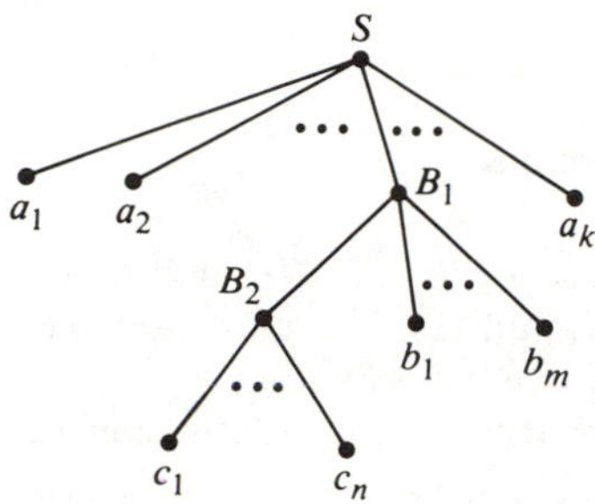

FIG. 1.5

Then a derivation tree is of the form shown in Fig. 1.6.

If the grammar is right linear, then the generation trees have an even more restricted form. At each level at most one node may have descendants, and this must be the rightmost node. Thus, Fig. 1.7 would be an example of a derivation tree for a right linear grammar.

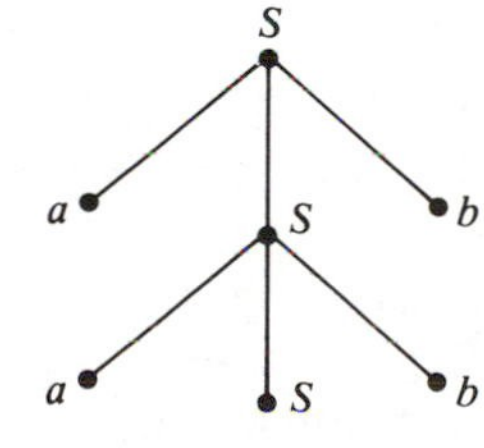

FIG. 1.6

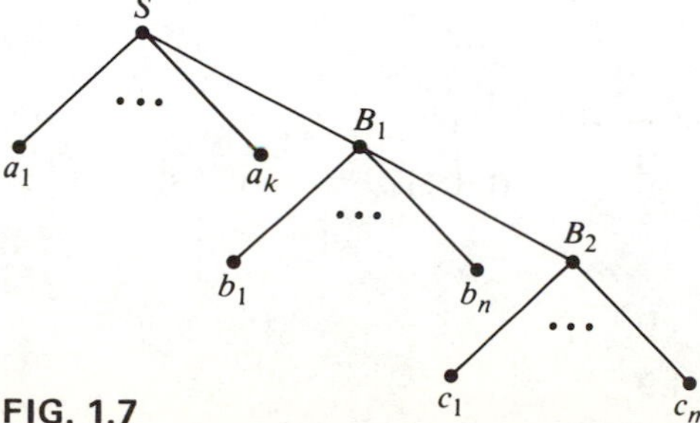

FIG. 1.7

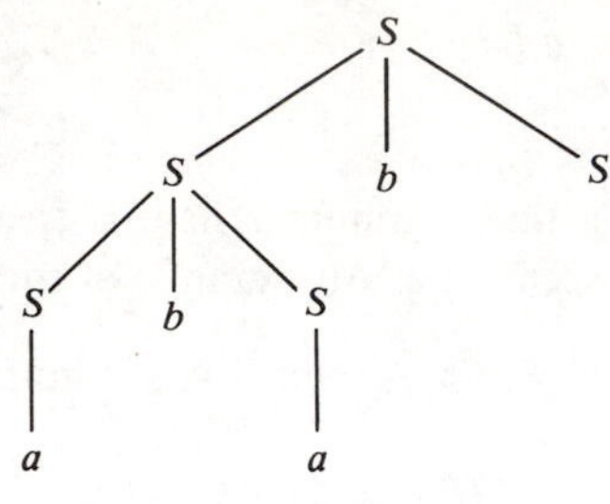

FIG. 1.8

PROBLEMS

1 Let G be the grammar

$$S \to SbS \mid a$$

and consider the tree shown in Fig. 1.8. We shall give a technique for numbering the tree. The root will be numbered (1). The successors are numbered (1, 1), (1, 2), (1, 3) in order, and the numbered tree looks like Fig. 1.9.

Using this idea, construct a formal definition of generation trees.

2 Using the definition of Problem 1, prove Theorem 1.6.1.

3 Show that the generation trees, as defined in problem 1, have the following properties:

i) there is exactly one root which no edge enters; i.e. it has in-degree 0;
ii) for each node N other than the root, there is a unique path from the root to N.

4 Show that if $G = (V, \Sigma, P, S)$ is a context-free grammar, then

$$A \overset{*}{\Rightarrow} \alpha \overset{*}{\Rightarrow} w$$

for some $\alpha \in V^*$, $w \in \Sigma^*$, if and only if there is a grammatical tree T such that the root is labeled by A, $\mathbf{fr}(T) = w$, and $\alpha = \lambda(\xi)$, for some cross section ξ in T.

5 Let T be a set. Define a "tree structure" $(T, \alpha, \lambda, x_0)$ over T by the following axioms:

i) α and λ are partial orders on T.
ii) $\alpha \cup \lambda \cup (\alpha \cup \lambda)^{-1} = T \times T$, where for any relation ρ, ρ^{-1} denotes the inverse (or converse relation); that is, $(x, y) \in \rho^{-1}$ if and only if $(y, x) \in \rho$.

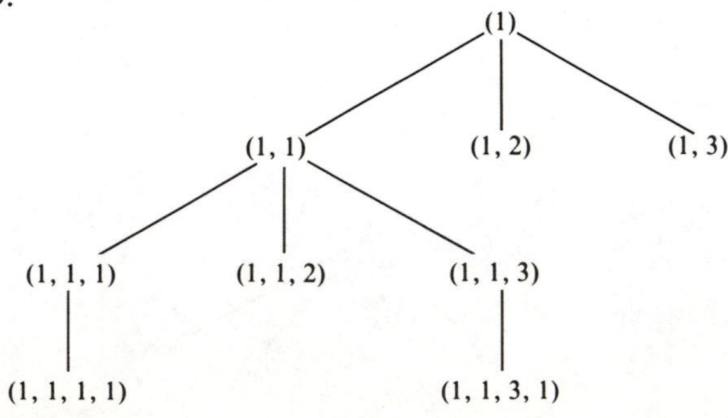

FIG. 1.9

iii) $\lambda' = \alpha^{-1}\lambda'\alpha$, where $\lambda' = \lambda - \{(x, x) \mid x \in T\}$.
iv) $x_0 \in T$, and for any $y \in T$, $x_0 \alpha y$.

Intuitively, $x\alpha y$ means that x is an "ancestor" of y while $x\lambda y$ means x is to the left of y. Do our grammatical trees satisfy these axioms? Do these axioms capture the essence of "tree structures?"

6 Let T be any tree. Define a *canonical cross section* (*of level n*, for $n \geqslant 0$) *in T* inductively as follows:

i) The sequence $\xi = (x_0)$ consisting of the root x_0 of T, is a canonical cross section (*of level* 0) in T.
ii) Let

$$\xi_0 = (x_1, \ldots, x_k, \ldots, x_m)$$

be a canonical cross section of level h, in which x_k is the rightmost node which is internal in T. Let $y_1, y_2, \ldots, y_r$ be all the immediate descendants of x_k in T and let $y_1 \sqsubset y_2 \sqsubset \cdots \sqsubset y_r$. Then the sequence

$$\xi_1 = (x_1, \ldots, x_{k-1}, y_1, \ldots, y_r, x_{k+1}, \ldots, x_m)$$

is a canonical cross section (*of level* $h+1$) in T.

a) Show that every canonical cross section is a cross section.
b) Show that no two distinct canonical cross sections in a tree can be of the same level.

7 Let T be a derivation tree of any grammar G, and let $\xi = (x_1, \ldots, x_m)$ and $\xi' = (x'_1, \ldots, x'_{m'})$ be two canonical cross sections in T, of level h and h', respectively. Define $\lambda(\xi) = \lambda(x_1) \cdots \lambda(x_m) \in V^*$, and similarly $\lambda(\xi')$. Show that $\lambda(\xi) \underset{R}{\Rightarrow} \lambda(\xi')$ if $h' = h + 1$. Also show that if T is a derivation tree with $\text{fr}(T) = S$ of G, then $\lambda(\xi)$ is a canonical sentential form in G; and that, conversely, for every canonical sentential form α, there is a grammatical tree with a canonical cross section ξ such that $\lambda(\xi) = \alpha$.

8 Prove the following useful proposition.

Proposition Let T be a derivation tree of some unambiguous grammar G and let ξ, ξ' be two canonical cross sections in T. Assume that if $\mathbf{rt}(T) = A$, then $S \overset{*}{\Rightarrow} x\,A\,y$ for some $x, y \in \Sigma^*$. Then $\lambda(\xi) = \lambda(\xi')$ implies $\xi = \xi'$.

1.7* RAMSEY'S THEOREM

Let $\Sigma = \{a, b\}$. It turns out that any string in Σ^* of length at least 4 has two consecutive identical subwords. To see that, let's try to find a counterexample x. The string x must start with a letter, say a. The second letter cannot be a for, if it were we would have $x = aa \cdots$ and that would satisfy the condition. Similarly, the next character must be an a and again the same reasoning forces the fourth letter to be b. Thus, x begins

$$abab = (ab)^2,$$

and the result is verified.

Now let us consider another more general situation. Let Σ be a nonempty set and suppose that Σ^+ is partitioned into two classes; that is, $\Sigma^+ = A \cup B$ with $A \cap B = \emptyset$. Any string of length at least 4 has two consecutive nonempty substrings, which are both in A or both in B. It clearly suffices to deal with a string of length 4. Suppose w is a string of length 4, which does not have the desired property $w = abcd$

with $a, b, c, d \in \Sigma$. Suppose $a \in A$. Then we must have $b \in B$, $c \in A$, and $d \in B$. To which set does the subword bc belong? If it belongs to A, then $\underline{a}\,\underline{bc}$ is a contradiction and if $bc \in B$ then $\underline{bc}\,\underline{d}$ is a contradiction.

We now state a very general theorem due to Ramsey, and examine special cases of it. The theorem will show that these examples are special cases of a more general situation.

Theorem 1.7.1 (*Ramsey*) Let $q_1, \ldots, q_t$, r be given positive integers such that $1 \leqslant r \leqslant q_1, \ldots, q_t$. There exists a minimal positive integer $N(q_1, \ldots, q_t, r)$ such that for all integers $n \geqslant N(q_1, \ldots, q_t, r)$, the following is true.

Let S be a set with† $|S| = n$, and suppose that $P_r(S)$, the set of all subsets of S of size r, is expressed as

$$P_r(S) = \{U \subseteq S \mid |U| = r\} = A_1 \cup \cdots \cup A_t,$$

with $A_i \cap A_j = \emptyset$ for $i \neq j$. Then there exists $F \subseteq S$ and j such that $|F| = q_j$ and

$$P_r(F) \subseteq A_j.$$

The theorem is sufficiently complex that some examples may help to clarify the result before we prove it.

Example Consider the statement when $r = 1$. The statement is:

Let $q_1, \ldots, q_t \geqslant 1$. There exists a minimum positive integer $N(q_1, \ldots, q_t, 1)$ so that, for all integers $n \geqslant N(q_1, \ldots, q_t, 1)$, the following is true: If $S = A_1 \cup \cdots \cup A_t$, $|S| = n$, $A_i \cap A_j = \emptyset$ if $i \neq j$, then S has a subset T such that $|T| = q_j$ and $T \subseteq A_j$ for some j.

This is a familiar statement in which we can rephrase the second part as follows:

If there is a set of n balls and t boxes with $n \geqslant N(q_1, \ldots, q_t, 1)$, then there is a subset of q_j balls which go into box A_j.

This form is more familiar and is known as *Dirichlet's principle* (or the "drawer" or "shoe box" principle).

Let us estimate $N(q_1, \ldots, q_t, 1)$. The largest case in which this would not be true is taken:

$$N(q_1, \ldots, q_t, 1) = (q_1 - 1) + \ldots + (q_t - 1).$$

(If $q_1 = \ldots = q_t = q$, then we could have $q - 1$ balls in each box and the principle would not be true.) Adding one more point gives the desired result, so:

$$N(q_1, \ldots, q_t, 1) = 1 + \sum_{i=1}^{t} (q_i - 1) = q_1 + \ldots + q_t - t + 1.$$

† For any set S, the *cardinality* of S, or the number of elements in S, is denoted by $|S|$.

Example Consider the theorem with $q_1 = \ldots = q_t = q \geqslant r \geqslant 1$. The statement is roughly that, if $|S| = n$, which is sufficiently large, and

$$P_r(S) = A_1 \cup \cdots \cup A_t,$$

then there exists $F \subseteq S$, $|F| = q$, and $P_r(F) \subseteq A_j$.

The statement is equivalent to Ramsey's theorem. In one direction, this is trivial. Conversely, suppose the assertion of this example to be valid. In the general case $1 \leqslant r \leqslant q_1, \ldots, q_t$, and define $q = \max\{q_i\}$. Then, by the above statement, there is a subset F with $|F| = q$ and $P_r(F) \subseteq A_j$. Take any subset $F' \subseteq F$ such that $|F'| = q_j$, and we have that $P_r(F') \subseteq P_r(F) \subseteq A_j$, and so Ramsey's theorem is satisfied.

Now we begin the proof of Ramsey's Theorem.

Proof We begin by induction on t.

Basis. $t = 1$. The result is trivial since $P_r(S) = A_1$ and we need only take $N(q_1, r) = q_1$.

Induction step. $t \geqslant 2$

We first show that it suffices to prove the result for $t = 2$. Suppose that we can prove the theorem in that case. We will now show that the result is true for $t + 1$. We can write

$$P_r(S) = A_1 \cup \ldots \cup A_{t+1} = A_1 \cup (A_2 \cup \ldots \cup A_{t+1}).$$

Let $q_2' = N(q_2, \ldots, q_{t+1}, r)$. If $n \geqslant N(q_1, q_2', r)$, then S must contain a subset F with the property that:

i) $|F| = q_1$ and $P_r(F) \subseteq A_1$, or
ii) $|F| = q_2'$ and $P_r(F) \subseteq A_2 \cup \cdots \cup A_{t+1}$.

If the first alternative holds, we are done. Otherwise, take $S' = F$ so that $|S'| = q_2' = N(q_2, \ldots, q_{t+1}, r)$ and $P_r(S') = A_2' \cup \ldots \cup A_{t+1}'$ where $A_j' = A_j \cap P_r(S')$ for $2 \leqslant j \leqslant t + 1$. By the induction hypothesis, there is a subset $G \subseteq S'$ so that $|G| = q_i$ and $P_r(G) \subseteq A_i' \subseteq A_i$ for some i. This completes the proof of sufficiency.

Next, we return to a proof of the result for $t = 2$. It has already been established in an example that:

$$N(q_1, q_2, 1) = q_1 + q_2 - 1.$$

Claim $N(q_1, r, r) = q_1$ and $N(r, q_2, r) = q_2$.

Proof The second result follows from the first by symmetry. To see the first result, let $q_2 = r$ and $n \geqslant q_1$. If $A_2 \neq \emptyset$, then let $\{a_1, \ldots, a_r\}$ be an r-combination of A_2. Then $F = \{a_1, \ldots, a_r\}$ is a subset of S (since $|S| = n \geqslant q_1 \geqslant r$) such that $P_r(F) \subseteq A_2$. If $A_2 = \emptyset$, then $P_r(S) = A_1$; and if S is any set with $|S| = n \geqslant q_1$, then any subset F of q_1 elements has $P_r(F) \subseteq A_1$. This completes the proof of the claim.

The main argument with $t = 2$ is completed by induction. Assume that we have $1 < r < q_1, q_2$. The induction hypothesis asserts that there exists integers $N(q_1 - 1, q_2, r)$, $N(q_1, q_2 - 1, r)$, and $N(q_1', q_2', r-1)$ for all q_1', q_2' which satisfy $1 \leqslant r-1 \leqslant q_1', q_2'$. We shall show the existence of $N(q_1, q_2, r)$. This is valid because we can fill out the following array for each r; for example, for $r = 2$, we have:

$$\begin{array}{lll} N(2,2,2) & N(2,3,2) & \cdots \\ N(3,2,2) & N(3,3,2) & \cdots \\ N(4,2,2) & N(4,3,2) & \cdots \\ \vdots & \vdots & \end{array}$$

This will imply the existence of $N(q_1, q_2, 3)$, etc.

Assume the existence of $p_1 = N(q_1 - 1, q_2, r)$, $p_2 = N(q_1, q_2 - 1, r)$, and $N(p_1, p_2, r-1)$, and we shall prove the existence of $N(q_1, q_2, r)$. Moreover, it will be shown that

$$N(q_1, q_2, r) \leqslant N(p_1, p_2, r-1) + 1. \tag{1.7.1}$$

Suppose $n \geqslant N(p_1, p_2, r-1) + 1$. Let S be a set with $a \in S$ and $|S| = n$. Define $T = S - \{a\}$. Then

$$P_r(S) = A_1 \cup A_2,$$

with $A_1 \cap A_2 = \emptyset$. Define

$$P_{r-1}(T) = B_1 \cup B_2, \tag{1.7.2}$$

where $B_i = \{U \in P_{r-1}(T) | U \cup \{a\} \in A_i\}$ for $i = 1, 2$.

Clearly, $|T| \geqslant N(p_1, p_2, r-1)$, since $T = S - \{a\}$. By the induction hypothesis, there exists a set F so that

i) $|F| = p_1$ and $p_{r-1}(F) \subseteq B_1$, or
ii) $|F| = p_2$ and $p_{r-1}(F) \subseteq B_2$.

We assume the first case. (Case (ii) is analogous.) Since $p_1 = N(q_1 - 1, q_2, r)$, F contains a subset G so that:

iii) $|G| = q_1 - 1$ with $P_r(G) \subseteq A_1$, or
iv) $|G| = q_2$ with $P_r(G) \subseteq A_2$,

by the induction hypothesis.

If (iv) holds, then the induction is completed, so we assume that (iii) holds. Then $H = G \cup \{a\}$ has the property that $|H| = q_1$; and now we consider the r-combinations of H. If an r-combination of H does not contain a, then it is an r-combination of F and, by (iii), it is in A_1. If an r-combination of H contains a, then it consists of a and an $(r-1)$-combination of G. But G has all its $r-1$ subsets in B_1. By the definition of the B-decomposition, our r-combination is in A_1. Thus, H is a subset of cardinality q_1 and $P_r(H) \subseteq A_1$. Thus the induction is extended and the theorem is proven. □

There is an interesting application of Ramsey's theorem to graph theory. In the vernacular, the following result asserts that, at a sufficiently large party, there exist m individuals who are all strangers to each other, or a clique of m people all of whom know each other.

Theorem 1.7.2 For any m there exists $N(m)$ so that, if $n \geqslant N(m)$, any graph with n vertices either contains a set of m isolated vertices or contains the complete subgraph on m points.

Proof Let $N(m) = N(m, m, 2)$ with $P_2(S) = A_1 \cup A_2$, where A_2 is the set of edges and $A_1 = P_2(S) - A_2$. □

Another important application of Ramsey's theorem concerns repeated patterns in strings.

Theorem 1.7.3 Let $\Sigma^+ = A_1 \cup A_2 \cup \ldots \cup A_t$, $A_i \cap A_j = \emptyset$, if $i \neq j$. For each natural number n, there exists a minimum positive integer $N_t(n)$ such that each word w, where $\lg(w) \geqslant N_t(n)$, is in $\Sigma^* A_j^n \Sigma^*$ for some j with $1 \leqslant j \leqslant t$.

Proof Let $N_t(n) = N(\overbrace{n, \ldots, n}^{t}, 2)$ and let $w = a_1 \ldots a_m$, $a_i \in \Sigma$, $m \geqslant N_t(n)$. Let $S = \{0, 1, 2, \ldots, m\}$. For each pair (i, j), with $i, j \in S$ and $i < j$, associate a unique word $w_{i,j} = a_{i+1} \cdots a_j$. Thus there is a partition on $P_2(S)$ induced by the A_i. By Ramsey's theorem, there is a set $F = \{p_0, \ldots, p_n\} \subseteq S$ with $p_i < p_{i+1}$ such that

$$\{w_{p_i p_j} \mid p_i < p_j; \quad i, j \in F\} \subseteq A_\ell.$$

Thus the consecutive subwords of w (the words are consecutive since $i, j \in F$)

$$w_{p_0, p_1}, w_{p_1, p_2}, \ldots, w_{p_{n-1}, p_n}$$

are all in A_ℓ, and so $w \in \Sigma^* A_\ell^n \Sigma^*$. □

Now we can estimate the number $N_t(n)$. We begin by an example.

Example 1 $N_2(2) \leqslant 4$. This is the example which was given before.

Example 2 Suppose $N_2(2) = 3$. Then take $\Sigma = \{0, 1\}$, $A_1 = \{0\}$, $A_2 = \Sigma^+ - \{0\}$. The string $w = 010$ fails to be in one of the desired sets, since its factorizations are

$$\underbrace{\overbrace{0 \quad 1}^{A_2}}_{} \quad \quad \overbrace{1 \quad 0}^{A_2}$$

$$\begin{array}{ccc} 0 & 1 & 0 \\ A_1 & A_2 & A_1 \end{array}$$

One can study this case in more detail and show that $N_t(n) = n^t$.

PROBLEMS

1 Prove the following geometric proposition:

Suppose there are five points in the plane and no three of them are collinear. Then four of the points are the vertices of a convex quadrilateral.

2 Prove the following fact:

Let $m \geqslant 4$. If m points in the plane have no three points collinear, and if all the quadrilaterals formed from the m points are convex, then the m points are the vertices of a convex m-gon.

3 Using Problems 1 and 2, prove the following theorem:

Let $m \geqslant 4$. There exists a minimal positive integer N_m so that the following is true for all $n \geqslant N_m$: If n points in the plane have no three points collinear, then m of the points are the vertices of a convex m-gon.

*4 Ramsey's Theorem becomes easier to prove in the infinite case. Prove the following form of the result:

Let $t, r \geqslant 1$. Let S be an infinite set and suppose that

$$P_r(S) = A_1 \cup \ldots \cup A_t$$

with $A_i \cup A_j = \emptyset$ if $i \neq j$. Then there is an infinite set $F \subseteq S$ so that $P_r(F) \subseteq A_i$ for some i.

1.8* NONREPETITIVE WORDS

For the moment, let Σ be a binary alphabet. Any string of length at least 4 must have two identical subwords, as we argued in the last section. It turns out that over a three-letter alphabet, one can construct strings of infinite length such that no two consecutive subwords are identical. Such a string will now be constructed. There are many applications of these sequences, particularly in mathematical games.

The construction is made in the following way: Define

$$\xi_0 = a$$

and

$$\xi_{i+1} = \phi(\xi_i)$$

for each $i \geqslant 0$, where ϕ is the homomorphism:

$$\begin{aligned} \phi a &= abcab &&= \alpha, \\ \phi b &= acabcb &&= \beta, \\ \phi c &= acbcacb &&= \gamma. \end{aligned}$$

The desired string is the limit of the ξ_i's. For instance,

$$\begin{aligned} \xi_0 &= a \\ \xi_1 &= abcab \\ \xi_2 &= abcabacabcbacbcacbabcabacabcb \end{aligned}$$

etc.

The argument proceeds by examining these words closely.

Proposition 1.8.1

a) Each of α, β, and γ (which will be called *blocks*) begins with an a and is a product of two words, each beginning with an a (which will be called *half-blocks*).

b) All blocks and half-blocks are distinct.

c) For each x in $\{\alpha, \beta, \gamma\}^*$, if $x = w_1 auaw_2$, where the number of a's in u is 0 (written $\#_a(u) = 0$), then $\lg(u) \leqslant 3$.

d) For any x in $\{\alpha, \beta, \gamma\}^*$, if $x = w_1 auaw_2$ and $\#_a(u) = 0$, then u uniquely determines the block to which the first a belongs and whether it is the first or second a in that block.

Proof Only (d) requires explanation. In view of (c), the only cases that may arise are those shown in Table 1.3.

TABLE 1.3

aua	*First a belongs to:*	*First or second a?*
$\ldots aba \ldots$	α	Second
$\ldots aca \ldots$	β	First
$\ldots abca \ldots$	α	First
$\ldots acba \ldots$	γ	Second
$\ldots abcba \ldots$	β	Second
$\ldots acbca \ldots$	γ	First

□

Now we prove a key lemma.

Lemma 1.8.1 If η is a nonrepetitive sequence and $\theta = \phi(\eta)$, then θ is a nonrepetitive sequence.

Proof Suppose θ has a repetition; that is,

$$\theta = \phi(\eta) = w_1 t_1 t_2 w_2$$

where $t_1 = t_2$. It will be shown that η has a repetition.

CASE 1. Suppose $\#_a(t_1) \geqslant 2$. Let X be the block to which the first a belongs. One possible picture is shown in Fig. 1.10. More generally, X need not be contained in t_1.

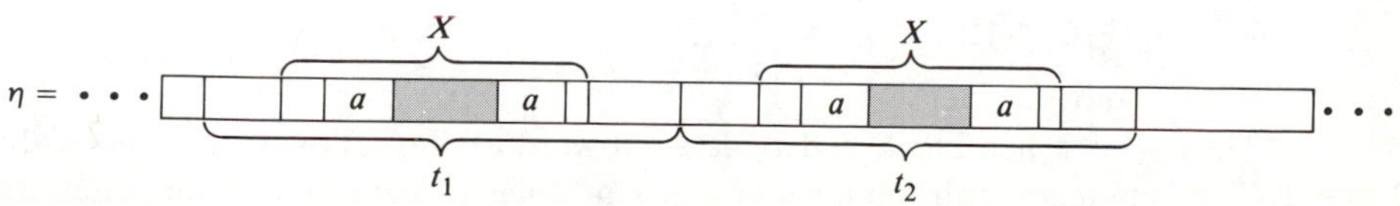

FIG. 1.10

The block X and its position in t_1 (respectively, t_2) is determined by the string between the first two a's in t_1. (This is cross-hatched in Fig. 1.10.)

If the two blocks were together, then we would have

$$t_1 = t_2 = X \qquad \text{and} \qquad \theta = w_1XXw_2$$

which implies

$$\eta = w'_1ddw'_2$$

where $\phi(d) = X$ and $\varphi(w'_i) = w_i$ for $i = 1, 2$. That would finish the proof.

	X	$y_1 \cdots y_n$	X	$y_1 \cdots y_n \cdots$
	t_1		t_2	

FIG. 1.11

Now suppose the X-blocks are not adjacent. Then the picture is shown in Fig. 1.11, where $Y_1, \ldots, Y_n$ are the blocks between the X-blocks. Note that Y_n may overlap t_2 but all the a's in $Y_1 \cdots Y_n$ are in t_1 because we singled out the first a in t_1 and $t_1 = t_2$. These blocks are uniquely determined by the part of t_1 to the right of X. Compare Figs. 1.8 and 1.9. The corresponding part of t_2 determines the same sequence of blocks and

$$\eta = w'_1dy_1 \cdots y_ndy_1 \cdots y_nw'_2$$

where $\phi(w'_i) = w_i$, $\phi d = X$, $\phi y_j = Y_j$ for $i = 1, 2; j = 1, \ldots, n$.

CASE 2. $\#_a(t_1) = 1$. Thus

$$\#_a(t_2) = \#_a(t_1) = 1.$$

Thus the two a's are consecutive in $\theta = \phi(\eta)$. Since the second a in each block is preceded by c and since each block ends in b, the only way we can have consecutive a's in θ is to have them following different letters in θ. The only way that this is compatible with membership in t_1 and t_2 is for t_1 and t_2 to begin with a, as is shown in Fig. 1.12.

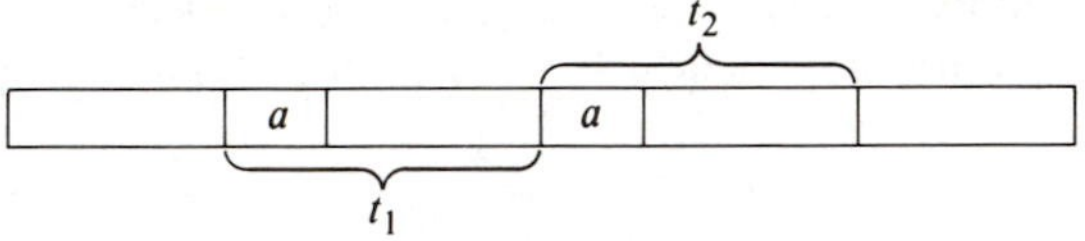

FIG. 1.12

Thus t_1 is a half-block and t_2 is a subword of the following half-block. In Table 1.4, we enumerate all the possible cases in order to determine which ones are actually feasible.

Inspection of the table shows only two possibilities. Either:

1 t_1 is the second half-block of α and t_2 is a subword of the first half-block of α; or

2 t_1 is the second half-block of γ and t_2 is a subword of the first half-block of γ.

In the event that (1) holds, η contains *aa*; and if (2) holds, η contains *cc*.

TABLE 1.4 Feasible matches between t_1 and $t_2 w_2''$

t_1	$t_2 w_2''$	*Feasible?*
abc	*ab*	No
ab	*abc*	Yes
ab	*ac*	No
ab	*acbc*	No
ac	*abcb*	No
abcb	*abc*	No
abcb	*ac*	No
abcb	*acbc*	No
acbc	*acb*	No
acb	*abc*	No
acb	*ac*	No
acb	*acbc*	Yes

CASE 3. $\#_a(t_1) = 0$. Then $\#_a(t_2) = 0$ also. Since there are at most three letters of the sequence between any two consecutive a's, the only possibility is that

$$\lg(t_1) = \lg(t_2) = 1,$$

but this is impossible, because no two consecutive letters are equal. □

With the aid of this lemma, the main theorem follows easily.

Theorem 1.8.1 Let $\Sigma = \{a, b, c\}$. There is a "doubly-infinite"-length string over Σ which is nonrepetitive; i.e., has no two consecutive identical subwords.

Proof Define the sequence

$$\xi_0 = a,$$

$$\xi_{i+1} = \phi(\xi_i).$$

Then

$$\xi_1 = \phi a = \alpha = abcab$$

$\xi_1 = \alpha$ contains $a = \xi_0$ as a strictly proper subword [i.e., the first and last letters of ξ_1 are not in ξ_0]. Repeating ξ_2 has ξ_1 as such a subword and, in general, ξ_n contains ξ_{n-1} as a strictly proper subword. There is a unique infinite-length Σ-sequence $\xi = \lim_{n\to\infty} \xi_n$ such that each prefix of ξ of length $\lg(\xi_k)$ is ξ_k. ξ does not contain any repetition of any subword because $\xi_0 = a$ does not and by the Lemma. □

PROBLEMS

***1** Generalize the result of this section to show that there exist sequences of unbounded length over an alphabet of five letters, which are *strongly nonrepetitive*; i.e., such that there are not two consecutive words t_1 and t_2 such that t_2 is obtained by t_1 by a permutation of the letters. [*Hint.* Let $\Sigma = \{a, b, c, d, e\}$ and let σ be the cycle $(a\ b\ c\ d\ e)$. Define a homomorphism ϕ by:

$$\begin{aligned} \phi a &= bacaeacadaeadab = \alpha, \\ \phi b &= \sigma(\alpha), \\ \phi c &= \sigma^2(\alpha), \\ \phi d &= \sigma^3(\alpha), \\ \phi e &= \sigma^4(\alpha), \end{aligned}$$

Now define

$$\begin{aligned} \xi_0 &= a \\ \xi_{i+1} &= \phi(\xi_i), \end{aligned}$$

to obtain the desired result.] Can you take the limit of the ξ_i to obtain an infinite sequence?

2 Taking the sequences constructed in Problem 1, show that asymptotically each symbol occurs with density $\frac{1}{5}$.

3 Show that if $k \leqslant 3$, any string over an alphabet of k symbols of length greater than $2^k - 1$ has two consecutive subwords, one of which is a permutation of the other.

4 (*Open problem*). Do there exist infinite sequences over a four-letter alphabet which are strongly nonrepetitive?

5 Let S be a semigroup. An element $0 \in S$ is a *zero* for S if $s0 = 0s = 0$ for each $s \in S$. S is *nilpotent* if there exists an integer k such that $S^k = \{0\}$. Construct a semigroup S which is nonnilpotent, has three generators, and the square of each element in S is 0.

1.9* THE LAGRANGE INVERSION FORMULA AND ITS APPLICATION

There is an old inversion formula due to Lagrange which is occasionally useful in language theory. We sketch a derivation of the formula and omit all considerations of convergence, as is customary in the combinatorial applications of generating functions and power series.

Suppose that

$$x = yf(x), \tag{1.9.1}$$

and that $f(x)$ can be expanded as a power series in x:

$$f(x) = \sum_{i=0}^{\infty} f_i x^i, \tag{1.9.2}$$

where $f_0 \neq 0$. We wish to solve not just for x as a power series in y, but for some function $g(x)$. That is, one seeks $a_0, a_1, \ldots,$ such that:

$$g(x) = \sum_{i=0}^{\infty} a_i y^i. \tag{1.9.3}$$

Since (1.9.3) implies that $x = 0$ if $y = 0$, then $a_0 = g(0)$. Moreover,

$$y = x(f(x))^{-1} = \sum_{i=1}^{\infty} b_i x^i. \tag{1.9.4}$$

If Eq. (1.9.3) is differentiated, we get

$$g'(x) = \sum_{i=1}^{\infty} i a_i y^{i-1} \frac{dy}{dx}. \tag{1.9.5}$$

Multiplying (1.9.5) by $(f(x))^n$ yields:

$$g'(x)(f(x))^n = \sum_{i=1}^{\infty} i a_i y^{i-1} (f(x))^n \frac{dy}{dx}. \tag{1.9.6}$$

By using (1.9.1), we get:

$$g'(x)(f(x))^n = \sum_{i=1}^{\infty} i a_i y^{i-n-1} x^n \frac{dy}{dx}. \tag{1.9.7}$$

Let us now evaluate

$$\frac{d^{n-1}}{dx^{n-1}} (f(x))^n g'(x)\Big|_{x=0}$$

by using Eq. (1.9.7). Clearly, the result is:

$$(n-1)!\,[\text{Coefficient of } x^{n-1} \text{ in } (1.9.7)]. \tag{1.9.8}$$

This gives rise to two cases.

CASE 1. $i = n$. The general term of (1.9.7) becomes:

$$i a_i y^{i-n-1} x^n \frac{dy}{dx} = n a_n x^n \frac{1}{y} \frac{dy}{dx}, \tag{1.9.9}$$

$$= n a_n x^n \frac{\sum_{i=1}^{\infty} i b_i x^{i-1}}{\sum_{i=1}^{\infty} b_i x^i} \qquad \text{(By using (1.9.4))} \tag{1.9.10}$$

$$= n a_n x^{n-1}(1 + c_1 x + c_2 x^2 + \ldots).$$

Therefore the coefficient of x^{n-1} is:

$$n a_n. \tag{1.9.11}$$

CASE 2. $i \neq n$. The general term is

$$i a_i x^n y^{i-n-1} \frac{dy}{dx} = i a_i x^n \frac{1}{i-n} \frac{d}{dx} [y^{i-n}]. \tag{1.9.12}$$

Note that there does not exist any power of x (even negative ones) which has a derivative $1/x$; consequently $(d/dx)\ [y^{i-n}]$ does not contain x^{-1} and Case 2 contributes no terms in x^{n-1}.

Thus

$$\sum_{i=1}^{\infty} ia_i x^n y^{i-n-1} \frac{dy}{dx} = \ldots + na_n x^{n-1} + \ldots, \tag{1.9.13}$$

and therefore

$$\frac{d^{n-1}}{dx^{n-1}} [g'(x)(f(x))^n] \bigg|_{x=0} = (n-1)!na_n = n!a_n.$$

The expression for a_n is:

$$a_n = \frac{1}{n!} \frac{d^{n-1}}{dx^{n-1}} (g'(x)(f(x))^n) \bigg|_{x=0} \tag{1.9.14}$$

if $n \geqslant 1$ and

$$a_0 = g(0). \tag{1.9.15}$$

Summarizing the above discussion, we have proved a famous theorem of Lagrange. Actually we shall state a slightly stronger theorem than we proved, and leave the generalization to the reader. Instead of forcing our original relation to be homogeneous, we shall allow a constant term. The changes to the statement and theorem are minor.

Theorem 1.9.1 Let

$$x = c + yf(x). \tag{1.9.16}$$

Then

$$g(x) = g(c) + \sum_{n=1}^{\infty} \frac{y^n}{n!} \left[\frac{d^{n-1}}{dx^{n-1}} g'(x)(f(x))^n \right]_{x=c}. \tag{1.9.17}$$

First, we give a purely mathematical example of the use of Lagrange's Theorem.

Example Let

$$x = ye^x. \tag{1.9.18}$$

Then $(f(x))^n = e^{nx}$ and take $g(x) = x$. Computing, we get:

$$\frac{d^{n-1}}{dx^{n-1}} e^{nx} = n^{n-1} e^{nx}$$

so that

$$a_0 = 0,$$

$$a_n = n^{n-1}$$

and

$$x = \sum_{n=1}^{\infty} \frac{n^{n-1}}{n!} y^n. \tag{1.9.19}$$

One may check that (1.9.19) is a solution of x in terms of y by substituting in (1.9.18)

Now let us consider an example from language theory. Consider the grammar G:

$$S \to SbS \mid a$$

The language $L(G) = \{(ab)^n a \mid n \geqslant 0\}$ is ambiguously generated by G. We seek the number of derivations of $(ab)^n a$. Let us rewrite the grammar as an equation:

$$S = a + SbS. \tag{1.9.20}$$

One may now derive the power-series solution of (1.9.20) iteratively but we need not do so here. If we map Eq. (1.9.20) into the ring of polynomials in the natural way (actually mapping from the noncommutative case into the commutative one), we get a mapping:

$$S \mapsto x,$$

$$b \mapsto y,$$

$$a \mapsto 1.$$

Thus (1.9.20) becomes:

$$x = yx^2 + 1. \tag{1.9.21}$$

Thus $f(x) = x^2$. For $g(x)$, we choose:

$$g(x) = x.$$

Now we evaluate

$$\frac{d^{n-1}}{dx^{n-1}}(x^{2n}) = (2n)(2n-1)\cdots(n+2)x^{n+1}$$

and

$$a_n = \frac{(2n)\cdots(n+2)}{n!}\frac{(n+1)!}{(n+1)!} = \frac{2n!}{(n+1)(n!)^2} = \frac{\binom{2n}{n}}{(n+1)}.$$

Therefore

$$x = 1 + \sum_{n=1}^{\infty}\left(\frac{\binom{2n}{n}}{n+1}\right)y^n$$

$$= \sum_{n=0}^{\infty}\left(\frac{\binom{2n}{n}}{n+1}\right)y^n.$$

This tells us that there are $\binom{2n}{n}/(n+1)$ derivation trees of $(ab)^n a$. One could also derive the result from the grammar by generating function techniques, but the present approach is easier and more general.

PROBLEMS

1 Carry out the nonhomogeneous proof of Theorem 1.9.1.

2 Was it necessary to use the nonhomogeneous form of Lagrange's theorem in working the last example of the section?

3 Let $1 - x + yx^{\beta} = 0$. Use Lagrange's theorem to solve for x^{α} as a function of y. By judicious choices of α and β, a number of classical identities involving binomial coefficients may be derived.

4 Consider the grammar

$$S \to aSa \mid bSb \mid aa \mid bb \mid \Lambda$$

Show directly that the number of strings of length i in this grammar is given by δ_i, where

$$\delta_i = \begin{cases} 0 & \text{if } i \text{ is odd,} \\ 2^j & \text{if } i = 2j. \end{cases}$$

5 Suppose we have a triangle ABC. By placing a new point in the interior and joining this point to each of the vertices A, B, and C, we can decompose the triangle into three elementary triangles. This construction may be iterated with some other triangle. The diagrams in Fig. 1.13 show the "triangulations of a triangle" with 1, 3, and 5 elementary triangles. Find the number of triangulations of a triangle into n elementary triangles. [*Hint*. Construct a map from triangulations to parenthesized strings. Construct an appropriate grammar which generates these strings such that the degree of ambiguity is the desired number.]

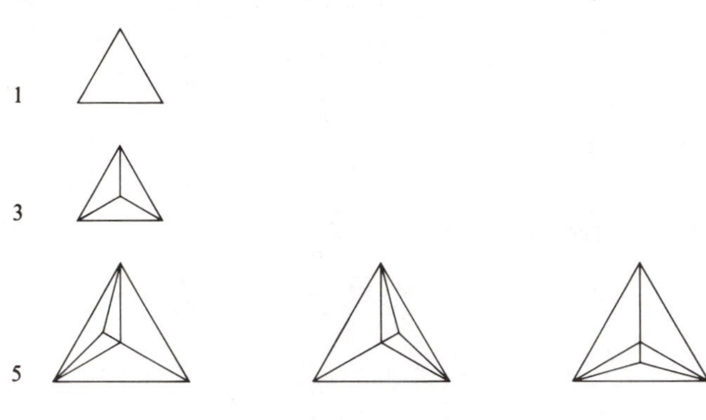

FIG. 1.13

1.10 HISTORICAL SURVEY

The origins of formal language theory may be found in the work of Chomsky [1959a, 1963, 1964, 1965]. A number of important early contributions are due to Bar-Hillel and his colleagues, and may be found in Bar-Hillel [1964]. There are a number of other general books on this subject. Aho and Ullman [Vol. I, 1972] cover many of the basic facets of the theory in a book oriented toward theories of translating and compiling. Book and Greibach [1973] present the basic theory in a style oriented towards a general abstract study. Ginsburg [1966] is a text that emphasizes the mathematical aspects of the context-free case. Hopcroft and Ullman [1969] give a very general coverage, as well as a number of related topics. The book by Salomaa [1973] covers a wide variety of topics concerning formal languages, also.

Theorem 1.2.1 is from Levi [1944]. Much of the material from Section 1.3 may be found in Lentin [1972] and Schützenberger [1967]. In particular, Theorem 1.3.3 is from Fine and Wilf [1965]. Theorem 1.7.1 is from Ramsey [1930]. The proof given follows Ryser [1963] and Erdös and Szerkeres [1935]. The latter reference contains the geometric results given in the problems. Theorem 1.8.1 is from Pleasants [1970]. Our proof of the Lagrange inversion formula follows Stanton [1961].

Applications of simple language theory to compiling may be found in the textbooks by Gries [1971] and Aho and Ullman [1977].

two

Finite Automata and Linear Grammars

2.1 INTRODUCTION

In this chapter, regular events, or the sets accepted by finite automata, are discussed. In particular they are characterized by a class of context-free grammars as well. This fills in one of the pieces of the Chomsky Hierarchy. A number of simple but useful results are obtained both in the text and in the exercises.

It has been assumed that the reader has had some familiarity with elementary automata theory and so the coverage in this chapter is quite concise. Readers who experience difficulty are advised to consult some of the general references given in Section 2.7.

2.2 ELEMENTARY FINITE AUTOMATA THEORY – ULTIMATELY PERIODIC SETS

The techniques and results of finite automata theory are necessary for our development. The subject is treated very concisely here and the reader is referred to the literature for a more leisurely discussion.

Definition A *finite automaton* is a 5-tuple $A = (Q, \Sigma, \delta, q_0, F)$, where:

i) Q is a finite nonempty set of *states*.
ii) Σ is a finite nonempty set of *inputs*.
iii) δ is a function from $Q \times \Sigma$ into Q called the *direct transition function*.
iv) $q_0 \in Q$ is the *initial state*.
v) $F \subseteq Q$ is the set of *final states*.

Next, it is necessary to extend δ to allow A to accept sequences of inputs.

Definition Let $A = (Q, \Sigma, \delta, q_0, F)$ be a finite automaton. For each $(q, a, x) \in Q \times \Sigma \times \Sigma^*$, define

$$\delta(q, \Lambda) = q \qquad \text{and} \qquad \delta(q, ax) = \delta(\delta(q, a), x).$$

Note the following simple identities:

For each $q \in Q; x, y, z \in \Sigma^*$,

$$\delta(q, xy) = \delta(\delta(q, x), y); \tag{2.2.1}$$

$$\delta(q, x) = \delta(q, y) \quad \text{implies} \quad \delta(q, xz) = \delta(q, yz). \tag{2.2.2}$$

The notation $rp(y) = \delta(q_0, y)$, the "response" to y, is sometimes used, and denotes the state A reaches after reading y.

Finally, A *accepts* a string $x \in \Sigma^*$ if A, starting in q_0 at the left end of x, goes through some computation and reads all of x, and stops in some final state. The set of all accepted strings is denoted as $T(A)$. More compactly,

$$T(A) = \{x \in \Sigma^* \mid \delta(q_0, x) \in F\}.$$

Definition A set $L \subseteq \Sigma^*$ is called *regular* if there is some finite automaton A such that $L = T(A)$.

Example Let $L = \{a^i b^j \mid i \geqslant 0, j \geqslant 0\} = a^* b^*$. We shall show that L is regular by constructing a finite automaton A which accepts x. To avoid excessive formalism, we draw the "state diagram" of A as in Fig. 2.1. The initial state is q_0 and the set of final states is $F = \{q_0, q_1\}$.

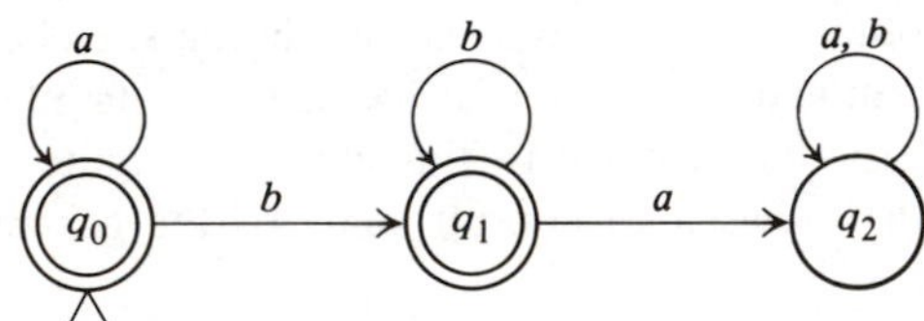

FIG. 2.1

In our discussions of families of languages, we want to show that certain sets are not definable. For this reason, we need to find a set that is not regular.

Theorem 2.2.1 The set $L = \{a^i b^i \mid i \geqslant 0\}$ is not regular.

Proof Suppose $L = \{a^i b^i \mid i \geqslant 0\}$ is regular. Then there exists a finite automaton $A = (Q, \Sigma, \delta, q_0, F)$ so that $L = T(A)$. Consider the set $\{\delta(q_0, a^i) \mid i \geqslant 0\}$. There are infinitely many tapes a^i, $i \geqslant 0$, and only finitely many states in Q. Therefore, there exist i, j, with $i > j$, so that

$$\delta(q_0, a^i) = \delta(q_0, a^j).$$

By setting $z = b^i$ in Eq. (2.2.2), we have:

$$\delta(q_0, a^i b^i) = \delta(q_0, a^j b^i).$$

If $\delta(q_0, a^i b^i) = q$ is in F, then $a^j b^i$ is in $T(A)$, which is a contradiction since $i > j$. If $q \notin F$, then $a^i b^i \notin T(A)$, which is again a contradiction. Therefore, L cannot be regular. □

We shall now establish a necessary condition on strings in a regular set. This theorem and its generalization for more powerful classes of sets is an important tool in proving that certain sets do *not* belong to the family in question.

Theorem 2.2.2 (*Iteration theorem for regular sets*) Let $A = (Q, \Sigma, \delta, q_0, F)$ be a finite automaton with n states. Let $w \in T(A)$ and $\lg(w) \geqslant m$. If $m \geqslant n$, then there exist x, y, z, such that $w = xyz, y \neq \Lambda$, and $xy^k z \in T(A)$ for each $k \geqslant 0$.

Proof Let $w = a_1 \cdots a_m$. Consider the set $\tilde{Q} = \{rp(a_1 \cdots a_i) \mid 0 \leqslant i \leqslant m\}$. We have $|\tilde{Q}| = m + 1 > n = |Q|$. Then there must be p, r, such that $0 \leqslant p < r \leqslant n$ so that $q_p = q_r$ where $q_i = rp(a_1 \cdots a_i)$ for $i \geqslant 0$. Take $x = a_1 \cdots a_p$, $y = a_{p+1} \cdots a_r$, $z = a_{r+1} \cdots a_m$. Note that $\lg(y) = r - p > 0$. Thus $w = xyz \in T(A)$. Also, $rp(x) = rp(xy)$.

We claim that

$$rp(x) = rp(xy^k) \qquad \text{for each } k \geqslant 0.$$

Proof of claim by induction on k $k = 0$ is trivial. Then,

$$rp(xy^{k+1}) = \delta(rp(xy^k), y).$$

By the induction hypothesis,

$$rp(xy^{k+1}) = \delta(rp(x), y) = rp(xy) = rp(x)$$

and the claim is verified. Therefore

$$\begin{aligned} rp(w) &= rp(xyz) = \delta(rp(xy), z) \\ &= \delta(rp(xy^k), z) = rp(xy^k z). \end{aligned}$$

Thus, if $w \in T(A)$, then $xy^k z \in T(A)$ for each $k \geqslant 0$. □

Next we turn to the question of dealing with regular sets over the one-letter alphabet.

Definition 1 A set X of natural numbers is said to be *ultimately periodic* if X is finite or if there exist two integers $N_0 \geqslant 0, p \geqslant 1$, so that if $x \geqslant N_0$, then $x \in X$ if and only if $x + p \in X$.

Example The sets X_1 and X_2 are clearly ultimately periodic:

$$X_1 = \{10, 12, 14, 16, 18, \ldots\}, \qquad N_{01} = 10, \qquad p_1 = 2;$$

$$X_2 = \{5, 8, 11, 14, 17, \ldots\}, \qquad N_{02} = 5, \qquad p_2 = 3.$$

Also $X_3 = X_1 \cup X_2$ is ultimately periodic. Find N_{03} and p_3.

It is useful to establish a canonical form for ultimately periodic sets.

Theorem 2.2.3 Let X be an ultimately periodic set with N_0 and p as in the above definition. Let

$$A = X \cap \{i \mid 0 \leqslant i < N_0\}$$

and

$$B = \bigcup_{j=1}^{s} \{g(j) + pi \mid i \geqslant 0\},$$

where

$$\begin{aligned} G &= \{g(1), \ldots, g(s)\} \\ &= X \cap \{i \mid N_0 \leqslant i < N_0 + p\}. \end{aligned}$$

Then $X = A \cup B$.

Proof First we show the following proposition.

Claim 1 $B = \bigcup_{j=1}^{s} \{g(j) + pi \mid i \geqslant 0\} = \{x \in X \mid x \geqslant N_0\} = X_{N_0}$.

Proof that $B \subseteq X_{N_0}$ Note that for any j, $g(j) \in X$ and $N_0 \leqslant g(j) < N_0 + p$. Then $g(j) \in X_{N_0}$ and $g(j) + p \in X_{N_0}$.

Claim 2 If $y \in X$ and $y \geqslant N_0$, then $y + ip \in X$ for all i, $i \geqslant 0$.

Proof of Claim 2 The argument is a trivial induction on i.

Returning to the proof of Claim 1, note that $g(j) + ip \in X_{N_0}$ and the first part of that proof is complete, because we have now shown that $B \subseteq X_{N_0}$.

Conversely, suppose that $x \in X_{N_0}$. Then $x \in X$ and $x \geqslant N_0$. Consider

$$\{x \mid x \geqslant N_0\} = \bigcup_{i=0}^{\infty} Y_i,$$

where

$$Y_i = \{y \mid N_0 + ip \leqslant y < N_0 + (i+1)p\}.$$

This can always be done as we are dividing an interval into a countable number of subintervals which do not overlap.

Claim 3 If $x \in X_{N_0} \cap Y_i$, then $x = g(j) + ip$ for some j, $1 \leqslant j \leqslant s$. Moreover, $x \in B$.

Proof of Claim 3 The argument is an induction on i.

Basis. $i = 0$. $x \in X_{N_0}$ and $N_0 \leqslant x < N_0 + p$. Thus, $x = g(j)$ for some j, $1 \leqslant j \leqslant s$. Therefore $x = g(j) + 0 \cdot p$ and the basis is complete.

Induction step. Assume the result for $i = k$. Suppose that $x \in X_{N_0}$ and $N_0 + (k+1)p \leqslant x < N_0 + (k+2)p$. Subtracting p from all parts of the inequality gives $N_0 + kp \leqslant x - p < N_0 + (k+1)p$. Thus $x - p \in X_{N_0} \cap Y_k$ and, by the induction hypothesis, $x - p = g(j) + kp$ for some j. Now we know that $x = g(j) + (k+1)p$, and the induction has been extended. Note that $x \in B$ because B contains numbers of this form.

Now the proof of Claim 1 can be finished. Recall that we assumed that $x \in X$ and $x \geqslant N_0$. Then $x \in Y_i$ for some i and, by Claim 3, $x = g(j) + pi$ for some j, so that $x \in B$.

To do the main proof is now easy. Clearly, if $x \in A \cup B$, then $x \in X$, since $A \subseteq X$ and by Claim 1. On the other hand, suppose $x \in X$. If $x < N_0$, then $x \in A$. If $x \geqslant N_0$, then $x \in Y_i$ for some i, and Claim 3 implies that $x \in B$. □

We can also discuss ultimately periodic sequences as well as sets.

Definition 1 An infinite sequence $\{x_n\}$ of natural numbers is *ultimately periodic* if there exist integers $N'_0 \geqslant 0$ and $p' \geqslant 1$ such that $x_{n+p'} = x_n$ for each $n \geqslant N'_0$.

Example $(3, 2, 1, 1, 2, 2, 1, 1, 2, 2, 1, 1, 2, \ldots)$ is an ultimately periodic sequence.

This allows us to give a second definition of ultimately periodic sets.

Definition 2 A set X of natural numbers is said to be *ultimately periodic* if X is finite or if the sequence $(y_1, y_2 - y_1, \ldots, y_{n+1} - y_n, \ldots)$ is an ultimately periodic sequence where $(y_1, y_2, \ldots)$ are the elements of X in increasing order.

Example Consider the set X_3 defined at the beginning of this section. A simple calculation shows that the desired sequence occurs in the previous example and so X_3 is ultimately periodic.

Of course it must be shown that these definitions are equivalent.

Theorem 2.2.4 Definition 1 is equivalent to Definition 2.

Proof The argument is left to the reader.

Definition 2 is more convenient than Definition 1 in showing that particular sets are not ultimately periodic.

Now we are ready to prove the main result about this topic.

Theorem 2.2.5 A set $L \subseteq \{a\}^*$ is regular if and only if X is ultimately periodic where $X = \{i \mid a^i \in L\}$.

Proof Assume that X is an ultimately periodic set of natural numbers. By Theorem 2.2.3, $X = A \cup B$ where A is finite and

$$B = \bigcup_{j=1}^{s} \{g(j) + pi \mid i \geqslant 0\}.$$

Thus

$$L = \{a^i \mid i \in X\} = \{a^i \mid i \in A\} \cup \bigcup_{j=1}^{s} \{a^{g(j)+ip} \mid i \geqslant 0\}.$$

The first set is regular since A is finite. The second set is the finite union of sets of the form $\{a^{g(j)+ip} \mid i \geqslant 0\} = a^{g(j)}(a^p)^*$, and so these are regular sets and L is regular.

Conversely, suppose that $L \subseteq \{a\}^*$ is regular. $L = T(A)$, where $A = (Q, \{a\}, \delta, q_0, F)$. Write $L = \{a^i \mid i \in X\}$. If L is finite, then X is finite and hence ultimately periodic, and we are done. Suppose L is infinite. Then let N_0 be the least number such that $a^{N_0} \in L$ and $N_0 \geqslant |Q|$. By the iteration theorem, we know that $a^{N_0} = a^j a^p a^{\ell}$, $p \geqslant 1$, and moreover $rp(a^{N_0}) = rp(a^j (a^p)^n a^{\ell}) \in F$ for any $n \geqslant 0$. When $n = 2$, we have $rp(a^{N_0}) = rp(a^{N_0+p})$.

To show that X is ultimately periodic, let $i \geqslant N_0$ so that $i = N_0 + s$ for some $s \geqslant 0$. We must show that $i \in X$ if and only if $i + p \in X$. We compute

$$\begin{aligned} rp(a^i) &= rp(a^{N_0+s}) = \delta(rp(a^{N_0}), a^s) \\ &= \delta(rp(a^{N_0+p}), a^s) = rp(a^{N_0+s+p}) \\ &= rp(a^{i+p}). \end{aligned}$$

Therefore $i \in X$ if and only if $i + p \in X$. Thus X is ultimately periodic. □

One important use of this result is to show that certain sets cannot be regular.

Example $\{a^{n^2} \mid n \geqslant 1\}$ is not regular. Let $X = \{n^2 \mid n \geqslant 1\}$. Suppose that X were ultimately periodic. Then the sequence $(y_1, y_2 - y_1, \ldots)$ would be ultimately periodic. But this sequence is $(1, 3, 5, 7, 9, 11, \ldots, 2n+1, \ldots)$. In order for the sequence to be ultimately periodic, we need to have $y_{n+1} - y_n = y_{n+p'+1} - y_{n+p'}$ for some p'. This implies $2n + 1 = 2(n + p') + 1$, which implies $p' = 0$, which contradicts $p' \geqslant 1$.

PROBLEMS

1 Design a finite automaton that accepts the set

$$L = \{w \in \{a, b\}^* \mid w \text{ does not contain the subword } bab\}.$$

2 Let $x \in \Sigma^*$. Construct a finite automaton that accepts $\{x\}$. How many states are there in the minimal finite automaton for this set?

3 Let $R \subseteq \Sigma \times \Sigma$ be given. Define

$$H_R = \{a_1 \cdots a_k \mid k \geqslant 2, \quad (a_i, a_{i+1}) \in R \text{ for each } i,\ 1 \leqslant i < k\}.$$

Show that H_R is regular.

4 Let $X, Y \subseteq \Sigma^*$. Define

$$XY^{-1} = \{w \mid wy \in X \quad \text{for some } y \in Y\}.$$

Show that if X is regular and Y is arbitrary, then XY^{-1} is regular.

5 Show that the set $\{xx \mid x \in \{a, b\}^*\}$ is not regular.

6 Show that the following sets are not regular.

a) $\{a^{2^n} \mid n \geqslant 1\}$ b) $\{a^p \mid p \text{ is prime}\}$ c) $\{a^{n!} \mid n \geqslant 1\}$

7 Let R be an equivalence relation on a set. Let $rk(R)$, the *rank* of equivalence relation R, be the number of equivalence classes induced by R. Let E_1 and E_2 be equivalence relations on X. We say E_1 *refines* E_2 if $E_1 \subseteq E_2$ (that is, xE_1y implies that xE_2y). Show that if E_1 and E_2 are equivalence relations on X, it follows that, if $E_1 \subseteq E_2$, then $rk(E_1) \geqslant rk(E_2)$.

8 Let R be an equivalence relation on Σ^*. R is a *right congruence relation* if xRy implies that, for any word $z \in \Sigma^*$, $(xz)R(yz)$; that is,

$$(x, y) \in R \text{ implies } (xz, yz) \in R \quad \text{for all } z \in \Sigma^*.$$

Furthermore let $L \subseteq \Sigma^*$. Then R *refines* L iff $(x, y) \in R$ implies that $x \in L$ if and only if $y \in L$. That is, if xRy, then either x and y are both in L or x and y are both not in L. Show that R refines L if and only if L is a union of some of the equivalence classes of R.

9 Let $L \subseteq \Sigma^*$. Define R_L, the *right congruence relation induced by the set L*, as follows:

$$(x, y) \in R_L \quad \text{if and only if for each } z \in \Sigma^*$$
$$[xz \in L \quad \text{if and only if } yz \in L].$$

Prove the following proposition.

Theorem
a) R_L is a right congruence relation.
b) R_L refines L.
c) If R is any right congruence relation that refines L, then $R \subseteq R_L$.

10 Prove the following proposition:

Theorem Let $L \subseteq \Sigma^*$. The following statements are equivalent.
a) L is regular.
b) There is a right congruence relation on Σ^* of finite rank which refines L.
c) R_L has finite rank.

11 Prove Fermat's little theorem. That is, for any prime p and nonnegative integer a,

$$a^p \equiv a \bmod p.$$

Let us fix $\Sigma = \{0, 1\}$ and define a mapping from Σ^* into the natural numbers, as follows:

$$x \mapsto \underline{x}$$

where $\underline{x}$ is the integer represented by x as a binary string. If $x = a_{n-1} \cdots a_0$, then

$$\underline{x} = \sum_{i=0}^{n-1} a_i 2^i.$$

For example,

$$\underline{1} = 1 \qquad \underline{101} = 5$$
$$\underline{10} = 2 \qquad \underline{\Lambda} = 0$$

12 Prove the following facts:

a) The map $x \mapsto \underline{x}$ is a one-to-one map from $\{1\}\Sigma^*$ onto the positive integers.

b) For any $x, y \in \Sigma^*$,

$$\underline{xy} = 2^{\lg(y)}\underline{x} + \underline{y}.$$

c) For any $x \in \Sigma^+$ and $k \geq 1$,

$$(\underline{x^k}) = \underline{x}\left[\frac{2^{k \lg(x)} - 1}{2^{\lg(x)} - 1}\right].$$

13 Prove the following result.

Theorem Let $\Sigma = \{0, 1\}$ and p be an odd prime. If $x, y, z \in \Sigma^*$, so that $2^{\lg(y)} \not\equiv 1 \bmod p$, then

$$\underline{xy^{p-1}z} \equiv \underline{xz} \bmod p.$$

14 Prove the following result: Let $\Sigma = \{0, 1\}$ with $x, y, z \in \Sigma^*$. Let $p = \underline{xy^kz}$ be an odd prime and assume $2^{\lg(y)} \not\equiv 1 \bmod p$. Then

$$\underline{xy^ky^{p-1}z} \equiv \underline{xy^kz} \equiv 0 \bmod p.$$

15 Is the hypothesis that $2^{\lg(y)} \not\equiv 1 \bmod p$ actually needed in Problems 13 and 14?

Now the previous problems can be combined to show that no infinite set of prime numbers can be regular if they are represented in this fashion.

16 Prove the following result.

Theorem Let $\Sigma = \{0, 1\}$. Let $\mathscr{P}$ be any infinite subset of $\{1\}\Sigma^*$ such that $w \in \mathscr{P}$ implies that $\underline{w}$ is prime. Then $\mathscr{P}$ is not regular.

2.3 TRANSITION SYSTEMS

For our purposes it is convenient to consider a more complex type of device than a finite automaton. Let us describe our new device by a state graph, i.e., a finite directed labelled graph. Consider the graph shown in Fig. 2.2. Note that this graph has two arrows labelled 0 leaving q_0 and even has two initial states. Formally, we have the following definition:

Definition A *transition system* is a 5-tuple $A = (Q, \Sigma, \delta, Q_0, F)$ where Q, Σ, and F are as in a finite automaton, $\emptyset \neq Q_0 \subseteq Q$ and δ is a finite subset of $Q \times \Sigma^* \times Q$.

Note that every finite automaton is a transition system.

Definition A transition system $A = (Q, \Sigma, \delta, Q_0, F)$ *accepts* $w \in \Sigma^*$ if there exist $r \geq 0$, $w = u_1 \cdots u_r$, $u_i \in \Sigma^*$, $q_0, \ldots, q_r \in Q$ such that

i) $q_0 \in Q_0$,

ii) $(q_i, u_{i+1}, q_{i+1}) \in \delta$ for $0 \leq i < r$,

iii) $q_r \in F$.

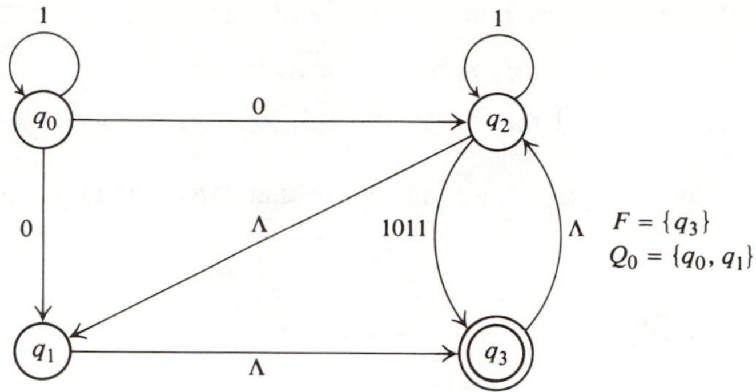

FIG. 2.2

Write $T(A) = \{w | \ A \text{ accepts } w\}$. Intuitively, A accepts w if there is a path in the graph from some initial state to some final state and the concatenation of all the labels on the path is w.

Note that if A is a finite automaton, $T(A)$ is the same as when A is regarded as a transition system.

Example In the previous example, $101011 \in T(A)$. There are infinitely many different paths from q_0 to q_3 with that label.

Since every finite automaton is a transition system, these devices accept all the regular sets and possibly more. We now show that these devices are no more powerful than finite automata.

Theorem 2.3.1 (Myhill) For each transition system $A = (Q, \Sigma, \delta, Q_0, F)$, $T(A)$ is regular.

Proof We may assume that each element of δ is a member of $Q \times (\Sigma \cup \{\Lambda\}) \times Q$. [For if $(q, x, q') \in \delta$ with $\lg(x) > 1$, we write $x = a_1 \cdots a_k, k \geqslant 2$. Delete (q, x, q') from δ and add to δ the triples

$$(q, a_1, q_1)$$
$$(q_1, a_2, q_2)$$
$$\vdots$$
$$(q_{k-2}, a_{k-1}, q_{k-1})$$
$$(q_{k-1}, a_k, q')$$

where the q_i are all new state symbols.]

Define $B = (2^Q, \Sigma, \delta_B, Q_0', F_B)$ where $F_B = \{X \subseteq Q | \ X \cap F \neq \emptyset\}$. Define the direct spontaneous transition relation, P_0, on Q by:

$$(q, q') \in P_0 \quad \text{if and only if} \quad (q, \Lambda, q') \in \delta;$$

then let $P = P_0^*$ be the reflexive transitive closure of P. Define

$$Q_0' = \{q \mid q_0 P q \qquad \text{for some } q_0 \in Q_0\}.$$

Finally, for each $V \subseteq Q$, define $\delta_B(V, a) = \{q' \mid (v, a, w) \in \delta,\ wPq' \text{ for some } (w, v) \in Q \times V\}$.

To complete the proof, we must argue that $T(B) = T(A)$. It suffices to show the following:

Claim $q \in \delta_B(Q_0', x)$ if and only if there exist

$$r, q_0, \ldots, q_r \text{ in } Q; \qquad b_1, \ldots, b_r \text{ in } \Sigma \cup \{\Lambda\}$$

such that:

i) $x = b_1 \cdots b_r$,

ii) $q_0 \in Q_0$,

iii) $(q_i, b_{i+1}, q_{i+1}) \in \delta$ for $0 \leqslant i < r$,

iv) $q_r = q$.

The argument is an induction on $m = \lg(x)$:

Basis $m = 0$, $x = \Lambda$. Then $q \in \delta_B(Q_0', \Lambda)$ if and only if $q \in Q_0'$. Thus all $b_i = \Lambda$, and the basis is established.

Induction step. Suppose the result true for all sequences x of length k. We will show it true for xa, $a \in \Sigma$, which has length $k + 1$. Let $V = \delta'(Q_0', x)$. Then

$$\begin{aligned} q' \in \delta_B(Q_0', xa) &= \delta_B(\delta_B(Q_0', x), a) = \delta_B(V, x) \\ &= \{t \mid (v, a, w) \in \delta, \quad wPt \text{ for some } (w, v) \in Q \times V\}. \end{aligned}$$

But $v \in V$ implies that claims (i) through (iv) hold for v. Note that wPt implies a finite number of additional Λ-rules (all of type (iii)) ending at q'. Thus there exists a sequence of the desired type.

Conversely, if such a sequence occurs ending at q', we have $q' \in rp_B(xa)$. Thus the claim is verified.

Finally, we verify that $T(B) = T(A)$:

$$x \in T(B)$$

if and only if

$$\delta_B(Q_0', x) \in F_B.$$

This holds if and only if

$$\delta_B(Q_0', x) \cap F \neq \emptyset.$$

In turn, this is equivalent to the existence of $r \geqslant 0, b_1, \ldots, b_r$ in $\Sigma \cup \{\Lambda\}, q_0, \ldots, q_r \in Q$ such that:

i) $x = b_1 \cdots b_r$,

ii) $q_0 \in Q_0$,

iii) $(q_i, b_{i+1}, q_{i+1}) \in \delta$ for $0 \leqslant i < r$,

iv) $q_r \in F$.

Therefore, $x \in T(B)$ if and only if $x \in T(A)$. □

Some applications of transition systems will now be given.

Theorem 2.3.2 X is regular implies X^T is regular.

Proof Let $X = T(A)$, where $A = (Q, \Sigma, \delta, q_0, F)$ is a finite automaton. Define $B = (Q, \Sigma, \delta_B, F, \{q_0\})$, where $\delta_B = \{(q', a, q) | \ q' = \delta(q, a)\}$. Note that B is not necessarily a finite automaton but is a transition system. We claim that for each $x = a_1 \cdots a_m$, $a_i \in \Sigma$ for $1 \leqslant i \leqslant m$, $q \in Q$, $\delta(q, x) = q'$ if and only if there exist $q_1, \ldots, q_{m+1}$ so that:

i) $q_{m+1} = q'$,

ii) $(q_{i+1}, a_i, q_i) \in \delta_B$ for $1 \leqslant i \leqslant m$,

iii) $q_1 = q$.

Proof of claim by induction on lg(x).

Basis. $x = \Lambda$ so $\delta(q, \Lambda) = q$. But $q = q_1 = q_{0+1} = q'$ and the basis is verified.

Induction step. Assuming the result for all tapes of length m, we have that

$$\delta(q, xa) = \delta(\delta(q, x), a).$$

By the induction hypothesis, $x = a_1 \cdots a_m$, and the definition of δ_B, there exist $q_1, \ldots, q_{m+1}$ so that:

i) $q_{m+1} = \delta(q, x)$,

ii) $(q_{i+1}, a_i, q_i) \in \delta_B$ for $1 \leqslant i \leqslant m$,

iii) $q_1 = q$,

iv) $(\delta(q, xa), a, \delta(q, x)) \in \delta_B$.

Taking $q_{m+2} = \delta(q, xa)$, $a_{m+1} = a$, the result follows.

It is now easy to verify that $T(B) = (T(A))^T = X^T$. Let $x = a_1 \cdots a_m$ with $a_i \in \Sigma$ for $1 \leqslant i \leqslant m$.

$x \in T(B)$ if and only if there exist $q_1, \ldots, q_{m+1} \in Q$ such that

i) $q_1 \in F$,

ii) $(q_i, a_i, q_{i+1}) \in \delta_B$, $\quad 1 \leqslant i \leqslant m$,

iii) $q_{m+1} = q_0$.

This holds

if and only if $\delta(q_0, x^T) = q_1 \in F$,

if and only if $x^T \in X$,

if and only if $x \in X^T$.

Thus $T(B) = X^T$ is regular. □

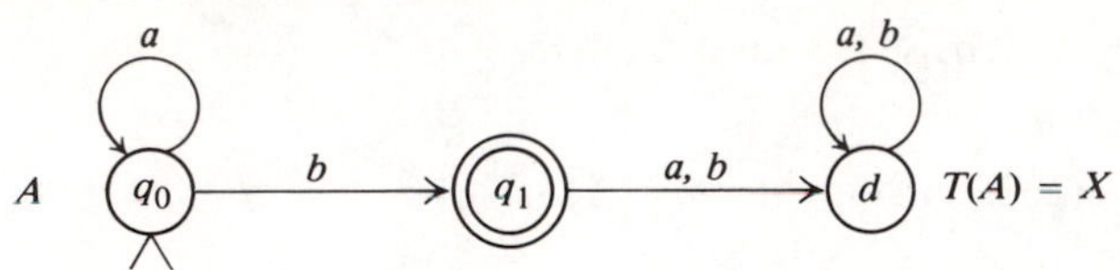

FIG. 2.3

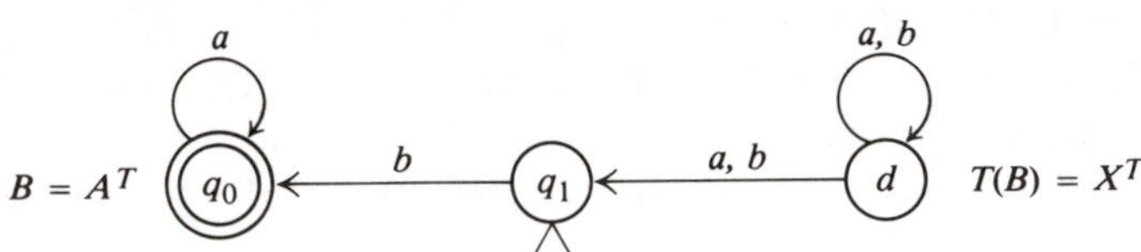

FIG. 2.4

Example $X = \{a\}^* \{b\}$, $X^T = \{b\}\{a\}^*$. X is regular, since it is recognized by the finite automaton A. (See Fig. 2.3.)

Construct the transition system B from A by converting all final states to initial states, the initial state to a final state, and reversing all arrows. (See Fig. 2.4.)

Next we show closure of the regular sets under product and star.

Theorem 2.3.3 If X and Y are regular sets, then XY is regular and X^* is regular.

Proof Suppose $X = T(A_1)$, $Y = T(A_2)$, where each $A_i = (Q_i, \Sigma, \delta_i, q_{0i}, F_i)$ for $i = 1, 2$ denotes a finite automaton. Assume, without loss of generality, that $Q_1 \cap Q_2 = \emptyset$. First we construct a new transition system A, as follows:

$$A = (Q_1 \cup Q_2, \Sigma, \delta_A, \{q_{01}\}, F_2),$$

where $\delta_A = \delta_1 \cup \delta_2 \cup \{(q, \Lambda, q_{02}) | \ q \in F_1\}$. The intuitive picture of this construction is shown in Fig. 2.5.

Thus there is a path from q_{01} to a final state in F_2 under $w = xy$ if and only if there is a path q_{01} to a final state in A_1 under x and a path from q_{02} to some final state of F_2 under y. Formally, it is easily seen that

$$T(A) = T(A_1)T(A_2) = XY,$$

and therefore XY is regular.

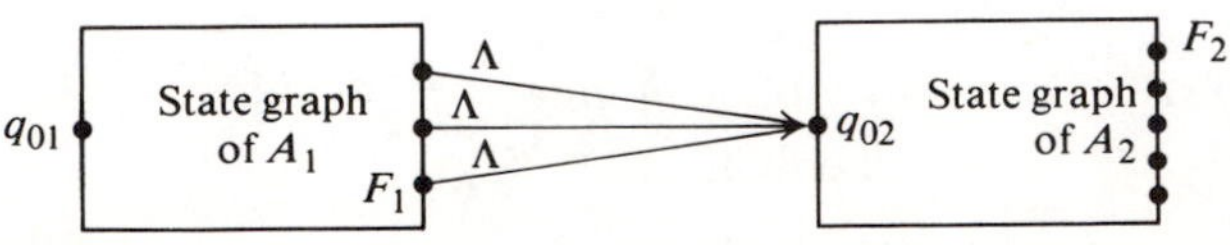

FIG. 2.5

Next we construct a transition system B which can accept X^*. Let $B = (Q_1 \cup \{\bar{q}_0\}, \Sigma, \delta_B, \{\bar{q}_0\}, \{\bar{q}_0\})$ where $\bar{q}_0$ is a new state not in Q_1.

$$\delta_B = \delta_1 \cup \{(\bar{q}_0, \Lambda, q_0)\} \cup \{(q, \Lambda, \bar{q}_0) \mid q \in F_1\}.$$

The intuitive picture is shown in Fig. 2.6.

It is easily verified that $T(B) = (T(A_1))^* = X^*$ and hence X^* is regular. □

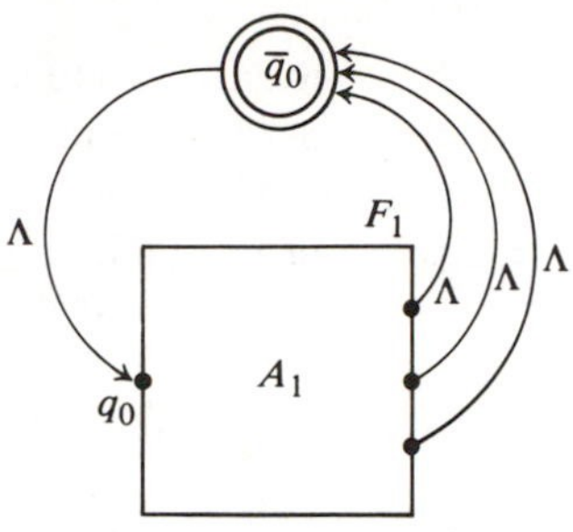

FIG. 2.6

PROBLEMS

1 It is easier to design a transition system to recognize a regular set than to do it with a finite automaton. In this problem, we shall attempt to see how much easier. Find a regular set X_n, $n \geqslant 1$, such that X_n can be accepted by a transition system with n states but any ordinary finite automaton takes 2^n states.

2 Show that if $L \subseteq \Sigma^*$ is regular and φ: $\Sigma^* \to \Delta^*$ is a homomorphism, then $\varphi L = \{\varphi x \mid x \in L\}$ is also regular.

3 Show that if $L \subseteq \Delta^*$ is regular and φ: $\Sigma^* \to \Delta^*$ is a homomorphism, then $\varphi^{-1} L = \{x \in \Sigma^* \mid \varphi x \in L\}$ is also regular.

4 Show that the family of regular sets is closed under union.

5 Are the following propositions true or false? Support your answer by giving proofs or counterexamples.

a) If $L_1 \cup L_2$ is regular and $|L_1| = 1$, then L_2 is regular.

b) If $L_1 \cup L_2$ is regular and L_1 is finite, then L_2 is regular.

c) If $L_1 \cup L_2$ is regular and L_1 is regular, then L_2 is regular.

d) If $L_1 L_2$ is regular and $|L_1| = 1$, then L_2 is regular.

e) If $L_1 L_2$ is regular and L_1 is finite, then L_2 is regular.

f) If $L_1 L_2$ is regular and L_1 is regular, then L_2 is regular.

g) If L^* is regular, then L is regular.

2.4 KLEENE'S THEOREM

The family of regular sets has a lovely set-theoretic characterization due to Kleene.

Theorem 2.4.1 The family of regular sets (over Σ) is the smallest family containing $\{a\}$ for each $a \in \Sigma$ and which is closed under union, concatenation, and *.

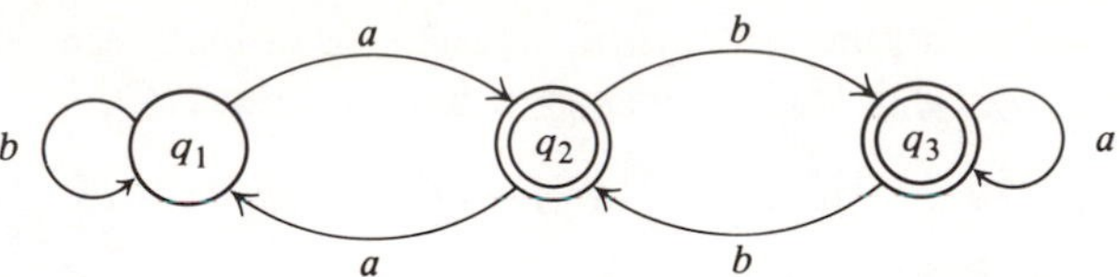

FIG. 2.7

Proof Let $\mathscr{R}$ be the family of regular sets and let $\mathscr{K}$ be the least family containing the sets $\{a\}$, $a \in \Sigma$, and closed under $\cup$, $\cdot$, and *. Clearly $\mathscr{K} \subseteq \mathscr{R}$ since every set $\{a\}$ is regular and by Theorem 2.3.3 and Problem 4 of Section 2.3. Conversely, one must show that $\mathscr{R} \subseteq \mathscr{K}$. One technique for doing this is to let $A = (Q, \Sigma, \delta, q_1, F)$ be a finite automaton with $Q = \{q_1, \ldots, q_n\}$, $\Sigma = \{0, 1\}$, and $F = \{q_{\ell_1}, q_{\ell_2}, \ldots, q_{\ell_r}\}$.

Definition For all i, j, k, with $1 \leqslant i, j \leqslant n$ and $0 \leqslant k \leqslant n$, define the set $\alpha_{ij}^{(k)}$ inductively by:

$$\alpha_{ij}^{0} = \{a \in \Sigma \cup \{\Lambda\} | \ \delta(q_i, a) = q_j\}.$$

Then

$$\alpha_{ij}^{(k)} = \alpha_{ij}^{(k-1)} \cup (\alpha_{ik}^{(k-1)}(\alpha_{kk}^{(k-1)})^* \alpha_{kj}^{(k-1)}).$$

Example See Fig. 2.7.

$$\begin{aligned} \alpha_{12}^{(1)} &= \alpha_{12}^{(0)} \cup \alpha_{11}^{(0)}(\alpha_{11}^{(0)})^* \alpha_{12}^{(0)} \\ &= a \cup (b \cup \Lambda)(b \cup \Lambda)^* a \\ &= a \cup b^* a = b^* a. \end{aligned}$$

Claim 1 Let $R_{ij}^{(k)} = \{x \in \Sigma^* | \ \delta(q_i, x) = q_j$ and for each $x, z \in \Sigma^+$, $x = yz$, $\delta(q_i, y) = q_\ell$ implies $\ell \leqslant k\}$. Then $\alpha_{ij}^{(k)} = R_{ij}^{(k)}$. That is, $\alpha_{ij}^{(k)}$ is the set of all words which take A from state i to state j without going through (i.e., *both* entering and leaving) any state q_ℓ with $\ell > k$.

Proof By induction on k.

Base of induction: $k = 0$. The definition of $\alpha_{ij}^{(0)}$ implies that $\alpha_{ij}^{(0)} = \{a \in \Sigma \cup \{\Lambda\} | \delta(q_i, a) = q_j\}$. Since it is impossible to factor $a \in \Sigma \cup \{\Lambda\}$ into $a = yz$ with $y, z \in \Sigma^+$, we have $\alpha_{ij}^{(0)} \subseteq R_{ij}^{(0)}$. Let $x \in R_{ij}^{(0)}$. Then $\delta(q_i, x) = q_j$. Assume that $x = yz$ with $y, z \in \Sigma^+$. Then $\delta(q_i, y) = q_\ell$ with $\ell \leqslant 0$. But there is no $q_\ell \in Q$ with $\ell \leqslant 0$. Thus it is impossible to factor x as above. Then x must be in $\Sigma \cup \{\Lambda\}$. Therefore $x \in \{a \in \Sigma \cup \{\Lambda\} | \ \delta(q_i, a) = q_j\} = \alpha_{ij}^{(0)}$. Thus $\alpha_{ij}^{(0)} \supseteq R_{ij}^{(0)}$, so $\alpha_{ij}^{(0)} = R_{ij}^{(0)}$.

Induction step. Assume $\alpha_{ij}^{(k-1)} = R_{ij}^{(k-1)}$ for all $1 \leqslant i, j \leqslant n$. Then

$$\begin{aligned} \alpha_{ij}^{(k)} &= \alpha_{ij}^{(k-1)} \cup (\alpha_{ik}^{(k-1)})(\alpha_{kk}^{(k-1)})^* \alpha_{kj}^{(k-1)} \\ &= R_{ij}^{(k-1)} \cup R_{ik}^{(k-1)}(R_{kk}^{(k-1)})^* R_{kj}^{(k-1)} \qquad \text{(by induction hypothesis).} \end{aligned}$$

To show that $\alpha_{ij}^{(k)} \subseteq R_{ij}^{(k)}$, assume that $x \in \alpha_{ij}^{(k)}$. Then $x \in R_{ij}^{(k-1)}$ or $x \in R_{ik}^{(k-1)}(R_{kk}^{(k-1)})^* R_{kj}^{(k-1)}$. In the first case, $x \in R_{ij}^{(k)}$, since $R_{ij}^{(k-1)} \subseteq R_{ij}^{(k)}$ (easy consequence of definition of $R_{ij}^{(k)}$. In the second case, $x = yzw$, where $y \in R_{ik}^{(k-1)}$,

$z \in (R_{kk}^{(k-1)})^*$, and $w \in R_{kj}^{(k-1)}$. Then $q_j = \delta(\delta(\delta(q_i, y), z), w) = \delta(q_i, yzw) = \delta(q_i, x)$. Now suppose $x = x'x''$, with $x', x'' \in \Sigma^+$. An analysis of the cases $\lg(x') < \lg(y)$, $\lg(x') = \lg(y)$, $\lg(y) < \lg(x') < \lg(yz)$, $\lg(x') = \lg(yz)$, and $\lg(yz) < \lg(x') < \lg(yzw)$ indicates that $\delta(q_i, x') = q_\ell$ with $\ell = k$. Thus $x \in R_{ij}^{(k)}$, which means that $\alpha_{ij}^{(k)} \subseteq R_{ij}^{(k)}$.

We must now show that $R_{ij}^{(k)} \subseteq \alpha_{ij}^{(k)}$. Assume $x \in R_{ij}^{(k)}$. Then $\delta(q_i, x) = q_j$ and, for every y, $z \in \Sigma^+$, such that $x = yz$, $\delta(q_i, y) = q_\ell$ with $\ell \leqslant k$. If for every y, $z \in \Sigma^+$, the previous sentence holds with $\ell < k$, then $x \in R_{ij}^{(k-1)} = \alpha_{ij}^{(k-1)}$ by the induction hypothesis. Suppose this stronger condition does not hold. Then there exist y, $z \in \Sigma^+$ such that $x = yz$ and $\delta(q_i, y) = q_k$. Let us further restrict y and z so that y is minimal in the sense that if $y = uv$, u, $v \in \Sigma^+$, $\delta(q_i, u) = q_\ell$ then $\ell < k$. This simply means that $y \in R_{ik}^{(k-1)}$. Now factor z into two words $z = z'z''$ with $\delta(q_k, z') = q_k$ and $z'' \neq \Lambda$ (we can always do this at first by picking $z' = \Lambda$, $z'' = z$).

Furthermore, choose z' and z'' so that z' is the maximal prefix of z such that $\delta(q_k, z') = q_k$ and $\lg(z') < \lg(z)$. Thus $z' \in (R_{kk}^{(k-1)})^*$ and $z'' \in R_{kj}^{(k-1)}$.

Summarizing, we have shown that if $x \in R_{ij}^{(k)}$, then either $x \in R_{ij}^{(k-1)}$ or else x can be factored into $x = yz'z''$ with $y \in R_{ik}^{(k-1)}$, $z' \in (R_{kk}^{(k-1)})^*$, and $z'' \in R_{kj}^{(k-1)}$. But this means that $x \in R_{ij}^{(k-1)} \cup R_{ik}^{(k-1)}(R_{kk}^{(k-1)})^* R_{kj}^{(k-1)} = \alpha_{ij}^{(k)}$. Thus $R_{ij}^{(k)} \subseteq a_{ij}^{(k)}$ implying $R_{ij}^{(k)} = \alpha_{ij}^{(k)}$ and the theorem follows by induction. The situation can be summarized by the diagram in Fig. 2.8.

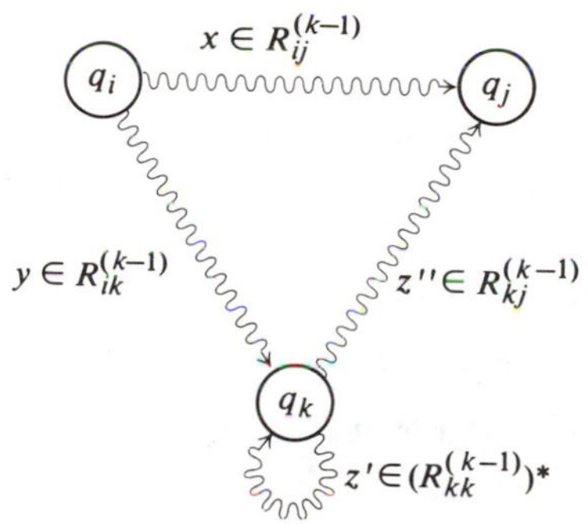

FIG. 2.8

Claim 2 Let A be a finite automaton as above. Then

$$T(A) = \begin{cases} |\emptyset| & \text{if } r = 0 \quad \text{(i.e., no final states)}, \\ \alpha_{1\ell_1}^{(n)} \cup \alpha_{1\ell_2}^{(n)} \cup \cdots \cup \alpha_{1\ell_r}^{(n)} & \text{otherwise.} \end{cases}$$

Proof If A has no final states, then $T(A) = \emptyset$. Suppose $r \neq 0$. By the previous theorem,

$$\begin{aligned} \alpha_{ij}^{(n)} &= \{x \in \Sigma^* \mid \delta(q_i, x) = q_j \text{ and for each } x, z \in \Sigma^+, x = yz, \delta(q_i, y) = q_\ell \text{ implies } \ell \leqslant n\} \\ &= \{x \in \Sigma^* \mid \delta(q_i, x) = q_j\} \qquad \text{(since } \ell \leqslant n \text{ for all } q_\ell \in Q). \end{aligned}$$

Now, $x \in T(A)$

$$\begin{aligned}
&\text{if and only if} \quad \delta(q_1, x) = q_{\ell_i} \quad \text{for some } i,\ 1 \leqslant i \leqslant r,\\
&\text{if and only if} \quad x \in \alpha_{1\ell_i}^{(n)} \quad \text{for some } i,\ 1 \leqslant i \leqslant r,\\
&\text{if and only if} \quad x \in \bigcup_{1 \leqslant i \leqslant r} \alpha_{1\ell_i}^{(n)} = \alpha_{1\ell_1}^{(n)} \cup \cdots \cup \alpha_{1\ell_r}^{(n)}.
\end{aligned}$$

Therefore,

$$T(A) = \alpha_{1\ell_1}^{(n)} \cup \cdots \cup \alpha_{1\ell_r}^{(n)}.$$

Note that the form of the regular set obtained by this method is not unique, since it depends upon the numbering of the states.

This argument shows that $L \in \mathscr{R}$ is also in $\mathscr{K}$, so that

$$\mathscr{R} = \mathscr{K},$$

and the proof is complete. □

PROBLEMS

1 Show that:

a) $\alpha_{ij}^{(i)} = (\alpha_{ii}^{(i-1)})^* \alpha_{ij}^{(i-1)}$;

b) $\alpha_{ij}^{(j)} = \alpha_{ij}^{(j-1)}(\alpha_{jj}^{(j-1)})^*$;

c) $\alpha_{ii}^{(i)} = (\alpha_{ii}^{(i-1)})^*$.

2 Give a procedure for constructing a finite automaton directly from a "regular expression," i.e., a description of the regular set in terms of Kleene's theorem. [*Hint*: Use transition systems.]

3 Let L be a regular set. Let

$$M_L = \{y \mid xyz \in L \text{ for some } x, z \in \Sigma^* \text{ such that } \lg(x) = \lg(y) = \lg(z)\}.$$

Show that M_L, the set of middle thirds of L, is regular.

2.5 RIGHT LINEAR GRAMMARS AND LANGUAGES

We are already in a position to characterize the right linear languages. The argument can be broken down into two lemmas. The first deals with the "power" of this class of grammars, and shows that any regular set can be generated by some right linear grammar.

Lemma 2.5.1 If L is a regular set, then $L = L(G)$ for some right linear grammar G.

Proof Since L is regular, there exists a finite automaton

$$A = (Q, \Sigma, \delta, q_1, F)$$

such that $L = T(A)$. (q_1 has been chosen as an initial state for technical convenience.)

Since, by a suitable renaming of Q, we can make $\Sigma \cap Q = \emptyset$, we can assume, without loss of generality, that Σ and Q are disjoint.

Define

$$G = (V, \Sigma, P, q_1),$$

where

$$V = \Sigma \cup Q,$$

$$P = \{q \to a\delta(q,a) \mid (q,a) \in Q \times \Sigma\} \cup \{q \to \Lambda \mid q \in F\},$$

the set of variables being Q and the start symbol $q_1 \in Q_1$.

Since $\delta\colon Q \times \Sigma \to Q$, we have immediately that G is a right linear grammar. All that must be shown is that $L(G) = T(A)$.

Claim For all $y \in \Sigma^*$, there exists a unique derivation of the form

$$q_1 \overset{*}{\Rightarrow} yq$$

with $q \in Q$. Moreover, $q = \delta(q_1, y)$.

Proof This is an obvious consequence of the fact that y determines a unique path through the automaton. A formal proof is included as an example of how such proofs are carried out. Hereafter, if the proofs are straightforward, they will be left to the reader.

The proof is by induction on $\lg(y)$.

Basis. $\lg(y) = 0$ implies $y = \Lambda$; but, by definition,

$$\delta(q_1, \Lambda) = q_1.$$

Therefore, $q_1 \overset{0}{\Rightarrow} q_1 = \Lambda q_1 = \Lambda\delta(q_1, \Lambda)$ is in P, where the derivation is unique since A has no Λ-rules. Therefore,

$$q_1 \overset{*}{\Rightarrow} \Lambda q_1 \qquad \text{uniquely.}$$

Induction step. Assume that, for all $y \in \Sigma^*$, if $\lg(y) \leqslant n$, then there exists a unique derivation

$$q_1 \overset{*}{\Rightarrow} yq$$

and $q = \delta(q_1, y)$. Let $w \in \Sigma^*$ and $\lg(w) = n + 1$. Then w can be written

$$w = ya \qquad a \in \Sigma, \qquad y \in \Sigma^*, \qquad \lg(y) = n.$$

By the induction hypothesis, there exists a unique derivation

$$q_1 \overset{*}{\Rightarrow} yq$$

and $q = \delta(q_1, y)$. But

$$\delta(q_1, y) \to a\delta(\delta(q_1, y), a)$$

is in P and is unique since δ is a function. Therefore,

$$q_1 \overset{*}{\Rightarrow} y\delta(q_1, y) \Rightarrow ya\delta(\delta(q_1, y), a).$$

Now, using the fact that

$$\delta(\delta(q_1, y), a) = \delta(q_1, ya)$$

and

$$w = ya$$

we have

$$q_1 \overset{*}{\Rightarrow} w\delta(q_1, w) \text{ uniquely,}$$

which proves the claim. Therefore,

$$q_1 \overset{*}{\Rightarrow} y\delta(q_1,y) \Rightarrow y$$

if and only if $\delta(q_1,y) \to \Lambda$ is in P. But, from the definition of P, we have

$$\delta(q_1,y) \to \Lambda \quad \text{is in } P$$

if and only if $\delta(q_1,y) \in F$. Therefore,

$$q_1 \overset{*}{\Rightarrow} y \qquad \text{if and only if} \quad \delta(q_1,y) \in F,$$

or, equivalently,

$$y \in L(G) \qquad \text{if and only if} \quad y \in T(A),$$

which proves the lemma. □

Corollary Every regular set is an unambiguous context-free language.

Example Let G be

$$S \to SbS \mid a$$

We have seen that G is ambiguous. But $L(G) = (ab)^*a$ is regular, and hence there exists an unambiguous right linear grammar G' such that $L(G') = (ab)^*a$. For instance, G' could be taken to be

$$S \to abS \mid a$$

Now we turn to the reverse direction of simulating a right linear grammar by a finite automaton. Such a direct construction would be tedious because there is much more "freedom" in what the grammar may do than there is in a finite automaton; but the proof becomes transparent with the aid of transition systems.

Lemma 2.5.2 If L is generated by a right linear grammar, then L is regular.

Proof Let $L = L(G)$, where

$$G = (V, \Sigma, P, S)$$

is a right linear grammar. Now define a transition system:

$$C = (Q, \Sigma, \delta, \{S\}, F),$$

$$Q = (V - \Sigma) \cup \{q\}, \qquad q \notin V,$$

$$F = \{q\},$$

$$\delta = \{(q_i, u, q_j) \mid q_i \to uq_j \text{ is in } P\} \cup \{(q_i, u, q) \mid q_i \to u \text{ is in } P\}.$$

Clearly, C is a transition system, and all that must be shown is $L(G) = T(C)$. As is typical in these constructions, it is easier to prove more.

Claim Let $r \geqslant 1$. $S = w_0 \Rightarrow w_1 \Rightarrow w_2 \Rightarrow \cdots \Rightarrow w_r = w \in L(G)$ if and only if there exist $u_i \in \Sigma^*$ for $0 \leqslant i \leqslant r$; $q_i \in Q$ for $0 \leqslant i < r$, such that:

i) $w_i = u_1 \cdots u_i q_i$ for $0 \leqslant i < r$,

ii) $w_r = u_1 \cdots u_r$

iii)$'$ (q_i, u_{i+1}, q_{i+1}) is in δ for $0 \leqslant i < r-1$, and

iv)$'$ (q_{r-1}, u_r, q) is in δ.

Proof of the claim It is easy to see, by induction on r, that

$$S = w_0 \Rightarrow w_1 \Rightarrow \cdots \Rightarrow w_r = w \in L(G)$$

if and only if there exist $u_i \in \Sigma^*$ for $0 \leqslant i \leqslant r$; $q_i \in Q$ for $0 \leqslant i < r$, such that

i) $w_i = u_1 \cdots u_i q_i$ for $0 \leqslant i < r$,

ii) $w_r = u_1 \cdots u_r$

iii) $q_i \rightarrow u_{i+1} q_{i+1}$ is in P for $0 \leqslant i < r-1$, and

iv) $q_r \rightarrow u_r$ is in P.

But by the construction, (iii)$'$ and (iv)$'$ are equivalent to (iii) and (iv). But the second half of the biconditional, together with the fact that the initial set of states is $\{S\}$ and $q \in F$, gives us

$$S \overset{*}{\Rightarrow} w, \qquad w \in \Sigma^* \qquad \text{if and only if} \qquad w \in T(G).$$

Therefore,

$$L(G) = T(C).$$

Since C is a transition system, $L(G)$ is regular. □

Combining this with Lemma 2.5.2 leads to the main result of this section.

Theorem 2.5.1 L is a right linear language if and only if L is a regular set.

Corollary Every regular set is a context-free language.

Consider the grammar G with production

$$S \rightarrow aSb \mid \Lambda$$

G is a linear grammar with only one variable and

$$L(G) = \{a^i b^i \mid i \geqslant 0\}.$$

We know that $L(G)$ is not regular. Therefore, there are linear languages which are not right linear languages.

Theorem 2.5.2 The family of right linear languages (regular sets) is a proper subfamily of the family of linear context-free languages.

Corollary The family of regular sets is properly contained in the family of context-free languages.

We will establish other properties of these classes of grammars in later sections when more techniques are available.

PROBLEMS

1 Show that every linear context-free language may be generated by a context-free grammar $G = (V, \Sigma, P, S)$, where each rule is of the form:

$$A \to a$$

$$A \to aB$$

or

$$A \to Ba$$

where $A, B \in N$, $a \in \Sigma \cup \{\Lambda\}$. This is sometimes called *linear normal form.*

2 Prove the following fact:

Fact $L \subseteq \Sigma^*$ is a linear context-free language if and only if there exists a set Σ', a regular set $U \subseteq (\Sigma')^*$ and two homomorphisms φ_1 and φ_2 from $(\Sigma')^*$ into Σ^* so that $L = \{\varphi_1(w)\varphi_2(w^T) \mid w \in U\}$.

3 Show that a language L is left linear if and only if L is regular.

4 A context-free grammar is *metalinear* if each rule is of the form:

$$S \to A_1 \cdots A_m \qquad A_i \in N - \{S\};$$

$$A \to u_1 B u_2 \qquad B \in N - \{S\}; u_1, u_2 \in \Sigma^*;$$

$$A \to u \qquad u \in \Sigma^*.$$

A set L is *metalinear* if $L = L(G)$ for some metalinear grammar. Show that L is metalinear if and only if L is a finite union of products of linear context-free languages.

5 Consider an automaton which has a nondeterministic finite-state control, two read-only input tapes equipped with right end markers, and which computes as follows: It starts with input pair $(w_1\$, w_2\$)$, reading the left end of both tapes. At each instant of time, the read head of one tape (assume it is associated with the current state) advances one square to the right and a state change occurs. The device accepts by final state when one tape has been entirely read. We say the device accepts (x, y) if $(x\$, y\$)$ leads to an accepting configuration. Such a device accepts a binary relation on words. Formalize such devices. Show that if L is a relation accepted by such a device, then

$$\Pi_1(L) = \{x \in \Sigma^* \mid (x, y) \in L \quad \text{for some } y \in \Sigma^*\}$$

is regular.

6 Show that L is a linear context-free language if every string $z \in L$ can be represented as $z = xy$ and the set

$$\{(x, y^T) \mid z = xy \in L\}$$

is accepted by a nondeterministic two-tape finite automaton. (Cf. Problem 5.)

7 Let $L \subseteq \Sigma^* c \Sigma^*$ with $c \notin \Sigma$. Is it true that if L is a linear context-free language, then $\{x \mid xcy \in L \text{ for some } y \in \Sigma^*\}$ is a regular set?

8 Show that, for $k \geq 1$, $L_k = a_1^* \cdots a_k^*$ may be generated by a right linear grammar which has k variables. Show that there is no right linear grammar with fewer than k variables that generates L_k.

2.6 TWO-WAY FINITE AUTOMATA

We now consider finite automata which can move both ways on their input tapes. Intuitively, such devices should be able to accept more than just regular sets, since they can revisit certain parts of the input.

Definition A *two-way finite automaton* is a 5-tuple $A = (Q, \Sigma, \delta, q_0, F)$, where Q, Σ, q_0, F are as in a finite automaton; δ is a map from $Q \times \Sigma$ into $\{-1, 0, 1\} \times Q$.

Intuitively, $\delta(q, a) = (d, q')$ means that, if A is in a state q reading input a, then A goes to the left when $d = -1$, remains stationary if $d = 0$, or goes to the right if $d = 1$ and enters state q'.

Definition Let $A = (Q, \Sigma, \delta, q_0, F)$ be a two-way finite automaton. Assume, without loss of generality, that $Q \cap \Sigma = \emptyset$. An *instantaneous description* (or *ID*) of A is an element of $\Sigma^* Q \Sigma^*$.

Example The ID $a_1 \cdots a_{i-1} q a_i \cdots a_n$ describes the machine as drawn below:

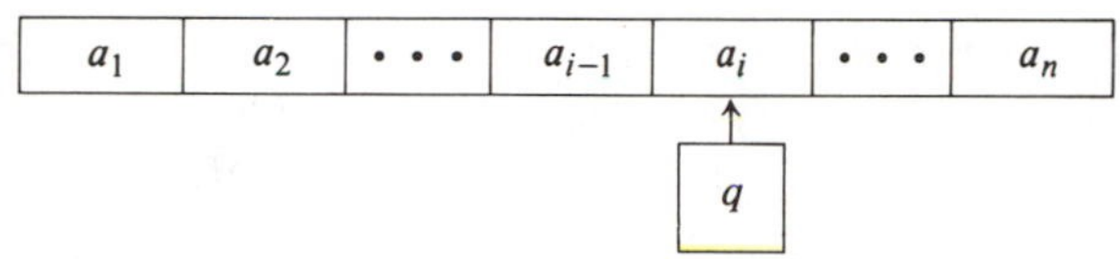

Definition The move relation $\vdash$ of ID's of a two-way finite automaton $A = (Q, \Sigma, \delta, q_0, F)$ is defined as follows: For any $q \in Q; a_1, \ldots, a_n \in \Sigma$,

$$a_1 \cdots q a_i \cdots a_n \vdash a_1 \cdots q' a_{i+d} \cdots a_n$$

if $\delta(q, a_i) = (d, q')$, where $n \geqslant 1$, $1 \leqslant i \leqslant n$, and $a_{n+1} = \Lambda$. Moreover, if $i = 1$, then $d \geqslant 0$.

The convention $a_{n+1} = \Lambda$ allows A to leave the righthand end of its input tape. The last condition prevents A from going left from the first square of the tape.

As usual, $\overset{*}{\vdash}$ denotes the reflexive–transitive closure of $\vdash$. It is interesting to compare the following two relationships.

a) $qz \overset{*}{\vdash} qz$,

b) $xqz \overset{*}{\vdash} xqz$.

If (a) holds, it means that A starts on the lefthand symbol of z, computes within z, and returns to the same place. Thus, if (a) holds, one can say that (b) holds. On the other hand, if (b) holds, A starts at the same place but the computation may involve visiting x as well as z, and one cannot conclude that (a) holds.

Next, we can define acceptance.

Definition Let $A = (Q, \Sigma, \delta, q_0, F)$ be a two-way finite automaton. Define

$$T(A) = \{x \in \Sigma^* \mid q_0 x \overset{*}{\vdash} xq \quad \text{for some } q \in F\}.$$

Example Let A be as shown in Fig. 2.9.

	0	1
q_0	$1, q_1$	$-1, q_1$
q_1	$-1, q_0$	$0, q_2$
q_2	$-1, q_1$	$1, q_2$

$F=\{q_2\}$

FIG. 2.9

Clearly,

$$\begin{aligned} q_0 011 &\vdash 0q_1 11 \\ &\vdash 0q_2 11 \\ &\vdash 01q_2 1 \\ &\vdash 011q_2. \end{aligned}$$

Thus, $011 \in T(A)$. The reader should verify that $00 \notin T(A)$ and 00 causes A to go into an infinite loop.

Since every finite automaton is a special case of a two-way finite automaton, these new devices can accept every regular set and possibly more. Our next definition is useful in analyzing the behavior of two-way finite automata.

Definition Let $A = (A, \Sigma, \delta, q_0, F)$ be a two-way finite automaton and suppose $0 \notin Q$. For each $x \in \Sigma^*$, define a map τ_x from $Q \cup \{0\}$ into $Q \cup \{0\}$, where:

i) If $x = x'a$ for some $a \in \Sigma$ and $x'qa \overset{*}{\vdash} x'aq'$, then $\tau_x(q) = q'$. Otherwise, $\tau_x(q) = 0$.
ii) If $q_0 x \overset{*}{\vdash} xq'$, then $\tau_x(0) = q'$.
iii) Otherwise, $\tau_x(0) = 0$.

In words, condition (i) means that A is started on the rightmost symbol of an input x in state q. If A ultimately leaves the entire input word in a state q', then $\tau_x(q) = q'$. Otherwise, $\tau_x(q) = 0$.

Condition (ii) means that if A is started on the left end of input x in state q_0 and it finally goes off the right end of x in state q', then $\tau_x(0) = q'$. Otherwise, $\tau_x(0) = 0$.

In order to analyze the computations, we shall examine computations which "return to the same place."

Definition Let $A = (Q, \Sigma, \delta, q_0, F)$ be a two-way finite automaton. For each x, $z \in \Sigma^*$; q, $q' \in Q$ define $xqz \underset{s}{\overset{+}{\vdash}} xq'z$ if there exist $n > 1$, x_i, $z_i \in \Sigma^*$, where $1 \leqslant i \leqslant n$ and

$$x_1 q_1 z_1 \vdash x_2 q_2 z_2 \vdash \cdots \vdash x_n q_n z_n$$

with:

i) $x_i z_i = xz$ for all i, $1 \leqslant i \leqslant n$,
ii) $x_1 q_1 z_1 = xqz$,

iii) $x_n q_n z_n = xq'z$, and

iv) for all i, $1 < i < n, x_i \neq x$ and $z_i \neq z$.

Thus, $xqz \overset{+}{\underset{s}{\vdash}} xq'z$ describes the *shortest* non-null computation which starts with the input head on the first square of z and returns to that position.

We now begin to relate the τ functions to computations.

Lemma 2.6.1 Let $A = (Q, \Sigma, \delta, q_0, F)$ be a two-way finite automaton. For all $x, y \in \Sigma^*$, if $\tau_x = \tau_y$, then, for any $z \in \Sigma^*; q, q' \in Q$,

$$xqz \overset{+}{\underset{s}{\vdash}} xq'z \qquad \text{if and only if} \quad yqz \overset{+}{\underset{s}{\vdash}} yq'z.$$

Proof Figure 2.10 illustrates computations on xz and yz if we assume that $\tau_x = \tau_y$. Note that $xq_2z \overset{+}{\underset{s}{\vdash}} xq_3z$ and $yq_2z \overset{+}{\underset{s}{\vdash}} yq_3z$, even though the computations are different.

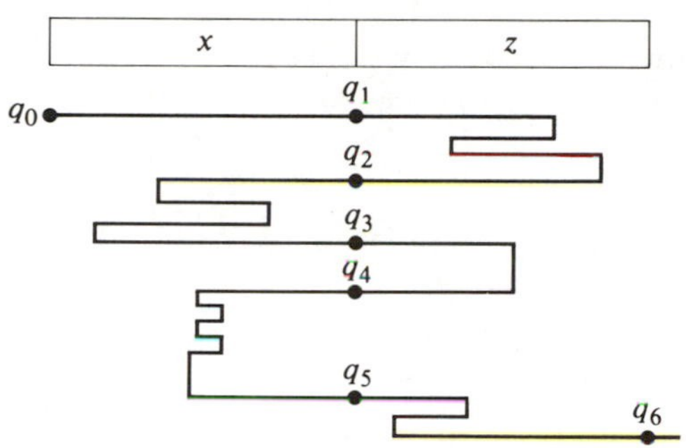

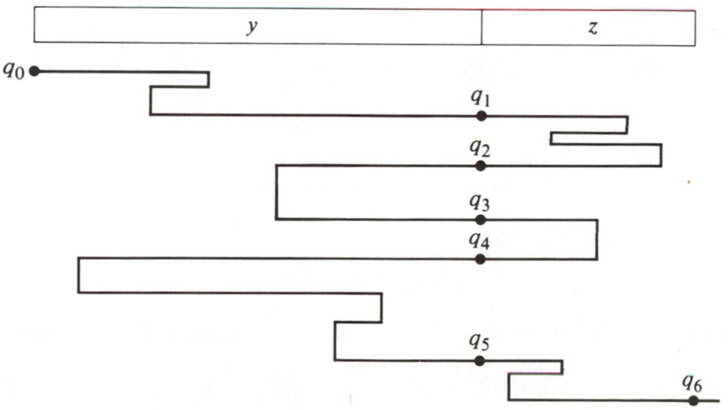

FIG. 2.10 The traces of a computation on xz and on yz if $\tau_x = \tau_y$.

If $x = \Lambda$, then

$$\tau_x(0) = q_0 \qquad \text{and} \qquad \tau_x(q'') = 0$$

for all $q'' \in Q$, by the definition of τ_x. Assume that $y \neq \Lambda$; that is, $y = y'a$ for some $a \in \Sigma$. Since $\tau_x = \tau_y$, we know that $\tau_y(0) = q_0$ and

$$q_0 y \overset{*}{\vdash} y q_0 \qquad \text{implies} \qquad q_0 y' a \overset{*}{\vdash} y' a q_0,$$

which implies

$$q_0 y' a \overset{*}{\vdash} y' q'' a \overset{*}{\vdash} y' a q_0 \qquad \text{for some } q'' \in Q,$$

But then

$$\tau_y(q'') = q_0 \neq 0 = \tau_x(q''),$$

which is a contradiction. Thus, $y = \Lambda$.

Combining the previous argument with symmetry, we see that the following is true:

Fact $x = \Lambda$ if and only if $y = \Lambda$.

By the symmetry between x and y, it suffices to prove the result in one direction. Suppose $xqz \overset{+}{\vdash}_s xq'z$. Then, by definition,

$$x_1 q_1 z_1 \vdash x_2 q_2 z_2 \vdash \cdots \vdash x_n q_n z_n. \tag{2.6.1}$$

At the first step of the computation, we move left or we do not. From Eq. (2.6.1) and this observation, there are two disjoint cases:

i) All the x_i are prefixes of x, at least one of which is proper (the first move went left);

ii) All the z_i are suffixes of z (the first move had $d \geqslant 0$).

CASE i. Assume that all the x_i are prefixes of x and at least one of them is proper.

Let $x, y \neq \Lambda$, so that $x = x'a$ and $y = y'b$ for some $a, b \in \Sigma$. Using the assumption of Case (i) and (2.6.1), we have:

$$x' a q_1 z \vdash x' q_2 a z \tag{2.6.2}$$

and

$$x' q_2 a \overset{*}{\vdash} x' a q_n = x q_n. \tag{2.6.3}$$

From (2.6.2), it clearly follows that:

$$y' b q_1 z \vdash y' q_2 b z, \tag{2.6.4}$$

since A is deterministic. Since $\tau_x(q_2) = \tau_y(q_2)$, it follows from (2.6.3) that:

$$y' q_2 b \overset{*}{\vdash} y' b q_n = y q_n = y q'. \tag{2.6.5}$$

Combining (2.6.4) and (2.6.5), we have:

$$yqz \overset{+}{\vdash}_s yq'z,$$

and Case (i) is proven.

CASE ii. All the z_i are prefixes of z. Then,

$$q_1z_1 \vdash \cdots \vdash q_nz_n,$$

which implies that

$$yq_1z \vdash \cdots \vdash yq_nz;$$

that is,

$$yqz \overset{+}{\underset{s}{\vdash}} yq'z. \qquad \square$$

In our next result, we extend the computations beyond merely $\overset{+}{\underset{s}{\vdash}}$.

Lemma 2.6.2 Let $A = (Q, \Sigma, \delta, q_0, F)$ be a two-way finite automaton. For each $x, y \in \Sigma^*$, if $\tau_x = \tau_y$, then, for each $z \in \Sigma^*, q \in Q$,

$$q_0xz \overset{*}{\vdash} xqz \qquad \text{if and only if} \qquad q_0yz \overset{*}{\vdash} yqz.$$

Proof By the symmetry between x and y, it suffices to prove one direction. Suppose $q_0xz \overset{*}{\vdash} xqz$. Then either

$$q_0x \overset{*}{\vdash} xq \qquad \text{(never use the interior of } z) \tag{2.6.6}$$

or

$$q_0x \overset{*}{\vdash} xq_1 \qquad \text{and} \qquad xq_1z \overset{+}{\underset{s}{\vdash}} xq_2z \overset{+}{\underset{s}{\vdash}} \cdots \overset{+}{\underset{s}{\vdash}} xq_nz \tag{2.6.7}$$

for some $n > 1$, some $q_i \in Q$, with $q_n = q$.

To see that these are the only two cases, examine the original computation sequence; that is,

$$q_0xz \vdash x'_1q'_1z'_1 \vdash x'_2q'_2z'_2 \vdash \cdots \vdash x'_mq'_mz'_m \vdash xqz. \tag{2.6.8}$$

If no ID $x'_iq'_iz'_i$ occurs with $x'_i = x$ and $z'_i = z$, then (2.6.6) holds. Otherwise, we may consider only the IDs in (2.6.8) with $x'_i = x$ and $z'_i = z$ and connect these by $\overset{+}{\underset{s}{\vdash}}$ to get (2.6.7).

Now we analyze the two cases.

CASE 1. Assume (2.6.6) holds. Then

$$\tau_y(0) = \tau_x(0) = q,$$

so that $q_0y \overset{*}{\vdash} yq$, which implies that:

$$q_0yz \overset{*}{\vdash} yqz.$$

CASE 2. Assume that (2.6.7) holds. By an argument identical to Case 1,

$$q_0yz \overset{*}{\vdash} yq_1z. \tag{2.6.9}$$

By use of Lemma 2.6.1 applied to (2.6.7), we have:

$$yq_1z \overset{+}{\underset{s}{\vdash}} yq_2z \overset{+}{\underset{s}{\vdash}} \cdots \overset{+}{\underset{s}{\vdash}} yq_nz = yqz. \tag{2.6.10}$$

Combining (2.6.9) and (2.6.10) produces:

$$q_0yz \overset{*}{\vdash} yqz,$$

and the proof is complete. $\square$

Now we are ready to relate a two-way finite automaton A to the induced right congruence relation $R_{T(A)}$ of Problem 9 of Section 2.2.

Lemma 2.6.3 Let $A = (Q, \Sigma, \delta, q_0, F)$ by a two-way finite automaton. If $\tau_x = \tau_y$, where $x, y \in \Sigma^*$, then $(x, y) \in R_{T(A)}$. $R_{T(A)}$ is the right congruence relation induced by $T(A)$.

Proof Assume $\tau_x = \tau_y$. Then, for any $z \in \Sigma^*$,

$$\begin{aligned} xz \in T(A) &\Leftrightarrow q_0xz \overset{*}{\vdash} xzq_f \quad \text{for some } q_f \in F, \\ &\Leftrightarrow q_0xz \overset{*}{\vdash} xqz, qz \overset{*}{\vdash} zq_f \quad \text{for some } q \in Q, q_f \in F, \\ &\Leftrightarrow q_0yz \overset{*}{\vdash} yqz, qz \overset{*}{\vdash} zq_f \quad \text{for some } q \in Q, q_f \in F \qquad \text{(by Lemma 2)}, \\ &\Leftrightarrow q_0yz \overset{*}{\vdash} yzq_f \quad \text{for some } q_f \in F, \\ &\Leftrightarrow yz \in T(A). \end{aligned}$$

Thus, $(x, y) \in R_{T(A)}$. □

Now we present the main theorem of this section.

Theorem 2.6.1 For each two-way finite automaton $A = (Q, \Sigma, \delta, q_0, F)$, $T(A)$ is a regular set.

Proof Since $\tau_x = \tau_y$ implies $(x, y) \in R_{T(A)}$, then $rk(R_{T(A)}) \leqslant |\{\tau_x \mid x \in \Sigma^*\}|$. If $|Q| = n$, then the number of different τ_x functions is at most $(n+1)^{n+1}$. Thus, $R_{T(A)}$ has finite rank and $T(A)$ is regular. □

Remark 1. The family of sets accepted by two-way finite automata with endmarkers is the same as those accepted without endmarkers.

Proof $\{¢\}\, X\, \{\$\}$ is regular if and only if X is regular. The "if part" is obvious, and the "only if part" follows from closure under homomorphism. □

Remark 2. Let $A = (Q, \Sigma, \delta, q_0, F)$ be a two-way finite automaton. Consider the sets

$$R(A) = \{x \in \Sigma^* \mid q_0x \overset{*}{\vdash} xq \quad \text{for some } q \in Q - F\}$$

and

$$L(A) = \{x \in \Sigma^* \mid q_0x \overset{*}{\vdash} xq \quad \text{for no } q \in Q\}.$$

$R(A)$ is the set of tapes rejected by a two-way finite automaton, in that the device leaves the right end of the input in a nonfinal state. $L(A)$ is the set of tapes that cause A to never leave the input tape. Since $\Sigma^* = T(A) \cup R(A) \cup L(A)$, we have that $L(A) = \Sigma^* - (T(A) \cup R(A))$, since the sets are disjoint. Therefore, both $R(A)$ and $L(A)$ are regular sets.

Remark 3. If A is a nondeterministic two-way finite automaton, then $T(A)$ is regular and, moreover, Remarks 1 and 2 hold for A.

PROBLEMS

1 Let us change the formal definition of the manner in which a two-way finite automaton A works, so that it may leave the input tape at either end. Define $T_L(A)$ as the set of tapes A accepts by starting at the left end and going off the *left* end in some final state. Show that $T_L(A)$ is regular. Can you give an algorithm for constructing an ordinary finite automaton for this set?

2 Find a regular set Y_n $(n \geqslant 1)$ such that Y_n is accepted by a two-way finite automaton which has a linear number of states, while the reduced connected automaton for Y_n has an exponential number of states.

3 Find a family of sets L_n such that:

i) Each L_n is accepted by a cn-state transition system, where c is some constant independent of n; and

ii) for each $n \geqslant 2$, no L_n is accepted by any two-way deterministic finite automaton with fewer than $dn^2/\log n$ states; d is a constant independent of n.

2.7 HISTORICAL SURVEY

There are a number of texts that cover finite automata theory in some detail. Salomaa [1969a] is an excellent general text. Eilenberg [1974] gives an elegant mathematical treatment, although his terminology is unique.

The paper by Rabin and Scott [1959] is the source for the classical treatment of finite automata and is still worth reading. Exercises 9 and 10 of Section 2.2 are based on the work of Nerode [1958]. The material on the nonrecognizability of the primes follows Hartmanis and Shank [1968]. Transition systems follow an idea of Myhill [1957], and are a variation of the nondeterministic automata of Rabin and Scott [1959]. Kleene's theorem may be found in Kleene [1956]. Our proof uses techniques due to McNaughton and Yamada [1960]. Theorem 2.5.1 may be essentially found in Chomsky and Miller [1958], and Bar-Hillel and Shamir [1960]. Exercise 6 of Section 2.5 is from Rosenberg [1967]. The results of Section 2.6 follow the paper by Shepherdson [1959].

three

Some Basic Properties of Context-Free Languages

3.1 INTRODUCTION

A number of basic results will be established here. It is possible to eliminate variables that can never occur in a sentential form as well as variables that can never generate a terminal string. A "factorization lemma" is proved for derivations, and this lemma is used to prove a number of simple but useful little theorems.

It may be shown that substituting context-free languages into context-free languages gives context-free languages. Another characterization of regular sets is presented that involves self-embedding grammars.

3.2 REDUCED GRAMMARS

It can sometimes happen that grammars contain variables that cannot generate any terminal strings. Consider the following example:

Example

$$E \to E+E|T|F$$

$$F \to F*E|(T)|a$$

$$T \to E-T$$

where $\Sigma = \{a, +, *, (,), -\}$.

The only rule with T on the lefthand side has T also on the righthand side, so it appears that T will never derive a terminal string. Surely such a situation is undesirable, and an algorithm for eliminating such variables would be useful.

Theorem 3.2.1 For each context-free grammar $G = (V, \Sigma, P, S)$, one can effectively construct a context-free grammar $G' = (V', \Sigma, P', S)$ such that $L(G) = L(G')$. Moreover, if $L(G) = \emptyset$, then $P' = \emptyset$, and if $L(G) \neq \emptyset$, then for each $A \in N'$ there exists $x \in \Sigma^*$ such that

$$A \overset{*}{\underset{G'}{\Rightarrow}} x$$

Proof The first part of the proof consists of a construction that determines the set of variables which derive terminal strings. The proof is a paradigm for future proofs and is given in (tedious) detail.

Define

$$W_1 = \{A \in N \mid A \to x \text{ is in } P \quad \text{for some } x \in \Sigma^*\}$$

$$W_{k+1} = W_k \cup \{A \in N \mid A \to \alpha \text{ is in } P \quad \text{for some } \alpha \in (\Sigma \cup W_k)^*\}.$$

Intuitively, W_k contains those variables that will derive some string of terminals in a derivation tree of height less than or equal to k.

i) $W_k \subseteq W_{k+1}$, by construction.

ii) If there exists an i such that $W_i = W_{i+1}$, then

$$W_i = W_{i+m}, \qquad \text{for all } m \geq 0.$$

Proof By induction on m.

Basis. $W_i = W_{i+0}$.

Induction step. Suppose $W_i = W_{i+m}$. Then

$$\begin{aligned} A \in W_{i+m+1} &\Leftrightarrow A \in W_{i+m} \quad \text{or} \quad A \to \alpha \text{ is in } P \text{ for some } \alpha \in (\Sigma \cup W_{i+m})^* \\ &\Leftrightarrow A \in W_i \quad \text{or} \quad A \to \alpha \text{ is in } P \text{ for some } \alpha \in (\Sigma \cup W_i)^* \\ &\Leftrightarrow A \in W_{i+1} \\ &\Leftrightarrow A \in W_i. \end{aligned}$$

This completes the proof of (ii).

Note that the above proof would generalize for any sequence of sets defined in this manner and for any predicate that depends on its predecessors in a similar fashion.

iii) $W_n = W_{n+1}$ where $n = |N|$.

Proof From (i) we have

$$W_1 \subseteq W_2 \subseteq W_3 \subseteq \cdots \subseteq W_n \subseteq W_{n+1} \subseteq \cdots.$$

But for all i, $W_i \subseteq N \Rightarrow |W_i| \leq |N|$. Therefore, by a trivial counting argument,

$$W_n = W_{n+1}.$$

iv) $A \in W_i$ if and only if $A \overset{*}{\Rightarrow} x$ where $x \in \Sigma^*$ in a derivation tree of height $\leq i$.

Proof The argument is an induction on i.

Basis. $i = 1$. The result is immediate.

Induction step. Assume the result for i. Then by the construction, $A \in W_{i+1}$ if and only if $A \in W_i$ or $A \to \alpha$ is in P for some $\alpha \in (\Sigma \cup W_i)^*$. The induction hypothesis will take care of the first possibility. In the other case, let

$$\alpha = u_0 C_1 u_1 \cdots u_{k-1} C_k u_k,$$

where $k \geqslant 0$, $C_j \in W_i$, and $u_j \in \Sigma^*$ for all j. By the induction hypothesis, there exist $z_j \in \Sigma^*$ such that $C_j \overset{*}{\Rightarrow} z_j$ in a tree of height $\leqslant i$.

If one notes that the tree in Fig. 3.1 is of height $\leqslant i + 1$, then we can conclude the following: $A \in W_{i+1}$ if and only if $A \overset{*}{\Rightarrow} x$ for some $x \in \Sigma^*$ by a tree of height $\leqslant i + 1$. This completes the proof of (iv).

v) $W_n = \{A \mid A \overset{*}{\Rightarrow} x \quad \text{for some } x \in \Sigma^*\}$ where $n = |N|$.

Proof If $A \in W_n$, then A is in the righthand side of (v). Conversely suppose $A \overset{*}{\Rightarrow} x$. Let i be the height of a derivation tree of x from A. If $i \leqslant n$, then

$$A \in W_i \subseteq W_n.$$

If $i > n$, write $i = n + m$. Then, by (ii) and (iii),

$$A \in W_{n+m} = W_n,$$

and the proof of (v) is complete.

Now we can finish the proof by constructing G'. If $L(G) \neq \emptyset$, define

$$G' = (V', \Sigma, P', S),$$

$$V' = W_n \cup \Sigma \cup \{S\},$$

$$P' = \{A \to \alpha \mid A, \alpha \in (\Sigma \cup W_n)^*, \quad \text{and} \quad A \to \alpha \text{ is in } P\}.$$

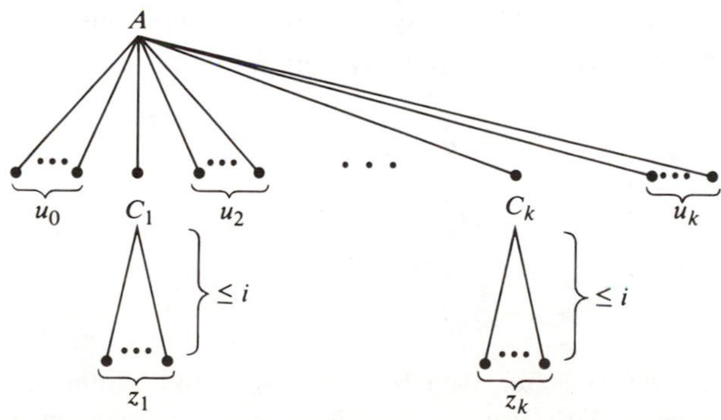

FIG. 3.1

In the extreme case where $L(G) = \emptyset$, we'll have $S \notin W_n$. By convention, G' will not have any rules; that is, $P' = \emptyset$. If $L(G) \neq \emptyset$, then, for any $A \in N'$, there is $x \in \Sigma^*$ so that

$$A \overset{*}{\underset{G'}{\Rightarrow}} x$$

This follows from the construction and (v). All that remains for us to do is to show that

$$L(G) = L(G').$$

Since $P' \subseteq P$, every G' derivation is a G derivation and $L(G') \subseteq L(G)$. Conversely, suppose $w \in L(G)$. Then $S \overset{*}{\Rightarrow} w$ and $w \in \Sigma^*$. For every variable A_j that appears in the tree, $A_j \overset{*}{\Rightarrow} u_j$, $u_j \in \Sigma^*$. Thus $A_j \in W_n$ by (v), and the first production used was of the form $\pi_j = A_j \to \alpha_j$ and it must be the case that $\alpha_j \in (\Sigma \cup W_n)^*$. Therefore, each such $\pi_j \in P'$, and hence we have a G' derivation of w. Thus $L(G) \subseteq L(G')$, and therefore:

$$L(G) = L(G'). \qquad \square$$

Example Consider the grammar

$$E \to E + E \mid T \mid F$$
$$F \to F * E \mid (T) \mid a$$
$$T \to E - T$$

The algorithm works in a bottom-up fashion:

$W_1 = \{F\}$ since $F \to a$ is a production;

$W_2 = \{F, E\}$ since $E \to F$ is a production;

$W_3 = W_2$.

The new grammar has rules:

$$E \to E + E \mid F$$
$$F \to F * E \mid a$$

There is another problem to be considered in examining the structure of a grammar. The following example illustrates the problem.

Example

$$S \to aBa$$
$$B \to Sb \mid bCC$$
$$C \to abb$$
$$D \to aC$$

If S is the start symbol, then D cannot occur in a sentential form; i.e., it is not "reachable" from S. We begin our consideration of this phenomenon by defining *reachability*.

Definition Let $G = (V, \Sigma, P, S)$ be a context-free grammar, and let $A \in N$ and $B \in V$. B is said to be *reachable* from A if

$$A \overset{*}{\Rightarrow} \alpha B \beta \qquad \text{for some } \alpha, \beta \in V^*.$$

A construction is now given to eliminate unreachable symbols.

Theorem 3.2.2 For each context-free grammar $G = (V, \Sigma, P, S)$, one can effectively construct $G' = (V', \Sigma', P', S)$ such that $L(G') = L(G)$ and each symbol in V' is reachable from S.

Proof For each $A \in N$, define

$$W_1(A) = \{A\};$$

$$W_{k+1}(A) = W_k(A) \cup \{C \in V \mid \text{there exist } \alpha, \beta \in V^* \text{ and } B \in W_k(A) \text{ so that } B \to \alpha C \beta \text{ is in } P\}.$$

Intuitively, $W_k(A)$ contains all symbols reachable from A by a derivation of fewer than k steps.

The $W_k(A)$ have the following properties:

i) $W_k(A) \subseteq W_{k+1}(A)$;

ii) If $W_k(A) = W_{k+1}(A)$, then for all $m \geq 0$, $W_k(A) = W_{k+m}(A)$;

iii) $W_n(A) = W_{n+1}(A)$ where $n = |N|$;

iv) $W_n(A) = \{B \in V \mid A \overset{*}{\Rightarrow} \alpha B \beta,\ \ \alpha, \beta \in V^*\}$.

The proof of these facts completely parallels that used in Theorem 3.2.1 and is omitted.

To obtain G', we use $W_n(S)$ in the following way. Let

$$G' = (V', \Sigma', P', S),$$

$$V' = W_n(S) \quad \text{and} \quad \Sigma' = V' \cap \Sigma,$$

$$P' = \{A \to \alpha \text{ in } P \mid A \in W_n(S)\}.$$

Every symbol in V' is in $W_n(S)$ and by (iv) is reachable from S. To complete the proof, it must only be checked that G and G' are equivalent. Since $P' \subseteq P$, any G' derivation is a G derivation, and so $L(G') \subseteq L(G)$. Conversely, if $w \in L(G)$, then

$$S \underset{G}{\overset{*}{\Rightarrow}} w \tag{3.2.1}$$

Every symbol in each step is in $W_n(S)$ and so each production used in (3.2.1) is in P'. Thus, (3.2.1) may be written:

$$S \underset{G'}{\overset{*}{\Rightarrow}} w$$

and $L(G) \subseteq L(G')$, which completes the proof. □

Example Let us return to the previous example and consider G where P consists of the following productions:

$$S \to aBa$$
$$B \to Sb \mid bCC$$
$$C \to abb$$
$$D \to aC$$

Let us compute $W_4(S)$:

$$W_1(S) = \{S\},$$
$$W_2(S) = \{S, B, a\},$$
$$W_3(S) = \{S, B, C, a, b\} = W_4(S).$$

Thus, D cannot be reached from S and the construction produces G', where:

$$\Sigma' = \{a, b\} \qquad N = \{S, B, C\}$$
$$S \to aBa$$
$$B \to Sb \mid bCC$$
$$C \to abb$$

In our discussion about reachability, our examples stressed the case of unreachable variables. Actually, the discussion is relevant to terminal symbols that are not reachable from S. The reader should now recheck the previous discussion to see how that case was accommodated.

We may combine the ideas of Theorems 2.3.1 and 2.3.2 to yield the following concept of a reduced grammar:

Definition A context-free grammar $G = (V, \Sigma, P, S)$ is *reduced* if $P = \emptyset$ or, for every $A \in V$, $S \overset{*}{\Rightarrow} \alpha A \beta \overset{*}{\Rightarrow} w$ for some $\alpha, \beta \in V^*$, $w \in \Sigma^*$.

The main result is that every language has a reduced grammar.

Theorem 3.2.3 For each context-free grammar $G = (V, \Sigma, P, S)$, one can effectively construct a context-free grammar G' such that $L(G') = L(G)$ and G' is reduced.

Proof Given a grammar G, we may use Theorem 3.2.1, and we may assume that every variable (except possibly S) produces a terminal string. Next we apply the construction of Theorem 3.2.2. It is easily checked that this transformation does not undo the effects of the first transformation, since we are just deleting rules. Now the resulting grammar is equivalent to G and is reduced.

There is only one case that has not been explained. Suppose that the original grammar G generated the empty set. Then all variables except S would be eliminated by these transformations and all S-productions would be eliminated by the first transformation. G' would end up with $P' = \emptyset$ and that is desirable since $\emptyset$ is a context-free language. □

By an earlier remark, a reduced grammar with $P \neq \emptyset$ has no unused symbols whether they are terminals or variables.

PROBLEMS

1 Let us reconsider the proof of Theorem 3.2.1. Define a sequence of sets

$$W'_0 = \emptyset,$$

$$W'_{k+1} = \{A \in N \mid A \to \alpha \text{ is in } P \quad \text{for some } \alpha \in (\Sigma \cup W'_k)^*\}.$$

Relate the sets W'_k to the W_k defined in the original proof.

2 Construct a reduced grammar equivalent to the grammar shown below. Let G be

$$S \to aBa$$

$$B \to Sb \mid bCC \mid DaB$$

$$C \to abb \mid DD$$

$$E \to aC$$

$$D \to aDB$$

3 Construct a reduced grammar for the following grammar G where $G = (V, \Sigma, P, S)$ and P is:

$$S \to aSbS$$

$$A \to bBSa \mid bBaB$$

$$B \to ABaA \mid C$$

$$C \to ABS \mid ab$$

4 Can you reformulate the construction given in Theorem 3.2.2 as a transitive closure problem?

5 Give an algorithm for deciding whether an arbitrary context-free grammar generates the empty set.

6 Let $G = (V, \Sigma, P, S)$ be a context-free grammar and let $\alpha, \beta \in V^*$. Give an algorithm for deciding whether $\alpha \overset{*}{\Rightarrow} \beta$. Note that when $\alpha = S$ and $\beta = w \in \Sigma^*$, this gives an algorithm for checking whether $w \in L(G)$ and shows that context-free languages are recursive sets.

7 Show that a reduced grammar for the context-free language $\{\Lambda\}$ cannot have any rule of the form

$$A \to \alpha a \beta$$

with $a \in \Sigma, \alpha, \beta \in V^*$.

3.3 A TECHNICAL LEMMA AND SOME APPLICATIONS TO CLOSURE PROPERTIES

There is a technical lemma which is very useful in writing proofs in context-free language theory. We will prove this easy lemma now, and use it in showing that the context-free languages are closed under transpose.

Lemma 3.3.1 Let $G = (V, \Sigma, P, S)$ be a context-free grammar and let $\alpha, \beta \in V^*$. If $\alpha \overset{r}{\Rightarrow} \beta$ for some $r \geqslant 0$ and if $\alpha = \alpha_1 \cdots \alpha_n$ for some $n \geqslant 1$, $\alpha_i \in V^*$ for

$1 \leqslant i \leqslant n$, then there exist $t_i \geqslant 0$, $\beta_i \in V^*$ for $1 \leqslant i \leqslant n$ such that $\beta = \beta_1 \cdots \beta_n$, $\alpha_i \overset{t_i}{\Rightarrow} \beta_i$, and

$$\sum_{i=1}^{n} t_i = r.$$

Proof We induct on r, the length of the derivation.

Basis. Let $\alpha = \alpha_1 \cdots \alpha_n \overset{0}{\Rightarrow} \beta$. Then $\alpha = \beta$, so let $\beta_i = \alpha_i$ and $t_i = 0$. Hence, $\alpha_i \overset{0}{\Rightarrow} \beta_i$ and:

$$\sum_{i=1}^{n} t_i = 0 = r.$$

Induction step. Our induction hypothesis is that if $\alpha = \alpha_1 \cdots \alpha_n \overset{r}{\Rightarrow} \beta$, then there exist $t_i \geqslant 0, \beta_i \in V^*$ such that $\beta = \beta_1 \cdots \beta_n, \alpha_i \overset{t_i}{\Rightarrow} \beta_i$ and $\Sigma_{i=1}^{n} t_i = r$.

Now consider

$$\alpha = \alpha_1 \cdots \alpha_n \overset{r+1}{\Rightarrow} \beta$$

Then there exists $\gamma \in V^*$ such that $\alpha = \alpha_1 \cdots \alpha_n \Rightarrow \gamma \overset{r}{\Rightarrow} \beta$. Because G is a context-free grammar, the rule used in $\alpha \Rightarrow \gamma$ was of the form $A \to \xi$. Let α_k, $1 \leqslant k \leqslant n$, contain the A that was rewritten in $\alpha \Rightarrow \gamma$. Then $\alpha_k = \alpha' A \beta'$ for some $\alpha', \beta' \in V^*$. Let

$$\gamma_i = \begin{cases} \alpha_i & \text{if } i \neq k, \\ \alpha' \xi \beta' & \text{if } i = k. \end{cases}$$

Then $\alpha_i \overset{0}{\Rightarrow} \gamma_i$ if $i \neq k$ and $\alpha_k \overset{1}{\Rightarrow} \gamma_k$. Thus

$$\alpha = \alpha_1 \cdots \alpha_n \Rightarrow \gamma_1 \cdots \gamma_n \overset{r}{\Rightarrow} \beta$$

By the induction hypothesis, there exist t_i, β_i so that $\beta = \beta_1 \cdots \beta_n$, $\gamma_i \overset{t_i}{\Rightarrow} \beta_i$ and $\Sigma_{i=1}^{n} t_i = r$. Combining the derivations, we find

$$\alpha_i \overset{0}{\Rightarrow} \gamma_i \overset{t_i}{\Rightarrow} \beta_i \quad \text{for } i \neq k$$

and

$$\alpha_k \Rightarrow \gamma_k \overset{t_k}{\Rightarrow} \beta_k$$

Let

$$t_i' = \begin{cases} t_i & \text{if } i \neq k, \\ t_k + 1 & \text{if } i = k. \end{cases}$$

Thus we know $t_i' \geqslant 0, \beta_i \in V^*$, so that

$$\beta = \beta_1 \cdots \beta_n$$

$$\alpha_i \overset{t_i'}{\Rightarrow} \beta_i$$

We compute $\Sigma_{i=1}^{n} t_i' = 1 + \Sigma_{i=1}^{n} t_i = r + 1$. □

Next we turn to proving a closure property of context-free languages.

Theorem 3.3.1 If L is a context-free language, then

$$L^T = \{x^T \mid x \in L\}$$

is a context-free language.

Proof Let $L = L(G)$, where $G = (V, \Sigma, P, S)$ is a context-free grammar. Define

$$G^T = (V, \Sigma, P^T, S),$$

where

$$P^T = \{A \to \alpha^T \mid A \to \alpha \text{ is in } P\}.$$

Claim For each $A \in N, A \overset{*}{\underset{G}{\Rightarrow}} \alpha, \alpha \in V^*$ if and only if $A \overset{*}{\underset{G^T}{\Rightarrow}} \alpha^T$.

Proof of claim We will show by induction on the length r of a derivation in G that if $A \overset{r}{\Rightarrow} \alpha, \alpha \in V^*$ then $A \overset{r}{\underset{G^T}{\Rightarrow}} \alpha^T$. The reverse direction follows from the observation that we could replace G by G^T, and vice versa, in the proof. Note that $(G^T)^T = G$.

Basis. For any $A \in N, A \overset{0}{\underset{G}{\Rightarrow}} A$ implies $A \overset{0}{\underset{G^T}{\Rightarrow}} A$.

Induction step. Assume that for all $A \in N$, if $A \overset{t}{\underset{G}{\Rightarrow}} \alpha$, $\alpha \in V^*$, and $t \leqslant r$, then $A \overset{t}{\underset{G^T}{\Rightarrow}} \alpha^T$. If $A \overset{r+1}{\underset{G}{\Rightarrow}} \beta$, then $A \underset{G}{\Rightarrow} \alpha \overset{r}{\underset{G}{\Rightarrow}} \beta$. Let

$$\alpha = u_1 A_1 u_2 A_2 \cdots u_n A_n u_{n+1} \qquad u_i \in \Sigma^*, \qquad A_i \in N.$$

Now since $A \underset{G}{\Rightarrow} \alpha$ is in P implies $A \underset{G}{\Rightarrow} \alpha^T$ is in P',

$$A \underset{G^T}{\Rightarrow} \alpha^T = u_{n+1}^T A_n u_n^T A_{n-1} \cdots u_2^T A_1 u_1^T$$

But $u_1 A_1 u_2 A_2 \cdots u_n A_n u_{n+1} \overset{r}{\underset{G}{\Rightarrow}} \beta$. By the preceding lemma, there exist $\gamma_i \in V^*$, $t_i \geqslant 0$ so that $A_i \overset{t_i}{\Rightarrow} \gamma_i$, $\beta = u_1 \gamma_1 u_2 \gamma_2 \cdots \gamma_n u_{n+1}$; and $\Sigma_{i=1}^n t_i = r$. Thus each $t_i \leqslant r$ and the induction hypothesis holds for $A_i \overset{t_i}{\Rightarrow} \gamma_i$ so that $A \overset{t_i}{\underset{G^T}{\Rightarrow}} \gamma_i^T$. Therefore

$$A \underset{G^T}{\Rightarrow} u_{n+1}^T A_n \cdots A_1 u_1^T \overset{r}{\underset{G^T}{\Rightarrow}} u_{n+1}^T \gamma_n^T \cdots \gamma_1^T u_1^T = \beta^T$$

which extends the induction and proves the claim.

In particular, for $w \in \Sigma^*$,

$$S \overset{*}{\underset{G}{\Rightarrow}} w \qquad \text{if and only if} \qquad S \underset{G^T}{\Rightarrow} w^T$$

Therefore

$$(L(G))^T = L(G^T).$$

□

Corollary L is a regular set if and only if L is a left linear language.

Proof This is an immediate consequence of the following observations.

a) L is regular if and only if L is a right linear language. Cf. Theorem 2.5.1.

b) If G is right linear, then G^T is left linear.

c) If L is regular, then L^T is regular. Cf. Theorem 2.3.2. □

PROBLEMS

1 Show that the language

$$L = \{w \in \{a, b\}^* \mid \#_a(w) = \#_b(w)\}$$

is an unambiguous context-free language.

2 Is L, given in Problem 1, also linear and unambiguous?

3 Show that Lemma 3.3.1 becomes false for transitive closure ($\overset{+}{\Rightarrow}$) rather than $\overset{*}{\Rightarrow}$. That is, if we assume $r \geqslant 1$ and require $t_i \geqslant 1$ for each $1 \leqslant i \leqslant n$, then the result is no longer true.

3.4 THE SUBSTITUTION THEOREM

Intuitively we know that if a context-free grammar G generates $\{a^n b^n\}$, then $\{0^n 1^n\}$ is also context-free, because we could go through the grammar and replace a by 0 and b by 1. This would suggest that if we replaced a and b by any strings x, y, and possibly by any two "reasonable" sets of strings, we would still have a context-free language. In this section we will treat this situation in its full generality.

Definition Let Σ be a fixed alphabet. For any $a \in \Sigma$, let Σ_a be an alphabet and let $\varphi(a) \subseteq \Sigma_a^*$ be a set. Such a mapping φ is a *substitution mapping* if

$$\varphi(\Lambda) = \{\Lambda\}$$

and if for all a_i, $1 \leqslant i \leqslant k$,

$$\varphi(a_1 \cdots a_k) = \varphi(a_1) \cdots \varphi(a_k).$$

Note. (i) φ is a set-valued function.

(ii) If $\varphi(a)$ is a singleton, then φ reduces to the usual definition of a semigroup homomorphism.

We extend φ to sets in an obvious way, namely if $L \subseteq \Sigma^*$,

$$\varphi(L) = \bigcup_{x \in L} \varphi(x).$$

Let us work more examples in order to understand this operation. Let

$$L = \{a^n b c^n \mid n \geqslant 1\}.$$

Define $\varphi a = L_1$, $\varphi b = L_2$, and $\varphi c = L_3$, where L_1, L_2, and L_3 are any three fixed context-free languages. Then

$$\varphi L = \bigcup_{n \geqslant 1} L_1^n L_2 L_3^n.$$

Now, we shall give the main theorem of this section.

Theorem 3.4.1 If L is a context-free language and φ is a substitution map such that for every $a \in \Sigma$, $\varphi(a)$ is a context-free language, then $\varphi(L)$ is a context-free language.

Proof

$$L = L(G_L), \qquad G_L = (V_L, \Sigma_L, P_L, S),$$

and for every $a \in \Sigma_L$, since $L_a = \varphi(a)$ is a context-free language, let

$$L_a = L(G_a), \qquad G_a = (V_a, \Sigma_a, P_a, S_a).$$

By appropriate renaming of variables we can ensure that for each $a, b \in \Sigma$,

$$N_a \cap V_b = \emptyset \qquad \text{and} \qquad N_b \cap V_L = \emptyset \qquad \text{and} \qquad \Sigma_a \cap N_L = \emptyset.$$

Therefore we can assume, without loss of generality, that these conditions hold. Now define a mapping

$$\tau\colon V_L \to N_L \cup \left(\bigcup_{a \in \Sigma_L} \{S_a\} \right)$$

by

$$\tau(a) = \begin{cases} a & \text{if } a \in N_L, \\ S_a & \text{if } a \in \Sigma_L. \end{cases}$$

Next extend τ to strings by letting

$$\tau(\Lambda) = \Lambda$$

and if $x \in V_L^*, x = x_1 \cdots x_n, x_i \in V_L$, then

$$\tau(x) = \tau(x_1)\tau(x_2) \cdots \tau(x_n).$$

Now let

$$\begin{aligned} G_{L'} &= (V_{L'}, \Sigma_{L'}, P_{L'}, S), \\ \Sigma_{L'} &= \bigcup_{a \in \Sigma_L} \{S_a\}, \\ V_{L'} &= N_L \cup \Sigma_{L'}, \\ P_{L'} &= \{A \to \tau(\alpha) |\ A \to \alpha \text{ is in } P\}. \end{aligned}$$

Claim 1 For each $A \in N_L, A \overset{*}{\underset{G_L}{\Rightarrow}} \alpha$ if and only if $A \overset{*}{\underset{G_{L'}}{\Rightarrow}} \tau(\alpha)$.

Proof This is intuitively obvious, since τ corresponds to a simple renaming of Σ_L. A formal proof by induction on the length of the derivation, using the Lemma 3.3.1, is straightforward and is left as an exercise.

In particular we have

$$S \overset{*}{\underset{G_L}{\Rightarrow}} a_1 \cdots a_n \in L(G_L) \quad \text{if and only if } S \overset{*}{\underset{G_{L'}}{\Rightarrow}} S_{a_1} \cdots S_{a_n}, \quad a_i \in \Sigma_L, \quad 1 \leqslant i \leqslant n.$$

Now let

$$\begin{aligned} G &= (V, \Sigma, P, S), \\ V &= V_{L'} \cup \left(\bigcup_{a \in \Sigma_L} V_a \right), \\ \Sigma &= \bigcup_{a \in \Sigma_L} \Sigma_a, \\ P &= P_{L'} \cup \left(\bigcup_{a \in \Sigma_L} P_a \right). \end{aligned}$$

Claim 2 $S_{a_1} \cdots S_{a_n} \overset{*}{\underset{G}{\Rightarrow}} w \in L(G) \subseteq \Sigma^*$ if and only if there exists $w_i \in \Sigma^*$ $(1 \leqslant i \leqslant n)$ such that

$$S_{a_i} \overset{*}{\underset{G_{a_i}}{\Rightarrow}} w_i \in L(G_{a_i}) \qquad \text{and} \qquad w = w_1 \cdots w_n.$$

Proof This is a direct consequence of Lemma 3.3.1 and the fact that, since all the grammars are disjoint,

$$S_{a_i} \underset{G}{\overset{*}{\Rightarrow}} w_i \qquad \text{if and only if} \quad S_{a_i} \underset{G_{a_i}}{\overset{*}{\Rightarrow}} w_i$$

and, for each $a \in \Sigma$,

$$N_a \cap \Sigma = \emptyset.$$

Claim 3 $S \underset{G}{\overset{*}{\Rightarrow}} w$, $w \in L(G)$ if and only if there exists a derivation of the form

$$S \underset{G_{L'}}{\overset{*}{\Rightarrow}} S_{a_1} \cdots S_{a_n} \underset{G}{\overset{*}{\Rightarrow}} w$$

Proof Since $P_{L'} \subseteq P$ if $S \underset{G_{L'}}{\overset{*}{\Rightarrow}} S_{a_1} \cdots S_{a_n} \underset{G}{\overset{*}{\Rightarrow}} w$ then $S \underset{G}{\overset{*}{\Rightarrow}} w$. Conversely, let $S \underset{G}{\overset{*}{\Rightarrow}} w$. Since all the grammars involved are disjoint, rules from different grammars commute. Therefore we may "rearrange" the derivation $S \underset{G}{\overset{*}{\Rightarrow}} w$ in such a way that all rules from $P_{L'}$ precede those from the P_{a_i}. Thus there exists a derivation of the form

$$S \underset{G_{L'}}{\overset{*}{\Rightarrow}} \alpha \underset{G}{\overset{*}{\Rightarrow}} w \qquad \alpha \in V_{L'}^*$$

such that $\alpha \overset{*}{\Rightarrow} w$ uses no rule from $P_{L'}$. Since $V_{L'} \cap \Sigma = \emptyset$ and $w \in \Sigma^*$, all of α must be rewritten in the derivation $\alpha \underset{G}{\overset{*}{\Rightarrow}} w$. Now, since this derivation contains no rules from $P_{L'}$, α must be of the form:

$$\alpha = S_{a_1} S_{a_2} \cdots S_{a_n}$$

which proves the claim.

Combining these three facts we have:

$$\begin{aligned} S \underset{G}{\overset{*}{\Rightarrow}} w \in L(G) \qquad & \text{if and only if } S \underset{G_{L'}}{\overset{*}{\Rightarrow}} S_{a_1} S_{a_2} \cdots S_{a_n} \underset{G}{\overset{*}{\Rightarrow}} w \\ & \text{if and only if there exists } w_i \text{ such that} \\ & \qquad S_{a_i} \underset{G_{a_i}}{\overset{*}{\Rightarrow}} w_i \in L(G_{a_i}) \quad \text{and} \\ & \qquad S \underset{G_L}{\overset{*}{\Rightarrow}} a_1 \cdots a_n \in L(G_L) \qquad \text{(by claim 2)}, \\ & \text{if and only if } w \in \varphi(L). \end{aligned}$$

Therefore $\varphi(L) = L(G)$, which proves the theorem. □

Corollary 1 If L_1 and L_2 are context-free languages, then

i) $L_1 \cup L_2$,

ii) $L_1 L_2$,

iii) L_1^*

are context-free languages.

Proof (i) Let $L = \{a, b\}$, which is context-free. (Any finite set is context-free.) Let

$$\varphi(a) = L_1, \qquad \varphi(b) = L_2.$$

Then

$$\varphi(L) = L_1 \cup L_2.$$

ii) Let $L = \{ab\}$ and φ be as in (i). Then

$$\varphi(L) = L_1L_2.$$

iii) Let $L = \{a\}^*$. Since L is regular, it is context-free. Again let $\varphi(a) = L_1$. Then

$$\varphi(L) = L_1^*.$$

Corollary 2 If L is a context-free language and φ is any homomorphism, then $\varphi(L)$ is a context-free language.

We already know that every regular set is context-free, by the characterization theorem for right linear languages (Theorem 2.5.1). The substitution theorem gives us another proof.

Corollary 3 Every regular set is context-free.

Proof By Kleene's theorem (Theorem 2.4.1), the family of regular sets is the least collection which contains $\emptyset$, $\{a\}$, $a \in \Sigma$, and is closed under finite applications of $\cup$, $\cdot$, and *. Since $\emptyset$ is context-free, and so is $\{a\}$ for any $a \in \Sigma$, we know that every regular set is context-free, from Corollary 1. □

Now we can also show that the substitution theorem holds for the family of regular sets.

Theorem 3.4.2 If L is a regular set and φ is a substitution map such that for every $a \in \Sigma$, $\varphi(a)$ is regular, then $\varphi(L)$ is regular.

Proof Using Kleene's theorem, we know that every regular set can be obtained from $\emptyset$ and $\{a\}$, $a \in \Sigma$, by a finite number of applications of union, product, and star. Since φ maps each singleton into a set that can be obtained by a finite number of applications of union, product, and Kleene closure, replacing each $\{a\}$ in the regular expression for L by $\varphi(a)$ still gives only a finite number of applications of union, product, and closure. Hence, $\varphi(L)$ is regular. □

3.5 REGULAR SETS AND SELF-EMBEDDING GRAMMARS

Another grammatical characterization of regular sets can be given.

Definition A context-free grammar $G = (V, \Sigma, P, S)$ is *self-embedding* if there exists $A \in N$ such that

$$A \overset{*}{\Rightarrow} \alpha A \beta$$

for some $\alpha, \beta \in V^+$. A context-free language L is self-embedding if *every* context-free grammar for L is self-embedding.

This definition is equivalent to: A context-free language L is not self-embedding if and only if there exists a context-free grammar G for L that is not self-embedding.

If a variable is self-embedding, then

$$A \overset{*}{\Rightarrow} \alpha A \beta \tag{3.5.1}$$

and (3.5.1) may be iterated to yield

$$A \overset{*}{\Rightarrow} \alpha^i A \beta^i \qquad \text{for all } i \geqslant 0. \tag{3.5.2}$$

If one further assumes a reduced grammar, then strings are produced with coordinated substrings like

$$v_2^i v_3 v_4^i.$$

Sets that contain such strings give the appearance of nonregular sets. This provides some insight for the belief that self-embedding grammars may generate nonregular sets. That is not true in general, as the following example shows:

$$S \rightarrow aSa \mid a \mid \Lambda$$

This grammar generates $L(G) = a^*$. Our intuition is not completely wrong, as the following theorem shows.

Theorem 3.5.1 A set L is regular if and only if L is a context-free language and is not self-embedding.

Proof If L is regular, then $L = L(G)$ for some right linear grammar G. Since every production of G is one of the forms

$$A \rightarrow uB$$

$$A \rightarrow u$$

where $A, B \in N$, $u \in \Sigma^*$, then G is not self-embedding.

Assume $L = L(G)$, whence

$$G = (V, \Sigma, P, S)$$

is a non-self-embedding, context-free grammar. Further, without loss of generality, we may assume that G is reduced. Consider the following two cases.

CASE 1. For each $A \in N$, there exist α, β in V^* such that $A \overset{*}{\Rightarrow} \alpha S \beta$. Note that, since $S \overset{*}{\Rightarrow} S$ is always true, any grammar with exactly one variable satisfies Case 1.

Now every production in P is of at least one of the following forms:

i) $A \rightarrow \alpha B \beta$

ii) $A \rightarrow \alpha B$

iii) $A \rightarrow B \beta$

iv) $A \rightarrow B$

v) $A \rightarrow u$

where $A, B \in N$, $\alpha, \beta \in V^+$, and $u \in \Sigma^*$.

Rules of type (iv) and type (v) cause no difficulty and will not be considered further.

We now prove a series of facts which show that G is either right linear or left linear.

Fact 1 P contains no rules of type (i).

Proof Assume that P contains a production of type (i). Then

$$A \Rightarrow \alpha B\beta \qquad \alpha, \beta \in V^+.$$

Now, since we are in case 1,

$$B \overset{*}{\Rightarrow} \alpha_1 S\beta_1 \qquad \alpha_1, \beta_1 \in V^*.$$

Since G is reduced, there exist α_2, β_2 in V^* such that

$$S \overset{*}{\Rightarrow} \alpha_2 A\beta_2.$$

Combining these, we get

$$A \Rightarrow \alpha B\beta \overset{*}{\Rightarrow} \alpha\alpha_1 S\beta_1\beta \overset{*}{\Rightarrow} \alpha\alpha_1\alpha_2 A\beta_2\beta_1\beta$$

But $\alpha, \beta \in V^+$ implies $\alpha\alpha_1\alpha_2, \beta_2\beta_1\beta \in V^+$. The situation is depicted by Fig. 3.2. But this is a contradiction, since G is not self-embedding. Hence P contains no productions of type (i).

Fact 2 P does not contain productions of both type (ii) and type (iii).

Proof Assume

$$A \to \alpha B \qquad C \to D\beta \qquad \alpha, \beta \in V^+,$$

are in P. Since we are in case 1, there exist α_1, β_1 in V^* such that

$$B \overset{*}{\Rightarrow} \alpha_1 S\beta_1$$

But G is reduced, and hence there exist α_2, β_2 in V^* such that

$$S \overset{*}{\Rightarrow} \alpha_2 C\beta_2$$

Similarly, there exist α_3, α_4, β_3, β_4 in V^* so that

$$D \overset{*}{\Rightarrow} \alpha_3 S\beta_3 \qquad \text{and} \qquad S \overset{*}{\Rightarrow} \alpha_4 A\beta_4$$

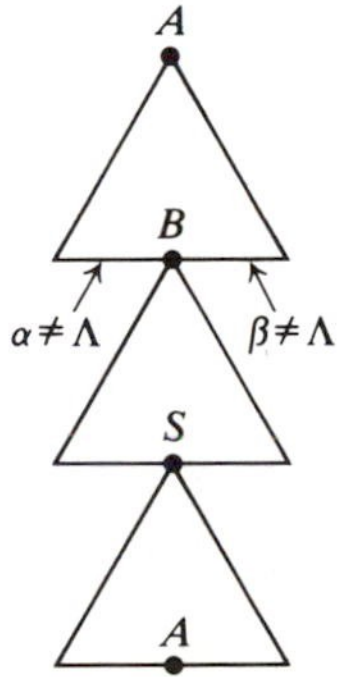

FIG. 3.2

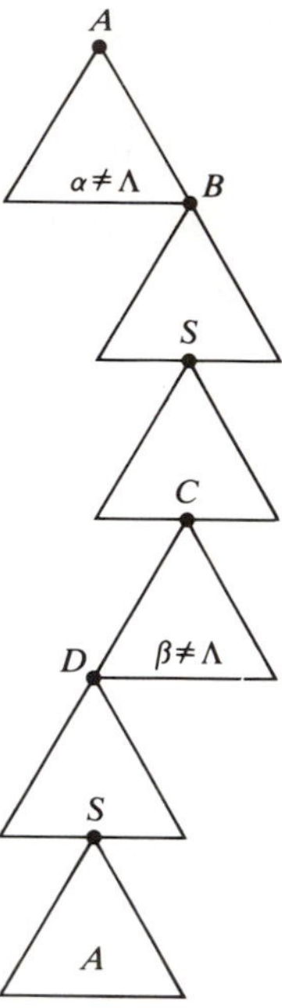

FIG. 3.3

Combining these we have

$$A \Rightarrow \alpha B \overset{*}{\Rightarrow} \alpha\alpha_1 S\beta_1 \overset{*}{\Rightarrow} \alpha\alpha_1\alpha_2 C\beta_2\beta_1 \Rightarrow \alpha\alpha_1\alpha_2 D\beta\beta_2\beta_1 \overset{*}{\Rightarrow} \alpha\alpha_1\alpha_2\alpha_3 S\beta_3\beta\beta_2\beta_1$$
$$\overset{*}{\Rightarrow} \alpha\alpha_1\alpha_2\alpha_3\alpha_4 A\beta_4\beta_3\beta\beta_2\beta_1$$

But again $\alpha, \beta \in V^+$ implies $\alpha\alpha_1\alpha_2\alpha_3\alpha_4$ and $\beta_4\beta_3\beta\beta_2\beta_1 \in V^+$. The tree is shown in Fig. 3.3. This contradicts the fact that G is not self-embedding and hence G cannot have productions of both type (ii) and type (iii).

Fact 3 If P contains a rule of type (ii) (type (iii)), $A \to \alpha B$ (respectively, $A \to B\alpha$), then $\alpha \in \Sigma^*$.

Proof We prove this only for rules of type (ii), since the proof for rules of type (iii) is completely symmetric.

Let $A \to \alpha B$ and assume $\alpha \notin \Sigma^*$. Then there exist $\gamma_1, \gamma_2 \in V^*$ and $C \in N$, such that

$$\alpha = \gamma_1 C \gamma_2$$

There are two cases to consider:

a) $\gamma_1 \neq \Lambda$. Then

$$A \to \gamma_1 C \gamma_2 B \quad \text{is in } P;$$

But γ_1, $\gamma_2 B \in V^+$, and thus P would have a rule of type (i), which contradicts Fact 1.

b) $\gamma_1 = \Lambda$. Then

$$A \to C\gamma_2 B \quad \text{is in } P;$$

but this is a rule of type (ii) and type (iii), which contradicts Fact 2. Therefore $\alpha \in \Sigma^*$.

Combining these three facts, we see that G is either a right linear grammar or a left linear grammar. In either case, L is regular, which completes Case 1.

CASE 2. There is some $A \in N$ such that for no $\alpha, \beta \in V^*$ does

$$A \overset{*}{\Rightarrow} \alpha S \beta$$

We will show by induction on the number of variables in G that $L(G)$ is regular.

Basis. $|N| = 1$. Any grammar with one variable satisfies Case 1 and the basis is vacuously satisfied.

Induction step. Assume that if $|N| = k$ and there exists $A \in N$ such that for no $\alpha, \beta \in V^*$ does

$$A \overset{*}{\Rightarrow} \alpha S \beta$$

then $L(G)$ is regular.

Now consider a grammar G in which $|N| = k + 1$. Consider the following grammars:

$$G_1 = (V, \Sigma \cup \{A\}, P_1, S),$$
$$P_1 = \{B \to \alpha \text{ in } P \mid B \in (N - \{A\})\}.$$

In G_1, we treat A as a terminal.

Now we define G_2 to be like G but S is dropped and A is the new start variable:

$$G_2 = (V - \{S\}, \Sigma, P_2, A),$$
$$P_2 = \{B \to \alpha \text{ in } P \mid B \in (N - \{S\}), \alpha \in (V - \{S\})^*\}.$$

Claim $L(G_1)$ and $L(G_2)$ are regular.

Proof If $G_1(G_2)$ satisfies the condition of Case 1, then $L(G_1)$ (respectively, $L(G_2)$) is regular. Otherwise Case 2 applies. But $|N_1|$ (and also $|N_2|) = k$ and hence, by the induction hypothesis, $L(G_1)$ (respectively, $L(G_2)$) is regular.

Now let φ be the substitution map

$$\varphi(a) = \begin{cases} L(G_2), & a = A, \\ a, & a \in \Sigma. \end{cases}$$

Since $L(G_1)$ and $L(G_2)$ are regular, $\varphi(L(G_1))$ is regular and all that must be shown is $\varphi(L(G_1)) = L(G)$.

Fact 4 For any $\alpha \in V^*$, $A \overset{*}{\underset{G}{\Rightarrow}} \alpha$ if and only if $A \overset{*}{\underset{G_2}{\Rightarrow}} \alpha$. (Recall that this is the fixed A in the definition of Case 2.)

Proof This is a direct consequence of the following.

a) If $\alpha \in V^*$ and $A \overset{*}{\underset{G}{\Rightarrow}} \alpha$ then α does not contain S, since we are in Case 2.

b) P_2 consists of precisely those rules that do not have an S in them.

Fact 5 $x \in L(G)$ if and only if there exists a derivation of the form

$$S \overset{*}{\underset{G_1}{\Rightarrow}} u_1 A u_2 A \cdots u_n A u_{n+1} \overset{*}{\underset{G}{\Rightarrow}} u_1 w_1 u_2 \cdots u_n w_n u_{n+1}$$
$$u_i, w_i \in \Sigma^*,$$

where $x = u_1 w_1 u_2 \cdots u_n w_n u_{n+1}$ and $A \overset{*}{\underset{G}{\Rightarrow}} w_i$.

Proof Clearly if such a derivation exists, $x \in L(G)$. Now suppose $x \in L(G)$. Then

$$x \in \Sigma^* \qquad \text{and} \qquad S \overset{*}{\underset{G}{\Rightarrow}} x$$

Consider a new derivation obtained from this by:

a) First rewrite *all* variables except A and its descendants, in each case using the same rule as was used in the original derivation.

b) Complete the derivation by using the remaining steps in exactly the same order as they occurred in the original derivation.

Since in (a) no rules with A on the lefthand side are used, they are all in P_1. Therefore,

$$S \overset{*}{\underset{G_1}{\Rightarrow}} u_1 A u_2 \cdots A u_{n+1} \overset{*}{\underset{G}{\Rightarrow}} x \qquad u_i \in \Sigma^*.$$

Now by Lemma 3.3.1 there exist w_i in Σ^* such that:

$$x = u_1 w_1 u_2 \cdots u_n w_n u_{n+1}$$

and

$$A \overset{*}{\underset{G}{\Rightarrow}} w_i$$

or, equivalently,

$$S \overset{*}{\underset{G_1}{\Rightarrow}} u_1 A u_2 \cdots u_n A u_{n+1} \overset{*}{\underset{G}{\Rightarrow}} u_1 w_1 u_2 \cdots u_n w_n u_{n+1}$$

This completes the proof of Claim 5. To complete the proof we have $x \in L(G)$ if and only if there exists a derivation of the form

$$S \overset{*}{\underset{G_1}{\Rightarrow}} u_1 A u_2 \cdots u_n A u_{n+1} \overset{*}{\underset{G}{\Rightarrow}} x = u_1 w_1 u_2 \cdots u_n w_n u_{n+1}$$

and

$$A \overset{*}{\underset{G}{\Rightarrow}} w_i \qquad u_i, w_i \in \Sigma^*$$

from Fact 5. This holds if and only if

$$S \overset{*}{\underset{G_1}{\Rightarrow}} u_1 A u_2 \cdots u_n A u_{n+1} \in L(G_1)$$

and

$$A \overset{*}{\underset{G_2}{\Rightarrow}} w_i \in L(G_2),$$

using Fact 4. In turn, this holds if and only if

$$x \in \varphi(L(G_1)),$$

by the definition of φ. Thus $L(G) = \varphi(L(G_1))$, and therefore $L(G)$ is regular, by the substitution theorem. □

PROBLEMS

1 Explain why the case structure of the proof of Theorem 3.5.1 is necessary. That is, why not just induct on the number of variables, as in Case 2?

3.6 HISTORICAL SURVEY

Almost all of the results given here may be found in the fundamental paper by Bar-Hillel, Perles, and Shamir [1961]. Theorem 3.5.1 is from Chomsky [1959a, 1959b].

four

Normal Forms for Context-Free Grammars

4.1 INTRODUCTION

This chapter is devoted to showing that there are many different types of context-free grammars which can generate all of the context-free languages. Results of this type are of general interest because, if one wishes to show that some set is context-free, it is easier if one can employ the full generality of context-free grammars so that one can exploit Λ-rules, chain rules, left recursion, etc. On the other hand, if one wishes to show that some property does *not* hold, it is convenient to be able to restrict the type of grammar severely, since the complexity of a proof can be reduced.

We shall be interested in exhibiting a number of normal forms which generate all the context-free languages. Moreover, we are interested in transformations for putting a given grammar into these forms, as well as analyzing how much time and/or space is required. As one might expect, there are some algorithms that are easy to describe but very inefficient.

A number of the normal forms used here are important in practical applications to parsing, while almost all of them will occur later in this book in simplifying some proof or other.

4.2 NORMS, COMPLEXITY ISSUES, AND REDUCTION REVISITED

As we consider various normal forms for grammars, constructions will be given for achieving these transformations. One question of interest is the efficiency of these methods. A full discussion of these matters would take us into the theory of computational complexity and the differences between Turing machines, random-access machines (RAMs, for short), and bit vector machines. While this is not the appropriate place for such a treatment (cf. Chapter 9), we do wish to mention enough of the ideas to permit the reader to be aware of the issues.

In order to discuss these concepts, we need to clarify the notion of the *size* of a context-free grammar.

Definition Let $G = (V, \Sigma, P, S)$ be a context-free grammar. Define

$$|G| = \sum_{\substack{A \to \alpha \\ \text{in } P}} \lg(A\alpha) \tag{4.2.1}$$

and

$$\|G\| = |G| \cdot \log_2 |V|. \tag{4.2.2}$$

$|G|$ is read as the *size* of G and $\|G\|$ the *norm* of G.

The *size* of G is simply the number of characters involved in productions. The *norm* of G is a more realistic measure because it not only counts the size of the grammar but includes a measure of the size of the alphabet used. The log occurs because one should count the amount of information in V, or the number of bits required to encode V.

For example, suppose we have some algorithm that scans the entire production set and checks, for each production,

$$A \to \alpha$$

in P, whether or not $A \in N$. Should we use $|G|$ or $\|G\|$ in evaluating the work done? Naturally the second measure is more realistic, since it accounts for the size of the alphabet and if N is large, checking to see whether $A \in N$ should enter into the accounting. On the other hand, for many purposes, $|G|$ will suffice.

First, we estimate the relationship between $|V|$ and the size of a grammar $G = (V, \Sigma, P, S)$.

Lemma 4.2.1 For any context-free grammar $G = (V, \Sigma, P, S)$ such that if $L(G) \neq \emptyset$, $L(G) \neq \{\Lambda\}$, and if every letter in V occurs in at least one production, then

i) $2 \leqslant |V| \leqslant |G|$;

ii) $|V| \leqslant 2n/(\log n)$, where $n = \|G\| = |G| \log |V|$. (All logs are to the base 2.)

Proof Since $S \in N$, $|N| \geqslant 1$. Since $\Sigma \neq \emptyset$, we have

$$|V| = |N| + |\Sigma| \geqslant 1 + 1 = 2.$$

The upper bound of (i) follows from the assumption that each symbol of V appears in at least one production.

From (i), we have

$$n = |G| \log |V| \geqslant |V| \log |V| \geqslant 2 \log 2.$$

Consider the function

$$f(x) = 2\sqrt{x} - \log x. \tag{4.2.3}$$

If (4.2.3) is differentiated,

$$f'(x) = \frac{1}{\sqrt{x}} - \frac{c}{x} = \frac{\sqrt{x} - c}{x},$$

where

$$c = \frac{1}{\ell\text{n } 2} = 1.44269\ldots$$

Thus

$$f'(x) > 0$$

if $x > c^2 = 2.0813\ldots$ The minimum of the function is at c^2 and is $f(c^2) = 1.8278\ldots$ The function f is monotonically increasing for all $x > c^2$. Since our concern is only at positive integer values, the above argument shows that

$$f(n) > f(3)$$

for all integers $n > 3$. It is also true that

$$f(3) = 1.8791\ldots > 1.8284 = f(2).$$

Hence

$$f(n) \geqslant f(2) = 2\sqrt{2} - 1 > 0$$

or, for all $n \geqslant 2$,

$$2\sqrt{n} - \log n > 0. \tag{4.2.4}$$

From (4.2.4), for all $n \geqslant 2$,

$$2\sqrt{n} > \log n.$$

Taking logs,

$$\log(2\sqrt{n}) > \log\log n,$$

$$\log 2 + \tfrac{1}{2}\log n > \log\log n,$$

$$\log 2 + \log n - \log\log n > \tfrac{1}{2}\log n,$$

$$\log\left(\frac{2n}{\log n}\right) > \frac{1}{2}\log n.$$

Multiplying by $(2n/(\log n))$ – (which is always positive in this range), we get:

$$\frac{2n}{\log n}\log\left(\frac{2n}{\log n}\right) > n;$$

but

$$n \geqslant |V| \log |V|,$$

so

$$\frac{2n}{\log n}\log\left(\frac{2n}{\log n}\right) > |V| \log |V|.$$

It follows immediately that if $x, y > 1$ and $x \log x > y \log y$, then $x > y$. Taking $x = (2n/(\log n))$ and $y = |V|$, then we have shown that

$$\frac{2n}{\log n} > |V| \qquad \square$$

Many of the current investigations into the complexity of computations give us only "order of magnitude" information about the time or the space required. Such statements are useful, and so we introduce some terminology which is convenient.

Definition Let

$\mathcal{O}(f(n)) = \{g(n) \mid$ There exist positive constants c, N_0, such that

$$|g(n)| \leqslant cf(n) \quad \text{for all } n \geqslant N_0\};$$

$\Omega(f(n)) = \{g(n) \mid$ There exist positive constants c and N_0 such that

$$g(n) \geqslant cf(n) \quad \text{for all } n \geqslant N_0\};$$

$\Theta(f(n)) = \{g(n) \mid$ There exist positive constants c, c', and N_0, such that

$$cf(n) \leqslant g(n) \leqslant c'f(n) \quad \text{for all } n \geqslant N_0\}.$$

One can read $\mathcal{O}(f(n))$ to be "order at most $f(n)$"; $\Omega(f(n))$ as "order at least $f(n)$"; $\Theta(f(n))$ as "order exactly $f(n)$".

These definitions are used in a peculiar but customary way. One writes

$$\binom{n}{2} = \mathcal{O}(n^2)$$

instead of $\binom{n}{2} \in \mathcal{O}(n^2)$. Using equality signs in this context requires care because $=$ is no longer reflexive. For instance, it is true that

$$1 + O(n^{-1}) = \mathcal{O}(1),$$

but

$$\mathcal{O}(1) = 1 + \mathcal{O}(n^{-1})$$

is false.

Now, let us examine the computation of W_n in the reduction algorithm, Theorem 3.2.1.

Theorem 4.2.1 Let $G = (V, \Sigma, P, S)$ be a context-free grammar. The computation of $W = W_n$ given in Theorem 3.2.1 requires time

$$\mathcal{O}(|N| \cdot \|G\|) \leqslant \mathcal{O}\left(\frac{\|G\|^2}{\log \|G\|}\right).$$

Proof It is clear that to compute W_i requires time proportional to the size of G. That means $|G|$ if that measure is used, or $\|G\|$ if that is used. We will work with $\|G\|$. Moreover, the computation may take at most $|N|$ iterations, so the total bound is $\mathcal{O}(|N| \cdot \|G\|)$. By Lemma 4.2.1,

$$\mathcal{O}(|N| \cdot \|G\|) \leqslant \mathcal{O}(|V| \cdot \|G\|) \leqslant \mathcal{O}\left(\frac{\|G\|^2}{\log \|G\|}\right). \qquad \square$$

Now we shall show how to do better. It will be assumed that we work on a computer with a random-access memory, which we refer to as a RAM. For the reader unfamiliar with this concept, imagine a typical general-purpose computer with an unbounded random-access memory. Each word of memory can hold an arbitrary number, and the instruction set is sufficient to compute any partial recursive function. It suffices to write programs for such a machine in a high-level language. (One can read Chapter 9 for more details about this class of machines.)

Our program will be organized as follows.

Data Structures

W is a subset of N; *stack* will denote a typical pushdown store, and we will have the usual *push* and *pop* procedures. For each $B \in N$, *position*(B) is a list of positions where B appears in the righthand side of a production; *nongen*($A \to \alpha$) is an integer for each production.

The program now follows, see Fig. 4.1.

```
begin
  W: = ∅;
  stack: = ∅;
  for all B ∈ N do position(B): = ∅;
  for all A → α in P do
  begin
    if α ∈ Σ* then
    begin
      if A ∉ W then
        begin
          W: = W ∪ {A};
          push(A)
        end
    end else
    comment α = α₀B₁ ··· αₙ₋₁Bₙαₙ where n ≥ 1, αᵢ ∈ Σ* and Bᵢ ∈ N;
    begin
      nongen(A → α): = number of variables in α;
      for all Bᵢ, 1 ≤ i ≤ n, do
      position(Bᵢ): = position(Bᵢ) ∪ {(A → α, i)}
    end
  end;
  while stack ≠ empty do
  begin
    B: = pop;
    for all (A → α, i) in position(B) do
    begin
      nongen(A → α): = nongen(A → α) − 1;
      if nongen(A → α) = 0 and A ∉ W then
        begin
          W: = W ∪ {A};
          push(A)
        end
    end
  end
end.
```

FIG. 4.1 An Improved Program to Calculate W.

It is not difficult to see that this program always terminates and calculates $W = \{A \in N \mid A \overset{*}{\Rightarrow} x \text{ for some } x \in \Sigma^*\}$. Moreover, the time required is proportional to the size of G, but that argument is more complicated.

PROBLEMS

1 Prove the claims made about the program given in this section.

2 In the argument of Lemma 4.2.1, Part (i), where are the hypotheses that $L(G) \neq \emptyset$, $L(G) \neq \{\Lambda\}$ needed? Show that (i) is false without the hypothesis. Explain.

3 Let $k \geqslant 1$ and $L_k = \{a^{4^k}\}$. Show that, for any context-free grammar G such that $L(G) = L_k$, we must have that $|G| \geqslant 5k$. The argument is rather complex and so a sketch is given here. If the reader can prove the claims, the result will follow.

Let $G = (V, \Sigma, P, S)$ be a context-free grammar and let $P = \{A_i \to \alpha_i \mid 1 \leqslant i \leqslant p\}$. Assume G minimizes $|G|$.

a) If $L(G)$ is finite, show that there is no loss of generality in assuming that there are no recursive variables. ($A \overset{*}{\Rightarrow} \alpha A \beta$ never occurs.)

b) Show that we may assume that G is Λ-free if $L(G)$ has cardinality one.

c) Show that, if $L(G) = \{x\}$, then

$$\lg(x) \leqslant \prod_{i=1}^{p} \lg(\alpha_i).$$

d) Show that there is no context-free grammar G_1 which can generate $\{a^4\}$ with $|G_1| < 5$.

e) Show that there do not exist nonnegative integers p and x_i, $1 \leqslant i \leqslant p$, such that

$$\prod_{i=1}^{p} x_i \geqslant 4^k$$

and

$$\sum_{i=1}^{p} (x_i + 1) < 5k.$$

4.3 ELIMINATION OF NULL AND CHAIN RULES

Our first goal is to show that null rules may be eliminated from a context-free grammar. If we do this carefully, the language $L(G)$ will not be altered if $\Lambda \notin L(G)$. If $\Lambda \in L(G)$, then we could eliminate all null rules and get a grammar for $L(G) - \{\Lambda\}$. Instead, we'll eliminate all null rules except $S \to \Lambda$ and further restrict the new grammar so that S appears on no righthand side of a production.

An essential part of a proof of this result is an algorithm to determine which variables can generate Λ. The first algorithm is the "classical" one due to Bar-Hillel, Perles, and Shamir [1961].

Theorem 4.3.1 Let $G = (V, \Sigma, P, S)$ be a context-free grammar. There is an algorithm for producing a context-free grammar $G' = (V', \Sigma, P', S')$, so that

i) $L(G') = L(G)$;

ii) $A \to \Lambda$ is in P' if and only if $\Lambda \in L(G)$ and $A = S'$;

iii) S' does not occur on the righthand side of any production in P'.

Proof Let $n = |N|$ and $W_1 = \{A \mid A \to \Lambda\}$. For each $k \geqslant 1$, let

$$W_{k+1} = W_k \cup \{A \mid A \to \alpha \text{ is in } P \text{ for some } \alpha \in W_k^*\}.$$

It is easy to see that:

1 $W_i \subseteq W_{i+1}$ for each $i \geqslant 1$;

2 If $W_i = W_{i+1}$, then $W_i = W_{i+m}$ for each $m \geqslant 1$;

3 $W_{n+1} = W_n$;

4 $W_n = \{A \in N \mid A \overset{*}{\Rightarrow} \Lambda\}$;

5 $\Lambda \in L(G)$ if and only if $S \in W_n$.

To construct the new grammar, define $G' = (V \cup \{S'\}, \Sigma, P', S')$, where

$$P' = \{S' \to S\} \cup \{S' \to \Lambda \mid S \in W_n\} \cup \{A \to A_1 \cdots A_k \mid k \geqslant 1;\ \ A_i \in V;$$
$$\text{there exist } \alpha_1, \ldots, \alpha_{k+1} \in W_n^* \text{ so that } A \to \alpha_1 A_1 \ldots \alpha_k A_k \alpha_{k+1} \text{ is in } P\}.$$

Clearly, S' does not appear on the righthand side of any production in P'. Moreover, $\Lambda \in L(G')$ if and only if $S' \to \Lambda$ is in P' if and only if $S \in W_n$ if and only if $S \overset{*}{\Rightarrow} \Lambda$ if and only if $\Lambda \in L(G)$.

It only remains for us to show that $L(G') = L(G)$. First, we see that, for each production $A \to A_1 \cdots A_k$ in P', there must have been a production $A \to \alpha_1 A_1 \cdots \alpha_k A_k \alpha_{k+1}$ in P, where $\alpha_i \in W_n^*$ for $1 \leqslant i \leqslant k+1$. Thus, $\alpha_i \underset{G}{\overset{*}{\Rightarrow}} \Lambda$, and so

$$A \underset{G}{\Rightarrow} \alpha_1 A_1 \cdots \alpha_k A_k \alpha_{k+1} \underset{G}{\overset{*}{\Rightarrow}} A_1 \cdots A_k$$

Thus every production in G' can be simulated in G by a derivation so that $L(G') \subseteq L(G)$.

To see that $L(G) \subseteq L(G')$, we shall prove, by induction on the length h of a derivation, that if $A \underset{G}{\overset{h}{\Rightarrow}} w$, $w \in \Sigma^+$, then $A \underset{G'}{\overset{*}{\Rightarrow}} w$.

Basis. $h = 1$. If $A \to w$ is in P, then, since $w \neq \Lambda$, $A \to w$ is in P'.

Induction step. If $A \underset{G}{\Rightarrow} A_1 \cdots A_k \underset{G}{\overset{t}{\Rightarrow}} w$, $w \in \Sigma^+$, $t \leqslant h$, then, by Lemma 3.3.1, there exist $w_i \in \Sigma^*$ so that $w = w_1 \cdots w_k$ and $A_i \underset{G}{\overset{t'}{\Rightarrow}} w_i$ for some $t' \leqslant h$. If $w_i \in \Sigma^+$, then $A_i \underset{G'}{\overset{*}{\Rightarrow}} w_i$ by the induction hypothesis. If $w_i = \Lambda$, then $A_i \in W_n$ and $A \to A_{j_1} \cdots A_{j_p}$ is in P', where $1 \leqslant p \leqslant k$ and $A_{j_1} \cdots A_{j_p}$ is the subsequence of $A_1 \cdots A_k$ obtained by deleting those A_i whose $w_i = \Lambda$. Therefore,

$$A \underset{G'}{\Rightarrow} A_{j_1} \cdots A_{j_p} \underset{G'}{\overset{*}{\Rightarrow}} w_{j_1} \cdots w_{j_p}$$

where $w_{j_1} \cdots w_{j_p} = w$. □

Corollary There is an algorithm which decides whether $\Lambda \in L(G)$ for any context-free grammar G.

Proof From (v), $\Lambda \in L(G)$ if and only if $S \in W_n$. □

Example We can illustrate the construction with the following grammar, where $\Sigma = \{a, b, x\}$:

$$S \rightarrow aOb$$
$$O \rightarrow P|aOb|OO$$
$$P \rightarrow x|E$$
$$E \rightarrow \Lambda$$

The grammar is part of ALGOL. To see this, make the following associations:

S	stands for	⟨string⟩;
O	stands for	⟨open string⟩;
P	stands for	⟨proper string⟩;
E	stands for	⟨empty⟩;
a	stands for	‘
b	stands for	’
x	stands for	⟨any sequence of basic symbols not containing”⟩

Here we regard x as a terminal, for simplicity. We compute:

$$W_1 = \{E\},$$
$$W_2 = \{E, P\},$$
$$W_3 = \{E, P, O\},$$

and $W_4 = W_3$. The new grammar is:

$$S' \rightarrow S$$
$$S \rightarrow aOb|ab$$
$$O \rightarrow P|aOb|OO|O|ab$$
$$P \rightarrow x|E$$

Note that the new grammar contains many redundancies. When it is reduced it may not even resemble the original one. Note that these changes all came merely from the single rule $E \rightarrow \Lambda$. In more complex examples, the grammars are changed drastically.

Now that we have developed this grammatical transformation, it is easy to see how to pass from any context-free grammar G to a Λ-free grammar which generates $L(G) - \{\Lambda\}$.

Example The next example will help us understand the complexity of this algorithm.

$$S \rightarrow A_1 \cdots A_k$$
$$A_i \rightarrow a_i|\Lambda \qquad \text{for all } i,\ 1 \leqslant i \leqslant k.$$

Note that $|\Sigma| = k$, $|V| = 2k+1$, $|G| = 4k+1$, and $\|G\| = (4k+1)\log(2k+1)$. If we compute G', we find that P' is as follows:

$$
\begin{aligned}
S' &\to S \mid \Lambda \\
S &\to X_1 \cdots X_k \qquad X_i \in \{A_i, \Lambda\} \quad \text{and} \quad X_1 \cdots X_k \neq \Lambda, \\
A_i &\to a_i \qquad 1 \leqslant i \leqslant k,
\end{aligned}
$$

where $|V'| = 2k+2$. To compute $|G'|$, we merely count the symbols in each production. This results in

$$
\begin{aligned}
|G'| = {} & 2 + \\
& 1 + \\
& \sum_{i=0}^{k} \binom{k}{i}(1+i) - 1 + 2k
\end{aligned}
$$

Thus,

$$
\begin{aligned}
|G'| &= 2k + 2 + \sum_{i=0}^{k} \binom{k}{i} + \sum_{i=0}^{k} i\binom{k}{i} \\
&= 2k + 2 + 2^k + k2^{k-1} \\
&= (k+2)2^{k-1} + 2k + 2.
\end{aligned}
$$

This algorithm takes exponential time no matter how the set of variables that derive Λ is computed, because it takes that long to even write down G'.

It is possible to do much better. One can in fact show that this can be done in essentially linear time.

The next case to be considered is the elimination of "chain rules."

Definition Let $G = (V, \Sigma, P, S)$ be a context-free grammar. A production $A \to B$ in P is called a *chain rule* if $A, B \in N$.

Now we present an algorithm to eliminate both chain and Λ-rules.

Theorem 4.3.2 For each context-free grammar $G = (V, \Sigma, P, S)$, there is a grammar $G' = (V, \Sigma, P', S)$ so that $L(G') = L(G)$ and P' has only productions of the form

$$
\begin{aligned}
S &\to \Lambda \\
A &\to \alpha \qquad \alpha \in (V - \{S\})^+, \ \lg(\alpha) \geqslant 2, \\
A &\to a \qquad a \in \Sigma.
\end{aligned}
$$

Proof We may assume, without loss of generality, that $G = (V, \Sigma, P, S)$ satisfies the conditions of Theorem 4.3.1. Let $A \in N$ and we shall eliminate all chain rules $A \to B$, $B \in N$, by the following construction. Define

$$W_0(A) = \{A\}$$

and, for each $i \geqslant 0$,

$$W_{i+1}(A) = W_i(A) \cup \{B \in N \mid C \to B \text{ is in } P \text{ for some } C \in W_i(A)\}.$$

The following facts are immediate:

i) For each $i \geqslant 0$, $W_i(A) \subseteq W_{i+1}(A)$;

ii) If $W_i(A) = W_{i+1}(A)$, then, for all $m \geqslant 0$, $W_i(A) = W_{i+m}(A)$;

iii) $W_n(A) = W_{n+1}(A)$, where $n = |N|$;

iv) $W_n(A) = \{B \in N | \ A \overset{*}{\Rightarrow} B\}$.

Next, we define $G' = (V, \Sigma, P', S)$, where

$$P' = \{A \to \alpha | \ \alpha \notin N \text{ and } B \to \alpha \text{ is in } P \quad \text{for some } B \in W_n(A)\}.$$

It is clear that G' satisfies the conditions of the theorem. It is straightforward to verify that $L(G') = L(G)$. □

Example

$$E \to E + T | T$$
$$T \to T * F | F$$
$$F \to (E) | a$$

Clearly, $W_3(F) = \{F\}$, $W_3(T) = \{T, F\}$, $W_3(E) = \{E, T, F\}$. The new grammar is:

$$E \to E + T | T * F | (E) | a$$
$$T \to T * F | (E) | a$$
$$F \to (E) | a$$

Let us also consider the grammar show below.

Example Consider the grammar

$$A_i \to A_{i+1} | a_i A_{i+1} \qquad \text{for each } i,\ 1 \leqslant i < k,$$
$$A_k \to a_k$$

The start variable is A_1. For this grammar G, $|G| = 5k - 3$ and so $\|G\| = O(k \log k)$. If we apply the transformation given in Theorem 4.3.2, we get G', as shown below:

$$A_i \to a_j A_{j+1} \qquad \text{for each } i, j,\ 1 \leqslant i \leqslant j < k,$$
$$A_i \to a_k \qquad \text{for each } i,\ 1 \leqslant i \leqslant k.$$

Clearly,

$$|G'| = 2k + 3 \sum_{j=1}^{k-1} j$$
$$= \frac{k(3k+1)}{2},$$

or

$$\|G'\| = O(k^2 \log k) = O\left(\frac{\|G\|^2}{\log \|G\|}\right).$$

This example shows that the transformation can enlarge G' by a factor of $\|G\|/(\log \|G\|)$.

PROBLEMS

1 Show that the nested-set algorithm given in Theorem 4.3.1 to compute W_n takes time less than a constant times

$$\frac{\|G\|^2}{\log \|G\|}.$$

2 Devise a new algorithm which computes W_n of Theorem 4.3.1 and which takes a length of time that is linear in the size of the grammar. [*Hint*: One approach requires a stack and for each $B \in N$, a list of all places in the righthand sides of productions at which B occurs. One also needs to keep a count of how many symbols in a righthand side cannot produce Λ.]

3 Devise a new algorithm for computing a Λ-free equivalent of G which works in linear time (using the $|G|$ measure), assuming that W_n is computable in linear time.

4 Prove (if it is true) that the constructions given in this section preserve the unambiguity of the original grammar. Do these constructions change the "degree of ambiguity" of a grammar?

5 State and prove a result for chain-rule elimination in the presence of null rules.

6 Consider the last example of Λ-rule elimination in this section. Estimate $\|G'\|$ as a function of $\|G\|$.

Let us extend our notions of complexity from grammars to languages. Define $|L|$, for L a context-free language, to be:

$$|L| = \min\{|G|: \quad G \text{ is a context-free grammar} \quad \text{and} \quad L(G) = L\}.$$

Although the same notation is used for the cardinality of L, we shall distinguish between the two concepts whenever the context is not clear. A similar definition holds for $\|L\|$.

7 Let us define

$$|L|_\Lambda = \min\{|G|: \quad G \text{ is a } \Lambda\text{-free, context-free grammar} \quad \text{and} \quad L(G) = L\},$$

where L is any context-free language with $\Lambda \notin L$. Show that for any context-free language L with $\Lambda \notin L$, we have

$$|L|_\Lambda \leqslant c|L|$$

for some constant c, where $|L|$ is defined above. Would a similar result be true if we changed our definition of $|G|$ to be the number of productions?

4.4 CHOMSKY NORMAL FORM AND ITS VARIANTS

In a context-free grammar, there is no *a priori* bound on the size of a righthand side of a production. Many proofs can be simplified if these righthand sides are bounded to be of length at most 2; then no grammatical tree ever has more than binary branching. There are many ways to achieve this effect, and different normal forms arise. We mention several of these here. There exist applications for each in which none of the others would suffice.

Definition A context-free grammar $G = (V, \Sigma, P, S)$ is said to be in *canonical two form* if each rule is of the form

i) $A \to BC$ with $B, C \in N$

ii) $A \to B$ with $B \in N$

iii) $A \to a$ with $a \in \Sigma$

iv) $S \to \Lambda$

Furthermore, if $S \to \Lambda$ is in P, then $B, C \in N - \{S\}$ in (i) and (ii).

This form guarantees that we have at most binary branching but we may still have chains, as shown below in Fig. 4.2.

There is another normal form which eliminates that possibility.

Definition A context-free grammar $G = (V, \Sigma, P, S)$ is in *Chomsky normal form* if each rule is of the form

i) $A \to BC$ with $B, C \in N$,

ii) $A \to a$ with $a \in \Sigma$,

iii) $S \to \Lambda$.

Furthermore, if $S \to \Lambda$ is in P, then B, C in $N - \{S\}$ in (i).

Next we show that any context-free language may be generated by a grammar in Chomsky normal form.

Theorem 4.4.1 For each context-free grammar $G = (V, \Sigma, P, S)$, there is a grammar $G' = (V', \Sigma, P', S)$ so that $L(G') = L(G)$ and G' is in Chomsky normal form.

Proof We may assume that G satisfies the conditions of Theorem 4.3.2. Furthermore, for each production in P, $A \to B_1 \cdots B_r$, $B_i \in V$, $r \geq 2$, we may assume that each $B_i \in N$; for, if some $B_j \in \Sigma$, replace B_j by a new nonterminal symbol C and add a production $C \to B_j$. (Recall that $B_j \in \Sigma$.) This is repeated for all such instances in all the rules.

Now we can construct P'.

1 If $A \to \alpha$ is in P and $\lg(\alpha) \leq 2$, then $A \to \alpha$ is in P'.

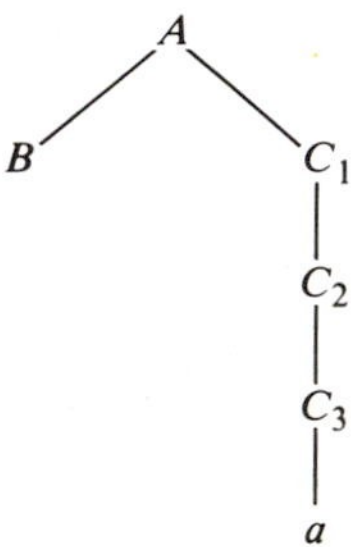

FIG. 4.2

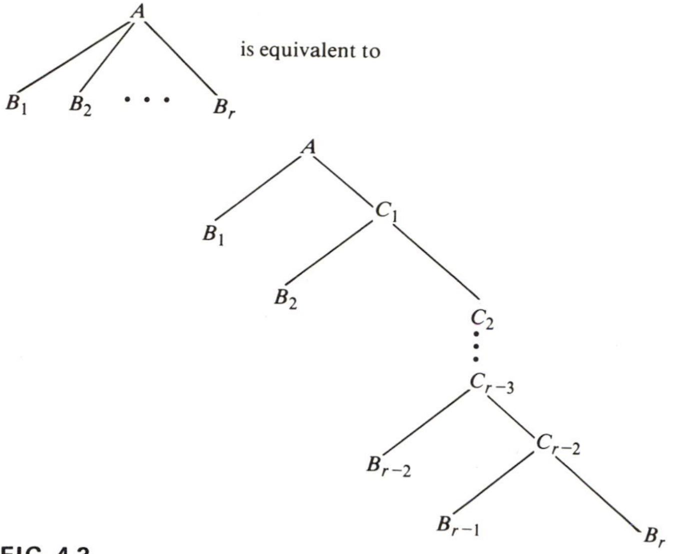

FIG. 4.3

2 Let $A \to B_1 \cdots B_r, r \geqslant 3, B_i \in N$ be in P. Then P' contains:

$$\begin{aligned} A &\to B_1C_1 \\ C_1 &\to B_2C_2 \\ &\vdots \\ C_{r-3} &\to B_{r-2}C_{r-2} \\ C_{r-2} &\to B_{r-1}B_r \end{aligned}$$

where $C_1, \ldots, C_{r-2}$ are all new symbols. [Note that if $r = 3$, the rules are $A \to B_1C_1$ and $C_1 \to B_2B_3$.] This transformation is illustrated in Fig. 4.3. It is now a straightforward matter to verify that $L(G') = L(G)$. □

Example Consider the following grammar:

$$\begin{aligned} S &\to TbT \\ T &\to TaT \mid ca \end{aligned}$$

First, we eliminate terminals on the right, and produce:

$$\begin{aligned} S &\to TBT \\ T &\to TAT \\ T &\to CA \\ B &\to b \\ A &\to a \\ C &\to c \end{aligned}$$

Only the first two rules need modification to achieve Chomsky normal form. Thus we have

$$T \to CA \qquad S \to TD_1$$
$$B \to b \qquad D_1 \to BT$$
$$A \to a \qquad T \to TD_2$$
$$C \to c \qquad D_2 \to AT$$

A similar theorem may be stated for the canonical two form.

Theorem 4.4.2 For each context-free grammar G, one may effectively construct an equivalent context-free grammar in canonical two form.

Another form may be employed in which the generation trees always have binary branching.

Definition Let $G = (V, \Sigma, P, S)$ be a context-free grammar, G is said to be in *binary standard form* if each rule is of the form

$$A \to BC$$

where $A \in N; B, C \in V$.

We leave to the reader (Problem 2, below) the task of formulating and proving the theorem which tells how general the binary standard form is.

PROBLEMS

1 Prove Theorem 4.4.2.

2 State as general a theorem as possible about the binary standard form.

3 Place the following grammar into Chomsky normal form, canonical two form and binary standard form.

$$S \to aAC$$
$$A \to aB \mid bAB$$
$$B \to b$$
$$C \to c$$

4. Let $G = (V, \Sigma, P, S)$ be a context-free grammar in Chomsky normal form. Suppose $w \in L(G)$ and $S \overset{i}{\Rightarrow} w$. Find a relationship between i and $\lg(w)$.

5 Show that if G is an unambiguous context-free grammar and if G' is the Chomsky normal-form grammar for G constructed by Theorem 4.4.1, then G' is unambiguous.

6 Suppose $G = (V, \Sigma, P, S)$ is a context-free grammar. Show that one can find an equivalent grammar G' which is in canonical two form, where every variable in G is in G', and where $|G'|$ is proportional to $|G|$. Is the result also true for $\|G\|$?

7 Is the result of Problem 6 also valid for Chomsky normal form?

8 Work out the relationship between $|G|$ (and $\|G\|$) and $|G'|$ (respectively, $\|G'\|$) where G' is the binary standard form grammar of G.

4.5 INVERTIBLE GRAMMARS

The motivation for studying the next class of grammars comes from the theory of bottom-up parsing. Crudely speaking, bottom-up parsing consists of (i) successively finding phrases and (ii) reducing them to their parents. In a certain sense, each half of this process can be made simple but only at the expense of the other. Invertible grammars allow reduction decisions to be made simply.

Definition A context-free grammar $G = (V, \Sigma, P, S)$ is said to be *invertible* if $A \to \alpha$ and $B \to \alpha$ in P implies $A = B$.

Thus invertible grammars have unique righthand sides of the productions and the reduction phase of parsing becomes a matter of table lookup. The reason for this name is that P^{-1} is a function exactly when G is invertible.

Next we show that each context-free language can be given an invertible grammar.

Theorem 4.5.1 For each context-free grammar $G = (V, \Sigma, P, S)$, there is an invertible context-free grammar $G' = (V', \Sigma, P', S)$ such that $L(G') = L(G)$.

Proof The proof is an example of trivialization. That is, there is an unnatural argument which proves the result in such a way as to destroy the potential utility of the theorem. Let $G = (V, \Sigma, P, S)$, where $N = \{A_1, \ldots, A_n\}$. Let R be a new symbol not in V and define

$$G' = (V', \Sigma, P', S),$$

where $N' = N \cup R$ and $P' = \{A_i \to \alpha R^i |\ A_i \to \alpha \text{ is in } P\} \cup \{R \to \Lambda\}$. Clearly, G' is invertible and $L(G') = L(G)$. □

The trivialization occurs in the previous proof because null rules are used to encode the index of the variable in unary. We prefer to allow Λ-rules only if absolutely necessary. Now we show how to prove the previous theorem without this trick. The argument becomes more complex but the result is more useful.

Theorem 4.5.2 For each context-free grammar $G = (V, \Sigma, P, S)$, there is an invertible context-free grammar $G' = (V', \Sigma, P', S')$ so that $L(G') = L(G)$. Moreover

i) $A \to \Lambda$ is in P' if and only if $\Lambda \in L(G)$ and $A = S'$.

ii) S' does not appear on the righthand side of any rule in P'.

Proof Let us assume, without loss of generality, that $G = (V, \Sigma, P, S)$ is Λ-free and chain-free. [If $\Lambda \in L(G)$, then $L_1 = L(G) - \{\Lambda\}$ has a grammar $G' = (V', \Sigma, P', S')$, which is Λ-free and chain-free. If the result has been proved for G', take $G'' = (V' \cup \{S''\}, \Sigma, P'', S'')$, where $P'' = P' \cup \{S'' \to \Lambda,\ S'' \to S'\}$. Clearly, $L(G'') = L(G)$ and G'' will be invertible if G' is.]

Let $G' = (V', \Sigma, P', S')$ and let $N' = \{S'\} \cup N''$, where N'' consists of all nonempty subsets of N.

P' is defined to include exactly:

1 $S' \to A$ is in P' where A is any subset of N containing S.

2 For each production $B \to x_0 B_1 x_1 \cdots B_n x_n$ with $n \geqslant 0$, $B_1, \ldots, B_n \in N$, and $x_0, \ldots, x_n \in \Sigma^*$, then for each $A_1, \ldots, A_n \in N' - \{S'\}$, P' contains

$$A \to x_0 A_1 x_1 \cdots A_n x_n$$

where

$$A = \{C \mid C \to x_0 C_1 x_1 \cdots C_n x_n \text{ is in } P \quad \text{for some } C_1, \ldots, C_n \text{ with each } C_i \in A_i\}.$$

If $C \to y_0 C_1 y_1 \cdots C_n y_n$ is in P with $y_0, \ldots, y_n \in \Sigma^*$, $C_i \in V - \Sigma$, we call the string $y_0 - y_1 - \cdots - y_n$ the *stencil* of the production (variables replaced by dashes).

Note that P and P' have the same set of stencils if we exclude the rules of the form (1) from P'. Assume without loss of generality that G' is reduced.

Before embarking on a proof that $L(G') = L(G)$, we give an example of the construction.

Example Consider the following grammar

$$S \to 0A \mid 1B$$

$$A \to 0A \mid 0S \mid 1B$$

$$B \to 1 \mid 0$$

Applying the construction of the theorem leads to the following grammar:

$$\{B\} \to 1 \mid 0$$

$$\{A\} \to 0\{S\} \mid 0\{S, B\}$$

$$\{A, S\} \to 0\{A\} \mid 0\{A, B\} \mid 0\{A, S\} \mid 0\{A, S, B\} \mid 1\{B\} \mid 1\{B, A\} \mid 1\{B, A, S\} \mid 1\{B, S\}$$

$$S' \to \{S\} \mid \{A, S\} \mid \{B, S\} \mid \{A, B, S\}$$

Reducing the grammar leads to

$$S' \to \{A, S\}$$

$$\{B\} \to 1 \mid 0$$

$$\{A, S\} \to 0\{A, S\} \mid 1\{B\}$$

To finish the proof, note that G' is invertible. Now we begin the proof that $L(G') = L(G)$.

Claim 1 For each $A \in N'$ and each $x \in \Sigma^*$,

$$A \stackrel{*}{\Rightarrow} x \text{ in } G'$$

implies

$$B \stackrel{*}{\Rightarrow} x \text{ in } G \quad \text{for each } B \in A.$$

Proof The argument is an induction on ℓ, the length of a derivation in G'.

Basis. Suppose $\ell = 1$. Then $A \Rightarrow x \in \Sigma^*$ in G' and $A \to x$ is in P'. By the construction, $A = \{C \in N \mid C \to x \text{ is in } P\}$. Thus $A \to \alpha$ is in P' if and only if $B \to x$ is in P for each $B \in A$.

Induction step. Suppose $\ell \geqslant 2$ and Claim 1 holds for all derivations of length less than ℓ. Then suppose $A \Rightarrow x_0 A_1 x_1 \cdots A_n x_n \overset{\ell-1}{\Rightarrow} x$ in G'. This implies that for each i, $1 \leqslant i \leqslant n$,

$$A_i \overset{*}{\Rightarrow} y_i \in \Sigma^* \qquad \text{and} \qquad x_0 y_1 x_1 \cdots y_n x_n = x.$$

By the construction, for each $B \in A$ there exist $B_i \in A_i$ so that $B \to x_0 B_1 x_1 \cdots B_n x_n$ is in P. Moreover, the induction hypothesis implies that $B_i \overset{*}{\Rightarrow} y_i$ in G, and therefore

$$B \underset{G}{\Rightarrow} x_0 B_1 x_1 \cdots B_n x_n \underset{G}{\overset{*}{\Rightarrow}} x_0 y_1 x_1 \cdots y_n x_n = x$$

Note that Claim 1 implies that

$$L(G') \subseteq L(G).$$

To complete the proof, the following result is needed.

Claim 2 For each $x \in \Sigma^*$, let $X_x = \{C \in N \mid C \overset{*}{\Rightarrow} x \text{ in } G\}$. If $B \overset{*}{\Rightarrow} x$ in G, then $A \overset{*}{\Rightarrow} x$ in G' for some A such that $B \in A \subseteq X_x$.

Proof The argument is an induction on ℓ, the length of a derivation in G.

Basis. $\ell = 1$. Suppose $B \Rightarrow x \in \Sigma^*$ so $B \to x$ is in P. Then $A \to x$ is in P' with $B \in A = \{C \in N \mid C \to x \text{ is in } P\}$.

Induction step. Suppose $B \Rightarrow x_0 B_1 x_1 \cdots B_n x_n \overset{*}{\Rightarrow} x_0 y_1 x_1 \cdots y_n x_n = x \in \Sigma^*$ in G is a derivation of length ℓ, where $B, B_1, \ldots, B_n \in N$; $x_0, \ldots, x_n, y_1, \ldots, y_n \in \Sigma^*$. There are derivations $B_i \overset{*}{\Rightarrow} y_i$, all of which have length $< \ell$. By the induction hypothesis, there are $A_i \in N'$ so that

$$A_i \overset{*}{\Rightarrow} y_i \text{ in } G' \qquad \text{and} \qquad B_i \in A_i.$$

By the construction, $A \to x_0 A_1 x_1 \cdots A_n x_n$ is in P' with $B \in A$. Thus

$$A \Rightarrow x_0 A_1 x_1 \cdots A_n x_n \overset{*}{\Rightarrow} x_0 y_1 x_1 \cdots y_n x_n = x \text{ in } G'.$$

By Claim 2, $L(G') \supseteq L(G)$, and hence $L(G') = L(G)$. □

The construction given seems to be exponential in nature. The following example will confirm it.

Example Let k be a positive even integer. Let $\Sigma = \{a, b, c\}$ and $N = \{A_1, \ldots, A_k\}$. Let $\sigma_a = (1, 2, \ldots, k)$ and $\sigma_b = (1, 2)$ be two permutations written in cyclic notation. These two permutations generate the symmetric group on k-letters; that is, the group of all permutations of the letters $\{1, \ldots, k\}$. Define P by:

$$A_i \to aA_{\sigma_a(i)} \mid bA_{\sigma_b(i)} \qquad \text{for each } i, \quad 1 \leqslant i \leqslant k;$$

$$A_i \to c \qquad \text{for each odd } i, \quad 1 \leqslant i < k.$$

For $G=(V,\Sigma,P,A_1)$, we have

$$|V| = k+3 \qquad \text{and} \qquad |G| = 7k.$$

Now the variables of G' will be sets of variables such as $\{A_1, A_3, \ldots\}$. To simplify the notation, we will write $\{1, 3, \ldots\}$ instead. If the computation of G' is carried out and reduced, we get $N' = \{B \subseteq N\colon |B| = k/2\} \cup \{S'\}$ and

$$\begin{aligned} P' = {} & \{S' \to B \mid A_1 \in B \subseteq N, \quad |B| = k/2\} \\ & \cup \{B \to aB', B \to bB'' \mid B \subseteq N, \quad |B| = k/2, \quad B' = \sigma_a(B), \quad B'' = \sigma_b(B)\} \\ & \cup \{\{1, 3, \ldots, k-1\} \to c\}. \end{aligned}$$

Clearly,

$$|V'| = \binom{k}{k/2} + 4 > 2^{k/2},$$

$$|P'| = 2 + 6\binom{k}{k/2} + \binom{k}{k/2} > 7 \cdot 2^{k/2}.$$

One can show that

$$\|G'\| = O\left(\frac{n}{\log n} \cdot 2^{n/\log n}\right), \tag{4.5.1}$$

where $n = \|G\|$.

PROBLEMS

1 Why did we assume that G was chain-free in the proof of Theorem 4.5.2?

2 If we assume that G is unambiguous, then does the following stronger correspondence hold in the proof of Theorem 4.5.2?

Proposition $B \overset{*}{\Rightarrow} x$ in G if and only if $\{B\} \overset{*}{\Rightarrow} x$ in G'.

3 Show that, for any context-free grammar G, there is a context-free grammar G' such that $L(G) = L(G')$ which is invertible and chain-free.

4 Show that there exist context-free grammars G with $\Lambda \notin L(G)$ for which there do not exist equivalent grammars that are invertible, chain-free, and Λ-free.

5 Continuing the last example of Section 4.5,

a) Prove Eq. (4.5.1).

b) Find an equivalent invertible grammar of size k^2.

c) Note that $L(G)$ is regular. Find a finite automaton for $L(G)$ of "size" proportional to k. [The *size* of a finite automaton may be thought of as the length of all its transitions when written out as a string.]

6 There is an intimate relationship between invertibility and determinism in the case of one-sided linear grammars. Can you expand on this insight?

4.6 GREIBACH NORMAL FORM

In this section, another normal form is considered which has important implications in both theory and practice.

The most important practical applications of this form are to top-down parsing. A problem occurs in top-down parsing when we have "left recursive" variables.

Definition Let $G = (V, \Sigma, P, S)$ be a context-free grammar. A variable $A \in N$ is said to be *left recursive* (*right recursive*) if $A \overset{+}{\Rightarrow} A\alpha$ for some $\alpha \in V^*$ (respectively, $A \overset{+}{\Rightarrow} \alpha A$). A grammar is *left* (*right*) *recursive* if it has at least one left (right) recursive variable.

In "recursive descent" parsers, the presence of left recursion causes the device to go into an infinite loop. Thus the elimination of left recursion is of practical importance in such parsers. It will turn out that a grammar in the form we are now introducing is never left recursive. Thus, the main theorem of this section will solve this looping problem in top-down parsers. We begin by considering two lemmas, even before the normal form is introduced.

Lemma 4.6.1 Let $G = (V, \Sigma, P, S)$ be a context-free grammar. Let $\pi = A \to \alpha_1 B \alpha_2$ be a production in P and $B \to \beta_1 | \cdots | \beta_r$ be the only BNF rule in P with B on the lefthand side. Define $G_1 = (V, \Sigma, P_1, S)$, where

$$P_1 = (P - \{\pi\}) \cup \{A \to \alpha_1 \beta_1 \alpha_2 \mid \alpha_1 \beta_2 \alpha_2 \mid \cdots \mid \alpha_1 \beta_r \alpha_2\}.$$

Then $L(G_1) = L(G)$.

Proof Clearly, $L(G_1) \subseteq L(G)$, since if $A \to \alpha_1\beta_i\alpha_2$ is used in a G_1-derivation, then $A \underset{G}{\Rightarrow} \alpha_1 B \alpha_2 \underset{G}{\Rightarrow} \alpha_1\beta_i\alpha_2$ can occur in G.

Conversely, note that $A \to \alpha_1 B\alpha_2$ is the only production of G not in G_1. If $A \to \alpha_1 B \alpha_2$ is used in a G-derivation of a terminal string, then B must be rewritten by some $B \to \beta_i$. These two steps are combined in G_1. Therefore, $L(G) \subseteq L(G_1)$. □

The next lemma involves certain regular sets.

Lemma 4.6.2 Let $G = (V, \Sigma, P, S)$ be a Λ-free, context-free grammar. Let

$$A \to A\alpha_1 | \cdots | A\alpha_r$$

where $\alpha_i \neq \Lambda$ for all i, $1 \leqslant i \leqslant r$, be all the rules with A on the left such that the leftmost symbol of the righthand side of the rule is A. Let

$$A \to \beta_1 | \cdots | \beta_s$$

be the remaining rules with A on the left. Let $G_1 = (V \cup \{Z\}, \Sigma, P_1, S)$, where Z is a new nonterminal symbol and P_1 is the set of productions in P with all the productions having A on the left replaced by

$$A \to \beta_1 Z | \cdots | \beta_s Z | \beta_1 | \cdots | \beta_s$$

$$Z \to \alpha_1 Z | \cdots | \alpha_r Z | \alpha_1 | \cdots | \alpha_r$$

Then $L(G_1) = L(G)$.

Proof The effect of this construction is to eliminate the left recursion in the variable A. In each place, we have a new right recursive variable Z. Note that none of the new A-rules are directly left recursive because none of the β_i begin with A. Since $\beta_i \neq \Lambda$, we cannot get left recursion on A by "going through" Z. Also, note that Z is not a left recursive variable because $\alpha_i \neq \Lambda$ for all i and because none of the α_i begin with Z.

To complete the proof, note that the original productions in G with A on the left generate the regular set

$$\{\beta_1, \ldots, \beta_s\}\{A\alpha_1, \ldots, A\alpha_r, \alpha_1, \ldots, \alpha_r\}^* \cup \{A\}.$$

Moreover, this is the set generated by A (with the help of Z) in G_1. With the aid of this remark, it is straightforward to verify that $L(G_1) = L(G)$. We omit the details. □

Now the grammatical form is introduced.

Definition A context-free grammar $G = (V, \Sigma, P, S)$ is said to be in *Greibach normal form* if each rule is of one of the forms

$$A \to aB_1 \cdots B_n$$

$$A \to a$$

$$S \to \Lambda$$

where $B_1, \ldots, B_n \in N - \{S\}$, $a \in \Sigma$. A grammar is said to be in *m-standard form* if G is in Greibach form, as above, and $n \leqslant m$.

Thus a grammar is in Greibach form if and only if it is in m-standard form for some m.

There are a number of alternative definitions of Greibach form. In certain textbooks, all rules are required to be of the form

$$A \to a\alpha$$

with $a \in \Sigma$, $\alpha \in N^*$. Such a definition rules out Λ from being in the language. In other places, the rules may be of the form

$$A \to a\beta$$

where $a \in \Sigma$ and $\beta \in V^*$; that is, terminals and variables may be in β. One must be quite careful in quoting theorems from the literature that involve this grammatical form.

This form has a number of important implications. Ignoring $S \to \Lambda$, all other rules have righthand sides that begin with a terminal. If G is in Greibach normal form and $w \in L(G)$, $w \neq \Lambda$, then every derivation of w from S in G has exactly $\lg(w)$ steps. The following proposition generalizes this fact and states it precisely.

Theorem 4.6.1 Let $G = (V, \Sigma, P, S)$ be a context-free grammar in Greibach normal form. If $w \in \Sigma^*$, $\alpha \in N^*$, and $S \overset{+}{\Rightarrow} w\alpha$ then every derivation of $S \overset{+}{\Rightarrow} w\alpha$ has exactly $\max\{1, \lg(w)\}$ steps.

We are now in a position to prove the main result.

Theorem 4.6.2 Every context-free language may be generated by a context-free grammar in Greibach normal form.

Proof Suppose, without loss of generality, that $L = L(G)$, where $G = (V, \Sigma, P, S)$ is reduced, in Chomsky normal form, and assume (for the moment) that G is Λ-free. Let $N = \{A_1, \ldots, A_m\}$ with $S = A_1$.

We begin by modifying the grammar so that if $A_i \to A_j\alpha$ is in P, then $j > i$. Suppose that this has been done for all rules starting with A_1 and proceeding to A_k. Inductively, we may suppose that $A_i \to A_j\alpha$ for $1 \leqslant i \leqslant k$ implies $j > i$. We now deal with the rules that have A_{k+1} on the left. If $A_{k+1} \to A_j\alpha$ is a production with $j < k+1$, we generate a new set of productions by substituting for A_j the righthand side of each of the A_j rules according to Lemma 4.6.1. By repeating this operation at most k times, we will obtain rules of the form

$$A_{k+1} \to A_\ell\alpha \quad \text{with } \ell \geqslant k+1.$$

The rule with $\ell = k+1$ are replaced according to Lemma 4.6.2 in which we introduce a new nonterminal Z_{k+1}.

Repeating the construction for each original nonterminal gives rules of the following forms:

1 $A_k \to A_\ell\alpha$ with $\ell > k$, $\alpha \in ((N - \{S\}) \cup \{Z_1, \ldots, Z_n\})^+$;

2 $A_k \to a\alpha$ where $a \in \Sigma$, $\alpha \in ((N - \{S\}) \cup \{Z_1, \ldots, Z_n\})^+$;

3 $Z_k \to \alpha$ where $\alpha \in ((N - \{S\}) \cup \{Z_1, \ldots, Z_n\})^+$.

The reader should verify that the exact quantification given above is correct. This requires a separate proof and employs the fact that G was in Chomsky normal form.

Note that the leftmost symbol on the righthand side of any A_m production must be terminal by rule (1) and the fact that there is no higher indexed nonterminal.

For A_{m-1}, the leftmost symbol generated is terminal or A_m. If it is A_m, generate new rules by use of Lemma 4.6.1. These new rules all begin with a terminal symbol. Repeat the process for $A_{m-1}, \ldots, A_1$. Finally, examine the $Z_1, \ldots, Z_n$ rules. These rules begin with an A_i. For each A_i, use Lemma 4.6.1 again. Because G was in Chomsky normal form, the only terminal on the righthand side of any rule is the first one.

To complete the proof, we must deal with the case where $\Lambda \in L$. If this occurs, let $G = (V, \Sigma, P, S)$ be the Greibach normal-form grammar for $L - \{\Lambda\}$. Define $G' = (V \cup \{S'\}, \Sigma, P', S')$, where $P' = P \cup \{S' \to S\} \cup \{S' \to \Lambda\}$. Use Lemma 4.6.1 once on the rule $S' \to S$. Clearly, the resulting grammar G' is in Greibach normal form and generates L. □

Corollary Every context-free language may be given a context-free grammar which is not left recursive.

Example Consider G as shown below:

$$A_1 \to A_2A_3$$
$$A_2 \to A_1A_2 \mid 1$$
$$A_3 \to A_1A_3 \mid 0$$

Applying Lemma 4.6.1 to A_2 yields:

$$A_1 \to A_2A_3$$
$$A_2 \to A_2A_3A_2 | 1$$
$$A_3 \to A_1A_3 | 0$$

Now Lemma 4.6.2 can be applied to the second production:

$$A_1 \to A_2A_3$$
$$A_2 \to 1Z_1 | 1$$
$$Z_1 \to A_3A_2Z_1 | A_3A_2$$
$$A_3 \to A_1A_3 | 0$$

Focussing on A_3, we use Lemma 4.6.1 to obtain:

$$A_1 \to A_2A_3$$
$$A_2 \to 1Z_1 | 1$$
$$Z_1 \to A_3A_2Z_1 | A_3A_2$$
$$A_3 \to A_2A_3A_3 | 0$$

Now Lemma 4.6.1 is used again on A_3,

$$A_1 \to A_2A_3$$
$$A_2 \to 1Z_1 | 1$$
$$Z_1 \to A_3A_2Z_1 | A_3A_2$$
$$A_3 \to 1Z_1A_3A_3 | 1A_3A_3 | 0$$

Now it is possible to begin the process of back-substitution. A_3 and A_2 are already in Greibach form, but A_1 is not:

$$A_1 \to 1Z_1A_3 | 1A_3$$
$$A_2 \to 1Z_1 | 1$$
$$A_3 \to 1Z_1A_3A_3 | 1A_3A_3 | 0$$
$$Z_1 \to A_3A_2Z_1 | A_3A_2$$

If we substitute for A_3 in the Z_1 rules, we obtain:

$$A_1 \to 1Z_1A_3 | 1A_3$$
$$A_2 \to 1Z_1 | 1$$
$$A_3 \to 1Z_1A_3A_3 | 1A_3A_3 | 0$$
$$Z_1 \to 1Z_1A_3A_3A_2Z_1 | 1A_3A_3A_2Z_1 | 0A_2Z_1 | 1Z_1A_3A_3A_2 | 1A_3A_3A_2 | 0A_2$$

This grammar is in Greibach form.

Now consider the following grammar which will help us to estimate the size of a grammar in Greibach normal form. Let G be:

$$B_i \to B_{i+1}B_{k+1} \mid B_{i+1}B_{k+2} \quad \text{for all } i, \quad 1 \leqslant i < k,$$

$$B_k \to a \mid b$$

$$B_{k+1} \to a$$

$$B_{k+2} \to b$$

where $\Sigma = \{a, b\}$, $N = \{B_1, \ldots, B_{k+2}\}$, and $S = B_1$. Then $|V| = k + 4$, $|G| = 6k + 2$. If the construction is carried out, we get G' with productions

$$B_{k+1} \to a$$

$$B_{k+2} \to b$$

$$B_{k+1-i} \to \alpha$$

for each α in $\{a, b\}\{B_{k+1}, B_{k+2}\}^{i-1}$ and for each i, $1 \leqslant i \leqslant k$. Clearly for each i, $1 \leqslant i \leqslant k$, we will have 2^i righthand sides (with B_{k+1-i} on the left), and each such rule has length $i + 1$. Thus:

$$|G'| = 4 + \sum_{i=1}^{k} (i+1)2^i = 2k2^k + 4.$$

The latter equality may be easily verified by induction.

Note that G' is exponentially larger than the original grammar. Moreover, G was not even left recursive originally. If we reduce G', we get G'' shown below:

$$B_{k+1} \to a$$

$$B_{k+2} \to b$$

$$B_1 \to \alpha$$

for each $\alpha \in \{a, b\}\{B_{k+1}, B_{k+2}\}^{k-1}$. Thus:

$$|G''| = 2^k + 5,$$

which is still exponential in the size of G.

PROBLEMS

1 Give an algorithm for detecting left-recursive variables.

2 Although the algorithm given in the proof of Theorem 4.6.2 starts from Chomsky normal form, show that chain rules may occur in the middle of the computation. Would the algorithm work if we started from canonical two form?

3 Does the construction given in this section preserve unambiguity?

4 Place the following grammar in Greibach normal form

$$E \to E + T \mid T$$

$$T \to T * F \mid F$$

$$F \to (E) \mid a$$

5 A context-free grammar $G = (V, \Sigma, P, S)$ is in *reverse Greibach form if* all rules are of the form

$$A \to \alpha a \qquad \alpha \in (N - \{S\})^*$$
$$A \to a \qquad a \in \Sigma$$
$$S \to \Lambda$$

Show that any context free language has a grammar in reverse Greibach form.

6 A context-free grammar $G = (V, \Sigma, P, S)$ is in *double Greibach form* if each rule is in one of the following forms

$$S \to \Lambda$$
$$A \to a \qquad a \in \Sigma$$
$$A \to a\alpha b \qquad a, b \in \Sigma; \alpha \in (N - \{S\})^*$$

Show that every context-free language has a grammar in double Greibach form.

7 The following "proof" of Problem 6 has been proposed. If the sketch presented here is correct, write a complete proof. If there is a flaw in the approach, explain the problem in detail.

Suppose we are given a context-free grammar G; place G in Greibach normal form and call your new grammar G_1. Define G_2 as G_1^T, that is, if $G_1 = (V_1, \Sigma, P_1, S_1)$, define $G_2 = (V_1, \Sigma, P_1^T, S_1)$, where

$$P_1^T = \{A \to \alpha^T \mid A \to \alpha \text{ in } P_1\}.$$

Place G_2 in Greibach normal form and call the resulting grammar G_3. Now form $G_4 = G_3^T$. It is claimed that $L(G_4) = L(G)$ and that G_4 is in double Greibach form.

4.7 2-STANDARD FORM

In the previous section, we showed that any context-free grammar could be placed in Greibach form or, equivalently, in m-standard form for some m. In the present section, we shall attempt to minimize m and yet still generate all the context-free languages. If $m = 1$, we would have rules of the form

$$A \to aB \qquad B \in N - \{S\}$$
$$A \to a \qquad a \in \Sigma$$
$$S \to \Lambda$$

But these are right linear rules and so we can generate only regular sets. Thus, we must have $m \geqslant 2$ if we are to succeed in generating all the context-free languages.

Theorem 4.7.1 For each context free grammar $G = (V, \Sigma, P, S)$, there exists a context-free grammar G' such that G' is in 2-standard form and $L(G) = L(G')$.

Proof We may assume, without loss of generality, that G is in m-standard form for some m; that is, G is in Greibach form where:

$$A \to a\alpha \qquad \alpha \in (N - \{S\})^*, \quad \lg(\alpha) \leqslant m,$$
$$A \to a$$
$$S \to \Lambda$$

Thus it suffices to show that if G is in m-standard form for some $m \geqslant 3$, then we can find a grammar G' in $(m-1)$-standard form such that $L(G) = L(G')$. Let

$$G = (V, \Sigma, P, S)$$

be in m-standard form, $m \geqslant 3$. Define

$$G' = (V', \Sigma, P', S),$$

where

$$V' = V \cup \{(A, B) |\ A, B \in N\}$$

and P' is given by

$$\begin{aligned} P' = &\ \{A \to \alpha |\ A \to \alpha \text{ is in } P \text{ and } \lg(\alpha) \leqslant m\} \\ &\cup \{A \to aB_1 \cdots B_{m-2}(B_{m-1}, B_m) |\ A \to aB_1 \cdots B_m \text{ is in } P\} \\ &\cup \{(A, B) \to \alpha B |\ A \to \alpha \text{ is in } P \text{ and } \lg(\alpha) \leqslant m-1\} \\ &\cup \{(A, B) \to aB_1 \cdots B_{m-2}(B_{m-1}, B) |\ A \to aB_1 \cdots B_{m-1} \text{ is in } P\} \\ &\cup \{(A, B) \to aB_1 \cdots B_{m-3}(B_{m-2}, B_{m-1})(B_m, B) | A \to aB_1 \cdots B_m \text{ is in } P\}. \end{aligned}$$

Definition If $A \to \alpha$ is a rule, then we shall call $\lg(\alpha)$ the *width* of the rule.

The intuition behind the construction is not difficult. If we have a rule of width $m+1$, we replace it by a rule of width m whose last variable is a pair; see Fig. 4.4.

Now, however, the rules with paired variables must be defined. If

$$B_{m-1} \to \alpha \text{ is in } P$$

with $\lg(\alpha) < m$, then clearly we will have

$$(B_{m-1}, B_m) \to \alpha B_m$$

If the righthand side of α is too long, more paired variables are introduced.

It is certainly clear that G' is in $(m-1)$-standard form, but it is less clear that $L(G') = L(G)$.

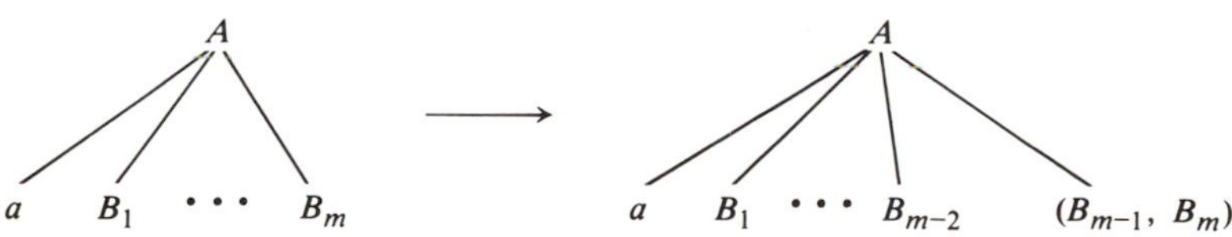

FIG. 4.4

Claim 1

a) If $\gamma, \alpha \in V^*$ and $\gamma \overset{*}{\underset{G}{\Rightarrow}} \alpha$ using only rules of width less than m, then

$$\gamma \overset{*}{\underset{G'}{\Rightarrow}} \alpha \tag{4.7.1}$$

b) If $A \overset{+}{\underset{G}{\Rightarrow}} \alpha$ with $\alpha \in V^*$ using only rules of width less than m, then

$$(A, B) \overset{+}{\underset{G'}{\Rightarrow}} \alpha B$$

for any $B \in N$.

Proof To prove (a) it suffices to note that if A is some variable occurring in γ, then since each rule used in the derivation $A \overset{+}{\underset{G}{\Rightarrow}} \alpha$ is of width less than m, there is a corresponding rule in P', and hence

$$A \overset{+}{\underset{G'}{\Rightarrow}} \alpha$$

The generalization to (4.7.1) then follows directly from Lemma 3.3.1.

To prove (b), let the derivation $A \overset{+}{\underset{G}{\Rightarrow}} \alpha$ be of the form

$$A \underset{G}{\Rightarrow} \gamma \overset{*}{\underset{G}{\Rightarrow}} \alpha, \qquad \lg(\gamma) < m.$$

Thus the rule

$$A \to \gamma \text{ is in } P$$

and $\lg(\gamma) \leqslant m - 1$. Therefore the rule

$$(A, B) \to \gamma B \text{ is in } P'.$$

Furthermore, since

$$\gamma \overset{*}{\underset{G}{\Rightarrow}} \alpha$$

by (4.7.1), we have

$$\gamma \overset{*}{\underset{G'}{\Rightarrow}} \alpha$$

Combining these results gives

$$(A, B) \underset{G'}{\Rightarrow} \gamma B \overset{*}{\underset{G'}{\Rightarrow}} \alpha B$$

Claim 2 If

$$A \overset{+}{\underset{G}{\Rightarrow}} x \quad \text{with} \quad x \in \Sigma^*,$$

then i) $A \overset{+}{\underset{G'}{\Rightarrow}} x$

ii) $(A, B) \overset{+}{\underset{G'}{\Rightarrow}} xB$ for any $B \in N$.

Proof Let p be the number of rules of width greater than $m - 1$ in the derivation $A \overset{+}{\underset{G}{\Rightarrow}} x$. We induct on p.

Basis. $p = 0$. Claim 2 reduces to a special case of Claim 1 which we have proven.

Induction step. Assume that if $\ell \leqslant p$ and

$$A \overset{+}{\underset{G}{\Rightarrow}} x$$

using ℓ rules of width greater than $m-1$, then

$$A \overset{+}{\underset{G'}{\Rightarrow}} x$$

$$(A, B) \overset{+}{\underset{G'}{\Rightarrow}} xB$$

Now let

$$A \overset{+}{\underset{G}{\Rightarrow}} x$$

using $p+1$ rules of width greater than $m-1$. Then the derivation is of the form

$$\begin{aligned} A &\overset{*}{\underset{G}{\Rightarrow}} \gamma A'\eta && (4.7.2) \\ &\underset{G}{\Rightarrow} \gamma a B_1 \cdots B_k \eta \qquad k \geqslant m-1, \\ &\overset{*}{\underset{G}{\Rightarrow}} x_0 a x_1 \cdots x_k x_{k+1} = x \end{aligned}$$

where the derivation (4.7.2) uses no rules of width greater than $m-1$, and hence, by Claim 1,

$$\begin{aligned} A &\overset{*}{\underset{G'}{\Rightarrow}} \gamma A'\eta \\ \gamma &\overset{*}{\underset{G}{\Rightarrow}} x_0 \\ B_i &\overset{*}{\underset{G}{\Rightarrow}} x_i \qquad \text{for each } i,\ 1 \leqslant i \leqslant k, \\ \eta &\overset{*}{\Rightarrow} x_{k+1} \end{aligned}$$

each with at most p rules of width greater than $m-1$. Therefore,

$$\begin{aligned} \gamma &\overset{*}{\underset{G'}{\Rightarrow}} x_0 \\ B_i &\overset{*}{\underset{G'}{\Rightarrow}} x_i \qquad 1 \leqslant i \leqslant k, \\ \eta &\overset{*}{\underset{G'}{\Rightarrow}} x_{k+1} \end{aligned}$$

by the induction hypothesis.

There are now two cases.

CASE 1 $k = m-1$. In this case, the rule

$$A' \to aB_1 \cdots B_k \text{ is in } P',$$

and thus, by combining the above results, we have

$$\begin{aligned} A &\overset{*}{\underset{G'}{\Rightarrow}} \gamma A'\eta \\ &\underset{G'}{\Rightarrow} \gamma a B_1 \cdots B_k \eta \\ &\overset{*}{\underset{G'}{\Rightarrow}} x_0 a x_1 \cdots x_k x_{k+1} = x \end{aligned}$$

CASE 2. $k = m$. Then the rule

$$A' \to aB_1 \cdots (B_{m-1}, B_m) \text{ is in } P'.$$

Now, since

$$B_{m-1} \overset{+}{\underset{G}{\Rightarrow}} x_{m-1} \qquad \text{and} \qquad B_m \overset{+}{\underset{G}{\Rightarrow}} x_m$$

using at most p rules of width greater than $m-1$, by parts (ii) and (i) of the induction hypothesis, we have:

$$(B_{m-1}, B_m) \underset{G'}{\overset{+}{\Rightarrow}} x_{m-1}B_m \underset{G'}{\overset{+}{\Rightarrow}} x_{m-1}x_m$$

Combining these results gives

$$\begin{aligned} A &\underset{G'}{\overset{*}{\Rightarrow}} \gamma A'\eta \\ &\underset{G'}{\Rightarrow} \gamma a B_1 \cdots B_{m-2}(B_{m-1}, B_m)\eta \\ &\underset{G'}{\overset{*}{\Rightarrow}} x_0 a x_1 \cdots x_m x_{m+1} = x \end{aligned}$$

which completes the proof of (i).

To prove (ii), let the derivation $A \underset{G}{\overset{+}{\Rightarrow}} x$ be of the form

$$A \Rightarrow \gamma \overset{*}{\Rightarrow} x$$

There are three cases to consider.

CASE 3. $\lg(\gamma) \leqslant m-1$. Then the rule

$$(A, B) \to \gamma B \text{ is in } P'.$$

Using Lemma 3.3.1 and part (i) of Claim 2, we have

$$\gamma \underset{G'}{\overset{*}{\Rightarrow}} x$$

Thus

$$(A, B) \underset{G'}{\Rightarrow} \gamma B \underset{G'}{\overset{*}{\Rightarrow}} xB$$

CASE 4. $\lg(\gamma) = m$. Then the derivation is of the form

$$A \underset{G}{\Rightarrow} aB_1 \cdots B_{m-1} \underset{G}{\overset{*}{\Rightarrow}} ax_1 \cdots x_{m-1}$$

Thus we have:

1 $$B_i \underset{G}{\overset{*}{\Rightarrow}} x_i \qquad 1 \leqslant i \leqslant m-1,$$

using at most p rules of width greater than $m-1$, since the first rule is of width m.

2 The rule

$$(A, B) \to aB_1 \cdots B_{m-2}(B_{m-1}, B)$$

is in P'.

3 By the induction hypothesis,

$$B_i \underset{G'}{\overset{*}{\Rightarrow}} x_i \qquad 1 \leqslant i \leqslant m-2,$$

and

$$(B_{m-1}, B) \underset{G'}{\overset{*}{\Rightarrow}} x_{m-1}B$$

Combining gives

$$\begin{aligned} (A, B) &\underset{G'}{\Rightarrow} aB_1 \cdots B_{m-2}(B_{m-1}, B) \\ &\underset{G'}{\overset{*}{\Rightarrow}} ax_1 \cdots x_{m-1}x_m B = xB \end{aligned}$$

CASE 5. $\lg(\gamma) = m + 1$. Then, similarly to Case 4, we have that

$$A \to aB_1 \cdots B_{m-3}(B_{m-2}, B_{m-1})(B_m, B)$$

is in P' and

$$B_i \underset{G'}{\overset{*}{\Rightarrow}} x_i \qquad 1 \leqslant i \leqslant m-3,$$

$$(B_{m-2}, B_{m-1}) \underset{G'}{\overset{*}{\Rightarrow}} x_{m-2}B_{m-1} \underset{G'}{\overset{*}{\Rightarrow}} x_{m-2}x_{m-1}$$

$$(B_m, B) \underset{G'}{\overset{*}{\Rightarrow}} x_m B$$

Thus

$$\begin{aligned}(A, B) &\underset{G'}{\Rightarrow} aB_1 \cdots B_{m-3}(B_{m-2}, B_{m-1})(B_m, B) \\ &\underset{G'}{\overset{*}{\Rightarrow}} ax_1 \cdots x_{m-2}x_{m-1}x_m B = xB\end{aligned}$$

which completes the induction.

Now, taking $A = S$ in Claim 2 gives:

Claim 3. For each x in Σ^*, if $S \underset{G}{\overset{*}{\Rightarrow}} x$, then $S \underset{G'}{\overset{*}{\Rightarrow}} x$. Thus

$$L(G) \subseteq L(G')$$

Claim 4. $L(G') \subseteq L(G)$.

Proof. Define a map φ: $V' \to V$, by:

$$\varphi(a) = a \qquad \text{for each } a \in V,$$

$$\varphi((A, B)) = AB \qquad \text{for each } (A, B) \in N \times N.$$

Now extend φ to be a homomorphism from $(V')^*$ to V^* in the natural way. It is then straightforward to prove by induction that, for each α, β in $(V')^*$,

$$\text{if} \qquad \alpha \underset{G'}{\overset{*}{\Rightarrow}} \beta$$

$$\text{then} \qquad \varphi(\alpha) \underset{G}{\overset{*}{\Rightarrow}} \varphi(\beta).$$

Thus if $S \underset{G'}{\overset{*}{\Rightarrow}} x, x \in \Sigma^*$, then

$$\varphi(S) = S \underset{G}{\overset{*}{\Rightarrow}} \varphi(x) = x$$

or, equivalently, $L(G') \subseteq L(G)$, which completes the proof of the theorem. □

PROBLEMS

1 Estimate the size of G' as a function of the size of G. Can you improve the construction given in Theorem 4.7.1?

2 Put the following grammar into 2-standard form:

$$S \to SaA \mid SA \mid b$$

$$A \to Ad \mid ASa \mid aS \mid c$$

4.8 OPERATOR GRAMMARS

One of the most important normal forms used in precedence analysis is the operator form.

Definition A context-free grammar $G = (V, \Sigma, P, S)$ is said to be in *operator form* if $P \subseteq N \times (V^* - V^*N^2V^*)$.

This means that each rule in P is of one of the following forms:

i) $A \to B$ for $A \in N, B \in V_\Lambda$, or

ii) $A \to \alpha BC\beta$ where for all $\alpha, \beta \in V^*, B, C \in V$, either $B \in \Sigma$ or $C \in \Sigma$.

The main point is that there are never two adjacent variables in the righthand side of a rule in an operator grammar.

We can now show that every context-free language has a grammar in this form. It is not too difficult to prove this result with the aid of Greibach normal form [2-standard form is particularly convenient]. We shall give a proof that does not use this form because, in other applications, the construction will be needed. Note that the case in which $\Lambda \in L$ is handled somewhat separately because it does not generalize in the applications to precedence parsing.

Theorem 4.8.1 Let $G = (V, \Sigma, P, S)$ be a Λ-free, context-free grammar. There is a context-free grammar $G = (V', \Sigma, P', S)$ in operator form such that $L(G') = L(G)$.

Proof There is no loss of generality in assuming that $G = (V, \Sigma, P, S)$ is Λ-free and in canonical two form. Define $G' = (V', \Sigma, P', S)$ where $V' = \Sigma \cup \{S\} \cup (N \times \Sigma)$. Define $P' = P_1 \cup P_2 \cup P_3 \cup P_4$, where

$$P_1 = \{S \to (S, a)a \mid a \in \Sigma\}$$

$$P_2 = \{(A, a) \to \Lambda \mid A \in N; a \in \Sigma; A \to a \text{ in } P\}$$

$$P_3 = \{(A, a) \to (B, a) \mid A, B \in N; a \in \Sigma; A \to B \text{ in } P\}$$

$$P_4 = \{(A, a) \to (B, b)b(C, a) \mid A, B, C \in N; a, b \in \Sigma; A \to BC \text{ in } P\}$$

The idea of the construction is to imagine that we are at some internal node of a derivation tree of G which is labelled by A. The leading terminal of the subtree properly to the right of A is encoded into the variable A (cf. Fig. 4.5). Note that G' is in operator form.

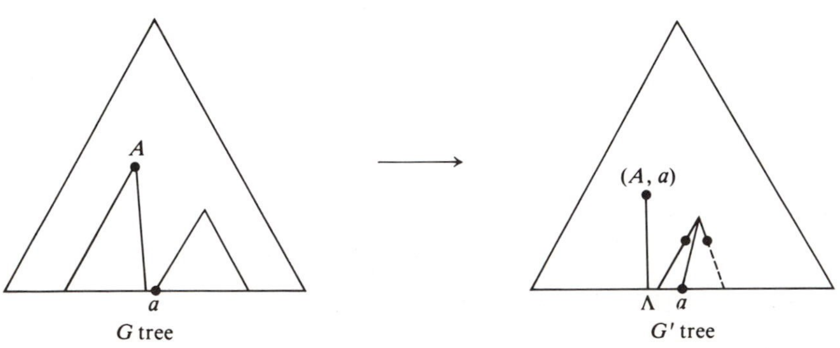

FIG. 4.5

Let us define a mapping ϕ from $P_2 \cup P_3 \cup P_4$ into P as follows:

$$\phi((A,a) \to \Lambda) = A \to a \quad \text{if } (A,a) \to \Lambda \text{ is in } P_2$$

$$\phi((A,a) \to (B,a)) = A \to B \quad \text{if } (A,a) \to (B,a) \text{ is in } P_3$$

$$\phi((A,a) \to (B,b)b(C,a)) = A \to BC \quad \text{if } (A,a) \to (B,b)b(C,a) \text{ is in } P_4$$

Extend ϕ to a homomorphism from $(P_2 \cup P_3 \cup P_4)^*$ into P^*. We can now state the exact correspondence between derivations in G and in G'.

Proposition For each $a \in \Sigma$, $x \in \Sigma^*$, $A \in N$, and for each sequence $\pi_1, \ldots, \pi_n$ of productions in P,

$$A \overset{*}{\underset{G}{\Rightarrow}} xa \qquad \text{by canonical derivation } (\pi_1, \ldots, \pi_n)$$

if and only if there exist $\pi_1', \ldots, \pi_n'$ in P' such that

$$\phi(\pi_i') = \pi_i \qquad \text{for all } i, 1 \leqslant i \leqslant n,$$

and

$$(A,a) \overset{*}{\underset{G'}{\Rightarrow}} x$$

by canonical derivation $(\pi_1', \ldots, \pi_n')$.

The proof of the proposition involves an induction on n and is left to the reader.

From the proposition it follows that for any $x \in \Sigma^*, a \in \Sigma$,

$$S \overset{*}{\underset{G}{\Rightarrow}} xa \qquad \text{by canonical derivation } (\pi_1, \ldots, \pi_n)$$

if and only if

$$(S,a) \overset{*}{\Rightarrow} x \qquad \text{by canonical derivation } (\pi_1', \ldots, \pi_n')$$

and $\phi(\pi_i') = \pi_i$. Using a rule from P_1 it follows easily that $L(G) = L(G')$. □

Now we consider the case in which G is not Λ-free.

Theorem 4.8.2 If $G = (V, \Sigma, P, S)$ is any context-free grammar, then there is another grammar $G' = (V', \Sigma, P', S')$ so that G' is in operator form and $L(G') = L(G)$.

Proof If $\Lambda \notin L(G)$, there is nothing new to prove. If $\Lambda \in L(G)$, then $L - \{\Lambda\}$ is context-free. Apply Theorem 4.8.1 to a Λ-free grammar for $L - \{\Lambda\}$, and let $G'' = (V'', \Sigma, P'', S)$ be the resulting operator grammar. Define $G' = (V', \Sigma, P', S')$, where $V' = V'' \cup \{S'\}$ and S' is a new symbol. Then $P' = P'' \cup \{S' \to \Lambda, S' \to S\}$. Clearly, G' is in operator form and $L(G') = L$. □

Example Let G be given as follows:

$$S \to SA \mid SB \mid a$$

$$A \to a$$

$$B \to b$$

If we apply the construction of Theorem 4.8.1 to G and then reduce it, we get the following grammar:

$$S \to (S,a)a \mid (S,b)b$$

$$(S,a) \to (S,a)a(A,a) \mid (S,b)b(A,a) \mid \Lambda$$

$$(S,b) \to (S,a)a(B,b) \mid (S,b)b(B,b)$$

$$(A,a) \to \Lambda$$

$$(B,b) \to \Lambda$$

For example, we show the derivation of *aab* in both grammars G and G' in Fig. 4.6.

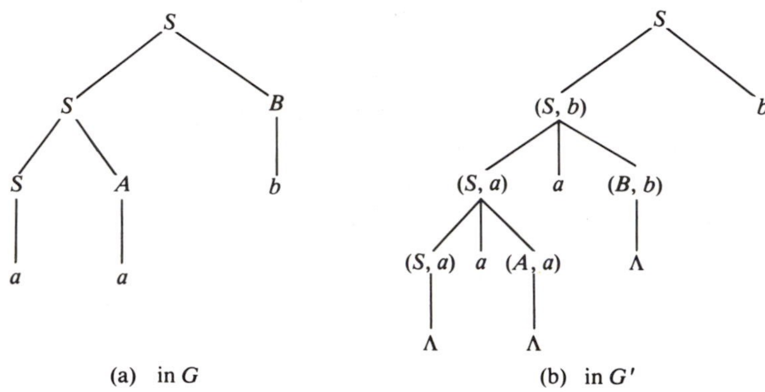

(a) in G (b) in G'

FIG. 4.6

PROBLEMS

1 Prove the proposition stated in the proof of Theorem 4.8.1.

2 The construction used in proving Theorem 4.8.1 uses Λ-rules even when G is Λ-free. Give a new construction that does not have that property.

3 Can you give a simpler proof of Theorem 4.8.1 with the aid of the 2-standard form?

4 One can strengthen the definition of operator form by demanding that the rules be of the following forms:

$S \to \Lambda$	
$A \to a$	$a \in \Sigma$,
$A \to B$	$B \in N - \{S\}$,
$A \to \alpha BC\beta$	where $\alpha, \beta \in (V - \{S\})^*$, $B, C \in V - \{S\}$, and either $B \in \Sigma$ or $C \in \Sigma$.

Modify the construction to achieve this form as well.

4.9 FORMAL POWER SERIES AND GREIBACH NORMAL FORM

It is possible to view a context-free grammar in terms of some traditional mathematical concepts such as equations and formal power series. For example, consider a grammar with the production shown below:

$$S \to SbS \mid a$$

Let us rewrite this grammar as an equation:

$$S = a + SbS \tag{4.9.1}$$

In some sense, we want to solve (4.9.1) for S. To do this, we approximate by taking S to be empty. Then we get a first approximation:

$$\sigma_0 = \emptyset.$$

A second approximation may be made by substituting σ_0 into (4.9.1) to obtain σ_1:

$$\sigma_1 = a$$

Continuing, we get

$$\begin{aligned} \sigma_2 &= a + aba \\ \sigma_3 &= a + (a + aba)b(a + aba) \\ &= a + aba + 2ababa + abababa \\ &\vdots \end{aligned}$$

Now, these operations have been carried out and we have tacitly assumed a number of properties of + and · such as distributivity. These were fortuitous choices, since these conventions led to a situation where the coefficients of the term x in the σ_i were the number of derivation trees of x of height $\leqslant i$. In the limit, σ_∞ could be written:

$$\sigma = \sigma_\infty = \sum_{x \in \Sigma^*} \sigma(x)x,$$

where $\sigma(x)$ is the *degree of ambiguity of* x, that is, the number of canonical derivations of x.

The example indicates that these ideas give a useful interpretation to the action of a grammar. It is therefore worthwhile to make these definitions precise and to understand any underlying assumptions.

Definition Let Σ be an alphabet. A *formal power series* is a map from Σ^* into the integers and is written $\sigma: x \to \sigma(x)$, or as

$$\sigma = \sum_{x \in \Sigma^*} \sigma(x)x$$

This is a power series in variables which are the elements of Σ; they are associative but not commutative.

The *support* of a formal power series σ is written as $\text{supp}(\sigma)$ and defined by

$$\text{supp}(\sigma) = \{x \in \Sigma^* \mid \sigma(x) \neq 0\}.$$

Thus, the support gives a language from a formal power series.

Because the underlying set is the integers, it is easy to define useful operations such as plus and product on formal power series. (This is done mainly in the exercises.) Many other classes of power series can be defined. For instance, a power series arising from a grammar will have coefficients that are nonnegative integers. It is worthwhile to study power series which have negative coefficients, or even to generalize to power series whose coefficients are in an arbitrary ring. Further applications may be found in the exercises and the literature.

It is useful to explain the process of associating a formal power series with a grammar. Our first example, while very intuitive, hid several issues because of its simplicity.

Let $G=(V,\Sigma,P,S)$ be a context-free grammar and let $N=\{A_1,\ldots,A_k\}$ with $S=A_1$. For each $A_i\in N$, let α_j^i, $1\leqslant j\leqslant m_i$, be all the righthand sides of A_i rules. G may be specified by the equations:

$$A_i = \alpha_1^i + \cdots + \alpha_{m_i}^i$$

for $1\leqslant i\leqslant k$. If we assume G is Λ-free and chain-free, then for each $x\in\Sigma^*$, there will be only a finite number of derivation trees for x. Let $\sigma(x)$ be this number, and define

$$\sigma = \sum_{x\in\Sigma^*} \sigma(x)x$$

Here σ may be computed by simultaneous approximation of all variables. We shall illustrate this by an example.

Example

$$A_1 \to A_1a|A_2b$$
$$A_2 \to a|b$$

In the form of equations, we have:

$$A_1 = A_1a + A_2b$$
$$A_2 = a + b$$

We approximate with ordered pairs of sets:

$$\sigma_0 = (\emptyset,\emptyset) = (\sigma_{01},\sigma_{02}),$$
$$\sigma_1 = (\emptyset,a+b) = (\sigma_{11},\sigma_{12}),$$
$$\sigma_2 = (ab+bb,a+b) = (\sigma_{21},\sigma_{22}),$$
$$\sigma_3 = (aba+bba+ab+bb,a+b) = (\sigma_{31},\sigma_{32}),$$
$$\sigma_4 = (abaa+bbaa+aba+bba+ab+bb,a+b) = (\sigma_{41},\sigma_{42}),$$
$$\vdots \qquad\qquad \vdots$$

To obtain σ, we compute

$$\sigma = \lim_{k\to\infty}\sigma_k = (\lim_{k\to\infty}\sigma_{k1}, \lim_{k\to\infty}\sigma_{k2}).$$

It is easy to prove that σ exists, and a procedure like this may be used in a more general context where the underlying equations were not generated by a grammar.

Formal power series and the associated equations that they satisfy are useful in deriving an alternative method for placing a grammar into Greibach normal form. Let $G=(V,\Sigma,P,S)$ be a context-free grammar. Assume that $N=\{A_1,\ldots,A_k\}$, $S=A_1$, and that G is Λ-free and chain-free. We take variable A_i and partition the righthand sides associated with A_i into those in NV^+ and those in ΣV^*. That is, we write:

$$A_i \rightarrow \alpha_i^1 | \cdots | \alpha_i^{n_i}$$

where $1 \leqslant i \leqslant k$, $n_i \geqslant 0$, and $\alpha_i^\ell \in \Sigma V^*$ for $1 \leqslant \ell \leqslant n_i$, and for each $1 \leqslant i, j \leqslant k$, we write

$$A_j \rightarrow A_i\alpha_{ij}^1 | \cdots | A_i\alpha_{ij}^{m_{ij}}$$

where $m_{ij} \geqslant 0$ and $\alpha_{ij}^\ell \in V^+$ for $1 \leqslant \ell \leqslant m_{ij}$. To simplify the notation, we write

$$r_{ij} = \alpha_{ij}^1 + \cdots + \alpha_{ij}^{m_{ij}}$$

$$b_i = \alpha_i^1 + \cdots + \alpha_i^{n_i}$$

where $1 \leqslant i, j \leqslant k$ and $n_i > 0$, $m_{ij} > 0$. If (say) $m_{ij} = 0$, then $r_{ij} = \emptyset$. Now we may represent G as:

$$\mathbf{A} = \mathbf{A}\mathbf{R} + \mathbf{b}, \tag{4.9.2}$$

where $\mathbf{A} = [A_1, \ldots, A_k]$, $\mathbf{b} = [b_1, \ldots, b_k]$, and $\mathbf{R} = (r_{ij})$. The r_{ij} and b_i notation can be extended by defining

$$r_{ij}^\ell = \alpha_{ij}^\ell \qquad \text{and} \qquad b_i^\ell = \alpha_i^\ell$$

An example will show that the process is less arcane than the notation might suggest.

Example Consider a grammar G given by:

$$A_1 \rightarrow A_1aA_2 | A_2A_2 | b$$

$$A_2 \rightarrow A_2d | A_2A_1a | aA_1 | c$$

In matrix form, this becomes

$$[A_1 \quad A_2] = [A_1 \quad A_2] \begin{bmatrix} aA_2 & \emptyset \\ A_2 & d + A_1a \end{bmatrix} + [b \quad aA_1 + c].$$

Now we are ready to state an algorithm for transforming a grammar into Greibach normal form.

Algorithm 4.9.1 Let $G=(V,\Sigma,P,S)$ be a Λ-free and chain-free context-free grammar. Assume $N=\{A_1,\ldots,A_k\}$ and $S=A_1$.

1 Express G by equations of the form (4.9.2); that is,

$$\mathbf{A} = \mathbf{A}\mathbf{R} + \mathbf{b}$$

2 Let $\mathbf{H} = (H_{ij})$ be a $k \times k$ matrix, each of whose entries is a new variable.

Construct a new system of equations:

$$\mathbf{A} = \mathbf{bH} + \mathbf{b}, \tag{4.9.3a}$$

$$\mathbf{H} = \mathbf{RH} + \mathbf{R}. \tag{4.9.3b}$$

3 Replace every word in $\mathbf{R}$ that is in NV^* by substituting the righthand sides for the leading variables. That is, if we have a word $A_p\alpha$ for some $1 \leqslant p \leqslant k$, then, from (4.9.3a), the A_p productions are:

$$A_p \to b_{j'}^{\ell} H_{j'p} \qquad \text{for } 1 \leqslant \ell \leqslant m_{j'},\ 1 \leqslant j' \leqslant k,$$

and

$$A_p \to b_p^{\ell} \qquad \text{for } 1 \leqslant \ell \leqslant m_p.$$

This results in a new system of equations:

$$\mathbf{A} = \mathbf{bH} + \mathbf{b}, \tag{4.9.4a}$$

$$\mathbf{H} = \mathbf{KH} + \mathbf{K}, \tag{4.9.4b}$$

where $\mathbf{K}$ is derived from $\mathbf{R}$ by making the above substitution.

4 The Greibach form grammar of G is now given by Eqs. (4.9.4a) and (4.9.4b).

If we apply this algorithm to our running example, step 2 gives us

$$[A_1 \quad A_2] = [b \quad aA_1 + c] \begin{bmatrix} H_{11} & H_{12} \\ H_{21} & H_{22} \end{bmatrix} + [b \quad aA_1 + c]$$

and

$$\begin{bmatrix} H_{11} & H_{12} \\ H_{21} & H_{22} \end{bmatrix} = \begin{bmatrix} aA_2 & \emptyset \\ A_2 & d + A_1 a \end{bmatrix} \begin{bmatrix} H_{11} & H_{12} \\ H_{21} & H_{22} \end{bmatrix} + \begin{bmatrix} aA_2 & \emptyset \\ A_2 & d + A_1 a \end{bmatrix}.$$

Note that the $(2, 1)$ and $(2, 2)$ entries of $\mathbf{R}$ require further modification. To derive $\mathbf{K}$ from $\mathbf{R}$, we carry out the substitutions, noting in advance that H_{12} must be a useless variable. We get

$$\mathbf{H} = \mathbf{KH} + \mathbf{K},$$

where

$$\mathbf{K} = \begin{bmatrix} aA_2 & \emptyset \\ aA_1H_{22} + cH_{22} + aA_1 + c & d + bH_{11}a + aA_1H_{21}a + cH_{21}a + ba \end{bmatrix}.$$

Now the Greibach form is obtained from Eqs. (4.9.4) and gives us:

$A_1 \to bH_{11} | aA_1H_{21} | cH_{21} | b$

$A_2 \to aA_1H_{22} | cH_{22} | aA_1 | c$

$H_{11} \to aA_2H_{11} | aA_2$

$H_{21} \to aA_1H_{22}H_{11} | cH_{22}H_{11} | aA_1H_{11} | cH_{11} | dH_{21} | bH_{11}aH_{21} | aA_1H_{21}aH_{21} | cH_{21}aH_{21} | baH_{21} |$
$\qquad aA_1H_{22} | cH_{22} | aA_1 | c$

$H_{22} \to dH_{22} | bH_{11}aH_{22} | aA_1H_{21}aH_{22} | cH_{21}aH_{22} | baH_{22} | d | bH_{11}a | aA_1H_{21}a | cH_{21}a | ba$

The method for achieving Greibach form developed in Section 4.6 led to grammars which were exponential in the size of G. We shall now show that this method does much better.

Theorem 4.9.1 Let G' be the Greibach normal-form grammar produced from G by Algorithm 4.9.1. Then

$$|G'| \leqslant c|G|^3$$

for some constant c.

Proof Assume that the number of **R** words is u and their total length is ℓ_u. Similarly, suppose the total length of the b words is ℓ_v and v is the number of such words. The rules which arise from Eq. (4.9.2) are

$$A_i \to A_j r_{ji}^{\ell} \qquad \text{with } 1 \leqslant \ell \leqslant m_{ji}, \quad 1 \leqslant i,j \leqslant k,$$

and

$$A_i \to b_i^{\ell} \qquad \text{with } 1 \leqslant \ell \leqslant n_i, \quad 1 \leqslant i \leqslant k.$$

There are u rules of the first type, so A_i and A_j contribute $2u$ to $|G|$. The r_{ji} contribute ℓ_u. A similar analysis for the second type of rules yields that

$$|G| = \ell_u + 2u + \ell_v + v. \tag{4.9.5}$$

Now the productions arising from (4.9.4a) are:

$$A_i \to b_j^{\ell} H_{ji} \qquad \text{for } 1 \leqslant \ell \leqslant n_j, \quad 1 \leqslant i,j \leqslant k,$$

and

$$A_i \to b_i^{\ell} \qquad \text{for } 1 \leqslant \ell \leqslant n_i, \quad 1 \leqslant i \leqslant k.$$

Each b_j^{ℓ} may appear in at most k rules of the first type and one of the second type. The contribution of (4.9.4a) is at most:

$$k(\ell_v + 2v) + \ell_v + v. \tag{4.9.6}$$

Now suppose **K** has w words of total length ℓ_w and recall that **K** is derived from **R**. In particular, each word $A_p\alpha$ in **R** may be replaced by the summation of all words $b_j^{\ell} H_{jp}\alpha$, where $1 \leqslant \ell \leqslant n_j$, $1 \leqslant j \leqslant k$, and $b_p^{\ell}\alpha$, where $1 \leqslant \ell \leqslant n_p$. The number of words in each category is at most v because each **b** word can appear at most once in each type of rule. The total length of words of the first type (involving b_j^{ℓ}, H_{jp}, and α) is at most:

$$\ell_v + v(1 + \lg(\alpha)). \tag{4.9.7}$$

A similar analysis for the second type yields the bound:

$$\ell_v + v(1 + \lg(\alpha)) + \ell_v + v \leqslant 2\ell_v + 2v\lg(r_{ij}^{\ell}), \tag{4.9.8}$$

since $r_{ij}^{\ell} = A_p\alpha$ and using a bound $2v$ for the number of words. Since such substitutions can be made for at most u words of **R**,

$$w \leqslant 2uv \tag{4.9.9}$$

and

$$\begin{aligned} \ell_w &= \sum_{\substack{i,j,\ell,\\ 1 \leqslant \ell \leqslant m_{ij},\\ 1 \leqslant i,j \leqslant k}} 2\ell_v + 2v\lg(r_{ij}^{\ell}) \\ &= 2\ell_v u + 2v \sum_{i,j,\ell} \lg(r_{ij}^{\ell}) \\ &= 2\ell_v u + 2v\ell_u \leqslant 4\ell_u\ell_v, \end{aligned} \tag{4.9.10}$$

using $u \leqslant \ell_u$ and $v \leqslant \ell_v$.

The contribution to $|G'|$ from (4.9.4b) is at most:

$$k(\ell_w + 2w) + \ell_w + w, \tag{4.9.11}$$

as for (4.9.4a).

Finally, the size of G' is determined by (4.9.4a) and (4.9.4b), so (4.9.6) and (4.9.11) yield:

$$|G'| \leqslant k(\ell_v + 2v) + \ell_v + v + k(\ell_w + 2w) + \ell_w + w. \tag{4.9.12}$$

Now, using (4.9.9) and (4.9.10), we have:

$$|G'| \leqslant k(\ell_v + 2v) + \ell_v + v + k(4\ell_u\ell_v + 2 \cdot 2uv) + 4\ell_u\ell_v + 2uv.$$

It follows easily that there is some constant c so that

$$|G'| \leqslant ck\ell_u\ell_v.$$

Now $\ell_u \leqslant |G|$, $\ell_v \leqslant |G|$, and $k = |N| \leqslant |V|$ so that

$$|G'| \leqslant c|G|^2 \cdot |V| \leqslant c|G|^3$$ □

To see that the bound given in the previous theorem is achieved, consider $G = (V, \Sigma, P, S)$, where $\Sigma = \{a_1, \ldots, a_k\}$, $k > 1$, $N = \{A_1, \ldots, A_k\}$, $S = A_1$, and:

$$P = \{A_i \to A_{i+1}^2 \mid 1 \leqslant i < k\} \cup \{A_k \to a_j \mid 1 \leqslant j \leqslant k\}.$$

Note that $|V| = 2k$ and $|G| = 5k - 3$. Algorithm 4.9.1 will produce the grammar:

$$\begin{array}{lll}
A_i \to a_j H_{ki} & 1 \leqslant j \leqslant k, & 1 \leqslant i \leqslant k, \\
A_k \to a_j & 1 \leqslant j \leqslant k, & \\
H_{ij} \to a_\ell H_{ki} H_{i-1,j} & 2 \leqslant i \leqslant k, & 1 \leqslant \ell, j \leqslant k, \\
H_{kj} \to a_\ell H_{k-1,j} & 1 \leqslant j \leqslant k, & 1 \leqslant \ell \leqslant k, \\
H_{i,i-1} \to a_\ell H_{ki} & 2 \leqslant i \leqslant k, & 1 \leqslant \ell \leqslant k, \\
H_{k,k-1} \to a_\ell & 1 \leqslant \ell \leqslant k. &
\end{array}$$

Clearly, $|V'| = k^2 + 2k$. After some work,

$$|G'| = 4k^3 + 5k^2 + k.$$

Let us reduce this grammar to see whether that changes its size substantially. We get:

$$\begin{array}{llll}
A_1 \to a_\ell H_{k1} & 1 \leqslant \ell \leqslant k, & & \\
H_{ij} \to a_\ell H_{ki} H_{i-1,j} & j+1 < i < k, & j \geqslant 1, & 1 \leqslant \ell \leqslant k, \\
H_{kj} \to a_\ell H_{k-1,j} & 1 < j < k-1, & 1 \leqslant \ell \leqslant k, & \\
H_{i,i-1} \to a_\ell H_{ki} & 2 \leqslant i < k, & 1 \leqslant \ell \leqslant k, & \\
H_{k,k-1} \to a_\ell & 1 \leqslant \ell \leqslant k. & &
\end{array}$$

Now we find that $|V'| = (k^2 + k + 2)/2$, and

$$|G'| = 2k^3 - 4k^2 + 5k.$$

Thus there are grammars for which this algorithm produces results on the order of $|G|^3$.

Our study of the complexity of grammatical transformations has led to a number of good algorithms but we have not yet proved a lower bound on the complexity of a transformation. Such a bound is now derived.

Theorem 4.9.2 There is a context-free language L_k with $\Lambda \notin L$ such that, for any context-free grammar G in Greibach form such that $L(G) = L_k$, it must be the case that:

$$|G| \geqslant 5k^2.$$

Moreover, there is a grammar G_k for L_k such that $|G_k| = 7k$.

Proof Let $L_k = \{a_1, \ldots, a_k\}^{4^k}$. Let G_k have the productions:

$$A_i \to A_{i+1}^4 \qquad \text{for} \quad 1 \leqslant i \leqslant k,$$

$$A_{k+1} \to a_1 | \cdots | a_k$$

Clearly,

$$|G_k| = 5k + 2k = 7k.$$

This proves the last statement of the theorem.

Let $G = (V, \Sigma, P, S)$ be a reduced grammar in Greibach normal form which generates L. Assume that G is a minimal grammar which generates L with respect to $|G|$. The k strings $a_1^{4^k}, \ldots, a_k^{4^k}$ are all in L, so simultaneously consider a derivation of each string. Because G is in Greibach form, the productions used in any pair of these derivations are disjoint since the terminal strings produced involve different letters. Let P_i be the productions used in the derivation of $a_i^{4^k}$. Define $G_i = (V, \Sigma, P_i, S)$. It is easy to see that

$$L(G_i) = \{a_i^{4^k}\}.$$

Thus each G_i is a Greibach-form grammar generating $\{a_i^{4^k}\}$. By Problem 3 of Section 4.2, we have:

$$|G_i| \geqslant 5k.$$

Now, since each of the k grammars G_i has pairwise disjoint productions, we know that:

$$|G| \geqslant \sum_{i=1}^{k} |G_i| \geqslant 5k^2. \qquad \square$$

PROBLEMS

Let

$$\sigma = \sum_{x \in \Sigma^*} \sigma(x)x \qquad \text{and} \qquad \tau = \sum_{x \in \Sigma^*} \tau(x)x$$

be formal power series and let n be an integer. Define

$$n\sigma = \sum_{x \in \Sigma^*} n\sigma(x)x,$$

$$\sigma + \tau = \sum_{x \in \Sigma^*} (\sigma(x) + \tau(x))x,$$

and

$$\sigma\tau = \sum_{x \in \Sigma^*} \rho(x)x,$$

where

$$\rho(x) = \sum_{x=yz} \sigma(y)\tau(z).$$

Thus $\sigma\tau$ is the product (or Cauchy product) of σ and τ.

1 Show that the set of all formal power series is a ring with respect to + and · of power series.

2 Show that, if σ and τ are formal power series,

$$\operatorname{supp}(\sigma + \tau) = \operatorname{supp}(\sigma) \cup \operatorname{supp}(\tau),$$
$$\operatorname{supp}(\sigma\tau) = \operatorname{supp}(\sigma)\operatorname{supp}(\tau).$$

3 If σ is a formal power series and $k \geqslant 1$, verify that σ^k is well defined. Using that notation and assuming that $\sigma(\Lambda) = 0$, define:

$$\sigma^+ = \lim_{n \to \infty} \sum_{m=1}^{n} \sigma^m.$$

Here σ^+ is called the *quasi-inverse* of σ. Show that:

a) σ^+ exists;

b) σ^+ satisfies $\sigma + \sigma^+\sigma = \sigma + \sigma\sigma^+ = \sigma^+$;

c) $\operatorname{supp}(\sigma^+) = (\operatorname{supp}(\sigma))^+$.

A collection $\mathscr{H}$ of formal power series is said to be *rationally closed* if, for every $\sigma \in \mathscr{H}$ such that $\sigma(\Lambda) = 0$, we have $\sigma^+ \in \mathscr{H}$.

The family of (positive) rational power series is the least rationally closed family which contains Λ (the power series where $\Lambda(x) = 1$ if $x = \Lambda$ and $\Lambda(x) = 0$ if $x \neq \Lambda$), each $a \in \Sigma$ is regarded as a power series $a(x) = 1$ if $x = a$ and $a(x) = 0$ if $x \neq a$, and is closed under sum, product, and multiplication by (nonnegative) integers n.

4 Show that a language L is regular if and only if $L = \operatorname{supp}(\rho)$, where ρ is in the family of positive rational power series.

Let μ be any map from Σ into $n \times n$ matrices whose entries are nonnegative integers. Extend μ to a homomorphism by defining:

$$\mu(\Lambda) = \mathbf{I}, \qquad \text{the } n \times n \text{ identity matrix,}$$

and

$$\mu(ax) = \mu(a)\mu(x),$$

where $a \in \Sigma$ and $x \in \Sigma^*$. A power series σ is said to admit a *matrix representation* if there exist $n \geqslant 1$ and a map μ such that for all $x \in \Sigma^+$, $\sigma(x) = (\mu(x))_{1,n}$ (that is, the $(1, n)$ entry in $\mu(x)$).

5 Characterize the family of formal power series that admit matrix representations.

6 Prove that Algorithm 4.9.1 works.

7 Show that if one starts from a grammar in Chomsky normal form and applies Algorithm 4.9.1, then the resulting grammar is in 2-standard form.

4.10 HISTORICAL SURVEY

A general reference on algorithmic complexity is Aho, Hopcroft, and Ullman [1974]. The approach adopted here is related to work by Hunt, Szymanski, and Ullman [1974], who have been studying the complexity of many problems related to grammars. Theorem 4.2.1 and Problem 2 of Section 4.3 are due to A. Yehudai. Theorems 4.3.1 and 4.3.2 are from Bar-Hillel, Perles, and Shamir [1961]. Chomsky normal form appears in Chomsky [1959a]. Canonical two-form first appeared in Gray and Harrison [1969, 1972]. Invertibility was first studied in McNaughton [1967] for parenthesis grammars, and Fischer [1969] for operator-precedence grammars. The fact that it holds for all context-free grammars first appears in Gray and Harrison [1969].

Greibach normal form and Theorem 4.6.2 are from Greibach [1965]. Our proof of Theorem 4.7.1 follows Hopcroft and Ullman [1969]. Other proofs and generalizations may be found in Wood [1969a, 1970]. 2-Standard form is mentioned in Greibach [1965]. Operator form first occurs in Floyd [1963]. The material in Section 4.9 on power series is from the work of Schützenberger. The matrix technique for placing a grammar in GNF is due to Rosenkrantz [1967]. Problems 3 of Section 4.2 and 7 of Section 4.3 are due to Gruska. The lower bound on achieving GNF is due to Pirická-Kemenová [1975] and to Yehudai.

five
Pushdown Automata

5.1 INTRODUCTION

The major result of this chapter is the characterization of context-free languages in terms of *pushdown automata.* This is an important and satisfying theorem, in that our intuition about which sets are context-free will be greatly strengthened. Whenever one is faced with some new context-free set, it is generally much easier to describe a pushdown automation to accept it than to try to produce a grammar.

Another important family is introduced, the *deterministic* context-free languages. These languages are all unambiguous and, moreover, are recognizable in linear time. It has turned out that this family is a very practical one for compiler writers and those interested in fast parsing techniques. The relationship between fast parsing and this family is taken up again in Chapter 13.

An interesting family of pushdown automata is defined by bounding the number of times the direction of a pushdown can change. Thus "finite-turn pushdown automata" are introduced in Section 5.7 and some basic results obtained. Others will occur later when we have additional tools at our disposal.

5.2 BASIC DEFINITIONS

There is a class of devices, called pushdown automata, which is very important since its study leads to an important characterization of the context-free languages. Intuitively, a pushdown automaton consists of three parts, a read-only input tape, a read–write pushdown store, and a finite state control. (See Fig. 5.1.)

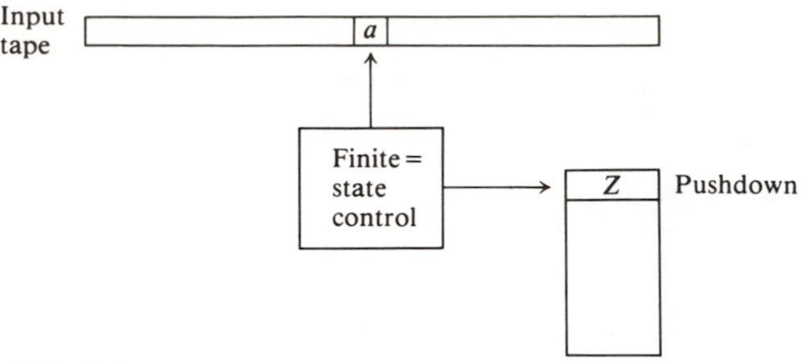

FIG. 5.1

Depending on the state the automaton is in, the input symbol it is reading, and the symbol on the top of the pushdown store, the automaton may make a transition to any one of a finite set of states, writing a finite number of symbols on its pushdown store. (Writing the null string corresponds to erasing the topmost symbol.)

In addition, the automaton may make transitions and write on its store *without* reading an input symbol. Such transitions will be called Λ-moves. Later we will prove that Λ-moves do not increase the power of the automaton in the sense that, for each automaton with Λ-moves, there exists an automaton without Λ-moves which accepts the same set.

We will assume that there must be some symbol on the pushdown in order for the automaton to make a move (i.e., the automaton must halt when it empties its store). We will show that, in exactly the same sense as with Λ-moves, this assumption leads to no loss of generality.

It should be noted that the automaton has a potentially unbounded memory, and it is only the fact that its access to this memory is highly restricted that prevents it from being equivalent to a Turing machine.

We now proceed to make these ideas precise.

Definition A *pushdown automaton* (*pda* for short) is a 7-tuple

$$A = (Q, \Sigma, \Gamma, \delta, q_0, Z_0, F),$$

where

Q is a finite nonempty set of *states*,
Σ is a finite nonempty set of *input symbols*,
Γ is a finite nonempty set of *pushdown symbols*,
$q_0 \in Q$ is the *initial state*,
$Z_0 \in \Gamma$ is the *initial symbol* on the pushdown store,
$F \subseteq Q$ is a *set of final states*,
$\delta: Q \times (\Sigma \cup \Lambda) \times \Gamma \rightarrow$ finite subsets of $Q \times \Gamma^*$.

We will write $(q', \alpha) \in \delta(q, a, Z)$ to indicate a particular transition.

To describe the automaton at any given time we need to know three things: the state it is in, what remains on the input tape, and what is on the pushdown store.

Definition Let $A = (Q, \Sigma, \Gamma, \delta, q_0, Z_0, F)$ be a pda. An *instantaneous description* (abbreviated *ID*) of A is an element of $Q \times \Sigma^* \times \Gamma^*$. An *initial ID* is a member of $\{q_0\} \times \Sigma^* \times \{Z_0\}$.

Thus

$$(q, ax, \alpha Z), \quad q \in Q, \quad x \in \Sigma^*, \quad a \in \Sigma_\Lambda, \quad \alpha \in \Gamma^*, \quad \text{and} \quad Z \in \Gamma,$$

would be an ID for an automaton in state q, currently reading input a, and having Z on the top of the stack.

Note that a may be Λ, in which case the device will make a Λ-move; that is, the input is not advanced. Also, the topmost symbol on the stack will be written at the righthand end of the third coordinate of the ID's.

Definition Let $A = (Q, \Sigma, \Gamma, \delta, q_0, Z_0, F)$ be a pda. Define a relation $\vdash$ called the *move relation* by:

$$(q, ax, \alpha Z) \vdash (q', x, \alpha\beta)$$

if

$$(q', \beta) \in \delta(q, a, Z)$$

for any $q, q' \in Q$; any a in $\Sigma \cup \{\Lambda\}$; any $x \in \Sigma^*$; $\alpha, \beta \in \Gamma^*$, and $Z \in \Gamma$. Let $\overset{*}{\vdash}$ be the reflexive transitive closure of $\vdash$.

Note that $\lg(\alpha Z) \geqslant 1$, which corresponds to the assumption that the automaton cannot make a move if the pushdown store is empty. Moreover the case $\beta = \Lambda$ allows the top symbol on the pushdown to be erased.

Note that if, for some $q, q' \in Q; x \in \Sigma^*; \alpha, \beta \in \Gamma^*$,

$$(q, x, \alpha) \overset{*}{\vdash} (q', \Lambda, \beta),$$

then, for any $y \in \Sigma^*$,

$$(q, xy, \alpha) \overset{*}{\vdash} (q', y, \beta).$$

The converse is also true.

For the pushdown, the operation is slightly different. For any $q, q' \in Q$; $\beta, \gamma \in \Gamma^*$, and $x, y \in \Sigma^*$, if:

$$(q, xy, \beta) \overset{*}{\vdash} (q', y, \gamma),$$

then, for any $\alpha \in \Gamma^*$,

$$(q, xy, \alpha\beta) \overset{*}{\vdash} (q', y, \alpha\gamma).$$

Here the converse is false. The above situation is shown pictorially in Fig. 5.2. The failure of the converse is shown in Fig. 5.3.

For future reference, we summarize these observations in a formal statement.

Proposition 5.2.1 Let $A = (Q, \Sigma, \Gamma, \delta, q_0, Z_0, \emptyset)$ be a pda. Let $q, q' \in Q$, $\beta, \gamma \in \Gamma^*$, $x \in \Sigma^*$. If

$$(q, x, \beta) \overset{*}{\vdash} (q', \Lambda, \gamma),$$

then, for any $y \in \Sigma^*, \alpha \in \Gamma^*$,

$$(q, xy, \alpha\beta) \overset{*}{\vdash} (q', y, \alpha\gamma).$$

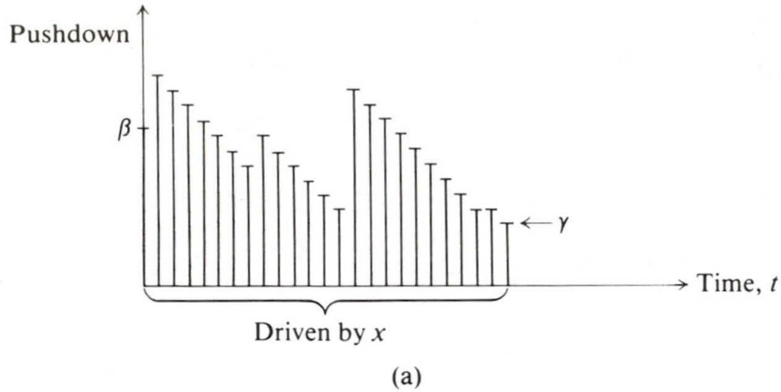

(a)

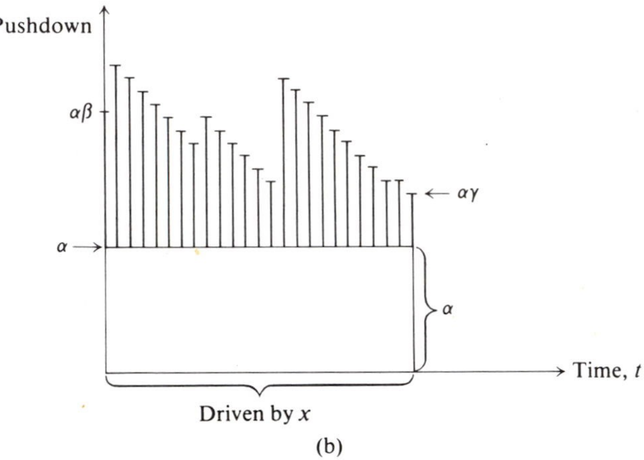

(b)

FIG. 5.2

It is important to observe that the *converse* of Proposition 5.2.1 is false. We illustrate this in Fig. 5.3.

The idea of Fig. 5.3 is that, in a computation $(q, xy, \alpha\beta) \overset{*}{\vdash} (q', y, \alpha\gamma)$, it is possible that some of α is destroyed and then rewritten. If we ran the same computation without α on the pushdown, then the computation would "block" at point * in Fig. 5.3.

We must now define what we mean by saying that a pda accepts a set.

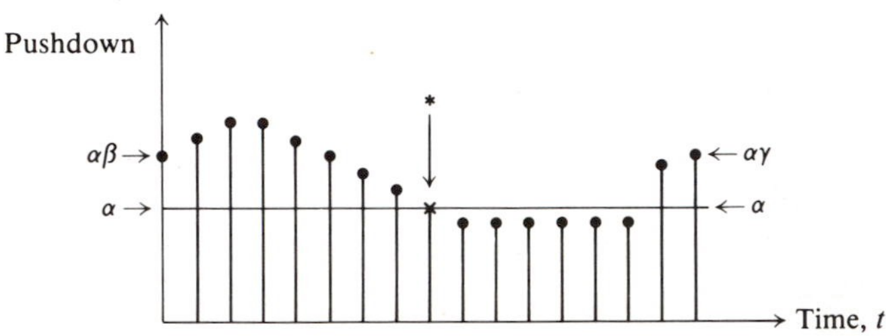

FIG. 5.3

Definition Let $A = (Q, \Sigma, \Gamma, \delta, q_0, Z_0, F)$ be a pda. Define:

$$T(A) = \{w \in \Sigma^* \mid (q_0, w, Z_0) \overset{*}{\vdash} (q, \Lambda, \alpha) \quad \text{for some } q \in F, \alpha \in \Gamma^*\}$$

and

$$N(A) = \{w \in \Sigma^* \mid (q_0, w, Z_0) \overset{*}{\vdash} (q, \Lambda, \Lambda) \quad \text{for some } q \in Q\}$$

and

$$L(A) = \{w \in \Sigma^* \mid (q_0, w, Z_0) \overset{*}{\vdash} (q, \Lambda, \Lambda) \quad \text{for some } q \in F\}.$$

$T(A)$ is the set *accepted* by automaton A *by final state.* $N(A)$ is the set *accepted* by automaton A *by empty store.* $L(A)$ is the set *accepted by both final state and empty store*.

Intuitively, A accepts by final state if there exists *some* finite sequence of moves that exhausts the input and leaves A in a final state. (Note that, since A may have Λ-moves, it may not halt even though it accepts.) On the other hand, A accepts by empty store if there exists *some* finite sequence of moves that exhausts the input and empties the pushdown store. (In this case the automaton will stop since it cannot make any move if its store is empty.)

Finally, we would like to define a "deterministic pda." To ensure that a pda is deterministic, not only must we restrict the "choice" of a next state to at most one state, but we must also take into account Λ-moves. In order to permit the automaton to perform operations on its pushdown store without reading its input, instead of simply disallowing Λ-moves, we permit a Λ-move from a given state if and only if there is no "regular" (non-Λ) move. Hence,

Definition A pda $A = (Q, \Sigma, \Gamma, \delta, q_0, Z_0, F)$ is *deterministic* (dpda for short) if for all $(q, a, Z) \in Q \times (\Sigma \cup \{\Lambda\}) \times \Gamma$,

1. $|\delta(q, a, Z)| \leqslant 1$;
2. If $\delta(q, \Lambda, Z) \neq \emptyset$, then $\delta(q, a, Z) = \emptyset$ for each $a \in \Sigma$.

Definition A set L is called a *deterministic context-free language* if there is some dpda A such that $L = T(A)$. we say that two dpda's A and A' are *equivalent* if $T(A) = T(A')$.

Before proceeding to a mathematical analysis of pda's, we give two examples to illustrate the ideas and notation.

Example 1 Let G be the grammar

$$S \to aSa \mid bSb \mid c$$

(It may be premature to call a set a "deterministic" context-free language before the connection between pda's and these languages has been established but we shall do so.)

Then

$$L_c = L(G) = \{wcw^T \mid w \in \{a, b\}^*\}.$$

That is, L_c is the set of palindromes with a center marker. We want to construct a pda A which accepts L_c.

Intuitively, A will copy each symbol of its input onto its pushdown until it encounters the center marker. It will then go into a new state, in which it will compare the top symbol on the pushdown with the input. If they fail to match, it will halt; otherwise it will erase the top symbol on the pushdown and repeat the process with the next symbol of the input. Finally, if it exhausts its input and only the start symbol remains on the pushdown, it will go into an accepting state.

Let

$$A = (Q, \Sigma, \Gamma, \delta, q_0, Z_0, F),$$

where

$$\begin{aligned} Q &= \{q_0, q_1, q_2\}, \\ \Sigma &= \{a, b, c\}, \\ \Gamma &= \{a, b, Z_0\}, \\ F &= \{q_2\}, \end{aligned}$$

and δ is given by:*

For all $d, A \in \{a, b\}$,

$\delta(q_0, d, Z_0) = (q_0, Z_0 d)$		Stack first input letter.
$\delta(q_0, d, A) = (q_0, Ad)$		Continue stacking.
$\delta(q_0, c, B) = (q_1, B)$	for all $B \in \Gamma$	Center found.
$\delta(q_1, d, d) = (q_1, \Lambda)$		Compare and erase.
$\delta(q_1, \Lambda, Z_0) = (q_2, Z_0)$		Accept.

To show how the automaton works, consider the input *aabcbaa*:

$$\begin{aligned} (q_0, aabcbaa, Z_0) &\vdash (q_0, abcbaa, Z_0 a) \\ &\vdash (q_0, bcbaa, Z_0 aa) \\ &\vdash (q_0, cbaa, z_0 aab) \\ &\vdash (q_1, baa, Z_0 aab) \\ &\vdash (q_1, aa, Z_0 aa) \\ &\vdash (q_1, a, Z_0 a) \\ &\vdash (q_1, \Lambda, Z_0) \\ &\vdash (q_2, \Lambda, Z_0), \end{aligned}$$

at which point the machine halts, since q_2 is not in the domain of δ.

Note $c \in L_c$ and $(q_0, c, Z_0) \overset{*}{\vdash} (q_2, \Lambda, Z_0)$.

The automaton is clearly deterministic, and hence $L_c = T(A)$ is a deterministic, context-free language.

---

* Note that in a dpda, we write $\delta(q, a, Z) = (q', \alpha)$, instead of $\delta(q, a, Z) = \{(q', \alpha)\}$.

Example 2 Let G be the grammar

$$S \to aSa \mid bSb \mid \Lambda$$

Then

$$P = L(G) = \{ww^T \mid w \in \{a, b\}^*\}$$

is clearly context-free. P is the set of even-length palindromes (without a center marker).

P differs from L_c only in that there is no center marker. Hence, if we could construct a pda which could find the center of the input, we could proceed as before. A little thought should convince the reader that, since the input is one-way and the length of the input is unbounded, a deterministic pda cannot find the center of the input. (Can you prove that rigorously?) Therefore we will construct a pda that will "guess" at where the center is and then proceed as before. Clearly, if the pda "guesses" correctly, it will work properly. All that must be checked is that, when the automaton makes a wrong guess, it does not accept the input.

CASE 1. If the automaton "guesses" too soon, then, although the pda could empty its pushdown, the input would not be exhausted and hence the string will not be accepted.

CASE 2. If the automaton "guesses" too late, then it could exhaust its input, but the pushdown would not be empty and therefore the string will not be accepted.

Formally, let

$$C = (Q, \Sigma, \Gamma, \delta, q_0, Z_0, \emptyset),$$

where

$$Q = \{q_0, q_1\},$$
$$\Sigma = \{a, b\},$$
$$\Gamma = \{a, b, Z_0\},$$

and δ is given by:

For all $c, A \in \{a, b\}$,

$\delta(q_0, c, Z_0) = \{(q_0, Z_0c)\}$	Stack first letter.
$\delta(q_0, c, A) = \{(q_0, Ac)\}$	Continue stacking.
$\delta(q_0, \Lambda, Z_0) = \{(q_1, \Lambda)\}$	Accept Λ.
$\delta(q_0, c, c) = \{(q_0, cc), (q_1, \Lambda)\}$	Guess what to do.
$\delta(q_1, c, c) = \{(q_1, \Lambda)\}$	Compare and pop.
$\delta(q_1, \Lambda, Z_0) = \{(q_1, \Lambda)\}$	Accept.

To show how the pda works, consider the input $abba$. There are two possible sequences of ID's:

$$\begin{aligned}(q_0, abba, Z_0) &\vdash (q_0, bba, Z_0a)\\ &\vdash (q_0, ba, Z_0ab)\\ &\vdash (q_0, a, Z_0abb)\\ &\vdash (q_0, \Lambda, Z_0abba)\end{aligned}$$

and

$$\begin{aligned}(q_0, abba, Z_0) &\vdash (q_0, bba, Z_0a)\\ &\vdash (q_0, ba, Z_0ab)\\ &\vdash (q_1, a, Z_0a)\\ &\vdash (q_1, \Lambda, Z_0)\\ &\vdash (q_1, \Lambda, \Lambda)\end{aligned}$$

Since the second of these ends with an empty pushdown and null input, the string is accepted. (The reader should verify that a string like *abbb* is not accepted.)

Thus C accepts P by empty store. It should be noted that C is nondeterministic. Later we will prove that there is no deterministic pda that accepts P.

Before embarking on the proof of equivalence between pda and context-free grammars, we associate timing conditions with these devices.

Definition A pda $A = (Q, \Sigma, \Gamma, \delta, q_0, Z_0, F)$

i) *operates with delay k*, $k \geqslant 0$, if for all $q, q' \in Q$; $\alpha, \beta \in \Gamma^*$,

$$(q, \Lambda, \alpha) \overset{n}{\vdash} (q', \Lambda, \beta) \qquad \text{implies } n \leqslant k.$$

[Intuitively, A can have at most k consecutive Λ-moves.]

ii) *operates in quasi-realtime* (is *quasi-realtime*) if there is $k \geqslant 0$ such that A operates with delay k. [Intuitively, A can have at most a bounded number of Λ-moves.]

iii) *operates in linear time* if there exists $k \geqslant 0$ such that for all $q, q' \in Q$; $\alpha, \beta \in \Gamma^*$, and $w \in \Sigma^+$, if

$$(q, w, \alpha) \overset{n}{\vdash} (q', \Lambda, \beta),$$

then $n \leqslant k \lg(w)$. [Intuitively, every non-null input can be processed in time proportional to its length.]

iv) is *Λ-free* if for all $q \in Q$, $Z \in \Gamma$,

$$\delta(q, \Lambda, Z) = \emptyset.$$

v) *operates in realtime* if A is deterministic and operates with delay 0,

vi) is *unambiguous* if, for each $w \in \Sigma^*$, there is at most one computation

$$C_0 \vdash C_1 \vdash \cdots \vdash C_n$$

where C_0 is an initial ID involving w and C_n is an accepting ID. [Note that the form of a final ID depends on whether we are dealing with $L(A)$, $N(A)$, or $T(A)$.]

Looking ahead to Lemma 5.6.5, we will prove the following result.

Proposition 5.2.2 Every dpda is equivalent to an unambiguous pda.

Every Λ-free pda operates with delay 0. Each pda that operates in quasi-realtime operates in linear time. The converse is false. To see this, imagine a dpda A that accepts a^*b^*c. As this set is regular, the dpda need not even consult its stack, but let us suppose that A stacks all its input up to the c. Then if the input is of the proper form, A will accept as $L(A)$ by erasing its pushdown. This will take a number of consecutive Λ-moves that is linear in the length of the input. Thus A would be a linear-time dpda but not quasi-realtime.

Example Returning to Example 1 and examining the pda A, we note that A is deterministic and operates with delay one. What can you say about Example 2?

PROBLEMS

1 Show that, if $L \subseteq \Sigma^*$, then $L = L(A)$ for some pda A if and only if $L = T(B)$ for some pda B if and only if $L = N(C)$ for some pda C.

2 Can you modify the pda in Example 1 to work in realtime?

3 Show that the set $L = \{w \in \{a, b\}^* \mid \#_a(w) = \#_b(w)\}$ can be accepted by a dpda.

4 Show that the set $L = \{a^n b^m \mid 1 \leqslant n \leqslant m < 2n\}$ can be accepted by a pda.

5 Given any pda A, one can construct a new pda B such that if $(q', \alpha) \in \delta_B(q, a, Z)$, then $\lg(\alpha) \leqslant 2$. That is, B never tries to add more than one character at a time. In what sense is B "equivalent" to A? That is, is $N(B) = N(A)$? If A is realtime, is B? etc.

6 There is another way in which dpda's can be used to accept languages. Let $A = (Q, \Sigma, \Gamma, \delta, q_0, Z_0, F)$ be a dpda. If

$$(q, x, \alpha)$$

is an ID, we say that $(q, \alpha^{(1)})$ is the *mode*. We now let $\tilde{F}$ be a set of modes. Show that

$$L = \{w \in \Sigma^* \mid (q_0, w, Z_0) \overset{*}{\vdash} (q, \Lambda, \alpha) \quad \text{for some } (q, \alpha^{(1)}) \in \tilde{F}\}$$

is a deterministic context-free language.

7 Show that every regular set accepted by a finite automaton with n states may be accepted by

i) a dpda with n states and one pushdown symbol, or
ii) a dpda with one state and n pushdown symbols.

Be sure to state which type of acceptance is being used.

8 Show that a dpda A, with q states and t pushdown symbols and maximum length r to be stacked, has an equivalent dpda with q states and at most one symbol added to the stack at a time.

5.3 EQUIVALENT FORMS OF ACCEPTANCE

Given a pda A, a set may be accepted as $T(A)$, $N(A)$, and $L(A)$. We shall study the relation between sets defined in these ways.

Definition For a fixed alphabet Σ, let:

$$\mathscr{T}_\Sigma = \{L \subseteq \Sigma^* \mid L = T(A) \quad \text{for some pda } A\},$$
$$\mathscr{N}_\Sigma = \{L \subseteq \Sigma^* \mid L = N(A) \quad \text{for some pda } A\},$$
$$\mathscr{L}_\Sigma = \{L \subseteq \Sigma^* \mid L = L(A) \quad \text{for some pda } A\}.$$

$\mathscr{T}_\Sigma$ is the set of languages accepted by final state, $\mathscr{N}_\Sigma$ is the set of languages accepted by empty store, and $\mathscr{L}_\Sigma$ is the set of languages accepted by both final state and empty pushdown. In this section, we prove that $\mathscr{T}_\Sigma = \mathscr{N}_\Sigma = \mathscr{L}_\Sigma$.

We begin by showing that $\mathscr{N}_\Sigma \subseteq \mathscr{T}_\Sigma$.

Theorem 5.3.1 For each (deterministic) pda $A = (Q, \Sigma, \Gamma, \delta, q_0, Z_0, \emptyset)$, there exists a (deterministic) pda $B = (Q', \Sigma, \Gamma', \delta_B, \bar{q}_0, Y_0, \{f\})$ such that $N(A) = T(B) = N(B) = L(B)$. Moreover

$$(q_0, x, Z_0) \overset{*}{\underset{A}{\vdash}} (q, \Lambda, \Lambda) \quad \text{for some } q \in Q$$

if and only if $(\bar{q}_0, x, Y_0) \overset{*}{\underset{B}{\vdash}} (f, \Lambda, \Lambda)$.

Proof Let

$$B = (Q \cup \{\bar{q}_0, f\}, \Sigma, \Gamma \cup \{Y_0\}, \delta_B, \bar{q}_0, Y_0, \{f\})$$

where $\bar{q}_0, f \notin Q$, $Y_0 \notin \Gamma$, and δ_B is given by:

1 $\delta_B(\bar{q}_0, \Lambda, Y_0) = \{(q_0, Y_0 Z_0)\}$ Add a new bottom symbol.

2 For all $(q, a, Z) \in Q \times (\Sigma \cup \{\Lambda\}) \times \Gamma$, $\delta_B(q, a, Z) = \delta(q, a, Z)$ Simulate A.

3 $\delta_B(q, \Lambda, Y_0) = \{(f, \Lambda)\}$ for all $q \in Q$. Erase Y_0 and accept.

Note. B is deterministic if and only if A is deterministic.

Intuitively, B enters Z_0 on the pushdown, simulates A until A's stack is empty, and then makes a transition to f, erasing its start symbol.

We now proceed to show $N(A) = T(B)$.

Claim 1 If $x \in N(A)$, then $(\bar{q}_0, x, Y_0) \overset{*}{\underset{B}{\vdash}} (f, \Lambda, \Lambda)$.

Proof If $x \in N(A)$, then

$$(q_0, x, Z_0) \overset{*}{\underset{A}{\vdash}} (q, \Lambda, \Lambda) \quad \text{for some } q \in Q.$$

But, since $\delta_A \subseteq \delta_B$, we have

$$(q_0, x, Z_0) \overset{*}{\underset{B}{\vdash}} (q, \Lambda, \Lambda).$$

Now, since the pushdown could only have been emptied on the last move, we have

$$(\bar{q}_0, x, Y_0) \underset{B}{\vdash} (q_0, x, Y_0 Z_0) \overset{*}{\underset{B}{\vdash}} (q, \Lambda, Y_0) \underset{B}{\vdash} (f, \Lambda, \Lambda),$$

or, equivalently,

$$\text{If } x \in N(A), \text{ then } (\bar{q}_0, x, Y_0) \overset{*}{\underset{B}{\vdash}} (f, \Lambda, \Lambda).$$

Claim 2 If $(\bar{q}_0, x, Y_0) \overset{*}{\underset{B}{\vdash}} (f, \Lambda, \Lambda)$, then $x \in N(A)$.

Proof If $(\bar{q}_0, x, Y_0) \overset{*}{\underset{B}{\vdash}} (f, \Lambda, \Lambda)$, then, from the construction of B, the computation must be of the form

$$(\bar{q}_0, x, Y_0) \underset{B}{\vdash} (q_0, x, Y_0Z_0) \overset{*}{\underset{B}{\vdash}} (q, \Lambda, Y_0) \underset{B}{\vdash} (f, \Lambda, \Lambda) \quad \text{for some } q \in Q.$$

Now, since Y_0 could not have been rewritten in the computation

$$(q_0, x, Y_0Z_0) \overset{*}{\underset{B}{\vdash}} (q, \Lambda, Y_0),$$

we must have

$$(q_0, x, Z_0) \overset{*}{\underset{B}{\vdash}} (q, \Lambda, \Lambda).$$

This computation uses only states from Q. Therefore

$$(q_0, x, Z_0) \overset{*}{\underset{A}{\vdash}} (q, \Lambda, \Lambda)$$

or $x \in N(A)$. Thus,

$$(\bar{q}_0, x, Y_0) \overset{*}{\underset{B}{\vdash}} (f, \Lambda, \Lambda) \quad \text{implies } x \in N(A).$$

Also, since f is a final state, $x \in L(B)$ and $x \in T(B)$. B empties its stack if and only if B enters a final state. Together with Claims 1 and 2, we have

$$N(A) = T(B) = N(B) = L(B)$$

and

$$(q_0, x, Z_0) \overset{*}{\underset{A}{\vdash}} (q, \Lambda, \Lambda) \qquad \text{if and only if} \quad (\bar{q}_0, x, Y_0) \overset{*}{\underset{B}{\vdash}} (f, \Lambda, \Lambda). \qquad \square$$

Corollary (a) $\mathscr{N}_\Sigma \subseteq \mathscr{T}_\Sigma$; (b) $\mathscr{N}_\Sigma \subseteq \mathscr{L}_\Sigma$.

Next we show that $\mathscr{T}_\Sigma \subseteq \mathscr{N}_\Sigma$.

Theorem 5.3.2 If $L = T(A)$ for some pda A, then there exists a pda B such that $L = N(B) = L(B)$.

Proof Let

$$A = (Q, \Sigma, \Gamma, \delta, q_0, Z_0, F).$$

We will construct B from A as follows: B has a special stack marker Y_0 (its start symbol), which can only be erased from a special state d. On a given input, B will

a) Place A's start symbol on the pushdown (using a Λ-move) from a special initial state;
b) Simulate A until A enters a final state;
c) If A enters a final state, B may either (i) go into the special state d, erase its store and halt, or (ii) continue simulating A until another final state is reached.

Formally, we have

$$B = (Q \cup \{d, q_0'\}, \Sigma, \Gamma \cup \{Y_0\}, \delta_B, q_0', Y_0, \{d\}),$$

where $d, q_0' \notin Q$, $Y_0 \notin \Gamma$, and δ_B is given by:

1 $\delta_B(q_0', \Lambda, Y_0) = \{(q_0, Y_0Z_0)\}$ Add Z_0 to stack.
2 $\delta_B(q, a, Z) = \delta(q, a, Z)$ for all (q, a, Z), $q \notin F$, or $a \neq \Lambda$. Simulate A.

3 If $q \in F$, $\delta_B(q, \Lambda, Z) = \delta(q, \Lambda, Z) \cup \{(d, \Lambda)\}$ for all $Z \in \Gamma \cup \{Y_0\}$. In a final state, guess whether or not it is the end. Erase everything from d.

4 $\delta_B(d, \Lambda, Z) = \{(d, \Lambda)\}$ for all $Z \in \Gamma \cup \{Y_0\}$.

Note. B may be nondeterministic even if A is deterministic.

We now must show that $N(B) = T(A)$.

Claim 1 $T(A) \subseteq N(B)$.

Proof If $x \in T(A)$, then $(q_0, x, Z_0) \overset{*}{\underset{A}{\vdash}} (q, \Lambda, \alpha)$, for some $q \in F$, $\alpha \in \Gamma^*$. Since $\delta \subseteq \delta_B$, we have

$$(q_0, x, Z_0) \overset{*}{\underset{B}{\vdash}} (q, \Lambda, \alpha) \qquad \text{for some } q \in F, \alpha \in \Gamma^*.$$

Now, since, in the above computation, B could not have annihilated its store (except possibly on the last step), we have, by (1) above,

$$(q'_0, x, Y_0) \underset{B}{\vdash} (q_0, x, Y_0Z_0) \overset{*}{\underset{B}{\vdash}} (q, \Lambda, Y_0\alpha).$$

But

$$(q, \Lambda, Y_0\alpha) \underset{B}{\vdash} \begin{cases} (d, \Lambda, \Lambda) & \text{if } \alpha = \Lambda \\ (d, \Lambda, Y_0\alpha') & \text{if } \alpha = \alpha' Z \quad \text{for some } Z \in \Gamma, \end{cases}$$

whence

$$(d, \Lambda, Y_0\alpha') \overset{*}{\underset{B}{\vdash}} (d, \Lambda, \Lambda).$$

Combining we have: If $x \in T(A)$, then $(q'_0, x, Y_0) \overset{*}{\underset{B}{\vdash}} (d, \Lambda, \Lambda)$ or

$$T(A) \subseteq N(B).$$

Claim 2 $N(B) \subseteq T(A)$.

Proof If $x \in N(B)$, then

$$(q'_0, x, Y_0) \overset{*}{\underset{B}{\vdash}} (d, \Lambda, \Lambda).$$

The above computation must end in d since it is the only state that can erase Y_0. From the construction of B, this is possible only if the computation is of the form

$$(q'_0, x, Y_0) \underset{B}{\vdash} (q_0, x, Y_0Z_0) \overset{*}{\underset{B}{\vdash}} (q, \Lambda, Y_0\alpha) \overset{*}{\underset{B}{\vdash}} (d, \Lambda, \Lambda) \qquad \text{for some } q \in F \text{ and } \alpha \in \Gamma^*.$$

But since Y_0 could not have been rewritten in the computation

$$(q_0, x, Y_0Z_0) \overset{*}{\underset{B}{\vdash}} (q, \Lambda, Y_0\alpha),$$

we must have

$$(q_0, x, Z_0) \overset{*}{\underset{A}{\vdash}} (q, \Lambda, \alpha), \qquad q \in F.$$

Therefore $x \in N(B)$ implies $x \in T(A)$ or

$$T(A) \supseteq N(B).$$

Combining Claims (1) and (2), we have:

$$T(A) = N(B),$$

which proves the theorem. Also, $N(B) = L(B)$. □

Combining these theorems with Problem 5, we have:

Theorem 5.3.3 $\mathscr{T}_\Sigma = \mathscr{N}_\Sigma = \mathscr{L}_\Sigma$. That is, acceptance by final state or by empty store or by both simultaneously leads to the same family of accepted sets.

Proof We have actually shown that

$$\mathscr{T}_\Sigma = \mathscr{N}_\Sigma \subseteq \mathscr{L}_\Sigma.$$

The proof that $\mathscr{L}_\Sigma \subseteq \mathscr{T}_\Sigma$ is left for Problem 5. □

PROBLEMS

1 Suppose that the proof of Theorem 5.3.2 were changed and a new start state q_0' was not added. [Change q_0' to q_0 in (1) above.] Would the construction still work?

2 Congratulations! You have just purchased a standard pda or dpda. The following options are available at a slight extra cost. Which of these features increase the power of your pda (dpda)? Prove your answers.

a) The ability to move on input strings rather than on elements of Σ_Λ.
b) The ability to define δ on strings from Γ^+ instead of just Γ, and hence to erase strings in one move.
c) The ability to move on Λ on the pushdown as well as on elements of Γ.

3 Design a dpda to accept the following set by empty store:

$$L = \{a^{i_1} b \cdots a^{i_{r-1}} b a^{i_r} c^s a^{i_{r-s+1}} \mid r \geqslant 1,\ 1 \leqslant i_j \quad \text{for all } j,\ 1 \leqslant j \leqslant r,\ 1 \leqslant s \leqslant r\}.$$

4 Design the simplest Λ-free pda you can which accepts L as defined in Problem 3. Can you do it with a realtime dpda? Can you do it with a deterministic multitape Turing machine that works in realtime?

5 Explain why it does not follow immediately that $\mathscr{L}_\Sigma \subseteq \mathscr{T}_\Sigma$. Now give the necessary construction.

6 A pushdown automaton $A = (Q, \Sigma, \Gamma, \delta, q_0, a, F)$ is said to be a *counter* if $|\Gamma| = 1$. Show that, for each counter A, there exists a counter B such that

$$N(A) = L(B).$$

7 Let $L = \{a^n b^m c \mid n \geqslant m \geqslant 1\}$. Construct a counter A such that $L(A) = L$. Show that there is no counter B such that $N(B) = L$.

8 Show that, for counters, the families $\mathscr{T}$ and $\mathscr{N}$ are incomparable.

For future reference, a *counter language* is any set $L \subseteq \Sigma^*$ which is accepted as $L(A)$ for some counter A. Now, counter languages are very restricted because a pda may not move on an empty store. Thus the only information we can get from the stack is when it is empty and then the computation stops. To remedy this, we allow detection of a zero count as well.

A pushdown automaton $A = (Q, \Sigma, \Gamma, \delta, q_0, Z_0, F)$ is an *iterated counter* if $\Gamma = \{Z_0, a\}$, and

$$\delta(q, b, a) \subseteq Q \times \{a\}^*$$

and

$$\delta(q, b, Z_0) \subseteq (Q \times Z_0 a^*) \cup (Q \times \{\Lambda\})$$

for each $q \in Q$ and $b \in \Sigma \cup \{\Lambda\}$. Thus, an iterated counter may count down to zero more than once. Of course, every counter language is an iterated counter language.

9 Show that, for the family of iterated counters,

$$\mathscr{N} = \mathscr{L} = \mathscr{T}.$$

5.4 CHARACTERIZATION THEOREMS

Our purpose in studying pushdown automata is to characterize context-free languages in terms of them. Without further ado, we begin this task.

Definition Let

$$\mathscr{C}_\Sigma = \{L \subseteq \Sigma^* \mid L \text{ is a context-free language}\}.$$

Then $\mathscr{C}_\Sigma$ is the *family of context-free languages* (over Σ).

In the last section, we showed that $\mathscr{N}_\Sigma = \mathscr{T}_\Sigma = \mathscr{L}_\Sigma$. In this section we will prove that $\mathscr{N}_\Sigma = \mathscr{C}_\Sigma$; that is, the family of context-free languages is the same as the family of languages accepted by empty store by pda's. Thus we will have

$$\mathscr{C}_\Sigma = \mathscr{N}_\Sigma = \mathscr{T}_\Sigma = \mathscr{L}_\Sigma.$$

giving a very nice characterization of the context-free languages, which we will use extensively.

The proof that $\mathscr{N}_\Sigma = \mathscr{C}_\Sigma$ is very important, not only for the result obtained, but also for the technique employed, since similar constructions occur elsewhere in both the theory and the applications of context-free languages.

Theorem 5.4.1 For each context-free language L, there exists a pda A such that $L = N(A)$.

Proof Let $L = L(G)$ for some context-free grammar

$$G = (V, \Sigma, P, S).$$

Now, construct a pda

$$A = (\{q\}, \Sigma, V, \delta, q, S, \emptyset),$$

where δ is given by

i) $\delta(q, \Lambda, Z) = \{(q, \alpha^T) \mid Z \to \alpha \text{ is in } P\}$;

ii) For each $a \in \Sigma$, $\delta(q, a, a) = \{(q, \Lambda)\}$.

Intuitively, A performs a standard top-down parse. There is no left recursion problem because A is nondeterministic. To illustrate this, consider:

Example Let G be the grammar with

$$S \to aSb \mid \Lambda$$

as productions. Then

$$\delta(q, \Lambda, S) = \{(q, bSa), (q, \Lambda)\},$$
$$\delta(q, a, a) = \delta(q, b, b) = \{(q, \Lambda)\}.$$

Now consider the string aab. The reader may easily verify that the possible computations are

i) $(q, aab, S) \overset{*}{\vdash} (q, ab, b)$;
ii) $(q, aab, S) \overset{*}{\vdash} (q, aab, \Lambda)$;
iii) $(q, aab, S) \overset{*}{\vdash} (q, b, bbbSa)$;
iv) $(q, aab, S) \overset{*}{\vdash} (q, \Lambda, b)$.

Thus $aab \notin N(A)$. On the other hand,

$$\begin{aligned}(q, ab, S) &\vdash (q, ab, bSa)\\ &\vdash (q, b, bS)\\ &\vdash (q, b, b)\\ &\vdash (q, \Lambda, \Lambda).\end{aligned}$$

Thus, $ab \in N(A)$.

We now proceed to prove the theorem.

Claim 1 If $S \underset{L}{\overset{*}{\Rightarrow}} u\alpha$, with $u \in \Sigma^*, \alpha \in NV^* \cup \{\Lambda\}$, then, for each $w \in \Sigma^*$,

$$(q, uw, S) \overset{*}{\vdash} (q, w, \alpha^T).$$

Proof By induction on the length of the derivation.

Basis $S \overset{0}{\Rightarrow} S$, so $u = \Lambda$ and $\alpha = S$. Then

$$(q, w, S) \overset{0}{\vdash} (q, w, S),$$

and the basis is complete.

Induction step. Suppose that we have a leftmost derivation of length $n + 1$,

$$S \underset{L}{\overset{n}{\Rightarrow}} uB\gamma \underset{L}{\Rightarrow} ux\beta\gamma$$

where $B \to x\beta$ is in P, $u, x \in \Sigma^*$, $\gamma \in V^*$, and $\beta \in NV^* \cup \{\Lambda\}$. By the induction hypothesis, we have, for any $w \in \Sigma^*$,

$$(q, uxw, S) \overset{*}{\vdash} (q, xw, \gamma^T B).$$

Since $B \to x\beta$ is in P, there is a rule of type (i), so that for any $w \in \Sigma^*$

$$\begin{aligned}(q, uxw, S) &\overset{*}{\vdash} (q, xw, \gamma^T B)\\ &\vdash (q, xw, \gamma^T \beta^T x^T)\\ &\overset{*}{\vdash} (q, w, \gamma^T \beta^T).\end{aligned}$$

We were able to conclude the above computation using rules of type (ii) above, since $x \in \Sigma^*$. Thus the induction is extended and the claim is proven.

In particular, if $S \overset{*}{\underset{L}{\Rightarrow}} x \in \Sigma^*$, then, by taking

$$u = x, \qquad w = \Lambda, \qquad \alpha = \Lambda,$$

we have

$$(q, x, S) \overset{*}{\vdash} (q, \Lambda, \Lambda).$$

Therefore

$$L \subseteq N(A).$$

Claim 2 If $(q, uw, S) \overset{*}{\vdash} (q, w, \alpha^T)$, $u, w \in \Sigma^*$, $\alpha \in V^*$, then $S \overset{*}{\underset{L}{\Rightarrow}} u\alpha$.

Proof By induction on the number of steps in the computation.

Basis. If $(q, w, S) \overset{0}{\vdash} (q, w, S)$, then $u = \Lambda$ and $\alpha = S$. Therefore, $S \overset{0}{\Rightarrow} S$ completes the basis.

Induction step. Assume that if

$$(q, uw, S) \overset{n}{\vdash} (q, w, \alpha^T), \qquad u, w \in \Sigma^*, \alpha \in V^*,$$

then

$$S \overset{*}{\underset{L}{\Rightarrow}} u\alpha$$

Now let $(q, uw, S) \overset{n+1}{\vdash} (q, w, \alpha^T)$. There are two cases to consider.

CASE 1. The last move is type (ii). Then if we let $u = u'a$, with $a \in \Sigma$,

$$(q, uw, S) = (q, u'aw, S) \overset{n}{\vdash} (q, aw, \alpha^T a)$$
$$\vdash (q, w, \alpha^T).$$

By the induction hypothesis,

$$S \overset{*}{\underset{L}{\Rightarrow}} u'a\alpha = u\alpha$$

CASE 2. The last move is type (i). Then

$$(q, uw, S) \overset{n}{\vdash} (q, w, \beta^T B) \vdash (q, w, \beta^T \gamma^T) = (q, w, \alpha^T).$$

By the construction, $B \to \gamma$ is in P and $\alpha = \gamma\beta$. By the induction hypothesis,

$$S \overset{*}{\underset{L}{\Rightarrow}} uB\beta$$

Now, using $B \to \gamma$, we have

$$S \overset{*}{\underset{L}{\Rightarrow}} uB\beta \underset{L}{\Rightarrow} u\gamma\beta = u\alpha$$

which completes the proof of Claim 2.

In particular, if $x \in \Sigma^*$ and

$$(q, x, S) \overset{*}{\vdash} (q, \Lambda, \Lambda),$$

then, by taking $u = x$, $w = \Lambda$, $\alpha = \Lambda$, we have

$$S \overset{*}{\underset{L}{\Rightarrow}} x$$

Therefore, $N(A) \subseteq L$. Now, using the result of the previous claim, we get

$$L = N(A),$$

which proves the theorem. □

The construction that we have given allows us to draw some even stronger conclusions. We shall state them here as a theorem and leave the proof for the exercises. We will feel free to employ these facts in the future.

Theorem 5.4.2 For each context-free language L, there is a pda $A = (Q, \Sigma, \Gamma, \delta, q_0, S, F)$ such that $N(A) = L(A) = L$, and

i) $|Q| = 2$;
ii) for all $q, q' \in Q, a \in \Sigma_\Lambda, Z \in \Gamma, \alpha \in \Gamma^*$, if
$$(q', \alpha) \in \delta(q, a, Z),$$
then
$$\lg(\alpha) \leqslant 2;$$
iii) for all $w \in \Sigma^+, \alpha \in \Gamma^*, q \in Q$,
$$(q_0, w, S) \overset{*}{\vdash} (q, \Lambda, \alpha)$$
implies $q \neq q_0$.
iv) If L is an unambiguous context-free language, then A is an unambiguous pda.
v) A operates in linear time.

We shall shortly investigate the role of Λ-moves in pda's.

Next we turn to showing that $N(A)$ is context-free. This construction has many important applications.

Theorem 5.4.3 If A is an (unambiguous) pda, then $N(A)$ is an (unambiguous) context-free language.

Proof Let $A = (Q, \Sigma, \Gamma, \delta, q_0, Z_0, F)$.

We may assume without loss of generality that there exists a unique state $f \in Q$ such that $F = \{f\}$ and

$$(q_0, x, Z_0) \overset{*}{\vdash} (q, \Lambda, \Lambda) \qquad \text{if and only if } q = f,$$

since, if A does not satisfy this condition, we can construct

$$A' = (Q \cup \{\bar{q}_0, f\}, \Sigma, \Gamma \cup \{Y_0\}, \delta', \bar{q}_0, Y_0, \{f\}),$$

where $\delta \subseteq \delta'$ and

$$\delta'(\bar{q}_0, \Lambda, Y_0) = \{(q_0, Y_0 Z_0)\},$$
$$\delta'(q, \Lambda, Y_0) = \{(f, \Lambda)\} \quad \text{for all } q \in Q.$$

Clearly, A' satisfies the condition and $N(A) = N(A') = L(A') = T(A')$.

Now define

$$G = (V, \Sigma, P, S),$$

where

$$V = \Sigma \cup (Q \times \Gamma \times Q),$$

$$S = (q_0, Z_0, f),$$

and P is given by:

i) For all $k \geqslant 1$, each $a \in \Sigma_\Lambda$, each $Z, Z_1, \ldots, Z_k \in \Gamma$, each $q, p, q_1, \ldots, q_k \in Q$,

$$(q, Z, q_k) \to a(p, Z_1, q_1)(q_1, Z_2, q_2) \cdots (q_{k-2}, Z_{k-1}, q_{k-1})(q_{k-1}, Z_k, q_k)$$

if

$$(p, Z_k \cdots Z_1) \in \delta(q, a, Z).$$

ii) $$(q, Z, p) \to a \qquad \text{if } (p, \Lambda) \in \delta(q, a, Z).$$

The idea of the construction is to encode information into the variables (q, Z, p). In (q, Z, p), the first coordinate tells us that the pda is currently in state q. The second coordinate indicates that the top of the pushdown is Z. Let us imagine that the pda A is in state q and reading Z at the top of the pushdown. Let us consider strings $w \in \Sigma^*$ which cause the pda to ultimately erase Z from the top of pushdown. The third component p is a "guess" that we will be in state p when that Z is erased as above.

Before giving a proof that $L(G) = N(A)$, we work an example.

Example We will construct A and G for the set

$$L = \{a^n b^m a^n \mid n, m \geqslant 1\} \cup \{a^n b^m c^m \mid n, m \geqslant 1\}.$$

The idea behind A's processing of the set is simple.

a) Stack the a's and then b's.
b) If next input is a, erase all b's from stack and match up the remaining a's in the input with the stacked a's.
c) If next input is c, match up the c's with the b's and then erase the a's from the stack.

A can accept this set as

$$L = L(A).$$

Formally

$$A = (Q, \Sigma, \Gamma, \delta, 0, c, \{2\}),$$

where

$$Q = \{0, 1, 2\},$$

$$\Sigma = \Gamma = \{a, b, c\}.$$

Table 5.1 gives

$$\delta : Q \times (\Sigma \cup \{\Lambda\}) \times \Gamma \to Q \times \Gamma^*.$$

The second half of the table gives the productions associated with each move of A. (Some of the unnecessary productions have been omitted.)

Let $q_0 = 0, Z_0 = c$, and

$$(q', \alpha) \in \delta(q, a, Z),$$

where $q, q' \in Q, \alpha \in \Gamma^*, Z \in \Gamma$, and $a \in \Sigma$.

TABLE 5.1

q	a	Z	q'	α	*Productions*
0	a	c	0	ca	$(0, c, 2) \to a(0, a, 1)(1, c, 2) \mid a(0, a, 2)(2, c, 2)$
0	a	a	0	aa	$(0, a, 1) \to a(0, a, 1)(1, a, 1) \qquad (0, a, 2) \to a(0, a, 2)(2, a, 2)$
0	b	a	0	b	$(0, a, 1) \to b(0, b, 1) \qquad (0, a, 2) \to b(0, b, 2)$
0	b	b	0	bb	$(0, b, 1) \to b(0, b, 1)(1, b, 1) \qquad (0, b, 2) \to b(0, b, 2)(2, b, 2)$
0	a	b	1	Λ	$(0, b, 1) \to a$
1	Λ	b	1	Λ	$(1, b, 1) \to \Lambda$
1	a	a	1	Λ	$(1, a, 1) \to a$
1	Λ	c	2	Λ	$(1, c, 2) \to \Lambda$
0	c	b	2	Λ	$(0, b, 2) \to c$
2	c	b	2	Λ	$(2, b, 2) \to c$
2	Λ	a	2	Λ	$(2, a, 2) \to \Lambda$
2	Λ	c	2	Λ	$(2, c, 2) \to \Lambda$

Note. The start symbol in G is $(0, c, 2)$.

Now consider the computation

$$\begin{aligned}(0, abba, c) &\vdash (0, bba, ca)\\ &\vdash (0, ba, cb)\\ &\vdash (0, a, cbb)\\ &\vdash (1, \Lambda, cb)\\ &\vdash (1, \Lambda, c)\\ &\vdash (2, \Lambda, \Lambda)\end{aligned}$$

The corresponding (leftmost) derivation of *abba* in G is shown in Fig. 5.4.

The correspondence between a partial computation of A and its associated generation can best be seen by example:

$$(0, abba, c) \overset{3}{\vdash} (0, a, cbb).$$

On the other hand, concatenating the frontier of the generation tree at the third step in the derivation gives

$$abb(0, b, 1)(1, b, 1)(1, c, 2).$$

The string *abb* is that part of the input string used and *cbb* (the reversal of the string obtained by concatenating the center symbol of each variable) is the state of the pushdown at the corresponding point in the computation.

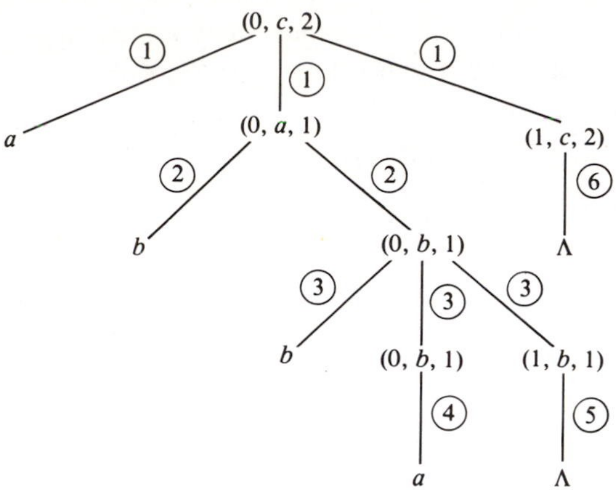

FIG. 5.4

A similar statement holds in general, and it is just this statement which we must make precise and prove to show that $L(G) = N(A)$. Hence, we define

$$H = \{\alpha \in (Q \times \Gamma \times Q)^* \mid \text{If } \alpha = \alpha_1 (q_1, Z_1, q_1')(q_2, Z_2, q_2')\alpha_2, \quad \text{then } q_1' = q_2\}.$$

Thus H is a set of strings of triples where the triples are "internally linked," as shown below.

Example Continuing from the previous example, let

$$\alpha = (0, b, 1)(1, b, 1)(1, c, 2).$$

Clearly, $\alpha \in H$.

Next, we define a mapping $\varphi : H \to \Gamma^*$, where:

$$\varphi(\Lambda) = \Lambda,$$

$$\varphi(\alpha(q, Z, q')) = Z\varphi(\alpha) \qquad \text{for all } \alpha(q, Z, q') \in H.$$

Note that, for any α, β, we have

$$\varphi(\alpha\beta) = \varphi(\beta)\varphi(\alpha).$$

The purpose of φ is to decode the center components of its argument and to reverse them.

Example If $\alpha = (0, b, 1)(1, b, 1)(1, c, 2)$, then $\varphi\alpha = cbb$.

Claim For each $w, y \in \Sigma^*$, each p, q, q' in Q, each $\alpha \in N^*$, and for all $n \geqslant 1$,

$$(q, Z, q') \overset{n}{\underset{\text{L}}{\Rightarrow}} w\alpha$$

if and only if

$$(q, wy, Z) \overset{n}{\vdash} (p, y, \varphi(\alpha))$$

and either†

$$\alpha \in (\{p\} \times \Gamma \times Q)H \cap H(Q \times \Gamma \times \{q'\}) \cap H$$

or

$$\alpha = \Lambda \qquad \text{and} \qquad p = q'.$$

Proof By induction on n.

Basis. $n = 1$; then,

$$(q, Z, q') \overset{1}{\Rightarrow} w\alpha \qquad \text{if and only if} \qquad (q, Z, q') \to w\alpha \text{ is in } P.$$

There are two possible cases.

CASE 1. The rule $(q, Z, q') \to w\alpha$ is type (i). This can occur if and only if

$$\alpha \in (\{p\} \times \Gamma \times Q)H \cap H(Q \times \Gamma \times \{q'\}) \cap H.$$

Suppose

$$\alpha = (p, Z_1, q_1) \cdots (q_{k-1}, Z_k, q')$$

for some $q_1, \ldots, q_{k-1} \in Q; Z_1, \ldots, Z_k \in \Gamma$. Thus,

$$(q, Z, q') \overset{1}{\Rightarrow} w\alpha$$

if and only if

$$(q, Z, q') \to w(p, Z_1, q_1) \cdots (q_{k-1}, Z_k, q') \text{ is in } P$$

if and only if

$$(p, Z_k \cdots Z_1) \in \delta(q, w, Z)$$

if and only if

$$(q, wy, Z) \vdash (p, y, Z_k \cdots Z_1).$$

But

$$\varphi(\alpha) = \varphi((p_1, Z_1, q_1)(q_1, Z_2, q_2) \cdots (q_{k-1}, Z_k, q')) = Z_k Z_{k-1} \cdots Z_1.$$

Thus

$$(q, Z, q') \overset{1}{\Rightarrow} w\alpha$$

by a rule of type (i) if and only if

$$(q, wy, Z) \overset{1}{\vdash} (p, y, \varphi(\alpha))$$

and

$$\alpha \in (\{p\} \times \Gamma \times Q)H \cap H(Q \times \Gamma \times \{q'\}) \cap H.$$

---

† This condition means that either

$$\alpha = (p, Z_1, q_1)\beta(q_2, Z_2, q') \in H$$

for some $q_1, q_2 \in Q$, $Z_1, Z_2 \in \Gamma$, and some $\beta \in H$ (that is, the first component of the first triple is p while the last component of the last triple is q'), or

$$\alpha = \Lambda \qquad \text{and} \qquad p = q'.$$

CASE 2. The rule $(q, Z, q') \to w\alpha$ is type (ii). This can happen if and only if

$$\alpha = \Lambda$$

Thus

$$(q, Z, q') \overset{1}{\Rightarrow} w$$

if and only if

$$(q, Z, q') \to w \text{ is in } P$$

if and only if

$$(q', \Lambda) \in \delta(q, w, Z)$$

if and only if

$$(q, wy, Z) \overset{1}{\vdash} (q', y, \Lambda).$$

Now, since $\varphi(\alpha) = \varphi(\Lambda) = \Lambda$, we have

$$(q, Z, q') \overset{1}{\Rightarrow} w\alpha \qquad \text{if and only if} \quad (q, wy, Z) \overset{1}{\vdash} (p, y, \varphi(\alpha))$$

and

$$\alpha = \Lambda \qquad \text{and} \qquad p = q'.$$

Induction Step. Assume the claim holds for $k \leqslant n$. Note that

$$(q, Z, q') \overset{n+1}{\underset{L}{\Rightarrow}} w\alpha$$

will hold if and only if

$$(q, Z, q') \overset{n}{\underset{L}{\Rightarrow}} w_1 Y \alpha_2 \overset{1}{\underset{L}{\Rightarrow}} w_1 a \alpha_1 \alpha_2$$

where

$$w = w_1 a, \qquad \alpha = \alpha_1 \alpha_2, \qquad Y \to a\alpha_1 \text{ is in } P.$$

Let

$$Y = (q'', Z', p').$$

Now, applying the induction hypothesis, we have

$$(q, Z, q') \overset{n}{\underset{L}{\Rightarrow}} w_1 Y \alpha_2$$

if and only if

$$(q, w_1 ay, Z) \overset{n}{\vdash} (q'', ay, \varphi(Y\alpha_2)) = (q'', ay, \varphi(\alpha_2)Z'),$$

where the equality follows from

$$\varphi(Y\alpha_2) = \varphi(\alpha_2)\varphi(Y) = \varphi(\alpha_2)Z'.$$

By the induction hypothesis, $Y\alpha_2 \in (\{q''\} \times \Gamma \times Q)H \cap H(Q \times \Gamma \times \{q'\})$, and hence

a) $\alpha_2 = \Lambda$ and $p' = q'$

or

$\alpha_2 \neq \Lambda$ and $Y\alpha_2 \in H(Q \times \Gamma \times \{q'\}) \cap H$.

But this gives

b) $\alpha_2 \in (\{p'\} \times \Gamma \times Q)H \cap H(Q \times \Gamma \times \{q'\}) \cap H$, since $Y = (q'', Z', p')$.

Now, since $Y \to a\alpha_1$ is in P,

$$Y = (q'', Z', p') \overset{1}{\Rightarrow} a\alpha_1$$

Applying the induction hypothesis a second time gives

$$(q'', Z', p') \overset{1}{\Rightarrow} a\alpha_1$$

if and only if

$$(q'', ay, Z') \overset{1}{\vdash} (p, y, \varphi(\alpha_1))$$

with either

c) $\alpha_1 = \Lambda$ and $p = p'$

or

d) $\alpha_1 \in (\{p\} \times \Gamma \times Q)H \cap H(Q \times \Gamma \times \{p'\}) \cap H.$

Now, combining, we have

$$(q, Z, q') \overset{n+1}{\Rightarrow} w\alpha$$

if and only if

$$(q, w_1 ay, Z) \overset{n}{\vdash} (q'', ay, \varphi(\alpha_2)Z') \overset{1}{\vdash} (p, y, \varphi(\alpha_2)\varphi(\alpha_1)),$$

where we may combine the computations by Proposition 5.2.1.

Now, using the fact that

$$w = w_1 a \qquad \alpha = \alpha_1 \alpha_2$$

and

$$\varphi(\alpha_2)\varphi(\alpha_1) = \varphi(\alpha_1\alpha_2) = \varphi(\alpha),$$

we have

$$(q, Z, q') \underset{L}{\overset{n+1}{\Rightarrow}} w\alpha \qquad \text{if and only if} \quad (q, wy, Z) \overset{n+1}{\vdash} (p, y, \varphi(\alpha)).$$

To get the conditions on α, there are four cases to consider:

CASE 3. $\alpha_1 = \alpha_2 = \Lambda$. Then, from (a) and (c) above, we have:

$$p' = q', \qquad p = p'.$$

Thus,

$$\alpha = \alpha_1\alpha_2 = \Lambda \qquad \text{and} \qquad p = q'.$$

CASE 4. $\alpha_1 \neq \Lambda, \alpha_2 = \Lambda$. Then, from (a) and (d), we have:

$$\alpha = \alpha_1 \in (\{p\} \times \Gamma \times Q)H \cap H(Q \times \Gamma \times \{q'\}) \cap H.$$

CASE 5. $\alpha_1 = \Lambda, \alpha_2 \neq \Lambda$. Then, from (b) and (c),

$$\alpha = \alpha_2 \in (\{p\} \times \Gamma \times Q)H \cap H(Q \times \Gamma \times \{q'\}) \cap H.$$

CASE 6. $\alpha_1 \neq \Lambda$ and $\alpha_2 \neq \Lambda$. Then, from (b) and (d),

$$\alpha = \alpha_1\alpha_2 \in [(\{p\} \times \Gamma \times Q)H \cap H(Q \times \Gamma \times \{p'\}) \cap H]$$

$$[(\{p'\} \times \Gamma \times Q)H \cap H(Q \times \Gamma \times \{q'\}) \cap H],$$

or

$$\alpha \in (\{p\} \times \Gamma \times Q)H \cap H(Q \times \Gamma \times \{q'\}) \cap H,$$

which proves the claim.

Now let

$$q = q_0, \qquad Z = Z_0, \qquad \alpha = y = \Lambda, \qquad p = q' = f$$

in the above claim and we get

$$S = (q_0, Z_0, f) \overset{n}{\Rightarrow} w \in \Sigma^* \qquad \text{if and only if} \qquad (q_0, w, Z_0) \overset{n}{\vdash} (f, \Lambda, \Lambda).$$

Therefore,

$$L(G) = N(A) = L(A) = T(A).$$

By the claim, if A is unambiguous, then so is G. □

We may now combine several of our previous results to state one of the main results of this book.

Theorem 5.4.4 Let an alphabet Σ be fixed. Then

$$\mathscr{T}_\Sigma = \mathscr{N}_\Sigma = \mathscr{L}_\Sigma = \mathscr{C}_\Sigma.$$

Corollary Every deterministic context-free language is unambiguous.

PROBLEMS

1 Prove Theorem 5.4.2.

2 Is Theorem 5.4.2, part (v), true if we replace the linear time condition by the condition of operating with delay 0; that is, if we require a Λ-free pda? Explain in detail.

3 Show that the following sets are context-free

a) $L = \{a^i b^j c^j \mid i, j \geq 1\} \cup \{a^i b^i c^j \mid i, j \geq 1\}$;

b) $L = \{a^i b^j \mid i \geq 1, i \leq j < 2i\}$;

c) $L = \{xcy \mid x, y \in \Sigma^*, x \neq y\}$, where $c \notin \Sigma$.

Hint. Find suitable context-free languages L_1, L_2, L_3 so that $L = L_1 \cup L_2 \cup L_3$, and the sets are not pairwise disjoint.

Let us generalize the concept of a pushdown automaton to allow two-way motion on the input. Formally, a *two-way nondeterministic pushdown automaton* is a 7-tuple $A = (Q, \Sigma, \Gamma, \delta, q_0, Z_0, F)$, where Q, Γ, q_0, Z_0, and F have their customary meanings. Σ, the input alphabet, is now assumed to contain two distinguished symbols ¢ and \$, which serve as the left and right endmarkers, respectively. δ is a mapping from $Q \times \Sigma \times \Gamma$ into finite subsets of $\{-1, 0, 1\} \times Q \times \Gamma^*$. The idea is that

$$(d, q', \gamma) \in \delta(q, a, Z)$$

means that the device may go into state q', write γ on the pushdown, and move right if $d = 1$, move left if $d = -1$, and remain stationary on the input if $d = 0$. If $(d, q', \gamma) \in \delta(q, a, Z)$ implies $d \geq 0$, then A is a one-way pda.

If $|\delta(q, a, Z)| \leq 1$ for all (q, a, Z), then A is *deterministic*. As an abbreviation, we can write 1-pda or 2-pda to stand for a one-way or two-way pda, and write 1-dpda or 2-dpda to stand for one-way or two-way deterministic pushdown automata.

An ID of a 2-pda is a quadruple of the form

$$(q, ¢w\$, i, \gamma),$$

where $q \in Q$, $w \in (\Sigma - \{¢, \$\})^*$, $0 \leq i \leq \lg(w) + 2$, and $\gamma \in \Gamma^*$. Thus an ID tells us the state of the device, the location of the read head on the input, and the complete contents of the pushdown store.

One defines

$$(q, ¢w\$, i, \alpha Z) \vdash (q', ¢w\$, i + d, \alpha\gamma)$$

if $(d, q', \gamma) \in \delta(q, a, Z)$ and $1 \leq i + d \leq n$. A 2-pda A *accepts* $w \in (\Sigma - \{¢, \$\})^*$ if

$$(q_0, ¢w\$, 2, Z_0) \overset{*}{\vdash} (q, ¢w\$, n, \alpha)$$

for some $q \in F$. Let $T(A) = \{w \mid A \text{ accepts } w\}$.

4 Show that any 2-pda A' may be simulated by a 2-pda A with the following properties.

On any move which adds to the stack (there is also no loss of generality in assuming that additions to the stack are of length 1),

a) the input head is not moved, and
b) the move is independent of the input.

More formally, if $(d, q', \gamma) \in \delta(q, a, Z)$ implies

c) $\gamma = \Lambda$, or
d) $\gamma = ZZ'$ with $Z, Z' \in \Gamma$, $d = 0$, and $(d, q', \gamma) \in \delta(q, b, Z)$ for every $b \in \Sigma$.

5.5 Λ-MOVES IN PDA'S AND THE SIZE OF A PDA

We shall briefly consider the role of Λ-moves in pda's. One might conjecture that every context-free language can be accepted by a Λ-free pda. If "accepted" is used to mean by $N(A)$ or $L(A)$, then there is a minor problem with Λ. If $\Lambda \in L$, then the pda must have at least one Λ-move in order to erase Z_0 from the pushdown store. This argument is one justification of those authors who allow pda's to move on empty pushdowns. We begin by assuming that $\Lambda \notin L$.

Theorem 5.5.1 $L \subseteq \Sigma^+$ is a context-free language if and only if $L = N(A)$ for some Λ-free pda A.

Proof

a) If $L = N(A)$ for some Λ-free pda, then the result follows directly from Theorem 5.4.4.

b) Suppose $L = L(G)$, where

$$G = (V, \Sigma, P, S).$$

We may assume, without loss of generality, that G is in Greibach normal form. Let

$$A = (\{q\}, \Sigma, V, \delta, q, S, \emptyset),$$

where

$$\delta(q, a, Z) = \{(q, \alpha^T) \mid Z \to a\alpha \text{ is in } P\}.$$

Clearly, A is Λ-free and the proof that $N(A) = L(G)$ is exactly the same as in Theorem 5.4.1. □

Now we turn to acceptance by final state. Final states easily eliminate the previous problem with Λ.

Theorem 5.5.2 $L \subseteq \Sigma^*$ is a context-free language if and only if $L = T(A)$ for some Λ-free pda A.

Proof If $L = T(A)$, then L is a context-free language, by Theorem 5.4.4. Let $L = L(G)$, where

$$G = (V, \Sigma, P, S)$$

is in Greibach form.

Define

$$A = (\{q_0, q, f\}, \Sigma, V', \delta, q_0, S', F),$$

where

$$V' = V \cup \{A' \mid A \in N\}.$$

Then

i) $\delta(q, a, Z) = \{(q, \alpha^T) \mid Z \to a\alpha \text{ is in } P\}$;

ii) $\delta(q, a, Z') = \{(q, B'\alpha^T) \mid Z \to a\alpha B \text{ is in } P\} \cup \{(f, \Lambda) \mid Z \to a \text{ is in } P\}$;

iii) $\delta(q_0, a, S') = \{(q, B'q^T) \mid S \to a\alpha B \text{ is in } P\} \cup \{(f, \Lambda) \mid S \to a \text{ is in } P\}$;

and

$$F = \{f\} \cup \{q_0 \mid S \to \Lambda \text{ is in } P\}.$$

Note. The state q_0 allows $\Lambda \in L$.

The proof that $L(G) = T(A)$ is straightforward and is left as an exercise. □

Corollary Every context-free language may be accepted by a nondeterministic pda with delay 0.

We may restate these results in a still more vivid form.

Theorem 5.5.3 For each pda A, one can construct a Λ-free pda B so that $T(A) = T(B)$.

Proof Given a pda A, we use Theorem 5.4.4 to get a context-free grammar G_1 for $T(A)$. By Theorem 5.5.2, we can find a Λ-free pda B so that $T(B) = T(A)$. □

The theorems of this section are really nontrivial in spite of their short proofs. The reason that the proofs are so simple is that the hard work was done in the grammatical transformation. The skeptical reader may try to prove Theorem 5.5.3 directly without the aid of Greibach form.

Many pda constructions are greatly simplified by the presence of null moves. In the future, we shall use them extensively.

In Chapter 4, we discussed the size of a grammar and now we wish to consider the size of a pda. There are at least two different ways to define the size. By analogy with $|G|$, we could define $|A|$ to be the length of the string which results if all of the entries in δ are written out as a word. The formal definition now follows.

Definition Let $A = (Q, \Sigma, \Gamma, \delta, q_0, Z_0, F)$ be a pda. Define

$$|A| = \sum_{(q',\alpha)\in\delta(q,a,Z)} (\lg(\alpha) + \lg(a) + 3).$$

While this is a natural definition, it is cumbersome to compute. One would like to use a measure like $|Q| \times |\Sigma| \times |\Gamma|$, but this measure seems too crude. For example, we could write down two pda's having the same Q, Σ, and Γ, and yet one writes long strings on each stack move while the other does not. For this reason, it is necessary to impose a restriction on the class of pda's being considered.

Definition A pda $A = (Q, \Sigma, \Gamma, \delta, q_0, Z_0, F)$ is *moderate* if $(q', \alpha) \in \delta(q, a, Z)$ implies $\lg(\alpha) \leq 2$.

We already know something about moderate pda's.

Theorem 5.5.4 For each (deterministic) pda A, there is a moderate (deterministic) pda B which is equivalent to A in whichever form of acceptance is being used.

Proof The technique of adding states works in the deterministic case as well. □

For moderate pda's, $|A|$ actually grows proportionally to the number of rules, as the following result shows.

Theorem 5.5.5 Let $A = (Q, \Sigma, \Gamma, \delta, q_0, Z_0, F)$ be a moderate pda. Then

$$3|\delta| \leq |A| \leq 6|\delta|,$$

and hence

$$|A| = \theta(|\delta|).$$

Proof Since A is moderate, $(q', \alpha) \in \delta(q, a, Z)$ implies $\lg(\alpha) \leq 2$. Therefore

$$|A| = \sum_{(q', \alpha) \in \delta(q, a, Z)} (\lg(a\alpha) + 3) \leq 6|\delta|.$$

The lower bound is obvious also. □

Now we can consider another definition of size:

Definition Let $A = (Q, \Sigma, \Gamma, \delta, q_0, Z_0, F)$ be a moderate pda. Let

$$\text{Size}(A) = |Q \times \Sigma \times \Gamma|.$$

This is an attractive measure of size, since it is independent of δ.

Now we can begin to relate these measures to each other.

Theorem 5.5.5 There exists a constant c such that for any moderate pda $A = (Q, \Sigma, \Gamma, \delta, q_0, Z_0, F)$, where $m = |Q \times \Sigma \times \Gamma|$ and $n = |A|$, we have

$$n \leq cm^3,$$

where c depends only on the coding of the rules.

Proof Let $|Q| = q, |\Sigma| = s$, and $|\Gamma| = t$. Then

$$m = qst.$$

To prove that $n \leqslant cm^3$, we construct the largest possible moderate pda. We include every allowable type of rule, i.e., for each

$$(q', \alpha) \in \delta(q, a, Z)$$

for all $q, q' \in Q$, $Z \in \Gamma$, $a \in \Sigma \cup \{\Lambda\}$, $\alpha \in \Lambda \cup \Gamma \cup \Gamma^2$, we have a rule. Since A is a moderate pda,

$$n \leqslant |\delta|(2 + 1 + 3) = 6|\delta|,$$

by the definition of $n = |A|$. Thus

$$\begin{aligned} n \leqslant 6|\delta| &\leqslant 6q(1 + t + t^2)\, q(s + 1)t \\ &= 6q^2(t + t^2 + t^3)\,(s + 1) \\ &\leqslant 6q^3(3t^3)\, 2s^3 = 36m^3, \end{aligned}$$

so $c = 36$ will do. □

PROBLEMS

1 Show that, for any context-free language L, there is a deterministic pda A and a homomorphism φ such that A operates in realtime and $\varphi(L(A)) = L$.

2 Consider the following "proof" of Theorem 5.5.2. Explain in detail exactly what goes wrong.

Let $L = L(G)$, where $G = (V, \Sigma, P, S)$ is in 2-standard form. Let $A = (\{q_0, q_1\}, \Sigma, V, \delta, q_0, S, F)$, where $F = \{q_1\} \cup \{q_0 \mid S \to \Lambda \text{ is in } P\}$. Here, δ is defined as follows:

$$\begin{aligned} \delta(q_0, a, A) &= \delta(q_1, a, A) \\ &= \{(q_1, \Lambda) \mid A \to a \text{ is in } P\} \\ &\quad \cup \{(q_1, B) \mid A \to aB \text{ is in } P\} \\ &\quad \cup \{(q_1, CB) \mid A \to aBC \text{ is in } P\}. \end{aligned}$$

Clearly, A is Λ-free and it is straightforward to verify that $T(A) = L(G)$.

3 Prove the following result.

Proposition For each context-free language L there is a pda $A = (Q, \Sigma, \Gamma, \delta, q_0, Z_0, F)$ such that:

a) $L = \{w \in \Sigma^* \mid (q_0, w, Z_0) \overset{*}{\vdash} (q, \Lambda, \Lambda) \text{ for some } q \in F\}$.

b) If $\Lambda \in L$, then $\delta(q_0, \Lambda, Z_0) = \{(q_0, \Lambda)\}$ and $q_0 \in F$. If $\Lambda \notin L$, then $\delta(q_0, \Lambda, Z_0) = \emptyset$.

c) If $q \in Q - \{q_0\}$ or $Z \in \Gamma - \{Z_0\}$, $\delta(q, \Lambda, Z) = \emptyset$.

d) For each $(q, a, Z) \in Q \times \Sigma \times \Gamma$, if $(q', \alpha) \in \delta(q, a, Z)$, then $\lg(\alpha) \leqslant 2$.

4 Show that, if a finite set is recognized by a deterministic (nondeterministic) pda with q states and t pushdown symbols, then it can be recognized by a (non)-deterministic finite automaton with a number of states proportional to

$$t^{(qt)^2}.$$

5 Show that, for each $n > 0$, there is an infinite regular set L_n which is accepted by a reduced finite automaton that has at least 2^{2^n} states but can be accepted by a dpda of size proportional to n^3.

6 Find a lower bound for m in terms of n for moderate pda's, which would be a counterpart of Theorem 5.5.5. Are additional hypotheses required on the pda?

5.6 DETERMINISTIC LANGUAGES CLOSED UNDER COMPLEMENTATION

Although the full family of context-free languages is not closed under complementation (as we shall see shortly), the deterministic languages are. This important result will often be used in the sequel, even before dpda's are studied in detail. The proof of the result is fairly complicated.

Our intuition about how to prove this result is strong. One wishes to replace F by $Q-F$ and design a "complementary machine." The problem is that Λ-moves complicate the action of dpda's. A dpda might go into an infinite Λ-cycle in the middle of processing an input.

First we ensure that our dpda's always have a next move. This could fail to happen either if a transition was not defined or if the pushdown were emptied prematurely. The idea of the first lemma is to make δ as "total as possible."

Lemma 5.6.1 Let $A = (Q, \Sigma, \Gamma, \delta, q_0, F)$ be a dpda. There is an equivalent dpda $A' = (Q', \Sigma, \Gamma', \delta', q_0', Z_0', F)$ such that

1 For all (q, a, Z) in $Q' \times \Sigma \times \Gamma'$,

$$|\delta'(q, a, Z)| + |\delta'(q, \Lambda, Z)| = 1.$$

2 If $\delta'(q, a, Z_0') = (q', \alpha)$ for some $a \in \Sigma_\Lambda$, then $\alpha = Z_0'\beta$ for some $\beta \in (\Gamma')^*$.

Proof We construct A', in which Z_0' acts as a bottom-of-stack marker so that the pushdown is never erased, and we add any missing transitions.

Define $A' = (Q', \Sigma, \Gamma', \delta', q_0', Z_0', F)$, where $\Gamma' = \Gamma \cup \{Z_0'\}$, $Q' = Q \cup \{q_0', d\}$ and δ' is defined by four cases:

1 $\delta'(q_0', \Lambda, Z_0') = (q_0, Z_0'Z_0)$

2 For all $(q, a, Z) \in \operatorname{dom} \delta$,

$$\delta'(q, a, Z) = \delta(q, a, Z).$$

3 If $\delta(q, \Lambda, Z) = \emptyset$ and $\delta(q, a, Z) = \emptyset$ for some $a \in \Sigma$, then

$$\delta'(q, a, Z) = (d, Z).$$

4 For all $Z \in \Gamma'$, $a \in \Sigma$,

$$\delta'(d, a, Z) = (d, Z).$$

5 For all $q \in Q, a \in \Sigma$,

$$\delta'(q, a, Z'_0) = (d, Z'_0).$$

Clearly, A' is a dpda which satisfies cases (1) and (2). For any $x \in \Sigma^*$, $q \in F$,

$$(q_0, x, Z_0) \overset{*}{\underset{A}{\vdash}} (q, \Lambda, \alpha)$$

if and only if

$$(q'_0, x, Z'_0) \underset{A'}{\vdash} (q_0, x, Z'_0 Z_0)$$
$$\overset{*}{\underset{A'}{\vdash}} (q, \Lambda, Z'_0 \alpha).$$

Therefore,

$$T(A') = T(A). \qquad \square$$

One of the problems to be dealt with concerns the possibility that a dpda will get into a Λ-loop and the computation will not terminate.

Definition An ID (q, Λ, α) of a dpda $A = (Q, \Sigma, \Gamma, \delta, q_0, Z_0, F)$ is *immortal* if, for all integers i, there is an ID (q_i, Λ, β_i) such that $\lg(\beta_i) \geqslant \lg(\alpha)$ and $(q, \Lambda, \alpha) \overset{i}{\vdash} (q_i, \Lambda, \beta_i)$.

Intuitively, an ID is immortal if A can make an infinite number of Λ-moves and also never shorten its pushdown below its initial height. This would mean that the pushdown might grow infinitely, or might cycle between different strings of the same length.

Some of the basic facts about immortal ID's are summarized in the following proposition.

Proposition 5.6.1 Let $A = (Q, \Sigma, \Gamma, \delta, q_0, Z_0, F)$ be a dpda, and let $q \in Q, Z \in \Gamma, \alpha, \alpha' \in \Gamma^*$. Then,

a) If (q, Λ, α) is immortal, then for any $w \in \Sigma^*$ and $i \geqslant 0$, there exist $q_i \in Q$, $\beta_i \in \Gamma^*$ such that

$$(q, w, \alpha) \overset{i}{\vdash} (q, w, \beta_i).$$

b) For any $\alpha \in \Gamma^*$, (q, Λ, Z) is immortal if and only if $(q, \Lambda, \alpha Z)$ is immortal.

c) If

$$(q_1, w_1, \alpha_1) \overset{*}{\vdash} (q, w, \alpha) \overset{*}{\vdash} (q', w', \alpha')$$

and (q, Λ, α) is immortal, then $w' = w$.

d) If there exists $a \in \Sigma$ such that

$$(q, a, Z) \overset{*}{\vdash} (q', \Lambda, \alpha_1),$$

then (q, Λ, Z) is not immortal.

Proof

a) If (q, Λ, α) is immortal, then

$$(q, \Lambda, \alpha) \overset{i}{\vdash} (q_i, \Lambda, \beta_i)$$

for some $q_i \in Q$ and $\beta_i \in \Gamma^*$. By Proposition 5.2.1, (a) follows.

b) The argument is trivial since the immortal computation never emptied the pushdown so α would not even be read.

c) This follows from the determinism of A and the definition of immortality, since, once an immortal ID is reached, no additional input is read.

d) This is a variant of (c), since, if a true input gets read, the ID that started the computation could not have been immortal, by the determinism of A. The formal details are left to the reader. □

Because of (a), it is convenient to refer to ID's of the form (q, w, α) as being immortal also.

Before deriving an algorithm for detecting immortal ID's, we need more definitions.

Definition Let $A = (Q, \Sigma, \Gamma, \delta, q_0, Z_0, F)$ be a pda and let $q \in Q$, $Q_1 \subseteq Q$, and $\alpha \in \Gamma^*$. Define:

$$T(A, q, \alpha, Q_1) = \{w \in \Sigma^* \mid (q, w, \alpha) \overset{*}{\vdash} (q', \Lambda, \beta) \quad \text{for some } \beta \in \Gamma^* \text{ and some } q' \in Q_1\}$$

and

$$L(A, q, \alpha, Q_1) = \{w \in \Sigma^* \mid (q, w, \alpha) \overset{*}{\vdash} (q', \Lambda, \Lambda) \quad \text{for some } q' \in Q_1\}.$$

These sets are context-free, in general.

Lemma 5.6.2 Let $A = (Q, \Sigma, \Gamma, \delta, q_0, Z_0, F)$ be a pda and let $q \in Q$, $Q_1 \subseteq Q$, and $\alpha \in \Gamma^*$. Then $T(A, q, \alpha, Q_1)$ and $L(A, q, \alpha, Q_1)$ are context-free languages.

Proof Define $B_{q,\alpha,Q_1} = (Q \cup \{q_0'\}, \Sigma, \Gamma, \delta', q_0', Z_0, Q_1)$, where δ' is defined as follows:

1 $\delta'(q_0', \Lambda, Z_0) = (q, \alpha)$

2 $\delta'(p, a, Z) = \delta(p, a, Z)$ for all (p, a, Z) in the domain of δ.

B is deterministic if A is. Clearly,

$$T(B) = T(A, q, \alpha, Q_1)$$

and

$$L(B) = L(A, q, \alpha, Q_1)$$

are context-free languages. □

Now $T(A, q, \alpha, Q)$ and $L(A, q, \alpha, Q)$ are used to provide a test for immortal configurations.

Lemma 5.6.3 Let $A = (Q, \Sigma, \Gamma, \delta, q_0, Z_0, F)$ be a dpda and let $q \in Q$ and $Z \in \Gamma$. If A satisfies condition (1) of Lemma 5.6.1, then (q, Λ, Z) is immortal if and only if

$$T(A, q, Z, Q) = \{\Lambda\}$$

and

$$\Lambda \notin L(A, q, Z, Q).$$

Moreover, this is decidable in polynomial time.

Proof Suppose (q, Λ, Z) is immortal. Then

$$A \notin L(A, q, Z, Q)$$

because, if it were, then

$$(q, \Lambda, Z) \vdash^{*} (q', \Lambda, \Lambda),$$

which violates the immortality of (q, Λ, Z). Also, if there exists $x \in \Sigma^+$ which is in $T(A, q, Z, Q)$, then

$$(q, x, Z) \vdash_{A}^{*} (q', \Lambda, \beta). \tag{5.6.1}$$

But, since at least one true input was used in computation (5.6.1), then (q, x, Z) could not have initiated an infinite Λ-loop; that is, (q, Λ, Z) is not immortal. Cf. Proposition 5.6.1(d).

Conversely, assume that (q, Λ, Z) is not immortal; then there exist $i \geqslant 0$, $q' \in Q$, and $\gamma \in \Gamma^*$, such that

$$(q, \Lambda, Z) \vdash^{i} (q', \Lambda, \gamma),$$

and there is no $q'' \in Q, \gamma' \in \Gamma^*$ with

$$(q', \Lambda, \gamma) \vdash (q'', \Lambda, \gamma').$$

This can occur in one of two cases, namely:

1 $\gamma = \Lambda$, or

2 $\gamma = \alpha Z'$ and $\delta(q', \Lambda, Z') = \emptyset$.

If (1) holds, then $\Lambda \in L(A, q, Z, Q)$. If (2) holds, then, since A satisfies the first condition of Lemma 5.6.1, there exist $a \in \Sigma$, $q''' \in Q$, $\gamma''' \in \Gamma^*$, such that

$$\delta(q', a, Z') = (q''', \gamma'''),$$

and consequently,

$$(q, a, Z) \vdash^{i+1} (q''', \Lambda, \alpha\gamma''').$$

Then

$$a \in T(A, q, Z, Q).$$

In either case, one of the conditions is violated.

To analyze the running time of the algorithm, let us proceed as follows. The size of a pda for $L(A, q, Z, Q)$ is proportional to the size of A. Assume that all our pda's never add more than one symbol to the stack at a time ((q', α) in $\delta(q, a, Z)$ implies $\lg(\alpha) \leqslant 2$). There is no loss of generality in this assumption because we may break down a long addition of symbols into many additions of length 1.

To check whether $\Lambda \notin L(A, q, Z, Q)$, convert from the dpda to a context-free grammar for the same set. The grammar G will be of size proportional to the size of the pda. One can test whether the grammar generates Λ in time proportional to $\|G\|$.

For $T(A, q, Z, Q)$, pass to a pda C (not necessarily deterministic) which accepts this set as $N(C)$. The size of C is polynomial in the size of A. Again pass to a grammar for this language. This grammar will be polynomial in the size of C. Reduce the grammar in linear time. There exists $x \neq \Lambda$ in $T(A, q, Z, Q)$ if and only if there is a righthand side that contains a terminal. (Cf. Problem 3.2.7.) □

Now we are in a position to detect which immortal ID's go through final states.

Lemma 5.6.4 Let $A = (Q, \Sigma, \Gamma, \delta, q_0, Z_0, F)$ be a dpda. Let $C_1 = \{(q, Z) | q \in Q, Z \in \Gamma$, and (q, Λ, Z) is an immortal ID, and there exists no $q' \in F$ such that $(q, \Lambda, Z) \overset{*}{\vdash} (q', \Lambda, \alpha)$ for any $\alpha \in \Gamma^*\}$ and $C_2 = \{(q, Z) | q \in Q, Z \in \Gamma$, and (q, Λ, Z) is an immortal ID and $(q, \Lambda, Z) \overset{*}{\vdash} (q', \Lambda, \alpha)$ for some $q' \in F$ and $\alpha \in \Gamma^*\}$. Let (q, Λ, Z) be an immortal ID. Then

a) $(q, Z) \in C_1$ if and only if $T(A, q, Z, F) = \emptyset$.

b) $(q, Z) \in C_2$ if and only if $T(A, q, Z, F) = \{\Lambda\}$.

Proof Consider $T(A, q, Z, F)$. Since (q, Λ, Z) is immortal,

$$T(A, q, Z, F) = \begin{cases} \emptyset & \text{if } (q, Z) \in C_1, \\ \{\Lambda\} & \text{if } (q, Z) \in C_2. \end{cases}$$ □

Corollary There is an algorithm for testing membership in C_1 or C_2 in time which is polynomial in the size of A.

Proof The proof of Lemma 5.6.3 gives a polynomial time test for the emptiness of $T(A, q, Z, F)$ and for membership of Λ. □

Before continuing, a different form of acceptance is required.

Definition Let $A = (Q, \Sigma, \Gamma, \delta, q_0, Z_0, F)$ be a dpda. We define a relation $\overset{*}{\Vdash} \subseteq \overset{*}{\vdash}$ as follows: For all $q, q' \in Q$, $w, w' \in \Sigma^*$, and $\gamma, \gamma' \in \Gamma^*$,

$$(q, w, \gamma) \overset{*}{\Vdash} (q', w', \gamma')$$

if and only if

i) $(q, w, \gamma) \overset{*}{\vdash} (q', w', \gamma')$ and

ii) $\delta(q', \Lambda, \gamma'^{(1)})$ is undefined (in particular, if $\gamma' = \Lambda$).

Intuitively, $(q, w, \gamma) \overset{*}{\Vdash} (q', w', \gamma')$ if and only if $(q, w, \gamma) \overset{*}{\vdash} (q', w', \gamma')$ in a computation which cannot be extended by Λ-moves. That is, A has gone as far as it could go in computing on (q, w, γ) without reading the first symbol of w'.

The computations defined with $\overset{*}{\Vdash}$ are sometimes called *d-computations* (d for deterministic). We can define "d-acceptance" by

$$T_d(A) = \{w \in \Sigma^* | (q_0, w, Z_0) \overset{*}{\Vdash} (q, \Lambda, \alpha) \quad \text{for some } q \in F, \alpha \in \Gamma^*\}.$$

Note that a dpda A may have many different opportunities to accept w since $w = w\Lambda^i$ for any i but only one opportunity to d-accept w.

Next we introduce a special type of dpda.

Definition A dpda $A = (Q, \Sigma, \Gamma, \delta, q_0, Z_0, F)$ is *loop-free* if for all $w \in \Sigma^*$ there exists $q \in Q$ and $\alpha \in \Gamma^*$ such that $(q_0, w, Z_0) \Vdash^* (q, \Lambda, \alpha)$.

The q and α in the definition of loop-free are uniquely determined by w. Thus, a loop-free dpda always exhausts its input string and stops. Note that a loop-free dpda cannot go into an immortal ID after the input is processed. That is, suppose

$$(q_0, w, Z_0) \Vdash^* (q, \Lambda, \alpha).$$

Could (q, Λ, α) be immortal, or in other words, could this computation continue indefinitely? This could not happen because, if it did, strings like wa, where $a \in \Sigma$ would violate the definition of loop-free since

$$(q_0, wa, Z_0) \vdash^* (q', \Lambda, \beta)$$

for no $q' \in Q$ and $\beta \in \Gamma^*$, so

$$(q_0, wa, Z_0) \Vdash^* (q', \Lambda, \beta)$$

is impossible as well.

Lemma 5.6.5 For any dpda A, there is a dpda A' which is loop-free and $T(A') = T(A)$. A' may be effectively constructed from A.

Proof We may assume, without loss of generality, that $A = (Q, \Sigma, \Gamma, \delta, q_0, Z_0, F)$ satisfies the conditions of Lemma 5.6.1. (Intuitively, A always has a next move.) Define $A' = (Q', \Sigma, \Gamma, \delta', q_0, Z_0, F')$ where $Q' = Q \cup \{f, d\}$ and $F' = F \cup \{f\}$. δ' is defined by five cases.

1 For all $(q, a, Z) \in (Q \times \Sigma \times \Gamma)$,

$$\delta'(q, a, Z) = \delta(q, a, Z).$$

(All moves on true inputs are simulated.)

2 For all q, Z such that (q, Λ, Z) is not an immortal ID, let

$$\delta'(q, \Lambda, Z) = \delta(q, \Lambda, Z),$$

(All Λ-moves that terminate are included).

3 For all $(q, Z) \in C_1$ of Lemma 5.6.4, let

$$\delta'(q, \Lambda, Z) = (d, Z).$$

(We broke an infinite Λ-loop in which the stack never shortened and which never went through a final state and instead went directly to a new non-final state.)

4 For all $(q, Z) \in C_2$ of Lemma 5.6.4, let

$$\delta'(q, \Lambda, Z) = (f, Z).$$

(In this step, we broke an infinite Λ-loop in which the stack never shortened and which involved a final state and instead went directly to a new final state.)

5 For all $(a, Z) \in \Sigma \times \Gamma$,

$$\delta'(f, a, Z) = (d, Z),$$

$$\delta'(d, a, Z) = (d, Z).$$

By Lemmas 5.6.3 and 5.6.4, one can decide whether an ID is immortal or not and test membership in C_1 or C_2 and so A' may be effectively constructed from A. It is straightforward to check that A' is a dpda because A is and because $C_1 \cap C_2 = \emptyset$.

Claim 1 A' is loop-free.

Proof Suppose A' is not loop-free. There exists $w_0 \in \Sigma^*$ such that, for all $q \in Q$ and $\alpha \in \Gamma^*$, it is not the case that

$$(q_0, w_0, Z_0) \overset{*}{\underset{A'}{\Vdash}} (q, \Lambda, \alpha).$$

Since A' satisfies the conditions of Lemma 5.6.1, this means that, for all $i \geqslant 0$, there exist $q_i \in Q$, $\alpha_i \in \Gamma^+$, and w_i, a suffix of w_0, such that

$$(q_0, w_0, Z_0) \overset{i}{\vdash} (q_i, w_i, \alpha_i).$$

Now $\lg(w_i) \geqslant 0$ for all i and $\lg(w_i)$ is nonincreasing, so let i_0 be chosen such that for all $i \geqslant i_0$, $\lg(w_i) = \lg(w_{i_0})$. Thus, for all $i \geqslant i_0$, $w_i = w_{i_0}$ and

$$(q_{i_0}, \Lambda, \alpha_{i_0}) \overset{i-i_0}{\vdash} (q_i, \Lambda, \alpha_i).$$

Now for all $i \geqslant i_0$, $\lg(\alpha_i) > 0$, so there is $i_1 \geqslant i_0$ such that for all $i \geqslant i_1$, $\lg(\alpha_i) \geqslant \lg(\alpha_{i_1})$. Let $Z \in \Gamma$ and $\alpha \in \Gamma^*$ be such that

$$\alpha Z = \alpha_{i_1}$$

and let β_i be such that

$$\alpha\beta_i = \alpha_i$$

for all $i \geqslant i_1$; it is clear that

$$(q_{i_1}, \Lambda, Z) \overset{i-i_1}{\vdash} (q_i, \Lambda, \beta_i)$$

and $\lg(\beta_i) \geqslant 1$.

Since for all $Z \in \Gamma$,

$$\delta'(d, \Lambda, Z) = \delta'(f, \Lambda, Z) = \emptyset,$$

it must be true that for all $i \geqslant i_1$, we have $q_i \in Q$. This, in turn, implies that, for all $i > i_1$, if

$$\beta_i = \beta Z_i$$

and

$$\beta_{i+1} = \beta\beta'$$

for some β', then

$$(q_{i+1}, \beta') \in \delta(q_i, \Lambda, Z_i),$$

because the only entries in $\delta' - \delta$ involve d and f. Thus

$$(q_{i_1}, \Lambda, Z) \overset{i-i_1}{\underset{A}{\vdash}} (q_i, \Lambda, \beta_i).$$

This implies that $(q_{i_1}, Z) \in C_1 \cup C_2$ whence

$$\delta'(q_{i_1}, \Lambda, Z) \in \{(d, Z), (f, Z)\},$$

which contradicts

$$(q_{i_1}, \Lambda, Z) \overset{1}{\underset{A'}{\vdash}} (q_{i_1+1}, \Lambda, \beta_{i_1+1})$$

since $q_{i_1+1} \in Q$. Therefore A' is loop-free after all.

Claim 2 If

$$(q_0, w_0, \gamma_0) \underset{A}{\vdash} (q_1, w_1, \gamma_1) \underset{A}{\vdash} \cdots \underset{A}{\vdash} (q_k, w_k, \gamma_k), \tag{5.6.2}$$

where $\gamma_0 = Z_0$ and no immortal ID occurs in (5.6.2) (except possibly (q_k, w_k, γ_k)), then

$$(q_0, w_0, \gamma_0) \underset{A'}{\vdash} \cdots \underset{A'}{\vdash} (q_k, w_k, \gamma_k).$$

Proof The argument is a straightforward induction on k because the construction of A' includes all the moves used in (5.6.2).

Now we consider "successful" computations of A involving immortal ID's.

Claim 3 If there exists some $k \geqslant 0$ such that

$$(q_0, w_0, \gamma_0) \underset{A}{\vdash} (q_1, w_1, \gamma_1) \underset{A}{\vdash} \cdots \underset{A}{\vdash} (q_k, w_k, \gamma_k) \vdash \cdots \tag{5.6.3}$$

where $\gamma_0 = Z_0, w_k = \Lambda$, and (q_k, w_k, γ_k) is immortal but (q_j, w_j, γ_j) is not, for $j < k$, then

$$(q_0, w_0, \gamma_0) \underset{A'}{\vdash} \cdots \underset{A'}{\vdash} (q, \Lambda, \gamma),$$

where

$$q = \begin{cases} f & \text{if } q_j \in F \quad \text{for some } j \geqslant k, \\ d & \text{otherwise.} \end{cases}$$

Proof By Claim 2,

$$(q_0, w_0, \gamma_0) \overset{*}{\underset{A'}{\vdash}} (q_k, w_k, \gamma_k).$$

By the construction of A'

$$(q_k, w_k, \gamma_k) \underset{A'}{\vdash} \begin{cases} (f, \Lambda, \gamma) & \text{for some } \gamma \in \Gamma^* & \text{if } q_j \in F \text{ for some } j \geqslant k, \\ (d, \Lambda, \gamma') & \text{for some } \gamma' \in \Gamma^* & \text{if } q_j \notin F \text{ for all } j \geqslant k. \end{cases}$$

The proof is completed by pasting together these A' computations. □

Our next task is to relate computations in A' to those in A.

Claim 4 If there exists $k \geqslant 0$ such that

$$(q_0, w_0, \gamma_0) \underset{A'}{\vdash} \cdots \underset{A'}{\vdash} (q_k, w_k, \gamma_k), \tag{5.6.4}$$

where $\gamma_0 = Z_0$, $w_k = \Lambda$, and $q_k \in F \cup \{f\}$, then either

i) $(q_0, w_0, \gamma_0) \underset{A}{\vdash} \cdots \underset{A}{\vdash} (q_k, w_k, \gamma_k)$ with $q_k \in F$ and $w_k = \Lambda$ [i.e., no immortal ID's encountered in A], or

ii) there exist $q \in F, \gamma \in \Gamma^*$ such that

$$(q_0, w_0, \gamma_0) \overset{*}{\underset{A}{\vdash}} (q_{k-1}, w_{k-1}, \gamma_{k-1}) \overset{*}{\underset{A}{\vdash}} (q, \Lambda, \gamma)$$

and $w_{k-1} = \Lambda$ [an immortal ID in C_2 encountered by A].

Proof of Claim 4 Consider (5.6.4). All the ID's of A' are ID's of A unless an immortal ID was encountered by A' when started on (q_0, w_0, γ_0). If none were encountered then (i) holds. If there exists $0 \leqslant i < k$ such that $(q_i, w_i, \gamma_i^{(1)})$ is immortal in A, then clearly $q_k = f$ and $i = k - 1$. But, by rule (4) of the construction, we have

$$(q_0, w_0, \gamma_0) \overset{k-1}{\underset{A'}{\vdash}} (q_{k-1}, \Lambda, \gamma_{k-1}) \underset{A'}{\vdash} (f, \Lambda, \gamma_k).$$

$(q_{k-1}, \gamma_{k-1}^1)$ is in C_2, and so there exist $q \in F, \gamma \in \Gamma^*$ so that $(q_{k-1}, \Lambda, \gamma_{k-1}) \overset{*}{\vdash} (q, \Lambda, \gamma)$. Therefore,

$$(q_0, w_0, \gamma_0) \overset{k-1}{\underset{A}{\vdash}} (q_{k-1}, \Lambda, \gamma_{k-1}) \overset{*}{\vdash} (q, \Lambda, \gamma).$$

Our last claim relates the behaviors of A and A'.

Claim 5 $T(A') = T(A)$.

Proof By Claims 2, 3, and 4. □

Note that Proposition 5.2.2 follows from the preceding theorem.

We can now put together all our results into the main theorem of this section.

Theorem 5.6.1 If L is a deterministic context-free language, then $\bar{L} = \Sigma^* - L$ is also a deterministic context-free language.

Proof Suppose $L = T(A)$, where $A = (Q, \Sigma, \Gamma, \delta, q_0, Z_0, F)$ is a dpda. By Lemma 5.6.5, there is no loss of generality in supposing that A is loop-free. Define $A' = (Q', \Sigma, \Gamma, \delta', q_0', Z_0, F')$, where

$$Q' = \{(q, i) \mid q \in Q, i \in \{0, 1, 2\}\};$$

$$q_0' = (q_0, i_0) \qquad \text{where } i_0 = \begin{cases} 0 & \text{if } q_0 \notin F, \\ 1 & \text{if } q_0 \in F; \end{cases}$$

$$F' = Q \times \{2\};$$

and δ' is defined by cases:

1 If $(q, a, Z) \in Q \times \Sigma \times \Gamma$, then

$$\delta'((q, 1), a, Z) = \delta'((q, 2), a, Z) = ((q', i), \alpha)$$

where $\delta(q, a, Z) = (q', \alpha)$ and

$$i = \begin{cases} 0 & \text{if } q' \notin F, \\ 1 & \text{if } q' \in F. \end{cases}$$

2 If $(q, Z) \in Q \times \Gamma$ and $\delta(q, \Lambda, Z) = (q', \alpha)$, then

$$\delta'((q, 1), \Lambda, Z) = ((q', 1), \alpha)$$

and

$$\delta'((q, 0), \Lambda, Z) = ((q', i), \alpha)$$

where

$$i = \begin{cases} 0 & \text{if } q' \notin F, \\ 1 & \text{if } q' \in F. \end{cases}$$

3 If $\delta(q, \Lambda, Z) = \emptyset$, then

$$\delta'((q, 0), \Lambda, Z) = ((q, 2), Z).$$

The idea of the construction is to use three copies of the set of states of Q. A state of the form $(q, 0)$ means that A has not been in a final state since it last made a move on a true input. A state of the form $(q, 1)$ indicates that A has entered a final state in that time interval. The states of the form $(q, 2)$ are used only for final states.

The detailed argument will proceed by consideration of a number of claims.

Claim 1 A' is a dpda and $T_d(A') = T(A')$.

Proof It is clear that A' is a dpda from the construction. It is always true that $T_d(A') \subseteq T(A')$. If $w \in T(A')$, then

$$(q_0', w, Z_0) \overset{*}{\underset{A'}{\vdash}} ((q, 2), \Lambda, \alpha)$$

for some $q \in Q$ and $\alpha \in \Gamma^*$. But, for all $q \in Q$, $Z \in \Gamma$,

$$\delta((q, 2), \Lambda, Z) = \emptyset,$$

so

$$(q_0', w, Z_0) \overset{*}{\underset{A'}{\Vdash}} ((q, 2), \Lambda, \alpha),$$

and therefore $w \in T_d(A')$.

Claim 2 For any $q, q' \in Q$, $\gamma, \gamma' \in \Gamma^*$, and $i \geqslant 0$,

$$((q, 1), \Lambda, \gamma) \overset{i}{\underset{A'}{\vdash}} ((q', 1), \Lambda, \gamma')$$

if and only if

$$(q, \Lambda, \gamma) \overset{i}{\underset{A}{\vdash}} (q', \Lambda, \gamma').$$

Proof The argument is an induction on i. The basis when $i = 0$ is trivial.

Induction step. Assume the result for all computations of length k. Now

$$((q, 1), \Lambda, \gamma) \overset{k+1}{\underset{A'}{\vdash}} ((q', 1), \Lambda, \gamma') \tag{5.6.5}$$

if and only if there exist $Z \in \Gamma$ and $\gamma'' \in \Gamma^*$ such that

$$((q, 1), \Lambda, \gamma) \overset{k}{\underset{A'}{\vdash}} ((q'', 1), \Lambda, \gamma''Z) \underset{A'}{\vdash} ((q', 1), \Lambda, \gamma'). \tag{5.6.6}$$

Note that we know the intermediate state $(q'', 1)$ has second component 1 because no Λ-move can change the 1 in $(q, 1)$ to a 0 or a 2. By the induction hypothesis applied to (5.6.6) and by the definition of δ', this condition holds if and only if

$$(q, \Lambda, \gamma) \overset{k}{\underset{A}{\vdash}} (q'', \Lambda, \gamma''Z)$$
and
$$\delta(q'', \Lambda, Z) = (q', \alpha) \tag{5.6.7}$$
and
$$\gamma' = \gamma''\alpha.$$

Thus, (5.6.7) holds if and only if

$$(q, \Lambda, \gamma) \overset{k}{\underset{A}{\vdash}} (q'', \Lambda, \gamma''Z) \underset{A}{\vdash} (q', \Lambda, \gamma')$$
or
$$(q, \Lambda, \gamma) \overset{k+1}{\underset{A}{\vdash}} (q', \Lambda, \gamma').$$

The induction has been extended.

Claim 3 For any $q, q' \in Q, \gamma, \gamma' \in \Gamma^*$, and $i \geqslant 0$,

$$((q, 0), \Lambda, \gamma) \overset{i}{\underset{A'}{\vdash}} ((q', 0), \Lambda, \gamma')$$
if and only if
$$(q, \Lambda, \gamma) \overset{i}{\underset{A}{\vdash}} (q', \Lambda, \gamma').$$

Proof The argument is similar to the proof of Claim 2. The difference is that we may observe that an intermediate state must have second component 0, for if it were a 1 or a 2 it could not be reconverted to a 0 in a Λ-computation.

Now we consider how the second component in the states of A' might change.

Claim 4 For any $q, q' \in Q, \gamma, \gamma' \in \Gamma^*$,

$$((q, 0), \Lambda, \gamma) \overset{i}{\underset{A'}{\vdash}} ((q', 1), \Lambda, \gamma')$$

if and only if there exist $j \leqslant i$, $q'' \in F$, and $\gamma'' \in \Gamma^*$, so that

$$(q, \Lambda, \gamma) \overset{j}{\underset{A}{\vdash}} (q'', \Lambda, \gamma'') \overset{i-j}{\underset{A}{\vdash}} (q', \Lambda, \gamma').$$

Proof The argument is another induction on i in which the basis is omitted.

Induction step. Suppose the result holds for k and consider

$$((q, 0), \Lambda, \gamma) \overset{k+1}{\underset{A'}{\vdash}} ((q', 1), \Lambda, \gamma'). \tag{5.6.8}$$

This holds if and only if there exist $q'' \in Q, \ell \in \{0, 1\}, \gamma'' \in \Gamma^*, Z \in \Gamma$, such that

$$((q, 0), \Lambda, \gamma) \overset{k}{\underset{A'}{\vdash}} ((q'', \ell), \Lambda, \gamma''Z) \underset{A'}{\vdash} ((q', 1), \Lambda, \gamma'). \tag{5.6.9}$$

Note that $\ell \neq 2$ since A' cannot move from a 2-state to a 1-state under Λ. In turn, (5.6.9) holds if and only if

$$(q, \Lambda, \gamma) \overset{k}{\underset{A}{\vdash}} (q'', \Lambda, \gamma''Z) \tag{5.6.10}$$

and either

$$\ell = 0, \qquad \delta(q'', \Lambda, Z) = (q', \alpha), \qquad q' \in F \qquad \text{and} \qquad \gamma' = \gamma''\alpha$$

or

$$\ell = 1, \qquad \delta(q'', \Lambda, Z) = (q', \alpha), \qquad \gamma' = \gamma''\alpha \qquad \text{and}$$
$$(q, \Lambda, \gamma) \overset{j}{\underset{A}{\vdash}} (q''', \Lambda, \gamma''') \quad \text{for some } q''' \in F, j \leqslant k.$$

The equivalence of (5.6.9) and (5.6.10) uses the induction hypothesis and Claim 3. Using (5.6.10) we see that (5.6.8) holds if and only if

$$(q, \Lambda, \gamma) \mathrel{\vdash_A^{m}} (q_1, \Lambda, \beta) \mathrel{\vdash_A^{k+1-m}} (q', \Lambda, \gamma'),$$

where $m =$ **if** $\ell = 1$ **then** j **else** $k + 1$. The values of q_1 and β may be obtained from (5.6.10) and $q_1 \in F$. This extends the induction and completes the proof of Claim 4.

Claim 5 For any $q, q' \in Q, q \notin F, \gamma, \gamma' \in \Gamma^*$, and $i \geqslant 0$,

$$((q, 0), \Lambda, \gamma) \mathrel{\vdash_{A'}^{i+1}} ((q', 2), \Lambda, \gamma')$$

if and only if

$$(q, \Lambda, \gamma) \mathrel{\vdash_A^{i}} (q', \Lambda, \gamma'), \qquad \delta(q', \Lambda, (\gamma')^{(1)}) = \emptyset,$$

and for any $p \in F$, $\gamma'' \in \Gamma^*$,

$$(q, \Lambda, \gamma) \mathrel{\not\vdash_A^{*}} (p, \Lambda, \gamma'').$$

Proof The argument is an induction on i.

Basis. $i = 0$. Then,

$$((q, 0), \Lambda, \gamma) \mathrel{\vdash_{A'}} ((q', 2), \Lambda, \gamma')$$

if and only if (by rule (3))

$$q = q', \qquad \gamma = \gamma' \qquad \text{and} \qquad \delta(q, \Lambda, \gamma^{(1)}) = \emptyset,$$

which holds if and only if

$$(q, \Lambda, \gamma) \mathrel{\vdash_A^{0}} (q', \Lambda, \gamma')$$

and, since $q \notin F$, then $q' = q \notin F$, and so

$$(q, \Lambda, \gamma) \mathrel{\not\vdash_A^{*}} (q'', \Lambda, \gamma'')$$

for any $q'' \in F$.

Induction step. Assume the result for $i = k$. Let us consider

$$((q, 0), \Lambda, \gamma) \mathrel{\vdash_{A'}^{k+2}} ((q', 2), \Lambda, \gamma').$$

This holds if and only if

$$((q, 0), \Lambda, \gamma) \mathrel{\vdash_{A'}} ((q'', 0), \Lambda, \gamma'') \mathrel{\vdash_A^{k+1}} ((q', 2), \Lambda, \gamma'). \tag{5.6.11}$$

The second state has second component 0 because if it were a 2, we could not move further on Λ. If it were a 1, it would not be possible to ultimately reach a 2-state on Λ's. Now (5.6.11) holds if and only if $q'' \notin F$, $\delta(q, \Lambda, \gamma^{(1)}) = (q'', \alpha)$, $\gamma = \beta\gamma^{(1)}$, $\gamma'' = \beta\alpha$, and, by the induction hypothesis,

$$(q'', \Lambda, \gamma'') \mathrel{\vdash_A^{k}} (q', \Lambda, \gamma')$$

$q' \notin F$, and $\delta(q', \Lambda, (\gamma')^{(1)}) = \emptyset$, and for any $p \in F, \gamma''' \in \Gamma^*$,

$$(q'', \Lambda, \gamma'') \mathrel{\not\vdash^{*}} (p, \Lambda, \gamma''').$$

This holds if and only if

$$(q, \Lambda, \gamma) \underset{A}{\vdash} (q'', \Lambda, \gamma'') \overset{k}{\vdash} (q', \Lambda, \gamma'),$$

$\delta(q', \Lambda, (\gamma'')^{(1)}) = \emptyset$, and for any $p \in F, \gamma''' \in \Gamma^*$,

$$(q, \Lambda, \gamma) \overset{*}{\not\vdash} (p, \Lambda, \gamma''').$$

This extends the induction.

Claim 6 For any $q, q' \in Q, \gamma, \gamma' \in \Gamma^*$, and $i \in \{0, 1, 2\}$, if

$$((q, i), \Lambda, \gamma) \overset{*}{\underset{A'}{\Vdash}} ((q', i'), \Lambda, \gamma'),$$

then $i' \in \{1, 2\}$.

Proof If $i = 2$, then $i' = 2$ because $\overset{*}{\Vdash}$ reduces to $\overset{0}{\vdash}$. If $i = 1$, then $i' = 1$ for any number of Λ-moves. If $i = 0$, then it may be changed to a 1 and would remain so because a 1-state cannot change to a 0-state under Λ's. If $i = 0$, it may be changed to a 2. In the only remaining case, we would have

$$((q, 0), \Lambda, \gamma) \overset{*}{\underset{A'}{\Vdash}} ((q', 0), \Lambda, \gamma').$$

This holds if and only if

$$((q, 0), \Lambda, \gamma) \overset{*}{\underset{A'}{\vdash}} ((q', 0), \Lambda, \gamma')$$

and

$$\delta'((q', 0), \Lambda, (\gamma')^{(1)}) = \emptyset. \tag{5.6.12}$$

But if $\delta(q', \Lambda, (\gamma')^{(1)}) = \emptyset$, then (5.6.12) is contradicted by part (3) of the construction. On the other hand if $\delta(q', \Lambda, (\gamma')^{(1)}) \neq \emptyset$, then (5.6.12) is contradicted by part (2) of the construction.

Claim 7 For any $w \in \Sigma^*, q \in Q, \gamma \in \Gamma^*, i_0 \in \{0, 1\}$, if

$$((q, i_0), w, \gamma_0) \overset{*}{\underset{A'}{\Vdash}} ((q', i), \Lambda, \gamma),$$

then

$$(q, w, \gamma_0) \overset{*}{\underset{A}{\vdash}} (q', \Lambda, \gamma)$$

and if $q = q_0$ and $\gamma_0 = Z_0$, then $i = 1$ holds if and only if $w \in T(A)$.

Proof The argument is an induction on $\lg(w)$.

Basis. $\lg(w) = 0$, so $w = \Lambda$, and we have

$$((q, i_0), \Lambda, \gamma_0) \overset{*}{\underset{A'}{\Vdash}} ((q', i), \Lambda, \gamma).$$

There are several possibilities:

CASE 1 If $i_0 = 1$, then $i = 1$, since a "1-state" cannot be changed to a "0-state" under Λ's nor can it go to a "2-state" without becoming a "0-state" first. By Claim 2,

$$(q, \Lambda, \gamma_0) \overset{*}{\underset{A}{\vdash}} (q', \Lambda, \gamma).$$

Since $q = q_0, \gamma_0 = Z_0$, and $i_0 = 1$ imply $q_0 \in F$, then this in turn implies $\Lambda \in T(A)$. This completes the proof of Case 1.

CASE 2 $i_0 = 0$. By Claim 6, $i = 1$ or $i = 2$. Assume $i = 1$. Then, for some $k \geqslant 0$,

$$((q, 0), \Lambda, \gamma_0) \Vdash_{A'}^{k} ((q', 1), \Lambda, \gamma).$$

By Claim 4, there exist

$$(q, \Lambda, \gamma_0) \vdash_{A}^{j} (q'', \Lambda, \gamma') \vdash_{A}^{k-j} (q', \Lambda, \gamma)$$

for some $j \leqslant k, q'' \in F$. Thus, if $q = q_0, \gamma_0 = Z_0$, then $w = \Lambda \in T(A)$.

Now assume $i = 2$. Then

$$((q, 0), \Lambda, \gamma_0) \Vdash_{A'}^{*} ((q', 2), \Lambda, \gamma)$$

implies that there is some $k \geqslant 0$ such that

$$((q, 0), \Lambda, \gamma_0) \Vdash_{A'}^{k+1} ((q', 2), \Lambda, \gamma).$$

Note that $q \notin F$ since $i_0 = 0$. By claim 5,

$$(q, \Lambda, \gamma_0) \vdash_{A}^{k} (q', \Lambda, \gamma),$$

and for no $p \in F, \gamma' \in \Gamma^*$ do we have

$$(q, \Lambda, \gamma_0) \vdash_{A}^{*} (p, \Lambda, \gamma').$$

Therefore, $q = q_0$, $\gamma_0 = Z_0$ implies that $w \notin T(A)$. The proof of the basis is now complete.

Induction step. Assume the result true for all $w \in \Sigma^*$ such that $0 \leqslant \lg(w) \leqslant k$. Let

$$((q, i_0), w, \gamma_0) \Vdash_{A'}^{*} ((q', i), \Lambda, \gamma), \tag{5.6.13}$$

where $\lg(w) = k + 1 \geqslant 1$. Then we factor this computation as

$$((q, i_0), w, \gamma_0) \vdash_{A'}^{*} ((q_1, i_1), a, \gamma_1) \tag{5.6.14}$$

and

$$((q_1, i_1), a, \gamma_1) \vdash_{A'} ((q_2, i_2), \Lambda, \gamma_2) \vdash_{A'}^{*} ((q', i), \Lambda, \gamma), \tag{5.6.15}$$

where $w = w'a$ where $w' \in \Sigma^*, a \in \Sigma$, and $\delta(q', \Lambda, \gamma^{(1)}) = \emptyset$, because the original computation (5.6.13) involved $\Vdash^*$.

Consider computation (5.6.14). We have

$$((q, i_0), w', \gamma_0) \vdash_{A'}^{*} ((q_1, i_1), \Lambda, \gamma_1' Z),$$

where $\gamma_1 = \gamma_1' Z, \gamma_1' \in \Gamma^*$, and $Z \in \Gamma$. Furthermore,

$$\delta'((q_1, i_1), a, Z) \neq \emptyset,$$

so that $\delta'((q_1, i_1), \Lambda, Z) = \emptyset$, since A' is deterministic. Then

$$((q, i_0), w', \gamma_0) \Vdash_{A'}^{*} ((q_1, i_1), \Lambda, \gamma_1),$$

where $\lg(w') \leqslant k$, so the induction hypothesis applies, to yield

$$(q, w', \gamma_0) \vdash_{A}^{*} (q_1, \Lambda, \gamma_1) \tag{5.6.16}$$

and $w' \in T(A)$ if and only if $i_1 = 1$ when $q = q_0$ and $\gamma_0 = Z_0$.

Now, we consider the computation of (5.6.15). By the construction of A',

$$(q_1, a, \gamma_1) \underset{A}{\vdash} (q_2, \Lambda, \gamma_2). \tag{5.6.17}$$

Since

$$((q_2, i_2), \Lambda, \gamma_2) \overset{*}{\underset{A'}{\Vdash}} ((q', i), \Lambda, \gamma), \tag{5.6.18}$$

which follows from (5.6.15), and by the construction of A', we have that

$$i_2 = 1 \qquad \text{if and only if} \qquad q_2 \in F.$$

By the induction hypothesis applied to (5.6.18), we have:

$$(q_2, \Lambda, \gamma_2) \overset{*}{\underset{A}{\vdash}} (q', \Lambda, \gamma). \tag{5.6.19}$$

But (5.6.16) and (5.6.17), together with (5.6.19), yield

$$(q, w, \gamma_0) \overset{*}{\underset{A}{\vdash}} (q', \Lambda, \gamma).$$

It follows that $q = q_0$, $\gamma_0 = Z_0$, and $i = 1$ hold if and only if $w \in T(A)$. □

Claim 8 For any $w \in \Sigma^*$, $q \in Q$, and $\gamma \in \Gamma^*$,

$$(q_0, w, Z_0) \overset{*}{\underset{A}{\Vdash}} (q, \Lambda, \gamma)$$

implies

$$((q_0, i_0), w, Z_0) \overset{*}{\underset{A'}{\Vdash}} ((q, i), \Lambda, \gamma)$$

for some i.

Proof The argument is an induction on $\lg(w)$.

Basis. $\lg(w) = 0$. From the definition of A', $i_0 = 0$ or $i_0 = 1$. By Claim 6, $i = 1$ or $i = 2$. Now, every possible case that can arise is dealt with by Claims 2, 4, or 5.

Induction step. Assume the result for all $w \in \Sigma^*$ such that $0 \leqslant \lg(w) \leqslant k$. If

$$(q_0, w, Z_0) \overset{*}{\underset{A}{\Vdash}} (q, \Lambda, \gamma),$$

where $\lg(w) = k + 1$, then

$$(q_0, w, Z_0) \overset{*}{\underset{A}{\Vdash}} (q_1, a, \gamma_1) \underset{A}{\vdash} (q_2, \Lambda, \gamma_2) \overset{*}{\underset{A}{\Vdash}} (q, \Lambda, \gamma)$$

for some $w' \in \Sigma^*$, $a \in \Sigma$, so that $w = w'a$, some $q_1, q_2 \in Q$, and some $\gamma_1, \gamma_2 \in \Gamma^*$. This implies

$$((q_0, i_0), w', Z_0) \overset{*}{\underset{A'}{\Vdash}} ((q_1, i_1), \Lambda, \gamma_1)$$

and $i_1 \in \{1, 2\}$, by the induction hypothesis. Hence

$$((q_0, i_0), w, Z_0) \overset{*}{\underset{A'}{\Vdash}} ((q_1, i_1), a, \gamma_1) \underset{A'}{\vdash} ((q_2, i_2), \Lambda, \gamma_2)$$

with $i_2 = 0$ or 1, by the construction of A'. Moreover,

$$((q_2, i_2), \Lambda, \gamma_2) \overset{*}{\underset{A'}{\Vdash}} ((q, i), \Lambda, \gamma)$$

by Claims 2, 4, 5, or 6. Combining the subcomputations, we have:

$$((q_0, i_0), w, Z_0) \overset{*}{\underset{A'}{\Vdash}} ((q, i), \Lambda, \gamma).$$

We now arrive at our last proposition.

Claim 9 $T(A') = \Sigma^* - T(A)$

Proof Since A is loop-free, for any $w \in \Sigma^*$, there exist q and γ such that

$$(q_0, w, Z_0) \Vdash_A^* (q, \Lambda, \gamma)$$

Hence, by Claim 8

$$((q_0, i_0), w, Z_0) \Vdash_{A'}^* ((q, i), \Lambda, \gamma)$$

By Claim 7, $i = 2$ if and only if $w \notin T(A)$. Thus $w \notin T(A)$ if and only if $w \in T_d(A') = T(A')$. Therefore,

$$T(A') = \Sigma^* - T(A). \qquad \square$$

PROBLEMS

Let $A = (Q, \Sigma, \Gamma, \delta, q_0, Z_0, F)$ be a dpda and let $q \in Q$, $Q_1 \subseteq Q$, for any $\alpha \in \Gamma^*$. Define:

$$L(A, q, \alpha, Q_1) = \{w \in \Sigma^* \mid (q, w, \alpha) \vdash^* (q', \Lambda, \Lambda) \quad \text{for some } q' \in Q_1\};$$

$$L_d(A, q, \alpha, Q_1) = \{w \in \Sigma^* \mid (q, w, \alpha) \Vdash^* (q', \Lambda, \Lambda) \quad \text{for some } q' \in Q_1\};$$

$$T_d(A, q, \alpha, Q_1) = \{w \in \Sigma^* \mid (q, w, \alpha) \Vdash^* (q', \Lambda, \beta) \quad \text{for some } q' \in Q_1, \beta \in \Gamma^*\}.$$

1 Show that, if A is a dpda, then $L_d(A, q, \alpha, Q_1)$ and $T_d(A, q, \alpha, Q_1)$ are context-free languages. Show that one can decide whether they are nonempty and whether a given string belongs to them in time that is polynomial in the size of A.

2 Let $A = (Q, \Sigma, \Gamma, \delta, q_0, Z_0, F)$ be a dpda. Show that A is loop-free if and only if

$$\Sigma^* = (T_d(A, q_0, Z_0, F) \cup T_d(A, q_0, Z_0, Q - F)).$$

3 Let $A = (Q, \Sigma, \Gamma, \delta, q_0, Z_0, F)$ be a loop-free dpda. Is it true or false that

$$T_d(A, q_0, Z_0, Q - F) = \Sigma^* - T(A)?$$

Justify your answer.

4 Let $A = (Q, \Sigma, \Gamma, \delta, q_0, F)$ be a dpda. A pair (q, α) with $q \in Q$, $\alpha \in \Gamma^*$, is *accessible* if there exists $w \in \Sigma^*$ such that

$$(q_0, w, Z_0) \vdash^+ (q, \Lambda, \alpha).$$

Is there an algorithm to decide which configurations are accessible? Suppose A were nondeterministic. Would the result still hold?

***5** Let $A = (Q, \Sigma, \Gamma, \delta, q_0, Z_0, \emptyset)$ be a dpda. Let

$$r = \max\{1, \lg(\gamma) \mid \delta(q, a, Z) = (q', \gamma)\}$$

and let

$$N = \begin{cases} (r^{|Q||\Gamma|} - 1)/(r - 1) & \text{if } r > 1, \\ |Q||\Gamma| & \text{if } r = 1. \end{cases}$$

Show that (q, Λ, Z) is an immortal ID if and only if there exists $j > N$ such that

$$(q, \Lambda, Z) \overset{j}{\vdash} (q', \Lambda, \gamma)$$

for some $q' \in Q, \gamma \in \Gamma^*$.

6 Show that in a dpda, Λ-moves can be essential only in computations that cause the stack to decrease in height.

7 Show that it is never necessary for a dpda to change states in computations where the stack is increasing in height.

8 In Lemma 5.6.5, is it true or false that:

a) $T_d(A') = T_d(A)$? b) $T(A') = T_d(A)$? c) $T(A') = T_d(A')$?

9 Let $L \subseteq \Sigma^*$ be a deterministic context-free language and let $c \notin \Sigma$. Construct a deterministic loop-free dpda A such that

$$L(A) = L_d(A) = T(A) = T_d(A) = Lc.$$

10 Show that any deterministic context-free language may be accepted by a dpda A such that for each input string w of length n, the computation of A on w takes time proportional to n.

11 Define a pda A to be a deterministic (iterated) counter if A is deterministic and is a(n) (iterated) counter. (Counters and iterated counters are defined in the exercises in Section 5.3.) Show that the family of deterministic iterated counter languages is closed under complementation. Is the same result true for counter languages?

5.7 FINITE-TURN PDA'S

We have seen that restricting pda's to be deterministic has led to a useful family of languages. Another restriction will be considered here and some simple implications will be derived. In later sections when more tools are available, we shall return to this family and characterize it in several simple and elegant ways.

To illustrate the restriction we have in mind, consider the set

$$L = \{a^n b^n \mid n \geqslant 0\}\{c\}\{a^n b^n \mid n \geqslant 0\}.$$

A pda accepting this set might stack a's and pop on b's and then repeat this strategy for the second half of the set. A graph of the pushdown would look like Fig. 5.5.

We shall say that, in this computation, there were 3 "turns" or places where the length of the pushdown reversed. The restriction we shall study is to bound the number of turns in a computation. Formalism is needed if we are to be precise about this restriction.

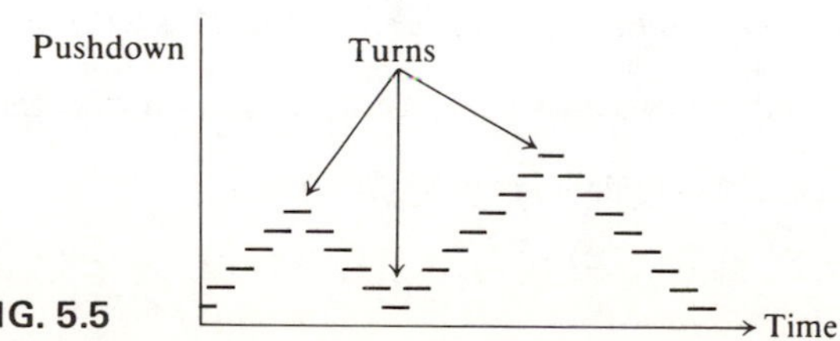

FIG. 5.5

Definition Let $A = (Q, \Sigma, \Gamma, \delta, q_0, Z_0, \emptyset)$ be a pda. A *sweep* is a computation

$$(q_0, w, Z_0) \overset{*}{\vdash} (q, \Lambda, \Lambda)$$

for any $w \in \Sigma^*$ and $q \in Q$.

Thus a sweep is any computation that empties the pushdown. Next we classify the moves of the pda.

Definition Let $A = (Q, \Sigma, \Gamma, \delta, q_0, Z_0, \emptyset)$ be a pda and let $(q', \beta) \in \delta(q,a,Z)$ for some $q \in Q$, $a \in \Sigma \cup \{\Lambda\}$, and $Z \in \Gamma$. A move $(q, ax, \alpha Z) \vdash (q', x, \alpha\beta)$ is called

Nondecreasing if $\lg(\beta) \geqslant 1$,

Nonincreasing if $\lg(\beta) \leqslant 1$,

Increasing if $\lg(\beta) > 1$,

or

Decreasing if $\beta = \Lambda$.

Next the notion of "increasing" is applied to sweeps.

Definition Let $(q_0, x_0, \gamma_0) \vdash \cdots \vdash (q_k, x_k, \gamma_k)$, where $\gamma_0 = Z_0$, $\gamma_k = \Lambda$, and $x_k = \Lambda$, be a sweep. The concept of an increasing (decreasing) sweep is defined recursively as follows:

i) The *length* of (q_0, x_0, γ_0) is defined to be *increasing*;

ii) Inductively, if the length at (q_i, x_i, γ_i) is increasing and if the move $(q_i, x_i, \gamma_i) \vdash (q_i, x_{i+1}, \gamma_{i+1})$ is nondecreasing (decreasing), then the length at $(q_{i+1}, x_{i+1}, \gamma_{i+1})$ is said to be *increasing* (*decreasing*);

iii) If the length at (q_i, x_i, γ_i) is decreasing and the move $(q_i, x_i, \gamma_i) \vdash (q_{i+1}, x_{i+1}, \gamma_{i+1})$ is nonincreasing (increasing), then the length at $(q_{i+1}, x_{i+1}, \gamma_{i+1})$ is said to be decreasing (increasing).

Now, a "turn" can be precisely defined.

Definition Let A be a pda and suppose we have

$$(q_i, x_i, \gamma_i) \vdash (q_{i+1}, x_{i+1}, \gamma_{i+1}).$$

If the length at (q_i, x_i, γ_i) is increasing (decreasing) while the length at $(q_{i+1}, x_{i+1}, \gamma_{i+1})$ is decreasing (increasing), then the length has had a *turn* at (q_i, x_i, γ_i).

Definition A sweep is a $(2k-1)$-turn sweep if it has exactly $(2k-1)$ turns. A pda is a $(2k-1)$-*turn pda* if every sweep has at most $2k-1$ turns. A pda A is said to be a *finite turn* if there is some $k \geqslant 1$ so that A is a $(2k-1)$ turn pda.

Let us single out the sweeps with a bounded number of turns.

Definition Let A be a pda and let $k \geqslant 1$. Define

$$N_{2k-1}(A) = \{x \in \Sigma^* \mid (q_0, x, Z_0) \overset{*}{\vdash} (q, \Lambda, \Lambda) \text{ for some } q \in Q \text{ is a } (2i-1) \text{ sweep for some } i \leqslant k\}.$$

Our first little result is to show that $N_{2k-1}(A)$ is always a context-free language.

Lemma 5.7.1 For each pda A and any $k \geq 1$, there is a $(2k-1)$-turn pda A' such that

$$N(A') = N_{2k-1}(A).$$

Proof Let $A = (Q, \Sigma, \Gamma, \delta, q_0, Z_0, F)$ be a pda. We shall construct a pda A' with $2k$ copies of the states of A, which will simulate A and keep track of the $(2k-1)$-turn sweeps. Define $A' = (Q', \Sigma, \Gamma, \delta', (q_0, 1), \emptyset)$, where $Q' = Q \times \{i \mid 1 \leq i \leq 2k\}$. δ' is given by cases:

CASE 1 $((q', i), \alpha) \in \delta'((q, i), a, Z)$ if and only if

$(q', \alpha) \in \delta(q, a, Z)$ and either i is odd and $\lg(\alpha) \geq 1$

or i is even and $\lg(\alpha) \leq 1$.

(Thus a move from (q, i) to (q', i) is nondecreasing if i is odd and nonincreasing if i is even.)

CASE 2 $((q', 2i), \Lambda) \in \delta'((q, 2i-1), a, Z)$ if and only if

$(q', \Lambda) \in \delta(q, a, Z)$.

(Moves from a state $(q, 2i-1)$ to $(q', 2i)$ are decreasing moves.)

CASE 3 $((q', 2i+1), \alpha) \in \delta'((q, 2i), a, Z)$ if and only if

$(q', \alpha) \in \delta(q, a, Z)$ and $\lg(\alpha) \geq 2$.

(Moves from $(q, 2i)$ to $(q', 2i+1)$ are increasing moves.)

It is now a straightforward matter to verify that each turn in a sweep of A' corresponds to a move from a state of the form (q, i) to one of the form $(q', i+1)$. Therefore, A' is a $(2k-1)$-turn pda. Note that any $(2i-1)$ sweep of A (where $1 \leq i \leq k$) corresponds to a sweep of A'. Since the converse of this is also true, it follows that

$$N_{2k-1}(A) = N(A'). \qquad \square$$

Corollary $N_{2k-1}(A)$ is a context-free language for each pda A.

One of our ultimate goals will be to characterize the finite-turn languages grammatically. The following definition will prove to be equivalent to these languages but it will take some effort before the characterization is achieved.

Definition A context-free grammar $G = (V, \Sigma, P, S)$ is *ultralinear* if there exists a finite number of (possibly empty) pairwise disjoint sets $X_0, \ldots, X_n$ such that

$$N = V - \Sigma = \bigcup_{i=0}^{n} X_i$$

and for each X_i and each $A \in X_i$, either

1 $A \to w$ is in P

where $w \in (\Sigma \cup X_0 \cup \cdots \cup X_{i-1})^*$, or

2 $A \to uBv$ is in P

with $u, v \in \Sigma^*$ and $B \in X_i$.

Note that every linear language is ultralinear by taking $X_0 = \emptyset$ and $X_1 = N$. We are now ready to prove half of our characterization theorem.

Theorem 5.7.1 If A is a finite-turn pda, then $N(A)$ is an ultralinear language.

Proof Let $A = (Q, \Sigma, \Gamma, \delta, q_0, Z_0, \emptyset)$ be a finite-turn pda. There is no loss of generality in assuming that A satisfies the following properties:

i) $Q = Q_1 \cup \cdots \cup Q_{2k}$ with $q_0 \in Q_1$.
ii) Every move from a state of Q_{2i-1} is either a nondecreasing move to a state of Q_{2i-1} or a decreasing move to a state of Q_{2i}.
iii) Every move from a state of Q_{2i} is either a nonincreasing move to a state of Q_{2i} or an increasing move to a state of Q_{2i+1}.
iv) $(q', \alpha) \in \delta(q, a, Z)$ for any $q \in Q$, $a \in \Sigma \cup \{\Lambda\}$, and $Z \in \Gamma$ implies $\lg(\alpha) \leqslant 2$.

(i), (ii) and (iii) follow from Lemma 5.7.1. Property (iv) may be assumed because we could add extra states to achieve it if necessary. Such additions would result in a new pda A' such that $N(A') = N(A)$, and if A is a $(2k-1)$-turn pda, then so is A'.

Now for any state $q \in Q$, define $\nu(q) = i$, where $q \in Q_i$. Note that $\nu(q_0) = 1$ and $\nu(q) \leqslant 2k$ for all $q \in Q$.

Define $G = (V, \Sigma, P, S)$, where

$$V = \Sigma \cup \{S\} \cup \bigcup_{1 \leqslant i < j \leqslant 2k} (Q_i \times \Gamma \times Q_j \times (\Gamma \cup \{\Lambda\})).$$

and P is given by the following productions: For all $q, q', q'', p \in Q$; $a \in \Sigma \cup \{\Lambda\}$; $Y, Z, Z' \in \Gamma$; $X \in \Gamma \cup \{\Lambda\}$. Then,

1 $S \to (q_0, Z_0, q', \Lambda)$;

2 $(q, Z, q', \Lambda) \to a$ if $(q', \Lambda) \in \delta(q, a, Z)$;

3 $(q, Z, q'', X) \to a(q', Y, q'', X)$ if $(q', Y) \in \delta(q, a, Z)$;

4 $(q'', X, q', Y) \to (q'', X, q, Z)a$ if $(q', Y) \in \delta(q, a, Z)$;

5 $(q, Z, q'', Z') \to a(q', Y, q'', \Lambda)$ if $(q', Z'Y) \in \delta(q, a, Z)$;

6 $(q'', Z', q', \Lambda) \to (q'', Z', q, Z)a$ if $(q', \Lambda) \in \delta(q, a, Z)$;

7 $(q, Z, q', X) \to (q, Z, p, Y)(p, Y, q', X)$ for all $p \in Q$ such that $\nu(q) < \nu(p) < \nu(q')$

The basic idea of the construction is embodied in the following observations and the claim.

The first rule indicates a goal of obtaining all words in $N(A)$. Rule 2 is a terminal rule, which corresponds to a decreasing move of the pda and will only be applicable when $\nu(q)$ is odd and $\nu(q')-\nu(q)=1$. Productions (3) and (4) correspond to length-preserving moves of the pda. Production (5) corresponds to an increasing move of the pda. It can occur only when $\nu(q')$ is odd and $\nu(q')<\nu(q'')$. Similarly, (6) represents a decreasing move of the pda, which can only apply when $\nu(q')$ is even and $\nu(q'')<\nu(q)$. Rule 7 corresponds to a sequence of moves of the pda such that there is a state p such that

$$\nu(q)<\nu(p)<\nu(q'),$$

at which the length of the pushdown is exactly one. The following claim summarizes the correspondence between the variables and the pda's computation.

Claim For each $q, q' \in Q$, $Z \in \Gamma$, and $Y \in \Gamma \cup \{\Lambda\}$,

$$(q, Z, q', Y) \overset{*}{\Rightarrow} w \qquad w \in \Sigma^*$$

if and only if

$$(q, w, Z) \overset{*}{\vdash} (q', \Lambda, Y).$$

Proof The argument involves an induction and case analysis in each direction and is omitted.

It follows from the claim that

$$L(G) = N(A).$$

To complete the proof, we need only verify that G is ultralinear. Define

$$X_i = \{(q, Z, q', Y) \mid \nu(q')-\nu(q)=i\} \quad \text{for } 1 \leqslant i \leqslant 2k-1$$

and

$$X_{2k} = \{S\}.$$

It is now easy to verify that G is ultralinear. □

Corollary If A is a one-turn pda, then $N(A)$ is a linear language.

Proof If $k=1$, then the grammar G uses no productions of type (7). Thus G is in linear normal form (Problem 2.5.1). □

PROBLEMS

1 Complete the proof of the claim in Theorem 5.7.1.

A context-free grammar $G=(V, \Sigma, P, S)$ is said to be *nonterminal bounded* if there exists an integer $k \geqslant 1$ such that, for any derivation $A \overset{*}{\Rightarrow} \alpha$, $\alpha \in V^*$, the number of occurrences of variables in α is at most k. A language is called *nonterminal bounded* if it is generated by a nonterminal bounded grammar. If G is such a grammar and $\alpha \in V^*$ define $\rho(\alpha)$, the *rank of* α, to be the largest integer r such that there is a word $\beta \in V^*$ with r occurrences of variables such that

$$\alpha \overset{*}{\Rightarrow} \beta.$$

2 Prove that:

a) For $w \in \Sigma^*$, $\rho(w) = 0$.

b) $\rho(A_1 \cdots A_n) = \sum_{i=1}^{n} \rho(A_i)$ for $A_1, \ldots, A_n \in V$, $n \geqslant 0$.

c) $\rho(A) \geqslant 1$ for each $A \in N$.

d) If A is a variable of rank r, there exists a word $\alpha \in V^*$ such that:

i) $A \overset{*}{\Rightarrow} \alpha$

ii) α has r occurrences of variables, and

iii) each variable in α has rank 1.

e) Every nonterminal bounded grammar contains variables of rank 1.

3 Prove that a context-free grammar G is ultralinear if and only if G is nonterminal bounded.

4 Is the set $L = (\{a^n b^n \mid n \geqslant 0\}c)^*$ nonterminal bounded or not? Can you prove your answer?

5 Show that if L_1 and L_2 are finite-turn languages, then so are

$$L_1 \cup L_2$$

and

$$L_1 L_2.$$

6 Show that every regular set is a finite-turn language.

5.8 HISTORICAL SURVEY

The close connection between context-free languages and pushdown automata was established by Chomsky and Schützenberger. Cf. Chomsky [1962] and Schützenberger [1963]. Another early reference is Evey [1963]. Theorem 5.6.1 is due to Haines [1965]. The theory of deterministic context-free languages originated in Haines [1965] and Ginsburg and Greibach [1966a]. Related results are in Schützenberger [1963]. The theory of finite-turn pda's is due to Ginsburg and Spanier [1966].

SIX

The Iteration Theorem, Nonclosure and Closure Results

6.1 INTRODUCTION

This chapter begins with an iteration theorem for context-free languages. Use of this result allows us to give direct proofs that certain sets are not context-free. The theorem also shows that, over the one-letter terminal alphabet, there is no difference between context-free and regular sets. Next, the closure properties of the context-free languages are explored. One particularly important result is that context-free languages are closed under "sequential transducer mappings."

Section 6.6 digresses by giving a closure result whose proof is not constructive. Section 6.7 discusses the relationship of programming languages to context-free languages and indicates the programming language features that are incompatible with the context-free languages. A theorem is established in Section 6.8 that enables us to prove that there are "nonlinear" context-free languages. The proof is rather a nice blend of the different techniques used in this chapter. A natural map of context-free languages into n-ary relations on natural numbers is given in Section 6.9, and Parikh's Theorem is proved.

6.2 THE ITERATION THEOREM

We will now establish one of the most important theorems of context-free language theory. It is a necessary condition on the set of strings of a language. The notation of Section 1.6 will be needed in our development.

Definition Let $w \in \Sigma^*$. Any sequence $\varphi = (v_1, \ldots, v_n) \in (\Sigma^*)^n$ such that

$$w = v_1 \cdots v_n$$

is called a *factorization* of w. Any integer i, $1 \leqslant i \leqslant \lg(w)$ is called a *position* of w.

Let K be a set of positions in w. Any factorization φ induces a "partition" of K, which we write as

$$K/\varphi = (K_1, \ldots, K_n),$$

where for each i, $1 \leqslant i \leqslant n$,

$$K_i = \{k \in K \mid \lg(v_1, \ldots, v_{i-1}) < k \leqslant \lg(v_1, \ldots, v_i)\}.$$

Note that some K_i may be empty, so this is not a true partition.

Examples

a) Let $w = a_1 \cdots a_n, a_i \in \Sigma$, and $K = \{1, \ldots, n\}$.

i) If we take $\varphi = (a_1, a_2, \ldots, a_n)$, then

$$K/\varphi = \{K_i\} \qquad \text{where } K_i = \{i\}.$$

ii) If we take $\varphi = (a_1 a_2 \cdots a_n)$, then

$$K/\varphi = K_1 = K.$$

b) Let $w = a^p b^p c^p, \varphi = (a^p, b^p, c^p)$ and $K = \{p+1, \ldots, 2p\}$; then

$$K_1 = K_3 = \emptyset, \qquad K_2 = K.$$

Notation. To mark a set of positions we will underline them. Thus, in (b) above, the set of positions would be written as:

$$a^p \; \underline{b^p} \; c^p.$$

We can now state and prove an iteration theorem for context-free languages. The theorem we prove is stronger than the "pumping lemma" ("*xuwvy* theorem") found in some standard texts. The additional power of the iteration theorem stems from the use of positions. This forces the factorization of a string to be restricted and cuts down on the number of cases that can arise.

Theorem 6.2.1 (*The Iteration Theorem*) Let $L = L(G)$ be a context-free language and $G = (V, \Sigma, P, S)$ be a grammar for L. There exists a number $p(G)$ such that for each $w \in L$ and any set K of positions in w, if $|K| \geqslant p(G)$, then there is a factorization

$$\varphi = (v_1, \ldots, v_5) \quad \text{of } w$$

such that:

i) There exists $A \in N$ such that

$$S \overset{*}{\Rightarrow} v_1 A v_5$$

$$A \overset{*}{\Rightarrow} v_2 A v_4$$

$$A \overset{*}{\Rightarrow} v_3$$

ii) For each $q \geqslant 0$, $v_1 v_2^q v_3 v_4^q v_5 \in L$.

iii) If $K/\varphi = \{K_1, \ldots, K_5\}$, then

a) either $K_1, K_2, K_3 \neq \emptyset$ or $K_3, K_4, K_5 \neq \emptyset$; and

b) $|K_2 \cup K_3 \cup K_4| \leqslant p(G)$.

Part (iii) means, in part, that $K_3 \neq \emptyset$ and either K_2 or $K_4 \neq \emptyset$. Thus either $v_2 \neq \Lambda$ or $v_4 \neq \Lambda$. Condition (iii) (b),

$$|K_2 \cup K_3 \cup K_4| \leqslant p(G),$$

is necessary in order to prohibit trivial factorizations in which $w = v_2 v_3 v_4$.

Proof Let

$$r = \max\{2, \lg(\alpha) \mid A \to \alpha \text{ is in } P\},$$

and define

$$v = |N|, \qquad p(G) = r^{2v+3}.$$

Observe that one can actually compute $p(G)$ and that it depends on the grammar. This will be needed later when this theorem arises in certain decidability questions.

Let w be in L and let K be any set of positions in w such that $|K| \geqslant p(G)$. Let T be a generation tree for $S \overset{*}{\Rightarrow} w$ and let $y_1, \ldots, y_{\lg(w)}$ be the sequence of non-null terminal nodes in T. That is, using the notation from Section 1.6,

$$y_i \overset{+}{\sqsubset} y_{i+1} \quad \text{for } 1 \leqslant i \leqslant \lg(w),$$

$$w = \lambda(y_1) \cdots \lambda(y_{\lg(w)}),$$

and

$$\lambda(y_i) \in \Sigma.$$

Now define two sets:

$$D = \{x \text{ in } T \mid x \overset{*}{\ulcorner} y_i \quad \text{for some } i \in K\},$$

$$B = \{x \text{ in } T \mid x \ulcorner x_1 \text{ and } x \ulcorner x_2 \quad \text{for some } x_1, x_2 \in D, x_1 \neq x_2\}.$$

Intuitively, a node is in D if there is a path from the node to a position. A node is in B if it has at least two immediate descendants, each of which has a path to a position. (Nodes in D (B) will be referred to as D- (B)-nodes.)

Claim 1 If every path in T, the tree for w, contains $\leqslant i$ B-nodes, then w has $\leqslant r^i$ positions in K.

Proof The maximum number of positions would occur if each B-node had maximum "fan out" and each of the successors of a B-node was a D-node. Since the maximum "fan out" of any node in the tree is r, the maximum number of positions in w is r^i.

Now choose a path $s = (s_0, \ldots, s_t)$ in T such that:

a) s_0 is the root of T;

b) s_t is a leaf;

c) s contains the maximum number of B-nodes taken over all such paths.

Claim 2 s contains at least $(2v+3)$ B-nodes.

Proof Assume s has $\leqslant (2v+2)$ B-nodes. Then, since s has a maximal number of B-nodes, every path in T from s_0 to a leaf must have $\leqslant (2v+2)$ B-nodes. By Claim 1, w would have $\leqslant r^{2v+2}$ positions in K; but w was chosen to have at least r^{2v+3} positions in K. Hence s must have at least $(2v+3)$ B-nodes. □

Now define a set C_s of nodes on s by:

i) $C_s \subseteq B$;

ii) For each $x \in C_s, x \overset{*}{\ulcorner} y, y \in B$ imply $y \in C_s$;

iii) $|C_s| = 2v+3$.

Intuitively, C_s contains the "lowest" $(2v+3)$ B-nodes on s.

Claim 3 If $C_s = C_L \cup C_R$ for any sets C_L and C_R, then either

$$|C_L| \geqslant v+2 \quad \text{or} \quad |C_R| \geqslant v+2.$$

Proof Assume that this is not the case. Then

$$|C_s| \leqslant |C_L| + |C_R| \leqslant 2v+2 < 2v+3.$$

But this is a contradiction. Hence, either $|C_R|$ or $|C_L| \geqslant v+2$.

We now define two sets

$$C_L = \{x \in C_s | x \ulcorner y \quad \text{and} \quad y \overset{+}{\sqsubset} s_t \quad \text{for some } y \in D\}$$

and

$$C_R = \{x \in C_s | x \ulcorner y \quad \text{and} \quad s_t \overset{+}{\sqsubset} y \quad \text{for some } y \in D\}.$$

Intuitively, $x \in C_L$ (respectively, C_R) if it is in C_s and has an immediate descendant y which has a descendant that is a position strictly to the left (right) of s_t.

Example See Fig. 6.1.

Note. C_L and C_R are not necessarily disjoint.

Claim 4 $C_s = C_L \cup C_R$.

Proof

a) $C_L \cup C_R \subseteq C_s$, by definition of C_L and C_R.

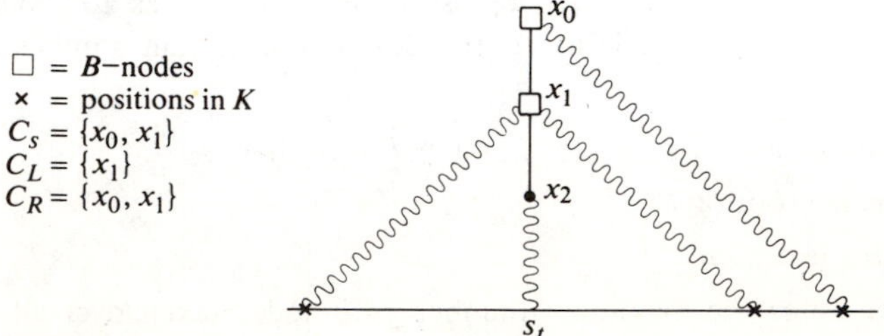

FIG. 6.1

b) On the other hand, if $x \in C_s$, then x has at least two descendants which are positions in K, since x is a B-node. One of these might be s_t, but at least one must lie either to the left or to the right of s_t. Hence, x is an element of either C_L or C_R. Thus $C \subseteq C_L \cup C_R$, and therefore

$$C_s = C_L \cup C_R,$$

which completes the proof of Claim 4.

By Claim 3 there are now two dual cases to consider, namely

$$|C_L| \geqslant v+2 \qquad \text{or} \qquad |C_R| \geqslant v+2.$$

We will assume that

$$|C_L| \geqslant v+2.$$

The argument in the other case completely parallels this one and is omitted.

Thus we have

$$C_L = \{x_1, \ldots, x_m\},$$

where

$$x_i \overset{+}{\sqsubset} x_{i+1} \quad \text{for } 1 \leqslant i < m.$$

Now, since $m \geqslant (v+2)$, there exists j, k, and there is $A \in N$ such that

$$1 < j < k \leqslant m$$

and

$$\lambda(x_j) = \lambda(x_k) = A.$$

But this gives

$$S \overset{*}{\Rightarrow} v_1 A v_5 \quad \text{for some } v_1, v_5 \in \Sigma^*,$$

$$A \overset{*}{\Rightarrow} v_2 A v_4 \quad \text{for some } v_2, v_4 \in \Sigma^*,$$

$$A \overset{*}{\Rightarrow} v_3 \quad \text{for some } v_3 \in \Sigma^*.$$

This is illustrated in Fig. 6.2.

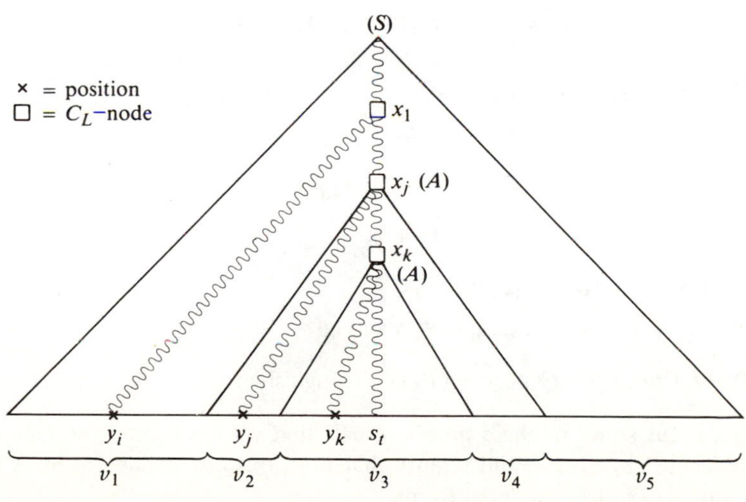

FIG. 6.2

Now, by iterating the second sequence of productions $q \geqslant 0$ times, we get

$$S \overset{*}{\Rightarrow} v_1 A v_5 \overset{*}{\Rightarrow} v_1 v_2^q A v_4^q v_5 \Rightarrow v_1 v_2^q v_3 v_4^q v_5 \in L.$$

Since $x_1, x_j, x_k \in C_L$, there exist y_i, y_j, and y_k such that $i, j, k \in K$, and

$$x_1 \overset{*}{\ulcorner} y_i, \qquad x_j \overset{*}{\ulcorner} y_j, \qquad x_k \overset{*}{\ulcorner} y_k,$$

and

$$y_i \overset{+}{\llcorner} y_j \overset{+}{\llcorner} y_m \overset{+}{\llcorner} s_t$$

(where we have also used the fact that T is a tree).

Letting φ be the factorization

$$\varphi = (v_1, v_2, v_3, v_4, v_5)$$

and

$$K/\varphi = \{K_1, \ldots, K_5\},$$

we have

$$i \in K_1, \qquad j \in K_2, \qquad k \in K_3.$$

Thus, $K_1, K_2, K_3 \neq \emptyset$.

Finally, since s was chosen to have the maximum number of B-nodes and that part of the path starting at x_1 has exactly $(2v + 3)$ B-nodes, no other path starting at x_1 can have more than $(2v + 3)$ B-nodes. Further, any path starting at x_j can be extended to be a path starting at x_1, and hence must have $\leqslant (2v + 3)$ B-nodes.

Thus, by Claim 1, the subtree rooted at x_j can have at most

$$r^{2v+3} = p(G) = p$$

positions in K. Since this subtree derives $v_2 v_3 v_4$, we must have

$$|K_2 \cup K_3 \cup K_4| \leqslant p. \qquad \square$$

Corollary (*The Pumping Lemma*) Let L be a context-free language generated by $G = (V, \Sigma, P, S)$. There exists a number $p(G)$ such that, if $w \in L$ and $\lg(w) \geqslant p(G)$, then there exists a factorization

$$\varphi = (v_1, v_2, v_3, v_4, v_5) \quad \text{of } w$$

such that:

i) There exists $A \in N$ so that

$$S \overset{*}{\Rightarrow} v_1 A v_5$$

$$A \overset{*}{\Rightarrow} v_2 A v_4$$

$$A \overset{*}{\Rightarrow} v_5$$

ii) For each $q \geqslant 0$, $v_1 v_2^q v_3 v_4^q v_5 \in L$;

iii) $v_1, v_2, v_3 \neq \Lambda$ or $v_3, v_4, v_5 \neq \Lambda$ and $\lg(v_2 v_3 v_4) \leqslant p(G)$.

Proof Choose every position to be distinguished. $\square$

A careful study of these proofs reveals that we never used the fact that the leaves were labeled by Σ. (We did require that positions *not* be labeled by Λ.) Therefore, the result is valid for sentential forms.

Theorem 6.2.2 (*The Iteration Theorem for Sentential Forms*) Let $L(G) \subseteq \Sigma^*$ be a context-free language generated by $G = (V, \Sigma, P, S)$. There exists a number $p(G)$ such that, for any sentential form α of G and any set K of positions in α, if $|K| \geqslant p(G)$, then there is a factorization

$$\varphi = (\beta_1, \beta_2, \beta_3, \beta_4, \beta_5) \quad \text{of } w$$

such that:

i) There exists $A \in N$ such that:

$$S \overset{*}{\Rightarrow} \beta_1 A \beta_5$$

$$A \overset{*}{\Rightarrow} \beta_2 A \beta_4$$

$$A \overset{*}{\Rightarrow} \beta_3$$

ii) For each $q \geqslant 0$, $\beta_1 \beta_2^q \beta_3 \beta_4^q \beta_5$ is a sentenial form of G;

iii) If $K/\varphi = \{K_1, \ldots, K_5\}$, then:

a) either $K_1, K_2, K_3 \neq \emptyset$ or $K_3, K_4, K_5 \neq \emptyset$; and

b) $|K_2 \cup K_3 \cup K_4| \leqslant p(G)$.

Using the iteration theorem, we can now show that there exist languages that are not context-free.

Theorem 6.2.3 $N = \{a^n b^n a^n \mid n \geqslant 1\}$ is not context-free.

Proof Suppose N is context-free. Then, from the iteration theorem, there exists a p such that conclusions of the theorem hold.

Let

$$w = a^p \underline{b^p} a^p$$

where the underlined bs are distinguished. That is,

$$K = \{p+1, \ldots, 2p\}.$$

Then there exists a factorization

$$\varphi = (v_1, v_2, \ldots, v_5),$$

and we may assume, without loss of generality, from the symmetry of w that $K_1, K_2, K_3 \neq \emptyset$.

Thus,

$$v_1 = a^p b^i, \qquad i > 0$$

$$v_2 = b^j, \qquad j > 0$$

$$v_3 = b^k v, \qquad k > 0, \quad v \in b^* a^*.$$

Now consider

$$w_2 = v_1 v_2^2 v_3 v_4^2 v_5 = a^p b v' \quad \text{for some } v' \in b^+ a^* \text{ because } w_2 \in N;$$

$$= a^p b^p a^p$$

But $\lg(w_2) = \lg(a^p b^p a^p) = 3p$. On the other hand,

$$\lg(w_2) = \lg(w) + \lg(v_2 v_4) \geqslant 3p + 1,$$

which is a contradiction. Hence N is not context-free. □

It is of some interest to compare the pumping lemma with the iteration theorem, As we shall later see, the use of positions greatly restricts the number of possible factorizations of a string and reduces the labor involved in showing a set to be noncontext-free. We shall now give an example of a noncontext-free language that can be shown to be noncontext-free by the iteration theorem but not by the pumping lemma.

Theorem 6.2.4 Let $L = \{a^*bc\} \cup \{a^p ba^n ca^n \mid p \text{ prime}, n \geqslant 0\}$. L is not a context-free language, but the conclusions of the pumping lemma hold for L.

Proof The iteration theorem may be used to show that L is not context-free. Let p be any prime larger than the constant p_0 of the iteration theorem. Consider

$$w = \underline{a^p}\, ba^p ca^p,$$

where the underlined a's are distinguished. All possible factorizations lead to a contradiction. We omit the details because a more elegant proof that L is not context-free will be given in Section 6.5.

Now let us show that the pumping lemma is too weak to show that L is not context-free.

CASE 1. Let $w = a^m bc$, where $\lg(w) \geqslant p_0$, the constant of the pumping lemma. Then we have a factorization:

$$v_1 = a^{m-1}$$

$$v_2 = a$$

$$v_3 = bc$$

$$v_4 = \Lambda$$

$$v_5 = \Lambda$$

Clearly, $v_1 v_2^q v_3 v_4^q v_5 \in L$ for all $q \geqslant 0$.

CASE 2. Let $w = a^p ba^n ca^n$, where $\lg(w) \geqslant p_0, n \geqslant 1$. Take the factorization

$$v_1 = a^p ba^{n-1}$$

$$v_2 = a$$

$$v_3 = c$$

$$v_4 = a$$

$$v_5 = a^{n-1}$$

Then $v_1 v_2^q v_3 v_4^q v_5 \in L$ for all $q \geqslant 0$. Thus the pumping lemma is satisfied. □

PROBLEMS

1 Use the iteration theorem to show that the set L given in Theorem 6.2.4 is not context-free.

2 If you try to prove an iteration theorem for regular sets using right linear grammars, what is your strongest result?

3 Prove the strongest iteration theorem you can get for the family of linear context-free languages by specializing the argument in this section.

4 In Problem 8 of Section 2.5, it was shown that every linear context-free language was representable as

$$L = \{\varphi_1(w)\varphi_2(w^T) \mid w \in R\},$$

where φ_1, φ_2 are homomorphisms and R is regular. Can you use this characterization to obtain an iteration theorem for the linear context-free languages?

5 Give a pda proof of the iteration theorem.

6 Using the result of Problem 5, can you find an iteration theorem for deterministic context-free languages?

7 By the use of the iteration theorem, show that the set L given below is noncontext-free. Show that this result cannot be obtained with the pumping lemma.

$$L = \{a^i b^j c^k \mid i \neq j \neq k \neq i\}.$$

8 Is the set L given below context-free or not?

$$L = \{a^i b^j c^k \mid i, j \geqslant 1, k > \max\{i, j\}\}.$$

9 Let $G = (V, \Sigma, P, S)$ be a reduced context-free grammar. A variable $A \in N$ is said to be *recursive* if $A \overset{*}{\Rightarrow} uAv$ for some $u, v \in \Sigma^*$, where $uv \neq \Lambda$. Show that $L(G)$ is infinite if and only if G has a recursive variable.

10 Are the following sets context-free or not? Prove your answer.

$L_1 = \{a^i b^j a^i b^j \mid i, j \geqslant 1\}$;

$L_2 = \{xx \mid x \in \{a, b\}^*\}$;

$L_3 = \{n_1 c n_2^T \mid n_1, n_2 \in 1\{0, 1\}^*,\quad c \notin \{0, 1\},$ and $\underline{n_1} < \underline{n_2}$ where $\underline{n_i}$ denotes the binary number represented by n_i for $i = 1, 2\}$;

$L_4 = \{a^n b^n a^j \mid n \leqslant j < 2n, n \geqslant 1\}$.

***11** Find an iteration theorem for the family of counter languages.

12 Recall from problems 13 through 16 in Section 2.2 that, if $\Sigma = \{0, 1\}$, the map $x \mapsto \underline{x}$ is a one-to-one map from $\{1\}\Sigma^*$ onto the positive integers. Prove the following result.

Proposition Let $\Sigma = \{0, 1\}$, $v_1 \in \{1\}\Sigma^*$, v_2, v_3, v_4, $v_5 \in \Sigma^*$, be such that $2^{\lg(v_2)} \not\equiv 1 \bmod p$ and $2^{\lg(v_4)} \not\equiv 1 \bmod p$, where p is an odd prime. Then

$$\underline{v_1 v_2^{p-1} v_3 v_4^{p-1} v_5} \equiv \underline{v_1 v_3 v_5} \bmod p.$$

Hint: Recall Problem 14 of Section 2.2.

13 Prove the following result.

Proposition Let $\Sigma = \{0, 1\}$, $v_1 \in \{1\}\Sigma^*$, v_2, v_3, v_4, v_5 be in Σ^*. Let $k \geqslant 0$ be such that $\underline{v_1 v_2^k v_3 v_4^k v_5} = p$ is an odd prime, $2^{\lg(v_2)} \not\equiv 1 \bmod p$ and $2^{\lg(v_4)} \not\equiv 1 \bmod p$. Then

$$\underline{v_1 v_2^k v_2^{p-1} v_3 v_4^k v_4^{p-1} v_5} \equiv \underline{v_1 v_2^k v_3 v_4^k v_5} \equiv 0 \bmod p.$$

14 Let $\Sigma = \{0, 1\}$. If $\mathscr{P}$ is an infinite subset of $\{1\}\Sigma^*$ which represents primes (i.e., $w \in \mathscr{P}$ implies $\underline{w}$ is a prime), then $\mathscr{P}$ is not context-free.

6.3* CONTEXT-FREE LANGUAGES OVER A ONE-LETTER ALPHABET

The following theorem characterizes the context-free language over a one-letter alphabet.

Theorem 6.3.1 Every context-free language $L \subseteq \{a\}^*$ is regular.

Proof Let $L \subseteq \{a\}^*$ be a context-free language generated by some grammar G, and let $N_0 = p(G)$ be the constant given by the iteration theorem. Then, for each

$$w \in L \cap \Sigma^{N_0} \Sigma^+,$$

there exists a factorization

$$\varphi = (v_1, v_2, v_3, v_4, v_5)$$

such that

a) $w = v_1 v_2 v_3 v_4 v_5$,

b) $\lg(v_2 v_3 v_4) \leqslant N_0$,

c) $v_2 v_4 \neq \Lambda$.

From (b) and (c) we have

$$v_2 v_4 = a^j \qquad \text{for some } j,\ 1 \leqslant j \leqslant N_0.$$

Further, since $\Sigma = \{a\}$, any two words commute:

$$w_k = v_1 v_2^k v_3 v_4^k v_5 = v_1 v_3 v_5 (a^j)^k \in L, \qquad 0 \leqslant k.$$

Claim 1 Let p be the least common multiple of $\{1, \ldots, N_0\}$. Then, for all $w \in L \cap \Sigma^{N_0} \Sigma^+$, we have that $w(a^p)^* \subseteq L$.

Proof Each word in $w(a^p)^*$ is of the form

$$w(a^p)^i = v_1 v_2 v_3 v_4 v_5 a^{pi} = v_1 v_3 v_5 a^j a^{pi} = v_1 v_3 v_5 a^{j+pi}.$$

Now, since p is the least common multiple of $\{1, \ldots, N_0\}$ and $1 \leqslant j \leqslant N_0$, j divides p. Therefore,

$$j + pi = j(1 + (p/j)i),$$

where the second factor is an integer. Thus

$$w(a^p)^i = v_1 v_3 v_5 a^{(1+(p/j)i)j} = v_1 v_3 v_5 (v_2 v_4)^{1+(p/j)i},$$

which is an element of L by the iteration theorem.

Now define

$$A_i = a^{N_0+i}(a^p)^* \cap L, \qquad 1 \leqslant i \leqslant p.$$

Note that A_i may be empty for some i. Let y_i be a word of minimal length in A_i if $A_i \neq \emptyset$. Otherwise, let y_i be undefined.

Claim 2
$$L = \left(L \cap \left(\bigcup_{i=0}^{N_0} \Sigma^i\right)\right) \cup \left(\bigcup_{i=1}^{p} y_i(a^p)^*\right).$$

Proof

a)
$$\left(L \cap \left(\bigcup_{i=0}^{N_0} \Sigma^i\right)\right) \cup \left(\bigcup_{i=1}^{p} y_i(a^p)^*\right) \subseteq L.$$

Since: i) $L \cap (\bigcup_{i=0}^{N_0} \Sigma^i) \subseteq L$;

ii) $y_i \in L$ and, by Claim 1, $y_i(a^p)^* \subseteq L$.

b) To show that

$$L \subseteq \left(L \cap \left(\bigcup_{i=0}^{N_0} \Sigma^i\right)\right) \cup \left(\bigcup_{i=1}^{p} y_i(a^p)^*\right)$$

let x be any element of L. There are two cases.

CASE 1. If $\lg(x) \leqslant N_0$, then

$$x \in L \cap \left(\bigcup_{i=0}^{N_0} \Sigma^i\right).$$

CASE 2. If $\lg(x) > N_0$, then

$$\lg(x) = N_0 + k \quad \text{for some } k.$$

Let

$$k = qp + r, \qquad 1 \leqslant r \leqslant p.$$

Then

$$x = a^{N_0+r}(a^p)^q.$$

Thus

$$A_r = (a^{N_0+r}(a^p)^* \cap L) \neq \emptyset,$$

and A_r has a minimal element y_r. Let

$$y_r = a^{N_0+r}(a^p)^s \quad \text{for some } s \geqslant 0.$$

This gives

$$x = y_r(a^p)^{q-s},$$

where $q - s \geqslant 0$ since y_r was minimal, which completes the proof of Claim 2.

Therefore L is regular, since it can be written as a regular expression. □

Recalling the definition of an ultimately periodic set from Section 2.2, we can prove the following theorem.

Theorem 6.3.2 For $L \subseteq \Sigma^*$, where $|\Sigma| = 1$, the following conditions are equivalent:

1 L is a context-free language.

2 L is a regular set.

3 $I_L = \{i \mid a^i \in L\}$ is an ultimately periodic set.

Proof (1) implies (2) by Theorem 6.3.1. (2) implies (3) by Theorem 2.2.5. If I_L is ultimately periodic, then L is regular, by Theorem 2.2.5, and context-free by the Corollary to Theorem 2.5.1. □

PROBLEMS

1 Show that, if $L \subseteq \Sigma^*$ is any context-free language, then $\{\lg(x) \mid x \in L\}$ is an ultimately periodic set of natural numbers.

2 Show that $L = \{a^{f(n)} \mid n \geqslant 1\}$, where $f(n)$ is a polynomial of degree at least 2, is not an ultimately periodic set.

3 If $L \subseteq a_1^* \cdots a_n^*$, where $\Sigma = \{a_1, \ldots, a_n\}$, define

$$I(L) = \{(i_1, \ldots, i_n) \mid a_1^{i_1} \cdots a_n^{i_n} \in L\}.$$

Show that, if L is a context-free language, then $I(L)$ may be expressed as a finite union of sets of the form:

$$\{c + i_1 p_1 + \cdots + i_m p_m \mid i_1, \ldots, i_m \geqslant 0\}.$$

The symbols $c, p_1, \ldots, p_m$ are n-tuples of nonnegative integers and none of the p_i contain more than two nonzero components.

4 Let f be a function on the natural numbers and $L \subseteq \Sigma^*$. Define

$$L(f) = \{x \in \Sigma^* \mid xy \in L \quad \text{for some } y \in \Sigma^* \text{ and } \lg(y) = f(\lg(x))\}.$$

Here f is said to be a *context-free preserving function* if, for each L that is context-free, $L(f)$ is also context-free. Show that if f is a context-free preserving function, then:

a) for each $r \geqslant 0$, $\{i \mid f(i) = r\}$ is ultimately periodic;

b) for each $d \geqslant 1$ and for each $r < d$, $\{i \mid (f(i))_{\mathrm{mod}\, d} = r\}$ is ultimately periodic; and

c) for each $k \geqslant 1$, $\{i \mid f(i) \leqslant ki\}$ is ultimately periodic.

5 Show that if f is a context-free preserving function, then for $k \geqslant 1$,

$$\{m \mid f(n) = m \quad \text{and} \quad f(n) \leqslant kn \quad \text{for some } n\}$$

is a finite set.

*6 Show that f is a context-free preserving function if and only if:

a) for each $r \geqslant 0$, $\{i \mid f(i) = r\}$ is ultimately periodic;

b) for each $d \geqslant 1$ and each $r < d$, $\{i \mid (f(i))_{\mathrm{mod}\, d} = r\}$ is ultimately periodic;

c) for each $k \geqslant 1$, $\{m \mid f(n) = m$ and $f(n) \leqslant kn$ for some $n\}$ is finite.

7 Using the result of Problem 6, show that the class of context-free preserving functions is closed under composition, addition, multiplication, and exponentiation.

8 Is every context-free preserving function also a total recursive function?

6.4 REGULAR SETS AND SEQUENTIAL TRANSDUCERS

In studying the closure properties of context-free languages, it is possible to give very simple proofs by using pushdown automata.

We have already shown that the context-free languages are closed under union, product, Kleene closure, substitution mapping, homomorphism, and reversal. We now show that they are closed under intersection with a regular set. Later it will be shown that the intersection of two context-free languages is not necessarily a context-free language.

Theorem 6.4.1 If L is a (deterministic) {unambiguous} context-free language and R is a regular set, then $L \cap R$ is a (deterministic) {unambiguous} context-free language.

Proof Let $L = T(A)$ for some pda A:

$$A = (Q, \Sigma, \Gamma, \delta_A, q_{0A}, Z_0, F_A)$$

and $R = T(B)$ for some finite automaton

$$B = (Q_B, \Sigma, \delta_B, q_{0B}, F_B).$$

Let C be a pda defined by

$$C = (Q_A \times Q_B, \Sigma, \Gamma, \delta, (q_{0A}, q_{0B}), Z_0, F_A \times F_B),$$

where, for each $(q_1, q_2) \in Q_A \times Q_B$, each $a \in \Sigma_\Lambda$ and each $Z \in \Gamma$,

$$\delta((q_1, q_2), a, Z) = \{((q', \delta_B(q_2, a)), \alpha) \mid (q', \alpha) \in \delta_A(q, a, Z)\}.$$

Intuitively, C simulates A and B in parallel and accepts if and only if they both accept. Note that, since for each $q_2 \in Q_B$,

$$\delta_B(q_2, \Lambda) = q_2,$$

the two machines remain in "synchronization."

Claim For each (q_1, q_2), $(q_1', q_2') \in Q_A \times Q_B$, each $w \in \Sigma^*$, and each α, $\beta \in \Gamma^*$,

$$((q_1, q_2), w, \alpha) \overset{*}{\underset{C}{\vdash}} ((q_1', q_2'), \Lambda, \beta)$$

if and only if

$$(q_1, w, \alpha) \overset{*}{\underset{A}{\vdash}} (q_1', \Lambda, \beta) \qquad \text{and} \qquad q_2' = \delta_B(q_2, w).$$

Proof The proof, by induction on the number of moves, is left as an exercise.

Thus,

$$x \in T(C) \qquad \text{if and only if} \qquad x \in T(A) \quad \text{and} \quad x \in T(B).$$

Therefore,

$$T(C) = L \cap R,$$

which proves the theorem. Note that C is deterministic {unambiguous} if A is. □

Corollary If L is a (deterministic) {unambiguous} context-free language and R is regular, then $L - R$ is a (deterministic) {unambiguous} context-free language.

Proof If R is regular, then $\Sigma^* - R$ is regular. But we have

$$L - R = L \cap (\Sigma^* - R). \qquad \square$$

This result does not generalize to the intersection of two deterministic context-free languages, as the following example shows. Let

$$L_1 = \{a^i b^j a^j \mid i, j \geqslant 1\}$$

and

$$L_2 = \{a^i b^i a^j \mid i, j \geqslant 1\}.$$

Clearly, L_1 and L_2 are deterministic context-free languages. Then

$$L_1 \cap L_2 = \{a^i b^i a^i \mid i \geqslant 1\}$$

would be context-free but this is not so. Thus we have shown:

Theorem 6.4.2 The family of (deterministic) context-free languages is not closed under intersection. The family of context-free languages is not closed under complement. There is a context-free language which is not deterministic.

Proof The second sentence follows because

$$L_1 \cap L_2 = \Sigma^* - ((\Sigma^* - L_1) \cup (\Sigma^* - L_2)).$$

If every context-free language were deterministic, the family $\mathscr{C}$ would be closed under complementation, by Theorem 5.6.1. $\square$

In Section 3.4, the idea of a homomorphism was generalized to the concept of a substitution. Another direction would be to have a powerful kind of transducer into which a context-free language could be sent. Such devices will now be introduced.

Definition A *sequential transducer* is a 5-tuple

$$S = (Q, \Sigma, \Delta, \delta, q_0),$$

where

Q is a finite nonempty set of *states*,

Σ is a finite nonempty *input alphabet*,

Δ is a finite nonempty *output alphabet*,

$q_0 \in Q$ is the *start state*, and

δ is a finite subset of $Q \times \Sigma^* \times \Delta^* \times Q$.

Intuitively, if $(q, u, v, q') \in \delta$, the machine in state q under the influence of input $u \in \Sigma^*$ will make a transition to state q', outputting $v \in \Delta^*$. This may be represented graphically as:

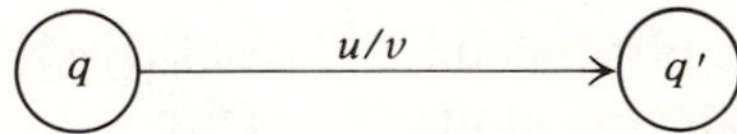

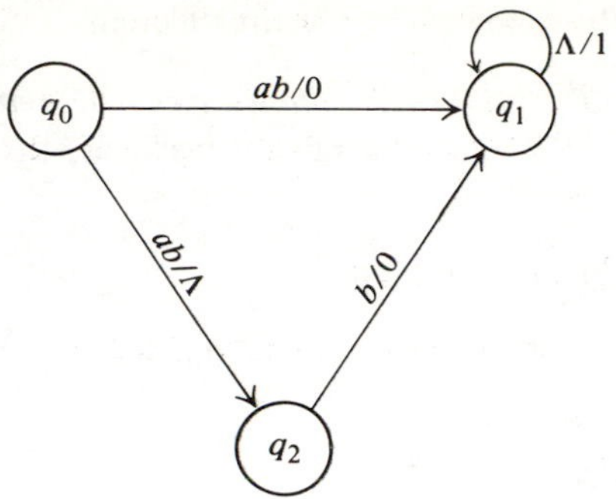

FIG. 6.3

Thus there is a natural correspondence between sequential transducers and labeled directed graphs.

Example See Fig. 6.3.

The sequential transducer functions like a nondeterministic finite automaton (i.e., given an input, one can follow any path through the automaton which corresponds to that input). Thus, in the example,

$$S(ab) = \{\Lambda\} \cup \{01^*\}.$$

We now give formal definition of the output of S.

Definition Let $Q = (Q, \Sigma, \Delta, \delta, q_0)$ be a sequential transducer. For $u \in \Sigma^*$, we say $v \in S(u)$ if and only if there exist $u_1, \ldots, u_k \in \Sigma^*$; $v_1, \ldots, v_k \in \Delta^*, q_1, \ldots, q_k \in Q$, such that

i) $u = u_1 \cdots u_k$,

ii) $v = v_1 \cdots v_k$,

iii) $(q_i, u_{i+1}, v_{i+1}, q_{i+1}) \in \delta$ for each $i, 0 \leqslant i < k$.

If $L \subseteq \Sigma^*$, then

$$S(L) = \bigcup_{u \in L} S(u).$$

Finally, if $L \subseteq \Delta^*$, then

$$S^{-1}(L) = \{w \in \Sigma^* \mid S(w) \subseteq L\}.$$

Note that, if $S = (Q, \Sigma, \Delta, \delta, q_0)$ is a sequential transducer, then:

a) If $\delta \subseteq Q \times \Sigma \times \Delta \times Q$ and satisfies the condition that whenever (q, a, v, q') $\in \delta$ and $(q, a, v', q'') \in \delta$, then $v = v'$ and $q' = q''$, then S corresponds to a "sequential machine."

b) If φ: $\Sigma \to \Delta^*$ is any homomorphism, then, if one takes the one-state machine defined by

$$\delta = \{(q_0, a, \varphi(a), q_0) \mid \text{ for each } a \in \Sigma_\Lambda\},$$

then $S(x) = \varphi(x)$ for each $x \in \Sigma^*$.

We now prove the following important theorem.

Theorem 6.4.3 (*The Sequential Transducer Theorem*) If L is a context-free language (regular set) and S is a sequential transducer, then $S(L)$ is a context-free language (regular set).

Proof Let $L = T(A)$ for some pda

$$A = (Q_1, \Sigma, \Gamma, \delta_1, q_0, Z_0, F_1)$$

satisfying the following condition:

For all $(q, a) \in Q \times \Sigma_\Lambda$,

$$\text{if } (q', \alpha) \in \delta_1(q, a, Z_0), \qquad \text{then } \alpha \neq \Lambda.$$

The condition ensures that the start symbol Z_0 is never erased. The method of Lemma 5.6.1 may be employed here to ensure that this condition is satisfied. Let

$$S = (Q_2, \Sigma, \Delta, \delta_2, s_0).$$

Now let

$$m = \max\{1, \lg(u), \lg(v) \mid (q, u, v, q') \in \delta_2\}$$

and

$$\Sigma_m = \bigcup_{i=0}^{m} \Sigma^i, \qquad \Delta_m = \bigcup_{i=0}^{m} \Delta^i.$$

Define a new pda B, which simulates both the original pda A and the sequential transducer S.

$$B = (\bar{Q}, \Delta, \Gamma, \delta, (q_0, s_0, \Lambda, \Lambda), Z_0, \bar{F}),$$

where

$$\bar{Q} = Q_1 \times Q_2 \times \Sigma_m \times \Delta_m,$$

$$\bar{F} = F_1 \times Q_2 \times \{\Lambda\} \times \{\Lambda\},$$

and δ has three types of rules:

Type 1. For all $(q, Z) \in Q_1 \times \Gamma$ and for all $s \in Q_2$,

$$\delta((q, s, \Lambda, \Lambda), \Lambda, Z) = \{((q, s', u, v), Z) \mid (s, u, v, s') \in \delta_2\}.$$

Type 2. For all $(q, s, a) \in Q_1 \times Q_2 \times (\Sigma \cup \{\Lambda\})$, and for all $(x, y) \in \Sigma_m \times \Delta_m$ such that $\lg(ax) \leqslant m$,

$$\delta((q, s, ax, y), \Lambda, Z) = \{((q', s, x, y), \alpha) \mid (q', \alpha) \in \delta_1(q, a, Z)\}.$$

Type 3. For all $(q, s, b) \in Q_1 \times Q_2 \times \Delta$ and for all $y \in \Delta_m$ such that $\lg(y) < m$,

$$\delta((q, s, \Lambda, by), b, Z) = \{((q, s, \Lambda, y), Z)\}.$$

Although B looks rather formidable, the idea involved is simple. If (q, s, u, v) is a state, then q and s correspond to the state of A and S, respectively, at that point in the computation, and u and v are input and output "buffers" for S (used in a manner described below). In accepting a string, B performs the following sequence of steps.

Step 1 (*Move of type 1*). B "guesses" that S in state s will map u into v and transfer to state s':

$$((q, s, \Lambda, \Lambda), x, \beta) \vdash_{\overline{B}} ((q, s', u, v), x, \beta).$$

Note that a Type-1 move occurs only when both the input and output buffers are empty. Also, the state of the pda, the pushdown, and the input all remain unchanged.

Step 2 (*Move of type 2*). B now simulates A started in state q with β on the pushdown and input u:

$$((q, s', u, v), x, \beta) \vdash_{\overline{B}}^{*} ((q', s', \Lambda, v), x, \beta').$$

The state of the transducer, the output buffer and the input remained unchanged during this computation.

Step 3 (*Moves of type 3*). B then checks whether the output v of S generated in Step 1 corresponds to the input string:

$$((q', s', \Lambda, v), vx, \beta') \vdash_{\overline{B}}^{*} ((q', s', \Lambda, \Lambda), x, \beta').$$

If $x \neq \Lambda$, then B goes back to Step 1; otherwise the input string is accepted if and only if $q' \in F_1$. Note that the states of A and S and the pushdown store remain unchanged.

We now prove a series of claims which show that B operates as described.

Claim 1 For each $q, q' \in Q_1$, each $s, s' \in Q_2$, each $u \in \Sigma_m$, each $v \in \Delta_m$, each $w, w' \in \Delta^*$, each $\alpha', \beta \in \Gamma^*$, and each $Z \in \Gamma$,

$$((q, s, \Lambda, \Lambda), w, \beta Z) \vdash_{\overline{B}} ((q', s', u, v), w', \alpha')$$

by a move of Type 1 if and only if

$$q' = q, \qquad w' = w, \qquad \alpha' = \beta Z, \qquad \text{and} \qquad (s, u, v, s') \in \delta_2.$$

Proof Follows directly from the definition of moves of Type 1.

Claim 2 For each $q, q' \in Q_1$, each $s, s' \in Q_2$; each $ux \in \Sigma_m$, each $v, v' \in \Delta_m$, each $w, w' \in \Delta^*$, each $\beta \in \Gamma^*$, $\beta' \in \Gamma^+$, and $Z \in \Gamma$,

$$((q, s, ux, v), w, \beta Z) \vdash_{\overline{B}}^{n} ((q', s', x, v'), w', \beta'),$$

using only moves of Type 2 if and only if

$$s' = s, \qquad v' = v, \qquad w' = w, \qquad \text{and} \qquad (q, u, \beta Z) \vdash_{\overline{A}}^{n} (q', \Lambda, \beta').$$

Proof We prove the *only if* direction by induction on n.

Basis. $n = 0$. Then,

$$((q, s, ux, v), w, \beta Z) \vdash_{\overline{B}}^{0} ((q', s', x, v'), w', \beta'),$$

$$q' = q, \quad s' = s, \quad u = \Lambda, \quad v' = v, \quad w' = w, \quad \text{and} \quad \beta' = \beta Z.$$

But

$$(q, u, \beta Z) \vdash_{\overline{A}}^{0} (q, u, \beta Z).$$

Induction step. Assume that the *only if* direction of the claim holds for all computations of length n. Let

$$((q,s,ux,v),w,\beta Z) \vdash_B^{n+1} ((q',s',x,v'),w',\beta').$$

Then

$$((q,s,u'ax,v),w,\beta Z) \vdash_B^{n} ((q_1,s_1,ax,v_1),w_1,\beta_1 Z_1), \tag{6.4.1}$$

$$\vdash_B ((q',s',x,v'),w',\beta_1\beta_2), \tag{6.4.2}$$

where

$$u = u'a, \qquad a \in \Sigma \cup \{\Lambda\}, \qquad \text{and} \qquad \beta' = \beta_1\beta_2.$$

Applying the induction hypothesis to (6.4.1) gives:

$$s_1 = s, \qquad v_1 = v, \qquad w_1 = w, \qquad (q,u',\beta Z) \vdash_A^{n} (q_1,\Lambda,\beta_1 Z).$$

Now (6.4.2) is a move of Type 2. Hence,

$$s' = s_1, \qquad v' = v_1, \qquad w' = w_1, \qquad (q',\beta_2) \in \delta(q_1,a,Z).$$

Combining these results gives:

$$s' = s, \qquad v' = v, \qquad w' = w,$$

and

$$(q,u,\beta Z) = (q,u'a,\beta Z) \vdash_A^{n} (q_1,a,\beta_1 Z_1)$$

$$\vdash_A (q',\Lambda,\beta_1\beta_2) = (q',\Lambda,\beta'),$$

which completes the induction.

The *if* direction follows directly from the fact that, for each move in A, there is a corresponding Type-2 move in B. A formal proof by induction is left as Exercise 1.

Claim 3 For each $q,q' \in Q_1$, each $s,s' \in Q_2$, each $ux \in \Sigma_m$, each $w,w' \in \Delta^*$, $vy \in \Delta_m$, $\beta' \in \Gamma^+$, $\beta \in \Gamma^*$, and $Z \in \Gamma$,

$$((q,s,ux,vy),w,\beta Z) \vdash_B^{*} ((q',s',x,y),w',\beta'),$$

with no moves of Type 1 if and only if $s' = s$, $w = vw'$, and

$$(q,u,\beta Z) \vdash_A^{*} (q',\Lambda,\beta').$$

Proof The *only if* direction will be proved by induction on n.

Basis. $\lg(v) = 0$. Then $v = \Lambda$ and

$$((q,s,ux,y),w,\beta Z) \vdash_B^{*} ((q',s',x,y),w',\beta').$$

Since only moves of Type 2 could be used, we have, by Claim 2, that

$$s' = s, \qquad w' = w, \qquad \text{and} \qquad (q,u,\beta Z) \vdash_A^{*} (q',\Lambda,\beta').$$

Induction step. Assume that the *only if* direction of the claim holds for $\lg(v) = n$.

Let $\lg(v) = n+1$. Then,

$$v = v'a, \qquad a \in \Delta \qquad \lg(v') = n.$$

The computation of B must be of the form:

$$((q,s,u_1u_2x,v'ay),w,\beta Z) \vdash_B^* ((q_1,s_1,u_2x,ay),w_1,\beta_1Z_1) \tag{6.4.3}$$

$$\vdash_B ((q_2,s_2,u_2x,y),w_2,\beta_2Z_2) \tag{6.4.4}$$

$$\vdash_B^* ((q',s',x,y),w',\beta'), \tag{6.4.5}$$

where $u=u_1u_2$.

In line (6.4.3), only moves of Type 2 and Type 3 are used and $\lg(v')=n$. Thus, by the induction hypothesis,

$$s_1 = s, \qquad w = v'w_1, \qquad \text{and} \qquad (q,u_1,\beta Z) \vdash_A^* (q_1,\Lambda,\beta_1Z_1).$$

Move (6.4.4) is a Type-3 move and thus,

$$q_2 = q_1, \qquad s_2 = s_1, \qquad w_1 = aw_2, \qquad \beta_2Z_2 = \beta_1Z_1.$$

Finally, (6.4.5) consists of only moves of Type 2. Again applying Claim 2 gives

$$s' = s_2, \qquad w' = w_2, \qquad (q_2,u_2,\beta_2Z_2) \vdash_A^* (q',\Lambda,\beta').$$

Combining these results gives

$$s' = s, \qquad w = v'aw' = vw$$

and

$$(q,u_1u_2,\beta Z) \vdash_A^* (q_2,u_2,\beta_2Z_2) \vdash_A^* (q',\Lambda,\beta'),$$

proving this direction of Claim 3.

Conversely, it suffices to prove that, for all $q \in Q_1$, $s \in Q_2$, $u \in \Delta_m$, $\lg(u) < m$, if $w = vw'$, then:

$$((q,s,u,vy),w,\beta Z) \vdash_B^* ((q,s,u,y),w',\beta Z).$$

This is a straightforward proof by induction on $\lg(v)$. Then the desired result follows directly from Claim 2.

Claim 4 For each $q,q' \in Q_1$, $s,s' \in Q_2$, $w,y \in \Delta^*$, $\beta \in \Gamma^*$, $\beta' \in \Gamma^+$, and $Z \in \Gamma$,

$$((q,s,\Lambda,\Lambda),wy,\beta Z) \vdash_B^+ ((q',s',\Lambda,\Lambda),y,\beta'),$$

using $k \geq 1$ moves of Type 1 if and only if there exist $w_1,\ldots,w_k$ in Δ^*, there exist $s_0,\ldots,s_k$ in Q_2, there exist $u_1,\ldots,u_k$ in Σ^* such that

$$w = w_1 \cdots w_k,$$

$$s_0 = s, \qquad s_k = s',$$

$$(s_i,u_{i+1},w_{i+1},s_{i+1}) \in \delta_2, \qquad 0 \leq i \leq k,$$

$$(q,u_1\cdots u_k,\beta Z) \vdash_A^* (q',\Lambda,\beta').$$

Proof The argument in the *only if* direction is an induction on k.

Basis. $k=1$. If

$$((q,s,\Lambda,\Lambda),wy,\beta Z) \vdash_B^+ ((q',s',\Lambda,\Lambda),y,\beta'),$$

using only one move of Type 1, then the computation must be of the form:

$$((q, s, \Lambda, \Lambda), wy, \beta Z) \vdash_B^* ((q_1, s_1, \Lambda, \Lambda), x_1, \beta_1 Z_1) \quad (6.4.6)$$

$$\vdash_B ((q_2, s_2, u, v), x_2, \beta_2 Z_2) \quad (6.4.7)$$

$$\vdash_B^* ((q', s', \Lambda, \Lambda), y, \beta'), \quad (6.4.8)$$

where $s_1, s_2 \in Q_2, x_1, x_2 \in \Delta^*$.

The computation (6.4.6) has only Type-2 moves, since no Type-3 moves are possible when the output buffer is empty. By Claim 2.

$$s_1 = s, \qquad x_1 = wy,$$

and

$$(q, \Lambda, \beta Z) \vdash_A^* (q_1, \Lambda, \beta_1 Z_1).$$

Now (6.4.7) is the single Type-1 move, and hence, by Claim 1,

$$q_2 = q_1, \qquad x_2 = x_1, \qquad \beta_2 Z_2 = \beta_1 Z_1,$$

$$(s_1, u, v, s_2) \in \delta_2.$$

Finally, (6.4.8) has no Type-1 moves and thus, by Claim 3,

$$s' = s_2, \qquad x_2 = vy,$$

$$(q_2, u, \beta_2 Z_2) \vdash_A^* (q', \Lambda, \beta').$$

Combining these results gives

$$v = w, \qquad s_1 = s, \qquad s_2 = s',$$

$$(s, u, w, s') \in \delta_2,$$

$$(q, u, \beta Z) \vdash_A^* (q_1, u, \beta_1 Z_1) \vdash_A^* (q', \Lambda, \beta').$$

Thus, by taking

$$s_0 = s, \qquad s_1 = s', \qquad u_1 = u, \qquad \text{and} \qquad w_1 = w,$$

we will have proved the basis.

Induction step. Assume that the *only if* direction of the claim holds for a computation with $k \geqslant 1$ moves of Type 1. Let

$$((q, s, \Lambda, \Lambda), wy, \beta Z) \vdash_B^+ ((q', s', \Lambda, \Lambda), y, \beta'),$$

with $k + 1$ moves of Type 1. Then

$$((q, s, \Lambda, \Lambda), w'w''y, \beta Z) \vdash_B^+ ((q_1, r_1, \Lambda, \Lambda), w''y, \beta_1 Z_1) \quad (6.4.9)$$

$$\vdash_B^+ ((q', s', \Lambda, \Lambda), y, \beta'), \quad (6.4.10)$$

where $w = w'w''$ and (6.4.9) uses only k moves of Type 1. Such a "factorization" of the computation must exist since the last move of Type 1 cannot be made unless both the input and output buffers are empty.

Thus the induction hypothesis applies to (6.4.9) and there exist

$$w_1, \ldots, w_k \text{ in } \Delta^*, s_0, \ldots, s_k \text{ in } Q_2, u_1, \ldots, u_k \text{ in } \Sigma^*,$$

such that

$$w' = w_1 \cdots w_k,$$

$$s_0 = s, \qquad s_k = r_1,$$

$$(s_i, u_{i+1}, w_{i+1}, s_{i+1}) \in \delta_2, \qquad 0 \leqslant i < k,$$

$$(q, u_1 \cdots u_k, \beta Z) \overset{*}{\underset{A}{\vdash}} (q_1, \Lambda, \beta_1 Z_1).$$

But (6.4.10) uses only one move of Type 1 and thus, by the basis of the induction, there is some $u \in \Sigma^*$ such that

$$(r_1, u, w'', s') \in \delta_2$$

and

$$(q_1, u, \beta_1 Z_1) \overset{*}{\underset{A}{\vdash}} (q', \Lambda, \beta').$$

Therefore, if we let

$$s_{k+1} = s', \qquad w_{k+1} = w'', \qquad u_{k+1} = u,$$

we will have

$$w = w'w'' = w_1 \cdots w_{k+1},$$

$$s_0 = s, \qquad s_{k+1} = s',$$

$$(s_i, u_{i+1}, w_{i+1}, s_{i+1}) \in \delta_2, \qquad 0 \leqslant i < k+1,$$

$$(q, u_1 \cdots u_k u_{k+1}, \beta Z) \overset{*}{\underset{A}{\vdash}} (q_1, u_{k+1}, \beta_1 Z_1)$$

$$\overset{*}{\underset{A}{\vdash}} (q', \Lambda, \beta'),$$

which completes the proof of the necessity of Claim 4.

Using Claims 1, 2, and 3, the proof of the converse is straightforward and is left as an exercise.

Now, taking

$$q = q_0, \qquad s = s_0, \qquad \beta = y = \Lambda, \qquad Z = Z_0$$

in Claim 4 gives

$$((q_0, s_0, \Lambda, \Lambda), w, Z_0) \overset{+}{\underset{B}{\vdash}} ((q', s', \Lambda, \Lambda), \Lambda, \beta')$$

if and only if there exist $w_1, \ldots, w_k$ in $\Delta^*, s_0, \ldots, s_k$ in Q_2, $u_1, \ldots, u_k$ in Σ^* such that

$$w = w_1 \cdots w_k,$$

$$s_0 = s_0, \qquad s_k = s',$$

$$(s_i, u_{i+1}, w_{i+1}, s_{i+1}) \in \delta_2 \quad \text{for } 0 \leqslant i < k.$$

$$(q_0, u_1 \cdots u_k, Z_0) \overset{*}{\underset{A}{\vdash}} (q', \Lambda, \beta').$$

Thus, $w \in T(B)$ if and only if $w \in S(L)$, which proves the theorem for context-free languages.

For regular sets, it suffices to note that exactly the same construction works without using the pushdown store. In this case, B will be a nondeterministic finite automaton but $T(B)$ is still a regular set. □

PROBLEMS

1 Give a formal proof of the *if* direction in the proof of Claims 2 and 3 in the proof of Theorem 6.4.3.

2 Show that, for each sequential transducer $S = (Q, \Sigma, \Delta, \delta, q_0)$, there is a sequential transducer $S' = (Q', \Sigma, \Delta, \delta', q_0')$ such that $\delta' \subseteq Q' \times \Sigma_\Lambda \times \Delta^* \times Q'$ and $S(u) = S'(u)$ for all $u \in \Sigma^*$.

It is often useful to discuss *a-transducers* or *accepting transducers.* The idea is to define $S = (Q, \Sigma, \Delta, \delta, q_0, F)$, where $F \subseteq Q$ and the rest is as usual in a sequential transducer. We change the definition to define $S(w)$ as before, except that the computation must end in a final state.

3 Show that, if S is an a-transducer and L is a context-free language, then $S(L)$ is a context-free language.

4 Show that if L is a linear context-free language and S is a sequential transducer, then $S(L)$ is a linear context-free language.

5 Extend the previous problem to the case where L is metalinear. Cf. Problem 4 of Section 2.5 for the definition of metalinear.

6 Give a context-free grammar proof of the sequential-transducer theorem.

7 Let G be the following linear grammar:

$$S \rightarrow aSa \mid bSb \mid dSa \mid dSb \mid dS \mid c$$

Describe $L(G)$ and show that the complement of $L(G)$ is not context-free.

8 Let $L_1, L_2 \subseteq \Sigma^*$, and define the set of *shuffles* of L_1 and L_2 as

$$\text{shuf}(L_1, L_2) = \{x_1y_1 \cdots x_ky_k \mid k \geq 1, x_1 \cdots x_k \in L_1, y_1 \cdots y_k \in L_2, \quad x_i, y_j \in \Sigma^*\}.$$

Show that

$$\text{shuf}(L_1 \cup L_2, L_1' \cup L_2') = \bigcup_{i,j \in \{1, 2\}} \text{shuf}(L_i, L_j').$$

Prove or disprove:

$$\text{shuf}(L_1, L_2) = \text{shuf}(L_2, L_1).$$

9 Show that, if L is context-free (regular) and R is regular, then

$$\text{shuf}(L, R)$$

is context-free (regular).

10 Find two context-free languages L_1 and L_2 such that $\text{shuf}(L_1, L_2)$ is not context-free. Make L_1 and L_2 as "simple" as possible.

6.5 APPLICATIONS OF THE SEQUENTIAL-TRANSDUCER THEOREM

Using the sequential-transducer theorem from the previous section, we can obtain further closure properties of context-free languages. We first define a restricted form of the sequential transducer which is sufficiently powerful for many applications.

Definition A *generalized sequential machine* (*gsm*) is a 6-tuple

$$S = (Q, \Sigma, \Delta, \delta, \lambda, q_0)$$

where

Q is a finite nonempty set of *states*,

Σ is a finite nonempty *input alphabet*,

Δ is a finite nonempty *output alphabet*,

$q_0 \in Q$ is the *start state*,

$\delta : Q \times \Sigma \to Q$ is the *transition function*, and

$\lambda : Q \times \Sigma \to \Delta^*$ is the *output function.*

The functions δ and λ are extended to Σ^* in the usual way, namely: For each $q \in Q, x \in \Sigma^*, a \in \Sigma$,

$$\delta(q, \Lambda) = q,$$

$$\delta(q, ax) = \delta(\delta(q, a), x),$$

$$\lambda(q, \Lambda) = \Lambda,$$

$$\lambda(q, ax) = \lambda(q, a)\lambda(\delta(q, a), x).$$

The definition of a gsm is not standardized in the literature. One must exercise care because some authors define this device with final states.

The gsm can be thought of as a sequential machine with not necessarily length-preserving outputs. Although many of the results for sequential machines carry over to gsm's, some do not. For instance, given two sequential machines M_1 and M_2, then it is decidable whether or not there is an $x \in \Sigma^+$ such that $M_1(x) = M_2(x)$ (where $M(x)$ designates the response of M to input x). If M_1 and M_2 are gsm's, then this is no longer the case.

Also, every homomorphism can be represented by a one-state gsm.

Definition Let $L \subseteq \Sigma^*$ and let S be a gsm. We define two sets

$$S(L) = \{S(x) \mid x \in L\},$$

and

$$S^{-1}(L) = \{x \mid S(x) \in L\}.$$

Theorem 6.5.1 If L is a context-free language (regular set) and S is a generalized sequential machine, then $S(L)$ is a context-free language (regular set).

Proof Let

$$S = (Q, \Sigma, \Delta, \delta, q_0)$$

be a gsm. Define a sequential transducer

$$S' = (Q, \Sigma, \Delta, \delta', q_0),$$

where

$$\delta' = \{(q, a, \lambda(q, a), \delta(q, a)) \mid \text{for each } (q, a) \in Q \times \Sigma\} \cup \{(q_0, \Lambda, \Lambda, q_0)\}.$$

Claim $S(L) = S'(L)$.

Proof By induction on the length of the input. The argument is left as an exercise.

Thus, by the sequential-transducer theorem, we have completed the proof. □

Corollary If L is a context-free language (regular set) and φ is a homomorphism, then $\varphi(L)$ is a context-free language (regular set).

Example Let

$$L = \{a^*bc\} \cup \{a^p ba^n ca^n \mid p \text{ prime}, n \geqslant 0\}.$$

L is the noncontext-free set used in Theorem 6.2.4 to distinguish between the iteration theorem and the pumping lemma. Now an elegant proof that L is not context-free will be given.

Suppose that L were context-free. Then

$$L_1 = L - \{a^*bc\}$$

would be context-free. Define the gsm S by:

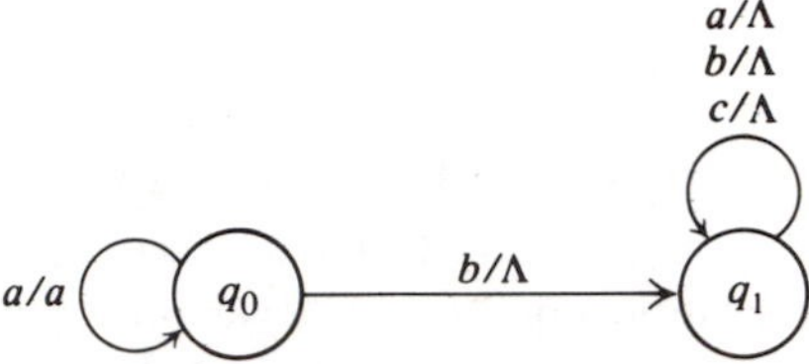

Then

$$S(L_1) = \{a^p \mid p \text{ prime}\}$$

would be a context-free language. This is a contradiction of Theorem 6.3.1, and shows L to be noncontext-free.

Now, let us consider inverse gsm mappings.

Theorem 6.5.2 If L is a context-free language (regular set) and S is a gsm mapping, then $S^{-1}(L)$ is a context-free language (regular set).

Proof Let

$$S = (Q, \Sigma, \Delta, \delta, \lambda, q_0).$$

Define a sequential transducer

$$S' = (Q, \Delta, \Sigma, \delta', q_0),$$

where

$$\delta' = \{(q, \lambda(q,a), a, \delta(q,a)) \mid (q,a) \in Q \times \Sigma\} \cup \{(q_0, \Lambda, \Lambda, q_0)\}.$$

Claim $S'(L) = S^{-1}(L)$.

Proof By induction. The argument is left as an exercise.

Thus, again applying the sequential-transducer theorem, we have the desired result. □

Corollary If $L \subseteq \Delta^*$ is a context-free language (regular set) and $\varphi: \Sigma^* \to \Delta^*$ is a homomorphism, then $\varphi^{-1}(L)$ is a context-free language (regular set).

It turns out that the family of context-free languages is not closed under S^{-1} if S is a sequential transducer.

Theorem 6.5.3 There is a deterministic context-free language L and a sequential transducer S such that $S^{-1}(L)$ is not context-free. The family of context-free languages is not closed under inverse sequential transducer mappings.

Proof Let S be the following sequential transducer.

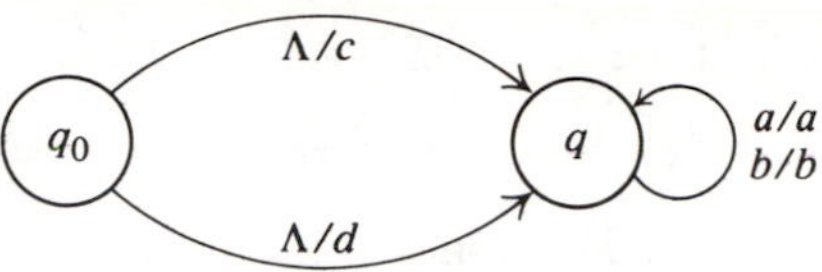

Then, for all $w \in \{a, b\}^*$,

$$S(w) = \{cw, dw\}.$$

Now let

$$L = \{ca^ib^ja^j \mid i,j \geqslant 1\} \cup \{da^ib^ia^j \mid i,j \geqslant 1\}.$$

Clearly, L is a deterministic context-free language. But

$$\begin{aligned} S^{-1}(L) &= \{w \mid S(w) \subseteq L\} \\ &= \{w \mid dw \in L \quad \text{and} \quad cw \in L\} \\ &= \{a^ib^ja^k \mid i = j \text{ and } j = k\} \\ &= \{a^nb^na^n \mid n \geqslant 1\} \end{aligned}$$

is not context-free. □

Next we turn to a set-theoretic operation on sets.

Definition Let $X, Y \subseteq \Sigma^*$. Define

$$X^{-1}Y = \{w \in \Sigma^* \mid xw \in Y \quad \text{for some } x \in X\},$$

$$YX^{-1} = \{w \in \Sigma^* \mid wx \in Y \quad \text{for some } x \in X\}.$$

YX^{-1} ($X^{-1}Y$) is the *right* (*left*) *quotient* of Y by X.

We now prove that context-free languages are closed under right quotient with regular sets. The proof is interesting since it is based only on the closure properties of context-free languages and hence would apply to any family of languages that satisfy the necessary closure properties.

Theorem 6.5.4 If L is a context-free language and R is a regular set, then LR^{-1} is a context-free language.

Proof Let $L, R \subseteq \Sigma^*$ and $c \notin \Sigma$. Let

$$S = (\{q_0, q_1\}, \Sigma \cup \{c\}, \Sigma, \delta, q_0),$$

where

$$\delta = \{(q_0, a, a, q_0) \mid a \in \Sigma\} \cup \{(q_0, c, \Lambda, q_1)\} \cup \{(q_1, a, \Lambda, q_1) \mid a \in \Sigma \cup \{c\}\}.$$

Graphically, S is given by:

a/a (q_0) —c/Λ→ (q_1) a/Λ, c/Λ

a denotes any letter in Σ

It is easily seen that, for each $x \in \Sigma^*, y \in (\Sigma \cup \{c\})^*$,

$$S(x) = x, \qquad S(xcy) = x.$$

Now let φ: $(\Sigma \cup \{c\})^* \to \Sigma^*$ be the homomorphism given by

$$\varphi(a) = \begin{cases} a, & a \in \Sigma, \\ \Lambda, & a = c. \end{cases}$$

Claim $S(\varphi^{-1}(L) \cap \Sigma^* cR)$ is context-free.

Proof

i) $\Sigma^* cR$ is regular.

ii) Since φ is a homomorphism, φ^{-1} is an inverse homomorphism. Thus $\varphi^{-1}(L)$ is context-free.

iii) $\varphi^{-1}(L) \cap \Sigma^* cR$ is context-free, since the intersection of a context-free language with a regular set is context-free.

iv) $S(\varphi^{-1}(L) \cap \Sigma^* cR)$ is context-free, by the sequential-transducer theorem.

Claim $LR^{-1} = S(\varphi^{-1}(L) \cap \Sigma^* cR)$.

Proof $x \in S(\varphi^{-1}(L) \cap \Sigma^* cR)$ if and only if there is $y \in \Sigma^*$ so that

$$xcy \in \varphi^{-1}(L) \cap \Sigma^* cR.$$

This holds if and only if there is $y \in \Sigma^*$ such that

$$xcy \in \varphi^{-1}(L) \qquad \text{and} \qquad y \in R.$$

But this holds if and only if there is $y \in \Sigma^*$ such that

$$y \in R \qquad \text{and} \qquad \varphi(xcy) = xy \in L \qquad \text{and} \qquad y \in R;$$

i.e., if and only if

$$x \in LR^{-1}.$$ □

Corollary If L is a context-free language and R a regular set, then $R^{-1}L$ is a context-free language.

Proof

$$R^{-1}L = (L^T(R^T)^{-1})^T,$$

and both regular sets and context-free languages are closed under reversal.

Corollary If L is a context-free language, then

a) $\text{init}(L) = \{u \mid uv \in L \quad \text{for some } v \in \Sigma^*\}$,

b) $\text{fin}(L) = \{u \mid vu \in L \quad \text{for some } v \in \Sigma^*\}$, and

c) $\text{subwords}(L) = \{v \mid uvw \in L \quad \text{for some } u, w \in \Sigma^*\}$

are context-free languages.

Proof

a) $\text{init}(L) = L(\Sigma^*)^{-1}$,

b) $\text{fin}(L) = (\Sigma^*)^{-1}L$,

c) $\text{subwords}(L) = \text{fin}(\text{init}(L))$. □

Now we shall show that the full family of context-free languages is not closed under quotient.

Theorem 6.5.5 There exist two deterministic context-free languages L_1 and L_2 such that $L_1^{-1}L_2$ is not a context-free language.

Proof Let

$$L_1 = a\{b^i a^i \mid i \geq 1\}^*$$

and

$$L_2 = \{a^i b^{2i} \mid i \geq 1\}^*.$$

Clearly, L_1 and L_2 are deterministic context-free languages, and

$$L_1^{-1}L_2 = \{w \mid yw \in L_2 \quad \text{for some } y \in L_1\}.$$

Now

$$w \in L_1^{-1}L_2 \tag{6.5.1}$$

if and only if there exist $k > \ell \geq 0, i_1, \ldots, i_k \geq 1, j_1, \ldots, j_\ell \geq 1$ such that

$$yw = a^{i_1}b^{2i_1}a^{i_2}b^{2i_2}\cdots a^{i_k}b^{2i_k} \tag{6.5.2}$$

and

$$y = ab^{j_1}a^{j_1}b^{j_2}a^{j_2}\cdots b^{j_\ell}a^{j_\ell}. \tag{6.5.3}$$

In turn this holds if and only if there exist $k > \ell \geq 0, i_1, \ldots, i_k \geq 1, j_1, \ldots, j_\ell \geq 1$, such that

$$j_r = 2^r \quad \text{for each } \ell \geq r \geq 1, \tag{6.5.4}$$

and

$$i_r = 2^{r-1} \quad \text{for each } \ell \geq r \geq 1. \tag{6.5.5}$$

It now follows easily from these propositions that

$$(L_1^{-1}L_2) \cap b^+ = \{b^{2^m} \mid m \geq 1\}.$$

If $L_1^{-1}L_2$ were context-free, then, by Theorem 6.4.1, $\{b^{2^m} \mid m \geq 1\}$ would be regular; but that would contradict Theorem 6.3.1. The result about right quotient follows from the identity.

$$L_1L_2^{-1} = (L_2^T(L_1^T)^{-1})^T. \qquad \square$$

We shall later see that Theorem 6.5.5 is a trivially weak result. Actually any recursively enumerable set may be obtained as the quotient of two context-free languages.

PROBLEMS

1 Show that, if $L \subseteq \Delta^*$ is a deterministic context-free language and S is a gsm, then $S^{-1}(L)$ is also a deterministic context-free language. Hence, the deterministic context-free languages are closed under inverse gsm mappings.

2 Let $L \subseteq \Delta^*$ and let $S = \{Q, \Sigma, \Delta, \delta, q_0)$ be a sequential transducer. By definition, $S^{-1}(L) = \{w \mid S(w) \subseteq L\}$ and it has been shown that $\mathscr{C}$ is not closed under S^{-1}. Suppose we had defined S^{-1} by the following relationship:

$$S^{-1}(L) = \{w \in \Sigma^* \mid S(w) \cap L \neq \emptyset\}.$$

Is $\mathscr{C}$ now closed under S^{-1}?

3 Let $X, Y, Z \subseteq \Sigma^*$. Show that:

a) $(XZ^{-1})Y^{-1} = X(YZ)^{-1}$,

b) $(X^{-1}Y)Z^{-1} = X^{-1}(YZ^{-1})$,

c) $(XY)^{-1}Z = Y^{-1}(X^{-1}Z)$.

Now we consider a-transducers, which were defined in the problems at the end of Section 6.4.

Definition An a-transducer $S = (Q, \Sigma, \Delta, \delta, q_0, F)$ is *1-bounded* if

$$\delta \subseteq Q \times (\Sigma \cup \{\Lambda\}) \times (\Delta \cup \{\Lambda\}) \times Q.$$

4 Show that, for each a-transducer $S = (Q, \Sigma, \Delta, \delta, q_0, F)$, there is a 1-bounded a-transducer $S' = (Q', \Sigma, \Delta, \delta', q_0, F)$, such that

$$S'(w) = S(w) \qquad \text{for each } w \in \Sigma^*.$$

Let $S = (Q, \Sigma, \Delta, \delta, q_0, F)$ be an a-transducer and let λ be any function from F into subsets of Σ^*. Define:

$$S(\lambda) = \{u_1 \cdots u_r \lambda(q_r) v_r \cdots v_1 \mid \text{There exist } r \geq 0, q_1, \ldots, q_r, q_r \in F, \text{ such that } (q_i, u_{i+1}, v_{i+1}, q_{i+1}) \in \delta \quad \text{for } 0 \leq i < r\}.$$

5 Show the following useful result.

Lemma Let $S = (Q, \Sigma, \Delta, \delta, q_0, F)$ be an a-transducer. If for each $q \in F$, $\lambda(q)$ is a context-free language, then $S(\lambda)$ is also context-free. Moreover, if each $\lambda(q)$ is ultralinear, then so is $S(\lambda)$.

6 Show that the class of ultralinear languages is the least family which contains the finite sets and is closed under finitely many applications of union, product, and $S(\lambda)$ (where the image of $S(\lambda)$ is contained in the family).

7 Show that a set L is ultralinear if and only if there is a finite-turn pda A such that $L = N(A)$.

8 Show that L is linear if and only if L is accepted by a 1-turn pda.

Let Σ and Δ be two alphabets and let R_1, R_2 be subsets of $\Sigma^* \times \Delta^*$. Define

$$R_1 R_2 = \{(x_1 x_2, y_1 y_2) \mid (x_1, y_1) \in R_1, (x_2, y_2) \in R_2\}.$$

Define

$$R^0 = \{(\Lambda, \Lambda)\},$$

and, for each $k \geqslant 0$, define

$$R^{k+1} = R^k R.$$

Then write

$$R^* = \bigcup_{i=0}^{\infty} R^i.$$

A relation R is said to be *regular* if R is obtained from the set

$$\{(a, \Lambda), (\Lambda, b) | \; a \in \Sigma, b \in \Delta\}$$

by finitely many applications of $\cup$, $\cdot$, and *. Also define a *transduction* to be any mapping from Σ^* into Δ^*, but we shall write it as a relation.

9 Prove the following important theorem.

Theorem (*Nivat*) A transduction from Σ^* into Δ^* is regular if and only if there exists an alphabet Γ, a regular set $R \subseteq \Gamma^*$, a homomorphism φ from Γ^* into Σ^*, a homomorphism ψ from Γ^* into Δ^*, such that, for each $x \in \Sigma^*$,

$$\tau x = \psi(\varphi^{-1}(x) \cap R).$$

Let Σ and Δ be alphabets and let the members of Σ be interpreted as *elementary messages.* The *coding problem* is to find suitable mappings φ from Σ^+ into Δ^* so that right inverses exist, i.e., so that $\varphi\varphi^{-1} = 1$. For our purposes, define an encoding as any one-to-one homomorphism from Σ^+ into Δ^+. Define

$$A_0 = \varphi(\Sigma)$$

and

$$A = \varphi(\Sigma^+).$$

A_0 is called the set of all code words or just the *code*, while A is the set of all *encoded messages.*

Recall that a semigroup S is *freely generated* by a set S_0 if every element of S has a unique representation as a product of elements of S_0. S is *free* if there is a set S_0 which freely generates S.

10 Show that

a) $A = A_0^+$

b) A is a free semigroup of Δ^+ generated by A_0.

11 Show that, if A is an arbitrary free semigroup of Δ^+, then there exists a set Σ, and an encoding φ: $\Sigma^+ \to \Delta^+$ such that $A = \varphi(\Sigma^+)$.

Let S be any semigroup and $A, B \subseteq S$. Define

$$A^{-1}B = \{s \in S | \; as \in B \quad \text{for some } a \in A\}$$

and

$$AB^{-1} = \{s \in S | \; sa \in B \quad \text{for some } a \in A\}.$$

For Problems 12 through 14, let $A_0 \subseteq \Delta^+$ and $A = (A_0)^+$. Define

$$A_1 = A_0^{-1} A_0$$

and

$$A_{n+1} = A_0^{-1} A_n \cup A_n^{-1} A_0$$

for each $n \geqslant 0$.

12 Show that A is freely generated by A_0 if and only if, for each $n \geqslant 1$,

$$A_n \cap A_0 = \emptyset.$$

13 Show that, if $A_n = A_{n+k}$ for some $n, k \geqslant 1$, then

$$A_{n+jk+r} = A_{n+r}$$

for all $j \geqslant 0$ and all $r, 0 \leqslant r < k$.

14 Show that, if A_0 is finite, then there exists a natural number N_0 such that, for all $n > N_0$, there exists $m \leqslant N_0$ such that

$$A_n = A_m.$$

15 Show that there is an algorithm for deciding whether a regular set is a code. Does your method work for context-free sets?

6.6* PARTIAL ORDERS ON Σ^*

By introducing partial orders on Σ^*, some surprising properties will be derived. The methods of this section will be nonconstructive and the reader should watch for the occurrence of such techniques.

In Chapter 1, we studied various partial orders on Σ^*. For example, we might write $x \leqslant_1 y$ if and only if $y = y_1 x y_2$, which is the familiar relation "x is a subword of y." $(\Sigma^*, \leqslant_1)$ is a partially ordered set.

Recall that, in any partially ordered set $(S, \leqslant)$, x and y are said to be *incomparable* if $x \nleqslant y$ and $y \nleqslant x$.

Example 1 The set $\{ab^n a \mid n \geqslant 1\}$ is an infinite set of pairwise incomparable elements of the partially ordered set $(\Sigma^*, \leqslant_1)$.

Next we shall consider another partial ordering, namely that of subsequences.

Definition Let x and y be in Σ^*. We write $x \leqslant y$ if $x = x_1 \cdots x_n$ and $y = y_1 x_1 \cdots y_n x_n y_{n+1}$ for some $n \geqslant 0, x_i, y_j \in \Sigma^*$, where $1 \leqslant i \leqslant n$ and $1 \leqslant j \leqslant n+1$.

Lemma 6.6.1 $(\Sigma^*, \leqslant)$ is a partially ordered set.

Proof It is clear that $\leqslant$ is reflexive and transitive. To prove the antisymmetric property, assume that $x \leqslant y$, which implies that

$$x = x_1 \cdots x_n,$$

and

$$y = y_1 x_1 \cdots y_n x_n y_{n+1}, \tag{6.6.1}$$

and hence that

$$\lg(y) = \lg(x) + \lg(y_1 \cdots y_{n+1}) \tag{6.6.2}$$

and, *a fortiori*,

$$\lg(y) \geqslant \lg(x). \tag{6.6.3}$$

Also assume that $y \leqslant x$, so that

$$y = y_1' \cdots y_k',$$

$$x = x_1' y_1' \cdots x_k' y_k' x_{k+1}',$$

and hence that

$$\lg(x) = \lg(y) + \lg(x_1' \cdots x_{k+1}'),$$

and, *a fortiori*,

$$\lg(x) \geqslant \lg(y). \tag{6.6.4}$$

But (6.6.3) and (6.6.4) imply $\lg(x) = \lg(y)$, which implies (using (6.6.2)) that

$$\lg(y_1 \cdots y_{n+1}) = 0,$$

so that $y_1 \cdots y_{n+1} = \Lambda$, and, by (6.6.1), $y = x$.

The following observation will also turn out to be useful.

Fact 1 For each $u \in \Sigma^*$, there are only finitely many $x \in \Sigma^*$ such that $x \leqslant u$.

Next we consider a lemma which will be applied in our main theorem.

Lemma 6.6.2 If Σ is an alphabet which has the property that every set of pairwise incomparable elements of Σ^* is finite, then every infinite subset of Σ^* has an infinite chain.

Proof Let L be an infinite subset of Σ^* and suppose that every chain in L is finite. Consider the set X of maximum elements of maximal chains. If $x, y \in X$, then x and y are incomparable. By assumption X is finite and $|X| =$ the number of maximal elements of L. But L is infinite, so that infinitely many distinct chains have the same maximal element u. But we then have $x \leqslant u$ for infinitely many x, which contradicts Fact 1. □

We are now ready to prove an important result.

Theorem 6.6.2 Every set of pairwise incomparable elements of $(\Sigma^*, \leqslant)$ is finite.

Proof We induct on $|\Sigma|$.

Basis. $|\Sigma| = 1$. The result is trivial.

Induction step. Suppose the result holds for all alphabets Δ with $|\Delta| = n$. Let $|\Sigma| = n + 1$, and let $Y = \{y_1, y_2, \ldots\}$ be an infinite set of pairwise incomparable elements.

Claim 1 There is $x \in \Sigma^*$ such that $x \nleqslant y_i$ for all i.

Proof Suppose the contrary; i.e., that for each $x \in \Sigma^*$, there is an i so that $x \leqslant y_i$. Consider a string $x = y_1 a$, where $a \in \Sigma^*$. Then $x \nleqslant y_1$ so there must be some $j > 1$ so that $y_1 a = x \leqslant y_j$. But then $y_1 \leqslant x \leqslant y_j$, which contradicts the incomparability of y_1 and y_j.

We may assume there is a shortest x which satisfies Claim 1. Among all infinite sets of pairwise incomparable elements, suppose that Y is chosen so that x has minimum length.

Let

$$x = x_1 \cdots x_k,$$

where $x_j \in \Sigma$ for $1 \leqslant j \leqslant k$. Note that $k \neq 0$, for then x would be null and $\Lambda = x \leqslant y_i$ for all i. If $k = 1$, then $y_i \in (\Sigma - \{x_1\})^*$ for all $i \geqslant 1$ [by the incomparability condition]. But this would contradict the induction hypothesis for $\Sigma - \{x_1\}$.

Claim 2 $x_1 \cdots x_{k-1} \leqslant y_i$ for all but finitely many i.

Proof Suppose $x_1 \cdots x_{k-1} \nleqslant y_j$ for infinitely many j, say $j_1, \ldots$ Define

$$Y_0 = \{y_{j_1}, y_{j_2}, \ldots \mid y_{j_i} \in Y \quad \text{and} \quad x_1 \cdots x_{k-1} \nleqslant y_{j_i}\}.$$

Then Y_0 is an infinite set of pairwise incomparable elements which has a string $x' = x_1 \cdots x_{k-1}$ satisfying Claim 1, where $\lg(x') < \lg(x)$, and that would be a contradiction, since x was chosen to be minimal.

By relabeling subscripts of the y_i, we may assume that

$$x_1 \cdots x_{k-1} \leqslant y_i \qquad \text{for all } i \geqslant \ell.$$

Moreover, for each $i \geqslant \ell$, there exist unique words, $y_{i1}, \ldots, y_{ik}$ such that

$$y_i = y_{i1} x_1 y_{i2} x_2 \cdots y_{ik-1} x_{k-1} y_{ik}$$

and $x_j \nleqslant y_{ij}$ for all $1 \leqslant j < k$; that is, $y_{ij} \in (\Sigma - \{x_j\})^*$. Moreover, we have $x_k \nleqslant y_{ik}$ for all $i \geqslant \ell$. [Suppose $x_k \leqslant y_{ik}$ for some $i \geqslant \ell$; then $x_1 \cdots x_k = x \leqslant y_i$ which would contradict our choice of x.]

Claim 3 There exist infinite index sets $N_1, \ldots, N_k$ such that

a) $N_{j+1} \subseteq N_j$ for $1 \leqslant j < k$.

b) If $p, q \in N_j$ for some j, $1 \leqslant j \leqslant k$ and $p < q$, then $y_{pj} \leqslant y_{qj}$.

Proof Let $N_0 = \{i \mid i \geqslant \ell\}$. The existence of N_j will follow from the existence of the N_{j-1} for $1 \leqslant j \leqslant k$. Let

$$Y_j = \{y_{ij} \mid i \in N_{j-1}\} \qquad \text{for } 1 \leqslant j \leqslant k. \tag{6.6.5}$$

CASE 1. Y_j is finite.

If Y_j is finite, then, since N_{j-1} is infinite, we have that $I_w = \{i \in N_{j-1} \mid y_{ij} = w\}$ for some fixed $w \in \Sigma^*$ must be infinite. In other words, from (6.6.5), as i runs through N_{j-1}, infinitely many of the y_{ij} must be the same. Define N_j to be any such I_w. Clearly, this N_j is infinite and satisfies (a) and (b) since N_{j-1} did.

CASE 2. Y_j is infinite.

In this case, since $Y_j \subseteq (\Sigma - \{x_j\})^*$ the induction hypothesis applies. By Lemma 6.6.2, Y_j has an infinite chain

$$y_{s_1 j} < y_{s_2 j} < \cdots. \tag{6.6.6}$$

Let $t_1, t_2, \ldots$ be an infinite strictly increasing subsequence of $s_1, s_2, \ldots$ and define $N_j = \{t_i | \ i \geqslant 1\}$. Clearly, N_j is infinite and $N_j \subseteq N_{j-1}$. To see (b), suppose $p, q \in N_j$ and $p < q$. By (6.6.6), we know that $y_{pj} \leqslant y_{qj}$. This completes the proof of Claim 3.

If $p < q$ and $p, q \in N_k$, then $p, q \in N_j$ for $1 \leqslant j < k$ so that for each j, $1 \leqslant j \leqslant k$, $y_{pj} \leqslant y_{qj}$. Therefore

$$\begin{aligned} y_p &= y_{p1}x_1y_{p2}x_2 \cdots y_{pk-1}x_{k-1}y_{pk} \\ &\leqslant y_{q1}x_1y_{q2}x_2 \cdots y_{qk-1}x_{k-1}y_{qk} = y_q. \end{aligned}$$

But $y_p \leqslant y_q$ contradicts the definition of Y. □

Corollary (*The König Infinity Lemma*) Each set of pairwise incomparable elements of $(\mathbb{N}^k, \leqslant)$ is finite where $\mathbb{N}$ is the set of natural numbers and $(n_1, \ldots, n_k) \leqslant (n'_1, \ldots, n'_k)$ if $n_i \leqslant n'_i$ for each i, $1 \leqslant i \leqslant$ k.

Proof Consider the mapping φ: $(n_1, \ldots, n_k) \rightarrow a_1^{n_1} \cdots a_k^{n_k}$. φ is an isomorphism. If X is an infinite set of pairwise incomparable elements of $(\mathbb{N}^k, \leqslant)$ then $\varphi(X)$ is an infinite subset of $\{a_1\}^* \cdots \{a_n\}^* \subseteq \{a_1, \ldots, a_n\}^*$. But if u and v are incomparable elements of $\mathbb{N}^k$, then $\varphi(u)$ and $\varphi(v)$ are incomparable elements of $(\{a_1, \ldots, a_n\}^*, \leqslant)$. This contradicts Theorem 6.6.2. □

We introduce the operations of taking subsequences and supersequences of sets.

Definition Let $L \subseteq \Sigma^*$ and $\leqslant$ be the "subsequence" ordering defined at the start of this section. Define

$$\tilde{L} = \{x \in \Sigma^* | \ y \leqslant x \quad \text{for some } y \text{ in } L\}$$

and

$$\underset{\sim}{L} = \{x \in \Sigma^* | \ x \leqslant y \quad \text{for some } y \text{ in } L\}.$$

In words, $\tilde{L}$ is called the set of *supersequences* of L while $\underset{\sim}{L}$ is the set of *subsequences* of L.

Some algebraic identities concerning these sets are listed below.

Lemma 6.6.3 For any $L \subseteq \Sigma^*$,

1 $L \subseteq \tilde{L}$;

2 $L \subseteq \underset{\sim}{L}$;

3 $\underset{\approx}{L} = \underset{\sim}{L}$.

Proof (1) and (2) are immediate from the definitions. For (3), note that $\underset{\sim}{L} \subseteq \underset{\approx}{L}$ by (2). Suppose $x \in \underset{\approx}{L}$. Then $x \leqslant y$ for some $y \in \underset{\sim}{L}$. Again by the definition, $y \leqslant z$ for some $z \in L$. By transitivity, $x \leqslant z$, so that $x \in \underset{\sim}{L}$. □

Before passing to our main results, we need one more definition.

Definition Let $(S, \leqslant)$ be any partially ordered set. $x \in S$ is said to be *minimal* if $y \leqslant x$ and $y \in S$ imply $y = x$.

We recall a trivial fact about minimal elements.

Fact Let $(S, \leqslant)$ be any partially ordered set. If x and y are distinct minimal elements, then x and y are incomparable.

Proof Immediate

Now we are ready to prove a useful lemma.

Lemma 6.6.4 Let $L \subseteq \Sigma^*$.

a) There exists a finite subset $F \subseteq \Sigma^*$ so that $\widetilde{L} = \widetilde{F}$.

b) There exists a finite subset $G \subseteq \Sigma^*$ so that

$$\underset{\sim}{L} = \Sigma^* - \widetilde{G}.$$

Proof a) Let F be the set of minimal elements of L. By the previous fact, the elements of F are pairwise incomparable. By Theorem 6.6.1, F is finite. We must prove that $\widetilde{L} = \widetilde{F}$.

Suppose $x \in \widetilde{F}$. Then $y \leqslant x$ for some $y \in F \subseteq L$. Thus, $x \in \widetilde{L}$ and $\widetilde{F} \subseteq \widetilde{L}$.

Suppose $x \in \widetilde{L}$. Then $y \leqslant x$ for some $y \in L$. There is $y' \in F$ so that $y' \leqslant y \leqslant x$. [If y is minimal, then $y' = y$. If not, the definition of minimality guarantees the existence of y'.] Thus $x \in \widetilde{F}$ and $\widetilde{L} \subseteq \widetilde{F}$. Therefore, $\widetilde{L} = \widetilde{F}$.

b) Let $M = \Sigma^* - \underset{\sim}{L}$.

Claim $M = \widetilde{M}$.

Proof We already know that $M \subseteq \widetilde{M}$. Suppose that $\widetilde{M} \nsubseteq M$; i.e., there is $x \in \widetilde{M}$ and $x \notin M = \Sigma^* - \underset{\sim}{L}$. That is, $x \in \widetilde{M}$ and $x \in \underset{\sim}{L}$. Since $x \in \widetilde{M}$, $x \geqslant y$ for some $y \in M$. Since $x \in \underset{\sim}{L}$ and $x \geqslant y$, we conclude that $y \in \underset{\approx}{L} = \underset{\sim}{L}$. But we have established that $y \in \underset{\sim}{L}$ and $y \in M = \Sigma^* - \underset{\sim}{L}$, which is a contradiction. This completes the proof of the claim.

By part (a) of the Lemma, there is a finite subset G so that $\widetilde{M} = \widetilde{G}$. However,

$$\widetilde{G} = M = \Sigma^* - \underset{\sim}{L} = \widetilde{G},$$

so that

$$\underset{\sim}{L} = \Sigma^* - \widetilde{G}. \qquad \square$$

Now we come to our main result.

Theorem 6.6.3 For any set $L \subseteq \Sigma^*$, $\widetilde{L}$ and $\underset{\sim}{L}$ are regular sets.

Proof For any word, $w \in \Sigma^*$, write

$$w = w_1 \cdots w_n,$$

where $w_i \in \Sigma \cup \{\Lambda\}$ for $1 \leqslant i \leqslant n$. Clearly, $\widetilde{w}$ is regular since $\widetilde{w} = \Sigma^*\{w_1\}\Sigma^* \cdots \Sigma^* \{w_n\}\Sigma^*$. Moreover, for any finite set $W \subseteq \Sigma^*$, $\widetilde{W}$ is regular since

$$\widetilde{W} = \bigcup_{w \in W} \{\widetilde{w}\},$$

and a finite union of regular sets is regular.

Let $L \subseteq \Sigma^*$ and let F and G be as given by the previous lemma. Then

$$\tilde{L} = \tilde{F}$$

is regular by the above remark and

$$\underset{\sim}{L} = \Sigma^* - \tilde{G}$$

is regular since the complement of a regular set is regular. □

This theorem is amazing because there are no constraints on the set L. It might not even be recursive, and still $\underset{\sim}{L}$ and $\tilde{L}$ are regular.

PROBLEMS

Definition Let $k \geqslant 1$ and let $x, y \in \Sigma^*$. We define $x \leqslant_k y$ if $x = x_1 \cdots x_k$ and $y = y_1 x_1 \cdots y_k x_k y_{k+1}$ for some x_i and y_j in Σ^* where $1 \leqslant i \leqslant k$ and $1 \leqslant j \leqslant k+1$. Thus $x \leqslant_k y$ if a factorization of x into k parts occurs in y.

1 Is $(\Sigma^*, \leqslant_k)$ a partially ordered set?

2 Is a constructive proof of Theorem 6.6.3 possible if L is recursively enumerable? If L were context-sensitive, could one construct a right linear grammar for $\underset{\sim}{L}$?

3 Show that no matter how one partitions an infinite n-ary expansion of any real number into blocks of finite length, one block is necessarily a subsequence of another.

6.7 PROGRAMMING LANGUAGES ARE NOT CONTEXT-FREE

Since much of the motivation for studying context-free languages came from programming languages, it is desirable to ask whether existing languages are context-free or not. To understand this question, one must ask "What is a programming language?" Let us take ALGOL as an example because it was one of the earliest languages that was carefully designed. The set of valid ALGOL programs is the set of strings that (i) satisfies the syntactic conditions of ALGOL and (ii) satisfies the semantic conditions. Since the syntax is written in BNF, there is no doubt that the set of strings which satisfy (i) is context-free. The semantic conditions for ALGOL were written in English and it is not immediately clear whether the set of strings which satisfy (i) and (ii) is context-free. Note that there is a distinction between the specification of a language and some implementation restriction of a compiler. In ALGOL, an identifier has unbounded length while, in a particular compiler, the length may be at most 10 characters. Our interest is in the language definition, not a particular implementation.

Theorem 6.7.1 ALGOL 60 is not a context-free language.

Proof Let L be the set of (syntactically and semantically) valid ALGOL 60 programs. If L were context-free, then so would

$$M = L \cap (\{\mathbf{begin}\}\{\mathbf{real}\}\{x\}^*\{;\}\{x\}^*\{:=\}\{x\}^*\{\mathbf{end}\})$$

since it would be the intersection of a context-free language and a regular set. But

$$M = \{\mathbf{begin\ real}\ x^i; x^j := x^k\ \mathbf{end} \mid i = j = k, i \geqslant 1\},$$

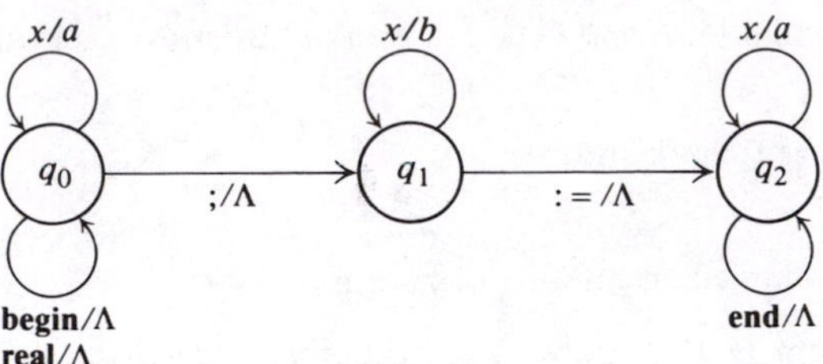

FIG. 6.4

where the condition $i = j = k$ follows from the semantic rule that every variable that occurs in a valid ALGOL program must be previously declared. Also, $i \geqslant 1$, since there is no bound on the length of identifiers in ALGOL. Let S be the gsm shown in Fig. 6.4.

Then $S(M) = \{a^n b^n a^n \mid n \geqslant 1\}$, which is a contradiction since context-free languages are closed under sequential-transducer maps. Thus L is not context-free. □

Now let us turn to another language.

Theorem 6.7.2 FORTRAN, as specified below, is not a context-free language.

Proof Let F be the set of all valid ASA FORTRAN programs with the assumption that there is no bound on the number of continuation cards.

Let R be the following set, where the representation of R is written on separate lines to make it more intuitive.†

$$R = \{ \text{ WRITE (6, 1)}$$

$$1 \text{ FORMAT(1}\}\{0\}^*\{H\}\{X\}^*\{)$$

$$\text{END}\}$$

Clearly, R is a regular set. If F were context-free, then $L = F \cap R$ would be, but we have that

$$L = \{ \text{ WRITE (6, 1)}$$

$$1 \text{ FORMAT(}10^n\text{HX}^{10^n}\text{)}$$

$$\text{END} \mid n \geqslant 0\}$$

Define the homomorphism φ by $\varphi(X) = X$ and $\varphi(a) = \Lambda$ otherwise. Then

$$\varphi(L) = \{x^{10^n} \mid n \geqslant 0\}$$

would be context-free but it isn't. This contradiction establishes that F is not context-free. □

Now we turn to PL/I, which is a descendant of both ALGOL and FORTRAN. The argument used for ALGOL will not work for PL/I, since it is not necessary to

---

† The characters {and} are meta characters not in the FORTRAN character set.

declare every identifier. However, the generality of structures in PL/I allows the number of dimensions of an array to be unbounded.

Theorem 6.7.3 PL/I is not context-free.

Proof Let P be the class of valid PL/I programs and suppose P were context-free. Consider

$$M = P \cap (\{\text{MAH: PROCEDURE OPTIONS (MAIN): DECLARE A(1:4}\}\{,1:4\}^*\{\text{);}$$
$$\text{A(2}\}\{,2\}^*\{\text{)} = \text{A(3}\}\{,3\}^*\{\text{; END MAH;}\})$$

The quantity in parentheses is regular so that M is context-free. Thus

$$\begin{aligned} \text{M} = \{&\text{MAH: PROCEDURE OPTIONS (MAIN);}\\ &\text{DECLARE A(1:4}\{,1:4\}^i\text{);}\\ &\text{A(2}\{,2\}^i\text{)} = \text{A(3}\{,3\}^i\text{);}\\ &\text{END MAH;} \mid i \geq 0\} \end{aligned}$$

This follows because (i) there is no bound on the number of dimensions in PL/I and (ii) each reference to the array must have the same number of indices.

Define a homomorphism φ as follows:

$$\begin{aligned} \varphi 4 &= a\\ \varphi 2 &= b\\ \varphi 3 &= c\\ \varphi x &= \Lambda \qquad \text{in all other cases.} \end{aligned}$$

Clearly, $\varphi M = \{a^j b^j c^j \mid j \geq 1\}$, which would be context-free if P were. This contradiction establishes that PL/I is not context-free. □

PROBLEMS

1 In Theorem 6.7.2, no bound was placed on the number of continuation cards in FORTRAN. Suppose this quantity were bounded. Would FORTRAN be context-free? Explain.

2 Is ALGOL 68 a context-free language?

3 Is PASCAL a context-free language?

4 Is COBOL a context-free language?

6.8* THE PROPER CONTAINMENT OF THE LINEAR CONTEXT-FREE LANGUAGES IN $\mathcal{C}$

The techniques of using closure properties which have been presented in this chapter are of great value. To illustrate this, we return to the case of linear languages and prove a theorem from which it follows that there are context-free languages which are not linear.

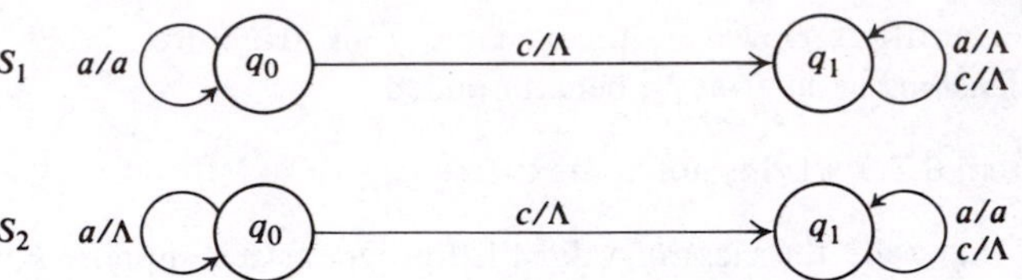

FIG. 6.5 The definition of S_1 and S_2; a denotes any letter of Σ.

Theorem 6.8.1 Let Σ be a finite nonempty set, $c \notin \Sigma$ and $R, X \subseteq \Sigma^*$. If RcX is a linear context-free language, then either R or X is regular.

Proof Let

$$L(G) = RcX = L,$$

where

$$G = (V, \Sigma \cup \{c\}, P, S)$$

is a linear context-free grammar. Assume, without loss of generality, that G is reduced.

Now define two gsm's S_1 and S_2 by Fig. 6.5.

The reader may easily verify that

$$S_1(RcX) = R \qquad S_2(RcX) = X.$$

Now define a set of variables

$$C = \{A \in N | \; A \overset{*}{\Rightarrow} w \quad \text{for some } w \in \Sigma^* c \Sigma^*\}.$$

Since each $w \in L$ contains exactly one c, if $A \overset{*}{\Rightarrow} \alpha \in V^*$, then either

1 α contains no c and at most one variable which belongs to C; or

2 α contains a c and no variables which belong to C.

Now we partition P into four disjoint sets

$$P_0 = \{A \to u | \; u \in \Sigma^*\} \cup \{A \to uBv | \; B \in N, \quad u, v \in \Sigma^*\},$$

$$P_1 = \{A \to ucv | \; u, v \in \Sigma^*\},$$

$$P_2 = \{A \to u_1 c u_2 B v | \; B \in N, u_1, u_2, v \in \Sigma^*\},$$

$$P_3 = \{A \to uBv_1 c v_2 | \; B \in N, u, v_1, v_2 \in \Sigma^*\}.$$

The variables that occur on the righthand side of rules in $P_2 \cup P_3$ are not in C, since, if they were, one could derive a word in L with two c's.

Define three grammars:

$$G_1 = (V, \Sigma \cup \{c\}, P_0 \cup P_1, S),$$

$$G_2 = (V, \Sigma \cup \{c\}, P_0 \cup P_2, S)$$

$$G_3 = (V, \Sigma \cup \{c\}, P_0 \cup P_3, S)$$

and let

$$L_i = L(G_i), \qquad 1 \leqslant i \leqslant 3.$$

Again, using the fact that if $w \in L$, it has exactly one c, we have that every derivation in G uses exactly one rule in $P_1 \cup P_2 \cup P_3$. Thus

$$L = L_1 \cup L_2 \cup L_3.$$

Claim 1 $S_1(L_1), S_1(L_2)$, and $S_2(L_3)$ are regular.

Proof We give a right linear grammar

$$G'_1 = (V, \Sigma, P'_1, S)$$

such that $S_1(L_1) = L(G'_1)$. Let

$$\begin{aligned} P'_1 &= \{A \to u \mid A \to u \text{ is in } P_0 \text{ and } u \in \Sigma^*\} \\ &= \cup \{A \to uB \mid A \to uBv \text{ is in } P_0, B \in N\} \\ &= \cup \{A \to u \mid A \to ucv \text{ is in } P_1\}. \end{aligned}$$

To show that $L(G'_1) = S_1(L_1)$ it suffices to prove:

Claim $S \underset{G_1}{\overset{*}{\Rightarrow}} ucv$ if and only if $S \underset{G'_1}{\overset{*}{\Rightarrow}} u$.

Proof The argument is omitted.

Thus $L(G'_1) = S_1(L_1)$. Since G'_1 is right linear, $L(G'_1)$ is regular and therefore $S_1(L_1)$ is regular.

Similar proofs show that $S_1(L_2)$ and $S_2(L_3)$ are regular, which proves the claim.

Now, since

$$L = RcX = L_1 \cup L_2 \cup L_3,$$

then

$$R = S_1(L) = S_1(L_1) \cup S_1(L_2) \cup S_1(L_3). \tag{6.8.1}$$

Also, since

$$X = S_2(L) = S_2(L_1) \cup S_2(L_2) \cup S_2(L_3),$$

then

$$S_2(L_3) \subseteq X. \tag{6.8.2}$$

It will suffice to prove the next claim because then we will have that R is regular or X is.

Claim 2 Either $R = S_1(L_1) \cup S_1(L_2)$ or $X = S_2(L_3)$.

Proof From (6.8.1) we have

$$S_1(L_1) \cup S_1(L_2) \subseteq R.$$

Now suppose $S_1(L_1) \cup S_1(L_2) \subsetneq R$. Then there exists a w such that

$$w \in R - (S_1(L_1) \cup S_1(L_2)).$$

Since $w \in R$,

$$wcX \subseteq RcX = L. \tag{6.8.3}$$

But

$$wcX \cap (L_1 \cup L_2) = \emptyset, \tag{6.8.4}$$

since

$$S_1(wcX) = w \notin (S_1(L_1) \cup S_1(L_2)).$$

From (6.8.3) and (6.8.4) and the fact that $L = L_1 \cup L_2 \cup L_3$ we have

$$wcX \subseteq L_3.$$

Therefore,

$$S_2(wcX) = X \subseteq S_2(L_3).$$

Thus, from (6.8.2), we get:

$$S_2(L_3) = X,$$

which proves Claim 2.

Claims 1 and 2 show that either R or X is regular, and this proves the theorem. □

Corollary Let Σ be a finite nonempty set, $c \notin \Sigma$, and $R \subseteq \Sigma^*$. If RcR is a linear context-free language, then R is regular.

Theorem 6.8.2 There exist context-free languages which are not linear.

Proof Let G be the context-free grammar given by

$$S \to TcT$$

$$T \to aTb \mid \Lambda$$

Then

$$L(G) = \{a^ib^i \mid i \geqslant 0\}\{c\}\{a^jb^j \mid j \geqslant 0\}.$$

By the above corollary, if $L(G)$ were linear, then

$$R = \{a^ib^i \mid i \geqslant 0\}$$

would be regular. But, from Theorem 2.2.1, R is not regular. Therefore $L(G)$ is not linear. □

PROBLEMS

1 Let $R \subseteq \Sigma^*$ be a regular set and $c \notin \Sigma$. Show that

$$L = \{xcx^T \mid x \in R\}$$

is a linear context-free language

2 L is said to be a *ucv-language* if $L \subseteq \Sigma^* c \Sigma^*$, where $c \notin \Sigma$. If L is such a language, let $u, v \in \Sigma^*$, and define

$$f_L(u) = \{w \mid ucw \in L\},$$

$$g_L(v) = \{w \mid wcv \in L\},$$

$$U(L) = \{w \mid f_L(w) \neq \emptyset\},$$

$$V(L) = \{w \mid g_L(w) \neq \emptyset\}.$$

Prove the following result.

Proposition Let L be a *ucv* context-free language. If, for each $u \in \Sigma^*$, $f_L(u)$ is finite, then $V(L)$ is regular. If, for each $v \in \Sigma^*$, $g_L(v)$ is finite, then $U(L)$ is regular.

3 Use the result of Problem 2 to show that if a regular set gets run into a pda, the contents of the pushdown store is regular. More formally, let $A = (Q, \Sigma, \Gamma, \delta, q_0, Z_0, \emptyset)$ be a pda and let $R \subseteq \Sigma^*$ be a regular set. Show that

$$P_R = \{\alpha \in \Gamma^* \mid (q_0, w, Z_0) \overset{*}{\vdash} (q, \Lambda, \alpha) \quad \text{for some } q \in Q \text{ and } w \in R\}.$$

[*Hint*: Consider $L_q = \{wc\alpha \mid (q_0, w, Z_0) \overset{*}{\vdash} (q, \Lambda, \alpha), \text{ where } w \in \Sigma^*\}$ but watch out for the possibly infinitely many Λ-moves.]

4 Show that the linear languages are not closed under product.

5 Let $R, X \subseteq \Sigma^*$, and $c \notin \Sigma$. Show that, if R and X are linear context-free languages and either R or X is regular, then RcX is a linear context-free language.

6 Let $X \subseteq \Sigma^*$ and $c \notin \Sigma$. Show that XcX is a linear context-free language if and only if X is regular.

7 Let $G = (V, \Sigma, P, S)$ be a metalinear grammar, as defined in Problem 4 of Section 2.5. The *width* of G is defined as

$$\max \{m \mid S \rightarrow A_1 \cdots A_m \text{ is in } P\}.$$

L is said to be *metalinear of width* k if $L = L(G)$ for some metalinear grammar of width k. Let $X_i \subseteq \Sigma^*$ for $1 \leqslant i \leqslant m, m \geqslant 2$, and let $c \notin \Sigma$. Show that if $X_1cX_2 \cdots cX_m$ is metalinear of width $k > 1$ and if X_1 is not regular, then $X_2cX_3 \cdots cX_m$ is metalinear of width at most $k - 1$.

8 Let $X_i \subseteq \Sigma^*$ for $1 \leqslant i \leqslant m$ and let $c \notin \Sigma$. Show that if $X_1c \cdots cX_m$ is metalinear and of width k, then at most k of the X_i are not regular.

9 Let $X \subseteq \Sigma^*$ and $c \notin \Sigma$. Show that $(Xc)^*X$ is metalinear if and only if X is regular.

10 Let Σ be an alphabet and $c \notin \Sigma$. If $L \subseteq \Sigma^*$, then define

$$N(L) = \{xcy \mid x, y \in L, x \neq y\}.$$

Show that, if L is regular, then $N(L)$ is context-free.

11 Is it true that $N(L)$ context-free implies L is regular?

12 Show that an affirmative answer to Problem 11 gives an elegant proof that English is not context-free. [*Hint*: Consider sentences like "John is more successful as a 'y' than Bill is as a 'z'."]

6.9* SEMILINEAR SETS AND PARIKH'S THEOREM

In this section, a natural mapping from sets of strings into sets of n-tuples of natural numbers will be explored. The resulting theorem is a classical one in language theory. The applications of this theorem will be found in the exercises in future sections. We approach the proof by first stating a result which follows easily from the Iteration Theorem.

Lemma 6.9.1 (*The Pairing Lemma*) For each context-free grammar $G = (V, \Sigma, P, S)$ there is an integer p such that, for any $k \geq 1$, if $w \in L(G)$ and $\lg(w) \geq p^k$, then there exist strings $v_1, v_3, v_5, v_{21}, \ldots, v_{2k}, v_{41}, \ldots, v_{4k} \in \Sigma^*$ and $A \in N$ such that:

i) $$\begin{aligned} S &\overset{*}{\Rightarrow} v_1 A v_5 \overset{*}{\Rightarrow} v_1 v_{21} A v_{41} v_5 \\ &\overset{*}{\Rightarrow} v_1 v_{21} v_{22} A v_{42} v_{41} v_5 \\ &\vdots \\ &\overset{*}{\Rightarrow} v_1 v_{21} \cdots v_{2k} A v_{4k} \cdots v_{41} v_5 \\ &\overset{*}{\Rightarrow} v_1 v_{21} \cdots v_{2k} v_3 v_{4k} \cdots v_{41} v_5 = w \end{aligned}$$

ii) $v_{2i} v_{4i} \neq \Lambda$ for each i, $1 \leq i \leq k$; and

iii) $\lg(v_{21} \cdots v_{2k} v_3 v_{4k} \cdots v_{41}) \leq p^k$.

Proof When $k = 1$, the lemma is a minor modification of the pumping lemma. The proof of the Pairing Lemma merely follows that of the Iteration Theorem except that, because $\lg(w) \geq p^k$, the crucial path in the generation tree for w has k repetitions of some variable A. It is not necessary to even worry about positions. □

A fair amount of notation must be built up in order to state the main theorem. Let $\mathbb{N}$ be the set of natural numbers as well as the commutative monoid consisting of $\mathbb{N}$ under $+$. $\mathbb{N}^n$ denotes the cartesian product of $\mathbb{N}$ with itself n times. Let $x = (x_1, \ldots, x_n)$ and $y = (y_1, \ldots, y_n)$ be in $\mathbb{N}^n$ and define

$$x + y = (x_1 + y_1, \ldots, x_n + y_n)$$

and for $m \geq 0$, define

$$mx = (mx_1, \ldots, mx_n).$$

Definition A set of the form

$$\{\alpha_0 + n_1\alpha_1 + \cdots + n_m\alpha_m \mid n_j \geq 0 \quad \text{for } 1 \leq j \leq m\},$$

where $\alpha_0, \ldots, \alpha_m$ are elements of $\mathbb{N}^n$, is said to be a *linear* subset of $\mathbb{N}^n$. A *semilinear set* is a finite union of linear sets.

Let us fix $\Sigma = \{a_1, \ldots, a_n\}$ and define a mapping from Σ^* into $\mathbb{N}^n$ given by

$$\psi(w) = (\#_{a_1}(w), \ldots, \#_{a_n}(w)),$$

where $\#_{a_i}(w)$ denotes the number of occurrences of a_i in the word w. Note that, for any $x, y \in \Sigma^*$,

$$\psi(xy) = \psi(x) + \psi(y) = \psi(y) + \psi(x) = \psi(yx).$$

ψ is sometimes called a *Parikh mapping.* For any $L \subseteq \Sigma^*$, define

$$\psi(L) = \{\psi(x) \mid x \in L\}.$$

Sometimes $\psi(L)$ is referred to as the "commutative image" of L.

Example Let $L = \{a_1^i a_2^i \mid i \geqslant 0\}$. Then

$$\psi(L) = \{(i, i) \mid i \geqslant 0\} = \{i(1, 1) \mid i \geqslant 0\}.$$

Thus, $\psi(L)$ is a linear subset of $\mathbb{N}^2$.

We sometimes say that a language $L \subseteq \Sigma^*$ has a *semilinear image* if $\psi(L)$ is semilinear.

A mapping like ψ can induce an equivalence relation on languages, as follows:

Definition Two languages L_1 and L_2 contained in Σ^* are called *letter-equivalent* if $\psi L_1 = \psi L_2$.

The languages with a semilinear image can be characterized quite simply.

Theorem 6.9.1 A set $L \subseteq \Sigma^*$ has a semilinear image if and only if L is letter-equivalent to a regular set.

Proof Suppose L has a semilinear image; that is,

$$\psi L = M_1 \cup \cdots \cup M_m,$$

where each

$$M_i = \{\alpha_{i0} + n_{i1}\alpha_{i1} + \cdots + n_{ir_i} \mid n_{ij} \geqslant 0 \quad \text{for } 1 \leqslant j \leqslant r_i\}.$$

Let $y_{i0}, y_{i1}, \ldots, y_{ir_i}$ be strings in Σ^* whose images under ψ are, respectively, α_{i0}, $\alpha_{i1}, \ldots, \alpha_{ir_i}$. Then define G by the productions:

$$S \to A_1 | \cdots | A_m$$

$$A_i \to A_i y_{ij} | y_{i0} \qquad \text{for all } i, j, \quad 1 \leqslant i \leqslant m, \quad 1 \leqslant j \leqslant r_i.$$

Since G is left linear, $L(G)$ is regular and, clearly,

$$\psi(L(G)) = \psi(L).$$

Conversely, we shall show that any regular set has a semilinear image by Kleene's Theorem. It is clear that

$$\psi\emptyset = \emptyset$$

and that $\psi\{\alpha_i\}$ is semilinear.

CASE 1. If ψL_1 and ψL_2 are semilinear, then $\psi L_1 \cup \psi L_2$ is semilinear.

Proof If $\psi L_i = L_{i1} \cup \cdots \cup L_{ik_i}$ for $i = 1, 2$, then

$$\psi(L_1 \cup L_2) = \bigcup_{i=1}^{2} \bigcup_{j=1}^{k_i} L_{ij}$$

is a semilinear representation of $L_1 \cup L_2$.

CASE 2. If L_1 and L_2 have semilinear images, then so does $L_1 L_2$.

Proof Since concatenation distributes over union and we have closure under union, it suffices to assume that $\psi L_1 = M_1$ and $\psi L_2 = M_2$, where M_1 and M_2 are linear. Let

$$M_i = \{\alpha_i + n_{i1}\alpha_{i1} + \cdots + n_{im_i}\alpha_{im_i} | n_i \geqslant 0\} \qquad \text{for } i = 1, 2.$$

It is easy to verify that

$$\psi(L_1L_2) = M_1 + M_2$$
$$= \{\alpha_1 + \alpha_2 + n_{11}\alpha_{11} + \cdots + n_{1m_1}\alpha_{1m_1} + n_{21}\alpha_{21} + \cdots + n_{2m_2}\alpha_{2m_2} | n_{ij} \geqslant 0\}.$$

The proof for * is a little tricky so it is convenient to do a special case first.

CASE 3. If ψL is linear, then ψL^* is semilinear.

Proof Suppose

$$\psi L = M = \{\alpha_0 + n_1\alpha_1 + \cdots + n_m\alpha_m \mid n_i \geqslant 0\}.$$

Note that

$$\psi(L^*) = \{\mathbf{0}\} \cup \{\alpha_0 + n_0\alpha_0 + n_1\alpha_1 + \cdots + n_m\alpha_m \mid n_i \geqslant 0\},$$

where $\mathbf{0}$ denotes the zero vector in $\mathbb{N}^n$.

CASE 4. If ψL has a semilinear image, then so does ψL^*.

Proof Let $L = L_1 \cup \cdots \cup L_k$, where each $L_i \subseteq \Sigma^*$ is a set whose image is a linear set in $\mathbb{N}^n$. By Cases 2 and 3,

$$L_1^* \cdots L_k^*$$

has a semilinear image. The proof of Case 4 now follows easily from the observation that

$$\psi L^* = \psi((L_1 \cup \cdots \cup L_k)^*) = \psi(L_1^* \cdots L_k^*).$$

The converse now follows from Kleene's theorem. □

We are now ready to prove the main result of the section.

Theorem 6.9.2 (*Parikh's Theorem*) For each context-free language L, ψL is semilinear. Equivalently, each context-free language is letter-equivalent to a regular set.

Proof Let $G = (V, \Sigma, P, S)$ be a context-free grammar such that $L(G) = L$, and let p be the constant from the pairing lemma.

For any $\alpha \in V^*$, define $\nu(\alpha) = \{A \in N | \alpha = \beta A \gamma \text{ for some } \beta, \gamma \in V^*\}$. That is, $\nu(\alpha)$ is the set of variables that occur in α. We extend ν to derivations. That is, if θ is a derivation,

$$\theta \colon \alpha_1 \Rightarrow \cdots \Rightarrow \alpha_n,$$

define

$$\nu(\theta) = \bigcup_{i=1}^{n} \nu(\alpha_i).$$

Now let U be any set of variables containing S. Define L_U to be the subset of L consisting of words derivable from S in which the only variables used were from U. More precisely,

$$L_U = \{w \in L \mid \text{For some } \theta\colon S \overset{*}{\Rightarrow} w, \nu(\theta) = U\}.$$

Claim 1 It suffices to prove that each L_U has a semilinear image or, equivalently, that each L_U is letter-equivalent to a regular set.

Proof There are only finitely many sets U and hence sets L_U. Moreover;

$$L = \bigcup_U L_U,$$

so that Claim 1 follows.

Consider a set L_U. Let $k = |U|$ and define

$$F = \{w \in L_U \mid \lg(w) < p^k\}.$$

Now consider the set

$$\{xy \in \Sigma^* \mid \theta\colon A \overset{*}{\Rightarrow} xAy, \nu(\theta) \subseteq U, \lg(xy) \leqslant p^k\}.$$

Because the length of xy is bounded, this is a finite set, so let

$$s_1, \ldots, s_m$$

be any fixed enumeration of the elements of the set.

Claim 2 $\qquad \psi(L_U) \subseteq \psi(Fs_1^* \cdots s_m^*).$

Proof The argument proceeds by strong induction on $\lg(w)$, where $w \in L_U$. Let $n_0 \geqslant 0$ be fixed and suppose that

$$\psi(z) \in \psi(Fs_1^* \cdots s_m^*)$$

for all $z \in L_U$, with $\lg(z) < n_0$. Now suppose $w \in L_U$ and $\lg(w) = n_0$. If $\lg(w) < p^k$, then $w \in F$, so that $\psi(w) \in \psi(Fs_1^* \cdots s_m^*)$.

Suppose $\lg(w) \geqslant p^k$. Since $w \in L_U$, there is some derivation

$$\theta\colon S \overset{*}{\Rightarrow} w$$

with $\nu(\theta) = U$. Since $\lg(w) \geqslant p^k$, the pairing lemma yields a derivation θ' such that

$$\begin{aligned} S &\underset{\theta_0}{\overset{*}{\Rightarrow}} v_1 A v_5 \\ &\underset{\theta_0}{\overset{*}{\Rightarrow}} v_1 v_{21} A v_{41} v_5 \\ &\ \ \vdots \\ &\underset{\theta_k}{\overset{*}{\Rightarrow}} v_1 v_{21} \cdots v_{2k} A v_{4k} \cdots v_{41} v_5 \\ &\underset{\theta_{k+1}}{\overset{*}{\Rightarrow}} v_1 v_{21} \cdots v_{2k} v_3 v_{4k} \cdots v_{41} v_5 = w \end{aligned}$$

where $A \in U$ and $1 \leqslant \lg(v_{21} \cdots v_{2k} v_3 v_{4k} \cdots v_{41}) \leqslant p^k$. Certain subderivations of θ' have been distinguished. Note that $\nu(\theta') = \nu(\theta) = U$. Since

$$\nu(\theta') = \bigcup_{i=0}^{k+1} \nu(\theta_i) = U,$$

each variable in $U - \{A\}$ is in at least one $\nu(\theta_i)$ for some i, $0 \leqslant i \leqslant k+1$. For each variable in $U - \{A\}$, arbitrarily choose some i, $0 \leqslant i \leqslant k+1$, such that $\nu(\theta_i)$ contains that variable. Some values of i may be chosen more than once. Since there are only $k-1$ variables in $U - \{A\}$ and k values between 1 and k, some value of i, $1 \leqslant i \leqslant k$ is not chosen at all. Let i_0 be such an index. That is, $\nu(\theta_{i_0})$ contains only A. Now delete the subdrivation θ_{i_0} from θ' to yield

$$\theta'' \colon S \overset{*}{\Rightarrow} v_1 v_{21} \cdots v_{2i_0-1} v_{2i_0+1} \cdots v_{2k} v_3 v_{4k} \cdots v_{4i_0+1} v_{4i_0-1} \cdots v_{41} v_5 = w'.$$

From the choice of i_0, every variable in $U - \{A\}$ is in $\nu(\theta'')$. Clearly, $A \in \nu(\theta'')$, so $\nu(\theta'') = U$. Hence, $w' \in L_U$. Since $\lg(w') < \lg(w) = n_0$,

$$\psi(w') \in \psi(Fs_1^* \cdots s_m^*)$$

by the induction hypothesis. Since $w' v_{2i_0} v_{4i_0}$ is a permutation of w,

$$\psi(w) = \psi(w' v_{2i_0} v_{4i_0}) \in \psi(Fs_1^* \cdots s_m^* v_{2i_0} v_{4i_0}).$$

But $v_{2i_0} v_{4i_0}$ is in $\{s_1, \ldots, s_m\}$, so

$$\psi(w) \in \psi(Fs_1^* \cdots s_m^* v_{2i_0} v_{4i_0}) = \psi(Fs_1^* \cdots s_m^*).$$

Claim 3 $\psi(Fs_1^* \cdots s_m^*) \subseteq \psi(L_U)$.

Proof Let $w \in L_U$, and we prove that $\psi(ws_i) \in \psi(L_U)$ for any i. From the definition of the s_i, we can write $s_i = v_2 v_4$ for some v_2 and v_4, and there is some $B \in N$ and some derivation

$$\theta \colon B \overset{*}{\Rightarrow} v_2 B v_4$$

with $\nu(\theta) = U$. Since $w \in L_U$, there is a derivation of w in which B occurs; for example,

$$S \overset{*}{\Rightarrow} xBz \overset{*}{\Rightarrow} xyz = w$$

but then

$$S \overset{*}{\Rightarrow} xBz \overset{*}{\Rightarrow} xv_2Bv_4z \overset{*}{\Rightarrow} xv_2yv_4z = w'$$

Now $w' \in L_U$ and $\psi(w') = \psi(ws_i)$. Thus,

$$\psi(L_U s_i) \subseteq \psi(L_U) \qquad \text{for each } s_i$$

and since

$$F \subseteq L_U,$$

this shows that

$$\psi(ws_i) = \psi(w') \in \psi(Fs_1^* \cdots s_m^*) \subseteq \psi(L_U s_1^* \cdots s_m^*) \subseteq \psi(L_U).$$

By Claims 3 and 4,

$$\psi(L_U) = \psi(Fs_1^* \cdots s_m^*).$$

Since $Fs_1^* \cdots s_m^*$ is clearly regular, the proof is complete. □

PROBLEMS

1 Show that a set of n-tuples of natural numbers is linear if and only if it is a coset of a finitely generated subsemigroup of $\mathbb{N}^n$.

2 Show that the family of semilinear sets of $\mathbb{N}^n$ is closed under intersection and complementation. Show that if $L_1 \subseteq \mathbb{N}^m$ and $L_2 \subseteq \mathbb{N}^n$ are semilinear sets, then $L_1 \times L_2$ is a semilinear subset of $\mathbb{N}^{n+m}$.

3 Find a set $L \subseteq \Sigma^*$ which is not a context-free language but which has a semilinear image.

4 Use Parikh's Theorem to show that every context-free language $L \subseteq a^*$ is regular.

We begin to build a logical system involving addition and the logical connectives. The formulas will express statements about natural numbers. The *set of Presburger formulas*, $\mathscr{P}$, is the least class of formulas satisfying the following conditions.

a) For given nonnegative integers n_i, n_i', $0 \leqslant i \leqslant m$,

$$n_0 + \sum_{i=1}^{m} n_i x_i = n_0' + \sum_{i=1}^{m} n_i' x_i$$

is a formula in $\mathscr{P}$ with free variables $x_1, \ldots, x_n$.

b) If $P_1, P_2 \in \mathscr{P}$, then so is $P_1 \cap P_2$.

c) If $P_1, P_2 \in \mathscr{P}$, then so is $P_1 \cup P_2$.

d) If P is in $\mathscr{P}$, then so is $\neg P$.

e) If $P(x_1, \ldots, x_n)$ is in $\mathscr{P}$ and $1 \leqslant i \leqslant n$, then $(\forall x_i)P(x_1, \ldots, x_n) \in \mathscr{P}$.

f) If $P(x_1, \ldots, x_n)$ is in $\mathscr{P}$ and $1 \leqslant i \leqslant n$, then the formula

$$(\exists x_i)P(x_1, \ldots, x_n)$$

is in $\mathscr{P}$.

A formula with no free variables is called a *sentence*.

***5** Show that it is decidable whether or not a Presburger sentence is true.

If $P(x_1, \ldots, x_n)$ is a Presburger formula, it defines a relation as follows:

$$A_p = \{(a_1, \ldots, a_n) \mid P(a_1, \ldots, a_n) \quad \text{is true}\}.$$

A *Presburger set* $A \subseteq \mathbb{N}^n$ is of the form A_p for some Presburger formula $P(x_1, \ldots, x_n)$.

6 Show that the family of Presburger sets in $\mathbb{N}^n$ is identical with the family of semilinear sets in $\mathbb{N}^n$.

6.10 HISTORICAL SURVEY

The pumping lemma first appears in Bar-Hillel, Perles, and Shamir [1961]. The iteration theorem is from Ogden [1968]. The example used in Theorem 6.2.4 is due to Wise. Problems 10 through 12 in Section 6.2 are from Hartmanis and Shank [1968]. The $L \cap R$ theorem is due to Bar-Hillel, Perles, and Shamir [1961], although our machine proof is much simpler than the original argument. Theorem 6.3.1 is from

Ginsburg and Rice [1962]. While gsm's and context-free languages were first studied in Ginsburg and Rose [1963], our development follows Ginsburg, Greibach, and Harrison [1967]. Problems 4–7 of Section 6.3 are from Kosaraju [1975].

Theorem 6.6.3 is from Haines [1969]. Our notation for quotient follows that of the "French school"; cf. Eilenberg [1974]. Exercise 9 from Section 6.3 is from Nivat [1967].

Theorem 6.8.1 is from Greibach [1966]. At the end of Section 6.8, Problem 2 is from Bar-Hillel, Perles, and Shamir [1961], and Problem 3 is from Greibach [1967]. Parikh's theorem occurred originally in Parikh [1961] and was republished in Parikh [1966] due to its importance and the inaccessibility of the original note. Our proof follows Goldstine [1977].

seven
Ambiguity and Inherent Ambiguity

7.1 INTRODUCTION

In earlier sections, ambiguous context-free grammars have been introduced, and we defined a language to be inherently ambiguous if every one of its infinitely many context-free grammars was ambiguous. *Either* such languages exist *or* for every ambiguous grammar there is an equivalent unambiguous grammar. In either event, this is an interesting phenomenon. It turns out that the former case holds, and in Section 7.2, this is proved with the aid of the iteration theorem.

In Section 7.3, we strengthen the above result by showing that there are inherently ambiguous languages that have an exponential number of derivation trees in the length of the string. Since the number of factorizations of a string of length n is exponential in n, this is as many as possible.

Section 7.4 is devoted to showing that certain operations preserve or do not preserve unambiguity or inherent ambiguity. While those results are simple to prove, they turn out to be very useful.

7.2 INHERENTLY AMBIGUOUS LANGUAGES EXIST

Our earlier discussion of inherently ambiguous languages was very brief and consisted merely of a definition. Now we shall use the iteration theorem to prove that they exist. The first step in the proof is to examine phrases.

Definition Let $G=(V,\Sigma,P,S)$ be a context-free grammar and suppose $\eta,\beta\in V^*$. β is said to be a *phrase* of η if there exist $\alpha,\gamma\in V^*, A\in N$, so that

$$S\overset{*}{\Rightarrow}\alpha A\gamma \qquad A\overset{n}{\Rightarrow}\beta \quad \text{for some } n\geqslant 1 \text{ and } \eta=\alpha\beta\gamma$$

β is a *simple phrase* of η if β is a phrase of η as above, in which $n=1$.

Definition Let α and β be subwords of γ, where $\alpha,\beta,\gamma\in V^*$. α and β are said to be *disjoint* if there exist $\rho,\sigma,\tau\in V^*$ so that $\gamma=\rho\alpha\sigma\beta\tau$ or $\gamma=\rho\beta\sigma\alpha\tau$.

The following simple result is needed.

Theorem 7.2.1 Let $G=(V,\Sigma,P,S)$ be an unambiguous context-free grammar, let $x\in L(G)$, and let x_1 and x_2 be phrases of x. Either:

i) x_1 and x_2 are disjoint,
ii) x_1 is a subword of x_2, or
iii) x_2 is a subword of x_1.

Proof Consider the (unique) rightmost derivation for x:

$$S=\beta_0\underset{R}{\Rightarrow}\beta_1\underset{R}{\Rightarrow}\cdots\underset{R}{\Rightarrow}\beta_n=x$$

Since x_1 in Σ^* is a phrase of x, there is an index i such that $\beta_i=\alpha_iAv_i$ and $A\overset{*}{\underset{R}{\Rightarrow}}x_1$. Since the derivation is rightmost, $v_i\in\Sigma^*$. Similarly, there is a number j so that $\beta_j=\alpha_jBv_j$, $B\overset{*}{\underset{R}{\Rightarrow}}x_2$ and $v_j\in\Sigma^*$.

There are 3 cases: $i=j$, $i>j$, and $i<j$. The third case will follow from the second by symmetry. Let z_1 be the node of the tree labeled A while z_2 has label B. If $i=j$, then $z_1=z_2$ and $\alpha_i=\alpha_j$, $A=B$, and $v_i=v_j$. Thus $x_1=x_2$.

Now assume $j<i$. In the derivation for x, we have either one of two choices. Since $\beta_j\overset{+}{\underset{R}{\Rightarrow}}\beta_i$ or $\alpha_jBv_j\overset{+}{\underset{R}{\Rightarrow}}\alpha_iAv_i$, our two choices for subderivations of the derivation in question are

$$B\overset{+}{\underset{R}{\Rightarrow}}\gamma Ay \quad \text{for some } \gamma\in V^* \text{ and } y\in\Sigma^*$$

or

$$\alpha_j\overset{+}{\underset{R}{\Rightarrow}}\gamma' Ay' \quad \text{for some } \gamma'\in V^* \text{ and } y'\in\Sigma^*.$$

These cases are represented by Fig. 7.1.

CASE 1. Suppose $B\overset{+}{\underset{R}{\Rightarrow}}\gamma Ay$ for some $\gamma\in V^*$ and $y\in\Sigma^*$. Then we have

$$B\overset{+}{\underset{R}{\Rightarrow}}\gamma Ay\overset{*}{\underset{R}{\Rightarrow}}\gamma x_1y\overset{*}{\underset{R}{\Rightarrow}}x_2$$

because $B\overset{*}{\underset{R}{\Rightarrow}}x_2$ and $A\overset{*}{\underset{R}{\Rightarrow}}x_1$ and both are in Σ^*. Therefore, x_1 is a subword of x_2.

CASE 2. Suppose $\alpha_j\overset{+}{\underset{R}{\Rightarrow}}\gamma' Ay'$ for some $\gamma'\in V^*$ and some $y'\in\Sigma^*$. Then

$$S\overset{*}{\underset{R}{\Rightarrow}}\alpha_jBv_j\overset{*}{\underset{R}{\Rightarrow}}\alpha_jx_2v_j\overset{*}{\underset{R}{\Rightarrow}}\gamma' Ay'x_2v_j\overset{*}{\underset{R}{\Rightarrow}}\gamma' x_1y'x_2v_j\overset{*}{\underset{R}{\Rightarrow}}x$$

Thus, x_1 and x_2 are disjoint phrases of x. □

Corollary Let $G=(V,\Sigma,P,S)$ be a context-free grammar. Let $x\in L(G)$ and x_1,x_2 be phrases of x. If x_1 and x_2 are incomparable (with respect to $\leqslant$, that is, one

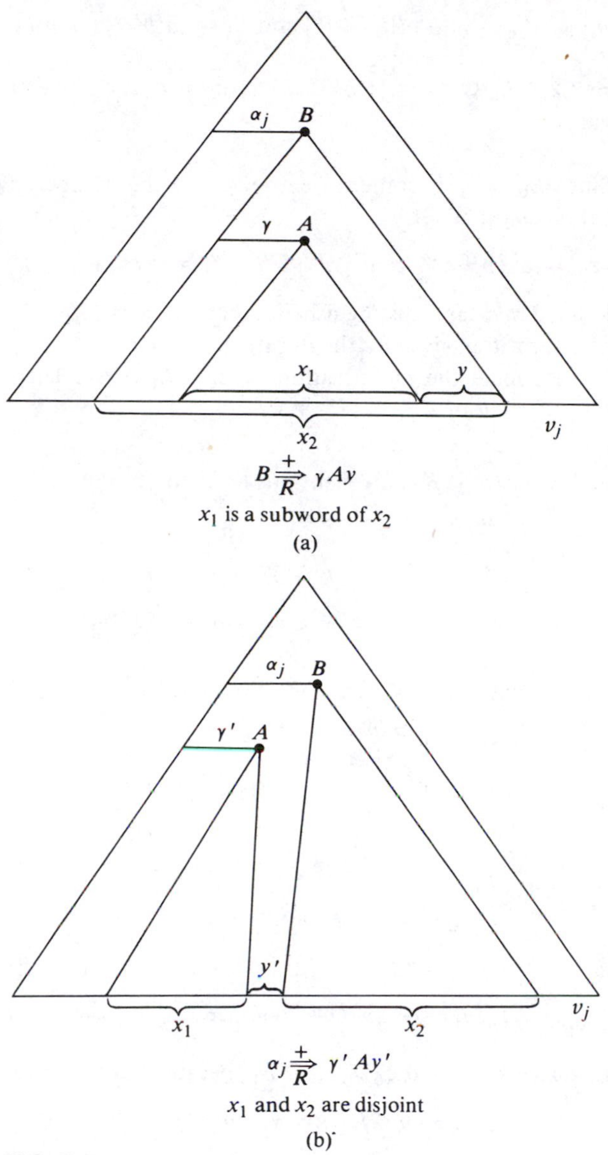

$B \overset{+}{\underset{R}{\Rightarrow}} \gamma A y$

x_1 is a subword of x_2

(a)

$\alpha_j \overset{+}{\underset{R}{\Rightarrow}} \gamma' A y'$

x_1 and x_2 are disjoint

(b)

FIG. 7.1

is not a subword of the other) and they are not disjoint, then G is ambiguous; that is, if x_1 and x_2 "overlap," then G is ambiguous.

Now the idea of our proof that there exist inherently ambiguous languages can be explained. We shall take two languages L_0 and L_1 and show that $L_0 \cup L_1$ is inherently ambiguous. We will study a string z_0 in $L_0 - L_1$ and determine the form of its factorization. Another string z_1 in $L_1 - L_0$ will be studied in its factorization determined. By pumping these strings we shall obtain overlapping phrases of a string in $L_0 \cup L_1$ and conclude that the grammar must be ambiguous.

Notation Let $L_0 = \{a^i b^i c^j | i, j \geqslant 1\}$ and $L_1 = \{a^i b^j c^j | i, j \geqslant 1\}$.

Theorem 7.2.2 $L_0 \cup L_1 = \{a^i b^j c^k | i = j \text{ or } j = k\}$ is an inherently ambiguous context-free language.

Proof Since $L_0 \cup L_1$ is context-free, let p_0 be the number give by the iteration theorem. Let $p = p_0!$ and let

$$z_0 = a^{2p} b^{2p} c^{3p} = a^{2p} b^p \underline{b^p} c^{3p} = x_0 u_0 w_0 v_0 y_0$$

where the underlined b's are distinguished; that is, $K = \{3p+1, \ldots, 4p\}$, and $x_0 u_0 w_0 v_0 y_0$ is a factorization given by the iteration theorem.

We must determine the factorization of $z_0 \in L_0 - L_1$. There are two cases according as $K_1, K_2, K_3 \neq \emptyset$ or $K_3, K_4, K_5 \neq \emptyset$.

CASE 1. Suppose $K_1, K_2, K_3 \neq \emptyset$. This leads to:

$$\begin{aligned} x_0 &= a^{2p} b^{p+j} && j > 0, \\ u_0 &= b^k && k > 0, \\ w_0 &= b^{p-(j+k)} w' && k < p_0 \leqslant p \text{ and } j + k < p. \end{aligned}$$

CASE 1a. Suppose $v_0 \in b^*$. Then we would have:

$$\begin{aligned} x_0 &= a^{2p} b^{p+j} && j > 0, \\ u_0 &= b^k && k > 0, \\ w_0 &= b^{\ell} && \ell > 0, \\ v_0 &= b^m && m \geqslant 0, \\ y_0 &= b^{p-(j+k+\ell+m)} c^{3p} \end{aligned}$$

But then

$$x_0 w_0 y_0 = a^{2p} b^{p+j+\ell} b^{p-(j+k+\ell+m)} c^{3p} = a^{2p} b^{2p+k+m} c^{3p}$$

But $x_0 w_0 y_0 \notin L_0$, since $k > 0$ and $x_0 w_0 y_0 \notin L_1$, because $\ell > 0$ implies that:

$$k + m < j + k + \ell + m \leqslant p.$$

CASE 1b. $v_0 \in b^+ c^+$. The factorization is:

$$\begin{aligned} x_0 &= a^{2p} b^{p+j} && j > 0, \\ u_0 &= b^k && k > 0, \\ w_0 &= b^{\ell} && \ell > 0, \\ v_0 &= b^{p-(j+k+\ell)} c^m && m > 0, j + k + \ell < p_0 \leqslant p, \\ y_0 &= c^{3p-m} \end{aligned}$$

Then

$$x_0u_0^2w_0v_0^2y_0 = a^{2p}b^{p+j}b^{2k}b^{\ell}b^{p-(j+k+\ell)}c^m b^{p-(j+k+\ell)}c^m c^{3p-m} \in a^+b^+c^+b^+c^+$$

and therefore $x_0u_0^2 w_0 v_0^2 y_0 \notin L_0 \cup L_1$.

CASE 1c. $v_0 \in c^*$. Then the factorization becomes:

$$\begin{aligned}
x_0 &= a^{2p}b^{p+j} && j>0,\\
u_0 &= b^k && p-2>k>0,\\
w_0 &= b^{p-(j+k)}c^{\ell} && k<p_0 \leqslant p, \ell \geqslant 0,\\
v_0 &= c^m && m \geqslant 0,\\
y_0 &= c^{3p-(\ell+m)}
\end{aligned}$$

Consider $x_0w_0y_0 = a^{2p}b^{2p-k}c^{3p-m}$, $x_0w_0y_0 \notin L_0$, since $2p-k<2p$ because $k>0$. But $x_0w_0y_0 \in L_0 \cup L_1$ by the iteration theorem, so that $x_0w_0y_0 \in L_1$. This implies that $2p-k=3p-m$, or that

$$m = p+k.$$

However, let us consider

$$\begin{aligned}
x_0u_0^2w_0v_0^2y_0 &= a^{2p}b^{2p+k}c^{3p+m}\\
&= a^{2p}b^{2p+k}c^{4p+k}
\end{aligned}$$

But $x_0u_0^2w_0v_0^2y_0 \notin L_0 \cup L_1$, since $k>0$, and $2p+k \neq 4p+k$ since $p>0$. This shows that Case 1 cannot hold.

CASE 2. $K_3, K_4, K_5 \neq \emptyset$. We must have that:

$$\begin{aligned}
y_0 &= b^ic^{3p} && i>0,\\
v_0 &= b^j && j>0,\\
w_0 &= w'b^k && k>0.
\end{aligned}$$

CASE 2a. $u_0 \in b^*$. Then the factorization would be:

$$\begin{aligned}
y_0 &= b^ic^{3p} && i>0,\\
v_0 &= b^j && j>0,\\
w_0 &= b^k && k>0,\\
u_0 &= b^{\ell} && \ell \geqslant 0,\\
x_0 &= a^{2p}b^{2p-(\ell+k+j+i)}
\end{aligned}$$

But then

$$\begin{aligned}
x_0w_0y_0 &= a^{2p}b^{2p-(i+j+k+\ell)}b^kb^ic^{3p}\\
&= a^{2p}b^{2p-(j+\ell)}c^{3p}
\end{aligned}$$

Since $j>0$, $x_0w_0y_0 \notin L_0 \cup L_1$, which contradicts that $u_0 \in b^*$.

CASE 2b. $u_0 \in a^+b^+$. In this case, $x_0u_0^2w_0v_0^2y_0 \in a^+b^+a^+b^+c^+$, which would be a contradiction.

CASE 2c. $u_0 \in a^*$. This leads to the factorization:

$$\begin{aligned} y_0 &= b^ic^{3p} && i>0, \\ v_0 &= b^j && j>0, \\ w_0 &= a^{\ell}b^{2p-(j+i)} && i+j<p, \ell \geqslant 0, \\ u_0 &= a^k && 0 \leqslant k \leqslant 2p-\ell, \\ x_0 &= a^{2p-(k+\ell)} \end{aligned}$$

To complete our picture of the factorization, suppose $k \neq j$. But then

$$x_0u_0^2w_0v_0^2y_0 = a^{2p+k}b^{2p+j}c^{3p}$$

But $x_0u_0^2w_0v_0^2y_0 \notin L_0$, since $k \neq j$, and $x_0u_0^2w_0v_0^2y_0 \notin L_1$, since $2p+j<3p$. Therefore, we have the following factorization, in which we have subscripted all the indices for future applications:

$$\begin{aligned} x_0 &= a^{2p-(j_0+\ell_0)} \\ u_0 &= a^{j_0} && j_0>0, \\ w_0 &= a^{\ell_0}b^{2p-(i_0+j_0)} && p-(i_0+j_0)<p_0 \leqslant p, \ell_0 \geqslant 0, \\ v_0 &= b^{j_0} && p_0>j_0>0, \\ y_0 &= b^{i_0}c^{3p} && p-1>i_0>0. \end{aligned}$$

Note that $j_0<p_0$, since otherwise $|K_4|>p_0$ would contradict the iteration theorem. Thus $j_0|p$ and $q_0=(p/j_0)+1$ is an integer. We have that

$$S \overset{*}{\Rightarrow} x_0A_0y_0 \overset{*}{\Rightarrow} x_0u_0^{q_0}A_0v_0^{q_0}y_0 \overset{*}{\Rightarrow} x_0u_0^{q_0}w_0v_0^{q_0}y_0 = a^{3p}b^{3p}c^{3p} = z$$

and that

$$A_0 \overset{*}{\Rightarrow} u_0^{q_0}w_0v_0^{q_0} = a^{p+j_0+\ell_0}b^{3p-i_0} \tag{7.2.1}$$

Next we consider the word

$$z_1 = a^{3p}b^{2p}c^{2p} = a^{3p}\underbrace{b^p}\,b^pc^{2p},$$

where $K=\{3p+1,\ldots,4p\}$. The problem of obtaining a factorization of z_1 is "dual" to the problem of factoring z_0. To see this duality, we reverse z_0 and interchange a's and c's. (Note that the symmetry of the iteration theorem under reversal plays a role here.) Thus it follows that $z_1=x_1u_1w_1v_1y_1$ and $K_1,K_2,K_3 \neq \emptyset$. The factorization is:

$$\begin{aligned} x_1 &= a^{3p}b^{i_1} && p-1>i_1>0, \\ u_1 &= b^{j_1} && p_0>j_1 \geqslant 1, \\ w_1 &= b^{2p-(i_1+j_1)}c^{k_1} && i_1+j_1<p, k_1 \geqslant 0, \\ v_1 &= c^{j_1} \\ y_1 &= c^{2p-(j_1+k_1)}. \end{aligned}$$

Let $q_1 = (p/j_1) + 1$. Since $j_1 < p_0$, q_1 is an integer. We have that

$$S \overset{*}{\Rightarrow} x_1 A_1 y_1 \overset{*}{\Rightarrow} x_1 u_1^{q_1} A_1 v_1^{q_1} y_1 \overset{*}{\Rightarrow} x_1 u_1^{q_1} w_1 v_1^{q_1} y_1 = a^{3p} b^{3p} c^{3p}$$

and

$$A_1 \overset{*}{\Rightarrow} u_1^{q_1} w_1 v_1^{q_1} = b^{3p-i_1} c^{p+j_1+k_1} \tag{7.2.2}$$

Now let us consider the string $a^{3p}b^{3p}c^{3p}$. We know that we may "pump up" our factorization of z_0 and z_1 to get factorizations of $a^{3p}b^{3p}c^{3p}$ (see Fig. 7.2). We must now see how the phrases that derive from A_0 and A_1 fit into the picture. Recall that

$$A_0 \overset{*}{\Rightarrow} a^{p+j_0+\ell_0} b^{3p-i_0} \tag{7.2.3}$$

and

$$A_1 \overset{*}{\Rightarrow} b^{3p-i_1} c^{p+j_1+k_1} \tag{7.2.4}$$

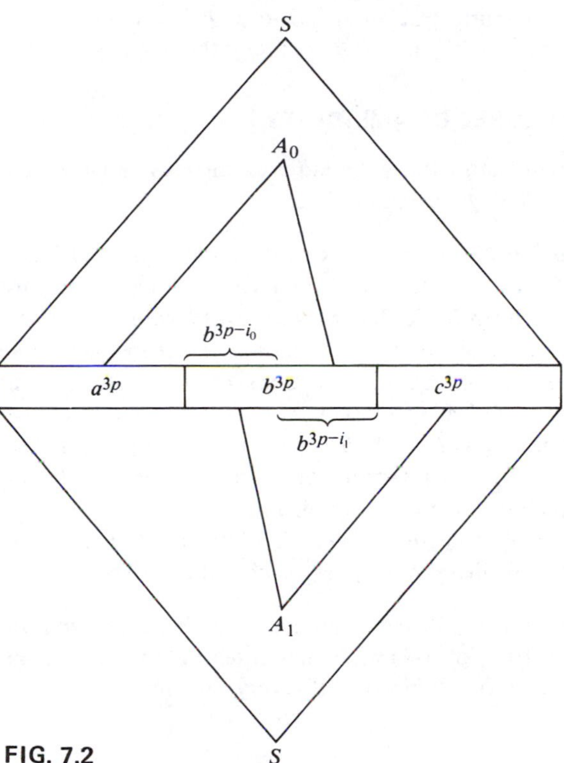

FIG. 7.2

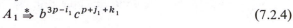

But it is clear that the phrases (7.2.3) and (7.2.4) overlap, since the minimum length of the b's in the righthand side of (7.2.3) is:

$$3p - i_0 > 3p - p = 2p,$$

while the minimum length of the b's on the lefthand side of (7.2.4) is:

$$3p - i_1 > 3p - p = 2p.$$

There is no way to partition $(3p)$ b's into two classes each of which has size greater than $2p$ without overlap, as can be seen from Fig. 7.2. Therefore the arbitrary grammar G is ambiguous, and hence $L_0 \cup L_1$ is an inherently ambiguous context-free language. □

PROBLEMS

1 Show that $\{\alpha\alpha^T \mid \alpha \in \{a, b\}^*\}^2$ is an inherently ambiguous context-free language. (*Hint*. Start with $z_0 = aba^{2p}bba^{2p}baaba^{3p}bba^{3p}ba$.)

2 Find a minimal linear language L which is inherently ambiguous among the class of minimal linear grammars yet L has an unambiguous linear grammar.

3 Let $M = \{a^i ba^{i+1} b \mid i \geqslant 0\}$ and define $L_0 = abM^*$ and $L_1 = M^*a^*b$. Show that $L_0 \cup L_1$ is inherently ambiguous.

4 A set $L \subseteq \Sigma^*$ is *bounded* if there exist $w_1, \ldots, w_r \in \Sigma^*$ so that $L \subseteq w_1^* \cdots w_r^*$. Settle the following question by providing a proof or a counterexample.

For each inherently ambiguous language L, is there some bounded regular set $R \subseteq w_1^* \cdots w_r^*$ such that $L \cap R$ is inherently ambiguous?

7.3 THE DEGREE OF AMBIGUITY

Now that we know that inherently ambiguous languages exist, let us take a more refined view of ambiguous generation.

Definition Let $k \geqslant 1$. A context-free grammar G is *ambiguous of degree k* if each string in $L(G)$ has at most k distinct derivation trees (equivalently, leftmost derivations). If $k \geqslant 2$, then L is called *inherently ambiguous of degree k* if L cannot be generated by any grammar that is ambiguous of degree less than k but can be generated by a grammar which is ambiguous of degree k. L is *finitely inherently ambiguous* if there is some k and some G so that G is inherently ambiguous of degree k.

For example, $L_0 \cup L_1 = \{a^i b^j c^k \mid i = j \text{ or } j = k\}$ is inherently ambiguous of degree 2. Since a grammar which is ambiguous of degree 1 is unambiguous, it only makes sense to use the phrase "inherently ambiguous of degree k" when $k \geqslant 2$. Also note that if G is ambiguous of degree k, then $k = \sup\{\sigma(x) \mid x \in \Sigma^*\}$,† where $\sigma(x)$ is the coefficient of x in the formal power series, as described in Section 4.9.

Definition A context-free grammar G is *infinitely ambiguous* if, for each $i \geqslant 1$, there exists a string in $L(G)$ which has at least i leftmost derivations. A language L is *infinitely inherently ambiguous* if every grammar generating L is infinitely ambiguous.

Example Consider the grammar G:

$$S \to SS \mid \Lambda$$

where $L(G) = \{\Lambda\}$. G is infinitely ambiguous but $L(G)$ is an unambiguous language.

We begin our development by reconsidering $L_0 \cup L_1$ of Section 7.2.

---

† Suppose S is a partially ordered set with respect to $\leqslant$ and $S_0 \subseteq S$. An element $s \in S$ is an *upper bound* for S_0 if $s_0 \leqslant s$ for every $s_0 \in S_0$. An element $s^* \in S$ is a *least upper bound* for S_0 if $s^* \leqslant s$ for every upper bound s of S_0. We also write $s^* = \sup(S)$. A similar definition holds for *lower bounds* and *greatest lower bounds*, and the notation used is $\inf(S)$. If φ is a function with domain X, one writes

$$\sup \varphi(x) \quad \text{for} \quad \sup\{\varphi(x) \mid x \in X\}.$$

Theorem 7.3.1 For any $n \geqslant 1, (L_0 \cup L_1)^n$ is inherently ambiguous of degree 2^n.

Proof Let p_0 be the constant of the iteration theorem for $(L_0 \cup L_1)^n$ and let $p = p_0!$; by a straightforward generalization of the proof of Theorem 7.2.2, we can prove the following: If

$$w_2 a^{2p} b^p \underline{b^p} c^{3p} w_3 \in (L_0 \cup L_1)^n \text{ with } w_{i+1} \in (L_0 \cup L_1)^{k_i}$$

for some k_i, $i = 1, 2$, then:

$$w_2 a^{2p} b^{2p} c^{3p} w_3 = x_0 u_0 w_0 v_0 y_0,$$

where

$$\begin{aligned} x_0 &= w_2 a^{2p-(j_0+\ell_0)} & & \\ u_0 &= a^{j_0} & & \\ w_0 &= a^{\ell_0} b^{2p-(i_0+j_0)} & & \ell_0 \geqslant 0, \\ v_0 &= b^{j_0} & & p \geqslant p_0 > j_0 > 0, \\ y_0 &= b^{i_0} c^{3p} w_3 & & p-1 > i_0 > 0. \end{aligned}$$

Moreover, if we take $q_0 = (p/j) + 1$, then

$$x_0 u_0^{q_0} w_0 v_0^{q_0} y_0 = w_2 a^{3p} b^{3p} c^{3p} w_3 \in (L_0 \cup L_1)^n.$$

Similarly, if we consider

$$w_2 a_3^{3p} \underline{b^p} b^p c^{2p} w_3 = x_1 u_1 w_1 v_1 y_1,$$

then we find that

$$\begin{aligned} x_1 &= w_2 a^{3p} b^{i_1} & & p-1 > i_1 > 0, \\ u_1 &= b^{j_1} & & p \geqslant p_0 > j_1 > 0, \\ w_1 &= b^{2p-(i_1+j_1)} c^{k_1} & & i_1 + j_1 < p, k_1 \geqslant 0, \\ v_1 &= c^{j_1} & & \\ y_1 &= c^{2p-(j_1+k_1)} w_3 & & \end{aligned}$$

Taking $q_1 = (p/j_1) + 1$, we have that

$$x_1 u_1^{q_1} w_1 v_1^{q_1} y_1 = w_2 a^{3p} b^{3p} c^{3p} w_3 \in (L_0 \cup L_1)^n.$$

Using these factorizations, we are ready to prove the following result.

Claim For any $w_{i+1} \in (L_0 \cup L_1)^{k_i}$, $i = 1, 2$, $k_1, k_2 \geqslant 0$, the string $w_2 a^{3p} b^{3p} c^{3p} w_3 \in (L_0 \cup L_2)^n$ has at least two derivations.

Proof We have already seen (in the proof of Theorem 7.2.2) that the two phrases $u_0^{q_0} w_0 v_0^{q_0}$ and $u_1^{q_1} w_1 v_1^{q_1}$ overlap, so that $w_2 a^{3p} b^{3p} c^{3p} w_3$ has at least two derivations.

If we consider the string $(a^{3p}b^{3p}c^{3p})^n$, then we see that this string has at least 2^n distinct derivations since we may generate any of the n subwords $a^{3p}b^{3p}c^{3p}$ in at least two ways.

A straightforward argument shows that L is of degree exactly 2^n. □

Next we turn to showing that there is a context-free language with an unbounded degree of inherent ambiguity.

Theorem 7.3.3 $(L_0 \cup L_1)^*$ is a context-free language which is infinitely inherently ambiguous.

Proof Let p_0 be the constant of the iteration theorem for $(L_0 \cup L_1)^*$ and let $p = p_0!$; we note that the claim of the previous theorem applies in this case as well. Therefore, for any $n \geqslant 0$, the string $(a^{3p}b^{3p}c^{3p})^n$ has 2^n trees. Since $(L_0 \cup L_1)^*$ contains $(L_0 \cup L_1)^n$ for any n, we can proceed as follows. Let i be any fixed integer and let n be such that $2^n > i$. Then $(L_0 \cup L_2)^n \subseteq (L_0 \cup L_1)^*$ and has a degree of ambiguity that is greater than i. □

PROBLEMS

1 Show that $L = \{ww^T \mid w \in \{a, b\}^*\}^2$ is infinitely inherently ambiguous.

2 Let Σ be an alphabet with $|\Sigma| \geqslant 2$ and $c \notin \Sigma$. Show that

$$L = \{ucv_1u^Tv_2 \mid u, v_1, v_2 \in \Sigma^*\}$$

is infinitely inherently ambiguous.

3 Is there a (minimal) linear language that is infinitely inherently ambiguous?

4 Show that, for each $k \geqslant 2$, there exists an inherently ambiguous grammar of degree k.

5 Let $G = (V, \Sigma, P, S)$ be a reduced context-free grammar. Let π denote the production $A \to B_1 \cdots B_k$ and let $x \in \Sigma^*$. The *degree of direct ambiguity* of (π, x) is the number of different factorizations such that

$$A \Rightarrow B_1 \cdots B_k \overset{*}{\Rightarrow} x_1 \cdots x_k$$

where for each j, $1 \leqslant j \leqslant k$, $B_j \in V$, and

$$B_j \overset{*}{\Rightarrow} x_j$$

and

$$x = x_1 \cdots x_k$$

The *degree of direct ambiguity* of $G = (V, \Sigma, P, S)$ is $k \geqslant 1$ if k is the least integer such that any pair (π, x) with $\pi \in P$ and $x \in L(G)$ has degree of direct ambiguity $\leqslant k$. A grammar has an *infinite degree of direct ambiguity* if for each i, there is some pair (π, x) with degree of direct ambiguity $\geqslant i$. Similar definitions hold for languages. Show that the degree of direct ambiguity of a grammar is less than or equal to the degree of ambiguity.

6 Find a linear context-free language (i.e., give its grammar) which is infinitely ambiguous but has degree of inherent direct ambiguity equal to 1.

7 Let Σ be an alphabet, $|\Sigma| \geqslant 2$, and let $c, d \notin \Sigma$. Show that

$$L = \{u_1cv_1u_1^Tu_2^Tv_2du_2 \mid u_1, u_2, v_1, v_2 \in \Sigma^*\}$$

is a language which is infinitely inherently directly ambiguous; i.e., every grammar for L has an unbounded degree of direct ambiguity.

8 (*Open question due to Shamir*). Are there any languages whose degree of direct ambiguity is not 1 and not infinite?

9 Extend the concept of an unambiguous pda to obtain a family of pda's which correspond to the finitely inherently ambiguous languages.

7.4* THE PRESERVATION OF UNAMBIGUITY AND INHERENT AMBIGUITY BY OPERATIONS

For a number of applications, it is necessary to know which operations do or do not preserve unambiguity and inherent ambiguity. Many of the basic facts about this have been studied when we studied the relevant closure operations, and it is a comparatively simple problem to combine our results.

Our first proposition restates some facts which have been proven earlier in a different form.

Proposition 7.4.1

a) If L is a context-free language whose intersection with some regular set is inherently ambiguous, then L is inherently ambiguous.

b) If L_1 and L_2 are disjoint unambiguous context-free languages, then $L_1 \cup L_2$ is unambiguous.

c) If L is an unambiguous context-free language and R is a regular set, then $L - R$ and $L \cup R$ are both unambiguous.

d) If L is an inherently ambiguous context-free language and R is a regular set with $L \cap R = \emptyset$, then $L \cup R$ is inherently ambiguous.

Now we study gsm's.

Theorem 7.4.1 If L is an unambiguous context-free language and S is a gsm which is one-to-one on L, then $S(L)$ is also an unambiguous context-free language.

Proof The argument is merely a careful re-examination of the proof of Theorem 6.4.3 in the case where S is a gsm. Assume that L is unambiguous so that A (using the notation of the proof of Theorem 6.4.3) is an unambiguous pda. Moreover, S is a gsm which is one-to-one on L. Now Claim 4 in the proof of Theorem 6.4.3 becomes the following proposition.

Claim 4′ For each $q, q' \in Q_1, s, s' \in Q_2, w, y \in \Delta^*, \beta \in \Gamma^*, \beta' \in \Gamma^+$, and $Z \in \Gamma$,

$$((q, s, \Lambda, \Lambda), wy, \beta Z) \overset{+}{\underset{B}{\vdash}} ((q', s', \Lambda, \Lambda), y, \beta'),$$

using $k \geqslant 1$ moves of Type 1 if and only if there exist $u_1, \ldots, u_k$ in Σ such that

$$s_0 = s,$$

$$s' = \delta_2(s, u_1 \cdots u_k)$$

$$S(u_1 \cdots u_k) = \lambda_2(s, u_1 \cdots u_k) = w,$$

and

$$(q, u_1 \cdots u_k, \beta Z) \overset{+}{\underset{A}{\vdash}} (q', \Lambda, \beta').$$

Using Claim 4′ and the facts that S' is one-to-one on L and that A is unambiguous, one can show that B is an unambiguous pda so that $S(L)$ is unambiguous. We omit the details. □

Next, we turn to a consideration of inverse gsm's.

Theorem 7.4.2 If L is an unambiguous context-free language and T is a gsm, then $T^{-1}(L)$ is an unambiguous context-free language.

Proof Again, we use Theorem 6.4.3. Let $L \subseteq \Delta^*$ and let the sequential transducer of Theorem 6.4.3 be T^{-1} as defined in the proof of Theorem 6.5.2. Claim 4, from Theorem 6.4.3, becomes:

Claim 4″ For each $q, q' \in Q_1$, $s, s' \in Q_2$, $w, y \in \Sigma^*$, $\beta \in \Gamma^*$, $\beta' \in \Gamma^+$, and $Z \in \Gamma$,

$$((q, s, \Lambda, \Lambda), wy, \beta Z) \overset{+}{\underset{B}{\vdash}} ((q', s', \Lambda, \Lambda), y, \beta'),$$

using $k \geq 1$ moves of Type 1 if and only if there exist $u_1, \ldots, u_k$ in Δ^* such that

$$s' = \delta_2(s, u_1 \cdots u_k)$$

$$T(w) = \lambda_2(s, w) = u_1 \cdots u_k$$

and

$$(q, u_1 \cdots u_k, \beta Z) \overset{+}{\underset{A}{\vdash}} (q', \Lambda, \beta').$$

From Claim 4″ and the unambiguity of the pda A, it follows that B is an unambiguous pda, so $T^{-1}(L)$ is unambiguous. □

Corollary 1 If L is an unambiguous context-free language and φ is a homomorphism, then $\varphi^{-1}L$ is an unambiguous context-free language.

Proof Every homomorphism is a one-state gsm mapping. □

Corollary 2 If $L \subseteq \Sigma^*$ is inherently ambiguous and S is a gsm which is one-to-one on Σ^*, then $S(L)$ is inherently ambiguous.

Proof If $S(L)$ were unambiguous, then

$$S^{-1}(S(L)) = L$$

would be unambiguous and that would be a contradiction. □

Corollary 3 Let $L \subseteq \Sigma^+$ be an unambiguous (inherently ambiguous) context-free language and let $w \in \Sigma^*$. Then wL and Lw are both unambiguous (inherently ambiguous).

Proof One can design a gsm S which maps L into wL and S is one-to-one on Σ^*. By Theorem 7.4.1, wL is unambiguous if L is and by Corollary 2 of Theorem 7.4.2, inherent ambiguity is preserved also. The case of Lw follows that of wL by the preservation of these properties under transpose. (Cf. Problem 1 of Section 7.4.) □

The next theorem will have an application in proving a metatheorem about decidability.

Theorem 7.4.3

a) The finitely inherently ambiguous languages are closed under inverse gsm mappings.

b) The finitely inherently ambiguous languages are closed under quotients with singletons on both the left and right.

Proof The argument for (a) is an extension of the proof of Theorem 7.4.2. If L is finitely inherently ambiguous, the pda A has a bounded number of accepting sequences and so does the pda B.

The argument for (b) involves giving a machine construction for $L\{w\}^{-1}$. It will be clear that this set is finitely inherently ambiguous if L is. The details are left to the reader. □

The previous theorem is rather weak. Since an unambiguous language is finitely inherently ambiguous, the result only says that these operations will not produce an infinitely inherently ambiguous language. The theorem does not even imply that these operations preserve inherent ambiguity. (Cf. Problem 2 of Section 7.4.)

In general, any form of "recoding" destroys ambiguity and inherent ambiguity. We prove a simple result now and leave similar cases for the problems.

Theorem 7.4.4 Neither unambiguity nor inherent ambiguity is preserved under projections (i.e., homomorphisms φ which map Σ into Δ) nor under product by a two-word set.

Proof Let $M = \{da^ib^ic^j \mid i,\ j \geqslant 1\} \cup \{ea^ib^j\ c^j \mid\ i, j \geqslant 1\}$. M is clearly unambiguous. Define a projection φ by the condition that, for all $x \in \Sigma$,

$$\varphi x = \begin{cases} e & \text{if } x = d \quad \text{or} \quad x = e, \\ x & \text{otherwise.} \end{cases}$$

Clearly,

$$\varphi(M) = e(L_0 \cup L_1) = \{ea^ib^jc^k \mid i = j \quad \text{or} \quad j = k\}.$$

By Corollary 2 of Theorem 7.4.2, M is inherently ambiguous.

On the other hand, define ψ such that

$$\psi x = a$$

for all $x \in \Sigma$. Then

$$\psi(L_0 \cup L_1) = \{a^i \mid i \geqslant 3\} = a^3a^*.$$

Thus $L_0 \cup L_1$ is inherently ambiguous and $\psi(L_0 \cup L_1)$ is unambiguous because it is regular.

Turning to the second operation, define

$$N = \{a^ib^ic^j \mid i,j \geqslant 1\} \cup \{da^ib^jc^j \mid i,j \geqslant 1\}.$$

N is surely unambiguous. Now we form

$$\{d, d^2\}N$$

and assume it to be unambiguous. Note that since $d^2a^*b^*c^*$ is a regular set, then

$$\{d, d^2\}N \cap (d^2a^*b^*c^*) = d^2(L_0 \cup L_1)$$

would be unambiguous. But by Corollary 2 of Theorem 7.4.3, it is inherently ambiguous.

Let

$$L' = a^*b^*c^* \cup d^2d^*a^*b^*c^* \cup d(L_0 \cup L_1).$$

L' is inherently ambiguous because

i) $d(L_0 \cup L_1)$ is inherently ambiguous, by Corollary 2 of Theorem 7.4.3;

ii) $a^*b^*c^* \cup d^2d^*a^*b^*c^*$ is a regular set disjoint from $d(L_0 \cup L_1)$; and

iii) by Proposition 7.4.1(d).

But

$$\{d, d^2\}L' = d^+a^*b^*c^*$$

is regular and hence unambiguous. This shows nonclosure of inherent ambiguity under product with a two-word set. □

PROBLEMS

1 Show that L is an unambiguous context-free language if and only if L^T is.

2 Show that, if L is inherently ambiguous and φ is a homomorphism, then $\varphi^{-1}(L)$ is not necessarily inherently ambiguous.

3 Show that there is an inherently ambiguous language L and a gsm S which is one-to-one on L, such that $S(L)$ is unambiguous. Actually S can even be a *sequential machine,* which means that $\lambda: Q \times \Sigma \to \Delta$.

4 Show that neither unambiguity nor inherent ambiguity is preserved by init or by subwords.

5 Show that the set

$$L = \{a^p b^q c^r d^s e^t \mid (p = q \text{ and } r = s) \quad \text{or} \quad (q = r \text{ and } s = t); p, q, r, s, t \geq 1\}$$

is an inherently ambiguous language. Moreover, $\bar{L} = \{a, b, c, d, e\}^* - L$ is also a context-free language.

6 Find an unambiguous context-free language L whose complement is not context-free.

7.5 HISTORICAL SURVEY

Parikh [1961] first showed the existence of inherently ambiguous languages. Our argument derives from the iteration theorem and uses techniques of Ogden [1968]. The notion of direct ambiguity is due to Earley [1968]. Problem 7 of Section 7.4 is from Shamir [1971]. Most of the results from Section 7.4 are due to Ginsburg and Ullian [1966]. Problems 5 and 6 are from Hibbard and Ullian [1966].

eight
Decision Problems for Context-Free Grammars

8.1 INTRODUCTION

In this chapter, we look at context-free grammars and languages from the point of view of actually computing certain information. Do there exist algorithms to determine (say) whether $L(G) = \emptyset$ or $L(G_1) = \Sigma^*$? Section 8.2 is devoted to some solvable problems, i.e., ones for which algorithms exist. Regrettably, that is a short section because most of the questions that arise do not have algorithmic solutions.

In Section 8.3, the halting problem for Turing machines is reviewed informally. The Post correspondence problem is defined and shown to be unsolvable by reduction to the halting problem. Then this problem is encoded into some context-free languages.

In Section 8.4, it is shown that one can't decide whether $L_1 \cap L_2 = \emptyset$ for two context-free languages L_1 and L_2. One cannot decide whether $L(G) = \Sigma^*$. It is not possible to decide whether a context-free grammar G is ambiguous or not. A similar result holds for deciding whether $L(G)$ is inherently ambiguous.

In Section 8.5, we consider problems like "given a context-free language $L(G)$, can we decide whether $L(G)$ is deterministic?" That problem is unsolvable. If we replace "deterministic" by (say) "finitely inherently ambiguous," then the answer is the same. A general theorem is proved which deals with the decision question concerning whether

$$L(G) \in \mathscr{S}, \text{ (or not)},$$

where $\mathscr{S}$ is an appropriate family of sets.

8.2 SOLVABLE DECISION PROBLEMS FOR CONTEXT-FREE GRAMMARS AND LANGUAGES

A number of basic decision questions about context-free grammars and languages will be investigated. In this section, the decidable questions are considered. It is somewhat discouraging that most natural questions are undecidable, but these negative results are important, because they indicate which problems can have no algorithmic solutions. Among the solvable questions, the complexity of carrying out the basic computations will be studied.

First, we turn to the very important question of "recognition." Given a context-free grammar $G = (V, \Sigma, P, S)$ and a string $w \in \Sigma^n$, is $w \in L(G)$ or not? This problem will be analyzed in great detail in a later chapter, where a variety of algorithms will be given. These algorithms run in under cubic time as a function of n, the length of the string to be recognized. For the moment, we content ourselves with proving that the problem is solvable and we give a simple (but computationally terrible) algorithm.

Theorem 8.2.1 There is an algorithm to determine, for a context-free grammar $G = (V, \Sigma, P, S)$ and a string $w \in \Sigma^*$, whether or not $w \in L(G)$.

Proof Assume, without loss of generality, that G is in Chomsky normal form. (Cf. Theorem 4.4.1.) If $w = \Lambda$, then $w \in L(G)$ if and only if $S \to \Lambda$ is in P. Assume $w \in \Sigma^+$, where $\lg(w) = n \geqslant 1$. Then $S \stackrel{t}{\Rightarrow} w$ implies $t \leqslant 2n - 1$, since G is in Chomsky normal form. (Cf. Problem 4 of Section 4.4.) We can decide whether $w \in L(G)$ by enumerating all derivations of length $\leqslant 2n - 1$. □

We now show that there is an algorithm that can be used to decide whether a context-free language is empty, finite, or infinite. In later sections, it will be shown that almost all other general questions of interest about context-free languages are not decidable.

Theorem 8.2.2 There is an algorithm to determine whether an arbitrary context-free language is empty, finite, or infinite.

Proof Let $L = L(G)$, where $G = (V, \Sigma, P, S)$; $L(G)$ is nonempty if and only if $S \in W_n$, where W_n is the set constructed in the proof of Theorem 3.2.1.

From the pumping lemma, we know that there exists a computable number $p = p(G)$ such that $L(G)$ is infinite if and only if there exists $w \in L(G)$ such that $\lg(w) \geqslant p$. Let

$$L_p = L \cap \left(\bigcup_{i<p} \Sigma^i \right) = \{w \in L \mid \lg(w) < p\}.$$

L_p is computable since $\bigcup_{i<p} \Sigma^i$ is finite.

We also know that $L - L_p$ is a context-free language since L_p is finite. But

$$|L(G)| = \infty \quad \text{if and only if} \quad L - L_p \neq \emptyset.$$

From the first part of this theorem, we have an algorithm for determining whether $L - L_p$ is empty. □

We can also decide whether a deterministic context-free language equals a regular set.

Theorem 8.2.3 Let L be a deterministic context-free language and let R be a regular set. It is decidable whether or not $L = R$.

Proof $L = R$ if and only if

$$L \subseteq R \tag{8.2.1}$$

and

$$R \subseteq L. \tag{8.2.2}$$

That is, if and only if

$$L \cap \bar{R} = \emptyset \tag{8.2.3}$$

and

$$\bar{L} \cap R = \emptyset. \tag{8.2.4}$$

But $L \cap \bar{R}$ is a context-free language, since $\bar{R}$ is regular if R is. On the other hand, $\bar{L}$ is a deterministic context-free language, since L is, and hence $\bar{L} \cap R$ is context-free. By Theorem 8.2.1, (8.2.3) and (8.2.4) are solvable. □

PROBLEMS

1 Let $L = T(A)$, where A is a dpda, and let $R = T(B)$, where B is a finite automaton. Show that the following problems are solvable in polynomial time as a function of $|A|$ and $|B|$.

a) $L \subseteq R$ b) $R \subseteq L$ c) $L = R$ d) $L \cap R = \emptyset$

2 Let $G = (V, \Sigma, P, S)$ be a context-free grammar and let $\alpha, \beta \in V^*$. Show that it is decidable whether or not $\alpha \overset{*}{\Rightarrow} \beta$ and whether or not $\alpha \underset{L}{\overset{*}{\Rightarrow}} \beta$.

3 Let $G = (V, \Sigma, P, S)$ be a context-free grammar. A variable $A \in N$ is *recursive* if

$$A \overset{*}{\Rightarrow} uAv$$

for some $u, v \in \Sigma^*$ and $uv \neq \Lambda$. Give an algorithm which determines whether a given variable is recursive.

4 Show directly (without using grammars) that there is an algorithm for testing whether or not $T(A) = \emptyset$, where A is a pda.

8.3 TURING MACHINES, THE POST CORRESPONDENCE PROBLEM, AND CONTEXT-FREE LANGUAGES

Although it is assumed that Turing machines are familiar to the reader,† we shall give a quick sketch of a proof of the halting problem for Turing machines. Although this is a familiar example of an unsolvable problem, there is another problem called the Post Correspondence Problem which is more natural in the context of language theory because it involves strings of symbols.

---

† Chapter 9 contains some material on Turing machines and computational complexity. It is not needed here.

For the purposes of the present discussion, imagine a Turing machine working over some fixed alphabet, and let us assume that the input is regarded as a nonnegative integer. Let us assume that we have some mapping g which is a Gödel numbering; that is, g maps from the positive integers onto the set of all Turing machines. Moreover, g is a totally computable function. Thus, given $n, g(n)$ denotes the nth Turing machine, which will also be written A_n. If machine A_n is run on input x, there are two possible outcomes: Either $A_n(x)$ eventually halts and gives some output, or it runs forever.

Definition The *halting problem* is the problem of deciding, for any number n, whether $A_n(n)$ halts or not.

Theorem 8.3.1 The halting problem is recursively unsolvable.

Proof Suppose it were solvable. Then there would be an algorithm P which decides the halting problem. We could define a new algorithm Q based on P as follows: For a given n, decide whether $A_n(n)$ halts, using P. If $A_n(n)$ halts, then go into an infinite loop; else stop. This procedure Q is clearly an algorithm, so that there is a Turing machine A_k which computes Q; that is, $Q(x) = A_k(x)$ for all x. Let us diagonalize and examine $A_k(k)$:

$$A_k(k) \text{ halts} \quad \text{implies} \quad Q(k) \text{ loops} \quad \text{implies} \quad A_k(k) \text{ loops.}$$

On the other hand,

$$A_k(k) \text{ loops} \quad \text{implies} \quad Q(k) \text{ halts} \quad \text{implies} \quad A_k(k) \text{ halts.}$$

Therefore, $A_k(k)$ halts if and only if $A_k(k)$ loops. Clearly, this is a contradiction. □

Now we turn our attention to a problem which is very useful in language theory.

Definition Let $\mathbf{x} = (x_1, \ldots, x_n)$ and $\mathbf{y} = (y_1, \ldots, y_n)$ be two lists of nonnull words from a common alphabet Σ. The *Post Correspondence Problem* (*PCP* for short) is to determine whether or not there exist $i_1, \ldots, i_k$, where $1 \leqslant i_j \leqslant n$ such that

$$x_{i_1} \cdots x_{i_k} = y_{i_1} \cdots y_{i_k}$$

If there exists a solution to a PCP, then there are infinitely many, since one may iterate a solution any number of times to obtain another solution.

Examples

1.
$$\mathbf{x} = (a, b^2a, a^2b),$$
$$\mathbf{y} = (ba, a^3, ba).$$

In this case there is no solution, since any solution must start with some index i and x_i and y_i must have a common nonnull initial subword.

2.
$$\mathbf{x} = (b^3, ab^2),$$
$$\mathbf{y} = (b^2, bab^3).$$

Then $(1, 2, 1)$ is a solution since

$$b^3ab^2b^3 = b^2bab^3b^2$$

3.
$$\mathbf{x} = (ba, ab^2, bab),$$
$$\mathbf{y} = (bab, b^2, abb).$$

Any solution must have $i_1 = 1$. Then

$$x_1 = ba$$
$$y_1 = bab$$

Now the choice for x_{i_2} must begin with a b. Therefore, $i_2 = 1$ or 3. If $i_2 = 1$, then

$$x_1 x_1 = baba$$
$$y_1 y_1 = babbab$$

which fails. Thus, $i_2 \neq 1$. If $i_2 = 3$, one gets

$$x_1 x_3 = babab$$
$$y_1 y_3 = bababb$$

By exactly the same reasoning as above, $i_3 = 3$, $i_4 = 3$, etc. But the sequence will continue indefinitely and hence there can be no solution, because the x-word cannot catch up with the y-word.

It is convenient to use an intermediate problem to prove that the correspondence problem is unsolvable.

Definition Let $\mathbf{x} = (x_1, \ldots, x_n)$ and $\mathbf{y} = (y_1, \ldots, y_n)$ be two lists of non-null words from some common alphabet Σ. The *Modified Post Correspondence Problem* (MPCP, for short) is to determine whether or not there exist $i_1, \ldots, i_k$ where $1 \leqslant i_j \leqslant n$, such that

$$x_1 x_{i_1} \cdots x_{i_k} = y_1 y_{i_1} \cdots y_{i_k}$$

The only difference between the MPCP and the PCP is the condition that the first strings used in the MPCP be x_1 and y_1.

Lemma 8.3.1 If the Post Correspondence Problem were solvable, then the Modified Post Correspondence Problem would also be solvable.

Proof Let

$$\mathbf{x} = (x_1, \ldots, x_n)$$

and

$$\mathbf{y} = (y_1, \ldots, y_n)$$

be two lists of words over some alphabet Σ. Assume that this is the instance of MPCP that we wish to solve. Now an "equivalent" PCP will be constructed. Let $\Sigma' = \Sigma \cup \{¢, \$\}$ where ¢ and \$ are new symbols. Define two homomorphisms φ_L and φ_R by the conditions

$$\varphi_L(a) = ¢a$$
$$\varphi_R(a) = a¢$$

for each $a \in \Sigma$. Define

$$\mathbf{x}' = (x'_1, \ldots, x'_{n+2}),$$

where

$$x'_1 = ¢\varphi_R(x_1)$$

$$x'_{i+1} = \varphi_R(x_i)$$

for each i, $1 \leqslant i \leqslant n$, and

$$x'_{n+2} = \$$$

Also, define

$$\mathbf{y}' = (y'_1, \ldots, y'_{n+2}),$$

where

$$y'_1 = \varphi_L(y_1)$$

$$y'_{i+1} = \varphi_L(y_i)$$

for each i, $1 \leqslant i \leqslant n$, and

$$y'_{n+2} = ¢\$$$

The lists $\mathbf{x}'$ and $\mathbf{y}'$ represent an instance of a PCP. We shall show that the PCP for $\mathbf{x}'$ and $\mathbf{y}'$ has a solution if and only if the MPCP for $\mathbf{x}$ and $\mathbf{y}$ has a solution.

It is clear that if $1, i_1, \ldots, i_k$ is a solution to the MPCP with lists $\mathbf{x}$ and $\mathbf{y}$, then

$$1, i_1 + 1, \ldots, i_k + 1, n + 2$$

is a solution to the PCP with lists $\mathbf{x}'$ and $\mathbf{y}'$.

Suppose $i_1, \ldots, i_k$ is a solution to the PCP with lists $\mathbf{x}'$ and $\mathbf{y}'$. Then clearly, $i_1 = 1$, since that is the only index for which both terms start with ¢. Also $i_k = n + 2$, since that is the only index for which both terms end in the same character. Let j be the least integer such that $i_j = n + 2$. Then, it is not hard to see that $i_1, \ldots, i_j$ is also a solution. It should now be clear that:

$$1, i_2 - 1, \ldots, i_{j-1} - 1$$

is a solution to the MPCP for lists $\mathbf{x}$ and $\mathbf{y}$. Therefore, if there were an algorithm to solve the PCP, then we could also solve the MPCP. □

Now we are ready to prove the main theorem.

Theorem 8.3.2 For $|\Sigma| \geqslant 2$, the Post Correspondence Problem is unsolvable. That is, there is no algorithm which takes $\mathbf{x}$ and $\mathbf{y}$ as input and determines whether or not an index sequence $i_1, \ldots, i_k$ exists such that

$$x_{i_1} \cdots x_{i_k} = y_{i_1} \cdots y_{i_k}$$

Proof It suffices to show that if the MPCP were solvable, then the halting problem would be solvable, by Lemma 8.3.1. Given a Turing machine A and an input w, an instance of the MPCP will be constructed that has a solution if and only if A halts on w.

Let $A = (Q, \Sigma, \Gamma, B, \delta, q_0, \{\bar{q}\})$ be a Turing machine, and assume that A has a unique "halting state," say $\bar{q}$. The idea of the construction is that A's halting computation on w will look like:†

---

† $\alpha q \beta$ denotes an ID of the Turing machine A and indicates that A is in internal state q, the tape is $\alpha\beta$, and A is reading the first character of β.

$$q_0w \vdash \alpha_1 q_1 \beta_1 \vdash \cdots \vdash \alpha_k q_k \beta_k,$$

where $q_k = \bar{q}$. In that case, a solution of the MPCP will be as follows:

$$\# q_0 w \# \alpha_1 q_1 \beta_1 \# \cdots \# \alpha_k q_k \beta_k \#$$

The construction proceeds by giving the pertinent lists in Table 8.1.

TABLE 8.1 Lists for the MPCP

Number	**x**	**y**	
1	$\#$	$\# q_0 w \#$	
2	$\bar{q}\#\#$	$\#$	
3	$\#$	$\#$	
4	a	a	for each $a \in \Sigma - \{B\}$
For each $q \in Q - \{\bar{q}\}$, each $q' \in Q$, each $a, b, c \in \Sigma - \{B\}$,			
	qa	$q'b$	if $\delta(q, a) = (q', b, 0)$
	qa	bq'	if $\delta(q, a) = (q', b, 1)$
	cqa	$q'cb$	if $\delta(q, a) = (q', b, -1)$
	$q\#$	$bq'\#$	if $\delta(q, B) = (q', b, 1)$
	$cq\#$	$q'cb\#$	if $\delta(q, B) = (q', b, -1)$
	$q\#$	$q'b\#$	if $\delta(q, B) = (q', b, 0)$
	$a\bar{q}b$	$\bar{q}$	
	$a\bar{q}\#$	$\bar{q}\#$	
	$\#\bar{q}b$	$\#\bar{q}$	

In order to analyze the MPCP, the following definition is helpful.

Definition Let **x** and **y** be two lists over an alphabet Σ for an MPCP. A pair of strings (u, v), where $u, v \in \Sigma^*$, is said to be a *partial solution* to the MPCP if u is a prefix of v, and u and v are formed by concatenating corresponding strings from **x** and **y**, respectively. If $v = uu'$, then u' is said to be the *remainder* of the partial solution (u, v).

Claim If

$$q_0w \vdash \alpha_1 q_1 \beta_1 \vdash \cdots \vdash \alpha_k q_k \beta_k, \tag{8.3.1}$$

where none of $q_0, \ldots, q_{k-1}$ are equal to $\bar{q}$, then there is a partial solution

$$(u, v) = (\# q_0 w \# \alpha_1 q_1 \beta_1 \# \cdots \# \alpha_{k-1} q_{k-1} \beta_{k-1} \#, \# q_0 w \# \alpha_1 q_1 \beta_1 \# \cdots \# \alpha_k q_k \beta_k \#). \tag{8.3.2}$$

Moreover, this is the only partial solution whose second coordinate is as long as $\lg(v)$.

Proof The argument is an induction on k.

Basis. $k = 0$. Since this is a MPCP, we must choose the first pair and we get

$$(\#, \# q_0 w \#).$$

Induction step. Suppose the claim is true for some k and $q_k \neq \bar{q}$. We will show it true for $k+1$. The remainder of the partial solution (u, v) is $u' = \alpha_k q_k \beta_k \#$. We must match this from list x in the next move. Note that there can be at most one pair in Table 8.1 that is consistent with this requirement. Moreover this pair corresponds to a move of the Turing machine. The other symbols of u' come from items 3 and 4 in the lists. This provides a new partial solution

$$(u'', u''\alpha_{k+1} q_{k+1} \beta_{k+1} \#),$$

where this is the configuration A can reach from $\alpha_k q_k \beta_k$. There is no other partial solution whose second component is so long. This completes the induction proof.

If $q_k = \bar{q}$, then pairs from 2, 3, 4, and the last 3 items on the list may be added to the partial solution to give a total solution to the MPCP. On the other hand, if A never reaches $\bar{q}$, then there are partial solutions which are not total solutions.

Therefore there is a solution to the MPCP if and only if M halts on w. But this is unsolvable. □

Our next task is now to "code" the PCP into some languages. For ease in the construction, we use a three-letter alphabet $\Sigma = \{a, b, c\}$. All of the results may also be proved for a two-letter alphabet by suitably encoding the three-letter alphabet. The encoding to a binary alphabet is left for the problems.

First we define three languages which will be used extensively. Let

$$\mathbf{x} = (x_1, x_2, \ldots, x_n), \qquad \mathbf{y} = (y_1, y_2, \ldots, y_n), \qquad x_i, y_i \in \{a, b\}^+.$$

Let

$$L(\mathbf{x}) = \{ba^{i_k}b \cdots ba^{i_1}cx_{i_1} \cdots x_{i_k} \mid k \geq 1, \quad 1 \leq i_j \leq n, \quad 1 \leq j \leq k\}.$$

The idea behind $L(\mathbf{x})$ is simple. The integers $i_1, \ldots, i_k$ are encoded as blocks of a's separated by b's in reverse order; c acts as a "center" marker and is followed by $x_{i_1}x_{i_2} \cdots x_{i_k}$.

Proposition 8.3.1

a) Let w be a word in $L(\mathbf{x})$; given the part of the word up to c in w, the remainder is uniquely determined.

b) It is possible that different index sequences give rise to the same x and y words. That is, it is possible that

$$ba^{i_k} \cdots ba^{i_1} \neq ba^{j_r} \cdots ba^{j_1}$$

and yet

$$x_{i_1} \cdots x_{i_k} = x_{j_1} \cdots x_{j_r}.$$

Example $\mathbf{x} = (a, b, b^2)$. Then

$$ba^2ba^2 \neq ba^3 \qquad \text{but} \qquad x_2x_2 = b^2 = x_3.$$

Next let

$$\begin{aligned} L(\mathbf{x}, \mathbf{y}) &= L(\mathbf{x})\{c\}(L(\mathbf{y}))^T \\ &= \{ba^{i_k} \cdots ba^{i_1}cx_{i_1} \cdots x_{i_k}cy_{j_\ell}^T \cdots y_{j_1}^T ca^{j_1}b \cdots a^{j_\ell}b \mid \text{ where} \\ &\quad k, \ell \geq 1, 1 \leq i_p, j_q \leq n, 1 \leq p \leq k, 1 \leq q \leq \ell\}, \end{aligned}$$

and

$$L_s = \{w_1cw_2cw_2^Tcw_1^T \mid w_1, w_2 \in \{a, b\}^+\}.$$

Theorem 8.3.3 $L(\mathrm{x}, \mathrm{y})$ and L_s are deterministic context-free languages.

Proof We give an informal description of dpda's which accept $L(\mathrm{x}, \mathrm{y})$ and L_s, and leave as an exercise the formal proof that the constructions are correct.

The construction for $L(\mathrm{x}, \mathrm{y}) = L(\mathrm{x})\{c\}(L(\mathrm{y}))^T$ now follows:

1 Copy everything up to the first c onto the stack.

2 Erase the top block of a's from the stack, counting them. This is possible since the number of a's in a valid block is $\leqslant n$. If more than n a's are found, the string is rejected.

3 Now advance on the input, checking to see whether the input is x_{i_j}, where i_j is the number determined in Step 2. Again this is possible since there are only a finite number of x_{i_j}.

4 If input symbol is not a c, go back to Step 2.

5 Copy everything up to the next c onto the stack.

6 Count the number of a's in the current block of a's, from the input.

7 Now check to see whether the top of the stack is $y_{i_j}^T$, where i_j is the number of a's counted in Step 6.

8 If the stack is Z_0, then accept by erasing Z_0 and going to a final state under Λ; else return to Step 6 and continue. If the input is not exhausted, go back to Step 6.

Now the technique for $L_s = \{w_1cw_2cw_2^Tcw_1^T \mid w_1, w_2 \in \{a, b\}^+\}$ is given:

1 Copy everything up to the second c onto the stack.

2 Compare the rest of the input with the stack. □

The next lemma plays a key role in subsequent applications.

Lemma 8.3.2 $L(\mathrm{x}, \mathrm{y}) \cap L_s$ contains no infinite context-free language.

Proof

$$L(\mathrm{x}, \mathrm{y}) \cap L_s = \{t_1ct_2ct_2^Tct_1^T \mid t_1 = ba^{i_k} \cdots ba^{i_1}; t_2 = x_{i_1} \cdots x_{i_k} = y_{i_1} \cdots y_{i_k}\}.$$

Fact t_1 uniquely determines $t_1ct_2ct_2^Tct_1^T$.

Proof t_1 uniquely determines t_2 by the encoding of $L(\mathrm{x}, \mathrm{y})$.

Now suppose L is an infinite context-free language and $L \subseteq L(\mathrm{x}, \mathrm{y}) \cap L_s$. Then, by the iteration theorem, there exists a constant p such that the conclusions of that theorem hold.

Let

$$w = t_1ct_2ct_2^Tct_1^T \in L$$

with $\lg(t_2) \geqslant p$. This is possible since, for L to be infinite, it must contain arbitrarily long words and if

$$t_1 = ba^{i_p} \cdots ba^{i_1},$$

then $\lg(t_2) \geqslant p$, since $x_i \neq \Lambda$, $1 \leqslant i \leqslant n$.

Now let all the positions in t_2 be distinguished as shown below:

$$w = t_1 c \underline{t_2} c t_2^T c t_1^T.$$

Then, by the iteration theorem, there exists a factorization

$$\varphi = (v_1, v_2, v_3, v_4, v_5)$$

such that

$$v_1 v_2^q v_3 v_4^q v_5 \in L \quad \text{for all } q \geqslant 0,$$

and either $K_1, K_2, K_3 \neq \emptyset$ or $K_3, K_4, K_5 \neq \emptyset$. Assume $K_1, K_2, K_3 \neq \emptyset$. (The case $K_3, K_4, K_5 \neq \emptyset$ is similar to this one.) Then

$$v_1 = t_1 c v_1' \quad \text{for some } v_1',$$

$$v_2 \neq \Lambda,$$

and

$$v_1 v_3 v_5 \in L.$$

Thus

$$v_1 v_3 v_5 = t_1 c v_1' v_3 v_5 \in L.$$

But, by the fact proved above,

If

$$t_1 c v_1' v_3 v_5 \in L,$$

then

$$t_1 c v_1' v_3 v_5 = t_1 c t_2 c t_2^T c t_1^T = z$$

Therefore,

$$v_1 v_2 v_3 v_4 v_5 = w = v_1 v_3 v_5$$

This is a contradiction, since $v_2 \neq \Lambda$, and therefore L cannot be both infinite and context-free. □

PROBLEMS

1 Extend the theorems of this section to the case of a two-letter alphabet. Encode $L(\mathbf{x}, \mathbf{y})$ and L_s into a binary alphabet.

2 Show that the Post Correspondence Problem is solvable if $|\Sigma| = 1$.

Let $|\Sigma| \geqslant 2$ and let $\mathbf{x} = (x_1, \ldots, x_n)$ and $\mathbf{y} = (y_1, \ldots, y_n)$ be two lists of nonnull Σ-words.

3 Is the Post Correspondence Problem solvable

a) if $n = 1$?

b) if $n = 2$?

c) if $n \geqslant 1$ and for each i, $1 \leqslant i \leqslant n$, $\lg(x_i) = \lg(y_i)$?

4 Show that there exists some positive integer n_0 such that the Post Correspondence Problem with $n = n_0$ is unsolvable.

5 Is the following problem unsolvable or not? Given $|\Sigma| \geq 2$ and let $\mathbf{x} = (x_1, \ldots, x_n)$ and $\mathbf{y} = (y_1, \ldots, y_n)$ be lists of nonnull Σ-words; do there exist $k \geq 1$, $\ell \geq 1$, $i_1, \ldots, i_k$, $j_1, \ldots, j_\ell$, such that $1 \leq i_p, j_q \leq n$ for $1 \leq p \leq k$, $1 \leq q \leq \ell$, and

$$x_{i_1} \cdots x_{i_k} = y_{j_1} \cdots y_{j_\ell}?$$

6 Is the following problem unsolvable or not? Given $|\Sigma| \geq 2$ and let $\mathbf{x} = (x_1, \ldots, x_n)$ and $\mathbf{y} = (y_1, \ldots, y_n)$ be two lists of nonnull Σ-words; do there exist $k \geq 1$, $i_1, \ldots, i_k$, $j_1, \ldots, j_k$, such that $1 \leq i_p, j_q \leq n$ for $1 \leq p, q \leq k$, and

$$x_{i_1} \cdots x_{i_k} = y_{j_1} \cdots y_{j_k}?$$

7 Let $A = (Q, \Sigma, \Gamma, B, \delta, q_0, \{f\})$ be a Turing machine, given that B is the blank symbol and is in Σ; f is the unique "stopping state." Assume $Q \cap \Sigma = \emptyset$. A *computation* of A is a sequence

$$\alpha_0 \vdash \alpha_1 \vdash \cdots \vdash \alpha_n,$$

where $\alpha_i \in \Sigma^* Q \Sigma^+$ and $\alpha_i \vdash \alpha_{i+1}$, as specified by δ. Let $c \notin \Sigma$ and define

$$L_1 = \{\alpha c \beta^T c \mid \alpha \underset{A}{\vdash} \beta\}^* c$$

and

$$L_2 = \{q_0 w c \mid w \in \Sigma^*\}\{\alpha^T c \beta c \mid \alpha \underset{A}{\vdash} \beta\}^* \{(xfy)^T \mid x, y \in \Sigma^*\}\{cc\}.$$

Show that L_1 and L_2 are deterministic context-free languages. Are they real-time as well?

8 Show that there is an algorithm which takes as input a Turing machine A and produces a context-free grammar G_A such that

$$L(G_A) = \Sigma^* - \{\alpha_1 c \alpha_2^T c \cdots c \alpha_{2k}^T cc \mid \alpha_1 = q_0 w \quad \text{for some } w \in \Sigma^*, \alpha_{2k} = xfy \text{ and } \alpha_1 \vdash \alpha_2 \vdash \cdots \vdash \alpha_{2k}\}.$$

9 Show that there is a context-free language L such that the set of prefixes of $\Sigma^* - L$ is not recursive but is recursively enumerable.

10 Fix $\Sigma = \{a, b\}$. Construct a family $\{G_n \mid n \geq 0\}$ of context-free grammars such that:

i) For each $n \geq 0$, G_n may be effectively constructed from n;

ii) $\Lambda \in L(G_n)$ for each n;

iii) $|\Sigma^* - L(G_n)| \leq 1$;

iv) $\{n \mid L(G_n) \neq \Sigma^*\}$ is not recursive.

Hint: Take a Turing machine A which accepts a nonrecursive set over Σ^*. Encode (non)computations such that there is a set $J(A, n)$ which lacks one member from $\{a, b\}^*$ if and only if A accepts n.

11 Show that every recursively enumerable set L may be represented as $L_1 L_2^{-1}$ for some context-free languages L_1 and L_2. *Hint*: Represent $L = T(A)$ for some Turing machine $A = (Q, \Sigma, \Gamma, B, \delta, q_0, \{f\})$.

12 Refer to the proof of Theorem 8.3.2. Show that A halts on $w \in \Sigma^*$ if and only if there exists $k \geq 0$, $3 \leq i_1, \ldots, i_k \leq n$ such that

$$x_1 x_{i_1} \cdots x_{i_k} x_2 = y_1 y_{i_1} \cdots y_{i_k} y_2$$

13 Show that, for any recursive function f and for arbitrarily large integers n, there is a context-free grammar G so that $|G| = n$, $L(G)$ is a regular set, and the reduced finite automaton accepting $L(G)$ has at least $f(n)$ states. [*Hint.* Cf. Problem 8.]

8.4 BASIC UNSOLVABLE PROBLEMS FOR CONTEXT-FREE GRAMMARS AND LANGUAGES

In Section 8.3, we worked out the properties of two deterministic context-free languages. With the aid of these sets, we shall very easily develop the basic negative results about the context-free languages and grammars. In what follows, the results are claimed for all alphabets with at least two symbols. In fact, the proofs are given only for alphabets with at least three symbols. In Problem 1, the reader is asked to extend the result to a binary alphabet.

We begin our development by noting the form of strings in $L(\mathbf{x}, \mathbf{y}) \cap L_s$.

Lemma 8.4.1 It is recursively unsolvable to determine for arbitrary lists of words $\mathbf{x}$ and $\mathbf{y}$ whether

$$L(\mathbf{x}, \mathbf{y}) \cap L_s \neq \emptyset.$$

Proof

$$L(\mathbf{x}, \mathbf{y}) \cap L_s = \{t_1 c t_2 c t_2^T c t_1^T \mid t_1 = ba^{i_k} \cdots ba^{i_1}; \quad t_2 = x_{i_1} \cdots x_{i_k} = y_{i_1} \cdots y_{i_k}\}$$

Therefore, $L(x, y) \cap L_s \neq \emptyset$ if and only if there exists a solution to the Post Correspondence Problem. But the Post Correspondence Problem is recursively unsolvable, which proves the lemma. □

This establishes the following result.

Theorem 8.4.1 Let $|\Sigma| \geqslant 2$. It is recursively unsolvable to determine whether $L_1 \cap L_2 = \emptyset$ for (deterministic) context-free languages L_1 and L_2.

Proof Lemma 8.4.1 gives the result for $|\Sigma| \geqslant 3$ by taking $L_1 = L(\mathbf{x}, \mathbf{y})$ and $L_2 = L_s$. The case $|\Sigma| \geqslant 2$ is left to Exercise 1. □

Next we learn that we cannot even decide whether $L_1 \cap L_2$ is context-free.

Theorem 8.4.2 Let $|\Sigma| \geqslant 2$. It is recursively unsolvable to determine whether $L_1 \cap L_2$ is a context-free language for arbitrary context-free languages L_1 and L_2.

Proof

$$L(\mathbf{x}, \mathbf{y}) \cap L_s \neq \emptyset$$

if and only if there exists a solution to the Post Correspondence Problem. By an earlier observation, we know that if there is one solution to the Post Correspondence Problem, there are infinitely many. But we have shown that $L(\mathbf{x}, \mathbf{y}) \cap L_s$ contains no infinite context-free language. Therefore $L(\mathbf{x}, \mathbf{y}) \cap L_s$ is a context-free language if and only if it is empty. But by Lemma 8.4.1 this is undecidable. □

Now, we wish to show that one cannot decide whether a context-free language is regular. To do this, we need a simple lemma.

Lemma 8.4.2 Let $|\Sigma| \geqslant 2$. Let $M(\mathrm{x}, \mathrm{y}) = \Sigma^* - (L(\mathrm{x}, \mathrm{y}) \cap L_s)$. $M(\mathrm{x}, \mathrm{y})$ is a context-free language and it is recursively unsolvable to determine whether or not $M(\mathrm{x}, \mathrm{y}) = \Sigma^*$.

Proof

$$\begin{aligned} M(\mathrm{x}, \mathrm{y}) &= \Sigma^* - (L(\mathrm{x}, \mathrm{y}) \cap L_s) \\ &= (\Sigma^* - L(\mathrm{x}, \mathrm{y})) \cup (\Sigma^* - L_s) \\ &= \bar{L}(\mathrm{x}, \mathrm{y}) \cup \bar{L}_s. \end{aligned}$$

We know that $L(\mathrm{x}, \mathrm{y})$ and L_s are deterministic context-free languages and so are $\bar{L}(\mathrm{x}, \mathrm{y})$ and $\bar{L}_s$, by Theorem 5.6.1. Thus $M(\mathrm{x}, \mathrm{y})$ is a union of two deterministic context-free languages and hence is a context-free language. But

$$M(\mathrm{x}, \mathrm{y}) = \Sigma^*$$

if and only if

$$L(\mathrm{x}, \mathrm{y}) \cap L_s = \emptyset.$$

Now, using the fact that $L(\mathrm{x}, \mathrm{y}) \cap L_s = \emptyset$ is undecidable, we have that $M(\mathrm{x}, \mathrm{y}) = \Sigma^*$ is undecidable. □

Theorem 8.4.3 Let $M(\mathrm{x}, \mathrm{y})$ be as in Lemma 8.4.2 above. $M(\mathrm{x}, \mathrm{y})$ is regular if and only if $M(\mathrm{x}, \mathrm{y}) = \Sigma^*$. Thus, it is recursively unsolvable to determine whether an arbitrary context-free language over an alphabet Σ, $|\Sigma| \geqslant 3$, is regular.

Proof Again we use the fact that $L(\mathrm{x}, \mathrm{y}) \cap L_s$ is either empty or infinite. Since $L(\mathrm{x}, \mathrm{y}) \cap L_s$ contains no infinite context-free languages, it contains no infinite regular sets.

Recall that

$$M(\mathrm{x}, \mathrm{y}) = \Sigma^* - (L(\mathrm{x}, \mathrm{y}) \cap L_s)$$

and

$$\Sigma^* - M(x, y) = L(\mathrm{x}, \mathrm{y}) \cap L_s.$$

We claim that $M(\mathrm{x}, \mathrm{y})$ is regular if and only if $M(\mathrm{x}, \mathrm{y}) = \Sigma^*$. The *if* direction is trivial. If $M(\mathrm{x}, \mathrm{y})$ is regular, then $\Sigma^* - M(\mathrm{x}, \mathrm{y}) = L(\mathrm{x}, \mathrm{y}) \cap L_s$ is regular. Since $L(\mathrm{x}, \mathrm{y}) \cap L_s$ cannot be infinite, we must have $L(\mathrm{x}, \mathrm{y}) \cap L_s = \emptyset$, which implies $M(\mathrm{x}, \mathrm{y}) = \Sigma^*$. By Lemma 8.4.2, one cannot decide whether $M(\mathrm{x}, \mathrm{y}) = \Sigma^*$. □

Corollary For $|\Sigma| \geqslant 2$, it is recursively unsolvable whether or not an arbitrary context-free language is regular.

Proof Cf. Problem 1 at the end of this section. □

Now we shall consider the containment and equality problems for context-free languages.

Theorem 8.4.4 Let $|\Sigma| \geqslant 2$. It is recursively unsolvable to determine whether, for arbitrary context-free languages L_1 and L_2,

$$L_1 \subseteq L_2,$$

$$L_1 = L_2.$$

Proof Recall that

$$M(\mathbf{x}, \mathbf{y}) = \Sigma^* - (L(\mathbf{x}, \mathbf{y}) \cap L_s).$$

Let

$$L_1 = \Sigma^*$$

$$L_2 = \Sigma^* - (L(\mathbf{x}, \mathbf{y}) \cap L_s) = M(\mathbf{x}, \mathbf{y}).$$

Both L_1 and L_2 are context-free languages, and

$$L_1 \subseteq L_2 \quad \text{if and only if } M(\mathbf{x}, \mathbf{y}) = \Sigma^*.$$

But it is recursively unsolvable to determine whether $M(\mathbf{x}, \mathbf{y}) = \Sigma^*$.

Take $L_1 = M(\mathbf{x}, \mathbf{y})$ and $L_2 = \Sigma^*$. The unsolvability of the equality problem follows from Lemma 8.4.2. □

Next we turn to a potentially useful idea. Could we find an algorithm to decide whether a context-free grammar is ambiguous?

Theorem 8.4.5 Let $|\Sigma| \geqslant 4$. It is recursively unsolvable to determine whether an arbitrary context-free grammar over Σ is ambiguous or not.

Proof Let

$$\mathbf{x} = (x_1, \ldots, x_n),$$

$$\mathbf{y} = (y_1, \ldots, y_n)$$

be two lists of nonnull words over $\{a, b\}^*$. Consider G where

$$S \to S_1 | S_2$$

$$S_1 \to x_i S_1 dc^i | x_i dc^i \quad \text{for } 1 \leqslant i \leqslant n,$$

$$S_2 \to y_i S_2 dc^i | y_i dc^i \quad \text{for } 1 \leqslant i \leqslant n.$$

Clearly,

$$L(G) = \{x_{i_1} \cdots x_{i_m} dc^{i_m} \cdots dc^{i_1} \mid m \geqslant 1, x_j \in \{a, b\}^*, 1 \leqslant i_j \leqslant n, \quad \text{for all } 1 \leqslant j \leqslant m\}$$

$$\cup \{y_{j_1} \cdots y_{j_p} dc^{j_p} \cdots dc^{j_1} \mid p \geqslant 1, y_k \in \{a, b\}^*, 1 \leqslant j_\ell \leqslant n, \quad \text{for all } 1 \leqslant \ell \leqslant p\}.$$

Moreover, the context-free languages generated by $G_i = (V, \Sigma, P, S_i)$ are both unambiguous. Thus, G is ambiguous if and only if

$$\{x_{i_1} \cdots x_{i_m} dc^{i_m} \cdots dc^{i_1}\} \cap \{y_{j_1} \cdots y_{j_p} dc^{j_p} \cdots dc^{j_1}\} \neq \emptyset.$$

Thus, G is ambiguous if and only if $m = p$; $(i_1, \ldots, i_m) = (j_1, \ldots, j_m)$, and $x_{i_1} \cdots x_{i_m} = y_{i_1} \cdots y_{i_m}$, that is, if and only if the Post Correspondence Problem has a solution; but the Post Correspondence Problem is recursively unsolvable. Therefore it is recursively unsolvable to determine whether an arbitrary context-free grammar is ambiguous. □

Lastly, we consider inherent ambiguity.

Theorem 8.4.6 There is no algorithm to decide whether a context-free language is inherently ambiguous.

Proof Let x, y be nonnull lists of words over $\{a, b\}^*$. Define

$$L = \{a^i b^i c^j \mid i, j \geqslant 1\}\{d\}L(\mathrm{x}, \mathrm{y}) \cup \{a^i b^j c^j \mid i, j \geqslant 1\}\{d\}L_s.$$

L is surely a context-free language. Moreover, each term is an unambiguous context-free language.

Claim L is inherently ambiguous if and only if

$$L(\mathrm{x}, \mathrm{y}) \cap L_s \neq \emptyset.$$

Proof of the claim If L is inherently ambiguous, then there must be some string in each term and surely $L(\mathrm{x}, \mathrm{y}) \cap L_s \neq \emptyset$. If $L(\mathrm{x}, \mathrm{y}) \cap L_s \neq \emptyset$, then let $z \in L(\mathrm{x}, \mathrm{y}) \cap L_s$. Define $R = a^*b^*c^*dz$, which is a regular set. Suppose that L were unambiguous. Then

$$L \cap R = L_2 = \{a^i b^i c^j \mid i, j \geqslant 1\}\{dz\} \cup \{a^i b^j c^j \mid i, j \geqslant 1\}\{dz\} = (L_0 \cup L_1)dz$$

would be unambiguous, by Theorem 6.4.1. But, by Theorem 7.2.2, $L_0 \cup L_1$ is inherently ambiguous. Applying Theorem 7.4.3,

$$(L_0 \cup L_1)\{dz\} = L_2$$

is also inherently ambiguous. But this contradicts that L_2 is unambiguous.

It now follows that we can decide whether L is inherently ambiguous if and only if $L(\mathrm{x}, \mathrm{y}) \cap L_s \neq \emptyset$. But this is undecidable, by Lemma 8.4.1. □

There are additional questions about context-free languages which are recursively unsolvable but which are not included here. The above theorems should be sufficient to provide the reader with a "feel" for the types of questions which are undecidable and the methods used in proving that a given question is undecidable.

PROBLEMS

1 Extend all the results of this section to a binary alphabet.

2 Show that, given a context-free grammar G, there is no effective way to construct G' such that

$$L(G') = L(G) - \{\Lambda\}$$

and $|G'| = \min \{|G_1|: L(G_1) = L(G) - \{\Lambda\}, G_1 \text{ is } \Lambda\text{-free}\}$.

3 Show that it is undecidable to determine, of two context-free grammars, whether or not they have the same set of sentential forms.

4 There is an interesting class of decision problems called "birdie" problems." We already know that one cannot decide whether a context-free language is regular. Suppose a birdie tells us that $L(G)$ is regular. Show that one cannot construct a finite automaton A so that

$$L(G) = T(A).$$

[*Hint*: Cf. Problem 11 of Section 8.3.]

5 Is it decidable whether or not $L \subseteq R$ for a context-free language L and a regular set R?

6 A context-free language L is *prefix-free* if, for any $u, v \in \Sigma^*$, we have that $uv \in L$ and $u \in L$ imply $v = \Lambda$. Show that it is undecidable whether or not L is prefix-free. [*Hint*: Reduce to $L_1 \cap L_2 = \emptyset$.]

7 Show that there is an algorithm to decide whether an arbitrary pda A is finite-turn or not (cf. Section 5.7). Show that if A is finite-turn, it is solvable to find the least integer k_0 such that each sweep of A has $(2k-1)$ turns for some $k \leqslant k_0$.

8.5* A POWERFUL METATHEOREM

In the previous section, certain problems were proved to be unsolvable. Given a context-free grammar, we cannot decide whether it is unambiguous or regular, etc. We will consider many other questions such as, "is $L(G)$ a deterministic context-free language," or "unambiguous," or "precedence." These problems are often undecidable, and the proofs are sufficiently similar that one suspects that the subject can be unified so that proving one theorem will distill the essence of the argument. This section is devoted to such a theorem.

We will need some properties of the "bounded sets." These sets were first studied because it was noticed that many of our examples were of the form of subsets of $a^*b^*c^*$. It is useful to generalize the concept as follows:

Definition A set $L \subseteq \Sigma^*$ is *bounded* if there exist $k \geqslant 0$, $w_1, \ldots, w_k \in \Sigma^*$, such that:

$$L \subseteq w_1^* \cdots w_k^*.$$

A set that is not bounded is called *unbounded.*

For example,

$$L_0 \cup L_1 = \{a^ib^jc^k \mid i = j \quad \text{or} \quad j = k, \quad i, j, k \geqslant 1\}$$

is bounded. Also,

$$\{(aba)^i c (aba)^i \mid i \geqslant 0\}$$

is bounded but

$$\{a, b\}^*$$

is unbounded.

We need the following lemma about unbounded regular sets and finite automata.

Lemma 8.5.1 Let $a, b \in \Sigma$ and let $L \subseteq \Sigma^*$, where $L = T(A)$ for some reduced finite automaton $A = (Q, \Sigma, \delta, q_0, F)$. Either:

1 L is bounded, or

2 There exist $a \neq b$ in $\Sigma, x_1, x_2, x_3, x_4$ in Σ^*, and $q \in Q$ such that

$$\delta(q_0, x_1) = q, \tag{8.5.1}$$

$$\delta(q, ax_2) = q, \tag{8.8.2}$$

$$\delta(q, bx_3) = q, \tag{8.8.3}$$

and

$$\delta(q, x_4) \in F. \tag{8.5.4}$$

Proof Let $|Q| = k$ and we induct on k.

Basis. $k = 1$. $T(A) = \emptyset$ or $T(A) = \Sigma^*$. If $L = T(A) = \emptyset$, then L is bounded. If $T(A) = \Sigma^*$, then $q_0 \in F$ and $x_1 = x_2 = x_3 = x_4 = \Lambda$ satisfy Condition 2 of the lemma.

Induction step. Assume the result for all finite automata with k or fewer states and assume $|Q| = k + 1$. Suppose (2) is false. That is, for all $x_1, \ldots, x_4 \in \Sigma^*$, the conjunction of (8.5.1), (8.5.2), (8.5.3), and (8.5.4) is false. Now choose $x_1 = \Lambda$, which forces $q_0 = q$. Choose any x_4 such that (8.5.4) is true (why does such an x_4 exist?). This means that at most one of (8.5.2) and (8.5.3) can be true; i.e., there exists $a \in \Sigma, x = x_2$, such that

$$\delta(q, ax_2) = \delta(q_0, ax) = q_0.$$

Moreover, by choosing x to be minimal among the set of all nonnull y, so that $\delta(q_0, y) = q_0$, the string ax is unique. For each $c \in \Sigma$, define

$$A_c = (Q - \{q_0\}, \Sigma, \delta', \delta(q_0, c), F - \{q_0\}),$$

where

$$\delta' = \delta \cap ((Q - \{q_0\}) \times \Sigma \times (Q - \{q_0\})).$$

If $\delta(q_0, c) = q_0$, define A_c to be a one-state finite automaton which accepts $\emptyset$. Now

$$T(A) = \begin{cases} (ax)^* \bigcup_{c \in \Sigma} cT(A_c) & \text{if } q_0 \notin F, \\ ((ax)^* \bigcup_{c \in \Sigma} cT(A_c)) \cup (ax)^* & \text{if } q_0 \in F. \end{cases}$$

By the induction hypothesis, $T(A_c)$ is a bounded set. But the bounded sets are closed under finite union and products, so that $T(A)$ is bounded. □

The previous lemma is employed to prove the following useful theorem.

Theorem 8.5.1 Let L be any regular set over $\Sigma = \{a, b\}$. The following three conditions are equivalent.

a) L is unbounded.

b) There exist u, v, x, y in Σ^* such that

$$x\{au, bv\}^* y \subseteq L.$$

c) There exist u, v, x, y in Σ^* such that

$$x\{ua, vb\}^* y \subseteq L.$$

Proof Parts (b) and (c) are clearly equivalent, since L is (un)bounded if and only if L^T is (un)bounded. (Cf. Problem 1 at the end of this section.)

Next, we show that (a) implies (b). Since L is regular and unbounded, it follows, from Lemma 8.5.1, that there exist $x = x_1$, $u = x_2$, $v = x_3$, and $y = x_4$, so that

(8.5.1) through (8.5.4) of the lemma are satisfied. Pasting together the computation of A in Lemma 8.5.1 gives that

$$x\{au, bv\}^* y \subseteq L.$$

To show that (b) implies (a), we proceed by a sequence of claims.

Claim 1

a) If L contains an unbounded set, then L is unbounded.

b) If L is unbounded, then so is $\{x\}L$, where $x \in \Sigma^*$.

c) If L is unbounded, then so is $\{x\}L\{y\}$ for $x, y \in \Sigma^*$.

Proof (a) follows from Problem 8.5.1 by contraposition. (b) follows by induction on $\lg(x)$. (c) follows from (b) and the closure of the bounded sets under reversal (Problem 1 again).

Claim 2 In order to show that (b) implies (a), it suffices to show that

$$\{au, bv\}^*$$

is unbounded.

Proof Suppose that $\{au, bv\}^*$ were unbounded. By Claim 1(c),

$$x\{au, bv\}^* y$$

is unbounded. But, by (b), if $x\{au, bv\}^* y \subseteq L$, then Claim 1(a) implies that L is unbounded and we would be done.

Suppose now

$$\{au, bv\}^* \subseteq w_1^* \cdots w_k^*$$

for some $w_1, \ldots, w_k \in \Sigma^*$. Let $\ell_i = \lg(w_i)$ and let ℓ be the least common multiple of $\ell_1, \ldots, \ell_k$. Consider the string

$$((au)^\ell (bv)^\ell)^k \;=\; w_1^{i_1} \cdots w_k^{i_k} \tag{8.5.5}$$

and let us call a string $(au)^\ell (bv)^\ell$ a *block.*

Claim 3 Each block of (8.5.5) must contain (as a subword) w_i and w_j, where $i \neq j$.

Proof If not,

$$(au)^\ell (bv)^\ell \;=\; w_j^{p_j} \quad \text{for some } p_j;$$

but

$$\lg(w_j) \mid \ell \lg(au)$$

and

$$\lg(w_j) \mid \ell \lg(bv).$$

Thus Fig. 8.1 describes the factorizations.

But it is clear that the first character of w_j must be an a (cf. the left arrow in Fig. 8.1). On the other hand, the first character of w_j must be a b, by the second arrow in Fig. 8.1. This contradiction establishes Claim 3.

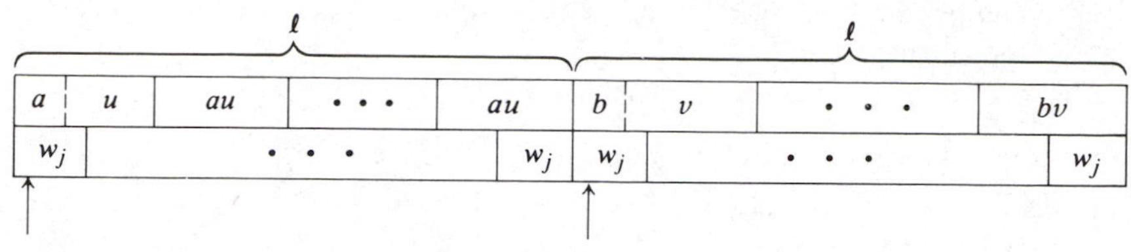

FIG. 8.1

To finish the proof, Claim 3 establishes the need for two distinct words in each block. So we have k blocks, and we must assign $w_1 \cdots w_k$ to the word

$$((au)^{\ell}(bv)^{\ell})^k,$$

using two different w_i in each block. The best way we could do this is shown below.

	Block 1	Block 2	. . .	Block $k-1$	Block k
Assignment	1, 2	2, 3		$k-1, k$	$k, k+1$

But we need $k+1$ words w_i and we have only k of them. This contradiction establishes the result. □

In order to state our main result, it will be necessary to introduce predicates on languages.

Definition Let X be any set. A *predicate* $\mathscr{P}$ is any function from X into $\{true, false\}$. $\mathscr{P}$ is *nontrivial* if there exist $x_1, x_2 \in X$ so that $\mathscr{P}(x_1) = true$ and $\mathscr{P}(x_2) = false$.

Now some special predicates are introduced on a family of languages over the alphabet $\{a, b\}$.

Definition Let $\Sigma = \{a, b\}$ and let $\mathscr{P}$ be a predicate on a class of languages over Σ^*. Let $u, v, x, y \in \Sigma^*$. Define the one-to-one homomorphism φ where

$$\varphi(a) = au$$
$$\varphi(b) = bv$$

Then define

$$\mathscr{L}(\mathscr{P}, x, u, v, y) = \{L' \mid L' = \varphi^{-1}(w^{-1}(x^{-1}Ly^{-1})), w \in \{au, bv\}^+, \mathscr{P}(L) = true\}.$$

Define the one-to-one homomorphism ψ by

$$\psi(a) = ua$$
$$\psi(b) = vb$$

Then

$$\mathscr{R}(\mathscr{P}, x, u, v, y) = \{L' \mid L' = \psi^{-1}(x^{-1}Ly^{-1})w^{-1}, w \in \{ua, vb\}^+, \mathscr{P}(L) = true\}.$$

Note that $\mathscr{L}(\mathscr{P}, x, u, v, y)$ and $\mathscr{R}(\mathscr{P}, x, u, v, y)$ are in fact families of languages over $\{a, b\}$.

Example Suppose one has a predicate on languages, which is always *false* except for the language

$$L = abb\{aba, b^4, aa\}^* ab.$$

Here $x = abb, u = ba, v = b$, and $y = ab$. Then

$$x^{-1}Ly^{-1} = \{aba, b^4, aa\}^*.$$

Then

$$\begin{aligned} M &= \{L' \mid L' = w^{-1}(x^{-1}Ly^{-1}), w \in \{aba, bb\}^+\} \\ &= \{\{aba, b^4, aa\}^*, bb\{aba, b^4, aa\}^*\}. \end{aligned}$$

Putting the pieces together yields

$$\mathscr{L}(\mathscr{P}, x, u, v, y) = \{\{a, bb\}^*, b\{a, bb\}^*\}.$$

Our next technical lemma contains the essence of the proof of the main result.

Lemma 8.5.2 Let $\mathscr{P}$ be any predicate on the family of context-free languages over $\Sigma = \{a, b\}$. If there exists a context-free language L_0 and strings x, u, v, y in $\{a, b\}^*$ such that either:

a) $\mathscr{P}(L_0) = true$,

b) $x\{au, bv\}^* y \subseteq L_0$, and

c) $\mathscr{L}(\mathscr{P}, x, u, v, y)$ is a proper subfamily of the context-free languages over Σ^*;

or

d) $\mathscr{P}(L_0) = true$,

e) $x\{ua, vb\}^* y \subseteq L_0$, and

f) $\mathscr{R}(\mathscr{P}, x, u, v, y)$ is a proper subfamily of the context-free languages over Σ^*;

then, for any arbitrary context-free grammar G, the predicate $\mathscr{P}(L(G))$ is undecidable.

Proof Let $\mathscr{P}$ be any predicate over the context-free languages that satisfies (a), (b), and (c). (There is a dual proof for (d), (e), and (f), which will be omitted.) From (c), there is a context-free language $L' \subseteq \Sigma^*$ that is not in $\mathscr{L}(\mathscr{P}, x, u, v, y)$. Define two one-to-one homomorphisms φ_1 and φ_3 by:

$$\begin{aligned} \varphi_1 a &= au \\ \varphi_1 b &= bv \\ \varphi_3 a &= auau \\ \varphi_3 b &= aubv \end{aligned}$$

Let G be an arbitrary context-free grammar over Σ:

$$\begin{aligned} L_1 &= x\varphi_3(L(G))bvau\{au, bv\}^* y \\ L_2 &= x\{auau, aubv\}^* bvau\varphi_1(L')y \\ L_3 &= L_0 \cap (\Sigma^* - \{x\{auau, aubv\}^* bvau\{au, bv\}^* y\}) \end{aligned}$$

Clearly, L_1, L_2, and L_3 are context-free languages. Then $L_1 \cup L_2 \cup L_3$ is a context-free language and let G_1 be a context-free grammar such that

$$L(G_1) = L_1 \cup L_2 \cup L_3. \tag{8.5.6}$$

Since G is given, G_1 can be effectively constructed.†

Claim $\mathscr{P}(L(G_1)) = true$ if and only if $L(G) = \Sigma^*$.

Proof of claim Suppose

$$L(G) = \{a, b\}^*.$$

Then

$$\varphi_3(L(G)) = \{auau, aubv\}^*$$

and

$$L_1 \cup L_3 = L_0.$$

To see (8.57), note that, if $z \in L_3$, then $z \in L_0$. If $z \in L_1$, then, since $L_1 \subseteq x\{au, bv\}^*y \subseteq L_0$ by (b) of the lemma, so $z \in L_0$. Thus $L_1 \cap L_3 \subseteq L_0$. Conversely, assume $z \in L_0$. If z is the form in L_1, then we are done; otherwise it is in $L_0 \cap (\Sigma^* - L_1) = L_3$. This proves (8.5.7). From (8.5.7) and the fact that $L_2 \subseteq L_0$, we have that

$$L(G_1) = L_1 \cup L_2 \cup L_3 = L_0 \cup L_2 = L_0,$$

and so

$$\mathscr{P}(L(G_1)) = true.$$

Conversely, assume that $L(G) \notin \{a, b\}^*$. Then there exists

$$z \in \{a, b\}^* - L(G). \tag{8.5.8}$$

Then

$$\varphi_3(z) \in \{auau, aubv\}^* - \varphi_3(L(G)).$$

Let

$$w = \varphi_3(z)bvau.$$

Clearly,

$$xw\Sigma^* \cap L_1 = \emptyset, \tag{8.5.9}$$

because if $xws \in L_1$, then, since $w = \varphi_3(z)bvau$, we would have $z \in L(G)$, which contradicts (8.5.8).

Define

$$T = \{t \mid xwty \in L_3\}.$$

We claim that

$$T \cap \{au, bv\}^* = \emptyset, \tag{8.5.10}$$

because $t \in T \cap \{au, bv\}^*$ implies that

$$xwty \in x\{auau, aubv\}^*\, bvau\{au, bv\}^*y = M,$$

so that

$$xwty \notin L_3 = L_0 \cap (\Sigma^* - M),$$

which contradicts the definition of T.

---

† That is, there is some recursive function that produces G_1 from G. However, we don't know which recursive function does so unless we have an effective presentation of L'.

We claim that

$$w^{-1}(x^{-1}L(G_1)y^{-1}) = \varphi_1(L') \cup T. \tag{8.5.11}$$

To see this, suppose $t \in w^{-1}(x^{-1}L(G_1)y^{-1})$. Then

$$xwty \in L(G_1). \tag{8.5.12}$$

If $xwty \in L_3$, then $t \in T$ and we are done. Assume that $xwty \notin L_3$. By (8.5.6) and (8.5.12),

$$xwty \in L_1 \cup L_2. \tag{8.5.13}$$

But $xwty \notin L_1$ because of (8.5.9). Thus (8.5.13) leads to

$$xwty \in L_2. \tag{8.5.14}$$

From the definition of L_2 and (8.5.14), we have

$$t \in \varphi_1(L').$$

The argument can be reversed and this completes the proof of (8.5.11).

Applying, φ_1^{-1} to (8.5.11) yields:

$$\varphi_1^{-1}(w^{-1}(x^{-1}L(G_1)y^{-1})) = \varphi_1^{-1}(\varphi_1(L') \cup T). \tag{8.5.15}$$

Since φ_1 is one-to-one,

$$\varphi_1^{-1}\varphi_1(L') = L',$$

and moreover

$$\varphi_1^{-1}(T) = \emptyset,$$

since $t \in \varphi_1^{-1}(T)$ would imply $\varphi_1 t \in \{au, bv\}^* \cap T$, which contradicts (8.5.10). Thus (8.5.15) becomes

$$\varphi_1^{-1}(w^{-1}(x^{-1}L(G_1)y^{-1})) = L'.$$

If $\mathscr{P}(L(G_1)) = true$, then L' would be in $\mathscr{L}(\mathscr{P}, x, u, v, y)$, which would be a contradiction. Therefore, $\mathscr{P}(L(G_1)) = false$, and the proof of the claim is complete.

The predicate $\mathscr{P}(L(G_1))$ is undecidable because it is undecidable whether or not $L(G) = \{a, b\}^*$, by Lemma 8.4.2. But given G, one can effectively obtain G_1, so $\mathscr{P}(L(G))$ is undecidable. □

Now, we are able to state the main result of this section.

Theorem 8.5.2 Let $\mathscr{S}$ be any subfamily of the finitely inherently ambiguous context-free languages over $\Sigma = \{a, b\}$ such that there is some language L_0 in $\mathscr{S}$ which has an unbounded regular subset. For an arbitrary context-free grammar, the predicate

$$L(G) \in \mathscr{S}$$

is undecidable.

Proof By Theorem 7.4.3, the finitely inherently ambiguous context-free languages are closed under inverse homomorphisms and quotients with singleton sets on both the left and the right. Define the predicate $\mathscr{P}$ by

$$P(L) = \begin{cases} true & \text{if } L \in \mathscr{S}, \\ false & \text{if } L \notin \mathscr{S} \end{cases}$$

Then, for all $x, u, v, y \in \Sigma^*$, $\mathscr{L}(\mathscr{P}, x, u, v, y)$ is a subset of the context-free languages of finite degree of inherent ambiguity. There exist context-free languages L' which are infinitely inherently ambiguous, by Theorem 7.3.3; and so (c) of Lemma 8.5.2 is satisfied. Moreover, by assumption, there exists $L_0 \in \mathscr{S}$ with an unbounded regular set. By Theorem 8.5.1, (b) is satisfied. Since $L_0 \in \mathscr{S}$, $\mathscr{P}(L_0) = \mathit{true}$ and (a) is satisfied. Since the hypotheses of Lemma 8.5.2 are satisfied, the conclusion holds. □

We list a few corollaries of this theorem. In the future, we shall make extensive use of the result. Note that the simplest example of an unbounded regular subset is $\{a, b\}^*$.

Theorem 8.5.3 For the following families $\mathscr{S}$ of context-free languages over $\Sigma = \{a, b\}$ and for arbitrary context-free grammars G, it is undecidable whether or not

$$L(G) \in \mathscr{S}.$$

1 the finitely inherently ambiguous context-free languages;

2 the finitely directly inherently ambiguous context-free languages;

3 for any $k \geqslant 1$, the context-free languages of degree of inherent ambiguity $\leqslant k$;

4 the unambiguous context-free languages;

5 the regular sets;

6 the deterministic context-free languages;

7 the transpose of any of the above classes.

PROBLEMS

1 Show that the collection of bounded sets over Σ is closed under product, transpose, and union. Show that a subset of bounded sets is bounded.

2 Show that if $|\Sigma| \geqslant 2$, then Σ^* is not bounded.

3 Verify that Theorem 8.5.2 holds if the languages are specified by pushdown automata rather than by context-free grammars.

4 Show that, if L_0 is any fixed context-free language which contains an unbounded regular subset, then it is undecidable whether or not $L(G) = L_0$.

5 Show that, for any arbitrary context-free grammar G, one can decide whether or not

$$L(G) = \{wcw^T \mid w \in \{a, b\}^*\}.$$

6 Show that one cannot decide whether a given context-free language can be parsed in linear time.

7 Show that R is a bounded regular set if and only if R belongs to the smallest family of sets which contains all regular subsets of w^*, $w \in \Sigma^*$, and which is closed under finite union and finite product.

8 A set L is *commutative* if, for all words $x, y \in L$, $xy = yx$. Show that a set is commutative if and only if $L \subseteq w^*$.

9 Let $u, v \in \Sigma^*$. Show that $uv \neq vu$ implies $\{u, v\}^*$ is unbounded. This gives another proof of Problem 2.

10 Show that every context-free language L is commutative or else L^* contains an unbounded regular set.

11 Show that it is undecidable whether or not $L(G)$ is linear, or metalinear, or ultralinear.

8.6 HISTORICAL SURVEY

The basic decision questions in this chapter date back to Bar-Hillel, Perles, and Shamir [1961]. The unsolvability of the halting problem is due to Turing [1936]. The Post Correspondence Problem is from Post [1946]. Our proof follows Hopcroft and Ullman [1969]. Exercises 7, 8, and 9 of Section 8.3 are based on Hartmanis [1967a]; problems 10 and 11 are from Ullian [1967]. Problem 2 of Section 8.4 is from Gruska [1975], while Problem 3 was proved by Blattner [1973], Salomaa [1973b], and Rozenberg [1972]. "Birdie problems" like Problem 4 of Section 8.4 were systematically studied by Ullian [1967]. Problem 6 of Section 8.4 is due to Englefriet [1973], and Problem 7 is due to Ginsburg and Spanier [1966].

The main results of Section 8.5 are derived from the work of Hunt and Rozenkrantz [1978]. Bounded languages were introduced by Ginsburg and Spanier [1964]. Lemma 8.5.1 is due to Hopcroft [1969]. Problem 4 is also from Hopcroft [1969].

nine
Context-Sensitive and Phrase-Structure Languages

9.1 INTRODUCTION

It is possible to characterize both the context-sensitive languages and the phrase-structure languages in terms of Turing machines. For the context-sensitive case, one needs to restrict attention to nondeterministic, linearly space-bounded devices. This focuses attention on both time- and space-bounded computations of nondeterministic as well as deterministic Turing machines. While the general topic of machine complexity is outside the scope of this book, some of the open questions in language theory are related to questions in machine complexity theory. The serious student of language theory is well advised to learn this subject in more depth than can be provided here.

In Section 9.2, we begin by considering a number of alternative forms of phrase-structure grammars. All of these are useful in one application or another. Section 9.3 is devoted to a study of the basic properties of the context-sensitive languages. For instance, every context-sensitive language is recursive but there are recursive sets that are not context-sensitive. Section 9.4 is devoted to time- and tape-bounded Turing machines. A few of the basic theorems of machine-based complexity theory are proved there, such as Savitch's Theorem (9.4.3), which relates space-bounded nondeterministic and deterministic computations. In Section 9.5, machine characterizations of the context-sensitive and phrase-structure languages are given.

9.2 VARIOUS TYPES OF PHRASE-STRUCTURE GRAMMARS

In Sections 1.4 and 1.5, a number of types of grammars were introduced for both the context-sensitive languages and the phrase-structure languages. We shall now introduce one more grammatical definition. This family of grammars also generates the phrase-structure languages.

Definition A *nonterminal rewriting grammar* (or *NR grammar*) is a 4-tuple $G = (V, \Sigma, P, S)$, where V, Σ, and S are as in a phrase-structure grammar. P is a finite set of productions of the form

$$x_0 A_1 x_1 \cdots x_{n-1} A_n x_n \to x_0 \beta_1 x_1 \cdots x_{n-1} \beta_n x_n$$

with $n > 0, x_i \in \Sigma^*, \beta_i \in V^*$, and $A_i \in N$.

Note that, in a nonterminal rewriting grammar, the terminals are not displaced once they are generated.

If we abbreviate each class of grammars by its initials, Fig. 9.1 displays the grammar class containments.

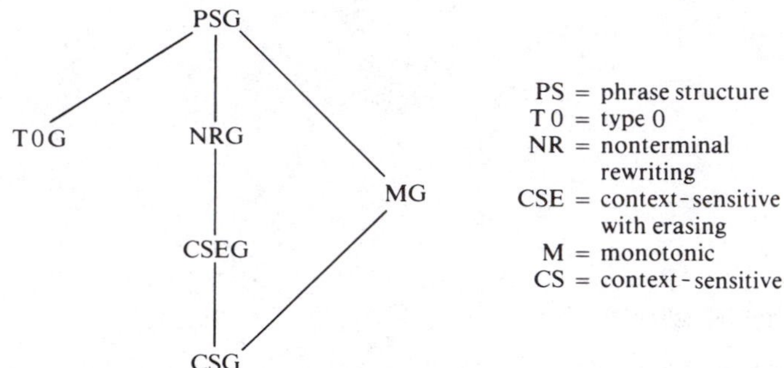

FIG. 9.1

We shall now quickly show that the following classes of languages are coextensive.

$$\text{PSL} = \text{T0L} = \text{NRL} = \text{CSEL}$$

and

$$\text{CSL} = \text{ML}.$$

To show how these families interrelate, a sequence of easy results will be proven.

Lemma 9.2.1 For each phrase-structure (respectively, context-sensitive with erasing, context-sensitive, monotonic, NR) grammar $G = (V, \Sigma, P, S)$, there is a phrase-structure (respectively, context-sensitive with erasing, context-sensitive, monotonic, NR) grammar $G' = (V', \Sigma, P', S)$ such that

$$L(G') = L(G)$$

and each rule in P' is of the form

$$\alpha \to \beta$$

with $\alpha \in N^+, \beta \in N^*$, or

$$A \to a$$

with $A \in N$ and $a \in \Sigma$.

Proof Let $G = (V, \Sigma, P, S)$ be a grammar of the desired type. Define a map $\varphi: V \to V' = V \cup \{A_a \mid a \in \Sigma\}$, such that:

$$\varphi(A) = A \qquad \text{if } A \in N,$$

$$\varphi(a) = A_a \qquad \text{if } a \in \Sigma,$$

and extend φ to be a homomorphism. Define $G' = (V', \Sigma, P', S)$, where

$$P' = \{\varphi(\alpha) \to \varphi(\beta) \mid \alpha \to \beta \text{ is in } P\} \cup \{A_a \to a \mid a \in \Sigma\}.$$

It is a straightforward matter to verify that $L(G') = L(G)$ and G' is of the same type as G. □

Corollary 1 The class of phrase-structure languages equals the class of type 0 languages.

Proof G' is a type 0 grammar. □

In order to deal with the other classes, we need a reduction lemma.

Definition For any phrase-structure grammar $G = (V, \Sigma, P, S)$, let the *weight* of a production $\pi = \alpha \to \beta$ be $\lg(\beta)$ and let the weight of G be $\max\{\lg(\beta) \mid \alpha \to \beta \text{ is in } P\}$.

Lemma 9.2.2 For each type 0 (monotonic) grammar $G = (V, \Sigma, P, S)$, there is a type 0 (monotonic) grammar $G' = (V', \Sigma, P', S)$ of weight at most 2, so that $L(G') = L(G)$. Furthermore, if G is of type 0, then the only length-decreasing rules in G' have the form $A \to \Lambda$ for $A \in V' - \Sigma$; if G is monotonic, then every rule in G' has the form $\alpha \to \beta$ for $\alpha \in N^+$ and $\beta \in V^*$.

Proof First we must modify G so that it has no length-decreasing rules except Λ-rules of the form $A \to \Lambda$. This step is not necessary for monotonic grammars.

Define a new grammar $G' = (V', \Sigma, P', S)$, where $V' = V \cup \{R\}$ and P' is defined as follows.

1 If $\alpha \to \beta$ is in P and $\lg(\alpha) \leq \lg(\beta)$, then $\alpha \to \beta$ is in P'.

2 If $A_1 \cdots A_m \to B_1 \cdots B_n$ is in P with $A_1, \ldots, A_m \in N$, $B_1, \ldots B_n \in V$, and $n < m$, then
$$A_1 \cdots A_m \to B_1 \cdots B_n R^{m-n}$$
is in P'.

3 P' contains $R \to \Lambda$.

Note that a rule $ABC \to \Lambda$ in G is transformed to $ABC \to RRR$ in G'.

Clearly, $L(G') = L(G)$, G' is type 0, and G' has context-free Λ-rules but no other length-decreasing rules.

Now assume that we have a grammar $G = (V, \Sigma, P, S)$ which is monotonic or is the result of the previous construction. In the former case, we may assume (by Lemma 9.2.1) that every rule in P has the form $\alpha \to \beta$ where $\alpha \in N^+, \beta \in V^*$.

Let π be a production in P. If the weight of π is less than 3, then π is in P'. If the weight of π is at least 3, then

$$\pi = A_1 \cdots A_m \to B_1 \cdots B_n$$

where $m \leqslant n$ and $n \geqslant 3$. Perform the following steps.

1 If $m = n$, then go to step 2. Let P' contain:

$$A_1 \cdots A_m \to B_1 \cdots B_{m-1} X_{\pi,1}$$

$$X_{\pi,1} \to B_m \cdots B_n$$

This rule provides either rules whose left- and righthand sides have the same length, or rules of reduced weight.

2 For rules $\sigma = C_1 \cdots C_m \to D_1 \cdots D_m$, where $m \geqslant 3$ and each $D_i \in V - \Sigma$, P' contains:

$$C_1 C_2 \to D_1 Y_{\sigma,1}$$

$$Y_{\sigma,i} C_{i+2} \to D_{i+1} Y_{\sigma,i+1} \quad \text{for } 1 \leqslant i < m-2$$

$$Y_{\sigma,m-2} C_m \to D_{m-1} D_m$$

All of these rules are of weight 2. Thus steps 1 and 2 start with a production of weight n and produce only productions of lesser weight. Repeat the construction until all the rules associated with the original production have weight 2. The argument is repeated for all productions whose weight is at least 3. □

Now we may apply this result to establish an equivalence between context-sensitive and monotonic languages.

Theorem 9.2.1 For each type 0 (monotonic) grammar $G = (V, \Sigma, P, S)$, there is a context-sensitive grammar with erasing (context-sensitive grammar) $G' = (V', \Sigma, P', S)$ such that $L(G') = L(G)$.

Proof By Lemma 9.2.2, assume without loss of generality that the weight of G is at most 2, that G contains no length-decreasing rules except those of the form $A \to \Lambda$, and that every rule in P has the form $\alpha \to \beta$ for some $\alpha \in N^+$ and $\beta \in V^*$.

i) If a production $\pi \in P$ has only one nonterminal on its lefthand side, then $\pi \in P'$;

ii) If $\pi = AB \to CD$ and $C = A$ or $D = B$, then $\pi \in P'$;

iii) If $\pi = AB \to CD$ with $C \neq A$ and $D \neq B$, then the following productions are in P':

$$AB \to (\pi, A)B$$

$$(\pi, A)B \to (\pi, A)(\pi, B)$$

$$(\pi, A)(\pi, B) \to C(\pi, B)$$

$$C(\pi, B) \to CD$$

where (π, A) and (π, B) are new variables.

It is clear that G' is context-sensitive (with erasing if G was not monotonic). An easy induction verifies that $L(G') = L(G)$. □

Corollary 1 The family of context-sensitive languages with erasing equals the family of phrase-structure languages.

Corollary 2 The family of monotonic languages equals the family of context-sensitive languages.

Corollary 3 The family of nonterminal rewriting languages equals the family of phrase-structure languages.

PROBLEMS

1 Show by examples that Fig. 9.1 cannot have any lines added. That is, there is a line between two grammar classes XG and YG in Fig. 9.1 if and only if

$$XG \subseteq YG \qquad \text{where } X, Y \in \{PS, T0, NR, CSE, M, CS\}.$$

9.3 ELEMENTARY DECIDABLE AND CLOSURE PROPERTIES OF CONTEXT-SENSITIVE LANGUAGES

There are some very simple properties of the context-sensitive grammars that will be developed here. Since only grammatical arguments are now available, we shall use them as much as is reasonable. There are a number of closure results that are intuitively clear when an automaton theoretic characterization is available. These results could be proven with grammars but would be less intuitive.

Our first goal will be to give an algorithm that tests whether a given string belongs to a context-sensitive language.

Definition Let $G = (V, \Sigma, P, S)$ be a context-sensitive grammar and let $w \in \Sigma^n$ for some $n \geqslant 1$. Define a sequence of sets $W_i \subseteq V^*$ as follows:

$$W_0 = \{S\}$$

and for each $i \geqslant 0$,

$$W_{i+1} = W_i \cup \{\beta \in V^+ \mid \alpha \Rightarrow \beta \text{ in } G, \alpha \in W_i, \text{and } \lg(\beta) \leqslant n\}.$$

The next claim summarizes the properties of the W_i.

Proposition 9.3.1 Let $G = (V, \Sigma, P, S)$, w, and the W_i be as in the previous definition.

i) For each $i \geqslant 0$, $W_i \subseteq W_{i+1}$;

ii) If $W_k = W_{k+1}$ for some $k \geqslant 0$, then

$$W_k = W_{k+m} \qquad \text{for all } m \geqslant 1;$$

iii) For each $i \geqslant 0$,

$$W_i = \{\beta \in V^+ \mid S \overset{\ell}{\Rightarrow} \beta, \lg(\beta) \leqslant n, \ell \leqslant i\};$$

iv) There exists $k < \max\{2|V|^n, n+1\}$ such that

$$W_k = W_{k+1};$$

v) Let k be the least integer such that $W_k = W_{k+1}$. Then

$$W_k = \{\beta \in V^+ \mid S \overset{*}{\Rightarrow} \beta, \lg(\beta) \leqslant n\}.$$

Proof Part (i) is trivial. Part (ii) is a trivial induction on m. Part (iii) is clear, or could be verified by induction on i.

To prove (iv), note that, from (iii),

$$W_i \subseteq \bigcup_{j=1}^{n} V^j \tag{9.3.1}$$

for each i. Taking cardinalities

$$|W_i| \leqslant \left| \bigcup_{j=1}^{n} V^j \right| = \sum_{j=1}^{n} |V|^j \leqslant \max\{2|V|^n, n+1\}.$$

Cf. Problem 1. Since $|V|$ and n are fixed, the W_i are of uniformly bounded size; and since $W_i \subseteq W_{i+1}$, it is clear that:

$$W_k = W_{k+1}$$

for some k where $k < \max\{2|V|^n, n+1\}$.

Part (v) follows easily because, if $S \overset{*}{\Rightarrow} \beta$, $\lg(\beta) \leqslant n$, then $S \overset{\ell}{\Rightarrow} \beta$ for some $\ell \geqslant 0$. If $\ell \leqslant k$, then $\beta \in W_\ell \subseteq W_k$. If $\ell > k$, then, since $W_\ell = W_k$ by (ii), we know that $\beta \in W_k$. □

We can now show that there is an algorithm to decide whether $w \in L(G)$, where G is an arbitrary context-sensitive grammar.

Theorem 9.3.1 Let $G = (V, \Sigma, P, S)$ be a context-sensitive grammar. Then $L(G)$ is recursive; i.e. there is an algorithm which, given any $w \in \Sigma^*$, decides whether or not $w \in L(G)$.

Proof Let $w = a_1 \cdots a_n$, $n \geqslant 0$, $a_i \in \Sigma$ for $1 \leqslant i \leqslant n$. If $n = 0$, $\Lambda \in L(G)$ if and only if

$$S \to \Lambda$$

is in P. Now assume that $n \geqslant 1$. Let $W = W_k$ of Proposition 9.3.1, where k is the smallest nonnegative integer such that $W_k = W_{k+1}$. By (v) of Proposition 9.3.1, $w \in L(G)$ if and only if $w \in W$. Since W is finite and has been effectively constructed, the result follows. □

Now we shall show that the context-sensitive languages are a proper subset of the class of recursive sets. The argument is a straightforward "diagonalization." The reader not familiar with the technique should study it carefully, because it is very powerful and widely applicable.

Theorem 9.3.2 There are recursive sets which are not context-sensitive languages.

Proof Let Σ be an alphabet. Let $x_1, x_2, \ldots$ be an effective enumeration (without repetition) of Σ^*. Let $G_1, G_2, \ldots$ be an effective enumeration (without repetition) of the context-sensitive grammars with terminal alphabet Σ. Define

$$L = \{x_i \mid x_i \notin L(G_i)\}. \tag{9.3.2}$$

Claim 1 L is recursive.

Proof Given $w \in \Sigma^*$, by using the effective enumeration of Σ^*, we can determine the i for which $x_i = w$.

Now using the effective enumeration of the grammars, we can find G_i.

By Theorem 9.3.1 it is decidable whether or not $x_i \in L(G_i)$.

Claim 2 L is not a context-sensitive language.

Proof Assume that L is a context-sensitive language. Then

$$L = L(G_j) \quad \text{for some } j \tag{9.3.3}$$

But now consider string x_j;

$$x_j \in L$$

if and only if (by (9.3.3))

$$x_j \in L(G_j),$$

which holds if and only if (by (9.3.2))

$$x_j \notin L.$$

We have shown that $x_j \in L$ if and only if $x_j \notin L$, which is a contradiction. Therefore, L is not a context-sensitive language. □

Now we turn to the second main topic of this section, elementary closure properties of the context-sensitive languages. Our purpose here is to establish a few easy results which are best proven by elementary grammatical constructions. Since some of the same constructions work for phrase-structure languages, those will be proved at the same time.

Theorem 9.3.3 The families of context-sensitive and phrase-structure languages are closed under $\cup$, $\cdot$, *, and transpose.

Proof The arguments are all quite trivial and are omitted. Cf. Theorem 3.3.1 for similar constructions in the context-free case. □

In a later section, it will be seen that the context-sensitive languages are not closed under homomorphisms. Moreover, it is the case where $\Lambda \in \varphi(\Sigma)$ that causes problems. We now consider a restriction on homomorphisms which does allow preservation of context-sensitive languages.

Definition A homomorphism φ on a set $L \subseteq \Sigma^*$ is said to be *k-limited* ($k \geqslant 1$ is an integer), if for each $w \in L$, if $w = xyz$ for some $x, y, z \in \Sigma^*$ and $\varphi(y) = \Lambda$ then $\lg(y) \leqslant k$.

The intuition behind this definition is that for any $w \in L$, φ never erases more than k adjacent letters within w.

Example Let

$$L_1 = \{a^p b^q c^r \mid p, q, r \geqslant 1\},$$

$$L_2 = \{a^p b^2 c^q \mid p, q \geqslant 1\}$$

and define φ by

$$\varphi d = \begin{cases} \Lambda & \text{if } d = b \\ d & \text{otherwise.} \end{cases}$$

Now φ is not k-limited on L_1 for any k. To see that, suppose it were. Then consider

$$w = ab^{k+1}c \in L_1.$$

Let $x = a$, $y = b^{k+1}$, and $z = c$. Then $\varphi(y) = \Lambda$ but $\lg(y) > k$. On the other hand, φ is 2-limited for L_2 since no word of L_2 has more than two b's.

Theorem 9.3.4 The family of context-sensitive languages is closed under k-limited homomorphisms.

Proof Let $G = (V, \Sigma, P, S)$ be a context-sensitive grammar. There is no loss of generality in assuming that G is in the form specified by Lemma 9.2.1. Let φ be a k-limited homomorphism on $L(G)$. Note that $\varphi : \Sigma^* \to \Delta^*$. Define

$$r = \max \{k + 1, \lg(\beta) \mid \alpha \to \beta \text{ is in } P\}.$$

Define $G = (V', \Sigma', P', S')$, where

$$\Sigma' = \{b \in \Delta \mid \varphi(\Sigma) \cap \Delta^* b \Delta^* \neq \emptyset\};$$

that is, Σ' consists of all letters of Δ that occur in $\varphi(\Sigma)$. Then,

$$N' = \{[\alpha] \mid \alpha \in V^*, \lg(\alpha) < 2r\},$$

$$S' = [S],$$

$$V' = N' \cup \Sigma',$$

P' is defined as follows:

1 If $S \to \Lambda$ is in P or if there exists $x \in L(G)$ such that $\varphi(x) = \Lambda$ then

$$[S] \to \Lambda$$

is in P'.

2 If $\alpha \Rightarrow \beta$ in G and $[\alpha]$, $[\beta] \in N'$, then

$$[\alpha] \to [\beta]$$

is in P'.

3 For any $[\alpha], [\beta_1], \ldots, [\beta_m] \in N'$ such that

$$\alpha \Rightarrow \beta_1 \cdots \beta_m \text{ in } G$$

where $\lg(\beta_i) = r$ for each i, $1 \leqslant i \leqslant m$, and $r \leqslant \lg(\beta_m) < 2r$, then

$$[\alpha] \rightarrow [\beta_1] \cdots [\beta_m]$$

is in P'.

4 For any $[\alpha_1], [\alpha_2], [\beta_1], \ldots, [\beta_m]$ in N' such that

$$\alpha_1 \alpha_2 \underset{G}{\Rightarrow} \beta_1 \cdots \beta_m$$

where $\lg(\beta_i) = r$ for each i, $1 \leqslant i < m$, and

$$r \leqslant \lg(\beta_i) < 2r \qquad \text{and} \qquad r \leqslant \lg(\alpha_1), \lg(\alpha_2) < 2r,$$

then

$$[\alpha_1]\,[\alpha_2] \rightarrow [\beta_1] \cdots [\beta_m]$$

is in P'.

5 For each $[x] \in N', x \in \Sigma^*, \varphi(x) \neq \Lambda$,

$$[x] \rightarrow \varphi(x)$$

is in P'.

All the rules of P' are context-free except those of (4). G' is monotonic, so by Theorem 9.2.1, $L(G')$, is context-sensitive. Moreover, G' is effectively constructable since, in part (1), we *can* check[†] to see whether there exists $x \in L(G)$ such that $\varphi(x) = \Lambda$, because φ is k-limited on $L(G)$ and we need check only those strings x where $\lg(x) \leqslant k$. This can be done by Theorem 9.3.1. The tests required in parts (2), (3), and (4) can be carried out, so G' is effectively constructable from G.

We leave to the reader the verification that $L(G') = \varphi(L(G))$. □

Corollary The family of context-sensitive languages is closed under Λ-free homomorphisms.

PROBLEMS

1 Show that

$$\sum_{j=1}^{n} |V|^j < \begin{cases} 2|V|^n & \text{if } |V| > 1, \\ n+1 & \text{if } |V| = 1. \end{cases}$$

2 In subsequent sections, we shall learn that there are phrase-structure languages which are not recursive. Where do the proofs of Theorem 9.3.1 and Proposition 9.3.1 break down if G was assumed to be an arbitrary phrase-structure grammar?

---

† Later we will see that the question $L(G) = \emptyset$ is unsolvable for context-sensitive grammars G.

3 What is the recognition time of the algorithm given in Theorem 9.3.1? Give this as a function of n, the length of the input.

4 Show that the family of phrase-structure languages is closed under

a) substitution (and hence homomorphisms);

b) gsm mappings;

c) inverse gsm mappings.

5 Show that the family of context-sensitive languages is closed under

a) Λ-free substitution; [φ is a Λ*-free* substitution if for each $a \in \Sigma$, $\Lambda \notin \varphi(a)$.]

b) inverse gsm mappings.

6 Complete the proof of Theorem 9.3.4 by showing that $L(G') = \varphi(L(G))$.

7 Formulate suitable restrictions on the type of substitution mappings under which the context-sensitive languages are closed.

8 Give effective enumerations of Σ^* and of the context-sensitive grammars over Σ, as described in the proof of Theorem 9.3.2.

9 Does it matter whether or not there are repetitions in the enumerations used in the proof of Theorem 9.3.2?

9.4 TIME- AND TAPE-BOUNDED TURING MACHINES — $\mathscr{P}$ AND $\mathscr{NP}$

In this section, we shall take a close look at Turing machines and examine some implications of nondeterminism versus determinism. We shall also consider time- and tape-bounded computations, as well as two particularly important classes of sets called $\mathscr{P}$ and $\mathscr{NP}$.

Our coverage of these topics will not be thorough, as we need only a few results for our purposes. This general topic is important and textbooks should become available on this subject soon.

We begin with an intuitive version of a k-tape nondeterministic Turing machine. Such a device is illustrated in Fig. 9.2.

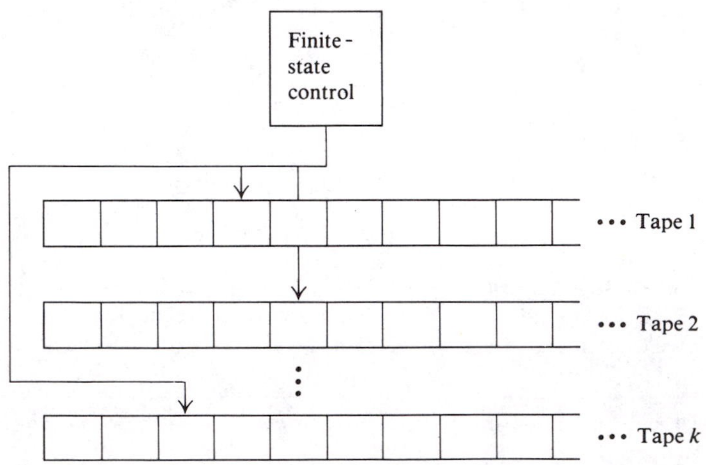

FIG. 9.2

In this version, the k-work tapes are semi-infinite (to the right) and the first tape will contain the input. It can be shown that the results to be obtained are very insensitive to these details.

It is now necessary to give a precise definition.

Definition A *k-tape nondeterministic Turing machine* is a 7-tuple $A = (Q, \Sigma, \Gamma, B, \delta, q_0, F)$, where:

i) Q is a finite nonempty set of *states*;

ii) Σ is a finite nonempty set of *input letters*;

iii) Γ is a finite nonempty set of *work symbols* and $\Sigma \subseteq \Gamma$;

iv) $B \in \Gamma - \Sigma$ is the *blank symbol*;

v) $q_0 \in Q$ is the *initial state*;

vi) $F \subseteq Q$ is the set of *final* or accepting states;

vii) δ is a mapping from $Q \times \Gamma^k$ into subsets of $Q \times (\Gamma \times \{-1, 0, 1\})^k$. δ is called the *transition function*.

Such a device is called a *k-tape deterministic Turing machine* if

$$|\delta(q, a_1, \ldots, a_k)| \leqslant 1 \text{ for each } q \in Q; a_1, \ldots, a_k \in \Gamma.$$

Next, we define an instantaneous description or ID of a k-tape Turing machine. Intuitively, an ID must tell us what state the device is in, the contents of each work tape, and the head position on each tape.

Definition Let $A = (Q, \Sigma, \Gamma, B, \delta, q_0, F)$ be a k-tape nondeterministic Turing machine. An *instantaneous description* or *ID* of A is any element of $Q(\Gamma^*\{\upharpoonleft\}\Gamma^+)^k$, where we assume that $Q \cap \Gamma = \emptyset$ and that $\upharpoonleft$ is a new symbol not in $Q \cup \Gamma$.

Thus a typical ID is of the form

$$q(\alpha_1 \upharpoonleft \beta_1, \ldots, \alpha_k \upharpoonleft \beta_k),$$

which indicates that the contents of the ith tape is $\alpha_i\beta_i$ and that the read-write head on this tape is scanning the first letter of β_i. For single-tape Turing machines, one sometimes writes the ID as $\alpha q \beta$.

Now we are ready to indicate how the device works. This is done by defining a "move" relation on ID's. To avoid a surplus of notation, an informal definition is given.

Definition Let $A = (Q, \Sigma, \Gamma, B, \delta, q_0, F)$ be a k-tape nondeterministic Turing machine. If α is an ID of A, where

$$\alpha = q(u_1 \upharpoonleft a_1 v_1'', \ldots, u_k \upharpoonleft a_k v_k'')$$

and

$$(q', (b_1, d_1), \ldots, (b_k, d_k)) \text{ is in } \delta(q, a_1, \ldots, a_k),$$

then A rewrites each a_i by b_i and moves one position to the right (left) on tape i if $d_i = +1$ (-1), while, if $d_i = 0$, the head position on tape i does not change. If any $v_i'' = \Lambda$ and $d_i = +1$, then the contents of tape i is represented by $u_i b_i \upharpoonleft B$ in β. If β is the resulting ID, we write $\alpha \vdash \beta$. As usual, $\overset{*}{\vdash}$ is the reflexive-transitive closure of $\vdash$.

An ID is called *initial* if it is of the form $q_0(\restriction w, \restriction B, \ldots, \restriction B)$, where† $w \in \Sigma^+ \cup \{B\}$. An *accepting ID* is any element of $F(\Gamma^* \{\restriction\} \Gamma^+)^k$.

Now we can discuss acceptance by a nondeterministic Turing machine.

Definition Let $A = (Q, \Sigma, \Gamma, B, \delta, q_0, F)$ be a k-tape nondeterministic Turing machine and let $w \in \Sigma^+ \cup \{B\}$. *A accepts w* (or when $w = B$, A accepts Λ), if

$$q_0(\restriction w, \restriction B, \ldots, \restriction B) \overset{*}{\vdash} q(\alpha_1, \ldots, \alpha_k) \qquad \text{for some } q \in F$$
$$\text{and some } \alpha_1, \ldots, \alpha_k \in \Gamma^* \{\restriction\} \Gamma^+.$$

We also write $T(A) = \{w \in \Sigma^* \mid A \text{ accepts } w\}$.

Next, we name the sets defined by a Turing machine.

Definition A set L is said to be *recursively enumerable* (or *r.e.*, for short) if $L = T(A)$ for some Turing machine A.

It can easily be seen that this definition is insensitive to whether or not A is deterministic or has multiple tapes, etc. Thus an r.e. set has the property that there is a procedure which returns the value *true* if the string is in the set but, if the string is not in the set, the procedure may return the value *false* or it may fail to halt. Of course, we can't determine whether a Turing machine will stop or not.

Definition A set L is *recursive* if both L and $\bar{L} = \Sigma^* - L$ are r.e.

Thus, a recursive set is one for which we can determine whether *or not* a given string is a member. This corresponds to our previous informal usage of the phrase.

This formalism and the ideas involved can be appreciated by studying a detailed example.

Example Let $L = \{xzyz^T \mid x, y, z \in \{a, b\}^*, \ z \neq \Lambda\}$. We shall design a 2-tape nondeterministic Turing machine which accepts L. The idea is quite simple. We shall read the input, which is on the first tape. We shall guess when z begins and ends, and during z, we write it on tape 2. After this is done, we skip merrily along ignoring y. When we guess that z^T begins, we compare the input against tape 2. We have $\Sigma = \{a, b\}$, $\Gamma = \Sigma \cup \{c, B\}$, $F = \{q_5\}$, and δ is defined as follows.

i) For each $d \in \Sigma$,

$$\delta(q_0, d, B) = (q_1, (d, 0), (c, 1)).$$

Mark left end of tape 2 with a c.

† An initial ID in which $w = \Lambda$ is represented by $(\restriction B, \ldots)$.

ii) For each $d \in \Sigma$,

$$\delta(q_1, d, B) = \{(q_1, (d, 1), (B, 0)), (q_2, (d, 1), (d, 1))\}.$$

The first alternative is a guess that the input letter is part of x and should be skipped over. The second alternative is to assume that it is part of z and should be written on tape 2.

iii) For each $d \in \Sigma$,

$$\delta(q_2, d, B) = \{(q_2, (d, 1), (d, 1)), (q_3, (d, 0), (B, -1))\}.$$

The first alternative continues to write z on tape 2 while the second one prepares to consider that y is next.

iv) For each $d, e \in \Sigma$,

$$\delta(q_3, d, e) = \{(q_3, (d, 1), (e, 0)), (q_4, (d, 0), (e, 0))\}.$$

Either skip over y or prepare to check z^T against tape 2.

v) For each $d \in \Sigma$,

$$\delta(q_4, d, d) = (q_4, (d, 1), (d, -1)).$$

Go right on tape 1 and left on tape 2 to check for z^T.

vi) Stop and accept.

$$\delta(q_4, B, c) = (q_5, (B, 0), (c, 0)).$$

The reader should follow several computations of this Turing machine on a given input. For instance, it is worth checking that there is no computation sequence that accepts *ab*.

There are many variants of Turing machines. One of the most common is a Turing machine with a separate input tape which is delimited by endmarkers. This input tape may be read but not written. Another variation concerns whether or not a Turing machine must halt in order to accept. In some instances this is desirable, while for other results just passing through a final state is sufficient. Halting is represented by having a final state q_f such that $\delta(q_f, a_1, \ldots, a_k) = \emptyset$ for all $a_1, \ldots, a_k \in \Gamma$.

Another variant in the way in which a Turing machine accepts concerns "on-line" versus "off-line" computation. Let A be a Turing machine with a separate read-only input tape. We equip the device with an output tape on which it may write a zero or a one. A computation of A on input $a_1 \cdots a_n$ is *on-line* if A never goes left on the input and writes a one or zero on the output after reading a_i (indicating whether $a_1 \cdots a_i$ was accepted or rejected) but before reading a_{i+1}. A computation is sometimes said to be *off-line* if it is not on-line. It is much easier to prove lower bounds on on-line computations, because the form that the computation takes is so restricted.

Next we deal with measuring the time or space complexity of a computation.

Definition Let A be a k-tape Turing machine and let S and T be functions from $\mathbb{N}$ into $\mathbb{N}$ where $\mathbb{N}$ denotes the set of natural numbers. A is said to be of *time complexity* $T(n)$ if, for each accepted input of length n, there exists some computation sequence of at most $T(n)$ moves which leads to an accepting ID. Similarly, A is of *space* or *tape complexity* $S(n)$ if, for every accepted input of length n, there is some accepting computation in which at most $S(n)$ different squares are scanned by any read-write head.

Example If we return to the previous example, it is clear that $T(n) = n + 4$ and $S(n) = n + 1$.

When we have a Turing machine with a separate read-only input, we measure only the space used on the work tapes as the input tape cannot be changed. Thus we may talk about accepting a set in, say, $\log n$ space.

One may wonder which functions could be the space bound of a computation.

Definition A function S from $\mathbb{N}$ into $\mathbb{N}$ is a *measurable space function,* or *measurable*, if there is a Turing machine A which has one work tape and a read-only input tape and which visits exactly $S(n)$ squares on its work tape, where n is the length of the input.

For example, it is easy to see that $\log n$ is measurable. So is any polynomial in n or in $\log n$, as well as functions like 2^n. Of course, nonmeasurable functions exist, by a counting argument. Techniques for exhibiting them will occur in the exercises.

The first result to be proved here will be useful in estimating the tape complexity of language recognition problems.

Theorem 9.4.1 If a set L is accepted by a deterministic k-tape Turing machine A with space bound $S(n)$, then L is accepted by some deterministic one-tape Turing machine C with space bound $S(n)$.

Proof The proof is quite intuitive, so we content ourselves with a sketch. In Fig. 9.3, we show what A looks like at some given time. Figure 9.4 shows how C represents all of this information on a single tape.

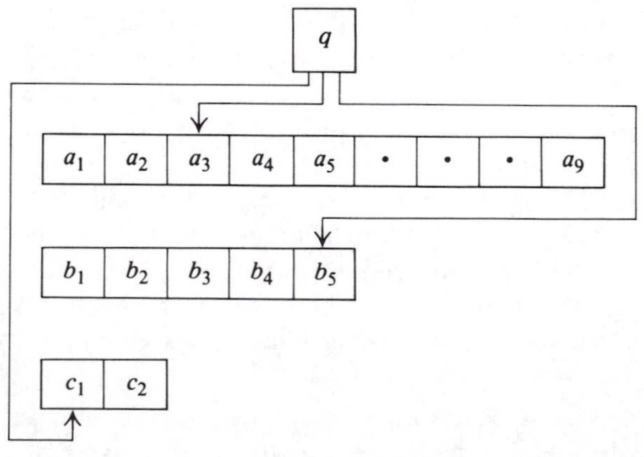

FIG. 9.3 A three-tape Turing machine.

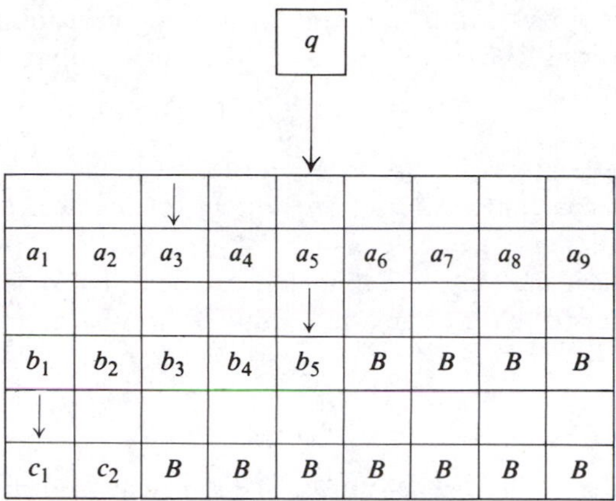

FIG. 9.4 A single-tape Turing machine which simulates a three-tape machine; q is only one component of the state.

To simulate a move of A, C must visit each of the cells which are pointed at, recording in its state the symbol scanned by each of A's heads. When all this information is available, C determines A's move. C then goes back to each tape, changes the symbol scanned, and moves the pointers as A would require. It should be clear that $T(C) = T(A)$. □

Our next development shows that constant factors do not matter in computing space bounds. The analogous result for time is left for Exercise 2.

Theorem 9.4.2 Let $\epsilon > 0$ be any real number. If L is accepted by a deterministic k-tape Turing machine A with space complexity $S(n)$, then there is a deterministic k-tape Turing machine C which accepts L and has space complexity $\epsilon S(n)$.

Proof The argument merely involves recoding the tape alphabet of A to use, as basic symbols, blocks of length r where r is the least integer such that $r\epsilon \geqslant 1$. □

In preparation for the next theorem, a lemma about space-bounded Turing machines is useful.

Lemma 9.4.1 Let $A = (Q, \Sigma, \Gamma, B, \delta, q_0, F)$ be a k-tape Turing machine of tape complexity $S(n)$, and $w \in \Sigma^*$ be an input of length n.

i) The number of different ID's which can arise from w is at most $c^{S(n)}$, where c is a constant independent of n.

ii) If A accepts w, then there is an accepting computation

$$\alpha_0 = q_0(\uparrow w, \uparrow B, \ldots, \uparrow B) \vdash \alpha_1 \vdash \cdots \vdash \alpha_{k-1},$$

where

$$(1)\ \alpha_i \neq \alpha_j \text{ for all } i \neq j \text{ and } (2)\ k \leqslant c^{S(n)}.$$

Proof Since $\lg(w) = n$, A can visit at most $S(n)$ squares on any work tape. Thus the total number of ID's which can occur during the computation is

$$|Q|(|\Gamma| + 1)^{kS(n)}(S(n))^k,$$

because there are $|Q|$ choices for the state, and for each one of k tapes, there are at most $(|\Gamma| + 1)^{S(n)}$ tape contents,† and $S(n)$ places for the head to be (and so a total of $(S(n))^k$ head positions).

It is now clear that any accepting computation of A on w can be converted to one which satisfies (ii) because any duplicate ID's involve a "loop", which can be omitted.

Note that

$$|Q|(|\Gamma| + 1)^{kS(n)}(S(n))^k \leqslant c^{S(n)}$$

for a suitable constant c independent of n. The same constant may be used in both parts of the lemma. □

It is a well-known fact that nondeterministic and deterministic Turing machines are equivalent in accepting power, and this is proved in any course on the subject. We prove a stronger result, namely, the relationship between the space complexity of the nondeterministic and deterministic machines.

Theorem 9.4.3 (*Savitch's Theorem*) Let $S(n) \geqslant n$ be a measurable space function. If a set L is accepted by a nondeterministic Turing machine A of tape complexity $S(n)$, then L is accepted by some deterministic Turing machine C of tape complexity $(S(n))^2$.

Proof Suppose we have $w \in T(A)$ and $\lg(w) = n$. Then

$$\alpha \overset{k}{\vdash} \gamma,$$

where α is the initial ID, γ is some accepting ID, and $k \geqslant 0$. Now this computation takes place if and only if there exists an ID β so that

$$\alpha \overset{\lceil k/2 \rceil}{\vdash} \beta \overset{\lfloor k/2 \rfloor}{\vdash} \gamma.$$

Recall that $\lceil k/2 \rceil + \lfloor k/2 \rfloor = k$ for all k.

The idea of the proof is to check for such a β (there are only finitely many of them, by part (i) of Lemma 9.4.1). If we were working on a model of computation which allowed us to have recursive programs, the result would be trivial. As it is, we must carry out the analysis far enough to see that all the computations can be done on a Turing machine. Let us define a predicate $P(\eta, \sigma, k)$, which is supposed to be true if there is a computation of A from η to σ of length k which uses at most space $S(n)$. P is defined for all ID's η and σ which use at most space $S(n)$ and all $k \geqslant 0$, as follows:

---

† If we used exactly $S(n)$ squares of tape, the bound would be $|\Gamma|^{S(n)}$, but we could use less, so the bound is

$$|\Gamma| + \cdots + |\Gamma|^{S(n)} \leqslant (|\Gamma| + 1)^{S(n)}.$$

$$P(\eta, \sigma, k) = \begin{cases} \textit{true} & \text{if } k = 0 \text{ and } \eta = \sigma, \\ \textit{true} & \text{if } k = 1 \text{ and } \eta \vdash \sigma, \\ \textit{true} & \text{if } k > 1, P(\eta, \theta, \lceil k/2 \rceil) \text{ which uses no more than tape} \\ & S(n), \text{ and } P(\theta, \sigma, \lfloor k/2 \rfloor) \text{ for some ID } \theta. \\ \textit{false} & \text{in all other cases.} \end{cases}$$

It is easy to see that P may be calculated because all of the ID's which use at most space $S(n)$ may be enumerated.

Let $f(\eta, \sigma, k)$ be the number of intermediate ID's that must be stored in evaluating $P(\eta, \theta, k)$. It is easy to check by induction that this quantity is $\leqslant \lceil \log_2 k \rceil$; and when storage is also provided for η and σ, the bound is $2 + \lceil \log_2 k \rceil$.

The strategy for constructing the deterministic simulating machine C now becomes clear. In view of Lemma 9.4.1, we can restrict ourselves to accepting computations of length $\leqslant c^{S(n)}$. C will deterministically compute $P(\alpha, \gamma, c^{S(n)})$ for all possible accepting configurations which use at most $S(n)$ tape. (We know the number of these, by Lemma 9.4.1 again.) The number of ID's to be stored is at most

$$2 + \mathcal{O}\lceil \log c^{S(n)} \rceil = \mathcal{O}(S(n)).$$

On the other hand, the length of an ID is $\mathcal{O}(S(n))$ and the total space which will be used is $\mathcal{O}((S(n))^2)$. Use of Theorem 9.4.2 allows all constants to be reduced to unity. □

Some notation is useful in dealing with the various classes of languages accepted by time- and tape-bounded Turing machines. The notation facilitates the classification of languages and the study of relationships between classes.

Definition Fix some countably infinite alphabet and assume that all the machines which are discussed have input alphabets which are finite subsets of this alphabet.

a) DTIME($T(n)$) (respectively, NTIME($T(n)$)) is the family of all sets accepted by deterministic (respectively, nondeterministic) Turing machines which operate within time-bound $T(n)$.

b) DSPACE($S(n)$) (respectively, NSPACE($S(n)$)) is defined analogously to part (a), except that "time" is replaced by "space".

c) $\mathcal{P} = \bigcup_{k=1}^{\infty} \text{DTIME}(n^k)$

d) $\mathcal{NP} = \bigcup_{k=1}^{\infty} \text{NTIME}(n^k)$

e) $\mathcal{P}\text{-SPACE} = \bigcup_{k=1}^{\infty} \text{DSPACE}(n^k)$

For instance, Savitch's theorem asserts that

$$\text{NSPACE}(S(n)) \subseteq \text{DSPACE}((S(n))^2).$$

From this, it follows that

$$\mathcal{P}\text{-SPACE} = \bigcup_{k=1}^{\infty} \text{NSPACE}(n^k).$$

One reason for the importance of these concepts is that various problems can be coded into languages and then we may speak of reducing one problem to another. More precisely, we have the following.

Definition A language $L_1 \subseteq \Sigma^*$ is *polynomially reducible* or *p-reducible* to a language $L_2 \subseteq \Delta^*$, written $L_1 \leqslant_p L_2$ if there is a function $f: \Sigma^* \to \Delta^*$ computed by a deterministic polynomially time-bounded Turing machine such that

$$x \in L_1 \quad \text{if and only if} \quad f(x) \in L_2.$$

Proposition 9.4.1

a) If $L_2 \in \mathscr{P}$ and $L_1 \leqslant_p L_2$ then $L_1 \in \mathscr{P}$.

b) The relation $\leqslant_p$ is transitive; that is, if $L_1 \leqslant_p L_2$ and $L_2 \leqslant_p L_3$, then $L_1 \leqslant_p L_3$.

Next, we define the important notions of "hard" and "complete."

Definition A set L is *$\mathscr{NP}$-hard* if, for each $L' \in \mathscr{NP}$, we have $L' \leqslant_p L$. L is *$\mathscr{NP}$-complete* if $L \in \mathscr{NP}$ and L is $\mathscr{NP}$-hard.

Proposition 9.4.2

a) Let L_1 be $\mathscr{NP}$-complete. If $L_2 \in \mathscr{NP}$ and $L_1 \leqslant_p L_2$, then L_2 is also $\mathscr{NP}$-complete.

b) Let L be $\mathscr{NP}$-complete. $L \in \mathscr{P}$ if and only if $\mathscr{P} = \mathscr{NP}$.

Part (b) focuses attention on an open question, namely, whether $\mathscr{P} = \mathscr{NP}$. It turns out that a large number of important problems can be shown to be $\mathscr{NP}$-complete. If any of these problems can be shown to be in $\mathscr{P}$, then they all will be.

PROBLEMS

1 Design a deterministic Turing machine to accept $L = \{xzyz^T \mid x, y, z \in \{a, b\}^*, z \neq \Lambda\}$. What time and tape complexity does your machine have?

2 Given a deterministic k-tape Turing machine A with $k > 1$, which accepts a set L with time complexity $T(n)$, and given any real number ϵ, show that there is a k-tape Turing machine B which accepts L and has time complexity $n + \epsilon T(n)$.

3 Does the speed-up theorem of Problem 2 imply that a linear time computation ($T(n) = c_1 n + c_2$) can be speeded up to a real-time computation ($T(n) = n$)?

4* Speed-up theorems have been extensively studied and proved in abstract form for arbitrary measures of computations that include time and space. We state a general version of the result below for space. Prove the result.

Theorem Let $A_0, A_1, \ldots$ be an enumeration of deterministic Turing machines with a fixed input alphabet. For any recursive function r, there exists a recursive set L such that if A_i (the ith Turing machine) accepts L in space $S_i(n)$, then there exists Turing machine A_j which accepts L in space $S_j(n)$ and

$$r(S_j(n)) \leqslant S_i(n)$$

almost everywhere (i.e., with only finitely many exceptions).

5 Show that, for each recursive function r, there is a recursive function T which is monotone increasing, $T(n) \geqslant r(n)$, such that any language L recognizable in time $h(T(n))$, where h is any recursive function, is also recognizable in time $T(n)$. This result is called the "gap theorem" because it shows that there are arbitrarily large gaps among the recursive functions which contain no running times.

6 Give an example of a nonmeasurable space function.

7 The proof of Savitch's theorem is merely a sketch. Complete the argument by giving a detailed construction and the necessary proof. Extend the theorem to the case where $S(n) \geqslant \log n$.

8 Extend Savitch's theorem to nonmeasurable space functions.

A Turing machine is said to be *realtime* if it is a deterministic Turing machine with time bound $T(n) = n$ and has a separate input tape. In problems 9–13, the input tape is not counted among the work tapes.

9 Can a realtime Turing machine accept any deterministic context-free language?

10 Find large classes of functions computed by realtime Turing machines.

11* Show that the set $L \subseteq \Sigma^*$, where $\Sigma = \{a, b, c, d, e, f\}$, given by

$$L = \{uveu^T \mid u \in \{a, b\}^*, v \in \{c, d\}^*\} \cup \{uvfv^T \mid u \in \{a, b\}^*, v \in \{c, d\}^*\},$$

can be accepted by a realtime Turing machine with two work tapes, but by no realtime Turing machine with one work tape.

12* (*Very difficult*) Find a family of sets $\{L_k\}$ such that L_k can be recognized in real time by a k-tape Turing machine but not by any $(k-1)$-tape realtime Turing machine.

13* Let $\Sigma_n = \{a_1, \ldots, a_n, \bar{a}_1, \ldots, \bar{a}_n\}$. Consider the set O_n which encodes the "origin-crossing problem" defined by

$$\mathrm{O}_n = \{w \in \Sigma_n^* \mid \text{For each } i,\ 1 \leqslant i \leqslant n,\ \#_{a_i}(w) = \#_{\bar{a}_i}(w)\}.$$

The name of this set derives from thinking of a_i (respectively, $\bar{a}_i$) as an instruction to take one step to the right (left) along the ith axis in n-space. Show that O_n is real time recognizable by a Turing machine with one work tape.

14 Consider the following set $L \subseteq \Sigma^*$, where $\Sigma = \{a, b, c\}$:

$$L = \{w_1 c \cdots c w_{2^k} c u_1 c \cdots c u_\ell \mid w_i, u_j \in \{a, b\}^*, \lg(w_i) = k = \lg(u_j) \text{ for all } i, j; \ell, k \geqslant 1; \text{there exists some } j, 1 \leqslant j \leqslant 2^k \text{ such that } u_\ell = w_j\}.$$

Show that any on-line deterministic multitape Turing machine that accepts L requires time $T(n)$, where

$$T(n) \geqslant c(n^2/(\log n)^2) \text{ infinitely often}$$

for some constant c. [*Hint*: Count the number of different ID's which could exist after all the w_i's are read.]

15 Show that if there exists a real number $r \geqslant 1$ such that $\mathrm{DSPACE}(n^r) \subseteq \mathscr{P}$, then

$$\mathscr{P} = \mathscr{NP} = \mathscr{P}\text{-SPACE}.$$

16 Show that there exists no pair of real numbers r and s, $1 \leqslant r \leqslant s$, such that

$$\mathrm{DSPACE}(n^r) \subseteq \mathscr{P} \subseteq \mathrm{DSPACE}(n^s)$$

or

$$\mathrm{NSPACE}(n^r) \subseteq \mathscr{P} \subseteq \mathrm{NSPACE}(n^s).$$

A similar result holds for $\mathscr{N}\mathscr{P}$.

17 Show that, for any real number $r \geqslant 1$,

a) $\mathscr{P} \neq \mathrm{DSPACE}(n^r)$ b) $\mathscr{P} \neq \mathrm{NSPACE}(n^r)$

c) $\mathscr{N}\mathscr{P} \neq \mathrm{DSPACE}(n^r)$ d) $\mathscr{N}\mathscr{P} \neq \mathrm{NSPACE}(n^r)$

9.5 MACHINE CHARACTERIZATIONS OF THE CONTEXT-SENSITIVE AND PHRASE-STRUCTURE LANGUAGES

Similar characterizations of the phrase-structure and context-sensitive languages can be given. The former family is exactly the class of sets accepted by unrestricted Turing machines. The other family is accepted by nondeterministic linearly space-bounded Turing machines. The proofs of the characterizations are so similar that we shall consider them at the same time.

Definition A *linear bounded automaton*, or *lba*, for short, is a one-tape nondeterministic Turing machine which is $(S(n) = n + 1)$-space bounded, which accepts by leaving the input tape at the right end in a final state.

The fact that $S(n) = n + 1$ instead of $S(n) = n$ in the space bound arises from the fact that a Turing machine must scan the blank to the right of the last symbol of the input in order to detect the right end of the input string.

Since we know that constants do not change a space-complexity class (by Theorem 9.4.2), an lba has a linear amount of space at its disposal.

Our first result will be to show that each set accepted by an lba is a context-sensitive language.

Lemma 9.5.1 For each lba C, there is a monotonic grammar G such that $L(G) = T(C)$.

Proof Let $L = T(C)$, where $C = (Q, \Sigma, \Gamma, B, \delta, q_0, F)$ is an lba. Construct $G = (V, \Sigma, P, S)$, where

$$V = \{(S, A\} \cup \Sigma \cup \times \Gamma)(\Gamma \cup \Gamma') \times \Gamma) \cup ((Q \cup \{T\}) \times (\Gamma \cup \Gamma'),$$

with T a new symbol not in Q. Γ' denotes a primed copy of Γ. The rules of P are given by cases.

(Tape generation) For each $a \in \Sigma$, P contains:

$$S \to (q_0, a, a)A$$
$$A \to (a, a)A$$
$$A \to (a', a)$$
$$S \to (q_0, a', a)$$
$$S \to \Lambda \quad \text{if } q_0 \text{ is in } F.$$

(Stay) If $(q, b, 0) \in \delta(p, a)$ then, for each $c \in \Sigma$, P contains

$$(p, a, c) \to (q, b, c)$$
$$(p, a', c) \to (q, b', c)$$

(Move left) If $(q, b, -1) \in \delta(p, a)$, then, for each $c \in \Sigma, d, c \in \Gamma$, P contains

$$(d, e)(p, a, c) \to (q, d, c)(b, c),$$
$$(d, e)(p, a', c) \to (q, d, e)(b', c)$$

(Move right) If $(q, b, 1) \in \delta(p, a)$, then, for each $c, e \in \Sigma, d \in \Gamma$, P contains

$$(p, a, c)\,(d, e) \to (b, c)\,(q, d, e)$$
$$(p, a, c)(d', e) \to (b, c)(q, d', e)$$

(Accept) If $(q, b, 1) \in \delta(p, a)$, and $q \in F$, then, for each $c \in \Sigma$, P contains $(p, a', c) \to (T, a, c)$.

(Retrieve original input) For each $b, d \in \Sigma, a, c \in \Gamma$, P contains

$$(a, b)(T, c, d) \to (T, a, b)(T, c, d)$$

and

$$(T, a, b) \to b$$

Rather than give a formal proof that the construction works and $L(G) = T(C)$, we shall explain each phase of the construction.

1. S generates a string $(q_0, a_1, a_1)(a_2, a_2) \cdots (a_{\ell-1}, a_{\ell-1})(a'_\ell, a_\ell)$. In this string, (q_0, a_1, a_1) denotes that C is scanning a_1 in state q_0.

2–4. These rules simply simulate the action of C on the tape. The first coordinate of each ordered pair is used to record the changes that C makes to its tape.

5. When the device has entered a final state, we have

$$S \overset{*}{\Rightarrow} (b_1, a_1) \cdots (b_{\ell-1}, a_{\ell-1})(T, b_\ell, a_\ell)$$

6. Then T sends a signal and we get Ts throughout, that is,

$$(T, b_1, a_1) \cdots (T, b_\ell, a_\ell).$$

Finally, $a_1 \cdots a_\ell$ is produced as the terminal string. Note that the construction is still valid if $\ell \leqslant 1$.

Note that if C "guessed wrong," the grammar will not generate anything since it will have a string with variables in it that cannot be rewritten as terminals. □

Now, we prove a similar result for r.e. sets.

Lemma 9.5.2 If $L = T(A)$ for some Turing machine A, then there is a phrase-structure grammar G, such that $L = L(G)$.

Proof Let $L = T(A)$, where $A = (Q, \Sigma, \Gamma, B, \delta, q_0, F)$ is a Turing machine. There is no loss of generality in assuming that A is deterministic and has one tape. We construct a phrase-structure grammar $G = (V, \Sigma, P, S)$, such that $L(G) = L$. G will nondeterministically generate some word in Σ^* and simulate the action of A on it. Let $V = \Sigma \cup ((\Sigma \cup \{\Lambda\}) \times \Gamma) \cup Q \cup \{S, T, U\}$. P consists of the following productions.

1 $S \to q_0 T$

2 $T \to [a, a] T$ for each $a \in \Sigma$

3 $T \to U$

4 $U \to [\Lambda, B]\, U$ (Recall that B is the blank)

5 $U \to \Lambda$

6 $p\,[a, C] \to [a, D]\, q$ for each $a \in \Sigma \cup \{\Lambda\}$, $q \in Q$, and $C \in \Gamma$, so that $\delta(p, C) = (q, D, 1)$

7 $p\,[a, C] \to q\,[a, D]$ for each $a \in \Sigma \cup \{\Lambda\}$, $q \in Q$, and $C \in \Gamma$, so that $\delta(p, C) = (q, D, 0)$

8 $[b, E]\, p\,[a, C] \to q\,[b, E]\,[a, D]$ for each $a, b \in \Sigma \cup \{\Lambda\}$, E, $C \in \Gamma$, and $q \in Q$, so that $\delta(p, C) = (q, D, -1)$

9 $[a, C]\, q \to qaq$
$q\,[a, C] \to qaq$
$q \to \Lambda$ for each $a \in \Sigma \cup \{\Lambda\}$, $C \in \Gamma$, and $q \in F$.

A generation must begin with rules (1) and (2), and yields

$$S \overset{*}{\Rightarrow} q_0\,[a_1, a_1]\ [a_2, a_2] \cdots [a_n, a_n]\, T$$

with each $a_i \in \Sigma$. If A accepts $a_1 \cdots a_n$, then it stops and so never uses more than some m cells to the right of the input. Next, use rule (3), then rule (4) m times, and then rule (5). This yields

$$S \overset{*}{\Rightarrow} q_0\,[a_1, a_1] \cdots [a_n, a_n]\ [\Lambda, B]^m$$

Only rules (6), (7), and (8) are used until a final state is reached. Note that the first components of the tape symbols are never changed. We claim the following.

Claim If $q_0 a_1 \cdots a_n \overset{*}{\vdash} X_1 \cdots X_{r-1} q X_r \ldots X_{n+m}$, then

$$q_0\,[a_1, a_1]\,[a_2, a_2] \cdots [a_n, a_n]\,[\Lambda, B]^m$$
$$\overset{*}{\Rightarrow} [a_1, X_1]\,[a_2, X_2] \cdots [a_{r-1}, X_{r-1}]\,q\,[a_r, X_r] \cdots [a_{n+m}, X_{n+m}]$$

where $a_i = \Lambda$ for $i > n$ and $X_j \in \Gamma$ for $1 \leqslant j \leqslant n + m$.

Proof of claim The argument is a straightforward induction on the number of moves and is omitted.

By (9), $q \in F$ implies that:

$$[a_1, X_1] \cdots [a_{r-1}, X_{r-1}]\, q\, [a_r, X_r] \cdots [a_{n+m}, X_{n+m}] \stackrel{*}{\Rightarrow} a_1 \cdots a_n$$

Thus, $T(A) \in L(G)$. The reverse argument is again an induction, which is omitted. □

Now we turn to the arguments which take us from grammars to automata.

Lemma 9.5.3 If L is a context-sensitive language, then $L = T(A)$ for some lba A.

Proof Let $L = L(G)$, where $G = (V, \Sigma, P, S)$ is context-sensitive. The lba A is constructed to work in the following way. Suppose, without loss of generality, that A has endmarkers. This is justified in Problem 1 at the end of this section. A will work as follows:

1 (*Initialization*) A divides the input into two channels. Channel 1 contains the original input string, while channel 2 is for scratch work. A writes S on channel 2 at the lefthand end (next to the endmarker).

2 (*Search*) A slides back and forth across the tape until it finds some string α on channel 2 such that $\alpha \to \beta$ is in P.

3 (*Replace*) Replace α by β and slide the symbols on the rest of channel 2 to the right if necessary. It will not be necessary to move symbols to the left. (Why?) If it is necessary to move a symbol past the right endmarker, A goes to a "dead" state and halts without accepting.

4 (*Decide*) A guesses whether to continue or quit. If it continues, it goes back to 2 and repeats the cycle. Otherwise it goes to 5.

5 (*Compare*) A moves to the left end of the input and then compares channels 1 and 2. If they agree, A accepts. Otherwise A halts without accepting.

It is easily seen that this construction works and that $T(A) = L$. □

Combining our results leads to the following important theorem.

Theorem 9.5.1 L is a context-sensitive language if and only if there is an lba A such that $L = T(A)$.

We can define a deterministic lba in the obvious way and define a deterministic context-sensitive language to be a set accepted by such a device. It can easily be seen that the family of deterministic context-sensitive languages has many attractive features. For example, it is a boolean algebra. It is not known whether or not the deterministic and nondeterministic lba's are equivalent in computation power.

Now we finish our simulations of grammars by automata.

Lemma 9.5.4 If L is generated by a phrase-structure grammar, then $L = T(A)$ for some Turing machine A.

Proof The argument is quite similar to the proof of the previous lemma and may be safely omitted. □

Combining the previous results leads to a characterization of phrase-structure languages.

Theorem 9.5.2 The following conditions are equivalent.

1 L is a phrase-structure language.

2 L is accepted as $T(A)$ for some nondeterministic (or deterministic) multitape (or single-tape) Turing machine A.

3 L is recursively enumerable.

Now that both the phrase-structure languages and the context-sensitive languages have been given machine characterizations, our coverage of the Chomsky hierarchy is complete.

There are two classical open questions about the context-sensitive languages which should be stated. Is every context-sensitive language accepted by a deterministic lba? In other words, is it the case that

$$\text{NSPACE}(n) = \text{DSPACE}(n)?$$

Another question of interest is whether the context-sensitive languages are closed under complementation. We know that DSPACE(n) is closed under complementation so that if NSPACE(n) = DSPACE(n), then we have closure of NSPACE(n) under complementation. It could be the case that context-sensitive languages are closed under complementation but that DSPACE(n) $\subsetneq$ NSPACE(n).

While these problems are interesting in their own right, they can be viewed as special cases of open problems in machine-based complexity theory. For instance, we know of no function $S(n) \geqslant \log n$ such that the question

$$\text{DSPACE}(S(n)) = \text{NSPACE}(S(n))?$$

has been resolved.

PROBLEMS

1 Show that, for any (deterministic) lba A with endmarkers, there is an equivalent lba C without endmarkers.

2 Show that every context-free language is accepted by some deterministic lba. Symbolically,

$$\mathscr{C} \subseteq \text{DSPACE}(n).$$

A stronger result will be proved later, namely, that $\mathscr{C} \subseteq \text{DSPACE}((\log n)^2)$.

3* (*Open question*) Is

$$\mathscr{C} \subseteq \text{NSPACE}(\log n)?$$

4 Show that, for each lba A, there is an lba B which is equivalent and which always halts.

5 Work out the closure properties of the r.e. sets, the context-sensitive languages, and the deterministic context-sensitive languages. Be sure to include nega-

tive results such as the fact that the context-sensitive languages are not closed under homomorphism.

Let us fix an alphabet Σ with $\Sigma = \{a_0, \ldots, a_{m-1}\}$, and use the notation $xy = z$ to stand for the concatenation predicate $\{(x, y, z) | x, y, z \in \Sigma^* \text{ and } xy = z\}$. We construct a formal logical system $\mathscr{R}$, starting from the concatenation predicate, and allowing the following operations:

a) If P_1 and P_2 are in $\mathscr{R}$, then $P_1 \vee P_2$ is in $\mathscr{R}$ (disjunction).

b) If P is in $\mathscr{R}$ then $\neg P$ is in $\mathscr{R}$ (negation).

c) If $P(x_1, \ldots, x_n)$ is in $\mathscr{R}$, then

$$Q(y_1, \ldots, y_m) \Leftrightarrow P(z_1, \ldots, z_n)$$

is in $\mathscr{R}$, where each z_i is either one of the y_i or a string from Σ^*, or even a concatenation of such terms. This operation is called *explicit transformation* and allows us to form a new predicate from an old one by interchanging variables, identifying them, replacing a variable by a constant, etc.

d) If $P(x_1, \ldots, x_n, y)$ is an $(n + 1)$-ary predicate in $\mathscr{R}$, then

$$(\exists z)_{z \leqslant y} \, P(x_1, \ldots, x_n, z) \qquad (*)$$

is in $\mathscr{R}$. This is called *bounded existential quantification* and means that $(*)$ is true if and only if there is a string $z \in \Sigma^*$ such that $z \leqslant y$ for which $P(x_1, \ldots, x_n, z)$ holds. We interpret $z \leqslant y$ as follows: Since $z, y \in \Sigma^*$, regard them as numbers in m-adic notation, since $\leqslant$ is thus the usual "less than or equal to" relationship between natural numbers.

e) Nothing else is in $\mathscr{R}$.

Thus $\mathscr{R}$ is a formal logical system and we can define relations or sets on Σ^*. These sets or relations are called *rudimentary*.

6 Show that each rudimentary set can be accepted by a deterministic lba.

7 Show that every regular set is rudimentary.

8 Show that any context-free language is rudimentary.

9 Show that the rudimentary sets (i.e., definable by 1-place rudimentary predicates) are coextensive with the least family which contains the context-free languages and is closed under boolean operations and length-preserving homomorphisms.

10 Give a machine characterization of the rudimentary sets.

11 Show that there is no algorithm which can determine, of a given context-sensitive grammar G, whether or not $L(G) = \emptyset$. (Thus the problem is unsolvable for phrase-structure grammars also.)

12 Show that there is no algorithm which can determine, of a context-sensitive grammar G, whether or not $L(G)$ is infinite.

13 Show that there is an algorithm which takes a given context-sensitive grammar $G = (V, \Sigma, P, S)$ and two strings α and β in V^* and which decides whether or not

$$\alpha \overset{*}{\Rightarrow} \beta$$

14 Show that the problem mentioned in the previous exercise becomes unsolvable if G is a phrase-structure grammar.

15 Show that there is no algorithm which can decide whether a given production is ever used in a derivation of a string in a context-sensitive language.

16 We can effectively enumerate the lba's over an alphabet Σ as $A_1, \ldots$ Let φ be a fixed homomorphism which maps strings in Σ^* into a fixed alphabet, say $\{0, 1, \#\}^*$, such that $\lg(\varphi(a)) \geqslant |\Gamma_i|$ for each $a \in \Sigma$ and where Γ_i is the work alphabet of A_i.

$$L_0 = \{\# A_i \# \varphi(w) \# \mid w \in \Sigma^*, \# \notin \Sigma, \text{ and } w \in T(A_i)\}.$$

Prove the following three statements.

a) L_0 is a context-sensitive language.

b) $L_0 \in \text{DSPACE}(n)$ if and only if $\text{NSPACE}(n) = \text{DSPACE}(n)$.

c) $\overline{L}_0 \in \text{NSPACE}(n)$ if and only if the family of context-sensitive languages is closed under complementation.

The previous problem asserts that L_0 could be thought of as a "hardest context-sensitive language" with respect to space. It is also a hardest language with respect to time.

17 Show that every context-sensitive language is in $\mathscr{P}$ if and only if $L_0 \in \mathscr{P}$.

18 Let LINEAR denote the set of linear context-free languages. Show that

$$\text{LINEAR} \subseteq \text{NSPACE}(\log n).$$

19 Define $E_1 = L(G)$, where G is given by

$$S \to a_1 S \bar{a}_1 \mid a_2 S \bar{a}_2 \mid \Lambda$$

Define

$$L(E_1) = \{cx_1 y_1 z_1 cx_2 y_2 z_2 c \cdots cx_k y_k z_k c \mid k \geqslant 1, c \notin \Sigma = \{a_1, a_2, \bar{a}_1, \bar{a}_2\},$$
$$y_1 \cdots y_k \in E_1, x_i \in (\Sigma \cup \{c\})^* \{c\} \cup \{\Lambda\}, y_i \in \{c\} (\Sigma \cup \{c\})^* \cup \{\Lambda\}.\}$$

Show that $L(E_1)$ is a linear context-free language.

20* Show that, for any ϵ, $0 \leqslant \epsilon < 1$, the following statements are equivalent:

a) $\text{LINEAR} \subseteq \text{DSPACE}(\log n)^{(1+\epsilon)}$

b) $L(E_1) \in \text{DSPACE}(\log n)^{(1+\epsilon)}$

c) $\text{NSPACE}(S(n)) \subseteq \text{DSPACE}([S(n)]^{1+\epsilon})$ for all $S(n) \geqslant \log n$.

21 Can you find a recursive set of phrase-structure grammars $\mathscr{G} = \{G_i\}$ such that $\mathscr{L} = \{L(G) \mid G \in \mathscr{G}\}$ is exactly the family of recursive sets?

9.6 HISTORICAL SURVEY

The basic material on phrase-structure and context-sensitive grammars is due to Chomsky [1959]. Linear bounded automata were studied by Myhill [1960]. Connections with context-sensitive languages were established by Landweber [1963] and Kuroda [1964]. Some closure results about context-sensitive languages were derived by Ginsburg and Greibach [1966b]. The importance of time- and space-complexity classes of Turing-machine computations was first noted by Hartmanis and Stearns [1965]. Theorem 9.4.3 is from Savitch [1970]. Cook [1971] was the first to realize the importance of $\mathscr{P}$ and $\mathscr{NP}$. Karp [1972] systematically reduced many combinatorial problems to the $\mathscr{P} = \mathscr{NP}$ question. Speed-up theorems such as Problem 4 at the end of Section 9.4 were first proved by Blum [1967]. Problem 5 is from Borodin [1972]. Problem 11 is from Rabin [1963], while Problem 12 is from Aanderaa [1974]. Problem 13 is from Fischer and Rosenberg [1968]. Problem 14 is from Hennie [1966], while Problems 15 through 17 are from Book [1972b].

Problem 6 of Section 9.5 is from Myhill [1960]. Problems 7 and 8 are from the work of Jones [1969], while Problems 9 and 10 are due to Yu [1970]. A number of decision questions about context-sensitive languages come from Landweber [1964].

Problems 16 and 17 are from Hartmanis and Hunt [1973]. Problems 18 through 20 are from the work of Sudborough [1975ab, 1976ab].

ten

Representation Theorems for Languages

10.1 INTRODUCTION

In this section, a number of characterization theorems for classes of languages will be proved. All of the results are important and are used extensively.

There have been a number of papers in the literature which place various restrictions on phrase-structure grammars or on their derivations, so that the languages that are generated are exactly the context-free languages. Section 10.2 is devoted to proving one theorem which captures the essential idea of such constructions. Then, we shall obtain a number of the results from the literature as corollaries.

Section 10.3 is devoted to showing that any r.e. set L may be represented as

$$L = \varphi(L_1 \cap L_2),$$

where L_1 and L_2 are deterministic context-free languages and φ is a homomorphism. Some applications for this result are given.

In Section 10.4, the semi-Dyck and Dyck sets are introduced. These are sets with several types of left and right brackets, which are balanced according to one-sided or two-sided cancellation rules. It will be shown that each context-free language L is of the form

$$L = \varphi(D \cap R),$$

where D is a semi-Dyck set, R is a regular set, and φ is a homomorphism.

Section 10.5 is devoted to proving that there is one context-free language L_0 such that any other context-free language L may be written

$$L = \varphi^{-1} L_0,$$

where φ is a homomorphism. The importance of this result will be clear in Chapter 12 where it will be shown that L_0 is a "hardest" context-free language with respect to both time and space.

10.2* BAKER'S THEOREM

In this section, we shall start from NR grammars of Section 9.2, which are known to generate exactly the family of phrase-structure languages. By placing suitable restrictions on the rules, one can get context-free languages. The main theorem in this section has, as corollaries, almost every other result of this type that is known.

Next we introduce an important property of NR grammars.

Definition Let $G = (V, \Sigma, P, S)$ be an NR grammar. G is *terminal bounded* if each rule in P is of the form

$$x_0 A_1 x_1 \cdots x_{n-1} A_n x_n \rightarrow y_0 B_1 \cdots y_{m-1} B_m y_m$$

where each $x_i, y_i \in \Sigma^*$, $A_i, B_i \in N$, and either $n = 1$ or there is some j, $0 \leqslant j \leqslant m$, such that, for every k, $1 \leqslant k < n$, $\lg(y_j) > \lg(x_k)$.

This definition says that either a rule is context-free ($n = 1$) or that there is some terminal string y_j which is strictly longer than any of the terminal strings $x_1, \ldots, x_{n-1}$; that is, y_j is longer than any string that can appear between two variables in the lefthand side.

Example

$$AaB \rightarrow BaCbb$$

This is a terminal bounded rule since $\lg(bb) = 2 > \lg(a) = 1$.

Notation. For any NR grammar $G = (V, \Sigma, P, S)$, define

$$N(G) = \sum_{\substack{\alpha \rightarrow \beta \\ \text{is in } P}} (\lg(\alpha) - 1).$$

$N(G)$ measures the excess of symbols on the lefthand side of rules over that which would be present in a context-free grammar with the same number of rules.

Fact Let $G = (V, \Sigma, P, S)$ be an NR grammar, $N(G) = 0$ if and only if G is context-free.

Example If we consider the rule in the previous example as an entire grammar, then

$$N(G) = 2.$$

We need one more definition before we can begin to prove a lemma.

Definition Let $G = (V, \Sigma, P, S)$ be an arbitrary NR grammar. Define

$$L_G = \max\{0, \lg(x) | \; x\gamma \to \beta \text{ is in } P \quad \text{for some } \gamma, \beta \in V^*, x \in \Sigma^*\};$$

$$R_G = \max\{0, \lg(x) | \; \gamma x \to \beta \text{ is in } P \quad \text{for some } \gamma, \beta \in V^*, x \in \Sigma^*\};$$

$$B_G = \max\{0, \lg(x) | \; \gamma_1 A_1 x A_2 \gamma_2 \to \beta \text{ is in } P \text{ for some } x \in \Sigma^*, A_1, A_2 \in N, \gamma_1, \gamma_2 \in V^*\}.$$

Thus L_G (respectively, R_G) is the largest length of a terminal string appearing on the left (right) end of a rule in P. B_G is the maximum length of a string appearing between two variables in the lefthand side of a rule in P.

We are now ready for a nontrivial lemma.

Lemma 10.2.1 Let $G = (V, \Sigma, P, S')$ be a terminal bounded grammar with $N(G) > 0$. Then there exists a terminal bounded grammar G_1, a regular set R, and a gsm S such that

$$L(G) = S(L(G_1) \cap R),$$

and

$$N(G_1) < N(G).$$

Proof There are basically two cases in the proof.

CASE 1 $L_G > B_G$ or $R_G > B_G$.

The idea will be to take a rule of G which has in its left side a terminal string that is too long to appear between variables in any rule, and shorten the terminal context of this rule.

Assume, without loss of generality, that $R_G \geqslant L_G$ and $R_G > B_G$. (For $L_G > R_G$, the construction would yield a G_1 symmetric to the present one.)

The idea is to consider a string AwB where $w \in \Sigma^*$ and $\lg(w) = R_G > B_G$, $A, B \in V$. No rule of P can span AwB, so that, if some initial part of a derivation produces w, then any later step must apply a rule to the left of w independent of what occurs to the right of w, or to the right of w independent of what occurs to the left of w.

We shall replace a single rule in P whose lefthand side contains a terminal string of length R_G by a rule with shorter terminal context. But this could allow derivations in which the new rule could be applied when the old rule was not applicable. Accordingly, a special symbol \$ will be used with the new rule to flag unwanted derivations.

Define $G_1 = (V_1, \Sigma \cup \{\$\}, P_1, S')$, where $V_1 = V \cup \{\$\}$. Choose a rule $\gamma w \to \beta w$ in P, where $w \in \Sigma^*$ and $\lg(w) = R_G$. Define

$$P_1 = (P - \{\gamma w \to \beta w\}) \cup \{\gamma \to \beta w\$\}.$$

G_1 is terminal bounded since G was. Since $\lg(w) = R_G > 0$, $\lg(\gamma) < \lg(\gamma w)$, so that

$$N(G_1) < N(G).$$

Given a string $\sigma\gamma w\rho$, we can use $\gamma w \to \beta w$ in G to produce $\sigma\beta w\rho$. w is available as context for the further rewriting of β or of ρ. In G_1 if we start with $\sigma\gamma w\rho$ and use $\gamma \to \beta w\$$ in P_1, we get $\sigma\beta w\$w\rho$ and again both β and ρ have the context w

with which to continue. But we have to restrict the context in which $\gamma \to \beta w\$$ is applied and to erase the extra $w\$$.

Let $R = (V \cup \{\$w\})^*$ and define the gsm S as follows: Let $w = w_1 \cdots w_n$, $w_i \in \Sigma$, and:

$$q_0 \xrightarrow{\$/\Lambda} q_1 \xrightarrow{w_1/\Lambda} q_2 \xrightarrow{w_2/\Lambda} q_3 \rightarrow \cdots \xrightarrow{w_{n-1}/\Lambda} q_n, \quad q_n \xrightarrow{w_n/\Lambda} q_0, \quad q_0 \xrightarrow{a/a} q_0 \ (a \neq \$)$$

To complete the proof, we must prove the following claim.

Claim 1 $L(G) = S(L(G_1) \cap R)$.

Proof We shall only sketch the argument here but will give the essential parts so that the details can be easily supplied. The argument proceeds by first showing that $L(G) \subseteq S(L(G_1) \cap R)$. To prove this, it suffices to prove Claim 1(a).

Claim 1(a) For any $y \in \Sigma^*$, if

$$S' \overset{n}{\underset{G}{\Rightarrow}} y = u_1 w u_2 w \cdots u_k w u_{k+1}$$

where $n > 0, k \geqslant 0$, and each

$$u_i \in V^* - V^* w V^*,$$

then there exist $i_1, \ldots, i_k \geqslant 0$ such that

$$S' \overset{n}{\underset{G_1}{\Rightarrow}} z = u_1 (w\$)^{i_1} w u_2 (w\$)^{i_2} \cdots u_k (w\$)^{i_k} w u_{k+1}$$

Proof The argument is an easy induction on n and is omitted.

Note that Claim 1(a) is sufficient to prove that $L(G) \subseteq S(L(G_1) \cap R)$ since $z \in R$ and $y = S(z)$.

The reverse direction is more interesting. There are derivations of strings in $L(G_1) \cap R$ which cannot be simulated exactly in G [$\gamma \to \beta w\$$ may be applicable to a string while $\gamma w \to \beta w$ is not]. One can show that, for each $y \in L(G_1) \cap R$, there is some derivation of y in which $\gamma \to \beta w\$$ is applied only when context w has already been generated to the right of γ. This derivation is "almost" a G-derivation and it is easy to construct a G-derivation of $S(y)$ which imitates it. The argument proceeds in a sequence of steps.

Claim 1(b) If $y \in L(G_1) \cap R$, then G_1 has a derivation

$$S' \underset{G_1}{\Rightarrow} \alpha_1 \underset{G_1}{\Rightarrow} \cdots \underset{G_1}{\Rightarrow} \alpha_n = y$$

and each $\alpha_i \in R$.

Proof The argument involves labeling all occurrences of \$ in y and considering where each subscripted \$ was introduced. A straightforward case analysis proves the result, and details are left to the reader.

Claim 1(c) If, for some $n \geqslant 0$,

$$S' \underset{G_1}{\Rightarrow} \alpha_0 \underset{G_1}{\Rightarrow} \alpha_1 \underset{G_1}{\Rightarrow} \cdots \underset{G_1}{\Rightarrow} \alpha_n$$

and each $\alpha_i \in R$, then

$$S' = S(\alpha_0) \underset{G}{\Rightarrow} S(\alpha_1) \underset{G}{\Rightarrow} \cdots \underset{G}{\Rightarrow} S(\alpha_n)$$

Proof The argument is a straightforward induction on n.

Claims 1(a) and 1(b) prove that

$$S(L(G_1) \cap R) \subseteq L(G)$$

and that completes the proof of Claim 1.

CASE 2 $L_G \leqslant B_G$ and $R_G \leqslant B_G$.

The idea is similar to Case 1 except that we must consider a string w of length $B_G + 1$. Choose a rule

$$x_0 A_1 x_1 \cdots x_{n-1} A_n x_n \rightarrow x_0 \gamma_1 x_1 \cdots x_{n-1} \gamma_n x_n$$

where each $x_i \in \Sigma^*$, $A_i \in N$, $\gamma_i \in V^*$, and there exists j, $1 \leqslant j \leqslant n-1$, so that $\lg(x_j) = B_G$. We claim $n \geqslant 2$. Otherwise, $n = 1$ and all rules have one variable on the left, so that $B_G = L_G = R_G = 0$, and thus $N(G) = 0$. Since G is terminal bounded, the righthand side of this rule has a terminal substring w of length $> B_G$. Since $B_G \geqslant L_G$ and $B_G \geqslant R_G$, $\lg(w) > \lg(x_i)$ for any i, $0 \leqslant i \leqslant n$.

Thus some part of the γ's must be included in w. Let us say that γ_k must be included in w. (By symmetry, assume $k < n$.) We rewrite the rule as

$$\sigma A_k x_k A_{k+1} \rho \rightarrow \beta_1 w \beta_2$$

where $\lg(\beta_1) < \lg(x_0 \gamma_1 \cdots \gamma_{k-1} x_{k-1} \gamma_k)$. Define $G_1 = (V_1, \Sigma \cup \{¢, \$\}, P_1, S')$ where $V_1 = V \cup \{¢, \$\}$, and let $P' = \{\sigma A_k \rightarrow \beta_1 w \$, x_k A_{k+1} \rho \rightarrow x_k ¢ w \beta_2\}$.

Then

$$P_1 = (P - \{\sigma A_k x_k A_{k+1} \rho \rightarrow \beta_1 w \beta_2\}) \cup P'.$$

G_1 is surely terminal bounded. Clearly, $N(G_1) < N(G)$.

Let $R = (V \cup \{\$ x_k ¢ w\})^*$ and define a gsm as indicated in Fig. 10.1. Let $x_k = x'_1 \cdots x'_p$, and $w = w_1 \cdots w_r$, when $x'_i, w_j \in \Sigma$.

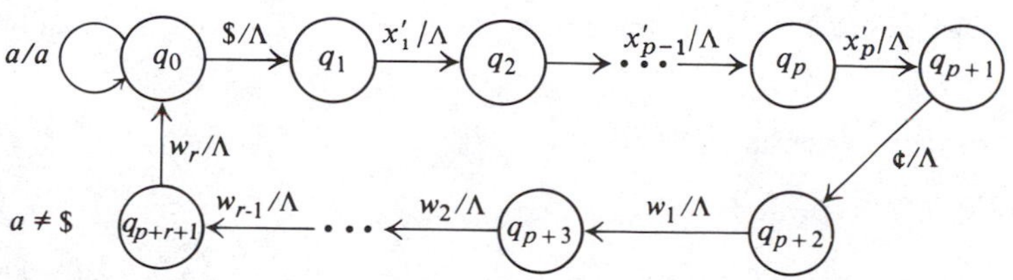

FIG. 10.1

Again the completion of the argument depends on the following result.

Claim 2 $L(G) = S(L(G_1) \cap R)$.

Proof The argument will be sketched by giving an outline.

Claim 2(a) For any y, if $S' \overset{n}{\underset{G}{\Rightarrow}} y$ then there exists $z \in R$ such that

$$S' \overset{*}{\underset{G_1}{\Rightarrow}} z$$

and

$$S(z) = y$$

Proof The argument is a straightforward induction on n.

As in Claim 1, it is the reverse direction that is more complex. Take y in $L(G_1) \cap R$, and index occurrences of ¢ and \$, so that

$$y = \gamma_0 \$_1 x_k ¢_1 \gamma_1 \$_2 X_k ¢_2 \cdots \gamma_{p-1} \$_p x_k ¢_p \gamma_p$$

Claim 2(b) If $y \in L(G_1) \cap R$, then

$$S' \underset{G_1}{\Rightarrow} \alpha_1 \underset{G_1}{\Rightarrow} \cdots \underset{G_1}{\Rightarrow} \alpha_n = y$$

such that for all j, $¢_j$ first appears in α_{r+1} if $\$_j$ first appears in α_r.

Proof The argument is a case study of how symbols may be generated. The reader should provide the details.

Claim 2(c) If

$$S' = \alpha_0 \overset{*}{\underset{G_1}{\Rightarrow}} \alpha_1 \overset{*}{\underset{G_1}{\Rightarrow}} \cdots \overset{*}{\underset{G_1}{\Rightarrow}} \alpha_m = y$$

where, for each $i < m$, $\alpha_i \overset{*}{\underset{G_1}{\Rightarrow}} \alpha_{i+1}$ by a single rule of P or via consecutive applications of the two rules of P', then

$$S' = S(\alpha_0) \underset{G}{\Rightarrow} \cdots \underset{G}{\Rightarrow} S(\alpha_m) = S(y).$$

Proof Induction on m.

The argument above completes the proof of Claim 2. The main proof is now complete. □

We are now going to show that terminal bounded grammars can generate only context-free languages. Intuitively, this seems clear since the long terminal context prevents reapplication of a rule and hence destroys the ability to transmit information.

Theorem 10.2.1 (Baker's theorem) If $G = (V, \Sigma, P, S')$ is a terminal bounded grammar, then $L(G)$ is context-free.

Proof We induct on $N(G)$.

Basis. If $N(G) = 0$, then G is context-free.

Induction step. Assume the result for all grammars G' such that $N(G') < k$. Consider $G = (V, \Sigma, P, S')$ with $N(G) = k$. By Lemma 10.2.1, there exists a regular set R, a gsm S, and a terminal bounded grammar G_1 such that $N(G_1) < k$ and $L(G) = S(L(G_1) \cap R)$. By the induction hypothesis, $L(G_1)$ is context-free. Therefore

$$L(G) = S(L(G_1) \cap R)$$

is also context-free and the proof is complete. □

Now we begin a sequence of corollaries of this theorem. Each of the corollaries is nontrivial and interesting in its own right.

Corollary 1 If $G = (V, \Sigma, P, S)$ is a phrase-structure grammar with each rule of the form $\alpha \to \beta$ with $\alpha \in N^+$ and $\beta \in V^* \Sigma V^*$, then $L(G)$ is context-free.

Corollary 2 If $G = (V, \Sigma, P, S)$ is a context-sensitive grammar with erasing, such that each rule is of the form $\alpha \to \beta$ with $\alpha \in \Sigma^* N \Sigma^*$, then $L(G)$ is context-free.

Corollary 3 If $G = (V, \Sigma, P, S)$ is a context-sensitive grammar with erasing, in which each rule is of the form $xA\beta \to x\gamma\beta$, where $A \in N$, $x \in \Sigma^*$, $\beta \in V^*$, and $\lg(x) \geqslant \lg(\beta)$, then $L(G)$ is context-free.

Corollary 4 If $G = (V, \Sigma, P, S)$ is a context-sensitive grammar with erasing, such that each rule is of the form $\alpha A \gamma \to \alpha\beta\gamma$, where either

i) $\alpha \in \Sigma^*$ and $\lg(\alpha) \geqslant \lg(\gamma)$

or ii) $\gamma \in \Sigma^*$ and $\lg(\gamma) \geqslant \lg(\alpha)$,

then $L(G)$ is context-free.

Corollary 5 Let $G = (V, \Sigma, P, S)$ be an NR grammar and let $<$ be a partial ordering on V. Suppose that each rule is of the form

$$A_1 \cdots A_n \to B_1 \cdots B_m$$

where each $A_i \in N$ and there is some k, $1 \leqslant k \leqslant m$, such that for all i, $1 \leqslant i \leqslant n$, $A_i < B_k$. Then $L(G)$ is context-free.

Proof The argument is involved and is left for Problem 2 at the end of the section, where some hints are given.

Definition Let $G = (V, \Sigma, P, S)$ be an NR grammar. If $x \in \Sigma^*$, $\alpha \to \beta$ is in P, and $\gamma \in V^*$, write

$$x\alpha\gamma \underset{L}{\Rightarrow} x\beta\gamma \quad \text{and} \quad \gamma\alpha x \underset{R}{\Rightarrow} \gamma\beta x.$$

Define

$$\text{Left}(G) = \{w \in \Sigma^* \mid S \overset{*}{\underset{L}{\Rightarrow}} w\}$$

and

$$\text{Two-way}(G) = \{w \in \Sigma^* \mid S \overset{*}{\underset{L \cup R}{\Rightarrow}} w\},$$

where $\overset{*}{\underset{L \cup R}{\Rightarrow}}$ means that each rewriting is either a leftmost one (by $\underset{L}{\Rightarrow}$) or a rightmost one (by $\underset{R}{\Rightarrow}$).

Corollary 6 If $G = (V, \Sigma, P, S)$ is an NR grammar, then Left (G) and Two-way (G) are context-free.

Proof We shall first construct a new terminal bounded grammar G' such that $L(G') = \text{Two-way } (G')$ and $\varphi L(G') = \text{Two-way } (G)$, where φ is a homomorphism. Let $q = \max \{\lg(\alpha) \mid \alpha \to \beta \text{ is in } P\}$. Let d, L, R, and S_1 be new symbols. Define $G' = (V', \Sigma', P', S_1)$, where $\Sigma' = \Sigma \cup \{d\}$, and $V' = V \cup \{d, L, R, S_1\}$. P' is defined as follows.

i)

$$L \to \Lambda$$

$$R \to \Lambda$$

$$S_1 \to d^q LSRd^q$$

are all in P.

ii) If $u\alpha v \to w\beta x$ is in P and $u, v, w, x, y \in (\Sigma')^*$, $\alpha, \beta \in \{\Lambda\} \cup N(\Sigma^* N)^*$ with $\lg(y) = q$, then

$$yuL\alpha v \to ywL\beta x$$

$$u\alpha Rvy \to w\beta Rxy$$

$$yuL\alpha Rv \to ywL\beta Rx$$

are all in P'.

The idea is to add markers L and R to designate the leftmost and rightmost variables at any point in a derivation. To also make G' terminal bounded, extra terminal context is added on the left or right side of each rule; this terminal context does not interfere with the application of rules, since each rule can be applied only where there are no nonterminals on at least one side.

It is now easy to see that

$$L(G') = \text{Two-way } (G').$$

Let φ be the homomorphism given by

$$\varphi d = \Lambda$$

$$\varphi a = a \quad \text{if } a \neq d.$$

A straightforward argument shows that

$$\varphi(L(G')) = \text{Two-way } (G).$$

Since G' is terminal bounded, Two-way (G) is context-free. □

PROBLEMS

1 Show that if G is an NR grammar, then Left (G) is context-free.

2 Prove Corollary 5. *Hint*. Assume that $<$ is a total order and that S is the least element in this ordering. Also assume that, if $\alpha \to \beta$ is a rule, then either $\beta \in N^*$ or $\beta \in \Sigma$. Let d, E, and S_1 be new symbols. Define $\Sigma_1 = \Sigma \cup \{d\}$, $V_1 = V \cup \{d, E, S_1\}$, and let

$$p = \max \{\lg(\beta) \mid \alpha \to \beta \text{ is in } P\}.$$

Define φ to be a homomorphism given by

$$\varphi A = Ad^{p^i}$$

if $A \in V$ and A is greater than exactly i elements in V. Define P_1 to consist of the following rules:

a) $S_1 \to SdE$
   $E \to d$

b) If $\alpha \to \beta$ is in P and $Y \in N$, then add to P_1

$$\varphi(\alpha)Y \to \varphi(\beta)Y$$

Show that $G_1 = (V_1, \Sigma_1, P_1, S_1)$ is an NR grammar and is terminal bounded. Define a homomorphism ψ: $V_1^* \to V^*$ by

$$\psi A = \begin{cases} \Lambda & \text{if } A = d, \\ A & \text{otherwise.} \end{cases}$$

Show that

$$\psi(L(G_1)) = L(G)$$

and hence $L(G)$ is context-free.

10.3* DETERMINISTIC LANGUAGES GENERATE RECURSIVELY ENUMERABLE SETS

Any recursively enumerable (or phrase-structure) language L may be generated as

$$L = \varphi(L_1 \cap L_2),$$

where L_1 and L_2 are deterministic context-free languages and φ is a homomorphism. This result turns out to be extremely useful when investigating new families of languages. For example, if one is investigating a new family of languages that is subrecursive, and one knows that the family is closed under homomorphism and contains the deterministic context-free languages, then the new family cannot be closed under intersection.

The construction is not very hard at all. Let

$$G = (V, \Sigma, P, S)$$

be a phrase-structure grammar. Assume that G has k rules for some k. Define

$$L_1'(G) = \{\gamma_1\alpha_i d_i \gamma_2 c \gamma_2^T \beta_i^T \gamma_1^T c \mid \gamma_1, \gamma_2 \in V^*,\ \alpha_i \to \beta_i \text{ is in } P,\ 1 \leqslant i \leqslant k\}^+,$$

where $d_1, \ldots, d_k$ and c are new symbols, not in V.

Lemma 10.3.1 $L_1'(G)$ is a deterministic context-free language for each phrase-structure grammar G.

Proof For $\alpha_i \to \beta_i$ in P, $1 \leqslant i \leqslant k$, let $\alpha_i = \alpha_{i1} \cdots \alpha_{im(i)}$ and $\beta_i = \beta_{i1} \cdots \beta_{in(i)}$, each α_{ij} and β_{ij} in V.

Note. By the definition of a phrase-structure grammar, $m(i) \geqslant 1$ and $n(i) \geqslant 0$.

Let $A = (Q, \Sigma', \Gamma, \delta, Z_0, \{f\})$ be the deterministic pda with $\Sigma' = V \cup \{c, d_1, \ldots, d_k\}$. Then

$$Q = \{q_0, q_1, q_2, d, f\} \cup \{s_{ij} \mid 1 \leqslant i \leqslant k, 0 \leqslant j < m(i)\} \cup \{t_{ij} \mid 1 \leqslant i \leqslant k, 0 \leqslant j < n(i)\};$$

and $\Gamma = \Sigma' \cup \{Z_0\}$, Z_0 being a new symbol, and δ defined as follows:

i) $\delta(q_0, a, Z_0) = (q_0, Z_0 a)$ for each a in V;
$\delta(q_0, a, b) = (q_0, ba)$ for each a and b in $V \cup \{d_i \mid 1 \leqslant i \leqslant k\}$;
$\delta(q_0, c, b) = (q_1, b)$ for each b in $V \cup \{d_i \mid 1 \leqslant i \leqslant k\}$.

ii) $\delta(q_1, a, a) = (q_1, \Lambda)$ for each a in V;
$\delta(q_1, \Lambda, d_i) = (s_{i0}, \Lambda)$ for each $1 \leqslant i \leqslant k$.

iii) $\delta(s_{ij}, \Lambda, \alpha_{i(m(i)-j)}) = (s_{i(j+1)}, \Lambda)$ for each $1 \leqslant i \leqslant k$, $0 \leqslant j < m(i) - 1$;
$\delta(s_{i(m(i)-1)}, \Lambda, \alpha_{i1}) = (t_{i0}, \Lambda)$ for each $1 \leqslant i \leqslant k$.

iv) $\delta(t_{ij}, \beta_{i(n(i)-j)}, a) = (t_{i(j+1)}, a)$ for each a in $V \cup \{Z_0\}$, $1 \leqslant i \leqslant k$, $0 \leqslant j < n(i) - 1$;
$\delta(t_{i(n(i)-1)}, \beta_{i1}, a) = (q_2, a)$ for each $1 \leqslant i \leqslant k$, a in $V \cup \{Z_0\}$, If $n(i) = 0$, this becomes $\delta(t_{i0}, \Lambda, a) = (q_2, a)$.

v) $\delta(q_2, a, a) = (q_2, \Lambda)$ for each a in V;
$\delta(q_2, c, Z_0) = (f, Z_0)$.

vi) $\delta(f, \Lambda, Z_0) = (q_0, Z_0)$.

vii) $\delta(q, a, b) = (d, b)$ for all (q, a, b) not previously specified.

The dpda A operates as follows:

1 In (i), A copies the input onto the stack until the symbol c is read.

2 In (ii), it checks the input against the stack until some d_i is read on the stack. The d_i is then erased.

3 Without moving the input, A checks in (iii) to see whether the word α_i is on the stack (erasing α_i in the process).

4 In (iv), A sees whether β_i is on the input while not altering the stack.

5 In (v), A matches the input against the stack until c is read.

6 In (v), A goes to an accepting state if c is read on the input and Z_0 on the stack.

7 In (vi), A then goes to the start state, the cycle (beginning at step (1)) being repeated.

It is a straightforward matter to verify that $T(A) = L_1'(G)$. □

The following notation is useful.

Notation. For a in Σ, let $\hat{a}$ be a new symbol. Let $\hat{\Lambda} = \Lambda$ and $\hat{w} = \hat{a}_1 \cdots \hat{a}_k$ for each $w = a_1 \cdots a_k$, all a_i in Σ. For each $U \subseteq \Sigma^*$, let $\hat{U} = \{\hat{u} \mid u \text{ in } U\}$. For each phrase-structure grammar G, let $L_1(G) = L_1'(G)(\hat{\Sigma})^*$.

Corollary $L_1(G)$ is a deterministic context-free language.

Proof Since strings over $(\hat{\Sigma})^*$ involve a new alphabet, it is clear that $L'_1(G)\,(\hat{\Sigma})^*$ is a deterministic context-free language.

Now, a second encoding must be prepared.

Notation. Let V be a finite set containing S, $k \geqslant 1$, and let $c, d_1, \ldots, d_k$ be $k+1$ new symbols. Let

$$L(k, V) = \{Sd_ic \mid 1 \leqslant i \leqslant k\}\{\alpha_1\alpha_2 c\alpha_2^T d_j \alpha_1^T c \mid 1 \leqslant j \leqslant k, \alpha_1 \text{ and } \alpha_2 \text{ in } V^*\}^* \{\beta c \hat{\beta}^T \mid \beta \text{ in } V^*\}.$$

Lemma 10.3.2 $L(k, V)$ is a deterministic context-free language.

Proof Let A be the deterministic pda $(Q, \Sigma', \Gamma, \delta, q_0, Z_0, \{f_1, f_2\})$, where

$$Q = \{q_0, q_1, q_2, d, f_1, f_2\} \cup \{s_i \mid 0 \leqslant i \leqslant 4\},$$
$$\Sigma' = V \cup \hat{\Sigma} \cup \{c, d_1, \ldots, d_k\},$$
$$\Gamma = V \cup \hat{V} \cup \{Z_0\},$$

Z_0 being a new symbol, and δ is defined as follows (a and b are arbitrary elements in V):

i) $\delta(q_0, S, Z_0) = (q_1, Z_0)$;
$\delta(q_1, d_i, Z_0) = (q_2, Z_0)$ for $1 \leqslant i \leqslant k$;
$\delta(q_2, c, Z_0) = (s_0, Z_0)$.

ii) $\delta(s_0, a, Z_0) = (s_0, Z_0 a)$;
$\delta(s_0, a, b) = (s_0, ba)$;
$\delta(s_0, c, a) = (s_1, a)$.

iii) $\delta(s_1, a, a) = (s_2, \Lambda)$;
$\delta(s_1, \hat{a}, a) = (s_3, \Lambda)$.

iv) $\delta(s_2, a, a) = (s_2, \Lambda)$;
$\delta(s_2, d_j, a) = (s_4, a)$, $\delta(s_2, d_j, Z_0) = (s_4, Z_0)$.

v) $\delta(s_3, \hat{a}, a) = (s_3, \Lambda)$;
$\delta(s_3, \Lambda, Z_0) = (f_1, Z_0)$.

vi) $\delta(s_4, a, a) = (s_4, \Lambda)$;
$\delta(s_4, c, Z_0) = (s_0, Z_0)$.

vii) $\delta(s_0, c, Z_0) = (f_2, Z_0)$;
$\delta(f_2, d_i, Z_0) = (s_4, Z_0)$ for $1 \leqslant i \leqslant k$.

viii) $\delta(q, a', Z) = (d, Z)$ for all (q, a', Z) in $Q \times \Sigma' \times \Gamma$ not previously defined.

Note that the rules in (vii) are needed in case $\alpha_1\alpha_2 = \Lambda$ or $\beta = \Lambda$.

Intuitively, A operates as follows:

1 In (i), A checks to see whether the first three input symbols are Sd_ic for some i.

2 In (ii), A copies the input symbols onto the stack until the symbol c is read.

3 In (iii) and (iv), it matches the input against the stack until some d_j is read on the input.

4 In (iv), the d_j is read on the input without altering the stack.

5 In (vi), the input is again matched against the stack until the symbol c is read.

6 A then goes to s_0 and cycles.

7 If, at step (3), a symbol $\hat{a}$ is read, then A goes to s_3, where it compares, in (v), $\hat{a}$ on the input with a on the stack.

8 A accepts if, after reading the input, the stack is empty except for Z_0.

It is a straightforward matter to formally verify that $T(A) = L(k, V)$. The details are omitted. □

We now obtain the desired representation theorem for recursively enumerable sets.

Theorem 10.3.1 For each recursively enumerable set $E \subseteq \Sigma^*$, there exist deterministic context-free languages L_1 and L_2, and a homomorphism φ such that

$$E = \varphi(L_1 \cap L_2).$$

Proof Let $E = L(G)$, where $G = (V, \Sigma, P, S)$ is a phrase-structure grammar. Let $L_1 = L_1(G)$ and $L_2 = L(k, V)$, where k is the number of productions in P. Let φ be the homomorphism defined by $\varphi(\hat{a}) = a$ for each $\hat{a}$ in $\hat{\Sigma}$ and $\varphi(a) = \Lambda$ for each a in $V \cup \{c, d_1, \ldots, d_k\}$.

Let x be a word in E. Then there exist $\gamma_{j1}, \gamma_{j2}, \alpha_{g(j)}, \beta_{g(j)}$ for $0 \leqslant j \leqslant m$, such that

$$\gamma_{01} = \gamma_{02} = \Lambda, \quad \alpha_{g(0)} = S, \quad \gamma_{m1}\beta_{g(m)}\gamma_{m2} = x,$$

and

$$\gamma_{j1}\alpha_{g(j)}\gamma_{j2} \quad \text{implies that} \quad \gamma_{j1}\beta_{g(j)}\gamma_{j2},$$

with $\alpha_{g(j)} \to \beta_{g(j)}$ in P, for $0 \leqslant j \leqslant m$, and

$$\gamma_{j1}\beta_{g(j)}\gamma_{j2} = \gamma_{(j+1)1}\alpha_{g(j+1)}\gamma_{(j+1)2}$$

for $1 \leqslant j \leqslant m-1$. For each γ_1, i, and γ_2, let

$$s(\gamma_1, i, \gamma_2) = \gamma_2^T\gamma_1^T c\gamma_1 d_i \gamma_2 c$$

and

$$t(\gamma_1, i, \gamma_2) = \gamma_1\alpha_i d_i \gamma_2 c \gamma_2^T \beta_i^T \gamma_1^T c.$$

Then

$$z = t(\gamma_{01}, g(0), \gamma_{02})t(\gamma_{11}, g(1), \gamma_{12}) \cdots t(\gamma_{m1}, g(m), \gamma_{m2})\hat{x}$$

is in $L_1(G)$. However,

$$z = Sd_{g(0)}cs(\gamma_{11}\alpha_{g(1)}, g(1), \gamma_{12}) \cdots s(\gamma_{m1}\alpha_{g(m)}, g(m), \gamma_{m2})x^T c\hat{x}.$$

Therefore, z is in $L(k, V)$; that is, z is in $L_1 \cap L_2$. Then $x = \varphi(z)$ is in $\varphi(L_1 \cap L_2)$; that is, $E \subseteq \varphi(L_1 \cap L_2)$.

Suppose that X is in $\varphi(L_1 \cap L_2)$. Thus $x = \varphi(z)$ for some z in $L_1 \cap L_2$. Then

$$z = t(\gamma_{01}, g(0), \gamma_{02}) \cdots t(\gamma_{m1}, g(m), \gamma_{m2})\hat{x}$$

for some $\gamma_{01}, \gamma_{02}, \ldots, \gamma_{m1}, \gamma_{m2}, g(0), \ldots, g(m)$. Similarly,

$$z = Sd_{f(0)}cs(\xi_{11}, f(1), \xi_{12}) \cdots s(\xi_{n1}, f(n), \xi_{n2})x^T c\hat{x}$$

for some $\xi_{11}, \xi_{12}, \ldots, \xi_{n1}, \xi_{n2}, f(0), \ldots, f(n)$. Then $m = n$ (since there are exactly $2m + 2$ and $2n + 2$ occurrences of c in z). By observing the occurrences of d_j in z, we see that $f(i) = g(i)$ for $0 \leqslant i \leqslant m$. We also see that

$$\gamma_{01} = \gamma_{02} = \Lambda, \qquad \alpha_{g(0)} = S, \qquad \gamma_{i1}\alpha_{g(i)} = \xi_{i1}, \qquad \gamma_{i2} = \xi_{i2},$$

and

$$\gamma_{(i-1)1}\beta_{g(i-1)}\gamma_{(i-1)2} = \xi_{i1}\xi_{i2} = \gamma_{i1}\alpha_{g(i)}\gamma_{i2}$$

for $0 \leqslant i \leqslant m$, and $\gamma_{m1}\beta_{g(m)}\gamma_{m2} = x$. Thus

$$S \Rightarrow \gamma_{01}\beta_{g(0)}\gamma_{02} \Rightarrow \gamma_{11}\beta_{g(1)}\gamma_{12} \Rightarrow \cdots \Rightarrow \gamma_{m1}\beta_{g(m)}\gamma_{m2} = x;$$

that is, x is in E. Then $\varphi(L_1 \cap L_2) \subseteq E$ and the proof is complete. □

The application that was discussed earlier can now be formalized.

Theorem 10.3.2 Let $\mathscr{L}$ be any family of recursive sets that contains the family of deterministic context-free languages.

a) If $\mathscr{L}$ is closed under intersection, then $\mathscr{L}$ is not closed under homomorphism.

b) If $\mathscr{L}$ is closed under homomorphism, then $\mathscr{L}$ is not closed under intersection.

Other variations are possible as well.

Theorem 10.3.3 Let $\mathscr{L}$ be any family of recursive sets such that there is a nonempty language in $\mathscr{L}$. If $\mathscr{L}$ is closed under intersection and homomorphism, then $\mathscr{L}$ does not contain the family of deterministic context-free languages.

PROBLEMS

1 Extend Theorem 10.3.1 to the following: Given Σ, let $\Sigma_0 = \hat{\Sigma} \cup \{a, b\}$, a and b being two new symbols. There exists a homomorphism φ of Σ_0^* onto Σ^* with the following property: For each recursively enumerable set $E \subseteq \Sigma^*$, there exist deterministic context-free languages $L_1 \subseteq \Sigma_0^*$ and $L_2 \subseteq \Sigma_0^*$ such that $E = \varphi(L_1 \cap L_2)$.

2 Give a Turing-machine proof of Theorem 10.3.1.

3 Let $A = (Q, \Sigma, \Lambda, \delta, q_0, Z_0, F)$ be a pda and let $L \subseteq \Sigma^*$. Define

$$H_L = \{\alpha \in \Gamma^* \mid (q_0, w, Z_0) \overset{*}{\vdash} (q, \Lambda, \alpha) \qquad \text{for some } w \in L\}.$$

Thus H_L is the set of all pushdown contents that can occur when L is fed into A. If L is context-free, is H_L regular or context-free? In general, describe what kind of sets can occur as H_L.

4 Show that an arbitrary deterministic Turing machine may be simulated by a deterministic device with two pushdown stores.

5 Show, with the help of the previous problem, that any deterministic Turing machine may be simulated by a deterministic device with four iterated counters (i.e., they can count to zero more than once).

6 Show that a deterministic Turing machine may be simulated by a deterministic device with two iterated counters.

7 Show that, for each Turing machine A, there exists a finite alphabet Γ and two deterministic iterated counter languages L_1 and L_2 over Γ such that A halts on some input if and only if $L_1 \cap L_2 = \emptyset$.

8 Show that it is undecidable whether or not $L = \Sigma^*$ where L is an iterated one-counter language. Thus the equality problem is unsolvable for this family of languages.

9 Show that it is undecidable whether or not $L_1 \subseteq L_2$ for deterministic iterated counter languages L_1 and L_2.

10.4 THE SEMI-DYCK SET AND CONTEXT-FREE LANGUAGES

An algebraic characterization of the context-free languages will be obtained in this section. It hinges on the semi-Dyck set, which is a particular deterministic context-free language.

To motivate the semi-Dyck set, let us imagine a terminal alphabet consisting of left and right parentheses, (and). Define D_1 to be the set of all well-balanced parentheses, for example,

$$(\,) \in D_1,$$

$$(\,)(\,) \in D_1,$$

and

$$((\,)((\,))) \in D_1,$$

but

$$)(\notin D_1.$$

D_1 is a (deterministic) context-free language, as we shall see very soon. An alternative way to describe D_1 is to code (as a_1 and) as $\bar{a}_1$ [or a_{-1}]. Then D_1 is the set of all strings of $\{a_1, \bar{a}_1\}^*$ subject to the relation

$$a_1\bar{a}_1 = \Lambda$$

[respectively, $a_1 a_{-1} = \Lambda$].

Correspondingly, one could allow two-sided cancellation, which would give us the "two-sided" or simply the "Dyck Set," D_1'.

Example

$$)(\in D_1',$$

$$)((\,))(\in D_1'.$$

The last relation is more natural if we write

$$\bar{a}_1 a_1 a_1 \bar{a}_1 \bar{a}_1 a_1 \in D_1'.$$

If we think of $\bar{a}_1$ as the inverse of a_1, it is like group theory. In the exercises, we shall see that the analogy is appropriate.

We shall soon introduce the semi-Dyck set on r letters. Many of the results to be given hold for D_r' as well with similar proofs but these will be omitted and left for the problems.

The terminal alphabet of D_r, the semi-Dyck set on r letters, will be $\Sigma_r \cup \bar{\Sigma}_r$, where $\Sigma_r = \{a_1, \ldots, a_r\}$ and $\bar{\Sigma}_r = \{\bar{a}_i \mid a_i \in \Sigma_r\}$.

We may define

$$\Sigma = \Sigma_r \cup \bar{\Sigma}_r$$

and consider Σ^* which is a free monoid. We can define relations on Σ^*, first defining

$$\rho_0 = \{(a_i\bar{a}_i, \Lambda) \mid a_i \in \Sigma_r\} \cup \{(\Lambda, a_i\bar{a}_i) \mid a_i \in \Sigma_r\}.$$

Let $\simeq$ be the least two-sided congruence relation that contains ρ_0. Not only is $\simeq$ an equivalence relation on Σ^* but

$$xa_i\bar{a}_iy \simeq xy$$

for all i, $1 \leqslant i \leqslant r$, and all $x, y \in \Sigma^*$. Intuitively, if $x, y \in \Sigma^*$, then $x \simeq y$ if and only if x can be obtained from y by introducing or cancelling adjacent pairs $a_i\bar{a}_i$ or vice versa (meaning that y can be obtained from x in this fashion).

Example Let $r = 2$. Then,

$$a_1\bar{a}_1a_1a_2a_1 \simeq a_2\bar{a}_2a_1a_1\bar{a}_1a_2a_1\bar{a}_1a_1.$$

It is convenient to have a normal form for such words.

Definition Let $\Sigma = \Sigma_r \cup \bar{\Sigma}_r$ for some $r \geqslant 1$. A word $w \in \Sigma^*$ is *reduced* (for D_r) if w contains no consecutive pairs $a_i\bar{a}_i$ for any i, $1 \leqslant i \leqslant r$. A word w is *reduced* for D_r' if w contains no consecutive pairs $a_i\bar{a}_i$ or $\bar{a}_ia_i$ for any i, $1 \leqslant i \leqslant r$.

Given any word in $(\Sigma)^*$, we may reduce it by cancelling consecutive pairs. We shall now carry out this process carefully.

Definition Let $\Sigma = \Sigma_r \cup \bar{\Sigma}_r$ for some $r \geqslant 1$. Define a mapping μ from Σ^* into Σ^* as follows:

$$\mu(\Lambda) = \Lambda,$$

$$\mu(xa_i) = \mu(x)a_i \quad \text{for each } i, \quad 1 \leqslant i \leqslant r,$$

$$\mu(x\bar{a}_i) = \begin{cases} \mu(x)\bar{a}_i & \text{if } \mu(x) \notin \Sigma^*a_i, \quad 1 \leqslant i \leqslant r, \\ x' & \text{if } \mu(x) = x'a_i. \end{cases}$$

Examples

$$\mu(\Lambda) = \Lambda,$$

$$\mu(a_i) = a_i,$$

$$\mu(\bar{a}_i) = \bar{a}_i,$$

$$\mu(a_1a_2\bar{a}_2a_1\bar{a}_1a_2) = \mu(a_1a_2\bar{a}_2a_1\bar{a}_1)a_2 = \mu(a_1a_2\bar{a}_2)a_2 = \mu(a_1)a_2 = a_1a_2.$$

We summarize the pertinent properties of μ in the following proposition.

Proposition 10.4.1 Let $\Sigma = \Sigma_r \cup \bar{\Sigma}_r$ for some $r \geqslant 1$ and let $u, v, w, x, y \in \Sigma^*$

a) $\mu(xa_i\bar{a}_i) = \mu(x)$ for any i, $1 \leqslant i \leqslant r$.
b) $\mu(w)$ is reduced.
c) $\mu(w) \simeq w$.
d) If u is reduced, $\mu(u) = u$.
e) $\mu(\mu(w)) = \mu(w)$.
f) $\mu(xy) = \mu(\mu(x)y)$.
g) $\mu(xy) = \mu(\mu(x)\mu(y))$.
h) If $\mu(x) = \mu(y)$, then $\mu(uxv) = \mu(uyv)$.
i) $\mu(xa_i\bar{a}_i y) = \mu(xy)$ for any i, $1 \leqslant i \leqslant r$.
j) $\mu(x) = \mu(y)$ if and only if $x \simeq y$.
k) Let $w \in \Sigma^*$. If $y \in \Sigma^*$, y is reduced and $y \simeq w$, then $y = \mu(w)$.

Proof The proof of (a) is a straightforward induction on the length of x. The proofs of (b) and (c) are easy inductions on the length of w. A trivial induction on the length of u proves (d).

To show (e), let $w \in \Sigma^*$. By (b), $\mu(w)$ is reduced. By (d),

$$\mu(\mu(w)) = \mu(w).$$

Now (f) will be shown by induction on y.

Basis. $y = \Lambda$. Then

$$\mu(x) = \mu(\mu(x))$$

and the basis follows from (e).

Induction step. Assume the result for all words y and consider ya with $a \in \Sigma$. There are two cases, depending on whether $a \in \Sigma_r$ or $a \in \bar{\Sigma}_r$.

CASE 1 $a = a_i \in \Sigma_r$.

$$\begin{aligned} \mu(xya) &= \mu(xya_i) \\ &= \mu(xy)a_i && \text{by definition of } \mu, \\ &= \mu(\mu(x)y)a_i && \text{by the induction hypothesis,} \\ &= \mu(\mu(x)ya_i) && \text{by the definition of } \mu. \end{aligned}$$

The induction is now extended in Case 1.

CASE 2 $a = \bar{a}_i \in \bar{\Sigma}_r$.

There are two cases here, depending on whether or not

$$\mu(xy) = \begin{cases} zb & \text{for some } b \neq a_i, \\ za_i. \end{cases}$$

CASE 2(a) $\mu(xy) = zb$, where $b \neq a_i$.

Then

$$\begin{aligned}\mu(xy\bar{a}_i) &= \mu(xy)\bar{a}_i && \text{by definition of } \mu,\\ &= \mu(\mu(x)y)\bar{a}_i && \text{by the induction hypothesis.}\end{aligned}$$

Since $\mu(\mu(x)y) = \mu(xy) = zb$, $b \neq a_i$, we may invoke the definition of μ again and

$$\mu(\mu(x)y)\bar{a}_i = \mu(\mu(x)y\bar{a}_i),$$

and the induction is extended in Case 2(a).

CASE 2(b) $\mu(xy) = za_i$.

$$\begin{aligned}\mu(xy\bar{a}_i) &= \mu((xy)\bar{a}_i)\\ &= \mu(\mu(xy)\bar{a}_i) && \text{by the induction hypothesis,}\\ &= \mu(za_i\bar{a}_i) = \mu(z) = z.\end{aligned}$$

Note that za_i and z are reduced because za_i is in the range of μ. The only way that z could fail to be reduced would be to have some cancellation at the right end, but that is impossible, by the one-sided nature of our system. On the other hand,

$$\mu(\mu(x)y\bar{a}_i) = z$$

because $\mu(\mu(x)y) = \mu(xy) = za_i$; the induction is extended and the entire proof of (f) is complete.

The proofs of (g) and (h) are left to the reader; (i) follows from (g) and (a), because

$$\begin{aligned}\mu(xa_i\bar{a}_iy) &= \mu(\mu(xa_i\bar{a}_i)\mu(y))\\ &= \mu(\mu(x)\mu(y))\\ &= \mu(xy).\end{aligned}$$

The proof of (j) follows in a straightforward manner from (i). To show (k), note that $y \simeq w$ implies

$$\mu(y) = \mu(w)$$

but, since y is reduced,

$$\mu(w) = \mu(y) = y.$$

□

The μ function is quite helpful in dealing with the semi-Dyck set.

Definition Let $r \geqslant 1$ and define $G_r = (V_r, \Sigma, P, S)$, where $\Sigma = \Sigma_r \cup \bar{\Sigma}_r$, $V_r = \Sigma \cup \{S\}$, and P consists of the following productions:

$$S \to Sa_iS\bar{a}_iS \mid \Lambda$$

for each i, $1 \leqslant i \leqslant r$. The *semi-Dyck set* is formally defined by

$$D_r = L(G_r).$$

We may think of the a_i, $1 \leqslant i \leqslant r$, as r different kinds of left brackets, and the $\bar{a}_i$ for $1 \leqslant i \leqslant r$, as their respective right brackets.

It is clear that

$$D_r = \{w \in \Sigma^* \mid \mu(w) = \Lambda\}.$$

Our first result is that D_r is a deterministic context-free language.

Theorem 10.4.1 D_r is a deterministic context-free language.

Proof Let $A = (\{q_0, q_1\}, \Sigma, \Sigma \cup \{Z_0\}, \delta, q_0, Z_0, \{q_0\})$, where $\Sigma = \Sigma \cup \bar{\Sigma}_r$. Define:

$\delta(q_0, a_i, Z_0) = (q_1, Z_0 a_i)$ for each i, $1 \leqslant i \leqslant r$;

$\delta(q_1, a_i, a_j) = (q_1, a_j a_i)$ stack first letter for all $1 \leqslant i, j \leqslant r$;

$\delta(q_1, \bar{a}_i, a_i) = (q_1, \Lambda)$ for each i, $1 \leqslant i \leqslant r$; cancel $a_i\bar{a}_i$;

$\delta(q_1, \Lambda, Z_0) = (q_0, Z_0)$ accept and prepare to repeat.

Corollary D_r is an unambiguous context-free language.

Now we list some basic properties of D_r.

Proposition 10.4.2 Let D_r be the semi-Dyck set.

a) If $x, y \in D_r$, then $xy \in D_r$.
b) If $x \in D_r$, then $a_i x \bar{a}_i \in D_r$ for all i, $1 \leqslant i \leqslant r$.
c) For each word $x \in D_r$, either $x = \Lambda$ or $x = a_i y \bar{a}_i z$ for some i, $1 \leqslant i \leqslant r$, and some $y, z \in D_r$.
d) If $a_i \bar{a}_i z \in D_r$, then $z \in D_r$.
e) If $yz \in D_r$ and $y \in D_r$, then $z \in D_r$.
f) $x \in \operatorname{init}(D_r) = \{w \in \Sigma^* \mid wy \in D_r \text{ for some } y \in \Sigma^*\}$ if and only if $\mu(x) \in \Sigma_r^*$ (that is, w has no letters in $\bar{\Sigma}_r$).

Proof Since $w \in D_r$ if and only if $\mu(w) = \Lambda$, Proposition 10.4.1 can be used to prove (a) through (e) elegantly. As an example, consider (e).

$$y \in D_r \text{ implies } \mu(y) = \Lambda,$$

$$yz \in D_r \text{ implies } \mu(yz) = \Lambda.$$

But

$$\mu(yz) = \mu(\mu(y)z) = \mu(z) = \Lambda,$$

so

$$z \in D_r.$$

To see (f), suppose $x = x_1 \cdots x_\ell$, $\mu(x) = x_{i_1} \cdots x_{i_k}$, $\ell \geqslant k \geqslant 0$, and each $x_{i_j} \in \Sigma_r$. Define $y = \bar{x}_{i_k} \cdots \bar{x}_{i_1}$, where $\bar{x}_{i_j}$ is a barred copy of x_{i_j}. Clearly,

$$\mu(xy) = \mu(\mu(x)y) = \mu(x_{i_1} \cdots x_{i_k} \bar{x}_{i_k} \cdots \bar{x}_{i_1}) = \Lambda,$$

so $xy \in D_r$, which means that $x \in \operatorname{init}(D_r)$. This proves the *if* direction.

Conversely, suppose $x \in \text{init}(D_r)$. There exists $y \in \Sigma^*$ so that

$$xy \in D_r.$$

We show that $\mu(x) \in \Sigma_r^*$ by induction on the length of x. The basis is trivial.

Induction step. Assume the result for a string x. If $y = \Lambda$, we are done. Let a be the first letter of y.

CASE 1 $a \in \Sigma_r$. By the induction hypothesis, $\mu(x) \in \Sigma_r^*$; and by the definition of μ,

$$\mu(xa) = \mu(x)a \in \Sigma_r^*,$$

which extends the induction.

CASE 2 $a \in \bar{\Sigma}_r$. Let $a = \bar{a}_i$. By the induction hypothesis, $\mu(x) \in \Sigma_r^*$. Since $\mu(xy) = \Lambda$, it follows that

$$\mu(x) = x'a_i, \qquad a_i \in \Sigma_n, \qquad x' \in \Sigma_r^*.$$

But, clearly,

$$\mu(xa) = \mu(x\bar{a}_i) = \mu(x'a_i\bar{a}_i) = \mu(\mu(x')\mu(a_i\bar{a}_i)) = x' \in \Sigma_r^*.$$

The induction has been extended and the proof is complete. □

We are now in a position to state and prove the main theorem of this section, which is a characterization of context-free languages in terms of D_r. The result says that every context-free language L may be written as

$$L = \varphi(D_r \cap R),$$

where D_r is the semi-Dyck set on r-letters, R is a regular set, and φ is a homomorphism. Of course, for any homomorphism φ, and any regular set, it follows that $\varphi(D_r \cap R)$ is a context-free language, by our closure properties.

Theorem 10.4.2 (Chomsky-Schützenberger Theorem) For each context-free language L, there is an integer r, a regular set R, and a homomorphism φ such that $L = \varphi(D_r \cap R)$.

Proof Let $L = L(A)$, where $A = (Q, \Sigma, \Gamma, \delta, q_0, Z_0, F)$ is a pda satisfying the conditions of Problem 3 of Section 5.5. That is,

a) $L = L(A)$.
b) If $\Lambda \in L$, then $\delta(q_0, \Lambda, Z_0) = \{(q_0, \Lambda)\}$ and $q_0 \in F$; otherwise, $\delta(q_0, \Lambda, Z_0) = \emptyset$.
c) If $q \in Q - \{q_0\}$ or $Z \in \Gamma - \{Z_0\}$, then $\delta(q, \Lambda, Z) = \emptyset$.
d) If $(q', \alpha) \in \delta(q, a, Z)$, then $\lg(\alpha) \leqslant 2$.

Assume that Q, Σ, and Γ are pairwise disjoint and that $|\Sigma \cup \Gamma| = r$. The alphabet for the semi-Dyck set will be $\Sigma_r \cup \bar{\Sigma}_r$; but in order to retain notational consistency, we will write

$$\Sigma_0 = (\Sigma \cup \Gamma) \cup (\bar{\Sigma} \cup \bar{\Gamma}).$$

Define φ as the homomorphism from Σ_0^* into Σ^* determined by

$$\varphi(a) = a, \qquad \varphi(\bar{a}) = \Lambda \qquad \text{if } a \in \Sigma,$$
$$\varphi(Z) = \varphi(\bar{Z}) = \Lambda \qquad \text{if } Z \in \Gamma.$$

Let D_r be the semi-Dyck set over Σ_0.

Define a grammar $G = (Q \cup \Sigma_0 \cup \{S\}, \Sigma_0, P, S)$, where S is a new symbol and P is given as follows:

i) $S \to Z_0 q_0$ is in P.

ii) If $\delta(q_0, \Lambda, Z_0) = \{(q_0, \Lambda)\}$, then

$$S \to q_0$$

is in P.

iii) If $(q', \alpha) \in \delta(q, a, Z)$ for $q, q' \in Q$, $A \in \Sigma$, $Z \in \Gamma$, $\alpha \in \Gamma^*$, then

$$q \to a\bar{a}\bar{Z}\alpha q'$$

is in P.

iv) If $q \in F$, then

$$q \to \Lambda$$

is in P.

Since G is right linear, then $R = L(G)$ is regular.

It only remains for us to show that

$$L = \varphi(D_r \cap R).$$

Define $G_q = (Q \cup \Sigma_0 \cup \{S\}, \Sigma_0, P, q)$ and then $L(G_q) = \{x \in \Sigma_0^* \mid q \overset{*}{\Rightarrow} x\}$.

First we prove that $L \subseteq \varphi(D_r \cap R)$. Suppose $x \in L$. If $x = \Lambda$, then, by our assumption about the pda A,

$$\delta(q_0, \Lambda, Z_0) = \{(q_0, \Lambda)\} \text{ with } q_0 \in F.$$

By rules (ii) and (iii) in the definition of P, we have

$$S \Rightarrow q_0 \Rightarrow \Lambda$$

so $\Lambda \in R$. Since $\Lambda \in D_r$, we have that

$$\Lambda \in \varphi(D_r \cap R).$$

If $x \neq \Lambda$, then

$$(q_0, x, Z_0) \overset{*}{\vdash} (q_f, \Lambda, \Lambda) \quad \text{with } q_f \in F.$$

To establish the desired result, we need the following result.

Claim 1 For any $q \in Q$, $x \in \Sigma^+$, $\alpha \in \Gamma^+$, and $q_f \in F$, if

$$(q, x, \alpha) \overset{+}{\vdash} (q_f, \Lambda, \Lambda),$$

then

$$x \in \varphi(D_r \cap \alpha L(G_q)).$$

Proof The argument is an induction on the length of the computation sequence.

Basis. If $(q, x, \alpha) \vdash (q_f, \Lambda, \Lambda)$, then $x \in \Sigma \cup \{\Lambda\}$ and $\alpha \in \Gamma$. Then A contains the rule $(q_f, \Lambda) \in \delta(q, x, \alpha)$ with $q_f \in F$. By construction, P contains the rule

$$q_f \to \Lambda$$

and

$$q \to x\bar{x}\bar{\alpha}q_f$$

Clearly,

$$q \Rightarrow x\bar{x}\bar{\alpha}q_f \Rightarrow x\bar{x}\bar{\alpha}$$

Hence, $\alpha x\bar{x}\bar{\alpha} \in D_r \cap \alpha(L(G_q))$ and

$$x = \varphi(\alpha x\bar{x}\bar{\alpha}) \in \varphi(D_r \cap \alpha(L(G_q))).$$

Induction step. Suppose that $(q, x, \alpha) \overset{(n-1)}{\vdash} (q_f, \Lambda, \Lambda)$ with $q_f \in F$ implies $x \in \varphi(D_r \cap \alpha(L(G_q)))$. Assume $(q, ax, \alpha Z) \vdash (q', x, \alpha\alpha')$ by the rule $(q', \alpha') \in \delta(q, a, Z)$ and let $(q', x, \alpha\alpha') \overset{(n-1)}{\vdash} (q_f, \Lambda, \Lambda)$ with $n > 1, q_f \in F, a \in \Sigma$ (by our assumption about the pda). Then

$$q \to a\bar{a}\bar{Z}\alpha' q'$$

is in P by part (iii). Clearly,

$$a\bar{a}\bar{Z}\alpha' L(G_{q'}) \subseteq L(G_q),$$

which implies that

$$\alpha Z a\bar{a}\bar{Z}\alpha' L(G_{q'}) \subseteq \alpha Z L(G_q).$$

By intersecting with D_r and applying φ, we have

$$\varphi(D_r \cap \alpha Z a\bar{a}\bar{Z}\alpha' L(G_{q'})) \subseteq \varphi(D_r \cap (\alpha Z L(G_q))).$$

By the induction hypothesis, $x \in \varphi(D_r \cap \alpha\alpha' L(G_{q'}))$. So

$$ax \in a\varphi(D_r \cap \alpha\alpha' L(G_{q'})).$$

Now, we claim the following is true.

Claim 1(a) For each $q' \in Q$, $\alpha \in \Gamma^+$, $\alpha' \in \Gamma^*$, $a \in \Sigma$,

$$a\varphi(D_r \cap \alpha\alpha' L(G_{q'})) \subseteq \varphi(D_r \cap \alpha Z a\bar{a}\bar{Z}\alpha' L(G_{q'})).$$

Proof of Claim 1(a) If $y \in a\varphi(D_r \cap \alpha\alpha' L(G_{q'}))$, then there is z such that $y = a\varphi(\alpha\alpha' z)$, with $\alpha\alpha' z \in D_r$ and $z \in L(G_{q'}))$. Moreover, note that

$$y = a\varphi(\alpha\alpha' z) = a\varphi(z),$$

since $\varphi(\alpha) = \varphi(\alpha') = \Lambda$, because $\varphi(\Gamma) = \Lambda$. Consider

$$\alpha Z a\bar{a}\bar{Z}\alpha' z.$$

This string is obviously in $\alpha Z a\bar{a}\bar{Z}\alpha' L(G_{q'})$, since z is in $L(G_{q'})$. It is surely in D_r since $\alpha\alpha' z$ is. But

$$\varphi(\alpha Z a\bar{a}\bar{Z}\alpha' z) = \varphi(\alpha) a\varphi(\alpha')\varphi(z) = a\varphi(z) = a\varphi(\alpha\alpha' z) = y.$$

Thus y is in the righthand side.

Returning to the main proof, we have that

$$ax \in \varphi(D_r \cap \alpha Za\bar{a}\bar{Z}\alpha' L(G_{q'})) \subseteq \varphi(D_r \cap \alpha Z L(G_q)),$$

which completes the induction proof of Claim 1.

Using Claim 1, we can show that $L \subseteq \varphi(D_r \cap R)$ as follows: If $x \in L$ and $\lg(x) > 0$, then $(q_0, x, Z_0) \overset{*}{\vdash} (q_f, \Lambda, \Lambda)$, with $q_f \in F$. By claim 1, $x \in \varphi(D_r \cap Z_0 L(G_{q_0}))$. Since $S \to Z_0 q_0$ is always a rule of P, $Z_0 L(G_{q_0}) \subseteq L(G)$. Therefore, $x \in \varphi(D_r \cap Z_0 L(G_{q_0})) \subseteq \varphi(D_r \cap L(G)) = \varphi(D_r \cap R)$.

We must now deal with the reverse direction. Suppose $x \in \varphi(D_r \cap R)$; then $x = \varphi(y)$, where $y \in D_r \cap R$. Since $y \in R$, $S \overset{*}{\Rightarrow} y$. There are two possibilities for the generation of y. Either

1 $S \Rightarrow q_0 \overset{*}{\Rightarrow} y$

or

2 $S \Rightarrow Z_0 q_0 \overset{*}{\Rightarrow} y$

CASE 1 If $S \Rightarrow q_0 \overset{*}{\Rightarrow} y$ and $y \in D_r \cap R$, then $y = \Lambda$ and $\Lambda \in L$.

Proof $S \to q_0$ is in P if and only if $\delta(q_0, \Lambda, Z_0) = \{(q_0, \Lambda)\}$ and $q_0 \in F$, which implies $\Lambda \in L$. Consider the derivation $q_0 \overset{*}{\Rightarrow} y$. Assume that $y \neq \Lambda$. Then the derivation begins as

$$q_0 \Rightarrow a\bar{a}\bar{Z}\alpha q' \overset{*}{\Rightarrow} y'$$

where $a \in \Sigma$, $Z \in \Gamma$, $\alpha \in \Gamma^*$, and $q' \in Q$. Thus $y = a\bar{a}\bar{Z}\alpha y'$ where $y' \in L(G_{q'})$. But y is not in D_r because there is no way to cancel $\bar{Z}$. This contradiction establishes that $y = \Lambda$.

CASE 2 Suppose that

$$S \Rightarrow Z_0 q_0 \overset{*}{\Rightarrow} y$$

with $y \in D_r \cap R$. We wish to show that $\varphi(y)$ is in L. This is accomplished with the following result.

Claim 2 For each $q \in Q$, $\alpha \in \Gamma^*$, $z \in \Sigma_0^*$, if $\alpha q \overset{*}{\Rightarrow} \alpha z$ with $z \in L(G_q)$, and $\alpha z \in D_r$, then

$$(q, \varphi(z), \alpha) \overset{*}{\vdash} (q_f, \Lambda, \Lambda) \quad \text{for some } q_f \in F.$$

Proof of Claim 2 The argument is an induction on the length of a generation of $\alpha q \overset{*}{\Rightarrow} \alpha z$.

Basis. Suppose $\alpha q \Rightarrow \alpha z$ with $z \in L(G_q)$ and $\alpha z \in D_r$. By the definition of G_q, we must have that $q \to \Lambda$ is a rule of P and $z = \Lambda$. (This is the only string in Σ^* that G_q can generate.) Then $\alpha z \in D_r$ implies $\alpha \in D_r$. But $\alpha \in D_r$ implies that $\alpha = \Lambda$, since $\Gamma^* \cap \Sigma^* = \{\Lambda\}$. Since $q \to \Lambda$ is in P, then $q \in F$. Thus $(q, \varphi(z), \alpha) = (q, \Lambda, \Lambda)$ $\overset{*}{\vdash} (q, \Lambda, \Lambda)$ with $q \in F$ and the basis is complete.

Induction step. Suppose that $\alpha q \overset{(n-1)}{\Rightarrow} \alpha z$, $n > 1$, $z \in L(G_q)$; then $\alpha z \in D_r$ implies that $(q, \varphi(z), \alpha) \overset{*}{\vdash} (q_f, \Lambda, \Lambda)$ with $q_f \in F$.

Suppose that

$$\alpha q \Rightarrow \alpha a\bar{a}\bar{X}\alpha' q' \overset{(n-1)}{\Rightarrow} \alpha z$$

where $a \in \Sigma; X \in \Gamma; \alpha, \alpha' \in \Gamma^*; z \in L(G_q)$, and $\alpha z \in D_r$. Clearly,

$$z = a\bar{a}\bar{X}\alpha' z'$$

where $z' \in L(G_{q'})$. Thus

$$\alpha q \Rightarrow \alpha a\bar{a}\bar{X}\alpha' q' \overset{(n-1)}{\Rightarrow} \alpha a\bar{a}\bar{X}\alpha' z'$$

where $z' \in L(G_{q'})$ and $\alpha a\bar{a}\bar{X}\alpha' z' \in D_r$. But $\alpha a\bar{a}\bar{X}\alpha' z' \in D_r$ implies that there exists β in Γ^* such that $\alpha = \beta X$ and $\beta\alpha' z' \in D_r$. (The form of the rules in G prevents us from having $\alpha = \beta X\gamma$ with $\gamma \in D_r$.)

Rewriting the primary derivation again,

$$\beta X q \Rightarrow \beta X a\bar{a}\bar{X}\alpha' q' \overset{(n-1)}{\Rightarrow} \beta X a\bar{a}\bar{X}\alpha' z'$$

where $z' \in L(G_{q'})$ and $\beta X a\bar{a}\bar{X}\alpha' z' \in D_r$. This implies that

$$\beta\alpha' q' \overset{(n-1)}{\Rightarrow} \beta\alpha' z'$$

where $z' \in L(G_{q'})$ and $\beta\alpha' z' \in D_r$ (since $\beta X a\bar{a}\bar{X}\alpha' z' \in D_r$). By the induction hypothesis,

$$(q', \varphi(z'), \beta\alpha') \overset{*}{\vdash} (q_f, \Lambda, \Lambda)$$

with $q_f \in F$. But since we have a rule $q \to a\bar{a}\bar{X}\alpha' q'$ in P, then $(q', \alpha') \in \delta(q, a, X)$. Therefore,

$$\begin{aligned}(q, \varphi(z), \alpha) &= (q, \varphi(a\bar{a}\bar{X}\alpha' z'), \beta X)\\ &= (q, a\varphi(z'), \beta X)\\ &\vdash (q', \varphi(z'), \beta\alpha')\\ &\overset{*}{\vdash} (q_f, \Lambda, \Lambda)\end{aligned}$$

with $q_f \in F$. This completes the induction proof of Claim 2.

To complete the entire proof, we need only show that $\varphi(D_r \cap R) \subseteq L$. Suppose that

$$S \Rightarrow Z_0 q_0 \overset{*}{\Rightarrow} y$$

and $y \in D_r \cap R$. Then $y = Z_0 y'$, where $y' \in L(G_{q_0})$ and $Z_0 y' \in D_r$. By Claim 2,

$$(q_0, \varphi(y), Z_0) \overset{*}{\vdash} (q_f, \Lambda, \Lambda),$$

which means that $\varphi(y) \in L$. Hence,

$$\varphi(D_r \cap R) \subseteq L,$$

and the proof is complete. □

The result can now be sharpened by coding D_r into D_2.

Theorem 10.4.3 If L is context-free, then there is a regular set R, and two homomorphisms φ_1 and φ_2 such that

$$L = \varphi_2(\varphi_1^{-1}(D_2) \cap R).$$

Proof Let D_2 be the semi-Dyck set on $\{0, 1, \bar{0}, \bar{1}\}$, and let $A = (Q, \Sigma, \Gamma, \delta, q_0, Z_0, F)$ be the pda of the previous theorem. Let $\Sigma = \{a_1, \ldots, a_k\}$ and $\Gamma = \{A_1, \ldots, A_m\}$. Define φ_1 which maps $(\Sigma \cup \Gamma)^*$ into $\{0, 1, \bar{0}, \bar{1}\}^*$ by

$$\left.\begin{aligned} \varphi_1(a_i) &= 10^i 1 \\ \varphi_1(\bar{a}_i) &= \bar{1}\bar{0}^i \bar{1} \end{aligned}\right\} \quad \text{for each } i,\ 1 \leqslant i \leqslant k,$$

and

$$\left.\begin{aligned} \varphi_1(A_i) &= 10^{i+k} 1 \\ \varphi_1(\bar{A}_i) &= \bar{1}\bar{0}^{i+k} \bar{1} \end{aligned}\right\} \quad \text{for each } i,\ 1 \leqslant i \leqslant m.$$

Note that $\varphi_1(a_i\bar{a}_i) = \varphi_1(A_i\bar{A}_i) = \Lambda$ for each i. Moreover, if $r = |\Sigma \cup \Gamma|$, then

$$D_r = \varphi_1^{-1}(D_2).$$

By the proof of the previous theorem,

$$L = \varphi_2(D_r \cap R) = \varphi_2(\varphi_1^{-1}(D_2) \cap R). \qquad \square$$

PROBLEMS

1 Show that D_r and D_r' are not regular sets.

2 Define $\simeq$ reduction, and μ' in the case of the Dyck set, i.e., for two-sided cancellation. Reprove all the results of this chapter for D_r' noting carefully where and how things change.

3 Note that μ (and μ') determine relations $\simeq$ and $\simeq'$ on Σ^* by

$$x \simeq y \quad \text{if and only if } \mu(x) = \mu(y).$$

These relations are congruence relations. What sort of algebraic structure is $\Sigma^*/\simeq$? Show that $\Sigma^*/\simeq'$ is isomorphic to the free group on r generators. Note that D_r' is the kernel of a free group.

4 Give an unambiguous grammar for D_r and D_r'. Does G_r suffice for D_r? Prove your answer.

5 Let G be a group which is finitely presented. The *word problem* for (the presentation of) G is to give an algorithm which determines whether or not a given word in the generators of G defines the identity. Show that the word problem for the free group with generators $a_1, \ldots, a_r$ is decidable.

6 Let $G = (V, \Sigma, P, S)$ be a context-free grammar. Define a homomorphism $\varphi: V^* \to N^*$,

$$\varphi(A) = \begin{cases} A & \text{if } A \in N, \\ \Lambda & \text{if } A \in \Sigma. \end{cases}$$

Let D be any derivation of G,

$$D : S = \alpha_0 \Rightarrow \alpha_1 \Rightarrow \cdots \Rightarrow \alpha_n$$

Define the index of D as

$$\text{index}(D, G) = \max\{\lg(\varphi(\alpha_i)) \mid 0 \leqslant i \leqslant n\}.$$

If $w \in L(G)$, then define

$$\text{index}(w, G) = \min\{\text{index}(D, G) \mid D \text{ is a derivation of } w\}.$$

Also, the notion can be extended to grammars by defining

$$\text{index}(G) = \text{lub}\{u \mid \text{index}(w, G) \leqslant u \text{ for all } w \in L(G)\}.$$

G is of *finite index* if index (G) is finite. Show that the following grammar for D_1 has infinite index:

$$S \rightarrow SS|\Lambda|\, a_1 S \bar{a}_1$$

7 Show that, for each positive integer k, there is some context-free grammar of index k.

8 Using Problem 6 as a guide, define the concept of "leftmost index." Produce a context-free grammar G which is of index 2 but has infinite leftmost index.

9 Define the index of a context-free language L by

$$\text{index}(L) = \min\{\text{index}(G) \mid L(G) = L\}.$$

Show that D_1 has infinite index.

10 Show that, for each positive integer k, there is some context-free language of index k.

11 Prove that every context-free language is a homomorphic image of a deterministic context-free language.

12 Characterize phrase-structure languages in terms of Dyck sets, homomorphisms, and regular sets. (There are many ways to do this.)

13 A set $L \subseteq \Sigma^*$ is a *standard regular set* if there exist two binary relations ρ_1 and ρ_2 on Σ (not Σ^*) such that $x \in L$ if and only if

i) $x \in a\Sigma^* \cap \Sigma^* b$ for some $(a, b) \in \rho_1$, and
ii) $x \notin \Sigma^* ab \Sigma^*$, where $(a, b) \in \rho_2$.

Show that, for every regular set $L \subseteq \Delta^*$, there is some alphabet Σ, a homomorphism $\varphi: \Sigma^* \rightarrow \Delta^*$, and a standard regular set R such that $L = \varphi(R)$.

14 Show that every context-free language L may be represented as $L = \varphi(D_r \cap R)$ for some r, some homomorphism φ, and some *standard* regular set R.

***15** Give algebraic characterizations similar to Theorem 10.4.2 for the families of:

a) minimal linear languages,
b) linear languages,
c) metalinear languages.

16 Let $\Delta_1 = \{a_1, a_1\}$. Define a mapping $\nu(a_1) = 1$ and $\nu(\bar{a}_1) = -1$, and extend ν to be a homomorphism of Δ_1^* into the integers. Define the set:

$$Ł = \{x \in \Delta_1^* \mid \nu x = -1 \text{ and, for each proper prefix } x' \text{ of } x, \nu x' \geqslant 0\}.$$

Ł is called the *Łukasiewicz language,* and it is closely related to "Polish" or parenthesis-free notation. We can generalize to $\Delta_n = \{a_0, \ldots, a_n\}$ and define $\nu(a_i) = i - 1$ for each i, $0 \leqslant i \leqslant n$. Then

$$Ł_n = \{x \in \Delta_n^* \mid \nu x = -1 \text{ and } \nu x' \geqslant 0 \text{ for each proper prefix } x' \text{ of } x\}.$$

Show that $Ł_n$ is an iterated counter language.

17 Show that a necessary and sufficient condition for $L \subseteq \Sigma^*$ to be a counter language is that there exists a regular transduction τ from $\{a_1, \bar{a}_1\}^*$ into Σ^* such that

$$L = \tau(D_1).$$

Cf. the problems in Section 6.5 for the definition of regular transductions.

18 Show that D_1' is not a counter language.

19 Show that the family of iterated counter languages is exactly the least family containing D_1 and closed under union, inverse homomorphism, intersection with regular sets, concatenation, $^+$, and arbitrary homomorphisms.

20 A language L is *stack bounded of order p* if there is a pda A such that $L = N(A)$ and each stack contents is an element of $Z_0 A_{i_1}^* \cdots A_{i_p}^*$, where each $A_{i_j} \in \Gamma - \{Z_0\}$. L is *stack bounded* if L is stack bounded of order p for some p. Show that the set of stack bounded languages is exactly the closure of the iterated counter languages under substitution.

***21** Show that any iterated counter language that is not nonterminal bounded must contain an infinite regular set.

22 Show that the semi-Dyck set can be accepted by a deterministic Turing machine with space function $S(n) = \log n$.

***23** Extend the result in Problem 22 to the Dyck set (i.e., allow two-sided cancellation).

Let F be a field. A *linear group* (over F) is any group which is isomorphic to the group of $k \times k$ invertible matrices over F for some $k \geqslant 1$.

***24** Show that the word problem for finitely generated linear groups over a field is solvable in log space (i.e., by a Turing machine which runs in space $S(n) = \log n$). Relate to Problems 5 and 23.

There are a number of other interesting ways to utilize parentheses in language theory.

Definition A *parenthesis grammar* is a grammar $G = (V, \Sigma, P, S)$ where

i) The symbols (and) are in Σ, and

ii) Each rule is of the form

$$A \rightarrow (\alpha)$$

where $\alpha \in (V - \{(,)\})^*$.

A set L is a *parenthesis language* if L is generated by some parenthesis grammar.

25 Show that a parenthesis language may be recognized in deterministic log space.

***26** Show that there is an algorithm to decide whether $L(G_1) \subseteq L(G_2)$, where G_1 and G_2 are parenthesis grammars. Hence the equality problem is also solvable.

***27** Show that there is an algorithm to decide whether a given context-free language is a parenthesis language.

A *general two-type bracketed grammar* is a 7-tuple $G = (N, \Sigma, I, B_1, B_2, S, P)$, and where N, Σ, I are finite nonempty sets called *nonterminals, terminals,* and *intermediate symbols*, respectively. B_1 contains only indexed square brackets while B_2 contains only indexed round brackets. $S \in N$ is the *start symbol.* P is a finite set of productions of the following forms:

a) $A \to \eta$ where $A \in N$ and $\eta \in (\Sigma \cup N \cup I \cup B_1)^*$

b) $\alpha \to [_i X\beta(_i$

c) $\alpha \to]_i X\beta)_i$

where $\alpha \in I$, $X \in (N \cup \Sigma)^*$, $\beta \in I \cup \{\Lambda\}$, and all square brackets are in B_1 and all round brackets are in B_2.

Example $G = (\{S, A\}, \{a, b, c\}, \{\alpha, \beta\}, \{[_1, [_2,]_1,]_2\}, \{(_1, (_2,)_1,)_2\}, S, P)$ where P is given by

$$S \to [_1 A]_1 \qquad \alpha \to]_2 b\alpha)_2 \qquad \beta \to [_2\beta(_2$$

$$A \to a[_2 A]_2 c \qquad \alpha \to]_1\beta)_1 \qquad \beta \to [_2(_2$$

$$A \to a[_2\alpha]_2 c \qquad \beta \to [_1\beta(_1$$

The rules in such a grammar are used as context-free rules except that the brackets and parentheses "commute with terminals" and "cancel each other" if properly nested. To make this precise, define a form as any string in $(N \cup \Sigma \cup I \cup B_1 \cup B_2)^*$. A form η_2 is a *normalization* of a form η_1 if there is a $\tau \in B_1 \cup B_2, a \in \Sigma$, and forms η_3, η_4 such that $\eta_1 = \eta_3\tau a\eta_4$ and $\eta_2 = \eta_3 a\tau\eta_4$. A form will be called *normalized* if there is no other form which is a normalization of it (e.g., if $\eta_1 = a(_3)_3 A[_1 aB]_1 c[_2 D]_2$ with $a, c \in \Sigma, A, B, D \in N$, a normalization of it would be $\eta_2 = a(_3)_3 Aa[_1 B]_1 c[_2 D]_2$. A normalization of η_2 is $\eta_3 = a(_3)_3 Aa[_1 Bc]_1 [_2 D]_2$; η_3 is normalized).

A form η_2 is a *reduction* of a form η_1 if there are forms η_3, η_4 such that either $\eta_1 = \eta_2[_i]_i\eta_4$ or $\eta_1 = \eta_3(_j)_j\eta_4$, and $\eta_2 = \eta_3\eta_4$. Note that in any case the vanishing brackets have the same index.

A form will be called *reduced* if there is no other form which is a reduction of it (e.g., if $\eta_2 = a(_3)_3 Aa[_1 B]_1 c[_2 D]_2$ as in the previous example, then $\eta_4 = aAa[_1 B]_1 c[_2 D]_2$ is a reduction of η_2; η_4 is also reduced).

A form will be said to be in *canonical form* if it is both normalized and reduced.

A form ξ is called the *canonical form of a form* θ if ξ is in canonical form and there is a sequence $\eta_1, \eta_2, \ldots, \eta_m$ of forms such that $\theta = \eta_1, \xi = \eta_m$ and for each i, $1 \leqslant i \leqslant m$, η_{i+1} is either a reduction or a normalization of η_i.

28 Show that any substring of a reduced form is also a reduced form.

29 Show that the canonical form of a form η is unique. It will be denoted by $\mathrm{cf}\{\eta\}$. Also show that

$$\mathrm{cf}\{\eta_1\rho\eta_2\} = \mathrm{cf}\{\eta_1\}\rho\,\mathrm{cf}\{\eta_2\} \quad \text{if } \rho \in I \cup N.$$

A form η_1 which is in canonical form is said to *directly derive* a form η_2, written $\eta_1 \Rightarrow \eta_2$, if there is a form η_3 such that η_3 is obtained from η_1 by replacing a symbol u ($u \in N \cup I$) of η_1 by the righthand side of a production in P having the symbol u on the lefthand side, and $\eta_2 = \text{cf}\{\eta_3\}$.

30 Show that for the example grammar G defined before Problem 28, we have

$$L(G) = \{a^n b^n c^n \mid n \geqslant 1\}.$$

31 Show that every recursively enumerable set L can be generated by a general two-type bracketed grammar.

10.5 CONTEXT-FREE LANGUAGES AND INVERSE HOMOMORPHISMS

We shall show that there is one context-free language L_0 from which any context-free language L may be obtained by an inverse homomorphism. That is, for each context-free $L \subseteq \Sigma^*$, there exists a homomorphism φ so that $L = \varphi^{-1}(L_0)$. This result has a number of implications that are not at all obvious. It will turn out, when we study parsing, that L_0 is a "hardest context-free language." Any context-free language can be parsed in whatever time or space it takes to recognize L_0.

The key to finding L_0 is to use the semi-Dyck set. Choosing $L_0 = D_2$ could not work because D_2 is deterministic and hence unambiguous. For any homomorphism φ, $\varphi^{-1}D_2$ is unambiguous, and we could not generate the inherently ambiguous languages in this way. We shall choose a nondeterministic version of D_2 as a "generator."

Definition Let $\Sigma = \{a_1, a_2, \bar{a}_1, \bar{a}_2, ¢, c\}$. Define

$$L_0 = \{\Lambda\} \cup \{x_1 c y_1 c z_1 d \cdots x_n c y_n c z_n d \mid n \geqslant 1, \quad y_1 \cdots y_n \in ¢D_2, x_i, z_i \in \Sigma^* \text{ for all } i, 1 \leqslant i \leqslant n, \quad y_i \in \{a_1, a_2, \bar{a}_1, \bar{a}_2\}^* \text{ for all } i \geqslant 2\}.$$

(Note that the x_i's and z_i's can contain c's and ¢'s.)

It is easy to see that L_0 is context-free. Imagine a pushdown automaton which "guesses" a substring y_1 in the first block and processes it in the natural way a pushdown automaton would work on the Dyck set (i.e., stack everything and pop when the top of the stack is a_i and the input is $\bar{a}_i$). The computation is repeated for each block as delimited by d's.

We are now ready to begin the main argument.

Theorem 10.5.1 If L is a context-free language, then there is a homomorphism φ so that $L = \varphi^{-1}(L_0)$ if $\Lambda \in L$ and $L = \varphi^{-1}(L_0 - \{\Lambda\})$ if $\Lambda \notin L$.

Proof There is no loss of generality in assuming that Λ is not in L. (If $\Lambda \in L$, then the argument to be given works for $L - \Lambda$. Since $\varphi\Lambda = \Lambda \in L_0$ and $\varphi x = \Lambda$ if and only if $x = \Lambda$ for our φ, the construction also works for L.) We may also assume, without loss of generality, that $L = L(G)$, where $G = (V, \Sigma, P, S)$ is in Greibach form. Thus every rule π_i of P is of the form

$$A \to a\alpha,$$

where $A \in N$, $a \in \Sigma$, and $\alpha \in (N - \{S\})^*$. Let us index N as $\{A_1, \ldots, A_n\}$, where $A_1 = S$.

The idea of the construction is to encode productions. We shall do this by only encoding the variables in the production, not the terminals. Then, when φ is defined on a terminal a, it will encode all possible productions whose righthand sides start with a.

We begin by defining two mappings from P into Σ_2^*. If π_k is $A_i \to a$, then

$$\bar{\tau}\pi_k = \bar{a}_1 \bar{a}_2^i \bar{a}_1.$$

If π_k is $A_i \to aA_{j_1} \cdots A_{jm}$ for some $m \geqslant 1$, then

$$\bar{\tau}\pi_k = \bar{a}_1 \bar{a}_2^i \bar{a}_1 \; a_1 a_2^{j_m} a_1 \cdots a_1 a_2^{j_1} a_1 .$$

To define τ, we recall that i is the index of the lefthand side and

$$\textbf{if } i \neq 1 \textbf{ then } \tau\pi_k = \bar{\tau}\pi_k$$

$$\textbf{else} \quad \tau\pi_k = ¢a_1 a_2 a_1 \bar{\tau}\pi_k$$

Since τ and $\bar{\tau}$ encode only the nonterminals in the production and not the terminal, we let $P_a = \{\pi_{p_1}, \ldots, \pi_{p_k}\}$ be the set of all productions whose righthand side begins with $a \in \Sigma$. We define the homomorphism φ by

$$\varphi a = \textbf{if } P_a \neq \emptyset \textbf{ then } c\tau(\pi_{p_1}) \cdots c\tau(\pi_{p_m})cd$$

$$\textbf{else} \quad ¢¢$$

It only remains for us to show that $L = \varphi^{-1}(L_0 - \{\Lambda\})$. The following claim is the key to the proof and gives the exact correspondence between a derivation in G and the structure of L_0.

Claim For each $b_1, \ldots, b_k$ in Σ; $A_{i_1}, \ldots, A_{i_r}$ in $N - \{S\}$, we have that

$$S \overset{*}{\underset{L}{\Rightarrow}} b_1 \cdots b_k \, A_{i_1} \cdots A_{i_r}$$

under production sequence $(\pi_{p_1}, \ldots, \pi_{p_k})$ if and only if there exist x_i, y_i, z_i, $1 \leqslant i \leqslant k$, such that

i) $\varphi(b_1 \cdots b_k) = x_1 c y_1 c z_1 d \cdots d x_k c y_k c z_k d$

ii) $y_1 \cdots y_k \in \operatorname{init}(¢D_2) = \{x \mid xw \in ¢D_2 \text{ for some } w \in \Sigma^*\}$

iii) $\mu(y_1 \cdots y_k) = ¢a_1 a_2^{i_r} a_1 \cdots a_1 a_2^{i_1} a_1$, where, for each w, $\mu(w)$ is the unique reduced word that can be obtained from w by cancellation; cf. Section 10.3.

Before proving the claim, let us work an example which will illustrate the construction.

Example Consider a grammar with productions

$$\pi_1 : A_1 \to aA_2A_2$$

$$\pi_2 : A_2 \to a$$

$$\pi_3 : A_2 \to bA_2$$

$$\pi_4 : A_2 \to b$$

First we compute τ:

$$\tau(\pi_4) = \bar{\tau}(\pi_4) = \bar{a}_1\bar{a}_2^2\bar{a}_1$$

$$\tau(\pi_3) = \bar{\tau}(\pi_3) = \underbrace{\bar{a}_1\bar{a}_2^2\bar{a}_1}_{\text{Code for parent } A_2} \quad \underbrace{a_1a_2^2a_1}_{\text{Code for } A_2 \text{ on the right}}$$

$$\tau(\pi_2) = \bar{\tau}(\pi_2) = \bar{a}_1\bar{a}_2^2\bar{a}_1$$

$$\tau(\pi_1) = ¢a_1a_2a_1\ \bar{a}_1\bar{a}_2\bar{a}_1\ a_1a_2^2a_1\ a_1a_2^2a_1$$

Clearly,

$$\varphi a = c\tau(\pi_1)\, c\tau(\pi_2)cd$$

$$\varphi b = c\tau(\pi_3)\, c\tau(\pi_4)cd$$

Now

$$A_1 \overset{*}{\underset{L}{\Rightarrow}} aabA_2$$

under production sequence (π_1, π_2, π_3). Let us verify how the derivation corresponds to conditions of the claim:

$$\begin{aligned}\varphi(aab) = {} & c¢a_1a_2a_1\bar{a}_1\bar{a}_2\bar{a}_1a_1a_2^2a_1a_1a_2^2a_1c\bar{a}_1\bar{a}_2^2\bar{a}_1cd\\ & c¢a_1a_2a_1\bar{a}_1\bar{a}_2\bar{a}_1a_1a_2^2a_1a_1a_2^2a_1c\bar{a}_1\bar{a}_2^2\bar{a}_1cd\\ & c\bar{a}_1\bar{a}_2^2\bar{a}_1a_1a_2^2a_1c\bar{a}_1\bar{a}_2^2\bar{a}_1cd\end{aligned}$$

and (i) of the claim is clearly true. Within each block (or line), there are different ways to choose x_i, y_i, and z_i. In the last line, we could choose

$$x_3 = c\bar{a}_1\bar{a}_2^2\bar{a}_1a_1a_2^2a_1c$$

$$x_3 = \bar{a}_1\bar{a}_2^2\bar{a}_1$$

$$z_3 = \Lambda$$

or we could have chosen

$$x_3 = c$$

$$y_3 = \bar{a}_1\bar{a}_2^2\bar{a}_1a_1a_2^2a_1$$

$$z_3 = c\bar{a}_1\bar{a}_2^2\bar{a}_1c$$

To be concrete, choose

$$y_1 = ¢a_1a_2a_1\bar{a}_1\bar{a}_2\bar{a}_1a_1a_2^2a_1a_1a_2^2a_1 = \tau(\pi_1)$$

$$y_2 = \tau(\pi_2)$$

and

$$y_3 = \tau(\pi_3)$$

This will determine x_i and z_i for $1 \leqslant i \leqslant 3$. To check whether $y_1 \cdots y_3 \in \text{init}(¢D_2)$, we use part (f) of Proposition 10.4.2. So both parts (ii) and (iii) of the claim require computing $\mu(y_1y_2y_3)$. But that is fun, as the reader who does it will learn. The answer is

$$\mu(y_1y_2y_3) = ¢a_1a_2^2a_1$$

Now we return to the proof and note that the claim suffices to prove the theorem. This is because (ii) and (iii) hold if and only if $y_1 \cdots y_k \in ¢D_2$; we have that $w \in L$ if and only if there exist x_i, y_i, z_i, $1 \leqslant i \leqslant k$ such that

i) $\varphi w = x_1cy_1cz_1d \cdots x_kcy_kcz_kd$

ii) $y_1 \cdots y_k \in ¢D_2$

iii) $y_i = \tau\pi_{p_i} \in \Sigma_2^*$ for $i \geqslant 2$,

which holds if and only if $w \in L_0 - \{\Lambda\}$.

Now we shall prove the claim by induction on k.

Basis. $k = 1$.

CASE 1 The derivation is

$$A_1 \Rightarrow a$$

where this production is π_{p_i}. Then, applying τ to this production gives

$$\tau\pi_{p_i} = ¢a_1a_2a_1\bar{a}_1\bar{a}_2\bar{a}_1$$

If $P_a = \{\pi_{p_1}, \ldots, \pi_{p_m}\}$, we have

$$\varphi a = c\tau(\pi_{p_1}) \cdots c\tau(\pi_{p_m})cd = x_1cy_1cz_1d$$

If we let $y_1 = \tau(\pi_{p_i})$, then $\mu(y_1) = ¢$ and so $y_1 \in \text{init}(¢D)$, and all the properties of the claim are established. Conversely, if each part of the claim is satisfied, there must be a derivation $A_1 \Rightarrow a$ and Case 1 has been verified.

CASE 2 The derivation is

$$A_1 \Rightarrow aA_{j_1}A_{j_2} \cdots A_{jm}$$

where $m \geqslant 1$, and the production is π_{p_i}. By definition,

$$\tau\pi_{p_i} = ¢a_1a_2a_1\bar{a}_1\bar{a}_2\bar{a}_1a_1a_1^{j_m}a_1 \cdots a_1a_2^{j_1}a_1$$

If $P_a = \{\pi_{p_1}, \ldots, \pi_{pm}\}$, then

$$\varphi a = c\tau(\pi_{p_1}) \cdots c\tau(\pi_{pm})cd = x_1cy_1cz_1d$$

satisfying property (i) of the claim. As in Case 1, we let $y_1 = \tau(\pi_{p_i})$. Then

$$\mu(y_1) = ¢a_1 a_2^{j_m} a_1 \cdots a_1 a_2^{j_1} a_1$$

satisfying property (iii). Consequently, $y_1 \in \text{init}(¢D)$, satisfying property (ii). Conversely, if each part of the claim is satisfied, there must be a derivation

$$A_1 \Rightarrow aA_{j_1} A_{j_2} \cdots A_{jm}$$

and the basis has been verified.

Induction step. Assume the result for $k \geqslant 1$. Suppose we have

$$S \overset{*}{\underset{L}{\Rightarrow}} b_1 \cdots b_k A_{i_1} \cdots A_{i_r}$$

the production π_p is $A_{i_1} \to b_{k+1} A_{j_1} \cdots A_{jt}$ and $\varphi(b_1 \cdots b_k) = x_1 c y_1 c z_1 d \cdots d x_k c y_k c z_k d$, where $\mu(y_1 \cdots y_k) = ¢a_1 a_2^{i_r} a_1 \cdots a_1 a_2^{i_1} a_1$. Let $y_{k+1} = \tau(\pi_p) = \bar{a}_1 \bar{a}_2^{i_1} \bar{a}_1 a_1 a_2^{j_t} a_1 \cdots a_1 a_2^{j_1} a_1$ and $\varphi(b_{k+1}) = x_{k+1} c y_{k+1} c z_{k+1} cd$. We compute

$$\begin{aligned} \mu(y_1 \cdots y_{k+1}) &= \mu(a_1 a_2^{i_r} a_1 \cdots a_1 a_2^{i_1} a_1 y_{k+1}) \\ &= a_1 a_2^{i_r} a_1 \cdots a_1 a_2^{i_2} a_1 a_1 a_2^{j_t} a_1 \cdots a_1 a_2^{j_1} a_1 \end{aligned}$$

while

$$S \overset{*}{\underset{L}{\Rightarrow}} b_1 \cdots b_k A_{i_1} \cdots A_{i_r} \underset{L}{\Rightarrow} b_1 \cdots b_k b_{k+1} A_{j_1} \cdots A_{jt} A_{i_2} \cdots A_{i_r}$$

This establishes one direction of the proof.

On the other hand, suppose $\varphi(b_1 \cdots b_k) = x_1 c y_1 c z_1 d \cdots d x_{k+1} c y_{k+1} c z_{k+1} d$ and $\mu(y_1 \cdots y_{k+1}) \in ¢\{a_1, a_2\}^*$. By the construction of φ, the only way this can happen is if

$$\mu(y_1 \cdots y_k) = ¢a_1 a_2^{i_r} a_1 \cdots a_1 a_2^{i_1} a_1$$

and

$$\mu(y_{k+1}) = \tau(\pi_p) = \bar{a}_1 \bar{a}_2^{s} \bar{a}_1 a_1 a_2^{j_t} a_1 \cdots a_1 a_2^{j_1} a_1$$

where π_p must be a production

$$A_s \Rightarrow b_{k+1} A_{j_1} \cdots A_{jt} \tag{10.5.1}$$

But since $\mu(y_1 \cdots y_{k+1}) \in ¢\{a_1, a_2\}^*$, there must be some cancellation between $\mu(y_1 \cdots y_k)$ and $\mu(y_{k+1})$; that is, $s = i_1$. By the induction hypothesis,

$$S \overset{*}{\underset{L}{\Rightarrow}} b_1 \cdots b_k A_{i_1} \cdots A_{i_r}$$

and by using equation (10.5.1), we have

$$S \overset{*}{\underset{L}{\Rightarrow}} b_1 \cdots b_k A_{j_1} \cdots A_{jt} A_{i_2} \cdots A_{i_r}$$

Therefore the induction has been extended. □

Corollary 1 L_0 is an inherently ambiguous language.

Proof If L_0 were unambiguous, then for any homomorphism φ, $\varphi^{-1}(L_0)$ would be unambiguous. By the theorem, every context-free language would be unambiguous and that contradicts Theorem 7.2.2.

Corollary 2 L_0 is not a deterministic context-free language.

Proof If it were, it would be unambiguous and would contradict Corollary 1.

PROBLEMS

1 Write a context-free grammar for L_0.

2 How would you recognize strings of L_0? Can you give a polynomial-time algorithm for recognition of strings in L_0? There is a great deal of interest in efficient recognition of strings in L_0.

**3 Find a set $\hat{L}_0$ (not context-free) with the property that $\mathscr{P} = \mathscr{NP}$ if and only if $\hat{L}_0 \in \mathscr{P}$. [*Hint.* Take three copies of L_0, shuffle them (cf. Problem 8 at the end of Section 6.4), and find a suitable restriction on the result. Relate to the family of sets accepted by nondeterministic Turing machines in quasi-realtime.]

10.6 HISTORICAL SURVEY

Theorem 10.2.1 is from Baker [1974]. Corollary 1 of that result is due to Ginsburg and Greibach [1966]. Corollaries 2 and 3 are due to Book [1972]. Corollary 5 is from Hibbard [1966]. Corollary 6 was proved by Matthews [1967].

Theorem 10.3.1 is from Ginsburg, Greibach, and Harrison [1967]. Problem 6 of Section 10.3 is due to Minsky [1961].

Theorem 10.4.2 is from Chomsky and Schützenberger [1963]. The concept of index, and relevant results about it, appear in Yntema [1967], Nivat [1967], Brainerd [1968], and Salomaa [1969]. Problems 13 through 15 of Section 10.4 derive from the paper by Chomsky and Schützenberger [1963]. The exercises on counters are from Boasson [1971, 1973, 1974] and Greibach [1969, 1975a]. Ritchie and Springsteel [1972] appear to have been the first to recognize the semi-Dyck set in log space. Problem 24 is from Lipton and Zalcstein [1976]. Problem 25 was suggested by the work of Mehlhorn [1975] and Lynch [1976].

The equivalence problems for parenthesis grammars are due to McNaughton [1967] and Knuth [1967]. Various kinds of bracketed grammars are given in Schkolnick [1968] and Harrison and Schkolnick [1971]. Exercise 31 is from Santos [1972].

Theorem 10.5.1 is from Greibach [1973].

eleven

Basic Theory of Deterministic Languages

11.1 INTRODUCTION

Deterministic context-free languages are one of the most important classes of languages because it is possible to construct efficient parsers for them. In this chapter, we begin a systematic study of this family.

We start by studying the closure properties of the class. It takes a great deal of work to prove that, if L is deterministic and R is regular, then LR^{-1} is also deterministic. That result implies that adding or removing a right endmarker does not affect the class of deterministic languages.

Section 11.3 is devoted to simple closure and nonclosure results. One gains a certain amount of advantage by studying the more tractable subfamily of strict deterministic languages. This study is begun in Section 11.4, and machine characterizations are obtained in Section 11.5. It turns out that a language is strict deterministic if and only if it is both deterministic and prefix-free.

In Section 11.6, an infinite hierarchy of strict deterministic languages is established, based on degrees or on the number of states of dpda's accepting them.

Next, the length of time required to accept deterministic languages is considered. The real-time strict deterministic languages are defined and studied in Section 11.7; and it is shown that there are some (strict) deterministic languages that cannot be accepted in realtime even on a multitape Turing machine.

In Section 11.8, the trees that occur in strict deterministic grammars are characterized. Using this characterization, it is possible to prove iteration theorems for both strict deterministic and deterministic languages.

In Section 11.10, we look at the family of simple languages, i.e., those accepted by one-state realtime dpda's which accept by empty store. It will be shown that this family has an unsolvable inclusion problem but a solvable equivalence problem.

11.2 CLOSURE OF DETERMINISTIC LANGUAGES UNDER RIGHT QUOTIENT BY REGULAR SETS

Our goal is to show that if L is a deterministic context-free language and R is a regular set, then LR^{-1} is also a deterministic context-free language. The proof proceeds in an indirect manner; and first we define tables which will be used as push-down symbols.

Definition Let $A = (Q, \Sigma, \Gamma, \delta, q_0, Z_0, F)$ be a dpda and let $n = |Q|$. For each $\alpha \in \Gamma^*$, define an $n \times n$ matrix $T(\alpha)$, called a *transition matrix for* α, such that

$$(T(\alpha))_{pq} = \begin{cases} 1 & \text{if } (p, w, \alpha) \overset{*}{\vdash} (q, \Lambda, \Lambda) \quad \text{for some } w \in \Sigma^*, \\ 0 & \text{otherwise.} \end{cases}$$

Let $\mathscr{T}$ be the set of all such matrices for A. Note that, for a dpda A, there are at most 2^{n^2} such matrices; and our first question concerns their effective construction from A. Note that the matrix $T(\Lambda)$ is the $n \times n$ identity matrix.

Lemma 11.2.1 Let $A = (Q, \Sigma, \Gamma, \delta, q_0, Z_0, F)$ be a dpda and let $\mathscr{T}$ be the set of all transition tables for A. If f is the function from $\mathscr{T} \times \Gamma^*$ into $\mathscr{T}$ defined by

$$f(T(\alpha), \beta) = T(\alpha\beta)$$

for $\alpha, \beta \in \Gamma^*$, then f may be effectively computed from A.

Proof First, we must show that f is well defined. More precisely, we have:

Claim 1 For any $\alpha_1, \alpha_2, \beta \in \Gamma^*$ if $T(\alpha_1) = T(\alpha_2)$, then $f(T(\alpha_1), \beta) = f(T(\alpha_2), \beta)$.

Proof Assume $T(\alpha_1) = T(\alpha_2)$, where $\alpha_1, \alpha_2 \neq \Lambda$. The special cases where $\alpha_1 = \Lambda$ or $\alpha_2 = \Lambda$ may be handled separately later. For any $p, q \in Q$ if $T(\alpha_1, \beta)_{pq} = 1$, then there exists $w \in \Sigma^*$ so that

$$(p, w, \alpha_1\beta) \overset{*}{\vdash} (q, \Lambda, \Lambda).$$

Since $\alpha_1 \neq \Lambda$, there exist $w_1, w_2 \in \Sigma^*, q' \in Q$ such that

$$w = w_1 w_2$$

$$(p, w, \alpha_1\beta) \overset{*}{\vdash} (q', w_2, \alpha_1) \overset{*}{\vdash} (q, \Lambda, \Lambda).$$

Moreover, we may choose w_1, w_2, q' such that in

$$(p, w, \alpha_1\beta) \overset{*}{\vdash} (q', w_2, \alpha_1) \qquad (11.2.1)$$

no part of α_1 is ever read. Thus we may conclude from (11.2.1) that

$$(p, w_1, \beta) \overset{*}{\vdash} (q', \Lambda, \Lambda).$$

But

$$(q', w_2, \alpha_1) \stackrel{*}{\vdash} (q, \Lambda, \Lambda)$$

implies

$$T(\alpha_1)_{q'q} = 1.$$

From $T(\alpha_1) = T(\alpha_2)$, we have

$$T(\alpha_2)_{q'q} = 1.$$

Thus there exists $w_3 \in \Sigma^*$ such that

$$(q', w_3, \alpha_2) \stackrel{*}{\vdash} (q, \Lambda, \Lambda).$$

Hence

$$(p, w_1 w_3, \alpha_2 \beta) \stackrel{*}{\vdash} (q', w_3, \alpha_2) \stackrel{*}{\vdash} (q, \Lambda, \Lambda).$$

Therefore $T(\alpha_2\beta)_{pq} = 1$.

Conversely, if $T(\alpha_2\beta)_{pq} = 1$, then $T(\alpha_1\beta)_{pq} = 1$, so that

$$T(\alpha_1\beta) = T(\alpha_2\beta).$$

This argument also shows that, if we have $T(\alpha)$ and $T(\beta)$, we may effectively compute

$$f(T(\alpha), \beta) = T(\alpha\beta).$$

We need only show how to compute $T(\alpha)$ from A, where $\alpha \in \Gamma^*$. For any $p, q \in Q$,

$$T(\alpha)_{pq} = \begin{cases} 1 & \text{if } \{w \in \Sigma^* \mid (p, w, \alpha) \stackrel{*}{\vdash} (q, \Lambda, \Lambda)\} \neq \emptyset, \\ 0 & \text{otherwise.} \end{cases}$$

We know from Section 5.6 that

$$L(A, p, \alpha, q) = \{w \in \Sigma^* \mid (p, w, \alpha) \stackrel{*}{\vdash} (q, \Lambda, \Lambda)\}$$

is a context-free language which is effectively constructible from A. Moreover, its emptiness is decidable, so that $T(\alpha)$ is computable from A. □

It is important to observe that the computation of f depends on $T(\alpha)$ and not on α.

Corollary Let $A = (Q, \Sigma, \Gamma, \delta, q_0, Z_0, F)$ be a dpda with $p, q \in Q$. Define

$$R_{pq} = \{\alpha \in \Gamma^* \mid (p, w, \alpha) \stackrel{*}{\vdash} (q, \Lambda, \Lambda) \text{ for some } w \in \Sigma^*\}.$$

R_{pq} is a regular set.

Proof Define a relation τ on Γ^* by

$$(\alpha_1, \alpha_2) \in \tau \Leftrightarrow T(\alpha_1) = T(\alpha_2).$$

τ is a right congruence relation on Γ^*. τ has finite rank since there are only a finite number of such matrices. Moreover

$$R_{pq} = \bigcup_{\substack{\alpha \in \Gamma^* \\ T(\alpha)=1}} [\alpha]_\tau,$$

where $[\alpha]_\tau$ denotes the equivalence class of α under τ. Therefore, R_{pq} is regular. (Cf. Problem 10 of Section 2.2.) □

Our next result not only is useful by itself, but is an important intermediate result in showing closure under quotient.

Theorem 11.2.1 If $L \subseteq \Sigma^*$ is a deterministic context-free language, then so is $\text{init}(L) = L(\Sigma^*)^{-1}$.

Proof By Problem 8 of Section 5.5, if $c \notin \Sigma$, then there is a dpda $A_1 = (Q_1, \Sigma \cup \{c\}, \Gamma_1, \delta, q_0, F_1)$ such that

$$Lc = L(A_1) = \{w \in (\Sigma \cup \{c\})^* \mid (q_0, w, Z_0) \overset{*}{\vdash} (q, \Lambda, \Lambda) \text{ for some } q \in F_1\}.$$

There is no loss of generality in assuming that

$$\delta(q, a, Z) = (q', \alpha)$$

implies that $\lg(\alpha) \leqslant 2$.

Let $\mathscr{T}$ be the set of transition tables for A_1. Let $f\colon \mathscr{T} \times \Gamma_1^* \to \mathscr{T}$ be the function defined by

$$f(T(\alpha), \beta) = T(\alpha\beta)$$

for α, $\beta \in \Gamma_1^*$. f is well defined and is computable by Lemma 11.2.1. Construct $A_2 = (Q_2, \Sigma, \Gamma_2, \delta_2, r_0, \bar{Z}_0, F_2)$, where

$$Q_2 = \{(q, i) \mid q \in Q_1, i \in \{0, 1, 2\}\} \cup \{r_0\},$$

$$\Gamma_2 = \Gamma_1 \times \mathscr{T} \cup \{\bar{Z}_0\} \qquad \text{where } \bar{Z}_0 \text{ is a new symbol,}$$

$$F_2 = \{(q, 2) \mid q \in Q_1\} \cup \{r_0 \mid L \neq \emptyset\}$$

δ_2 is defined by cases as shown below.

CASE 1. For any $a \in \Sigma \cup \{\Lambda\}$, if $\delta(q_0, a, Z_0) = (q, \alpha)$, then:

a) if $\alpha = \Lambda$, let $\delta_2(r_0, a, \bar{Z}_0) = ((q, 0), \bar{Z}_0)$;

b) if $\alpha = A \in \Gamma_1$, let $\delta_2(r_0, a, \bar{Z}_0) = ((q, 0), \bar{Z}_0(A, T(\Lambda)))$;

c) if $\alpha = A_2A_1$, let $\delta_2(r_0, a, \bar{Z}_0) = ((q, 0), \bar{Z}_0(A_2, T(\Lambda))(A_1, T(A_2)))$.

For any $a \in \Sigma \cup \{\Lambda\}$, $Z \in \Gamma_1$, let $\delta(q, a, Z) = (p, \alpha)$.

CASE 2 (*Simulation of erase rules in* $(q, 1)$ *or* $(q, 2)$.) If $\alpha = \Lambda$, then for all $S \in \mathscr{T}$, let:

$$\delta_2((q, 1), a, (Z, S)) = \delta_2((q, 2), a, (Z, S)) = ((p, 0), \Lambda).$$

CASE 3. (*Preservation of tables.*) If $\alpha = Z_1 \in \Gamma_1$, then, for all $S \in \mathscr{T}$, let

$$\delta_2((q, 1), a, (Z, S)) = \delta_2((q, 2), a, (Z, S)) = ((p, 0), (Z_1, S)).$$

CASE 4. (*Use transition tables to predict what will happen next.*) If $\alpha = A_2A_1$, where $A_1, A_2 \in \Gamma_1$, then for all $S \in \mathscr{T}$, let

$$\begin{aligned}\delta_2((q, 1), a, (Z, S)) &= \delta_2((q, 2), a, (Z, S))\\ &= ((p, 0), (A_2, S)(A_1, f(S, A_2)).\end{aligned}$$

CASE 5. (*Deciding to accept.*) For each $A \in \Gamma_1$, $S \in \mathscr{T}$, and $q \in Q_1$, let

$$\delta_2((q,0),\Lambda,(A,S)) = \begin{cases} ((q,2),(A,S)) & \text{if } S' = f(S,A) \text{ and there is} \\ & \quad p \in F_1 \text{ such that } (S')_{qp} = 1, \\ ((q,1),(A,S)) & \text{if } S' = f(S,A) \text{ and for all} \\ & \quad p \in F, (S')_{qp} = 0. \end{cases}$$

States $(q,1)$ and $(q,2)$ are the states in which input is processed. Only Λ-moves are done in states $(q,0)$. When in state $(q,0)$, A_2 determines whether A_1 would accept under some future input. If such an input exists, A_2 continues in states of the form $(q,2)$; and if not, it uses states of the form $(q,1)$.

We shall prove that the construction works, by a series of simple claims.

Claim 1 For each $q \in Q_1, n \geqslant 1, A_i \in \Gamma_1, w \in \Sigma^*$,

$$(q_0, w, Z_0) \overset{k}{\underset{A_1}{\vdash}} (q, \Lambda, A_n \cdots A_1)$$

if and only if

$$(r_0, w, \bar{Z}_0) \overset{2k-1}{\underset{A_2}{\vdash}} ((q,0),\Lambda,\alpha),$$

where $\alpha = \bar{Z}_0(A_n, T(\Lambda))(A_{n-1}, T(A_n)) \cdots (A_2, T(A_3 \cdots A_n))(A_1, T(A_2 \cdots A_n))$.

Proof The argument is a straightforward induction on k. The basis involves only part (1) of the construction, while the induction step uses parts (2), (3), (4), and (5). Details are left for Problem 2 at the end of the section.

Claim 2 $r_0 \in F_2$ if and only if $L \neq \emptyset$ if and only if $\Lambda \in \text{init}(L)$.

Claim 3

$$\begin{aligned} \text{init}(L) &= L(\Sigma^*)^{-1} \\ &= [Lc((\Sigma \cup \{c\})^*)^{-1}] \cap \Sigma^* \\ &= [L(A_1)((\Sigma \cup \{c\})^*)^{-1}] \cap \Sigma^*. \end{aligned}$$

Claim 4

$$T(A_2) \subseteq \text{init}(L).$$

Proof Let $w \in T(A_2)$. If $w = \Lambda$ and $r_0 \in F_2$, then $L \neq \emptyset$, by Claim 2, and so $\Lambda \in \text{init}(L)$. The case $r_0 \notin F_2$ is left for the problems. Suppose $w \neq \Lambda$. Then there exist $q \in Q_1, \alpha_2 \in \Gamma_2^*, A \in \Gamma_1, S \in \mathscr{T}$, such that

$$(r_0, w, \bar{Z}_0) \overset{*}{\underset{A_2}{\vdash}} ((q,0),\Lambda,\alpha_2(A,S)) \underset{A_2}{\vdash} ((q,2),\Lambda,\alpha_2(A,S)).$$

Note that $\alpha_2 = \bar{Z}_0$ if and only if $S = T(\Lambda)$. By Claim 1, there exists $\alpha_1 \in \Gamma_1^*$ such that

$$(q_0, w, Z_0) \overset{*}{\vdash} (q, \Lambda, \alpha_1 A)$$

and

$$S = \begin{cases} T(\alpha_1) & \text{if } \alpha_1 \neq \Lambda, \\ T(\Lambda) & \text{if } \alpha_1 = \Lambda. \end{cases}$$

By Claim 1, $\alpha_1 = \Lambda$ if and only if $\alpha_2 = \bar{Z}_0$. Let $S' = f(S, A)$. If $\alpha_1 = \Lambda$, then $\alpha_2 = \bar{Z}_0$ and $S = T(\Lambda)$. Thus

$$S' = f(S, A) = f(T(\Lambda), A) = T(A) = T(\alpha_1 A).$$

If $\alpha_1 \neq \Lambda$, then

$$S' = f(T(\alpha_1), A) = T(\alpha_1 A).$$

By part (5) of the construction of δ_2, if $\delta_2((q, 0), \Lambda, (A, S)) = ((q, 2), (A, S))$, then there exists $p \in F_1$ so that

$$(S')_{qp} = 1.$$

Thus there exists $w' \in \Sigma_c^*$ such that

$$(q_0, ww', Z_0) \underset{A_1}{\overset{*}{\vdash}} (q, w', \alpha_1 A)$$
$$\underset{A_1}{\overset{*}{\vdash}} (p, \Lambda, \Lambda) \qquad \text{where } p \in F_1.$$

Thus

$$ww' \in L(A_1)$$

and so

$$w \in [L(A_1)((\Sigma \cup \{c\})^*)^{-1}] \cap \Sigma^* = \text{init}(L)$$

by Claim 3. Therefore

$$T(A_2) \subseteq \text{init}(L).$$

Claim 5 $\quad \text{init}(L) \subseteq T(A_2)$

If $w \in \text{init}(L)$ and $w = \Lambda$, then $L \neq \emptyset$ and $r_0 \in F_2$ by Claim 2. Thus $w \in T(A_2)$. Now suppose $w \neq \Lambda$ is in init(L). There exist $w' \in \Sigma^*$ so that

$$ww' \in L$$

and

$$ww'c \in L(A_1).$$

Hence there exist $q \in Q_1, p \in F_1, A \in \Gamma_1$ and $\alpha_1 \in \Gamma_1^*$ such that

$$(q_0, ww'c, Z_0) \underset{A_1}{\overset{*}{\vdash}} (q, w'c, \alpha_1 A) \tag{11.2.2}$$
$$\underset{A_1}{\overset{*}{\vdash}} (p, \Lambda, \Lambda).$$

But (11.2.2) implies that

$$(q_0, w, Z_0) \underset{A_1}{\overset{*}{\vdash}} (q, \Lambda, \alpha_1 A)$$

and allows us to use Claim 1 to conclude that

$$(r_0, w, \bar{Z}_0) \underset{A_2}{\overset{*}{\vdash}} (q, 0), \Lambda, \alpha_2(A, S))$$

for some $\alpha_2 \in \Gamma_2^*$. Moreover,

$$S = \begin{cases} T(\Lambda) & \text{if } \alpha_1 = \Lambda, \\ T(\alpha_1) & \text{if } \alpha_1 \neq \Lambda. \end{cases}$$

Again, note that $\alpha_1 = \Lambda$ if and only if $\alpha_2 = \bar{Z}_0$. Let $S' = f(S, A)$ and so $S' = T(\alpha_1 A)$. We already know that

$$(q, w'c, \alpha_1 A) \underset{A_1}{\overset{*}{\vdash}} (p, \Lambda, \Lambda)$$

where $p \in F_1$. Thus

$$(S')_{qp} = 1.$$

By part (5) of the construction of δ_2,

$$\delta_2((q, 0), \Lambda, (A, S)) = ((q, 2), (A, S)),$$

so that $w \in T(A_2)$. Therefore, $\text{init}(L) \subseteq T(A_2)$.

This completes the entire proof. □

The next step in showing closure under right quotient is to show closure under removal of the right endmarker. The idea is similar to what is done in the proof of Theorem 11.2.1, but that construction will not work directly. We wish to consider the computation

$$(q, c, \alpha A) \overset{*}{\vdash} (p, \Lambda, \Lambda). \tag{11.2.3}$$

There are two different ways in which (11.2.3) can occur, namely:

i) The letter c can erase A and α can be erased by the null string,

or ii) Λ can erase A and c can erase α.

It is necessary to generalize transition tables to keep track of these possibilities.

Definitions Let $A = (Q, \Sigma, \Gamma, \delta, q_0, Z_0, F)$ be a dpda. Let $n = |Q|$, $c \notin \Sigma$, and $\alpha \in \Gamma^*$. A *c-transition table for* α is an $n \times n$ matrix $T_c(\alpha)$ defined by

$$(T_c(\alpha))_{pq} = (i, j),$$

where

$$i = \begin{cases} 1 & \text{if } (p, c, \alpha) \overset{*}{\vdash} (q, \Lambda, \Lambda), \\ 0 & \text{otherwise,} \end{cases}$$

and

$$j = \begin{cases} 1 & \text{if } (p, \Lambda, \alpha) \overset{*}{\vdash} (q, \Lambda, \Lambda), \\ 0 & \text{otherwise.} \end{cases}$$

Let $\mathscr{T}_c$ denote all c-transition tables for A.

Given a dpda, one can effectively compute the set of transition tables.

Lemma 11.2.2 Let $A = (Q, \Sigma, \Gamma, \delta, q_0, Z_0, F)$ be a dpda and let $\mathscr{T}_c$ be the set of all c-transition tables for A. If $f_c\colon \mathscr{T}_c \times \Gamma^* \to \mathscr{T}_c$ is the function defined by

$$f_c(T_c(\alpha), \beta)) = T_c(\alpha\beta)$$

for $\alpha, \beta \in \Gamma^*$, then f_c is computable from A.

Proof The argument is similar to that of Lemma 11.2.1 and is left as Exercise 4 at the end of the section. □

With the aid of c-transition tables, the right endmarkers may be removed.

Theorem 11.2.2 Let c be a letter not in Σ. If $L \subseteq \Sigma^* c$ is a deterministic context-free language, then so is $L(c^{-1})$.

Proof Assume that

$$L = T(A_1) = T_d(A_1)$$

for some loop-free dpda A_1. Construct a dpda A_2 such that

$$L = L(A_2) = T(A_2).$$

By using c-transition tables and f_c from Lemma 11.2.2, construct A_3 from A_2 such that

$$T(A_3) = Lc^{-1}.$$

A construction similar to that employed in the proof of Theorem 11.2.1 will work to produce A_3 from A_2. ☐

Finally, the main result can be proved.

Theorem 11.2.3 If L is a deterministic context-free language and R is a regular set, then LR^{-1} is also a deterministic context-free language.

Proof Assume $L, R \subseteq \Sigma^*$ and let $c \notin \Sigma$. Define

$$\varphi\colon (\Sigma \cup \{c\})^* \to \Sigma^*$$

to be a homomorphism defined by

$$\varphi a = \begin{cases} a & \text{if } a \in \Sigma, \\ \Lambda & \text{if } a = c. \end{cases}$$

Now

$$L_1 = \varphi^{-1}(L) \cap \Sigma^* c R$$

is a deterministic context-free language by Problem 1 of Sec. 6.5 and Theorem 6.4.1. Note that

$$L_1 = \{wcy \mid wy \in L \text{ and } y \in R\}.$$

Define

$$L_2 = (\text{init}(L_1)) \cap \Sigma^* c.$$

$\text{init}(L_1)$ is a deterministic context-free language and hence so is L_2. But

$$\begin{aligned} L_2 &= \{wc \mid wcy \in L_1 \quad \text{for some } y \in R\} \\ &= \{wc \mid wy \in L \quad \text{for some } y \in R\} = (LR^{-1})c. \end{aligned}$$

By Theorem 11.2.3, LR^{-1} is a deterministic context-free language since $L_2 = (LR^{-1})c$ is. ☐

PROBLEMS

1 Do Lemma 11.2.1 and its Corollary hold for nondeterministic pda's as well as deterministic ones?

2 Prove Claim 1 in the proof of Theorem 11.2.1.

3 The proof of Claim 4 in Theorem 11.2.1 does not explicitly deal with the case where $w = \Lambda$ and $r_0 \notin F_2$. Analyze this case.

4 Prove Lemma 11.2.2.

5 Complete the details of the proof of Theorem 11.2.2.

11.3 CLOSURE AND NONCLOSURE PROPERTIES OF DETERMINISTIC LANGUAGES

It is necessary for us to know which operations do or do not preserve deterministic context-free languages.

We recall from Theorem 6.4.1 that if L is deterministic and R is regular, then $L \cap R$ is a deterministic context-free language. We also know that, if L is a deterministic language and S is a gsm, then $S^{-1}(L)$ is also a deterministic language. (Cf. Problem 1 at the end of the section.) It follows as a corollary of this result that the family of deterministic context-free languages is closed under inverse homomorphisms. The first new operation that we shall study here is product with regular sets.

Theorem 11.3.1 If L is a deterministic context-free language and R is a regular set, then LR is also a deterministic context-free language.

Proof Let $A_1 = (Q_1, \Sigma, \Gamma, \delta_1, q_1, F_1)$ be a dpda such that $T(A_1) = L$. There is no loss of generality in assuming that A_1 is loop-free, by Lemma 5.6.5. Let $A_2 = (Q_2, \Sigma, \delta_2, q_2, F_2)$ be a finite automaton such that $T(A_2) = R$. We construct a dpda A_3 for LR as follows. Let $A_3 = (Q_3, \Sigma, \Gamma, \delta_3, q_3, Z_0, F_3)$, where

$$Q_3 = Q_1 \times 2^{Q_2},$$

$$q_3 = (q_1, \emptyset),$$

$$F_3 = Q_1 \times \{Q \subseteq Q_2 \mid Q \cap F_2 \neq \emptyset\}.$$

δ_3 is defined by cases as shown below.

CASE 1. For $Z \in \Gamma$, q, $q' \in Q_1$, $Q \subseteq Q_2$, $\alpha \in \Gamma^*$ if $\delta_1(q, \Lambda, Z) = (q', \alpha)$, define

$$\delta_3((q, Q), \Lambda, Z) = \begin{cases} (q', Q \cup \{q_2\}), \alpha) & \text{if } q' \in F_1, \\ ((q', Q), \alpha) & \text{if } q' \notin F. \end{cases}$$

As A_1 goes to a final state, place the start state of A_1 into the finite control of A_1.

CASE 2. For $Z \in \Gamma, q, q' \in Q_1, Q \subseteq Q_2, a \in \Sigma, \alpha \in \Gamma^*$, if $\delta_1(q, a, Z) = (q', \alpha)$, then define

$$\delta_3((q, Q), a, Z) = \begin{cases} ((q', \{q_2\} \cup \delta_2(Q, a)), \alpha) & \text{if } q' \in F_1, \\ ((q', \delta_2(Q, a)), \alpha) & \text{if } q' \notin F_1. \end{cases}$$

We simulate all possible computations of A_2 in the second component and continue to add the start state every time A_1 hits a final state.

Note that A_3 is a deterministic pda because A_1 is.

To complete the proof, we must show that $T(A_3) = LR$. The argument is given in several simple claims.

Claim 1 Let $q,\ q' \in Q_1,\ p \in Q_2,\ w \in \Sigma^*,\ \alpha,\ \beta \in \Gamma^*$, and $S,\ S' \subseteq Q_2$. If $((q, S), w, \alpha) \overset{*}{\underset{A_3}{\vdash}} ((q', S'), \Lambda, \beta)$ and if $p \in S$, then $\delta_2(p, w) \in S'$.

Proof The argument follows easily by induction on lg(w).

The next claim states a correspondence between A_1 and A_3 computations.

Claim 2 For any $w_1, w_2 \in \Sigma^*$, for any $k, \ell \geq 0$, any $q, q' \in Q$, any $\alpha, \beta \in \Gamma^*$, and any $S, S' \subseteq Q_2$,

$$(q_1, w_1 w_2, Z_0) \overset{k}{\underset{A_1}{\vdash}} (q', w_2, \alpha) \overset{\ell}{\underset{A_1}{\vdash}} (q'', \Lambda, \beta)$$

if and only if

$$((q_1, \emptyset), w_1 w_2, Z_0) \overset{k}{\underset{A_3}{\vdash}} ((q', S), w_2, \alpha) \overset{\ell}{\underset{A_3}{\vdash}} ((q'', S'), \Lambda, \beta).$$

Proof The argument is an induction on $k + \ell$ and is omitted.

In our next claim, we show that $LR \subseteq T(A_3)$;

Claim 3 $\qquad LR \subseteq T(A_3).$

Proof $\qquad w \in LR$

if and only if there exist $w_1, w_2 \in \Sigma^*$ so that

$$w = w_1 w_2$$

$$w_1 \in L,$$

and

$$w_2 \in R.$$

This holds if and only if

$$(q_1, w_1, Z_0) \overset{*}{\underset{A_1}{\vdash}} (q', \Lambda, \alpha) \tag{11.3.1}$$

and

$$\delta(q_2, w_2) \in F_2, \tag{11.3.2}$$

where $q' \in F_1$. Since A_1 is loop-free and because (11.3.1) holds, we have

$$(q_1, w_1 w_2, Z_0) \overset{*}{\underset{A_1}{\vdash}} (q', w_2, \alpha) \overset{*}{\underset{A_1}{\vdash}} (q'', \Lambda, \beta)$$

for some $q' \in F_1$, some $\beta \in \Gamma^*$, and some $q'' \in Q_1$. By Claim 2,

$$((q_1, \emptyset), w_1 w_2, Z_0) \overset{*}{\underset{A_3}{\vdash}} ((q', S), w_2, \alpha) \overset{*}{\underset{A_3}{\vdash}} ((q'', S'), \Lambda, \beta). \tag{11.3.3}$$

Since $q' \in F_1$, we have

$$q_2 \in S$$

by the construction. Moreover, by Claim 1,

$$\delta(q_2, w_2) \in S'.$$

But we assumed that $w_2 \in R$, so

$$\delta(q_2, w_2) \in F_2.$$

Thus

$$(q'', S') \in F_3$$

and (11.3.3) is an accepting computation of A_3 on $w_1 w_2$. Therefore $w_1 w_2 \in T(A_3)$.

In order to prove the converse, an intermediate proposition is helpful.

Claim 4 For any $k \geq 0$, $w \in \Sigma^*$, $\beta \in \Gamma^*$, $q' \in Q_1$, $S' \subseteq Q_2$ if there exists $q'' \in S'$ and

$$((q_1, \emptyset), w, Z_0) \underset{A_3}{\overset{k}{\vdash}} ((q', S'), \Lambda, \beta),$$

then there exist $w_1, w_2 \in \Sigma^*, q \in Q_1, S \subseteq Q_2$, and $\alpha \in \Gamma^*$ such that

$$w = w_1 w_2$$

$$((q_1, \emptyset), w_1 w_2, Z_0) \underset{A_3}{\overset{*}{\vdash}} ((q, S), w_2, \alpha) \underset{A_3}{\overset{*}{\vdash}} ((q', S'), \Lambda, \beta),$$

where

$$q \in F_1,$$

$$q_2 \in S,$$

and

$$\delta(q_2, w_2) = q''.$$

Proof The argument is a straightforward induction on k and is omitted.

Claim 5 $$T(A_3) \subseteq LR.$$

Proof Assume that $w \in T(A_3)$. Then,

$$((q_1, \emptyset), w, Z_0) \underset{A_3}{\overset{*}{\vdash}} ((q', S'), \Lambda, \beta) \tag{11.3.4}$$

for some $\beta \in \Gamma^*$, and some $(q', S') \in F_3$. This means that $S' \cap F_2 \neq \emptyset$, so let $q'' \in S' \cap F_2$. By Claim 4 there exist $w_1, w_2 \in \Sigma^*, q \in Q_1, S \subseteq Q_2, \alpha \in \Gamma^*$, such that

$$((q_1, \emptyset), w_1 w_2, Z_0) \underset{A_3}{\overset{*}{\vdash}} ((q, S), w_2, \alpha) \underset{A_3}{\overset{*}{\vdash}} ((q', S'), \Lambda, \beta),$$

where $q \in F_1, q_2 \in S$, and $\delta_2(q_2, w_2) = q''$. By Claim 2,

$$(q_1, w_1, Z_0) \underset{A_1}{\overset{*}{\vdash}} (q, \Lambda, \alpha)$$

with $q \in F_1$ and

$$\delta_2(q_2, w_2) = q'' \in F_2.$$

Thus, $w = w_1 w_2$ with $w_1 \in L$ and $w_2 \in R$, and therefore $T(A_3) \subseteq LR$. □

Next we study product on the left with a single string.

Lemma 11.3.1 Let Σ be an alphabet, let $a \in \Sigma$ and let $c \notin \Sigma$. The following conditions are equivalent.

1 cL is a deterministic context-free language.

2 L is a deterministic context-free language.

3 aL is a deterministic context-free language.

Proof Suppose cL is a deterministic context-free language. Assume, without loss of generality, that $cL = T(A)$, where $A = (Q, \Sigma, \Gamma, \delta, q_0, Z_0, F)$ is a loop-free deterministic pda. Define $B = (Q, \Sigma - \{c\}, \Gamma, \delta_B, \bar{q}_0, \bar{Z}_0, F)$, where

$$\delta_B(q, a, Z) = \delta(q, a, Z) \quad \text{for all } (q, a, Z) \in Q \times ((\Sigma \cup \{\Lambda\}) - \{c\}) \times \Gamma.$$

The initial state $\bar{q}_0$ and the initial symbol $\bar{Z}_0$ are determined by the condition $(q_0, c, Z_0) \overset{*}{\Vdash} (\bar{q}_0, \Lambda, \alpha\bar{Z}_0)$ for some $\alpha \in \Gamma^*$. It is now a straightforward matter to verify that $L = T(B)$, which is still a deterministic language.

To prove (2) implies (3) is a trivial dpda construction and is omitted.

To show that (3) implies (1), assume that aL is a deterministic context-free language. Define a homomorphism φ by

$$\varphi b = b \quad \text{if } b \in \Sigma$$

and

$$\varphi c = a.$$

Then

$$\varphi^{-1}(aL) \cap c\Sigma^* = cL$$

is deterministic by the closure of deterministic languages under inverse homomorphism and under intersection with regular sets. □

We can use this lemma repeatedly as follows.

Theorem 11.3.2 Let $L \subseteq \Sigma^*$ and $w \in \Sigma^*$. L is a deterministic context-free language if and only if wL is.

Proof Let $w = a_1 \cdots a_n$, where $n \geqslant 0$, $a_k \in \Sigma$ for $1 \leqslant k \leqslant n$. The proof follows from using the lemma n times. □

Now we turn to showing that the deterministic context-free languages are not closed under certain operations. We recall that they are not closed under union.

Theorem 11.3.3

1 The family of deterministic context-free languages, Δ_0, is a proper subfamily of the family of context-free languages.

2 Δ_0 is not closed under homomorphisms. More strongly, Δ_0 is not closed under "projections"; that is, maps from Σ into Δ extended to be homomorphisms.

3 Δ_0 is not closed under concatenation. More strongly, Δ_0 is not closed under concatenation on the left by two element sets.

4 Δ_0 is not closed under * (or $^+$ either).

5 Δ_0 is not closed under transposition.

Proof Since every deterministic context-free language is unambiguous, it follows from the existence of inherently ambiguous languages that Δ_0 is a proper subfamily of the context-free languages.

To see (2), recall that D_r, the semi-Dyck set, is deterministic. For any regular set R, $D_r \cap R$ is deterministic; and if Δ_0 were closed under homomorphism, then

$$L = \varphi(D_r \cap R)$$

would be deterministic. By Theorem 10.4.2, every context-free language would be deterministic, which would contradict (1).

It is convenient to define

$$L_0 = \{a^i b^i a^j \mid i, j \geqslant 1\},$$

$$L_1 = \{a^i b^j a^j \mid i, j \geqslant 1\},$$

$$L_2 = L_0 \cup L_1.$$

Recall that L_2 is inherently ambiguous and hence not a deterministic context-free language. (Cf. Section 7.2.)

To prove part (3) of the theorem, let

$$L = cL_0 \cup L_1.$$

It is clear that L is deterministic. Let $R = \{c, c^2\}$. Suppose that RL were deterministic. Then

$$RL \cap c^2a^*b^*a^* = c^2L_2$$

would be deterministic. Using Theorem 11.3.2 allows us to conclude that L_2 is deterministic, which is false.

To show (4), define

$$L = L_0 \cup cL_1 \cup \{c\}.$$

Suppose that L^* were deterministic. Then

$$L^* \cap c^2a^+b^*a^* = c^2L_2$$

would be, and that was already shown to be impossible.

To show (5), let

$$L = cL_1 \cup c^2L_0.$$

Clearly, L is deterministic. Suppose L^T were deterministic. Then

$$(L^T\{c, c^2\}^{-1}) \cap \Sigma^* = L_0 \cup L_1 = L_2$$

would be deterministic by Theorem 11.2.4. But this is a contradiction. □

PROBLEMS

1 Show that if L is a deterministic context-free language and R is a regular set, then

$$L \cup R,$$

$$L - R,$$

and

$$R - L$$

are all deterministic context-free languages.

2 Let Σ be an alphabet and $¢ \neq \$ \notin \Sigma$. If $L_1, L_2 \subseteq \Sigma^*$, then $¢L_1 \cup \$L_2$ is called the *marked union* of L_1 and L_2. The *marked concatenation* of L_1 and L_2 is $L_1 ¢ L_2$ while the *marked star* is $(L_1\$)^*$. Show that the family of deterministic context-free languages is closed under marked union, marked product, and marked star.

3 Show that, if L is a deterministic context-free language and R is a regular set then

$$\operatorname{div}(L, R) = \{u \mid uR \subseteq L\}$$

is also a deterministic context-free language.

4 Find a context-free language L and a regular set R such that $\operatorname{div}(L, R)$ is not even context-free. R can even be chosen to have cardinality two if L is chosen correctly.

5 Let $x, y \in \Sigma^*$. Recall that $x < y$ if $y = xy'$ for some $y' \in \Sigma^+$. Define

$$\min(L) = \{y \in L \mid \text{If } x < y, \text{ then } x \notin L\}.$$

That is, y is in $\min(L)$ if $y \in L$ and no proper prefix of y is in L. Show that if L is a deterministic context-free language, then so is $\min(L)$.

6 Show that, if L is a context-free language, then $\min(L)$ may not be context-free.

7 If $L \subseteq \Sigma^*$, define

$$\max(L) = \{y \in L \mid \text{If } y < x, \text{ then } x \notin L\}.$$

Thus $y \in \max(L)$ means that $y \in L$ and no continuation of y is in L. Show that, if L is a deterministic context-free language, then so is $\max(L)$.

8 Give an example of a context-free language L so that $\max(L)$ is not context-free.

9 Extend the proof of Theorem 11.3.2 to cover projections.

10 Show that, if L is a deterministic context-free language, then $L - \min(L)$ is also a deterministic context-free language.

11 Are the deterministic context-free languages closed under left quotient with regular sets?

12 Show that it is unsolvable to determine, of two deterministic context free languages L_1 and L_2, whether or not:

a) $L_1 \cup L_2$ is deterministic;

b) $L_1 \subseteq L_2$;

c) $L_1 L_2$ is deterministic;

d) L_1^* is deterministic.

11.4 STRICT DETERMINISTIC GRAMMARS

In this section, a new family of grammars will be introduced and related to the deterministic languages. The intuition behind this family is technical and its use will simplify many arguments.

Notation. Let $\alpha \in V^*$ and $n \geqslant 0$. ${}^{(n)}\alpha$ denotes the prefix of α of length $\min\{n, \lg(\alpha)\}$. The notation $\alpha^{(n)}$ is used for the suffix of α of length $\min\{n, \lg(\alpha)\}$.

Definition 11.4.1 Let $G = (V, \Sigma, P, S)$ be a context-free grammar and let π be a partition of the set V of terminal and nonterminal letters of G. Such a partition π is called *strict* if:

1 $\Sigma \in \pi$; and

2 For any $A, A' \in N$ and $\alpha, \beta, \beta' \in V^*$ if $A \to \alpha\beta$ and $A' \to \alpha\beta'$ are in P and $A \equiv A' \pmod{\pi}$, then either:

  i) both $\beta, \beta' \neq \Lambda$ and ${}^{(1)}\beta \equiv {}^{(1)}\beta' \pmod{\pi}$, or

  ii) $\beta = \beta' = \Lambda$ and $A = A'$.

In most cases, the partition π will be clear from the context and we shall write simply $A \equiv B$ instead of $A \equiv B \pmod{\pi}$, and $[A]$ instead of $[A]_\pi = \{A' \in V \mid A' \equiv A \pmod{\pi}\}$.

Definition Any grammar $G = (V, \Sigma, P, S)$ is called *strict deterministic* if there exists a strict partition π of V. A language L is called a *strict deterministic language* if $L = L(G)$ for some strict deterministic grammar G.

The motivation behind this definition is that we wish to make certain restrictions on the simultaneous occurrences of substrings in different productions. Intuitively, if $A \to \alpha\beta$ is a production in our grammar, then "partial information" about A, together with complete information about a prefix α of $\alpha\beta$, yields similar partial information about the next symbol of β when $\beta \neq \Lambda$, or the complementary information about A when $\beta = \Lambda$. In the formal definition, the intuitive notion of "partial information" is precisely represented by means of the partition π.

Example 1 Let G_1 be a grammar with the productions

$$\begin{aligned} S &\to aA \mid aB \\ A &\to aAa \mid bC \\ B &\to aB \mid bD \\ C &\to bC \mid a \\ D &\to bDc \mid c \end{aligned}$$

The blocks of a strict partition are: Σ, $\{S\}$, $\{A, B\}$, $\{C, D\}$. The language is $L(G_1) = \{a^n b^k a^n, a^k b^n c^n \mid k, n \geqslant 1\}$.

Example 2 Our second example is a grammar for a set of simple arithmetic expressions (enclosed in parentheses). A natural grammar for them might have productions

$$S \to (E)$$

$$E \to E + T \mid T$$

$$T \to T * F \mid F$$

$$F \to S \mid a$$

Unfortunately, this grammar has no strict partition. However, we can find an equivalent strict deterministic grammar G_2:

$$S \to (E$$

$$E \to T_1 E \mid T_2$$

$$T_1 \to F_1 T_1 \mid F_2$$

$$T_2 \to F_1 T_2 \mid F_3$$

$$F_1 \to (E * \mid a *$$

$$F_2 \to (E + \mid a +$$

$$F_3 \to (E) \mid a)$$

The blocks of a strict partition for G_2 are Σ, $\{S\}$, $\{E\}$, $\{T_1, T_2\}$, $\{F_1, F_2, F_3\}$.

Next, we turn to the problem of testing a grammar for the strict deterministic property. First we introduce a convenient concept.

Definition Let α, $\beta \in V^*$ and let A, B be two letters in V such that $A \neq B$ and we have $\alpha = \gamma A \alpha_1$ and $\beta = \gamma B \beta_1$ for some γ, α_1, $\beta_1 \in V^*$. Then the pair (A, B) is called the *distinguishing pair of* α *and* β. *A* distinguishing pair (A, B) is said to be *terminal* if $A, B \in \Sigma$.

From the definition, we can make the following observation.

Fact Any two strings α, $\beta \in V^*$, have a distinguishing pair if and only if either α is not a prefix of β or β is not a prefix of α. If they have a distinguishing pair, then it is unique.

We shall now give our algorithm.

Algorithm 11.4.1 The algorithm takes as input any context-free grammar G and determines whether G is strict deterministic or not. In the former case the algorithm produces the minimal† strict partition of V.

---

† The partition is minimal with respect to the standard lattice ordering of partitions; that is, $\pi_1 \leqslant \pi_2$ if $\equiv_1 \subseteq \equiv_2$.

Assume that the productions of G are consecutively numbered; that is,

$$P = \{A_i \to \alpha_i \mid i = 1, \ldots, |P|\}$$

and all productions are distinct.

```
begin
  π = {{A}|A ∈ N} ∪ Σ;
L: for i: = 1 to |P| − 1 do
   begin
     for j: = i + 1 to |P| do
     begin
       comment A_i → α_i and A_j → α_j are two distinct productions in P;
       if A_i ≡ A_j then
         if α_i and α_j have no distinguishing pair then return (fail)
         else
         begin
           let (B, C) be the unique distinguishing pair of α_i and α_j;
           if B ≠ C then
             if B ∉ Σ and C ∉ Σ then
             begin
               replace [B] and [C] in π by one new block [B] ∪ [C];
               goto L
             end else
             begin
               comment B ∈ Σ or C ∈ Σ but not both since B ≢ C;
               return (fail)
             end
         end
     end
   end;
   return (succeed)
end.
```

Proof of the correctness of the algorithm The algorithm is relatively simple and we give only an outline of a proof of its correctness. At a later time, we will need the properties that may prevent a grammar from being strict deterministic.

First let us check that the algorithm always halts. There are two **for** loops, each of which is bounded. Variables i and j are not changed inside of these loops. Branching inside of the **for**-loops is either:

i) forward,

ii) out of the loops, or

iii) restarts the loops.

The first case must terminate since the loops are bounded. The second case trivially halts. In case (iii), the cardinality of π is decreased. Once we get to $|\pi| = 2$, then, if $B \not\equiv C$, we have $B \in \Sigma$ or $C \in \Sigma$ (but not both). Thus the loops cannot be restarted.

Now, let us investigate how a grammar may fail to be strict deterministic. Under the hypothesis and notation of Definition 11.4.1, we note that, if $A = A'$ (in the initial stage of the algorithm) or if $A \equiv A'$ (as a result of preceding stages in any subsequent stage) and if $\beta, \beta' \neq \Lambda$ and ${}^{(1)}\beta, {}^{(1)}\beta' \in N$, the case (i) in Condition 2 of the definition can always be satisfied by forcing ${}^{(1)}\beta \equiv {}^{(1)}\beta'$ (the statement preceding the **goto** does the job). We do not obtain an essential failure under these circumstances. But the following three kinds of failure are essential. Assume $A \equiv A'$ (forced by preceding stages).

Failure I

$$A \to \alpha\beta_1$$
$$A' \to \alpha$$

where $\beta_1 \neq \Lambda$. Taking $\beta = \beta_1$ and $\beta' = \Lambda$ in Definition 11.4.1, neither (i) nor (ii) can occur. Algorithm 1 directly returns "fail" since $\alpha\beta_1$ and α have no distinguishing pair.

Failure II

$$A \to \alpha$$
$$A' \to \alpha$$

where $A \neq A'$. Taking $\beta = \beta' = \Lambda$, we obtain case (ii) with the contradictory requirement $A = A'$. Algorithm 1 halts in the same way as in the case of Failure I.

Failure III

$$A \to \alpha B\beta_1$$
$$A' \to \alpha a\beta_2$$

where $B \in N$ and $a \in \Sigma$. Taking $\beta = B\beta_1$ and $\beta' = a\beta_2$ in Definition 11.4.1, we obtain case (i) with the requirement $B \equiv a$, which contradicts condition 1. Algorithm 1 returns "fail" from the innermost **else** clause.

These are all the possible ways for a grammar to fail to be strict deterministic. If no failure occurs, G is strict deterministic. Also, Algorithm 11.4.1 cannot return "fail" and since it always terminates, it returns "success".

The fact that the partition produced is strict and minimal follows from the property of the algorithm that two letters are made equivalent if and only if it is required by Definition 11.4.1. □

We need to establish some simple but important properties of strict deterministic grammars, all of which are almost direct consequences of Definition 11.4.1.

Theorem 11.4.1 Any strict deterministic grammar is equivalent to a reduced strict deterministic grammar.

Proof The standard construction (cf. Section 3.2) for reducing a grammar consists only of deleting some productions. The result thus follows directly from the following claim.

Claim Let π be a strict partition for a grammar $G = (V, \Sigma, P, S)$, and let $G' = (V', \Sigma, P', S)$ be a reduced grammar for G constructed by the methods of Section 3.2. Then G' is also a strict deterministic grammar.

Proof of the claim In G', we have $V' \subseteq V$ and $P' \subseteq P$. Let π' be the partition obtained from π by deleting all symbols of $V - V'$. Then the only way that π' could fail to be strict would be to have two productions p_1 and p_2 for which a failure occurs. But then $p_1, p_2 \in P$ and the failure would occur in π also and π would not be strict. □

The following lemma extends the property of strict partitions from productions to certain derivations in the grammar.

Lemma 11.4.1 Let $G = (V, \Sigma, P, S)$ be a context-free grammar with a strict partition π. Then, for any $A, A' \in N$, $\alpha, \beta, \beta' \in V^*$ and $n \geqslant 1$, if $A \Rightarrow_L^n \alpha\beta$, $A' \Rightarrow_L^n \alpha\beta'$ and $A \equiv A'$, then either

i) both $\beta, \beta' \neq \Lambda$ and ${}^{(1)}\beta \equiv {}^{(1)}\beta'$

or iii) $\beta = \beta' = \Lambda$ and $A = A'$.

Proof The argument is an induction on n. The basis is immediate since, for $n = 1$, the assertion of the lemma is equivalent to condition 2 in Definition 11.4.1.

Inductive step. Assume the assertion of the lemma is true for a given $n \geqslant 1$ and consider the case of $n + 1$. We can write:

$$A \Rightarrow_L^n wB\beta_1 \Rightarrow_L w\beta_2\beta_1 = \alpha\beta$$

and

$$A' \Rightarrow_L^n w'B'\beta_1' \Rightarrow_L w'\beta_2'\beta_1' = \alpha\beta'$$

for some $B, B' \in N$, $w, w' \in \Sigma^*$ and $\beta_1, \beta_1', \beta_2, \beta_2' \in V^*$, and assume, without loss of generality, that $\lg(\beta_2') \geqslant \lg(\beta_2)$.

CASE 1. $0 \leqslant \lg(\alpha) < \lg(w)$. Then both ${}^{(1)}\beta$, ${}^{(1)}\beta' \in \Sigma$ and thus ${}^{(1)}\beta \equiv {}^{(1)}\beta'$.

For the remaining cases we make the following claim.

Claim In the above derivations, if w is a prefix of w', or w' is a prefix of w, then $w = w'$ and $B \equiv B'$.

Proof of claim Assume, without loss of generality, that w is a prefix of w'; that is, that $w' = ww''$ for some $w'' \in \Sigma^*$. We have $A \Rightarrow_L^n wB\beta_1$ and $A' \Rightarrow_L^n ww''B'\beta_1'$. Then, by the inductive hypothesis, ${}^{(1)}(B\beta_1) \equiv {}^{(1)}(w''B'\beta_1')$ and since, for any $a \in \Sigma$, $B \not\equiv a$ (by the property that $\Sigma \in \pi$), we conclude that $w' = \Lambda$, $w = w'$, and $B \equiv B'$. This completes the proof of the claim.

CASE 2. $\lg(w) \leqslant \lg(\alpha) < \lg(w\beta_2)$. In other words, we have $\alpha = w\gamma_1$ and $\beta_2 = \gamma_1\gamma_2$ for some $\gamma_1, \gamma_2 \in V^*$ where $\gamma_2 \neq \Lambda$. w is a prefix of w', or, conversely (because they are initial subwords of α), we have $w = w'$ and $B \equiv B'$ by the claim. Therefore we can write also $\beta_2' = \gamma_1\gamma_2'$ for some $\gamma_2' \in V^+$ (we have used the assumption that $\lg(\beta_2') \geqslant \lg(\beta_2)$). Now we have $B \to \gamma_1\gamma_2$, $B' \to \gamma_1\gamma_2'$, and $\gamma_2, \gamma_2' \neq \Lambda$. By the strictness of π (property 2(i) in Definition 11.4.1), we conclude that ${}^{(1)}\beta = {}^{(1)}\gamma_2 = {}^{(1)}\gamma_2' = {}^{(1)}\beta'$.

CASE 3. $\lg(w\beta_2) \leqslant \lg(\alpha) \leqslant \lg(w\beta_2\beta_1)$. Again, from the claim, we have $w = w'$ and $B \equiv B'$. Moreoever, β_2 is a prefix of β_2', or conversely. By the strictness of π (property 2(ii) in Definition 11.4.1), this is possible only if $\beta_2 = \beta_2'$ and $B = B'$. Thus $wB = wB'$ and the result follows from the inductive hypothesis. □

The following concept will start to appear regularly.

Definition A set $L \subseteq \Sigma^*$ is *prefix-free* if $uv \in L$ and $u \in L$ imply $v = \Lambda$.

That is, a set is prefix free if no prefix of a string in L is also in L.

The following simple theorem is important.

Theorem 11.4.2 Any strict deterministic language is prefix-free.

Proof Let $G = (V, \Sigma, P, S)$ be a strict deterministic grammar, and assume

$$S \overset{n}{\underset{L}{\Rightarrow}} w \qquad \text{and} \qquad S \overset{n'}{\underset{L}{\Rightarrow}} wu$$

for some $w, u \in \Sigma^*$ and $n, n' \geqslant 1$. If $n \leqslant n'$, we have

$$S \overset{n}{\underset{L}{\Rightarrow}} w \qquad \text{and} \qquad S \overset{n}{\underset{L}{\Rightarrow}} \alpha \overset{*}{\underset{L}{\Rightarrow}} wu \tag{11.4.1}$$

for some $\alpha \in V^*$. On the other hand, if $n' < n$, we have

$$S \overset{n'}{\underset{L}{\Rightarrow}} \alpha \overset{*}{\underset{L}{\Rightarrow}} w \qquad \text{and} \qquad S \overset{n'}{\underset{L}{\Rightarrow}} wu. \tag{11.4.2}$$

In either case, for any k, $0 \leqslant k < \lg(\alpha)$, ${}^{(k)}\alpha = {}^{(k)}w$ implies ${}^{(k+1)}\alpha \equiv {}^{(k+1)}w$, by Lemma 11.4.1. Moreover,

$${}^{(k+1)}\alpha = {}^{(k+1)}w$$

since any terminal prefix of α is (by the definition of $\Rightarrow_L$) a prefix of wu in (11.4.1) or of w in (11.4.2). But this shows that $\alpha = w$, and so $u = \Lambda$. □

Corollary If L is a strict deterministic language, then either $L = \{\Lambda\}$ or $\Lambda \notin L$.

The following result will often be applied in the sequel.

Theorem 11.4.3 Let $G = (V, \Sigma, P, S)$ be a reduced strict deterministic grammar. Then, for any $A, B \in N$ and $\alpha \in V^*$,

$$A \Rightarrow^+ B\alpha \quad \text{implies} \quad A \not\equiv B.$$

Proof Let G be as in the theorem and let $A \Rightarrow^+ B\alpha$ for some $A, B \in N$ and $\alpha \in V^*$. Then, for some $\alpha' \in V^*$ and $n \geqslant 1$, we have

$$A \overset{n}{\underset{L}{\Rightarrow}} B\alpha'.$$

Assume, for the sake of contradiction, that $A \equiv B$. Then, by Lemma 11.4.1, for any $A' \in [A]$, $A' \overset{n}{\underset{L}{\Rightarrow}} \beta$ implies ${}^{(1)}\beta \in [A]$, and we obtain, for arbitrarily large $k \geqslant 1$, a derivation

$$A \overset{kn}{\underset{L}{\Rightarrow}} \beta_k \qquad \text{where } \beta_k \in NV^*. \tag{11.4.3}$$

By the fact that G is reduced also

$$A \Rightarrow_L^m w \qquad \text{where } w \in \Sigma^* \text{ and } m \geqslant 1. \tag{11.4.4}$$

Applying Lemma 11.4.1 to (11.4.4) (and using the definition of $\Rightarrow_L$), we obtain that

$$\text{for any } m' \geqslant m \quad \text{and} \quad \gamma \in V^*, \quad A \Rightarrow_L^{m} \gamma \quad \text{implies } \gamma \in \Sigma V^* \quad \text{or } \gamma = \Lambda,$$

which contradicts (11.4.3). □

Corollary No reduced strict deterministic grammar is left recursive (i.e., for no $A \in N$ and $\alpha \in V^*$, does $A \Rightarrow^+ A\alpha$).

We shall now prove a useful grammatical normal-form result. Other results of this type are left for the exercises. The technique used in the proof is very instructive.

Theorem 11.4.4 Any strict deterministic grammar is equivalent to a strict deterministic grammar in Greibach normal form.

Proof Let $G = (V, \Sigma, P, S)$ be a context-free grammar with strict partition π. If $L(G) = \{\Lambda\}$, we take the grammar with the only production $S \to \Lambda$ and the result is immediate. Assume, now, that $L(G) \neq \{\Lambda\}$ and that G is reduced and Λ-free. There is no loss of generality in this assumption by Theorem 11.4.1 and Problem 3 at the end of the section. Moreover, we may assume that G is in canonical two form by Problem 5.

We shall fix our attention upon the leftmost derivations in G; the main idea of the proof is based on Lemma 11.4.1. First, we need the following auxiliary result.

Claim 1 For any $A \in N$, there is a unique integer $n_A \geqslant 1$ such that for any $\alpha \in V^*$,

$$A \Rightarrow_L^{n_A - 1} \alpha \quad \text{implies} \quad \alpha \in NV^* \tag{11.4.5}$$

and

$$A \Rightarrow_L^{n_A} \alpha \quad \text{implies} \quad \alpha \in \Sigma V^*. \tag{11.4.6}$$

Moreover, for any $A, A' \in N$,

$$A \equiv A' \quad \text{implies} \quad n_A = n_{A'}. \tag{11.4.7}$$

Proof of the claim Let $A \in N$. By the fact that G is reduced and Λ-free, we can find an integer $n \geqslant 1$ such that $A \Rightarrow_L^n \alpha$ for some $\alpha \in \Sigma V^*$; and with the property that for any $\beta \in V^*$, $A \Rightarrow_L^{n-1} \beta$ implies $\beta \in NV^*$ (it is enough to find a shortest leftmost derivation from A producing a string in ΣV^*). Denote $n_A = n$. We have already established (11.4.5). To prove (11.4.6), assume that $A \Rightarrow_L^{n_A} \alpha'$ for some arbitrary $\alpha' \in V^*$. By Lemma 11.4.1, we have immediately ${}^{(1)}\alpha \equiv {}^{(1)}\alpha'$ (note that $\alpha' \neq \Lambda$), and hence ${}^{(1)}\alpha' \in \Sigma$. This shows (11.4.6).

Now, let $A' \in N$, $A' \equiv A$, and assume that $n_{A'}$ satisfies (11.4.5) and (11.4.6) for A'. Assume, without loss of generality, that $n_{A'} \geqslant n_A$. Then we have $A \Rightarrow_L^{n_A} \alpha$ and $A' \Rightarrow_L^{n_A} \alpha' \Rightarrow_L^{k} \alpha''$, where $k = n_{A'} - n_A$ and $\alpha, \alpha', \alpha'' \in V^*$. By Lemma 11.4.1, then, ${}^{(1)}\alpha \equiv {}^{(1)}\alpha'$ and thus $\alpha' \in \Sigma V^*$. Hence, $n_{A'} \leqslant n_A$ and we conclude that $n_A = n_{A'}$. We have (11.4.7). The uniqueness of n_A for a given $A \in N$ is a consequence of (11.4.7), taking $A' = A$. This completes the proof of Claim 1.

We define the following finite relation $\hat{P} \subseteq N \times V^*$,

$$\hat{P} = \{(A, \alpha) | \ A \in N, \alpha \in V^* \text{ and } A \Rightarrow^{n_A} \alpha\}.$$

By Claim 1, $(A, \alpha) \in \hat{P}$ implies $\alpha \in \Sigma V^*$.

Let us now define a new grammar G' as follows:

$$G' = (V, \Sigma, \hat{P}, S).$$

Since $\hat{P}$ is finite, G' is well defined. Also, by (11.4.6), $A \to \alpha$ in G' implies $\alpha \in \Sigma V^*$ and therefore G' is in Greibach normal form.

Claim 2 $L(G') = L(G)$.

Proof of the claim We have $\hat{P} \subseteq \Rightarrow^*_{L,G} \subseteq \Rightarrow^*_G$ and therefore any G'-derivation is a G-derivation. Thus, for any $w \in \Sigma^*$, $S \Rightarrow^*_{G'} w$ implies $S \Rightarrow^*_G w$. Hence, $L(G') \subseteq L(G)$. For the converse, we note that any derivation of the form

$$S \Rightarrow^*_{L,G} w \tag{11.4.8}$$

where $w \in \Sigma^*$, can be written as a composition of one or more derivations of the form

$$uA\beta \Rightarrow^{n_A}_{L,G} u\alpha\beta \tag{11.4.9}$$

where $u \in \Sigma^*$, $A \in N$, $\alpha \in \Sigma V^*$ and $\beta \in V^*$. Here $(A, \alpha) \in \hat{P}$ and thus (11.4.9) can be written as $uA\beta \Rightarrow_{G'} u\alpha\beta$. Thus (11.4.8) implies $S \Rightarrow^*_{G'} w$. Hence $L(G) \subseteq L(G')$ and the claim is proved.

Claim 3 G' is strict deterministic.

Proof of the claim We shall show that the partition π which is strict for G is also strict for G'. But this is simple since the statement of Lemma 11.4.1 can be converted to the second condition of strictness (in Definition 11.4.1) by taking $n = n_A = n_{A'}$ and replacing $\Rightarrow^n_L$ by $\to_{G'}$. This proves Claim 3. □

PROBLEMS

1 Show that any strict deterministic language is unambiguous.

2 Show that there are strict deterministic grammars that do not have maximal strict partitions. Thus the family of strict partitions on a grammar forms a semilattice but not a lattice.

3 We know, from the Corollary to Theorem 11.4.2, that either a strict deterministic language L has the property that $L = \{\Lambda\}$ or $\Lambda \notin L$. Prove the following result.

Theorem Let G be a strict deterministic grammar. Then either $L(G) = \{\Lambda\}$ or there exists an equivalent Λ-free strict deterministic grammar G'.

You may find it more convenient not to use the standard construction.

4 Prove the following result. (Cf. Section 4.5.)

Theorem Every strict deterministic grammar G is equivalent to an invertible strict deterministic grammar G'.

5 Prove the following result. (Cf. Section 4.4)

Theorem Any strict deterministic grammar is equivalent to a strict deterministic grammar in canonical two form.

6 Can you extend Problem 5 to use Chomsky normal form as opposed to canonical two form?

7 Show that there is an algorithm to decide whether or not a given deterministic context-free language is prefix-free.

11.5 DETERMINISTIC PUSHDOWN AUTOMATA AND THEIR RELATION TO STRICT DETERMINISTIC LANGUAGES

In this section, we reconsider dpda's and note some different ways in which they may accept languages. This will give us some characterizations of strict deterministic languages.

Definition Let $A = (Q, \Sigma, \Gamma, \delta, q_0, Z_0, F)$ be a dpda and, for a given $K \subseteq \Gamma^*$, define the language $T(A, K) \subseteq \Sigma^*$ as follows:

$$T(A,K) = \{w \in \Sigma^* \mid (q_0, w, Z_0) \overset{*}{\vdash} (q, \Lambda, \alpha) \quad \text{for some } q \in F \text{ and } \alpha \in K\}.$$

In particular, let

$$T_0(A) = T(A, \Gamma^*),$$

$$T_1(A) = T(A, \Gamma),$$

and

$$T_2(A) = T(A, \Lambda).$$

We shall use these definitions to define three families of languages.

Definition We define the following three families of languages for $i = 0,1,2$:

$$\Delta_i = \{T_i(A) \mid A \text{ is a dpda}\}.$$

Δ_0 is our family of deterministic context-free languages. Note that Δ_2 does not even contain all regular events but only the prefix-free ones.

The family Δ_1 contains all regular languages. It can be shown that Δ_1 is a subfamily of the closure of Δ_2 under the Kleene operations.

First some simple facts about these families will be established.

Theorem 11.5.1

1 Every language in Δ_2 is prefix-free.

2 $\Delta_2 \subseteq \Delta_1 \subseteq \Delta_0$.

3 All inclusions in (2) are proper.

Proof Part (1) is an immediate consequence of the definition of $T_2(A)$, since if

$$(q_0, x, Z_0) \overset{*}{\vdash} (q, \Lambda, \Lambda),$$

then

$$(q_0, xy, Z_0) \overset{*}{\vdash} (q, y, \Lambda) \overset{*}{\vdash} (q', \Lambda, \Lambda)$$

is possible only if $y = \Lambda$ (and $q' = q$).

To prove $\Delta_2 \subseteq \Delta_1$, let $L \in \Delta_2$ and let $A = (Q, \Sigma, \Gamma, \delta, q_0, Z_0, F)$ be a dpda such that $L = T_2(A)$. We shall construct another dpda A' with the same behavior as A except that A' will have an additional initial pushdown letter Z'_0, which is never overwritten. Formally, let

$$A' = (Q \cup \{q'_0\}, \Sigma, \Gamma \cup \{Z'_0\}, \delta', q'_0, Z'_0, F),$$

where $q'_0 \notin Q, Z'_0 \notin \Gamma$, and

$$\delta'(q, a, Z) = \begin{cases} \delta(q, a, Z) & \text{if } q \in Q, a \in \Sigma_\Lambda, \text{ and } Z \in \Gamma; \\ (q_0, Z'_0 Z_0) & \text{if } q = q'_0, a = \Lambda, \text{ and } Z = Z'_0; \\ \text{undefined otherwise.} \end{cases}$$

Now, for any $x \in \Sigma^*$, first $(q'_0, x, Z'_0) \underset{A'}{\vdash} (q_0, x, Z'_0 Z_0)$; and afterwards, for any $q \in F$,

$$(q_0, x, Z'_0 Z_0) \overset{*}{\underset{A'}{\vdash}} (q, \Lambda, Z'_0) \quad \text{if and only if} \quad (q_0, x, Z_0) \overset{*}{\underset{A}{\vdash}} (q, \Lambda, \Lambda).$$

Since $q \in F$ implies that $q \neq q_0$, we have $\delta'(q, \Lambda, Z'_0) = \emptyset$, and therefore $x \in T_1(A')$ if and only if $x \in T_2(A)$. Hence, $L = T_1(A')$.

Next, we wish to show $\Delta_1 \subseteq \Delta_0$. It should be clear to the reader why a construction is necessary. Let $L \in \Delta_1$ and let $A = (Q, \Sigma, \Gamma, \delta, q_0, Z_0, F)$ be a dpda such that $L = T_1(A)$. We shall construct another dpda A' which possesses a special copy of each letter in Γ, to be able to distinguish the bottom of the store. A' simulates A but accepts only with a single letter on the store. Formally, let

$$A' = (Q', \Sigma, \Gamma', \delta', q_0, \bar{Z}_0, \bar{F}),$$

where

$$\bar{F} = \{\bar{q} \mid q \in F\},$$

$$Q' = Q \cup \bar{F},$$

$$\bar{\Gamma} = \{\bar{Z} \mid Z \in \Gamma\},$$

$$\Gamma' = \Gamma \cup \bar{\Gamma}.$$

δ' is defined by cases.

CASE 1. For each $q \in Q, Z \in \Gamma$, and $a \in \Sigma \cup \{\Lambda\}$,

$$\delta'(q, a, Z) = \delta(q, a, Z).$$

CASE 2. For each $\bar{q} \in \bar{F}, Z \in \Gamma$, and $a \in \Sigma \cup \{\Lambda\}$,

$$\delta'(\bar{q}, a, Z) = \delta(q, a, Z).$$

CASE 3. If $\delta(q, a, Z) = (q', Y\alpha)$ with $Y \in \Gamma, q \in Q - F$, then

$$\delta'(q, a, \bar{Z}) = (q', \bar{Y}\alpha).$$

CASE 4. If $\delta(q, a, Z) = (q', Y\alpha)$ with $Y \in \Gamma$ and $\bar{q} \in \bar{F}$, then

$$\delta'(\bar{q}, a, \bar{Z}) = (q', \bar{Y}\alpha).$$

CASE 5. If $q \in F$, then

$$\delta(q, \Lambda, \bar{Z}) = (\bar{q}, \bar{Z}).$$

It is easy to see that, for every $x \in \Sigma^*$,

$$(q_0, x, \bar{Z}_0) \overset{*}{\underset{A'}{\vdash}} (q, x, \bar{Z}\alpha)$$

if and only if

$$(q_0, x, Z_0) \overset{*}{\underset{A}{\vdash}} (q, \Lambda, Z\alpha).$$

Thus, $x \in T_1(A)$ if and only if $\alpha = \Lambda$ and $q \in F$. In turn, this holds if and only if

$$(q, \Lambda, Z\alpha) \overset{*}{\underset{A'}{\vdash}} (\bar{q}, \Lambda, \bar{Z}).$$

But this holds if and only if $x \in T_0(A')$. Therefore, $L = T_0(A')$.

To show that $\Delta_2 \neq \Delta_1$, let $L_1 = \{a\}^*$. L_1 is not prefix-free and hence L is not in Δ_2. It is clear that $L_1 = T_1(A)$, where

$$A = (\{q_0\}, \{a\}, \{Z_0\}, \delta, q_0, Z_0, \{q_0\}) \qquad \text{and} \qquad \delta(q_0, a, Z_0) = (q_0, Z_0).$$

To show $\Delta_1 \neq \Delta_0$, let

$$L_2 = \{a^n b^n \mid n \geqslant 1\} \cup a^*.$$

First, $L_2 = T_0(A)$, where $A = (Q, \Sigma, \Gamma, \delta, q_0, Z_0, F)$ is a dpda with $Q = \{q_0, q_1\}$, $\Sigma = \{a, b\}$, $\Gamma = \{Z_0, Z_1, Z_2\}$, $F = \{q_0\}$, and

$$\delta(q_0, a, Z) = \begin{cases} (q_0, Z_1) & \text{if } Z = Z_0; \\ (q_0, ZZ_2) & \text{if } Z \neq Z_0; \end{cases}$$

and for any $q \in Q$,

$$\delta(q, b, Z) = \begin{cases} (q_0, \Lambda) & \text{if } Z = Z_1; \\ (q_1, \Lambda) & \text{if } Z = Z_2; \\ \text{undefined} & \text{if } Z = Z_0. \end{cases}$$

Second, assume that $L_2 = T_1(A)$ for some dpda A. Since there are only a finite number of accepting configurations (q, Λ, Z) where $q \in F$ and $Z \in \Gamma$, there is a sufficiently large n such that, for some $k < n$,

$$(q_0, a^n, Z_0) \overset{*}{\vdash} (q, \Lambda, Z)$$

and

$$(q_0, a^k, Z_0) \overset{*}{\vdash} (q, \Lambda, Z),$$

where $q \in F$ and $Z \in \Gamma$. But, since, for some $q' \in F$ and $Z' \in \Gamma$,

$$(q_0, a^n b^n, Z_0) \overset{*}{\vdash} (q, b^n, Z) \overset{*}{\vdash} (q', \Lambda, Z'),$$

we also have

$$(q_0, a^k b^n, Z_0) \overset{*}{\vdash} (q, b^n, Z) \overset{*}{\vdash} (q', \Lambda, Z'),$$

and hence $a^k b^n \in L_2$, which is a contradiction since $k < n$. Therefore $L_2 \notin \Delta_1$. □

Our next result is quite simple but informative.

Theorem 11.5.2 $L \in \Delta_2$ if and only if L is prefix-free and $L \in \Delta_0$.

Thus Δ_2 coincides with the family of prefix-free deterministic languages.

Proof The *only if* direction is immediate from Theorem 11.5.1.

For the *if* direction, let $L \in \Delta_0$ and let $A = (Q, \Sigma, \Gamma, \delta, q_0, Z_0, F)$ be a dpda such that $L = T_0(A)$. We can construct another dpda A' which simulates A and erases all its store after A accepts. If L is prefix-free then $L = T_2(A')$.

Formally, let

$$A' = (Q \cup \{q_f\}, \Sigma, \Gamma \cup \{Y_0\}, \delta', q_0, Y_0, \{q_f\})$$

where $q_f \notin Q$ and $Y_0 \notin \Gamma$. δ' is defined as follows:

1 For each $q \in Q - F$ and $Z \in \Gamma$,

$$\delta'(q, a, Z) = \delta(q, a, Z).$$

2 For each $q \in F \cup \{q_f\}$ and $Z \in \Gamma \cup \{Y_0\}$,

$$\delta'(q, \Lambda, Z) = (q_f, \Lambda).$$

3 $\delta'(q_0, \Lambda, Y_0) = (q_0, Y_0 Z)$.

Assume that L is prefix-free. If

$$(q_0, xy, Z_0) \overset{*}{\underset{A}{\vdash}} (q, y, \alpha) \overset{*}{\underset{A}{\vdash}} (q', \Lambda, \alpha'),$$

then $q' \in F$ implies $q \notin F$ or $y = \Lambda$. Therefore, for any $x \in \Sigma^*$ and $q \in F$,

$$(q_0, x, Z_0) \overset{*}{\underset{A}{\vdash}} (q, \Lambda, \alpha) \quad \text{if and only if} \quad (q_0, x, Y_0 Z_0) \overset{*}{\underset{A'}{\vdash}} (q, \Lambda, Y_0 \alpha) \overset{*}{\underset{A'}{\vdash}} (q_f, \Lambda, \Lambda),$$

and thus $x \in T_0(A)$ if and only if $x \in T_2(A')$. Hence, $L \in \Delta_2$. □

We now begin the long argument to show that every language in Δ_2 is strict deterministic. Our first lemma puts a dpda into a more convenient form.

Lemma 11.5.1 Let $L \in \Delta_2$. Then $L = T_2(\hat{A})$ for some dpda $\hat{A}$ with a single final state.

Proof Assume $L = T_2(A)$ for some dpda $A = (Q, \Sigma, \Gamma, \delta, q_0, Z_0, F)$. Using a similar construction as in the proof that $\Delta_1 \subseteq \Delta_0$ in Theorem 11.5.1, we construct another dpda $\hat{A}$ which can distinguish the bottom of the store. Otherwise, it simulates A except that if A erases its store and accepts, $\hat{A}$ does the same by entering the single final state.

Formally, let

$$\hat{A} = (Q, \Sigma, \Gamma', \delta', q_0, \bar{Z}_0, \{q_f\})$$

where $\Gamma' = \Gamma \cup \bar{\Gamma} = \{Z, \bar{Z} \mid Z \in \Gamma\}$ and $q_f \in F$ is chosen arbitrarily. δ' is defined by cases. For each $q \in Q, a \in \Sigma$, and $Z \in \Gamma$,

CASE 1. $\delta'(q, a, Z) = \delta(q, a, Z)$;

$$\text{CASE 2. } \delta'(q, a, \bar{Z}) = \begin{cases} (q', \bar{Z}'\gamma) & \text{if } \delta(q, a, Z) = (q', Z'\gamma); \\ (q_f, \Lambda) & \text{if } \delta(q, a, Z) = (q', \Lambda) \text{ and } q' \in F; \\ \text{undefined otherwise.} \end{cases}$$

Now, for any $w \in \Sigma^*$,

$$\begin{aligned} w \in T_2(A') \quad & \text{if and only if} \quad (q_0, w, \bar{Z}_0) \overset{*}{\underset{A'}{\vdash}} (q, a, \bar{Z}) \underset{A'}{\vdash} (q_f, \Lambda, \Lambda) \\ & \qquad\qquad \text{for some } a \in \Sigma_\Lambda, Z \in \Gamma, \text{ and } q \in Q, \\ & \text{if and only if} \quad (q_0, w, Z_0) \overset{*}{\underset{A}{\vdash}} (q, a, Z) \underset{A}{\vdash} (q', \Lambda, \Lambda) \\ & \qquad\qquad \text{for some } q' \in F, \\ & \text{if and only if} \quad w \in T_2(A). \end{aligned}$$

□

The next phase in our proof is to pass from $\hat{A}$ to a grammar which generates the same set. We shall employ the standard construction used in Section 5.4. The reader should review that construction. We shall refer to the canonical grammar of $\hat{A}$ denoted by $G_{\hat{A}}$ as defined there.

Lemma 11.5.2 For any dpda $\hat{A}$ with a single final state, the canonical grammar $G_{\hat{A}}$ is strict deterministic.

Proof Let $G_{\hat{A}}$ be the canonical grammar as given in Theorem 5.4.3 for a given dpda $\hat{A}$ (with a single final state). Define an equivalence relation $\equiv$ on V such that:

$$\begin{aligned} A \equiv B \quad \text{if and only if} \quad & A, B \in \Sigma \text{ or } A = (q, Z, q') \\ & B = (q, Z, q'') \text{ for some } q, q', q'' \in Q, Z \in \Gamma. \end{aligned}$$

Let $\pi = V/\equiv$. Obviously, $\Sigma \in \pi$. Let

$$A = (q, Z, q') \rightarrow a\gamma = \alpha\beta$$

$$A' = (q, Z, q'') \rightarrow a'\gamma' = \alpha\beta'$$

where $a, a' \in \Sigma \cup \{\Lambda\}, \gamma, \gamma' \in (V - \Sigma)^*$. Let us make the following three observations.

Observation 1. Either $a = a' = \Lambda$ or both $a, a' \in \Sigma$.

Observation 2. If $a = a'$, then either $\gamma = \gamma' = \Lambda$ and $q' = q''$, or we have

$$\gamma = (p, Z_1, q_1)(q_1, Z_2, q_2) \cdots (q_{k-1}, Z_k, q')$$

$$\gamma' = (p, Z_1, q_1')(q_1', Z_2, q_2') \cdots (q_{k-1}', Z_k, q'')$$

for some $p, q_i, q_i' \in Q$, $Z_i \in \Gamma$, and $k \geq 1$. In either case, $\lg(\gamma) = \lg(\gamma')$. (This observation is a consequence of the construction and of the fact that δ is single-valued.)

Observation 3. Either $\beta = \beta' = \Lambda$ or $\beta, \beta' \neq \Lambda$.

Assume that $\beta = \Lambda$ but $\beta' \neq \Lambda$. Then $\alpha = \alpha\beta = a\gamma$ and $a'\gamma' = \alpha\beta' = a\gamma\beta'$. Thus $a' = a$ and, by Observation 2, $\lg(\gamma) = \lg(\gamma')$. But now $\lg(\alpha) = \lg(\alpha\beta')$, which contradicts that $\beta' \neq \Lambda$.

To prove the strictness of π, assume first that $\beta \neq \Lambda$. Then, by the last observation, $\beta' \neq \Lambda$.

CASE 1. $\alpha = \Lambda$ and $a \in \Sigma$. Then $a' \in \Sigma$ by Observation 1 and both ${}^{(1)}\beta$, ${}^{(1)}\beta' \in \Sigma$. Hence, ${}^{(1)}\beta \equiv {}^{(1)}\beta'$.

CASE 2. $\alpha = a \in \Sigma_\Lambda$. Then $a' = \alpha = a$ and, by Observation 2 (note that $\gamma \neq \Lambda$), we have ${}^{(1)}\beta = (p, Z_1, q_1) \equiv (p, Z_1, q_1') = {}^{(1)}\beta'$.

CASE 3. $\alpha \in \Sigma_\Lambda N^+$. Then again $a = a'$ and, by Observation 2, $\alpha^{(1)} = (q_{i-1}, Z_i, q_i) = (q_{i-1}, Z_i, q_i')$ for some i, $1 \leq i < k$. Thus $q_i = q_i'$ and ${}^{(1)}\beta = (q_i, Z_{i+1}, q_{i+1}) \equiv (q_i, Z_{i+1}, q_{i+1}') = {}^{(1)}\beta'$.

Now, assume that $\beta = \Lambda$ and thus $\beta' = \Lambda$. Then $a = a'$ and $\gamma = \gamma'$. By Observation 2, $q' = q''$. Hence, $A = A'$. □

We already know that

$$L(G_{\hat{A}}) = T_2(\hat{A})$$

from the proof of Theorem 5.4.3.

We now have half of our characterization theorem.

Theorem 11.5.3 Δ_2 is a subfamily of the family of all strict deterministic languages.

Proof Let $L \in \Delta_2$. Then $L = T_2(A)$ for some dpda A. Then, by Lemma 11.5.1, $L = T_2(\hat{A})$ for some dpda $\hat{A}$ with a single final state. Now the canonical grammar $G_{\hat{A}}$ is strict deterministic by Lemma 11.5.2 and $L = L(G_{\hat{A}})$. Thus L is a strict deterministic language. □

Now we turn to a proof of the converse. Although the construction we are about to give could be simplified in some ways, it has the advantage that its state set is in a natural correspondence with the strict partition of the grammar. This correspondence will be exploited later.

First we introduce certain notational conventions which will simplify our formalism.

Definition For any strict partition π on a given context-free grammar $G = (V, \Sigma, P, S)$, define the *size* of π as

$$\|\pi\| = \max_{V_i \in \pi - \{\Sigma\}} |V_i|.$$

Thus $\|\pi\|$ is the cardinality of the largest non-Σ block of π.

For our proof, let $G = (V, \Sigma, P, S)$ be a grammar with the strict partition

$$\pi = \{\Sigma, V_0, V_1, \ldots, V_m\}, \tag{11.5.1}$$

where $m \geqslant 0$ and $V_0 = [S]$. We use special indexed symbols A_{ij} for the nonterminals of G, so that, for all i $(0 \leqslant i \leqslant m)$, we have

$$V_i = \{A_{i0}, A_{i1}, \ldots, A_{in_i}\}, \tag{11.5.2}$$

where $n_i = |V_i| - 1$. (Note that $\max_i n_i = \|\pi\|$.) Moreover, let $A_{00} = S$.

Definition Let $G = (V, \Sigma, P, S)$ be a grammar with strict partition π for which we use the notation from (11.5.1) and (11.5.2). We define the *canonical dpda A_G for G* as follows:

$$A_G = (Q, \Sigma, \Gamma, \delta, q_0, Z_0, \{q_0\}), \tag{11.5.3}$$

where

$Q = \{q_j \mid 0 \leqslant j < \|\pi\|\}$,

$\Gamma = \Gamma_1 \cup \Gamma_2$,

$\Gamma_1 = \{(V_i, \alpha) \mid A \to \alpha\beta$ is in P for some $A \in V_i, \alpha, \beta \in V^*\}$,

$\Gamma_2 = \{(V_i, \alpha, V_j) \mid A \to \alpha B\beta$ is in P for some $A \in V_i, B \in V_j$, and $\alpha, \beta \in V^*\}$,

$Z_0 = ([S], \Lambda) = (V_0, \Lambda)$,

and δ is defined by means of four types of moves, as follows. For any $V_i, V_k \in \pi - \{\Sigma\}$, $\alpha \in V^*, a \in \Sigma$, and $q_j \in Q$, we have:

TYPE 1. $\delta(q_0, \Lambda, (V_i, \alpha)) = (q_0, (V_i, \alpha, V_k)(V_k, \Lambda))$ if $A \to \alpha B\beta$ is in P for some $A \in V_i, B \in V_k$, and $\beta \in V^*$;

TYPE 2. $\delta(q_0, a, (V_i, \alpha)) = (q_0, (V_i, \alpha a))$ if $A \to \alpha a\beta$ is in P for some $A \in V_i$ and $\beta \in V^*$;

TYPE 3. $\delta(q_0, \Lambda, (V_i, \alpha)) = (q_j, \Lambda)$ if $A_{ij} \to \alpha$ is in P;

TYPE 4. $\delta(q_j, \Lambda, (V_k, \alpha, V_i)) = (q_0, (V_k, \alpha A_{ij}))$.

Otherwise δ is not defined. Moves of Types 1, 2, and 3 are called *detection moves*; a move of Type 4 is called a *reduction move.*

First we have to verify that our definition is correct.

Lemma 11.5.3 For any strict deterministic grammar G, the object A_G is a well-defined dpda.

Proof We have to show that δ is single-valued and is deterministic. Assume that we have the following two moves:

$$\begin{array}{ccc} (q, a, Z) & & (q, a', Z) \\ \big\downarrow \delta & & \big\downarrow \delta \\ (p, \alpha) & \neq & (p', \alpha') \end{array} \tag{11.5.4}$$

We shall show that $a \neq a'$ (hence the single-valuedness) and, moreover, $a, a' \in \Sigma$.

CASE 1. Both moves in (11.5.4) are of the same type in the terminology of the definition of A_G. Then either $a = a' = \Lambda$ or $a, a' \in \Sigma$. Suppose $a = a'$. Then we obtain $(p, \alpha) = (p', \alpha')$ immediately for Types 2 and 4 or using the strictness of π for Types 1 and 3. Hence $a \neq a'$ and $a, a' \in \Sigma$.

CASE 2. The two moves in (11.5.4) are of different types. Then neither of them is Type 4 since that is the only type with $Z \in \Gamma_2$. Assume therefore that $q = q_0$, $Z = (V_i, \alpha)$. Now moves of Types 1 and 2 are incompatible since $B \equiv a$ is not possible for $B \in N$ and $a \in \Sigma$, and neither Type 1 nor Type 2 is compatible with Type 3 since $A \equiv A'$, $A \to \alpha\beta$, and $A' \to \alpha$ in P imply $\beta = \Lambda$ by the strictness of π. Hence, $a \neq a'$. □

The following result is intuitively obvious but the formal proof is rather lengthy.

Lemma 11.5.4 Let A_G be the canonical dpda for a strict deterministic grammar G. Then $T_2(A_G) = L(G)$.

Proof Let us partition the yield relation $\vdash$ in accordance with the four possible moves in the definition of A_G.

$$(q, aw, \gamma Z) \underset{i}{\vdash} (q', w, \gamma\alpha) \tag{11.5.5}$$

if and only if $\delta(q, a, Z) = (q', \alpha)$ is a move of type i, $i = 1, 2, 3, 4$.

Thus $\vdash = \bigcup_{i=1}^{4} \underset{i}{\vdash}$. Moreover, let us define

$$\models \; = (\underset{1}{\vdash} \cup \underset{2}{\vdash})^* \underset{3}{\vdash}. \tag{11.5.6}$$

(Intuitively, if we interpret A_G as a parsing algorithm, $\models$ is the *detection phase* and $\underset{4}{\vdash}$ the *reduction phase* of the algorithm.)

Let $\mathcal{Q}$ be the set of configurations of A_G and define two sets $\mathcal{Q}_d$, $\mathcal{Q}_r \subseteq \mathcal{Q}$ as follows:

$$\mathcal{Q}_d = Q \times \Sigma^* \times \Gamma_2^* \Gamma_1,$$

$$\mathcal{Q}_r = Q \times \Sigma^* \times \Gamma_2^*.$$

Using the definition of A_G, we can interpret relations $\underset{i}{\vdash}$ as partial functions ($\vdash$ is single-valued) as follows:

$$\begin{array}{ccc} \mathcal{Q}_d & \xrightarrow[p]{\underset{1}{\vdash},\underset{2}{\vdash}} & \mathcal{Q}_d \\ & {\scriptstyle \underset{4}{\vdash}\ \nwarrow p} \qquad {\scriptstyle p \swarrow\ \underset{3}{\vdash}} & \\ & \mathcal{Q}_r & \end{array} \tag{11.5.7}$$

Now (11.5.6) and (11.5.7) imply:

$$\mathcal{Q}_d \xrightarrow[p]{(\models \underset{4}{\vdash})^* \models} \mathcal{Q}_r$$

We have the following.

Fact If $c_1 \in \mathscr{C}_d$ and $c_2 \in \mathscr{C}_r$, then

$$c_1 \overset{*}{\vdash} c_2 \quad \text{implies} \quad c_1 (\models \vdash_4)^* \models c_2. \tag{11.5.8}$$

Further, we will need the following claim about the contents of the store of A_G.

Claim 1 For any (q, w, γ), $(q', w', \gamma') \in \mathscr{C}_r$ (that is, $\gamma, \gamma' \in \Gamma_2^*$), if $(q, w, \gamma) \overset{+}{\vdash} (q', w', \gamma')$, then γ is not a prefix of γ'.

Proof of the claim The argument is an induction on the length of γ. (For convenience, we use the notation $\gamma \vdash \gamma'$ as an abbreviation for "$(q, w, \gamma) \vdash (q', w', \gamma')$ for some $q, q' \in Q$ and $w, w' \in \Sigma^*$.")

Basis. The case $\gamma = \Lambda$ is vacuously true, since $\vdash$ is, in this case, undefined.

Inductive step. Assume the claim proved for all γ_1 shorter than some $\gamma \in \Gamma_2^+$. Now let

$$\gamma = \gamma_1(V, \alpha, V') \overset{+}{\vdash} \gamma'$$

for some $(V, \alpha, V') \in \Gamma_2$. Then, by the definition of A_G,

$$\gamma_1(V, \alpha, \alpha V) \vdash_4 \gamma_1(V, \alpha A) \overset{*}{\vdash} \gamma' \quad \text{for some } A \in V.$$

Now αA in (V, A) cannot be changed back to α in (V, α, V') without being erased, i.e., without an application of a move of Type 3. Hence, a necessary condition for γ being a prefix of γ' is

$$\gamma_1(V, a, V') \overset{*}{\vdash} \vdash_3 \gamma_1 \overset{*}{\vdash} \gamma'.$$

Since $\gamma_1 \neq \gamma'$, we have $\gamma_1 \overset{+}{\vdash} \gamma'$. By the induction hypothesis γ_1 is not a prefix of γ', and hence γ is not also. This completes the proof of Claim 1.

The following two claims are crucial in our proof.

Claim 2. Let $w \in \Sigma^*$ and $i, j \geqslant 0$. If $A_{ij} \Rightarrow^+ w$ then, for any $y \in \Sigma^*$ and $\gamma \in \Gamma_2^*$,

$$(q_0, wy, \gamma(V_i, \Lambda)) (\models \vdash_4)^* \models (q_j, y, \gamma).$$

Let $c_1 = (q_0, wy, \gamma(V_i, \Lambda))$ and $c_2 = (q_j, y, \gamma)$. Assume $A_{ij} \overset{n}{\Rightarrow} w$. The argument is an induction on $n \geqslant 1$.

Basis. $n = 1$. Then $A_{ij} \to w$ and if $w \neq \Lambda$ then for every factorization $w = w_1 a w_2$ ($w_1, w_2 \in \Sigma^*$ and $a \in \Sigma$), we have

$$(q_0, aw_2y, \gamma(V_i, w_1)) \vdash_2 (q_0, w_2y, \gamma(V_i, w_1a));$$

and in any event we subsequently have

$$(q_0, y, \gamma(V_i, w)) \vdash_3 (q_j, y, \gamma) = c_2.$$

Thus, $c_1 \overset{*}{\vdash_2} \vdash_3 c_2$ or, using (11.5.6), $c_1 \models c_2$.

Inductive step. Let $n > 1$ and assume the result proved for all $n' < n$. Let $\alpha \in V^*$ such that

$$A_{ij} \Rightarrow \alpha \Rightarrow^+ w$$

For any prefix α_1 of α, we have one of the following three cases:

CASE 1. α_1 is followed by $a \in \Sigma$; that is, $\alpha = \alpha_1 a \alpha_2$. Then, for some suffix w_2 of w we have $\alpha_2 \Rightarrow^* w_2$ and

$$(q_0, aw_2y, \gamma(V_i, \alpha_1)) \vdash_{2} (q_0, w_2y, \gamma(V_i, \alpha_1 a)).$$

CASE 2. α_1 is followed by $B \in N$; that is, $\alpha = \alpha_1 B \alpha_2$. Then, for some suffix $w_B w_2$ of w, we have $B \Rightarrow^{n'} w_B$ $(n' < n)$, $\alpha_2 \Rightarrow^* w_2$ and

$$(q_0, w_B w_2 y, \gamma(V_i, \alpha_1) \vdash_{1} (q_0, w_B w_2 y, \gamma(V_i, \alpha, [B])([B], \Lambda))$$

$$(\vDash \vdash_{4})^* \vDash (q_k, w_2 y, \gamma(V_i, \alpha_1, {}^{\cdot}[B]))$$

by the inductive hypothesis from $B \Rightarrow^{n'} w_B$ if $B = A_{ik} \in [B]$,

$$\vdash_{4} (q_0, w_2 y, \gamma(V_i, \alpha B)).$$

CASE 3. $\alpha_1 = \alpha$. Then

$$(q_0, y, \gamma(V_i, \alpha)) \vdash_{3} (q_j, y, \gamma) = c_2.$$

Now starting with configuration c_1, that is, $\alpha_1 = \Lambda$, we can combine Cases 1 and 2 depending on the form of $\alpha \in (\Sigma \cup N)^*$, until we finish with Case 3 in which $\alpha_1 = \alpha$. Therefore,

$$c_1 (\vdash_{2} \cup \vdash_{1} (\vDash \vdash_{4})^* \vDash \vdash_{4})^* \vdash_{3} c_2;$$

hence,

$$c_1 (\overset{*}{\vdash_{2}} \vdash_{1} (\vDash \vdash_{4})^* \vDash \vdash_{4})^* \overset{*}{\vdash_{2}} \vdash_{3} c_2$$

using the identity $(\rho \cup \sigma)^* = (\rho^* \sigma)^* \rho^*$ (cf. Problem 2); hence,

$$c_1 (\vDash \vdash_{4} (\vDash \vdash_{4})^*)^* \vDash c_2,$$

using (11.5.6) and the identity $\rho^* \rho = \rho \rho^*$; hence,

$$c_1 (\vDash \vdash_{4})^* \vDash c_2,$$

using the identity $(\rho\rho^*)^* = \rho^{**} = \rho^*$. This proves Claim 2.

Our last claim is essentially the converse of Claim 2.

Claim 3 Let $w, y \in \Sigma^*$, $\gamma \in \Gamma_2^*$ and $i, j \geqslant 0$. If

$$(q_0, wy, \gamma(V_i, \Lambda)) \overset{*}{\vdash} (q_j, y, \gamma) \text{ then } A_{ij} \Rightarrow^+ w.$$

Again, let $c_1 = (q_0, wy, \gamma(V_i, \Lambda))$, $c_2 = (q_j, y, \gamma)$, and let $c_1 \overset{*}{\vdash} c_2$. By (11.5.8), $c_1 (\vDash \vdash_{4})^n \vDash c_2$ for some $n \geqslant 0$. Then, by the definition of A_G and (11.5.6),

$$c_1 (\vDash \vdash_{4})^n (\vdash_{1} \cup \vdash_{2})^* c_3 \vdash_{3} c_2, \qquad (11.5.9)$$

where $c_3 = (q_0, y, \gamma(V_k, \gamma))$. First, we show that $V_k = V_i$. Indeed, if $V_k \neq V_i$, we would have (using the notation from the proof of Claim 1),

$$\gamma(V_i, \Lambda) \overset{*}{\vdash} \gamma(V_i, \beta) \vdash_3 \gamma \overset{*}{\vdash} \vdash_1 \gamma(V_k, \Lambda) \overset{*}{\vdash} \gamma(V_k, \alpha) \vdash_3 \gamma$$

for some $\beta \in V^*$ since this is the only way of replacing V_i by V_k in agreement with the definition of A_G. But here $\gamma \overset{+}{\vdash} \gamma$ is contrary to Claim 1. Therefore, $V_i = V_k$ and from $c_3 \vdash_3 c_2$ we have $A_{ij} \to \alpha$.

We proceed by induction on n in (11.5.9).

Basis. $n = 0$. Then $c_1 (\vdash_1 \cup \vdash_2)^* c_3$. Moreover, no move of Type 1 can occur (since that would increase the length of γ). Thus $c_1 \overset{*}{\vdash_2} c_3 \vdash_3 c_2$. This is possible only if all letters in α are terminal or if $c_1 = c_3$, which occurs if $\alpha = \Lambda$. Hence, $\alpha \in \Sigma^*, \alpha = w$ and $A_{ij} \to w$.

Inductive step. Let $n > 1$ and assume the result proved for all $n' < n$. From (11.5.9), the definition of A_G and $A_{ij} \to \alpha$, we conclude that, for every prefix α_1 of α, there is a unique configuration $c = (q_0, w_2 y, \gamma(V_i, \alpha_1))$ such that $c_1 \overset{*}{\vdash} c \overset{*}{\vdash} c_2$ (the uniqueness follows from Claim 1). Here w_2 is a suffix of w. Let $w = w_1 w_2$ and $w_1 \in \Sigma^*$. First we show that $\alpha_1 \Rightarrow^* w_1$ by induction on the length of α_1. This is immediate if $\alpha_1 = \Lambda \Rightarrow^* \Lambda = w_1$. Assume that $\alpha_1 \Rightarrow^* w_1$ was already proved and let $\alpha = \alpha_1 B \alpha_2$ ($B \in V$ and $\alpha_2 \in V^*$). Let us consider two configurations

$$\begin{aligned} c &= (q_0, w_2, \gamma(V_i, \alpha_1)), \\ c' &= (q_0, w_2', \gamma(V_i, \alpha_1 B)). \end{aligned}$$

There are two cases.

CASE 1. $B = a \in \Sigma$. Then, by the definition of A_G, $c \vdash_2 c'$, $w_2 = a w_2'$, and $\alpha_1 a \Rightarrow^* w_1 a$ is trivial.

CASE 2. $B \in N$. Then we have

$$\begin{aligned} c &\vdash_1 (q_0, w_2 y, \gamma(V_i, \alpha_1, [B])([B], \Lambda)) \\ &\overset{*}{\vdash} (q_k, w_2' y, \gamma(V_i, \alpha_1, [B])) \\ &\vdash_4 c' \end{aligned}$$

assuming that $B = A_{ik} \in [B]$. From (11.5.8), we see that the relation $\overset{*}{\vdash}$ can be replaced by $(\models \vdash)^{n'} \models$ for some $n' < n$. Moreover, w_2' is a suffix of w_2, say $w_2 = w_1' w_2'$. Then by the inductive hypothesis $B \Rightarrow^+ w_1'$ and therefore $\alpha_1 B \Rightarrow^+ w_1 w_1'$. This ends the inductive proof that $\alpha_1 \Rightarrow^+ w_1$.

Now, for $\alpha_1 = \alpha$ we have $A_{ij} \Rightarrow \alpha \Rightarrow^* w'$ where w' is a prefix of w. We shall show that $w' = w$. For, assume $w = w'w''$. By Claim 2, then,

$$c_1 = (q_0, w'w''y, \gamma(V_i, \Lambda)) \overset{*}{\vdash} (q_j, w''y, \gamma).$$

But then, to avoid $\gamma \overset{+}{\vdash} \gamma$, which would contradict Claim 1, we must have $(q_j, w''y, \gamma) = c_2$ and hence $w'' = \Lambda$. We conclude $A_{ij} \Rightarrow^+ w$, as asserted. This finishes the proof of Claim 3.

Now, to conclude the proof of the lemma, we combine Claims 2 and 3 and substitute $y = \gamma = \Lambda$, $i = j = 0$ (note that $S = A_{00}$ by convention). We obtain that, for any $w \in \Sigma^*$,

$$S \Rightarrow^+ w \quad \text{if and only if } (q_0, w, (V_0, \Lambda)) \overset{*}{\vdash} (q_0, \Lambda, \Lambda),$$

and therefore $w \in L(G)$ if and only if $w \in T_2(A_G)$. □

We can immediately apply the previous lemma.

Theorem 11.5.4 The family of all strict deterministic languages is a subfamily of Δ_2.

Proof The theorem is a direct consequence of the definition of a canonical dpda and of Lemmas 11.5.3 and 11.5.4. □

Now, combining Theorems 11.5.2, 11.5.3, and 11.5.4, we obtain one of our main results.

Theorem 11.5.5 The family of strict deterministic languages coincides with the family of prefix-free deterministic languages.

TABLE 11.1 Closure Properties of Δ_2, Δ_1, and Δ_0

		Δ_2	Δ_1	Δ_0
Operations with Regular Sets				
Product	LR	No	No	Yes
Intersection	$L_1 \cap R$	Yes	Yes	Yes
Quotient	LR^{-1}	No	No	Yes
Boolean Operations				
Union	$L_1 \cup L_2$	No	No	No
Intersection	$L_1 \cap L_2$	No	No	No
Complement	$\bar{L}$	No	No	Yes
Kleene Operations				
*	L^*	No	No	No
Product	$L_1 L_2$	Yes	No	No
Marked Operations				
Union	$c_1 L_1 \cup c_2 L_2$	Yes	Yes	Yes
Product	$L_1 \$ L_2$	Yes	Yes	Yes
Other Operations				
Min		Yes	Yes	Yes
Max		Yes	Yes	Yes
Reversal		No	No	No
Homomorphism		No	No	No
Inverse gsm		No	Yes	Yes

PROBLEMS

1 Consider the following equivalence relation.

Definition Let $L \subseteq \Sigma^*$ be a deterministic context-free language. We define the *relative right congruence relation induced by* L, R_L, as follows: For $x, y \in L$,

$$(x, y) \in R_L \quad \text{if and only if for all } z \in \Sigma^*,\ xz \in L \Leftrightarrow yz \in L.$$

Prove that if $L \in \Delta_1$ then R_L has finite rank. Can you prove the converse?

2 Prove the following identities for sets over Σ^* or for binary relations over a set:

a) $\rho^*\rho = \rho\rho^*$ b) $(\rho \cup \sigma)^* = (\rho^*\sigma)^*\rho^*$ c) $(\rho\rho^*)^* = \rho^{**} = \rho^*$

*3–47 Table 11.1 summarizes the closure operations for Δ_0, Δ_1, and Δ_2. Prove all entries that have not yet been done in the book.

11.6* A HIERARCHY OF STRICT DETERMINISTIC LANGUAGES

In the last section, we defined $\|\pi\|$ where π is a strict partition. We shall relate this to the number of states of a dpda accepting the language generated by such a grammar.

Theorem 11.6.1 Let L be any language and let $n \geqslant 1$. Then $L = L(G)$ for some strict deterministic grammar with partition π such that $\|\pi\| = n$ if and only if $L = T_2(A)$ for some dpda A with n states.

Proof The result is immediate in the *only if* direction from Theorem 11.5.4 and from the fact that the canonical automaton has, by definition, $\|\pi\|$ states. For the *if* direction, we first note that the construction of dpda $\hat{A}$ with $|F| = 1$ in the proof of Lemma 11.5.1, doesn't change the number of states. The rest then follows from the proof of Theorem 11.5.3, in particular, that the partition π used for proving the strict determinism of the canonical grammar has the property that $\|\pi\| = |Q|$. □

Let us recall from Section 11.4 that every strict deterministic grammar has a unique partition π_0 which is the minimal element in the semilattice of all strict partitions of G. Also, $\|\pi_0\| \leqslant \|\pi\|$ for any other strict partition G. This suggests the following definition.

Definition Let G be a strict deterministic grammar. We define the *degree of* G as the number

$$\deg(G) = \|\pi_0\|,$$

where π_0 is the minimal strict partition for G. For any language $L \in \Delta_2$, define its degree as follows:

$$\deg(L) = \min\{\deg(G) \mid G \text{ is strict deterministic and } L(G) = L\}.$$

Our next objective will be to show that strict deterministic languages form a nontrivial hierarchy with respect to their degree or, equivalently, with respect to the minimal number of states of the corresponding dpda. This result can be intuitively explained by pointing out that the main reason for having more states in a dpda is when a greater amount of information from the top part of the store has to be preserved while any letters beneath it are read. This consideration leads us to an example which will serve as a basis for the formal proof of the result.

Lemma 11.6.1 Let $\Sigma = \{a, b\}$. Define, for any $n \geqslant 1$, the language

$$L_n = \{a^m b^k a^m b^k \mid 1 \leqslant m, 1 \leqslant k \leqslant n\}.$$

Then $L_n = T_2(A)$ for some dpda A with n states.

Proof Let $A_n = (Q, \Sigma, \Gamma, \delta, q_0, Z_0, F)$ be a dpda where $Q = \{q_0, \ldots, q_{n-1}\}$. $\Gamma = \{Z_0, 0, 1, 2, 3\}, F = \{q_0\}$, and δ is defined as follows:

$$\begin{aligned}
\delta(q_0, a, Z_0) &= (q_0, 02),\\
\delta(q_0, a, 2) &= (q_0, 12),\\
\delta(q_0, b, 2) &= (q_0, 3),\\
\delta(q_i, b, 3) &= (q_{i+1}, 3) \quad \text{for } 0 \leqslant i < n-1,\\
\delta(q_i, a, 3) &= (q_i, \Lambda) \quad \text{for } 0 \leqslant i \leqslant n-1,\\
\delta(q_i, a, 1) &= (q_i, \Lambda) \quad \text{for } 0 \leqslant i \leqslant n-1,\\
\delta(q_i, b, 0) &= (q_{i-1}, 0) \quad \text{for } 0 < i \leqslant n-1,\\
\delta(q_0, b, 0) &= (q_0, \Lambda).
\end{aligned}$$

To show that $T_2(A_n) = L_n$, it is enough to observe that a computation leads to acceptance of a string $w \in \Sigma^*$ if and only if it has the following form for some $m \geqslant 1$, where $1 \leqslant k \leqslant n$:

$$\begin{aligned}
(q_0, w, Z_0) &\vdash (q_0, a^{-1}w, 02)\\
&\vdash^{m-1} (q_0, (a^m)^{-1}w, 01^{m-1}2)\\
&\vdash (q_0, (a^m b)^{-1}w, 01^{m-1}3)\\
&\vdash^{k-1} (q_{k-1}, (a^m b^k)^{-1}w, 01^{m-1}3)\\
&\vdash (q_{k-1}, (a^m b^k a)^{-1}w, 01^{m-1})\\
&\vdash^{m-1} (q_{k-1}, (a^m b^k a^m)^{-1}w, 0)\\
&\vdash^{k-1} (q_0, (a^m b^k a^m b^{k-1})^{-1}w, 0)\\
&\vdash (q_0, (a^m b^k a^m b^k)^{-1}w, \Lambda).
\end{aligned}$$

The proof is complete. □

Next we shall prove that n states are necessary for the acceptance of L_n (as defined in Lemma 11.6.1). The formal proof is by no means trivial since we have to prove this for all conceivable dpda's. First we need a lemma.

Lemma 11.6.2 Let $A = (Q, \Sigma, \Gamma, \delta, q_0, Z_0, F)$ be a loop-free dpda and let $a \in \Sigma$. Then either:

a) there exists $n_0 \geqslant 1$ such that for any $q \in Q$, $\gamma \in \Gamma^*$, and $m \geqslant 1$, if $(q_0, a^m, Z_0) \overset{*}{\vdash} (q, \Lambda, \gamma)$, then $\lg(\gamma) \leqslant n_0$ (that is, the size of the stack is bounded); or

b) there exist m_0, $f \geqslant 1$, $q \in Q$, $\gamma_0 \in \Gamma^*$, $\eta \in \Gamma^+$, and $Z \in \Gamma$ such that, for every $h \geqslant 0$,

$$(q_0, a^{m_0+hf}, Z_0) \overset{*}{\Vdash} (q, \Lambda, \gamma_0\eta^h Z) \tag{11.6.1}$$

and for any $k \geqslant 0$ and $\gamma \in \Gamma^*$,

$$(q_0, a^k, \gamma_0\eta^h Z) \overset{*}{\vdash} (q', \Lambda, \gamma) \quad \text{implies} \quad \gamma = \gamma_0\eta^h\gamma' \tag{11.6.2}$$

for some $\gamma' \in \Gamma^+$ (i.e., the stack is essentially ultimately periodic in some word η).

Proof Let us assume that (a) is not satisfied. A useful claim is established first.

Claim 1 For each $r \geqslant 1$ there exist $n_r \geqslant 1, n_{r+1} > n_r, Z_r \in \Gamma, q_r \in Q, \gamma_r \in \Gamma^*$ with $\lg(\gamma_r) \geqslant r$, such that:

$$(q_0, a^{n_r}, Z_0) \overset{*}{\Vdash} (q_r, \Lambda, \gamma_r Z_r) \tag{11.6.3}$$

and for each $s \geqslant 0$,

$$(q_r, a^s, Z_r) \overset{*}{\vdash} (p_s, \Lambda, \theta_s) \tag{11.6.4}$$

for some $p_s \in Q$ and $\theta_s \in \Gamma^*$.

Proof Suppose that Claim 1 were false. Then there exists $r \geqslant 1$ and for each s there exists a computation sequence

$$(q_{s0}, u_{s0}, \gamma_{s0}) \vdash \cdots \vdash (q_{sk_s}, u_{sk_s}, \gamma_{sk_s}), \tag{11.6.5}$$

where $q_{s0} = q_0$, $u_{s0} = a^{m_s}$, $\gamma_{s0} = Z_0$, $u_{sk_s} = \Lambda$, and $\lg(\gamma_{sk_s}) \leqslant r$. Note that, for each s, there exists an integer m_s and so there are infinitely many ID's $(q_{sk_s}, \Lambda, \gamma_{sk_s})$. But $Q \times \Gamma$ is finite, so there exist $s \neq t$ such that

$$(q_{sk_s}, \gamma_{sk_s}) = (q_{tk_t}, \gamma_{tk_t}). \tag{11.6.6}$$

CASE 1. Suppose $m_s = m_t$. There is no loss of generality in assuming that $k_s < k_t$. (If it were not so, we could switch notation.) But A is deterministic so for each $0 \leqslant i \leqslant k_s$,

$$q_{si} = q_{ti}, \qquad u_{si} = u_{ti}, \qquad \text{and} \qquad \gamma_{si} = \gamma_{ti}.$$

Then

$$\begin{array}{l} (q_{s0}, u_{s0}, \gamma_{s0}) \vdash \cdots \vdash (q_{sk_s}, u_{sk_s}, \gamma_{sk_s}) \\ \qquad \| \qquad\qquad\qquad\qquad \| \\ (q_{t0}, u_{t0}, \gamma_{t0}) \vdash \cdots \vdash (q_{tk_s}, u_{tk_s}, \gamma_{tk_s}) \vdash \cdots \vdash (q_{tk_t}, u_{tk_t}, \gamma_{tk_t}). \end{array} \tag{11.6.7}$$

Thus

$$(q_{tk_s}, \Lambda, \gamma_{tk_s}) \overset{+}{\vdash} (q_{tk_t}, \Lambda, \gamma_{tk_t}). \tag{11.6.8}$$

But from (11.6.6) and (11.6.7),

$$(q_{sk_s}, \gamma_{sk_s}) = (q_{tk_t}, \gamma_{tk_t}) = (q_{tk_s}, \gamma_{tk_s}). \tag{11.6.9}$$

Thus (11.6.8) represents an infinite Λ-loop and

$$(q_0, a^{m_s}, Z_0) \overset{*}{\Vdash} (q, \Lambda, \gamma)$$

is false for all $q \in Q$ and $\gamma \in \Gamma^*$. This proves that $m_s \neq m_t$.

CASE 2. $m_s \neq m_t$. There is no loss of generality in assuming that $m_s < m_t$. Since A is deterministic, $k_s < k_t$, and for each $0 \leqslant i \leqslant k_s$,

$$q_{si} = q_{ti}, \qquad u_{si} = u_{ti}, \qquad \text{and} \qquad \gamma_{si} = \gamma_{ti}.$$

But we have

$$\begin{array}{l} (q_{s0}, a^{m_s}, Z_0) \vdash \cdots \vdash (q_{sk_s}, \Lambda, \gamma_{sk_s}) \\ \qquad \| \qquad\qquad\qquad\qquad \| \\ (q_{t0}, a^{m_t}, Z_0) \vdash \cdots \vdash (q_{tk_s}, a^{m_t - m_s}, \gamma_{tk_s}) \overset{*}{\vdash} (q_{tk_t}, \Lambda, \gamma_{tk_t}). \end{array}$$

Thus from (11.6.9),

$$(q_{tk_t}, a^{m_t - m_s}, \gamma_{tk_t}) \overset{*}{\vdash} (q_{tk_t}, \Lambda, \gamma_{tk_t}).$$

Now let

$$n_0 = \max\{\lg(\gamma_{ti}) \mid 1 \leqslant i \leqslant k_t\} \leqslant r.$$

Thus we have a uniform bound and (a) is satisfied. This contradiction proves Claim 1.

Let $r \geqslant 1$ and let n_r, q_r, and Z_r be as in Claim 1. Since $Q \times \Gamma$ is finite, there exist $i < j$ such that $Z_i = Z_j$ and $q_i = q_j$. Since A is deterministic,

$$(q_0, a^{n_i}, Z_0) \overset{*}{\Vdash} (q_i, \Lambda, \gamma_i Z_i) \tag{11.6.10}$$

and

$$(q_0, a^{n_j}, Z_0) \overset{*}{\Vdash} (q_i, \Lambda, \gamma_i \eta Z_i)$$

for some $\eta \in \Gamma^*$. Moreover, $\eta \in \Gamma^+$, since otherwise we would be in case (a). Then,

$$(q_i, a^{n_j - n_i}, Z_i) \overset{*}{\Vdash} (q_i, \Lambda, \eta Z_i). \tag{11.6.11}$$

Now choose $m = n_i$ and $f = n_j - n_i$. For each $h \geqslant 0$, we have

$$\begin{aligned} (q_0, a^{m+hf}, Z_0) &\overset{*}{\Vdash} (q_i, a^{hf}, \gamma_i Z_i) && \text{from (11.6.10)} \\ &\overset{*}{\Vdash} (q_i, \Lambda, \gamma_i \eta^h Z_i) && \text{from (11.6.11).} \end{aligned}$$

Note that (11.6.11) also implies that if $k \geqslant 0, h \geqslant 0$, and

$$(q_i, a^k, \gamma_i \eta^h Z_i) \overset{*}{\vdash} (q', \Lambda, \gamma),$$

then $\gamma = \gamma_i \eta^h \gamma'$ where $\gamma' \neq \Lambda$. Therefore (b) holds and the proof is complete. □

Now, we shall start the long argument which shows that any dpda which accepts L_n (as $T_2(A)$) has at least n states.

Lemma 11.6.3 Let L_n be the language from Lemma 11.6.1 for some $n \geqslant 1$ and let A be a dpda such that $T_2(A) = L_n$. Then A has at least n states.

Proof Let $A = (Q, \Sigma, \Gamma, \delta, q_0, Z_0, F)$ be a dpda satisfying the assumptions of the lemma and assume that $|Q| < n$. We assume that $n \geq 2$, since for $n = 1$ the lemma is trivial. Our strategy will be to prove a sequence of claims about A which will eventually lead to a contradiction. We shall investigate an accepting computation of the form

$$(q_0, a^m b^k a^m b^k, Z_0) \vdash^* (q_f, \Lambda, \Lambda), \tag{11.6.12}$$

where $1 \leq m$, $1 \leq k \leq n$, and $q_f \in F$. Informally, we distinguish four phases of computation in (11.6.12) in a natural way: In each phase one block of the same letter (a^m or b^k) is read. A typical history of the store is illustrated in Fig. 11.1.

First we show that the content of the store after the first phase is periodic.

Claim 1 There exist $m_0, f \geq 1, q_1 \in Q, \gamma_0 \in \Gamma^*, \eta \in \Gamma^+$, and $Z_1 \in \Gamma$ such that, for every $h \geq 0$,

$$(q_0, a^{m_0 + hf}, Z_0) \Vdash^* (q_1, \Lambda, \gamma_0 \eta^h Z_1). \tag{11.6.13}$$

Proof of the claim To be able to apply Lemma 11.6.2, we need the loop-free property. Consider therefore a dpda $A_a = (Q, \{a\}, \Gamma, \delta_a, q_0, Z_0, F)$ obtained from A by restriction of input alphabet to $\{a\}$; that is, for all $q \in Q$ and $Z \in \Gamma$,

$$\delta_a(q, a', Z) = \begin{cases} \delta(q, a', Z) & \text{if } a' \in \{a, \Lambda\}; \\ \text{undefined} & \text{if } a' = b. \end{cases}$$

Clearly, for any $m \geq 0, q \in Q$, and $\gamma \in \Gamma^*$,

$$(q_0, a^m, Z_0) \Vdash^*_{A_a} (q, \Lambda, \gamma) \quad \text{if and only if } (q_0, a^m, Z_0) \Vdash^*_{A} (q, \Lambda, \gamma). \tag{11.6.14}$$

For any $m \geq 1$, since a^m is a prefix of an acceptable string (for example, $a^m b a^m b$), there exist $q \in Q$ and $\gamma \in \Gamma^*$ such that $(q_0, a^m, Z_0) \Vdash^*_A (q, \Lambda, \gamma)$. Hence, by (11.6.14), A_a is loop-free. We shall now apply Lemma 11.6.2 to A_a, since, for any $m \geq 1$, there must be a different configuration (q, Λ, γ) in (11.6.14) – otherwise we would have $a^{m'} b^k a^m b^k \in T_2(A)$ for some $m' \neq m$. Also, since Q and Γ are finite but m may be arbitrary, there is no bound on the length of γ. Thus we cannot have case (a) in Lemma 11.6.2 and we obtain Claim 1 as a consequence of (11.6.1).

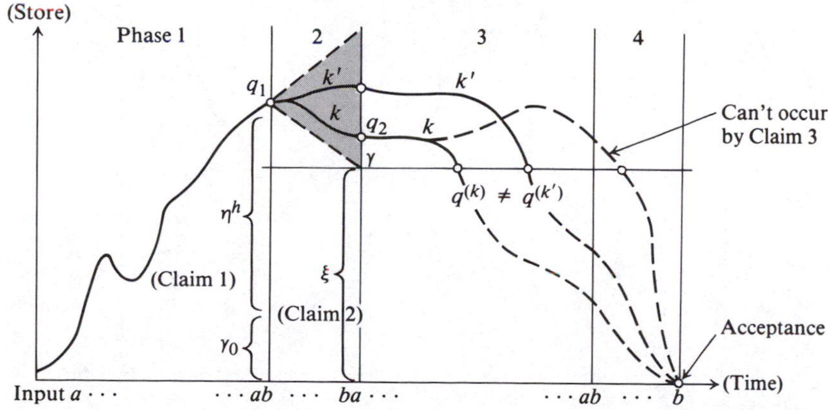

FIG. 11.1

For the rest of the proof we fix symbols m_0, f, γ_0, q_1, and Z_1 with the same meaning as in Claim 1. Our next claim is that during the second phase (during the reading of the b^k), only a bounded number of η's are erased from the store.

Claim 2 Let $1 \leqslant k \leqslant n$ and $h \geqslant 0$. Then

$$(q_1, b^k, \gamma_0\eta^h Z_1) \overset{*}{\Vdash} (q_2, \Lambda, \gamma_0\eta^{h-s}\gamma)$$

for some $q_2 \in Q, \gamma \in \Gamma^*$ and $s \leqslant n^2$.

Proof of the claim Let $q_2 \in Q$ and $\gamma' \in \Gamma^*$ be such that

$$c_1 = (q_1, b^k, \gamma_0\eta^h Z_1) \overset{*}{\Vdash} (q_2, \Lambda, \gamma'). \tag{11.6.15}$$

Such q_2 and γ' always exist, since otherwise A could not accept a string with the prefix $a^{m_0+hf}b^k$ (cf. (11.6.13)). It is enough to show that $\gamma_0\eta^{h-s}$ is a prefix of γ' for some $s \leqslant n^2$.

Assume, for the sake of contradiction, that this is not the case; that is, that $\gamma_0\eta^{h-n^2}$ is not a prefix of γ'. However, it is a prefix of $\gamma_0\eta^h Z_1$ in c_1 and therefore there exists a configuration c_1' such that (11.6.15) can be written in the form

$$c_1 \overset{*}{\vdash} c_1' \overset{*}{\Vdash} (q_2, \Lambda, \gamma')$$

and the contents of the store in c_1' is exactly $\gamma_0\eta^{h-n^2}$ (cf. Fig. 11.3). We shall concentrate on those transitions in $c_1 \overset{*}{\vdash} c_1'$ which are associated with erasing a letter from the original contents of the store (i.e., a letter written before configuration c_1 was entered; cf. thick lines in Fig. 11.2). Let us call these transitions *proper erasing.* Since at most one pushdown letter can be erased at a time, there are at least $\lg(\eta^{n^2}Z_1) = n^2 \cdot \lg(\eta) + 1$ proper erasing transitions in $c_1 \overset{*}{\vdash} c_1'$. At most k of the erasing transitions correspond to non-Λ-moves of A, since only k input letters are

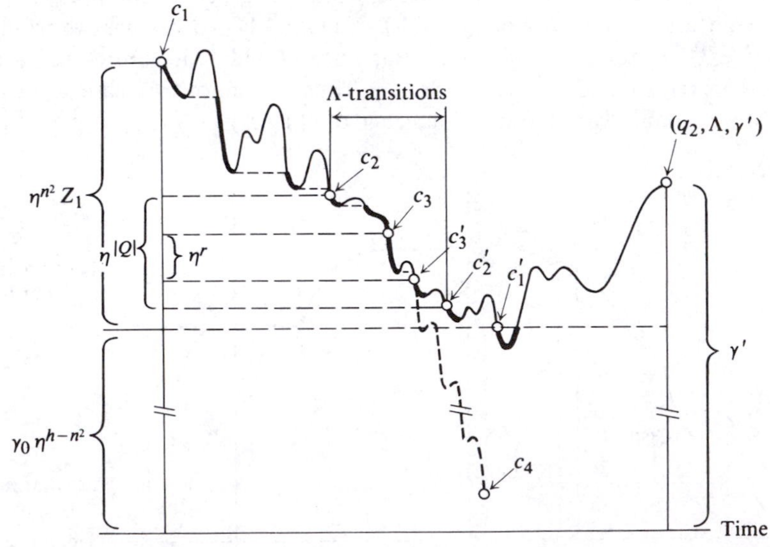

FIG. 11.2

read in (11.6.15). Consider the sequence of consecutive transitions corresponding to Λ-moves (we call them *Λ-transitions*) in $c_1 \overset{*}{\vdash} c_1'$ which contain the maximal number $N_{\max}$ of proper erasing transitions. Since $k \leqslant n$, $\lg(\eta) \geqslant 1$ and, using the fact that c_1 can be followed only by a non-Λ-transition (a consequence of (11.6.13)), we obtain the inequality $N_{\max} \geqslant n \cdot \lg(\eta)$. Now any suffix of $\gamma_0 \eta^h Z_1$ of length $N_{\max}$ contains at least $n-1$ repetitions of η or, using the assumption that $|Q| < n$, it contains at least $|Q|$ repetitions of η. Consequently, there exist two configurations c_2 and c_2' such that $c_1 \overset{*}{\vdash} c_2 \overset{+}{\vdash} c_2' \overset{*}{\vdash} c_1'$, where $c_2 \overset{+}{\vdash} c_2'$ consists entirely of Λ-transitions and exactly $|Q|$ repetitions of η are erased from the store during $c_2 \overset{+}{\vdash} c_2'$ (cf. Fig. 11.2). Formally, we have for some $p, p' \in Q$, $1 \leqslant j \leqslant k$, and $i \geqslant |Q|$,

$$c_1 \overset{*}{\vdash} c_2 = (p, b^j, \gamma_0 \eta^{h-i} \eta^{|Q|}) \overset{t}{\vdash} (p', b^j, \gamma_0 \eta^{h-i}) = c_2', \qquad (11.6.16)$$

where $t \geqslant |Q| \cdot \lg(\eta)$. Therefore at least two distinct configurations occur in $c_2 \overset{t}{\vdash} c_2'$ such that both have the same state and the same topmost string η in the store. In other words, for some $p'' \in Q$ and $1 \leqslant r \leqslant |Q|$,

$$c_2 \overset{*}{\vdash} c_3 = (p'', b^j, \gamma_0 \eta^{h-i} \eta^r) \overset{+}{\vdash} (p'', b^j, \gamma_0 \eta^{h-i}) = c_3' \overset{*}{\vdash} c_2'. \quad (11.6.17)$$

But this introduces a loop and (11.6.17) must repeat until almost all the periodic part of the store is erased:

$$c_3' \overset{*}{\vdash} (p'', b^j, \gamma_0 \eta^{r_0}) = c_4, \qquad (11.6.18)$$

where $r_0 \leqslant r$. Now let $h' = h + r$. Then

$$\begin{aligned}
(q_0, a^{m_0 + h'f} b^k, Z_0) &\overset{*}{\Vdash} (q_1, b^j, \gamma_0 \eta^{h'} Z_1) && \text{by Claim 1,}\\
&\overset{*}{\vdash} (p'', b^j, \gamma_0 \eta^{h'-i} \eta^r) && \text{by (11.6.16) and (11.6.17),-}\\
&\overset{*}{\vdash} (p'', b^j, \gamma_0 \eta^{h-i} \eta^r) = c_3 \overset{*}{\vdash} c_4 && \text{by (11.6.17) and (11.6.18),}\\
& && \text{using } h' = h + r.
\end{aligned}$$

Let $m = m_0 + hf$ and $m' = m_0 + h'f \neq m$. We have

$$(q_0, a^m b^k a^m b^k, Z_0) \overset{*}{\vdash} (p'', b^j a^m b^k, \gamma_0 \eta^{r_0}) \overset{*}{\vdash} (q_f, \Lambda, \Lambda)$$

on the one hand, and

$$(q_0, a^{m'} b^k a^m b^k, Z_0) \overset{*}{\vdash} (p'', b^j a^m b^k, \gamma_0 \eta^{r_0}) \overset{*}{\vdash} (q_f, \Lambda, \Lambda)$$

on the other hand, contradicting that $m' \neq m$ and $a^{m'} b^k a^m b^k \notin L_n = T_2(A)$. Thus $\gamma_0 \eta^{h-n^2}$ is a prefix of γ' which concludes the proof of Claim 2.

Thus for any $h \geqslant n^2$, $m = m_0 + hf$, and for any k, $1 \leqslant k \leqslant n$, we have a common prefix $\xi = \gamma_0 \eta^{h-n^2}$ of any possible contents of the pushdown store after the first two phases of the accepting computation,

$$(q_0, a^m b^k, Z_0) \overset{*}{\Vdash} (q_2, \Lambda, \xi\gamma), \qquad (11.6.19)$$

where $q_2 \in Q$ and $\gamma \in \Gamma^*$. Here γ is dependent only on k (cf. Fig. 11.2).

We shall turn our attention to the last two phases of the computation (11.6.12).

Claim 3 Let $1 \leqslant k \leqslant n$ and $m \geqslant 1$. There exist $m_k \leqslant m$ and $q^{(k)} \in Q$ such that

$$(q_2, a^{m_k}, \xi\gamma) \overset{*}{\vdash} (q^{(k)}, \Lambda, \xi), \tag{11.6.20}$$

where q_2, ξ, γ are the same as in (11.6.19).

Proof of the claim We have $(q_2, a^m b^k, \xi\gamma) \overset{*}{\vdash} (q_f, \Lambda, \Lambda)$ since $a^m b^k a^m b^k \in T_2(A)$. Therefore for some prefix w of $a^m b^k$ we have also $(q_2, w, \xi\gamma) \overset{*}{\vdash} (q^{(k)}, \Lambda, \xi)$ for some $q^{(k)} \in Q$. It is enough to show that $\lg(w) \leqslant m$. Suppose the converse; that is, $w = a^m b^j$ for some $1 \leqslant j \leqslant k$. Then we have

$$(q^{(k)}, b^{k-j}, \xi) \overset{*}{\vdash} (q_f, \Lambda, \Lambda). \tag{11.6.21}$$

Here $\xi = \gamma_0 \eta^{h-n^2}$ may be an arbitrarily long string since h is arbitrarily large. An argument similar to the proof of Claim 2 leads us to the conclusion that (11.6.21) contains a subsequence of Λ-transitions erasing more than $|Q| \cdot (k - \ell)$ occurrences of η in ξ and therefore erasing almost all ξ; but, since ξ was not changed during the second and third phases, we would have, as in Claim 2, that, for some $m' \neq m$,

$$(q_0, a^{m'} b^k a^m b^k, Z_0) \overset{*}{\vdash} (q^{(k)}, b^{k-j}, \xi') \overset{*}{\vdash} (q_f, \Lambda, \Lambda)$$

(where ξ' differs from ξ only in the number of repetitions of η; we omit the details, which are analogous to the arguments in the proof of Claim 2). This contradicts $T_2(A) = L_n$ and therefore $w = a^{m_k}$ for some $m_k \leqslant m$. This completes the proof of Claim 3.

The proof of Lemma 11.6.3 can now be completed without difficulty. Let $m \geqslant 1$, $1 \leqslant k \leqslant n$, and $1 \leqslant k' \leqslant n$. Let $q^{(k)}, q^{(k')} \in Q$ and $m_k, m_{k'}$ be as in Claim 3 (for k and k', respectively). Using (11.6.19) and (11.6.20), we can write

$$(q_0, a^m b^k a^m b^k, Z_0) \overset{*}{\vdash} (q^{(k)}, a^{m-m_k} b^k, \xi) = c \overset{*}{\vdash} (q_f, \Lambda, \Lambda)$$

and, for $m' = m + m_{k'} - m_k$,

$$(q_0, a^m b^{k'} a^{m'} b^k, Z_0) \overset{*}{\vdash} (q^{(k')}, a^{m-m_k} b^k, \xi) = c'.$$

By the assumption that $|Q| < n$, k and k' can be chosen in such a way that $k \neq k'$ but $q^{(k)} = q^{(k')}$. But then we have $c' = c \overset{*}{\vdash} (q_f, \Lambda, \Lambda)$ and thus $a^m b^{k'} a^{m'} b^k \in T_2(A)$ which is our final contradiction and establishes that A cannot have less than n states. □

Now we can state the main theorem of this section.

Theorem 11.6.2 For any $n \geqslant 1$ there is a language $L \in \Delta_2$ such that $\mathbf{deg}(L) = n$.

Proof Let $n \geqslant 1$ and consider the language L_n from Lemma 11.6.1. By Lemma 11.6.1 and Theorem 11.6.1, $L_n = L(G)$ for a grammar G with strict partition π, $\|\pi\| = n$. Since $\|\pi_0\| \leqslant \|\pi\|$ we have $\mathbf{deg}(L_n) \leqslant n$. Assume $\mathbf{deg}(L_n) < n$. By Theorem 11.6.1 there exists a dpda for L_n with less than n states, contradicting Lemma 11.6.3. □

Theorem 11.6.2 establishes a hierarchy of strict deterministic languages under their degree.

PROBLEMS

1 Check which of the transformations of strict deterministic grammars preserve degree.

2* (*Open problem*) Is the degree of a strict deterministic language effectively calculable?

11.7 DETERMINISTIC LANGUAGES AND REALTIME COMPUTATION

Our goal in this section is to investigate timing questions in dpda's. We already know that any deterministic context-free language may be accepted in linear time by a dpda from Problem 5.6.10. This tells us that a Turing machine would also accomplish this in linear time. We shall show, in this section, that there is a (strict) deterministic language L such that no realtime multitape Turing machine can accept L in realtime.

Notation. Let $L = \{a^{i_1}ba^{i_2}b \cdots a^{i_{r-1}}ba^{i_r}c^s a^{i_{r-s+1}} \mid r \geq 1,\ 1 \leq i_j \text{ for all } j,\ 1 \leq j \leq r, 1 \leq s \leq r\}$.

It is clear that $L \in \Delta_2 \subseteq \Delta_1 \subseteq \Delta_0$. We shall now show that L cannot be accepted in realtime. To do this, we consider a certain equivalence relation.

Definition Let $L \subseteq \Sigma^*$ and $k \geq 0$ be given. For any $x, y \in \Sigma^*$, define the relation $E_k(L)$, by the condition $(x,y) \in E_k(L)$ if and only if for each $z \in \Sigma^*$ with $\lg(z) \leq k$, we have $xz \in L$ if and only if $yz \in L$.

Clearly $E_k(L)$ is an equivalence relation on Σ^*.

Next we turn to the theorem which is the basis for this type of proof.

Theorem 11.7.1 Let $A = (Q, \Sigma, \Gamma, \delta, q_0, F)$ be a realtime Turing machine with m work tapes, $L = T(A)$, and let $k \geq 0$. Then

$$rk(E_k(L)) \leq |Q|\,|\Gamma|^{(2k+1)m}.$$

Proof Let $x, y \in \Sigma^*$ and suppose that $(x,y) \notin E_k(L)$. If we start A on x and on y, then let α_x and α_y be the last ID of A's computations. Clearly, $\alpha_x \neq \alpha_y$. [Otherwise, for any $z \in \Sigma^k$, $xz \in L$ if and only if $yz \in L$, which would contradict that $(x,y) \notin E_k(L)$.] As x, y range over Σ^* without limit, the number of ID's α_x and α_y grows without bound. Since A is realtime and $z \in \Sigma^k$, we must calculate the number of ID's that A can distinguish in k steps. This bound is

$$|Q|\,|\Gamma|^{(2k+1)m}$$

because an ID can contain any state, and in k steps, one can only move k positions on a work tape. Since this can involve k in either direction, we find that the number of different contents of a work tape is $|\Gamma|^{(2k+1)}$ and there are m work tapes.

To complete the argument, we note that if $rk(E_k(L)) = p$ were greater than the bound, then there would be p tapes which were pairwise inequivalent mod $E_k(L)$. These must lead to p distinct ID's which is more than A can distinguish in k steps, and leads to the contradiction that some two of them would have to be equivalent mod $E_k(L)$. □

Now we are ready to prove the desired result.

Theorem 11.7.2 L, as defined above, cannot be accepted by any realtime multitape Turing machine.

Proof Suppose, for the sake of contradiction, that $L = T(A)$ for some realtime multitape Turing machine with m tapes. Define

$$L_k = \{a^{i_1}b \cdots a^{i_{r-1}}ba^{i_r}c^s a^{i_{r-s+1}} \mid r \geqslant 1, 1 \leqslant i_j \leqslant k, 1 \leqslant j \leqslant r, 1 \leqslant s \leqslant r\}.$$

Thus we bound the number of successive a's to be k. Note that $L_k \subseteq L$. Next we consider the equivalence relation $E_{k+r}(L)$.

Claim $rk(E_{k+r}(L)) \geqslant k^r$.

Proof of the claim Consider two distinct prefixes of words in L_k,

$$x_1 = a^{i_1}b \cdots a^{i_{r-1}}ba^{i_r}$$

and

$$x_2 = a^{j_1}b \cdots a^{j_{r-1}}ba^{j_r},$$

where $x_1 \neq x_2$ and $1 \leqslant i_p, j_q \leqslant k$ for $1 \leqslant p, q \leqslant r$. Clearly, there exists a sequence $z = c^s a^t$, where $s + t \leqslant k + r$ such that

$$x_1 z \in L_k \qquad \text{but} \qquad x_2 z \notin L_k.$$

Thus $(x_1, x_2) \notin E_{k+r}(L)$. Thus there are at least as many classes of $E_{k+r}(L)$ as there are distinct prefixes of this form. Clearly, there are k values for each of $i_1, \ldots, i_r$ and each may be chosen independently. Therefore

$$|E_{k+r}(L)| \geqslant k^r$$

and the claim has been proven.

Now to complete the proof, we employ Theorem 11.7.1. We know that

$$k^r \leqslant rk(E_{k+r}(L)) < |Q|\,|\Gamma|^{(2(k+r)+1)m}. \tag{11.7.1}$$

In this inequality, k and r may grow but everything else is fixed. Thus (11.7.1) reduces to

$$k^r < c^{(k+r)} \tag{11.7.2}$$

for some constant c. As k and r grow, (11.7.2) is obviously violated for any constant c, and we have a contradiction. □

Corollary There exists a strict deterministic language which is not a realtime language.

Next we define some families of deterministic languages, recalling that quasi-realtime pda's have a bounded number of consecutive Λ-moves.

Definition A language L is called Δ_i-*(quasi) realtime* if $L = T_i(A)$ for some (quasi) realtime dpda A, $i = 0, 1, 2$.

With this definition, we can state another corollary of Theorem 11.7.2.

Corollary The family of Δ_i-realtime languages is properly contained in the family Δ_i for $i = 0, 1, 2$.

Proof Clearly, L as defined at the beginning of this section has the property that

$$L \in \Delta_2 \subseteq \Delta_1 \subseteq \Delta_0.$$

But it has been shown that L cannot be accepted by any realtime, on-line multitape Turing machine. Thus, L is not a realtime Δ_i language for $i = 0, 1, 2$. □

We begin to relate quasi-realtime and realtime languages. We shall do so for Δ_2 now.

Theorem 11.7.3 A language L is Δ_2-quasi-realtime if and only if it is Δ_2-realtime or $L = \{\Lambda\}$.

Proof The *if* direction is a direct consequence of the definition and the fact that $\{\Lambda\} = T_2(A)$ for any dpda A with a single move

$$\delta(q_0, \Lambda, Z_0) = (q_f, \Lambda) \qquad \text{for some } q_f \in F.$$

This dpda is quasi-realtime ($t = 1$).

For the *only if* direction, let $A = (Q, \Sigma, \Gamma, \delta, q_0, Z_0, F)$ be a dpda and assume A is quasi-realtime with time constant t. One can define an equivalent realtime dpda A' in such a way that (i) the pushdown letters of A' are codes for n-tuples ($n = 2t + 1$) of pushdown letters of A, and (ii) one move of A_i has the same effect as a sequence of at most n moves of A. A' must simulate the writing and erasing moves of A in its finite-state control and must transfer information to and from its pushdown storage in blocks of size n. We shall omit the formal construction and proof and leave the details for Problem 2 at the end of this section. □

It turns out to be valuable to have a grammatical characterization of the Δ_2-realtime languages.

Definition Let $G = (V, \Sigma, P, S)$ be a strict deterministic grammar with minimal strict partition π. G is called a *realtime strict deterministic* (or simply *realtime*) *grammar* if it is Λ-free and the following condition is satisfied for all $A, A', B, B' \in N$ and $\alpha, \beta \in V^*$.

$$\text{If } A \to \alpha B \text{ and } A' \to \alpha B'\beta \text{ are in } P, \text{ then } A \equiv A' \pmod{\pi} \text{ implies } \beta = \Lambda. \tag{11.7.3}$$

Note that if G is a realtime strict deterministic grammar, then for any A, $A' \in N$, if $A \to \alpha B$ is in P, $A' \to \alpha B'\beta$ is in P, and $A \equiv A'$, then $\beta = \Lambda$ and either $A = A'$ and $B = B'$ (so that there is but one rule involved) or $B \equiv B'$.

It is interesting to note that the requirement that π be minimal is necessary in this definition. Consider the following example:

$$S \to aAS \mid b$$

$$A \to aB$$

$$B \to aAB \mid aCA \mid b$$

$$C \to aD \mid c$$

$$D \to aAD \mid aCC$$

and let $\pi_0 = \{\Sigma, \{S\}, \{A, C\}, \{B, D\}\}$ and $\pi = \{\Sigma, \{S\}, \{A, B, C, D\}\}$. G is a realtime grammar. If the minimality condition were dropped from the definition, G would not be realtime with respect to π but would be with respect to π_0.

It is clear from the definition that the reduced form of any realtime grammar is also realtime.

Theorem 11.7.4 A language is a Δ_2-realtime language if and only if it is generated by some reduced realtime grammar.

Proof (*Only if*) First note that, since acceptance is by final state and empty pushdown, one can restrict attention to a dpda with one final state and there is no loss of time. More formally, the dpda $\hat{A}$ constructed in Lemma 11.5.1 is realtime if and only if A is realtime. By Lemma 11.5.2, $G_{\hat{A}}$ is strict deterministic under partition π defined in that proof. It is easily seen that π is minimal. Now let us recall that $G_{\hat{A}}$ has productions of two types as defined in the proof of Theorem 5.4.3. By the realtime property of $\hat{A}$ in both cases, we have $a \neq \Lambda$. Thus $G_{\hat{A}}$ is Λ-free and, moreover, in Greibach normal form. To prove (11.7.3), let $A \to \alpha B$ and $A' \to \alpha B'\beta$ be in P and assume $A = (q, Z, q') \equiv (q, Z, q'') = A'$. $G_{\hat{A}}$ is in Greibach normal form; hence $\alpha \neq \Lambda$ and ${}^{(1)}\alpha \in \Sigma$. By the determinism of $\hat{A}$ and the definition of $G_{\hat{A}}$, there is a unique $\gamma \in \Gamma^*$ (as well as $q' \in Q$) such that $\delta(q, {}^{(1)}\alpha, Z) = (q', \gamma)$. Consequently, $\lg(\alpha B) = \lg(\gamma) + 1 = \lg(\alpha B'\beta)$. Hence, $\beta = \Lambda$.

(*If*). Let $L = L(G)$ for some reduced realtime grammar G. Our strategy will be to modify the canonical dpda A_G in such a way that the resulting equivalent dpda A'_G will be quasi-realtime. This is sufficient for a proof that L is Δ_2-realtime language since the Λ-free property of G implies that $L \neq \{\Lambda\}$. To make it easier to follow the proof, we shall first examine the properties of A_G related to the occurrence of Λ-moves. We shall use the same notation as in the proof of Theorem 11.5.3. We have defined the δ-function of A by means of four types of moves: Types 1, 3, and 4 are Λ-moves, and Type 2 is always a non-Λ-move. Accordingly, we have distinguished four types of yield relations

$$(q, aw, \gamma Z) \vdash_i (q', w, \gamma\alpha) \quad \text{if and only if} \quad \delta(q, a, Z) = (q', \alpha) \text{ is a move of Type } i,$$

where $i = 1, 2, 3, 4$. Let c, c' be two configurations of A_G such that

$$c\,(\vdash_1 \cup \vdash_3 \cup \vdash_4)^m\, c' \tag{11.7.4}$$

for some $m \geqslant 0$, where c is the result of a Type 2 move. We are interested in finding a bound on the number m in (11.7.4). We shall see that such a bound exists after suitable modification of A_G. First we notice that (11.7.4) can be rewritten in the following form.

$$c\left[\prod_{i=1}^{n}\left(\overset{k_{1i}}{\underset{1}{\vdash}}\ \underset{3}{\vdash}\ \underset{4}{\vdash}\right)\overset{k_2}{\underset{1}{\vdash}}\right]c', \tag{11.7.5}$$

where $k_{1i}, k_2, n \geqslant 0, k_2 + \Sigma_{i=1}^{n}(k_{1i}+2) = m$, and Π denotes composition of relations.

Claim 1 If $G = (V, \Sigma, P, S)$ is a reduced realtime grammar and c, c' any two configurations of A_G satisfying a relation of the form (11.7.5), then $k_{1i} = 0$ for all i and $k_2 \leqslant |N|$.

Proof of the claim By definition, a Type 1 move can be followed by a Type 3 move if and only if there is a Λ-production in the grammar. Since G is Λ-free, $k_{1i} = 0$ for all i. Also, k_2 consecutive moves of Type 1 can occur if and only if $A \overset{k_2-1}{\underset{G}{\Rightarrow}} B\alpha$ for some $A, B \in N$ and $\alpha \in V^*$; but since there are only $|N|$ nonterminals and $A \overset{+}{\Rightarrow} A\alpha$ is not possible in a reduced strict deterministic grammar (the Corollary to Theorem 11.4.3), $k_2 \leqslant |N|$ (in fact, $k_2 \leqslant \|\pi\|$). The claim is proved.

As a consequence of Claim 1, only the number n in (11.7.5) can be unbounded. Therefore, we restrict our concern to the case $c\ (\underset{3}{\vdash}\ \underset{4}{\vdash})^n\ c'$, or, more conveniently,

$$c\ (\underset{4}{\vdash}\ \underset{3}{\vdash})^n\ c'$$

where c, c' are two configurations of A_G and $n \geqslant 0$. Directly from the definition of moves of Types 3 and 4, we have:

Claim 2 For any $q_j, q_\ell \in Q - \{q_0\}$; $V_k, V_i \in \pi$ and $\alpha \in V^*$,

$$(q_j, \Lambda, (V_k, \alpha, V_i))\ \underset{4}{\vdash}\ \underset{3}{\vdash}\ (q_\ell, \Lambda, \Lambda) \tag{11.7.6}$$

if and only if $A_{k\ell} \to \alpha A_{ij}$ is a production† in G.

Let us call any letter $(V_k, \alpha, V_i) \in \Gamma$ a *saturated letter* if and only if $A \to \alpha B$ is in P for some $A \in V_k$ and $B \in V_i$. Denote Γ_s the set of all saturated letters (we have $\Gamma_s \subseteq \Gamma_2$).

Claim 3 If $Z_1 = (V_k, \alpha, V_i)$ is saturated and $Z_2 = (V_k, \alpha\beta, V_j) \in \Gamma$, then $\beta = \Lambda$ and $j = i$.

Proof of the claim This claim is a consequence of property (11.7.3) of realtime grammars: Since Z_1 is saturated, we have $A \to \alpha B$ is in P for some $A \in V_k$ and $B \in V_i$; and since $Z_2 \in \Gamma_2$, we have $A' \to \alpha\beta C\theta$ for some $A' \in V_k, C \in V_j$, and $\theta \in V^*$. Then by the strict determinism of G, $\beta C\theta = B'\beta'$ for some $B' \in N$, $\beta' \in V^*$. But $\beta' = \Lambda$ by (11.7.3), and hence $C = B'$, $\beta = \Lambda$ and $V_i = [B'] = [C] = V_j$ by the strict determinism of G. The claim is proved.

---

† Recall the convention $V_i = \{A_{i0}, \ldots, A_{in_i}\}$ for $V_i \in \pi$.

By Claims 2 and 3, any saturated letter on the top of the store is always erased (never rewritten) and this is realized by a transition of the form $\vdash_4 \vdash_3$. Now, for any saturated letter $Z = (V_k, \alpha, V_i) \in \Gamma_s$, we can uniquely specify a partial function

$$f_Z \colon Q \underset{p}{\to} Q, \tag{11.7.7}$$

such that $f_Z(q_j) = q_\ell$ if and only if $q_j, q_\ell \neq q_0$ and one or the other side of equivalence (11.7.6) holds. We can extend (11.7.7) to:

$$f_\eta \colon Q \underset{p}{\to} Q \tag{11.7.8}$$

for $\eta \in \Gamma_s^+$ using (11.7.7) as a basis and defining inductively $f_{\eta Z} = f_\eta f_Z$, that is, for any $q \in Q$, $f_{\eta Z}(q) = f_\eta(f_Z(q))$ provided $f_Z(q)$ is defined. Note that there are only a finite number of distinct functions f_η. In fact, $|\{f_\eta |\ \eta \in \Gamma_s^+\}| \leqslant (|Q| + 1)^{|Q|}$.

Claim 4 For any $q, q' \in Q; \gamma, \gamma' \in \Gamma^*$ and $n \geqslant 1$,

$$(q, \Lambda, \gamma)\,(\vdash_3 \vdash_4)^n\,(q', \Lambda, \gamma') \quad \text{if and only if} \quad \gamma = \gamma'\eta$$

for some $\eta \in \Gamma_s^n$ and $q' = f_\eta(q)$.

This claim follows from Claims 2 and 3 by a straightforward induction on n.

Thus the only effect of $(\vdash_3 \vdash_4)^n$ is erasing a saturated string of length n from the store and changing the state of control. Claim 4 gives the basis for the elimination of an unbounded sequence of Λ-moves: instead of a saturated string η of length $\geqslant 1$, on the store of the modified dpda A'_G appears a single letter $\bar{f}_\eta$ representing the function f_η.

For the completeness we describe formally the construction of A'_G. For this, let $A_G = (Q, \Sigma, \Gamma, \delta, q_0, Z_0, \{q_0\})$ be the canonical dpda defined prior to Lemma 11.5.4. Define A'_G as follows:

$$A'_G = (Q', \Sigma, \Gamma', \delta', q_0, Z_0, \{q_0\}), \tag{11.7.9}$$

where $Q' = Q \cup \{q_Z |\ Z \in \Gamma_s\}$ (the new states are added for technical reasons only), $\Gamma' = \Gamma \cup \{f_\eta |\ \eta \in \Gamma_s^+\}$ and δ' is defined as follows: If $A \to \alpha B$ is in P for some $A \in V_i$ and $B \in V_k$, then define:

i) $\delta'(q_0, \Lambda, (V_i, \alpha)) = (q_Z, \Lambda)$ where $Z = (V_i, \alpha, V_k) \in \Gamma_s$;

ii) $\delta'(q_Z, \Lambda, f_\eta) = (q_0, f_{\eta Z}(V_k, \Lambda))$ for all $f_\eta \in \Gamma' - \Gamma$, $Z = (V_i, \alpha, V_k)$; and

iii) $\delta'(q_Z, \Lambda, Y) = (q_0, Yf_Z(V_k, \Lambda))$, where $Z = (V_i, \alpha, V_k)$, and for all $Y \in \Gamma$.

Moreover, for any $q_j \in Q - \{q_0\}$ and $f_\eta \in \Gamma' - \Gamma$, define

iv) $\delta'(q_j, \Lambda, f_\eta) = (f_\eta(q), \Lambda)$.

In all other cases define

v) $\delta'(q, a, Z) = \delta(q, a, Z)$.

Moves (i), (ii) and (iii) are new special cases of Type 1 moves of A_G; move (iv) is a special case of the Type 4 move. We observe that a saturated letter never appears in the store, and even if some Λ-moves were added, A'_G is quasi-realtime. It is easy to see that $T_2(A'_G) = T_2(A_G)$. Claim 4 suffices for that. □

PROBLEMS

1 Show that the following set L' cannot be accepted by any realtime multitape Turing machine:

$$L' = \{x_1dx_2 \cdots x_{r-1}dx_rcd^kcx_{r-k+1}^T \mid x_i \in \{a, b\}^*, 1 \leqslant i \leqslant r, 1 \leqslant k \leqslant r\}.$$

2 Give a detailed proof of Theorem 11.7.2.

3 Prove the following proposition about regular sets.

Proposition Let $L \subseteq \Sigma^*$ be a regular language. Then there exists a number $n \geqslant 1$ such that any string $x \in L$, where $\lg(x) \geqslant n$ can be written in the form $x = y_1zy_2$, where $y_1, y_2 \in \Sigma^*$, $z \in \Sigma^+$, $\lg(zy_2) \leqslant n$, and, for all $k \geqslant 0$, $y_1z^ky_2 \in L$.

4 Prove the following useful proposition:

Proposition Let $G = (V, \Sigma, P, S)$ be a reduced realtime grammar. Assume

$$S \underset{L}{\overset{*}{\Rightarrow}} uA\alpha$$

and

$$A \underset{L}{\overset{*}{\Rightarrow}} vA\beta$$

for some $A \in N$, $u \in \Sigma^*$, $\alpha \in V^*$, $v \in \Sigma^+$ and $\beta \in V^+$. Then for any $n \geqslant 0$ and $w \in \Sigma^*$,

$$S \overset{*}{\Rightarrow} uv^nw$$

implies $\lg(w) \geqslant n$.

5 Prove the following result:

Theorem Let G be any reduced realtime grammar. Then $L(G)$ is regular if and only if G is not self-embedding.

Hint. Problems 3 and 4 can be helpful.

6 Show that the result in Problem 5 is best possible in the following sense. Find a reduced, Λ-free, self-embedding, strict deterministic grammar G such that $L(G)$ is regular. Thus the result in Problem 5 cannot be extended to the full family of strict deterministic grammars.

Let $\mathscr{R}$ be the family of sets definable by realtime multitape Turing machines.

7 Show that $\mathscr{R}$ is closed under union, complementation, intersection, and product on the right with regular sets.

8 Show that $\mathscr{R}$ is not closed under product, *, transpose, homomorphism, either left or right quotient by regular sets, or max.

11.8* STRUCTURE OF TREES IN STRICT DETERMINISTIC GRAMMARS

In this section, the structural properties of derivation trees in strict deterministic grammars will be developed. In addition to the property of unambiguity, the strict deterministic grammars have a unique "partial" tree for every prefix of a terminal string. We utilize more general objects than derivation trees, namely, the grammatical trees (with roots labeled by any letter) in order to facilitate induction proofs. The uniqueness of the "partial" trees is the content of the Left-Part Theorem. This theorem will be also used to prove two deterministic iteration theorems.

Recall that our conventions in Section 1.6 were to use the term grammatical tree for a tree whose frontier is in V^*. A derivation tree has a frontier in Σ^*. For a given grammar G, $\mathscr{T}_G$ denotes the set of derivation trees of G while $\mathscr{T}_G(A)$ is the set of derivation trees whose root is A. (Cf. Section 1.6 for the rest of our notation involving trees.)

We are now ready to define the left-part of a grammatical tree.

Definition Let T be a derivation tree of some grammar G. For any $n \geqslant 0$, we define ${}^{(n)}T$, the *left n-part of T* (or the *left part* where n is understood) as follows.

Let $(x_1, \ldots, x_m)$ be the sequence of all terminal† nodes in T (from the left to the right); that is, $\{x_1, \ldots, x_m\} = \lambda^{-1}(\Sigma)$ and $x_1 \sqsubset^+ x_2 \sqsubset^+ \cdots \sqsubset^+ x_m$. Then

$${}^{(n)}T = \{x \text{ in } T \mid x \overset{*}{\sqsubset} \overset{*}{\ulcorner} x_n\} \quad \text{if } n \leqslant m, \text{ and}$$

$${}^{(n)}T = T \quad \text{if } n > m.$$

We consider ${}^{(n)}T$ to be a tree under the same relations $\ulcorner$, $\sqsubset$, and labeling λ as T.

Thus, for instance, the shaded area on Fig. 11.3 (including the path to x) is the left n-part of T if x is the nth terminal node in T. Note that, in general, ${}^{(n)}T$ may not be a derivation tree.

As immediate consequences of the definition, we have

Fact 1 ${}^{(n)}T = {}^{(n+1)}T$ if and only if ${}^{(n)}T = T$.

Fact 2 If ${}^{(n)}T = {}^{(n)}T'$, then ${}^{(j)}T = {}^{(j)}T'$ for any $j \leqslant n$.

Our principal result about the structure of derivation trees of a strict deterministic grammar can be informally stated as follows. A reduced grammar G has a

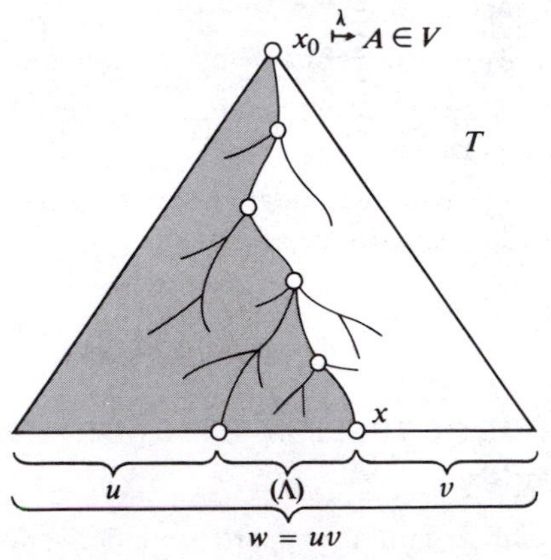

FIG. 11.3

† Note that the Λ-nodes are not being indexed.

strict partition π if and only if, given any $V \in \pi$, then each prefix u of any string $w = uv \in \Sigma^*$ generated by some symbol $A \in V_i$ *uniquely* determines the left partial subtree of tree T (cf. Fig. 11.3). T corresponds to a derivation $A \overset{*}{\Rightarrow} w$ up to the path to the terminal node (x) labeled by the first letter of v. We allow the labels of nodes on this particular path to be determined modulo the partition π (in particular, $\lambda(x) = \Sigma$). In the case when $v = \Lambda$, the complete tree is specified uniquely (and then it cannot be a proper subtree of any other tree with an equivalent root label).

For the formal statement of the theorem we first introduce the "left-part property" of a set of derivation trees.

Definition Let $\mathscr{T} \subseteq \mathscr{T}_G$ for some grammar $G = (V, \Sigma, P, S)$ and let π be an arbitrary partition on V, not necessarily strict. We say that $\mathscr{T}$ satisfies the *left-part property with respect to* π if and only if, for any $n \geq 0$ and $T, T' \in \mathscr{T}$ if

$$\mathbf{rt}(T) \equiv \mathbf{rt}(T') \pmod{\pi}$$

and

$${}^{(n)}\mathbf{fr}(T) = {}^{(n)}\mathbf{fr}(T'),$$

then

$${}^{(n+1)}T \cong {}^{(n+1)}T' \tag{11.8.1}$$

and, moreover, if $x \leftrightarrow x'$ is the structural isomorphism ${}^{(n+1)}T \leftrightarrow {}^{(n+1)}T'$, then for every x in ${}^{(n+1)}T$,

$$\lambda(x) = \lambda(x') \text{ if } x \sqsubset^+ y \text{ for some } y \in {}^{(n+1)}T \text{ or if } {}^{(n+1)}T = {}^{(n)}T \tag{11.8.2}$$

and

$$\lambda(x) \equiv \lambda(x') \pmod{\pi} \text{ otherwise.} \tag{11.8.3}$$

Note that the condition "$x \sqsubset^+ y$ for some $y \in {}^{(n+1)}T$" in (11.8.2) is equivalent to "x is not on the rightmost path in ${}^{(n+1)}T$".

An example of this kind of mapping can be obtained by considering grammar G_2 from Section 11.4. Let us consider the trees shown in Fig. 11.4.

If we let $n = 2$, we see that $\mathbf{rt}(T_1) = S \equiv S = \mathbf{rt}(T_2)$ and ${}^{(2)}\mathbf{fr}(T_1) = (a = {}^{(2)}\mathbf{fr}(T_2)$. Thus ${}^{(3)}T_1 \cong {}^{(3)}T_2$ and the path from S to $+$ in T_1 is "equivalent modulo π" to the path from S to $)$ in T_2.

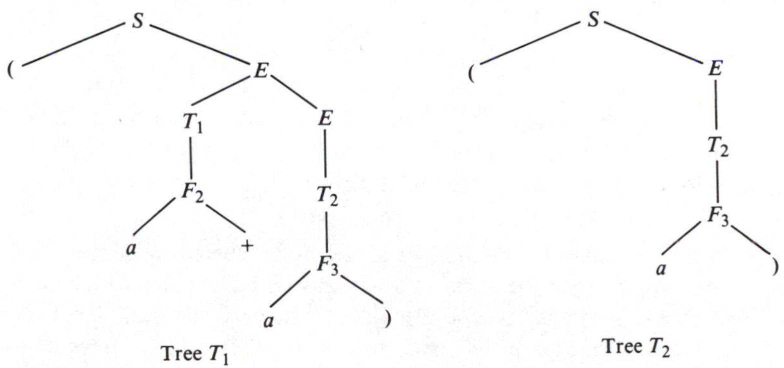

FIG. 11.4

Note that the left-part property is a *global property of trees* in distinction to the strictness of a grammar, which is a *local property* of derivation trees (being a property of their elementary subtrees).

Theorem 11.8.1 (*The Left-Part Theorem*) Let $G = (V, \Sigma, P, S)$ be a reduced grammar and let π be a partition on V such that $\Sigma \in \pi$. Then π is strict in G if and only if the set $\mathscr{T}_G$ of all derivation trees of G satisfies the left-part property with respect to π.

Proof (*The if direction*) Let G and π be as in the assumption of the theorem and assume $\mathscr{T}_G$ satisfies the left-part property with respect to π. We shall show that π is strict.

Let $A, A' \in N$, let $A \to \alpha\beta$ and $A' \to \alpha\beta'$ be in P and assume $A \equiv A' \pmod{\pi}$. Since G is reduced, we have $\alpha \overset{*}{\Rightarrow} w_\alpha$, $\beta \overset{*}{\Rightarrow} w_\beta$ and $\beta' \overset{*}{\Rightarrow} w_{\beta'}$ for some $w_\alpha, w_\beta, w_{\beta'} \in \Sigma^*$. Let us consider two derivation trees T, T' corresponding to derivations $A \Rightarrow \alpha\beta \overset{*}{\Rightarrow} w_\alpha w_\beta$ and $A' \Rightarrow \alpha\beta' \overset{*}{\Rightarrow} w_\alpha w'_\beta$, respectively. Let $n = \lg(w_\alpha)$. Then $\mathbf{rt}(T) = A \equiv A' = \mathbf{rt}(T')$ and ${}^{(n)}\mathbf{fr}(T) = {}^{(n)}\mathbf{fr}(T')$. Thus ${}^{(n+1)}T \cong {}^{(n+1)}T'$ by the left-part property of $\mathscr{T}_G$. Let $x \leftrightarrow x'$ be the structural isomorphism from ${}^{(n+1)}T$ to ${}^{(n+1)}T'$. We distinguish two cases:

CASE 1. $w_\beta \neq \Lambda$. Let x be the $(n+1)$st terminal node of T (labeled by ${}^{(1)}w_\beta$) and y the $(\lg(\alpha)+1)$st node among the immediate descendants of the root in T, counted from the left (that is, $\lambda(y) = {}^{(1)}\beta$). Clearly, y is in ${}^{(n+1)}T$ and by the structural isomorphism also y' is in ${}^{(n+1)}T'$, $\lambda(y') = {}^{(1)}\beta'$. Then ${}^{(1)}\beta \equiv {}^{(1)}\beta'$ by (11.8.2) or by (11.8.3) (depending on whether $y \sqsubset^{+} x$ or not).

CASE 2. $w_\beta = \Lambda$. Then ${}^{(n+1)}T = {}^{(n)}T$ and, by (11.8.2), $\lambda(x) = \lambda(x')$ for all x in ${}^{(n+1)}T$. Thus ${}^{(n+1)}T = {}^{(n+1)}T'$. Then also ${}^{(n)}T = {}^{(n)}T'$ by Fact 2 and using Fact 1 we conclude $T = T'$. Hence $A = A'$ and $\beta' = \beta = \Lambda$.

(*The only if direction*) Let G be a reduced grammar with strict partition π. Let $T, T' \in \mathscr{T}_G$ be two derivation trees such that

$$\mathbf{rt}(T) \equiv \mathbf{rt}(T') \pmod{\pi} \tag{11.8.4}$$

and

$${}^{(n)}\mathbf{fr}(T) = {}^{(n)}\mathbf{fr}(T') \tag{11.8.5}$$

for some $n \geqslant 0$. To show that ${}^{(n+1)}T$ and ${}^{(n+1)}T'$ satisfy (11.8.1), (11.8.2), and (11.8.3), we proceed by induction on the height h of the larger one of the two trees. Assume, without loss of generality, that the taller tree is T.

Basis. $h = 0$. Then T consists of a single node labeled by some $a \in \Sigma$. (Note that we cannot have $a = \Lambda$ since, in such a case, assumption (11.8.4) would be meaningless). Then by (11.8.4) and since $\Sigma \in \pi$ also, T' has a single node labeled by some $a' \in \Sigma$. Thus $T \cong T'$. Clearly, $a \equiv a'$ and, moreover, if $n \geqslant 1$, we have $a = a'$ from (11.8.5).

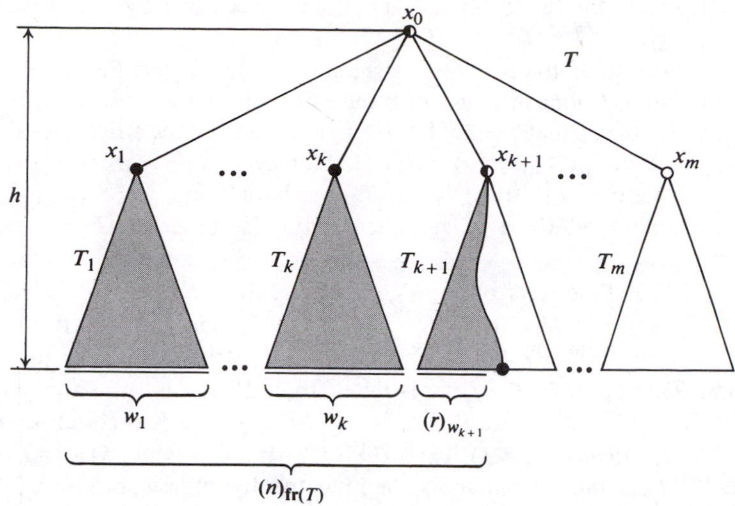

FIG. 11.5

Inductive step. Let $h > 0$ and assume the result; i.e., (11.8.1), (11.8.2), and (11.8.3), true for all trees with heights smaller than h. Let us denote this assumption (A). Let x_0 and x_0' be the roots of T and T', respectively, and let $x_0 \ulcorner x_1, \ldots, x_0 \ulcorner x_m$, $x_0' \ulcorner x_1', \ldots, x_0' \ulcorner x_{m'}'$, $x_1 \llcorner x_2 \llcorner \cdots \llcorner x_m$ and $x_1' \llcorner x_2' \llcorner \cdots \llcorner x_{m'}'$ (cf. Fig. 11.5).

Let us define, for $1 \leqslant i \leqslant m$ and $1 \leqslant j \leqslant m'$,

$$T_i = \{x \text{ in } T \mid x_i \overset{*}{\ulcorner} x\},$$
$$T_j' = \{x \text{ in } T' \mid x_j' \overset{*}{\ulcorner} x\}.$$

Clearly, all the T_i and T_j' are derivation trees of G and, because their heights are smaller than h, the inductive hypothesis (A) is applicable. Denote $w_i = \mathbf{fr}(T_i)$, $w_j' = \mathbf{fr}(T_j')$.

Claim If for some $k \leqslant m$, no tree among $T_1, \ldots, T_k$ contains the $(n+1)$st terminal node of T (in particular, if no such node exists), then $m' \geqslant k$ and $T_i = T_i'$ for $1 \leqslant i \leqslant k$.

The argument is an induction on k. The *basis* (in which $k = 0$) is vacuously true.

Inductive step. Assume the premise of the claim for some $k > 0$ and, as inductive hypothesis (B), the conclusion for $k-1$; that is, $m' \geqslant k-1$ and $T_i = T_i'$ $(1 \leqslant i \leqslant k-1)$. Then, in particular, $\lambda(x_i) = \lambda(x_i')$ for $1 \leqslant i \leqslant k-1$ and by the strictness of π, using (11.8.4), $\lambda(x_k) \equiv \lambda(x_k')$. Since $w_1 \cdots w_k$ is a prefix of $^{(n)}\mathbf{fr}(T) = {}^{(n)}\mathbf{fr}(T')$ and since $w_1 \cdots w_{k-1} = w_1' \cdots w_{k-1}'$ by inductive hypothesis (B), either $\mathbf{fr}(T_k)$ is a prefix of $\mathbf{fr}(T_k')$, or conversely. But since $\mathbf{rt}(T_k) = \lambda(x_k) \equiv \lambda(x_k') = \mathbf{rt}(T_k')$, and using inductive hypothesis (A), we conclude that $w_k = w_k'$ and $T_k = T_k'$. Therefore the claim follows.

Now if $n \geqslant \lg(\mathbf{fr}(T))$ (that is, if $^{(n)}\mathbf{fr}(T) = \mathbf{fr}(T)$), then by the claim, $T_i = T_i'$ $(1 \leqslant i \leqslant m \leqslant m')$. But then $\mathbf{fr}(T) = w_1 \cdots w_m = w_1' \cdots w_m'$ and by the strictness of

π we have $m = m'$; and since $\lambda(x_0) \equiv \lambda(x'_0)$, we have, again by the strictness of π, $\lambda(x_0) = \lambda(x'_0)$. Hence ${}^{(n+1)}T = T = T' = {}^{(n+1)}T'$.

For the rest of the proof, we assume $n < \lg(\mathbf{fr}(T))$ (cf. Fig. 11.3). Let y be the $(n + 1)$st terminal node in T and let k and r be such that y is the $(r + 1)$st terminal node in T_{k+1}. By the claim $T_i = T'_i$ $(1 \leq i \leq k)$ and thus, by the strictness of π, $m' > k$ and $\mathbf{rt}(T_{k+1}) = \lambda(x_{k+1}) \equiv \lambda(x'_{k+1}) = \mathbf{rt}(T'_k)$. Moreover, $w_1 \cdots w_k = w'_1 \cdots w'_k$ and since ${}^{(r)}w_{k+1}$ is a suffix of ${}^{(n)}\mathbf{fr}(T) = {}^{(n)}\mathbf{fr}(T')$, we have ${}^{(r)}w_{k+1} = {}^{(r)}(w'_{k+1} \cdots w'_{m'})$. The only possibility which is in agreement with the induction hypothesis (A) is ${}^{(r)}w_{k+1} = {}^{(r)}w'_{k+1}$.

Now, ${}^{(n+1)}T$ consists of $x_0, T_1, \ldots, T_k$, and ${}^{(r+1)}T_{k+1}$; ${}^{(n+1)}T'$ consists of $x'_0, T'_1, \ldots, T'_k$, and ${}^{(r+1)}T'_{k+1}$. Here ${}^{(r+1)}T_{k+1} \cong {}^{(r+1)}T'_{k+1}$ by the inductive hypothesis. Define a function f: ${}^{(n+1)}T \to {}^{(n+1)}T'$ such that f restricted to T_i is the structural isomorphism $T_i \mapsto T'_i$ $(0 \leq i \leq k)$, f restricted to ${}^{(r+1)}T_{k+1}$ is the structural isomorphism ${}^{(r+1)}T_{k+1} \mapsto {}^{(r+1)}T'_{k+1}$ and $f(x_0) = x'_0$. Now f is a structural isomorphism ${}^{(n+1)}T \mapsto {}^{(n+1)}T'$. Hence (11.8.1). Let $x \in {}^{(n+1)}T$. If $x \,\sqsubset^{+}\, y$, then $\lambda(x) = \lambda f(x)$, since either $x \in {}^{(r+1)}T_{k+1}$ and we can apply the inductive hypothesis; or else $x \in T_i$, $i \leq k$. Hence (11.8.2). Otherwise $\lambda(x) \equiv \lambda f(x)$, since either $x \in {}^{(r+1)}T_{k+1}$ and we can again apply the inductive hypothesis, or $x = x_0$ and $f(x) = x'_0$. Hence (11.8.3) and $\mathscr{T}_G$ satisfies the left-part property. □

Note that the assumption that G is reduced was not used in the *only if* part of the proof. On the other hand, in the *if* part, even if $\mathscr{T}_G$ satisfies the left-part property, the strictness of π may be violated for some useless production which does not appear in any grammatical tree. By Theorem 11.4.1, the requirement of a reduced grammar causes no loss of generality.

For reduced grammars we have the following result:

Fact 3 Let G be a reduced grammar. The left-part property is satisfied by $\mathscr{T}_G$ if and only if it is satisfied by $\mathscr{T}_G(S)$, the set of derivation trees in G.

The *only if* direction of this fact is trivial while the *if* direction follows from the observation that, in a reduced grammar, every grammatical tree is a subtree of some derivation tree.

The following two corollaries are immediate consequences of the Left-Part Theorem.

Corollary 1 Any strict deterministic grammar is unambiguous.

Corollary 2 If π is a strict partition on G, then for every $U \in \pi$, the set $\{w \in \Sigma^* \mid A \overset{*}{\Rightarrow} w \text{ for some } A \in U\}$ is prefix-free.

Thus, in particular, $L(G)$ is prefix-free, which we already know.

Our next objective is to give a machine-independent proof of a deterministic iteration theorem. The reader may wish to reread Section 6.2 before continuing, since our development will closely follow the earlier argument.

Theorem 11.8.2 (*Iteration Theorem for* Δ_2) Let $L \in \Delta_2$ and $L \subseteq \Sigma^*$. There is an integer $p(L)$ such that, for any string $w \in L$ and any set K of positions in w, if $|K| \geqslant p(L)$, then there is a factorization $\varphi = (v_1, \ldots, v_5)$ of w such that:

1 $v_2 \neq \Lambda$;

2 for each $n, m \geqslant 0, u \in \Sigma^*$,

$$v_1 v_2^{n+m} v_3 v_4^n u \in L \quad \text{if and only if} \quad v_1 v_2^m v_3 u \in L;$$

3 if $K/\varphi = \{K_1, \ldots, K_5\}$, then

i) $K_1, K_2, K_3 \neq \emptyset$ or $K_3, K_4, K_5 \neq \emptyset$;

ii) $|K_2 \cup K_3 \cup K_4| \leqslant p(L)$.

Corollary For each $n \geqslant 0$,

$$v_1 v_2^n v_3 v_4^n v_5 \in L.$$

Proof of the corollary Take $m = 1$ and $u = v_4 v_5$ in (11.8.2). This gives

$$v_1 v_2^{n+1} v_3 v_4^{n+1} v_5 \in L \quad \text{if and only if} \quad v_1 v_2 v_3 v_4 v_5 = w \in L.$$

Now take $m = 0$ and $u = v_5$ in (11.8.2). That gives:

$$v_1 v_2^n v_3 v_4^n v_5 \in L \quad \text{if and only if} \quad v_1 v_3 v_5 \in L.$$

Since $w = v_1 \cdots v_5$ is in L, the Corollary follows. □

Proof of Theorem 11.8.2 The argument mirrors the proof of Theorem 6.2.1. Let $G = (V, \Sigma, P, S)$ be a strict deterministic grammar generating L. Choose $p(L) = p(G)$ as in the proof of Theorem 6.2.1, and follow out that proof. That is, find $\varphi = (v_1, \ldots, v_5)$ satisfying the requirements of the proof.

Property (3) follows from the iteration theorem for context-free languages. To show property (1), suppose $v_2 = \Lambda$. Then we would have:

$$A \overset{+}{\Rightarrow} A v_4.$$

But left recursion is impossible in a strict deterministic grammar. Thus (3) has been satisfied.

To establish property (2), let $m, n \geqslant 0$. By the iteration theorem for context-free languages,

$$S \overset{*}{\Rightarrow} v_1 v_2^m A v_4^m v_5 \overset{*}{\Rightarrow} v_1 v_2^{m+n} v_3 v_4^{n+m} v_5 = w_1 v_4^m v_5 \tag{11.8.6}$$

where $w_1 = v_1 v_2^{m+n} v_3 v_4^n \in \Sigma^*$. Assume now

$$S \overset{*}{\Rightarrow} v_1 v_2^{m+n} v_3 v_4^n u = w_1 u \tag{11.8.7}$$

Let T, T' be two derivation trees corresponding to (11.8.6) and (11.8.7), respectively. Let $k = \lg(w_1)$. By the left-part theorem,

$$^{(k+1)}T \cong {}^{(k+1)}T'.$$

Let x be the node in T, which corresponds to the indicated occurrence of A in sentential form $v_1 v_2^m A v_4^m v_5$. Clearly, x is left of the $(k+1)$st terminal node in T (labeled with ${}^{(1)}v_4$). By the left-part property (2), the corresponding node in T' is also labeled with A. Therefore the following derivation corresponds to T':

$$S \overset{*}{\Rightarrow} v_1 v_2^m A u \overset{*}{\Rightarrow} w_1 u$$

Since $A \overset{+}{\Rightarrow} v_2^{n'} v_3 v_4^{n'}$ for any $n' \geq 0$, we have

$$v_1 v_2^{m+n'} v_3 v_4^{n'} u \in L, \qquad \text{any } n' \geq 0.$$

In particular, taking $n' = 0$, we obtain the *only if* part of property (2); taking $n = 0$ in (11.8.7) and n' arbitrary, we obtain the *if* direction of (2). □

The main purpose in proving an iteration theorem for Δ_2 was not to use it in showing sets to be non-strict deterministic. Our main purpose was to be able to prove a similar result for Δ_0. This result will be useful in showing that a number of particular sets are not deterministic.

Theorem 11.8.3 (*Iteration Theorem for* Δ_0) Let $L \subseteq \Sigma^*$ be a deterministic context-free language. There is an integer $p'(L)$ such that for every $w \in L$, and every set K of positions in w, if $|K| \geq p'(L)$, then there is a factorization

$$\varphi = (v_1, \ldots, v_5)$$

of w such that:

1 $v_2 \neq \Lambda$;

2 For all $n \geq 0$, $v_1 v_2^n v_3 v_4^n v_5 \in L$;

3 if $K/\varphi = \{K_1, \ldots, K_5\}$, then

i) $K_1, K_2, K_3 \neq \emptyset$ or $K_3, K_4, K_5 \neq \emptyset$,

ii) $|K_2 \cup K_3 \cup K_4| \leq p'(L)$;

4 if $v_5 \neq \Lambda$, then for each $m, n \geq 0$, $u \in \Sigma^*$,

$$v_1 v_2^{m+n} v_3 v_4^n u \in L \quad \text{if and only if} \quad v_1 v_2^m v_3 u \in L.$$

Proof Much of the previous proof and all of the proof of Theorem 6.2.1 still apply here. Thus (3) follows. Also, (2) follows easily. To complete the proof, let $L \in \Delta_0$. Then $L\$ \in \Delta_2$ and is subject to Theorem 11.8.2. Define $p'(L) = p(L\$)$ and let $w \in L$ with a set of positions K where $|K| \geq p'(L)$. Consider the factorization $\varphi' = (v_1, v_2, v_3, v_4, v_5')$ of $w\$$ obtained from Theorem 11.8.2 applied to $L\$$. Since \$ doesn't occupy any position from K, there are only two possibilities where it can occur: either $v_3 \in \Sigma^+\$$ and $v_4 = v_5' = \Lambda$, or $v_3 \in \Sigma^+$ and $v_5' = v_5\$$ for some $v_5 \in \Sigma^*$. In either event, (1) holds. Assume $v_5 \neq \Lambda$. We can restrict ourselves to the second possibility. Take $\varphi = (v_1, v_2, v_3, v_4, v_5)$ as the factorization of w. The result is now simple, since, for any $n, m \geq 0$ and $u \in \Sigma^*$, we have

$$\begin{aligned} v_1 v_2^{n+m} v_3 v_4^n u \in L \quad &\text{if and only if} \quad v_1 v_2^{n+m} v_3 v_4^n u\$ \in L\$ \\ &\text{if and only if} \quad v_1 v_2^m v_3 u\$ \in L\$ \\ &\text{if and only if} \quad v_1 v_2^m v_3 u \in L. \end{aligned}$$

This satisfies (4), and completes the proof. □

To illustrate the importance of the last theorem, some applications will be given.

Theorem 11.8.4 The set $L = \{a^n b^n \mid n \geq 1\} \cup \{a^n b^{2n} \mid n \geq 1\}$ is not a deterministic context-free language.

Proof Let $p = p(L)$ be an integer satisfying Theorem 11.8.3. Let $w = a^p \underline{b^p}$ and assume that all p positions which are b's are distinguished. By the theorem, there exist $v_1, \ldots, v_5$ such that $w = v_1 \cdots v_5$.

Claim 1 $v_2 \notin b^+$.

Proof If $v_2 = b^i$ for some $i \geq 1$, then:

$$v_1 = a^p b^h,$$

$$v_3 = b^j, \qquad j > 0,$$

$$v_4 = b^k,$$

and

$$v_5 = b^{p-(h+i+j+k)}.$$

Then

$$v_1 v_3 v_5 = a^p b^{p-(i+k)} \in L.$$

But this is a contradiction since $i > 0$ implies

$$p - (i + k) < p.$$

Claim 2 $v_2 \notin a^+ b^+$.

Proof This is clear.

Claim 3

$$\begin{aligned} v_1 &= a^i & i &\geq 0, \\ v_2 &= a^j & j &> 0, \\ v_3 &= a^{p-(i+j)} b^k & k &> 0, \\ v_4 &= b^j & & \\ v_5 &= b^{p-(k+j)} & & \end{aligned}$$

Proof This is clear except for the fact that $\lg(v_2) = \lg(v_4)$. Suppose that $v_4 = b^{j'}$ and $v_5 = b^{p-(k+j')}$, and we shall prove that $j = j'$. First, consider $v_1 v_3 v_5 = a^{p-j} b^{p-j'} \in L$. But, if $p - j = p - j'$, then $j = j'$. Then, suppose $2(p - j) = p - j'$, which implies that $j' = 2j - p$. An analysis of $v_1 v_2^2 v_3 v_4^2 v_5 \in L$ shows that either $j = j'$ or $j' > p$, which would contradict that $v_2 v_3 v_4$ can have at most p distinguished positions. Thus $j = j'$ and now Claim 3 is proven.

To complete the proof, we note that v_5 must have a distinguished position, by part 3(ii) of Theorem 11.8.3. Thus $v_5 \neq \Lambda$. By condition (4) of Theorem 11.8.3, let $u = v_5 b^p$. Note that:

$$v_1 v_2 v_3 v_4 u \in L.$$

Thus

$$v_1 v_3 v_5 b^p \in L.$$

But

$$v_1 v_3 v_5 b^p = a^{p-j} b^{2p-j} \in L.$$

The only way that this string is in L is if

$$p - j = 2p - j$$

or if

$$2(p-j) = 2p - j.$$

Neither of these conditions is consistent with $p > 0$ and $j > 0$. □

Another example will be given which is an even stronger implication.

Theorem 11.8.5 The language $L = \{ww^T \mid w \in \{a, b\}^*\}$ is not a finite union of deterministic languages.

Proof Assume, for the sake of contradiction, that

$$L = \bigcup_{i=1}^{N} L_i \qquad \text{for some } N \geqslant 1 \qquad \text{and} \qquad L_i \in \Delta_0.$$

Let

$$p = \max_{1 \leqslant i \leqslant N} p'(L_i),$$

where $p'(L_k)$ are the constants from Theorem 11.8.3 for every $i \leqslant N$. Consider the set

$$H = \{(ba^p b)^{2n} \mid n \geqslant 1\} \subseteq L.$$

H is infinite and therefore, for some L_i, $|H \cap L_i| \geqslant 2$ or, more specifically, there are two (even) numbers $n_1, n_2 \geqslant 2$ such that both $w = (ba^p b)^{n_1} \in L_i$ and $w' = w(ba^p b)^{n_2} \in L_i$. Applying the Iteration Theorem 11.8.3 to w, let

$$K = \{i \mid (n_1 - 1)(p+2) < i < n_1(p+2) = \lg(w)\}$$

(that is, K corresponds to the rightmost substring a^p in w). Clearly $|K| = p \geqslant p'(L_i)$. Let $(v_1, v_2, v_3, v_4, v_5)$ be the factorization of w from Theorem 11.8.3. By Property (3), and since strings in L_i are palindromes, we have $v_1 \in ba^+$, $v_5 \in a^+ b$ and $v_2 = v_4 = a^q$ for some q, $1 \leqslant q < p$. Define $u = v_4 v_5 (ba^p b)^{n_2}$. Now, taking $m = n = 1$ in 2 (note that $v_5 \neq \Lambda$), $v_1 v_2 v_3 u = w' \in L_i$ implies

$$v_1 v_2^2 v_3 v_4 u = ba^{p+q} b (ba^p b)^{n_1 - 2} ba^{p+q} b (ba^p b)^{n_2} \in L_i,$$

which is not a palindrome since $q, n_2 \neq 0$. We have a contradiction with $L_i \subseteq L$. □

Since L is an unambiguous language, we have the following consequence.

Corollary There exists an unambiguous context-free language which is not a finite union of deterministic languages.

PROBLEMS

1 The proof of Theorem 11.8.2 is not completely formal. Find the "hand-waving" part. Formulate and prove a lemma about cross sections and make the proof completely rigorous.

2 Extend Theorem 11.8.3 in that (2) is replaced by the following statement.

(2′) For each $n \geqslant 0$, $v_1 v_2^n v_3 v_4^n v_5 \in L$ if and only if $w \in L$.

A sequence of definitions is necessary before the next problems can be stated.

Definition A (finite) *tree automaton* is a system

$$\mathscr{A} = (Q, \Sigma, \alpha, F) \tag{1}$$

where Q is a finite nonempty set, $F \subseteq Q$, Σ is an alphabet, and α: $Q^* \times \Sigma \underset{p}{\rightarrow} Q$ is a function with the property that $\alpha^{-1}(q)$ is finite for all $q \in Q$.

Definition Let T be a tree with labels in Σ and let $\mathscr{A}$ be a tree automaton of the form (1). A function f: $T \rightarrow Q$ is called a *computation for T* if and only if:

i) if x is a leaf in T, then $f(x) = \alpha(\Lambda, \lambda(x))$; and

ii) if x is an internal node in T and $x_1, \ldots, x_n$ are all the immediate descendants of x such that $x_1 \sqsubset x_2 \sqsubset \cdots \sqsubset x_n$,

then $f(x) = \alpha(f(x_1)f(x_2) \cdots f(x_n), \lambda(x))$.

Define

$$L(\mathscr{A}) = \{\mathrm{fr}(T) \mid T \text{ is a tree with labels in } \Sigma \text{ and there is a computation } f\colon T \rightarrow Q \text{ such that } f(x_0) \in F \text{ where } x_0 \text{ is the root of } T\}.$$

It is not a coincidence that the following definition reminds us of the definition of a strict deterministic grammar.

Definition We shall say that a tree automaton $\mathscr{A} = (Q, \Sigma, \alpha, F)$ has the *strict deterministic property* if and only if $|F| = 1$ and there exists a partition π on Q such that, for any $\eta, \eta_1, \eta_2 \in Q^*$, $q_1, q_2 \in Q$, and $a, b \in \Sigma$, the following two implications hold:

i) If $\alpha(\eta q_1 \eta_1, a) \equiv \alpha(\eta q_2 \eta_2, b)$, then $q_1 \equiv q_2$;

ii) If $\alpha(\eta\eta_1, a) \equiv \alpha(\eta, b)$, then $\eta_1 = \Lambda$ and ($\eta \neq \Lambda$ implies $a = b$).

3 Prove the following result.

Theorem $L \in \Delta_2$ if and only if $L = \{\Lambda\}$ or $L = L(\mathscr{A})$ for some tree automaton with the strict deterministic property.

Definition A grammar $G = (V, \Sigma, P, S)$ is *deterministic* if and only if there is a partition π of V and a subset $E \subseteq V - \Sigma$ such that $\Sigma \in \pi$ and for every A, $A' \in V - \Sigma$ and $\alpha, \beta, \beta' \in V^*$,

a) if $A \rightarrow \alpha\beta$ is in P and $\alpha \in V^*E$, then $\beta = \Lambda$ and $A \in E$;

b) if $A \rightarrow \alpha\beta$ and $A' \rightarrow \alpha\beta'$ are in P and $A \equiv A' \pmod{\pi}$, then at least one of the following four cases is true:

i) $\beta, \beta' \neq \Lambda$ and ${}^{(1)}\beta \equiv {}^{(1)}\beta' \pmod{\pi}$;
ii) $\beta = \beta' = \Lambda$ and $A = A'$;
iii) $\beta = \Lambda$ and $A \in E$;
iv) $\beta' = \Lambda$ and $A' \in E$.

4 Note that, in the preceding definition, condition 1 is equivalent to the requirement

$$P \subseteq (V \times (V - E)^*) \cup (E \times (V - E)^* E),$$

and that we obtain a strict deterministic grammar as a special case when $E = \emptyset$. Prove the following result.

Theorem $L \in \Delta_0$ if and only if $L = L(G)$ for some deterministic grammar G.

11.9 INTRODUCTION TO SIMPLE MACHINES, GRAMMARS, AND LANGUAGES

In Section 11.6, we were able to construct a nontrivial hierarchy of strict deterministic languages. This hierarchy was based on the degree of a language, which was related to the number of states in a dpda. In this section, we shall restrict our attention to the "simplest" class of strict deterministic languages in the hierarchy, i.e., to the strict deterministic languages of degree one.

First we show a convenient characterization of strict deterministic grammars of degree 1. This characterization makes it easier to recognize these grammars.

Lemma 11.9.1 Let G be any context-free grammar. Then G is strict deterministic of degree 1 if and only if $A \to \alpha | \beta$ in G implies that either $\alpha = \beta$ or α, β have a terminal distinguishing pair.†

Proof Let G be strict deterministic, $\mathbf{deg}(G) = 1$ and let $A \to \alpha | \beta$ be in G, $\alpha \neq \beta$. If α, β have no distinguishing pair, one of them is a (proper) prefix of the other, which contradicts the strict determinism of G. Let (C, D) be the distinguishing pair of α, β. Then $C \equiv D$. By definition of distinguishing pairs, $C \neq D$. If $C, D \in N$, we have a contradiction of $\mathbf{deg}(G) = 1$. Hence, $C, D \in \Sigma$.

Assume that G has the above property. Recall Algorithm 11.4.1, which tests a given context-free grammar for the property of being strict deterministic. Now let us apply that Algorithm to G. Starting in Step 1 with partition π consisting of Σ and otherwise only of singletons, the algorithm never reaches Step 6 (Step 5 is always followed by Step 3 since $\Sigma \in \pi$), and thus π is not altered. The algorithm halts in Step 8 (Step 4 is never followed by Step 7 since $A_i \equiv A_j$ implies $A_i = A_j$, which implies $\alpha_i \neq \alpha_j$ by the assumption of the indices in the algorithm). Therefore, π is strict and $\|\pi\| = \|\pi_0\| = 1$. □

---

† Recall the definition (given in Section 11.4) of distinguishing pair.

Now let us introduce "simple" grammars.

Definition A context-free grammar $G = (V, \Sigma, P, S)$ in Greibach normal form is said to be a *simple grammar* (*s-grammar* for short) if for all $A \in N$, $a \in \Sigma$, and α, $\beta \in V^*$,

$$A \to a\alpha \quad \text{and} \quad A \to a\beta \text{ in } P$$

imply $\alpha = \beta$. A *simple language*, or *s-language*, for short, is a language generated by an *s*-grammar.

Example

$$S \to aSA \mid b$$

$$A \to a$$

This is clearly an *s*-grammar that generates the set $L(G) = \{a^n ba^n \mid n \geqslant 0\}$.

Consider the grammar

$$S \to aAd \mid aBe$$

$$A \to aAb \mid b$$

$$B \to aBc \mid c$$

This grammar is not an *s*-grammar. The language generated is

$$L = \{a^n b^n d \mid n \geqslant 1\} \cup \{a^n c^n e \mid n \geqslant 1\}.$$

It can be shown that L is not an *s*-language. L is, however, a realtime strict deterministic language.

Next, we relate strict deterministic languages of degree one to dpda's.

Lemma 11.9.2 L is a strict deterministic language and $\mathbf{deg}(L) = 1$ if and only if either $L = \{\Lambda\}$ or $L = T_2(A)$ for some realtime dpda A with one state.

Proof We note that $\{\Lambda\}$ is of degree 1. If $L = T_2(A)$ for some dpda with one state, then, by Theorem 11.6.1, L is strict deterministic of degree one.

Conversely, let G be a strict deterministic grammar of degree 1 and let $L(G) \neq \{\Lambda\}$. Assume, without loss of generality, that G is Λ-free. We shall show that G satisfies the main condition, from the definition of a realtime strict deterministic grammar. But this is immediate from the assumption that $\mathbf{deg}(G) = 1$; that is, $\|\pi_0\| = 1$, since then $A \equiv A' \pmod{\pi_0}$ implies $A = A'$. If we assume $A \equiv A'$, and $A \to \alpha B$ and $A' \to \alpha B'\beta$ are in P, then, since π_0 is strict,

$$B \equiv B',$$

so we have $B = B'$ by the degree 1 condition. Clearly, this implies $\beta = \Lambda$, by the strictness of π_0. Thus G is realtime. Clearly, L is accepted by a realtime dpda with only one state, as can be seen by a careful check of the proof of Theorem 11.7.4. $\square$

Next, we show that the realtime assumption is not necessary.

Lemma 11.9.3 $L = T_2(A')$ for some one-state realtime dpda A' if and only if $L = T_2(A)$ for some one-state dpda A and $L \neq \{\Lambda\}$.

Proof Only the *if* condition needs proof. Let $\{\Lambda\} \neq L = T_2(A)$ for some one-state dpda A. Then L is strict deterministic of degree 1, by Theorem 11.6.1. By Lemma 11.9.2, $L = T_2(A')$ for some one-state realtime dpda A'. □

Now the various results can be collected into one proposition.

Theorem 11.9.1 Let $L \subseteq \Sigma^*$. The following statements are equivalent:

a) L is simple.

b) L is strict deterministic of degree one.

c) L is accepted as $T_2(A)$ for some realtime dpda with one state or $L = \{\Lambda\}$.

d) L is accepted as $T_2(B)$ for some dpda with one state.

Proof By our lemmas, (b), (c), and (d) are already known to be equivalent. Clearly, if L is simple, it is strict deterministic of degree one.

Assume $\{\Lambda\} \neq L = T_2(A)$ for some one-state realtime dpda A. By the proof of Theorem 11.7.4, $L = L(G)$, where G is realtime, in Greibach form, and since A has one state, L is strict deterministic and of degree one. By Lemma 11.9.1, if we have

$$A \to a\alpha \qquad \text{and} \qquad A \to a\beta \text{ in } P$$

for $A \in N$, $a \in \Sigma$, and α, β in N^* (and all the rules are of this form), then $\alpha = \beta$. □

Now we turn to an important result about s-languages. We shall show that the inclusion question, that is, $L_1 \subseteq L_2$, is unsolvable for s-languages. There are two reasons why this result is noteworthy. First, the s-languages are very primitive and are contained in many of the other families of deterministic languages that have been studied. Thus it follows, as corollaries to this result, that the inclusion problem is unsolvable for all families that contain the s-languages.

There is a second reason why this inclusion result is important. There is an obvious relationship between the inclusion problem and the equality problem. If the inclusion problem is solvable, then the equality problem is also, since $L_1 = L_2$ if and only if $L_1 \subseteq L_2$ and $L_2 \subseteq L_1$. In the examples we have seen, such as regular sets or context-free languages, both problems have been solvable or both unsolvable. It could be the case that there is some family of languages that has an unsolvable inclusion problem but a solvable equality problem. The s-languages will turn out to be such a family.

In the argument which follows, some simple languages will be used and will be specified by dpda's. As we have only one state, it can be omitted from a description of a dpda, and we need only write:

$$A = (\Sigma, \Gamma, \delta, Z_0),$$

where

$$\delta\colon \Sigma \times \Gamma \to \Gamma^*$$

is a partial function, in order to specify an s-language.

Theorem 11.9.2 The inclusion problem for s-languages is recursively unsolvable; i.e., there is no algorithm which can decide, of two s-languages L_1 and L_2, whether or not $L_1 \subseteq L_2$.

Proof The argument will proceed by taking an arbitrary Turing machine A and input w to A. Two s-languages L_1 and L_2 will be constructed such that $L_1 \not\subseteq L_2$ if and only if A halts and accepts w. (This actually shows more; namely, that the inclusion problem is not partially decidable.)

Let $A = (Q, \Sigma, \Gamma, B, \delta, q_0, \{\bar{q}\})$ be any Turing machine and let $w \in \Sigma^*$. There is no loss of generality in assuming that A is totally defined on $Q - \{\bar{q}\}$ and that $\bar{q}$ is a unique final "halt" state. The idea of the proof will use the reduction from A to the MPCP done in Section 8.3. The reader is expected to be aware of the details of those arguments. Assume that the lists **x** and **y** given in Table 8.3.1 have been constructed.

For each integer i, $1 \leqslant i \leqslant n$, let f_i be a new symbol not in

$$\Delta = (\Sigma - \{B\}) \cup Q \cup \{\#\}.$$

Let ¢ and \$ be two new symbols not in $\Delta \cup \{f_1, \ldots, f_n\}$. Define a homomorphism φ: $\Delta^* \to (\Delta \cup \{¢\})^*$ defined by:

$$\varphi(a) = a¢$$

for each $a \in \Delta$. Now we define the first language of interest.

$$L_1 = \{f_2 f_{i_k} \cdots f_{i_1} f_1 \varphi(y_1 y_{i_1} \cdots y_{i_k} y_2)\$ \mid k \geqslant 0, 3 \leqslant i_1, \ldots, i_k \leqslant n\}.$$

We construct a one-state dpda A_1 such that $T_2(A_1) = L_1$. Let $A_1 = (\Delta \cup \{¢, \$, f_1, \ldots, f_n\}, \delta_1, \Gamma_1, Z_0)$, where

$$\Gamma_1 = \{Z_0, Z_1, C\} \cup \{[z] \mid z \in \Delta^+, \lg(z) \leqslant \max_i \{\lg(y_i)\}\}$$
$$\cup \{[z¢] \mid z \in \Delta^*, \lg(z) < \max_i \{\lg(y_i)\}\}.$$

The transition function is defined by cases.

CASE 1. Read the f_i's but stack the corresponding y_i's.

$$\delta_1(f_2, Z_0) = Z_1 [y_2^T] C,$$
$$\delta_1(f_i, C) = [y_i^T] C \quad \text{for each } i, 3 \leqslant i \leqslant n,$$
$$\delta_1(f_1, C) = [y_1^T].$$

For each $a \in \Delta$, $z \in \Delta^*$, $\lg(z) < \max_i \{\lg(y_i)\}$.

CASE 2. $\delta_1(a, [za]) = [z¢]$; Check whether symbols match.

CASE 3. $\delta_1(¢, [z¢]) = [z]$ if $z \neq \Lambda$.

CASE 4. $\delta_1(¢, [¢]) = \Lambda$.

CASE 5. $\delta_1(\$, Z_1) = \Lambda$.

(3) and (4) check whether every other symbol is a ¢. (5) checks that the last symbol is a \$.

It is not too difficult to see that $T_2(A_1) = L_1$.

The tricky part of the proof is the construction of an appropriate L_2. This set is

$$L_2 = \{f_2 f_{i_k} \cdots f_{i_1} f_1 \varphi(y_1 y_{i_1} \cdots y_{i_k} y_2)\$ \mid k \geqslant 0, 3 \leqslant i_1, \ldots, i_k \leqslant n, \quad x_1 x_{i_1} \cdots x_{i_k} x_2 \neq y_1 y_{i_1} \cdots y_{i_k} y_2\} \cup J$$

where J (an abbreviation for junk) is some set such that $J \cap L_1 = \emptyset$. Now we construct an appropriate machine $A_2 = (\Delta \cup \{¢, \$, f_1, \ldots, f_n\}, \Gamma_2, \delta_2, Z_0)$, where

$$\begin{aligned}\Gamma_2 = {} & \{Z_0, Z_1, A, C, D, E\} \\ & \cup \{[z] \mid z \in \Delta^+, \lg(z) \leqslant \max_i \{\lg(x_i)\} \\ & \cup \{[z¢] \mid z \in \Delta^*, \lg(z) < \max_i \{\lg(x_i)\}\}.\end{aligned}$$

δ_2 is defined by cases below.

CASE 1. $\delta_2(f_2, Z_0) = Z_1[x_2^T]C$.

CASE 2. $\delta_2(f_i, C) = [x_i^T]C$ for each $i, 3 \leqslant i \leqslant n$.

CASE 3. $\delta_2(f_1, C) = [x_1^T]$.

In steps (1) through (3), the f_i are read and the corresponding x_i are stacked.

For each $a \in \Delta$, $z \in \Delta^*$, $\lg(z) < \max_i \{\lg(x_i)\}$.

CASE 4. $\delta_2(a, [za]) = [z¢]$.

CASE 5. $\delta_2(¢, [¢]) = \Lambda$.

CASE 6. $\delta_2(¢, [z¢]) = [z]$ if $z \neq \Lambda$.

In (4) through (6), inputs are matched against the stack and it is checked that every other symbol in the input is a ¢.

CASE 7. $\delta_2(\$, Z_1) = E$. reject if final symbol is \$ and pushdown is only Z_1.

For each $a, b \in \Delta, a \neq b$, each $z, \bar{z} \in \Delta^*$, such that

$$\lg(z) < \max_i \{\lg(x_i)\},$$
$$\lg(\bar{z}) \leqslant \max_i \{\lg(x_i)\}.$$

CASE 8. $\delta_2(a, [zb]) = \Lambda$. If a mismatch occurs, pop the stack.

CASE 9. $\delta_2(¢, [\bar{z}]) = D$. If $\bar{z} \neq \Lambda$, use ¢ to encode D on the stack.

CASE 10. $\delta_2(a, D) = \Lambda$.

For each $c \in \Delta \cup \{¢\}$

CASE 11. $\delta_2(c, Z_1) = A$.

CASE 12. $\delta_2(c, A) = A$.

CASE 13. $\delta_2(\$, A) = \Lambda$.

In (11) through (13), if the bottom of the stack was encountered when a symbol other than A was read, the stack symbol A is used to encode that the input will be eventually accepted when \$ is finally read.

Claim 1

$$T_2(A_2) = L_2$$
$$= (L_1 - \{f_2 f_{i_k} \cdots f_{i_1} f_1 \varphi(x_1 x_{i_1} \cdots x_{i_k} x_2)\$ \mid k \geq 0, \quad 3 \leq i_1, \ldots, i_k \leq n\}) \cup J.$$

where J consists of some irrelevant strings so that

$$L_1 \cap J = \emptyset$$

Proof The proof of this claim is long and tedious and is left for Exercise 7 at the end of this section.

Claim 2 $L_1 \subseteq L_2$ if and only if

$$L_1 \cap \{f_2 f_{i_k} \cdots f_{i_1} f_1 \varphi(x_1 x_{i_1} \cdots x_{i_k} x_2)\$ \mid k \geq 0, 3 \leq i_1, \ldots, i_k \leq n\} = \emptyset$$

if and only if there is no sequence $i_1, \ldots, i_k, k \geq 0$, with $3 \leq i_1, \ldots, i_k \leq n$ such that

$$x_1 x_{i_1} \cdots x_{i_k} x_2 = y_1 y_{i_1} \cdots y_{i_k} y_2.$$

Proof From Claim 1, write $L_2 = (L_1 - X) \cup J$. Now

$$L_1 \subseteq L_2$$

if and only if

$$L_1 \cap \bar{L}_2 = \emptyset = L_1 \cap \overline{(L_1 - X) \cup J} = L_1 \cap \overline{(L_1 \cap \bar{X})} \cap \bar{J} = L_1 \cap (\bar{L}_1 \cup X) = L_1 \cap X$$

The second equivalence holds because of the structure of L_1 and X.

Claim 3 $L_1 \nsubseteq L_2$ if and only if the Turing machine halts on $w \in \Sigma^*$.

Proof The result follows from Claim 2 and Problem 12 of Section 8.3, in which it is shown that

$$x_1 x_{i_1} \cdots x_{i_k} x_2 = y_1 y_{i_1} \cdots y_{i_k} y_2$$

for some $k \geq 0$, $3 \leq i_1, \ldots, i_k \leq n$ if and only if A halts on w. Now the proof is complete. □

PROBLEMS

1 Let $R \subseteq \Sigma^*$ be an arbitrary regular set and let \$ be a new symbol not in Σ. Show that $R\$$ is a simple language.

2 Show that the family of s-languages is not closed under union, intersection, or complementation.

3 Show that the family of s-languages is closed under product.

4 Show that the family of s-languages is not closed under reversal.

5 Let D_r be the semi-Dyck set over $\Sigma_r \cup \bar{\Sigma}_r$ and let \$ be a new symbol not in $\Sigma_r \cup \bar{\Sigma}_r$. Show that $D_r\$$ is a simple language.

6 Show that it is undecidable to determine whether a given context-free language is an s-language or not.

7 Prove that $T_2(A_2) = L_2$ in the proof of Theorem 11.9.2.

8 Does Theorem 11.9.2 hold for single-turn simple machines?

9 Show that, for each s-grammar G, there is an equivalent s-grammar which is in 2-standard form.

11.10 THE EQUIVALENCE PROBLEM FOR SIMPLE LANGUAGES

In this section, we will show that the equivalence problem for s-languages is solvable. We shall assume that the two s-languages L_1 and L_2 are presented by s-grammars G_1 and G_2. If either $L_1 = \{\Lambda\}$ or $L_2 = \{\Lambda\}$, the problem is trivial, so we shall henceforth assume that G_1 and G_2 are Λ-free. The algorithm to be given will depend on the following definition of equivalence of strings.

Definition Let $G_i = (V_i, \Sigma, P_i, S_i)$, $i = 1, 2$, be two context-free grammars such that $N_1 \cap N_2 = \emptyset$ and let $\alpha, \beta \in (N_1 \cup N_2)^*$. We say that α is *equivalent* to β (written $\alpha \equiv \beta$), if for each $x \in \Sigma^*$, $\alpha \overset{*}{\Rightarrow} x$ if and only if $\beta \overset{*}{\Rightarrow} x$.

Note that since α and β may have variables from each grammar, the generations involved may employ productions from both grammars. Also note that $L(G_1) = L(G_2)$ if and only if $S_1 \equiv S_2$.

Example Let G_1 be the grammar

$$S_1 \rightarrow ab$$

and let G_2 have productions

$$S_2 \rightarrow Ab$$

$$A \rightarrow aB$$

$$B \rightarrow b$$

Note that $S_1 \not\equiv S_2$. However, it is easy to see that

$$S_1 B \equiv S_2.$$

Since our grammars are Λ-free and may be assumed to be reduced, we have that $\beta \equiv \Lambda$ if and only if $\beta = \Lambda$.

Our first result is that $\equiv$ is a congruence relation.

Lemma 11.10.1 Let $G_i = (V_i, \Sigma, P_i, S_i)$ be two context-free grammars with $N_1 \cap N_2 = \emptyset$ for $i = 1, 2$. The relation $\equiv$ is a congruence relation on $(N_1 \cup N_2)^*$; i.e., it is an equivalence relation, and furthermore, for any α, β, γ, δ in $(N_1 \cup N_2)^*$, if $\alpha \equiv \beta$ and $\gamma \equiv \delta$, then

$$\alpha\gamma \equiv \beta\delta.$$

Proof The proof that $\equiv$ is an equivalence relation is immediate. Suppose $\alpha \equiv \beta$ and $\gamma \equiv \delta$ for arbitrary strings α, β, γ, and δ in $(N_1 \cup N_2)^*$. For each $x \in \Sigma^*$,

$$\alpha\gamma \overset{*}{\Rightarrow} x$$

if and only if there exist $y, z \in \Sigma^*$ such that

$$x = yz, \qquad \alpha \overset{*}{\Rightarrow} y, \qquad \text{and} \qquad \gamma \overset{*}{\Rightarrow} z$$

This holds if and only if

$$x = yz, \qquad \beta \overset{*}{\Rightarrow} y \qquad \text{and} \qquad \delta \overset{*}{\Rightarrow} z$$

which, in turn, holds if and only if

$$\beta\delta \overset{*}{\Rightarrow} x$$

Thus $\alpha\gamma \equiv \beta\delta$. □

We shall always assume in what follows that the grammars to be considered are in Greibach normal form or, equivalently, in r-standard form for some $r \geqslant 2$. The lemmas we shall use in this section are being proved in a rather general form since they can be used in proving a number of different results. In the simplest case, any s-grammar may be placed in 2-standard form by Problem 11.9.9.

Definition Let $G = (V, \Sigma, P, S)$ be any grammar in Greibach form and let $A \in N$ and $a \in \Sigma$. Define

$$R(A, a) = \{\gamma \mid A \to a\gamma \text{ is in } P\}.$$

Note that, for any grammar in standard 2-form, it is always the case that $R(A, a) \subseteq N_\Lambda^2$. In an s-grammar,

$$R(A, a) = \emptyset \qquad \text{or} \qquad |R(A, a)| = 1.$$

We shall often write $R(A, a)$ for this unique string when no confusion can result.

We now know that the equivalence problem reduces to deciding if $S_1 \equiv S_2$. Let us introduce some terminology which helps to determine whether or not $\alpha \equiv \beta$.

Definition Let $G_i = (V_i, \Sigma, P_i, S_i)$ be two context-free grammars with $N_1 \cap N_2 = \emptyset$ and let α, β be in $(N_1 \cup N_2)^*$. We define the set of *witnesses* for α and β as

$$\bar{W}(\alpha, \beta) = \{x \in \Sigma^* \mid \alpha \overset{*}{\Rightarrow} x \quad \text{if and only if} \quad \beta \overset{*}{\not\Rightarrow} x\}.$$

The set of *shortest witnesses* is

$$W(\alpha, \beta) = \{x \in \bar{W}(\alpha, \beta) \mid \quad \text{for each } y \text{ in } \bar{W}(\alpha, \beta), \lg(x) \leqslant \lg(y)\}.$$

Thus a witness is a terminal string that distinguishes α from β.

Example Consider grammars G_1 and G_2 from the first example of this section and let $\alpha = S_1$ and $\beta = S_2$. Then

$$\bar{W}(S_1, S_2) = \{ab, abb\},$$
$$W(S_1, S_2) = \{ab\}.$$

Our algorithm for deciding whether $L_1 = L_2$ will work if we first consider $S_1 \equiv S_2$. Several transformations will be defined which map the pair (S_1, S_2) into a finite set of pairs to be tested, and the process will be repeated. Since there are a number of other algorithms of this type, we establish some preliminary lemmas which hold for general types of transformations.

To simplify technical definitions assume that two grammars $G_i = (V_i, \Sigma, P_i, S_i)$ are fixed with $N_1 \cap N_2 = \emptyset$. Let $N = N_1 \cup N_2$.

Definition A *transformation* T is a partial function from $N^* \times N^*$ into

$$\{\mathit{fail}\} \cup \{U \mid U \subseteq N^* \times N^*, U \text{ finite and nonempty}\}.$$

If $T(\alpha, \beta) = \mathit{fail}$, we say that T *failed on* (α, β). If $T \neq \mathit{fail}$ and is defined, then

$$T(\alpha, \beta) = \{(\alpha_1, \beta_1), \ldots, (\alpha_m, \beta_m) \mid \alpha_i, \beta_i \in N^* \quad \text{for all } i, 1 \leqslant i \leqslant m, \quad \text{where } m \geqslant 1\}.$$

Two important properties of transformations are now introduced, which are relevant in determining which transformations are useful in testing for equivalence.

Definition A transformation T is *valid* if, for each α, β at which T is defined,

1 $\alpha \equiv \beta$ implies $T(\alpha, \beta) = \{(\alpha_1, \beta_1), \ldots, (\alpha_m, \beta_m)\}$ for some $m \geqslant 1$ and $\alpha_i \equiv \beta_i$ for each i, $1 \leqslant i \leqslant m$, and

2 $\alpha \not\equiv \beta$ implies that either $T(\alpha, \beta) = \mathit{fail}$ or there exists $(\alpha_i, \beta_i) \in T(\alpha, \beta)$ and $\alpha_i \not\equiv \beta_i$.

The next property is a little more complicated.

Definition A transformation T is *monotone* if, for each $\alpha, \beta \in N^*$ such that $\alpha \not\equiv \beta$ and

$$T(\alpha, \beta) = \{(\alpha_1, \beta_1), \ldots, (\alpha_m, \beta_m)\},$$

and if y is a shortest witness of α and β, then there exist i, $1 \leqslant i \leqslant m$, and some shortest witness x for α_i and β_i such that $\lg(x) < \lg(y)$.

Now we introduce one of the transformations to be used in our final algorithm.

Definition Let $G_i = (V_i, \Sigma, P_i, S_i)$ be two s-grammars with $N_1 \cap N_2 = \emptyset$. For $\alpha, \beta \in N^+$, let $\alpha = A\alpha'$ and $\beta = B\beta'$ for some $A, B \in N$, $\alpha, \beta \in N^*$. The *A-transformation*, T_A, is defined by:

$$T_A(\alpha, \beta) = \begin{cases} \mathit{fail} & \text{if } |R(A, a)| + |R(B, a)| = 1 \quad \text{for some } a \in \Sigma, \\ \{(R(A, a)\alpha', R(B, a)\beta') \mid a \in \Sigma, R(A, a) \neq \emptyset, R(B, a) \neq \emptyset\} & \text{otherwise.} \end{cases}$$

Also, $T_A(a, \Lambda)$ and $T_A(\Lambda, \beta)$ are undefined.

Note that $T_A(\alpha, \beta) = \mathit{fail}$ if one of the sets is empty and the other is not.

Example Let G_1 be the s-grammar

$$S_1 \to aABC$$

$$A \to b$$

$$B \to c$$

$$C \to aC \mid \$$$

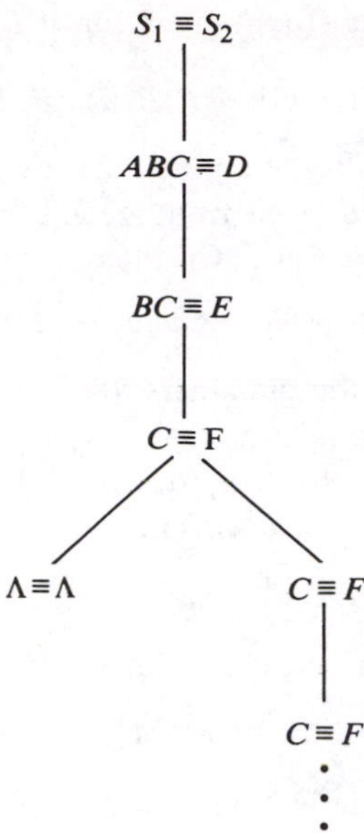

FIG. 11.6

and let G_2 be the s-grammar

$$S_2 \to aD$$
$$D \to bE$$
$$E \to cF$$
$$F \to aF \mid \$$$

We begin by applying T_A to (S_1, S_2), which yields (ABC, D), and continue. It is often helpful to represent this process by a tree, as shown in Fig. 11.6. The process may continue indefinitely.

Lemma 11.10.2 If the underlying grammars G_1 and G_2 are s-grammars, then T_A is both valid and monotone.

Proof The argument is subdivided into separate claims.

Claim 1 If $\alpha \equiv \beta$ and $T_A(\alpha, \beta)$ is defined, then $T_A(\alpha, \beta) = \{(\alpha_1, \beta_1), \ldots, (\alpha_m, \beta_m)\}$ for some $m \geqslant 1$ and $\alpha_i \equiv \beta_i$ for each i, $1 \leqslant i \leqslant m$.

Proof of Claim 1 Suppose $\alpha \equiv \beta$. It must be the case that both α and β are in N^+ for, if either α or β were Λ, then $\alpha = \beta = \Lambda$ and $T_A(\alpha, \beta)$ is undefined. Thus there exist $A, B \in N$, $\alpha', \beta' \in N^*$, such that

$$\alpha = A\alpha' \qquad \text{and} \qquad \beta = B\beta'.$$

Next we will argue that $T(\alpha, \beta) \neq fail$ for, if $T_A(\alpha, \beta) = fail$, then there would exist $a \in \Sigma$ for which

$$|R(A, a)| + |R(B, a)| = 1.$$

Without loss of generality, suppose $R(A, a) = \emptyset$ and $R(B, a) = \{\gamma\}$. Then no string that starts with a can be derived from A, and since the grammars are Λ-free, no such string can be derived from $\alpha = A\alpha'$. On the other hand,

$$\beta = B\beta' \Rightarrow a\gamma\beta' \Rightarrow axy$$

where $\gamma \overset{*}{\Rightarrow} x$ and $\beta' \overset{*}{\Rightarrow} y$, since the grammars are both reduced. Thus axy is a string that distinguishes α from β, contradicting that $\alpha \equiv \beta$.

Hence $T_A(\alpha, \beta) = \{(\alpha_1, \beta_1), \ldots, (\alpha_m, \beta_m)\}$ for some $m \geqslant 1$, and we must now show that $\alpha_i \equiv \beta_i$ for each i, $1 \leqslant i \leqslant m$. Let

$$\alpha_i = R(A, a)\alpha' \qquad \text{and} \qquad \beta_i = R(B, a)\beta',$$

from the definition of T_A. Let $\alpha_i \overset{*}{\Rightarrow} x \in \Sigma^*$. Then

$$\alpha = A\alpha' \Rightarrow aR(A, a)\alpha' \overset{*}{\Rightarrow} ax$$

But then $\beta \overset{*}{\Rightarrow} ax$. But this latter derivation must start with

$$\beta = B\beta' \Rightarrow aR(B, a)\beta' \overset{*}{\Rightarrow} ax$$

because the grammars are s-grammars, and so

$$\beta_i = R(B, a)\beta' \overset{*}{\Rightarrow} x$$

The same argument applied in the other direction yields that $\alpha_i \equiv \beta_i$, and the proof of Claim 1 is complete.

Claim 2 If $\alpha \not\equiv \beta$ and $T_A(\alpha, \beta) = \{(\alpha_1, \beta_1), \ldots, (\alpha_m, \beta_m)\}$ for some $m \geqslant 1$, then, for any $y \in \Sigma^+$, $y = ay'$ with $a \in \Sigma$ is in $\bar{W}(\alpha, \beta)$, if and only if there is some i, $1 \leqslant i \leqslant m$ such that $y' \in \bar{W}(\alpha_i, \beta_i)$.

Proof of claim 2 Let

$$\alpha = A\alpha' \qquad \text{and} \qquad \beta = B\beta'$$

for $A, B \in N$; $\alpha', \beta' \in N^*$. Then

$$\alpha \overset{*}{\Rightarrow} y \quad \text{if and only if} \quad \alpha = A\alpha' \underset{L}{\Rightarrow} aR(A, a)\alpha' \underset{L}{\Rightarrow} ay'$$

$$\text{if and only if} \quad R(A, a)\alpha' \overset{*}{\Rightarrow} y'$$

A similar argument holds for β. Thus y distinguishes α from β if and only if there is some i, $1 \leqslant i \leqslant m$, such that y' distinguishes $R(A, a)\alpha'$ from $R(B, a)\beta'$. But this proves Claim 2, by the definition of T_A.

Claims 1 and 2 combine to show that T_A is a valid transformation. In addition, Claim 2 implies that, if $\alpha \not\equiv \beta$ and $T_A(\alpha, \beta) = \{(\alpha_1, \beta_1), \ldots, (\alpha_m, \beta_m)\}$ for some $m \geqslant 1$ then $y = ay' \in \bar{W}(\alpha, \beta)$ if and only if there is some i, $1 \leqslant i \leqslant m$, such that $y' \in \bar{W}(\alpha_i, \beta_i)$. It is easy to verify that y is in $W(\alpha, \beta)$ if and only if $y' \in W(\alpha_i, \beta_i)$. This follows because, if there were a shorter witness for (α_i, β_i) than y', there would be a shorter witness than y for (α, β). The argument is reversible. $\square$

Next, we need a few more simple definitions.

Definition Let $G = (V, \Sigma, P, S)$ be any reduced context-free grammar. For each $A \in N$, define

$$\ell(A) = \min\{\lg(x) \mid A \overset{*}{\Rightarrow} x, x \in \Sigma^*\},$$
$$\ell = \max\{\ell(A) \mid A \in N\}.$$

When we deal with two grammars $G_i = (V_i, \Sigma, P_i, S_i)$, $i = 1, 2$, with $N_1 \cap N_2 = \emptyset$, we define

$$\ell = \max\{\ell_1, \ell_2\},$$

where $\ell_i = \max\{\ell(A) \mid A \in N_i\}$.

The following facts are useful.

Lemma 11.10.3 Let $G_i = (V_i, \Sigma, P_i, S_i)$ be two reduced Λ-free grammars.

1. For all $\alpha \in N^+$ and $x \in \Sigma^*$, if $\lg(x) < \lg(\alpha)$, then $\alpha \overset{*}{\not\Rightarrow} x$.
2. If $\beta \in N^+$, then there exists $x \in \Sigma^*$ such that $\beta \overset{*}{\Rightarrow} x$ and $\lg(x) \leq \ell \lg(\beta)$.
3. Let $\alpha, \beta \in N^+$. If $\lg(\alpha) > \ell \lg(\beta)$, then $\alpha \not\equiv \beta$.
4. Given $x \in \Sigma^*$ and $\beta \in N^*$, define β' to the shortest string such that $\beta = \beta'\beta''$ and $\beta' \underset{L}{\overset{*}{\Rightarrow}} x\gamma$ for some $\gamma \in N^*$. Then $\lg(\beta') \leq \lg(x)$.

Proof (1) is a trivial consequence of the fact that the grammars are reduced and Λ-free. Part (2) is a straightforward consequence of the fact that the grammars are reduced and Λ-free and using the definition of ℓ. To show (3), we know that there exists $x \in \Sigma^*$ such that $\beta \overset{*}{\Rightarrow} x$ and

$$\lg(x) \leq \ell \lg(\beta) < \lg(\alpha)$$

by (2) and the hypothesis of (3). By (1), $\alpha \overset{*}{\not\Rightarrow} x$, and so $x \in \overline{W}(\alpha, \beta)$. Therefore $\alpha \not\equiv \beta$.

To show (4), we use the definition of β' to write

$$\beta' = B_1 \cdots B_i, \qquad x = x_1 \cdots x_i, \qquad \text{and} \qquad B_j \in N,$$

for each j, $1 \leq j \leq i$, and $x_j \in \Sigma^*$ such that $B_j \underset{L}{\overset{*}{\Rightarrow}} x_j$ for each j, $1 \leq j < i$, and $B_i \underset{L}{\overset{*}{\Rightarrow}} x_i\gamma$. Since the grammars are Λ-free, we get that $\lg(x_j) \geq 1$ for $1 \leq j \leq i$. On the other hand,

$$\sum_{j=1}^{i} \lg(x_j) = \lg(x),$$

so that

$$\lg(\beta') = i \leq \lg(x). \qquad \square$$

Now the second type of transformation is introduced, the B-transformation, T_B.

Definition Let $G_i = (V_i, \Sigma, P_i, S_i)$ be two reduced Λ-free grammars with $N_1 \cap N_2 = \emptyset$ and $N = N_1 \cup N_2$. For all α, $\beta \in N^+$ with $\lg(\alpha) \geq 2$ and $\lg(\beta) > \ell$, let

$\alpha = A\alpha'$ and let x be the shortest terminal string generated by A. If $\beta' \in N^+$ is the shortest string such that there exists β'', $\gamma \in N^+$, with $\beta = \beta'\beta''$ and $\beta' \overset{*}{\underset{L}{\Rightarrow}} x\gamma$ then we say that

$$T_B(\alpha, \beta) = \{(\alpha', \gamma\beta''), (A\gamma, \beta')\}.$$

If no such β' exists, then

$$T(\alpha, \beta) = \textit{fail}.$$

T_B is undefined elsewhere.

Note that, since $\lg(\beta) > \ell$ and, by part (3) of Lemma 11.10.3,

$$\lg(\beta') \leqslant \lg(x),$$

it must be the case that $\beta'' \neq \Lambda$.

Note that the B-transformation may be applied to strings $\alpha \in N_1^+$ and $\beta \in N_2^+$. The resulting string $A\gamma$ is in $N_1 N_2^*$ and this is the reason that the symbols from the two grammars can be mixed together.

Example Let G_1 be the s-grammar

$$S_1 \to aAC$$
$$A \to aB \mid bAB$$
$$B \to b$$
$$C \to a$$

and let G be as follows:

$$S_2 \to aDE$$
$$D \to bDF \mid a$$
$$E \to bG$$
$$F \to b$$
$$G \to a$$

Let $\alpha = AB^5C$ and $\beta = DF^5E$. The shortest terminal string derivable from A is $x = ab$. We now attempt to derive $x = ab$ from β

$$\beta = DF^5E \Rightarrow aF^5E \Rightarrow abF^4E$$

This tells us that

$$\beta' = DF, \qquad \beta'' = F^4E, \qquad \text{and} \qquad \gamma = \Lambda$$

and thus,

$$T_B(\alpha, \beta) = \{(B^5C, F^4E), (A, DF)\}.$$

Next we show that the B-transformation is valid and monotone for s-grammars.

Lemma 11.10.4 Let G_1 and G_2 be reduced Λ-free grammars in Greibach normal form with $N_1 \cap N_2 = \emptyset$, $N = N_1 \cup N_2$, and let $\alpha, \beta \in N^*$ such that $\lg(\alpha) \geqslant 2$, $\lg(\beta) \geqslant \ell$. If

i) $\alpha = A\alpha'$ for some $A \in N$ such that $L(A) = \{w \in \Sigma^* \mid A \overset{*}{\Rightarrow} w\}$ is prefix-free, and if

ii) $\beta \underset{L}{\overset{*}{\Rightarrow}} z\delta$ for some $z \in \Sigma^+$, $\delta \in N^*$, and δ is unique†,

then the B-transformation is both valid and monotone.

Proof Again the argument is subdivided into separate claims.

Claim 1 If $\alpha \equiv \beta$ and $T_B(\alpha, \beta)$ is defined, then $T_B(\alpha, \beta) = \{(\alpha_1, \beta_1), (\alpha_2, \beta_2)\}$ and $\alpha_i \equiv \beta_i$ for $i = 1, 2$.

Proof of Claim 1 Let $\alpha \equiv \beta$, $\alpha = A\alpha'$ for some $A \in N$ and $\alpha' \in N^+$. Let x be a shortest terminal string derivable from A and assume that $T_B(\alpha, \beta)$ is defined. Let y be a shortest terminal string derived from α'. Then

$$\alpha = A\alpha' \overset{*}{\Rightarrow} xy$$

Since $\alpha \equiv \beta$, we have $\beta \underset{L}{\overset{*}{\Rightarrow}} xy$. Moreover, the derivation may be factored as

$$\beta \underset{L}{\overset{*}{\Rightarrow}} x\beta''' \underset{L}{\overset{*}{\Rightarrow}} xy$$

since the grammars are in Greibach normal form. Moreover, there must exist β', β'', and $\gamma \in N^*$ such that

$$\beta = \beta'\beta'' \qquad \text{and} \qquad \beta''' = \gamma\beta''$$

so that $\beta' \underset{L}{\overset{*}{\Rightarrow}} x\gamma$. (That is, β' is the shortest prefix of β which generates $x\gamma$.) Therefore

$$T_B(\alpha, \beta) = \{(\alpha', \gamma\beta''), (A\gamma, \beta')\}.$$

Next, it is necessary to show that $\alpha' \equiv \gamma\beta''$ and $A\gamma \equiv \beta'$. The first of the conditions is easy to check using the hypotheses of the lemma. For each $y' \in \Sigma^*$,

$$\alpha' \underset{L}{\overset{*}{\Rightarrow}} y'$$

if and only if

$$\alpha = A\alpha' \underset{L}{\overset{*}{\Rightarrow}} xy'$$

if and only if

$$\beta = \beta'\beta'' \underset{L}{\overset{*}{\Rightarrow}} xy'$$

because $\alpha \equiv \beta$. In turn, this holds if and only if

$$\beta'\beta'' \underset{L}{\overset{*}{\Rightarrow}} x\gamma\beta'' \underset{L}{\overset{*}{\Rightarrow}} xy'$$

if and only if

$$\gamma\beta \underset{L}{\overset{*}{\Rightarrow}} y'$$

For the second condition, assume, for the sake of contradiction, that $A\gamma \not\equiv \beta'$ and let y' be a shortest witness for $A\gamma$ and β'.

CASE 1. $A\gamma \underset{L}{\overset{*}{\Rightarrow}} y'$. Let z be a shortest terminal string derived from β''. Then

$$A\gamma\beta'' \underset{L}{\overset{*}{\Rightarrow}} y'z$$

---

† This means that $\beta \underset{L}{\overset{*}{\Rightarrow}} z\delta_1$ and $\beta \overset{*}{\Rightarrow} z\delta_2$ imply that $\delta_1 = \delta_2$.

Since we already know that $\alpha' \equiv \gamma\beta''$, we have that

$$\alpha = A\alpha' \underset{L}{\overset{*}{\Rightarrow}} y'z$$

and thus

$$\beta = \beta'\beta'' \underset{L}{\overset{*}{\Rightarrow}} y'z$$

since $\alpha \equiv \beta$. There must exist $y_1, y_2 \in \Sigma^*$ such that

$$y_1 y_2 = y'z$$

and

$$\beta' \overset{*}{\Rightarrow} y_1 \qquad \text{and} \qquad \beta'' \overset{*}{\Rightarrow} y_2$$

Since z is a shortest string derivable from β'', we get $\lg(z) \leqslant \lg(y_2)$. If $\lg(y_2) = \lg(z)$, then $y_2 = z$ and $y_1 = y'$, and thus

$$\beta' \underset{L}{\overset{*}{\Rightarrow}} y'$$

which contradicts that y' is a shortest witness of $A\gamma$ and β'. If $\lg(y_2) > \lg(z)$, then $\lg(y_1) < \lg(y')$ and so

$$\beta' \underset{L}{\overset{*}{\Rightarrow}} y_1$$

implies

$$A\gamma \underset{L}{\overset{*}{\Rightarrow}} y_1$$

which contradicts that $A\gamma'$ generates a prefix-free set, since y_1 is a prefix of y'.

CASE 2. $\beta' \underset{L}{\overset{*}{\Rightarrow}} y'$. Choose z as above, and obtain

$$\beta'\beta'' \underset{L}{\overset{*}{\Rightarrow}} y'z$$

Then

$$\alpha = A\alpha' \underset{L}{\overset{*}{\Rightarrow}} y'z$$

Since $\alpha' \equiv \gamma\beta''$, we get

$$A\gamma\beta'' \underset{L}{\overset{*}{\Rightarrow}} y'z$$

The argument now parallels that of Case 1, and a similar contradiction may be easily obtained.

Claim 2 Let $\alpha \not\equiv \beta$ and $T_B(\alpha, \beta) = \{(\alpha', \gamma\beta''), (A\gamma, \beta')\}$, where $\alpha', A, \beta', \beta'', \gamma$, and x are as in the definition of T_B. Then, for every $y' \in \Sigma^*$, we have $xy' \in \bar{W}(\alpha, \beta)$ if and only if $y' \in \bar{W}(\alpha', \gamma\beta'')$.

Proof of Claim 2 Since $L(A)$ is prefix-free and $A \overset{*}{\Rightarrow} x$ it follows that

$$\alpha = A\alpha' \overset{*}{\Rightarrow} xy' = y \quad \text{if and only if} \quad \alpha' \overset{*}{\Rightarrow} y'$$

If $\beta = \beta'\beta'' \underset{L}{\overset{*}{\Rightarrow}} xy'$, then, for some $\delta \in N^*$,

$$\beta = \beta'\beta'' \underset{L}{\overset{*}{\Rightarrow}} x\delta \underset{L}{\overset{*}{\Rightarrow}} xy' \tag{11.10.1}$$

Now

$$\beta = \beta'\beta'' \underset{L}{\overset{*}{\Rightarrow}} x\gamma\beta'' \tag{11.10.2}$$

But (11.10.1) and (11.10.2), together with hypothesis (ii) of the Lemma, imply

$$\delta = \gamma\beta'' \overset{*}{\Rightarrow} y'$$

Conversely, suppose

$$\gamma\beta'' \overset{*}{\Rightarrow} y'$$

Then, since $\beta' \overset{*}{\Rightarrow} x\gamma$, we have

$$\beta = \beta'\beta'' \overset{*}{\Rightarrow} x\gamma\beta'' \overset{*}{\Rightarrow} xy' = y$$

Thus we have shown that

$$\alpha \overset{*}{\Rightarrow} xy' = y \quad \text{if and only if } \alpha' \overset{*}{\Rightarrow} y'$$

and that

$$\beta \overset{*}{\Rightarrow} xy' = y \quad \text{if and only if } \gamma\beta'' \overset{*}{\Rightarrow} y'$$

Since $\alpha \not\equiv \beta$, $xy' \in \bar{W}(\alpha, \beta)$ if and only if exactly one of α or β generate y'. This holds if and only if exactly one of α' or $\gamma\beta''$ generates y', which holds if and only if $y' \in \bar{W}(\alpha', \gamma\beta'')$. This completes the proof of Claim 2.

Let us agree to say that two strings η and θ *agree on all strings of length less than or equal to k* if, for each $z \in \Sigma^*$, $\lg(z) \leqslant k$, $\eta \overset{*}{\Rightarrow} z$ if and only if $\theta \overset{*}{\Rightarrow} z$. We shall write $\eta \overset{k}{\equiv} \theta$, in this case. Also let $p = \lg(x)$.

Claim 3 For any $k \geqslant 1$, if all elements of $\bar{W}(\alpha, \beta)$ of length $\leqslant p + k$ are not of the form xy', then $\alpha' \overset{k}{\equiv} \gamma\beta''$. (That is, $\bar{W}(\alpha', \gamma\beta'')$ cannot contain any members of length less than or equal to k.)

Proof Suppose that $\alpha' \overset{k}{\equiv} \gamma\beta''$ is false. Then there exists $y' \in \Sigma^*, \lg(y') \leqslant k$, such that $y' \in \bar{W}(\alpha', \gamma\beta'')$. By Claim 2,

$$xy' \in \bar{W}(\alpha, \beta)$$

but

$$\lg(xy') = p + \lg(y') \leqslant p + k,$$

which is a contradiction.

The next claim gives additional information about witnesses.

Claim 4 Let G_1 and G_2 be as before. Assume that $\alpha \not\equiv \beta$ and $T_B(\alpha, \beta) = \{(\alpha', \gamma\beta''), (A\gamma, \beta')\}$. For any $k \geqslant 1$, suppose $\alpha' \overset{k}{\equiv} \gamma\beta''$. Then, for all $y \in \Sigma^*$, $\lg(y) \leqslant k + p$, we have $y \in \bar{W}(\alpha, \beta)$ if and only if there exist $y_1, y_2 \in \Sigma^*$ such that $y = y_1 y_2$, $y_1 \in \bar{W}(A\gamma, \beta')$, and $\beta'' \overset{*}{\Rightarrow} y_2 \neq \Lambda$.

Proof Let $y \in \Sigma^*$ with $\lg(y) \leqslant k + p$. Clearly, $\alpha \overset{*}{\Rightarrow} y$ if and only if

$$A \overset{*}{\Rightarrow} y'$$

and

$$\alpha' \overset{*}{\Rightarrow} y''$$

$$y = y'y''$$

for some $y', y'' \in \Sigma^*$. Since

$$\lg(y') \geqslant \lg(x) = p,$$

it follows that

$$\lg(y'') = \lg(y) - \lg(y') \leqslant k + p - p = k.$$

Since $\alpha' \overset{k}{\equiv} \gamma\beta''$, we have that $\alpha \overset{*}{\Rightarrow} y$ if and only if

$$A \overset{*}{\Rightarrow} y'$$

$$\gamma\beta'' \overset{*}{\Rightarrow} y''$$

and

$$y = y'y''$$

In turn, this holds if and only if

$$A \overset{*}{\Rightarrow} y'$$

$$\gamma \overset{*}{\Rightarrow} y_1''$$

$$\beta'' \overset{*}{\Rightarrow} y_2$$

and

$$y = y'y_1''y_2$$

This is all true if and only if

$$A\gamma \overset{*}{\Rightarrow} y'y_1'' = y_1$$

$$\beta'' \overset{*}{\Rightarrow} y_2$$

and

$$y = y_1y_2$$

On the other hand, $\beta \overset{*}{\Rightarrow} y$ if and only if there exist y_1, $y_2 \in \Sigma^*$ such that $\beta' \overset{*}{\Rightarrow} y_1$, $\beta'' \overset{*}{\Rightarrow} y_2$, $\beta = \beta'\beta''$, and $y = y_1y_2$. Since $\lg(\beta) > \ell$, $\lg(\beta') \leqslant \lg(x) \leqslant \ell$, so $\lg(\beta'') \geqslant 1$, which implies $y_2 \neq \Lambda$.

Thus we have shown that

i) $\alpha \overset{*}{\Rightarrow} y$ if and only if $A\gamma \overset{*}{\Rightarrow} y_1$, $\beta'' \overset{*}{\Rightarrow} y_2$, and $y = y_1y_2$, with $y_2 \neq \Lambda$; and

ii) $\beta \overset{*}{\Rightarrow} y$ if and only if $\beta' \overset{*}{\Rightarrow} y_1$, $\beta'' \overset{*}{\Rightarrow} y_2 \neq \Lambda$, and $y = y_1y_2$.

From the definition of $\overline{W}(\alpha, \beta)$, it follows that $y \in \overline{W}(\alpha, \beta)$ if and only if $y = y_1y_2$, $\beta'' \overset{*}{\Rightarrow} y_2$, and $y_1 \in \overline{W}(A\gamma, \beta')$. This completes the proof of Claim 4.

Now, the claims can be used to complete the proof of the Lemma. Let α, $\beta \in NN^+$ such that $T(\alpha, \beta)$ is defined. If $\alpha \equiv \beta$, then Claim 1 proves the first part of the validity. If $\alpha \not\equiv \beta$ and $T(\alpha, \beta) \neq$ *fail*, then two cases may arise.

CASE 1. There exists a shortest witness of the form xy' for α and β. By Claim 2, y' is a witness of α' and $\gamma\beta''$. Thus T_B is a valid transformation. To complete the proof of monotonicity, note that $\lg(y') < \lg(xy')$, since the grammars are reduced and Λ-free.

CASE 2. No shortest witness of the form xy' exists for α and β. Let y be any shortest witness for α and β. It must be the case that $\lg(y) > p$, so let $\lg(y) = p + k$ for some $k \geqslant 1$. By Claim 3, $\alpha' \overset{k}{\equiv} \gamma\beta''$. By Claim 4, there exist y_1, $y_2 \in \Sigma^*$ so that

$y_1 \in \bar{W}(A\gamma, \beta')$ and $\beta'' \overset{*}{\Rightarrow} y_2 \neq \Lambda$. This proves that T_B is valid in this case, also. Monotonicity also follows, for, if y is a shortest witness of α and β, we have that y_1 is a witness of $A\gamma$ and β'. y_1 is a shortest witness by the *if* part of Claim 4. (If z were a shorter witness of $A\gamma$ and β', then zy_2 would be a shorter witness of α, β than y.) Therefore, T_B is guaranteed to be valid and monotone. $\square$

Now that both T_A and T_B are available, we could start to use them on some sample grammars. However, situations can arise in which neither transformation is applicable. For example, suppose the pair $A \equiv \Lambda$ occurs. We augment our repertoire with two additional transformations so that for every pair in $N^* \times N^* - \{(\Lambda, \Lambda)\}$, there is always at least one applicable transformation.

Definition Let G_i be our underlying grammars. If $\alpha, \beta \in N^+$ and $\lg(\alpha) > \ell \lg(\beta)$, then

$$T_\ell(\alpha, \beta) = T_\ell(\beta, \alpha) = \textit{fail}.$$

T_ℓ is undefined elsewhere.

Definition If $\alpha \in N^+$, then

$$T_\Lambda(\alpha, \Lambda) = T_\Lambda(\Lambda, \alpha) = \textit{fail}.$$

T_Λ is undefined elsewhere.

Lemma 11.10.5 T_Λ and T_ℓ are valid and monotone transformations.

Proof If $\alpha \not\equiv \beta$ and $T_\Lambda(\alpha, \beta)$ is defined, then $T_\Lambda(\alpha, \beta) = \textit{fail}$. Part (1) of validity and monotonicity are vacuous. The proof of T_ℓ uses part (2) of Lemma 11.10.3 and is trivial. $\square$

Now the process of using transformations to form a tree is stated precisely.

Definition Let $G_i = (V_i, \Sigma, P_i, S_i)$, $i = 1, 2$, be two reduced Λ-free grammars with $N_1 \cap N_2 = \emptyset$ and $N = N_1 \cup N_2$. Let $\mathscr{T}$ be a set of transformations such that

$$N^* \times N^* - \{(\Lambda, \Lambda)\} \subseteq \bigcup_{T \in \mathscr{T}} \operatorname{dom}(T),$$

where $\operatorname{dom}(T)$ denotes the domain of T. A *$\mathscr{T}$-transformation tree* is a tree with a potentially infinite number of nodes, each labeled by elements of $N^* \times N^* \cup \{\textit{fail}\}$, where each elementary subtree corresponds to an application of $T \in \mathscr{T}$. If the root is labeled (α, β), we say that it is a *$\mathscr{T}$-transformation tree for* α, β.

Note that the only nodes of the tree which can be labeled *fail* are leaves. Also note that there are many different such trees for fixed $G_1, G_2, \mathscr{T}, \alpha$, and β, since the order in which transformations may be applied is not prescribed.

In the next lemma, the properties of such trees are explored.

Lemma 11.10.6 Let $\mathscr{T}$ be a set of valid and monotone transformations. Suppose $\alpha \not\equiv \beta$ and y is a shortest witness for α and β. For any $\mathscr{T}$-tree for α and β, there exists a finite path from the root to a leaf with successive labels

$$(\alpha_0, \beta_0), (\alpha_1, \beta_1), \ldots, (\alpha_t, \beta_t), \mathit{fail}$$

where $\alpha_0 = \alpha$, $\beta_0 = \beta$, and there exist strings $y = y_0, \ldots, y_t \in \Sigma^*$ such that

i) $t \leqslant \lg(y)$;

ii) for each i, $0 \leqslant i \leqslant t$, $\alpha_i \not\equiv \beta_i$ and y_i is a shortest witness for α_i and β_i; and

iii) for all i, $1 \leqslant i \leqslant t$, $\lg(y_i) < \lg(y_{i-1})$.

Proof The argument is an induction on $\lg(y)$.

Basis. $y = \Lambda$. By the definition of monotonicity, any $T \in \mathscr{T}$ can fail only on α and β. Thus $t = 0 \leqslant \lg(y)$. The other conditions are trivially satisfied.

Induction step. Assume the result true whenever $\lg(y) \leqslant k$ and $k > 0$. Let $\lg(y) = k + 1$, where y is a shortest witness for α, β. By validity, either $T(\alpha, \beta) = \mathit{fail}$, in which case the argument proceeds as in the basis; or else $T(\alpha, \beta) = \{(\alpha'_1, \beta'_1), \ldots, (\alpha'_m, \beta'_m)\}$. By monotonicity, there exists i, $1 \leqslant i \leqslant m$, $\alpha'_i \not\equiv \beta'_i$ and (α'_i, β'_i) has a shortest witness y' such that $\lg(y') < \lg(y)$. Let $(\alpha_1, \beta_1) = (\alpha'_i, \beta'_i)$ and $y_1 = y'$. The induction hypothesis applies to (α_1, β_1) with witness y_1 and yields the result. □

Corollary Let $\mathscr{T}$, α, β, and y be as in Lemma 11.10.6. Then a $\mathscr{T}$-tree for α, β must have a path from the root to a *fail* leaf with no two nodes labelled by the same pair (α_i, β_i).

Proof Two different nodes on the same path have shortest witnesses of different lengths. □

Next we show that valid transformations applied to equivalent pairs cannot fail.

Lemma 11.10.7 Let $G_i = (V_i, \Sigma, P_i, S)$, $i = 1, 2$, be two grammars with $N_1 \cap N_2 = \emptyset$ and let $N = N_1 \cup N_2$. Let α, $\beta \in N^*$ and $\mathscr{T}$ be any set of valid transformations. If $\alpha \equiv \beta$, then any $\mathscr{T}$-tree for α, β does not have a *fail*-leaf.

Proof The argument is an induction on the height n of a $\mathscr{T}$-tree for α, β.

Basis. $n = 0$. There is one node labeled $(\alpha, \beta) \neq \mathit{fail}$.

Induction step. Suppose the result is true for all α, β, $\alpha \equiv \beta$, and all (α, β)-trees of height $n \leqslant n_0$, where $n_0 > 0$. Let $n = n_0 + 1$. Consider a leaf s_n in a tree of height n. This node is on a path $(s_0, \ldots, s_n)$ from the root s_0.

Consider the subtree rooted at s_1, which also contains the leaf s_n. This is the shaded subtree in Fig. 11.7. Since all $\mathscr{T}$-transformations are valid, the pair (α_1, β_1) that labels s_1 must satisfy $\alpha_1 \equiv \beta_1$. The induction hypothesis applies to the subtree, so s_n is not labeled *fail.* □

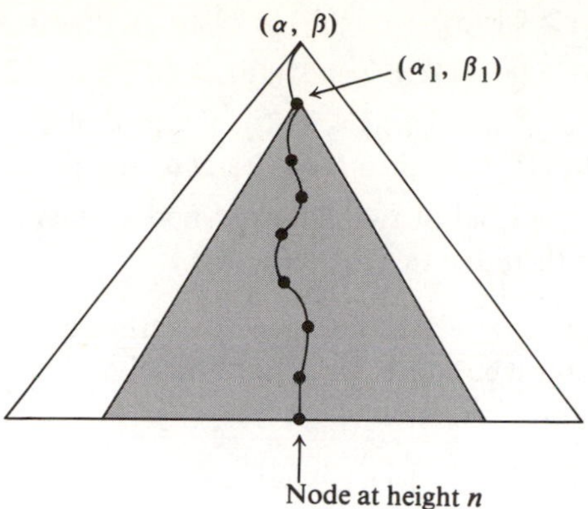

FIG. 11.7

Because the transformation trees we have been studying can be infinite, it is convenient to define a *partial transformation tree* as the finite tree which results by taking a transformation tree that has a cross section ξ and taking everything above and including ξ. An example is shown in Fig. 11.8.

There are many different ways to form partial trees. Let us fix the convention that no path in the tree is continued if it reaches a node label that has appeared earlier. That includes an earlier appearance as its own ancestor.

We are now ready to indicate how to solve the equivalence problem for s-grammars. For this purpose, we fix the class of the relevant transformations.

Definition Let $\mathscr{T}_s = \{T_A, T_B, T_{\mathfrak{L}}, T_\Lambda\}$. Note that $N^* \times N^* - \{(\Lambda, \Lambda)\} \subseteq \text{dom}(\mathscr{T}_s)$.

Now a special kind of equivalence tree is defined.

Definition Let $G_i = (V_i, \Sigma, P_i, S_i)$ be two s-grammars which are reduced, Λ-free, and in standard r-form for some $r \geqslant 2$. Assume $N_1 \cap N_2 = \emptyset$ and $N = N_1 \cup N_2$. Let $\alpha, \beta \in N^*$. An *equivalence tree* for α, β is a partial $\mathscr{T}_s$-transformation tree with the following restrictions:

i) If (α_1, β_1) is the label of the root of an elementary subtree and $T \in \mathscr{T}_s$ is the corresponding transformation, then

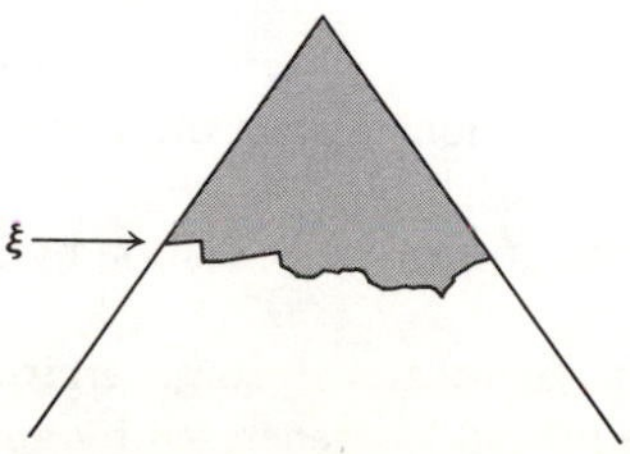

FIG. 11.8

a) if $\lg(\alpha_1) > \ell \lg(\beta_1)$, (or $\lg(\beta_1) > \ell \lg(\alpha_1)$), then $T = T_\ell$;

b) if $\lg(\alpha_1) > (r-1)\ell + 2$ and $\lg(\beta_1) > (r-1)\ell + 2$, then $T \neq T_A$;

c) if $T = T_B$, then $\lg(\alpha_1) \leqslant \lg(\beta_1)$. (Note that T_B may be applied when $\lg(\beta_1) < \lg(\alpha_1)$ but then the roles of α_1 and β_1 have to be reversed.

ii) If (α_1, β_1) is a label of two different nodes, then at least one of them is a leaf. (Note then that $(\alpha_1, \beta_1) = (\beta_1, \alpha_1)$.)

It is important to note that the previous definition constrains how the transformations are to be applied but does not do so uniquely. There are still a large number of choices as to which transformation to apply.

Example G_1 and G_2 are given below.

G_1	G_2
$S_1 \to aAC$	$S_2 \to aDE$
$A \to bAB \mid aB$	$D \to bDF \mid a$
$B \to b$	$E \to bG$
$C \to a$	$F \to b$
	$G \to a$

A straightforward calculation shows that $\ell = 4$. An equivalence tree for S_1, S_2 is shown in Fig. 11.9. Note that the leaf labeled $BC \equiv E$ has been circled to indicate that it has already been encountered in the tree and fully developed. There are a number of interesting points that occur in developing this tree. The reader should note the situation with the circled nodes, particularly $A \equiv DF$, in which the repetition occurs on the same path. This point will be clarified as additional properties of equivalence trees are established.

Lemma 11.10.8 Let $G_i = (V_i, \Sigma, P_i, S_i)$ be two s-grammars in standard r-form for some $r \geqslant 2$ with $N_1 \cap N_2 = \emptyset$ and $N = N_1 \cup N_2$. Let α, β be in N^*. In any equivalence tree for α, β, where $\lg(\alpha)$, $\lg(\beta) \leqslant (r-1)(\ell+1)+2$, any node labeled (α_1, β_1) has the property that either

$$\lg(\alpha_1) \leqslant (r-1)(\ell+1)+2$$

or

$$\lg(\beta_1) \leqslant (r-1)(\ell+1)+2.$$

Proof The argument is an induction on the shape of the tree.

Basis. The root clearly satisfies the condition by hypothesis.

Induction step. Suppose we are at some arbitrary node that satisfies the condition. A new node labeled (α_1, β_1) is generated by applying some transformation $T \in \mathscr{T}_s$ to the given node. If $T = T_\ell$ or $T = T_\Lambda$, the condition is vacuously satisfied.

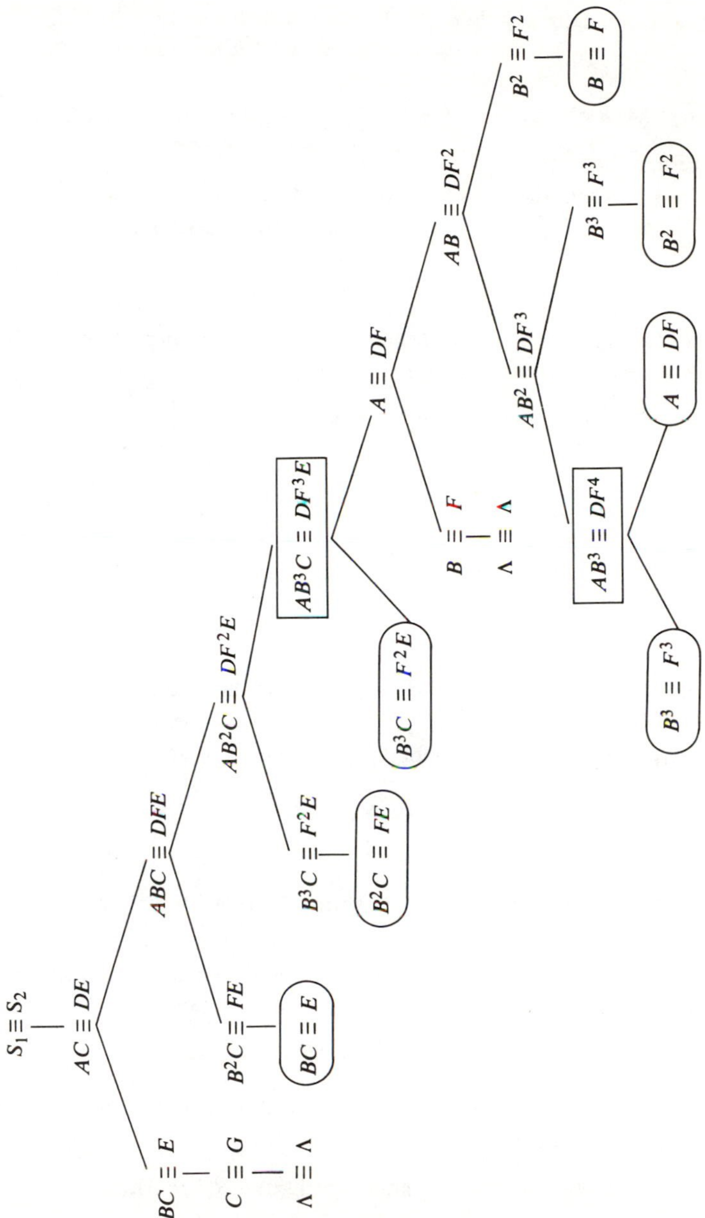
$S_1 \equiv S_2$
$AC \equiv DE$
$BC \equiv E$
$C \equiv G$
$\Lambda \equiv \Lambda$
$ABC \equiv DFE$
$B^2C \equiv FE$
$BC \equiv E$
$AB^2C \equiv DF^2E$
$B^3C \equiv F^2E$
$B^2C \equiv FE$
$AB^3C \equiv DF^3E$
$B^3C \equiv F^2E$
$A \equiv DF$
$B \equiv F$
$\Lambda \equiv \Lambda$
$AB \equiv DF^2$
$AB^2 \equiv DF^3$
$AB^3 \equiv DF^4$
$B^3 \equiv F^3$
$A \equiv DF$
$B^3 \equiv F^3$
$B^2 \equiv F^2$
$B^2 \equiv F^2$
$B \equiv F$

FIG. 11.9

If $T = T_A$, then the new node is labeled $(R(A,a)\alpha_1', R(B,a)\beta_1')$, where $\alpha_1 = A\alpha_1'$ and $\beta_1 = B\beta_1'$. By using part 1(b) of the definition of an equivalence tree, we get (without loss of generality by the symmetry) that

$$\lg(\alpha_1') = \lg(\alpha_1) - 1 \leqslant (r-1)\ell + 2 - 1.$$

Also, $\lg(R(A,a)) \leqslant r$, so that

$$\lg(R(A,a)\alpha_1') \leqslant (r-1)\ell + 2 - 1 + r = (r-1)(\ell+1) + 2,$$

and the condition holds.

If $T = T_B$, then the resulting node is labeled either $(\alpha', \gamma\beta'')$ or $(A\gamma, \beta')$, where $\beta_1 = \beta'\beta''$, $\alpha_1 = A\alpha'$, $\beta' \overset{*}{\underset{L}{\Rightarrow}} x\gamma$, and x is the shortest terminal string derived from A. Note that

$$\lg(\alpha_1) \leqslant (r-1)(\ell+1) + 2$$

by (i(c)) of the definition of an equivalence tree and the hypothesis of the lemma. Now β' is the shortest prefix of β for which the above is true, so that

$$\lg(\gamma) \leqslant (r-1)\lg(x) + 1 \leqslant (r-1)\ell + 1. \tag{11.10.3}$$

Clearly, we have

$$\lg(\alpha') = \lg(\alpha_1) - 1 \leqslant (r-1)(\ell+1) + 2$$

and

$$\lg(A\gamma) = \lg(\gamma) + 1 \leqslant (r-1)(\ell+1) + 2$$

from (11.10.3). □

Corollary 1 Let $G_i = (V_i, \Sigma, P_i, S_i)$, $i = 1, 2$, be two s-grammars in standard 2-form, with $N_1 \cap N_2 = \emptyset$ and $N = N_1 \cup N_2$. If α, $\beta \in N^+$ with $\lg(\alpha)$, $\lg(\beta) \leqslant \ell + 3$, then any node in an equivalence tree labeled (α_1, β_1) has either

$$\lg(\alpha_1) \leqslant \ell + 3$$

or

$$\lg(\beta_1) \leqslant \ell + 3.$$

Proof This follows directly from Lemma 11.10.8 by setting $r = 2$. □

Corollary 2 The number of nodes in an equivalence tree which are roots of elementary subtrees for T_A or T_B is at most

$$c|N|^{(\ell+1)(\ell+3)}.$$

Proof The labels of such nodes are all distinct, by (ii) of the definition of equivalence trees. If such a label is (α, β), then

$$\lg(\alpha) \leqslant \ell + 3 \qquad \text{and} \qquad \lg(\beta) \leqslant \ell(\ell+3),$$

or vice versa. The inequality for β follows from part (i(a)) of the definition of an equivalence tree. Thus,

$$\alpha \in N_\Lambda^{\ell+3} \qquad \text{and} \qquad \beta \in N_\Lambda^{\ell(\ell+3)}.$$

There are only

$$\frac{|N|^{\ell+4}-1}{|N|-1} \cdot \frac{|N|^{\ell(\ell+3)+1}-1}{|N|-1} \leqslant c_1|N|^{(\ell+1)(\ell+3)}$$

such labels for some constant c_1 if $|N|>1$. If $|N|=1$, there are fewer than $c_2\ell^3$ such labels for some constant c_2. □

Corollary 3 An equivalence tree has at most

$$d|N|^{(\ell+1)(\ell+3)}|\Sigma|$$

nodes, where d is a constant.

Proof For any node counted in Corollary 2, there are at most $\max\{|\Sigma|, 2\}$ immediate successors obtained by applying any transformation. Each of these nodes either is a leaf or may have one successor that is a leaf, so the number in Corollary 2 need be multiplied by at most $\max\{2|\Sigma|+1, 5\}$, as a bound on the total number of nodes. □

Now we can state and prove the main result.

Theorem 11.10.1 Let $G_i=(V_i, \Sigma, P_i, S_i)$, $i=1,2$, be two s-grammars with $N_1 \cap N_2 = \emptyset$ and $N=N_1 \cup N_2$, and let $\alpha, \beta \in N^*$. Then $\alpha \equiv \beta$ if and only if every equivalence tree for α and β does not have any leaf labeled *fail.*

Proof Let R be any equivalence tree for α and β. For any leaf labeled (α_1, β_1), where (α_1, β_1) does not label any ancestor of that leaf, it must be the case that (α_1, β_1) labels an internal node elsewhere in the tree. Modify R to form a new tree R_1 by appending to the leaf in question, a copy of the subtree rooted at the internal node. This is continued for all such leaves. The process cannot continue indefinitely since it cannot generate paths of length more than $c_1 N^{(\ell+1)(\ell+3)}$, by Corollary 2 to Lemma 11.10.8. R_1 includes every path from root to leaf of some $\mathcal{T}_s$ tree for α and β that has no label repeated twice. Moreover, R_1 has a *fail*-leaf if and only if R has a *fail*-leaf.

If $\alpha \equiv \beta$, then by Lemma 11.10.7, R_1 contains no *fail*-leaves and R cannot have any. Conversely, if $\alpha \not\equiv \beta$, then R_1 must have a *fail*-leaf, by Lemma 11.10.6. Note the condition that no label be repeated along the path. Therefore, R must have a *fail*-leaf. □

Corollary The equivalence problem for s-grammars is solvable.

Proof Construct an equivalence tree for $S_1 \equiv S_2$ and check it for *fail*-leaves. Since the tree is finite, this is an algorithm. □

PROBLEMS

1 In the definition of T_B, it was required that $\lg(\beta) > \ell$. It was explained in the text that this implies $\beta'' \neq \Lambda$. Show that the condition $\beta'' \neq \Lambda$ is necessary to ensure that T_B is monotone. Give an example of the application of T_B where $\beta'' = \Lambda$,

that would allow us to conclude that two strings are equivalent when in fact they are not.

2 Could we develop a decision procedure for equality of s-grammars by dropping T_B from our set of transformations? Prove your answer.

3 Let X, Y be nonempty sets of strings and suppose that X is prefix-free. Show that XY is prefix-free if and only if Y is prefix-free.

4 Let X, Y, Z be nonempty sets of strings and assume X is prefix-free. Show that if $XY = XZ$, then $Y = Z$.

5 Let X, Y, Z be nonempty sets of words and, furthermore, suppose that Y and Z are prefix-free. Show that if $YX = ZX$, then $Y = Z$.

6 Translate Problems 4 and 5 into results about cancellation of equivalent strings over N^*. Use these identities to find more shortcuts in dealing with equivalence trees.

7* Generalize the main result of this section by showing that it is decidable, of two deterministic languages, one of which is an s-language, whether or not they are equal. You should assume, for maximum generality, that the languages are presented by arbitrary dpda's.

11.11 HISTORICAL SURVEY

The LR^{-1} theorem (11.2.3) was originally proved in Ginsburg and Greibach [1966], as were many of the closure results in Section 11.3. Our proof of Theorem 11.2.3 follows Book and Greibach [1973], which in turn follows Hopcroft and Ullman [1968a]. The material on strict deterministic grammars follows Harrison and Havel [1972, 1973, 1974]. Problem 1 of Section 11.5 is from Geller and Harrison [1977].

Lemma 11.6.2 is from Ginsburg and Greibach [1966]. Theorem 11.7.1 and the exercises on realtime Turing-machine computations are derived from the work of Rosenberg [1967, 1968].

The unsolvability of the inclusion problem for simple languages is due to Friedman [1976], while the solvability of the equivalence problem is due to Korenjak and Hopcroft [1966]. Our proof follows Harrison, Havel, and Yehudai [1978].

twelve

Recognition and Parsing of General Context-Free Languages

12.1 INTRODUCTION

One of the most important applications of language theory concerns the recognition and parsing of context-free languages. Such recognizers are at the heart of many programs that take their input in natural-language form. Although some of these systems use more sophisticated types of grammars, like transformational grammars, even these rest on a context-free base.

In the present chapter, we begin by discussing machine models for recognition which are closer to actual computers than Turing machines. It is shown that there is a "hardest" context-free language with respect to recognition time and space. Section 12.3 is devoted to techniques for doing elementary operations on matrices, because it will turn out that one can reduce the recognition problem to computing the transitive closure of a matrix. The Cocke–Kasami–Younger algorithm appears in Section 12.4 and is analyzed in some detail. In Section 12.5, recognition is reduced to boolean matrix multiplication, in an algorithm due to Valiant. A very useful practical algorithm is given in Section 12.6, which is due to Graham, Harrison, and Ruzzo. Section 12.7 includes other related problems such as bounds on space required for general context-free recognition.

12.2 MATHEMATICAL MODELS OF COMPUTERS AND A HARDEST CONTEXT-FREE LANGUAGE

In order to avoid taking some tangents in our later development, we shall give some definitions and results here that will be used later in this chapter.

It will be important to determine the number of steps in a derivation of a string of length n. We will use this result in subsequent sections to analyze the number of steps required by certain parsing algorithms. Unless some restriction is placed on the grammar or the derivation, the length of a derivation may be unbounded.

Our purposes will be served by restricting the grammar to be of the following type:

Definiition A context-free grammar $G = (V, \Sigma, P, S)$ is *cycle-free* if, for each $A \in N$, $A \overset{+}{\Rightarrow} A$ is impossible.

Now we can state a result which says that, in a cycle-free grammar, the length of a derivation is linear in the length of the generated string.

Theorem 12.2.1 Let $G = (V, \Sigma, P, S)$ be a cycle-free, context-free grammar and let $\ell = \max\{\lg(\alpha) | A \to \alpha \text{ is in } P,\ A \in N\}$. There exist constants c_0, c_1, and c_2, which depend only on $|N|$ and ℓ such that $c_1 > c_2$, and for all $A \in N$, $\alpha \in V^*$, if $A \overset{i}{\Rightarrow} \alpha$, $\lg(\alpha) = n$, then

a) if $n = 0$, then $i \leqslant c_0$;

b) if $n > 0$, then $i \leqslant c_1 n - c_2$.

Proof We must consider the derivations of strings whose length is at most one.

Claim 1 Suppose $A \overset{i}{\Rightarrow} \alpha$ where $\lg(\alpha) < 1$. Then:

i) If $\alpha = \Lambda$, no path in the derivation tree is longer than $|N|$.

ii) If $\alpha = a \in \Sigma$, then the path from the root labeled A to the leaf labeled a is no longer than $|N|$.

iii) If $\alpha = B \in N$, then the path from the root to the leaf labeled B is no longer than $|N| - 1$.

Proof of Claim 1 Consider a path from the derivation tree of $A \overset{+}{\Rightarrow} \alpha$ as shown in Fig. 12.1.

Suppose the path from $A = A_1$ to α is of length k. Then we have

$$A = A_1 \overset{+}{\Rightarrow} A_2 \overset{+}{\Rightarrow} \cdots \overset{+}{\Rightarrow} A_k \overset{+}{\Rightarrow} \alpha$$

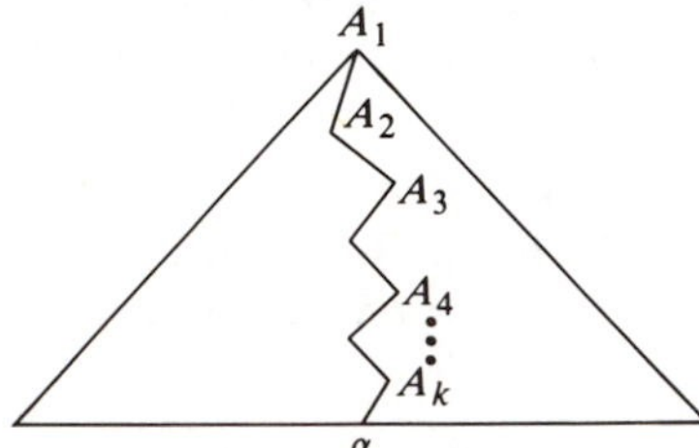

FIG. 12.1

Since $A_i \overset{+}{\Rightarrow} A_i$ is not possible, we must have that all of $A_1, \ldots, A_k$, and α are distinct. If $\alpha = B \in N$, then $k \leqslant |N| - 1$. If $\alpha = a \in \Sigma \cup \{\Lambda\}$, then $k \leqslant |N|$. This completes the proof of Claim 1.

Now we are in a position to complete the analysis of Λ-derivations. Note that a derivation $A \overset{i}{\Rightarrow} \Lambda$ has a tree of height $\leqslant |N|$. The number of nodes at height j in the tree is at most ℓ^j. Thus,

$$i \leqslant \sum_{j=0}^{|N|-1} \ell^j = c_0 = \begin{cases} 1 & \text{if } \ell = 0, \\ |N| & \text{if } \ell = 1, \\ \dfrac{\ell^{|N|} - 1}{\ell - 1} & \text{if } \ell > 1. \end{cases} \tag{12.2.1}$$

Let c_0 be this constant in eq. (12.2.1) which depends only on ℓ and $|N|$. Thus we have proved part (a) of the theorem.

Now we must work out the case where a nonterminal derives another nonterminal.

Claim 2 Suppose $A \overset{i}{\Rightarrow} B$, $B \in V$. If the length of the path from the root A to the leaf labelled B is k, then

$$i \leqslant k((\ell - 1)c_0 + 1).$$

Proof of Claim 2 The argument is an induction on k.

Basis $k = 0$ implies $i = 0$, and the basis is verified.

Induction step: Assume that $k > 0$ and that the result is true for the path to the node labeled B, of length $k - 1$. Then

$$A \Rightarrow A_1 \cdots A_m$$

where

$$A_d \overset{i_d}{\Rightarrow} B \qquad \text{for some } d,\ 1 \leqslant d \leqslant m,$$

and

$$A_j \overset{i_j}{\Rightarrow} \Lambda \qquad \text{if } j \neq d.$$

By the induction hypothesis,

$$i_d \leqslant (k - 1)\,((\ell - 1)c_0 + 1).$$

Moreover,

$$i_j \leqslant c_0 \qquad \text{if } j \neq d,$$

by our proof of (a). Therefore,

$$i = 1 + i_d + \sum_{j \neq d} i_j$$

$$i \leqslant 1 + (k - 1)\,((\ell - 1)c_0 + 1) + (\ell - 1)c_0 = k((\ell - 1)c_0 + 1),$$

using that $m \leqslant \ell$. This completes the proof of Claim 2.

If we combine Claims 1 and 2, we have already shown the following result:

Claim 3 Suppose $A \overset{i}{\Rightarrow} B$, $B \in V$. Then

$$i \leqslant \begin{cases} |N|\ell^{|N|} & \text{if } \ell > 1, \\ |N|((\ell - 1)c_0 + 1) & \text{if } B \in V, \\ (|N| - 1)((\ell - 1)c_0 + 1) & \text{if } B \in N. \end{cases}$$

Now we are ready for the main claim, which will complete the argument.

Claim 4 If $A \overset{i}{\Rightarrow} \alpha$, $\lg(\alpha) = n > 0$, then

$$i \leqslant c_1 n - c_2,$$

where

$$c_1 = 2|N|((\ell - 1)c_0 + 1) - c_0$$

and

$$c_2 = |N|((\ell - 1)c_0 + 1) - c_0.$$

Proof of Claim 4 The argument is an induction on n.

Basis. $n = 1$. We compute

$$c_1 \cdot 1 - c_2 = |N|((\ell - 1)c_0 + 1).$$

So $i \leqslant c_1 \cdot 1 - c_2$, by the second case of Claim 3.

Induction step. Assume the result true for all strings of length at least 1 and less than n. Suppose that $A \overset{i}{\Rightarrow} \alpha$, $\lg(\alpha) = n \geqslant 2$. The tree of this derivation must have a node with at least two immediate descendants producing nonnull strings, as shown in Fig. 12.2.

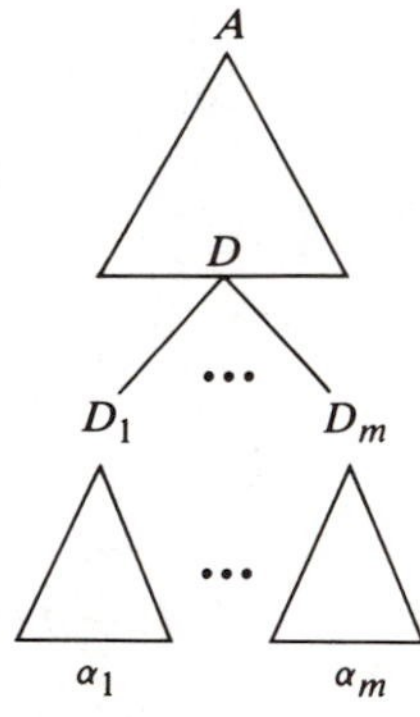

FIG. 12.2

Let D be the highest such descendant of A. Thus we have

$$A \overset{i^*}{\Rightarrow} D \Rightarrow D_1 \cdots D_m$$

where

$$D_j \overset{i_j}{\Rightarrow} \alpha_j, \qquad \lg(\alpha_j) = n_j$$

for each j, $1 \leqslant j \leqslant m$. Moreover,

$$\alpha_1 \cdots \alpha_m = \alpha \qquad \text{and} \sum_{j=1}^{m} n_j = n,$$

and there exist j_1, j_2 such that

$$\alpha_{j_1} \neq \Lambda \neq \alpha_{j_2}$$

since $\lg(\alpha) \geqslant 2$.

To simplify the notation of the proof, assume that there is some p, $2 \leqslant p \leqslant m$, such that

$$\alpha_1, \ldots, \alpha_r \neq \Lambda$$

and

$$\alpha_{p+1} = \cdots = \alpha_m = \Lambda$$

(There is no loss of generality in this assumption since, if this condition were not satisfied, we could introduce new indexing to make it so.)

Then

$$i = i^* + 1 + \sum_{j=1}^{m} i_j = i^* + 1 + \sum_{j=1}^{p} i_j + \sum_{j=p+1}^{m} i_j.$$

By the induction hypothesis,

$$\begin{aligned} i &\leqslant (|N| - 1)((\ell - 1)c_0 + 1) + 1 + \sum_{j=1}^{p} (c_1 n_j - c_2) + \sum_{j=p+1}^{m} c_0 \\ &= (|N| - 1)((\ell - 1)c_0 + 1) + 1 + c_1 n - pc_2 + (m - p)c_0 \\ &= c_1 n + (|N| - 1)((\ell - 1)c_0 + 1) + 1 + mc_0 - p[|N|((\ell - 1)c_0 + 1) - c_0 + c_0] \end{aligned}$$

by substituting the value of c_2. Continuing,

$$i \leqslant c_1 n + (|N| - 1)((\ell - 1)c_0 + 1) + 1 + mc_0 - p\,[|N|((\ell - 1)c_0 + 1].$$

Since $m \leqslant \ell$ and $p \geqslant 2$,

$$\begin{aligned} i &\leqslant c_1 n + (|N| - 1)((\ell - 1)c_0 + 1) + 1 + \ell c_0 - 2[|N|(\ell - 1)c_0 + 1] \\ &= c_1 n - (|N| + 1)((\ell - 1)c_0 + 1) + \ell c_0 + 1 \\ &= c_1 n - |N|((\ell - 1)c_0 + 1) - (\ell - 1)c_0 - 1 + \ell c_0 + 1 \\ &= c_1 n - [|N|((\ell - 1)c_0 + 1) - c_0] \\ &= c_1 n - c_2. \end{aligned}$$

Since the induction has been extended, the proof of Claim 4 and the proof of the theorem are complete. □

Because our fundamental goal in this chapter is to examine parsing and the resources that are required for its implementation, we must discuss how to implement it and how to compare algorithms. The usual technique is to implement algorithms on a standard model of a computer and then to estimate the time and storage requirements of each algorithm. For that approach, standardized models of computation must be used. There are two models in common usage which we shall employ, the Turing machine and the random-access machine (or RAM, for short). We already know about the use of Turing machines as language acceptors from Chapter 9.

Although Turing machines have an important role in the theory of computation, they are not natural models for algorithmic analysis. Turing-machine computations require a great deal of time moving back and forth along the tapes looking for information, and do not have the familiar random-access memory properties of computers. This suggest that another model is needed, and has led to the use of RAM's (named for *r*andom *a*ccess *m*emory model).

A RAM is a device of the type shown in Fig. 12.3. It has an input tape that can be read. Unlike a Turing-machine tape, every square may contain an integer, and there is no *a priori* bound on the size of the integers used. The output tape is of the same type, except that it can be written but not read.

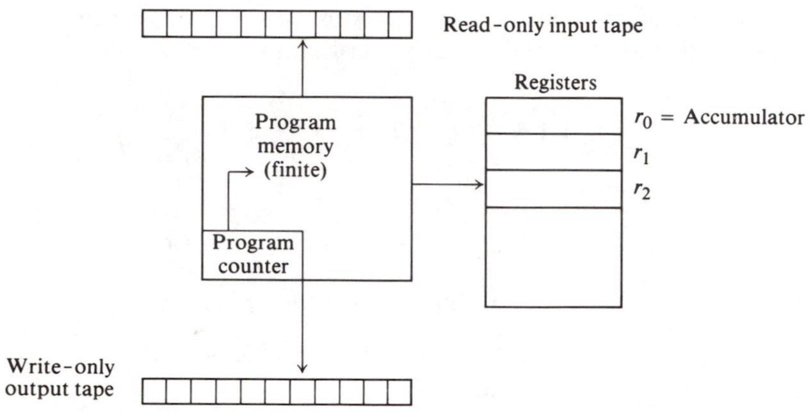

FIG. 12.3

The RAM has an unbounded number of registers, each of which is capable of storing an integer. The first register is thought of as the "accumulator." There is no bound on the size of the integers stored in a register, nor is there a bound on the number of registers that may be utilized. There is a program in a RAM which resides in a program memory that cannot be altered. Each register can be directly accessed by the program. A program counter indicates which instruction is currently being executed. The output is printed on a write-only output tape, each square of which can hold an arbitrary integer. There is an instruction set, which can be anything that is sufficient to compute any partial recursive function. For example, a simple instruction set might be:

LOAD σ
STORE σ
SUBTRACT σ
READ σ
WRITE σ
BRANCH ZERO ℓ

where ℓ labels an instruction in the program. On the other hand, σ may be (i) a nonnegative integer representing a register, (ii) a literal, which means that constants are available, or (iii) a tagged nonnegative integer used for indirection. The interpretations of these terms are familiar to those who have experience in assembly-language programming.

We are being deliberately vague about the actual instruction set. Cf. [Aho, Hopcroft, and Ullman [1974]] for a number of different choices. The reason we are vague is that we wish to use computers at a high level and so we shall write algorithms for a RAM in an ALGOL-like dialect. It would be a straightforward task to translate such a language into RAM code.

Example Suppose locations A_0 to A_{n-1} in our RAM each contain an integer. We wish to write a program to sort the integers into ascending order. Let *bit* have the values *true* or *false* and let *swap* exchange the values of its arguments.

```
procedure swap (x, y);
begin
  t: = x; x: = y; y: = t;
  comment the procedure is called by reference;
end;
begin
  repeat
    b: = false;
    for i: = 0 to n - 2 do
      if a_i > a_{i+1} then begin
        swap (a_i, a_{i+1});
        b: = true
        end
  until not (b)
end.
```

We leave it to the reader to analyze this algorithm, but note that, in the worst case, we might have $n(n-1)$ comparisons. Thus this is an algorithm that runs in quadratic time but linear space.

In our ALGOL dialect, program labels will have no computational significance, but will simply serve as reference points for the discussion. In addition to program variables containing integer or boolean values, we will allow variables to take on (unordered) sets as values. Our algorithms will often deal with two-dimensional matrices. The matrices will use *0-origin addressing.* That is, an $m \times n$ matrix will consist of rows 0 to $m-1$ and columns 0 to $n-1$. We will use the following matrix concepts. A matrix $\mathbf{M} = (m_{i,j})$ is (*strictly*) *upper triangular* if it consists only of elements $m_{i,j}$ where $i \leqslant j$ $(i < j)$. The *principal diagonal* of an $n \times n$ matrix $\mathbf{M}$ consists of the elements $m_{0,0}, m_{1,1}, \ldots, m_{n-1,n-1}$.

If we formalize what we have done in the example, the *time complexity* of a program is taken to be a function $f(n)$, which is the maximum over all inputs of size n of the sum of the time taken by each instruction executed.

For example, we could write a machine-language RAM program to subtract two numbers by writing:

```
READ 1
READ 2
LOAD 1
SUBTRACT 2
STORE 3
WRITE 3
HALT
```

There are 7 instructions executed, so the time complexity is 7. Our definition of time complexity could be considered to be unrealistic because the result is independent of the length of the numbers. In cases like this, it is said that the *uniform-cost criterion* is being used. We could charge log N to every instruction which uses integers of $\leqslant N$. In that case, the *logarithmic-cost criterion* is being employed. In many of our applications, the uniform-cost criterion is appropriate and will be used.

There is another type of model that is sometimes useful, the *bit-vector machine.* A bit-vector machine works like a RAM except that its memory utilizes bit vectors (of unbounded length). It is also convenient to have index registers and indirect addressing. A typical set of instructions for such a machine would be as follows:

Arithmetic Operations on index registers

$v_k := f(v_i, v_j)$,	where f is any boolean function of two variables extended to vectors by bitwise operation;
SHIFT L_v	Shift a word left
SHIFT R_v	or right
Transfer instructions for vectors and index registers	

As defined here, bit-vector machines are very powerful because many complex processes can be coded into very long binary strings, and a bit vector machine can perform its operations on these long strings in one step. When we use this model, we must argue that its use is realistic in a computational sense. For instance, if we are doing parsing of strings of length n and we are using bit vectors whose size is of length log n, that seems realistic because, in practice, most strings parsed are only a few hundred characters long at most. It would certainly be unrealistic to store strings of length n^2 in a single word.

Because of the way a bit-vector machine works, it is usually assumed that there are no input or output operations. One can recognize context-free languages on a bit-vector machine in time $(\log n)^3$. Now, that bound is less than linear time, and linear time is required to read the input in a reasonable model. So the method of achieving $(\log n)^3$ must be unrealistic.

Most of the discussion in this section has been descriptive. There is a mathematical result that we wish to establish. We wish to exhibit a single context-free language which has the property that, if one can parse this language in time $f(n) \geqslant n$

and/or space $g(n) \geqslant n$, then any context-free language can be parsed within these bounds. The significance of this result is that it is unnecessary to derive general time and space bounds for each of the parsing algorithms that will be studied. We could show instead that these algorithms have these bounds on just one particular grammar. We will not choose this approach, because the general techniques of algorithmic analysis are often more informative, and they lead us to notice significant special cases; but it is possible in principle.

Let A denote our favorite model of a computer, for instance, a random-access machine, a bit-vector machine, or some form of Turing machine.

Theorem 12.2.2 Let A be any computational model of the type just described that accepts $L \subseteq \Delta^*$ in time $p(n) \geqslant n$, where p is some polynomial. Let $\varphi: \Sigma^* \to \Delta^*$ be a homomorphism. The set

$$\varphi^{-1}(L) = \{w \in \Sigma^* | \varphi w \in L\}$$

can be accepted in time $p(n)$ by a device A' of the same type as A. The same result holds for space.

Proof We construct A' to work as follows:

1. Scan w and translate it to φw. This takes $k \lg(w)$ steps, for some constant k.
2. Simulate A on φw. This takes $p(\lg(\varphi w))$ steps.
3. Then w may be processed in

$$p(\lg(\varphi w)) + k \lg(w) \leqslant k' p(\lg(w))$$

steps for some constant k'. Note that a similar result holds for space. □

Let us now recall a specific context-free language, namely, L_0 of Section 10.5. Let $\Sigma = \{a_1, a_2, \bar{a}_1, \bar{a}_2, ¢, c\}$. Define

$$L_0 = \{\Lambda\} \cup \{x_1 c y_1 c z_1 d \cdots d x_n c y_n c z_n d | n \geqslant 1, y_1 \cdots y_n \in ¢ D_2, x_i, z_i \in \Sigma^*$$

for all i, $1 \leqslant i \leqslant n, y_i \in \{a_1, a_2, \bar{a}_1, \bar{a}_2\}^*$ for all $i \geqslant 2\}$. D_2 is the semi-Dyck set on two generators.

Theorem 12.2.3 L_0 is a "hardest" context-free language. That is, the time and tape complexity for recognizing any context-free language is identical to the time and tape bounds for L_0.

Proof The result follows immediately from Theorem 12.2.2 and Theorem 10.5.1. □

PROBLEMS

1 A weakened statement of Theorem 12.2.1 could be that, in a cycle-free grammar, there is a linear relationship between the length of string generated from A and the length of the derivation. Can you give a quick proof of this result by contradiction? If you succeed, why is the proof given in the text superior?

2 Suppose A is a k-tape Turing machine which accepts a set L with time complexity $T(n) \geqslant n$. Show that L can be accepted by a RAM program in time proportional to

$$T'(n) = \begin{cases} T(n) & \text{with uniform-cost criterion,} \\ T(n) \log T(n) & \text{with the logarithmic-cost criterion.} \end{cases}$$

3 Show that the converse of Problem 2 is false for the uniform-cost criterion. That is, there is a language L accepted by some RAM program P in time $T(n)$ under the uniform-cost criterion. There is no Turing machine A' which accepts L in time $p(T(n))$ for any polynomial $p(x)$.

4 Let L be a language accepted by a RAM program in time $T(n)$ under the logarithmic-cost criterion. Find the smallest possible polynomial $p(x)$ so that L is accepted by a Turing machine in time $p(T(n))$. For example, does $p(x) = x^3$ suffice?

5 If indirect addressing is removed as a feature in a RAM, what consequences follow?

6 Find a simple deterministic context-free language L_1 such that

$$\Delta_0 \subseteq \text{DSPACE } (\log n)$$

if and only if

$$L_1 \in \text{DSPACE } (\log n).$$

Recall that Δ_0 is the family of deterministic context-free languages. Simple is used in the sense of Section 11.9.

7 Consider the set L_1 in Problem 6. Is it fair to regard L_1 as a hardest deterministic context-free language?

12.3 MATRIX MULTIPLICATION, BOOLEAN MATRIX MULTIPLICATION, AND TRANSITIVE CLOSURE ALGORITHMS

A close connection between matrix multiplication, boolean matrix multiplication, and transitive closure algorithms will emerge in this chapter. Some classical results in this area are now recalled.

Let us first consider multiplication of matrices over an arbitrary ring. The key idea is to study the 2×2 case first, and then to reduce the general case to it.

Lemma 12.3.1 The product of two 2×2 matrices whose elements are from any ring can be computed with seven multiplications and fifteen additions.

Proof Let

$$\begin{bmatrix} a_{11} & a_{12} \\ a_{21} & a_{22} \end{bmatrix} \begin{bmatrix} b_{11} & b_{12} \\ b_{21} & b_{22} \end{bmatrix} = \begin{bmatrix} c_{11} & c_{12} \\ c_{21} & c_{22} \end{bmatrix}.$$

The following computation computes the c_{ij}. Each s_i term involves one addition and each m_i involves a single multiplication.

$$
\begin{aligned}
m_1 &= a_{11}b_{11} & m_2 &= a_{12}b_{21} \\
s_1 &= a_{11}-a_{21} & s_2 &= a_{21}+a_{22} \\
s_3 &= a_{22}-s_1 & s_4 &= a_{12}-s_3 \\
m_3 &= s_4 b_{22} & s_5 &= b_{22}-b_{12} \\
m_4 &= s_1 s_5 & s_6 &= b_{12}-b_{11} \\
m_5 &= s_2 s_6 & s_7 &= s_5+b_{11} \\
m_6 &= s_3 s_7 & s_8 &= b_{21}-s_7 \\
m_7 &= a_{22}s_8 & s_9 &= m_1+m_6
\end{aligned}
$$

$$
\begin{aligned}
c_{11} = s_{10} &= m_1+m_2 \\
s_{11} &= s_9+m_5 \\
c_{12} = s_{12} &= s_{11}+m_3 \\
s_{13} &= s_9+m_4 \\
c_{21} = s_{14} &= s_{13}+m_7 \\
c_{22} = s_{15} &= s_{13}+m_5
\end{aligned}
$$

It is a straightforward task to verify that these identities correctly compute c_{ij}. □

Now we shall treat general matrix multiplication in terms of the 2×2 case.

Theorem 12.3.2 Two $n \times n$ matrices whose elements come from an arbitrary ring can be multiplied in time proportional to $n^{2.81}$.

Proof Let us consider the case $n = 2^k$. Let us write the equation $\mathbf{C} = \mathbf{A} * \mathbf{B}$ involving $n \times n$ matrices as

$$
\begin{bmatrix} \mathbf{C}_{11} & \mathbf{C}_{12} \\ \mathbf{C}_{21} & \mathbf{C}_{22} \end{bmatrix} = \begin{bmatrix} \mathbf{A}_{11} & \mathbf{A}_{12} \\ \mathbf{A}_{21} & \mathbf{A}_{22} \end{bmatrix} \begin{bmatrix} \mathbf{B}_{11} & \mathbf{B}_{12} \\ \mathbf{B}_{21} & \mathbf{B}_{22} \end{bmatrix}, \tag{12.3.1}
$$

where each $\mathbf{C}_{ij}$, $\mathbf{A}_{ij}$, and $\mathbf{B}_{ij}$ is an $(n/2) \times (n/2)$ matrix. Thus we may regard $\mathbf{A}$, $\mathbf{B}$, and $\mathbf{C}$ as 2×2 matrices over a different ring. It is this observation that will allow us to use Lemma 12.3.1.

Let $M(n)$ be the number of scalar multiplications necessary to multiply two $n \times n$ matrices. Let $A(n)$ be the number of scalar additions necessary to multiply two $n \times n$ matrices. Let $T(n) = M(n) + A(n)$. Note that n^2 scalar additions are needed to *add* two $n \times n$ matrices. Using Eq. (12.3.1) and Lemma 12.3.1, we see that seven multiplications of $(n/2) \times (n/2)$ matrices and 15 additions of $(n/2) \times (n/2)$ matrices are needed; that is,

$$T(n) = 7T\left(\frac{n}{2}\right) + 15\left(\frac{n}{2}\right)^2.$$

Thus

$$M(n) = 7M\left(\frac{n}{2}\right)$$

and

$$A(n) = 7A\left(\frac{n}{2}\right) + 15\left(\frac{n}{2}\right)^2.$$

Using the initial conditions $M(2) = 7$ and $A(2) = 15$, we conclude that, if $n = 2^k$,

$$M(n) = 7^k$$

$$A(n) = 5(7^k - 4^k) \tag{12.3.2}$$

and

$$T(n) = 6 \cdot 7^k - 5 \cdot 4^k,$$

as the reader may easily verify by induction on k.

Note that $k = \log_2 n$ so that Eq. (12.3.2) is

$$M(n) = 7^k = 7^{\log_2 n} = n^{\log_2 7} = n^{2.81}.$$

Also observe that

$$T(n) = 6 \cdot n^{2.81} - 5 \cdot n^2 < 6 \cdot n^{2.81}. \tag{12.3.3}$$

Note that, if n is not a power of 2, one can pad the matrices out to the next larger power of 2. This can (at worst) double n, which involves increasing the constant by 6 in Eq. (12.3.3). □

We could instead assume, in Theorem 12.3.2, that $n = 2^k \cdot h$, where h is odd. It is then possible to derive an expression of the form

$$T(n) = c \cdot n^{2.81}$$

where $c < 6$. We leave this refinement for the reader.

Thus we have an $\mathcal{O}(n^{2.81})$ time bound for multiplication of $n \times n$ matrices over a ring. However, the product operation of a ring is associative but our applications will use nonassociative products. Consequently, we extend our previous result to multiplication of boolean matrices and then reduce our new product operation to boolean products.

Boolean matrices are $n \times n$ matrices whose elements are subsets of $\{0, 1\}$. The associated scalar operations $+$ and $*$, given by the following table for boolean addition and multiplication satisfy all the properties of a ring except that the element 1 has no additive inverse.

+	0	1
0	0	1
1	1	1

*	0	1
0	0	0
1	0	1

As usual, we define matrix multiplication by the "sum of products" rule.

Example

$$\begin{bmatrix} 1 & 1 \\ 0 & 1 \end{bmatrix} \begin{bmatrix} 1 & 1 \\ 1 & 0 \end{bmatrix} = \begin{bmatrix} 1 & 1 \\ 1 & 0 \end{bmatrix}.$$

Since we do not have a ring, we cannot apply our technique for fast multiplication to boolean matrices directly. Nevertheless, as the text theorem indicates, we can multiply boolean matrices within the same time bound.

Theorem 12.3.3 The product of two $n \times n$ boolean matrices can be computed in time proportional to $n^{2.81}$ steps.

Proof Given two $n \times n$ boolean matrices **A** and **B**, compute $\mathbf{C} = \mathbf{A} * \mathbf{B}$ by the algorithm given in Theorem 12.3.2, using $\mathbb{Z}_{n+1}$, the integers modulo $(n+1)$, as the ground ring. Note that, for $1 \leqslant i, j \leqslant n$, $0 \leqslant c_{i,j} \leqslant n$. Let **D** be the boolean product of **A** and **B**.

Claim $d_{i,j} = 1$ if and only if $1 \leqslant c_{i,j} \leqslant n$.

Proof of claim If $d_{i,j} = 0$, then there is no k such that $a_{i,k} b_{k,j} = 1$, and hence $c_{i,j} = 0$. If $d_{i,j} = 1$, then, for some value of k, $a_{i,k} = 1$ and $b_{k,j} = 1$. Therefore $1 \leqslant c_{i,j} \leqslant n$ and both the claim and the theorem follow. □

PROBLEMS

Transitive closure is an important and familiar operation on relations. It generalizes to graphs and matrices by the familiar connections among relations, matrices and graphs.

1 Let **A** be an $n \times n$ boolean matrix. Show that $\mathbf{A}^* = I \cup A \cup A^2 \cup \cdots = (I \cup \mathbf{A})^n$.

2 Another procedure for computing $\mathbf{A}^*$ or $\mathbf{A}^+$ involves Warshall's algorithm, shown below.

```
begin
    comment A is an n × n boolean matrix whose closure is to be
        computed. The answer is stored into B:
    for 1 ⩽ i, j ⩽ n do c_ij^(0) : = A[i, j];
    for k: = 1 to n do
        for 1 ⩽ i, j ⩽ n do
            c_ij^(k) : = c_ij^(k-1) ∪ c_ik^(k-1) · c_kj^(k-1);
    for 1 ⩽ i, j ⩽ n do B[i, j] : = c_ij^(n)
end.
```

Prove that Warshall's algorithm uses $\mathcal{O}(n^3)$ $\cup$ and $\cdot$ operations on a RAM and that $\mathbf{B} = \mathbf{A}^+$. Discuss appropriate cost functions for the computation.

3 Implement Warshall's algorithm on a bit-vector machine by storing rows (columns). What is the time bound achieved this way, and what is the appropriate cost function?

4 By a suitable encoding, show that the algorithm of Problem 3 can be implemented on a unit-cost RAM in time $n^2 \log n$. *Hint*: Map $(b_1, \ldots, b_n)$ into:

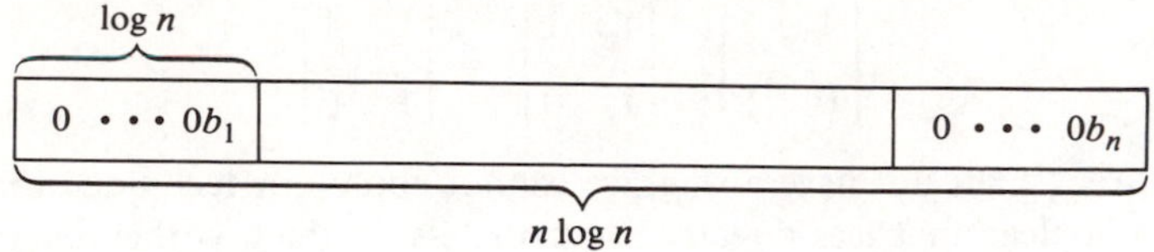

12.4 THE COCKE–KASAMI–YOUNGER ALGORITHM

The algorithm to be presented requires grammars in Chomsky normal form. As we saw in Theorem 4.4.1, there is no loss of generality in this assumption. The string Λ is in a language if and only if the Chomsky normal-form grammar for the language has a rule $S \rightarrow \Lambda$, where S is the start symbol. Furthermore, the rule $S \rightarrow \Lambda$ cannot be used in the derivation of any non-null strings. Consequently, without loss of generality, we can restrict our attention to non-null input strings and Λ-free grammars in Chomsky normal form.

The key to the Cocke–Kasami–Younger algorithm is to form a strictly upper triangular matrix of size $(n+1) \times (n+1)$, where n is the length of the input string. The entries in the matrix are subsets of variables. We can then determine membership in the language by inspecting one matrix entry. We can also use the matrix to generate a parse.

Algorithm 12.4.1 Let $G = (V, \Sigma, P, S)$ be a grammar in Chomsky normal form (without the rule $S \rightarrow \Lambda$) and let $w = a_1 a_2 \cdots a_n$, $n \geqslant 1$, be a string where, for $1 \leqslant k \leqslant n$, $a_k \in \Sigma$. Form the strictly upper-triangular $(n+1) \times (n+1)$ recognition matrix **T** as follows, where each element $t_{i,j}$ is a subset of $V - \Sigma$ and is initially empty.†

```
begin
loop_1:   for i: = 0 to n − 1 do
               t_{i,i+1} : = {A | A → a_{i+1} is in P};
loop_2:   for d: = 2 to n do
          for i: = 0 to n − d do
             begin j: = d + i;
               t_{ij}: = {A | there exists k, i + 1 ⩽ k ⩽ j − 1 such that
                  A → BC is in P for some B ∈ t_{i,k}, C ∈ t_{k,j}}
             end
end.
```

Example

$$S \rightarrow SS \mid AA \mid b \qquad\qquad w = aabb$$
$$A \rightarrow AS \mid AA \mid a$$

† Recall the 0-origin addressing convention for matrices.

The recognition matrix is

T =

	A	S, A	S, A	A, S
		A	A	A
			S	S
				S

In computing **T**, the superdiagonal stripe is filled in by loop 1. As the following diagram illustrates, the remaining computation is done down the diagonals ($j-i=d$) and working up to the righthand corner as $d=2,\ldots,n$. Thus the rows are filled left to right, and the columns are filled bottom to top.

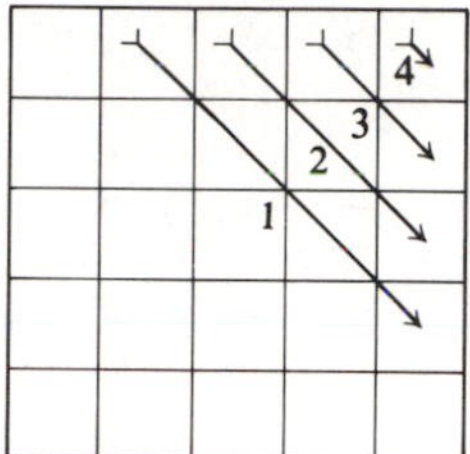

As shown in Fig. 12.4 the (i, j)th element of the matrix is computed by scanning across the ith row and down the jth column, always to the left and below the entry in question.

Thus we successively consider the pairs of entries

$$(i, i+1) \quad (i+1, j)$$
$$(i, i+2) \quad (i+2, j)$$
$$\vdots$$
$$(i, j-1) \quad (j-1, j)$$

Each matrix entry is a set of nonterminals. For each pair of entries, we find every grammar rule with a right part composed of a symbol from the first entry followed by a symbol from the second entry. The left parts of these rules constitute the (i,j)th entry in the recognition matrix.

The next theorem and its corollary show that the algorithm is correct, in that it recognizes all and only strings generated by the associated grammar.

Theorem 12.4.1 Let $G=(V, \Sigma, P, S)$ be a grammar in Chomsky normal form (without the rule $S \to \Lambda$). Let $w=a_1a_2 \cdots a_n, n \geqslant 1$, be a string, where for $1 \leqslant k \leqslant n$,

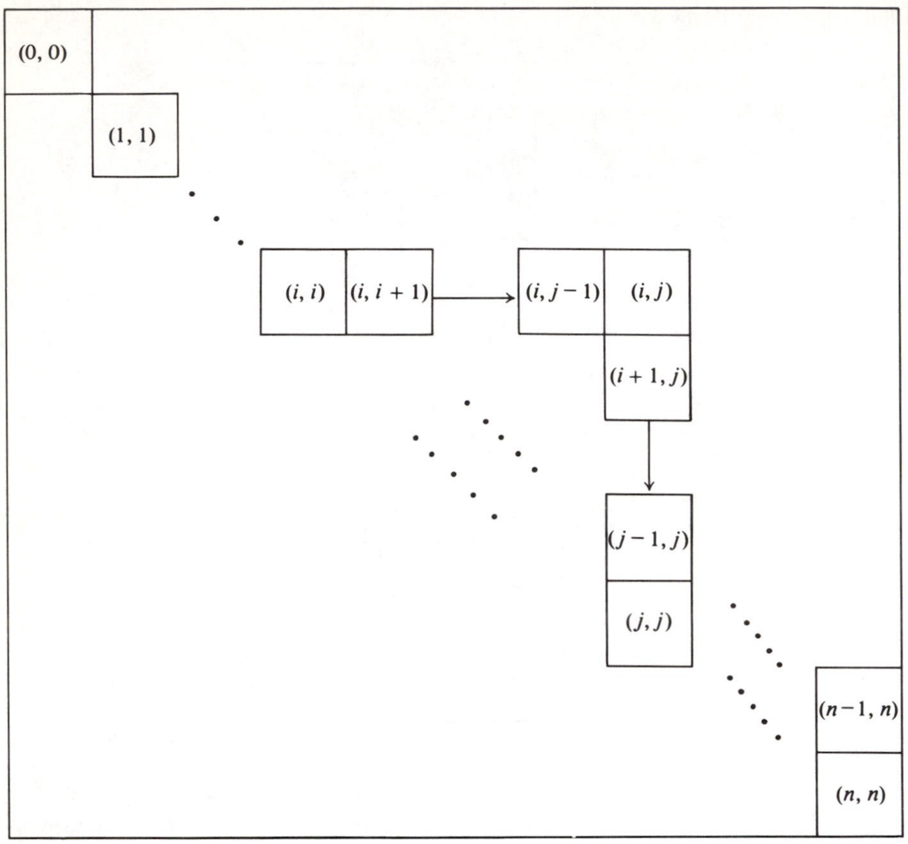

FIG. 12.4

$a_k \in \Sigma$, and let $\mathbf{T} = (t_{i,j})$ be the recognition matrix constructed by Algorithm 12.4.1. Then $A \in t_{i,j}$ if and only if $A \overset{+}{\Rightarrow} a_{i+1} a_{i+2} \cdots a_j$.

Proof Since the recognition matrix is strictly upper-triangular and $(n+1) \times (n+1)$, the algorithm must set entries t_{ij} where $0 \leqslant i \leqslant n-1$, $1 \leqslant j \leqslant n$, and $i < j$. Consequently, $1 \leqslant j - i \leqslant n$. The first loop handles the case $j - i = 1$. In the second loop, since $j = d + i$, we know that $d = j - i$. For a given value of d, we must have $j = d + i \leqslant n$. Consequently, $i \leqslant n - d$. It follows that Algorithm 12.4.1 sets every entry of the recognition matrix and each element is assigned a value only once. We show by induction on d that the values of $\mathbf{T}$ correspond appropriately to derivations.

Basis. $j - i = 1$, so $j - 1 = i$. Clearly, after the first loop, $A \in t_{i,i+1}$ if and only if $A \Rightarrow a_{i+1}$.

Induction step. For some $d = j - i$, $1 < d \leqslant n$, assume the result for all $d' < d$. After the second loop, $A \in t_{i,j}$ if and only if there exists k, $i < k < j$, such that $A \to BC$ is in P for some $B \in t_{i,k}$, $C \in t_{k,j}$.

Since $k < j$, we have

$$k - i < j - i = d,$$

and the induction hypothesis applies to $t_{i,k}$ since $k - i < d$. Also, since $i < k$,

$$j - k < j - i = d,$$

and, since $j - k < d$, the induction hypothesis holds for $t_{k,j}$ also.

$$B \in t_{i,k} \quad \text{if and only if } B \overset{+}{\Rightarrow} a_{i+1} \cdots a_k$$

$$C \in t_{k,j} \quad \text{if and only if } C \overset{+}{\Rightarrow} a_{k+1} \cdots a_j$$

Combining these results, we have

$$A \in t_{i,j} \quad \text{if and only if } A \Rightarrow BC \overset{+}{\Rightarrow} a_{i+1} \cdots a_j.$$

This extends the induction. □

Corollary $w \in L(G)$ if and only if $S \in t_{0,n}$.

Algorithm 12.4.1 is an "off-line" algorithm in the sense that all of the input is read at the beginning and the successive matrix entries computed correspond, by Theorem 12.4.1, to sets of successively longer substrings of the entire input string. An "on-line" algorithm would compute the matrix entries in such a way that, after reading a_i, the recognition matrix would indicate which nonterminals generate $a_1 a_2 \cdots a_i$. In fact, Algorithm 12.4.1 can be rewritten as an on-line algorithm. We present this algorithm so that the reader can compare it with other on-line algorithms.

Algorithm 12.4.2 Let $G = (V, \Sigma, P, S)$ be a grammar in Chomsky normal form (without the rule $S \to \Lambda$) and let $w = a_1 a_2 \cdots a_n$, $n \geqslant 1$, be a string, where for $1 \leqslant i \leqslant n$, $a_i \in \Sigma$. Form the strictly upper-triangular $(n + 1) \times (n + 1)$ recognition matrix **T** as follows, where each element $t_{i,j}$ is a subset of $V - \Sigma$:

begin

    for j: = 1 **to** n **do**

    begin

      $t_{j-1,j}$: = $\{A \mid A \to a_j$ is in $P\}$;

loop_2:   **for** i: = $j - 2$ **down to** 0 **do**

        $t_{i,j}$: = $\{A \mid$ there exists k, $i + 1 \leqslant k \leqslant j - 1$ such that

          $A \to BC$ is in P for some $B \in t_{i,k}$, $C \in t_{k,j}\}$

    end

end.

Note that this algorithm fills in the matrix column by column and the column elements are computed "bottom to top." We leave it to the reader to verify that Algorithm 12.4.1 and Algorithm 12.4.2 yield the same recognition matrix for any grammar and string.

Next we estimate the number of steps required by the algorithm, as a function of the length of the string being analyzed. Observe that, for a given terminal symbol a_{i+1}, computation of $\{A | A \to a_{i+1}$ is in $P\}$ takes a fixed amount of time. Similarly, for fixed i, j, and k, computation of $\{A | A \to BC$ is in P, $B \in t_{i,k}, C \in t_{k,j}\}$ takes an amount of time bounded by a constant with respect to the length of the string being analyzed.

Theorem 12.4.2 Algorithm 12.4.1 requires $\mathcal{O}(n^3)$ steps to compute the recognition matrix.

Proof Loop 1 takes $c_1 n$ steps to initialize the superdiagonal. The setting of $t_{i,j}$ in the body of loop 2 takes $c_2(d-1)$ steps, since k can take on $d-1$ values. Therefore the algorithm requires

$$c_1 n + c_2 \sum_{d=2}^{n} (d-1)(n-d+1) = c_1 n + \frac{c_2(n^3-n)}{6} = \mathcal{O}(n^3) \text{ steps.} \qquad \square$$

The space required by the algorithm is determined by the number of elements in the strictly upper-triangular matrix. Since each element contains a set of bounded size, we get immediately the next theorem.

Theorem 12.4.3 Algorithm 12.4.1 requires $n(n+1)/2$ cells of memory on a RAM.

Now that the recognition problem has been solved, a technique is needed for parsing. Algorithm 12.4.3, which follows, provides a means of obtaining a parse for a given string from its recognition matrix. The algorithm will also be used for the recognition matrices defined using other methods of recognition.

Algorithm 12.4.3 Let $G = (V, \Sigma, P, S)$ be a grammar in Chomsky normal form (without the rule $S \to \Lambda$) with the productions numbered $1, 2, \ldots, p$ and the ith production designated π_i. Let $w = a_1 a_2 \cdots a_n, n \geqslant 1$, be a string, where for $1 \leqslant k \leqslant n$, $a_k \in \Sigma$ and let $\mathbf{T} = (t_{i,j})$ be the recognition matrix for w constructed by Algorithm 2.1.1.

In order to produce a left parse for w, define the recursive procedure *parse*(i, j, A), which generates a left parse for $A \overset{+}{\Rightarrow} a_{i+1} a_{i+2} \ldots a_j$ by:

```
procedure parse(i, j, A);
begin
   if j − i = 1 and π_m = A → a_{i+1} is in P
   then output (m)
   else
   if k is the least integer i < k < j such that π_m = A → BC
        is in P where B ∈ t_{i,k} and C ∈ t_{k,j}
   then begin output (m); parse(i, k, B)
              parse(k, j, C)
        end
end;
```

Output a left parse for w as follows:

main program: **if** $S \in t_{0,n}$
then *parse*$(0, n, S)$
else output ("error").

Note that Algorithm 12.4.3 produces the leftmost parse "top down" with respect to the syntax trees. By contrast, Algorithm 12.4.1 builds the recognition matrix "bottom up." The reader can easily modify the algorithm to produce a rightmost parse.

We next verify that Algorithm 12.4.3 works and derive its running time. The theorem is followed by an example.

Theorem 12.4.4 Let $G = (V, \Sigma, P, S)$ be a grammar in Chomsky normal form (without the rule $S \to \Lambda$), with productions designated $\pi_1, \pi_2, \ldots, \pi_p$. If Algorithm 12.4.3 is executed with the string $w = a_1 a_2 \cdots a_n, n \geqslant 1$, where, for $1 \leqslant i \leqslant n, a_i \in \Sigma$, then the parsing algorithm terminates. If $w \in L(G)$, then the parsing algorithm produces a left parse; otherwise it announces error. The parsing algorithm takes time $\mathcal{O}(n^2)$.

Proof We establish the theorem by a sequence of partial results.

Claim 1 Whenever *parse*(i, j, A) is called, then $j > i$ and $A \in t_{i,j}$.

Proof of Claim 1 The procedure *parse* is called once from the main program and twice from within the body of *parse*. In all cases the call is conditional on the satisfaction of this property of the arguments.

Claim 2 *parse*(i, j, A) terminates and produces a left parse of the derivation $A \overset{+}{\Rightarrow} a_{i+1} a_{i+2} \cdots a_j$.

Proof of Claim 2 We induct on $j - i$.

Basis. $j - i = 1$. By claim 1, $A \in t_{i,i+1}$. It follows from Theorem 12.4.2 that $A \overset{+}{\Rightarrow} a_{i+1}$ and therefore that P contains a rule $\pi_m = A \to a_{i+1}$. Clearly, the procedure *parse* terminates and produces the left parse m.

Induction step. Assume the result for $j - i \leqslant d$. Consider *parse*(i, j, A), where $j - i = d + 1$. Since $j - i \neq 1$, the **else** portion of the conditional statement in *parse* is executed. It follows from Claim 1 and Theorem 12.4.2 that, for some B, C in $V - \Sigma$, $A \Rightarrow BC \overset{+}{\Rightarrow} a_{i+1} a_{i+2} \cdots a_j$ and, consequently, that P contains some rule $\pi_m = A \to BC$ where $B \in t_{i,k}$ and $C \in t_{k,j}$. Therefore, *parse* produces $(m,$ *parse*(i, k, B) *parse*$(k, j, C))$. By the induction hypothesis, *parse*(i, k, B) and *parse*(k, j, C) terminate and produce the appropriate left parses. Consequently, the **else** portion of *parse* terminates and produces a left parse of $A \overset{+}{\Rightarrow} a_{i+1} a_{i+2} \cdots a_j$.

Claim 3 For each d, $1 \leqslant d \leqslant n$, a call of *parse*$(i, j, A)$ takes at most cd^2 steps where $j - i = d$ and c is some constant.

Proof of Claim 3 We induct on d.

Basis. $d = 1$. *parse*$(i, i+1, A)$ takes one step.

Induction step. Assume the result for $j - i \leqslant d$. Suppose *parse* (i, j, A) is called with $j - i = d + 1$. Clearly, the **else** portion of the procedure is executed. Except for calls of *parse*, for some constant c_1, the **else** portion takes at most $c_1(j - i - 1) \leqslant c_1(j - i)$ steps, since k takes on $j - i - 1$ values. Therefore, if we choose $c = c_1$, then, including the recursive calls on *parse* and using the induction hypothesis, *parse* requires at most $c(j-i) + c(k-i)^2 + c(j-k)^2$ steps. Let $k = i + x$ and $j = i + x + y$. Then the number of steps is

$$c((j-i) + (k-i)^2 + (j-k)^2) = c(x + y + x^2 + y^2).$$

Using the elementary relationship

$$\frac{x+y}{2} \leqslant xy,$$

we get

$$x + y + x^2 + y^2 \leqslant x^2 + y^2 + 2xy = (x+y)^2 = (j-i)^2.$$

This completes the induction proof of Claim 3.

Putting the partial results together, it follows, from Theorem 12.4.2, that if $w \notin L(G)$, the $S \notin t_{0,n}$. Clearly, the algorithm terminates and announces error in this case. Otherwise the algorithm calls *parse*$(0, n, S)$. It follows from Claim 2 that the algorithm terminates and produces a left parse for $S \stackrel{+}{\Rightarrow} a_1 a_2 \cdots a_n = w$. It follows from Claim 3 that the algorithm takes $\mathcal{O}(n^2)$ steps. □

Example Continuing the previous example, we number the productions

1. $S \to SS$
2. $S \to AA$
3. $S \to b$
4. $A \to AS$
5. $A \to AA$
6. $A \to a$

The parse of $w = aaab$ is generated in the following way:

Since $S \in t_{0,4}$, *parse*$(0, 4, S)$ is called.

Since $\pi_2 = S \to AA$ is in P, $A \in t_{0,1}$, and $A \in t_{1,4}$, we get:

$(2, \textit{parse}(0, 1, A), \textit{parse}(1, 4, A)) = (2, 6, \textit{parse}(1, 4, A))$.

Since $\pi_4 = A \to AS$ is in P, $A \in t_{1,2}$, and $S \in t_{2,4}$, we get:

$(2, 6, 4, \textit{parse}(1, 2, A), \textit{parse}(2, 4, S)) = (2, 6, 4, 6, \textit{parse}(2, 4, S))$.

Since $\pi_1 = S \to SS$ is in P, $S \in t_{2,3}$, and $S \in t_{3,4}$, we get:

$(2, 6, 4, 6, 1, \textit{parse}(2, 3, S), \textit{parse}(3, 4, S))$

$\quad = (2, 6, 4, 6, 1, 3, \textit{parse}(3, 4, S))$

$\quad = (2, 6, 4, 6, 1, 3, 3)$,

which corresponds to the tree

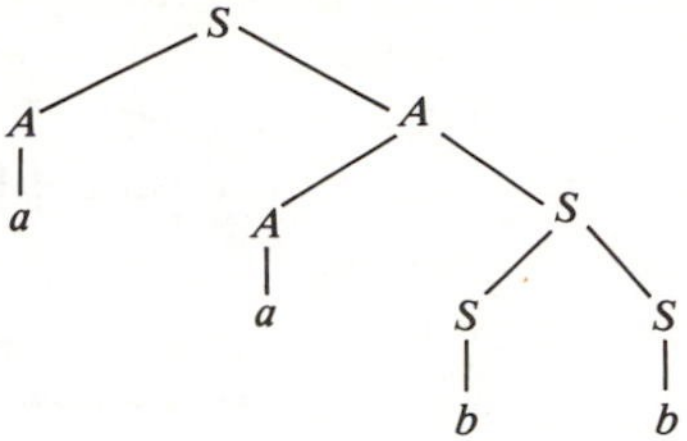

By combining our recognition and parsing results, we get a time bound for general context-free parsing.

Theorem 12.4.5 Every context-free language L can be parsed in time proportional to n^3 where n is the length of the string to be parsed and in space proportional to n^2.

Proof By Theorem 4.4.1, every context-free language $L \subseteq \Sigma^*$ is generated by a grammar $G = (V, \Sigma, P, S)$ in Chomsky normal form. For any string $w = a_1 a_2 \cdots a_n$, if $n = 0$, then $w = \Lambda$ is in L if $S \to \Lambda$ is in G. If $n > 0$, then, by Theorem 12.4.1, we can determine whether $w \in L$ by a computation which, by Theorem 12.4.2, requires at most $\mathcal{O}(n^3)$ steps. If $w \in L$, then, by Theorem 12.4.4, we can generate a parse for w in another $\mathcal{O}(n^2)$ steps. The space bound follows from Theorem 12.4.3. □

Although we have shown how Algorithm 12.4.1 recognizes strings in time $\mathcal{O}(n^3)$ on a RAM, it does not follow that this can be done on a Turing machine within the same time bound. It might be the case that the Turing machine cannot organize its tapes sufficiently well to avoid many bookkeeping steps that will change the time bound. In this section we show that, in fact, recognition can be done on a Turing machine in time $\mathcal{O}(n^3)$.

Our model will consist of a Turing machine with a read-only input tape and two work tapes.

Theorem 12.4.6 Let $G = (V, \Sigma, P, S)$ be a Λ-free, context-free grammar in Chomsky normal form and let $w = a_1 \cdots a_n$, $a_i \in \Sigma$, $1 \leqslant i \leqslant n$. There is a Turing machine A which computes the recognition matrix $\mathbf{T} = (t_{i,j})$ in time at most cn^3 for some constant c.

Proof The initial configuration of A is shown below,

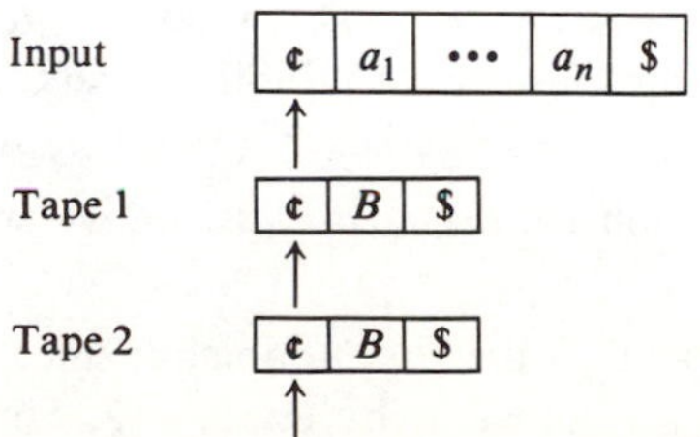

where ¢ and \$ are endmarkers on the tapes and B is a "blank" symbol.

The idea of the argument will be to have the upper-triangular entries of $t_{i,j}$ laid out on both tapes 1 and 2. On tape 1 the entries of **T** will be written by rows, while on tape 2 the entries will be by columns. The computation proceeds by filling in the matrix by diagonals, filling entries in the same order as does Algorithm 12.4.1.

The first phase of the computation is to initialize A to the configurations

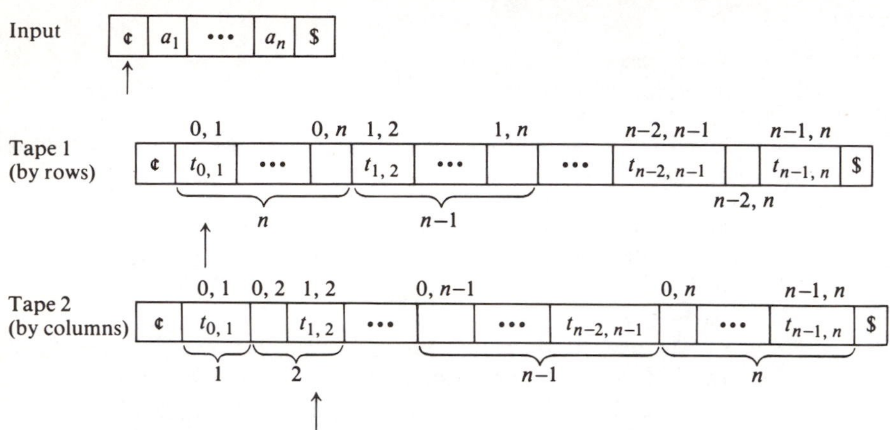

Since tape 1 and tape 2 each have $\mathcal{O}(n^2)$ entries, the initialization takes at least $\mathcal{O}(n^2)$ steps. It is left to the reader to show that the initialization can be done in time $\mathcal{O}(n^2)$.

We next show how to compute any element $t_{i,j}$ where $i+1<j\leqslant n$. The configuration just prior to the computation is shown below.

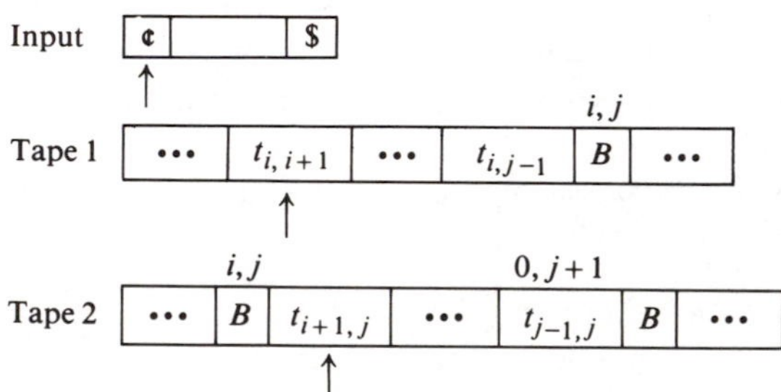

The procedure to compute $t_{i,j}$ is as follows, once we are in the position above.

> Move right on tapes 1 and 2, computing $t_{i,j}$ in the finite-state control until a blank is encountered on tape 1. This is square (i, j) on tape 1, so write the entry there. Move left on tape 2 to the first blank which is (i, j) and make the entry there. This computation takes $\mathcal{O}(j-i)$ steps.

Next we must get into position for the $t_{i+1,j+1}$ (if we weren't previously at the "end" of the diagonal).

> Move right on tape 1 to the first nonblank; since the rows are filled left to right, this is $t_{i+1,i+2}$. Move right on tape 2. Since the columns are filled bottom to top, the first blank we encounter is in square $(0, j+1)$ and the subsequent first nonblank is in position $(i+2, j+1)$.

If we reach \$ on the work tapes, then we have concluded a diagonal. Thus, the previously computed entry was $t_{i,n}$. The next entry to be computed will be $(0, n + 1 - i)$. To position the work tapes:

1 Move to ¢ on both tapes 1 and 2. If no blanks were encountered along the way, then look at the last entry $t_{i,j}$ in the finite-state control. This was $t_{0,n}$. If $S \in t_{0,n}$, then halt and accept; else halt and reject.

2 If there were blanks along the way, then move the head on tape 1 to the first square to the right of ¢. This is $t_{0,1}$. On tape 2, scan right and find the first blank; then go one square to the right on the blank. The blank is in position $(0, n + 1 - i)$. The square to the right is $t_{1,n+1-i}$. The tapes are then positioned correctly.

To estimate the number of steps, note that the computation of any element $t_{i,j}$, where $i + 1 < j \leqslant n$, takes at most cn steps. (One can compute c from studying the tape motion.) Since there are $\mathcal{O}(n^2)$ elements, at most $c_1 n^3$ steps are required to compute all the elements. In addition, we must consider the tape repositioning. To compute the next element in a diagonal requires $\mathcal{O}(n)$ steps for repositioning. For each of the n diagonals, we must reposition the heads over the entire work tapes. Consequently, repositioning requires $\mathcal{O}(n^3)$ steps. Thus, including the initialization, the entire computation takes

$$c_1 n^3 + c_2 n^3 + c_3 n^2 = \mathcal{O}(n^3) \text{ steps.} \qquad \square$$

Example Consider the grammar G used in the previous examples and shown below. Let $w = aabb$.

$$S \to SS \mid AA \mid b$$

$$A \to AS \mid AA \mid a$$

After initialization, the configuration of the Turing machine is

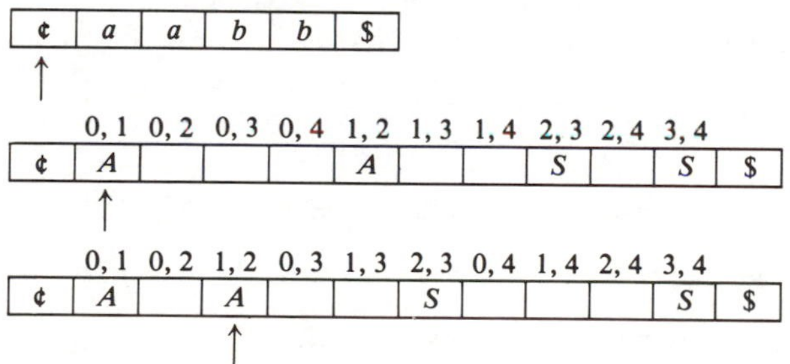

We scan right on both tapes to compute 0, 2. This is entered in the 0, 2 square of tape 1, which is the current position of the tape head. On tape 2, we scan left to the first blank to fill in the entry. Then we go right on tape 1 to the first nonblank. On tape 2, we go right on through one or more nonblanks and then through blanks and stop at $t_{2,3}$. This computation is repeated. The following is the configuration just before $t_{2,4}$ is computed.

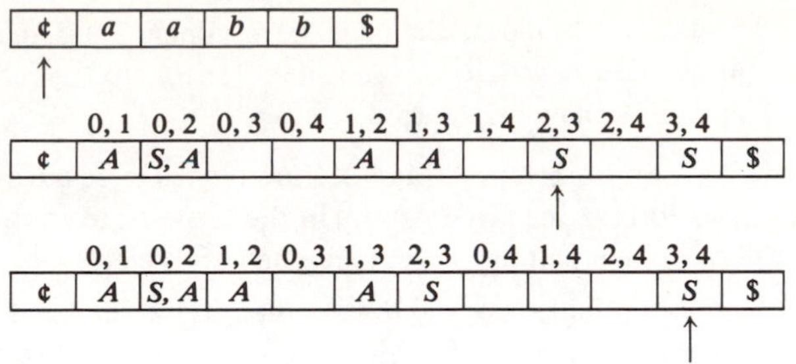

We compute $t_{2,4}$ as before, and make the entry. When we go right, we reach the endmarker and must move left. This yields:

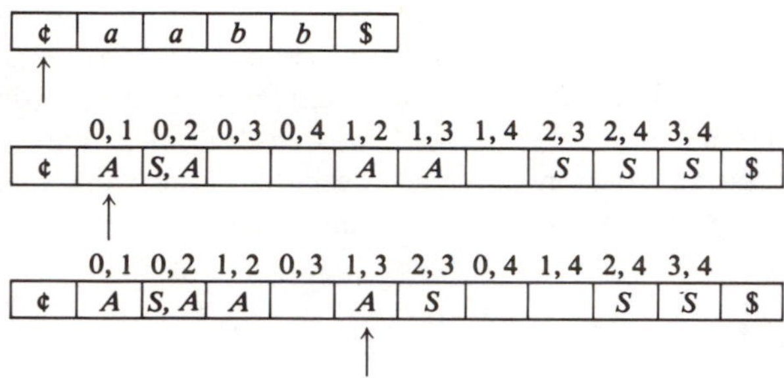

and so it goes . . . .

As is true in the random-access case, the recognition matrix can be computed on-line by a Turing machine, provided the bookkeeping is done slightly differently. We leave this construction to the reader.

As an interesting special case, let us assume that the underlying grammar G is linear. Recall (from Problem 2.5.1) that there is no loss of generality in assuming that $G = (V, \Sigma, P, S)$ is in linear normal form. That is, each rule is of one of the following types:

$$S \to \Lambda \qquad \text{if } \Lambda \in L(G)$$

$$A \to aB \qquad a \in \Sigma, A \in N, B \in N - \{S\}$$

$$A \to Ba \qquad a \in \Sigma, A \in N, B \in N - \{S\}$$

$$A \to a \qquad a \in \Sigma, A \in N$$

Now we are ready to prove that every linear context-free language can be parsed in time $O(n^2)$ by a form of the Cocke–Kasami–Younger algorithm. Algorithm 12.4.4 provides a variant of the recognition-matrix construction of Algorithm 12.4.1, which handles grammars in linear normal form. (Cf. Problem 1 of Section 2.5) The difference between the two algorithms is only in the way in which the $t_{i,j}$'s are computed in the second loop.

Algorithm 12.4.4 Let $G = (V, \Sigma, P, S)$ be a grammar in linear normal form (without the rule $S \rightarrow \Lambda$) and let $w = a_1 a_2 \cdots a_n$, $n \geqslant 1$, be a string, where, for $1 \leqslant i \leqslant n$, $a_i \in \Sigma$. Form the strictly upper-triangular $(n+1) \times (n+1)$ recognition matrix **T** as follows, where each element $t_{i,j}$ is a subset of $V - \Sigma$.

begin
loop_1: **for** $i := 0$ **to** $n - 1$ **do**
  $t_{i,i+1} := \{A \mid A \rightarrow a_{i+1}$ is in $P\}$;
loop_2: **for** $d := 2$ **to** n **do**
  for $i := 0$ **to** $n - d$ **do**
   begin $j := d + i$;
    $t_{i,j} := \{A \mid A \rightarrow a_{i+1} B$ is in P for some $B \in t_{i+1,j}\}$
     $\cup \{A \mid A \rightarrow B a_j$ is in P for some $B \in t_{i,j-1}\}$
   end
end.

Theorem 12.4.7 Let $G = (V, \Sigma, P, S)$ be a grammar in linear normal form (without the rule $S \rightarrow \Lambda$). Let $w = a_1 a_2 \cdots a_n, n \geqslant 1$, be a string, where for $1 \leqslant k \leqslant n$, $a_k \in \Sigma$, and let $\mathbf{T} = (t_{i,j})$ be the recognition matrix constructed by Algorithm 12.4.1. Then $A \in t_{i,j}$ if and only if $A \overset{+}{\Rightarrow} a_{i+1} \cdots a_j$.

Proof The argument parallels the proof of Theorem 12.4.2 except that, in analyzing a derivation, the first step is either $A \rightarrow a_{i+1}B$ or $A \rightarrow Ba_j$. The details are omitted. ☐

In order to obtain our time bounds, we simply analyze Algorithm 12.4.4.

Theorem 12.4.8 Every linear context-free language L can be parsed in time proportional to n^2, where n is the length of the string to be parsed. Additionally, every such language can be recognized using only a linear amount of space.

Proof By Problem 1 of Section 2.5, there is no loss of generality in assuming that L is generated by a grammar in linear normal form. Using Algorithm 12.4.4, an input string of length n is in the language if $S \in t_{0,n}$ (or if $n = 0$ and $S \rightarrow \Lambda$ is in the grammar). Following the timing analysis of Theorem 12.4.2, loop 1 requires $c_1 n$ steps. Since the setting of $t_{i,j}$ in loop requires inspection of only two matrix entries, it takes at most a constant c_2 number of steps. Therefore, the algorithm requires

$$c_1 n + c_2 \sum_{d=2}^{n} (n - d + 1) = c_1 n + \frac{c_2(n^2 - n)}{2} = \mathcal{O}(n^2) \text{ steps}$$

to construct the recognition matrix. Using Algorithm 12.4.3, it follows, from Theorem 12.4.4, that a parse can be produced in $\mathcal{O}(n^2)$ steps.

Since, in loop 2, each $t_{i,j}$ is computed using only entries from the previous diagonal, all that must be remembered for recognition are the previous diagonal (or the input) and the current diagonal. Since the diagonals have at most n elements, this is a linear space requirement. (However, it does not suffice if a parse is to be generated.) ☐

PROBLEMS

1 Complete the proof of Theorem 12.4.7.

2 Modify Algorithm 12.4.2 to obtain an on-line algorithm for recognition of strings in a linear context-free grammar which takes quadratic time and linear space.

3 Design an algorithm which meets the requirements of Problem 2 but runs on a Turing machine.

4 Construct an algorithm which obtains a parse from the recognition matrix and which requires linear time for a grammar in linear normal form. What is the space bound and which cost criterion is being used?

5 Devise a new algorithm to determine a parse of a string of length n from the recognition matrix which takes time proportional to $n \log n$.

6 Show how to achieve the configuration of the end of Phase 1 of the Turing-machine computation of Theorem 12.4.6, using time proportional to n^2.

7* Suppose that G is an unambiguous context-free grammar in Chomsky normal form. Can you prove a better time bound for Algorithm 12.4.1 in this case?

8 Show how to implement the Cocke–Kasami–Younger algorithm on a single-tape Turing machine which runs in time $O(n^4)$. [*Hint.* Code the recognition matrix onto the tape with the columns stored from left to right and from the bottom to the top. Use symbols to mark the top of each column. In working up column j, suppose $t_{i+1,j}$ has been computed and we are about to compute $t_{i,j}$. In computing $t_{i,j}$, the ith row of **T** is needed, so the earlier part of the computation stores $t_{k,j}$ in the same tape square as $t_{i,k}$. Thus, $t_{i,j}$ may be computed in a single left-to-right pass and stored in the next empty cell, which is $t_{i,j}$.].

12.5* VALIANT'S ALGORITHM

The Cocke–Kasami–Younger algorithm allowed us to recognize and parse in time proportional to n^3. We are now about to give a procedure due to Valiant, which will result in a time bound proportional to $n^{2.81}$. To achieve this, we will resort to techniques that are asymptotically superior but result in such huge constants that this method is only of theoretical interest. It is important in that it relates matrix multiplication, boolean matrix multiplication, transitive closure, and parsing algorithms.

We first give an overview of the ideas of the algorithm. Let $G = (V, \Sigma, P, S)$ be a context-free grammar in Chomsky normal form. Suppose w is a string of length n to be parsed. Our algorithm produces the same recognition matrix as Algorithm 12.4.1, but the computation proceeds in quite a different way. We form the same starting matrix as in the Cocke–Kasami–Younger algorithm. We note that one can naturally define a (nonassociative) product operation on nonterminals of the grammar. In a properly generalized sense, the recognition matrix can be found by taking the "transitive closure" of the starting matrix. It turns out that one can do this efficiently if one can take the "product" of two upper-triangular matrices efficiently. One can reduce computing this product to computing ordinary boolean matrix products. This, in turn, reduces to studying efficient methods for computing ordinary matrix products, which we have already done.

Given any binary operation on a set S, we can extend that operation to matrices whose elements are subsets of S in a natural way. Suppose $\mathbf{A} = (a_{ij})$, $\mathbf{B} = (b_{ij})$, and $\mathbf{C} = (c_{ij})$ are $n \times n$ matrices† whose elements are subsets of S. Then we define $\mathbf{C} = \mathbf{A} * \mathbf{B}$ by

$$c_{ij} = \bigcup_{k=0}^{n-1} a_{ik} * b_{kj} \qquad \text{for } 0 \leqslant i, j \leqslant n-1.$$

Also, by definition, $\mathbf{A} \subseteq \mathbf{B}$ if for all i and j, $a_{ij} \subseteq b_{ij}$. Of course, we define $\mathbf{C} = \mathbf{A} \cup \mathbf{B}$ by

$$c_{ij} = a_{ij} \cup b_{ij} \qquad \text{for } 0 \leqslant i, j \leqslant n-1.$$

Using any product operation for sets and ordinary set union, we define a transitive-closure operation on matrices whose elements are sets.

Definition Let $\mathbf{D}$ be an $n \times n$ matrix whose elements are subsets of a set S and let $*$ be any binary operation on S. Let $\mathbf{D}^{(1)} = \mathbf{D}$ and, for each $i > 1$, let

$$\mathbf{D}^{(i)} = \bigcup_{j=1}^{i-1} \mathbf{D}^{(j)} * \mathbf{D}^{(i-j)}.$$

The *transitive closure* of $\mathbf{D}$ is defined to be $\mathbf{D}^+ = \mathbf{D}^{(1)} \cup \mathbf{D}^{(2)} \cup \cdots$. We say that a matrix $\mathbf{D}$ is *transitively closed* if $\mathbf{D}^+ = \mathbf{D}$.

Since the underlying binary operation may be nonassociative, as is the operation to be used for constructing the recognition matrix, we have defined $\mathbf{D}^{(i)}$ so as to include all possible associations. Although we write

$$\mathbf{D}^+ = \mathbf{D}^{(1)} \cup \mathbf{D}^{(2)} \cup \mathbf{D}^{(t)} \cup \cdots$$

as an infinite union, if S is finite, then the number of unions is always finite, as the number of possible entries is finite and so there are only finitely many such matrices. We leave it to the reader to find an upper bound for t in this case so that $\mathbf{D}^+ = \mathbf{D}^{(1)} \cup \cdots \cup \mathbf{D}^{(t)}$.

Example Let $S = \{0, 1\}$ and define a binary product by the following table:

	0	1
0	0	0
1	0	1

Let $\mathbf{D}$ be any matrix over S. The transitive closure of $\mathbf{D}$ is the "standard transitive closure" treated in the literature. In the usual fashion, $\mathbf{D}$ describes a binary relation ρ and $\mathbf{D}^+$ corresponds in the same way to the transitive closure ρ^+ of ρ.

The heart of the algorithm for constructing the recognition matrix is the following binary operation on subsets of the nonterminals of a grammar.

† Recall our convention of 0-origin addressing for matrices.

Definition Let $G = (V, \Sigma, P, S)$ be a context-free grammar in Chomsky normal form. Let $N_1, N_2 \subseteq V - \Sigma$. Define:

$$N_1 \cdot N_2 = \{C \in V - \Sigma \mid C \to AB \text{ is in } P \quad \text{for some } A \in N_1, B \in N_2\}.$$

Example Let G contain the following rules:

$$C \to AB$$
$$D \to CE$$
$$F \to BE$$
$$E \to AF$$

There may be other rules as well but these need not concern us. Take $N_1 = \{A\}$, $N_2 = \{B\}, N_3 = \{E\}$. Note that:

$$N_1(N_2N_3) = \{E\} \neq \{D\} = (N_1N_2)N_3.$$

This establishes that this product of subsets is not associative.

Using the product operation just defined, we claim that the following algorithm computes the Cocke–Kasami–Younger recognition matrix. Note that we have not specified in detail how to compute $\mathbf{D}^+$. We leave the details for subsequent sections.

Algorithm 12.5.1 Let $G = (V, \Sigma, P, S)$ be a grammar in Chomsky normal form (without the rule $S \to \Lambda$) and let $w = a_1 a_2 \cdots a_n, n \geqslant 1$, be a string, where, for $1 \leqslant k \leqslant n, a_k \in \Sigma$.

Form the strictly upper-triangular $(n+1) \times (n+1)$ recognition matrix $\mathbf{T}$ as follows. Let $\mathbf{D}$ be a strictly upper-triangular $(n+1) \times (n+1)$ matrix, where each element $d_{i,j}$ is a subset of $V - \Sigma$ and initially the value of each element is $\emptyset$.

begin
  comment $\mathbf{D} = (d_{i,j})$ is an $(n+1) \times (n+1)$ square matrix;
  for $0 \leqslant i < j \leqslant n-1$ **do** $d_{i,j} := \emptyset$;
  for $i := 0$ **to** $n-1$ **do**
    $d_{i,i+1} := \{A \mid A \to a_{i+1} \text{ is in } P\}$;
  $T := \mathbf{D}^+$
end.

To show that the algorithm works, we establish the following result.

Theorem 12.5.1 Let $G = (V, \Sigma, P, S)$ be a context-free grammar in Chomsky normal form (without the rule $S \to \Lambda$) and let $w = a_1 a_2 \cdots a_n$, $n \geqslant 1$, be a string, where, for $1 \leqslant k \leqslant n$, $a_k \in \Sigma$. Let $\mathbf{D}^+$ be the matrix constructed by Algorithm 12.5.1 and let $\mathbf{T}$ be the Cocke–Kasami–Younger recognition matrix. Then $\mathbf{D}^+ = \mathbf{T}$.

Proof We first prove that the only nonempty elements of $\mathbf{D}^{(d)}$ are along the dth diagonal.

Claim In $\mathbf{D}^{(d)}$ we have

$$d_{i,j}^{(d)} = \begin{cases} t_{i,j} & \text{if } j-i = d, \\ \emptyset & \text{otherwise.} \end{cases}$$

Proof of claim The argument is an induction on $d = j - i$. The basis of the induction, namely, $d = j - i = 1$, is immediate.

Induction step. Consider forming the product $\mathbf{D}^{(d+1)}$. We have

$$d_{i,j}^{(d+1)} = \bigcup_{s=1}^{d} \bigcup_{k=0}^{n-1} d_{i,k}^{(s)} \cdot d_{k,j}^{(d+1-s)}.$$

It follows from the property that, for any subset of variables S, $S \cdot \emptyset = \emptyset \cdot S = \emptyset$, the only way we can get a nonzero entry is if there exists some s, $1 \leqslant s \leqslant d$, and some k, $0 \leqslant k < n$, so that $d_{i,k}^{(s)} \neq \emptyset$ and $d_{k,j}^{(d+1-s)} \neq \emptyset$. It follows, from the induction hypothesis, that, in such a case,

$$k - i = s$$

and

$$j - k = d + 1 - s.$$

Adding the equations produces

$$j - i = d + 1,$$

which shows that $d_{i,j}^{(d+1)} = \emptyset$ except if $j - i = d + 1$. If $j - i = d + 1$, it follows, from the definition of the product operation and the induction hypothesis, that

$$d_{i,j}^{(d+1)} = \{A \mid A \rightarrow BC \quad \text{where, for some } k, 0 \leqslant k \leqslant n, B \in t_{i,k}, C \in t_{k,j}\} = t_{i,j}.$$

This completes the proof of the claim.

Next, note that, as a corollary of the claim,

$$\mathbf{D}^{(d)} = \emptyset$$

if $d > n$. Therefore,

$$\mathbf{D}^{+} = \mathbf{D}^{(1)} \cup \mathbf{D}^{(2)} \cup \cdots \cup \mathbf{D}^{(n)} = \mathbf{T}.$$ □

Corollary 1 $B \in d_{i,j}^{+}$ if and only if

$$B \stackrel{+}{\Rightarrow} a_{i+1} \ldots a_j$$ □

Proof $d_{i,j}^{+} = t_{i,j}$ and we invoke Theorem 12.4.1.

Corollary 2 $w \in L(G)$ if and only if $S \in d_{0,n}^{+}$.

Example

$$S \rightarrow AB$$

$$A \rightarrow AA \mid a$$

$$B \rightarrow b$$

Let $w = aaab$. Thus we must form a 5×5 matrix $\mathbf{D}$:

$$\mathbf{D} = \begin{bmatrix} \emptyset & \{A\} & & \emptyset & \\ & \emptyset & \{A\} & & \\ & & \emptyset & \{A\} & \\ & & & \emptyset & \{B\} \\ & \emptyset & & & \emptyset \end{bmatrix}.$$

One can compute that

$$\mathbf{D}^{+} = \begin{bmatrix} \emptyset & \{A\} & \{A\} & \{A\} & \{S\} \\ & \emptyset & \{A\} & \{A\} & \{S\} \\ & & \emptyset & \{A\} & \{S\} \\ & & & \emptyset & \{B\} \\ & & & & \emptyset \end{bmatrix}.$$

Since we have established that Algorithm 12.5.1 yields the Cocke–Kasami–Younger recognition matrix, we can, of course, use the parsing Algorithm 12.4.3 on this matrix. Furthermore, using the proof of Theorem 12.5.1 as a guide, the reader can verify that a straightforward computation of $\mathbf{D}^{+}$ which takes advantage of the fact that only the product of nonempty sets yields a nonempty set, causes Algorithm 12.5.1 to be "stepwise equivalent" to Algorithm 12.4.1. Consequently, it is easily shown that Algorithm 12.5.1 can be carried out in $\mathcal{O}(n^3)$ steps. It remains to show that, when viewed as a transitive-closure problem, the time bound for this computation can be further improved.

We next give an algorithm which reduces matrix multiplication of the very general kind we have been considering to boolean matrix multiplication. Let S be any set and let $*$ be any binary operation on subsets of S. We demand only that $*$ satisfy the following distributive laws.

For any $X, Y, Z \subseteq S$,

$$X * (Y \cup Z) = X * Y \cup X * Z, \tag{D1}$$

$$(X \cup Y) * Z = X * Z \cup Y * Z. \tag{D2}$$

Suppose $S = \{A_1, A_2, \ldots, A_s\}$. Let $\mathbf{B} = (b_{i,j})$ be a matrix whose elements are subsets of S. Define a set of boolean matrices $\mathbf{B}_1, \mathbf{B}_2, \ldots, \mathbf{B}_s$, where, for $1 \leqslant k \leqslant s$, the $(i-j)$th element of $\mathbf{B}_k$ is 1 if $A_k \in b_{i,j}$ and 0 otherwise.

Example Let $S = \{A_1, A_2\}$ and $n = 3$. Then,

$$\mathbf{B} = \begin{bmatrix} \emptyset & \{A_1\} & \{A_1, A_2\} \\ \emptyset & \emptyset & \{A_2\} \\ \emptyset & \emptyset & \emptyset \end{bmatrix}.$$

Then

$$\mathbf{B}_1 = \begin{bmatrix} 0 & 1 & 1 \\ 0 & 0 & 0 \\ 0 & 0 & 0 \end{bmatrix} \quad \text{and} \quad \mathbf{B}_2 = \begin{bmatrix} 0 & 0 & 1 \\ 0 & 0 & 1 \\ 0 & 0 & 0 \end{bmatrix}.$$

Next we give an algorithm for $*$-multiplication of two such matrices.

Algorithm 12.5.2 Given two $n \times n$ matrices $\mathbf{B}$ and $\mathbf{C}$ whose entries are subsets of $S = \{A_1, \ldots, A_s\}$, our goal is to compute $\mathbf{B} * \mathbf{C}$.

1 Compute $\mathbf{B}_1, \ldots, \mathbf{B}_s$ and $\mathbf{C}_1, \ldots, \mathbf{C}_s$, where these are defined as above.

2 Compute the s^2 boolean products $\mathbf{B}_i * \mathbf{C}_j$ for $1 \leqslant i, j \leqslant s$.

3 Let $\mathbf{D} = (d_{i,j})$, where $d_{i,j} = \{E | E = \{A_p\}*\{A_q\}$, where $(\mathbf{B}_p * \mathbf{C}_q)_{i,j} = 1\}$.

Example Let $S = \{A_1, A_2\}$, $n = 3$, and define $*$ by the table:

	A_1	A_2
A_1	A_2	A_2
A_2	A_1	A_2

Let

$$\mathbf{B} = \begin{bmatrix} \emptyset & \{A_1\} & \{A_1, A_2\} \\ \emptyset & \emptyset & \{A_2\} \\ \emptyset & \emptyset & \emptyset \end{bmatrix}, \quad \mathbf{C} = \begin{bmatrix} \emptyset & \{A_1, A_2\} & \emptyset \\ \emptyset & \emptyset & \{A_1\} \\ \emptyset & \emptyset & \emptyset \end{bmatrix}.$$

Then, by using the definition of boolean-matrix products,

$$\mathbf{D} = \mathbf{B} * \mathbf{C} = \begin{bmatrix} \emptyset & \emptyset & \{A_2\} \\ \emptyset & \emptyset & \emptyset \\ \emptyset & \emptyset & \emptyset \end{bmatrix}.$$

By using Algorithm 12.5.2, we write:

$$\mathbf{B}_1 = \begin{bmatrix} 0 & 1 & 1 \\ 0 & 0 & 0 \\ 0 & 0 & 0 \end{bmatrix} \qquad \mathbf{B}_2 = \begin{bmatrix} 0 & 0 & 1 \\ 0 & 0 & 1 \\ 0 & 0 & 0 \end{bmatrix},$$

$$\mathbf{C}_1 = \begin{bmatrix} 0 & 1 & 0 \\ 0 & 0 & 1 \\ 0 & 0 & 0 \end{bmatrix}, \qquad \mathbf{C}_2 = \begin{bmatrix} 0 & 1 & 0 \\ 0 & 0 & 0 \\ 0 & 0 & 0 \end{bmatrix}.$$

Then

$$\mathbf{B}_1\mathbf{C}_1 = \begin{bmatrix} 0 & 0 & 1 \\ 0 & 0 & 0 \\ 0 & 0 & 0 \end{bmatrix}, \qquad \mathbf{B}_1\mathbf{C}_2 = \begin{bmatrix} 0 & 0 & 0 \\ 0 & 0 & 0 \\ 0 & 0 & 0 \end{bmatrix}$$

$$\mathbf{B}_2\mathbf{C}_1 = \begin{bmatrix} 0 & 0 & 0 \\ 0 & 0 & 0 \\ 0 & 0 & 0 \end{bmatrix} \qquad \mathbf{B}_2\mathbf{C}_2 = \begin{bmatrix} 0 & 0 & 0 \\ 0 & 0 & 0 \\ 0 & 0 & 0 \end{bmatrix}.$$

Since $(\mathbf{B}_1\mathbf{C}_1)_{02} = 1$, we have $d_{02} = A_1 * A_1 = A_2$, and both computations produce the same answer.

We leave it to the reader to verify that, for operations $*$ satisfying distributive laws (D1) and (D2), Algorithm 12.5.2 computes $\mathbf{D} = \mathbf{B} * \mathbf{C}$.

We can conclude that, if $M(n)$ is the time necessary to multiply two $n \times n$ matrices with elements that are subsets of some set S, and $BM(n)$ is the time to compute the boolean product of two $n \times n$ boolean matrices, then a relationship between the two quantities is given by the following result.

Theorem 12.5.2 $M(n) \leqslant cBM(n)$ for some constant c.

Having posed the recognition problem as a transitive-closure problem, and having reduced the multiplication aspect of that problem to fast boolean-matrix multiplication, it remains to reduce the transitive-closure problem to one with a time bound proportional to that for boolean-matrix multiplication. This will be done shortly.

Our next goal is to prove a lemma due to Valiant, on which the construction rests. In order to prove the lemma, it is necessary to develop a notation for nonassociative products in terms of binary trees.

In the discussion that follows, we will consider matrices whose elements are subsets of some set S. The multiplication operation $*$ defined on these subsets is assumed to have only the two distributive properties (D1) and (D2) to reduce matrix multiplication to boolean-matrix multiplication and the additional axiom

$$S * \emptyset = \emptyset * S = \emptyset. \tag{N1}$$

We will restrict our attention to strictly upper-triangular matrices. It will be convenient to use the following facts, which are immediate consequences of the axioms.

Lemma 12.5.1 If $\mathbf{A}$ and $\mathbf{B}$ are strictly upper-triangular matrices, then $\mathbf{A} * \mathbf{B}$ is also strictly upper-triangular and

$$\bigcup_{k=0}^{n-1} a_{ik} * b_{kj} = \bigcup_{k=i+1}^{j-1} a_{ik} * b_{kj}.$$

Proof Follows directly from Axiom N1.

Lemma 12.5.2 (*The distributive property*) Let S be any set and let $*$ be any binary operation on subsets of S satisfying axioms D1 and D2. Let $s_1, s_2, \ldots, s_t$, $t \geqslant 1$, be subsets of S, and let $\pi(s_1, s_2, \ldots, s_t)$ denote the ordered composition of $s_1, s_2, \ldots, s_t$ under $*$ and some order of association. If I is any family of subsets of S, then, for any $1 \leqslant k \leqslant t$,

$$\pi(s_1, s_2, \ldots, s_{k-1}, \bigcup_{i \in I} i, s_{k+1}, \ldots, s_t) = \bigcup_{i \in I} (s_1, s_2, \ldots, s_{k-1}, i, s_{k+1}, \ldots, s_t).$$

Proof Follows directly from distributive axioms D1 and D2. □

In order to describe the nonassociative products that we will deal with in Valiant's lemma, we first introduce a set of such products called *terms.* We then present a notation for terms and a sequence of propositions establishing the properties of the notation. The verification of these propositions is straightforward and is left for the reader.

Definition Let $\mathbf{B} = (b_{i,j})$ be an $n \times n$ matrix, whose elements are subsets of some set S. Let

$$b_{i_1, i_2}, b_{i_2, i_3}, \ldots, b_{i_t, i_{t+1}}$$

be any sequence of matrix elements. We say the sequence is *acceptable* in the case that, for $1 \leqslant j, k \leqslant t+1$, if $j < k$, then $i_j < i_k$.

The composition under $*$ of the elements of an acceptable sequence under some order of association is called a *term of* **B** or, more specifically, *an* (i_1, i_{t+1}) *term with t components.* The notation

$$\tau^*(b_{i_1, i_2}, b_{i_2, i_3}, \ldots, b_{i_t, i_{t+1}})$$

denotes any one of the terms of **B** with components $b_{i_1, i_2}, \ldots, b_{i_t, i_{t+1}}$ under the operation $*$. For example,

$$b_{12} * (b_{23} * b_{34})$$

and

$$(b_{23} * b_{35}) * b_{57}$$

are terms, but

$$b_{12} * b_{23} * b_{34}$$

is not a term because no order of association is given, and

$$b_{12} * b_{22}$$

is not a term because the indices do not increase.

Definition Two (i, j) terms are *formally distinct* if either they are composed of distinct sequences of elements or they have different orders of association. Let $\mathcal{T}^{(d)}_{(i,j)}(\mathbf{B})$ be the set of all formally distinct (i, j) terms having exactly d components from the matrix **B**. Let

$$\mathcal{T}^*(\mathbf{B}) = \bigcup_{d \geqslant 1} \bigcup_{i,j=0}^{n-1} \mathcal{T}^{(d)}_{(i,j)}(\mathbf{B})$$

be the set of all formally distinct terms with components from the matrix **B**. (We omit the explicit mention of **B** when the matrix is understood.)

Proposition 12.5.1 Let $\mathbf{B} = (b_{i,j})$ be an $n \times n$ matrix whose elements are subsets of S. Then, for all $0 \leqslant i, j \leqslant n-1$,

$$b_{i,j}^{(d)} = \bigcup_{\tau^* \in \mathscr{T}_{(i,j)}^{(d)}(\mathbf{B})} \tau^*$$

and

$$b_{i,j}^{+} = \bigcup_{d \geqslant 1} \quad \bigcup_{\tau^* \in \mathscr{T}_{(i,j)}^{(d)}} \tau^*.$$

The proof is straightforward and is left for the reader. □

A natural way to describe terms of the type just introduced is to use binary trees. For example, the (2, 7) term $(b_{2,3} * b_{3,5}) * b_{5,7}$ can be represented by a binary tree, as shown below.

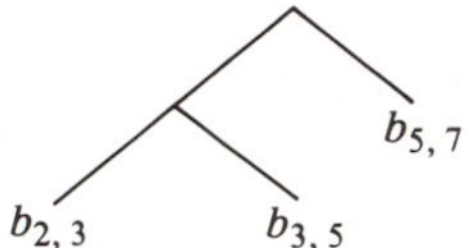

In order to precisely define the trees that describe terms, we introduce a functional notation. However, we shall continue to use the trees themselves as a descriptive device to explain the formalism.

We shall introduce functions $\tau(x_1, x_2, \ldots, x_t)$ which denote binary trees having t leaves labeled x_1 to x_t from left to right. If $\mathbf{B} = (b_{i,j})$ is an $n \times n$ matrix whose elements are subsets of some set S, then the subclass of trees $\tau(x_1, x_2, \ldots, x_t)$ we get by restricting $x_1, x_2, \ldots, x_t$ to be an acceptable sequence of elements from $\mathbf{B}$ will be in one-to-one correspondence with the terms of $\mathbf{B}$.

For example, the terms

$$\tau_1^*(x_1, x_2, x_3, x_4) = (x_1 * x_2) * (x_3 * x_4)$$

and

$$\tau_2^*(x_1, x_2, x_3, x_4) = x_1 * (x_2 * (x_3 * x_4))$$

will correspond to the functions $\tau_1(x_1, x_2, x_3, x_4)$ and $\tau_2(x_1, x_2, x_3, x_4)$ designating the binary trees

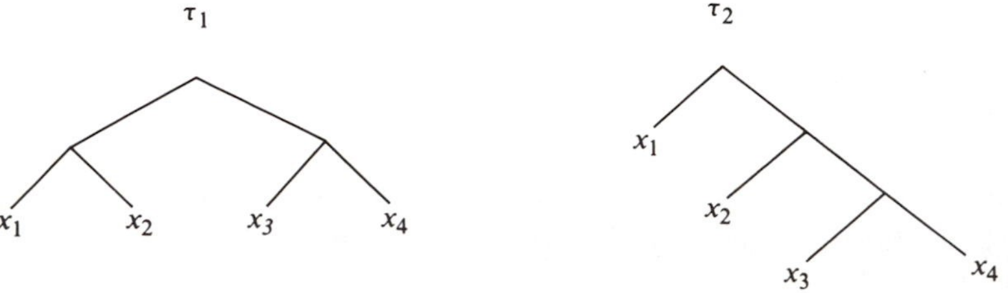

The formal definition of these functions is now given.

Definition Let $X = \{x_1, x_2, \ldots\}$ be a set. *The class* $\mathscr{T}$ *of binary trees* $\tau(x_{i_1}, x_{i_2}, \ldots, x_{i_t})$, $t \geqslant 1$ over X, is defined inductively as follows:

i) For any $x \in X$, $\tau(x) = x$ is in $\mathscr{T}$.

ii) For any x_{i_1}, x_{i_2} in X, $\tau(x_{i_1}, x_{i_2})$ is in $\mathscr{T}$.

iii) If $\tau_1(x_{i_1}, \ldots, x_{i_p})$, $\tau_2(x_{i_{p+1}}, \ldots, x_{i_t})$, and $\tau_3(x_{j_1}, x_{j_2})$ are in $\mathscr{T}$ for some $1 \leqslant p < t$, then

$$\tau(x_{i_1}, \ldots, x_{i_t}) = \tau_3(\tau_1(x_{i_1}, \ldots, x_{i_p}), \tau_2(x_{i_{p+1}}, \ldots, x_{i_t}))$$

is in $\mathscr{T}$.

iv) All elements of $\mathscr{T}$ are constructed from (i), (ii), and (iii).

By a suitable choice of elements, we get the class of trees corresponding to nonassociative products.

Definition Let $\mathbf{B} = (b_{i,j})$ be an $n \times n$ matrix, where each $b_{i,j}$ is a subset of some set S. The *acceptable class* $\mathscr{T}$ *of binary trees over* $\mathbf{B}$ is defined inductively by

i′) For any element $b_{i,j}$ of $\mathbf{B}$, $\tau(b_{i,j}) = b_{i,j}$ is in $\mathscr{T}$.

ii′) For any acceptable sequence y_1, y_2, $\tau(y_1, y_2)$ is in $\mathscr{T}$.

iii′) Let $x_1, x_2, \ldots, x_p, x_{p+1}, \ldots, x_t$ be an acceptable sequence of elements of $\mathbf{B}$. If $\tau_1(x_1, \ldots, x_p)$, $\tau_2(x_{p+1}, \ldots, x_t)$, and $\tau_3(y_1, y_2)$ are in $\mathscr{T}$, for some $1 \leqslant p < t$, then

$$\tau(x_1, \ldots, x_t) = \tau_3(\tau_1(x_1, \ldots, x_p), \tau_2(x_{p+1}, \ldots, x_t))$$

is in $\mathscr{T}$.

iv′) All elements of $\mathscr{T}$ are constructed from (i′), (ii′), and (iii′).

Clearly, an acceptable class of binary trees over a matrix is a special case of a class of binary trees over a set. These definitions are illustrated in Fig. 12.5. Figure 12.5(a) represents (i) or (ii). Figure 12.5(b) illustrates (iii) or (iii′).

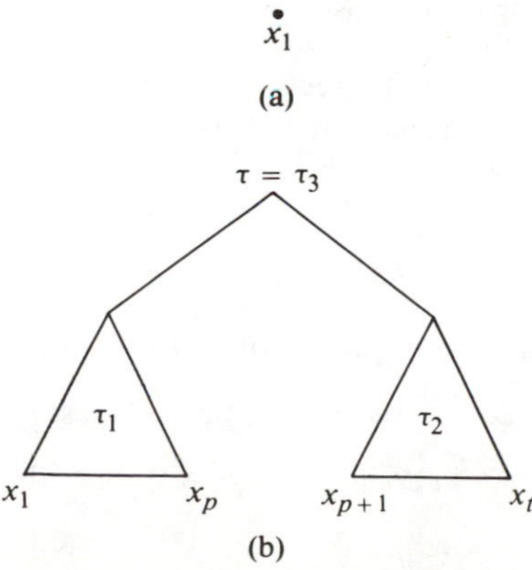

FIG. 12.5

The τ functions satisfy the following properties.

Proposition 12.5.2 Let $\mathscr{T}$ be an (acceptable) class of binary trees. For each $\tau(x_1, \ldots, x_t)$, $t > 1$, in $\mathscr{T}$, there exist k, $1 \leqslant k < t$, and three functions, τ_1, τ_2, and τ_3, all in $\mathscr{T}$, such that

$$\tau(x_1, \ldots, x_t) = \tau_3(\tau_1(x_1, \ldots, x_k), \tau_2(x_{k+1}, \ldots, x_t)).$$

This proposition is a restatement of the definition.

Our next principle, which is illustrated by Fig. 12.6, is familiar to us from language theory. We may describe it as a *composition principle.*

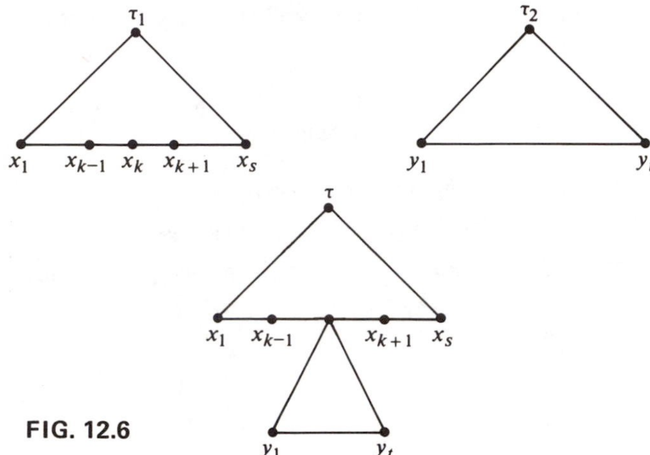

FIG. 12.6

Proposition 12.5.3 Let $\mathscr{T}$ be an (acceptable) class of binary trees. Given $\tau_1(x_1, \ldots, x_s)$ and $\tau_2(y_1, \ldots, y_t)$ in $\mathscr{T}$ and some k, where $1 \leqslant k \leqslant s$, then there exists a unique τ in T such that

$$\tau(x_1, \ldots, x_{k-1}, y_1, \ldots, y_t, x_{k+1}, \ldots, x_s) = \tau_1(x_1, \ldots, x_{k-1}, \tau_2(y_1, \ldots, y_t), x_{k+1}, \ldots, x_s).$$

We next introduce the notion of a factorization for binary trees.

Definition Let $\mathscr{T}$ be an (acceptable) class of binary trees. For any $\tau(x_1, \ldots, x_t)$ in $\mathscr{T}$ and any p, q such that $1 \leqslant p \leqslant q \leqslant t$, if, for some τ_1, τ_2, in $\mathscr{T}$,

$$\tau(x_1, \ldots, x_t) = \tau_1(x_1, \ldots, x_{p-1}, \tau_2(x_p, \ldots, x_q), x_{q+1}, \ldots, x_t),$$

then the quadruple (τ_1, τ_2, p, q) is a *factorization* of $\tau(x_1, \ldots, x_t)$.

Our next proposition is a unique factorization result for trees.

Proposition 12.5.4 Let $\mathscr{T}$ be an (acceptable) class of binary trees.

1 Given $\tau(x_1, \ldots, x_t)$ in $\mathscr{T}$ and $1 \leqslant p' \leqslant q' \leqslant t$, then there exist τ_1, τ_2, p, and q such that:

   a) $p \leqslant p'$,

   b) $q \geqslant q'$, and

   c) (τ_1, τ_2, p, q) is a factorization of $\tau(x_1, \ldots, x_t)$.

2 If there also exist τ'_1, τ'_2, r, and s such that:

d) $r \leqslant p'$,

e) $s \geqslant q'$, and

f) (τ'_1, τ'_2, r, s) is a factorization of $\tau\,(x_1, \ldots, x_t)$,

then either:

g) $r \leqslant p$ and $s \geqslant q$, or

h) $p \leqslant r$ and $q \geqslant s$.

3 There exists a unique factorization satisfying 1(a), 1(b), and 1(c) and such that $(q - p)$ is minimal.

Although we have written Proposition 12.5.4 out in great detail, the intuitive picture is shown in Fig. 12.7. By Case 2, we see that either τ_2 is nested inside of τ'_2, or vice versa.

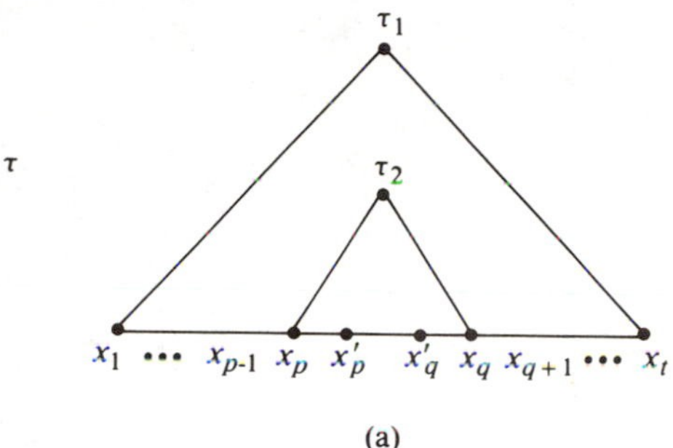

(a)

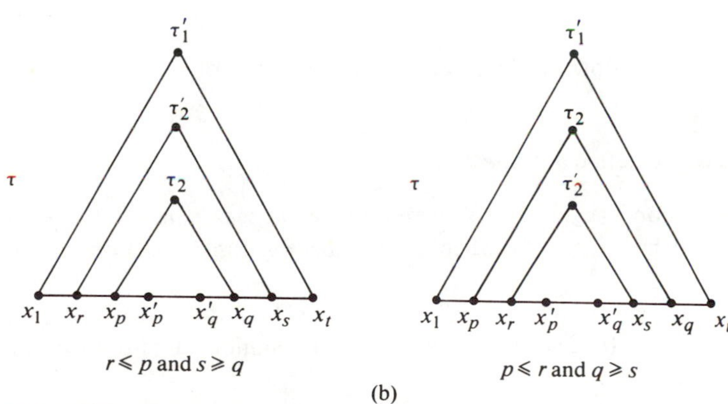

(b)

FIG. 12.7

This situation suggests the following definitions.

Definition A factorization of Case 3 in Proposition 12.5.4 is called the *smallest* (p', q') *factorization of* τ.

The smallest (p', q') factorization is exemplified in Fig. 12.8. In that figure, let us choose $p' = 5$ and $q' = 9$. The unique choices of p and q are $p = 4, q = 9$. The

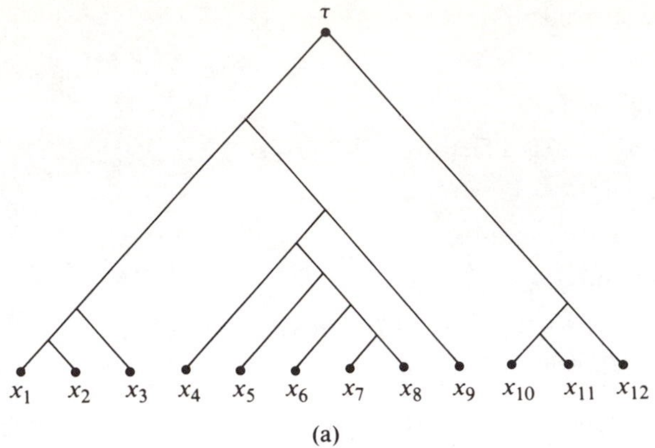

(a)

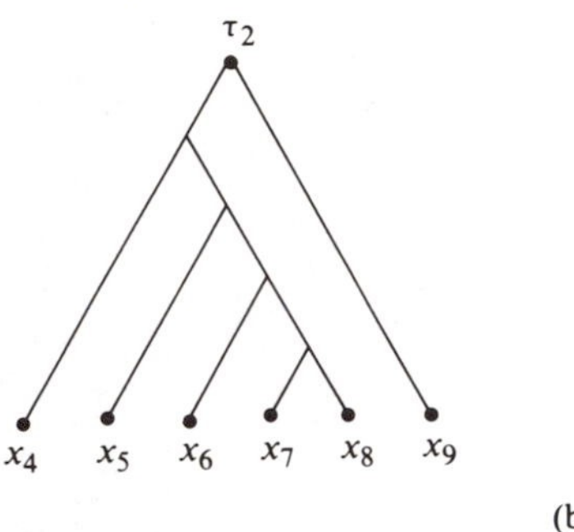

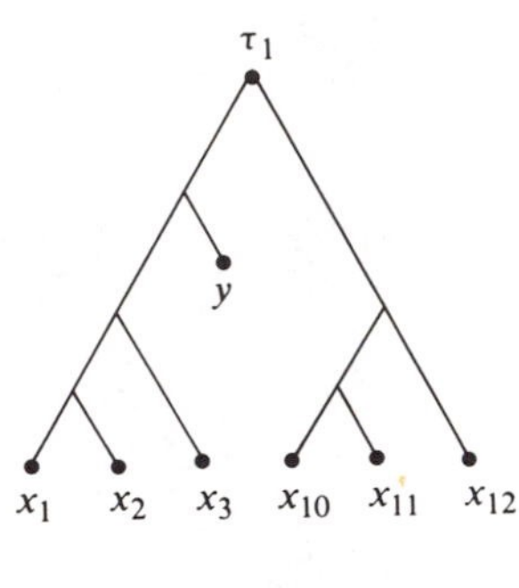

(b)

FIG. 12.8

trees τ_1 and τ_2 are shown in Fig. 12.8. Note that the root of τ_2 is the least common ancestor of x_5 and x_9.

Now, we define a *smallest tree.*

Definition $\tau(x_2, \ldots, x_t)$ is said to be *(u, v)-minimal* if the smallest (u, v) factorization of τ is $(i, \tau, 1, t)$, where i is the identity function of one variable, that is, $i(x) = x$.

Returning to Fig. 12.8(b), we note that the tree $\tau_2(x_4, \ldots, x_9)$ is $(8, 9)$-minimal. In a (u, v)-minimal tree, the least common ancestor of x_u and x_v is the root of the entire tree.

Now we present two lemmas concerning these minimal trees.

Lemma 12.5.3 Let

$$\tau(x_1, \ldots, x_t) = \tau_1(x_1, \ldots, x_{r-1}, \tau_2(x_r, \ldots, x_s), x_{s+1}, \ldots, x_t)$$

for some $t \geqslant 1$, $1 \leqslant r \leqslant s \leqslant t$. Then, for any $y_1, \ldots, y_{s-r+1}$, $\tau_2(y_1, \ldots, y_{s-r+1})$ is $(u - r + 1, v - r +)$-minimal if and only if (τ_1, τ_2, r, s) is the smallest (u, v) factorization of τ.

Proof The result follows directly from the definitions and Proposition 12.5.4. □

The next result is also an obvious property of these trees.

Lemma 12.5.4 Let $\mathscr{T}$ be an (acceptable) class of binary trees. Let τ_1, τ_2, τ_2' be in $\mathscr{T}$ and let $t \geqslant 1$, $1 \leqslant p \leqslant q \leqslant t$. Then

$$\tau_1(x_1, \ldots, x_{p-1}, \tau_2(x_p, \ldots, x_q), x_{q+1}, \ldots, x_t) = \tau_1(x_1, \ldots, x_{p-1}, \tau_2'(x_p, \ldots, x_q), x_{q+1}, \ldots, x_t),$$

if and only if $\tau_2 = \tau_2'$.

Now we extend the composition principle and the factorization notion to terms, by establishing a correspondence between trees and terms.

Proposition 12.5.5 Let $\mathbf{B} = (b_{i,j})$ be an $n \times n$ matrix whose elements are subsets of some set S. Let $\mathscr{T}$ be an acceptable class of binary trees over $\mathbf{B}$. Let $*$ be any binary operator on subsets of S satisfying axioms D1, D2, and N1. Then there is a one-to-one correspondence between the set of terms $\mathscr{T}^*$ and the set of trees $\mathscr{T}$. The correspondence is defined inductively by:

i) For any element $b_{i,j}$ of $\mathbf{B}$, $\tau(b_{i,j}) \leftrightarrow \tau^*(b_{i,j})$

ii) For any $\tau_1(b_{i_1,i_2}, b_{i_2,i_3}, \ldots, b_{i_{p-1},i_p})$ and $\tau_2(b_{i_p,i_{p+1}}, \ldots, b_{i_t,i_{t+1}})$,

$$\tau(\tau_1(b_{i_1,i_2}, \ldots, b_{i_{p-1},i_p}), \tau_2(b_{i_p,i_{p+1}}, \ldots, b_{i_t,i_{t+1}})) \leftrightarrow$$

$$\tau_1^*(b_{i_1,i_2}, \ldots, b_{i_{p-1},i_p}) * \tau_2^*(b_{i_p,i_{p+1}}, \ldots, b_{i_t,i_{t+1}}).$$

Using this correspondence, we extend the notion of minimality to terms in the obvious way.

Definition Let $\mathbf{B}$ be an $n \times n$ matrix whose elements are subsets of S. Let $\tau^*(b_{i_1,i_2}, \ldots, b_{i_t,i_{t+1}})$ be a term of $\mathbf{B}$. Then, for any p, q, $1 \leqslant p \leqslant q \leqslant t$, τ^* is (i_p, i_q)-*minimal* if the corresponding tree τ is (i_p, i_q)-minimal.

We next introduce two concepts related to matrices which are useful in conjunction with Valiant's Lemma and the transitive-closure algorithm. The first concept is the notion of a *central submatrix*. Intuitively, as shown in Fig. 12.9, a central submatrix is a matrix contained within a larger matrix such that the principal diagonal of the smaller matrix lies along the principal diagonal of the larger matrix.

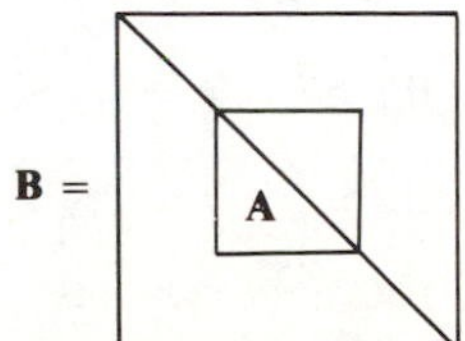

FIG. 12.9

Definition Let **B** be an $n \times n$ matrix. Then **A** is a *central submatrix* if there exists $m \geqslant 0$ and r, $0 \leqslant r \leqslant n-1$ such that $\mathbf{A} = (a_{i,j})$ is an $m \times m$ matrix and for $0 \leqslant i, j \leqslant m-1, a_{i,j} = b_{i+r-1,\ j+r-1}$.

The most important property of central submatrices for our purposes is given by the next theorem and its corollary.

Theorem 12.5.3 (*The Central Submatrix Theorem*) Let **B** be a strictly upper-triangular matrix. If **A** is a central submatrix of **B**, then, for any $d \geqslant 1$, the corresponding central matrix of $\mathbf{B}^{(d)}$ (or $\mathbf{B}^+$) is $\mathbf{A}^{(d)}$ (or $\mathbf{A}^+$).

Proof Let **B** be an $n \times n$ matrix and **A** be $m \times m$ with $a_{s,t} = b_{s+r-1,t+r-1}$ for each $0 \leqslant s, t \leqslant m-1$ as the indices range over **A**. These are the i, j positions of **B**, where $r \leqslant i, j < r+m$. Thus, let $i' = i - r + 1$ and $j' = j - r + 1$. We will show, by induction on d, that

$$b_{i,j}^{(d)} = a_{i',j'}^{(d)}.$$

Basis. $d = 1$. This is immediate.

Induction step. Suppose $d > 1$ and the result holds for $d-1$. It follows from the definitions and Lemma 12.5.1 that

$$b_{i,j}^{(d)} = \bigcup_{u=1}^{d-1} \bigcup_{k=i+1}^{j-1} b_{i,k}^{(u)} * b_{k,j}^{(d-u)}.$$

If we let $k' = k - r + 1$ and employ the induction hypothesis, then we get

$$b_{i,j}^{(d)} = \bigcup_{u=1}^{d-1} \bigcup_{k'=i'+1}^{j'-1} a_{i',k'}^{(u)} a_{k',j'}^{(d-u)} = a_{i',j'}^{(d)}.$$

This completes the proof for $\mathbf{B}^{(d)}$. For $\mathbf{B}^+$, note that

$$\mathbf{B}^+ = \bigcup_{t \geqslant 1} \mathbf{B}^{(d)}.$$

Corollary Let **B** be a strictly upper-triangular matrix which is transitively closed. If **A** is any central submatrix of **B**, then **A** is transitively closed.

The second useful concept is that of the reduction-closure operation on a matrix.

Definition Let $\mathbf{C} = (c_{i,j})$ be a strictly upper-triangular $n \times n$ matrix and let $n \geqslant r \geqslant n/2 \geqslant 1$. Define the $2(n-r) \times 2(n-r)$ matrix $\mathbf{D} = (d_{i,j})$ to be the *r-reduction* of **C** if

$$d_{i,j} = \begin{cases} c_{i,j} & \text{if } 0 \leqslant i, j \leqslant n-r-1, \\ c_{i',j} & \text{if } i > n-r-1, j \leqslant n-r-1, \\ c_{i,j'} & \text{if } i \leqslant n-r-1, j > n-r-1, \\ c_{i',j'} & \text{if } i, j > n-r-1, \end{cases}$$

where $i' = i + 2r - n, j' = j + 2r - n$.

The r-reduction of $\mathbf{C}$ is illustrated in Fig. 12.10(a). Intuitively, we form $\mathbf{D}$ by deleting the $(n - r + 1)$st to rth rows and columns.

Using the notion of the r-reduction of a matrix, we can define the reduction closure. Intuitively (as illustrated in Fig. 12.10(b)), we take the transitive closure of the r-reduced matrix and then restore each element to its original place in $\mathbf{C}$.

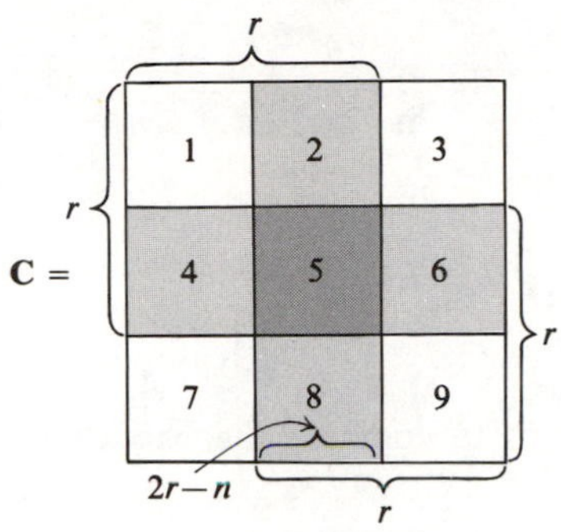

$\mathbf{D} =$

1	3
7	9

(a)

$\mathbf{D}^+ = \mathbf{E} =$

$\mathbf{E}_1$	$\mathbf{E}_3$
$\mathbf{E}_7$	$\mathbf{E}_9$

$\mathbf{C}^{+(r)} =$

$\mathbf{E}_1$	2	$\mathbf{E}_3$
4	5	6
$\mathbf{E}_7$	8	$\mathbf{E}_9$

(b)

FIG. 12.10

Definition Let $\mathbf{C} = (c_{i,j})$ be a strictly upper-triangular $n \times n$ matrix and let $n \geqslant r \geqslant n/2 \geqslant 1$. Let $\mathbf{D} = (d_{i,j})$ be the r-reduction of $\mathbf{C}$ and let $\mathbf{E} = (e_{i,j})$ be the transitive closure of $\mathbf{D}$. Define the $n \times n$ matrix $\mathbf{C}^{+(r)} = (c_{i,j}^{+(r)})$ to be the *reduction closure* of $\mathbf{C}$, where, for $0 \leqslant i, j \leqslant n-1$,

$$c_{i,j}^{+(r)} = \begin{cases} e_{i,j} & \text{if } i, j \leqslant n-r-1, \\ c_{i,j} & \text{if } n-r-1 < i \leqslant r-1 \\ & \quad \text{or } n-r-1 < i \leqslant r-1, \\ e_{i',j} & \text{if } i > r-1, j \leqslant n-r-1, \\ e_{i,j'} & \text{if } i \leqslant n-r-1, j > r-1, \\ e_{i',j'} & \text{if } i, j > r-1, \end{cases}$$

where $i' = i - (2r-n)$ and $j' = j - (2r-n)$.

Now we may begin to combine the partial results into a proof of the key lemma.

Lemma 12.5.5 (*Valiant's Lemma*) Let $\mathbf{B}$ a strictly upper-triangular $n \times n$ matrix, let $n \geqslant r \geqslant n/2 \geqslant 1$, and suppose that

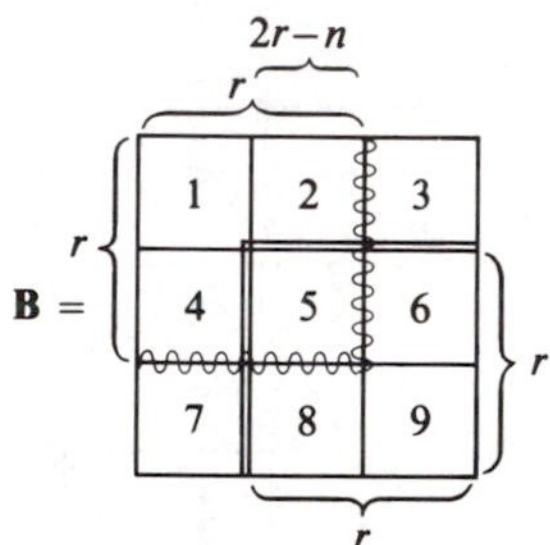

where the $r \times r$ submatrices

$$\mathbf{B}_1 = \begin{array}{|c|c|}\hline 1 & 2 \\ \hline 4 & 5 \\ \hline\end{array} \quad \text{and} \quad \mathbf{B}_2 = \begin{array}{|c|c|}\hline 5 & 6 \\ \hline 8 & 9 \\ \hline\end{array} \quad \text{of } \mathbf{B}$$

are transitively closed. Define $\mathbf{E}_r$ as the submatrix of $\mathbf{B}$ given by

$$\mathbf{E}_r = \begin{array}{|c|c|c|}\hline \emptyset & 2 & \emptyset \\ \hline \emptyset & \emptyset & 6 \\ \hline \emptyset & \emptyset & \emptyset \\ \hline\end{array}$$

where the shaded area above is taken from $\mathbf{B}$.

Then $\mathbf{B}^+ = (\mathbf{B} \cup \mathbf{E}_r^2)^{+(r)}$.

Proof The proof of the lemma is long and tedious. A sketch is given here with the detailed proofs of the claims relegated to the problems.

Since $\mathbf{B}_1$ and $\mathbf{B}_2$ are transitively closed, and since $\mathbf{B}$ is strictly upper triangular, the only part of $\mathbf{B}^+$ that is unknown is region 3, in which $0 \leqslant i \leqslant n-r-1$ and $r < j \leqslant n-1$. This follows from the Corollary to Theorem 12.5.3 on central submatrices.

Let $\mathscr{T}^*$ be the set of terms of $\mathbf{B}$ and let $\mathscr{T}$ be the corresponding set of acceptable trees.

Claim 1 Let τ^* be any (i_1, i_{t+1}) term of $\mathbf{B}$, where $i_1 \leqslant n-r-1$ and $i_{t+1} \geqslant r-1$. Then for some $i_p \leqslant n-r-1$ and $i_{q+1} \geqslant r$, τ^* contains a unique $(n-r-1, r-1)$-minimal (i_p, i_{q+1}) term τ_2^*. Moreover, either $p = q$ or, for some $\tau_3^*, \tau_4^* \in \mathscr{T}^*$ and for some i_s such that $n-r-1 < i_s \leqslant r-1$,

$$\tau_2^* = \tau_3^*(b_{i_p, i_{p+1}}, \ldots, b_{i_{s-1}, i_s}) * \tau_4^*(b_{i_s, i_{s+1}}, \ldots, b_{i_q, i_{q+1}}).$$

The proof of Claim 1 is left to Problem 2(a).

For any x, y, $0 \leqslant x \leqslant n-r-1 \leqslant r-1 \leqslant y \leqslant n-1$, let $U_{x,y}(\mathbf{B})$ be the set of all formally distinct $(n-r-1, r-1)$-minimal (x, y) terms of $\mathbf{B}$.

Claim 2 For any $x \leqslant n-r-1$ and $y > r-1$,

$$\bigcup_{\tau^* \in U_{x,y}(\mathbf{B})} \tau^* = b_{x,y} \cup \bigcup_{s=n-r}^{r-1} b_{x,s} * b_{s,y}. \qquad (12.5.1)$$

Proof of claim By Proposition 12.5.1, $b^+_{x,s}$ is the union of all formally distinct (x, s) terms of $\mathbf{B}$ and $b^+_{s,y}$ is the union of all formally distinct (s, y) terms of $\mathbf{B}$. Therefore, by Claim 1,

$$\bigcup_{\tau^* \in U_{x,y}(\mathbf{B})} \tau^* = b_{x,y} \cup \bigcup_{s=n-r}^{r-1} b^+_{x,s} * b^+_{s,y}.$$

Since $\mathbf{B}_1$ and $\mathbf{B}_2$ are transitively closed, $b_{x,s} = b^+_{x,s}$ and $b_{s,y} = b^+_{s,y}$ for all $x \leqslant n-r-1, n-r \leqslant s \leqslant r-1, y > r-1$.

Note that Eq. (12.5.1) can be computed by the following procedure.

1. Matrix-multiply partitions 2 and 6 of $\mathbf{B}$.
2. Form the union of the resulting $(n-r) \times (n-r)$ matrix with partition 3 of $\mathbf{B}$.

Let $\mathbf{C}$ be the $(n-r) \times (n-r)$ matrix which is in position 3 of $\mathbf{B} \cup \mathbf{E}_r^2$. We proceed to analyze $\mathbf{C}$.

It is clear from Claim 2 and the construction of $\mathbf{C}$ that the following is true.

Claim 3 For any $i \leqslant n-r-1, j > r-1$,

$$c_{i,j-r} = \bigcup_{\tau^* \in U_{i,j}(\mathbf{B})} \tau^*. \qquad (12.5.2)$$

In words, $c_{i,j-r}$ is the union of all $(n-r-1, r-1)$-minimal (i, j) terms of $\mathbf{B}$.

Note that, if $j = i + 2r - n$, Eq. (12.5.2) reduces to the following:

$$c_{i,i-n-r} = \bigcup_{\tau^* \in U_{i,i+2r-n}(\mathbf{B})} \tau^*.$$

Let $\mathbf{D}$ be the r-reduction of $\mathbf{B} \cup \mathbf{E}_r^2$ obtained by deleting the central $2r - n$ rows and columns. $\mathbf{D}$ is a $2(n-r) \times 2(n-r)$ matrix.

Clearly,

$$d^+_{i,j} = \bigcup_{u \geqslant 1} \bigcup_{\tau \in \tau^{(u)}_{i,j}(\mathbf{D})} \tau,$$

from Proposition 12.5.1. Moreover, each τ contains exactly one element from $\mathbf{C}$. This follows from the strict ordering of the subscripts on the terms and the method of construction of $\mathbf{D}$.

To finish the proof of the lemma requires establishing a correspondence between the terms of $\mathbf{D}$ and of $\mathbf{B}$.

Claim 4 Let $i \leqslant n - r - 1, j > r - 1$, and $j' = j - 2r + n$. Every (i, j') term of $\mathbf{D}$ is a union of some formally distinct (i, j) terms of $\mathbf{B}$.

The proof of Claim 4 is left as Problem 2(b).

In the reverse direction another claim is needed.

Claim 5 Let $i \leqslant n - r - 1, j > r - 1$, and $j' = j - 2r + n$. Every (i, j) term of $\mathbf{B}$ occurs in the formation of a unique (i, j') term of $\mathbf{D}$.

The proof of Claim 5 is relegated to Problem 2(c).

To complete the main proof, it follows from Claim 4 that $d^+_{i,j'}$ is a union of distinct (i, j) terms of $\mathbf{B}$. From Claim 5, every (i, j) term of $\mathbf{B}$ appears in $d^+_{i,j'}$. Thus $d^+_{i,j'}$ is exactly the union of all formally distinct (i, j) terms of $\mathbf{B}$. From Proposition 12.5.1,

$$d^+_{i,j'} = b^+_{i,j}$$

for all $i \leqslant n - r$, $j > r$, and $j' = j - 2r + n$. But this is exactly the region of $\mathbf{B}$ which had to be verified, and the proof is complete. □

Note that since

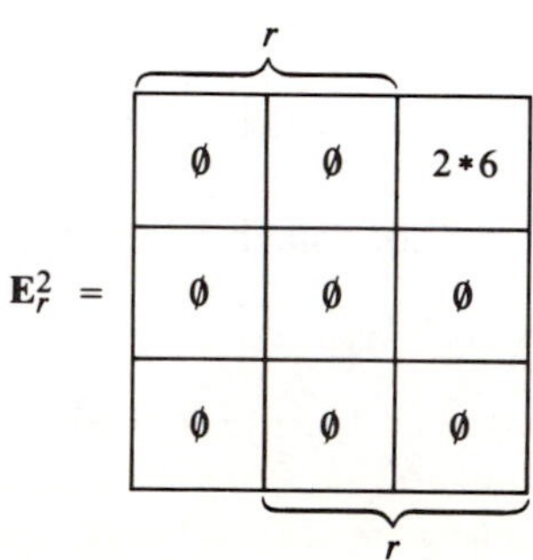

we have just shown that

$+(r)$

$\mathbf{B}^+ =$

1	2	$3 \cup 2 * 6$
4	5	6
7	8	9

This will provide a simple recursive method for the computation of $\mathbf{B}^+$.

Now we are ready to show how to compute $\mathbf{D}^+$ in less than cubic time. If $\mathbf{D}$ is a strictly upper-triangular matrix whose elements are subsets of some set S and $*$ is an arbitrary binary operation on S which satisfies axioms D1, D2, and N1, we wish to compute $\mathbf{D}^+$ as efficiently as possible. Since $*$ is not necessarily associative, techniques from the literature that assume associativity are useless here. It should be observed that our method will be as efficient as any that is known in the associative case. In what follows, it is convenient to assume that n is a power of 2. We shall return to this point later and will relax this assumption.

We now introduce a family of procedures that will be useful.

Definition We define the operation P_k of taking the transitive closure of an $n \times n$ strictly upper-triangular matrix $\mathbf{B}$ under the assumption that the $[n-(n/k)] \times [n-(n/k)]$ submatrices $\mathbf{B}_1$ and $\mathbf{B}_2$ (shown in Fig. 12.11) are already transitively closed.†

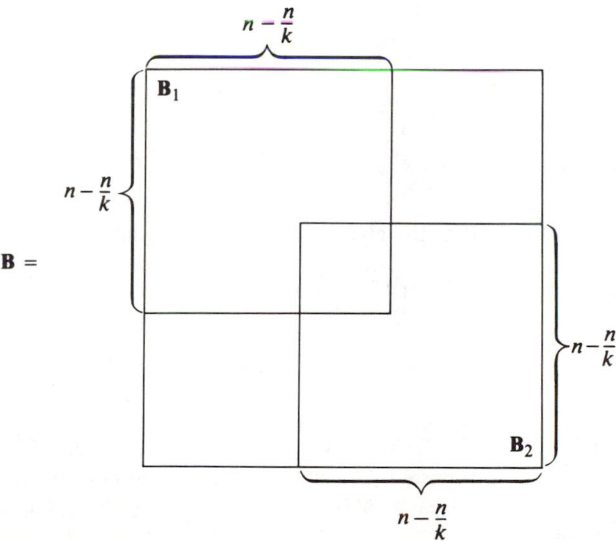

FIG. 12.11

† Recall that a matrix $\mathbf{D}$ is *transitively closed* if $\mathbf{D}^+ = \mathbf{D}$.

It will turn out that we need only construct P_2, P_3, and P_4.

Let $T_i(n)$ be the time required to compute P_i for an $n \times n$ matrix. Also, let $TR(n)$ be the time required to compute the transitive closure of an $n \times n$ matrix.

Now we give an algorithm to compute $\mathbf{D}^+$ in terms of P_2.

Algorithm 12.5.3 Let $\mathbf{A}$ be an $n \times n$ strictly upper-triangular matrix. We define a procedure *trans*($\mathbf{A}$) which returns the transitive closure of $\mathbf{A}$.

1 If $n = 2$, then $trans(\mathbf{A}) = \mathbf{A}$.

2 Consider $\mathbf{D} = \begin{array}{rcc} & \overbrace{\qquad}^{\frac{n}{2}} & \\ \frac{n}{2}\Big\{ & \mathbf{A}_1 & \mathbf{A}_3 \\ & \varnothing & \mathbf{A}_2 \Big\}\frac{n}{2} \\ & & \underbrace{\qquad}_{\frac{n}{2}} \end{array}$

3 Compute $trans(\mathbf{A}_1)$ and $trans(\mathbf{A}_2)$.

4 Let $\mathbf{B} = \begin{array}{|c|c|} \hline trans\ (\mathbf{A}_1) & \mathbf{A}_3 \\ \hline \varnothing & trans\ (\mathbf{A}_2) \\ \hline \end{array}$

5 Compute $P_2(\mathbf{B}) = \mathbf{A}^+$.

Now we will argue that the algorithm works, and analyze it.

Lemma 12.5.6 Algorithm 12.5.3 correctly computes $\mathbf{A}^+$ and

$$TR(n) = 2TR\left(\frac{n}{2}\right) + T_2(n) + \mathcal{O}(n^2).$$

Proof To see that $P_2(\mathbf{B}) = \mathbf{A}^+$, we induct on k where $n = 2^k$. Note that the result is true for $k = 1$. Suppose $k > 1$ and that *trans* works correctly for $n = 2^k$. Applying the algorithm to a matrix $\mathbf{A}$ of size 2^{k+1}, we correctly compute $trans(A_1)$ and $trans(\mathbf{A}_2)$ where

$$\mathbf{A} = \begin{array}{|c|c|} \hline \mathbf{A}_1 & \mathbf{A}_3 \\ \hline \varnothing & \mathbf{A}_2 \\ \hline \end{array}$$

by using the induction hypothesis. Let

$$\mathbf{B} = \begin{array}{|c|c|}\hline \mathbf{A}_1^+ & \mathbf{A}_3 \\ \hline \emptyset & \mathbf{A}_2^+ \\ \hline \end{array}$$

Now $\mathbf{B}$ has the square submatrices $\mathbf{A}_1^+$ and $\mathbf{A}_2^+$ of size 2^k. Applying P_2 yields the closure of $\mathbf{B}$, which is

$$\mathbf{B}^+ = \begin{array}{|c|c|}\hline \mathbf{A}_1^+ & \mathbf{A}_3^+ \\ \hline \emptyset & \mathbf{A}_2^+ \\ \hline \end{array} = \mathbf{A}^+$$

Clearly, the time bound is

$$TR(n) = 2TR\left(\frac{n}{2}\right) + T_2(n) + \mathcal{O}(n^2). \qquad \square$$

Next we turn to the interesting task of computing P_2.

Algorithm 12.5.4 Let $\mathbf{B}$ be an $n \times n$ matrix as shown below, where each square is of size $n/4$.

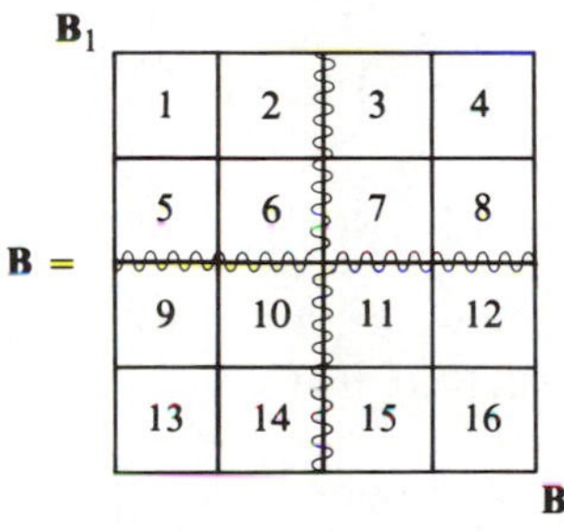

Assume that $\mathbf{B}_1 = \begin{array}{|c|c|}\hline 1 & 2 \\ \hline 5 & 6 \\ \hline \end{array}$ and $\mathbf{B}_2 = \begin{array}{|c|c|}\hline 11 & 12 \\ \hline 15 & 16 \\ \hline \end{array}$

are already transitive closed.

1 If $n = 2$, then $\mathbf{B}^+ = \mathbf{B}$.

2 Apply P_2 to $\mathbf{B}_3 = \begin{array}{|c|c|}\hline 6 & 7 \\ \hline 10 & 11 \\ \hline \end{array}$ to yield $\begin{array}{|c|c|}\hline 6 & 7' \\ \hline 10 & 11 \\ \hline \end{array} = \mathbf{B}_3^+$

3 Apply P_3 to $\mathbf{B}_4 =$

1	2	3
5	6	7′
9	10	11

to yield

1	2	3′
5	6	7′
9	10	11

$= \mathbf{B}_4^+$

4 Apply P_3 to $\mathbf{B}_5 =$

6	7′	8
10	11	12
14	15	16

to yield

6	7′	8′
10	11	12
14	15	16

$= \mathbf{B}_5^+$

5 Apply P_4 to

1	2	3′	4
5	6	7′	8′
9	10	11	12
13	14	15	16

to yield $\mathbf{B}^+$.

Lemma 12.5.7 The previous algorithm computes P_2 and

$$T_2(n) = T_2\left(\frac{n}{2}\right) + 2T_3\left(\frac{3n}{4}\right) + T_4(n).$$

Proof The equation is trivial to verify. □

To see that the algorithm works, note that we were allowed to assume that $\mathbf{B}_1$ and $\mathbf{B}_2$ were transitively closed. Note that

6

and

11

are transitively closed because they are central submatrices of transitively closed matrices. (Cf. the Corollary to Theorem 12.5.3.) Thus we apply P_2 to $\mathbf{B}_3$ to get $\mathbf{B}_3^+$. Next consider Step 3. To apply P_3 to $\mathbf{B}_4$, we must check to see whether

1	2
5	6

is transitively closed, and it is, by assumption. Moreover, we require that

6	7′
10	11

$= \mathbf{B}_3^+$

be transitively closed, which it is, by Step 2. Therefore, $P_3(\mathbf{B}_4) = \mathbf{B}_4^+$. Now we want to apply P_3 to $\mathbf{B}_5$. But

6	7′
10	11

$= \mathbf{B}_3^+$ and

11	12
15	16

$= \mathbf{B}_2^+$

are transitively closed by Step 2 and our assumption.

To invoke P_4 in Step 5 we need only check that $\mathbf{B}_4^+$ and $\mathbf{B}_5^+$ are transitively closed. But this is true, from Steps 2 and 4, respectively. Thus we obtain $\mathbf{B}^+$. □

With the aid of Valiant's Lemma, it is easy to give algorithms for P_3 and P_4.

Algorithm 12.5.5 (*Computation of* P_3) Given an $n \times n$ upper-triangular matrix $\mathbf{B}$. Let us represent $\mathbf{B}$ by

$\mathbf{B} =$

1	2	3
4	5	6
7	8	9

where each square is of size $n/3$. We may assume that

$\mathbf{B}_1 =$

1	2
4	5

$= \mathbf{B}_1^+$

and

$\mathbf{B}_2 =$

5	6
8	9

$= \mathbf{B}_2^+$

1 Compute $\mathbf{B} \cup \mathbf{E}_r * \mathbf{E}_r = \mathbf{C}$, where $r = 2n/3$. Recall that

$\mathbf{E}_r =$

∅	2	∅
∅	∅	6
∅	∅	∅

Thus

$\mathbf{C} =$

1	2	3′
4	5	6
7	8	9

2 Compute $\mathbf{C}^{+(r)}$ for $r = 2n/3$, using P_2, which means that we compute P_2 of

1	3′
7	9

This is permissible since | 1 | and | 9 | are closed.

The algorithm for P_4 is similar, with $r = 3n/4$.

Algorithm 12.5.6 (*Computation of* P_4) Let **B** be an $n \times n$ upper-triangular matrix, which is represented by

B =

1	2	3	4
5	6	7	8
9	10	11	12
13	14	15	16

where each entry is a matrix of size $n/4$. Assume that:

$\mathbf{B}_1$ =

1	2	3
5	6	7
9	10	11

$= \mathbf{B}_1^+$

and that:

$\mathbf{B}_2$ =

6	7	8
10	11	12
14	15	16

$= \mathbf{B}_2^+$

1 Compute $\mathbf{B} \cup \mathbf{E}_r * \mathbf{E}_r = \mathbf{C}$, where $r = 3n/4$, so

$\mathbf{E}_r$ =

∅	2	3	∅
∅	∅	∅	8
∅	∅	∅	12
∅	∅	∅	∅

Then

C =

1	2	3	4′
5	6	7	8
9	10	11	12
13	14	15	16

2 Compute $\mathbf{C}^{+(r)}$ for $r = 3n/4$, using P_2; i.e., apply P_2 to

1	4′
13	16

Now we begin to analyze these procedures.

Lemma 12.5.8 Algorithms 12.5.5 and 12.5.6 compute P_3 and P_4, respectively. Moreover,

$$T_3(n) = M(n) + T_2\left(\frac{2n}{3}\right) + \mathcal{O}(n^2),$$

$$T_4(n) = M(n) + T_2\left(\frac{n}{2}\right) + \mathcal{O}(n^2).$$

Proof Correctness follows, from Valiant's Lemma, while the equations follow trivially. □

At this point, we have reduced the computation of the transitive closure to the computation of the product of two upper-triangular matrices. We must estimate the time required to do this. Let $M(n)$ be the time necessary to multiply two such $n \times n$ matrices.

Lemma 12.5.9 If $n = 2^k$ for some $k \geqslant 1$, and there is some $\gamma \geqslant 2$ such that, for all m,

$$M(2^{m+1}) \geqslant 2^\gamma M(2^m),$$

then

$$T_2(n) \leqslant \begin{cases} c_1 M(n) & \text{for some constant } c_1 \quad \text{if } \gamma > 2, \\ c_2 M(n) \log n & \text{for some constant } c_2 \quad \text{if } \gamma = 2. \end{cases}$$

Proof If we substitute the result of Lemma 12.5.8 into the result of Lemma 12.5.7, we get

$$T_2(n) = 4T_2\left(\frac{n}{2}\right) + 2M\left(\frac{3n}{4}\right) + M(n) + \mathcal{O}(n^2). \tag{12.5.3}$$

By the monotonicity of M, $M(3n/4) \leqslant M(n)$ so

$$T_2(n) \leqslant 4T_2\left(\frac{n}{2}\right) + 3M(n) + \mathcal{O}(n^2). \tag{12.5.4}$$

The solution of (12.5.4) is claimed to be:

$$T_2(n) \leqslant \mathcal{O}(n^2 \log n) + 3M(n) \sum_{m=0}^{\log n} 2^{(2-\gamma)m}. \tag{12.5.5}$$

If we let $n = 2^k$, the claim becomes:

$$T_2(2^k) \leqslant c(k2^{2k}) + 3M(2^k) \sum_{m=0}^{k} 2^{(2-\gamma)m} \tag{12.5.6}$$

for some constant $c \geqslant c_1/4$, where c_1 is the constant in (12.5.4). We can verify this by induction on k. We shall just do the induction step here. Since $M(2^k) \leqslant 2^{-\gamma}M(2^{k+1})$, it follows that

$$T_2(2^{k+1}) \leqslant c(k+1)2^{2(k+1)} + 3M(2^{k+1}) \left[1 + 2^{(2-\gamma)} \sum_{m=0}^{k} 2^{(2-\gamma)m}\right]$$

or

$$T_2(2^{k+1}) \leqslant c(k+1)2^{2(k+1)} + 3M(2^{k+1}) \sum_{m=0}^{k+1} 2^{(2-\gamma)m}.$$

From inequality (12.5.4),

$$T_2(2^{k+1}) \leqslant 4T_2(2^k) + 3M(2^{k+1}) + c_1(2^{2k}).$$

By the induction hypothesis,

$$T_2(2^{k+1}) \leqslant 3M(2^{k+1}) + c_1(2^{2k}) + 4c(k2^{2k}) + 12M(2^k) \sum_{m=0}^{k} 2^{(2-\gamma)m}. \tag{12.5.7}$$

Since $c \geqslant c_1/4$, we have

$$4ck + c_1 \leqslant 4ck + 4c = 4c(k+1).$$

Multiplying both sides by 2^{2k} yields:

$$c_1 2^{2k} + 4ck2^k = c_1 2^{2k} + ck2^{k+2} \leqslant c(k+1)2^{2k+2}.$$

Substituting this in (12.5.7) yields:

$$T_2(2^{k+1}) \leqslant 3M(2^{k+1}) + 12M(2^k) \sum_{m=0}^{k} 2^{(2-\gamma)m} + c(k+1)2^{2k+2}.$$

This completes the induction proof of (12.5.5) and also establishes (12.5.4).

Since the series $\sum_{m=0}^{\infty} x_m$ converges if $|x| < 1$, then the result follows. □

Next we use the present result to estimate $TR(n)$.

Theorem 12.5.4 If there exists $\gamma \geqslant 2$ such that, for all m,

$$M(2^{m+1}) \geqslant 2^{\gamma} M(2^m),$$

then

$$TR(n) \leqslant \begin{cases} \mathcal{O}(M(n)) & \text{if } \gamma > 2, \\ \mathcal{O}(M(n)\log n) & \text{if } \gamma = 2. \end{cases}$$

Proof For the moment, we continue to assume that $n = 2^k$. It follows from Eq. (12.5.3), that

$$T_2(n) \geqslant 4T_2(n/2). \tag{12.5.8}$$

We claim that

$$TR(n) \leqslant \mathcal{O}(n^2) + T_2(n) \sum_{m=0}^{\log n} 2^{-m}. \tag{12.5.9}$$

Since $n = 2^k$, we shall show by induction on k that

$$TR(2^k) \leqslant T_2(2^k) \sum_{m=0}^{k} 2^{-m} + \mathcal{O}(2^{2k}).$$

We shall just do the induction step. Lemma 12.5.6 gives that

$$TR(2^{k+1}) = 2TR(2^k) + T_2(2^{k+1}) + \mathcal{O}(2^{2(k+1)}).$$

Applying the induction hypothesis yields

$$TR(2^{k+1}) \leqslant T_2(2^{k+1}) + 2\left[T_2(2^k) \sum_{m=0}^{k} 2^{-m}\right] + \mathcal{O}(2^{2(k+1)}).$$

Since $T_2(2^k) \leqslant T_2(2^{k+1})/4$, we have

$$TR(2^{k+1}) \leqslant T_2(2^{k+1}) \sum_{m=0}^{k+1} 2^{-m} + \mathcal{O}(2^{2(k+1)}).$$

This completes the induction step. It follows from (12.5.9) that:

$$TR(n) \leqslant 2T_2(n) + \mathcal{O}(n^2).$$

Applying Lemma 12.5.9 gives the result if $n = 2^k$.

Now we deal with nonpowers of 2. It may have seemed that we would run into difficulty with assuming that $n = 2^k$ and using P_3, which would seem to require that the size of the matrix be divisible by 3. Closer observation of P_2, which calls P_3, indicates that if $n = 2^k$, P_3 is applied to matrices of size $3n/4 = 3 \cdot 2^{k-2}$. When we take the "reduction by one third" operation, we deal with matrices of size 2^{k-2} and there is no problem.

To complete the proof, we merely pad out an $n \times n$ matrix to the next higher power of 2 if $n \neq 2^k$, which is $2^{\lceil \log_2 n \rceil}$. The method of padding is illustrated in Fig. 12.12.

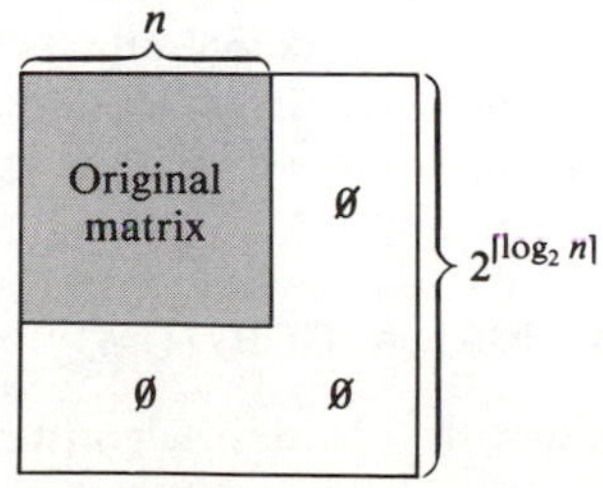

FIG. 12.12

Note that the padded matrix is still strict upper-triangular if the original one was. Note that there is a constant c so that, for all n,

$$cM(n) \geqslant M(2^{\lceil \log n \rceil}),$$

and the final result now holds for all n. □

Now we can combine our various results to obtain the following important theorem.

Theorem 12.5.5 Let S be a finite set and $*$ an arbitrary binary operation on S, which satisfies axioms D1, D2, and N1. If $\mathbf{D}$ is a strictly upper-triangular matrix whose entries are subsets of S, then the time required to compute $\mathbf{D}^+$ is $TR(n)$ and

$$TR(n) \leqslant \begin{cases} cBM(n) \leqslant cn^{2.81} & \text{if } BM(n) \geqslant n^{2+\epsilon} \quad \text{for some } \epsilon > 0, \\ cn^2 \log n & \text{if } BM(n) < n^{2+\epsilon} \quad \text{for any } \epsilon > 0. \end{cases}$$

Proof The result follows from Theorems 12.2.3, 12.5.2, and 12.5.4. □

We can now combine our individual results, to state the main result.

Theorem 12.5.6 Let $G = (V, \Sigma, P, S)$ be a context-free grammar in Chomsky normal form. The time needed to recognize a string of length n generated by G is at most a constant times

$$\begin{cases} BM(n) \leqslant n^{2.81} & \text{if } BM(n) \geqslant n^{2+\epsilon} \quad \text{for some } \epsilon > 0, \\ n^2 \log n & \text{if } BM(n) < n^{2+\epsilon} \quad \text{for any } \epsilon > 0. \end{cases}$$

Proof Algorithm 12.5.1 requires $\mathcal{O}(n^2)$ steps to initialize the matrix and $TR(n + 1)$ steps to compute the transitive closure. It is easily shown that the binary operation $\cdot$ defined in Section 4.1 satisfies axioms D1, D2, and N1. The time bound then follows, from Theorem 12.5.5. □

PROBLEMS

1 Prove Proposition 12.5.1.

2 Complete the following parts of the proof of Lemma 12.5.5:

a) Claim 1 b) Claim 4 c) Claim 5

3 In one abstract formulation in this section, we started from a binary operation $*$ on S and extended $*$ to work on subsets. Are the three axioms given exactly equivalent to this situation? That is, if we start out as above, do the axioms always hold? If the axioms hold, may $*$ be redefined as above?

12.6 A GOOD PRACTICAL ALGORITHM

In this section, another recognition algorithm is presented that is quite suitable for practical use. It works on any context-free grammar, so no initial transformations of the grammar are needed. It can be shown that the simplest variant of the algorithm runs in time cn^3, where c is proportional to $\|G\|$. It turns out that, in applications to the grammars which occur in natural language processing, dependence on $\|G\|$ is more critical than dependence on n. It also turns out that this method can be speeded up by a factor of $\log n$.

The algorithm to be presented will construct an $(n+1) \times (n+1)$ upper-triangular matrix. The entries in the matrix will be "dotted rules," which we now define.

Definition Let $G = (V, \Sigma, P, S)$ be a context-free grammar and let $\cdot$ be a symbol not in V. If $A \to \alpha\beta$ is in P, then we say that $A \to \alpha \cdot \beta$ is a *dotted rule* of G.

Our intuition tells us that the "dot" separates α and β; the α part of the rule has been found to be consistent with the input, while nothing is yet known about β. If $A \to \Lambda$ is in P, we write the dotted rule $A \to \cdot$ and let $\cdot$ concatenate with Λ.

The matrix will be filled in by using certain operations that will now be defined.

Definition Let $G = (V, \Sigma. P, S)$ be a context-free grammar. Let Q be a set of dotted rules, and let $R \subseteq V$. Define:

$$Q \times R = \{A \to \alpha B\beta \cdot \gamma \mid A \to \alpha \cdot B\beta\gamma \text{ is in } Q, \beta \overset{*}{\Rightarrow} \Lambda, \text{and } B \in R\};$$

$$Q * R = \{A \to \alpha B\beta \cdot \gamma \mid A \to \alpha \cdot B\beta\gamma \text{ is in } Q, \beta \overset{*}{\Rightarrow} \Lambda, B \overset{*}{\Rightarrow} C \text{ for some } C \in R\}$$

The idea of the $\times$ product is to extend the "product" of the Cocke–Kasami–Younger algorithm to the case in which Λ-rules exist. The $*$-product is a method of precomputing chain derivations. Next we extend these products to the case where both arguments are sets of dotted rules. Note that:

$$Q \times R \subseteq Q * R.$$

Definition Let $G = (V, \Sigma, P, S)$ be a context-free grammar and let Q, R be sets of dotted rules. Define

$$Q \times R = \{A \to \alpha B\beta \cdot \gamma \mid A \to \alpha \cdot B\beta\gamma \in Q, \beta \overset{*}{\Rightarrow} \Lambda, \text{and } B \to \eta \cdot \text{ is in } R\}$$

and

$$Q * R = \{A \to \alpha B\beta \cdot \gamma \mid A \to \alpha \cdot B\beta\gamma \in Q, \beta \overset{*}{\Rightarrow} \Lambda, B \overset{*}{\Rightarrow} C \text{ for some } C \in N \text{ and } C \to \eta \cdot \text{ is in } R\}.$$

Again, note that:

$$Q \times R \subseteq Q * R.$$

The algorithm that we shall give uses a predictor to guess which dotted rules may be needed next.

Definition Let $G = (V, \Sigma, P, S)$ be a context-free grammar and let $R \subseteq V$. Define

$$predict(R) = \{C \to \gamma \cdot \xi \mid C \to \gamma\xi \text{ is in } P, \gamma \overset{*}{\Rightarrow} \Lambda, B \overset{*}{\Rightarrow} C\eta \text{ for some } B \in R \text{ and some } \eta \in V^*\}.$$

If R is a set of dotted rules, then

$$predict(R) = predict(\{B \mid A \to \alpha \cdot B\beta \text{ is in } R\}).$$

It is important to note that *predict* depends only on the grammar and can be precomputed for each variable or dotted rule.

Example Consider the grammar

$$\begin{aligned} &S \to AB \\ &A \to \Lambda \\ &B \to CDC \\ &C \to \Lambda \\ &D \to a \end{aligned}$$

$$predict(\{S\}) = \{S \to \cdot AB, S \to A \cdot B, A \to \cdot, B \to \cdot CDC, B \to C \cdot DC, C \to \cdot, \\ D \to \cdot a\}$$

Let $Q = \{S \to A \cdot B\}$. Then

$$Q \times \{B\} = \{S \to AB\cdot\},$$

while

$$Q * \{D\} = \{S \to AB\cdot\}.$$

Now we can present the main algorithm.

Algorithm 12.6.1 Let $G = (V, \Sigma, P, S)$ be any context-free grammar. Let $w = a_1 \cdots a_n$, where $n \geqslant 0$ and $a_k \in \Sigma$ for each k, $1 \leqslant k \leqslant n$, be the string to be recognized. Form an $(n+1) \times (n+1)$ matrix $\mathbf{T} = (t_{ij})$, as follows:

begin
  $t_{0,0} := predict(\{S\})$;
  for $j := 1$ **to** n **do**
  begin
    comment build col. j, given cols. $0, \ldots, j-1$;
scanner:
    for $0 \leqslant i \leqslant j-1$ **do**
      $t_{i,j} := t_{i,j-1} \times \{a_j\}$:
completer:
    for $k := j-1$ **downto** 0 **do**
    begin $t_{k,j} := t_{k,j} \cup t_{k,k} * t_{k,j}$;
      for $i := k-1$ **downto** 0 **do**
        $t_{i,j} := t_{i,j} \cup t_{i,k} \times t_{k,j}$
    end;
predictor:
$$t_{j,j} := predict\left(\bigcup_{0 \leqslant i \leqslant j-1} t_{i,j}\right);$$
  end
end.

The order of computation will now be enumerated. Suppose we have built columns $0, \ldots, j-1$. To construct column j, the scanner puts partial information into the off-diagonal part of the column. The completer works up the column from $t_{j-1,j}$ to $t_{0,j}$. The computation of $t_{k,j}$ where $0 \leqslant k < j$, is done by first computing

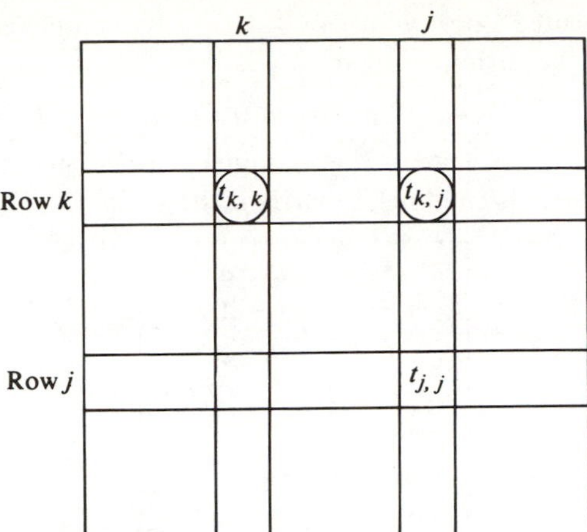

FIG. 12.13

$t_{k,j} := t_{k,j} \cup t_{k,k} * t_{k,j}$. That is, each entry $t_{k,j}$ is filled in by adding the $*$-product of the diagonal entry of that row to the original contents of $t_{k,j}$. This is illustrated in Fig. 12.13.

Next $t_{k,j}$ is cross-multiplied against $t_{i,k}$ and the result added to $t_{i,j}$ for all rows above $t_{k,j}$. Then we continue to the next entry, which is $t_{k-1,j}$. This is illustrated in Fig. 12.14.

Only after $t_{0,j}$ has been completed is the predictor used. The predictor fills in $t_{j,j}$.

Before studying the algorithm in detail, let us simply execute it on the first example of this section, when we try to recognize the input $w = a$. Since we have precomputed *predict*, the first executable statement yields:

$$t_{0,0} = \{S \to \cdot AB, A \to \cdot, S \to A \cdot B, B \to \cdot CDC, C \to \cdot, B \to C \cdot DC, D \to \cdot a\}.$$

The outer **for** loop is executed once, for $j = 1$. The scanner sets $t_{0,1}$ to $\{D \to a\cdot\}$. The

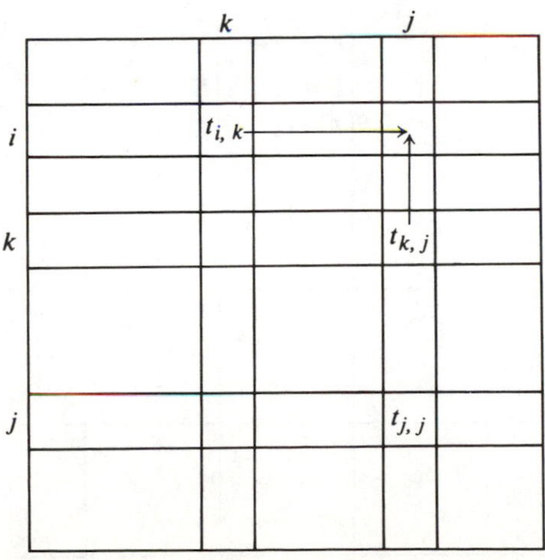

FIG. 12.14

inner **for** loop is executed once, with $k = 0$. Next, the completer adds to $t_{0,1}$ some new dotted rules, and the current value of $t_{0,1}$ is:

$$t_{0,1} = \{D \to a\cdot, S \to AB\cdot, B \to CD\cdot C, B \to CDC\cdot\}.$$

The next **for** loop is not executed. The computation is concluded in the predictor, where $t_{1,1}$ is set to $\{C \to \cdot\ \}$. The final T matrix is shown in Fig. 12.15.

$S \to \cdot AB$ $A \to \cdot$ $S \to A \cdot B$ $B \to \cdot CDC$ $C \to \cdot$ $B \to C \cdot DC$ $D \to \cdot a$	$D \to a \cdot$ $S \to AB \cdot$ $B \to CD \cdot C$ $B \to CDC \cdot$
	$C \to \cdot$

FIG. 12.15

As we shall see shortly, $w \in L(G)$, because $S \to AB\cdot$ is in $t_{0,1}$.

Example Let G be the grammar

$$E \to E * E | E + E | a$$

and let $w = a + a * a$. Note that the string w has two parses. We present the recognition matrix in Fig. 12.16, and ask the reader to verify the computation.

T =

$E \to \cdot E*E$ $E \to \cdot E+E$ $E \to \cdot a$	$E \to E \cdot *E$ $E \to E\cdot +E$ $E \to a\cdot$	$E \to E+\cdot E$	$E \to E+E\cdot$ $E \to E\cdot *E$ $E \to E\cdot +E$	$E \to E*\cdot E$	$E \to E+E\cdot$ $E \to E\cdot *E$ $E \to E\cdot +E$ $E \to E*E\cdot$
		$E \to \cdot E*E$ $E \to \cdot E+E$ $E \to \cdot a$	$E \to E\cdot *E$ $E \to E\cdot +E$ $E \to a\cdot$	$E \to E*\cdot E$	$E \to E*E\cdot$ $E \to E\cdot *E$ $E \to E\cdot +E$
				$E \to \cdot E*E$ $E \to \cdot E+E$ $E \to \cdot a$	$E \to E\cdot *E$ $E \to E\cdot +E$ $E \to a\cdot$

FIG. 12.16

Since $E \to E + E\cdot$ is in $t_{0,5}$ (and $E \to E * E\cdot$ is in $t_{0,5}$), we conclude that $w \in L(G)$.

Some new terminology is needed for the proof that the algorithm works.

Definition Let $G = (V, \Sigma, P, S)$ be a context-free grammar, let $w = a_1 \cdots a_n$, $a_k \in \Sigma$ for each $1 \leqslant k \leqslant n$, let $A \to \alpha\beta$ be in P, and let $1 \leqslant i, j \leqslant n$. A dotted rule $A \to \alpha \cdot \beta$ is called *(i, j)-consistent* if there exists $\gamma \in V^*$ such that

$$S \overset{*}{\Rightarrow} a_1 \cdots a_i A \gamma$$

and

$$\alpha \overset{*}{\Rightarrow} a_{i+1} \cdots a_j$$

A set of dotted rules is *(i, j)-consistent* if each rule in the set is. A set of (i, j)-*consistent* rules is *(i, j)-complete* if it contains all *(i, j)-consistent* rules.

There are only a finite number of (i, j)-consistent rules. Figure 12.17 shows the interpretation of an (i, j)-consistent rule.

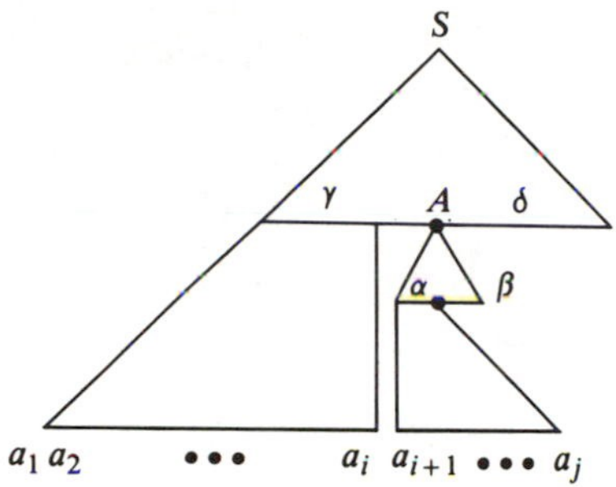

FIG. 12.17

It is convenient to prove a lemma about the preservation of consistency, which will substantially reduce the level of detail involved in carrying out the proof that the algorithm works.

Lemma 12.6.1 Let $G = (V, \Sigma, P, S)$ be a context-free grammar and let $w = a_1 \cdots a_n, n \geqslant 0$, where each $a_k \in \Sigma$ for $1 \leqslant k \leqslant n$. Let $0 \leqslant i, j \leqslant n$.

a) If $t_{i,j-1}$ is $(i, j-1)$-consistent, then $t_{i,j-1} \times \{a_j\}$ is (i, j)-consistent.

b) If $t_{i,i}$ and $t_{i,j}$ are (i, i)- and (i, j)-consistent, respectively, then $t_{i,i} * t_{i,j}$ is (i, j)-consistent.

c) For any k, $0 \leqslant k < j$, if $t_{i,k}$ and $t_{k,j}$ are (i, k)- and (k, j)-consistent, respectively, then $t_{i,k} \times t_{k,j}$ is (i, j)-consistent.

d)

$$\mathit{predict}\left(\bigcup_{0 \leqslant i < j} t_{i,j}\right)$$

is (i, j)-consistent if $t_{i,j}$ is (i, j)-consistent, where $i < j$.

Proof $A \to \alpha a_j \beta \cdot \gamma$ is in $t_{i,j-1} \times \{a_j\}$ if and only if

$$A \to \alpha \cdot a_j \beta\gamma \text{ is in } t_{i,j-1} \tag{12.6.1}$$

and

$$\beta \overset{*}{\Rightarrow} \Lambda \tag{12.6.2}$$

Since $t_{i,j-1}$ is $(i, j-1)$-consistent,

$$S \overset{*}{\Rightarrow} a_1 \cdots a_i A\theta \quad \text{for some } \theta \in V^* \tag{12.6.3}$$

and

$$\alpha \overset{*}{\Rightarrow} a_{i+1} \cdots a_{j-1} \tag{12.6.4}$$

Now,

$$\begin{aligned} \alpha a_j \beta &\overset{*}{\Rightarrow} a_{i+1} \ldots a_j \beta && \text{by (12.6.4),} \\ &\overset{*}{\Rightarrow} a_{i+1} \cdots a_j && \text{by (12.6.2).} \end{aligned}$$

This, together with (12.6.3), allows us to conclude that $t_{i,j-1} \times \{a_j\}$ is (i,j)-consistent, and completes the proof of part (a).

Next, we turn to part (b). $A \to \alpha B\beta \cdot \gamma$ is in $t_{i,i} * t_{i,j}$ if and only if

$$A \to \alpha \cdot B\beta\gamma \text{ is in } t_{i,i}$$

$$\beta \overset{*}{\Rightarrow} \Lambda \tag{12.6.5}$$

$$B \overset{*}{\Rightarrow} C \tag{12.6.6}$$

and

$$C \to \eta \cdot \text{ is in } t_{i,j}.$$

Since $t_{i,i}$ is (i, i)-consistent,

$$\alpha \overset{*}{\Rightarrow} \Lambda \tag{12.6.7}$$

and

$$S \overset{*}{\Rightarrow} a_1 \cdots a_i A\theta \tag{12.6.8}$$

for some θ. Since $C \to \eta \cdot$ is in $t_{i,j}$, we know that

$$\eta \overset{*}{\Rightarrow} a_{i+1} \cdots a_j \tag{12.6.9}$$

Combining (12.6.8) with (12.6.5), (12.5.6), (12.6.7), and (12.6.9) leads us to conclude that

$$\alpha B\beta \overset{*}{\Rightarrow} B\beta \overset{*}{\Rightarrow} C \overset{*}{\Rightarrow} \eta \overset{*}{\Rightarrow} a_{i+1} \cdots a_j$$

and so $A \to \alpha B\beta \cdot \gamma$ is (i, j)-consistent.

Now, we focus on part (c). $A \to \alpha B\beta \cdot \gamma$ is in $t_{i,k} \times t_{k,j}$ if and only if

$$A \to \alpha \cdot B\beta\gamma \text{ is in } t_{i,k} \tag{12.6.10}$$

$$\beta \overset{*}{\Rightarrow} \Lambda \tag{12.6.11}$$

and

$$B \to \eta \cdot \text{ is in } t_{k,j}. \tag{12.6.12}$$

By (12.6.10) and the consistency of $t_{i,k}$,

$$S \overset{*}{\Rightarrow} a_1 \cdots a_i A\theta \quad \text{for some } \theta \in V^* \tag{12.6.13}$$

$$\alpha \overset{*}{\Rightarrow} a_{i+1} \cdots a_k \tag{12.6.14}$$

By (12.6.12) and the consistency of $t_{k,j}$,

$$\eta \stackrel{*}{\Rightarrow} a_{k+1} \cdots a_j \tag{12.6.15}$$

We must derive some strings from $\alpha B \beta$. That is,

$$\begin{aligned} \alpha B \beta &\stackrel{*}{\Rightarrow} a_{i+1} \cdots a_k B \beta && \text{by (12.6.14)} \\ &\Rightarrow a_{i+1} \cdots a_k \eta \beta && \text{by (12.6.12)} \\ &\stackrel{*}{\Rightarrow} a_{i+1} \cdots a_k a_{k+1} \cdots a_j \beta && \text{by (12.6.15)} \\ &\stackrel{*}{\Rightarrow} a_{i+1} \cdots a_j && \text{by (12.6.11)} \end{aligned}$$

This derivation, together with (12.6.13), proves that $t_{i,k} \times t_{k,j}$ is (i,j)-consistent, and completes the proof of part (c).

Turning to part (d) of the lemma, $C \rightarrow \delta \cdot \xi$ is in $predict(\cup_{0 \leqslant i < j} t_{i,j})$ if and only if there exist $i < j$, and there is $B \in N$ such that

$$\delta \stackrel{*}{\Rightarrow} \Lambda \tag{12.6.16}$$

$$B \stackrel{*}{\Rightarrow} C\eta \qquad \text{for some } \eta \in V^* \tag{12.6.17}$$

$$A \rightarrow \alpha \cdot B\beta \quad \text{is in } t_{i,j}. \tag{12.6.18}$$

Since $t_{i,j}$ is assumed to be (i,j)-consistent,

$$S \stackrel{*}{\Rightarrow} a_1 \cdots a_i A \gamma \quad \text{for some } \gamma \in V^* \tag{12.6.19}$$

$$\alpha \stackrel{*}{\Rightarrow} a_{i+1} \cdots a_j \tag{12.6.20}$$

Note that

$$\begin{aligned} S &\stackrel{*}{\Rightarrow} a_1 \cdots a_i A \gamma && \text{by (12.6.17)} \\ &\Rightarrow a_1 \cdots a_i \alpha B \beta \gamma && \text{by (12.6.18)} \\ &\stackrel{*}{\Rightarrow} a_1 \cdots a_i a_{i+1} \cdots a_j B \beta \gamma && \text{by (12.6.20)} \\ &\stackrel{*}{\Rightarrow} a_1 \cdots a_j C \eta \beta \gamma && \text{by (12.6.17).} \end{aligned}$$

Using the last derivation with (12.6.16) allows us to conclude that $C \rightarrow \delta \cdot \xi$ is (j, j)-consistent, and completes the proof of the lemma. □

We are now ready to prove that the algorithm works. Understanding this proof is the key to modifying the algorithm to improve its performance.

Theorem 12.6.1 Let $G = (V, \Sigma, P, S)$ be a context-free grammar and let $w = a_1 \cdots a_n$, each $a_k \in \Sigma$ for $1 \leqslant k \leqslant n$. Let **T** be the recognition matrix produced by Algorithm 12.6.1. Then, for any $0 \leqslant i, j \leqslant n$, $t_{i,j}$ is both (i,j)-consistent and complete. Equivalently, $A \rightarrow \alpha \cdot \beta$ is in $t_{i,j}$ if and only if there exists $\gamma \in V^*$ such that

$$S \stackrel{*}{\Rightarrow} a_1 \cdots a_i A \gamma$$

and

$$\alpha \stackrel{*}{\Rightarrow} a_{i+1} \cdots a_j$$

Proof The argument will be an induction on the order in which the computation is carried out.

Basis. We must show that

$$predict(\{S\}) = t_{0,0}$$

is $(0,0)$-consistent and complete. It follows, from the definition of *predict*, that $t_{0,0}$ is $(0,0)$-consistent because, if $C \to \delta \cdot \xi$ is in $predict(\{S\})$, then $\delta \overset{*}{\Rightarrow} \Lambda$ and $S \overset{*}{\Rightarrow} C\eta$, and hence, $C \to \delta \cdot \xi$ is $(0,0)$-consistent. Conversely, if $C \to \delta \cdot \xi$ is $(0,0)$-consistent, then, by the definition of $(0,0)$-consistency, $\delta \overset{*}{\Rightarrow} \Lambda$ and there is some $\eta \in V^*$ such that $S \overset{*}{\Rightarrow} \Lambda C\eta = C\eta$, which implies that $C \to \delta \cdot \xi$ is in $predict(\{S\})$.

Induction step. Assume that we are about to make our final assignment to $t_{i,j}$ as specified below. As an induction hypothesis, assume that, after final assignment to all earlier entries $t_{i',j'}$, the $t_{i',j'}$ are (i',j')-consistent and complete.† We must show that, for $t_{i,j}$, the following propositions are true:

a) All dotted rules added to $t_{i,j}$ are (i,j)-consistent.

b) If $i<j$, then $t_{i,j}$ will be (i,j)-complete after execution of the program statement

$$t_{k,j} := t_{k,j} \cup t_{k,k} * t_{k,j},$$

when k and j have the values i and j, respectively.

c) The $t_{j,j}$ will be (j,j)-complete after execution of the statement labeled *predictor.*

The proof of part (a) follows immediately, because the induction hypothesis asserts that $t_{i,j-1}$ is $(i,j-1)$-consistent and Lemma 12.6.1(a) shows that

$$t_{i,j} = t_{i,j-1} \times \{a_j\}$$

is (i,j)-consistent. That assignment is done in the scanner. Similarly, the other parts of Lemma 12.6.1 assert that all additions to $t_{i,j}$ are (i,j)-consistent.

To show (b), let $i<j$ and let $A \to \alpha \cdot \beta$ be an (i, j)-consistent dotted rule. By (i,j)-consistency, it is known that

$$\alpha \overset{*}{\Rightarrow} a_{i+1} \cdots a_j \tag{12.6.21}$$

Since $i<j$, $a_{i+1} \cdots a_j \neq \Lambda$, and so there is some $X \in V$ which is the ancestor of a_j in (12.6.21):

$$\alpha = \alpha_1 X \alpha_2$$

for some $\alpha_1, \alpha_2 \in V^*$. Also there exists $k, i \leqslant k < j$, such that

† Our formulation of the induction step is complicated by the fact that some entries are partially completed before the final values are assigned. It is possible to state the exact characterization of the full matrix at any time during the execution of the algorithm, but it is cumbersome and involves extra notation. By stating the induction hypothesis this way, we can eliminate the extra notation.

$$\alpha_1 \stackrel{*}{\Rightarrow} a_{i+1} \cdots a_k \tag{12.6.22}$$

$$X \stackrel{*}{\Rightarrow} a_{k+1} \cdots a_j \tag{12.6.23}$$

$$\alpha_2 \stackrel{*}{\Rightarrow} \Lambda \tag{12.6.24}$$

It is easily checked that

$$A \rightarrow \alpha_1 \cdot X\alpha_2\beta$$

is (i, k)-consistent. Since $k < j$, the induction hypothesis applies, and $A \rightarrow \alpha_1 \cdot X\alpha_2\beta$ is in $t_{i,k}$.

There are now three cases to be considered.

CASE 1. $X \in \Sigma$. Then $X = a_j$ and $k = j - 1$, from (12.6.23). This case is illustrated in Fig. 12.18. Then

$$A \rightarrow \alpha_1 \cdot a_j\alpha_2\beta \text{ is in } t_{i,j-1}$$

so $A \rightarrow \alpha_1 a_j \alpha_2 \cdot \beta$ is in $t_{i,j-1} \times \{a_j\}$. Hence it is added to $t_{i,j}$ by the scanner.

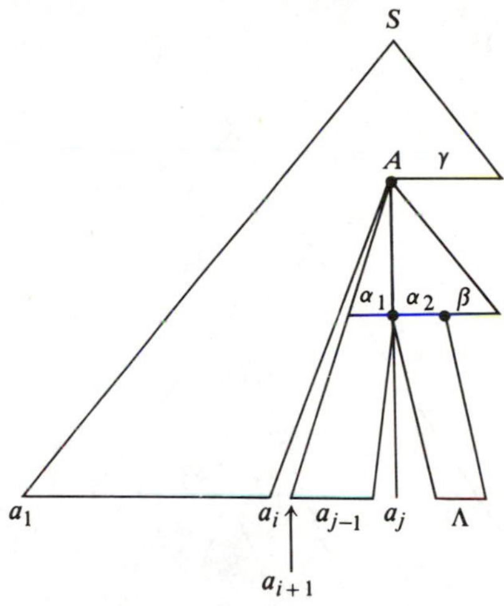

FIG. 12.18

CASE 2. $X \in N$ and $i < k$. This case is illustrated in Fig. 12.19. Rewriting (12.6.23), we have:

$$X \Rightarrow \delta \stackrel{*}{\Rightarrow} a_{k+1} \cdots a_j$$

and $X \rightarrow \delta$ is in P. It follows easily that $X \rightarrow \delta\,\cdot$ is (k, j)-consistent and must be in $t_{k,j}$, by the induction hypothesis, since $i < k$. But then $A \rightarrow \alpha \cdot \beta$ will be in $t_{i,k} \times t_{k,j}$, so it will be added to $t_{i,j}$ by the completer loop immediately after the computation of $t_{k,j}$ is finished.

CASE 3. $X \in N$ and $i = k$. Now we find that (12.6.22) and (12.6.23) become:

$$\alpha_1 \stackrel{*}{\Rightarrow} \Lambda$$

$$X \stackrel{*}{\Rightarrow} a_{i+1} \cdots a_j \neq \Lambda \tag{12.6.25}$$

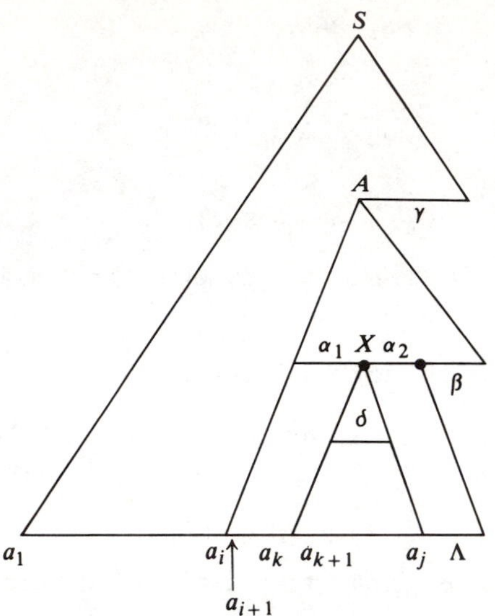

FIG. 12.19

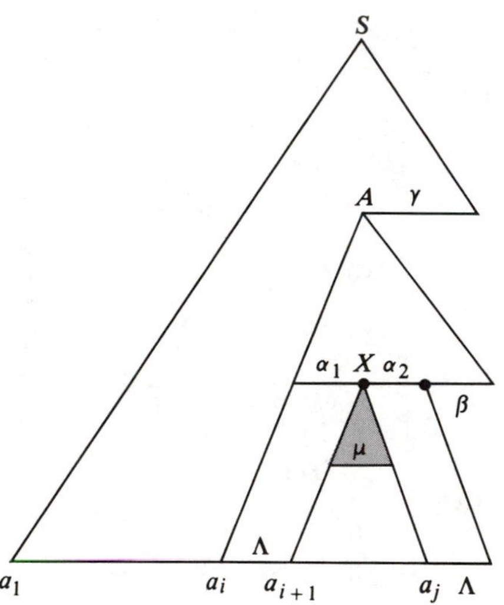

FIG. 12.20

The situation is illustrated in Fig. 12.20. Expanding (12.6.25), which is possible since $i < j$, we have:

$$X \Rightarrow \mu \overset{*}{\Rightarrow} a_{i+1} \cdots a_j \tag{12.6.26}$$

for some $\mu \in V^*$. Hence, $X \to \mu \cdot$ is (i, j)-consistent. Now, however, $t_{i,j}$ may not be complete when

$$t_{i,j} := t_{i,j} \cup t_{i,i} * t_{i,j} \tag{12.6.27}$$

is executed, so the induction hypothesis does not apply directly as it did in Cases 1 and 2. Let us examine a generation tree of (12.6.26). See Fig. 12.20. There will be an internal node in the tree, which is labeled Y and is the lowest common ancestor of a_{i+1} and a_j. That is

$$X \overset{*}{\Rightarrow} \theta_1 Y \theta_2$$
$$\theta_1 \overset{*}{\Rightarrow} \Lambda$$
$$\theta_2 \overset{*}{\Rightarrow} \Lambda$$
$$Y \to \delta \text{ is in } P$$

This situation is illustrated in Fig. 12.21.

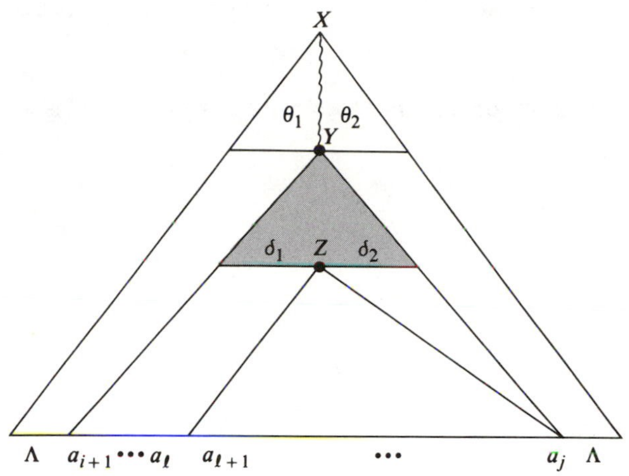

FIG. 12.21

There is some $Z \in V$ such that

$$\delta = \delta_1 Z \delta_2$$
$$\left.\begin{aligned}\delta_1 &\overset{*}{\Rightarrow} a_{i+1} \cdots a_\ell \\ Z &\overset{*}{\Rightarrow} a_{\ell+1} \cdots a_j\end{aligned}\right\} \text{ for some } i \leqslant \ell < j$$
$$\delta_2 \overset{*}{\Rightarrow} \Lambda$$

Note that $Z \in V$, so that $Z = a_j$ is included in this case. If $i + 1 = j$, then $\ell = i$ and $Z \overset{*}{\Rightarrow} a_j$. But then Z is a common ancestor of a_{i+1} $(= a_j)$ and a_j, which is a contradiction unless $Z = a_j$.

On the other hand, if $i + 1 < j$, then $i < \ell < j$, because $\ell = i$ would imply that Z is a lower common ancestor of a_{i+1} and a_j than Y. In either case $Y \to \delta\ \cdot$ is (i, j)-consistent. Moreover, $Y \to \delta\ \cdot$ falls under Case 1 or Case 2 above, respectively [with $Y \to \delta_1 Z \delta_2 \cdot$ in place of $A \to \alpha_1 X \alpha_2 \cdot \beta$, Z in place of X, and ℓ in place of k]. By the arguments used earlier, $Y \to \delta\ \cdot$ was added to $t_{i,j}$ *before* the statement

$$t_{i,j} := t_{i,j} \cup t_{i,i} * t_{i,j}$$

was executed.

Since $i<j$ and $A \to \alpha_1 \cdot X\alpha_2\beta$ is in $t_{i,i}$ by the induction hypothesis and

$$X \overset{*}{\Rightarrow} Y$$

we have that $A \to \alpha_1 X\alpha_2 \cdot \beta$ is in $t_{i,i} * t_{i,j}$, so that $A \to \alpha \cdot \beta$ will be in $t_{i,j}$ after execution of (12.6.27). This completes the proof of part (b).

To prove part (c), let $C \to \eta \cdot \theta$ be a dotted rule that is (j,j)-consistent. By definition,

$$S \overset{*}{\Rightarrow} a_1 \cdots a_j C\gamma \tag{12.6.28}$$

for some $\gamma \in V^*$ and

$$\eta \overset{*}{\Rightarrow} \Lambda. \tag{12.6.29}$$

Let the least common ancestor of a_j and C be a node labeled A, and the production

$$A \to \alpha B\beta$$

is used. See Fig. 12.22. α contains an ancestor of a_j while $B \in V$ is an ancestor of C.

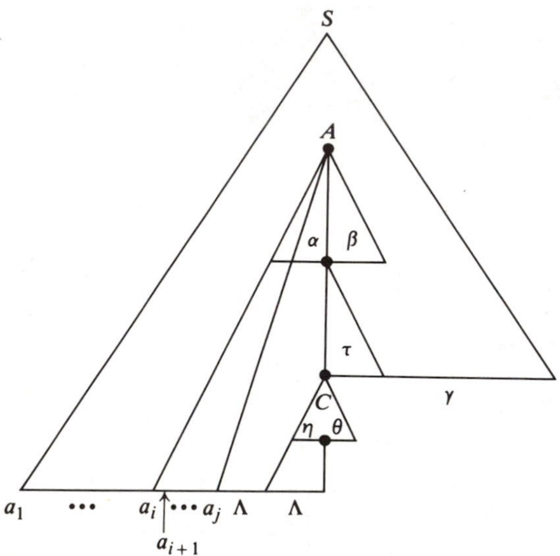

FIG. 12.22

Now $A \to \alpha \cdot B\beta$ must be (i,j)-consistent for some $i<j$. That is, there is some i so that

$$\alpha \overset{*}{\Rightarrow} a_{i+1} \cdots a_j$$

because α contains an ancestor of a_j. By the induction hypothesis,

$$A \to \alpha \cdot B\beta \text{ is in } t_{i,j} \subseteq \bigcup_{p=0}^{j-1} t_{p,j}.$$

Since B is an ancestor of C (but not of a_j), we have

$$B \overset{*}{\Rightarrow} C\tau$$

for some $\tau \in V^*$. Thus, $C \to \eta \cdot \theta$ must be in

$$predict\left(\bigcup_{p=0}^{j-1} t_{p,j}\right),$$

which completes the proof of (c) and of the theorem. □

Corollary Let G, w, $\mathbf{T}$ be as in Theorem 12.6.1. Then $w \in L(G)$ if and only if $S \to \alpha \cdot$ is in $t_{0,n}$ for some $\alpha \in V^*$.

Proof By the theorem, $S \to \alpha \cdot$ is in $t_{0,n}$ if and only if $S \Rightarrow \alpha \overset{*}{\Rightarrow} a_1 \cdots a_n = w$. □

Corollary Algorithm 12.6.1 is an on-line recognition algorithm.

Note that the algorithm would still work if $*$ were used instead of $\times$. This is true because $*$ preserves consistency, no extra dotted rules can occur, and none will be omitted.

In order to analyze the algorithm we have given, we shall modify it somewhat. The analysis will be simplified by using the $*$ operation in place of the $\times$ operation throughout the algorithm. Basically, this causes chain derivations to be handled as soon as possible, rather than as late as possible. As we remarked earlier, replacement of $\times$ by $*$ preserves the correctness of the algorithm.

We use $\mathbf{t}_j$ to denote the vector that is the jth column of $\mathbf{T}$; that is, the ith component of $\mathbf{t}_j$ is $t_{i,j}$. Union of two vectors, or $*$ of a vector by a scalar, is done componentwise. Algorithm 12.6.1 has been recast into vector notation below.

Algorithm 12.6.2 (*Vector version of Algorithm 12.6.1*)

begin

$$\mathbf{t}_0 := \begin{bmatrix} predict(\{S\}) \\ \emptyset \\ \vdots \\ \emptyset \end{bmatrix};$$

  for $j := 1$ **to** n **do**
  begin
scanner:
    $\mathbf{t}_j := \mathbf{t}_{j-1} * \{a_j\}$;
computer:
    for $k := j-1$ **downto** 0 **do**
      $\mathbf{t}_j := \mathbf{t}_j \cup \mathbf{t}_k * t_{k,j}$;
predictor:

$$t_{j,j} := predict\left(\bigcup_{0 \leqslant i < j} t_{i,j}\right);$$

  end
end.

First, we claim that this algorithm is also correct.

Theorem 12.6.2 Algorithm 12.6.2 is correct in that $A \to \alpha \cdot \beta$ is placed in $t_{i,j}$ if and only if $S \overset{*}{\Rightarrow} a_1 \cdots a_i A \gamma$ for some $\gamma \in V^*$ and $\alpha \overset{*}{\Rightarrow} a_{i+1} \cdots a_j$.

Proof The present algorithm is carrying out the same computation as Algorithm 12.6.1. Therefore, the result follows from Theorem 12.6.1. □

Now let us consider how to implement the "vector" algorithm on a bit-vector machine. For each dotted rule $A \to \alpha \cdot \beta$, let us define

$$\mathbf{t}_j^{(A \to \alpha \cdot \beta)} = \begin{bmatrix} \mathbf{t}_{0,j}^{A \to \alpha \cdot \beta} \\ \vdots \\ \mathbf{t}_{n,j}^{A \to \alpha \cdot \beta} \end{bmatrix}$$

where

$$t_{i,j}^{A \to \alpha \cdot \beta} = \begin{cases} 1 & \text{if } A \to \alpha \cdot \beta \text{ is in } t_{i,j}, \\ 0 & \text{otherwise.} \end{cases}$$

Corresponding to each column $\mathbf{t}_j$ is a sequence of vectors, one for each $t_j^{A \to \alpha \cdot \beta}$.

Example We use our first example again. First, we index all the dotted rules:

0.	$S \to \cdot AB$	6.	$B \to CD \cdot C$
1.	$S \to A \cdot B$	7.	$B \to CDC \cdot$
2.	$S \to AB \cdot$	8.	$C \to \cdot$
3.	$A \to \cdot$	9.	$D \to \cdot a$
4.	$B \to \cdot CDC$	10.	$D \to a \cdot$
5.	$B \to C \cdot DC$		

Then $\mathbf{t}_1$ (the matrix appears after Algorithm 12.6.1) is represented by

$$\mathbf{t}_1 \leftrightarrow \begin{bmatrix} 0 & 0 & 1 & 0 & 0 & 0 & 1 & 1 & 0 & 0 & 1 \\ 0 & 0 & 0 & 0 & 0 & 0 & 0 & 0 & 1 & 0 & 0 \end{bmatrix}.$$

The "one" in the bottom row means that $C \to \cdot$ is in $t_{1,1}$.

Note that the array has two rows and eleven columns. Although the number of columns is large, it depends, in general, on the grammar and not on the size of the input. In example, the row size is $n+1$, where n is the length of the input. Consequently, each column is stored in a bit-vector "word" and we shall use as many words as we have dotted rules.

Next, we must be able to perform operations on this representation of columns.

Lemma 12.6.2 Let $G = (V, \Sigma, P, S)$ be a context-free grammar, let $w = a_1 \cdots a_n$, and let $\mathbf{T} = (t_{ij})$ be the matrix computed by Algorithm 12.6.2. If the columns are represented as above, the following operations may be performed in constant time which is independent of n.

a) Compute the union of $\mathbf{t}_j$ and $\mathbf{t}_k$;

b) Compute a representation of $t_{i,j}$ from $\mathbf{t}_j$;

c) Test whether $A \to \alpha \cdot B\beta$ is in $\mathbf{t}_j$;

d) For any sequence of vectors $\mathbf{Q}$ and any set† R, compute

$$Q * R.$$

Proof Carrying out these computations is a straightforward programming exercise and will be left as Problem 2 at the end of the section. □

We are now ready to analyze the time bound for Algorithm 12.6.2.

Theorem 12.6.3 Algorithm 12.6.2 requires time $\mathcal{O}(n^2)$ when implemented on a bit-vector machine and uses words whose length is n. The algorithm may be implemented on a RAM and takes time $\mathcal{O}(n^3)$.

Proof By Lemma 12.6.2, all the operations used in Algorithm 12.6.2 require only constant time. If it takes time c_0 to compute $\mathbf{t}_0$ and time c_1 to execute the scanner, and time c_2 to execute the completer, then the entire program requires

$$c_0 + \sum_{j=1}^{n} c_1\left(\sum_{k=0}^{j-1} c_2\right) = c_0 + c_1 c_2 \sum_{j=1}^{n} j = \mathcal{O}(n^2).$$

Since only bit vectors of length n are used, one can simulate the whole process on a RAM in time $\mathcal{O}(n^3)$. □

Although the present algorithm seems quite different from the on-line version of the Cocke–Kasami–Younger algorithm, it turns out that the two algorithms are very closely related. The exact correspondence is brought out in the problems at the end of this section.

We now indicate how to use our new type of recognition matrix to parse as well as recognize. The algorithm that follows provides a means of obtaining, from the recognition matrix, a rightmost parse for a given string. The algorithm is similar to that used for the Cocke–Kasami–Younger recognition matrix.

Algorithm 12.6.3 Let $G = (V, \Sigma, P, S)$ be a cycle-free, context-free grammar with the productions designated $\pi_1, \pi_2, \ldots, \pi_p$. Let $w = a_1 a_2 \cdots a_n$, $n \geqslant 0$, be a string, where, for $1 \leqslant i \leqslant n$, $a_i \in \Sigma$; and let $\mathbf{T} = (t_{i,j})$ be the recognition matrix for w constructed by either Algorithm 12.6.1 or 12.6.2.

---

† This is to be interpreted for both the case $R \subseteq V$ and R a set of dotted rules.

Define the recursive procedure $parse(i, j, \pi_m)$ which generates a right parse for $A \Rightarrow \alpha \overset{*}{\Rightarrow} a_{i+1} \cdots a_j$, where $\pi_m = A \to \alpha$, as follows:

procedure $parse(i, j, \pi_m = A \to A_1 A_2 \cdots A_{p_m})$;
begin
  $output(m); j_0 := j$;
  for $\ell := p_m$ **downto** 1 **do**
  if $A_\ell \in \Sigma$
  then $j_0 := j_0 - 1$
  else
  if k is the greatest integer $i \leqslant k \leqslant j_0$ such that for some $\alpha \in V^*$,
    $A_\ell \to \alpha \cdot$ is in t_{k,j_0} and $A \to A_1 A_2 \cdots A_{\ell-1} \cdot A_\ell \cdots A_{p_m}$ is in $t_{i,k}$
    then begin $parse(k, j_0, A_\ell \to \alpha)$;
      $j_0 := k$;
    end;
end;

Output a right parse for w as follows:

main program: **if** for some $\alpha \in V^*$, $S \to \alpha \cdot$ is in $t_{0,n}$
then $parse(0, n, S \to \alpha)$
else *output*("error").

Example Consider the second example of this section with grammar

1. $E \to E * E$
2. $E \to E + E$
3. $E \to a$

and string $w = a + a * a$. Since $E \to E + E \cdot$ is in $t_{0,5}$, $parse(0, 5, \pi_2 = E \to E + E)$ is called, yielding $(2, parse(2, 5, \pi_1 = E \to E * E), parse(0, 1, \pi_3 = E \to a))$. Then $parse(2, 5, \pi_2 = E \to E * E)$ generates $(1, parse(4, 5, \pi_3 = E \to a), parse(2, 3, \pi_3 = E \to a))$, which yields $(1, 3, 3)$. $parse(0, 1, \pi_3 = E \to a)$ yields 3. Thus the output of the algorithm is $(2, 1, 3, 3, 3)$.

If the grammar contains cycles, then Algorithm 12.6.3 may not terminate. However, if we modify the algorithm so that, in the case that some t_{k,j_0} contains two or more dotted rules $A_\ell \to \alpha \cdot$ and $A_\ell \to \gamma \cdot$, we choose the dotted rule that was entered first by Algorithm 12.6.1, it can be shown that Algorithm 12.6.3 always terminates. We leave these details to the reader.

Theorem 12.6.4 Let $G = (V, \Sigma, P, S)$ be a cycle-free context-free grammar with productions designated $\pi_1, \pi_2, \ldots, \pi_p$. If Algorithm 12.6.3 is executed with the string $w = a_1 a_2 \cdots a_n$, $n \geqslant 0$, where, for $1 \leqslant i \leqslant n$, $a_i \in \Sigma$, then the algorithm terminates. If $w \in L(G)$, then the algorithm produces a right parse; otherwise it announces error. The algorithm takes time $\mathcal{O}(n^2)$.

Proof The proof follows that of Theorem 12.4.4. We outline the proof, giving only the details that differ significantly.

Claim 1 Whenever $parse(i, j, \pi_m = A \to \alpha)$ is called, then $j \geqslant i$ and $A \to \alpha \cdot$ is in $t_{i,j}$.

Claim 2 In the sequence of calls on *parse* during the execution of Algorithm 12.6.3, no call *parse*$(i, j, \pi_m = A \to A_1A_2 \cdots A_{p_m})$ generates another call *parse*$(i, j, \pi_m = A \to A_1A_2 \cdots A_{p_m})$.

Proof Given a call *parse*$(i, j, \pi_m = A \to A_1A_2 \cdots A_{p_m})$, each call *parse*$(k, j_0, A_\ell \to \alpha)$ directly generated has the property that $i \leqslant k \leqslant j_0$ and $j_0 \leqslant j$. It follows inductively that this property (namely, that successive values of j are nonincreasing and, for fixed values of j, successive values of i are nondecreasing) is true of the sequence of calls generated by *parse*$(i, j, \pi_m = A \to A_1A_2 \cdots A_{p_m})$. Suppose the call *parse*$(i, j, \pi_m = A \to A_1A_2 \cdots A_{p_m})$ directly generates the call *parse*$(i, j, \pi_r = B \to B_1B_2 \cdots B_{p_r})$. It follows that, for some ℓ, $1 \leqslant \ell \leqslant p_m$, $A_\ell = B$, and that $A \to A_1A_2 \cdots A_{\ell-1} \cdot A_\ell \cdots A_{p_m}$ is in $t_{i,i}$. It follows from Claim 1 and Theorem 12.6.1 that

$$\begin{aligned} A &\Rightarrow A_1A_2 \cdots A_{\ell-1}A_\ell \cdots A_{p_m} \\ &\stackrel{+}{\Rightarrow} A_1A_2 \cdots A_{\ell-1}a_{i+1} \cdots a_j A_{\ell+1} \cdots A_{p_m} \\ &\stackrel{+}{\Rightarrow} a_{i+1} \cdots a_j \end{aligned}$$

and that $A_1A_2 \cdots A_{\ell-1} \stackrel{+}{\Rightarrow} \Lambda$ and $A_{\ell+1} \cdots A_{p_m} \stackrel{+}{\Rightarrow} \Lambda$. Hence, $A \stackrel{+}{\Rightarrow} B$.

Inductively, if *parse*$(i, j, \pi_m = A \to A_1A_2 \cdots A_{p_m})$ generates a call with the same arguments, then $A \stackrel{+}{\Rightarrow} A$, contradicting the fact that G is cycle-free.

Claim 3 *parse*$(i, j, \pi_m = A \to \alpha)$ terminates and produces a right parse of $A \Rightarrow \alpha \stackrel{*}{\Rightarrow} a_{i+1} \cdots a_j$.

Proof Consider the sequence of calls on *parse* during the execution of Algorithm 12.6.3. It follows, from the argument in Claim 2, that the sequence of values for j is nonincreasing and that, for fixed j, the sequence of values for i is nondecreasing. It follows from Claim 1 that $0 \leqslant j$ and $0 \leqslant i$. Consequently, we conclude from Claim 2 that the number of calls is finite. Clearly, if *parse* does not make a call, then it terminates. Therefore the algorithm terminates. The production of a right parse then follows, by a straightforward induction on the number of calls on *parse*.

Claim 4 A call of *parse*$(i, j, \pi_m = A \to \alpha)$ takes at most $c(j-i)^2$ steps for some constant c if $j > i$, and c steps if $j = i$.

Proof We first analyze the number of steps required by the call on *parse*, excluding the recursive calls. The **for** loop is executed, at most, q times, where q is the length of the longest righthand side of a production. For each execution of the **for** loop, if $A_\ell \in \Sigma$, the number of steps is c_3 for some constant c_3. If $A_\ell \in N$, the number of steps, excluding recursive calls, is at most $c_4(j_0 - k + 1)$ for some constant c_4. Since $i \leqslant k$ and $j_0 \leqslant j$ for all values of k and j_0 during the call, the total number of steps, excluding recursive calls, is at most $qc_5(j-i+1)$, where $c_5 = \max(c_3, c_4)$. Since each recursive call has arguments j_0, k such that $i \leqslant k$ and $j_0 \leqslant j$, each recursive call requires at most $qc_5(j-i+1)$ steps, excluding its recursive calls.

By Claim 3, *parse*$(i, j, \pi_m = A \to \alpha)$ produces a right parse of $A \Rightarrow \alpha \stackrel{*}{\Rightarrow} a_{i+1} \cdots a_j$. Let p be the length of that derivation.

By Theorem 12.2.1, if $j = i$, then $p \leqslant c_0$ and if $j > i$, then $p \leqslant c_1(j-i) - c_2$ where c_0, c_1 and c_2 are constants. Since a production index is printed when and only when *parse* is called, this call on *parse* generates at most p recursive calls. Combining results, the total number of steps for the call on *parse* is at most

$$c_0 q c_5 \quad \text{if} \quad j = i$$

and

$$q c_5 (j-i+1)(c_1(j-i) - c_2) \quad \text{if} \quad j > i. \tag{12.6.30}$$

Simplifying Eq. (12.6.30) yields

$$\begin{aligned} qc_5(j-i+1)(c_1(j-i)-c_2) &= qc_5(c_1(j-i)^2 + (c_1-c_2)(j-i) - c_2) \\ &\leqslant qc_5(c_1(j-i)^2 + c_1(j-i)) \\ &\leqslant 2qc_5c_1(j-i)^2. \end{aligned}$$

Letting $c = \max\{c_0qc_5, 2qc_5c_1\}$ completes the claim. □

PROBLEMS

1 Give efficient algorithms for computing $\times$, $*$, and *predict*. Analyze the complexity of these algorithms.

2 Write the programs needed for the proof of Lemma 12.6.2.

3 Prove the following result:

Theorem Let $G = (V, \Sigma, P, S)$ be a context-free grammar in Chomsky normal form. Let $w = a_1 \cdots a_n$, $n \geqslant 0$, and $a_k \in \Sigma$ for $1 \leqslant k \leqslant n$. Let $\mathbf{T} = (t_{ij})$ be the matrix for G computed by Algorithm 12.6.1. Let $\mathbf{T}' = (t'_{ij})$ be the recognition matrix computed by the Cocke–Kasami–Younger algorithm. Then,

$$\{A \mid A \to BC\cdot \quad \text{or} \quad A \to a\cdot \text{ is in } t_{ij}\} \subseteq t'_{ij}$$

for each $0 \leqslant i < j \leqslant n$. In general, the containment is proper.

4 Let $G = (V, \Sigma, P, S)$ be any context-free grammar. We modify Algorithm 12.6.1 by "weakening" the predictor and changing that step of the program to be

$$t_{j,j} := predict(N).$$

Show that the new algorithm still works and is a correct recognizer. [*Hint.* Prove that $A \to \alpha \cdot \beta$ is in $t_{i,j}$ if and only if $\alpha \overset{*}{\Rightarrow} a_{i+1} \cdots a_j$.]

5* Consider the algorithm given in the previous problem. Show that the diagonal may be eliminated from the matrix by a suitable redefinition of $*$ and $\times$. What is the relationship between the resulting algorithm and the Cocke–Kasami–Younger algorithm?

6 Modify Algorithm 12.6.2 by noting that, as n grows, it is efficient to precompute the product of certain columns and q-tuples of sets. Show that such a modification can be made and that the resulting algorithm works.

7 Continuing with Problem 6, choose q so that the algorithm can run in time

$$\mathcal{O}\left(\frac{n^2}{\log n}\right) \text{ on a bit-vector machine,}$$

$$\mathcal{O}\left(\frac{n^3}{\log n}\right) \text{ on a RAM.}$$

8 Let us consider how to recognize a set defined by a 2-pda $A = (Q, \Sigma, \Gamma, \delta, q_0, Z_0, F)$. There is no loss of generality in assuming that A satisfies the conditions of Problem 4 of Section 5.4. Form a square matrix **T** such that (q, Z, q') is in t_{ij} if and only if

$$(q, ¢w\$, i, Z) \overset{*}{\vdash} (q', ¢w\$, j, \Lambda).$$

Note that this matrix is not upper-triangular, in general. Define a suitable product operation, and show that the problem of recognizing whether or not a string is in a 2-pda language L may be reduced to taking the transitive closure of **T**.

9 Show that $\mathbf{T}^+$ of Problem 8 may be computed in time proportional to n^3 and space proportional to n^2 on a RAM.

10 How fast can the operations of Problem 9 be carried out on a Turing machine?

11 What is the computational complexity of recognizing a set accepted by a 2-dpda?

12.7 GENERAL BOUNDS ON TIME AND SPACE FOR LANGUAGE RECOGNITION

We have considered a number of recognition algorithms, and, for each of these, we have computed the time and space requirements. In this section, we shall summarize the least upper bounds and greatest lower bounds now known for the time and memory used in context-free language recognition. These algorithms are sometimes extreme, in that time may be traded for space.

If we let $R(n)$ be the time required to recognize (or parse) a string of length n, then we have the following result:

Theorem 12.7.1 $n \leqslant R(n) \leqslant cBM(n)$.

Proof The upper bound follows from Valiant's algorithm. The lower bound is obvious, since we must read the entire string before giving an answer. □

Let us define $R'(n)$ to be the time required to recognize a string of length n by an *on-line* Turing machine. In this case, we must formulate the problem as in Section 9.4, to prevent the machine from copying the input to a work tape and then proceeding as in an off-line computation.

Theorem 12.7.2 For on-line computation,

$$\frac{n^2}{\log n} \leqslant R'(n) \leqslant \frac{n^3}{\log n} < n^3.$$

Proof The upper bound of n^3 follows from Algorithm 12.6.1 or Algorithm 12.4.2. The $n^3/\log n$ result can be obtained from Problem 7 at the end of Section 12.6. The lower bound is too complicated to be included here, but the idea can be mentioned briefly. Let

$$\Sigma = \{0,1\}, \quad c, s \notin \Sigma,$$

$$L = \{xyzcsu_1s \cdots su_ts \mid t \geqslant 1, x, y, z \in \Sigma^*, \lg(y) > 0, u_j \in \Sigma^* \text{ for } 1 \leqslant j \leqslant t,$$

$$\text{and } u_i = y^T \text{ for some } i, 1 \leqslant i \leqslant t\}.$$

It is interesting to note that L is a linear context-free language. The idea of the proof is to find another set L' (which is not context-free) that has essentially the same recognition time as L. It is possible to show that L' needs at least $n^2/\log n$ time for on-line recognition. □

Corollary There is a single context-free language which requires at least time $\mathcal{O}(n^2/\log n)$ for on-line recognition and can be recognized on-line in time $\mathcal{O}(n^2)$.

Let us now concentrate on the space requirements for recognition. Let $S(n)$ be the space required to recognize a string of length n.

Theorem 12.7.3 $\log n \leqslant S(n)$.

Proof There is no loss of generality in dealing with single-tape Turing machines, because of Theorem 9.4.1. Suppose we have an $L(n)$-tape-bounded, deterministic Turing machine with a read-only input and a single work tape. The instantaneous descriptions (IDs, for short) of such a machine are of the form (q, i, α), where q is a state, α is the portion of the work tape scanned so far, and i is the cell of the work tape being scanned (so $1 \leqslant i \leqslant \lg(\alpha)$). The maximum number of IDs is

$$r(n) = sL(n)t^{L(n)}, \tag{12.7.1}$$

where s is the number of states and $t > 1$ is the cardinality of the work alphabet. Let $C_1, \ldots, C_{r(n)}$ be an enumeration of all IDs. For each $n \geqslant 0$ and each $v \in \Sigma^*$, with $\lg(v) \leqslant n$, define a transition matrix $\mathbf{T}_n(v)$ to be an $r(n) \times r(n)$ matrix whose entries are from the set $\{00, 01, 10, 11\}$. Then $t_{i,j}$ is defined as follows:

1. The first digit of $t_{i,j}$ is 1 if and only if the Turing machine, started in tape configuration C_i while scanning the first cell of $v\$$, can reach ID C_j without moving the input head left out of $v\$$.
2. The second digit of $t_{i,j}$ is 1 if and only if, when started in C_i while scanning the first cell of $v\$$, the device can move the head left out of $v\$$ and can be in ID C_j the first time it does so.

Thus $\mathbf{T}_n(v)$ describes the behavior of the device on v when v is a suffix of the input. Then we have the following useful lemma:

Lemma 12.7.1 If $\lg(uv) \leqslant n$ for some $uv \in L$, where L is the language recognized by a single-tape Turing machine M and for some $v' \in \Sigma^*$, $\mathbf{T}_n(v) = \mathbf{T}_n(v')$, then $uv' \in L$.

Proof The argument is a straightforward "crossing sequence" proof and is omitted. □

Now, consider the language

$$L = \{wcw^T \mid w \in \{0, 1\}^*\}.$$

We shall shortly show that any on-line Turing machine requires at least $\log n$ tape to recognize L.

Let n be a fixed odd integer, and consider all strings in $S = \{0, 1\}^{n(n-1)/2}$.

Claim 1 No two strings in S have the same transition matrix.

Proof Suppose $w, w' \in S$ with $w \neq w'$ and $\mathbf{T}_n(w) = \mathbf{T}_n(w')$. Then $wcw^T \in L$ but, by Lemma 12.7.1, we have

$$wc(w')^T \in L,$$

which is a contradiction. If all such strings have distinct transition matrices and there are $2^{n(n-1)/2}$ such strings but only $4^{(r(n))^2}$ transition matrices, we must have

$$4^{(r(n))^2} \geqslant 2^{n(n-1)/2} \geqslant 2^{(n-1)/2}. \tag{12.7.2}$$

Taking logs of Eq. (12.7.2) yields:

$$2(r(n))^2 \geqslant \frac{n-1}{2}$$

or, using Eq. (12.7.1),

$$4(r(n))^2 = 4(sL(n)t^{L(n)})^2 \geqslant n - 1. \tag{12.7.3}$$

If $n > 1$, then $n - 1 \geqslant n/2$. Also, for all $L(n)$, $t^{L(n)} \geqslant L(n)$, since $t > 1$; so Eq. (12.7.3) becomes:

$$8s^2t^{4L(n)} \geqslant n. \tag{12.7.4}$$

Taking logs of Eq. (12.7.4) yields:

$$\log 8s^2 + 4L(n)\log t \geqslant \log n.$$

Thus

$$L(n) \geqslant \frac{\log n - \log 8s^2}{4 \log t}. \tag{12.7.5}$$

If $n > (8s^2)^2$, then $\log n > 2 \log 8s^2$, so Eq. (12.7.5) becomes:

$$L(n) \geqslant \frac{\log n}{8 \log t}$$

for $n > (8s^2)^2$. Thus, for infinitely many n (all odd $n > (8s^2)^2$), we have

$$L(n) \geqslant c \log n,$$

where $c = 1/(8 \log t)$. Therefore,

$$S(n) \geqslant \log n.$$

We note in passing that L can be recognized in $\log n$ space.

Claim 2 $L = \{wcw^T \mid w \in \{0, 1\}^*\}$ can be recognized in space $\log n$. This completes the proof of Theorem 12.7.3. □

Now we turn to an upper bound for $S(n)$. The next lemma shows a suitable way to "factor" a derivation.

Lemma 12.7.2 Let $G = (V, \Sigma, P, S)$ be a context-free grammar in Chomsky normal form. Let $A \in N$ and $\alpha \in V^3V^*$. If $A \overset{*}{\Rightarrow} \alpha$, then there exist β, γ, δ in V^* and $B \in N$ such that:

$$A \overset{*}{\Rightarrow} \beta B \delta \overset{*}{\Rightarrow} \beta\gamma\delta = \alpha$$

where

$$\left\lfloor \frac{n}{3} \right\rfloor < \lg(\gamma) \leqslant 2 \left\lfloor \frac{n}{3} \right\rfloor$$

and $n = \lg(\alpha)$.

Proof Suppose we have a derivation tree of $A \overset{*}{\Rightarrow} \alpha$. Each node of the tree is to be given a weight by the following procedure:

1 Every leaf has weight 1.

2 Every other node has a weight that is the sum of the weights of its immediate descendants.

Figure 12.23 illustrates a sample derivation and the corresponding labeling of the tree.

Example G is the grammar with productions

$$S \to AS \mid b$$

$$A \to SA \mid a$$

Note that the weight of the root is always n.

Now find a heaviest path s in the tree by starting at the root and taking, at each node, the branch to the heaviest subtree until a leaf is reached. Such a path is marked in Fig. 12.23. A path like s must start at the root with a weight of $n \geqslant 3$ (recall $\alpha \in V^3V^*$) and end at a leaf with weight 1.

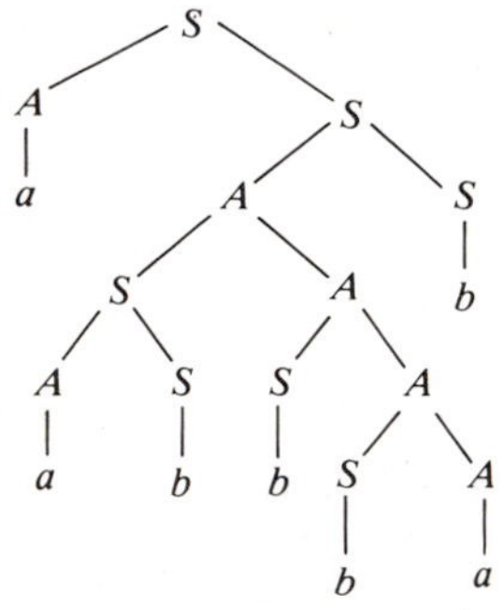

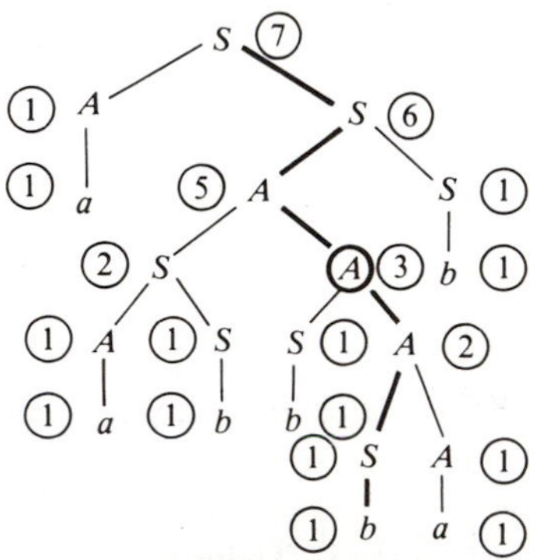

The circled node is the one promised by the lemma.

FIG. 12.23

Now trace up path s until the first node is encountered with weight $> \lfloor n/3 \rfloor$. This node cannot be a leaf, since a leaf has weight

$$1 = \left\lfloor \frac{3}{3} \right\rfloor \leqslant \left\lfloor \frac{n}{3} \right\rfloor.$$

Such a node must exist since the root has weight $n > \lfloor n/3 \rfloor$. As we progress up the path s, the weight at successive nodes will double (at most) since we have a Chomsky normal-form grammar and s is through the heaviest subtrees. Hence, this first node of weight $> \lfloor n/3 \rfloor$ follows a node of weight $\leqslant \lfloor n/3 \rfloor$, and so it itself has weight $\leqslant 2 \lfloor n/3 \rfloor$.

Let B be the label of this node. Its weight is $\lg(\gamma)$, where $A \stackrel{*}{\Rightarrow} \gamma$, and we have just shown that

$$\left\lfloor \frac{n}{3} \right\rfloor < \lg(\gamma) \leqslant 2 \left\lfloor \frac{n}{3} \right\rfloor.$$ □

Now we are in a position to prove a result that gives an upper bound on the space complexity of all context-free languages.

Theorem 12.7.4 Every context-free language can be recognized by a deterministic Turing machine that uses space $S(n) = (\log n)^2$.

Proof Let $L = L(G)$, where $G = (V, \Sigma, P, S)$ is some context-free grammar in Chomsky normal form. Let $N = \{A_1, \ldots, A_m\}$ with $S = A_1$. The construction of the Turing machine is quite complex, so an intuitive version is presented first.

It is necessary to determine whether $A \stackrel{*}{\Rightarrow} \alpha$, where $A \in N$ and $\alpha \in V^*$. If the $\lg(\alpha) \leqslant 3$ (for example), we can determine whether $A \stackrel{*}{\Rightarrow} \alpha$ by precomputing all such information and storing this in the finite-state control of the Turing machine.

If $\lg(\alpha) = k > 3$ and $A \stackrel{*}{\Rightarrow} \alpha$, then there exist $B \in N$, $\beta, \gamma, \delta \in V^*$, such that

$$A \stackrel{*}{\Rightarrow} \beta B \delta \Rightarrow \beta\gamma\delta = \alpha$$

where

$$\left\lfloor \frac{k}{3} \right\rfloor \leqslant \lg(\gamma) \leqslant 2 \left\lfloor \frac{k}{3} \right\rfloor.$$

The determination of $A \stackrel{*}{\Rightarrow} \alpha$ can be reduced to determining whether $B \stackrel{*}{\Rightarrow} \gamma$ and $A \stackrel{*}{\Rightarrow} \beta B \delta$.

Thus, to determine whether $A \stackrel{*}{\Rightarrow} \alpha$, the Turing machine will, for each $B \in N$ and each possible factorization of $\alpha = \beta\gamma\delta$ with $\lfloor k/3 \rfloor < \lg(\gamma) \leqslant 2 \lfloor k/3 \rfloor$, attempt the subproblem $B \stackrel{*}{\Rightarrow} \gamma$. If the subproblem is solved successfully, then the algorithm will attempt the complementary subproblem $A \stackrel{*}{\Rightarrow} \beta B \delta$. Since

$$\lg(\gamma) > \left\lfloor \frac{k}{3} \right\rfloor,$$

it follows that

$$\lg(\gamma) \geqslant \frac{k+1}{3},$$

and hence

$$\begin{aligned}\lg(\beta B\delta) &= \lg(\beta\gamma\delta) - \lg(\gamma) + \lg(B)\\ &\leqslant k - \frac{k+1}{3} + 1\\ &= \frac{2k+2}{3},\end{aligned}$$

since we also know that

$$\lg(\gamma) \leqslant 2\left\lfloor \frac{k}{3} \right\rfloor \leqslant \frac{2k}{3}.$$

Thus, if the original goal is of size $k = \lg(\alpha)$, then all possible subgoals are of size $\leqslant (2k+2)/3$. For $k \geqslant 3$,

$$2 = 2\cdot 1 \leqslant 2\cdot\frac{k}{3}$$

so

$$\frac{2k+2}{3} \leqslant \frac{2k+\frac{2}{3}k}{3} = \frac{8k}{9}.$$

Thus we have proved:

Claim 1 For $k \geqslant 3$, any goal of size k has all of its subgoals of size at most $\frac{8}{9}k$.

Next, we compute the number of levels of subgoals to break down the problem to one of size $\leqslant 3$.

Claim 2 The number p of levels of subgoals needed to bring the problem down to size $\leqslant 3$ satisfies

$$p \leqslant c \log_2 n,$$

where $c = 1/(\log_2(\frac{9}{8}))$.

Proof of Claim 2 After p levels, the goal of size k has been broken into subgoals of size $\leqslant (\frac{8}{9})^p k$. If we set this $\leqslant 3$ and take logs, we get

$$p \leqslant \frac{\log_2 k}{\log_2(\frac{9}{8})} = c\log_2 k.$$

To solve the problem at hand for an input of length n will require $O(\log n)$ space to record each current subgoal, and there will be $O(\log n)$ such subgoals, leading to a total bound of $O((\log n)^2)$.

The work tape is divided into blocks of

$$\lfloor \log n \rfloor + 1 \quad \text{cells.}$$

Each such block is long enough to contain a binary number from 0 to n. Imagine the tape split horizontally into channels or tracks. The top track of block i contains an integer denoted by *begin*(i). The second track contains an integer denoted by *end*(i). The third track contains an integer *size*(i). The fourth track contains a variable

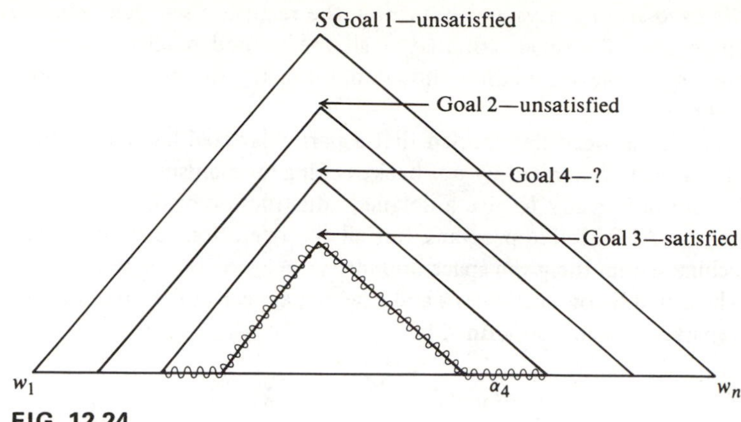

FIG. 12.24

called *variable(i)* (right justified) and a boolean variable (or bit) *sat(i)* (for satisfied). There are some other tracks to handle arithmetic and comparison operations as needed.

The meaning of the ith block can now be explained. Its purpose is to record information as to whether

$$variable(i) \overset{*}{\Rightarrow} \alpha_i \overset{*}{\Rightarrow} w_{begin(i)} \cdots w_{end(i)}$$

where $size(i) = \lg(\alpha_i)$ and each $w_k \in \Sigma$ for $begin(i) \leqslant k \leqslant end(i)$. Also

$$sat(i) = \begin{cases} true & \text{if } variable(i) \overset{*}{\Rightarrow} \alpha_i \text{ is known to be true,} \\ false & \text{otherwise.} \end{cases}$$

The approach we shall use is to break up a possible derivation of $S \overset{*}{\Rightarrow} w_1 \cdots w_n$ into subderivations of nearly equal parts. If $sat(i) = false$, then all succeeding blocks are partitions of the second half of the derivation, i.e., the inner subtree. If $sat(i) = true$, then subsequent blocks deal with the outer subtree. This is exemplified in Fig. 12.24.

The algorithm to be given is quite complicated. We wish to determine whether $S \overset{*}{\Rightarrow} w$, and we generalize that to the consideration of whether $A \overset{*}{\Rightarrow} w'$. If $\lg(w') \leqslant 3$, then table lookup is used; otherwise, we use recursion. The algorithm starts with the goal of determining whether $S \overset{*}{\Rightarrow} \alpha_1 = w$. An elaborate backtracking is begun, and w is factored into $\beta_1\gamma_1\delta_1$, where

$$\left\lfloor \frac{n}{3} \right\rfloor < \lg(\gamma_1) \leqslant 2\left\lfloor \frac{n}{3} \right\rfloor;$$

and a variable B_1 is stored into block 1 to indicate that it is possible that $B \overset{*}{\Rightarrow} \gamma_1$. Then γ_1 is stored by writing pointers to the first and last symbols of the input. (Since these input positions are between 1 and n, $\log n$ space is sufficient.) The determination of $B_1 \overset{*}{\Rightarrow} \gamma_1$ will be done recursively.

Now the process is continued on the subgoal in a similar fashion. There are several points which are different however. Subsequent α_i's may have several variables. For each α_i, we record the first and last indices of the subword of the input derived from α_i.

We have also been vague about how the recursion will take place, since that requires space also. The space for that is all the unused blocks to the right of the present one. A simple calculation shows that exactly the correct number of them exists at any time.

When it has been determined that a particular goal has failed, then the next case is systematically generated by our backtracking mechanism.

We are now ready to give a detailed construction of the device. The device is described by an ALGOL-like program, but all the operations can be carried out on a Turing machine within the given space bounds.

There will be two variables s and s' which appear in the program. Assume that these are separate procedures defined by:

$$s = size(i) - \sum_{k=i+1}^{j} (size(k) - 1)$$

and

$$s' = size(i) - \sum_{k=i+1}^{j-1} (size(k) - 1).$$

Every time that s and s' appear, imagine that they are recomputed.

In understanding the program, i is the last block for which $sat(i) = false$ and j is the last block. j may decrease, but it always is the case that $1 \leqslant i \leqslant j$.

begin

step_0: $i := 1$;
$j := 1$;
$begin(1) := 1$;
$end(1) := n$;
comment n may be computed on a first pass through the input;
$size(1) := n$;
$variable(1) := A_1$;
comment $A_1 = S$;
$sat(1) := false$;
if $n \leqslant 3$ and $variable(1) \overset{*}{\Rightarrow} a_1 \cdots a_n$ **then accept**;
comment The only goal here is to determine if $S \overset{*}{\Rightarrow} \alpha_1 = w$;

step_1: **comment** We are working on goal i and have finished subgoals $i+1, \ldots, j$. Each successfully completed subgoal k, $i+1 \leqslant k \leqslant j$ has established that size(k) symbols in α_i can be replaced by variable(k). Also s is the length of α_i after these replacements have been made;
if $s \leqslant 3$ **then goto** step_6;
comment We can test if goal i can be satisfied directly. Otherwise, a new subgoal must be built;
$j := j + 1$;
$begin(j) := begin(i)$;
$end(j) := begin(i) - 1$;
$size(j) := 0$;
$variable(j) := A_m$;

```
step_2:   comment advance the end pointers of subgoal j;
          repeat
              if end(j) = end(i) then goto step_3;
              end(j) := end(j) + 1;
              if (end(j) = begin(k)) and sat(k) for some† k, j − 1 ≥ k ≥ 1
                  then end(j) = end(k);
              size(j) := size(j) + 1;
          until size(j) > ⌊s'/3⌋ ;
          if size(j) > 2⌊s'/3⌋ then goto step_3;
          i := j;
          sat(i) := false;
          goto step_1;
step_3:   comment advance begin pointer for subgoal j;
          if begin(j) = begin(k) and sat(k) for some† k, j − 1 ≥ k ≥ 1
              then begin(j) := end(k);
          if begin(j) ≠ end(i) then
              begin
                  end(j) := begin(j);
                  begin(j) := end(j) + 1;
                  size(j) := 0;
                  goto step_2
              end;
step_4:   comment advance the variable stored in block j and continue back-
                  tracking;
          if variable(j) = A_k and (k > 1) then
              begin
                  variable(j) := A_{k-1};
                  begin(j) := begin(i);
                  end(j) := begin(i) − 1;
                  size(j) := 0;
                  goto step_2
              end;
step_5:   comment back up on block j;
          if (j = 2) and (i = 1) then quit;
          comment the above condition means that w is not in L;
          j := j − 1;
          repeat i := i − 1 until not sat(i);
          comment goal i has failed and we backtrack to a previous goal.
                  Since not sat(1) this will always work;
          goto step_2;
```

† Count downwards so the largest such k is used.

```
step_6:   comment The subgoal is now so small that it can be done with a direct
                    test;
          r := 0;
          q := begin(i);
          while q ≤ end(i) do
          begin
              if q = begin(k) for some† k, j ≥ k ≥ 1 and sat(k) then
              begin
                  a_{r+1} := var(k);
                  q := end(k)
              end
          else a_{r+1} := w_q;
          r := r + 1;
          q := q + 1;
          end;
          if var(i) ⇏* a_1 ··· a_r then
                                  begin
                                      i := i − 1;
                                      goto step_2
                                  end;
          comment If the test fails then we must continue backtracking. Whenever
                    we get here r = s ≤ 3 and the predicate may be checked in
                    the finite state control;
          if i = 1 then accept
          else
              begin
                  j := i;
                  repeat i := i − 1 until not sat(i);
                  sat(j) := true;
                  goto step_1;
              end
          end.
```

The tasks of showing that the program works and that only $\log^2 n$ storage is used on a Turing machine are left to the reader. □

Combining previous results leads to the following proposition.

Theorem 12.7.5 $\log n \leq S(n) \leq \log^2(n)$.

The situation for on-line tape bounds is quite simple.

Theorem 12.7.6 In the on-line case,

$$S'(n) = n.$$

Proof Note that we may copy the input on a work tape and use the upper bound of Theorem 12.7.3 for recognition. Thus, $S'(n) \leq n$.

---

† Count downwards so the largest k is used.

To handle the lower bound, again let

$$L = \{wcw^T \mid w \in \{0, 1\}^*\}.$$

There are 2^n words of length n for w such that $wcw^T \in L$. The ID's of the Turing machine when scanning the c must be different; otherwise we would accept wcw^T and $wc(w')^T$ when $w \neq w'$. But the number of different ID's would be

$$r(n) = sL(n)t^{L(n)} \geqslant 2^n.$$

By an analysis similar to that in the proof of Theorem 12.7.3, we find that

$$L(n) \geqslant n.$$

Thus, $S'(n) \geqslant n$, and therefore $S'(n) = n$. □

PROBLEMS

1 Give the best time bound you can for the recognition of any 2-pda language on a deterministic Turing machine with a single work tape and a read-only input tape.

2 Show that there exist nonregular context-free languages that can be accepted by a tape-bounded Turing machine which uses space $S(n) = \log\log(n)$.

3 Show that, if a language L is recognizable using space $S(n)$, and if

$$\inf_{n \to \infty} \frac{S(n)}{\log\log(n)} = 0,$$

then L is a regular set.

4 Show that it is recursively undecidable how much tape is required to recognize a nonregular context-free language. [*Hint.* Find a nonregular context-free language L_0 such that L_0 is recognizable in space $\log n$ if $L_1 \cap L_2 \neq \emptyset$, and in space $\log\log(n)$ if $L_1 \cap L_2 = \emptyset$, where L_1 and L_2 are variants of $L(\mathbf{x})$ and $L(\mathbf{y})$ of Section 8.3.

5* Show that for every nonregular, deterministic context-free language L, recognizing L or $\bar{L} = \Sigma^* - L$ requires space $\log(n)$ on a nondeterministic Turing machine.

6 Show that the language L defined in the proof of Theorem 12.7.6 can be recognized in linear time on a RAM.

7 Let $R(n)$ be the time required to test whether a string $w \in \Sigma^n$ is in L, where L is a context-free language. Let $CBM(n)$ be the time required to *check* whether $\mathbf{AB} = \mathbf{C}$ where $\mathbf{A}$, $\mathbf{B}$, and $\mathbf{C}$ are $n \times n$ boolean matrices. Show that

$$R(n) \geqslant \sqrt{CBM(n)}.$$

[*Hint.* Design a context-free language $L(\mathbf{A}, \mathbf{B}, \mathbf{C})$ whose complement consists of strings which represent that $\mathbf{A}$, $\mathbf{B}$, and $\mathbf{C}$ are $n \times n$ matrices and $\mathbf{AB} = \mathbf{C}$. Note that the time to recognize $L(\mathbf{A}, \mathbf{B}, \mathbf{C})$ and its complement is the same. Moreover, a reasonable encoding of $\bar{L}(\mathbf{A}, \mathbf{B}, \mathbf{C})$ is of order n^2, so that

$$CBM(n) \leqslant R(n^2) \leqslant (R(n))^2,$$

so

$$R(n) \geqslant \sqrt{CBM(n)}.$$

Describe $L(\mathbf{A}, \mathbf{B}, \mathbf{C})$, and show that it is a context-free language.

8 Based on Problem 7, devise a new context-free language $L(\mathbf{A}, \mathbf{B})$ which depends only on two $n \times n$ boolean matrices **A** and **B**. Show how an *on-line* recognizer for $L(\mathbf{A}, \mathbf{B})$ may be used to compute $\mathbf{AB} = \mathbf{C}$.

9 Using Problem 8, it follows that the time required by an on-line RAM to recognize a context-free language is:

$$R'(n) \geq \sqrt{BM'(n)}$$

where $BM'(n)$ is the time required to compute the boolean product of two matrices "on-line" (i.e., the jth column of the product is computed before the $j + 1$ column of **B** is read).

10 Write a recursive program to implement the algorithm given in the proof of Theorem 12.7.4.

12.8 HISTORICAL SURVEY

Theorem 12.2.1 is well known in one form or another. Our particularly sharp proof is due to A. Yehudai. Greibach [1973] found a hardest context-free language first. Problem 6 of Section 12.2 is from the work of Sudborough [1976]. The particular algorithm for multiplying 2×2 matrices used in Lemma 12.3.1 is credited to Winograd by Fischer and Probert [1974]. Strassen [1969] was the first to find an $n^{2.81}$ algorithm for the multiplication of $n \times n$ matrices. Problem 6 of Section 12.3 is from Warshall [1962]. The Cocke–Kasami–Younger algorithm may be found in many places, such as Kasami [1965] and Younger [1967]. Our version (and much of this chapter) derives from Graham and Harrison [1976].

Problem 8 of Section 12.4 is due to Taniguchi and Kasami [1969]. The hint given follows an unpublished construction of W.L. Ruzzo.

Section 12.5 derives from Valiant [1975]. The detailed proof of the key lemma is due to W.L. Ruzzo. Section 12.6 presents a new algorithm reported in Graham, Harrison, and Ruzzo [1976]. This algorithm in its simplest form is an adaptation of Earley's algorithm [1970]. The connection between this algorithm and the Cocke–Kasami–Younger algorithm is deeper than is hinted at in the problems of Section 12.6. Problem 8 is due to W.L. Ruzzo again.

The lower bound of Theorem 12.7.2 is due to Gallaire [1965]. Theorem 12.7.4 is due to Lewis, Stearns, and Hartmanis [1965]. Our proof is an adaptation of a "program" written by Ronald Hunsinger. Problem 5 of Section 12.7 is due to Alt and Mehlhorn [1975]. Problem 9 is due to Ruzzo.

thirteen

LR(*k*) Grammars and Languages

13.1 INTRODUCTION

In Chapter 12, we learned a variety of ways to parse general context-free languages. Such methods are not usually used in compiler construction because they require at best superlinear time. In practice, one wants a linear-time method and, moreover, one cannot tolerate large constants. An important class of grammars is known, called $LR(k)$ grammars, which have the property that they can be parsed in linear time. Also, the grammar class is large enough to allow us to accommodate "natural grammars" for programming languages. Any deterministic language has an $LR(k)$ grammar so that the family of languages is nontrivial and has desirable practical properties such as unambiguity.

In the next section, the basic definition of an $LR(k)$ grammar is presented. It is shown that every strict deterministic language is $LR(0)$ and that every deterministic language is $LR(1)$. In Section 13.3, an important characterization theorem for $LR(0)$ languages is proved.

Section 13.4 begins the treatment of parsing by defining table-driven LR-style parsers. Section 13.5 is a highly technical treatment of the generation of sets of $LR(k)$ items. In Section 13.6, consistency of a set of items is introduced. It is then possible to construct $LR(k)$ parsers and to prove exactly how they operate. Section 13.8 concludes by showing that $\Delta_0 = LR$.

13.2 BASIC DEFINITIONS AND PROPERTIES OF $LR(k)$ GRAMMARS

We are about to introduce $LR(k)$ grammars. In order to study this family, it is convenient to work with "handles" of canonical (or rightmost) sentential forms.

Definition Let $G = (V, \Sigma, P, S)$ be a context-free grammar and let $\gamma \in V^*$. A *handle* of γ is an ordered pair (ρ, i), where $\rho \in P$ and $i \geqslant 0$ such that there exist $A \in N$, $\alpha, \beta \in V^*$, and $w \in \Sigma^*$, such that:

i) $S \overset{*}{\underset{R}{\Rightarrow}} \alpha A w \underset{R}{\Rightarrow} \alpha\beta w = \gamma$

ii) ρ is $A \to \beta$

iii) $i = \lg(\alpha\beta)$.

Examples Let G_1 be the grammar

$$S \to aB \mid ab$$

$$B \to b$$

The string $\gamma = ab$ has handle $(S \to ab, 2)$ by the derivation

$$S \underset{R}{\Rightarrow} ab$$

On the other hand, γ has handle $(B \to b, 2)$ by derivation

$$S \underset{R}{\Rightarrow} aB \underset{R}{\Rightarrow} ab$$

Consider grammar G_2 shown below:

$$S \to Aa \mid aA$$

$$A \to a$$

The canonical sentential form $\gamma = aa$ has handles $(A \to a,\ 1)$ and $(A \to a,\ 2)$, as the reader may verify.

The idea behind an $LR(k)$ grammar is that a parsing device is reading some canonical sentential form. We wish the device to work by finding the handle $(A \to \beta, i)$ and replacing β by A. This gives a new canonical sentential form and the action is repeated. In order for this to work, our grammar must have the property that the handle is uniquely determined by what we have read up to now and by the next k characters ahead. The formal definition that follows says just this.

Definition 13.2.1 Let $k \geqslant 0$ and $G = (V, \Sigma, P, S)$ be a reduced context-free grammar such that $S \overset{+}{\underset{R}{\Rightarrow}} S$ is impossible in G. G is $LR(k)$ if, for each $w, w', x \in \Sigma^*$; $\gamma, \alpha, \alpha', \beta, \beta' \in V^*, A, A' \in N$, if

i) $S \overset{*}{\underset{R}{\Rightarrow}} \alpha A w \underset{R}{\Rightarrow} \alpha\beta w = \gamma w$ (That is, γw has handle $(A \to \beta, \lg(\alpha\beta))$.)

ii) $S \overset{*}{\underset{R}{\Rightarrow}} \alpha' A' x \underset{R}{\Rightarrow} \alpha'\beta' x = \gamma w'$ (That is, $\gamma w'$ has handle $(A' \to \beta', \lg(\alpha'\beta'))$.)

iii)† ${}^{(k)}w = {}^{(k)}w'$

then iv) $(A \to \beta, \lg(\alpha\beta)) = (A' \to \beta', \lg(\alpha'\beta'))$.

Example The grammar G_3 shown below is $LR(0)$.

$$S \to aAc$$

$$A \to Abb \mid b$$

---

† Recall that ${}^{(k)}w$ denotes the first k letters of w if $\lg(w) \geqslant k$, and all of w otherwise.

At this stage, we have not yet learned efficient tests for the $LR(0)$ property. We must enumerate all canonical sentential forms and verify that they have unique handles. The canonical sentential forms are listed below along with the corresponding handles.

Canonical Sentential Forms	Handles
aAc	$(S \to aAc, 3)$
$aAb^{2i}c$	$(A \to Abb, 4)$
$ab^{2i+1}c$	$(A \to b, 2)$

Note that $L(G_3) = \{ab^{2i+1}c \mid i \geqslant 0\}$.

Now let us consider a new grammar G_4, which generates the same language. G_4 consists of:

$$S \to aAc$$
$$A \to bAb \mid b$$

Consider the canonical sentential forms

$$abc \qquad \text{and} \qquad abbbc.$$

The first form has handle $(A \to b, 2)$, while the second one has handle $(A \to b, 3)$; yet, when we look back, we see $\gamma = ab$ and the same lookahead string, namely, Λ. Therefore, G_4 is not $LR(0)$.

The conclusion in Definition 13.2.1, that is, (iv), has several implications.

1 By the definition of equality of ordered pairs, we have $A = A'$, $\beta = \beta'$, and $\lg(\alpha\beta) = \lg(\alpha'\beta')$.

2 $\gamma = {}^{(\lg(\gamma))}\alpha'\beta' = {}^{(\lg(\alpha\beta))}\alpha'\beta' = {}^{(\lg(\alpha'\beta'))}\alpha'\beta' = \alpha'\beta'$. Thus, $\gamma = \alpha\beta = \alpha'\beta'$.

3 Since $\beta = \beta'$, from (2) we have $\alpha = \alpha'$.

4 $\alpha'\beta'x = \gamma w'$ implies $\alpha'\beta'x = \alpha'\beta'w'$ implies $x = w'$.

Note that, if G is $LR(k)$, then G is $LR(k')$ for all $k' \geqslant k$.

One of the properties that we wish a grammatical class to possess, in order that it constitute a useful class for parsing, is *unambiguity*. We show that the $LR(k)$ grammars are unambiguous.

The first lemma gives an equivalent formulation for equality of handles. This lemma does not require that the grammar be $LR(k)$.

Lemma 13.2.1 Let $G = (V, \Sigma, P, S)$ be a reduced context-free grammar. Assume that for $\alpha, \alpha', \beta, \beta' \in V^*$; $w, w' \in \Sigma^+$; $A, A' \in N$,

$$S \overset{*}{\underset{R}{\Rightarrow}} \alpha A w \underset{R}{\Rightarrow} \alpha\beta w$$

and

$$S \overset{*}{\underset{R}{\Rightarrow}} \alpha' A' w' \underset{R}{\Rightarrow} \alpha'\beta' w' = \alpha\beta w$$

Then, $\alpha A w = \alpha' A' w'$ if and only if

$$(A \to \beta, \lg(\alpha\beta)) = (A' \to \beta', \lg(\alpha'\beta')).$$

Proof Assume that:

$$(A \to \beta, \lg(\alpha\beta)) = (A' \to \beta', \lg(\alpha'\beta')).$$

Since $\alpha'\beta'w' = \alpha\beta w$ and $\lg(\alpha\beta) = \lg(\alpha'\beta')$, we have $\alpha\beta = \alpha'\beta'$ and $w = w'$. Since $\beta = \beta'$, we have $\alpha = \alpha'$. Also, $A = A'$. Thus, $\alpha A w = \alpha' A' w'$.

Conversely, assume that $\alpha A w = \alpha' A' w'$. By our quantification, since A and A' are the rightmost nonterminals in $\alpha A w$ and $\alpha' A' w'$, respectively, we have $A = A'$, $\alpha = \alpha'$, and $w = w'$. Since $\alpha\beta w = \alpha'\beta' w'$, we have $\beta = \beta'$. Thus,

$$(A \to \beta, \lg(\alpha\beta)) = (A' \to \beta', \lg(\alpha'\beta')). \qquad \square$$

The second lemma characterizes unambiguous grammars in terms of handles.

Lemma 13.2.2 Let $G = (V, \Sigma, P, S)$ be a reduced context-free grammar. Then G is unambiguous if and only if every canonical sentential form has exactly one handle except S, which has none.

Proof Assume that G is unambiguous.

Claim 1 S has no handle.

Proof Assume, for the sake of contradiction, that S has some handle. Then, for some $\alpha \in V^*$ and $w \in \Sigma^+$, $n \geqslant 0$, $m \geqslant 1$, since G is reduced, we have

$$S \underset{R}{\overset{n}{\Rightarrow}} \alpha \underset{R}{\Rightarrow} S \underset{R}{\overset{m}{\Rightarrow}} w$$

and also

$$S \underset{R}{\overset{m}{\Rightarrow}} w$$

Thus G is clearly ambiguous and we have a contradiction. Therefore S has no handle.

Claim 2 Every canonical sentential form except S has at least one handle.

Proof This follows directly from the definition of a canonical sentential form.

Claim 3 Every canonical sentential form except S has at most one handle.

Proof Assume, for the sake of contradiction, that this is not true. Then we have, for $\alpha, \alpha', \beta, \beta'' \in V^*$, $w, w', x \in \Sigma^*$, $\sigma, \sigma' \in P$, $\rho, \rho', \rho'' \in P^*$, $A, A' \in N$,

$$S \underset{R}{\overset{\rho'}{\Rightarrow}} \alpha A w \underset{R}{\overset{\sigma}{\Rightarrow}} \alpha\beta w \underset{R}{\overset{\rho}{\Rightarrow}} x$$

$$S \underset{R}{\overset{\rho''}{\Rightarrow}} \alpha' A' w' \underset{R}{\overset{\sigma'}{\Rightarrow}} \alpha'\beta' w' = \alpha\beta w \overset{\rho}{\Rightarrow} x$$

where $(A \to \beta, \lg(\alpha\beta)) \neq (A' \to \beta', \lg(\alpha'\beta'))$. Since G is unambiguous, $\rho'\sigma\rho = \rho''\sigma'\rho$. It follows that $\rho' = \rho''$; thus $\alpha A w = \alpha' A' w'$. Therefore, by Lemma 13.2.1, $(A \to \beta, \lg(\alpha\beta)) = (A' \to \beta', \lg(\alpha'\beta'))$, giving us a contradiction. Thus, every canonical sentential form except S has at most one handle.

Conversely, assume that every canonical sentential form has exactly one handle except S, which has none. Assume for the sake of contradiction that G is ambiguous. Then there exist m, n, $m \geqslant n \geqslant 1$, α_i, $\alpha_j' \in V^*$ for $0 \leqslant i \leqslant n$, $0 \leqslant j \leqslant m$, $w \in \Sigma^*$, and distinct derivations of w in G

$$S = \alpha_0 \underset{R}{\Rightarrow} \alpha_1 \cdots \underset{R}{\Rightarrow} \alpha_n = w$$

$$S = \alpha_0' \underset{R}{\Rightarrow} \alpha_1' \underset{R}{\Rightarrow} \cdots \underset{R}{\Rightarrow} \alpha_m' = w$$

We show how these derivations differ.

Claim There exists some i, $1 \leqslant i \leqslant n$, such that $\alpha_{n-i} \neq \alpha'_{m-i}$.

Proof Assume, for the sake of contradiction, that $\alpha_{n-i} = \alpha'_{m-i}$ for $1 \leqslant i \leqslant n$. If $m = n$, the two derivations are not distinct; therefore $m > n$. It follows that $\alpha_0 = \alpha'_{m-n}$, where $m - n \neq 0$. We know that $\alpha'_{m-n-1} \underset{R}{\Rightarrow} \alpha'_{m-n}$, so $\alpha'_{m-n} = S$ has a handle, which is contradiction.

We now let j, $1 \leqslant j \leqslant n$, be the smallest integer such that $\alpha_{n-j} \neq \alpha'_{m-j}$. It follows that $\alpha_{n-j+1} = \alpha'_{m-j+1}$. Since every canonical sentential form has at most one handle, Lemma 13.2.1 gives us that $\alpha_{n-j} = \alpha'_{m-j}$, which is a contradiction. □

Now we shall apply these results to verify that every $LR(k)$ grammar is unambiguous.

Theorem 13.2.1 Let $G = (V, \Sigma, P, S)$ be an $LR(k)$ grammar, $k \geqslant 0$. Then G is unambiguous.

Proof Assume, for the sake of contradiction, that $G = (V, \Sigma, P, S)$, an $LR(k)$ grammar, is ambiguous. By Lemma 13.2.2, we have either:

1 S has a handle;

2 some canonical sentential form besides S has no handle; or

3 some canonical sentential form has more than one handle.

CASE 1. Suppose S has a handle. Then, for some $\alpha \in V^*$, $x \in \Sigma^*$, we have

$$S \underset{R}{\overset{*}{\Rightarrow}} \alpha \underset{R}{\Rightarrow} S \underset{R}{\overset{*}{\Rightarrow}} x$$

Thus $S \underset{R}{\overset{+}{\Rightarrow}} S$ in G. But this contradicts the fact that G is $LR(k)$.

CASE 2. Assume that some canonical sentential form besides S has no handle. This is impossible, by the definition of a canonical sentential form.

CASE 3. Assume that some canonical sentential form has more than one handle. We have, for $\gamma, \alpha, \beta, \alpha', \beta' \in V^*$; $w, w' \in \Sigma^+$; $A, A' \in N$,

$$S \underset{R}{\overset{*}{\Rightarrow}} \alpha A w \underset{R}{\Rightarrow} \alpha\beta w = \gamma w$$

$$S \underset{R}{\overset{*}{\Rightarrow}} \alpha' A' w' \underset{R}{\Rightarrow} \alpha'\beta' w' = \alpha\beta w = \gamma w$$

where $(A \to \beta, \lg(\alpha\beta)) \neq (A' \to \beta', \lg(\alpha'\beta'))$.

Now, we know that ${}^{(k)}w = {}^{(k)}w'$. Thus, since G is $LR(k)$, $(A \to \beta, \lg(\alpha\beta)) = (A' \to \beta', \lg(\alpha'\beta'))$. But this is a contradiction. □

The following lemma tells us when a grammar is not $LR(k)$. Consequently the lemma is often useful in proofs by contradiction.

Lemma 13.2.3 Let $k \geqslant 0$ and $G = (V, \Sigma, P, S)$ be a reduced context-free grammar such that $S \underset{R}{\overset{+}{\Rightarrow}} S$ is impossible in G. G is not $LR(k)$ if and only if there exist $w, w', x \in \Sigma^*$; $A, A' \in N$; $\gamma', \gamma, \alpha, \alpha', \beta, \beta' \in V^*$, such that

i) $S \underset{R}{\overset{*}{\Rightarrow}} \alpha A w \underset{R}{\Rightarrow} \alpha\beta w = \gamma w$

ii) $S \underset{R}{\overset{*}{\Rightarrow}} \alpha' A' x \underset{R}{\Rightarrow} \alpha'\beta' x = \gamma' x = \gamma w'$

iii) ${}^{(k)}w = {}^{(k)}w'$

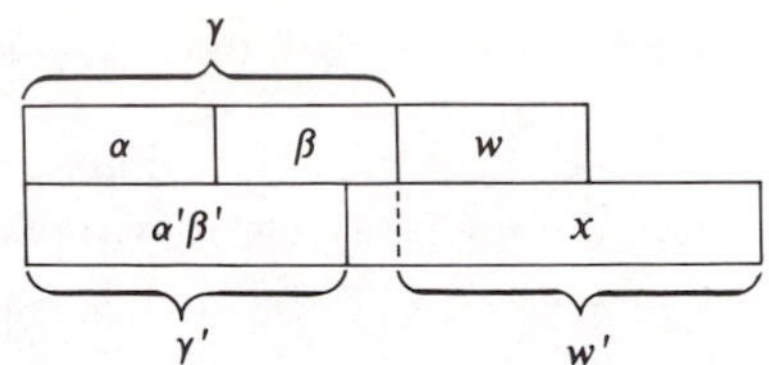

FIG. 13.1 The relations between the strings.

and iv) $(A \to \beta, \lg(\alpha\beta)) \neq (A' \to \beta', \lg(\alpha'\beta'))$, with

v) $\lg(\alpha'\beta') \geq \lg(\alpha\beta)$.

Proof If (i) through (v) hold, G is clearly not $LR(k)$. Conversely, assume that G is not $LR(k)$. Then, clearly, (i) through (iv) hold.

Suppose

$$\text{v}')\ \lg(\gamma') = \lg(\alpha'\beta') < \lg(\alpha\beta) = \lg(\gamma).$$

We shall show how, by reversing (i) and (ii), we can satisfy (v).

Figure 13.1 illustrates the relationships between the strings in (i) and (ii).

Now, let $y = {}^{(\lg(\gamma)-\lg(\gamma'))}x$. Clearly, $y \in \Sigma^*$. We now have, for $x, y, w \in \Sigma^*$; $\gamma', \alpha', \alpha, \beta', \beta \in V$, $A', A \in N$,

$$\text{i}')\ S \overset{*}{\underset{R}{\Rightarrow}} \alpha' A' x \underset{R}{\Rightarrow} \alpha'\beta' x = \gamma' x$$

From (i) we have:

$$\text{ii}')\ S \overset{*}{\underset{R}{\Rightarrow}} \alpha A w \underset{R}{\Rightarrow} \alpha\beta w = \gamma' y w$$

From (iii), we see that:

$$^{(k)}x = {}^{(k)}yw' = {}^{(k)}yw$$

Thus iii') $^{(k)}x = {}^{(k)}yw$

From (iv), we get:

$$\text{iv}')\ (A' \to \beta', \lg(\alpha'\beta')) \neq (A \to \beta, \lg(\alpha\beta)).$$

Thus (i') through (v') satisfy our lemma. □

The following theorem will be extremely useful in studying the class of $LR(0)$ languages. It is an inductive version of the definition of an $LR(k)$ grammar.

Theorem 13.2.2 (*Extended LR(k) theorem*) Suppose $G = (V, \Sigma, P, S)$ is an $LR(k)$ grammar and there exist $\alpha \in V^*; x_1, x_2, w \in \Sigma^*$, such that

i) $S \overset{*}{\underset{R}{\Rightarrow}} \alpha x_1 \overset{+}{\underset{R}{\Rightarrow}} w x_1$

ii) $S \overset{+}{\underset{R}{\Rightarrow}} w x_2$

iii) $^{(k)}x_1 = {}^{(k)}x_2$

iv) $x_2 \neq \Lambda$, $k > 0$, or $k = 0$ and there exists no $x \in \Sigma^*$ such that Sx is a sentential form of G with a handle whose second component is 1;†

then v) $S \overset{*}{\underset{R}{\Rightarrow}} \alpha x_2 \overset{+}{\underset{R}{\Rightarrow}} w x_2$.

† In most cases, we will use the fact that $x_2 \neq \Lambda$. The other possibilities will be useful later on and in the problems.

Proof We assume, for the sake of contradiction, that (i), (ii), (iii), and (iv) hold, but not (v). Suppose $\alpha x_1 \overset{+}{\underset{R}{\Rightarrow}} wx_1$ is a derivation of n steps, where $n \geqslant 1$, by the (unique) derivation

$$\alpha x_1 = \alpha_n x_1 \underset{R}{\Rightarrow} \alpha_{n-1} x_1 \underset{R}{\Rightarrow} \cdots \underset{R}{\Rightarrow} \alpha_1 x_1 = wx_1$$

with $\alpha_i \in V^*$, for $1 \leqslant i \leqslant n$. Let m be the number of steps in the derivation $S \overset{+}{\underset{R}{\Rightarrow}} wx_2$, and let $r = \min(m, n)$.

Now, suppose that the last r steps of the derivation $S \overset{+}{\underset{R}{\Rightarrow}} wx_2$ are

$$\alpha_r' \underset{R}{\Rightarrow} \alpha_{r-1}' \underset{R}{\Rightarrow} \cdots \underset{R}{\Rightarrow} \alpha_1' = wx_2$$

for some $\alpha_i \in V^*$, for $1 \leqslant i \leqslant r$.

Claim There exists some $\ell \leqslant r$ such that $\alpha_\ell' \neq \alpha_\ell x_2$.

Proof By contradiction. Suppose $\alpha_\ell' = \alpha_\ell x_2$ for all $\ell \leqslant r$.

CASE 1. $r < n$. Then $\alpha_r' = \alpha_r x_2 = S$. Thus $\alpha_r = S$ and $x_2 = \Lambda$. Since ${}^{(k)}x_1 = {}^{(k)}x_2$, we must have $k = 0$ or $x_1 = \Lambda$. If $x_1 = \Lambda$, then $S \overset{+}{\underset{R}{\Rightarrow}} S$, which contradicts the fact that G is $LR(k)$. Therefore, $k = 0$. However, we know that $\alpha_{r+1} x_1 \underset{R}{\Rightarrow} \alpha_r x_1 = Sx_1$. The handle of Sx_1 has second component 1, contradicting (iv).

CASE 2. $r = n$. Again $\alpha_r' = \alpha_r x_2$. We have $S \overset{*}{\underset{R}{\Rightarrow}} \alpha_r' = \alpha_r x_2 = \alpha_n x_2 = \alpha x_2 \overset{+}{\underset{R}{\Rightarrow}} wx_2$. But this is (v), which is assumed to be false. Thus, we have a contradiction and the claim is established.

Now let m be the smallest positive integer satisfying our claim. Clearly, $m > 1$, since $\alpha_1' = wx_2 = \alpha_1 x_2$.

Now, we know that there exist $\bar{\alpha}, \bar{\alpha}', \beta, \bar{\beta} \in V^*$; $\bar{A}, \bar{A}' \in N$ and $y, z \in \Sigma^*$ such that

i) $S \overset{*}{\underset{R}{\Rightarrow}} \alpha_m x_1 = \bar{\alpha}\bar{A}yx_1 \underset{R}{\Rightarrow} \bar{\alpha}\bar{\beta}yx_1 = \alpha_{m-1}x_1$

ii) $S \overset{*}{\underset{R}{\Rightarrow}} \alpha_m' = \bar{\alpha}'\bar{A}'z \underset{R}{\Rightarrow} \bar{\alpha}'\bar{\beta}'z = \alpha_{m-1}' = \alpha_{m-1}x_2 = \bar{\alpha}\bar{\beta}yx_2$

using the fact that $\alpha_{m-1}' = \alpha_{m-1}x_2$ from our minimality assumption about m.

Now let $\gamma = \bar{\alpha}\bar{\beta}$. We get:

i) $S \overset{*}{\underset{R}{\Rightarrow}} \bar{\alpha}\bar{A}yx_1 \underset{R}{\Rightarrow} \bar{\alpha}\bar{\beta}yx_1 = \gamma yx_1$

ii) $S \overset{*}{\underset{R}{\Rightarrow}} \bar{\alpha}'\bar{A}'z \underset{R}{\Rightarrow} \bar{\alpha}'\bar{\beta}'z = \gamma yx_2$

Now ${}^{(k)}x_1 = {}^{(k)}x_2$ implies ${}^{(k)}yx_1 = {}^{(k)}yx_2$. Since G is $LR(k)$, we have

$$(\bar{A} \to \bar{\beta}, \lg(\bar{\alpha}\bar{\beta})) = (\bar{A}' \to \bar{\beta}', \lg(\bar{\alpha}'\bar{\beta}')).$$

From (ii) $\alpha_m' = \bar{\alpha}'\bar{A}'z$, and, using the equality of handles, we have $\bar{\beta} = \bar{\beta}', \bar{A} = \bar{A}'$, and thus $\bar{\alpha}' = \bar{\alpha}$ and $z = yx_2$. Thus $\alpha_m' = \bar{\alpha}\bar{A}yx_2 = \alpha_m x_2$. But this contradicts our assumption that $\alpha_m' \neq \alpha_m x_2$. □

Now we must turn to relating Δ_2 to the family of $LR(0)$ languages. This will involve a detailed study of derivation trees and canonical cross sections. The reader may wish to reread the definitions given in the problems of Section 1.6. Our next lemma relates the canonical cross sections to the left part of a tree.

Lemma 13.2.4 Let T be a grammatical tree of some grammar, ${}^{(n)}T$ the left part of T for some $n \geqslant 0$, and $\xi = (x_1, \ldots, x_k, y_1, \ldots, y_m)$ a canonical cross section in T with exactly the nodes $x_1, \ldots, x_k$ in ${}^{(n)}T$. Then $\eta = (x_1, \ldots, x_k)$ is a canonical cross section in ${}^{(n)}T$.

Proof The argument is an induction on the level h of the cross section ξ.

Basis. The case when $h = 0$ is immediate, since $\xi = \eta = (x_0)$ where x_0 is the common root of T and ${}^{(n)}T$.

Inductive step. Assume the lemma true for canonical cross sections of level $h \geqslant 0$. Let ξ have level $h + 1$ and let ξ' be the (unique) canonical cross section of level h in T. Using the inductive hypothesis, let η' be the canonical cross section in ${}^{(n)}T$ which consists of all the nodes of ξ' which are in ${}^{(n)}T$. Now, to obtain ξ from ξ' we need the rightmost internal (with respect to T) node, say x, in ξ'. There are two cases. If x is not in ${}^{(n)}T$, then none of its descendants is in ${}^{(n)}T$ and $\eta = \eta'$. Hence, η is a canonical cross section in ${}^{(n)}T$. On the other hand, if x is in ${}^{(n)}T$, then it is the rightmost internal node not only in ξ' (with respect to T) but also in η' (with respect to ${}^{(n)}T$) and, by the definition of canonical cross section, we conclude that η is a canonical cross section in ${}^{(n)}T$. □

The next lemma is, in a certain sense, a converse of the previous lemma.

Lemma 13.2.5 Let T be a grammatical tree of some grammar and let ${}^{(n)}T$ be the left part of T for some $n \geqslant 0$. Let $\eta = (x_1, \ldots, x_k)$ be a canonical cross section in ${}^{(n)}T$ and let $y_1, \ldots, y_m$ be all the leaves in T which are right of x_k; that is, $x_k \sqsubset y_1 \sqsubset \cdots \sqsubset y_m$. Then the sequence $\xi = (x_1, \ldots, x_k, y_1, \ldots, y_m)$ is a canonical cross section in T.

Proof Again the argument is an induction, this time on the level h of canonical cross section η.

Basis. $h = 0$. Let x_0 be the root of ${}^{(n)}T$ (and of T). Then $\eta = (x_0)$ and the only possibility for ξ is $\xi = \eta = (x_0)$. Hence, ξ is a canonical cross section (of level 0) in T.

Inductive step. Assume the lemma true for canonical cross sections of level $h \geqslant 0$. Under the same notation as in Lemma 13.2.4, let $\eta = (x_1, \ldots, x_k)$ be of level $h + 1$ and let $\eta' = (x_1', \ldots, x_{k'}')$ be the (unique) canonical cross section of level h in ${}^{(n)}T$. By the induction hypothesis the sequence $\xi' = (x_1', \ldots, x_{k'}', y_j, \ldots, y_m)$ for some $j \geqslant 1$ is a canonical cross section in T. Since none of the nodes y_i $(j \leqslant i \leqslant m)$ is an internal node in T we can conclude† from the definition that $\xi = (x_1, \ldots, x_k, y_1, \ldots, y_m)$ is a canonical cross section in T. □

---

† We need only use the following observation: If $(x_1, \ldots, x_p, \ldots, x_m)$ is a canonical cross section where $x_{p+1}, \ldots, x_m$ are leaves and if $x_1', \ldots, x_q'$ are all the leaves in the subtree below x_p, then $(x_1, \ldots, x_{p-1}, x_1', \ldots, x_q', x_{p+1}, \ldots, x_m)$ is a canonical cross section.

We are now prepared to relate Δ_2 and $LR(0)$.

Theorem 13.2.3 Any reduced strict deterministic grammar is also an $LR(0)$ grammar.

Proof Let $G = (V, \Sigma, P, S)$ be a reduced strict deterministic grammar. First observe that $S \overset{+}{\underset{R}{\Rightarrow}} S$ cannot occur in P since that would contradict the Corollary to Theorem 11.4.3. Now, following Definition 13.2.1, assume that, for some $\alpha \in V^*$, $w, w' \in \Sigma^*, \rho, \rho' \in P$ and $n' \geq 0$, $(\rho, \lg(\alpha))$ and (ρ', n') are handles of αw and $\alpha w'$, respectively. We want to prove that these two handles are identical. Informally summarized, we shall prove this equivalence by first showing that each of the two handles appears in a certain position in a left part of a given derivation tree, and second, using the left-part theorem, that this left part is unique.

Since G is reduced, there is some $u \in \Sigma^*$ such that $\alpha \overset{*}{\underset{R}{\Rightarrow}} u$. Let T, T' be two derivation trees of G corresponding to derivations

$$S \overset{*}{\underset{R}{\Rightarrow}} \alpha w \overset{*}{\underset{R}{\Rightarrow}} uw \qquad \text{and} \qquad S \overset{*}{\underset{R}{\Rightarrow}} \alpha w' \overset{*}{\underset{R}{\Rightarrow}} uw'.$$

Since G is unambiguous (cf. Corollary 1 after Theorem 11.8.1), each of the two trees is unique. Moreover, since αw and $\alpha w'$ are canonical sentential forms (by Definition 13.2.1, this is a necessary condition for a sentential form to have a handle), there are canonical cross sections ξ_1 in T and ξ_1' in T' such that $\lambda(\xi_1) = \alpha w$ and $\lambda(\xi_1') = \alpha w'$; each canonical cross section is also unique in its respective tree (cf. Problem 7 of Section 11.6). We shall study these cross sections in detail (Fig. 13.2). Assume ξ_1 is of level h (in T) and ξ_1' of level h' (in T'). The existence of handles implies the existence of a canonical cross section ξ_0 of level $h-1$ in T and another canonical cross section ξ_0' of level $h'-1$ in T'. Corresponding to the definition of canonical cross section, let us write, for $1 \leq k \leq m$,

$$\xi_0 = (x_1, \ldots, x_k, \ldots, x_m), \tag{13.2.1}$$

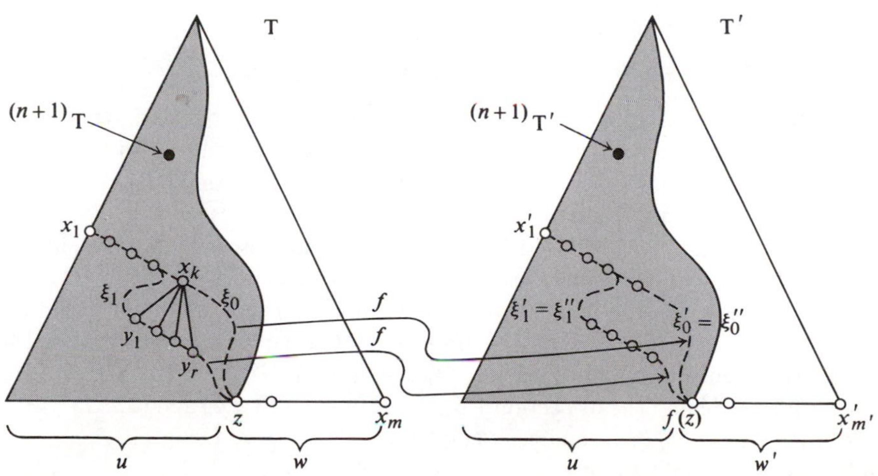

FIG. 13.2

and, for $r \geqslant 1$,

$$\xi_1 = (x_1, \ldots, x_{k-1}, y_1, \ldots, y_r, x_{k+1}, \ldots, x_m), \tag{13.2.2}$$

where

$$\lambda(x_1) \cdots \lambda(x_{k-1})\lambda(y_1) \cdots \lambda(y_r) = \gamma, \qquad \lambda(x_{k+1}) \cdots \lambda(x_m) = w. \tag{13.2.3}$$

Similarly, for ξ_0' and $1 \leqslant k' \leqslant m'$,

$$\xi_0' = (x_1', \ldots, x_{k'}', \ldots, x_{m'}'), \tag{13.2.4}$$

and for ξ_1' and $r' \geqslant 1$,

$$\xi_1' = (x_1', \ldots, x_{k'-1}', y_1', \ldots, y_{r'}', x_{k'+1}', \ldots, x_{m'}'). \tag{13.2.5}$$

In (13.2.1) and (13.2.4), x_k and $x_{k'}'$ are the rightmost internal nodes in ξ_0 and ξ_0', respectively.

Next we shall apply the Left-Part Theorem to T and T'. Assume first that $w \neq \Lambda$. Let $n = \lg(u)$ and let z be the $(n+1)$st terminal node in T; that is, $\lambda(z) = {}^{(1)}w$. From (11.2.3), we can see that z appears both in ξ_0 and ξ_1 or, more specifically, $z = x_\ell$ for some $\ell > k$. We have

$$^{(n)}fr(T) = u = {}^{(n)}fr(T'),$$

and the left-part property of the derivation trees of G yields the existence of a structural isomorphism f: $^{(n-1)}T \to {}^{(n+1)}T'$ and, moreover, for any x in T,

$$x \sqsubset^+ z \quad \text{implies} \quad \lambda(x) = \lambda(f(x)), \tag{13.2.6}$$

and for z itself,

$$\lambda(z) \equiv \lambda(f(z)) = {}^{(1)}w'. \tag{13.2.7}$$

Define

$$\eta_0 = (x_1, \ldots, x_k, \ldots, z),$$

$$\eta_1 = (x_1, \ldots, x_{k-1}, y_1, \ldots, y_r, x_{k+1}, \ldots, z).$$

(Note that $x_k \neq z$, but $x_{k+1} = z$ is possible.) By Lemma 13.2.4, η_0 and η_1 are canonical cross sections in $^{(n+1)}T$. Because canonical cross sections are invariant under structural isomorphism, the following are canonical cross sections in $^{(n+1)}T'$ (cf. Fig. 13.2).

$$f(\eta_0) = (f(x_1), \ldots, f(x_k), \ldots, f(z)),$$

$$f(\eta_1) = (f(x_1), \ldots, f(x_{k-1}), f(y_1), \ldots, f(y_r), \ldots, f(z)).$$

Extending $f(\eta_0)$ and $f(\eta_1)$ by all the leaves in T' on the right of $f(z)$ and using Lemma 13.2.5, we obtain two canonical cross sections ξ_0'' and ξ_1'' of T'. Now, by (13.2.6) and (13.2.7), $\lambda(\xi_1'') = \alpha w' = \lambda(\xi_1')$ and, since G is unambiguous, we have that $\xi_1'' = \xi_1'$ by Problem 8 of Section 11.6.

Now $y_1, \ldots, y_r$ in (13.2.2) are the immediate descendants of x_k in T (and thus in $^{(n+1)}T$) and therefore, using the structural isomorphism $^{(n+1)}T \cong {}^{(n+1)}T'$, $f(y_1), \ldots, f(y_r)$ are the immediate descendants of $f(x_k)$ in $^{(n+1)}T'$ (and, since $f(x_k) \sqsubset^+ f(z)$, this is also true in T'). Moreover, $f(x_k)$ is the rightmost internal node in $f(\eta_0)$ and hence in ξ_0''. Consequently, ξ_0'' has level $h' - 1$, which is possible only if $\xi_0'' = \xi_0'$ (cf. Problem 6(b) of Section 1.6). Therefore in (13.2.4) and (13.2.5), we have $k' = k$, $r' = r$, $x_{k'}' = f(x_k)$, and $y_i' = f(y_i)$ for $i = 1, \ldots, r$. Using (13.2.6), we conclude that $p' = p$ and $\lg(\alpha) = k - 1 + r = k' - 1 + r' = n'$.

It remains to verify the case $w = \Lambda$. In that case $T = T'$ by the Left-Part Theorem and the result is an immediate consequence of Problem 8 of Section 1.6. □

We are now in a position to prove a useful theorem. We shall show that every Δ_0 language has an $LR(1)$ grammar. When we learn how to accept every $LR(k)$ language by a dpda and some other techniques, we shall have proved that Δ_0 is coextensive with the $LR(k)$ languages.

One additional lemma is necessary.

Lemma 13.2.6. Let G be an $LR(0)$ grammar of the form $G = (V \cup \{\$\}, \Sigma \cup \{\$\}, P, S)$ where $P \subseteq N \times (V^* \cup V^*\$)$, $L(G) \subseteq \Sigma^*\$$, and there is no derivation $S \underset{R}{\overset{+}{\Rightarrow}} S\$$ in G. Define another grammar $G' = (V, \Sigma, P', S)$ where $P' = P_1 \cup P_2$,

$$P_1 = \{A \to \beta \mid A \to \beta \text{ in } P \text{ and } \beta \in V^*\},$$

$$P_2 = \{A \to \beta \mid A \to \beta\$ \text{ in } P\}.$$

Then G' is an $LR(1)$ grammar and $L(G')\$ = L(G)$.

Proof Assume, without loss of generality, that G is reduced. Clearly, there is no derivation $S \underset{R}{\overset{+}{\Rightarrow}} S$ in G' since $S \underset{R}{\overset{+}{\Rightarrow}} S\$$ cannot occur in G. We shall examine the handles in G'. Let $h = (A \to \beta, i)$ be a handle of γ in G' where $A \in N$, $\beta, \gamma \in V^*$, and $i \geqslant 0$. There are two possibilities. If $A \to \beta$ is in P_1, then h is also a handle of γ or $\gamma\$$ in G. On the other hand, if $A \to \beta$ is in P_2, then $(A \to \beta\$, i+1)$ is a handle of $\gamma\$$ in G.

Now, following Definition 13.2.1, let $\gamma \in V^*$, $w, w' \in \Sigma^*$, $\rho, \rho' \in P'$, $i \geqslant 0$, and let $h = (\rho, \lg(\gamma))$ and $h' = (\rho', i')$ be handles of γw and $\gamma w'$, respectively. Moreover, let ${}^{(1)}w = {}^{(1)}w'$. We shall show that $h = h'$. Assume that ρ and ρ' have the form $A \to \beta$ and $A' \to \beta'$, respectively, where $A, A' \in N$, $\beta, \beta' \in V^*$. We can distinguish four cases.

CASE 1. $\rho, \rho' \in P_1$. Then h is also a handle of γw or $\gamma w\$$ in G and h' is also a handle of $\gamma w'$ or $\gamma w'\$$ in G. In all cases we have $h = h'$ by the $LR(0)$ property of G.

CASE 2. $\rho, \rho' \in P_2$. Then $h_1 = (A \to \beta\$, \lg(\gamma)+1)$ is a handle of $\gamma w\$$ in G and $h_1' = (A' \to \beta'\$, i+1)$ is a handle of $\gamma w'\$$ in G. Here ${}^{(1)}w = {}^{(1)}w'$ implies ${}^{(1)}(w\$) = {}^{(1)}(w'\$)$ and thus $h_1 = h_1'$ by the $LR(0)$ property of G. Therefore, also, $h = h'$.

We shall see that the remaining two cases cannot occur. First, let us make the following observation, which is a direct consequence of Definition 13.2.1. If $h = (\rho, \lg(\gamma))$ is a handle of γw and if $\gamma w'$ is a canonical sentential form where $w, w' \in \Sigma^*$, then h is also a handle of $\gamma w'$. We proceed in our case analysis.

CASE 3. $\rho \in P_1$, $\rho' \in P_2$. Then h is a handle of γw or $\gamma w\$$ in G and $h_1 = (A' \to \beta'\$, i+1)$ is a handle of $\gamma w'\$$ in G. Here $\gamma w'\$$ is a canonical sentential form in G (otherwise it could not have a handle) and thus h is also a handle of $\gamma w'\$$ in G. Then, by the $LR(0)$ property, $h = h_1$. But this is not possible since \$ does not occur in β.

CASE 4. $\rho' \in P_1$, $\rho \in P_2$. Then h' is a handle of $\gamma w'$ or of $\gamma w'\$$ and $h_1 = (A \to \beta\$, \lg(\gamma)+1)$ is a handle of $\gamma w\$$. The form of h_1 implies that $w = \Lambda$. Since ${}^{(1)}w = {}^{(1)}w'$, also $w' = \Lambda$. Now h' is a handle of $\gamma\$$ (if it is a handle of γ, then it is also a handle of $\gamma\$$ since $\gamma\$$ is a canonical sentential form). But also h_1 is a handle of $\gamma\$$ and thus $h' = h_1$, which is again not possible.

We have proved that $h = h'$ and therefore G' satisfies the $LR(1)$ property. The fact that $L(G')\$ = L(G)$ is immediate from the definition of G'. □

We can now prove an important consequence of the previous result.

Theorem 13.2.4 Any deterministic language has an $LR(1)$ grammar.

Proof Let $L \subseteq \Sigma^*$ and $L \in \Delta_0$. Then $L\$ \in \Delta_2$ and, by Theorem 11.5.3, there exists a strict deterministic grammar $G = (V \cup \{\$\}, \Sigma \cup \{\$\}, P, S)$ such that $L(G) = L\$$. Using Theorem 11.4.1 and Problem 3 of Section 11.4, we may assume, without loss of generality, that G is reduced and Λ-free (note that $L(G) \neq \{\Lambda\}$). By Theorem 13.2.3, G is $LR(0)$. We shall check that G satisfies assumptions of Lemma 13.2.6. First, $P \subseteq N \times (V^* \cup V^*\$)$, or in other words, each production in P has the form $A \to \beta$ or $A \to \beta\$$, where $A \in N$ and $\beta \in V^*$. For, if $A \to \beta\$\delta$ where in P for some $\delta \neq \Lambda$, the fact that G is reduced and Λ-free would imply that $u\$v \in L\$$ for some $u, v \in \Sigma^*$ and $v \neq \Lambda$, which is not possible. Second, $S \overset{+}{\underset{R}{\Rightarrow}} S\$$ is impossible in G, since that would contradict the Corollary to Theorem 11.4.3 and the strict determinism of G. Now we can apply Lemma 13.2.6 and obtain an $LR(1)$ grammar G' such that $L(G') = L$. □

PROBLEMS

1 Is the following grammar $LR(k)$ and, if so, what is the least k for which it is true?

$$E \to E + T \mid T$$

$$T \to T * F \mid F$$

$$F \to (E) \mid a$$

2 Let $k \geqslant 0$. Find a family of grammars G_k such that G_k is not $LR(k)$ but is $LR(k+1)$.

3 Show that the restriction against derivations of the form $S \overset{+}{\underset{R}{\Rightarrow}} S$ in Definition 13.2.1 is necessary to preserve the unambiguity of $LR(k)$ grammars.

4 Another definition that has been proposed for $LR(k)$ grammars in Aho and Ullman [1972] is now given.

Definition Let $k \geqslant 0$ and $G = (V, \Sigma, P, S)$ be a reduced context-free grammar. Define the *augmented grammar* $G' = (V', \Sigma, P', S')$, where $V' = V \cup \{S'\}$ and $P' = P \cup \{S' \to S\}$, where S, a symbol not in V, is our new starting symbol. G is said to be $ALR(k)$ (augmented $LR(k)$) if and only if, in G',

For each $w, w', x \in \Sigma^*; \gamma, \alpha, \alpha', \beta, \beta'$ in $V'^*; A, A' \in V' - \Sigma$, if

i) $S' \overset{*}{\underset{R}{\Rightarrow}} \alpha A w \underset{R}{\Rightarrow} \alpha\beta w = \gamma w$ (That is, γw has handle $(A \to \beta, \lg(\alpha\beta))$)

and ii) $S' \overset{*}{\underset{R}{\Rightarrow}} \alpha' A' x \underset{R}{\Rightarrow} \alpha'\beta' x = \gamma w'$ (That is, $\gamma w'$ has handle $(A' \to \beta', \lg(\alpha'\beta'))$)

and iii) ${}^{(k)}w = {}^{(k)}w'$

then iv) $(A \to \beta, \lg(\alpha\beta)) = (A' \to \beta', \lg(\alpha'\beta'))$.

Show the following lemma.

Lemma Let $G = (V, \Sigma, P, S)$ be a reduced context-free grammar. For each $k \geqslant 0$, if G is $ALR(k)$, then G is $LR(k)$.

5 Prove the following partial converse of Problem 4.

Lemma Let $G = (V, \Sigma, P, S)$ be a reduced context-free grammar. If G is $LR(k)$ for some $k \geqslant 1$, then G is $ALR(k)$.

At this point, we know that the family of $LR(k)$ languages and grammars is the same for $k \geqslant 1$. Let us examine the case $k = 0$.

6 Prove the following result.

Lemma If $G = (V, \Sigma, P, S)$ is $LR(0)$ and $S \overset{+}{\underset{R}{\Rightarrow}} Sw$ is impossible in G for any $w \in \Sigma^+$, then G is $ALR(0)$.

7 Prove the following lemma.

Lemma Let $G = (V, \Sigma, P, S)$ be an $ALR(0)$ grammar. For any $w \in \Sigma^*$, $S \overset{+}{\underset{R}{\Rightarrow}} Sw$ is impossible in G.

8 Summarize the relationship between the families of $ALR(k)$ and $LR(k)$ grammars and languages.

Now let us consider a different variation on the $LR(k)$ definition.

Definition Let $k \geqslant 0$ and $G = (V, \Sigma, P, S)$ be a reduced context-free grammar. Define the *\$-augmented grammar* $G' = (V', \Sigma', P', S')$, where $V' = V \cup \{S', \$\}$, $\Sigma' = \Sigma \cup \{\$\}$, $P' = P \cup \{S' \to S\$\}$, where S' and \$ are new symbols not in V. G is said to be $\$LR(k)$ if and only if, in G',

For each $w, w', x \in \Sigma^*$; $\gamma, \alpha, \alpha', \beta, \beta'$ in V'^*, $A, A' \in N'$, if

i) $S' \overset{*}{\underset{R}{\Rightarrow}} \alpha A w \underset{R}{\Rightarrow} \alpha\beta w = \gamma w$ (That is, γw has handle $(A \to \beta, \lg(\alpha\beta))$)

and ii) $S' \overset{*}{\underset{R}{\Rightarrow}} \alpha' A' x \underset{R}{\Rightarrow} \alpha'\beta' x = \gamma w'$ (That is, $\gamma w'$ has handle $(A' \to \beta', \lg(\alpha'\beta'))$)

and iii) ${}^{(k)}w = {}^{(k)}w'$

then iv) $(A \to \beta, \lg(\alpha\beta)) = (A' \to \beta', \lg(\alpha'\beta'))$.

9 Let $G = (V, \Sigma, P, S)$ be a $\$LR(k)$ grammar and $k \geqslant 0$. Show that $S \overset{+}{\underset{R}{\Rightarrow}} S$ is impossible in G.

10 Let $G = (V, \Sigma, P, S)$ be a reduced context-free grammar. Show that, for each $k \geqslant 0$, if G is $\$LR(k)$, then G is $LR(k)$.

11 Let $G = (V, \Sigma, P, S)$ be a reduced context-free grammar. Show that, for each $k \geqslant 1$, if G is $LR(k)$, then G is $\$LR(k)$.

In order to work out the properties of the $\$LR(0)$ grammars, we need another definition.

Definition Let $G = (V, \Sigma, P, S)$ be a reduced context-free grammar. A production $\rho \in P$ is *pathological* if:

i) there exists a $T \in N$, $w \in \Sigma^*$, such that

$$\rho = (T \rightarrow S)$$

and

$$S \underset{R}{\overset{+}{\Rightarrow}} Tw \underset{R}{\Rightarrow} Sw$$

or ii) there exists an $A \in N$, $w \in \Sigma^*$ such that

$$\rho = (A \rightarrow \Lambda)$$

and

$$S \underset{R}{\overset{+}{\Rightarrow}} SAw \underset{R}{\Rightarrow} Sw$$

12 Prove the following result.

Lemma Let $G = (V, \Sigma, P, S)$ be a reduced context-free grammar. Then G has no pathological productions if and only if there exists no $w \in \Sigma^*$ such that Sw is a sentential form of G with a handle whose second component is 1.

13 Let $G = (V, \Sigma, P, S)$ be a reduced context-free grammar. Show that G is $\$LR(0)$ if and only if it is $LR(0)$ and has no pathological productions.

14 Prove a theorem which relates the families of $LR(k)$ and $\$LR(k)$ grammars for all $k \geq 0$.

15 Prove a theorem which relates the families of $\$LR(k)$ and $ALR(k)$ grammars for all $k \geq 0$.

Finally, another variation of the LR condition is given.

Definition Let $G = (V, \Sigma, P, S)$ be a reduced context-free grammar. Then G is $LLR(k)$ if and only if:

a) G is unambiguous, and

b) for all $w_1, w_2, w_3, w_3' \in \Sigma^*$, $A \in N$, if

i) $S \overset{*}{\Rightarrow} w_1 A w_3 \overset{*}{\Rightarrow} w_1 w_2 w_3$

ii) $S \overset{*}{\Rightarrow} w_1 w_2 w_3'$ and

iii) ${}^{(k)}w_3 = {}^{(k)}w_3'$ then

iv) $S \overset{*}{\Rightarrow} w_1 A w_3'$

16 Let $G = (V, \Sigma, P, S)$ be a $\$LR(k)$ grammar for some $k \geq 0$. Show that G is $LLR(k)$.

17 Show that every $LR(0)$ grammar is $LLR(1)$.

18 Let $G = (V, \Sigma, P, S)$ be an $LR(k)$ grammar, where $k \geq 1$. Show that G is an $LLR(k)$ grammar.

19 Show that, for any $k \geq 0$, there exists a grammar which is $LLR(0)$ but not $LR(k)$.

20 Prove the following useful result.

Theorem Let $G = (V, \Sigma, P, S)$ be a reduced context-free Λ-free grammar. Then G is $\$LR(k)$ if and only if G is $LLR(k)$.

21 Prove the following lemma about canonical cross sections.

Lemma Let T be any tree and ξ a canonical cross section in T of level $h \geqslant 1$. Let x, y be two nodes in ξ such that $x \sqsubset^* y$ and y is internal in T. There exists a node z in T such that $z \ulcorner x$ and $z \overset{+}{\ulcorner} y$.

Now we introduce an interesting family of grammars which is closely related to the LR grammars. In this family, the handle is uniquely determined by looking ahead k characters and looking behind ℓ characters.

Definition Let $G = (V, \Sigma, P, S)$ be a grammar with no derivations of the form $S \overset{+}{\underset{R}{\Rightarrow}} S$. Let $\ell, k \geqslant 0$. Then G is called a *BRC*(ℓ, k) *grammar* (bounded right context) if the following condition holds for all $\alpha, \alpha', \beta \in V^*$; $w, w' \in \Sigma^*$; $A \in N$; $\rho' \in P$ and $i' \geqslant \lg(\alpha'\beta)$. If $(A \to \beta, \lg(\alpha\beta))$ and (ρ', i') are handles of $\alpha\beta w$ and $\alpha'\beta w'$, respectively, and if $\alpha^{(\ell)} = \alpha'^{(\ell)}$ and ${}^{(k)}w = {}^{(k)}w'$, then ρ' has the form $A \to \beta$ and $i' = \lg(\alpha\beta)$.

22 Prove the following useful result.

Theorem Every strict deterministic grammar G is equivalent to some strict deterministic BRC$(\ell, 0)$ grammar G' for some $\ell \geqslant 0$. (*Hint*. Let $G = (V, \Sigma, P, S)$ be a strict deterministic grammar with partition π. Let $\pi - \Sigma = \{X_1, \ldots, X_m\} = X$, where X_i is a representative of the ith block.) Define $G' = (V \cup X, \Sigma, P', S)$ where

$$P' = \{X_i \to \Lambda \mid 1 \leqslant i \leqslant m\} \cup \{A \to X_i\alpha \mid A \to \alpha \text{ is in } P, A \in X_i\}.$$

Show that $L(G') = L(G)$, G' is strict deterministic, and (with the help of the previous problem) that G' is BRC$(\ell, 0)$ where $\ell = \max\{\lg(\alpha) \mid A \to \alpha \text{ is in } P\}$.

13.3 CHARACTERIZATION OF LR(0) LANGUAGES

Our main purpose in this section is to prove an important and very useful characterization theorem for $LR(0)$ languages.

Theorem 13.3.1 ($LR(0)$ *language characterization theorem*) Let $L \subseteq \Sigma^*$. The following four statements are equivalent.

a) L is an $LR(0)$ language.

b) $L \subseteq \Sigma^*$ is a deterministic context-free language and for all $x \in \Sigma^+$; w, $y \in \Sigma^*$, if $w \in L$, $wx \in L$, and $y \in L$, then $yx \in L$.

c) There exists a dpda $A = (Q, \Sigma, \Gamma, \delta, q_0, Z_0, F)$, where $F = \{q_f\}$ and there exists $Z_f \in \Gamma$ such that

$$L = T(A, Z_f) = T(A, \Gamma) = \{w \in \Sigma^* \mid (q_0, w, Z_0) \overset{*}{\vdash} (q_f, \Lambda, Z_f)\}.$$

d) There exist strict deterministic languages L_0 and L_1 such that $L = L_0 L_1^*$.

Proof We first prove that (a) implies (b). Assume that $G = (V, \Sigma, P, S)$ is an $LR(0)$ grammar and that $L = L(G)$. Furthermore, suppose that, for $w \in \Sigma^*$, $x \in \Sigma^+$, we have $w \in L$ and $wx \in L$. Thus, we have, in G, the derivations

i) $S \overset{*}{\underset{R}{\Rightarrow}} S \overset{+}{\underset{R}{\Rightarrow}} w$

and ii) $S \overset{*}{\underset{R}{\Rightarrow}} wx$

iii) ${}^{(0)}\Lambda = {}^{(0)}x = \Lambda$

and iv) $x \neq \Lambda$.

By the extended $LR(0)$ theorem (13.2.3), we get

v) $S \overset{*}{\underset{R}{\Rightarrow}} Sx \overset{+}{\underset{R}{\Rightarrow}} wx$

Now we assume that, for some $y \in \Sigma^*$, we have $y \in L$. Thus, we have $S \overset{+}{\underset{R}{\Rightarrow}} y$. Derivation (v) gives us

$$S \overset{*}{\underset{R}{\Rightarrow}} Sx \overset{+}{\underset{R}{\Rightarrow}} yx$$

Thus $yx \in L$, which completes the proof that (a) implies (b).

We now prove that (b) implies (c). This is the most involved part of the proof of this theorem, since several machine constructions are involved. We begin by considering the degenerate† languages that obey (b), namely $\emptyset$ and $\{\Lambda\}$. We then consider the prefix-free languages that satisfy (b). We next consider the languages that satisfy (b) that are not prefix-free.

Suppose $L = \emptyset$. Let $A = (\{q_0, q_f\}, \Sigma, \{Z_f\}, \emptyset, q_0, Z_f, \{q_f\})$, where $q_0 \neq q_f$. Clearly, $T(A, Z_f) = \emptyset$. Suppose $L = \{\Lambda\}$. Let $A = (\{q_f\}, \Sigma, \{Z_f\}, \emptyset, q_f, Z_f, \{q_f\})$. Clearly, $T(A, Z_f) = \{\Lambda\}$.

Now, we shall operate under the assumption that L is not degenerate. We know that there exists a dpda $A = (Q, \Sigma, \Gamma, \delta, q_0, Z_0, F)$ such that $L = T(A)$ since L is deterministic. We wish to modify A so that we obtain a new dpda such that L is accepted by a new machine with only Z_f on the pushdown. Our first step is to add a new "bottom of stack" marker to our machine. We let

$$A' = (Q', \Sigma, \Gamma', \delta', q_0', Z_b, F'),$$

where

$$Q' = Q \cup \{q_0'\}, \quad \text{where } q_0' \text{ is a new state not in } Q,$$

$$\Gamma' = \Gamma \cup \{Z_b\}, \quad \text{where } Z_b \text{ is a new symbol not in } \Gamma,$$

$$F' = F.$$

Define δ' as follows:

i) For all $q \in Q, a \in \Sigma, Z \in \Gamma$, let

$$\delta'(q, a, Z) = \delta(q, a, Z).$$

ii) Also let

$$\delta'(q_0', \Lambda, Z_b) = (q_0, Z_b Z_0).$$

Clearly, $T(A') = T(A)$.

We now choose any $x \in \Sigma^*$ such that $x \in \min(L)$. Since $L \neq \emptyset$, clearly, $\min(L) \neq \emptyset$. We shall now consider two cases. The first case will correspond to the strict deterministic languages. Observe carefully, however, that this does not follow directly from the statement of this case. Our construction will be much simpler in this case, than in Case 2, where our language is not prefix-free.

---

† A language L is said to be *degenerate* if $L = \emptyset$ or $L = \{\Lambda\}$.

CASE 1. Choose any $x \in \Sigma^*$ such that $x \in \min(L)$. For all $y \in \Sigma^+, xy \notin L$.

Claim L is strict deterministic.

Proof Assume, for the sake of contradiction, that L is not strict deterministic. Then there exist $w \in \Sigma^*$, $y \in \Sigma^+$ such that $w \in L$ and $wy \in L$ since L is not prefix-free. Since $x \in L, xy \in L$, by (b). But this contradicts the supposition for Case 1, giving us a contradiction. Thus L is strict deterministic.

We shall construct a machine that simulates the machine A' until a final state of A' is reached. It then erases the stack until a new bottom of stack marker is reached, and then goes to a special final state and puts the special accept symbol on the pushdown. We let

$$A'' = (Q'', \Sigma, \Gamma'', \delta'', q_0'', Z_b, F''),$$

where

$Q'' = Q'$,

$\Gamma'' = \Gamma' \cup \{Z_f\}$, where Z_f is a new symbol not in Γ', our special acceptance stack symbol,

$q_0'' = q_0'$,

$F'' = \{q_f\}$,

and δ'' is obtained from δ' as follows:

i) For $q \in Q' - F', a \in \Sigma_\Lambda, Z \in \Gamma$, let $\delta''(q, a, Z) = \delta'(q, a, Z)$.

ii) For all $q \in F', Z \in \Gamma' - Z_b$, we let

$$\delta''(q, \Lambda, Z) = (q, \Lambda).$$

iii) For $q \in F'$, we let

$$\delta''(q, \Lambda, Z_b) = (q_f, Z_f).$$

These cases have the following significance.

i) For nonfinal states, behave the same as A' behaves.

ii) When A'' reaches a final configuration for A', erase the stack until:

iii) The bottom marker is reached. Then go to the final configuration by replacing the bottom marker with the special accept symbol on the pushdown.

Since L is strict deterministic, we define no move for this configuration, making it a "dead configuration." Clearly,

$$T(A'', \Gamma'') = T(A'', Z_f) = T(A') = T(A) = L.$$

We now consider Case 2.

CASE 2. Let $x \in \Sigma^*$ be any string such that $x \in \min(L)$. For some $y \in \Sigma^+$, $xy \in L$. In this case, our machine cannot go to a dead configuration after reaching an accepting configuration. We shall construct a new machine A'', which, after accepting any string by $T(A'', Z_f)$, will pretend that it is, in fact, x that it has just accepted. Our first claim shows us how our machine will pretend that it has just accepted x. Our claim concerns the behavior of A' under the assumption of Case 2.

Claim There exists a $\bar{q} \in Q', \bar{\alpha} \in (\Gamma')^*, \bar{Z} \in \Gamma'$, such that, for our chosen x,

$$(q_0', x, Z_b) \overset{*}{\underset{A'}{\vdash}} (\bar{q}, \Lambda, Z_b\bar{\alpha}\bar{Z}),$$

where for some $\bar{a} \in \Sigma$, $\delta'(\bar{q}, \bar{a}, \bar{Z})$ is defined.

Proof This follows directly from the hypothesis of Case 2.

We now define A'' in terms of $A' = (Q', \Sigma, \Gamma', \delta', q_0', Z_b, F')$. We let

$$A'' = (Q'', \Sigma, \Gamma'', \delta'', q_0'', Z_b, F''),$$

where

$Q'' = Q' \cup \{q_f\}$, where q_f is a new symbol not in Q'.

$\Gamma'' = \Gamma' \cup \{Z_f\}$, where Z_f is a new symbol not in Γ' (Z_f will be our special acceptance stack symbol),

$q_0'' = q_0'$,

$F'' = \{q_f\}$.

We now define δ'' as follows:

i) For all $q \in F', Z \in \Gamma' - Z_b$, we let

$$\delta''(q, \Lambda, Z) = (q, \Lambda).$$

ii) For all $q \in F'$

a) $\delta''(q, \Lambda, Z_b) = (q_f, Z_f)$,

b) $\delta''(q, \Lambda, Z_f) = (q_f, Z_f)$.

iii) $\delta''(q_f, \Lambda, Z_f) = (q_f, Z_f\bar{\alpha}\bar{Z})$ where $\bar{\alpha}\bar{Z}$ is defined in the previous Claim.

iv) For all $a \in \Sigma, Z \in \Gamma' - Z_f, q \in Q', \alpha \in \Gamma^*$, if

$$\delta'(\bar{q}, a, Z) = (q, \alpha)$$

then

$$\delta''(q_f, a, Z) = (q, \alpha)$$

with $\bar{q}$ as defined in the previous Claim (note that $\delta'(\bar{q}, \Lambda, Z) = \emptyset$, since A' is deterministic).

v) For $q \in Q' - F', a \in \Sigma_\Lambda, Z \in \Gamma', q' \in Q', \alpha \in (\Gamma')^*$, if

$$\delta'(q, a, Z) = (q', \alpha)$$

then let

$$\delta''(q, a, Z) = (q', \alpha).$$

The sets of added rules have the following significance:

1 When an A'-accepting configuration is reached, the stack is erased until the bottom marker is reached.

2 When the bottom marker is reached, we go into an A''-accepting configuration.

3 The machine pretends that x has just been accepted and so adjusts its stack.

4 The machine proceeds under the assumption that it is in fact x that has just been accepted.

5 Otherwise, A'' proceeds as A'.

We must now show that A'' is a dpda such that $L = T(A'', Z_f) = T(A'', \Gamma'')$. We leave to the reader the task of showing that A'' is deterministic.

Next we must show that

$$L = T(A) = T(A') = T(A'', \Gamma'') = T(A'', Z_f) = L''.$$

First, we show that $L'' \subseteq L$. We assume that for some $w \in \Sigma^*$, we have $w \in L''$. Since $w \in L''$, we know that in A'' we have

$$(q_0'', w, Z_b) \overset{+}{\vdash} (q_f, \Lambda, Z_f).$$

By the determinism of A'', there exist $w_2, \ldots, w_n \in \Sigma^+$, $w_1 \in \Sigma^*$, $n \geqslant 1$, where $w = w_1 w_2 \cdots w_n$ such that

$$(q_0'', w_1 \cdots w_n, Z_b) \overset{+}{\vdash} (q_f, w_2 \cdots w_n, Z_f) \overset{*}{\vdash} \cdots \overset{+}{\vdash} (q_f, \Lambda, Z_f),$$

where our machine passes through q_f in only designated ID's. Since, in A'', we have

$$(q_0'', w_1, Z_b) \overset{*}{\vdash} (q_f, \Lambda, Z_f).$$

Thus $w_1 \in L(A'')$. Also in A', for some $\alpha \in (\Gamma')^*$, $q \in F'$, we have

$$(q_0', w_1, Z_b) \overset{+}{\vdash} (q, \Lambda, Z_b\alpha).$$

Thus $w_1 \in T(A') = L$.

Also, in A'', for $2 \leqslant i \leqslant n$, we have

$$(q_f, w_i, Z_f) \overset{+}{\vdash} (q_f, \Lambda, Z_f).$$

Thus in A'' we have

$$(q_f, w_i, Z_f) \vdash (q_f, w_i, Z_f\bar{\alpha}\bar{Z}) \overset{+}{\vdash} (q_f, \Lambda, Z_f).$$

Thus, in A', for some $q \in F'$, $\beta \in (\Gamma')^*$, we have

$$(\bar{q}, w_i, Z_b\bar{\alpha}\bar{Z}) \overset{+}{\vdash} (q, \Lambda, Z_b\beta),$$

since we have assumed that A'' only passes through q_f at the designated ID's, since A'' could get to the (q_f, Λ, Z_f) configuration only if A', the machine A'' is emulating, passed through a final state after reading w_i. We know that, in A',

$$(q_0', xw_i, Z_b) \overset{*}{\vdash} (\bar{q}, w_i, Z_b\bar{\alpha}\bar{Z}).$$

Thus $xw_i \in T(A') = L$.

We now show, by induction on i, that $w = w_1 \cdots w_i \in T(A') = L$, for $i \leqslant n$, where $w_1 \in \Sigma^*$ and $w_i \in \Sigma^+$ for $2 \leqslant i \leqslant n$.

Basis. $n = 1$. We have shown that $w_1 \in L$.

Induction step. Suppose $w_1 \cdots w_i \in L$. Now $x \in L$ and $xw_{i+1} \in L$; thus, since we are assuming that characterization (b) for $LR(0)$ languages holds, we have $w_1 \cdots w_i w_{i+1} \in L$. It is thus clear that $w = w_1 \cdots w_n \in L$.

We next show that $L = T(A') \subseteq L''$. Assume for some $w \in \Sigma^*$ that $w \in L$. Now, we know there exist $w_2, \ldots, w_n \in \Sigma^+$; $w_1 \in \Sigma^*$; $n \geqslant 1$, $w = w_1 \cdots w_n$, such that $w_1 \cdots w_i \in L$ for all i such that $1 \leqslant i \leqslant n$, and no other prefixes of w are in L.

Now consider any i such that $2 \leqslant i \leqslant n$.

Claim $xw_i \in L$.

Proof Since $w_1 \cdots w_{i-1} \in L$, $w_1 \cdots w_i \in L$, and $x \in L$, we know $xw_i \in L$. Therefore, in A' for some $q \in F'$, $\alpha \in (\Gamma')^*$,

$$(q_0', xw_i, Z_b) \overset{*}{\vdash} (\bar{q}, w_i, Z_b \bar{\alpha} \bar{Z}) \overset{+}{\vdash} (q, \Lambda, Z_b \alpha).$$

In A'' we get

$$(q_f, w_i, Z_f) \overset{+}{\vdash} (q_f, \Lambda, Z_f).$$

Also, since $w_1 \in L$, we know that in A'',

$$(q_0'', w_1, Z_b) \overset{+}{\vdash} (q_f, \Lambda, Z_f).$$

Thus in A'' we have

$$(q_0'', w_1 \cdots w_n, Z_b) \overset{+}{\vdash} (q_f, w_2 \cdots w_n, Z_f) \overset{+}{\vdash} \cdots \overset{+}{\vdash} (q_f, \Lambda, Z_f).$$

Thus $w = w_1 \cdots w_n \in T(A'', Z_f) = L''$.

By the construction of A'', we see that $T(A'', Z_f) = T(A'', \Gamma'')$. This completes the proof that (b) implies (c).

To help prove (c) implies (d), we first show that (c) implies (b). Assume there exists a dpda $A = (Q, \Sigma, \Gamma, \delta, q_0, Z, F)$, where $F = \{q_f\}$ and there exists $Z_f \in \Gamma$ such that $L = T(A, Z_f) = T(A, \Gamma)$. Clearly, $L \in \Delta_1$. By Theorem 11.5.1, $L \in \Delta_0$. Suppose that for $x \in \Sigma^+$; $w, y \in \Sigma^*$, we have $w \in L$, $wx \in L$, and $y \in L$. Then we have

$$(q_0, wx, Z_0) \overset{*}{\vdash} (q_f, x, Z_f) \overset{*}{\vdash} (q_f, \Lambda, Z_f)$$

and

$$(q_0, y, Z_0) \overset{*}{\vdash} (q_f, \Lambda, Z_f).$$

Therefore

$$(q_0, yx, Z_0) \overset{+}{\vdash} (q_f, x, Z_f) \overset{*}{\vdash} (q_f, \Lambda, Z_f).$$

Thus $yx \in L$. This completes the proof that (c) implies (b).

We now prove that (c) implies (d). We assume that there exists a dpda $A = (Q, \Sigma, \Gamma, \delta, q_0, Z_0, F)$, where $F = \{q_f\}$ and $L = T(A, \Gamma) = T(A, Z_f)$ for some $Z_f \in \Gamma$. Let $L_0 = \min(L)$. By Problem 11.3.5, L_0 is deterministic. By the definition of min, L_0 is prefix-free. Thus, by Theorem 11.5.5, L_0 is strict deterministic. We now consider two cases, when $L = L_0$ and when $L \neq L_0$.

CASE 1. $L = L_0$. Since L_0 is strict deterministic, $L = L_0(\emptyset)^*$.

CASE 2. $L \neq L_0$. Since $L \neq L_0$, there exist $x \in \Sigma^*$, $z \in \Sigma^+$ such that $x \in L$ and $xz \in L$. Let $L' = \{y \in \Sigma^* \mid xy \in L\}$. We shall show that L' is deterministic, and that $L = L_0 L'$.

We now construct a dpda to accept L'. Let $A' = (Q, \Sigma, \Gamma, \delta, q_f, Z_f, \{q_f\})$, where $A = (Q, \Sigma, \Gamma, \delta, q_0, Z_0, F)$ was previously defined. Clearly, A' is deterministic.

Claim $L = L_0 L'$.

Proof We first show that $L \subseteq L_0 L'$. Suppose that, for some $w \in \Sigma^*$, $w \in L$. Then, for some $w_0, w_1 \in \Sigma^*$, $w = w_0 w_1$, where $w_0 \in L_0 = \min(L)$.

If $w_1 = \Lambda$, clearly, $w_1 \in L'$; thus $w \in L_0 L'$.

Suppose $w_1 \neq \Lambda$. Since $w_0 \in L$, $w_0 w_1 \in L$, and $x \in L$, we know $x w_1 \in L$ by characterization (b) of $LR(0)$ languages. Recall that we are assuming (c), and (c) implies (b). Thus $w_1 \in L'$.

Conversely, we show that $L_0 L' \subseteq L$.

Suppose that, for some $w \in \Sigma^*$, $w \in L_0 L'$. Then, for some $w_0, w_1 \in \Sigma^*$, we have $w = w_0 w_1$, where $w_0 \in L_0$ and $w_1 \in L'$. Since $w_1 \in L'$, we know $x w_1 \in L$. Since $x \in L$, $x w_1 \in L$, and $w_0 \in L$, we know $w = w_0 w_1 \in L$, by characterization (b) of $LR(0)$ languages. Thus $L_0 L_1 \subseteq L$, and therefore we see that $L = L_0 L'$.

Now, let $L_1 = \min(L' - \{\Lambda\})$. Clearly, L_1 is strict deterministic, since L' is deterministic.

Claim $L' = L_1^*$.

We first show that $L' \subseteq L_1^*$. For some $w \in \Sigma^*$, assume that $w \in L'$. Suppose $w = \Lambda$. Then, clearly, $w \in L_1^*$. Assume $w \in \Sigma^+$. Then there exist $n \geq 1$, $w_i \in \Sigma^+$, for $1 \leq i \leq n$, where $w = w_1 \cdots w_n$ such that in machine A',

$$(q_f, w_1 \cdots w_n, Z_f) \overset{*}{\vdash} (q_f, w_2 \cdots w_n, Z_f) \overset{+}{\vdash} (q_f, w_3 \cdots w_n, Z_f) \overset{+}{\vdash} \cdots \overset{+}{\vdash} (q_f, \Lambda, Z_f),$$

where these are the only instances in which the machine A' goes through state q_f.

Thus, for $1 \leq i \leq n$,

$$(q_f, w_i, Z_f) \overset{+}{\vdash} (q_f, \Lambda, Z_f).$$

Thus $w_i \in L_1$ and hence $w \in L_1^*$.

We now show that $L_1^* \subseteq L'$. For some $w \in \Sigma^*$, assume $w \in L_1^*$. If $w = \Lambda$, clearly, $w \in L'$, by definition of L'. Assume $w \neq \Lambda$. Since $w \in L_1^*$, there exist $n \geq 1$, $w_i \in \Sigma^*$ such that $w_i \in L$ for $1 \leq i \leq n$, where $w = w_1 \cdots w_n$. We now have, in A',

$$(q_f, w_1 \cdots w_n, Z_f) \overset{*}{\vdash} (q_f, w_2 \cdots w_n, Z_f) \overset{*}{\vdash} \cdots \overset{*}{\vdash} (q_f, \Lambda, Z_f).$$

This gives us that

$$w = w_1 \cdots w_n \in L'.$$

Therefore,

$$L' = L_1^*.$$

Thus, we have $L = L_0 L_1^*$ with $L_0, L_1 \in \Delta_2$. This completes our proof that (c) implies (d).

Finally, we show that (d) implies (a). We assume that

$$L = L_0 L_1^* \qquad \text{where} \qquad L_0, L_1 \in \Delta_2.$$

We first consider the degenerate case. Suppose $L_0 = \emptyset$. Then $L = \emptyset$ and clearly is an $LR(0)$ language. Suppose $L_1 = \emptyset$ or $\{\Lambda\}$. Then $L = L_0$. Since L_0 is a strict deterministic language, L must be an $LR(0)$ language by Theorem 13.2.4.

Now, we handle the nondegenerate cases. We assume that

$$L_0, L_1 \neq \emptyset, \qquad L_1 \neq \{\Lambda\}.$$

Since L_i is a strict deterministic language, there exist strict deterministic, thus $LR(0)$, grammars $G_i = (V_i, \Sigma_i, P_i, S_i)$ such that $L_i = L(G_i)$, for $i = 0, 1$, with $N_0 \cap N_1 = \emptyset$.

Let $G = (V, \Sigma, P, S)$, where $V = V_0 \cup V_1 \cup \{S\}$, $S \cap \{V_0 \cup V_1\} = \emptyset$, $P = P_0 \cup P_1 \cup \{S \to SS_1, S \to S_0\}$, $\Sigma = \Sigma_0 \cup \Sigma_1$. Clearly, $L(G) = L$, since G lays down one word of L_0 followed by a series of strings of any length of words of L_1. We need only show that G is $LR(0)$. Since $L_1 \neq \{\Lambda\}$, and $L_1 \in \Delta_2$, we know $\Lambda \notin L_1$, by the Corollary to Theorem 11.4.2.

We assume now, for the sake of contradiction, that G is not an $LR(0)$ grammar. Then, by Lemma 13.2.3,

i) There exist $w, w', x \in \Sigma^*; \gamma, \gamma', \alpha, \alpha', \beta, \beta' \in V^*; A, A' \in N$, such that:

ii) $S \overset{*}{\underset{R}{\Rightarrow}} \alpha A w \underset{R}{\Rightarrow} \alpha\beta w = \gamma w$

iii) $S \overset{*}{\underset{R}{\Rightarrow}} \alpha' A' x \underset{R}{\Rightarrow} \alpha'\beta' x = \gamma' x = \gamma w'$

iv) ${}^{(0)}w = {}^{(0)}w' = \Lambda$

where v) $(A \to \beta, \lg(\alpha\beta)) \neq (A' \to \beta', \lg(\alpha'\beta'))$

and vi) $\lg(\alpha'\beta') \geqslant \lg(\gamma)$.

We now expand derivations (ii) and (iii). For some $y_1, \ldots, y_n, y_1', \ldots, y_m' \in \Sigma^+; y_0, y_0' \in \Sigma^*, n, m \geqslant 0$, (ii) gives us

$$S \underset{R}{\Rightarrow} SS_1 \overset{+}{\underset{R}{\Rightarrow}} Sy_n \underset{R}{\Rightarrow} SS_1y_n \overset{+}{\underset{R}{\Rightarrow}} Sy_{n-1}y_n \overset{*}{\underset{R}{\Rightarrow}} Sy_1 \cdots y_n \underset{R}{\Rightarrow} S_0y_1 \cdots y_n \overset{*}{\underset{R}{\Rightarrow}} y_0y_1 \cdots y_n$$

where $\alpha A w \underset{R}{\Rightarrow} \alpha\beta w$ are two consecutive canonical sentential forms in this derivation. (iii) gives us

$$S \underset{R}{\Rightarrow} SS_1 \overset{+}{\underset{R}{\Rightarrow}} Sy_m' \underset{R}{\Rightarrow} SS_1y_m' \overset{+}{\underset{R}{\Rightarrow}} Sy_{m-1}'y_m' \overset{*}{\underset{R}{\Rightarrow}} Sy_1' \cdots y_m' \underset{R}{\Rightarrow} S_0y_1' \cdots y_m' \overset{*}{\underset{R}{\Rightarrow}} y_0'y_1' \cdots y_m'$$

where $\alpha' A' x \underset{R}{\Rightarrow} \alpha'\beta' x$ are two consecutive canonical sentential forms in this derivation.

The productions in G come from either P_0, P_1, or from our two new productions. We thus now consider two cases, namely, ${}^{(1)}\gamma = S$ and ${}^{(1)}\gamma \neq S$. In the first case we will be working on a reduction in P_0 or on a new production; in the second case, we will be working on a reduction in P_1, or on a new production.

CASE 1. ${}^{(1)}\gamma = S$. We now have two subcases, which will turn out to represent a production in P_0 or a new production.

CASE 1(a). Suppose ${}^{(2)}\gamma = SS_1$. Then we know that, for some $\delta \in V_1^*$, we have $S_1 \overset{*}{\underset{R}{\Rightarrow}} S_1\delta$. But, since L_1 is strict deterministic, we must have $S_1 \overset{0}{\underset{R}{\Rightarrow}} S_1$ by the Corollary to Theorem 11.4.3, since strict deterministic grammars cannot be left-recursive. Then $\gamma = SS_1$ and

$$(A \to \beta, \lg(\alpha\beta)) = (A' \to \beta', \lg(\alpha'\beta')) = (S \to SS_1, 2).$$

But this is a contradiction of (v).

CASE 1(b). ${}^{(2)}\gamma \neq SS_1$. We have, for i such that $-1 \leqslant i \leqslant n-2$, $\alpha_1, \beta_1 \in V^*$, $w_1 \in \Sigma^*$, $A, A_1 \in N$,

$$S \overset{*}{\underset{R}{\Rightarrow}} SS_1 y_{n-i} \cdots y_n \overset{*}{\underset{R}{\Rightarrow}} S\alpha_1 A_1 w_1 y_{n-i} \cdots y_n = \alpha A w \underset{R}{\Rightarrow} \alpha\beta w = \gamma w$$
$$= S\alpha_1 \beta_1 w_1 y_{n-i} \cdots y_n$$

Also, for j such that $-1 \leqslant j \leqslant m-2$, $\alpha_1', \beta_1' \in V^*$, $x_1 \in \Sigma^*$, $A', A_1' \in N$,

$$S \overset{*}{\underset{R}{\Rightarrow}} SS_1 y_{m-j}' \cdots y_m' \overset{*}{\underset{R}{\Rightarrow}} S\alpha_1' A_1' x_1 y_{m-j}' \cdots y_m' = \alpha' A' x \underset{R}{\Rightarrow} \alpha'\beta' x = \gamma w'$$
$$= S\alpha_1' \beta_1' x_1 y_{m-j}' \cdots y_m'$$

Now, for $\gamma_1 \in V^*$, let $\gamma_1 = \gamma^{(\lg(\gamma)-1)}$, that is, γ without the leading S. Then, for some $w_1' \in \Sigma^*$, since $\lg(\alpha'\beta') \geqslant \lg(\gamma)$,

$$S_1 \overset{*}{\underset{R}{\Rightarrow}} \alpha_1 A_1 w_1 \underset{R}{\Rightarrow} \alpha_1 \beta_1 w_1 = \gamma_1 w_1$$
$$S_1 \overset{*}{\underset{R}{\Rightarrow}} \alpha_1' A_1' x_1 \underset{R}{\Rightarrow} \alpha_1' \beta_1' x_1 = \gamma_1 w_1'$$

Clearly, ${}^{(0)}w_1 = {}^{(0)}w_1'$. Thus, since G_1 is $LR(0)$, we have

$$(A_1 \to \beta_1, \lg(\alpha_1 \beta_1)) = (A_1' \to \beta_1', \lg(\alpha_1' \beta_1')).$$

Now $A = A_1$, $A' = A_1'$, $\beta = \beta_1$, $\beta' = \beta_1'$, and $\alpha_1 = S\alpha$, $\alpha_1' = S\alpha'$. Thus, $(A \to \beta, \lg(\alpha\beta)) = (A' \to \beta', \lg(\alpha'\beta'))$, contradicting (v).

CASE 2. ${}^{(1)}\gamma \neq S$. Again, we have two subcases.

Case 2(a). Suppose ${}^{(1)}\gamma = S_0$. We know that, for some $\delta \in V_0^*$, we have $S_0 \overset{*}{\underset{R}{\Rightarrow}} S_0\delta$. But, since L_0 is strict deterministic, as before, then we must have $S_0 \overset{0}{\underset{R}{\Rightarrow}} S_0$. Thus, we have $\gamma = S_0$, and

$$(A \to \beta, \lg(\alpha\beta)) = (A' \to \beta', \lg(\alpha'\beta')) = (S \to S_0, 1),$$

which contradicts (v).

CASE 2(b). Suppose ${}^{(1)}\gamma \neq S_0$. Then, for some α_1, $\beta_1 \in V^*$, $w_1 \in \Sigma^*$, $A_1 \in N$, we have

$$S \overset{*}{\underset{R}{\Rightarrow}} S_0 y_1 \cdots y_n \overset{*}{\underset{R}{\Rightarrow}} \alpha_1 A_1 w_1 y_1 \cdots y_n \underset{R}{\Rightarrow} \alpha_1 \beta_1 w_1 y_1 \cdots y_n$$

Also, for some $\alpha_1', \beta_1' \in V^*$, $x_1 \in \Sigma^*$, $A_1' \in N$, we have

$$S \overset{*}{\underset{R}{\Rightarrow}} S_0 y_1' \cdots y_n' \overset{*}{\underset{R}{\Rightarrow}} \alpha_1' A_1' x_1 y_1' \cdots y_m' \underset{R}{\Rightarrow} \alpha_1' \beta_1' x_1 y_1' \cdots y_n'$$

We have, for some $w_1' \in \Sigma^*$, since $\lg(\alpha_1'\beta_1') \geqslant \lg(\alpha_1\beta_1)$.

$$S_0 \overset{*}{\underset{R}{\Rightarrow}} \alpha_1 A_1 w_1 \underset{R}{\Rightarrow} \alpha_1 \beta_1 w_1 = \gamma w_1$$
$$S_0 \overset{*}{\underset{R}{\Rightarrow}} \alpha_1' A_1' x_1 \underset{R}{\Rightarrow} \alpha_1' \beta_1' x_1 = \gamma w_1'$$

Clearly, ${}^{(0)}w_1 = {}^{(0)}w_1'$. Since G_0 is $LR(0)$, we have

$$(A_1 \to \beta_1, \lg(\alpha_1 \beta_1)) = (A_1' \to \beta_1', \lg(\alpha_1' \beta_1')),$$

giving us a contradiction of (v). □

Condition (b) of the $LR(0)$ characterization theorem will prove most useful in checking whether or not a language is $LR(0)$. The following corollary to characterization (b) will be particularly useful.

Corollary Suppose $L \subseteq \Sigma^*$ is an $LR(0)$ language. For $w \in \Sigma^*$, $x \in \Sigma^+$, if $w \in L$ and $wx \in L$, then $wxx \in L$.

As an example of the utility of this corollary, consider the language $L = \{\Lambda, a\}$. We could prove directly that L is not an $LR(0)$ language, but the use of the corollary makes it even easier. Choose $w = \Lambda$ and $x = a$. If L were $LR(0)$, then aa would have to be in L, which is a contradiction.

The next theorem shows us that the factorization of an $LR(0)$ language, of the form given in the $LR(0)$ language-characterization theorem, is unique.

Recall that a language $L \subseteq \Sigma^*$ is degenerate if $L = \emptyset$ or $L = \{\Lambda\}$.

Theorem 13.3.2 (*Unique Factorization of LR(0) Languages*) Let $L = L_0 L_1^*$ be a nonempty $LR(0)$ language, where L_0, L_1 are strict deterministic languages. If there are two strict deterministic languages L_0', L_1' such that $L = L_0'(L_1')^*$, then $L_0 = L_0'$ and either

i) $L_1 = L_1'$

or ii) L_1, L_1' are degenerate.

Proof For the sake of a contradiction, we assume that there exist strict deterministic languages L_0, L_0', L_1, L_1' such that $L_0 L_1^* = L_0' L_1'^*$, where $L_0 \neq L_0'$ or $L_1 \neq L_1'$ and L_1 and L_1' are not degenerate.

CASE 1 $L_0 \neq L_0'$. We assume, without loss of generality, that there exists some $x \in \Sigma^*$ such that $x \in L_0'$ but $x \notin L_0$. This is possible since $L \neq \emptyset$ implies $L_0 \neq \emptyset$. Since $x \in L_0'$, we have $x \in L_0'(L_1')^*$. Thus, $x \in L$ and hence $x \in L_0 L_1^*$. Then, for some $x_0 \in \Sigma^*$, $x_1 \in \Sigma^+$, we have $x = x_0 x_1$, where $x_0 \in L_0$ and $x_1 \in L_1^*$. Since $x_0 \in L_0$, we know $x_0 \in L_0 L_1^*$; therefore, $x_0 \in L$. Now, we know that $x_0 \in L_0'(L_1')^*$. Clearly $x_0 \notin L_0'$, since x_0 is a proper prefix of x, $x \in L_0'$, and L_0' is prefix-free. Thus, there exist some $x_2 \in \Sigma^*$, $x_3 \in \Sigma^+$, such that $x_2 \in L_0'$, $x_3 \in L_1'^*$, where $x_0 = x_2 x_3$. We also know that $x = x_0 x_1 = x_2(x_3 x_1) \in L_0'$. Since $x_3 \neq \Lambda$, L_0 is not prefix-free. But this is a contradiction.

CASE 2 $L_0 = L_0'$. We have $L = L_0 L_1^* = L_0 L_1'^*$. We assume for the sake of contradiction, that $L_1 \neq L_1'$ and we do not have L_1 and L_1' degenerate. Without loss of generality, there exists a $y \in \Sigma^+$ such that $y \in L_1'$, but $y \notin L_1$. Since $L_0 \neq \emptyset$, there exists some $x \in \Sigma^*$ such that $x \in L_0$. Clearly, $xy \in L_0 L_1'^*$, giving us $xy \in L_0 L_1^*$. Therefore, $xy = x'y'$, where $x' \in L_0$ and $y' \in L_1^*$. Clearly, x must be a prefix of x' or x' a prefix of x. Since L_0 is prefix-free, we must have $x = x'$, and thus $y = y'$. Therefore, we see that $y \in L_1^*$. Now, since $y \notin L_1$, we know there exist $y_0 \in \Sigma^*$, $y_1 \in \Sigma^+$ such that $y = y_0 y_1$, where $y_0 \in L_1$. It follows that $xy_0 \in L$ and, hence, $xy_0 \in L_0 L_1'^*$. Thus $xy_0 = x'y_0'$ where $x' \in L_0$ and $y_0' \in L_1'^*$. Again, since L_0 is prefix-free, we have $x = x'$ and $y_0 = y_0'$, giving us $y_0 \in L_1'^*$. But we know $y_0 \notin L_1'$, since, if it were, we would have $y_0 \in L_1'$ and $y_0 y_1 \in L_1'$, where $y_1 \neq \Lambda$, contradicting the fact that L_1' is prefix-free. Now, since $y_0 \in L_1'^*$, there exist $y_2 \in \Sigma^*$, $y_3 \in \Sigma^+$ such that $y_0 = y_2 y_3$, where $y_2 \in L_1'$. Now we have $y = y_0 y_1 = y_2(y_3 y_1) \in L_1'$. But $y_3 y_1 \neq \Lambda_0$, and $y_2 \in L_1'$. But this contradicts the fact that L_1' is prefix-free. □

We conclude this section with an example of the use of the $LR(0)$ characterization theorem to show us immediately that a given language which is not strict deterministic is $LR(0)$. We shall show that the semi-Dyck language is contained in the class of $LR(0)$ languages.

Theorem 13.3.3 Let $D_r \subseteq \Sigma^*$ be the semi-Dyck language for some $r \geqslant 1$. Then D_r is an $LR(0)$ language, but not a strict deterministic language.

Proof $D_r = D$ is deterministic, by Theorem 10.4.1. Suppose that, for $x \in \Sigma^+$, $w, y \in \Sigma^*$, we have $w \in D$, $wx \in D$, and $y \in D$. By Proposition 10.4.2(e), we have $x \in D$. Since $y \in D$ and $x \in D$, we have $yx \in D$, by Proposition 10.4.2(a). By (b) of the $LR(0)$ language characterization theorem, D is an $LR(0)$ language. Since $a_1 a_1' \in D$ and $a_1 a_1' a_1 a_1' \in D$, D is not strict deterministic, since it is not prefix-free. □

PROBLEMS

All of these problems refer to concepts introduced in the problems of Section 13.2.

1 Show that L is an $ALR(0)$ language if and only if L is strict deterministic.

2 Show that L is a $\$LR(0)$ language if and only if L is an $LR(0)$ language.

3 Show that an $LR(0)$ grammar can have at most one pathological production.

4 Work out the closure properties for the $LR(0)$ languages, as was done for the families Δ_i, where $0 \leqslant i \leqslant 2$, in Problems 3 through 47 of Section 11.5.

5 Prove the following interesting result.

Theorem There is an algorithm to decide whether a deterministic language is $LR(0)$ if and only if there is an algorithm to decide whether two deterministic context-free languages are equal.

Hint for the *only if* direction: Let $L_1, L_2 \subseteq \Sigma^*$ be two deterministic context-free languages, and let $c_1, c_2, c_3, \$$ be four new symbols not in Σ. Consider the following set:

$$L = c_1(L_1\$)^* c_3 (L_2\$)^* \cup c_2(L_2\$)^* c_3 (L_1\$)^*.$$

6 Prove that there is an algorithm to decide whether a Δ_1 language is $LR(0)$ if and only if there is an algorithm to decide whether two deterministic context-free languages are equal.

13.4 LR-STYLE PARSERS

A parser that has many desirable practical features will now be described. The operation will be precisely specified and will depend on some special stack symbols, which are traditionally called "tables." In subsequent subsections, the existence of such tables will be derived for *LR*(k) grammars.

An "*LR*-style parser" has the following structure: There will be an input tape, an output tape, a pushdown stack, and some mechanism for "looking ahead" k characters on the input string. The pushdown symbols are alternately symbols of the grammar being parsed and certain tables. The action of the parser will be determined by the table at the top of the pushdown stack and the lookahead symbols. The table on top of the pushdown stack represents all the productions upon which the device may be working at a given stage of the parse. These tables determine whether to shift or reduce with the given lookahead, and if we are to reduce, what to "pop" from the top of the pushdown, and a choice of nonterminals to which we reduce. After we have popped the given number of symbols from the pushdown, the table appearing on top of the pushdown will uniquely tell us what reduction to make. The suitable nonterminal will then be placed on top of the pushdown, followed by the new appropriate table; and the number of the production being reduced by will be printed on the output tape (see Fig. 13.3).

The parser will accept a string by halting in a special **accept** state with the bottom-of-stack table on the pushdown, and with empty input tape. The parser will reject strings by halting in a special **error** state. Such a parser operates "properly" on a given grammar if, for every string over the alphabet over which the grammar is defined, the parser halts. Moreover, it must halt in the **error** state given a string not generated by the grammar. For a string generated by the grammar, the parser must halt in the **accept** state with the reversed canonical derivation of the string on the output tape.

The device shown in Fig. 13.3 is a type of deterministic pushdown "transducer" whose moves depend on the tables that are supplied.

The simplest way to formalize the parser is to begin with an instantaneous description (or ID). An *ID* of the parser is written as (γ, z, ρ), where

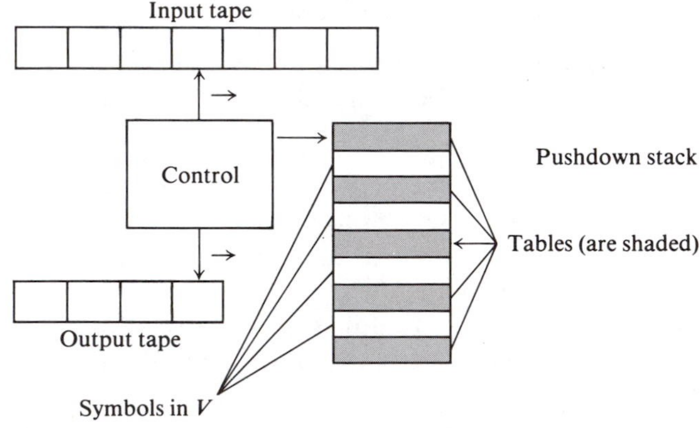

→ indicates head direction

FIG. 13.3 An LR style parser.

i) $z \in \Sigma^*$ is the contents of the (as yet unread) input.

ii) $\gamma \in T_0(VT)^*$ is the contents of the pushdown store. The "top" is assumed to be at the right. T_0 is a special "initial table."

iii) $\rho \in P^*$ is the contents of the output tape, the partial parse.

The initial ID is defined to be (T_0, z, Λ). In addition, there are two special ID's **error** and **accept**.

We are now ready to give a more formal description of the functions that control the parser.

Definition 13.4.1 Let $G = (V, \Sigma, P, S)$ be a reduced context-free grammar and $k \geq 0$. Let $\mathscr{T}$ be a set of tables.† Define two functions f and g as follows:

1 f, the *parsing action function,* is a map‡ from $\mathscr{T} \times \Sigma_\Lambda^k$ into {**shift, error**} $\cup$ {**reduce** $\pi \mid \pi \in P$};

2 g, the *goto function,* is a map from $\mathscr{T} \times V$ into $\mathscr{T} \cup$ {**error**}.

Example Assume $k = 1$. Let G be the grammar whose numbered productions are shown below:

1. $S \rightarrow aAd$
2. $S \rightarrow bAB$
3. $A \rightarrow cA$
4. $A \rightarrow c$
5. $B \rightarrow d$

For this grammar, $\mathscr{T} = \{T_0, \ldots, T_9\}$ and the functions f and g are given in Table 13.4.1.

TABLE 13.4.1 The f and g functions*

	f					g						
	a	b	c	d	Λ	a	b	c	d	A	B	S
T_0	shift	shift				T_1	T_2					
T_1			shift					T_3		T_4		
T_2			shift					T_3		T_5		
T_3			shift	reduce 4				T_3		T_8		
T_4				shift					T_6			
T_5				shift					T_9		T_7	
T_6					reduce 1							
T_7					reduce 2							
T_8				reduce 3								
T_9					reduce 5							

* A blank denotes error.

† The construction of tables that may be used by such a parser will be given later.

‡ Recall that $\Sigma_\Lambda^k = \{x \in \Sigma^* \mid \lg(x) \leq k\}$.

It is often convenient to express the goto function by a directed graph in which each node represents a table or "state". In our running example, we have the following diagram:

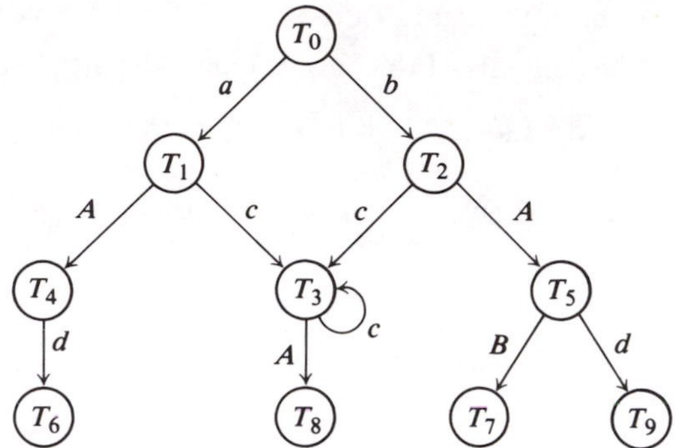

The goto graph for our parser

Now we shall indicate how the parsing device functions, by defining a move relation, $\vdash$, on ID's. The device is a pushdown-like automaton whose move will depend deterministically on its "state" (here, there is only one state), the first k letters of the input, and the topmost stack symbol.

Definition Suppose the parser is in ID $(\gamma T, z, \rho)$, where $T \in \mathscr{T}$, $z \in \Sigma^*$, and $\rho \in P^*$.

1 If $f(T, {}^{(k)}z) =$ **shift** then

a) if $z = \Lambda$ then $(\gamma T, z, \rho) \vdash$ **error**

b) if $z \neq \Lambda$ then we write $z = bz'$, $b \in \Sigma$, $z' \in \Sigma^*$. Moreover,
  (b_1) If $g(T, b) =$ **error** then $(\gamma T, bz', \rho) \vdash$ **error.**
  (b_2) If $g(T, b) \neq$ **error** then $(\gamma T, bz', \rho) \vdash (\gamma T b g(T, b), z', \rho)$.

That is, in step (b_2), we shift the next character of the input onto the stack and also stack the table determined by the topmost symbol and the input.

2 If $f(T, {}^{(k)}z) =$ **reduce** π where π is $A \to \beta$ then we wish to "pop" 2 lg(β) symbols. When we do so, let T' be the table we "uncover." More precisely, define $\gamma T = \gamma' T' \gamma''$, where $\lg(\gamma'') = 2\lg(\beta)$.

a) If $T' = T_0$, $S = A$, and $z = \Lambda$, then

$$(\gamma T, z, \rho) \vdash (T_0, \Lambda, \rho\pi) \vdash \textbf{accept}.$$

b) If $g(T', A) =$ **error** then $(\gamma T, z, \rho) \vdash$ **error.**

c) If neither case (a) nor case (b) holds, then

$$(\gamma' T' \gamma'', z, \rho) \vdash (\gamma' T' A g(T', A), \rho\pi).$$

In case 2(c), we remove the coded form of β, and replace it by its immediate ancestor A. The appropriate table is computed and stacked above A; the production used is added to the output.

3 If $f(T, {}^{(k)}z) =$ **error**, then $(\gamma T, z, \rho) \vdash$ **error**.

Finally, let $\overset{+}{\vdash}(\overset{*}{\vdash})$ be the (reflexive) transitive closure of $\vdash$.

The action of our sample parser on the following examples may be helpful. Let us use the parser on the string *bccd*, which is in $L(G)$.

$$\begin{aligned}(T_0, bccd, \Lambda) &\vdash (T_0bT_2, ccd, \Lambda)\\ &\vdash (T_0bT_2cT_3, cd, \Lambda)\\ &\vdash (T_0bT_2cT_3cT_3, d, \Lambda)\\ &\vdash (T_0bT_2cT_3AT_8, d, 4)\\ &\vdash (T_0bT_2AT_5, d, 43)\\ &\vdash (T_0bT_2AT_5dT_9, \Lambda, 43)\\ &\vdash (T_0bT_2AT_5BT_7, \Lambda, 435)\\ &\vdash (T_0, \Lambda, 4352)\\ &\vdash \textbf{accept}\end{aligned}$$

Since we have reached **accept**, a rightmost derivation of *bccd* is given by 2534, as can be seen by the following tree in Fig. 13.4.

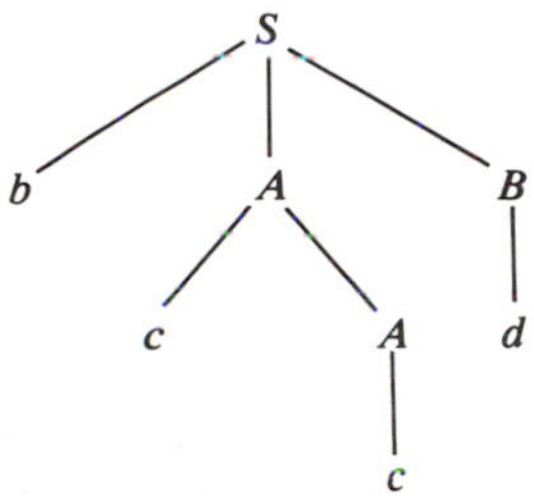

FIG. 13.4

Now, let us try to use the parser on a nonsentence, say *acb*. We have the computation

$$\begin{aligned}(T_0, acb, \Lambda) &\vdash (T_0aT_1, cb, \Lambda)\\ &\vdash (T_0aT_1cT_3, b, \Lambda)\\ &\vdash \textbf{error}\end{aligned}$$

because $f(T_3, b) =$ **error**.

This kind of parser has a number of attractive features, but there is a great deal that we do not know. Where did these tables come from? When and how can they be constructed? We shall learn how to construct such tables shortly. To do so, certain functions will be helpful.

Definition Let $G = (V, \Sigma, P, S)$ be a reduced context-free grammar. For α, $\beta \in V^*$, define

$$\text{FIRST}_k(\alpha) = \{x \in \Sigma_\Lambda^k \mid \alpha \overset{*}{\Rightarrow} y \quad \text{for some } y \in \Sigma^* \text{ and } x = {}^{(k)}y\},$$

and

$$\text{FOLLOW}_k(\beta) = \{x \in \Sigma_\Lambda^k \mid S \overset{*}{\Rightarrow} \theta\beta\gamma \quad \text{for some } \theta \in V^* \text{ and } x \in \text{FIRST}_k(\gamma)\}.$$

In our running example, it is easy to compute FIRST_1 and FOLLOW_1 although, in general, it takes some effort. Finding efficient algorithms for these tasks is left for the problems at the end of this section.

Example $\text{FIRST}_1(A) = \{c\}$ and $\text{FIRST}_1(B) = \{d\}$
$\text{FOLLOW}_1(A) = \{d\}$

in our running example.

PROBLEMS

1 Let $G = (V, \Sigma, P, S)$ be a reduced context-free grammar such that $L(G) \neq \emptyset$. Show that:

a) for $\alpha \in V^*$,

$$\text{FIRST}_k(\alpha) = \{x \in \Sigma_\Lambda^k \mid \alpha \underset{R}{\overset{*}{\Rightarrow}} y \quad \text{for some } y \in \Sigma^* \text{ and } x = {}^{(k)}y\};$$

b) for $A \in N$,

$$\text{FOLLOW}_k(A) = \{x \in \Sigma_\Lambda^k \mid S \underset{R}{\overset{*}{\Rightarrow}} \alpha A y \quad \text{where } y \in \Sigma^* \text{ and } x = {}^{(k)}y\}.$$

2 Derive an efficient algorithm for the computation of $\text{FIRST}_k(\alpha)$ and $\text{FOLLOW}_k(\alpha)$. Is it easier to determine whether some string belongs to these sets than to generate the sets?

3 The following function appears in the literature on *LR* parsing. For $\alpha \in V^*$, define

$$\text{EFF}_k(\alpha) = \{w \mid w \in \text{FIRST}_k(\alpha) \text{ and there is a derivation}$$
$$\alpha \underset{R}{\overset{*}{\Rightarrow}} \beta \underset{R}{\Rightarrow} wx \quad \text{where } \beta \neq Awx \text{ for all } A \in N\}.$$

Interpret the definition of EFF in terms of generation trees and then give an efficient algorithm for computing EFF.

13.5 CONSTRUCTING SETS OF LR(k) ITEMS

We now begin to construct certain sets which will be necessary in forming the tables that drive our parser.

Definition Let $G = (V, \Sigma, P, S)$ be a reduced context-free grammar, and let $k \geqslant 0$. An *LR(k) item* for G is a pair $(A \to \beta_1 \cdot \beta_2, u)$ where $A \in N$, $\beta_1, \beta_2 \in V^*$, $u \in \text{FOLLOW}_k(A)$, and $A \to \beta_1\beta_2$ is in P.

The intuition behind this definition is clear. It means that, in forming our tree, we have matched up to the dot and our lookahead is u. The situation is illustrated in Fig. 13.5.

An algorithm is now given for constructing sets of items. This construction will build sets that are reminiscent of the entries in the recognition matrices of Section 12.6.

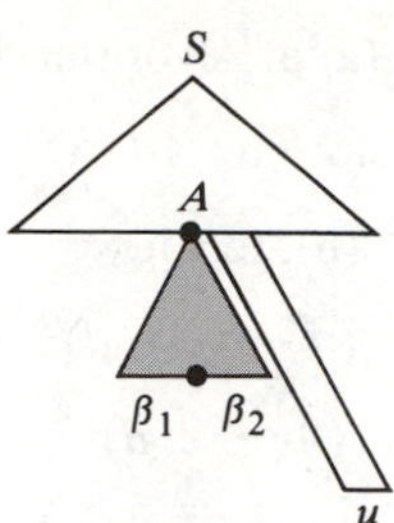

FIG. 13.5

Algorithm 13.5.1

Input $G = (V, \Sigma, P, S)$, a reduced context-free grammar, $k \geqslant 0$, and $\gamma \in V^*$.

Output We define the output to be a set $V_k(\gamma)$.†

Method

1 To construct $V_k(\Lambda)$,

a) If, for some $\alpha \in V^*$, $S \to \alpha$ is in P, add $(S \to \cdot\, \alpha, \Lambda)$ to $V_k(\Lambda)$.

b) If, for some $A, B \in N$, $\alpha, \beta \in V^*$, $u \in \Sigma^*$, we have $(A \to \cdot\, B\alpha, u)$ in $V_k(\Lambda)$, and $B \to \beta$ is in P, then, for all x such that‡ $x \in \text{FIRST}_k(\alpha u)$, add $(B \to \cdot\, \beta, x)$ to $V_k(\Lambda)$.

c) Repeat (b) until nothing new can be added to $V_k(\Lambda)$.

2 To construct $V_k(X_1 \cdots X_i)$ for some $i \geqslant 1$, $X_j \in V$ for $1 \leqslant j \leqslant i$.

a) If, for some $\alpha, \beta \in V^*, A \in N, u \in \Sigma^*$,

$(A \to \alpha \cdot X_i\beta, u)$ is in $V_k(X_1 \cdots X_{i-1})$,

then add

$(A \to \alpha X_i \cdot \beta, u)$ to $V_i(X_1 \cdots X_i)$.

b) If, for some $A, B \in N$, $\alpha, \beta, \delta \in V^*$, $u \in \Sigma^*$, $(A \to \alpha \cdot B\beta, u)$ has been placed in $V_k(X_1 \cdots X_i)$ and $B \to \delta$ is in P, then, for all $x \in \text{FIRST}_k(\beta u)$, add $(B \to \cdot\, \delta, x)$ to $V_k(X_1 \cdots X_i)$.

c) Repeat (b) until nothing new can be added to $V_k(X_1 \cdots X_i)$.

The algorithm clearly halts, since, for given k and G, only a finite number of $LR(k)$ items exist.

We now work out an example, starting with the running example of Section 13.4.

First, we compute

$$V_1(\Lambda): \quad \begin{cases} (S \to \cdot\, aAd, \Lambda) \\ (S \to \cdot\, bAB, \Lambda) \end{cases}$$

† Note that we write $V_k(\gamma)$ when the grammar in question is clear, as an abbreviation for $V_{G,k}(\gamma)$.

‡ FIRST is defined in Section 13.4.

We obtain $V_1(a)$ by applying part 2(a) of Algorithm 13.5.1 to $V_1(\Lambda)$. This adds

$$(S \to a \cdot Ad,\ \Lambda)$$

to $V_1(a)$, and allows us to use part 2(b), to add

$$(A \to \cdot\, cA,\ d)$$

and

$$(A \to \cdot\, c,\ d)$$

This completes the construction of $V_1(a)$. The reader should check that:

$$V_1(ac) \quad \text{is} \quad \begin{array}{l} (A \to c \cdot A,\ d) \\ (A \to c\ \cdot,\ d) \\ (A \to \cdot\, cA,\ d) \\ (A \to \cdot\, c,\ d) \end{array}$$

We now study the set of items generated by Algorithm 13.5.1. Our first lemma shows how having an item in a set of items corresponds to "moving across the righthand side of a production."

Lemma 13.5.1 Let $G = (V, \Sigma, P, S)$ be a reduced context-free grammar and $k \geqslant 0$. Then, for $A \in N$, $\alpha, \beta_1, \beta_2, \gamma \in V^*$, $u \in \text{FOLLOW}_k(A)$,

$$(A \to \cdot\, \beta_1\beta_2, u) \in V_k(\alpha), \quad \text{where } \alpha\beta_1 = \gamma$$

if and only if

$$(A \to \beta_1 \cdot \beta_2, u) \in V_k(\gamma).$$

Proof Assume that

$$(A \to \cdot\, \beta_1\beta_2, u) \in V_k(\alpha).$$

We use induction on $\lg(\beta_1)$.

Basis. Let $\lg(\beta_1) = 0$. Clearly,

$$(A \to \beta_1 \cdot \beta_2, u) = (A \to \cdot\, \beta_2, u) \in V_k(\alpha) = V_k(\alpha\beta_1).$$

Induction step. Assume that the lemma is true in this direction for $\lg(\beta_1) = \ell \geqslant 0$. We show that it is true for $\lg(\beta_1) = \ell + 1$. Let $\beta_1 = \beta_1' X$, where $\beta_1' \in V^*$, $X \in V$. By our induction hypothesis,

$$(A \to \beta_1' \cdot X\beta_2, u) \in V_k(\alpha\beta_1').$$

Therefore, $(A \to \beta_1' X \cdot \beta_2, u) \in V_k(\alpha\beta_1' X) = V_k(\alpha\beta_1)$ by 2(a) of Algorithm 13.5.1.

Now assume, conversely, that $(A \to \beta_1 \cdot \beta_2,\ u) \in V_k(\gamma)$. Again induct on $\lg(\beta_1)$.

Basis. $\lg(\beta_1) = 0$. Clearly,

$$(A \to \cdot\, \beta_1\beta_2, u) = (A \to \cdot\, \beta_2, u) \in V_k(\gamma) = V_k(\alpha),$$

where $\alpha\beta_1 = \gamma$.

Induction step. Assume that the lemma is true in this direction for $\lg(\beta_1) = \ell \geqslant 0$. We show that it is true for $\lg(\beta_1) = \ell + 1$. Let $\beta_1 = \beta_1' X$, where $\beta_1' \in V^*$, $X \in V$. Since $\beta_1' X \neq \Lambda$, clearly the item $(A \to \beta_1 \cdot \beta_2, u)$ had to be added to $V_k(\gamma)$ in Step 2(a) of Algorithm 13.5.1. Thus, for some $\gamma' \in V^*$ such that $\gamma = \gamma' X$, we have

$$(A \to \beta_1' \cdot X\beta_2, u) \in V_k(\gamma').$$

Now, by our induction hypothesis, there exists some $\alpha \in V^*$ such that $(A \to \cdot\, \beta_1\beta_2, u) \in V_k(\alpha)$, where $\alpha\beta_1' = \gamma'$. Therefore, $\alpha\beta_1' X = \alpha\beta_1 = \gamma' X = \gamma$. □

The following theorem shows that if, for one item in a set of items, β_1 precedes the dot, and for another item in this set of items, β_1' precedes the dot, then either β_1 is a suffix of β_1' or β_1' is a suffix of β_1.

Theorem 13.5.1 Let $G = (V, \Sigma, P, S)$ be a reduced context-free grammar and $k \geqslant 0$. Then, if A, $A' \in N$, γ, β_1, $\beta_1' \in V^+$, $\lg(\beta_1') \geqslant \lg(\beta_1)$, β_2, $\beta_2' \in V^*$, $w \in \mathrm{FOLLOW}_k(A)$, $w' \in \mathrm{FOLLOW}_k(A')$, and

$$(A \to \beta_1 \cdot \beta_2, w)$$

$$(A' \to \beta_1' \cdot \beta_2', w')$$

are in $V_k(\gamma)$, then there exists an $\alpha \in V^*$ such that $\beta_1' = \alpha\beta_1$.

Proof Since $(A \to \beta_1 \cdot \beta_2,\ w) \in V_k(\gamma)$, by Lemma 13.5.1, there exists some $\gamma' \in V^*$ such that $\gamma = \gamma'\beta_1$ and

$$(A \to \cdot\, \beta_1\beta_2, w) \text{ is in } V_k(\gamma').$$

Since $(A' \to \beta_1' \cdot \beta_2', w')$ is in $V_k(\gamma)$, by Lemma 13.5.1, there exists some $\gamma'' \in V^*$ such that $\gamma = \gamma''\beta_1'$ and

$$(A' \to \cdot\, \beta_1'\beta_2', w') \text{ is in } V_k(\gamma'').$$

Since $\gamma'\beta_1 = \gamma''\beta_1'$ and $\lg(\beta_1') \geqslant \lg(\beta_1)$, we let

$$\alpha = {}^{(\lg(\beta_1') - \lg(\beta_1))}\beta_1',$$

as shown in Fig. 13.6. Clearly, $\beta_1' = \alpha\beta_1$. □

Since there are only a finite number of possible $LR(k)$ items for any fixed grammar, there can be only a finite number of sets of items. Therefore, to compute the collection of distinct sets of items, we could systematically compute $V_k(\Lambda)$, $V_k(\gamma)$ for all γ such that $\lg(\gamma) = 1$, $V_k(\gamma)$ for all γ such that $\lg(\gamma) = 2, \ldots, V_k(\gamma)$ for all γ such that $\lg(\gamma) = \ell, \ldots$ This algorithm will eventually terminate, since, for some ℓ, we will eventually get no new sets of items. The algorithm we have just described is somewhat wasteful, since it will necessitate computing many empty sets of items. One can avoid computing many such sets of items by building up only the collection of nonempty sets of items.

γ'	α	β_1
γ''	β_1'	

FIG. 13.6

Algorithm 13.5.2

Input Reduced context-free grammar $G = (V, \Sigma, P, S)$ and $k \geq 0$.

Output We define the output to be $\mathscr{S}_k = \{V_k(\gamma) \neq \emptyset \mid \gamma \in V^*\}$.

Method Initially, $\mathscr{S}_k$ is empty.

1 If $V_k(\Lambda) \neq \emptyset$, place $V_k(\Lambda)$ in $\mathscr{S}_k$. The set $V_k(\Lambda)$ is initially unmarked.

2 If a set of $LR(k)$ items $V_k(\gamma)$ in $\mathscr{S}_k$ is unmarked,

  a) Compute $V_k(\gamma X)$ for each $X \in V$. If $V_k(\gamma X) \neq \emptyset$, add $V_k(\gamma X)$ to $\mathscr{S}_k$ as an unmarked set of items if it is not already there.

  b) Mark $V_k(\gamma)$.

3 Repeat Step (2) until all sets of items in $\mathscr{S}_k$ are marked.

Again, the algorithm is guaranteed to halt since we will eventually get no new sets of items.

We now use Algorithm 13.5.2 to compute all of the sets of items for our running example.

Example There are ten nonempty sets of items which are as follows:

$$V_1(\Lambda) = \begin{Bmatrix} (S \to \cdot\, aAd,\ \Lambda) \\ (S \to \cdot\, bAB,\ \Lambda) \end{Bmatrix}$$

$$V_1(a) = \begin{Bmatrix} (S \to a \cdot Ad,\ \Lambda) \\ (A \to \cdot\, cA,\ d) \\ (A \to \cdot\, c,\ d) \end{Bmatrix}$$

$$V_1(b) = \begin{Bmatrix} (S \to b \cdot AB,\ \Lambda) \\ (A \to \cdot\, cA,\ d) \\ (A \to \cdot\, c,\ d) \end{Bmatrix}$$

$$V_1(ac) = \begin{Bmatrix} (A \to c \cdot A,\ d) \\ (A \to c\, \cdot,\ d) \\ (A \to \cdot\, cA,\ d) \\ (A \to \cdot\, c,\ d) \end{Bmatrix}$$

$$V_1(aA) = \{(S \to aA \cdot d,\ \Lambda)\}$$

$$V_1(bA) = \begin{Bmatrix} (S \to bA \cdot B,\ \Lambda) \\ (B \to \cdot\, d,\ \Lambda) \end{Bmatrix}$$

$$V_1(aAd) = \{(S \to aAd\, \cdot,\ \Lambda)\}$$

$$V_1(bAB) = \{(S \to bAB\, \cdot,\ \Lambda)\}$$

$$V_1(acA) = \{(A \to cA\, \cdot,\ d)\}$$

$$V_1(bAd) = \{(B \to d\, \cdot,\ \Lambda)\}$$

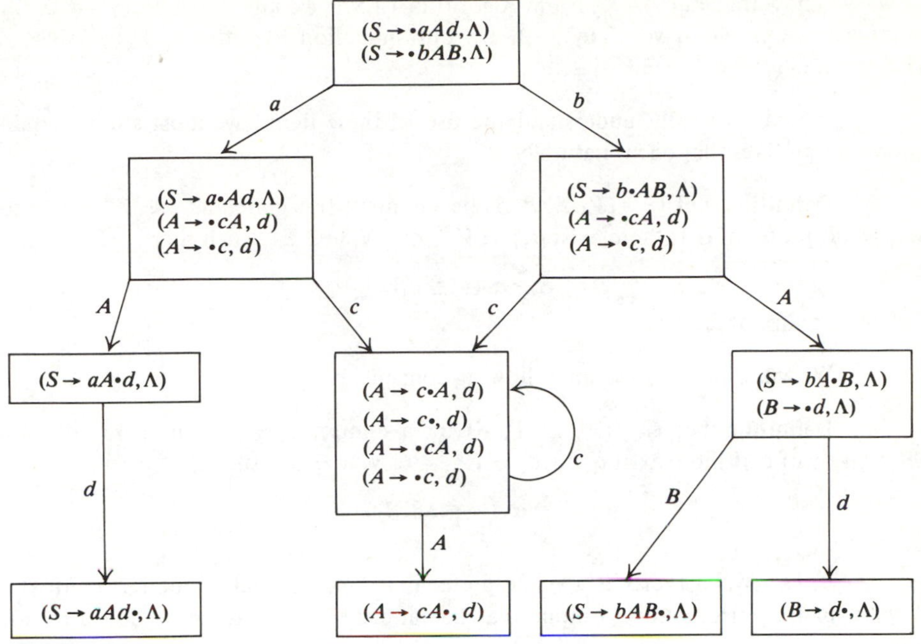

FIG. 13.7

It is an aid to our intuition to regard each set of items as a "state," and to draw a *state graph*. A state $V_k(\gamma)$ leads to state $V_k(\gamma X)$ under input $X \in V$. In our running example, we have the graph shown in Fig. 13.7. The reader should compare Fig. 13.7 with the goto graph in Section 13.4.

We now must show that Algorithm 13.5.2 generates the desired output.

Theorem 13.5.2 Let $G = (V, \Sigma, P, S)$ be a reduced, context-free grammar and $k \geqslant 0$. Let $\mathscr{S}_k$ be the collection of sets of items for G computed by Algorithm 13.5.2. Then

$$\mathscr{S}_k = \{V_k(\gamma) \neq \emptyset \mid \gamma \in V^*\}.$$

Proof We first show that $\mathscr{S}_k \subseteq \{V_k(\gamma) \neq \emptyset \mid \gamma \in V^*\}$. Suppose $I \in \mathscr{S}_k$. Then, for some $\gamma \in V^*$, $I = V_k(\gamma)$. By Algorithm 13.5.2, clearly, $V_k(\gamma) \neq \emptyset$, and thus $I \in \{V_k(\gamma) \neq \emptyset \mid \gamma \in V^*\}$. Therefore, $\mathscr{S}_k \subseteq \{V_k(\gamma) \neq \emptyset \mid \gamma \in V^*\}$.

Conversely, we must show that $\{V_k(\gamma) \neq \emptyset \mid \gamma \in V^*\} \subseteq \mathscr{S}_k$. Assume that $I = V_k(\gamma) \in \{V_k(\gamma') \neq \emptyset \mid \gamma' \in V^*\}$. We use induction on $\lg(\gamma)$.

Basis. $\lg(\gamma) = 0$. Then $\gamma = \Lambda$. Since $I \in \{V_k(\gamma) \neq \emptyset \mid \gamma \in V^*\}$, $V_k(\Lambda) \neq \emptyset$. By (1) of Algorithm 13.5.2, $I \in \mathscr{S}_k$.

Induction step. Assume that the theorem in this direction is true for $\lg(\gamma) \leqslant i$. We shall show that it is true for $\lg(\gamma) = i + 1$. Let $\gamma = \gamma' X$, where $X \in V$.

Now, we know that $V_k(\gamma) \neq \emptyset$. From Algorithm 13.5.1, we know that $V_k(\gamma') \neq \emptyset$, for otherwise we would have $V_k(\gamma) = \emptyset$. By our induction hypothesis, $V_k(\gamma') \in \mathscr{S}_k$. Therefore, $\{V_k(\gamma) \neq \emptyset \mid \gamma \in V^*\} \subseteq \mathscr{S}_k$. □

In order to fully understand the use of these items, we must study certain important prefixes that occur naturally.

Definition Let $G = (V, \Sigma, P, S)$ be a context-free grammar. $\gamma \in V^*$ is said to be a *viable prefix* of G is there exist $\alpha, \beta \in V^*, A \in N, w \in \Sigma^*$, such that

$$S \overset{*}{\underset{R}{\Rightarrow}} \alpha A w \underset{R}{\Rightarrow} \alpha\beta w$$

and γ is a prefix of $\alpha\beta$.

We will often also use the following concept.

Definition Let $G = (V, \Sigma, P, S)$ be a context-free grammar. $\gamma \in V^*$ is a *valid prefix* of G if there exist $\alpha, \beta_1, \beta_2 \in V^*, A \in N, w \in \Sigma^*$, such that

$$S \overset{*}{\underset{R}{\Rightarrow}} \alpha A w \underset{R}{\Rightarrow} \alpha\beta_1\beta_2 w$$

and $\gamma = \alpha\beta_1$.

Thus, a valid prefix is a viable prefix that "includes all of the left context." A valid prefix corresponds to input that has already been read and reduced by the parser.

Viable and valid prefixes turn out to be, in fact, equivalent concepts. The following lemma will be useful in showing the equivalence of these two concepts. The idea of the proof is that, if we look to some earlier steps in the derivation, viable prefixes turn out to be valid prefixes.

Lemma 13.5.2 Let $G = (V, \Sigma, P, S)$ be a reduced context-free grammar. Assume that, for some $A \in N, \alpha, \beta, \gamma, \delta \in V^*$, we have

$$S \overset{*}{\underset{R}{\Rightarrow}} \alpha A w \underset{R}{\Rightarrow} \alpha\beta w = \gamma\delta$$

where γ is a proper prefix of α. Then there exist $A' \in N, \alpha', \beta' \in V^*, w' \in \Sigma^*$, such that

$$S \overset{*}{\underset{R}{\Rightarrow}} \alpha' A' w' \underset{R}{\Rightarrow} \alpha'\beta' w' \overset{+}{\underset{R}{\Rightarrow}} \alpha\beta w$$

where, for some $\beta_1' \in V^*$, $\beta_2' \in V^+$, we have that $\beta' = \beta_1'\beta_2'$ and $\gamma = \alpha'\beta_1'$. Furthermore, if $\delta \in \Sigma V^*$, then ${}^{(1)}\beta_2' \in \Sigma$, and if $\delta \in \Sigma^*$, we have ${}^{(k)}\delta \in \mathrm{FIRST}_k(\beta_2' w')$ for any $k \geqslant 0$.

Proof Since $S \overset{*}{\underset{R}{\Rightarrow}} \alpha\beta w$ and γ is a proper prefix of α, we must have $\alpha \neq \Lambda$. Therefore

$$S \overset{+}{\underset{R}{\Rightarrow}} \alpha A w$$

Therefore, there exist $n \geqslant 2$, $\alpha_i \in V^*$ for $0 \leqslant i \leqslant n$, such that

$$S = \alpha_0 \underset{R}{\Rightarrow} \alpha_1 \underset{R}{\Rightarrow} \cdots \underset{R}{\Rightarrow} \alpha_{n-1} = \alpha A w \underset{R}{\Rightarrow} \alpha\beta w = \alpha_n$$

Intuitively, let i be the smallest integer such that α_i and all succeeding canonical sentential forms in the above derivation have γ as a prefix. Formally, define

<table>
<tr><td colspan="2">γ</td><td colspan="2">$\beta_i A_i w_i$</td></tr>
<tr><td>α'</td><td>β_1'</td><td>β_2'</td><td>w'</td></tr>
<tr><td></td><td colspan="2">β'</td><td></td></tr>
</table>

FIG. 13.8

i to be the least integer such that for all j, $n-1 \geqslant j \geqslant i$, there exist $A_j \in N$, $\beta_j \in V^+$, $w_j \in \Sigma^*$, and $\alpha_j = \gamma\beta_j A_j w_j$. Clearly, such an integer exists since $n-1 \geqslant 1$ and $\alpha_{n-1} = \alpha A w$, where $\lg(\gamma) < \lg(\alpha)$. Since $\alpha_i = S$ is impossible, we see that $i \geqslant 1$. Therefore, for some $A' \in N$, $\alpha', \beta' \in V^*$, $w' \in \Sigma^*$, we have

$$S \underset{R}{\overset{*}{\Rightarrow}} \alpha_{i-1} = \alpha' A' w' \underset{R}{\Rightarrow} \alpha'\beta' w' = \gamma\beta_i A_i w_i = \alpha_i \underset{R}{\overset{*}{\Rightarrow}} \alpha A w \underset{R}{\Rightarrow} \alpha\beta w$$

By our minimality assumption, $\lg(\gamma) \geqslant \lg(\alpha')$.

Now, since A_i is the rightmost variable in $\alpha'\beta' w'$, we know that $\lg(\gamma\beta_i A_i) \leqslant \lg(\alpha'\beta')$. Therefore, $\lg(\gamma) < \lg(\alpha'\beta')$. Thus, there exist $\beta_1' \in V^*$, $\beta_2' \in V^+$, where $\beta' = \beta_1'\beta_2'$ such that $\gamma = \alpha'\beta_1'$. (See Fig. 13.8.)

Now assume that $\delta \in \Sigma V^*$. We shall show that ${}^{(1)}\beta_2'$ cannot be written in this derivation. It will follow that ${}^{(1)}\beta_2' \in \Sigma$. Since we have the rightmost derivation

$$\gamma\beta_2' w' = \gamma\beta_i A_i w_i \underset{R}{\Rightarrow} \gamma\beta_{i+1} A_{i+1} w_{i+1} \underset{R}{\Rightarrow} \cdots \underset{R}{\Rightarrow} \gamma\beta_{n-1} A_{n-1} w_{n-1} \underset{R}{\Rightarrow} \gamma\beta_{n-1}\beta w_{n-1} = \gamma\delta$$

and $\beta_j \in V^+$ for all j such that $n-1 \geqslant j \geqslant i$, we must have

$${}^{(1)}\beta_2' = {}^{(1)}\beta_i = {}^{(1)}\beta_{i+1} = \cdots = {}^{(1)}\beta_{n-1} = {}^{(1)}\delta$$

Since ${}^{(1)}\delta \in \Sigma$, we have ${}^{(1)}\beta_2' \in \Sigma$. If $\delta \in \Sigma^*$, since we have $\beta_2' w' \underset{R}{\overset{+}{\Rightarrow}} \delta$, we must have ${}^{(k)}\delta \in \mathrm{FIRST}_k(\beta_2' w')$. □

The following example illustrates the Lemma.

Example Consider the grammar whose productions are

$$S \to abA$$
$$A \to c$$

Since

$$S \underset{R}{\overset{*}{\Rightarrow}} abA \underset{R}{\Rightarrow} abc$$

and a is a prefix of abc, we have that a is a viable prefix. However, since

$$S \underset{R}{\overset{*}{\Rightarrow}} S \underset{R}{\Rightarrow} abA$$

and a is a prefix of abA, we have that a is a valid prefix. Furthermore, $b \in \Sigma$ and ${}^{(k)}bc \in \mathrm{FIRST}_k\,(bA)$ for any $k \geqslant 0$.

The following theorem shows that valid and viable prefixes are equivalent. It will later prove extremely useful to go back and forth between these notions.

Theorem 13.5.3 Let $G = (V, \Sigma, P, S)$ be a reduced context-free grammar. Then $\gamma \in V^*$ is a valid prefix of G if and only if γ is a viable prefix of G.

Proof Assume that $\gamma \in V^*$ is a valid prefix of G. From the definitions it follows that γ is a viable prefix of G.

Conversely, assume that $\gamma \in V^*$ is a viable prefix of G. Then there exist $A \in N$, $\alpha, \beta \in V^*$, $w \in \Sigma^*$, such that

$$S \underset{R}{\overset{*}{\Rightarrow}} \alpha A w \underset{R}{\Rightarrow} \alpha\beta w$$

and γ is a prefix of $\alpha\beta$.

CASE 1. $\lg(\gamma) \geqslant \lg(\alpha)$. Then, clearly, γ is a valid prefix of G, by the definition.

CASE 2. $\lg(\gamma) < \lg(\alpha)$. If $\gamma = \Lambda$, then, for some $\delta \in V^*$,

$$S \underset{R}{\overset{*}{\Rightarrow}} S \underset{R}{\Rightarrow} \delta \underset{R}{\overset{*}{\Rightarrow}} \alpha\beta w$$

Thus Λ is a valid prefix of G.

Assume that $\gamma \neq \Lambda$. By Lemma 13.5.2, we have, for some $A' \in N$, $\alpha', \beta' \in V^*$, $w' \in \Sigma^*$,

$$S \underset{R}{\overset{*}{\Rightarrow}} \alpha' A' w' \underset{R}{\Rightarrow} \alpha'\beta' w'$$

where, for some $\beta_1' \in V^*$, $\beta_2' \in V^+$, we have $\beta' = \beta_1'\beta_2'$ and $\gamma = \alpha'\beta_1'$. Thus, γ is a valid prefix of G. □

The concept of a valid prefix leads to the corresponding notion of a valid *LR*(*k*) item. A valid *LR*(*k*) item for some $\gamma \in V^*$ specifies a production, and the place in that production, at which one might be working, after reading input that has been reduced to valid prefix γ.

Definition Let $G = (V, \Sigma, P, S)$ be a reduced context-free grammar and $k \geqslant 0$. For $\alpha, \beta_1, \beta_2 \in V^*$, $w, u \in \Sigma^*$, $A \in N$, $(A \to \beta_1 \cdot \beta_2, u)$ is a *valid LR(k) item for* $\alpha\beta_1$ if there exists a derivation in G such that

$$S \underset{R}{\overset{*}{\Rightarrow}} \alpha A w \underset{R}{\Rightarrow} \alpha\beta_1\beta_2 w$$

with $u = {}^{(k)}w$.

Example Again consider the sample grammar

$$S \to abA$$

$$A \to c$$

Since we have

$$S \underset{R}{\overset{*}{\Rightarrow}} S \underset{R}{\Rightarrow} abA$$

$(S \to a \cdot bA, \Lambda)$ is a valid *LR*(*k*) item for a for any $k \geqslant 0$.

Every valid *LR*(*k*) item for a string is an *LR*(*k*) item. Moreover, every valid prefix has at least one corresponding valid *LR*(*k*) item, as the following theorem shows.

Theorem 13.5.4 Let $G = (V, \Sigma, P, S)$ be a reduced context-free grammar. $\gamma \in V^*$ is a valid (viable) prefix of G if and only if there is at least one valid *LR*(*k*) item for γ.

Proof The theorem follows directly from the definitions involved and Theorem 13.5.3. □

We next show how the existence of a given production in a grammar guarantees the existence of certain valid $LR(k)$ items corresponding to that production.

Lemma 13.5.3 Let $G = (V, \Sigma, P, S)$ be a reduced context-free grammar. Assume that, for some $\beta_1, \beta_2 \in V^*$, $A \in N$, we have

$$A \to \beta_1\beta_2 \text{ in } P \qquad \text{and} \qquad u \in \text{FOLLOW}_k(A).$$

Then, for some $\alpha \in V^*$, $(A \to \beta_1 \cdot \beta_2, u)$ is a valid $LR(k)$ item for $\alpha\beta_1$.

Proof By Problem 13.4.1, there exist $\alpha \in V^*$, $w \in \Sigma^*$, such that

$$S \overset{*}{\underset{R}{\Rightarrow}} \alpha A w \underset{R}{\Rightarrow} \alpha\beta_1\beta_2 w,$$

where $u \in \text{FIRST}_k(w)$. Therefore, $(A \to \beta_1 \cdot \beta_2, u)$ is a valid $LR(k)$ item for $\alpha\beta_1$. □

Our ultimate goal in this section is to show that Algorithm 13.5.1 computes the set of valid $LR(k)$ items for any $\gamma \in V^*$. However, we first must prove a result which shows that, if some $\gamma \in V^*$ has a valid $LR(k)$ item with Λ preceding the dot, then there is another specified $LR(k)$ item for γ under most conditions.

Lemma 13.5.4 Let $G = (V, \Sigma, P, S)$ be a reduced context-free grammar and $k \geqslant 0$. For $\alpha, \beta \in V^*$, $u \in \Sigma^*$, $A \in N$, $(A \to \cdot\, \beta, u)$ is a valid $LR(k)$ item for α, where either $A \neq S$, $u \neq \Lambda$, or $\alpha \neq \Lambda$ if and only if there exists A', $B_0 \in N$, $\beta_1', \beta_2' \in V^*$, $u' \in \text{FOLLOW}_k(A')$ such that

1 $(A' \to \beta_1' \cdot B_0\beta_2', u')$ is a valid $LR(k)$ item for α. If $\alpha \neq \Lambda$, then $\beta_1' \in V^+$ while, if $\alpha = \Lambda$, then $u' = \Lambda$ and $S = A'$;

2 there exists an $n \geqslant 0$, $B_i \in N$, $\delta_i \in V^*$ for $1 \leqslant i \leqslant n$, with $B_n = A$ such that

$$B_0 \to B_1\delta_1$$
$$B_1 \to B_2\delta_2$$
$$\vdots$$
$$B_{n-1} \to B_n\delta_n$$
$$B_n \to \beta$$

are in P and $u \in \text{FIRST}_k(\delta_n \cdots \delta_1\beta_2'u')$.

Proof We assume that there exist $\alpha, \beta \in V^*$, $A \in N$, such that $(A \to \cdot\, \beta, u)$ is a valid $LR(k)$ item for α, where $A \neq S$, $u \neq \Lambda$, or $\alpha \neq \Lambda$. By definition, there exists a $w \in \Sigma^*$ such that

$$S \overset{*}{\underset{R}{\Rightarrow}} \alpha A w \underset{R}{\Rightarrow} \alpha\beta w$$

where $u = {}^{(k)}w$.

Since either $A \neq S$, $u \neq \Lambda$, or $\alpha \neq \Lambda$, we must have

$$S \overset{+}{\underset{R}{\Rightarrow}} \alpha A w \underset{R}{\Rightarrow} \alpha\beta w$$

Therefore, there exist $n \geqslant 2$, $\alpha_i \in V^*$ for $0 \leqslant i \leqslant n-1$ such that

$$S = \alpha_0 \underset{R}{\Rightarrow} \alpha_1 \underset{R}{\Rightarrow} \cdots \underset{R}{\Rightarrow} \alpha_{n-1} = \alpha A w \underset{R}{\Rightarrow} \alpha\beta w$$

Now let $i \geqslant 1$ be the smallest integer such that there exist $A_j \in N$, $\beta_j \in V^*$, $w_j \in \Sigma^*$ for all j such that $n-1 \geqslant j \geqslant i$, we have $\alpha_j = \alpha\beta_j A_j w_j$. Clearly, such an integer exists since $n-1 \geqslant 1$ and $\alpha_{n-1} = \alpha A w$. Therefore, for some $A' \in N$, α', $\beta' \in V^*$, $w' \in \Sigma^*$, we have

$$S \overset{*}{\underset{R}{\Rightarrow}} \alpha_{i-1} = \alpha' A' w' \underset{R}{\Rightarrow} \alpha'\beta' w' = \alpha\beta_i A_i w_i = \alpha_i \overset{*}{\underset{R}{\Rightarrow}} \alpha A w \underset{R}{\Rightarrow} \alpha\beta w$$

By the minimality of i, $\lg(\alpha) > \lg(\alpha')$, provided $\alpha \neq \Lambda$. If $\alpha = \Lambda$, then $\alpha' = \Lambda$ and $i = 1$.

Now, since A_i is the rightmost variable in $\alpha'\beta'w'$, we know that $\lg(\alpha\beta_i A_i) \leqslant \lg(\alpha'\beta')$. Therefore, $\lg(\alpha) < \lg(\alpha'\beta')$. Thus, there exist $\beta_1' \in V^*$, $\beta_2'' \in V^+$, where $\beta' = \beta_1'\beta_2''$ and $\alpha = \alpha'\beta_1'$. (The situation is similar† to Fig. 13.8.) Let $u' = {}^{(k)}w'$ and note that $u' \in \mathrm{FOLLOW}_k(A')$. Thus $(A' \to \beta_1' \cdot \beta_2'', u')$ is a valid $LR(k)$ item for α. Moreover,

i) $\beta_1 \in V^+$ if $\alpha \neq \Lambda$, and

ii) $A' = S$ and $u = w' = \Lambda$ if $\alpha = \Lambda$.

We now have

$$\alpha_i = \alpha'\beta' w' = \alpha\beta_i A_i w_i \overset{*}{\underset{R}{\Rightarrow}} \alpha\beta_{n-1} A_{n-1} w_{n-1} = \alpha A w \underset{R}{\Rightarrow} \alpha\beta w$$

We see that $B_j A_j \in NV^*$ for $i \leqslant j \leqslant n-1$, for otherwise we would have ${}^{(1)}\beta_j \in \Sigma$ for $i \leqslant j \leqslant n-1$. Therefore, ${}^{(1)}\beta_{n-1} = {}^{(1)}A \in \Sigma$, which is a contradiction. It is necessary to examine the sequence of derivations in which the variable immediately following α is changed. We now choose $i \leqslant i_0 \leqslant i_1 \leqslant \cdots \leqslant i_\ell = n-1$ such that $\beta_{i_j} = \Lambda$ for $0 \leqslant j \leqslant \ell$. We see, from our derivation, that $A_{i_0} = {}^{(1)}\beta_2''$. Therefore, for some $B_0 \in N$, $\beta_2' \in V^*$, we have $\beta_2'' = B_0\beta_2'$. We now consider the productions used in the steps $\alpha_{i_j} \Rightarrow \alpha_{i_j+1}$ for $0 \leqslant j \leqslant \ell$.

There exist $\delta_{i_j}' \in V^*$ for $0 \leqslant j \leqslant \ell$ such that

$$A_{i_j} \to \delta_{i_j}'$$

is in P. Since we can write $\alpha_{i_j+1} = \alpha\beta_{i_j+1} A_{i_j+1} w_{i_j+1}$, with $\beta_{i_j+1} A_{i_j+1} \in NV^*$, we must have ${}^{(1)}\delta_{i_j}' \in N$. Therefore, there exist $\delta_j \in V^*$, $B_j \in N$ such that $\delta_{i_j}' = B_j\delta_j$ for $0 \leqslant j \leqslant \ell$. We also know that $B_j = A_{i_j+1}$ from our derivation. This gives us a sequence of productions

$$\begin{aligned} B_0 &\to B_1\delta_1 \\ B_1 &\to B_2\delta_2 \\ &\vdots \\ B_{n-1} &\to B_n\delta_n \\ B_n &\to \beta \end{aligned}$$

† Replace β_2' in Fig. 13.8 by β_2'' and also γ by α.

From our derivation, we see that

$$u = {}^{(k)}w \in \mathrm{FIRST}_k(\delta_n \cdots \delta_1\beta_2'w')) = \mathrm{FIRST}_k(\delta_n \cdots \delta_1\beta_2'u').$$

Conversely, assume that there exist $A', B_0 \in N$, $\alpha, \beta_1', \beta_2' \in V^*$, and $u' \in \mathrm{FOLLOW}_k\ (A')$ such that $(A' \to \beta_1' \cdot B_0\beta_2', u')$ is a valid $LR(k)$ item for α, and there exist $n \geq 0, B_i \in N, \delta_i \in V^*$ for $1 \leq i \leq n$, with $B_n = A$, such that

$$\begin{aligned} B_0 &\to B_1\delta_1 \\ B_1 &\to B_2\delta_2 \\ &\vdots \\ B_{n-1} &\to B_n\delta_n \\ B_n &\to \beta \end{aligned}$$

are in P and $u \in \mathrm{FIRST}_k(\delta_n \cdots \delta_1\beta_2'u')$.

By a definition of a valid $LR(k)$ item, there exists a $w' \in \Sigma^*$, $\alpha' \in V^*$, such that $\alpha = \alpha'\beta_1'$, and

$$S \underset{R}{\overset{*}{\Rightarrow}} \alpha'A'w' \underset{R}{\Rightarrow} \alpha'\beta_1'B_0\beta_2'w'$$

where $u' = {}^{(k)}w'$.

Since $u \in \mathrm{FIRST}_k(\delta_n \cdots \delta_1\beta_2'u')$ and G is reduced, there exists some $w \in \Sigma^*$ such that

$$\delta_n \cdots \delta_1\beta_2'u' \underset{R}{\overset{*}{\Rightarrow}} w \qquad \text{where } u = {}^{(k)}w$$

Now we have

$$S \underset{R}{\overset{*}{\Rightarrow}} \alpha'\beta_1'B_0\beta_2'w' = \alpha B_0\beta_2'w'$$

since $\alpha = \alpha'\beta_1'$. Because $u' = {}^{(k)}w'$, we may write

$$w' = u'w''$$

for some $w'' \in \Sigma^*$. Then the above derivation becomes

$$S \underset{R}{\overset{*}{\Rightarrow}} \alpha B_0\beta_2'w' = \alpha B_0\beta_2'u'w'' \overset{*}{\Rightarrow} \alpha\beta\delta_n \cdots \delta_1\beta_2'u'w''$$

Since $u \in \mathrm{FIRST}_k(\delta_n \cdots \delta_1\beta_2'u')$, it is easy to see that

$$S \underset{R}{\overset{*}{\Rightarrow}} \alpha B_0\beta_2'w'' \underset{R}{\overset{*}{\Rightarrow}} \alpha\beta uw'' = \alpha\beta w$$

$$S \underset{R}{\overset{*}{\Rightarrow}} \alpha'\beta_1'B_0\beta_2'w' \underset{R}{\overset{*}{\Rightarrow}} \alpha'\beta_1'A\delta_n \cdots \delta_1w' \underset{R}{\overset{*}{\Rightarrow}} \alpha'\beta_1'Aw \underset{R}{\Rightarrow} \alpha'\beta_1'\beta w$$

Therefore, $(A \to \cdot\, \beta, u)$ is a valid $LR(k)$ item for α. □

We are now ready to prove that Algorithm 13.5.1 computes sets of valid $LR(k)$ items.

Theorem 13.5.5 Let $G = (V, \Sigma, P, S)$ be a reduced context-free grammar, $\gamma \in V^*$, and $k \geq 0$. An item is in $V_k(\gamma)$ after application of Algorithm 13.5.1 if and only if the item is a valid $LR(k)$ item for γ.

Proof By induction on $\lg(\gamma)$.

Basis. $\lg(\gamma) = 0$. Then $\gamma = \Lambda$. Assume that there exist $\beta \in V^*, A \in N, u \in \Sigma_\Lambda^k$ such that $(A \to \cdot\, \beta, u)$ is in $V_k(\Lambda)$ after application of Algorithm 13.5.1.

CASE 1. Assume $(A \to \cdot\, \beta, u)$ is added to $V_k(\Lambda)$ in Step 1(a). Then $A = S$ and $u = \Lambda$. Clearly, $(S \to \cdot\, \beta, \Lambda)$ is a valid $LR(k)$ item for Λ.

CASE 2. Assume $(A \to \cdot\, \beta, u)$ is added to $V_k(\Lambda)$ in Step 1(b). Then there exist $n \geqslant 0, B_i \in N, \delta_i \in V^*$ for $1 \leqslant i \leqslant n$, with $\beta_2' \in V^*$, $B_n = A$ such that

$$\begin{aligned} B_0 &\to B_1\delta_1 \\ B_1 &\to B_2\delta_2 \\ &\vdots \\ B_{n-1} &\to B_n\delta_n \\ B_n &\to \beta \end{aligned}$$

are in P and $u \in \text{FIRST}_k(\delta_n \cdots \delta_1\beta_2')$. It follows that $(S \to \cdot\, B_0\beta_2', \Lambda)$ is added to $V_k(\Lambda)$ in Step 1(a). By Lemma 13.5.4, $(A \to \cdot\, \beta, u)$ is a valid $LR(k)$ item for Λ.

Conversely, assume that $(A \to \cdot\, \beta, u)$ is a valid $LR(k)$ item for Λ. The case structure given below is from Lemma 13.5.4. The symbol α comes from Lemma 13.5.4, and $\alpha = \Lambda$ in the basis of the proof.

CASE 1. Assume $A = S$, $u = \Lambda$, and $\alpha = \Lambda$. Then, clearly, $(S \to \cdot\, \beta, u)$ must be added to $V_k(\Lambda)$ in Step 1(a) of Algorithm 13.5.1.

CASE 2. Assume $A \neq S$, $u \neq \Lambda$, or $\alpha \neq \Lambda$. By Lemma 13.5.4, there exist $B_0 \in N, \beta_2' \in V^*$ such that $(S \to \cdot\, B_0\beta_2', \Lambda)$ is a valid $LR(k)$ item for α and there exist an $n \geqslant 0, B_i \in N, \delta_i \in V^*$ for $1 \leqslant i \leqslant n$, with $B_n = A$, such that

$$\begin{aligned} B_0 &\to B_1\delta_1 \\ B_1 &\to B_2\delta_2 \\ &\vdots \\ B_{n-1} &\to B_n\delta_n \\ B_n &\to \beta \end{aligned}$$

are in P and $u \in \text{FIRST}_k(\delta_n \cdots \delta_1\beta_2')$. Therefore $(A \to \cdot\, \beta, u)$ will be placed in $V_k(\Lambda)$ in Step 1(b) of Algorithm 13.5.1.

Induction step Assume that the theorem is true for $\lg(\gamma) = j$. We show that it is true for $\lg(\gamma) = j + 1$. Consider some $LR(k)$ item $(A \to \beta_1 \cdot \beta_2, u)$ where $A \in N, \beta_1, \beta_2 \in V^*$, $u \in \text{FOLLOW}_k(A)$. Two cases must be considered.

CASE 1. $\beta_1 \neq \Lambda$. Let $\beta_1 = \beta_1'X$, where $\beta_1' \in V^*$, $X \in V$. We know, from the definition of valid $LR(k)$ items, that $(A \to \beta_1 \cdot \beta_2, u)$ is a valid $LR(k)$ item for γ if and only if $(A \to \beta_1' \cdot X\beta_2, u)$ is a valid $LR(k)$ item for γ', where $\gamma = \gamma'X$. By our induction hypothesis, $(A \to \beta_1' \cdot X\beta_2, u)$ is a valid $LR(k)$ item for γ' if and only if

$(A \to \beta_1' \cdot X\beta_2, u) \in V_k(\gamma')$. From Algorithm 13.5.1, it is clear that $(A \to \beta_1' \cdot X\beta_2, u) \in V_k(\gamma')$ if and only if $(A \to \beta_1 \cdot \beta_2, u) \in V_k(\gamma)$. Thus, $(A \to \beta_1 \cdot \beta_2, u)$ is a valid $LR(k)$ item for γ if and only if $(A \to \beta_1 \cdot \beta_2, u) \in V_k(\gamma)$.

CASE 2. $\beta_1 = \Lambda$. Assume that $(A \to \cdot\, \beta_2,\ u)$ is a valid $LR(k)$ item for γ. Therefore, there exist $A', B_0 \in N, \alpha_1, \beta_2' \in V^*, \beta_1' \in V^+, u' \in \text{FOLLOW}_k(A')$ such that $(A' \to \beta_1' \cdot B_0\beta_2',\ u')$ is a valid $LR(k)$ item for γ and an $n \geqslant 0$, $B_i \in N$, $\delta_i \in V^*$ for $1 \leqslant i \leqslant n$, with $B_n = A$, such that

$$B_0 \to B_1\delta_1$$
$$B_1 \to B_2\delta_2$$
$$\vdots$$
$$B_{n-1} \to B_n\delta_n$$
$$B_n \to \beta$$

are in P and $u \in \text{FIRST}_k(\delta_n \cdots \delta_n\beta_2'u')$. By Case 1,

$$(A' \to \beta_1' \cdot B_0\beta_2', u) \in V_k(\gamma).$$

Therefore, $(A \to \cdot\, \beta_2, u)$ is placed in $V_k(\gamma)$, by Algorithm 13.5.1 in Step 2(b).

Conversely, assume that $(A \to \cdot\, \beta_2,\ u) \in V_k(\gamma)$. Then there exist A', $B_0 \in N$, $\beta_2' \in V^*$, $\beta_1' \in V^+$, $u' \in \text{FOLLOW}_k(A')$ such that $(A' \to \beta_1' \cdot B_0\beta_2',\ u') \in V_k(\gamma)$ and there exist an $n \geqslant 0, B_i \in N, \delta_i \in V^*$ for $1 \leqslant i \leqslant n$, with $B_n = A$, such that

$$B_0 \to B_1\delta_1$$
$$B_1 \to B_2\delta_2$$
$$\vdots$$
$$B_{n-1} \to B_n\delta_n$$
$$B_n \to \beta$$

are in P and $u \in \text{FIRST}_k(\delta_n \cdots \delta_1\beta_2'u')$. By Case 1, $(A' \to \beta_1' \cdot B_0\beta_2',\ u')$ is a valid $LR(k)$ item for γ. Therefore, by Lemma 13.5.4, $(A \to \cdot\, \beta_2, u)$ is a valid $LR(k)$ item for γ. □

The following definition is useful for dealing with the collection of sets of items valid for the valid prefixes of a grammar.

Definition Let $G = (V, \Sigma, P, S)$ be a reduced context-free grammar and let $k \geqslant 0$. Then the *canonical collection of sets of LR(k) items for G* is defined as

$$\{\{i \mid i \text{ is a valid } LR(k) \text{ item for } \gamma\} \mid \gamma \in V^* \text{ is a valid prefix for } G\}.$$

We now use Algorithm 13.5.2 to get $\mathcal{S}_k$. We will now show that Algorithm 13.5.2 in fact produces the canonical collection of sets of $LR(k)$ items for G.

Theorem 13.5.6 Let $G = (V, \Sigma, P, S)$ be a reduced context-free grammar, $k \geqslant 0$. Then $\mathcal{S}_k$ = the canonical collection of sets of $LR(k)$ items for G.

Proof By Theorem 13.5.2, $\mathscr{S}_k = \{V_k(\gamma) \neq \emptyset \mid \gamma \in V^*\}$. By Theorem 13.5.5, $V_k(\gamma) \neq \emptyset$ if and only if γ has at least one valid $LR(k)$ item, and, by Theorem 13.5.4, this is true if and only if γ is a valid prefix. Therefore, $\mathscr{S}_k$ = the canonical collection of sets of $LR(k)$ items for G.

PROBLEMS

1 Construct the canonical collection of sets of $LR(k)$ items for the following grammars:

a) $k = 0$ and $S \to Sa \mid a$

b) $k = 1$ and $S \to aAc$
$A \to bAb \mid b$

c) $k = 0$ and $S \to aAc$
$A \to Abb \mid b$

d) $k = 1$ and $E \to E + T \mid T$
$T \to T * F \mid F$
$F \to (E) \mid a$

2 Which of the grammars in Problem 1 are $LR(k)$?

3 There can be a large number of elements in $\mathscr{S}_k$ even for a small $LR(k)$ grammar. Find an $LR(0)$ grammar G_n of size which is polynomial in n and yet where $|\mathscr{S}_0|$ is exponential in n.

13.6 CONSISTENCY AND PARSER CONSTRUCTION

The algorithms of the previous section may be applied to any context-free grammar, but the results may not be useful in constructing parsers. In this section, we shall introduce the important notion of *consistency*, which allows us to define parsers from our collection of sets of items. Then it will be shown which grammars yield parsers. It should not be a surprise to find that it is exactly the $LR(k)$ grammars which work.

In the parsers which were described in Section 13.4, all moves were made deterministically. We hope to be able to use the sets $V_k(\gamma)$ as the tables on the stack. In order to do so, these tables must satisfy certain conditions. For any move of our parser:

1 There must never be a conflict between a reduce and a shift move.

2 When we have a reduce move, the reduction to be performed must be uniquely determined.

This leads to the following definition.

Definition Let $G = (V, \Sigma, P, S)$ be a reduced, context-free grammar and let $k \geqslant 0$. A collection $\mathscr{S}$ of sets of $LR(k)$ items for G is *consistent* if, for all $I \in \mathscr{S}$, all

$A, A' \in N$, all $\beta, \beta_1, \beta_2 \in V^*$, where ${}^{(1)}\beta_2 \notin N$, and all $u, v \in \Sigma_\Lambda^k$ with $u \in \text{FIRST}_k(\beta_2 v)$, we have that

$$(A \to \beta \cdot, u) \in I \qquad \text{and} \qquad (A' \to \beta_1 \cdot \beta_2, v) \in I \quad \text{imply that}$$

$$(A' \to \beta_1 \cdot \beta_2, v) = (A \to \beta \cdot, u).$$

There are several things to note in this definition. The condition ${}^{(1)}\beta_2 \notin N$ means that $\beta_2 = \Lambda$ or ${}^{(1)}\beta_2 \in \Sigma$. The conclusion means that:

i) $u = v$

ii) $A = A'$

iii) $\beta_1 = \beta$ and $\beta_2 = \Lambda$

Example Returning to our running example from Section 13.5, it is easy to see that $\mathscr{S}_k$ is consistent. In fact, only the set

$$I = V_1(ac) = \begin{Bmatrix} (A \to c \cdot A, d) \\ (A \to c \cdot, d) \\ (A \to \cdot cA, d) \\ (A \to \cdot c, d) \end{Bmatrix}$$

might cause concern. But the first item can cause no problem, since $A \in N$. The third and fourth cannot be inconsistent with the second because both the third and fourth items have $\text{FIRST}_1(\beta_2 v) = \{c\}$ and no conflict can exist.

Our next task is to characterize the class of grammars which produce consistent grammars.

Theorem 13.6.1 Let $G = (V, \Sigma, P, S)$ be a reduced context-free grammar and let $k \geqslant 0$. G is $LR(k)$ if and only if the canonical collection of sets of $LR(k)$ items for G is consistent.

Proof Assume G is $LR(k)$. Assume, for the sake of contradiction, that the canonical collection of sets of $LR(k)$ items for G, denoted by $\mathscr{S}$, is not consistent. Then, for some $I \in \mathscr{S}$, we have some $A, B \in N, \beta, \beta_1, \beta_2 \in V^*, u, v \in \Sigma^*$, ${}^{(1)}\beta_2 \notin N$, $u \in \text{FIRST}_k(\beta_2 v)$ such that

$$(A \to \beta \cdot, u) \in I \qquad \text{and} \qquad (B \to \beta_1 \cdot \beta_2, v) \in I$$

where $(A \to \beta \cdot, u) \neq (B \to \beta_1 \cdot \beta_2, v)$. By definition of I, there exist $\alpha, \alpha'', \gamma \in V^*, w, x \in \Sigma^*$ such that $u = {}^{(k)}w$, $v = {}^{(k)}x$ and

$$S \overset{*}{\underset{R}{\Rightarrow}} \alpha A w \underset{R}{\Rightarrow} \alpha\beta w = \gamma w$$

$$S \overset{*}{\underset{R}{\Rightarrow}} \alpha'' B x \underset{R}{\Rightarrow} \alpha''\beta_1\beta_2 x = \gamma(\beta_2 x)$$

We are not yet ready to employ the $LR(k)$-ness of the grammar to force a contradiction, since we must have $\beta_2 \in \Sigma^*$ in order to use the $LR(k)$ definition. We therefore divide our proof into two cases, according to whether $\beta_2 \in \Sigma^*$ or $\beta_2 \notin \Sigma^*$.

CASE 1. $\beta_2 \in \Sigma^*$. Now we have

$$^{(k)}(\beta_2 x) = {}^{(k)}(\beta_2 v) = u$$

Since G is $LR(k)$ we therefore have

$$(A \to \beta, \lg(\alpha\beta)) = (B \to \beta_1\beta_2, \lg(\alpha''\beta_1\beta_2)).$$

It follows that $\lg(\alpha''\beta_1\beta_2) = \lg(\alpha\beta) = \lg(\gamma) = \lg(\alpha''\beta_1)$. Therefore $\beta_2 = \Lambda$. Since $\beta = \beta_1\beta_2$, we have $\beta = \beta_1$. Also, $v = {}^{(k)}x = {}^{(k)}(\beta_2 x) = u$. In addition, we have $A = B$. Therefore

$$(A \to \beta \cdot, u) = (B \to \beta_1 \cdot \beta_2, v),$$

which contradicts our hypothesis.

CASE 2. $\beta_2 \notin \Sigma^*$. We now rewrite β_2 in a rightmost fashion until we have a string of terminals. We know that there exists an $x' \in \Sigma^*$, $\rho \in P^+$ such that $\beta_2 \overset{\rho}{\underset{R}{\Rightarrow}} x'$ and $u = {}^{(k)}x'x$. Therefore we have

$$S \overset{*}{\underset{R}{\Rightarrow}} \gamma\beta_2 x \overset{\rho}{\underset{R}{\Rightarrow}} \gamma(x'x)$$

We consider the last step in this derivation, namely, there exist $A' \in N$, $\alpha' \in V^*$, $\beta', x'' \in \Sigma^*$ such that

$$S \overset{*}{\underset{R}{\Rightarrow}} \gamma\beta_2 x \overset{*}{\underset{R}{\Rightarrow}} \gamma\alpha' A' x'' \underset{R}{\Rightarrow} \gamma\alpha'\beta' x'' = \gamma(x'x)$$

Since ${}^{(1)}\beta_2 \notin N$ and $\beta_2 \neq \Lambda$, clearly ${}^{(1)}\alpha' = {}^{(1)}\beta_2 \in \Sigma$, and $\lg(\gamma\alpha'\beta') > \lg(\gamma)$. Since G is $LR(k)$, we now have

$$(A \to \beta, \lg(\gamma)) = (A' \to \beta', \lg(\gamma\alpha'\beta'))$$

This is clearly a contradiction; thus the canonical collection of sets of $LR(k)$ items for G must be consistent.

Conversely, assume that $\mathscr{S}$, the canonical collection of sets of $LR(k)$ items for G, is consistent. Assume, for the sake of contradiction, that G is not $LR(k)$. Then, by Lemma 13.2.3, there exist $u, w, w', x \in \Sigma^*$, $\gamma, \alpha, \alpha', \beta, \beta' \in V^*$, $A, A' \in N$ such that:

i) $S \overset{*}{\underset{R}{\Rightarrow}} \alpha A w \underset{R}{\Rightarrow} \alpha\beta w = \gamma w$

ii) $S \overset{*}{\underset{R}{\Rightarrow}} \alpha' A' x \underset{R}{\Rightarrow} \alpha'\beta' x = \gamma' x = \gamma w'$

iii) ${}^{(k)}w = {}^{(k)}w' = u$

iv) $(A \to \beta, \lg(\alpha\beta)) \neq (A' \to \beta', \lg(\alpha'\beta'))$, with

v) $\lg(\alpha'\beta') \geqslant \lg(\alpha\beta)$.

At this point, we know that if, in fact, $\lg(\gamma) \geqslant \lg(\alpha')$, then derivations (i) and (ii) will give us items that will lead us to a contradiction. However, in the case where $\lg(\gamma) < \lg(\alpha')$, we will have to examine an earlier step in the derivation of $\alpha'\beta' x$ to get our contradiction.

CASE 1. $\lg(\alpha') \leqslant \lg(\gamma)$. Then, for some $\beta_1', \beta_2' \in V^*$, $\beta' = \beta_1'\beta_2'$ and $\gamma = \alpha'\beta_1'$. Let $v = {}^{(k)}x$. Then $(A \to \beta \cdot, u)$ and $(A' \to \beta_1' \cdot \beta_2', v)$ are valid $LR(k)$ items for γ with $u = {}^{(k)}w' = {}^{(k)}(\beta_2' x) = {}^{(k)}(\beta_2' v)$. Since we have consistency,

$$(A \to \beta \cdot, u) = (A' \to \beta_1' \cdot \beta_2', v).$$

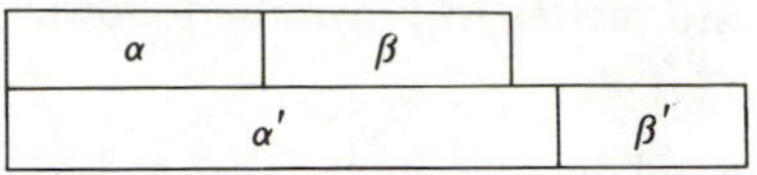

FIG. 13.9.

Therefore, $A = A'$, $\beta = \beta_1'$, $u = v$ and $\beta_2' = \Lambda$. Since $\alpha\beta = \alpha'\beta_1' = \alpha'\beta$, we have $\alpha = \alpha'$. Therefore, $(A \to \beta, \lg(\alpha\beta)) = (A' \to \beta', \lg(\alpha'\beta'))$, which contradicts (v).

CASE 2. $\lg(\gamma) < \lg(\alpha')$. We have the situation shown in Fig. 13.9. By Lemma 13.5.2 there exist $\alpha'', \beta'' \in V^*$, $w'' \in \Sigma^*$, $A'' \in N$, such that

$$S \underset{R}{\overset{*}{\Rightarrow}} \alpha''A''w'' \underset{R}{\Rightarrow} \alpha''\beta''w'' \underset{R}{\overset{+}{\Rightarrow}} \alpha'\beta'x = \gamma w'$$

where, for some $\beta_1'' \in V^*$, $\beta_2'' \in V^+$, we have $\beta'' = \beta_1''\beta_2''$, $u \in \text{FIRST}_k(\beta_2''w'')$ and $\gamma = \alpha''\beta_1''$. Since $w' \in \Sigma^*$, ${}^{(1)}\beta_2' \in \Sigma^+$, from this production, we see that

$$(A'' \to \beta_2'' \cdot \beta_2'', v)$$

is a valid $LR(k)$ item for γ where $v = {}^{(k)}w''$ and $u \in \text{FIRST}_k(\beta_2''v)$. Since $(A \to \beta\cdot, u)$ is also a valid $LR(k)$ item for γ, we have

$$(A \to \beta\cdot, u) = (A'' \to \beta_1' \cdot \beta_2'', v)$$

since $\mathscr{S}$ is consistent. Therefore, $\beta_2'' = \Lambda$. This, however, contradicts the quantification on β_2''. Therefore, G must be $LR(k)$. □

Corollary There is an algorithm which, if given a context-free grammar G and a nonnegative integer k, decides whether or not G is $LR(k)$.

Our next step is to build an LR parser from our sets $\mathscr{S}_k$. The set of tables that are necessary will consist of some new symbols to stand for the elements of $\mathscr{S}_k$. To be formal, define

$$\mathscr{T} = \mathscr{T}_k = \{T(I) \mid I \in \mathscr{S}_k\},$$

where $T(I)$ is a new symbol denoting I. $\mathscr{T}$ is called the *canonical collection of LR(k) tables for G*. Next, we must define the f and g functions of the parser.

Definition Let $G = (V, \Sigma, P, S)$ be an $LR(k)$ grammar and let $k \geq 0$. Let $\mathscr{T} = \mathscr{T}_k$ be the canonical collection of $LR(k)$ tables for G and assume that $\mathscr{T}$ is consistent. Define the parsing action function f and the goto function g as follows:

1 For each $T \in \mathscr{T}$ and $u \in \Sigma_\Lambda^k$, define

a) $f(T, u) =$ **shift** if there is some $\beta_1 \in V^*$, $\beta_2 \in \Sigma V^*$, $v \in \Sigma_\Lambda^k$ and $A \in N$ such that $(A \to \beta_1 \cdot \beta_2, v) \in T$ and $u \in \text{FIRST}_k(\beta_2 v)$;
b) $f(T, u) =$ **reduce** π if π is $A \to \beta$ and $(A \to \beta\cdot, u)$ is in T;
c) $f(T, u) =$ **error** otherwise.

2 For each $T = V_k(\gamma) \in \mathscr{T}$ and each $A \in V$, define

a) $g(V_k(\gamma), A) = V_k(\gamma A)$ if $V_k(\gamma A) \neq \emptyset$;
b) $g(V_k(\gamma), A) =$ **error** otherwise.

It is a straightforward matter to prove the following lemma and the proof is left for the exercises.

Lemma 13.6.1 The relations f and g defined in the previous definition are well defined functions if $\mathscr{S}$ is consistent.

Examples It is easy to see that the f and g functions in our running example of Section 13.4 were constructed by employing this definition.

As another example, let $k = 1$ and G be given by

1. $S \to aS$
2. $S \to a$

The sets of items and the g function may be "read" from the graph in Fig. 13.10.

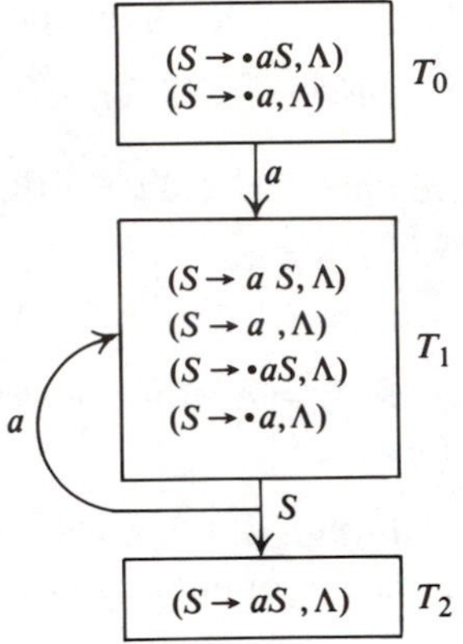

FIG. 13.10.

The f and g functions are given by the following table:

	f		g	
	a	Λ	a	S
T_0	shift		T_1	
T_1	shift	reduce 2	T_1	T_2
T_2		reduce 1		

Now our string of definitions and results are complete so that, given any $LR(k)$ grammar, we can use our algorithms to produce a consistent set of $LR(k)$ tables and an LR parser. However there is one more important task to accomplish. It must be shown that this parser works correctly. This means that any string in the language is accepted and, moreover, that any nonsentence is rejected in a finite time (i.e., the parser halts). A detailed analysis of the actions of the parser on nonsentences is useful for error recovery work.

We now show that, given a grammar $G = (V, \Sigma, P, S)$, the canonical $LR(k)$ parser for G does the following:

1. Given a string $x \in L(G)$, the parser halts in the **accept** state and outputs the parse for x in G.
2. Given a string $x \notin L(G)$, the parser halts in the **error** state.

The next theorem proves that our parser accepts strings in the language and outputs the correct parse.

Theorem 13.6.2 Let $G = (V, \Sigma, P, S)$ be an $LR(k)$ grammar, $k \geqslant 0$. Then, in the canonical $LR(k)$ parser for G with tables $\mathcal{T}_k$, for all $x \in L(G)$, $(T_0, x, \Lambda) \overset{+}{\vdash} (T_0, \Lambda, \rho) \vdash$ **accept**, where $S \overset{\rho^T}{\underset{R}{\Rightarrow}} x$.

Proof Let $x \in L(G)$. Then there exist $n \geqslant 0$, $\alpha_i \in V^*$, $w_i \in \Sigma^*$ for $0 \leqslant i \leqslant n+1$, $\rho_i \in P$, $A_i \in N$ for $0 \leqslant i \leqslant n$, $\alpha_{n+1} = A_{n+1} = \Lambda$ such that there is a unique derivation of x in G,

$$S = \alpha_0 A_0 w_0 \overset{\rho_0}{\underset{R}{\Rightarrow}} \alpha_0 \beta_0 w_0 = \alpha_1 A_1 w_1 \overset{\rho_1}{\underset{R}{\Rightarrow}} \alpha_1 \beta_1 w_1 =$$

$$\alpha_2 A_2 w_2 \underset{R}{\Rightarrow} \cdots \overset{\rho_n}{\underset{R}{\Rightarrow}} \alpha_n \beta_n w_n = \alpha_{n+1} A_{n+1} w_{n+1} = x$$

Claim 1 For $0 \leqslant i \leqslant n$, $\lg(\alpha_{i+1} A_{i+1}) \leqslant \lg(\alpha_i \beta_i)$.

Proof This is clear from the fact that A_{i+1} is the rightmost variable in $\alpha_i \beta_i w_i$.

Claim 1 allows us to do the following: For the $\alpha_i \beta_i$, $0 \leqslant i \leqslant n$, we order the prefixes of the $\alpha_i \beta_i$ as follows:

Row $n+1$	$\alpha_{n+1} A_{n+1}, \alpha_{n+1} A_{n+1}{}^{(1)} w_{n+1}, \ldots, {}^{\lg(\alpha_n \beta_n)}(\alpha_{n+1} A_{n+1} w_{n+1})$
Row n	$\alpha_n A_n, \alpha_n A_n{}^{(1)} w_n, \ldots, {}^{\lg(\alpha_{n-1} \beta_{n-1})}(\alpha_n A_n w_n)$
⋮	⋮
Row 1	$\alpha_1 A_1, \alpha_1 A_1{}^{(1)} w_1, \ldots, \alpha_1 A_1 w_1$
Row 0	$\alpha_0 A_0 = S$

We index each row from zero and we associate the pair (ℓ, m) with the mth element in row ℓ.

Next, we impose a linear ordering on these elements, defined by the order in which they have been listed, indexed from zero.

We now prepare for an induction proof, by defining *SP, IP,* and *OP,* which stand for the *stack part, input part,* and *output part,* as follows:

For $0 \leqslant i \leqslant t$, where t is the number of items ordered above, let

$$SP(i) = i\text{th element in the ordering.}$$

Assume that the pair (ℓ, m) is associated with this element. Let $SP(i) = \alpha_\ell A_\ell{}^{(m)} w_\ell$.

Also let

$$IP(i) = w_{\ell}^{(\lg(w_\ell)-m)}$$

$$OP(i) = \rho_n \cdots \rho_\ell.$$

We now make a very strong induction hypothesis which gives us the condition of every element of our parser at any given state of the parse.

Claim 2 After i steps, $0 \leqslant i \leqslant t$, the configuration of the parser is $(T_0 X_1 T_1 X_2 T_2 \cdots X_s T_s, y, \rho)$ where $x = x'y$ for $x', y \in \Sigma^*$, $T_j \in \mathscr{T}_k$ for $0 \leqslant j \leqslant s$, $X_j \in V$ for $1 \leqslant j \leqslant s$, $\rho \in P^*$ and

1 $X_1 \cdots X_s = SP(i)$,
2 $y = IP(i)$,
3 $\rho = OP(i)$,
4 $T_j = T(V_k(X_1 \cdots X_j))$ for $1 \leqslant j \leqslant s$.

Proof

Basis. $i = 0$. The initial ID of our parser is (x, T_0, Λ). We see that

1 $\Lambda = SP(0)$,
2 $y = x = IP(0)$,
3 $\Lambda = OP(0)$, and
4 Condition (4) is vacuously satisfied.

Induction step. Assume that, for $i = r$, (1), (2), (3), and (4) hold. Now assume that $i = r + 1$. After r moves, we have, by our induction hypothesis,

$$(T_0, x, \Lambda) \overset{*}{\vdash} (T_0 X_1 T_1 X_2 T_2 \cdots X_s T_s, y, \rho)$$

where $x = x'y$ with $x', y \in \Sigma^*$, $T_j \in \mathscr{T}_k$ for $0 \leqslant j \leqslant \ell$, $X_j \in V$ for $1 \leqslant j \leqslant s$, $\rho \in P^*$ with

1 $X_1 \ldots X_s = SP(r)$,
2 $y = IP(r)$,
3 $\rho = OP(r)$,
4 $T_j = T(V_k(X_1 \cdots X_j))$ for $1 \leqslant j \leqslant s$.

Assume that (ℓ, m) is associated with element r. By definition, we have

$$SP(r) = \alpha_\ell A_\ell ({}^{(m)}w_\ell)$$

$$IP(r) = w_\ell^{(\lg(w_\ell)-m)},$$

$$OP(r) = \rho_n \cdots \rho_\ell.$$

We now have two cases, one of which will amount to a shift move and the other to a reduce move.

CASE 1. $\lg(SP(r)) < \lg(\alpha_{\ell-1}\beta_{\ell-1})$. We know that

$$S \underset{R}{\overset{+}{\Rightarrow}} \alpha_\ell A_\ell w_\ell = \alpha_{\ell-1}\beta_{\ell-1}w_{\ell-1} = (SP(r))y$$

where $SP(r)$ is a proper prefix of $\alpha_{\ell-1}\beta_{\ell-1}$. We claim that there exist $A' \in N, \alpha'$, $\beta' \in V^*, w' \in \Sigma^*$ such that

$$S \underset{R}{\overset{*}{\Rightarrow}} \alpha' A' w' \underset{R}{\Rightarrow} \alpha'\beta' w' \underset{R}{\overset{+}{\Rightarrow}} \alpha_{\ell-1}\beta_{\ell-1}w_{\ell-1}$$

where, for some $\beta_1' \in V^*$, $\beta_2' \in V^+$ we have $\beta' = \beta_1'\beta_2'$ and $SP(r) = \alpha'\beta_1'$. If $SP(r)$ is not a proper prefix of $\alpha_{\ell-1}$, then this is immediate. Otherwise, it follows directly from Lemma 13.5.2. Therefore, $(A' \to \beta_1' \cdot \beta_2', {}^{(k)}w')$ is a valid $LR(k)$ item for $SP(r)$. Furthermore, by Lemma 13.5.2, ${}^{(1)}\beta_2' \in \Sigma$ and ${}^{(k)}y \in \text{FIRST}_k(\beta_2' w')$. It follows that $f_{T_s}({}^{(k)}y) =$ **shift**. Clearly, $\alpha_\ell A_\ell ({}^{(m+1)}w_\ell)$ is a valid prefix of G. It follows from Lemma 13.6.1 that the next move of our parser is well defined. Therefore

$$(T_0X_1T_1X_2T_2 \cdots X_sT_s, y, \rho)$$
$$\vdash (T_0X_1T_1X_2T_2 \cdots X_sT_s({}^{(1)}y)(T(V_k(X_1 \cdots X_s{}^{(1)}y))), y^{(\lg(y)-1)}, \rho).$$

Clearly,

1 $X_1 \cdots X_s({}^{(1)}y) = SP(r+1)$,
2 $y^{(\lg(y)-1)} = IP(r+1)$,
3 $\rho = OP(r+1)$,
4 $T_j = T(V_k(X_1 \cdots X_j))$ for $1 \leqslant j \leqslant s+1$, where $X_{s+1} = {}^{(1)}y$.

CASE 2. $\lg(SP(r)) = \lg(\alpha_{\ell-1}\beta_{\ell-1})$. We have

$$S \underset{R}{\overset{*}{\Rightarrow}} \alpha_{\ell-1}A_{\ell-1}w_{\ell-1} \underset{R}{\Rightarrow} \alpha_{\ell-1}\beta_{\ell-1}w_{\ell-1} = \alpha_\ell A_\ell w_\ell \overset{\rho^T}{\Rightarrow} x$$

Since $T_s = T(V_k(X_1 \cdots X_s))$, we have

$$(A_{\ell-1} \to \beta_{\ell-1} \cdot, {}^{(k)}w_{\ell-1}) = (A_{\ell-1} \to \beta_{\ell-1} \cdot, {}^{(k)}y) \in V_k(X_1 \cdots X_s).$$

Therefore, $f_{T_s}({}^{(k)}y) =$ **reduce** π where $\pi = (A_{\ell-1} \to \beta_{\ell-1})$. Clearly, $\alpha_{\ell-1}A_{\ell-1}$ is a viable prefix of G. Thus, by Lemma 13.6.1, we have the well-defined move

$$(T_0X_1T_1X_2T_2 \cdots X_sT_s, y, \rho)$$
$$\vdash (T_0X_1T_1X_2T_2 \cdots X_{\ell-\lg(\beta_{\ell-1})}T_{\ell-\lg(\beta_{\ell-1})}A_{\ell-1}T', y, \rho\pi),$$

where $T' = T(V_k(X_1 \cdots X_{\ell-\lg(\beta_{\ell-1})}A_{\ell-1})$. Therefore we have

1 $X_1 \cdots X_{\ell-\lg(\beta_{\ell-1})}A_{\ell-1} = SP(r+1)$,
2 $y = IP(r+1)$,
3 $\rho\pi = OP(r+1)$,
4 $T_j = T(V_k(X_1 \cdots X_j))$ for $1 \leqslant j \leqslant \ell - \lg(\beta_{\ell-1}) + 1$.

This completes the induction proof.

Now let $i = t-1$. We have parser configuration

$$(T_0X_1T_1X_2T_2 \cdots X_sT_s, \Lambda, \rho').$$

1 $X_1 \cdots X_s = SP(t-1) = \alpha_1 A_1 w_1$,
2 $\Lambda = IP(t-1)$,

3 $\rho' = OP(t-1) = \rho_n \cdots \rho_1$

4 $T_j = T(V_k(X_1 \cdots X_j))$ for $1 \leqslant j \leqslant s$.

We know, by our induction proof, that

$$SP(t) = \alpha_0\beta_0 w_0$$
$$IP(t) = \Lambda$$
$$OP(t) = \rho_n \cdots \rho_0$$

Since $\rho_0 = (S \to X_1 \cdots X_s) \in P$, then $(S \to X_1 \cdots X_s \cdot, \Lambda) \in T_s$. Therefore $f_{T_s}(\Lambda) =$ **reduce** π where $\pi = \rho_0$. Thus, by Lemma 13.6.1, the parser makes the well-defined move

$$(T_0X_1T_1X_2T_2 \cdots X_sT_s, \Lambda, \rho') \vdash (\Lambda, T_0, \rho'\pi) \vdash \textbf{accept}$$

where $S \overset{(\rho'\pi)^T}{\underset{\mathrm{R}}{\Rightarrow}} x$.

We now consider the behavior of our canonical $LR(k)$ parser on an input string not in the language. We wish to show that, when the parser is given a string that is not in the language, it will halt in a special **error** state; and moreover the parser will halt at the earliest step possible. That is, as soon as the input string thus far read could not have the given lookahead string if the string were in the language, the parser must halt and declare error. When $k = 0$, we must, in addition, consider the special case when the input string is a prefix of some string in the language.

Theorem 13.6.3 Let $G = (V, \Sigma, P, S)$ be an $LR(k)$ grammar, $k \geqslant 0$. Then in the canonical $LR(k)$ parser for G, with tables $\mathscr{T}_k$, for all $x \notin L(G)$, $(T_0, x, \Lambda) \overset{+}{\vdash} \textbf{error}$. Furthermore, the parser halts at the following point in the computation:

CASE 1. Let $x = x'x''$, where x' is the minimal-length prefix of x such that there exists no $y \in \Sigma^*$, with ${}^{(k)}y = {}^{(k)}x''$ and $x'y \in L(G)$. Then

$$(T_0, x, \Lambda) \overset{*}{\vdash} (\gamma, x'', \rho) \vdash \textbf{error}$$

where the next-to-last move of the parser is not a **reduce** move.

CASE 2. If $x \notin L(G)$ and Case 1 does not hold, then, for some $\gamma \in T_0(V\mathscr{T}_k)^*$, $\rho \in P^*$,

$$(T_0, x, \Lambda) \overset{*}{\vdash} (\gamma, \Lambda, \rho) \vdash \textbf{error}.$$

Proof We must consider two cases. In the first case, at some point the prefix of the string we have thus far read could not have the given lookahead for any string in the language. In the second case, the input string is a prefix of some string in the language.

CASE 1. In this case, it is assumed that there exist $x', x'' \in \Sigma^*$ such that $x = x'x''$ where x' is the minimal-length prefix of x such that there exists no $y \in \Sigma^*$, with ${}^{(k)}y = {}^{(k)}x''$ and $x'y \in L(G)$. We shall show that, immediately after reading the last letter of x', the parser declares an error. Since x' is the minimal-length prefix of

x such that there exists no $y \in \Sigma^*$ with ${}^{(k)}y = {}^{(k)}x''$ and $x'y \in L(G)$, by Theorem 4.1, the configuration of the parser after reading x' (or the initial configuration if $x' = \Lambda$) is

$$(T_0X_1T_1X_2T_2 \cdots X_sT_s, x'', \rho)$$

where $T_j \in \mathscr{T}_k$ for $0 \leqslant j \leqslant s$, $X_j \in V$ for $1 \leqslant j \leqslant s$, $\rho \in P^*$ and

1 $X_1 \cdots X_s = SP(i)$,

2 $x'' = IP(i)$,

3 $T_s = T(V_k(X_1 \cdots X_s))$.

Assume, for the sake of contradiction, that

$$(T_0X_1T_1X_2T_2 \cdots X_sT_s, x'', \rho) \vdash \textbf{error}$$

is false. Then there exist $A \in N, \beta_1, \beta_2 \in V^*, u \in \Sigma^*, {}^{(1)}\beta_2 \notin N$ such that $(A \to \beta_1 \cdot \beta_2, u)$ is a valid $LR(k)$ item for $X_1 \cdots X_s$ with ${}^{(k)}x'' \in \text{FIRST}_k(\beta_2 u)$. By definition, there exist $\alpha \in V^*, w \in \Sigma^*$, such that

$$S \overset{*}{\underset{R}{\Rightarrow}} \alpha A w \underset{R}{\Rightarrow} \alpha\beta_1\beta_2 w$$

and $u = {}^{(k)}w$. By (1), $\alpha\beta_1 \overset{*}{\underset{R}{\Rightarrow}} x'$. Thus, for some $u' \in \Sigma^*$, $\alpha\beta_1\beta_2 w \overset{*}{\underset{R}{\Rightarrow}} x'uu'$. But this contradicts the hypothesis of Case 1.

CASE 2. We therefore assume that, for some $y \in \Sigma^+, xy \in L(G)$ and ${}^{(k)}y = \Lambda$. Since $y \in \Sigma^+$ and ${}^{(k)}y = \Lambda$, we must have $k = 0$. Since $xy \in L$, by Theorem 13.6.2 for some $\gamma, \gamma' \in T_0(V\mathscr{T}_k)^*, \rho, \rho' \in P^*$,

$$(T_0, xy, \Lambda) \overset{*}{\vdash} (\gamma, y, \rho) \overset{*}{\vdash} (\gamma', \Lambda, \rho').$$

Therefore, given the input x, we will have

$$(T_0, x, \Lambda) \overset{*}{\vdash} (\gamma, \Lambda, \rho)$$

and after a finite number of steps, the parser will attempt to shift. By the definition of our parser, since the input stream will be empty, the parser will halt and declare **error**. □

PROBLEMS

1 Prove Lemma 13.6.1.

2 Prove the following proposition.

Lemma Let $G = (V, \Sigma, P, S)$ be a reduced context-free grammar, where $k \geqslant 0$. Let $I \in \mathscr{S}$, where $\mathscr{S}$ is the canonical collection of sets of $LR(k)$ items for G. Assume that, for some $B \in N$, $\beta_1 \in V^*$, $\beta_2 \in NV^*$, $v \in \text{FOLLOW}_k(B)$ we have $(B \to \beta_1 \cdot \beta_2, v) \in I$, with† $u \in \text{EFF}_k(\beta_2 v)$. Then there exist $C \in N$, $\delta \in \Sigma V^*$, $u' \in \text{FOLLOW}_k(C)$ such that

$$(C \to \cdot\, \delta, u') \in I$$

and $u \in \text{FIRST}_k(\delta u')$.

---

† EFF is defined in Problem 3 of Section 13.4 on page 530.

3 In the literature, one finds a different definition of consistency than the one used here.

Definition Let $G = (V, \Sigma, P, S)$ be a reduced context-free grammar and let $k \geqslant 0$. A collection $\mathscr{S}$ of sets of $LR(k)$ items for G is *$\mathscr{A}$-$\mathscr{U}$-consistent* if, for all $I \in \mathscr{S}$, $A, A' \in N, \beta, \beta_1, \beta_2 \in V^*$, and all $u, v \in \Sigma_\Lambda^k$ with $u \in \text{EFF}_k(\beta_2 v)$, we have that

$$(A \to \beta\cdot, u) \in I \qquad \text{and} \qquad (A' \to \beta_2 \cdot \beta_2, v) \in I$$

imply that

$$(A \to \beta\cdot, u) = (A' \to \beta_2 \cdot \beta_2, v).$$

Prove the following result.

Theorem Let $G = (V, \Sigma, P, S)$ be a reduced context-free grammar where $k \geqslant 0$. $\mathscr{S}$, the canonical collection of sets of $LR(k)$ items for G, is $\mathscr{A}$-$\mathscr{U}$-consistent if and only if it is consistent.

4 The way in which our parser is defined in Section 13.4 is complicated. In order for our parser to halt, three conditions must be satisfied, namely:

a) The input stream must be empty.
b) A reduction to S must be performed immediately before the parser halts.
c) After popping the stack for the final reduction, only T_0 may remain on the stack.

Show that each of these three conditions is necessary.

5 Fix $k \geqslant 0$. Analyze the time required to test a context-free grammar for the $LR(k)$ property if the consistency is checked.

***6** Find a method for testing a context-free grammar for the $LR(k)$ property which takes time proportional to n^{k+2} when k is fixed and where $n = |G|$.

13.7 THE RELATIONSHIP BETWEEN *LR*-LANGUAGES AND Δ_0

We have seen, in Theorems 13.2.4, that every deterministic language has an $LR(1)$ grammar. Our purpose here is to prove a converse and to characterize the deterministic context-free languages by *LR* grammars. To do this is not very difficult. We must merely convert the *LR* parser from Sections 13.4 and 13.6 into a dpda that accepts the language in question.

Theorem 13.7.1 Every $LR(k)$ language is a deterministic context-free language.

Proof The idea is simply to construct a dpda from the *LR* parser of the previous sections. The states of the dpda will consist of pairs, the first element of which is the table on the top of the stack while the second is the lookahead string. The final states will be those where the lookahead string, concatenated with a valid prefix corresponding to the set of items, produces a word in the language. More formally, let $G = (V, \Sigma, P, S)$ be an $LR(k)$ grammar. Define a dpda $A = (Q, \Sigma, \Gamma, \delta, q_0, T_0, F)$ where

$$\Gamma = V \cup \mathscr{T}$$

and $\mathscr{T} = \{\mathscr{T}_i\}$ is the set of $LR(k)$ tables produced by Algorithm 13.5.1.

$$\begin{aligned} Q = {} & (\mathscr{T} \times (\Sigma \cup \{\Lambda\})^k) \cup \{0, \ldots, k-1\} \times (\Sigma \cup \{\Lambda\})^k \\ & \cup (\Sigma \cup \{\Lambda\})^k \times \{t_j\} \\ & \cup \mathscr{T} \times \{t_{2p} \mid p = \lg(\alpha), A \to \alpha \text{ is in } P\}, \end{aligned}$$

and

$$q_0 = \begin{cases} (T_0, \Lambda) & \text{if } k = 0, \\ (0, \Lambda) & \text{otherwise.} \end{cases}$$

The final states are defined by cases:

$$F = \begin{cases} (T_0, t_{2p}) & \text{where } p = \lg(\alpha), S \to \alpha \text{ is in } P \text{ if } k = 0. \\ (i, x) & \text{if } k \geqslant 1, x \in L(G), \text{and } 0 \leqslant i < k. \\ (T, u) & \text{if } k \geqslant 1, u \in \Sigma^k, T = T(I) \text{ and there is some} \\ & (A \to \alpha \cdot a\beta, v) \in I \text{ for some } \alpha \in V^*, a \in \Sigma, \beta \in V^*, \\ & v \in (\Sigma \cup \{\Lambda\})^k \text{ and } u \in \text{FIRST}_{k+1}(a\beta v). \end{cases}$$

The δ function is defined by cases:

CASE 1. For each $a \in \Sigma$,

$$\delta((0, \Lambda), a, T_0) = \begin{cases} ((T_0, a), T_0) & \text{if } k = 1, \\ ((1, a), T_0) & \text{if } k > 1. \end{cases}$$

We start to fill a buffer with the lookahead string of length $k \geqslant 1$.

CASE 2. If $k > 1$, then for each $a \in \Sigma$, $(i, x) \in Q$ with $1 \leqslant i < k$,

$$\delta((i, x), a, T_0) = ((i+1, xa), T_0).$$

CASE 3. If $k > 1$ then, for each $x \in \Sigma^{(k-1)}$ and $a \in \Sigma$,

$$\delta((k-1, x), a, T_0) = ((T_0, xa), T_0).$$

Now the buffer is loaded.

CASE 4.

a) If† $f(T, u) = \textbf{shift}$, $k \geqslant 1$, $u = aU_2 \cdots U_k$, with $a \in \Sigma$, each $U_i \in \Sigma$, and $g(T, a) \neq \textbf{error}$ then

$$\delta((T, aU_2 \cdots U_k), b, T) = ((g(T, a), U_2 \cdots U_k b), Tag(T, a))$$

for all $b \in \Sigma$.

---

† f and g are the parsing action and goto functions associated with G and are defined in Section 13.6. Their effect on the parser is explained in Section 13.4.

b) If $k = 0$ and $f(T, u) = \textbf{shift}$, then

$$\delta((T, \Lambda), a, T) = ((g(T, a), \Lambda), Tag(T, a))$$

for any $a \in \Sigma$, provided $g(T, a) \neq \textbf{error}$.

CASE 5. If $f(T, u) = \textbf{reduce } \pi$, where π is $A \to \beta$, then let $p = \lg(\beta)$ and† for any $u \in (\Sigma \cup \{\Lambda\})^k$,

a) $\delta((T, u), \Lambda, T) = ((u, t_0), T)$

b) $\delta((u, t_{2i}), \Lambda, T) = ((u, t_{2i+1}), \Lambda)$ for each $T \in \mathscr{T}$, and each i, $0 \leqslant i < p$.

c) $\delta((u, t_{2i+1}), \Lambda, Y) = ((u, t_{2i+2}), \Lambda)$ for each i, $0 \leqslant i < p$, and each $Y \in V$.

d) If $k \geqslant 1$ and $g(T', a) \neq \textbf{error}$, then

$$\delta((u, t_{2p}), \Lambda, T') = ((g(T', A), u), T'Ag(T', A)).$$

e) If $k = 0$, then we have:

i) $\delta((\Lambda, t_{2p}), \Lambda, T') = ((T', t_{2p}), T')$,

ii) $\delta((T', t_{2p}), \Lambda, T') = ((g(T', A), \Lambda), T'Ag(T', A))$ provided $g(T', A) \neq$ **error**.

The extra move here is to be able to accept when $k = 0$.

This completes the construction. Note that the accepting condition has the property that, if the lookahead string u is concatenated to what has been read already, we have a string in the language.

It can be shown that $T(A) = L(G)$, but we shall not do so here because A is so close to the parser of Section 13.4 whose operation was proved to be correct in Section 13.6. □

The previous result can be combined with an earlier theorem to give an important characterization.

Theorem 13.7.2 L is a deterministic context-free language if and only if L is an $LR(k)$ language for some $k \geqslant 0$.

Proof The result follows from Theorems 13.7.1 and 13.2.4. □

Now we prove a very useful theorem which shows that the $LR(k)$ languages do not form a hierarchy with respect to k.

Theorem 13.7.3 Every $LR(k)$ language has an $LR(1)$ grammar and hence is an $LR(1)$ language.

Proof If $k = 0$ or $k = 1$, the result is trivial. Suppose L is an $LR(k)$ language with $k \geqslant 2$. Then $L \in \Delta_0$, by Theorem 13.7.1. By Theorem 13.2.4, L is $LR(1)$. □

---

† It is intended that different states t_i be used for different productions. This dependence is not shown in the notation, in order to simplify matters.

We have found an algorithm for testing whether a context-free grammar is $LR(k)$ when k is known. If k is not known, the problem is unsolvable.

Theorem 13.7.4 There is no algorithm which can decide, of a context free grammar G, whether or not G is $LR(k)$ for some k.

Proof See Knuth [1965] for the original proof, or Hunt and Szymanski [1976] for a metatheorem which covers a number of other important cases. □

PROBLEMS

1 Give a formal proof that $T(A) = L(G)$ in Theorem 13.7.1.

*2 Prove Theorem 13.7.2 by giving a direct grammatical transformation.

3 Show the following interesting result:

Theorem L is a deterministic context-free language if and only if L is a bounded-right-context language.

Hint. Show that any $LR(k)$ grammar is equivalent to a $BRC(1, k)$ grammar. Use Problem 21 of Section 13.2.

4 Prove the following result:

Theorem Every $LR(k)$ language with $k \geqslant 1$ may be given an $LR(1)$ grammar (and, hence, $LR(k)$) in Greibach normal form.

5 Find an $LR(0)$ language L for which there is no $LR(0)$ grammar which is in Greibach form.

6 Prove the following result. Pertinent definitions and results may be found in the problems of Section 13.2.

Lemma Let $G = (V, \Sigma, P, S)$ be an $LLR(k)$ grammar, $k \geqslant 0$. Then there exists an $LR(1)$ grammar G' such that $L(G) = L(G')$.

7 Prove the following result:

Theorem $L \subseteq \Sigma^*$ is a deterministic language if and only if L is an LLR language.

8 Prove the following result:

Theorem $L \subseteq \Sigma^*$ is an $LR(0)$ language if and only if L is an $LLR(0)$ language.

9 Let $L \subseteq \Sigma^*$ be in Δ_0. A string $x \in \Sigma^*$ is a *correct prefix* of L if there exists some $y \in \Sigma^*$ such that $xy \in L$. Define $I(L) = \{x | \ x = x'a$ for some $a \in \Sigma$, x' is a correct prefix of L but x is not$\}$. Let A be a dpda acting as a parser for L. A has the *correct prefix property* if, by changing the set of final states of A, we can produce a recognizer for $I(L)$. Show that the LR parser we have constructed in this chapter is a correct prefix parser.

13.8 HISTORICAL SURVEY

$LR(k)$ parsing was invented by Knuth [1965]. Our treatment of the fundamental concepts in Section 13.2 is from Geller and Harrison [1977a] while Theorem 13.2.3 is due to Harrison and Havel [1974]. The characterization of $LR(0)$ languages is also from Geller and Harrison [1977a]. The concept of $LLR(k)$ grammars is from Lewis and Stearns [1968]. The family of $BRC(\ell, k)$ grammars was introduced by Floyd [1964]. Problem 22 of Section 13.2 is from Harrison and Havel [1974].

The treatment of LR parsing is essentially the canonical subcase of the theory of characteristic parsing which is from Geller and Harrison [1977b and c]. Problem 6 of Section 13.6 is due to Hunt, Szymanski, and Ullman [1975a]. The proof of Theorem 13.7.1 is due to M.M. Geller. Problem 3 of Section 13.7 appears in Knuth [1965]; also see Graham [1971]. Problem 4 appears in Lomet [1973] and in Geller, Harrison, and Havel [1977] along with Problem 6.

References

AANDERAA, S.O., "On k-tape versus $(k-1)$ tape real time computation," SIAM–AMS Colloquium on Applied Mathematics, Vol. 7, *Complexity of Computation* (R. Karp, ed.), pp. 75–96, 1974.

AGUILAR, R., ed., *Formal Languages and Programming,* Amsterdam: North-Holland Publishing Co., 1976.

AHO, A.V., "Indexed grammars: an extension of the context-free grammars," *Journal of the Association for Computing Machinery,* **15**, pp. 647–671, 1968.

AHO, A.V., "Nested-stack automata," *Journal of the Association for Computing Machinery,* **16**, pp. 383–406, 1969.

AHO, A.V., DENNING, P.J., AND ULLMAN, J.D., "Weak and mixed-strategy precedence parsing," *Journal of the Association for Computing Machinery,* Vol. 19, pp. 225–243, 1972.

AHO, A.V., HOPCROFT, J.E., AND ULLMAN, J.D., "Time and tape complexity of pushdown automaton languages," *Information and Control,* **13**, pp. 186–206, 1968.

AHO, A.V., HOPCROFT, J.E., AND ULLMAN, J.D., *The Design and Analysis of Computer Algorithms,* Reading, Mass.: Addison-Wesley Publishing Co., 1974.

AHO, A.V., JOHNSON, S.C., AND ULLMAN, J.D., "Deterministic parsing of ambiguous grammars," *Communications of the Association for Computing Machinery,* **18**, pp. 441–452, 1975.

AHO, A.V., AND ULLMAN, J.D., *The Theory of Parsing, Translating, and Compiling,* Vols. I and II. Englewood Cliffs, N. J.: Prentice Hall, 1972 and 1973.

AHO, A.V., AND ULLMAN, J.D., "Optimization of $LR(k)$ parsers," *Journal of Computer and System Sciences,* **6**, pp. 573–602, 1972.

AHO, A.V., AND ULLMAN, J.D., *Compiler Design,* Reading, Mass.: Addison-Wesley Publishing Co., 1977.

AHO, A.V., ULLMAN, J.D., AND HOPCROFT, J.E., "On the computational power of pushdown automata," *Journal of Computer and System Sciences,* **4**, pp. 129–136, 1970.

ALLEN, D., "On a characterization of the nonregular set of primes," *Journal of Computer and System Sciences,* **1**, pp. 464–467, 1968.

ALT, H., AND MEHLHORN, K., "Untere Schranken für den Platzbedarf bei der kontext-freien Analyse," Fachbereich 10, *Angewandte Mathematik und Informatik der Universität des Saarlandes,* September 1975.

ALTMAN, E.B., AND BANERJI, R.B., "Some problems of finite representability," *Information and Control,* **8**, pp. 251–263, 1965.

AMAR, V., AND PUTZOLU, G., "On a family of linear grammars," *Information and Control,* **7**, pp. 283–291, 1964.

AMAR, V., AND PUTZOLU, G., "Generalizations of regular events," *Information and Control,* **8**, pp. 56–63, 1965.

ANGLUIN, D., "The four Russians' algorithm for boolean-matrix multiplication is optimal in its class," *SIGACT NEWS,* **8**, pp. 29–33, 1976.

ARBIB, M.A., *Theories of Abstract Automata,* Englewood Cliffs, N. J.: Prentice-Hall, 1969.

ARLAZAROV, V.L., DINIC, E.A., KRONOD, M.A., AND FARADZEV, I.A., "On economical construction of the transitive closure of an oriented graph," *Doklady Akad. Nauk* SSSR, **194**, pp. 487–488, 1970. *Also see* English translation in *Soviet Mathematics,* Vol. 11, pp. 1209–1210, 1970.

BACKUS, J.W., "The syntax and semantics of the proposed international algebraic language of the Zürich ACM–GAMM conference," *Proceedings of the International Conference on Information Processing,* UNESCO, Paris, June 1959.

BAKER, B.S., AND BOOK, R.V., "Reversal-bounded multipushdown machines," *Information and Control,* **24**, pp. 231–246, 1974.

BAKER, B.S. AND BOOK, R.V., "Reversal-bounded multipushdown machines," *Journal of Computer and System Sciences,* **8**, pp. 315–332, 1974.

BANERJI, R.B., "Phrase-structure languages, finite machines, and channel capacity," *Information and Control,* **6**, pp. 153–162, 1963.

BAR-HILLEL, Y., *Language and Information,* Reading, Mass.: Addison-Wesley Publishing Co., 1964.

BAR-HILLEL, Y., PERLES, M., AND SHAMIR, E., "On formal properties of simple phrase-structure grammars," *Zeitschrift für Phonetik, Sprachwissenschaft, und Kommunikationsforschung,* **14**, pp. 143–177, 1961.

BAR-HILLEL, Y., AND SHAMIR, E., "Finite-state languages: formal representations and adequacy problems," *The Bulletin of the Research Council of Israel,* **8F**, pp. 155–166, 1960.

BARNES, B., "A two-way automaton with fewer states than any equivalent one-way automaton," *IEEE Transactions on Computers,* **C-20**, pp. 474–475, 1971.

BEERI, C., "An improvement on Valiant's decision procedure for equivalence of deterministic finite-turn pushdown automata," *Journal of Computer and System Sciences*, **10**, pp. 317–339, 1975.

BEERI, C., "Two-way nested-stack automata are equivalent to two-way stack automata," *Journal of Computer and System Sciences,* **10**, pp. 317–339, 1975.

BENNETT, J.H., "On Spectra," Ph.D. Thesis, Dept. of Mathematics, University of Michigan, 1962.

BERSTEL, J., "Contribution à l'Etude des Propriétés Arithmétiques des Langages Formels," Sc.D. Thesis, University of Paris VII, January 1972.

BERSTEL, J., "Sur la densité asymptotique des langages formels," in *Automata, Languages, and Programming* (M. Nivat, ed.), pp. 345–358, Amsterdam North-Holland Publishing Co., 1973.

BIRD, M., "The equivalence problem for deterministic two-tape automata," *Journal of Computer and System Sciences,* **7**, pp. 218–236, 1973.

BLATTNER, M., "The unsolvability of the equality problem for sentential forms of context-free grammars," *Journal of Computer and System Sciences,* **7**, pp. 463–468, 1973.

BLATTNER, M., "Transductions of context-free languages into sets of sentential forms," in *Automata, Languages, and Programming* (J. Loeckx, ed.), **14**, "Lecture Notes in Computer Science," pp. 511–522, New York: Springer-Verlag, 1974.

BLATTNER, M., "Structural similarity in context-free grammars," *Information and Control,* **30**, pp. 267–294, 1976.

BLUM, E.K., "A note on free semigroups with two generators," *Bulletin of the American Mathematical Society,* **71**, pp. 678–679, 1965.

BLUM, M., "On the size of machines," *Information and Control,* **11**, pp. 257–265, 1967.

BLUM, M., "A machine-independent theory of the complexity of recursive functions," *Journal of the Association for Computing Machinery,* **14**, pp. 322–336, 1967.

BOASSON, L., "Cônes Rationnels et Familles Agréables de Langages – Application au Langage à Compteur," Thesis, University of Paris VII, 1971.

BOASSON, L., "Two iteration theorems for some families of languages," *Journal of Computer and System Sciences,* **7**, pp. 583–596, 1973.

BOASSON, L., "Un critère de rationalité des langages algébriques," in *Automata, Languages, and Programming* (M. Nivat, ed.), pp. 359–365, Amsterdam, North-Holland Publishing Co., 1973.

BOASSON, L., "Paires Itérantes et Langages Algébriques," Thesis, University of Paris VII, 1974.

BOASSON, L., "Langages algébriques, paires itérantes, et transductions rationnelles," *Theoretical Computer Science,* **2**, pp. 209–224, 1976.

BOOK, R.V., "Time-bounded grammars and their languages," *Journal of Computer and System Sciences,* **5**, pp. 397–429, 1971.

BOOK, R.V., "Terminal context in context-sensitive grammars," *SIAM Journal on Computing,* **1**, pp. 20–30, 1972a.

BOOK, R.V., "On languages accepted in polynomial time," *SIAN Journal on Computing,* **1**, pp. 281–287, 1972b.

BOOK, R.V., "On the structure of context-sensitive grammars," *Int. Journal of Computer and Information Sciences,* **2**, pp. 129–139, 1973.

BOOK, R.V., AND GREIBACH, S.A., "Quasi-real-time languages," *Mathematical Systems Theory,* **4**, pp. 97–111, 1970.

BOOK, R.V., AND GREIBACH, S.A., "Formal languages," unpublished manuscript, 1973.

BOOK, R.V., AND HARRISON, M.A., "Mutually divisible semigroups," *Discrete Mathematics,* **9**, pp. 329–332, 1974.

BORODIN, A., "Complexity classes of recursive functions and the existence of complexity gaps," *Proceedings of the First ACM Symposium on Theory of Computing,* pp. 67–78, 1969.

BORODIN, A., "Computational complexity and the existence of complexity gaps," *Journal of the Association for Computing Machinery,* **19**, pp. 158–174, 1972.

BORODIN, A., AND MUNRO, I., *The Computational Complexity of Algebraic and Numeric Problems,* New York: American Elsevier Publishing Co., 1975.

BOUCKAERT, M., PIROTTE, A., AND SNELLING, M., "Efficient parsing algorithms for general context-free parsers," *Information Sciences,* **8**, pp. 1–26, 1975.

BRAFFORT, P., AND HIRSCHBERG, D., *Computer Programming and Formal Systems,* Amsterdam, North-Holland Publishing Co., 1963.

BRAINERD, W.S., "An analog of a theorem about context-free languages," *Information and Control,* **11**, pp. 561–567, 1968.

BRAINERD, W.S., "Tree-generating regular systems," *Information and Control,* **14**, pp. 217–231, 1969.

BROSGOL, B.M., "Deterministic Translation Grammars," Ph.D. Thesis, Harvard University, 1974.

CANNON, R.L., "Phrase-structure grammars generating context-free languages," *Information and Control,* **29**, pp. 252–267, 1975.

CANTOR, D.G., "On the ambiguity problem of Backus systems," *Journal of the Association for Computing Machinery,* **9**, pp. 477–479, 1962.

CHANDRA, A.K., AND STOCKMEYER, L.J., "Alternation," *Proceedings of the 17th Annual Symposium on Foundations of Computer Science,* pp. 98–108, 1976.

CHEN, K.T., FOX, R.H., AND LYNDON, R.C., "Free differential calculus: IV. The quotient groups of the lower central series," *Annals of Mathematics,* **68**, pp. 81–95, 1958.

CHOMSKY, N., "Three models for the description of language," *IRE Transactions on Information Theory,* **IT2**, pp. 113–124, 1956.

CHOMSKY, N., "On certain formal properties of grammars," *Information and Control,* **2**, pp. 137–167, 1959a.

CHOMSKY, N., "A note on phrase-structure grammars," *Information and Control,* **2**, pp. 393–395, 1959b.

CHOMSKY, N., "Context-free grammars and pushdown storage," *MIT Research Lab of Electronics Quarterly Progress Report,* **65**, 1962.

CHOMSKY, N., "Formal properties of grammars," *Handbook of Mathematical Psychology,* Vol. 2 (Bush, Galanter, and Luce, eds.), New York: John Wiley, 1963.

CHOMSKY, N., *Syntactic Structures,* The Hague: Mouton & Co., 1964.

CHOMSKY, N., *Aspects of the Theory of Syntax,* Cambridge, Mass.: M.I.T. Press, 1965.

CHOMSKY, N., AND MILLER, G.A., "Finite-state languages," *Information and Control,* **1**, pp. 91–112, 1958.

CHOMSKY, N., AND SCHÜTZENBERGER, M.P., "The algebraic theory of context-free languages," in *Computer Programming and Formal Systems* (Braffort, P., and Hirschberg, D., eds.), Amsterdam: North-Holland, pp. 118–161, 1963.

CLIFFORD, A.H., AND PRESTON, G.B., *The Algebraic Theory of Semigroups,* Vols. I and II, Providence, R. I.: American Mathematical Society, 1967.

COBHAM, A., "On the base dependence of sets of numbers recognizable by finite automata," *Mathematical Systems Theory,* **3**, pp. 186–192, 1969.

COBHAM, A., "The instrinsic computational difficulty of functions," *Proceedings of the 1964 Congress for Logic, Mathematics, and Philosophy of Science,* Amsterdam: North-Holland Publishing Co., 1964; pp. 24–30.

COBHAM, A., "Uniform tag sequences," *Mathematical Systems Theory,* **6**, pp. 164–192, 1972.

COLE, S.N., "Real-time computation by iterative arrays of finite-state machines," Ph.D. Thesis, Harvard University, 1962.

COLE, S.N., "Deterministic pushdown store machines and real-time computation," *Journal of the Association for Computing Machinery,* **14**, pp. 453–460, 1971.

COLMERAUR, A., "Total precedence relations," *Journal of the Association for Computing Machinery,* **17**, pp. 14–30, 1970.

CONWAY, J.H., *Regular Algebra and Finite Machines.* London: Chapman and Hall, 1971.

COOK, S.A., "Characterizations of pushdown machines in terms of time-bounded computers," *Journal of the Association for Computing Machinery,* **18**, pp. 4–18, 1971.

COOK, S.A., "The complexity of theorem-proving procedures," *Proceedings of the Third Annual ACM Symposium on Theory of Computing,* pp. 151–158, 1971.

COOK, S.A., "An observation on time-storage tradeoff," *Journal of Computer and System Sciences,* **9**, pp. 308–316, 1974.

COURCELLE, B., "Une forme canonique pour les grammaires simples déterministes," *Revue Française d'Automatique, Informatique, and Recherche Opérationelle,* Série rouge, **8**, pp. 19–36, 1974.

COURCELLE, B., "Recursive schemes, algebraic trees, and deterministic languages," *Proceedings of the 15th Annual Symposium on Switching and Automata Theory,* pp. 52–62, 1974.

COURCELLE, B., "Sur les ensembles algébriques d'arbres et les langages déterministes," Ph.D. Thesis and IRIA Report, 1975.

CRESTIN, J.P., "Sur un langage quasi-rationnel d'ambiguité inhérente non bornée," Thèse de 3° Cycle, Faculty of Science, University of Paris, 1969.

CRESTIN, J.P., "Un langage non ambigu dont le carré est d'ambiguité non bornée," in *Automata, Languages, and Programming* (M. Nivat, ed.), pp. 377–390, Amsterdam: North-Holland Publishing Co., 1973.

CRESTIN, J.P., "Structure des grammaires d'ambiguité bornée," *Journal of Computer and System Sciences,* **8**, pp. 36–40, 1974.

CUDIA, D.F., "General problems of formal grammars," *Journal of the Association for Computing Machinery,* **17**, pp. 31–43, 1970.

ČULIK, K., AND COHEN, R., "*LR*-regular grammars – an extension of $LR(k)$ grammars," *Journal of Computer and System Sciences,* **7**, pp. 66–96, 1973.

DeREMER, F., "Practical Translators for $LR(k)$ Languages," Ph.D. Thesis and Project MAC Technical Report TR–65, M.I.T., 1965.

DeREMER, F., "Simple $LR(k)$ grammars," *Communications of the Association for Computing Machinery,* **14**, pp. 453–460, 1971.

DIKOVSKII, A. JA., "On the relationship between the class of all context-free languages and the class of deterministic context-free languages" (in Russian), *Algebra i Logika,* **8**, pp. 44–64, 1969.

EARLEY, J., "An efficient context-free parsing algorithm," *Communications of the Association for Computing Machinery,* **13**, pp. 94–102, 1970. *Also* Ph.D. thesis, Carnegie-Mellon University, 1968.

EICKEL, J., PAUL, M., BAUER, F.L., AND SAMELSON, K., "A syntax-controlled generator of formal language processors," *Communications of the Association for Computing Machinery,* **6**, pp. 451–455, 1963.

EILENBERG, S., *Automata, Languages, and Machines,* Vol. A, New York: Academic Press Inc., 1974.

EILENBERG, S., AND SCHÜTZENBERGER, M.P., "Rational sets in commutative monoids," *Journal of Algebra,* **13**, pp. 173–191, 1969.

ELGOT, C.C., "Decision problems of finite-automata design and related arithmetics," *Transactions of the American Mathematical Society,* **98**, pp. 21–51, 1961.

ELGOT, C.C., AND MEZEI, J.E., "On relations defined by generalized finite automata," *IBM Journal of Research and Development,* **9**, pp. 47–68, 1965.

ENGELFRIET, J., "Translation of simple program schemes," in *Automata, Languages, and Programming* (M. Nivat, ed.), pp. 215–223, Amsterdam: North-Holland Publishing Co., 1973.

ERDÖS, P., AND SZERKERES, G., "A combinatorial problem in geometry," *Compositio Mathematica,* **2**, pp. 463–470, 1935.

ESTENFELD, K., "Strukturelle Untersuchungen zur schwersten kontextfreien Sprache," Technical Report A76/06, Saarbrücken: Universität des Saarlandes, 1976.

EVEY, R.J., "The Theory and Application of Pushdown Store Machines," Ph.D. Thesis and Research Report, Mathematical Linguistics and Automatic Translation Project, Harvard University, NSF–10, May 1963.

FINE, N.J., AND WILF, H.S., "Uniqueness theorems for periodic functions," *Proceedings of the American Mathematical Society,* **16**, pp. 109–114, 1965.

FISCHER, M.J., "Grammars with Macrolike Productions," Ph.D. Dissertation, Harvard University, 1968.

FISCHER, M.J., "Two characterizations of context-sensitive languages," *IEEE Conference Record of 10th Annual Symposium on Switching and Automata Theory,* pp. 149–156, 1969.

FISCHER, M.J., "Some properties of precedence languages," *ACM Symposium on Theory of Computing,* pp. 181–190, 1969.

FISCHER, M.J., AND MEYER, A.R., "Boolean-matrix multiplication and transitive closure," *IEEE Conference Record of 12th Annual Symposium on Switching and Automata Theory,* pp. 129–131, 1971.

FISCHER, M.J., AND ROSENBERG, A.L., "Real-time solutions of the origin crossing problem," *Mathematical Systems Theory,* **2**, pp. 257–263, 1968.

FISCHER, P.C., "Turing machines with restricted memory access," *Information and Control,* **9**, pp. 364–379, 1966.

FISCHER, P.C., AND PROBERT, R.L., "Efficient procedures for using matrix algorithms," in *Automata, Languages and Programming* (J. Loeckx, ed.), Vol. 14, "Lecture Notes in Computer Science," Berlin: Springer-Verlag, 1974; pp. 413–428.

FISCHER, P.C., AND ROSENBERG, A., "Multitape one-way nonwriting automata," *Journal of Computer and System Sciences,* **2**, pp. 88–101, 1968.

FISCHER, P.C., MEYER, A.R., AND ROSENBERG, A.L., "Counter machines and counter languages," *Mathematical Systems Theory,* **2**, pp. 265–283, 1968.

FLIESS, M., "Transductions de séries formelles," *Discrete Mathematics,* **10**, pp. 57–74, 1974.

FLIESS, M., "Matrices de Hankel," *Journal of Pure and Applied Math,* **53**, pp. 197–222, 1974.

FLOYD, R.W., "Syntactic analysis and operator precedence," *Journal of the Association for Computing Machinery,* **10**, pp. 313–333, 1963.

FLOYD, R.W., "Bounded-context syntactic analysis," *Communications of the Association for Computing Machinery,* **7**, pp. 62–66, 1964a.

FLOYD, R.W., "The syntax of programming languages," *IEEE Transactions on Electronic Computers,* **EC-13**, pp. 346–353, 1964b.

FLOYD, R.W., "A machine-oriented recognition algorithm for context-free languages," unpublished manuscript, April 1969.

FRIEDMAN, E.P., "Deterministic Languages and Monadic Recursion Schemes," Ph.D. Thesis, Harvard University, Cambridge, 1974.

FRIEDMAN, E.P., "The inclusion problem for simple languages," *Theoretical Computer Science,* **1**, pp. 297–316, 1976.

GALIL, Z., "Some open problems in the theory of computation as questions about two-way deterministic pushdown automaton languages," *Mathematical Systems Theory,* **10**, pp. 211–218, 1977.

GALIL, Z., "Real-time algorithms for string matching and palindrome recognition," unpublished manuscript, Yorktown Heights, N.Y.: IBM Research Center, 1975.

GALIL, Z., "Two fast simulations which imply some fast string-matching and palindrome-recognition algorithms," *Information Processing Letters,* **4**, pp. 85–100, 1976.

GALIL, Z., AND SEIFERAS, J., "Recognizing certain repetitions and reversals within strings," *Proceedings of the 17th Annual Symposium on Foundations of Computer Science,* pp. 236–252, 1976.

GALLAIRE, H., "Recognition time of context-free languages by on-line Turing machines," *Information and Control,* **15**, pp. 288–295, 1969.

GELLER, M.M., GRAHAM, S.L., AND HARRISON, M.A., "Production prefix parsing" (extended abstract), *Automata, Languages, and Programming,* 2nd Colloquium (Jacques Loeckx, ed.), University of Saarbrücken, July 29–August 2, 1974, pp. 232–241.

GELLER, M.M., AND HARRISON, M.A., "Strict deterministic versus $LR(0)$ parsing," *Conference Record of the ACM Symposium on Principles of Programming Languages,* pp. 22–32, 1973.

GELLER, M.M., AND HARRISON, M.A., "Characterizations of $LR(0)$ languages," *Conference Record of the 14th Annual Symposium on Switching and Automata Theory,* pp. 103–108, 1973.

GELLER, M.M., AND HARRISON, M.A., "Characteristic parsing: A framework for producing compact deterministic parsers, I," *Journal of Computer and System Sciences,* **14**, pp. 265–317, 1977.

GELLER, M.M., AND HARRISON, M.A., "Characteristic parsing: A framework for producing compact deterministic parsers, II," *Journal of Computer and System Sciences,* **14**, pp. 318–343, 1977.

GELLER, M.M., AND HARRISON, M.A., "On $LR(k)$ grammars and languages," *Theoretical Computer Science,* **4**, pp. 245–276, 1977.

GELLER, M.M., HARRISON, M.A., AND HAVEL, I.M., "Normal forms of deterministic grammars," *Discrete Mathematics,* **16**, pp. 313–321, 1976.

GELLER, M.M., HUNT, H.B., SZYMANSKI, T.G., AND ULLMAN, J.D., "Economy of description by parsers, dpda's, and pda's," *Theoretical Computer Science,* **4**, pp. 143–159, 1977.

GINSBURG, S., *The Mathematical Theory of Context-Free Languages,* New York: McGraw-Hill Book Co., 1966.

GINSBURG, S., *Algebraic and Automata-Theoretic Properties of Formal Languages,* Amsterdam: North-Holland Publishing Co., 1975.

GINSBURG, S., GOLDSTINE, J., AND GREIBACH, S., "Uniformly erasable AFL," *Journal of Computer and System Sciences,* **10**, pp. 165–182, 1975.

GINSBURG, S., AND GREIBACH, S.A., "Deterministic context-free languages," *Information and Control,* **9**, pp. 602–648, 1966a.

GINSBURG, S., AND GREIBACH, S.A., "Mappings which preserve context-sensitive languages," *Information and Control,* **9**, pp. 620–649, 1966b.

GINSBURG, S., AND GREIBACH, S.A., "Abstract families of languages," *Memoirs of the American Mathematical Society,* **87**, 1969.

GINSBURG, S., GREIBACH, S.A., AND HARRISON, M.A., "Stack automata and compiling," *Journal of the Association for Computing Machinery,* **14**, pp. 172–201, 1967.

GINSBURG, S., GREIBACH, S.A., AND HARRISON, M.A., "One-way stack automata," *Journal of the Association for Computing Machinery,* **14**, pp. 389–418, 1967.

GINSBURG, S., AND HARRISON, M.A., "Bracketed context-free languages," *Journal of Computer and System Sciences,* **1**, pp. 1–23, 1967.

GINSBURG, S., AND HARRISON, M.A., "On the elimination of endmarkers," *Information and Control,* **12**, pp. 103–115, 1968.

GINSBURG, S., AND HARRISON, M.A., "One-way nondeterministic real-time list-storage languages," *Journal of the Association for Computing Machinery,* **15**, pp. 428–446, 1968.

GINSBURG, S., AND HARRISON, M.A., "On the closure of AFL under reversal," *Information and Control,* **17**, pp. 395–409, 1970.

GINSBURG, S., AND RICE, H.G., "Two families of languages related to ALGOL," *Journal of the Association for Computing Machinery,* **9**, pp. 350–371, 1962.

GINSBURG, S., AND ROSE, G.F., "Some recursively unsolvable problems in ALGOL-like languages," *Journal of the Association for Computing Machinery,* **10**, pp. 29–47, 1963.

GINSBURG, S., AND ROSE, G.F., "Operations which preserve definability in languages," *Journal of the Association for Computing Machinery,* **10**, pp. 175–195, 1963.

GINSBURG, S., AND ROSE, G.F., "The equivalence of stack-counter acceptors and quasi-real-time acceptors," *Journal of Computer and System Sciences,* **8**, pp. 243–269, 1974.

GINSBURG, S., AND SPANIER, E.H., "Quotients of context-free languages," *Journal of the Association for Computing Machinery,* **10**, pp. 487–492, 1963.

GINSBURG, S., AND SPANIER, E.H., "Bounded ALGOL-like languages," *Transactions of the American Mathematical Society,* **113**, pp. 333–368, 1964.

GINSBURG, S., AND SPANIER, E.H., "Finite-turn pushdown automata," *SIAM Journal on Control,* **4**, pp. 429–453, 1966.

GINSBURG, S., AND SPANIER, E.H., "Semigroups, Presburger formulas, and languages," *Pacific Journal of Mathematics,* **16**, pp. 285–296, 1966.

GINSBURG, S., AND SPANIER, E.H., "Bounded regular sets," *Proceedings of the American Mathematical Society,* **17**, pp. 1043–1049, 1966.

GINSBURG, S., AND SPANIER, E.H., "Derivation-bounded languages," *Journal of Computer and System Sciences,* **2**, pp. 228–250, 1968.

GINSBURG, S., AND ULLIAN, J.S., "Preservation of unambiguity and inherent ambiguity in context-free languages," *Journal of the Association for Computing Machinery,* **13**, pp. 364–368, 1966.

GINSBURG, S., AND ULLIAN, J., "Ambiguity in context-free languages," *Journal of the Association for Computing Machinery,* **13**, pp. 62–89, 1966.

GLADKII, A., "Grammars with linear memory," *Algebri i Logika Sem.,* **2**, pp. 43–55, 1963.

GLADKII, A., "On the complexity of derivations in phrase-structure grammars," *Algebri i Logika Sem.,* **3**, pp. 29–44, 1964.

GOLDSTINE, J., "Some independent families of one-letter languages," *Journal of Computer and System Sciences,* **10**, pp. 351–369, 1975.

GOLDSTINE, J., "A simplified proof of Parikh's theorem," *Discrete Mathematics,* **19**, pp. 235–240, 1977.

GRAHAM, S.L., "Extended precedence: bounded right-context languages and deterministic languages," *Proceedings of the Eleventh Symposium on Switching and Automata Theory,* pp. 175–180, 1970.

GRAHAM, S.L., "Precedence Languages and Bounded Right-Context Languages," Ph.D. Thesis and Technical Report CS–71–223, Department of Computer Science, Stanford University, 1971.

GRAHAM, S.L., "On bounded right-context languages and grammars," *SIAM Journal of Computing,* 3, pp. 224–254, 1974.

GRAHAM, S.L., AND HARRISON, M.A., "Parsing of general context-free languages," in *Advances in Computers,* Vol. 14 (M. Yovits and M. Rubinoff, eds.), pp. 77–185, New York: Academic Press, 1976.

GRAHAM, S.L., HARRISON, M.A., AND RUZZO, W.L., "On-line context-free recognition in less than cubic time," *Proceedings of the Eighth Annual ACM Symposium on Theory of Computing,* pp. 112–120, 1976.

GRAY, J.N., AND HARRISON, M.A., "The theory of sequential relations," *Information and Control,* **9**, pp. 435–468, 1966.

GRAY, J.N., AND HARRISON, M.A., "Single-pass precedence analysis," *Conference Record of the 10th Annual Symposium on Switching and Automata Theory,* pp. 106–117, 1969.

GRAY, J.N., AND HARRISON, M.A., "On the covering and reduction problems for context-free grammars," *Journal of the Association for Computing Machinery,* **19**, pp. 675–698, 1972.

GRAY, J.N., AND HARRISON, M.A., "Canonical precedence schemes," *Journal of the Association for Computing Machinery,* **20**, pp. 214–234, 1973.

GRAY, J.N., HARRISON, M.A., AND IBARRA, O.H., "Two-way pushdown automata," *Information and Control,* **11**, pp. 30–70, 1967.

GREIBACH, S.A., "Undecidability of the ambiguity problem for minimal linear grammars," *Information and Control,* **6**, pp. 119–125, 1963.

GREIBACH, S.A., "A new normal-form theorem for context-free, phrase-structure grammars," *Journal of the Association for Computing Machinery,* **12**, pp. 42–52, 1965.

GREIBACH, S.A., "The unsolvability of the recognition of linear context-free languages," *Journal of the Association for Computing Machinery,* **13**, pp. 582–587, 1966.

GREIBACH, S.A., "A note on pushdown-store automata and regular systems," *Proceedings of the American Mathematical Society,* **18**, pp. 263–268, 1967.

GREIBACH, S.A., "A note on undecidable properties of formal languages," *Mathematical Systems Theory,* **2**, pp. 1–6, 1968.

GREIBACH, S.A., "An infinite hierarchy of context-free languages," *Journal of the Association for Computing Machinery,* **16**, pp. 91–106, 1969.

GREIBACH, S.A., "Characteristic and ultrarealtime languages," *Information and Control,* **18**, pp. 65–98, 1971.

GREIBACH, S.A., "A generalization of Parikh's semilinear theorem," *Discrete Mathematics,* **2**, pp. 347–355, 1972.

GREIBACH, S.A., "The hardest context-free language," *SIAM Journal of Computing,* **2**, pp. 304–310, 1973.

GREIBACH, S.A., "Jump pda's and hierarchies of deterministic context-free languages," *SIAM Journal of Computing,* **3**, pp. 111–127, 1974.

GREIBACH, S.A., "One-counter languages and the IRS condition," *Journal of Computer and System Sciences,* **10**, pp. 237–247, 1975a.

GREIBACH, S.A., "Erasable context-free languages," *Information and Control,* **29**, pp. 301–326, 1975b.

GRIES, D., *Compiler Construction for Digital Computers,* New York: John Wiley and Sons, 1971.

GRIFFITHS, T.V., "Some remarks on derivations in general rewriting systems," *Information and Control,* **12**, pp. 27–54, 1968.

GRIFFITHS, T.V., "The unsolvability of the equivalence problem for Λ-free nondeterministic generalized machines," *Journal of the Association for Computing Machinery,* **15**, pp. 409–413, 1968.

GROSS, M., "Inherent ambiguity of minimal linear grammars," *Information and Control,* **7**, pp. 366–368, 1964.

GROSS, M., "Applications géometriques des langages formels," *ICC Bulletin,* **5-3**, 1966.

GROSS, M., AND LENTIN, A., *Notions sur les Grammaires Formelles,* Paris: Gauthier-Villars, 1967.

GRUSKA, J., "Some classifications of context-free languages," *Information and Control,* **14**, pp. 152–179, 1969.

GRUSKA, J., "Complexity and unambiguity of context-free grammars and languages," *Information and Control,* **18**, pp. 502–519, 1971.

GRUSKA, J., "A characterization of context-free languages," *Journal of Computer and System Sciences,* **5**, pp. 353–364, 1971.

GRUSKA, J., "On star-height hierarchies of context-free languages," *Kybernetika,* **9**, pp. 231–236, 1973.

GRUSKA, J., "Grammatical levels and subgrammars of context-free grammars," *Arch. Math 1, Scripta Fac. Sci. Nat. Ujep Bruneusis,* **IX**, pp. 19–21, 1973.

GRUSKA, J., "A note on ϵ-rules in context-free grammars," *Kybernetika,* **11**, pp. 26–31, 1975.

GRZEGORCZYK, A., "Some classes of recursive functions," *Rozprawy Matematyczne,* **IV**, pp. 1–46, 1954.

HAINES, L.H., "Note on the complement of a (minimal) linear language," *Information and Control,* **7**, pp. 307–314, 1964.

HAINES, L.H., "Generation and Recognition of Formal Languages," Ph.D. thesis, M.I.T., 1965.

HAINES, L.H., "On free monoids partially ordered by embedding," *Journal of Combinatorial Theory,* **6**, pp. 94–98, 1969.

HAINES, L.H., "Representation theorems for context-sensitive languages," unpublished manuscript, University of California, Berkeley, 1970.

HARRISON, M.A., *Introduction to Switching and Automata Theory,* New York: McGraw-Hill, 1965.

HARRISON, M.A., "On the relation between grammars and automata," in *Advances of Information Sciences 4* (J.T. Tou, ed.), pp. 39–92, New York: Plenum Press, 1972.

HARRISON, M.A., AND HAVEL, I.M., "Strict deterministic grammars," *Journal of Computer and Systems Sciences,* **7**, pp. 237–277, 1973.

HARRISON, M.A., AND HAVEL, I.M., "On the parsing of deterministic languages," *Journal of the Association for Computing Machinery,* **21**, pp. 525–548, 1974.

HARRISON, M.A., AND HAVEL, I.M., "Real-time strict deterministic languages," *SIAM Journal of Computing,* **1**, pp. 333–349, 1972.

HARRISON, M.A., AND HAVEL, I.M., "On a family of deterministic grammars," in *Automata, Languages, and Programming* (M. Nivat, ed.), pp. 413–442, Amsterdam: North-Holland Publishing Co., 1973.

HARRISON, M.A., AND IBARRA, O.H., "Multitape and multihead pushdown automata," *Information and Control,* **13**, pp. 433–470, 1968.

HARRISON, M.A., AND SCHKOLNICK, M., "A grammatical characterization of one-way nondeterministic stack languages," *Journal of the Association for Computing Machinery,* **18**, pp. 148–172, 1971.

HARTMANIS, J., "Context-free languages and Turing-machine computations," *Proceedings of a Symposium on Applied Mathematics,* **19**, *Mathematical Aspects of Computer Science*, pp. 42–51. Providence: American Mathematical Society, 1967a.

HARTMANIS, J., "On memory requirements for context-free language recognition," *Journal of the Association for Computing Machinery,* **14**, pp. 663–665, 1967b.

HARTMANIS, J., "Computational complexity of one-tape Turing-machine computations," *Journal of the Association for Computing Machinery,* **15**, pp. 325–339, 1968.

HARTMANIS, J., "On the complexity of undecidable problems in automata theory," *Journal of the Association for Computing Machinery,* **16**, pp. 160–167, 1969.

HARTMANIS, J., "Computational complexity of random-access stored-program machines," *Mathematical Systems Theory,* **5**, pp. 232–245, 1971.

HARTMANIS, J., "On nondeterminancy in simple computing devices," *Acta Informatica,* **1**, pp. 336–344, 1972.

HARTMANIS, J., AND HOPCROFT, J.E., "What makes some language-theory problems undecidable?" *Journal of Computer and System Sciences*, **3**, 196–217, 1969.

HARTMANIS, J., AND HOPCROFT, J.E., "An overview of computational complexity," *Journal of the Association for Computing Machinery,* **18**, pp. 444–475, 1971.

HARTMANIS, J., AND HUNT, H.B., III, "The lba problem and its importance in the theory of computing," in *Complexity of Computation* (R. Karp, ed.), Vol. VII, SIAM-AMS Proceedings, 1973; pp. 27–42.

HARTMANIS, J., AND SHANK, H., "On the recognition of primes by automata," *Journal of the Association for Computing Machinery,* **15**, pp. 382–389, 1968.

HARTMANIS, J., AND SHANK, H., "Two memory bounds for the recognition of primes by automata," *Mathematical Systems Theory,* **3**, pp. 125–129, 1969.

HARTMANIS, J., AND STEARNS, R.E., "Regularity-preserving modifications of regular expressions," *Information and Control,* **6**, pp. 55–69, 1963.

HARTMANIS, J., AND STEARNS, R.E., "On the computational complexity of algorithms," *Transactions of the American Mathematical Society,* **117**, pp. 285–306, 1965.

HARTMANIS, J., AND STEARNS, R.E., "Sets of numbers defined by finite automata," *American Mathematical Monthly,* **74**, pp. 539–542, 1967.

HARTMANIS, J., AND STEARNS, R.E., "Automata-based computational complexity," *Information Sciences,* **1**, pp. 173–184, 1969.

HENNIE, F.C., "One-tape, off-line Turing-machine computations," *Information and Control,* **8**, pp. 553–578, 1965.

HENNIE, F.C., "On-line Turing-machine computations," *IEEE Transactions on Electronic Computers,* **EC–15**, pp. 35–44, 1966.

HENNIE, F.C., AND STEARNS, R.E., "Two-tape simulation of multitape Turing machines," *Journal of the Association for Computing Machinery,* **13**, pp. 553–546, 1966.

HIBBARD, T.N., "Scan-limited automata and context-limited grammars," Ph.D. Thesis, Dept. of Mathematics, University of California at Los Angeles, 1966.

HIBBARD, T.N., "Context-limited grammars," *Journal of the Association for Computing Machinery,* **21**, pp. 446–453, 1974.

HIBBARD, T.N., AND ULLIAN, J., "The independence of inherent ambiguity from complementedness among context-free languages," *Journal of the Association for Computing Machinery,* **13**, pp. 588–593, 1966.

HOPCROFT, J.E., "On the equivalence and containment problems for context-free languages," *Mathematical Systems Theory,* **3**, pp. 119–124, 1969.

HOPCROFT, J.E., PAUL, W., AND VALIANT, L., "On time versus space and related problems," *Proceedings of the 16th Annual Symposium on Foundations of Computer Science,* pp. 57–64, 1975.

HOPCROFT, J.E., AND ULLMAN, J.D., *Formal Languages and Their Relation to Automata,* Reading, Mass.: Addison-Wesley Publishing Co., 1969.

HOPCROFT, J.E., AND ULLMAN, J.D., "An approach to a unified theory of automata," *Bell System Technical Journal,* **46**, pp. 1793–1829, 1967.

HOPCROFT, J.E., AND ULLMAN, J.D., "Deterministic stack automata and the quotient operator," *Journal of Computer and System Sciences,* **2**, pp. 1–12, 1968a.

HOPCROFT, J.E., AND ULLMAN, J.D., "Relations between time and tape complexities," *Journal of the Association for Computing Machinery,* **15**, pp. 414–427, 1968b.

HOTZ, G., "Sequentielle Analyse kontextfreier Sprachen," *Acta Informatica,* **4**, pp. 55–75, 1974.

HOTZ, G., "Normal-form transformations of context-free grammars," unpublished manuscript, 1976.

HOTZ, G., "Der Satz von Chomsky–Schützenberger und die schwerste kontextfreie Sprache von S. Greibach," unpublished manuscript, 1976.

HOTZ, G., AND CLAUS, V., "Automatentheorie und Formale Sprachen," Mannheim: Bib. Institut, 1972.

HOTZ, G., AND MESSERSCHMIDT, J., "Dyck Sprachen sind in Bandkomplexität log *n* analysierbar," Fachbereich 10, Saarbrücken: Universität des Saarlandes, 1975.

HUNT, H.B., III "A complexity theory of grammar problems," *Conference Record of the Third ACM Symposium on Principles of Programming Languages,* pp. 12–18, 1976.

HUNT, H.B., III, "On the complexity of finite, pushdown, and stack automata," *Mathematical Systems Theory,* **10**, pp. 33–52, 1976.

HUNT, H.B., III, "On the time and tape complexity of languages," *Proceedings of the 5th Annual Symposium on Theory of Computing*, pp. 10–19, 1973.

HUNT, H.B., III, AND RANGEL, J.L., "Decidability of equivalence, containment, intersection, and separability of context-free languages," *Proceedings of 16th Annual Symposium on Foundations of Computer Science,* pp. 144–150, 1975.

HUNT, H.B., III, AND ROSENKRANTZ, D.J., "Computational parallels between the regular and context-free languages," *SIAM Journal on Computing,* **7**, 1978.

HUNT, H.B., III, ROSENKRANTZ, D.J., AND SZYMANSKI, T.G., "The covering problem for linear context-free grammars," *Theoretical Computer Science,* **2**, pp. 361–382, 1976.

HUNT, H.B., III, AND ROZENKRANTZ, D.J., "On equivalence and containment problems for formal languages," *Journal of the Association for Computing Machinery,* **24**, pp. 387–396, 1977.

HUNT, H.B., III, AND SZYMANSKI, T.G., "Complexity metatheorems for context-free grammar problems," *Journal of Computer and System Sciences,* **13**, pp. 318–334, 1976.

HUNT, H.B., III, AND SZYMANSKI, T.G., "Dichotomization, reachability, and the forbidden-subgraph problem," *Proceedings of the Eighth Annual ACM Symposium on Theory of Computing,* pp. 126–135, 1976.

HUNT, H.B., III, SZYMANSKI, T.G., AND ULLMAN, J.D., "On the complexity of *LR*(*k*) Testing," *Communications of the Association for Computing Machinery,* **18**, pp. 707–716, 1975a.

HUNT, H.B., III, SZYMANSKI, T.G., AND ULLMAN, J.D., "Operations on sparse relations, with applications to grammar problems," *Proceedings of the Fifteenth Annual Symposium on Switching and Automata Theory,* pp. 127–132, 1974.

HUNT, H.B., III, SZYMANSKI, T.G., AND ULLMAN, J.D., "Operations on sparse relations," *Communications of the Association for Computing Machinery*, **20**, pp. 171–176, 1977.

IBARRA, O.H., "On two-way multihead automata," *Journal of Computer and System Sciences,* **7**, pp. 28–36, 1973.

IBARRA, O.H., AND KIM, C.E., "On 3-head versus 2-head finite automata," *Acta Informatica,* **4**, pp. 193–200, 1975.

IBARRA, O.H., AND KIM, C.E., "A useful device for showing the solvability of some decision problems," *Journal of Computer and System Sciences,* **13**, pp. 153–160, 1976.

ICHBIAH, J.D., AND MORSE, S.P., "A technique for generating almost optimal Floyd–Evans productions for precedence grammars," *Communications of the Association for Computing Machinery,* **13**, pp. 501–508, 1970.

IGARASHI, Y., AND HONDA, N., "On the extension of Gladkij's theorem and the hierarchy of languages," *Journal of Computer and System Sciences,* **7**, pp. 199–217, 1973.

JACOB, G., "Sur un théorème de Shamir," *Information and Control,* **27**, pp. 218–261, 1975a.

JACOB, G., "Représentations et Substitutions Matricielles dans la Théorie Algébriques des Transductions," Thesis, University of Paris VII, 1975b.

JONES, N.D., "Classes of automata and transitive closure," *Information and Control,* **13**, pp. 207–229, 1968.

JONES, N.D., "Context-free languages and rudimentary attributes," *Mathematical Systems Theory,* **3**, pp. 102–109, 1969.

JONES, N.D., "Space-bounded reducibility among combinatorial problems," *Journal of Computer and System Sciences,* **11**, pp. 68–85, 1975.

JONES, N.D., AND LAASER, W.T., "Complete problems for deterministic polynomial time," *Theoretical Computer Science,* **3**, pp. 105–118, 1976.

JONES, N.D., LAASER, W.T., AND LIEN, Y., "New problems complete for nondeterministic log space computability," *Mathematical Systems Theory,* **10**, pp. 19–32, 1976.

JONES, N.D., AND SELMAN, A.L., "Turing machines and the spectra of first-order formulas," *Journal of Symbolic Logic,* **39**, pp. 139–150, 1974.

JOSHI, A.K., LEVY, L.S., AND TAKAHASHI, M., "Tree-Adjunct Grammars," *Journal of Computer and System Sciences,* **10**, pp. 136–163, 1975.

KARP, R.M., "Reducibilities among combinatorial problems," in *Complexity of Computer Computations* (R. Miller and J. Thatcher, eds.), New York: Plenum Press, 1972; pp. 85–104.

KARP, R.M., "Automaton-based complexity theory," Class notes for CS 276, Computer Science Division, University of California, Berkeley, 1975.

KASAMI, T., "An efficient recognition and syntax-analysis algorithm for context-free languages," Science Report AFCRL–65–758, Air Force Cambridge Research Laboratory, Bedford, Mass., 1965.

KASAMI, T., AND TORII, K., "A syntax-analysis procedure for unambiguous context-free grammars," *Journal of the Association for Computing Machinery,* **16**, pp. 423–431, 1969.

KASAMI, T., "A note on computing time for recognition of languages generated by linear grammars," *Information and Control,* **10**, pp. 209–214, 1968.

KEMP, R., "An estimation of the set of states of the minimal $LR(0)$ acceptor," in *Automata, Languages, and Programming* (M. Nivat, ed.), pp. 563–574, Amsterdam: North-Holland Publishing Co., 1973.

KEMP, R., "Mehrdeutigkeiten kontextfreier Grammatiken," in *Automata, Languages, and Programming* (J. Loeckx, ed.), Vol. 14, Lecture notes in Computer Science," pp. 534–546, Berlin: Springer-Verlag, 1974.

KEMP, R., "*LR*(*k*) Analysatoren," Technical Report A73/02, Mathematisches Institut und Institut für Angewandte Mathematik, Saarbrücken, Universität des Saarlandes, 1973.

KLEENE, S.C., "Representation of events in nerve nets," in *Automata Studies* (C.E. Shannon and J. McCarthy, eds.), pp. 3–40, Princeton: Princeton University Press, 1956.

KNUTH, D.E., "On the translation of languages from left to right," *Information and Control,* **8**, pp. 607–639, 1965.

KNUTH, D.E., "A characterization of parenthesis languages," *Information and Control,* **11**, pp. 269–289, 1967.

KNUTH, D.E., "Fundamental Algorithms," Vol. I of *The Art of Computer Programming,* Reading, Mass.: Addison-Wesley Publishing Co., 1973.

KNUTH, D.E., "Top-down syntax analysis," *Acta Informatica,* **1**, pp. 79–110, 1971.

KNUTH, D.E., AND BIGELOW, R.H., "Programming languages for automata," *Journal of the Association for Computing Machinery,* **14**, pp. 615–635, 1967.

KNUTH, D.E., MORRIS, J.H., AND PRATT, V.R., "Fast pattern-matching in strings," *SIAM Journal on Computing,* **6**, pp. 323–350, 1977.

KNUTH, D.E., "Big omicron and big omega and big theta," *SIGACT NEWS,* **8**, pp. 18–24, 1976.

KORENJAK, A.J., "A practical method for constructing *LR*(*k*) processors," *Communications of the Association for Computing Machinery,* **12**, pp. 613–623, 1969.

KORENJAK, A.J., AND HOPCROFT, J.E., "Simple deterministic languages," *Conference Record of Seventh Annual Symposium on Switching and Automata Theory,* Berkeley, pp. 36–46, 1966.

KOSARAJU, S.R., "One-way stack automaton with jumps," *Journal of Computer and System Sciences,* **9**, pp. 164–176, 1974.

KOSARAJU, S.R., "Speed of recognition of context-free language by array automata," *SIAM Journal on Computing,* **4**, pp. 333–340, 1975.

KOSARAJU, S.R., "Context-free preserving functions," *Mathematical Systems Theory,* **9**, pp. 193–197, 1975.

KOSARAJU, S.R., "Recognition of context-free languages by random-access machines," unpublished manuscript, Fall, 1975.

KOZEN, D., "On parallelism in Turing machines," *Proceedings of the 17th Annual Symposium on Foundations of Computer Science,* pp. 89–97, 1976.

KRÁL, J., AND DEMNER, J., "A note on the number of states of the DeRemer's recognizer," *Information Processing Letters,* **2**, pp. 22–23, 1973.

KREIDER, D., AND RITCHIE, R.E., "A basis theorem for a class of two-way automata," *Zeitschrift für Mathematische Logik und Grundlagen der Mathematik,* **12**, pp. 243–255, 1966.

KURODA, S.Y., "Classes of languages and linear-bounded automata," *Information and Control,* **7**, pp. 207–223, 1964.

LALONDE, W.R., "On directly constructing *LR*(*k*) parsers without chain reductions," *Conference Record of the Third ACM Symposium on Principles of Programming Languages,* pp. 127–133, 1976.

LANDWEBER, P.S., "Three theorems on phrase-structure grammars of type 1," *Information and Control,* **6**, pp. 131–136, 1963.

LANDWEBER, P.S., "Decision problems of phase-structure grammars," *IEEE Transactions on Electronic Computers,* **EC-13**, pp. 354–362, 1964.

LEARNER, A., AND LIM, A.L., "A note on transforming grammars to Wirth–Weber precedence form," *Computer Journal,* **12**, pp. 142–144, 1970.

LEHMANN, D., "*LR*(k) grammars and deterministic languages," *Israel Journal of Mathematics,* **10**, pp. 526–530, 1971.

LENTIN, A., *Equations dans les Monoides Libres.* Paris: Gauthier–Villars, 1972.

LENTIN, A., AND SCHÜTZENBERGER, M.P., "A combinatorial problem in the theory of free monoids," in *Combinatorial Mathematics and Its Applications,* pp. 128–144, 1967; Proc. of conf. at Chapel Hill, N.C., April 10–14, 1967, Ed. by R.C. Bose and T.A. Dowling. Chapel Hill: University of No. Carolina Press, 1969.

LEVI, F.W., "On semigroups," *Bulletin of the Calcutta Mathematical Society,* **36**, pp. 141–146, 1944.

LEWIS, P.M., III, AND ROSENKRANTZ, D.J., "An ALGOL compiler designed using automata theory," *Proceedings of a Symposium on Computers and Automata,* Vol. 21. New York: Polytechnic Institute of Brooklyn, 1971; pp. 75–88.

LEWIS, P.M., III, AND STEARNS, R.E., "Syntax-directed transductions," *Journal of the Association for Computing Machinery,* **15**, pp. 465–488, 1968.

LEWIS, P.M., III, STEARNS, R.E., AND HARTMANIS, J., "Memory bounds for recognition of context-free and context-sensitive languages," *IEEE Conference Record on Switching Circuit Theory and Logical Design,* Ann Arbor, Michigan, pp. 191–202, 1965.

LIPTON, R.J., AND ZALCSTEIN, Y., "Word problems solvable in log space," *Journal of the Association for Computing Machinery,* **24**, pp. 522–526, 1977.

LIU, L.Y., AND WEINER, P., "A characterization of semilinear sets," *Journal of Computer and System Sciences,* **4**, pp. 299–307, 1970.

LOMET, D.B., "A formalization of transition diagram systems," *Journal of the Association for Computing Machinery,* **20**, pp. 235–237, 1973.

LYNCH, N., "Log space recognition and translation of parenthesis languages," *Journal of the Association for Computing Machinery,* **24**, pp. 583–590, 1977.

LYNDON, R.C., AND SCHÜTZENBERGER, M.P., "The equation $a^M = b^N c^P$ in a free group," *Michigan Mathematical Journal,* **9**, pp. 289–298, 1962.

MCNAUGHTON, R., "Parentheses grammars," *Journal of the Association for Computing Machinery,* **14**, pp. 490–500, 1967.

MCNAUGHTON, R., AND YAMADA, H., "Regular expressions and state graphs for automata," *IEEE Transactions on Electronic Computers,* **EC–9**, pp. 39–47, 1960.

MCWHIRTER, I.P., "Substitution expressions," *Journal of Computer and System Sciences,* **5**, pp. 629–637, 1971.

MAIBAUM, T.S.E., "A generalized approach to formal languages," *Journal of Computer and System Sciences,* **8**, pp. 409–439, 1974.

MARCUS, S., *Introduction Mathématique à la Linguistique Structurale.* Paris: Dunod, 1967.

MATTHEWS, G., "Discontinuity and asymmetry in phrase-structure grammars," *Information and Control,* **7**, pp. 137–146, 1963.

MATTHEWS, G., "A note on asymmetry in phrase-structure grammars," *Information and Control,* **7**, pp. 360–365, 1964.

MATTHEWS, G., "Two-way languages," *Information and Control,* **10**, pp. 111–119, 1967.

MAURER, H.A., "A direct proof of the inherent ambiguity of a simple context-free language," *Journal of the Association for Computing Machinery,* **16**, pp. 256–260, 1969.

MEHLHORN, K., "Bracket languages are recognizable in logarithmic space," Technical Report A 75/12. Saarbrücken: Universität des Saarlandes, 1975.

MEHTA, V., "Onward and upward with the arts: John is easy to please," *New Yorker,* **47**, pp. 44–87, May 8, 1971.

MEYER, A.R., and FISCHER, M.J., "Economy of description by automata, grammars, and formal systems," *Conference Record of 1971 Annual Symposium on Switching and Automata Theory,* pp. 188–191, 1971.

MICKUNAS, M.D., "On the complete covering problem for $LR(k)$ grammars," *Journal of the Association for Computing Machinery,* **23**, pp. 17–30, 1976.

MICKUNAS, M.D., LANCASTER, R.L., AND SCHNEIDER, B.B., "Transforming $LR(k)$ grammars to $LR(1)$, $SLR(1)$, and (1, 1) bounded right-context grammars," *Journal of the Association for Computing Machinery,* **23**, pp. 17–30, 1976.

MINSKY, M.L., "Recursive unsolvability of Post's problem of 'Tag' and other topics in the theory of Turing machines," *Annals of Mathematics,* **74**, pp. 437–455, 1961.

MINSKY, M.L., AND PAPERT, S., "Unrecognizable sets of numbers," *Journal of the Association for Computing Machinery,* **13**, pp. 281–286, 1966.

MORSE, M., AND HEDLUND, G.A., "Unending chess, symbolic dynamics, and a problem in semigroups," *Duke Mathematical Journal,* **11**, pp. 1–7, 1944.

MUNRO, I., "Efficient determination of the transitive closure of a directed graph," *Information Processing Letters,* **1**, pp. 56–58, 1971.

MYHILL, J., "Finite automata and the representation of events," WADD Technical Report 57–624, Wright–Patterson Air Force Base, November, 1957.

MYHILL, J., "Linear bounded automata," WADD Technical Note 60–165, Wright–Patterson Air Force Base, 1960.

NELSON, C., "One-way automata on bounded languages," Technical Report TR-14-76, Center for Research in Computing Technology, Harvard University, July, 1976.

NERODE, A., "Linear automaton transformations," *Proceedings of the American Mathematical Society,* **9**, pp. 541–544, 1958.

NIVAT, M., "Transductions des Langages de Chomsky," Ph.D. Thesis, University of Paris, 1967.

NIVAT, M., "Sur les automates à memoire pile." Institut de Programmation, 1970.

NIVAT, M., "On some families of languages related to the Dyck language," Institut de Programmation, 1970.

NIVAT, M., "Congruences de Thue et t-langages," *Studia Scientiarum Mathematicarum Hungarica,* **6**, pp. 243–249, 1971.

NIVAT, M., "On the interpretation of recursive program schemes," Rapport de Recherche No. 84, Institut de Recherche d'Informatique et d'Automatique, 1974.

NIVAT, M., "Extensions et restrictions des grammaires algébriques," in *Formal Languages and Programming* (R. Aguilar, editor), pp. 83–96, 1976.

OGDEN, W.F., "Intercalation Theorems for Pushdown Store and Stack Languages," Ph.D. thesis, Stanford University, 1968.

OGDEN, W.F., "A helpful result for proving inherent ambiguity," *Mathematical Systems Theory,* **2**, pp. 191–194, 1968.

PAGER, D., "A fast left-to-right parser for context-free grammars," Technical Report PE240, Information Sciences Program, University of Hawaii, January, 1972.

PAIR, C., "Trees, pushdown stores, and compilation," *Rev. Franç. Traitment Informatique,* Chiffres **7**; 3, pp. 199–216, 1964.

PAIR, C., AND QUERÉ, A., "Définition et étude des bilangages réguliers," *Information and Control,* **13**, pp. 565–593, 1968.

PARIKH, R.J., "Language-generating devices," *Quarterly Progress Report,* No. 60, Research Laboratory of Electronics, M.I.T., pp. 199–212, 1961.

PARIKH, R.J., "On context-free languages," *Journal of the Association for Computing Machinery,* **13**, pp. 570–581, 1966.

PATERSON, M.S., "Decision problems in computational models," in *Proceedings of the ACM Conference on Proving Assertions about Programs,* Las Cruces, New Mexico, 1972.

PAULL, M.C., AND UNGER, S.H., "Structural equivalence of context-free grammars," *Journal of Computer and System Sciences,* **2**, pp. 427–463, 1968.

PERROT, J.F., "Monoides syntactiques des langages algébriques," *Acta Informatica,* **7**, pp. 393–413, 1977.

PERROT, J.F., AND SAKAROVITCH, J., "Langages algébriques deterministes et groupes abéliens," *Second GI Fachtagung, Automaten theorie und formale Sprachen,* Kaiserslautern, pp. 20–30, May 1975.

PETERS, P.S., AND RITCHIE, R.W., "Context-sensitive immediate constituent analysis – context-free languages revisited," *Conference Record of the ACM Symposium on Theory of Computing,* pp. 1–8, 1969.

PILLING, D.L., "Commutative regular equations and Parikh's theorem," *Journal of the London Mathematical Society* (II) **6**, pp. 663–666, 1973.

PIRICKÁ-KELEMENOVÁ, A., "Greibach normal-form complexity," in *Mathematical Foundations of Computer Science 1975* (J. Bečvář, ed.), Vol. 32, "Lecture Notes in Computer Science," pp. 344–350. Berlin: Springer-Verlag, 1975.

PLEASANTS, P.A.B., "Nonrepetitive sequences," *Proceedings of the Cambridge Philosophical Society,* **68**, pp. 267–274, 1970.

POST, E.L., "A variant of a recursively unsolvable problem," *Bulletin of the American Mathematical Society,* **52**, pp. 264–268, 1946.

PRATT, V.R., RABIN, M.O., AND STOCKMEYER, L.J., "A characterization of the power of vector machines," *Conference Record of the Sixth ACM symposium on Theory of Computing,* pp. 122–134, 1974.

PRATT, V., "LINGOL – a progress report," *Fourth International Joint Conference on Artificial Intelligence,* Tbilisi, U.S.S.R., Vol. 1; 1975; pp. 422–428.

PRESBURGER, M., "Uber die Vollständigkeit eines gewissen Systems der Arithmetic ganzer Zahlen in welchem die Addition als einzige Operation hervortritt," *Sprawozdanie z I Kongresu Matematykow Krajow Slowanskieb,* Warsaw, pp. 92–101, 1930.

PUTZBACH, P., "Une famille de congruences de Thue pour lesquelles le problème de l'équivalence est decidable. Application a l'équivalence des grammaires séparées," in *Automata, Languages, and Programming* (M. Nivat, ed.), pp. 3–12. Amsterdam: North-Holland Publishing Co., 1973.

RABIN, M.O., "Degree of difficulty of computing a function and a partial ordering of recursive sets," Applied Logic Branch, Technical Report No. 2, Hebrew University, Jerusalem, 1960.

RABIN, M.O., "Real-time computation," *Israel Journal of Mathematics,* **1**, pp. 203–211, 1963.

RABIN, M.O., AND SCOTT, D., "Finite automata and their decision problems," *IBM Journal of Research and Development,* **3**, pp. 114–125, 1959.

RAMSEY, F.P., "On a problem of formal logic," *Proceedings of the London Mathematical Society,* 2nd Series, **30**, pp. 264–286, 1930.

RANEY, G.N., "Functional composition patterns and power-series reversion," *Transactions of the American Mathematical Society,* **94**, pp. 441–451, 1960.

REEDY, A., AND SAVITCH, W.J., "The Turing degree of the inherent ambiguity problem for context-free languages," *Theoretical Computer Science,* **1**, pp. 77–79, 1975.

RIORDAN, J., *Combinatorial Identities.* New York: John Wiley and Sons, Inc., 1968.

RITCHIE, R.W., "Classes of predictably computable functions," *Transactions of the American Mathematical Society,* **106**, pp. 139–173, 1963a.

RITCHIE, R.W., "Finite automata and the set of squares," *Journal of the Association for Computing Machinery,* **10**, pp. 528–531, 1963b.

RITCHIE, R.W., AND SPRINGSTEEL, F.N., "Language recognition by marking automata," *Information and Control,* **20**, pp. 313–330, 1972.

ROGERS, H., *The Theory of Recursive Functions and Effective Computability.* New York: McGraw-Hill Book Co., 1967.

ROSENBERG, A.L., "On multihead finite automata," *IBM Journal of Research and Development,* **10**, pp. 388–394, 1966.

ROSENBERG, A.L., "A machine realization of the linear context-free languages," *Information and Control,* **10**, pp. 175–188, 1967.

ROSENBERG, A.L., "Real-time definable languages," *Journal of the Association for Computing Machinery,* **14**, pp. 645–662, 1967.

ROSENBERG, A.L., "On the independence of realtime definability and certain structural properties of context-free languages," *Journal of the Association for Computing Machinery,* **15**, 672–679, 1968.

ROSENBERG, A.L., "A note on ambiguity of context-free languages and presentations of semilinear sets," *Journal of the Association for Computing Machinery,* **17**, pp. 44–50, 1970.

ROSENKRANTZ, D.J., "Matrix equations and normal forms for context-free grammar." *Journal of the Association for Computing Machinery,* **14**, pp. 501–507, 1967.

ROSENKRANTZ, D.J., "Programmed grammars and classes of formal languages," *Journal of the Association for Computing Machinery,* **16**, pp. 107–131, 1969.

ROSENKRANTZ, D.J., AND LEWIS, P.M., III, "Deterministic left-corner parsing," *Symposium on Switching and Automata Theory,* pp. 139–152, 1970.

ROSENKRATZ, D.J., AND STEARNS, R.E., "Properties of deterministic top-down grammars," *Information and Control,* **17**, pp. 226–255, 1970.

ROUNDS, W.C., "Mappings and grammars on trees," *Mathematical Systems Theory,* **4**, pp. 257–287, 1970.

ROZENBERG, G., "Direct proofs of the undecidability of the equivalence problem for sentential forms of linear context-free grammars and the equivalence problem for *OL* systems," *Information Processing Letters,* **1**, pp. 233–235, 1972.

RUOHONEN, K., "Some combinatorial mappings of words," *Annales Academiae Scientiarum Fennicae,* Sec. A, Helsinki, 1976.

RYSER, H.J., "Combinatorial Mathematics," Vol. 14, Carus Monograph Series, The Mathematical Association of America, 1963.

SALOMAA, A., *Theory of Automata.* New York: Pergamon Press, 1969a.

SALOMAA, A., "On grammars with restricted use of productions." *Annales Academiae Scientiarum Fennicae,* Series A.I., 454, Helsinki, 1969b.

SALOMAA, A., "On the index of a context-free grammar and language," *Information and Control,* **14**, pp. 474–477, 1969c.

SALOMAA, A., "On some families of formal languages obtained by regulated derivations," *Annales Academiae Scientiarum Fennicae,* Series A.I., 479. Helsinki, 1970.

SALOMAA, A., *Formal Languages,* New York: Academic Press, 1973a.

SALOMAA, A., "On sequential forms of context-free grammars," *Acta Informatica,* **2**, pp. 40–49, 1973b.

SANTOS, E.S., "A note on bracketed grammars," *Journal of the Association for Computing Machinery,* **19**, pp. 222–224, 1972.

SAVITCH, W.J., "Relationships between nondeterministic and deterministic tape complexities," *Journal on Computer and System Sciences,* **4**, pp. 177–192, 1970.

SAVITCH, W.J., "How to make arbitrary grammars look like context-free grammars," *SIAM Journal on Computing,* **2**, pp. 174–182, 1973.

SAVITCH, W.J., "Maze-recognizing automata and nondeterministic tape complexity," *Journal of Computer and System Sciences,* **7**, pp. 389–403, 1973.

SCHEINBERG, S., "Note on the boolean properties of context-free languages," *Information and Control,* **3**, pp. 372–375, 1960.

SCHKOLNICK, M., "Two-tape bracketed grammars," *Proceedings of the 9th Annual Symposium on Switching and Automata Theory,* pp. 315–326, 1968.

SCHÜTZENBERGER, M.P., "A remark on finite transducers," *Information and Control,* **4**, pp. 185–196, 1961a.

SCHÜTZENBERGER, M.P., "On the definition of a family of automata," *Information and Control,* **4**, pp. 245–270, 1961b.

SCHÜTZENBERGER, M.P., "Certain elementary families of automata," in *Proceedings of the Symposium on Mathematical Theory of Automata,* Polytechnic Institute of Brooklyn, pp. 139–153, 1962a.

SCHÜTZENBERGER, M.P., "On a theorem of R. Jungen," *Proceedings of the American Mathematical Society,* **13**, pp. 885–890, 1962b.

SCHÜTZENBERGER, M.P., "Finite counting automata," *Information and Control,* **5**, pp. 91–107, 1962c.

SCHÜTZENBERGER, M.P., "On context-free languages and pushdown automata," *Information and Control,* **6**, pp. 246–264, 1963.

SCHÜTZENBERGER, M.P., *Quelques Problèmes Combinatories de la Théorie des Automata;* Course notes. Paris: Institut de Programmation, 1967.

SCHÜTZENBERGER, M.P., "A remark on acceptable sets of numbers," *Journal of the Association for Computing Machinery,* **15**, pp. 300–303, 1968.

SCHÜTZENBERGER, M.P., "Le théorème de Lagrange selon Raney," in *Logiques et Automates.* Rocquencourt: Séminaires IRIA, 1971.

SCHÜTZENBERGER, M.P., "Une caractérisation des parties reconnaissables," in *Formal Languages and Programming* (R. Aguilar, ed.), 1976; pp. 77–82.

SCHÜTZENBERGER, M.P., "Sur une caractérisation des fonctions séquentielles," Research Report 176, IRIA, 1976.

SCOTT, D., "Some definitional suggestions for automata theory," *Journal of Computer and System Sciences,* **1**, pp. 187–212, 1967.

SEIFERAS, J.I., "A note on prefixes of regular languages," *ACM SIGACT News,* pp. 25–29, January 1974.

SEIFERAS, J.I., "Techniques for separating space complexity classes" and "Relating refined space complexity classes," *Journal of Computer and System Sciences,* **14**, pp. 73–99 and pp. 100–129, 1977.

SEIFERAS, J.I., AND MCNAUGHTON, R., "Regularity-preserving relations," *Theoretical Computer Science,* **2**, pp. 147–154, 1976.

SEKIMOTO, S., MUKAI, K., AND SUDO, M., "A method of minimizing $LR(k)$ parsers," *Systems, Computers, and Control,* **4**, pp. 73–80, 1973.

SEMONOV, A.L., "Algorithmic problems for power-series and context-free grammars," *Doklady Akademii Nauk SSSR,* **212**, pp. 50–52, 1973. Translated into English in *Soviet Math,* **14**, pp. 1319–1322, 1973.

SHAMIR, E., "A representation theorem for algebraic and context-free power series in noncommutating variables," *Information and Control,* **11**, pp. 239–254, 1967.

SHAMIR, E., "Some inherently ambiguous context-free languages," *Information and Control,* **18**, pp. 355–363, 1971.

SHEPHERDSON, J.C., "The reduction of two-way automata to one-way automata," *IBM Journal of Research and Development,* **3**, pp. 198–200, 1959.

SLISENKO, A.O., "Recognition of palindromes by multihead Turing machines," *Proceedings of the Steklov Mathematical Institute,* Acad. of Sciences of the U.S.S.R., **129**, pp. 30–202, 1973.

SMITH, A.R., "Real-time language recognition by one-dimensional cellular automata," *Journal of Computer and System Sciences,* **6**, pp. 233–253, 1972.

SMULLYAN, R.M., *Theory of Formal Systems.* Princeton: Princeton University Press, 1961.

STANAT, D.F., "A homomorphism theorem for weighted context-free grammars," *Journal of Computer and System Sciences,* **6**, pp. 217–232, 1972.

STANTON, R.G., *Numerical Methods for Science and Engineering.* Englewood Cliffs, N.J.: Prentice-Hall, Inc., 1961.

STEARNS, R.E., "A regularity test for pushdown machines," *Information and Control,* **11**, pp. 323–340, 1967.

STEARNS, R.E., HARTMANIS, J., AND LEWIS, P.M., III, "Hierarchies of memory-limited computations," *Conference Record on Switching Circuit Theory and Logical Design,* pp. 191–202, 1965.

STRASSEN, V., "Gaussian elimination is not optimal," *Numerische Mathematik,* **13**, pp. 354–456, 1969.

SUDBOROUGH, I.H., "A note on tape-bounded complexity classes and linear context-free languages," *Journal of the Association for Computing Machinery,* **22**, pp. 499–500, 1975.

SUDBOROUGH, I.H., "On tape-bounded complexity classes and multihead finite automata," *Journal of Computer and System Sciences,* **10**, pp. 62–76, 1975.

SUDBOROUGH, I.H., "One-way multihead writing finite automata," *Information and Control,* **30**, pp. 1–20, 1976.

SUDBOROUGH, I.H., "On deterministic context-free languages, multihead automata, and the power of an auxiliary pushdown store," *Proceedings of the Eighth Annual ACM Symposium on Theory of Computing,* pp. 141–148, 1976.

SZYMANSKI, T.G., AND ULLMAN, J.D., "Evaluating relational expressions with dense and sparse arguments," *SIAM Journal on Computing,* **6**, pp. 109–122, 1977.

SZYMANSKI, T.G., AND WILLIAMS, J.H., "Noncanonical extensions of bottom-up parsing techniques," *SIAM Journal on Computing,* **5**, pp. 231–250, 1976.

TANIGUCHI, K., AND KASAMI, T., "A note on computing time for the recognition of context-free languages by a single-tape Turing machine," *Information and Control,* **14**, pp. 278–284, 1969.

THATCHER, J.W., "Characterizing derivation trees of a context-free grammar through a generalization of finite-automata theory," *Journal of Computer and System Sciences,* **1**, pp. 317–322, 1967.

THATCHER, J.W., "Generalized 2-sequential transducers," *Journal of Computer and System Sciences,* **4**, pp. 339–367, 1970.

TOWNLEY, J.G., "The Measurement of Complex Algorithms," Ph.D. Thesis, Harvard University, Cambridge, Mass., October 1972. *Also available as* Report TR 14–73, Center for Research in Computing Technology, Harvard University.

TURING, A.M., "On computable numbers with an application to the Entscheidungsproblem," *Proceedings of the London Mathematical Society,* **2–42**, pp. 230–265, 1936.

ULLIAN, J., "Failure of a conjecture about context-free languages," *Information and Control,* **9**, pp. 61–65, 1966.

ULLIAN, J.S., "Partial-algorithm problems for context-free languages," *Information and Control,* **11**, pp. 80–101, 1967.

ULLMAN, J.D., "Halting stack automata," *Journal of the Association for Computing Machinery,* **16**, pp. 550–563, 1969.

ULLMAN, J.D., "Applications of Language Theory to Compiler Design," in *Theoretical Computer Science* (A.V. Aho, ed.). Englewood Cliffs, N.J.: Prentice-Hall, 1972.

ULLMAN, J.D., *Fundamental Concepts of Programming.* Reading, Mass.: Addison-Wesley Publishing Co., 1976.

URPONEN, T., "On axiom systems for regular expressions and on equations involving languages," *Annales Universitatis Turkuensis,* Series A, Turku, 1971.

URPONEN, T., "Equations with a Dyck-language solution," *Information and Control,* **30**, pp. 21–37, 1976.

VALIANT, L.G., "Decision Procedures for Families of Deterministic Pushdown Automata," Ph.D. Thesis, Department of Computer Science, University of Warwick, 1973.

VALIANT, L., "General context-free recognition in less than cubic time," *Journal of Computer and System Sciences,* **10**, pp. 308–315, 1975.

VALIANT, L.G., "Regularity and related problems for deterministic pushdown automata," *Journal of the Association for Computing Machinery,* **22**, pp. 1–10, 1975.

VALIANT, L.G., "A note on the succinctness of descriptions of deterministic languages," *Information and Control,* **32**, pp. 139–145, 1976.

VALIANT, L.G., AND PATERSON, M.S., "Deterministic one-counter languages," *Journal of Computer and System Sciences,* **10**, pp. 340–350, 1975.

VAN LEEUWEN, J., "A generalization of Parikh's theorem in formal language theory," in *Automata, Languages, and Programming* (J. Loeckx, ed.), Vol. 14, "Lecture Notes in Computer Science," pp. 17–26. Berlin: Springer-Verlag, 1974.

VAN LEEUWEN, J., AND SMITH, C.H., "An improved bound for detecting looping configurations in deterministic pda's," *Information Processing Letters,* **3**, pp. 22–24, 1974.

VAN LEEUWEN, J., "Variations of a new machine model," *Proceedings of the 17th Annual Symposium on Foundations of Computer Science,* pp. 228–235, 1976.

WARSHALL, S., "A theorem on boolean matrices," *Journal of the Association for Computing Machinery,* **9**, pp. 11–12, 1962.

WEGBREIT, B., "A generator of context-sensitive languages," *Journal of Computer and System Sciences,* **3**, pp. 456–461, 1969.

WEICKER, R., "General context-free language recognition by a RAM with uniform-cost criterion in time $n^2 \log n$," Technical Report No. 182, The Pennsylvania State University, 1976.

WILLIAMS, J.H., "Bounded-context parsable grammars," *Information and Control,* **28**, pp. 314–334, 1975.

WIRTH, N., "PL 360 – a programming language for the 360 computer," *Journal of the Association for Computing Machinery,* **15**, pp. 37–74, 1968.

WIRTH, N., AND WEBER, H., "EULER, a generalization of ALGOL, and its formal definition," *Communications of the Association for Computing Machinery,* **9**, pp. 13–25, pp. 88–89, 1966.

WISE, D.S., "Generalized overlap-resolvable grammars and their parsers," *Journal of Computer and System Sciences,* **6**, pp. 538–572, 1972.

WISE, D.S., "A strong pumping lemma for context-free languages," *Theoretical Computer Science,* **3**, pp. 359–369, 1976.

WOOD, D., "The normal-form theorem – another proof," *The Computer Journal,* **12**, pp. 139–147, 1969a.

WOOD, D., "A note on top-down deterministic languages," *BIT,* **9**, pp. 387–399, 1969b.

WOOD, D., "The theory of left-factored languages," *The Computer Journal,* **12**, pp. 349–356, 1969c, and **13**, pp. 55–62, 1970.

WOOD, D., "A generalised normal-form theorem for context-free grammars," *The Computer Journal,* **13**, pp. 272–277, 1970.

WOOD, D., "A further note on top-down deterministic languages," *The Computer Journal,* **14**, pp. 396–403, 1971.

WOOD, D., "Some remarks on the KH algorithm for s-grammars," *BIT,* **13**, pp. 476–489, 1973.

WOODS, W.A., "Context-sensitive parsing," *Communications of the Association for Computing Machinery,* **13**, pp. 437–445, 1970.

WRATHALL, C., "Subrecursive predicates and automata," Ph.D. Thesis, Harvard University, 1975. *Also* Research Report 56, Dept. of Computer Science, Yale University, 1975.

YAMADA, H., "Real-time computation and recursive functions not real-time computable," *IRE Professional Group on Electronic Computers,* **11**, pp. 753–760, 1962.

YAO, A.C., AND RIVEST, R.L., "$K + 1$ heads are better than K," *Proceedings of the 17th Annual Symposium on Foundations of Computer Science,* pp. 67–70, 1976.

YNTEMA, M.K., "Inclusion relations among families of context-free languages," *Information and Control,* **10**, pp. 572–597, 1967.

YOUNGER, D.H., "Recognition and parsing of context-free languages in time n^3," *Information and Control,* **10**, pp. 189–208, 1967.

YU, Y., "Rudimentary Relations and Formal Languages," Ph.D. Dissertation, University of California, Berkeley, 1970.

ZIMMER, R., "Soft precedence," *Information Processing Letters,* **1**, pp. 108–110, 1972.

Index